COMMON SYMBOLS AND NOTATION

α_k	Alpha (excess performance) of asset i
β_i	Beta of asset i with respect to the market
$\beta_{i,M}$	Long form of β_i
δ	Hedge ratio
bp	Basis points
BVE	Book value of equity
C_0	Cash or cash flow at time 0, usually invested
C_1	Cash or cash flow at time 1, usually returned
CAPM	Capital Asset Pricing Model
CF	Cash flow
$\mathcal{C}ov$	Covariance
$\tilde{e}$ or $\tilde{\epsilon}$	Noise
E/P	Earnings-price ratio
$\mathcal{E}$	Expected value
$\mathcal{E}(\tilde{C}_1)$	Expected (return of) cash at time 1
$\mathcal{E}(\tilde{g})$	Expected growth rate
$\mathcal{E}(\tilde{r})$	Expected rate of return, often used as cost of capital
$\mathcal{E}(\tilde{r}_{\text{Debt}})$	Debt cost of capital
$\mathcal{E}(\tilde{r}_{\text{Equity}})$	Equity cost of capital
$\mathcal{E}(\tilde{r}_{\text{Firm}})$	Firm's overall cost of capital (see also WACC)
$\mathcal{E}(\tilde{r}_M)$	Expected rate of return on overall market
EAC	Equivalent annual cost
FV	Future value
g	Growth rate, often of earnings or dividends
IRR	Internal rate of return
m	Small positive drift in random walk
MVE	Market value of equity
N	Number of years; see also T
NPV	Net present value
π	Inflation rate
P_0	Price at time 0 (today)
P_1	Price at time 1 (future)
P/E	Price-earnings ratio
P_{cum}	Stock price before dividend is paid out
P_{ex}	Stock price after dividend is paid out
PV	Present value
PVGO	Present value of growth opportunities
r	Rate of return
r_f	Risk-free rate of return
r_M	Rate of return on the market
$r_{s,t}$	Rate of return from time s to time t
r_t	Rate of return from time 0 to time t
$\mathcal{S}dv$	Standard deviation
$\mathcal{S}dv(\tilde{r})$	Standard deviation of rate of return; usually our measure of risk
SML	Security Market Line
T	Final period (time horizon)
t	Time t
τ	Tax rate
V	Value
$\mathcal{V}ar$	Variance
w	Weight (often used in a weighted average)
WACC	Weighted average cost of capital, usually the same as $\mathcal{E}(\tilde{r}_{\text{Firm}})$
YTM	Yield to maturity

CORPORATE FINANCE

An Introduction

The Prentice Hall Series in Finance

Alexander/Sharpe/Bailey
Fundamentals of Investments

Bear/Moldonado-Bear
Free Markets, Finance, Ethics, and Law

Berk/DeMarzo
Corporate Finance *

Berk/DeMarzo
Corporate Finance: The Core *

Berk/DeMarzo/Harford
Fundamentals of Corporate Finance *

Bierman/Smidt
The Capital Budgeting Decision: Economic Analysis of Investment Projects

Bodie/Merton/Cleeton
Financial Economics

Click/Coval
The Theory and Practice of International Financial Management

Copeland/Weston/Shastri
Financial Theory and Corporate Policy

Cox/Rubinstein
Options Markets

Dorfman
Introduction to Risk Management and Insurance

Dietrich
Financial Services and Financial Institutions: Value Creation in Theory and Practice

Dufey/Giddy
Cases in International Finance

Eakins
Finance in .learn

Eiteman/Stonehill/Moffett
Multinational Business Finance

Emery/Finnerty/Stowe
Corporate Financial Management

Fabozzi
Bond Markets: Analysis and Strategies

Fabozzi/Modigliani
Capital Markets: Institutions and Instruments

Fabozzi/Modigliani/Jones/Ferri
Foundations of Financial Markets and Institutions

Finkler
Financial Management for Public, Health, and Not-for-Profit Organizations

Francis/Ibbotson
Investments: A Global Perspective

Fraser/Ormiston
Understanding Financial Statements

Geisst
Investment Banking in the Financial System

Gitman
Principles of Managerial Finance *

Gitman
Principles of Managerial Finance—Brief Edition *

Gitman/Joehnk
Fundamentals of Investing *

Gitman/Madura
Introduction to Finance

Guthrie/Lemon
Mathematics of Interest Rates and Finance

Haugen
The Inefficient Stock Market: What Pays Off and Why

Haugen
Modern Investment Theory

Haugen
The New Finance: Overreaction, Complexity, and Uniqueness

Holden
Excel Modeling and Estimation in the Fundamentals of Corporate Finance

Holden
Excel Modeling and Estimation in the Fundamentals of Investments

Holden
Excel Modeling and Estimation in Investments

Holden
Excel Modeling and Estimation in Corporate Finance

Hughes/MacDonald
International Banking: Text and Cases

Hull
Fundamentals of Futures and Options Markets

Hull
Options, Futures, and Other Derivatives

Hull
Risk Management and Financial Institutions

Keown/Martin/Petty/Scott
Financial Management: Principles and Applications

Keown/Martin/Petty/Scott
Foundations of Finance: The Logic and Practice of Financial Management

Keown
Personal Finance: Turning Money into Wealth

Kim/Nofsinger
Corporate Governance

Levy/Post
Investments

May/May/Andrew
Effective Writing: A Handbook for Finance People

Madura
Personal Finance

Marthinsen
Risk Takers: Uses and Abuses of Financial Derivatives

McDonald
Derivatives Markets

McDonald
Fundamentals of Derivatives Markets

Megginson
Corporate Finance Theory

Melvin
International Money and Finance

Mishkin/Eakins
Financial Markets and Institutions

Moffett
Cases in International Finance

Moffett/Stonehill/Eiteman
Fundamentals of Multinational Finance

Nofsinger
Psychology of Investing

Ogden/Jen/O'Connor
Advanced Corporate Finance

Pennacchi
Theory of Asset Pricing

Rejda
Principles of Risk Management and Insurance

Schoenebeck
Interpreting and Analyzing Financial Statements

Scott/Martin/Petty/Keown/Thatcher
Cases in Finance

Seiler
Performing Financial Studies: A Methodological Cookbook

Shapiro
Capital Budgeting and Investment Analysis

Sharpe/Alexander/Bailey
Investments

Solnik/McLeavey
Global Investments

Stretcher/Michael
Cases in Financial Management

Titman/Martin
Valuation: The Art and Science of Corporate Investment Decisions

Trivoli
Personal Portfolio Management: Fundamentals and Strategies

Van Horne
Financial Management and Policy

Van Horne
Financial Market Rates and Flows

Van Horne/Wachowicz
Fundamentals of Financial Management

Vaughn
Financial Planning for the Entrepreneur

Welch
Corporate Finance: An Introduction *

Weston/Mitchel/Mulherin
Takeovers, Restructuring, and Corporate Governance

Winger/Frasca
Personal Finance

* denotes myfinancelab titles Log onto **www.myfinancelab.com** to learn more

CORPORATE FINANCE

An Introduction

Ivo Welch

BROWN UNIVERSITY

PRENTICE HALL

New York Boston San Francisco
London Toronto Sydney Tokyo Singapore Madrid
Mexico City Munich Paris Cape Town Hong Kong Montreal

Editor in Chief: Donna Battista
Executive Development Editor: Mary Clare McEwing
Managing Editor: Jeff Holcomb
Senior Production Supervisor: Kathryn Dinovo
Supplements Supervisor: Heather McNally
Director of Media: Susan Schoenberg
Senior Media Producer: Bethany Tidd
Associate Media Producer: Miguel Leonarte
Marketing Assistant: Ian Gold
Senior Author Support/Technology Specialist: Joe Vetere
Senior Prepress Supervisor: Caroline Fell
Rights and Permissions Advisor: Dana Weightman
Senior Manufacturing Buyer: Carol Melville
Senior Media Buyer: Ginny Michaud
Senior Designer: Barbara Atkinson
Text and Cover Designer: Leslie Haimes
Production Coordination, Composition, and Art: Windfall Software, using ZzTEX

1 2 3 4 5 6 7 8 9 10—CRK—12 11 10 09 08

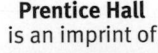

Prentice Hall
is an imprint of

PEARSON

www.pearsonhighered.com

ISBN-10: 0-321-58727-8
ISBN-13: 978-0-321-58727-5

About the Author

Ivo Welch is Professor of Financial Economics at Brown University, a position he has held since 2004. He previously held the same appointment at UCLA's Anderson School of Management (from 1989 to 2000) and Yale University's School of Management (from 2000 to 2004). He received his BA in computer science in 1985 from Columbia University, and both his MBA (1989) and PhD (1991) in finance from the University of Chicago. His work has been featured in many academic journals, as well as the popular press. More information about the author can be found at the book's Web site (www.prenhall.com/welch) and at the author's personal website (http://welch.econ.brown.edu).

To my parents, Arthur and Charlotte Welch

and to my wife, Lily

Preface

The author raises some thought-provoking questions beyond those found in most books of this genre.
—Marianne Plunkert
University of Colorado, Denver

Most corporate finance textbooks cover a similar canon of concepts, and my book is no exception. A quick glance at the table of contents will show you that most—though not all—of the topics in *Corporate Finance: An Introduction* overlap with those in traditional finance textbooks and syllabi. That said, this book is intentionally different. Although I cover similar territory, I also introduce many innovations in approach and emphasis. I hope that once you have seen them, there will be no going back.

INNOVATIONS IN APPROACH

The underlying philosophy of this book is based on a belief that any talented student can understand finance. I believe that our concepts are no more difficult than those in standard texts covering the principles of economics and that our mathematics is no more difficult than that in high school. I believe that finance is easiest when explained from basic principles and only gradually ramped up in complexity. I also believe that although it is important for students to learn how to solve traditional textbook problems, it is as important for them to learn how to think about and approach new problems that they will encounter in the real world.

I really like the approach starting from an ideal, simple market to more realistic and complex market conditions . . . [this is] one of the best written and easiest to understand texts I have ever read in finance.
—Kuo Tseng
California State University, Fresno

A LOGICAL PROGRESSION

The book starts with simple scenarios in which all the inputs are clear and progresses to more complex, real-world scenarios for which the solutions become more difficult. Within this architecture, chapters build organically on concepts learned earlier. This incremental progression allows students to reuse what they have learned and to understand the effect of each new change in and of itself.

One theme that binds the book together is the progression from the perfect-market, law-of-one-price ideal world (on which most finance formulas are based) to an imperfect market (in which formulas may need adjustment, explicitly or implicitly). The layout on pages xiv–xv showcases the building blocks of this approach.

NUMERICAL EXAMPLE LEADING TO FORMULA

I like this approach very much. This is, in fact, the optimal way to learn.
—Richard Fendler
Georgia State University

I learn best by numerical example, and I believe that students do, too. Whenever I want to understand an idea, I try to construct numerical examples for myself—the simpler, the better. Therefore, this book relies on simple numerical examples as its primary tutorial method. Instead of a "bird's eye" view of the formula first and application second, students will start with a "worm's eye" view and work their way up—from simple numbers, to more complex examples, and finally to abstract formulas. Each step is easy. At first glance, you may think this may be less "executive" or perhaps not as well-suited to students with only a cursory interest in finance. I assure you that neither of these is the case.

Critical questions such as, "What would this project be worth?" are answered in numerical step-by-step examples (printed in black), and right under the computations are the corresponding symbolic formulas (printed in red). I believe that the pairing of numerics with formulas will ultimately help students understand the material on a higher level and with more ease. The layout on pages xvi—xvii provides a small sample of the "numbers first" approach that I use throughout the book.

Without a doubt, this is the greatest strength of the text.
—Sharon Garrison
University of Arizona

The use of . . . simple numerical examples throughout . . . to explain essential concepts and formulas is outstanding.
—Effi Benmelech
Harvard University

PROBLEM SOLVING

A corollary to the numbers-first approach is my belief that formulaic memorization is a last resort. Such a rote approach leaves the house without a foundation. Instead of giving students canned formulas, I try to show them how to solve problems themselves. My goal is to teach students how to dissect new problems with a set of analytical tools that will stand them in good stead in their future careers.

SELF-CONTAINED FOR CLARITY

Many students come into class with a patchwork of background knowledge. Along the way, holes in their backgrounds cause some of them to get lost. I have therefore tried to keep this book self-contained. For example, all necessary statistical concepts are integrated in Chapter 8 (Investor Choice: Risk and Reward), and all necessary accounting concepts are explained in Chapter 13 (From Financial Statements to Economic Cash Flows).

I think [the] approach of integrating necessary material is perfect. It helps remind students [about] what they need to know and should bolster their confidence.
—Angela Lavin
University of South Dakota

INNOVATIONS IN CONTENT AND PERSPECTIVE

This book also offers numerous topical and expositional innovations, of which the following is a limited selection.

A STRONG DISTINCTION BETWEEN EXPECTED AND PROMISED CASH FLOWS

I clearly distinguish between the premium to compensate for default (credit risk)—a concept introduced in Chapter 6 (Uncertainty, Default, and Risk)—and the risk premium, which is introduced in Chapter 9 (The Capital Asset Pricing Model). Students should no longer make the mistake of thinking that they have taken care of credit risk when they discount a promised cash flow with a CAPM expected rate of return.

ROBUSTNESS

Throughout, I describe what finance practitioners can know clearly and what they can only guess at (with varying degrees of accuracy). In the application of a number of financial tools, I point out which of the guessed uncertainties are likely to have important repercussions and which are minor in consequence. I also try to be honest about where our academic knowledge is solid and where it is shaky.

Much more honest than other introductory books.
—Adam Gehr
DePaul University

A SPOTLIGHT ON THE PITFALLS OF CAPITAL BUDGETING

I really love the NPV Checklist. This alone makes the book stand high above the competition.
—Joe Walker
University of Alabama, Birmingham

A self-contained chapter (Chapter 12: Capital Budgeting Applications and Pitfalls) describes real-world difficulties and issues in applying capital budgeting techniques, ranging from externalities to real options, to agency issues, to behavioral distortions, and so on. The chapter ends with an "NPV Checklist."

FINANCIALS FROM A FINANCE PERSPECTIVE

The best discussion relating accounting to the financial inputs for valuation at this level that I have ever seen.
—Robert Hansen
Tulane University

A self-contained accounting chapter (Chapter 13: From Financial Statements to Economic Cash Flows) explains how earnings and economic cash flows relate. When students understand the logic of corporate financial statements, they avoid a number of common mistakes that have crept into financial cash flow calculations "by tradition." In addition, a synthesizing chapter on pro formas (Chapter 20: Pro Forma Financial Statements) combines all the ingredients from previous chapters—capital budgeting, taxes, the cost of capital, capital structure, and so on. Many students will be asked in their future jobs to construct pro formas, and our corporate finance curriculum has not always prepared them well enough to execute such assignments appropriately and thoughtfully.

COMPARABLES

A chapter on comparables (Chapter 14: Valuation from Comparables and Some Financial Ratios), usually not found in other corporate finance textbooks, shows that if used properly, the comparables valuation method is a good cousin to NPV.

AN UPDATED PERSPECTIVE ON CAPITAL STRUCTURE

The [capital structure] material is current and practical—much better done than other books I have seen.
—Richard Fendler
Georgia State University

The academic perspective on capital structure has been changing. Here are a few of the more novel points of emphasis in this book:

- Corporate claims do not just have cash flow rights but important control rights as well. This fact has many implications—that is, for the Modigliani-Miller perfect-market benchmark.
- Corporate liabilities are broader than just financial debt; in fact, on average, about two-thirds of firms' liabilities are nonfinancial. The value of the firm is thus the sum of its financial debt and equity *plus* its nonfinancial debt (often linked to operations). Again, this can be important in a number of applications.
- Adverse selection causes a pecking order, but so do other effects. Thus, the pecking order does not necessarily imply adverse selection.
- The debate about trade-off theory today has moved to how slowly it happens—whether it takes 5 years or 500 years for a firm to readjust.
- Historical stock returns are a major determinant of which firms today have high debt ratios and which have low debt ratios. A simple inspection of the evolution of IBM's capital structure from 2001 to 2003 in Chapter 15 makes this plainly obvious.
- Capital structure may not be a corporate control device. On the contrary, equity-heavy capital structures could be the result of a breakdown of corporate control.
- Preferred equity and convertibles have become rare among publicly traded corporations over the past decade.

• A unique synthesizing figure (Figure 18.5) in Chapter 18 (More Market Imperfections Influencing Capital Structure) provides a conceptual basis for thinking about capital structure in imperfect markets. It shows how APV and other non-tax-related imperfections hang together.

BASIC ORGANIZATION

Corporate Finance: An Introduction covers all the topics of the usual corporate finance curriculum. However, as noted above, the organizing principle of moving from perfect to imperfect markets unifies the core chapters. This progression from financial "utopia" to the complex real world is especially apparent in the first three parts of the book and is revisited multiple times in Part V on capital structure.

Part I: Value and Capital Budgeting shows how to work with rates of return and how to decide whether to take or reject projects in a perfect market under risk neutrality. Five chapters lay out the basics of the time value of money, net present value, valuation of perpetuities and annuities, capital budgeting, interest rates, and the concept of uncertainty in the absence of risk aversion.

. . . The transition from perfect to imperfect markets makes a lot of sense . . . and is consistent with the overall theme of the book, which is starting with simple concepts and gradually introducing more complex, realistic elements. I . . . like to structure my lectures according to similar logic.
—Evgeny Lyandres
Boston University

Part II: Risk and Return introduces risk aversion and shows how it creates a relation between risk and expected returns in a perfect market. It also provides a historical backdrop of rates of return on various asset classes and some institutional background. It then proceeds to the key concepts of risk, reward, and diversification from an investor's perspective, and culminates with a discussion of the Capital Asset Pricing Model.

Part III: Value and Market Efficiency in an Imperfect Market describes what happens if the perfect market assumptions do not hold in our messier real world. Although the perfect market assumptions form the basis of most finance formulas (such as NPV and the CAPM) and have facilitated the development of finance into a modern science, they are principally conceptual, not real. Thus, in this part, two chapters examine the reality of information differences, noncompetitive markets, transaction costs, and taxes. The differences between efficient and inefficient markets, and between rational and behavioral finance, are also explained.

Part IV: Real-World Application puts the theory to work in three chapters. It shows that although the financial concepts may be simple, their application can be complex. This part examine a wide swath of issues and pitfalls to consider when putting NPV and IRR to work, looks at financial statement analysis from a finance perspective, and considers the valuation technique of comparables.

Part V: Capital Structure and Payout Policy considers the capital structure that firms should choose. It starts again with a perfect-market theme and then shows in five chapters how this should play out in an imperfect world of corporate taxes and other issues. Some market imperfections should push firms toward more equity and others toward more debt.

Part VI: Projecting the Future shows how to think about the construction of pro formas. In a certain sense, it is what much of corporate finance is all about.

Part VII: Additional Topics contains six chapters for which the length of many corporate finance courses has little time. For those interested, there are treatments of capital structure dynamics, capital structure patterns in the United States, investment banking and M&A, corporate governance, international finance, and options. Moreover, the book's website (www.prenhall.com/welch) has a chapter on quantitative real option implementation.

Acknowledgments

I owe a great deal of gratitude to my publishing team, my colleagues, and my students. Other than myself, no one has put more love and care into this book than my development editor and project manager, Mary Clare McEwing. I am deeply indebted to her. This is the only text passage in this book that she did not get to edit. Thus, I am trying to acknowledge in the best way I know how much her editing has improved my presentation: It is impossible to overstate the positive influence she has had on this book. I hope that the publisher pays her twice as much as they do now. She deserves it.

My editor in chief Donna Battista was simply terrific. I could not have asked for anyone better. It is still a bit of a mystery to me how she can survive dealing with author prima donnas like me.

Kathryn Dinovo, Nancy Fenton, Jeff Holcomb, Heather McNally, and Paul Anagnostopoulos and his team of Rick Camp, Jennifer McClain, and Jacqui Scarlott did a great production job. At around my twelfth request to revise, they must have realized that they were not dealing with someone normal here. I also salute Susan Schoenberg, Miguel Leonarte, Barbara Atkinson, Kerri McQueen, and Bethany Tidd for the unique talents that they each brought to this project.

Marianne Plunkert, Joe Walker, Belinda Mucklow, and Michelle Moses not only found errors in earlier drafts of the book but also helped me to explain some of the concepts better. Mark McNabb helped greatly by writing the Instructor's Manual and PowerPoint slides. Kudos to all of them. Additional special thanks to Marianne Plunkert, who did a superb job in preparing the Test Bank and fleshing out many of the solutions to end-of-chapter problems as an aid to the student.

There are many colleagues who made a real intellectual contribution. First and foremost, there is Matthew Spiegel. He taught the introductory course at Yale when I joined the lineup, so I admit to having learned a lot from his notes, support, and advice. (Of course, Matt has used up all his brownie points with me by sending me too many RFS papers to referee.) Geert Rouwenhorst and Ira Millstein helped with the international finance and corporate governance chapters, respectively.

As early users of the book, Effi Benmelech and Diego Garcia provided expert feedback. Their positive reactions helped steer me through those moments when I had doubts about my sanity in spending 5 years of my life in writing a textbook. (I now believe that I have a much better sense of my sanity—not necessarily a good thing.)

Many other colleagues and students—too numerous to mention individually—contributed to honing the book's presentation along the way. I would like to single out Don Brown, Eric Talley, Tim Opler, Jay Ritter, Kathy Spiegel, and especially my wife, Lily Qiu. I am also grateful for the patience of many student victims, who had to act as beta testers during the book's evolution.

To all of these individuals, my profound thanks. You are all in this book.

—Ivo Welch

CONTRIBUTORS

I am most grateful to those fellow teachers who took the time to review, to be interviewed, and to take part in market research. Their input has been invaluable and has contributed enormously to improving the presentation. Although all provided well-considered input and thoughtful suggestions, I want to especially focus the spotlight on the following reviewers who gave above and beyond the scope of our review questions: Jennifer Conrad, University of North Carolina; Evgeny Lyandres, Rice University; Holger Mueller, New York University; Mitchell Petersen, Northwestern University; Marianne Plunkert, University of Colorado, Denver; William Reese, Tulane University; Robert Ritchey, Texas Tech University; Bruce Rubin, Old Dominion University; and Joe Walker, University of Alabama, Birmingham.

I also thank the following individuals who gave willingly of both their time and expertise:

Paul Adams, *University of Cincinnati*
Heitor Almeida, *New York University*
Ted Azarmi, *California State University, Long Beach*
Curtis Bacon, *Southern Oregon University*
Sung Bae, *Bowling Green State University*
Brad Barber, *University of California, Davis*
Chenchu Bathala, *Cleveland State University*
Deb Bauer, *University of Oregon*
Antonio Bernardo, *University of California, Los Angeles*
Sandro Brusco, *State University of New York at Stony Brook*
David Carter, *Oklahoma State University*
George Chang, *Bradley University*
Chao Chen, *California State University, Northridge*
Hsiang Lin Chih, *National Taipei University*
William Christie, *Vanderbilt University*
Patricia Clarke, *Simmons College*
Jonathan Clarke, *Georgia Institute of Technology*
Reid Click, *George Washington University*
Rebel Cole, *DePaul University*
Jennifer Conrad, *University of North Carolina, Chapel Hill*
Josh Coval, *Harvard Business School*
Stephen D'Arcy, *University of Illinois, Urbana-Champaign*
Richard DeMong, *University of Virginia*
Amy Dittmar, *University of Michigan*
Olubunmi Faleye, *Northeastern University*
Richard Fendler, *Georgia State University*
Thierry Foucault, *HEC School of Management, Paris*
Melissa Frye, *University of Central Florida*
Diego Garcia, *University of North Carolina, Chapel Hill*
Jon Garfinkel, *University of Iowa*
Sharon Garrison, *University of Arizona*
James Gatti, *University of Vermont*
Adam Gehr, *DePaul University*
Simon Gervais, *Duke University*
Thomas Geurts, *New York University*
Deborah Gregory, *University of Arizona*
Richard Gritta, *University of Portland*
Vidhan Goyal, *Hong Kong University of Science and Technology*
Terry Grieb, *University of Idaho*
Anurag Gupta, *Case Western Reserve University*
Abdul Habib, *Babson College*
Robert Hansen, *Tulane University*
Giora Harpaz, *CUNY Bernard Baruch*
Diana Harrington, *Babson College*
Milton Harris, *University of Chicago*
Jay Hartzell, *University of Texas, Austin*
J. Ronald Hoffmeister, *Arizona State University*
Jim Hsieh, *George Mason University*
Narayanan Jayaraman, *Georgia Institute of Technology*

Kurt Jesswein, *Sam Houston State University*
Wei Jiang, *Columbia University*
Fred Kaen, *University of New Hampshire*
Ayla Kayhan, *Louisiana State University*
Darren Kisgen, *Boston College*
Elinda Kiss, *University of Maryland, College Park*
Mark Klock, *George Washington University*
Brian Kluger, *University of Cincinnati*
Yrjo Koskinen, *Boston University*
Robert Krainer, *University of Wisconsin, Madison*
C.N.V. Krishnan, *Case Western Reserve University*
Karen Eilers Lahey, *University of Akron*
Paul Laux, *Case Western Reserve University*
Angeline Lavin, *University of South Dakota*
Mark Leary, *Cornell University*
Scott Lee, *Texas A&M University*
Sandy Leeds, *University of Texas, Austin*
Evgeny Lyandres, *Boston University*
Bala Maniam, *Sam Houston State University*
Brian Maris, *Northern Arizona University*
Ike Mathur, *Southern Illinois University, Carbondale*
Joseph McCarthy, *Bryant College*
Mark McNabb, *University of Cincinnati*
Richard Mendenhall, *University of Notre Dame*
John Mitchell, *Central Michigan University*
Bruce Mizrach, *Rutgers University, New Brunswick*
Tobias Moskowitz, *University of Chicago*
Belinda Mucklow, *University of Wisconsin, Madison*
Holger Mueller, *New York University*
Jim Musumeci, *Southern Illinois University, Carbondale*
James Nelson, *East Carolina University*
Henry Oppenheimer, *University of Rhode Island*
Michael Pagano, *Villanova University*
Don Panton, *University of Texas, Arlington*
Sarah Peck, *Marquette University*
Mitchell Petersen, *Northwestern University*
J. Michael Pinegar, *Brigham Young University*
Marianne Plunkert, *University of Colorado, Denver*
Andrew Pramschufer, *Calif. State University, Long Beach*
Cyrus Ramezani, *California State Poly, San Luis Obispo*
Raghavendra Rau, *Purdue University*
Ravi Ravichandran, *Loyola University of Chicago*
William Reese, Jr., *Tulane University*
Robert Ritchey, *Texas Tech University*
Brian Routledge, *Carnegie Mellon University*
Bruce Rubin, *Old Dominion University*
Salil Sarkar, *University of Texas, Arlington*
Husayn Shahrur, *Bentley College*
Jay Shanken, *Emory University*
Mark Simonson, *Arizona State University*
W. Gary Simpson, *Oklahoma State University*
Andrew Spieler, *Hofstra University*
Christopher Stivers, *University of Georgia*
Mark Hoven Stohs, *California State University, Fullerton*
Timothy Sullivan, *Bentley College*
Samuel Szewczyk, *Drexel University*
Robert Taggart, *Boston College*
Martin Thomas, *Drexel University*
John Thornton, *Kent State University*
K. C. Tseng, *California State University, Fresno*
Sorin Tuluca, *Fairleigh Dickinson University*
Harry Turtle, *Washington State University*
Joel Vanden, *Dartmouth College*
Belen Villalonga, *Harvard Business School*
Joseph Vu, *DePaul University*
Mahmoud Wahab, *University of Hartford*
Joe Walker, *University of Alabama, Birmingham*
Gwendolyn Webb, *CUNY Bernard Baruch*
Jill Wetmore, *Saginaw Valley State University*
John White, *Georgia Southern University*
Bob Wood, Jr., *Tennessee Tech University*
Yildiray Yildirim, *Syracuse University*
Jamie Zender, *University of Colorado, Boulder*
Mei Zhang, *Mercer University*

Innovations

PERFECT TO IMPERFECT MARKETS: AN ORGANIZING FRAMEWORK

The author structures a unique organizational framework that builds from perfect to imperfect markets—a novel, but natural, way to proceed from the simple to the complex. This approach springs from the fact that every important financial concept has been first derived in a perfect markets context.

WHERE IT'S DONE	HOW IT'S DONE	WHAT THEY'RE SAYING
CHAPTERS 2–4 TVM NPV Annuities & Perpetuities	**START WITH SIMPLICITY** Early on, the financial landscape is a risk-free world with no taxes, no transaction costs, no disagreements, and no limits to the number of buyers and sellers. We also assume, for convenience, that there is no uncertainty and no inflation and that interest rates are constant.	*In many ways it reflects the way in which we approach questions intuitively. We often teach concepts in this order, but without clearly explaining to students the progression that the perfect-to-imperfect approach makes so clear.* Gwendolyn Webb CUNY Baruch
CHAPTER 5 Time-varying rates of return, including Treasuries and yield curves	**ADD COMPLEXITY LAYER** Interest rates are no longer constant; they change over time.	*. . . a distinctive approach to introductory finance . . . a very clear and logical way to develop finance concepts, from the simplest case (where everything works) to the more complex (where application of the basic concepts becomes more problematic).* Robert Taggart Boston College
CHAPTER 6 Uncertainty	**ADD COMPLEXITY LAYER** There is now uncertainty. We no longer know the future and need statistics to describe the probabilities. The distinction between debt and equity is introduced, as well as the difference between debt and equity.	*Masterful in the way [the author] develops topics by first providing an intuitive base before going into more conceptual depth.* Bruce Rubin Old Dominion University

Where It's Done	How It's Done	What They're Saying
CHAPTERS 7–9 Historical investment Risk and reward Capital Asset Pricing Model	**ADD COMPLEXITY LAYER** The financial utopia becomes more complicated with the introduction of risk aversion. Portfolio optimization and then the CAPM are introduced.	*A breath of fresh air in the otherwise boring presentations found in competing products.* Kurt Jesswein Sam Houston State University
CHAPTERS 10–11 Market imperfections Efficient markets	**ADD COMPLEXITY LAYERS** The world now becomes truly imperfect with the advent of all sorts of frictions: disagreements, noncompetitive markets, transaction costs, and taxes.	*By discussing the limitations and challenges of perfect assumptions, the story becomes more complete and thus...more cohesive.* Mark McNabb University of Cincinnati
CHAPTERS 12–14 Applications	**ADD COMPLEXITY LAYERS** The real world is definitely messier than the perfect one!	*A fresh view on the classical questions discussed in finance textbooks.* Thierry Foucault HEC, Paris
CHAPTERS 15–16 Capital structure	**START WITH SIMPLICITY** We return to a perfect world for a consideration of debt and equity in an ideal sense.	*The book's progression . . . from a stylized and perfect capital market to one that resembles the real world by introducing additional layers of complexity . . . is refreshing and highly effective. . . . It is precisely how I teach corporate finance.* Holger Mueller New York University
CHAPTERS 17–19	**ADD COMPLEXITY LAYER** Taxes and other imperfections (some behavioral) ramp up the complexity.	*. . . A splendid job of integrating the dispersed materials of introductory finance courses. . . . Highly recommended.* Effi Benmelech Harvard University

Innovations

DISPELLING THE "FEAR OF FINANCE"

Students often enter the class with a fear of formulas, of theory, and of jargon. The author believes that deep down, finance is simple and that everyone can understand it. Welch wants to dispel such fears, and to that end, he approaches the subject in some unique ways.

Where It's Done	How It's Done	What They're Saying

NUMERICAL EXAMPLES

2.4A THE FUTURE VALUE OF MONEY

How much money will you receive in the future if t
invest $100 today? Turn around the rate of return foi
how money will grow over time given a rate of retur

$$20\% = \frac{\$120 - \$100}{\$100} \Leftrightarrow \$100 \cdot (1 + 20\%$$

$$r_1 = \frac{C_1 - C_0}{C_0} \Leftrightarrow C_0 \cdot (1 + r_1)$$

The $120 next year is called the future value (FV) o
the value of a present cash amount at some point in

Numerical examples come first and then lead to formulas. Numbers are displayed in black; formulas in red.
Students learn how to think about problems rather than mechanically apply formulas.
To tackle tough problems, they start with the simple and uncomplicated.
The goal is to enable students to solve all sorts of new problems on their own.

I like the way the math calculations are introduced/explained. Using numbers to build to the formula is a pleasant change from other books.

Melissa Frye
University of Central Florida

The use of numerical examples… will go a long way to building understanding and intuition for… difficult material.

Jaime Zender
University of Colorado

HOW BAD ARE MISTAKES?

How Bad Are Mistakes?

ERRORS IN CASH FLOWS VER
COST OF CAPITAL

Although it would be better to get everything pe
up with perfect cash flow forecasts and appropri
makes errors when outcomes in the world are unc
takes? Is it worse to commit an error in estimatin
of capital? To answer these questions, we will do
in which we consider a very simple project to lear
ter to the ultimate present value. Scenario analysi
need to learn how sensitive their estimated valu

In a feature called "How Bad Are Mistakes?" students see the relative magnitude of errors—some do not matter much and are tolerable, whereas others matter a great deal. The author also is upfront about where current theory may fall short.

The [How Bad Are Mistakes?] discussions are great. The quantitative aspects of the mistakes are not found in alternative books.

Evgeny Lyandres
Boston University

We owe it to students to explain when shortcuts will lead to small (tolerable) mistakes and when they lead to large (catastrophic) mistakes.

Mitchell Petersen
Northwestern University

Where It's Done	How It's Done	What They're Saying
SOLVE NOW! PROBLEMS	Students build confidence by working "Solve Now!" problems at the end of most sections, with complete solutions provided at the end of the chapter.	*The "Solve Nows" are great. This is better than just waiting until the end of the chapter.* Robert Ritchey, Texas Tech University

SOLVE NOW!

Q 2.35 Work out the present value of your tuiti
Assume that the tuition is $30,000 per
year. Your first tuition payment will occ
tuition payment will occur in 18 montl
interest rate of 6% per annum.

Q 2.35 The first tuition payment is worth $30,0(
$\$30{,}000/(1.06)^{3/2} \approx \$27{,}489$. Thus, the tc

Where It's Done	How It's Done	What They're Saying
IMPORTANT BOXES	"Important" boxes provide a compendium of all key points and observations; they are the equivalent of what the student would highlight in a given chapter.	*The "Important" feature and the sidebars that summarize the main points of the paragraphs are good pedagogical aids.* Marianne Plunkert, University of Colorado, Denver

IMPORTANT: In a perfect world, if you have all the right inputs to NPV, no other rule can make better decisions. Thus, it is the appropriate decision benchmark—and no other rule can beat it. This also means that information other than the NPV is redundant.

Where It's Done	How It's Done	What They're Saying
ANECDOTES	Anecdotes spice up the presentation with snippets from contemporary and historical finance.	*Anecdotes stress that finance is not an abstraction, but an agglomeration of ideas that have value in the conduct of everyday business and everyday life.* Mei Zhang, Mercer University

ANECDOTE Fibonacci and the Invention of Net Present Value

William Goetzmann argues that Leonardo of Pisa, commonly called Fibonacci, may have invented not only the famous "Fibonacci series" but also the concept of net present value.

Fibonacci's family were merchants in the Mediterranean in the thirteenth century, with trade relations to Arab merchants in Northern Africa. Fibonacci wrote about mathematics primarily as a tool to solve merchants' problems—in effect, to understand the pricing of goods and currencies relative to one another. Think about how rich you could get if you could determine faster than your competition which goods were worth more in relation to others! In fact, you should think of Fibonacci and other Pisan merchants as the "financial engineers" of the thirteenth century.

Fibonacci wrote his most famous treatise, *Liber Abaci*, at age 30, publishing it in 1202. We still are solving the same kinds of problems today that Fibonacci explained. One of them—which you will solve at the end of this chapter—is called "On a Soldier Receiving 300 Bezants for His Fief":

> A soldier is granted an annuity by the king of 300 bezants per year, paid in quarterly installments of 75 bezants. The king alters the payment schedule to an annual year-end payment of 300. The soldier is able to earn 2 bezants on 100 per month (over each quarter) on his investment. How much is his effective compensation after the terms of the annuity changed?

To solve this problem, you must know how to value payments at different points in the future—you must understand the time value of money. What is the value of 75 bezants in 1 quarter, 2 quarters, and so forth? What is the value of 300 bezants in 1 year, 2 years, and so on? Yes, money sooner is usually worth more than money later—but you need to determine by exactly how much in order to determine how good or bad the change is for the king and the soldier. To answer, you must use the interest rate Fibonacci gives and then compare the two different cash flow streams—the original payment schedule and the revised payment schedule—in terms of a common denominator. This common denominator will be the two streams' present values.

myfinancelab

Because practice with homework problems is crucial to learning finance, each copy of *Corporate Finance* is available with **MyFinanceLab**, a fully integrated homework and tutorial system.

Online Assessment Using End-of-Chapter Problems

The seamless integration among the textbook, assessment materials, and online resources sets a new standard in corporate finance education.

- **End-of-chapter problems** appear online. The values in the problems are algorithmically generated, giving students many opportunities for practice and mastery. Problems can be assigned by professors and completed online by students.

- **Helpful tutorial tools,** along with the same pedagogical aids from the text, support students as they study. Links to the eText direct students right to the material they most need to review.

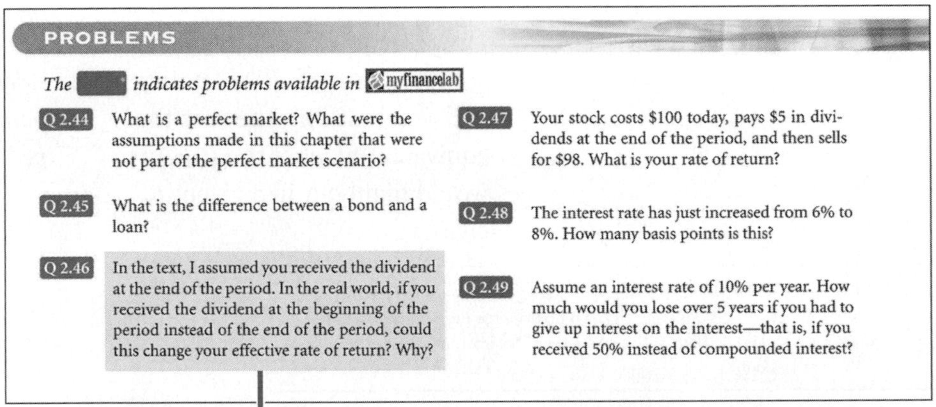

PROBLEMS

The ▬ *indicates problems available in* myfinancelab

Q 2.44 What is a perfect market? What were the assumptions made in this chapter that were not part of the perfect market scenario?

Q 2.45 What is the difference between a bond and a loan?

Q 2.46 In the text, I assumed you received the dividend at the end of the period. In the real world, if you received the dividend at the beginning of the period instead of the end of the period, could this change your effective rate of return? Why?

Q 2.47 Your stock costs $100 today, pays $5 in dividends at the end of the period, and then sells for $98. What is your rate of return?

Q 2.48 The interest rate has just increased from 6% to 8%. How many basis points is this?

Q 2.49 Assume an interest rate of 10% per year. How much would you lose over 5 years if you had to give up interest on the interest—that is, if you received 50% instead of compounded interest?

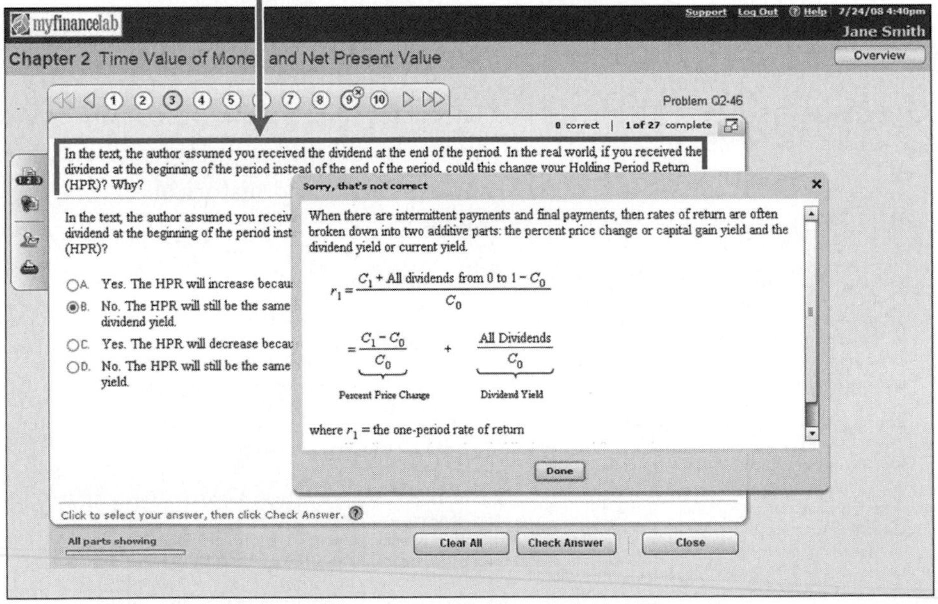

To learn more about MyFinanceLab, contact your local Prentice Hall representative or go online to www.myfinancelab.com

Hands-On Practice, Hands-Off Grading

- **Hands-on, Targeted Practice** Students can take pre-loaded practice tests for each chapter, and their test results will generate an individualized Study Plan. With the Study Plan, students learn to focus their energies on the topics they need to be successful in class, on exams, and, ultimately, in their future careers.

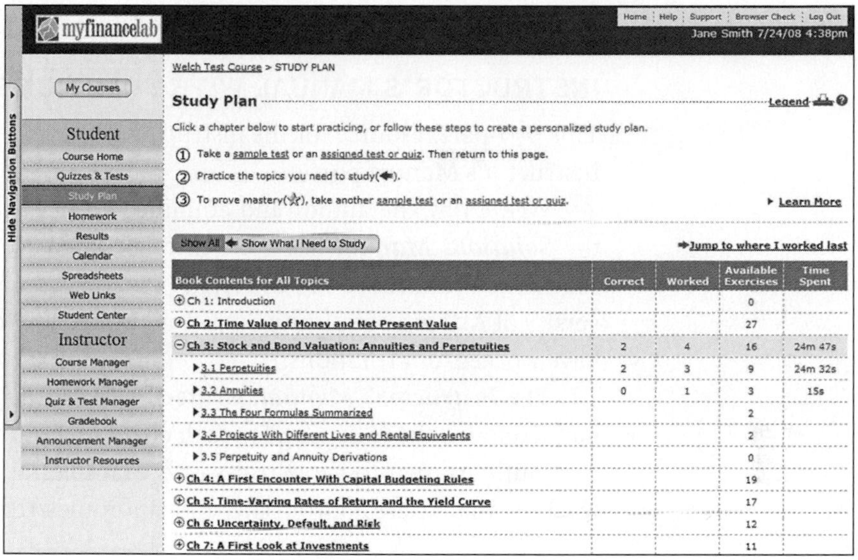

Powerful Instructor Tools

MyFinanceLab provides flexible tools that enable instructors to easily customize the online course materials to suit their needs.

- **Easy-to-Use Homework Manager** Instructors can easily create and assign tests, quizzes, or graded homework assignments. In addition to pre-loaded **MyFinanceLab** questions, the Test Bank is also available so that instructors have ample material with which to create assignments.

- **Flexible Gradebook** **MyFinanceLab** saves time by automatically grading students' work and tracking results in an online Gradebook.

- **Downloadable Classroom Resources** Instructors also have access to online versions of each instructor supplement, including the Instructor's Manual, PowerPoint Lecture Notes, and Test Bank.

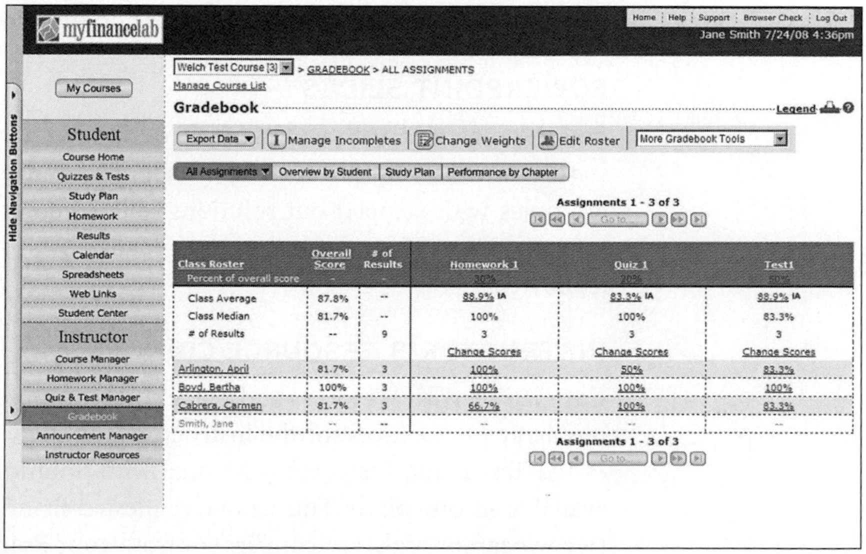

Resources for Instructor and Student

FOR THE INSTRUCTOR

INSTRUCTOR'S MANUAL WITH SOLUTIONS

This two-part resource for the instructor includes a Solutions Manual portion and an Instructor's Manual portion.

Written by the author and amplified with stepped solutions where appropriate, the ***Solutions Manual*** has gone through intensive rounds of accuracy checking by Marianne Plunkert of the University of Colorado at Denver, Joe Walker of the University of Alabama at Birmingham, and Michelle Moses. All end-of-chapter problems have worked-out solutions.

The ***Instructor's Manual***, written by Mark McNabb of the University of Cincinnati, contains the following for each chapter: a pithy chapter overview, extended lecture outlines, two to three real-world examples appropriate to the chapter content, teaching tips where appropriate, and landmines/trouble spots where warranted.

TEST BANK AND COMPUTERIZED TEST BANK

Written by Marianne Plunkert of the University of Colorado at Denver, the Test Bank features multiple-choice and short essay questions, some with a true-false orientation, for each chapter. Questions are carefully divided by major chapter sections and are identified by topic and level of difficulty. About 40 percent of all questions are numerical/mathematical in nature. All in all, there are approximately 1600 questions in the Test Bank, and all solutions have been checked for accuracy by Joe Walker of the University of Alabama at Birmingham. The Test Bank is available to professors as downloadable PDFs and Word files at **www.pearsonhighered.com/irc**. It is also available in printed form, and in the TestGen program—an easy-to-use testing software that allows instructors to view, edit, and add questions.

POWERPOINT SLIDES

PowerPoint slides, authored by Mark McNabb of the University of Cincinnati, contain lecture outlines, figures from the textbook, and an assortment of freshly worked examples with stepped-out solutions—all different from the text but based on the same concepts. These files can be downloaded by professors at **www.pearsonhighered.com/irc**.

INSTRUCTOR'S RESOURCE CD-ROM

Compatible with Windows and Macintosh computers, this CD-ROM offers a generous array of resources for the instructor. Complete files for the Test Bank, Computerized Test Bank, Instructor's Manual with Solutions, and PowerPoint slides are all available in one place. This can be requested from the Instructor's Resource Center (**www.pearsonhighered.com/irc**) or from your Pearson Professional and Career sales representative.

FOR THE STUDENT

MYFINANCELAB

This premium product gives students the practice and tutorial help they need to learn finance efficiently. A more detailed description can be found on pages xviii–xix.

SOLUTIONS MANUAL FOR THE STUDENT

This manual is the same as the solutions portion of the Instructor's Manual with Solutions. It is available for purchase or can be packaged with the text at a discount.

BOOK WEB SITE

The Web site accompanying the text at **www.prenhall.com/welch** has a number of features of interest to both students and instructors. All of the Web sites mentioned in the text have been hard-wired from the book site for convenience. The site includes one of the author's most interesting papers on "The Top Achievements, Challenges, and Failures of Finance" to pique student interest in the concept of finance as an evolving discipline.

Instructors will find an additional chapter on real options, which they may want to include in their courses, depending on time and interest. They will also find sample exams, with answers, from the author's own classes.

The author also maintains a Web site at **http://welch.econ.brown.edu**, where students and instructors can find additional relevant materials.

WALL STREET JOURNAL EDITION

When packaged with this text, Prentice Hall offers students a reduced-cost, 10- or 15-week subscription to the *Wall Street Journal* print edition and the *Wall Street Journal* Interactive Edition.

FINANCIAL TIMES EDITION

Featuring international news and analysis from journalists in more than 50 countries, the *Financial Times* provides insights and perspectives on financial and economic developments around the world. For a small charge, a 15-week subscription to the *Financial Times* can be included with each new textbook.

Brief Contents

Contents

1

Introduction

WHAT FINANCE IS ALL ABOUT

Finance is such an important part of modern life that almost everyone can benefit from understanding it better. What you may find surprising is that the financial problems facing *PepsiCo* or *Microsoft* are not really different from those facing an average investor, small business owner, entrepreneur, or family. On the most basic level, these problems are about how to allocate money. The choices are many: Money can be borrowed, saved, or lent. Money can be invested into projects. Projects can be undertaken with partners or with the aid of lenders. Projects can be avoided altogether if they do not appear to be valuable enough. Finance is about how best to decide among these and other investment alternatives—and this textbook will explain how.

1.1 THE GOAL OF FINANCE: RELATIVE VALUATION

There is one principal theme that carries through all of finance. It is *value*. What exactly is a particular object worth? To make smart decisions, you must be able to assess value—and the better you can assess value, the smarter your decisions will be.

Theme number one of this book is *value!* Make decisions based on value.

The main reason why you need to estimate value is that you will want to buy objects whose values are above their costs and avoid those where it is the reverse. Sounds easy? If it were only so. In practice, finding a good value (**valuation**) is often very difficult. But it is not the formulas that are difficult—even the most complex formulas in this book contain just a few symbols, and the overwhelming majority of finance formulas use only the five major operations (addition, subtraction, multiplication, division, and exponentiation). Admittedly, even if the formulas themselves are not sophisticated, there are a lot of them, and they have an intuitive economic meaning that requires experience to grasp. But if you managed to pass high-school algebra, and

Everyone needs to know how to value objects.

if you are motivated, you will be able to handle the math. It is *not* the math that is the real difficulty in valuation.

The tough aspect about valuation is the real world, not the theory.

Instead, the big difficulties lie in the real world, beyond finance theory. You often have to decide how you should judge the future—whether your gizmo will be a hit or a bust, whether the economy will enter a recession or not, where you will find product markets, how you can advertise, how interest rates or the stock market will move, and on and on. This book will explain what you should forecast and how you should use your forecasts in the best way, but it mostly remains up to you to make these forecasts. Putting this more positively, if forecasts and valuation were easy, a computer could take over this job. This will never happen. Valuation will always remain a matter of both art and science, which requires judgment and common sense. The formulas and finance in this book are only the necessary tools to convert your reasoned, informed, and intuitive estimates of the future into the information that you need today to make good decisions.

1.1A THE LAW OF ONE PRICE

The law of one price. Valuing objects is easier in relative terms.

So how do you assess value? Most of finance and thus most of this book is based in some form or another on the **law of one price**. It states that two identical items at the same venue should sell for the same price. Otherwise, why would anyone buy the more expensive item? This law of one price is the logic upon which virtually all valuation is based. It is important that you realize that this means that value in finance is defined in *relative* terms. The reason is that it is easier to determine whether an object is worth more or less than equivalent alternatives than it is to put an absolute value on it.

A car example.

For example, consider the value of a car—say, a 2007 Toyota Camry—that you own. If you can find other cars that are identical—at least along all dimensions that matter—to your Camry, then it should be worth the same and sell for the same price. Fortunately, for a 2007 Toyota Camry, this is not too difficult. There are many other 2007 Toyota Camries, as well as 2006 Toyota Camries, 2008 Toyota Camries, and 2007 Honda Accords, that you can readily purchase. If there are 10 other exact equivalents on the same block for sale, your valuation task is outright trivial.

Mistakes, both too low and too high, are costly.

What would happen if you make a mistake in valuing your Camry? If you put too low a value on your car, you would sell it too cheaply. If you put too high a value on your car, you would not be able to sell it. Naturally, you want to get the value right.

Don't forget opportunity costs.

A related way of thinking about your Camry versus the alternatives is that your Camry has an "opportunity cost." Your ownership of the Camry is not free. Ignoring transaction costs, your opportunity is to sell your car and purchase another Camry, or Accord, or anything else with this money. Let's say that the Accord is your alternative, and it is equivalent in all dimensions that matter. If someone were to offer to pay $1,000 above the Accord value for your Camry, the price would be above your opportunity cost. You should then sell the Camry, buy the Accord, and gain $1,000.

Approximations: Similar goods that are not perfectly the same.

The law of one price rarely applies perfectly. But it often applies "almost." For example, your Camry may have 65,334 miles on it, be green, and be located in Providence, RI. The comparable cars may have between 30,000 and 50,000 miles on them, feature different colors, and be located in other spots on the East Coast. In this case, the law of one price no longer works exactly. Instead, it should hold only approximately. That is, your car may not be worth the same exact amount as your compa-

ANECDOTE The Joy of Cooking: Positive Prestige Flows and Restaurant Failures

In New York City, two out of every five new restaurants close within 1 year. Nationwide, the best estimates suggest that about 90% of all restaurants close within 2 years. If successful, the average restaurant earns a return of about 10% per year. One explanation for why so many entrepreneurs are continuing to open up restaurants, despite seemingly low financial rates of return, is that restaurateurs enjoy owning a restaurant so much that they are willing to buy the prestige of owning one. If this is the case, then to value the restaurant, you must factor in how much the restaurateur is willing to pay for the prestige of owning it, just as you would factor in the revenues that restaurant patrons generate.

rables, but it should be worth a similar amount, perhaps using a few sensible price adjustments.

In the absence of similar objects, valuation is more difficult.

The task of valuing objects becomes more difficult when you are unable (or not allowed) to find similar objects for which you know the value. If you had to value your 2007 Camry based on knowledge of the value of plasma televisions, vacations, or pencils, then your valuation task would be much more difficult. It is just common sense that it is easier to value objects relative to close comparables than to objects that are very different. In the real world, some objects are intrinsically easy to value; others are very difficult to value.

SOLVE NOW!

Q 1.1 Discuss how easy it is to put a value on the following objects:
(a) An envelope containing foreign currency—say, 10,000 euros
(b) Paintings
(c) The Washington Monument
(d) Manhattan
(e) The Chrysler Building in New York
(f) Foreign stamps
(g) Love
(h) Yourself
(i) The species chimpanzee, or the Yangtze river dolphin

1.2 INVESTMENTS, PROJECTS, AND FIRMS

To value projects, make sure to use all costs and benefits, including opportunity costs and pleasure benefits.

The most basic object in finance is the project. As far as finance is concerned, every **project** is a set of flows of money (**cash flows**). Most projects require an upfront cash outflow (an **investment** or **expense** or **cost**) and are followed by a series of later cash inflows (**payoffs** or **revenues** or **returns**). It does not matter whether the cash flows come from hauling garbage or selling Prada handbags. Cash is cash. However, it is important that all costs and benefits are included as cash values. If you have to spend a lot of time hauling trash, which you find distasteful, then you have to translate your dislike into an equivalent cash negative. Similarly, if you want to do a project "for the fun of it," you must translate your "fun" into a cash positive. The discipline of finance takes over after all positives and negatives (inflows and outflows) from the project "black box" have been translated into their appropriate monetary cash values.

What is in the black box "project" is not trivial, but we won't cover much of it.

This does not mean that the operations of the firm—issues like manufacturing, inventory, sales, marketing, payables, working capital, competition, and so on—are unimportant. On the contrary, these business factors are all of the utmost importance in making the cash flows happen, and a good (financial) manager must understand them. After all, even if all you care about are cash flows, it is impossible to understand them well if you have no idea where they come from and how they could change in the future.

Cash flows must include (quantify) nonfinancial benefits.

Projects need not be physical. For example, a company may have a project called "customer relations," with real cash outflows today and uncertain future inflows. You (a student) can be viewed as a project: You pay for education (a cash outflow) and will earn a salary in the future (a cash inflow). If you value the prestige that the degree will offer, you should also put a cash value on it. Then, this too will count as another cash inflow. In addition, some of the payoffs from education are metaphysical rather than physical. If you like making friends in school or if knowledge provides you with pleasure, either today or in the future, then education yields a value that should be regarded as a positive cash flow. (The discipline of finance makes it easy on itself by asking *you* to put a hard cash value number on these or any other emotional factors.) Of course, for some students, the distaste of learning should be factored in as a cost (equivalent cash outflow)—but I trust that you are not one of them. All such nonfinancial flows must be appropriately translated into cash equivalents if you want to arrive at a good project valuation.

In finance, firms are basically collections of projects.

In finance, a **firm** is viewed as a collection of projects. This book assumes that the value of a firm is the value of all its projects' net cash flows, and nothing else. Actually, the metaphor can also extend to a family. Your family may own a house, a car, have tuition payments, education investments, and so on—a collection of projects.

The firm is the sum of all its inflows and all its outflows. Stocks and bonds are just projects with inflows and outflows.

There are two important specific kinds of projects that you may consider investing in—**bonds** and **stocks**, also called **debt** and **equity**. These are financial **claims** that the firm usually sells to investors. As you will learn later, you can mostly think of buying a stock as the equivalent of becoming an owner. You can think of buying a bond as the equivalent of lending money to the issuer. In effect, a bondholder is just a creditor. For example, a firm may sell a lender a $100 bond in exchange for a promised payment of $110 next year. (If the firm were to perform poorly, the bond would have to be paid off first, so it is less risky for an investor than the firm's equity. However, it has limited upside.) In addition, the firm usually has other obligations, such as money that it has to pay to its suppliers (called "payables"). Together, if you own all outstanding claims on the firm, that is, all obligations and all stock, then you own the firm. This logic is not deep—simply speaking, there is nobody else: "You are it."

$$\text{Entire Firm} = \text{All Outstanding Stocks} + \text{All Outstanding Liabilities}$$

As the 100% owner of a firm, you own all its stocks, bonds, and other obligations. Your entire firm then does its business and hopefully earns money. It does not need to pay out immediately what it earns, though. It can reinvest the money. Regardless of what the firm does, you still own it in its entirety. This means you own all net cash flows that the firm earns, after adjusting for all your necessary investments.

$$\text{Entire Firm} = \text{All Current and Future } \textit{Net} \text{ Earnings}$$

Yet another way to look at the firm is to recognize that you will receive all the net cash flows that the firm will pay out (e.g., interest payments or dividends), adjusting, of course, for all the money that you may put into the firm in the future.

$$\text{Entire Firm} = \text{All Current and Future Cash Inflows} - \text{Outflows}$$

It follows immediately that all the payments satisfying stocks and liabilities must be equal to all the firm's net cash flows, which must be equal to the firm's net payouts. All of these equalities really just state the same thing: "Value adds up."

We emphasize stocks and bonds.

Our book will spend a lot of time discussing claims, and especially the debt and equity forms of financing—but for now, you can consider both debt and equity to be just simple investment projects: You put money in, and they pay money out. For many stock and bond investments that you can buy and sell in the financial markets, it is reasonable to assume that most investors enjoy very few, if any, non-cash-based benefits (such as emotional attachment).

SOLVE NOW!

Q 1.2 In computing the cost of your M.B.A., should you take into account the loss of salary while going to school? Cite a few nonmonetary benefits that you reap as a student, too, and try to attach monetary value to them.

Q 1.3 If you purchase a house and live in it, what are your inflows and outflows?

1.3 FIRMS VERSUS INDIVIDUALS

We use the same principles in corporate finance as in "home economics."

This book is primarily about teaching concepts that apply to firms. In particular, if you are reading this, your goal will be to learn how you should determine projects' values, given appropriate cash flows. What is your best tool? The law of one price, of course.

Relative valuation often works well in the corporate world.

The same logic that applies to your Camry applies to corporate projects in the real world. They often have close comparables that make such relative valuation feasible. For example, say you want to put a value on a new factory that you would build in Rhode Island. You have many alternatives: You could determine the value of a similar factory that you could buy in Massachusetts, instead; or you could determine the value of a similar factory in Mexico; or you could determine how much it would cost you just to purchase the net output of a factory from another company; or you could determine how much money you could earn if you invest your money instead into the stock market or deposit it into a savings account. If you understand how to estimate your factory's value *relative to your other opportunities*, you then know whether you should build it or not. But not all projects are easy to value in relative terms. For example, what would be the value of building a tunnel across the

Atlantic, of controlling global warming, or of terraforming Mars to make it habitable for humans? There are no easy alternative objects to compare such projects to, so any valuation would inevitably be haphazard.

Value in the corporate context can depend on the quality of the market.

If a corporation can determine the value of projects, then it can determine whether it should take or pass up on them. In the first part of this book, where we assume that the world is perfect (which will be explained in a moment), you will learn that projects have a unique value and firms should take all projects that add value (in an absolute sense). Later on, the world will become more realistic, and you will recognize that projects can have a value that is different for some firms than it is for others. In this case, you must take your specific firm's position into account when deciding whether you should take or leave projects.

Separation of ownership and management (control).

An interesting aspect of corporate decision making is that the owners are often not the managers. Instead, the managers are hired professionals. For a publicly traded corporation that may have millions of shareholder owners, even the decision to hire managers is de facto no longer made by the owners, but by their representatives and by other managers.

Managers should do what owners want—value maximization!?

Unfortunately, it is just not feasible for managers simply to ask all the owners what they want. Therefore, one of the basic premises of finance is that owners expect their managers to maximize the value of the firm. You will learn that, in a perfect world, managers always know how to do this. However, in the world we live in, this can sometimes be difficult. How should a manager act if some owners dislike investing in cigarettes, some owners believe that the firm has great opportunities in selling green tea, some owners believe the firm should build warships, some owners believe the firm should just put all the money into the bank, and some owners believe the firm should return all their money to them? These are among the more intriguing problems that this book covers.

Ethical dilemmas.

The need for managers to decide on appropriate objectives also raises some interesting ethical concerns, most of which are beyond the scope of this book. But let me mention one, anyway. As I just noted, the standard view is that corporations are set up to maximize the wealth of their owners. It is the job of the government to create rules that constrain corporations to do so only within ethically appropriate boundaries. Thus, some will argue that it is the role of public institutions to pass laws that reduce the sale of products that kill (e.g., cigarettes), not the role of the corporation to abstain from selling them. If nothing else, they argue, if your corporation does not sell them, someone else almost surely will. (You can see this as a framework to help you understand corporations, not a normative opinion on what the moral obligations of companies should be. Nevertheless, it is also a view that many people have adopted as their normative perspective.) As if selling harmful products were not a complex enough dilemma, consider that laws are often passed by legislators who receive donations from tobacco corporations. (Indeed, public institutions are intentionally set up to facilitate such two-way "communications.") What are the moral obligations of tobacco firm owners, their corporations, and their managers now? Fortunately, you first need to learn about value maximization before you are ready to move on to these tougher questions. For the most part, this book sticks with the view that value maximization is the corporation's main objective.

Let's get rolling.

Let's begin looking at how you should estimate project value.

SOLVE NOW!

Q 1.4 Should you ever rely on the law of one price in your decision of whether to take or to reject projects?

Q 1.5 What is the main objective of corporate managers that this book assumes?

KEY TERMS

SOLVE NOW! SOLUTIONS

Q 1.1 Here are my own judgment calls.

(a) Easy. There are many foreign currency transactions, so you can easily figure out how many U.S. dollars you can get for 10,000 euros. You can find this exchange rate, e.g., at Yahoo! *Finance*.

(b) Depends. Some paintings are easier to value than others. For example, Warhol painted similar works repeatedly, and the price of one may be a good indication for the price of others. For other paintings, this can be very hard. What is the value of the *Mona Lisa,* for example? There are other da Vincis that may help, but ultimately, the *Mona Lisa* is unique.

(c) The Washington Monument is more than just the value of its closest alternative—which would be rebuilding it elsewhere. This may or may not be easy.

(d) Many individual buildings in Manhattan have sold, so you have good comparables for the individual components. However, no one has attempted to purchase a world center like Manhattan, which means that it may be difficult to estimate it accurately.

(e) The Chrysler Building would be relatively easy to value. There are many similar buildings that have changed hands in the last few years.

(f) Foreign stamps are harder to value than foreign currency, but probably not that much harder. Stamp collectors know and usually publish the prices at which the same stamps have traded in the past years.

(g) Love—oh, dear.

(h) Valuing yourself is a tough issue. You can look at yourself as a collection of cash flows, similar to other "walking cash flows," but doing so is highly error-prone. Nevertheless, having no other opportunities, this is how insurance companies attach a value to life in court. You may consider yourself more unique and irreplaceable. Still, you can infer your own value for your life by figuring out how willing you are to take the risk of losing it—e.g., by crossing the street, snowboarding, or motorcycling. I have also read that doctors work out what the value of all the proteins in your body are, which comes out to be many million dollars. Physicists, on the other hand, break down the proteins further and come up with an estimate that is less than a dollar.

(i) This is a very difficult task. We know that governments have spent a great amount of cash trying to preserve the environment in order to help species. The Yangtze river dolphin, however, just recently went extinct, primarily due to human activity. What is the value of this loss? Unfortunately, we don't have good comparables.

Q 1.2 Definitely yes. Forgone salary is a cost that you are bearing. This can be reasonably estimated, and many economic consulting firms regularly do so. As to (partly) nonmonetary benefits, there is the reputation that the degree offers you, the education that betters you, and the beer consumption pleasure, if applicable.

Q 1.3 Inflows: Value of implicit rent. Capital gain if house appreciates. Outflows: Maintenance costs. Transaction costs. Mortgage costs. Real estate tax. Uninsured potential losses. Capital loss if house depreciates. And so on.

Q 1.4 Absolutely yes. Indeed, the law of one price is the foundation upon which all project choice is based.

Q 1.5 Maximizing the value of the firm.

PROBLEMS

The indicates problems available in myfinancelab

Q 1.6 What is the law of one price?

Q 1.7 A degree program costs $50,000 in total expenses: $30,000 in tuition and $20,000 in housing and books. The U.S. government provides a grant for $10,000 of the tuition. Moreover, the university pays $20,000 of the $30,000 tuition in salary to your instructors. Being in the program is so much fun, you would be willing to pay a net of $5,000 for the pleasure, relative to your alternatives. What is the net cost of the education to you?

Q 1.8 What is the difference between investing in the stock and investing in the bond of a corporation? Which one is the less risky investment and why?

Q 1.9 What is the difference between the value of all outstanding obligations and all outstanding stocks versus the value of all underlying assets?

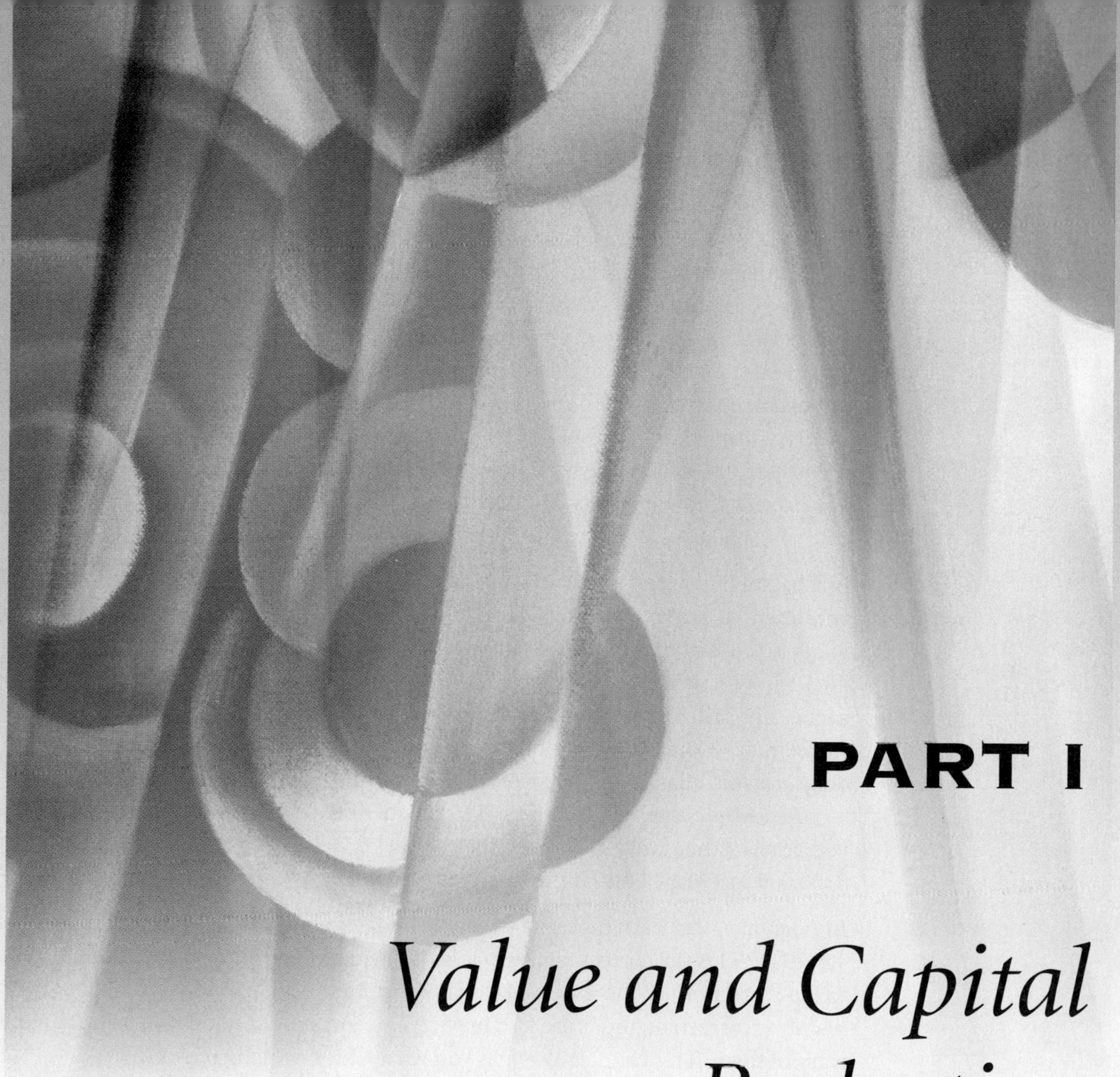

PART I

Value and Capital Budgeting

IN A PERFECT MARKET UNDER RISK NEUTRALITY

The two primary goals of this first part of the book (Chapters 2–6) are to explain how to work with rates of return and how to decide whether to accept or reject investment projects. We assume in this part that there are no taxes, no transaction costs, no disagreements, and no limits as to the number of sellers and buyers in the market. This is the so-called perfect market. I will explain later why a perfect market makes your life a lot easier.

WHAT YOU WANT TO LEARN IN THIS PART

- In Chapter 2, we start with the simplest possible scenario. In addition to the perfect market, we assume that there is no uncertainty: You know everything. And we assume that all rates of return in the economy are the same: A 1-year investment pays the same and perfectly known rate of return per annum as a 10-year investment. Under these assumptions, you learn how 1-year returns translate into multiyear returns and when you should accept or reject a project. The chapter introduces the important concept of "present value."

  Typical questions: If you earn 5% per year, how much will you earn over 10 years? If you earn 100% over 10 years, how much will you earn per year? What is the value of a project that will deliver $1,000,000 in 10 years? Should you buy this project if it cost you $650,000? What inputs do you need to decide this?

- In Chapter 3, you learn how to value particular kinds of projects—perpetuities and annuities—if the economy-wide interest rate remains constant. You then learn how to apply the formulas to the valuation of stocks and bonds. The popular Gordon dividend growth model for valuing stocks assumes that dividends are a simple growing perpetuity cash flow stream, which makes it a perfect application of the perpetuity formula. Mortgages and other bonds are good applications of pricing using the annuities formulas.

  Typical questions: If a firm pays $1/share dividends next year, growing by 3% per year forever, then what should its stock price be? What is the monthly payment for a $300,000 mortgage bond if the interest rate is 4% per year?

- In Chapter 4, you learn more about capital budgeting methods. Although net present value (NPV) is the correct method, at least one other common method often comes to the correct result: the internal rate of return. In the real world, a number of other, plainly incorrect, methods are also in wide use. You should know why you should be wary of them. This chapter also tells you what CFOs actually rely on.

  Typical questions: If a project has one investment outflow and two return inflows, how would you compute a "rate of return"? Can you accept projects whose rates of return are above their cost of capital? How bad is it when you use incorrect estimates—as you inevitably will—in your calculations? What are the big problems with a rule that accepts those projects that return money most quickly?

- In Chapter 5, you abandon the assumption that annual rates of return are the same regardless of the length of time of your investment. For example, 1-year investments may pay 2% per year, while 10-year investments may pay 5% per year. The scenario of time-varying rates of return is more realistic, but the questions that you want to answer still remain the same as those in Chapter 2. (The chapter then also explains more advanced aspects of bonds, such as the Treasury yield curve.)

  Typical questions: If you earn 5% in the first year and 10% in the second year, how much will you earn over both years? What is the meaning of a 4% annualized interest rate? What is the meaning of a 4% yield-to-maturity? How can you value projects if appropriate rates of return depend on different time horizons?

- In Chapter 6, you abandon the assumption that you know the future. To be able to study uncertainty in the real world, you must first learn how to describe it. This is done with statistics, the necessary aspects of which are explained here, too. The chapter then introduces risk neutrality, which is an assumption that can make it easier to understand some concepts in finance under uncertainty. Perhaps the two most important concepts are the difference between promised and expected rates of return and the difference between debt and equity. Under uncertainty, a project may not return the promised amount. Because of the possibility of default, the *stated* rate of return must be higher than the *expected* rate of return. Although you are interested in the latter, it is almost always only the former that you are quoted (promised). It is important that you always draw a sharp distinction between promised (stated) rates of return and expected rates of return. The second concept that this chapter explains is the difference between debt and equity—corporate claims that have a meaningful difference only under uncertainty.

Typical questions: If there is a 2% chance that your borrower will not return the money, how much extra interest should you charge? From an investment perspective, what is the difference between debt and equity? What is financing priority? What is a residual claim?

Looking ahead, Part II will continue with uncertainty scenarios in which investors are risk averse. Part III will explain what happens when financial markets or decision rules are not perfect.

The Time Value of Money and Net Present Value

THE MOTHER OF ALL FINANCE

We begin with the concept of a rate of return—the cornerstone of finance. You can always earn interest by depositing your money today into the bank. This means that money today is more valuable than the same amount of money next year. This concept is called the *time value of money*—\$1 in present value is better than \$1 in future value.

Investors make up just one side of the financial markets. They give money today in order to receive money in the future. Firms make up the other side. The process firms use to decide what to do with their money—which projects to take and which projects to pass up—is called *capital budgeting*. You will learn that there is one clear best method for making this critical decision. The firm should translate all *future* cash flows—both inflows and outflows—into their equivalent *present values* today, and then add them up to find the *net present value*, or NPV. The firm should take all projects that have positive net present values and reject all projects that have negative net present values.

This all sounds more complex than it is, so we'd better get started.

2.1 OUR BASIC SCENARIO: PERFECT MARKETS, CERTAINTY, CONSTANT INTEREST RATES

We start with a so-called perfect market.

As promised, we begin with the simplest possible scenario. In finance, this means that we assume that we are living in a so-called **perfect market**:

- There are no taxes.
- There are no transaction costs (costs incurred when buying and selling).

- There are no differences in information or opinions among investors.
- There are so many buyers and sellers (investors and firms) in the market that the presence or absence of just one (or a few) individuals does not have an influence on the price.

The perfect market allows us to focus on the basic concepts in their purest forms, without messy real-world factors complicating the exposition. We will use these assumptions as our sketch of how financial markets operate, though not necessarily how firms' product markets work. You will learn in Chapter 10 how to operate in a world that is not perfect. (This will be a lot messier.)

In early chapters only, we add even stronger assumptions.

In this chapter, we will make three additional assumptions (that are not required for a market to be considered "perfect") to further simplify the world:

- There is no risk or uncertainty. You have perfect foresight.
- There is no inflation.
- The interest rate per period is the same.

Of course, this financial utopia is unrealistic. However, the tools that you will learn in this chapter will also work in later chapters, where the world becomes not only progressively more realistic but also more difficult. Conversely, if any tool does not give the right answer in our simple world, it would surely make no sense in a more realistic world.

SOLVE NOW!

Q 2.1 What are the four perfect market assumptions?

2.2 LOANS AND BONDS

Finance jargon: interest, loan, bond, fixed income, maturity.

The material in this chapter is easiest to explain in the context of bonds and loans. A **loan** is the commitment of a borrower to pay a predetermined amount of cash at one or more predetermined times in the future (the final one called **maturity**), usually in exchange for cash up front today. Loosely speaking, the difference between the money lent and the money paid back is the **interest** that the lender earns. A **bond** is a particular kind of loan, so named because it "binds" the borrower to pay money. Thus, for an investor, "buying a bond" is the same as "extending a loan." Bond buying is the process of giving cash today and receiving a promise for money in the future. Similarly, from the firm's point of view, it is "giving a bond," "issuing a bond," or "selling a bond." Loans and bonds are also sometimes called **fixed income**, because they "promise" a fixed amount of payments to the holder of the bond.

Why learn bonds first? Because they are easiest.

You should view a bond as just another type of investment project—money goes in, and money comes out. In Chapter 5, you will learn more about Treasuries, which are bonds issued by the U.S. Treasury. The beauty of such bonds is that you know what the cash flows will be. Besides, much more capital in the economy is tied up in bonds and loans than is tied up in stocks, so understanding bonds well is very useful in itself.

Interest rates: limited upside. Rates of return: arbitrary upside.

You already know that the net return on a loan is called interest, and that the rate of return on a loan is called the **interest rate**—though we will soon firm up your knowledge about interest rates. One difference between an interest payment and a noninterest payment is that the former usually has a maximum payment, whereas the latter can have unlimited upside potential. However, not every rate of return is an interest rate. For example, an investment in a lottery ticket is not a loan, so it does not offer an interest rate, just a rate of return. In real life, its payoff is uncertain—it could be anything from zero to an unlimited amount. The same applies to stocks and many corporate projects. Many of our examples use the phrase "interest rate," even though the examples almost always work for any other rates of return, too.

Bond: defined by payment next year. Savings: defined by deposit this year.

Is there any difference between buying a bond for $1,000 and putting $1,000 into a bank savings account? Yes, a small one. The bond is defined by its future promised payoffs—say, $1,100 next year—and the bond's value and price today are based on these future payoffs. But as the bond owner, you know exactly how much you will receive next year. An investment in a bank savings account is defined by its investment today. The interest rate can and will change every day, so you do not know what you will end up with next year. The exact amount depends on future interest rates. For example, it could be $1,080 (if interest rates decrease) or $1,120 (if interest rates increase).

A bank savings account is like a sequence of 1-day bonds.

If you want, you can think of a savings account as a sequence of consecutive 1-day bonds: When you deposit money, you buy a 1-day bond, for which you know the interest rate this one day in advance, and the money automatically gets reinvested tomorrow into another bond with whatever the interest rate will be tomorrow.

SOLVE NOW!

Q 2.2 Is a deposit into a savings account more like a long-term bond investment or more like a series of short-term bond investments?

2.3 RETURNS, NET RETURNS, AND RATES OF RETURN

Defining return and our time. Our convention is that 0 means "right now."

The most fundamental financial concept is that of a return. The payoff or (dollar) **return** of an investment is simply the amount of cash (C) it returns. For example, an investment project that returns $12 at time 1 has

$$\text{Return at Time 1} = \$12$$
$$\text{Return}_1 = C_1$$

The subscript is an instant in time, usually abbreviated by the letter t. When exactly time 1 occurs is not important: It could be tomorrow, next month, or next year. But if we mean "right now," we use the subscript 0.

Defining net return and rate of return.

The net payoff, or **net return**, is the difference between the return and the initial investment. It is positive if the project is profitable and negative if it is unprofitable. For example, if the investment costs $10 today and returns $12 at time 1 with nothing in between, then it earns a net return of $2. Notation-wise, we really should use two subscripts on returns—the time when the investment starts (0) and when it ends (1). This would make it something like "Net Return$_{0,1}$." Yikes! Let's just omit the first subscript on such flows when it is zero.

$$\text{Net Return from Time 0 to Time 1} = \$12 - \$10 = \$2$$
$$\text{Net Return}_1 = C_1 - C_0$$

The **rate of return** is the net return expressed as a percentage of the initial investment.

$$\begin{array}{l} \text{Rate of Return} \\ \text{from Time 0 to Time 1} \end{array} = \frac{\$2}{\$10} = 20\%$$

$$r_1 = \frac{\text{Net Return from Time 0 to Time 1}}{\text{Purchase Price at Time 0}}$$

Often, it is convenient to calculate this as

$$r_1 = \frac{\$12 - \$10}{\$10} = \frac{\$12}{\$10} - 1 = 20\%$$

$$r_1 = \frac{C_1 - C_0}{C_0} = \frac{C_1}{C_0} - 1 \qquad (2.1)$$

Rates of return are used so often that they have their own unique letter, r. Percent (the symbol %) is a unit of 1/100. 20% is the same as 0.20.

How to compute returns with interim payments. Capital gains versus returns.

Many investments have interim payments. For example, many stocks pay interim cash **dividends**, many bonds pay interim cash **coupons**, and many real estate investments pay interim rent. How would you calculate the rate of return then? One simple method is to just add interim payments to the numerator. Say an investment costs \$92, pays a dividend of \$5 (at the end of the period), and then is worth \$110. Its rate of return is

$$r = \frac{\$110 + \$5 - \$92}{\$92} = \frac{\$110 - \$92}{\$92} + \frac{\$5}{\$92} = 25\%$$

$$r_1 = \frac{C_1 + \text{All Dividends from 0 to 1} - C_0}{C_0} = \underbrace{\frac{C_1 - C_0}{C_0}}_{\text{Percent Price Change}} + \underbrace{\frac{\text{All Dividends}}{C_0}}_{\text{Dividend Yield}}$$

When there are intermittent payments and final payments, then returns are often broken down into two additive parts. The first part, the price change or **capital gain**, is the difference between the purchase price and the final price, *not* counting interim payments. Here, the capital gain is the difference between \$110 and \$92, that is, the \$18 change in the price of the investment. It is often quoted in percent of the price, which would be \$18/\$92 or 19.6% here. The second part is the amount received in interim payments. It is the dividend or coupon or rent, here \$5. When it is divided by the price, it has names like **dividend yield**, **current yield**, **rental yield**, or **coupon yield**, and these are also usually stated in percentage terms. In our example, the dividend yield is \$5/\$92 ≈ 5.4%. Of course, if the interim yield is high, you might be experiencing a negative capital gain and still have a positive rate of return. For example, a bond that costs \$500, pays a coupon of \$50, and then sells for \$490, has a **capital loss** of \$10 (which comes to a −2% capital yield) but a rate of return of (\$490 + \$50 − \$500)/\$500 = +8%. You will almost always work with rates of return, not with capital gains. The only exception is when you have to work with taxes, because the IRS treats capital gains differently from interim payments. (We will cover taxes in Section 10.4.)

➤ Taxes on capital gains, Section 10.4, p. 321

People often use incorrect terms, but the meaning is usually clear, so this is harmless.

Most of the time, people (incorrectly but harmlessly) abbreviate a rate of return or net return by calling it just a return. For example, if you say that the return on your \$10,000 stock purchase was 10%, you obviously do not mean you received a unitless 0.1. You really mean that your rate of return was 10% and you received \$1,000. This is usually benign, because your listener will know what you mean. Potentially more harmful is the use of the phrase *yield*, which, strictly speaking, means *rate of return*. However, it is often misused as a shortcut for dividend yield or coupon yield (the percent payout that a stock or a bond provides). If you say that the yield on your stock was 5%, then some listeners may interpret it to mean that you earned a total rate of return of 5%, whereas others may interpret it to mean that your stock paid a dividend yield of 5%.

(Nominal) interest rates are usually nonnegative.

Interest rates should logically always be positive. After all, you can always earn 0% if you keep your money under your mattress—you thereby end up with as much money next period as you have this period. Why give your money to someone today who will give you less than 0% (less money in the future)? Consequently, interest rates are indeed almost always positive—the rare exceptions being both bizarre and usually trivial.

Basis points avoid an ambiguity in the English language: 100 basis points equals 1%.

Here is another language problem: What does the statement "the interest rate has just increased by 5%" mean? It could mean either that the previous interest rate, say, 10%, has just increased from 10% to 10% · (1 + 5%) = 10.5%, or that it has increased from 10% to 15%. Because this is unclear, the **basis point** unit was invented. A basis point is simply 1/100 of a percent. If you state that your interest rate has increased by 50 basis points, you definitely mean that the interest rate has increased from 10% to 10.5%. If you state that your interest rate has increased by 500 basis points, you definitely mean that the interest rate has increased from 10% to 15%.

IMPORTANT: 100 basis points constitute 1%. Basis points avoid "percentage ambiguities."

SOLVE NOW!

Q 2.3 A project offers a return of \$1,050 for an investment of \$1,000. What is the rate of return?

Q 2.4 A project offers a net return of \$25 for an investment of \$1,000. What is the rate of return?

Q 2.5 Is 10 the same as 1,000%?

Q 2.6 You purchase a stock for \$40 per share today. It will pay a dividend of \$1 next month. If you can sell it for \$45 right after the dividend is paid,

ANECDOTE Interest Rates over the Millennia

Historical interest rates are fascinating, perhaps because they look so similar to today's interest rates. Nowadays, typical interest rates range from 2% to 20% (depending on other factors). For over 2,500 years, from about the thirtieth century B.C.E. to the sixth century B.C.E., normal interest rates in Sumer and Babylonia hovered around 10–25% per annum, though 20% was the legal maximum. In ancient Greece, interest rates in the sixth century B.C.E. were about 16–18%, dropping steadily to about 8% by the turn of the millennium. Interest rates in ancient Egypt tended to be about 10–12%. In ancient Rome, interest rates started at about 8% in the fifth century B.C.E. but began to increase to about 12% by the third century A.C.E. (a time of great upheaval). When lending resumed in the late Middle Ages (twelfth century), personal loans in England fetched about 50% per annum, though they tended to hover between 10–20% in the rest of Europe. By the Renaissance, commercial loan rates had fallen to 5–15% in Italy, the Netherlands, and France. By the seventeenth century, even English interest rates had dropped to 6–10% in the first half, and to 3–6% in the second half. Mortgage rates tended to be lower yet. Most of the American Revolution was financed with French and Dutch loans at interest rates of 4–5%.

what would be its dividend yield, what would be its capital gain (also quoted as a capital gain yield), and what would be its total holding rate of return?

Q 2.7 If the interest rate of 9% increases to 12%, how many basis points did it increase?

Q 2.8 If the interest rate of 10% decreased by 20 basis points, what is the new interest rate?

2.4 THE TIME VALUE OF MONEY, FUTURE VALUE, AND COMPOUNDING

Because you can earn interest, a given amount of money today is worth more than the same amount of money in the future. After all, you could always deposit your money today into the bank and thereby get back more money in the future. This is an example of the concept of the **time value of money**, which says that a dollar today is worth more than a dollar tomorrow. This is one of the most basic and important concepts in finance.

2.4A THE FUTURE VALUE OF MONEY

Here is how to calculate future payoffs given a rate of return and an initial investment.

How much money will you receive in the future if the rate of return is 20% and you invest $100 today? Turn around the rate of return formula (Formula 2.1) to determine how money will grow over time given a rate of return:

$$20\% = \frac{\$120 - \$100}{\$100} \Leftrightarrow \$100 \cdot (1 + 20\%) = \$100 \cdot 1.2 = \$120$$

$$r_1 = \frac{C_1 - C_0}{C_0} \Leftrightarrow C_0 \cdot (1 + r_1) = C_1$$

The $120 next year is called the **future value (FV)** of $100 today. Thus, future value is the value of a present cash amount at some point in the future. It is the time value of money that causes the future value, \$120, to be higher than its present value (PV), \$100. Using the abbreviations FV and PV, you could also have written the above formula as

$$r_1 = \frac{\text{FV} - \text{PV}}{\text{PV}} \Leftrightarrow \text{FV} = \text{PV} \cdot (1 + r)$$

(If we omit the subscript on the r, it means a 1-period interest rate from now to time 1, i.e., r_1.) Please note that the time value of money is not the fact that the prices of goods may change between today and tomorrow (that would be inflation). Instead, the time value of money is based exclusively on the fact that your money can earn interest. Any amount of cash today is worth more than the same amount of cash tomorrow. Tomorrow, it will be the same amount plus interest.

➤ Section 5.2, "Inflation," p. 97

SOLVE NOW!

Q 2.9 A project has a rate of return of 30%. What is the payoff if the initial investment is \$250?

2.4B COMPOUNDING AND FUTURE VALUE

Now, what if you can earn the same 20% year after year and reinvest all your money? What would your 2-year rate of return be? Definitely *not* 20% + 20% = 40%! You know that you will have \$120 in year 1, which you can reinvest at a 20% rate of return from year 1 to year 2. Thus, you will end up with

Interest on interest (or rate of return on rate of return) means rates cannot be added.

$$\$100 \cdot (1 + 20\%)^2 = \$100 \cdot 1.2^2 = \$120 \cdot (1 + 20\%) = \$120 \cdot 1.2 = \$144$$

$$C_0 \cdot (1 + r)^2 = C_1 \cdot (1 + r) = C_2$$

This \$144—which is, of course, again a future value of \$100 today—represents a total 2-year rate of return of

$$r_2 = \frac{\$144 - \$100}{\$100} = \frac{\$144}{\$100} - 1 = 44\%$$

$$\frac{C_2 - C_0}{C_0} = \frac{C_2}{C_0} - 1 = r_2$$

This is more than 40% because the original net return of \$20 in the first year earned an additional \$4 in interest in the second year. You earn interest on interest! This is also called **compound interest**. Similarly, what would be your 3-year rate of return? You would invest \$144 at 20%, which would provide you with

$$C_3 = \$144 \cdot (1 + 20\%) = \$144 \cdot 1.2 = \$100 \cdot (1 + 20\%)^3 = \$100 \cdot 1.2^3 = \$172.80$$

$$C_3 = C_2 \cdot (1 + r) = C_0 \cdot (1 + r)^3 = C_3$$

Your 3-year rate of return from time 0 to time 3, call it r_3, would thus be

$$r_3 = \frac{\$172.80 - \$100}{\$100} = \frac{\$172.80}{\$100} - 1 = 72.8\%$$

$$\frac{C_3 - C_0}{C_0} = \frac{C_3}{C_0} - 1 = r_3$$

This formula translates the three sequential 1-year rates of return into one 3-year **holding rate of return**—that is, what you earn if you hold the investment for the entire period. This process is called **compounding**, and the formula that does it is the "one-plus formula":

$$(1 + 72.8\%) = (1 + 20\%) \cdot (1 + 20\%) \cdot (1 + 20\%)$$

$$(1 + r_3) = (1 + r) \cdot (1 + r) \cdot (1 + r)$$

or, if you prefer it shorter,

$$1.728 = 1.2^3$$

Figure 2.1 shows how your $100 would grow if you continued investing it at a rate of return of 20% per annum. The function is exponential—that is, it grows faster and faster as interest earns more interest.

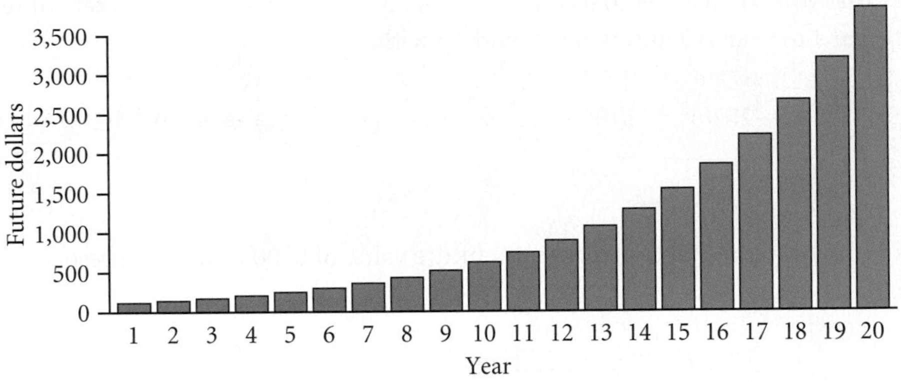

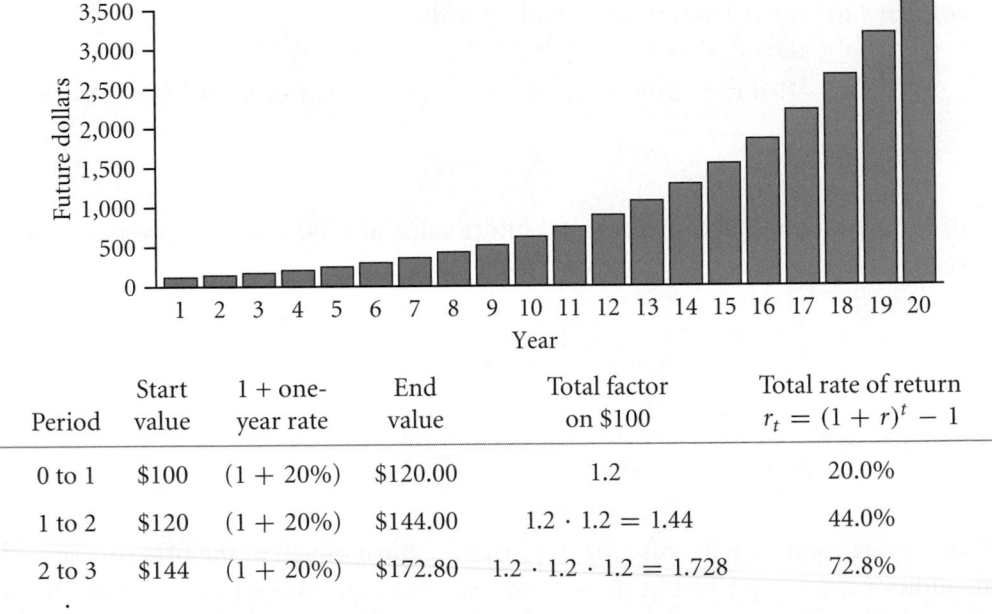

Period	Start value	1 + one-year rate	End value	Total factor on $100	Total rate of return $r_t = (1 + r)^t - 1$
0 to 1	$100	(1 + 20%)	$120.00	1.2	20.0%
1 to 2	$120	(1 + 20%)	$144.00	$1.2 \cdot 1.2 = 1.44$	44.0%
2 to 3	$144	(1 + 20%)	$172.80	$1.2 \cdot 1.2 \cdot 1.2 = 1.728$	72.8%
⋮					

Money grows at a constant rate of 20% per annum. If you compute the graphed value at 20 years out, you will find that each dollar invested right now is worth $38.34 in 20 years. The money at first grows in a roughly linear pattern, but as more and more interest accumulates and itself earns more interest, the graph accelerates steeply upward.

FIGURE 2.1 Compounding over 20 Years at 20% per Annum

IMPORTANT: The compounding formula translates sequential future rates of return into an overall holding rate of return:

$$\underbrace{(1+r_t)}_{\text{Multiperiod Holding Rate of Return}} = \underbrace{(1+r^t)}_{\text{Multiperiod Holding Rate of Return}} = \underbrace{(1+r)}_{\text{Current 1-Period Spot Rate of Return}} \cdot \underbrace{(1+r)}_{\text{Next 1-Period Rate of Return}} \cdots \underbrace{(1+r)}_{\text{Final 1-Period Rate of Return}}$$

The first rate is called the spot rate because it starts now (on the spot).

The compounding formula is so common that you must memorize it.

You can use the compounding formula to compute all sorts of future payoffs. For example, an investment project that costs \$212 today and earns 10% each year for 12 years will yield an overall holding rate of return of

Another example of a payoff computation.

$$\begin{aligned} r_{12} &= (1+10\%)^{12} - 1 = (1.1^{12} - 1) \approx 213.8\% \\ &(1+r)^t - 1 \qquad\qquad\qquad = r_{12} \end{aligned}$$

Your \$212 investment today would therefore turn into a future value of

$$\begin{aligned} C_{12} &= \$212 \cdot (1+10\%)^{12} = \$212 \cdot 1.1^{12} \approx \$212 \cdot (1+213.8\%) \approx \$665.35 \\ &C_0 \cdot (1+r)^{12} \qquad\qquad\qquad\qquad\qquad\qquad = C_{12} \end{aligned}$$

Now suppose you wanted to know what constant two 1-year interest rates (r) would give you a 2-year rate of return of 50%. It is not 25%, because $(1+25\%)\cdot(1+25\%) - 1 = 1.25^2 - 1 = 56.25\%$. Instead, you need to solve

"Uncompounding": Turn around the formula to compute individual holding rates.

$$(1+r)\cdot(1+r) = (1+r)^2 = 1+50\% = 1.50$$

The correct answer is

$$\begin{aligned} r &= \sqrt[2]{1.50} - 1 \approx 22.47\% \\ &= \sqrt[t]{1+r_t} - 1 = \quad r \end{aligned}$$

Check your answer: $(1+22.47\%)\cdot(1+22.47\%) = 1.2247^2 \approx (1+50\%)$. If the 12-month interest rate is 213.8%, what is the 1-month interest rate?

$$(1+r)^{12} \approx 1+213.8\%$$

$$r = \sqrt[12]{1+213.8\%} - 1 = (1+213.8\%)^{1/12} - 1 \approx 10\%$$

➤ Exponentiation, Book Appendix, p. A-1

Interestingly, compounding works even over fractional time periods. Say the overall interest rate is 5% per year, and you want to find out what the rate of return over half a year would be. Because $(1+r_{0.5})^2 = (1+r_1)$, you would compute

You can determine fractional time interest rates via compounding, too.

$$(1+r_{0.5}) = (1+r_1)^{0.5} = (1+5\%)^{0.5} \approx 1+2.4695\% = 1.024695$$

ANECDOTE Life Expectancy and Credit

Your life expectancy may be 80 years, but 30-year bonds existed even in an era when life expectancy was only 25 years—at the time of Hammurabi, around 1700 B.C.E. (Hammurabi established the Kingdom of Babylon and is famous for the Hammurabi Code, the first known legal system.) Moreover, four thousand years ago, Mesopotamians already solved interesting financial problems. A cuneiform clay tablet contains the oldest known interest rate problem for prospective students of the financial arts. The student must figure out how long it takes for 1 mina of silver, growing at 20% interest per year, to reach 64 minae. Because the interest compounds in an odd way (20% of the principal is accumulated until the interest is equal to the principal, and then it is added back to the principal), the answer to this problem is 30 years, rather than 22.81 years. This is not an easy problem to solve—and it even requires knowledge of logarithms!

Check—compounding 2.4695% over two (6-month) periods indeed yields 5%:

$$(1 + 2.4695\%) \cdot (1 + 2.4695\%) = 1.024695^2 \approx (1 + 5\%)$$
$$(1 + r_{0.5}) \cdot (1 + r_{0.5}) = (1 + r_{0.5})^2 = (1 + r_1)$$

You need logs to determine the time needed to get x times your money.

If you know how to use logarithms, you can also determine with the same formula how long it will take at the current interest rate to double or triple your money. For example, at an interest rate of 3% per year, how long would it take you to double your money?

$$(1 + 3\%)^x = (1 + 100\%) \Leftrightarrow x = \frac{\log(1 + 100\%)}{\log(1 + 3\%)} = \frac{\log(2.00)}{\log(1.03)} \approx 23.5$$
$$(1 + r)^t = (1 + r_t) \Leftrightarrow t = \frac{\log(1 + r_t)}{\log(1 + r)}$$

How Bad Are Mistakes?

ADDING OR COMPOUNDING INTEREST RATES?

Adding rather than compounding can make forgivably small mistakes in certain situations—but don't be ignorant of what you are doing.

Unfortunately, when it comes to interest rates in the real world, many users are casual, sometimes to the point where they are outright wrong. Some people mistakenly add interest rates instead of compounding them. When the investments, the interest rates, and the time periods are small, the difference between the correct and incorrect computation can be minor, so this practice can be acceptable, even if it is wrong. For example, when interest rates are 10%, compounding yields

$$(1 + 10\%) \cdot (1 + 10\%) - 1 = 1.1^2 - 1 = 21\%$$
$$(1 + r) \cdot (1 + r) - 1 = r_2$$
$$= 1 + r + r + r \cdot r - 1$$

which is not exactly the same as the simple sum of two r's, which comes to 20%. The difference between 21% and 20% is the "cross-term" $r \cdot r$. This cross-product is especially unimportant if both rates of return are small. If the interest rate were both

1%, the cross-term would be 0.0001. This is indeed small enough to be ignored in most situations, and therefore a forgivable approximation. However, when you compound over many periods, you will accumulate more and more cross-terms, and eventually the quality of your approximation will deteriorate.

SOLVE NOW!

Q 2.10 If the 1-year rate of return is 20% and interest rates are constant, what is the 5-year holding rate of return?

Q 2.11 If you invest $2,000 today and it earns 25% per year, how much will you have in 15 years?

Q 2.12 What is the holding rate of return for a 20-year investment that earns 5%/year each year? What would a $200 investment grow to?

Q 2.13 A project lost one-third of its value each year for 5 years. What was its total holding rate of return? How much is left if the original investment was $20,000?

Q 2.14 If the 5-year holding rate of return is 100% and interest rates are constant, what is the (compounding) annual interest rate?

Q 2.15 What is the quarterly interest rate if the annual interest rate is 50%?

Q 2.16 If the per-year interest rate is 5%, what is the 2-year total interest rate?

Q 2.17 If the per-year interest rate is 5%, what is the 10-year total interest rate?

Q 2.18 If the per-year interest rate is 5%, what is the 100-year total interest rate? How does this compare to 100 times 5%?

Q 2.19 At a constant rate of return of 6% per annum, how many years does it take you to triple your money?

2.4C HOW BANKS QUOTE INTEREST RATES

Banks and many other financial institutions use a number of conventions for quoting interest rates that may surprise you.

Banks add to the confusion, quoting interest rates using strange but traditional conventions.

An **annual percentage yield (APY)** is the simple rate of return. (It is what our book calls an interest rate. Your bank sometimes calls this an **annual equivalent rate** (AER) or an **effective annual rate.**) If you invest $100, and the APY is 10%, you end up with $110 at the end of the year.

The **interest rate** stated without qualification is not really a rate of return, but just a method of quoting. The true daily interest rate is this annual interest quote divided by 365 (or 360 by another convention). For example, if your bank quotes you an annual interest rate of 10%, it means that the daily interest rate is $10\%/365 \approx 0.0274\%$. This is also why your bank may call this the **annual rate, compounded daily.** Therefore, if you leave your money in the bank for 1 year, you earn a true

$$\text{Actual Rate of Return} = [1 + (10\%/365)]^{365} - 1 \approx 10.52\%$$

In sum, at a quoted bank interest rate of 10%, $100 turns into $110.52 after 1 year.

An **annual percentage rate** (**APR**) is the rate that a bank is required to quote on loans it extends, according to the Consumer Credit Act of 1980. This act requires lenders to quote an "annual rate, compounded monthly," thus rendering APR as a number similar to a plain interest quote (not an APY). For example, if the quote to you is 10% per annum, then the lender will collect $(1 + 10\%/12)^{12} - 1 \approx 10.47\%$ per year on the money lent to you. For every \$100 you borrow, you will have to pay the bank \$10.47 every year. However, in contrast to the simple interest quote, APR not only has a different compounding interval, but is also required to reflect other closing costs and fees in order to aid consumers. Yet even though APR is supposedly a standardized measure, there are still enough variations in common use that comparing APRs may not always be comparing apples to apples.

A **certificate of deposit** (**CD**) is a longer-term investment vehicle than a savings account deposit. If your bank wants you to deposit your money in a CD, do you think it will put the more traditional interest rate quote or the APY on its sign in the window? Because the APY of 10.52% looks larger and thus more appealing to depositors than the traditional 10% interest rate quote, most banks advertise the APY for deposits. If you want to borrow money from your bank, do you think your loan agreement will similarly emphasize the APY? No. Most of the time, banks leave this number to the fine print and focus on the APR (or the traditional interest rate quote) instead.

Interest rates are not intrinsically difficult but they can be tedious, and definitional confusions abound in their world. My best advice when money is at stake: If in doubt, ask how the interest rate is computed! Even better, ask for a simple illustrative calculation.

SOLVE NOW!

Q 2.20 If you earn an (effective) interest rate of 12% per annum, how many basis points do you earn in interest on a typical calendar day?

Q 2.21 If the bank quotes an interest rate of 12% per annum (not as an effective interest rate), how many basis points do you earn in interest on a typical day?

Q 2.22 If the bank states an *effective* interest rate of 12% per annum, and there are 52.15 weeks, how much interest do you earn on a deposit of \$100,000 over 1 week?

Q 2.23 If the bank quotes interest of 12% per annum, and there are 52.15 weeks, how much interest do you earn on a deposit of \$100,000 over 1 week?

Q 2.24 If the bank quotes interest of 12% per annum, and there are 52.15 weeks, how much interest do you earn on a deposit of \$100,000 over 1 year?

Q 2.25 If the bank quotes an interest rate of 6% per annum, what does a deposit of \$100 in the bank come to after 1 year?

Q 2.26 If the bank quotes a loan APR rate of 8% per annum, compounded monthly, and there are no fees, what do you have to pay back in 1 year if you borrow \$100 from the bank?

2.5 PRESENT VALUES, DISCOUNTING, AND CAPITAL BUDGETING

Now turn to the flip side of the future value problem: If you know how much money you will have next year, what does this correspond to in value *today*? This is especially important in a corporate context, where the question is, "Given that Project X will return $1 million in 5 years, how much should you be willing to pay to undertake this project today?" The process entailed in answering this question is called **capital budgeting** and is at the heart of corporate decision making. (The origin of the term was the idea that firms have a "capital budget," and that they must allocate capital to their projects within that budget.)

Capital budgeting: Should you budget capital for a project?

Start again with the rate of return formula

➤ Formula 2.1, p. 16

The "present value formula" *is* nothing but the rate of return definition—inverted to translate future cash flows into (equivalent) today's dollars.

$$r_1 = \frac{C_1 - C_0}{C_0} = \frac{C_1}{C_0} - 1$$

You only need to turn this formula around to answer the following question: If you know the prevailing interest rate in the economy (r_1) and the project's future cash flows (C_1), what is the project's value to you *today*? In other words, you are looking for the **present value (PV)**—the amount a future sum of money is worth today, given a specific rate of return. For example, if the interest rate is 10%, how much would you have to save (invest) to receive $100 next year? Or, equivalently, if your project will return $100 next year, what is the project worth to you today? The answer lies in the present value formula, which translates future money into today's money. You merely need to rearrange the rate of return formula to solve for the present value:

$$C_0 = \frac{\$100}{1 + 10\%} = \frac{\$100}{1.1} \approx \$90.91$$

$$C_0 = \frac{C_1}{1 + r_1} = \text{PV}(C_1)$$

Check this—investing $90.91 at an interest rate of 10% will indeed return $100 next period:

$$10\% \approx \frac{\$100 - \$90.91}{\$90.91} = \frac{\$100}{\$90.91} - 1 \Leftrightarrow (1 + 10\%) \cdot \$90.91 \approx \$100$$

$$r_1 = \frac{C_1 - C_0}{C_0} = \frac{C_1}{C_0} - 1 \Leftrightarrow (1 + r_1) \cdot C_0 = C_1$$

This is the **present value formula**, which uses a division operation known as **discounting**. (The term "discounting" indicates that we are reducing a value, which is exactly what we are doing when we translate future cash into current cash.) If you wish, you can think of discounting—the conversion of a future cash flow amount into its equivalent present value amount—as the *reverse* of compounding.

Discounting translates future cash into today's equivalent.

Thus, the present value (PV) of next year's $100 is $90.91—the value today of future cash flows. Let's say that this $90.91 is what the project costs. If you can borrow or lend at the interest rate of 10% elsewhere, then you will be indifferent between

Present value varies inversely with the cost of capital.

receiving \$100 next year and receiving \$90.91 for your project today. In contrast, if the standard rate of return in the economy were 12%, your specific project would not be a good deal. The project's present value would be

$$PV(C_1) = \frac{\$100}{1+12\%} = \frac{\$100}{1.12} \approx \$89.29$$
$$C_0 = \frac{C_1}{1+r_1} = PV(C_1)$$

which would be less than its cost of \$90.91. But if the standard economy-wide rate of return were 8%, the project would be a great deal. Today's present value of the project's future payoff would be

$$PV(C_1) = \frac{\$100}{1+8\%} = \frac{\$100}{1.08} \approx \$92.59$$
$$C_0 = \frac{C_1}{1+r_1} = PV(C_1)$$

which would exceed the project's cost of \$90.91. It is the present value of the project, weighed against its cost, that should determine whether you should undertake a project today or avoid it. The present value is also the answer to the question, "How much would you have to save at current interest rates today if you wanted to have a specific amount of money next year?"

The PV formula with 2 periods.

Let's extend the time frame in our example. If the interest rate were 10% per period, what would \$100 in 2 periods be worth today? The value of the \$100 is then

$$PV(C_2) = \frac{\$100}{(1+10\%)^2} = \frac{\$100}{1.21} \approx \$82.64$$
$$PV(C_2) = \frac{C_2}{(1+r)^2} = C_0 \tag{2.2}$$

Note the 21%. In 2 periods, you could earn a rate of return of $(1+10\%) \cdot (1+10\%) - 1 = 1.1^2 - 1 = 21\%$ elsewhere, so this is your appropriate comparable rate of return.

The interest rate can be called the "cost of capital."

This discount rate—the rate of return, r, with which the project can be financed—is often called the **cost of capital**. It is the rate of return at which you can raise money elsewhere. In a perfect market, this cost of capital is also the **opportunity cost** that you bear if you fund your specific investment project instead of the alternative next-best investment elsewhere. Remember—you can invest your money at this rate in another project instead of investing it in this one. The better these alternative projects in the economy are, the higher will be your cost of capital, and the lower will be the value of your specific investment project with its specific cash flows. An investment that promises \$1,000 next year is worth less today if you can earn 50% rather than 5% elsewhere. A good rule is to always add mentally the word "opportunity" before "cost of capital"—it is always your **opportunity cost of capital**. (In this part of our book, I will just tell you what the economy-wide rate of return is—here 10%—

for borrowing or investing. In later chapters, you will learn how this rate of return is determined.)

IMPORTANT: Always think of the r in the present value denominator as your "opportunity" cost of capital. If you have great opportunities elsewhere, your projects have to be discounted at high discount rates. The discount rate, the cost of capital, and the required rate of return are really all just names for the same factor.

The discount factor is a simple function of the cost of capital.

When you multiply a future cash flow by its appropriate **discount factor**, you end up with its present value. Looking at Formula 2.2, you can see that this discount factor is the quantity

$$\left(\frac{1}{1+21\%}\right) \approx 0.8264$$

$$\left(\frac{1}{1+r_2}\right)$$

In other words, the discount factor translates 1 dollar in the future into the equivalent amount of dollars today. In the example, at a 2-year 21% rate of return, a dollar in 2 years is worth about 83 cents today. Because interest rates are usually positive, discount factors are usually less than 1—a dollar in the future is worth less than a dollar today. (Sometimes, and less correctly, people call this the **discount rate**, but this name should be used for r_t instead.)

The discount rate is higher for years farther out, so the discount factor is lower.

Figure 2.2 shows how the discount factor declines when the cost of capital is 20% per annum. After about a decade, any dollar the project earns is worth less than 20 cents to you today. If you compare Figure 2.1 to Figure 2.2, you should notice how each is the "flip side" of the other.

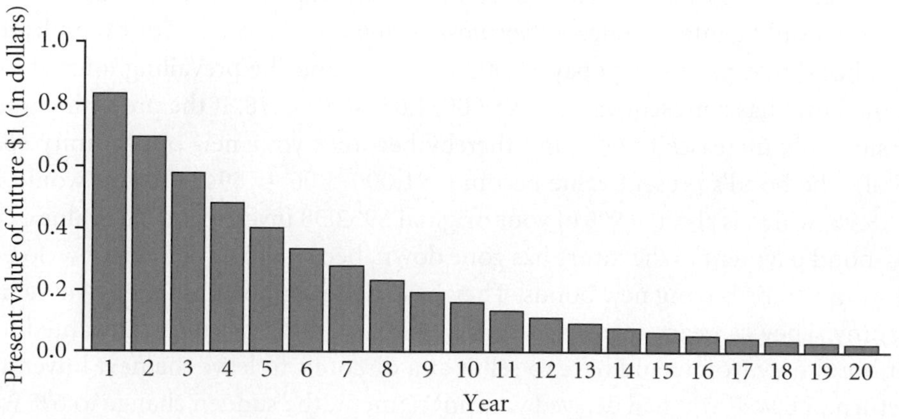

Each bar is $1/(1 + 20\%) \approx 83.3\%$ of the size of the bar to its left. After 20 years, the last bar is 0.026 in height. This means that $1 in 20 years is worth 2.6 cents in money today.

FIGURE 2.2 Discounting over 20 Years at a Cost of Capital of 20% per Annum

IMPORTANT: The cornerstones of finance are the following formulas:

$$\text{Rate of Return:} \qquad r_t = \frac{C_t - C_0}{C_0} = \frac{C_t}{C_0} - 1$$

Rearrange the formula to obtain the future value:

$$\text{Future Value:} \qquad \text{FV}_t = C_t = C_0 \cdot (1 + r_t) = C_0 \cdot (1 + r)^t$$

The process of obtaining r_t is called compounding, and it works through the "one-plus" formula:

$$\text{Compounding:} \qquad \underbrace{(1 + r_t)}_{\substack{\text{Total Holding} \\ \text{Rate of Return}}} = \underbrace{(1 + r)}_{\substack{\text{First Period} \\ \text{Rate of Return}}} \cdot \underbrace{(1 + r)}_{\substack{\text{Second Period} \\ \text{Rate of Return}}} \cdots \underbrace{(1 + r)}_{\substack{\text{Third Period} \\ \text{Rate of Return}}}$$

Rearrange the formula again to obtain the present value:

$$\text{Present Value:} \qquad \text{PV} = C_0 = \frac{C_t}{(1 + r_t)} = \frac{C_t}{(1 + r)^t}$$

The process of translating C_t into C_0—that is, the multiplication of a future cash flow by $1/(1 + r_t)$—is called discounting. The discount factor is:

$$\text{Discount Factor:} \qquad \frac{1}{(1 + r_t)} = \frac{1}{(1 + r)^t}$$

It translates 1 dollar at time t into its equivalent value today.

Bonds' present values and the prevailing interest rates move in opposite directions.

Remember how bonds are different from savings accounts? The former is pinned down by its promised fixed future payments, while the latter pays whatever the daily interest rate is. This induces an important relationship between the value of bonds and the prevailing interest rates—*they move in opposite directions*. For example, if you have a bond that promises to pay $1,000 in 1 year, and the prevailing interest rate is 5%, the bond has a present value of $1,000/1.05 ≈ $952.38. If the prevailing interest rate suddenly increases to 6% (and thereby becomes your new opportunity cost of capital), the bond's present value becomes $1,000/1.06 ≈ $943.40. You would have lost $8.98, which is about 0.9% of your original $952.38 investment. The value of your fixed-bond payment in the future has gone down, because investors can now do better than your 5% by buying new bonds. They have better opportunities elsewhere in the economy. They can earn a rate of return of 6%, not just 5%, so if you wanted to sell your bond now, you would have to sell it at a discount to leave the next buyer a rate of return of 6%. If you had delayed your investment, the sudden change to 6% would have done nothing to your investment. On the other hand, if the prevailing interest rate suddenly drops to 4%, then your bond will be more valuable. Investors would be willing to pay $1,000/1.04 ≈ $961.54, which is an immediate $9.16 gain. The inverse relationship between prevailing interest rates and bond prices is general and worth noting.

IMPORTANT: The price and the implied rate of return on a bond with fixed payments move in opposite directions. When the price of the bond goes up, its implied rate of return goes down. When the price of the bond goes down, its implied rate of return goes up.

SOLVE NOW!

Q 2.27 A project has a cost of capital of 30%. The final payoff is \$250. What should it cost today?

Q 2.28 A bond promises to pay \$150 in 12 months. The annual true interest rate is 5% per annum. What is the bond's price today?

Q 2.29 A bond promises to pay \$150 in 12 months. The bank quotes you interest of 5% per annum, compounded daily. What is the bond's price today?

Q 2.30 If the cost of capital is 5% per annum, what is the discount factor for a cash flow in 2 years?

Q 2.31 Interpret the meaning of the discount factor.

Q 2.32 What are the units on rates of return, discount factors, future values, and present values?

Q 2.33 Would it be good or bad for you, in terms of the present value of your liabilities, if your opportunity cost of capital increased?

Q 2.34 The price of a bond that offers a safe promise of \$100 in 1 year is \$95. What is the implied interest rate? If the bond's interest rate suddenly jumped up by 150 basis points, what would the bond price be? How much would an investor gain/lose if she held the bond while the interest rate jumped up by these 150 basis points?

2.6 NET PRESENT VALUE

Present values are alike and thus can be added, subtracted, compared, and so on.

An important advantage of present value is that all cash flows are translated into the same unit: cash today. To see this, say that a project generates \$10 in 1 year and \$8 in 5 years. You cannot add up these different future values to come up with \$18—it would be like adding apples and oranges. However, if you translate both future cash flows into their present values, you *can* add them. For example, if the interest rate was 5% per annum (so $(1 + 5\%)^5 = (1 + 27.6\%)$ over 5 years), the present value of these two cash flows together would be

$$\text{PV}(\$10 \text{ in 1 year}) = \frac{\$10}{1.05} \approx \$9.52$$

$$\text{PV}(\$8 \text{ in 5 years}) = \frac{\$8}{1.05^5} \approx \$6.27$$

$$\text{PV}(C_t) = \frac{C_t}{(1+r)^t}$$

Therefore, the total value of the project's future cash flows *today* (at time 0) is \$15.79.

The definition and use of NPV.

The **net present value** (**NPV**) of an investment is the present value of all its future cash flows minus the present value of its cost. It is really the same as present value, except that the word "net" up front reminds you to add and subtract *all* cash flows, including the *upfront* investment outlay today. The NPV calculation method is always the same:

1. Translate all future cash flows into today's dollars.
2. Add them all up. This is the present value of all future cash flows.
3. Subtract the initial investment.

NPV is the most important method for determining the value of projects. It is a cornerstone of finance. Let's assume that you have to pay \$12 to buy this particular project with its \$10 and \$8 cash flows. In this case, it is a positive NPV project, because

$$\text{NPV} = -\$12 + \frac{\$10}{1.05} + \frac{\$8}{1.05^5} \approx \$3.79$$

$$C_0 \quad + \frac{C_1}{1+r_1} + \frac{C_5}{(1+r)^5} = \text{NPV}$$

(For convenience, we omit the 0 subscript for NPV, just as we did for PV.)

Think about what NPV means, and how it can be justified.

There are a number of ways to understand net present value.

- One way is to think of the NPV of \$3.79 as the difference between the market value of the future cash flows (\$15.79) and the project's cost (\$12)—this difference is the "value added."
- Another way to think of your project is to compare its cash flows to an equivalent set of bonds that exactly *replicates* them. In this instance, you would want to purchase a 1-year bond that promises \$10 next year. If you save \$9.52—at a 5% interest rate—you will receive \$10. Similarly, you could buy a 5-year bond that promises \$8 in year 5 for \$6.27. Together, these two bonds exactly replicate the project cash flows. The **law of one price** tells you that your project should be worth as much as this bond project—the cash flows are identical. You would have had to put away \$15.79 today to buy these bonds, but your project can deliver these cash flows at a cost of only \$12—much cheaper and thus better than your bond alternative.

Yet another way to justify NPV: opportunity cost.

- There is yet another way to think of NPV. It tells you how your project compares to the alternative opportunity of investing in the capital markets. These opportunities are expressed in the denominator through the discount factor. What would you get if you took your \$12 and invested it in the capital markets instead of in your project? Using the future value formula, you know that you could earn a 5% rate of return from now to next year, and 27.6% from now to 5 years. Your \$12 would grow into \$12.60 by next year. You could take out the same \$10 cash flow that your project gives you and be left with \$2.60 for reinvestment. Over the next 4 years, at the 5% interest rate, this \$2.60 would grow into \$3.16. But your project would do better for you, giving you \$8. Thus, your project achieves a higher rate of return than the capital markets alternative would achieve.

The conclusion of this argument is not only the simplest but also the best capital budgeting rule: If the NPV is positive, as it is here, you should take the project. If it is negative, you should reject the project. If it is zero, it does not matter.

The correct capital budgeting rule: Take all positive NPV projects.

IMPORTANT:

- The **net present value formula** is

$$\text{NPV} = C_0 + \text{PV}(C_1) + \text{PV}(C_2) + \text{PV}(C_3) + \text{PV}(C_4) + \cdots$$
$$= C_0 + \frac{C_1}{1+r_1} + \frac{C_2}{1+r_2} + \frac{C_3}{1+r_3} + \frac{C_4}{1+r_4} + \cdots$$
$$= C_0 + \frac{C_1}{(1+r)} + \frac{C_2}{(1+r)^2} + \frac{C_3}{(1+r)^3} + \frac{C_4}{(1+r)^4} + \cdots$$

  The subscripts are time indexes, C_t is the net cash flow at time t (positive for inflows, negative for outflows), and r_t is the relevant interest rate for investments from now to time t. With constant interest rates, $r_t = (1+r)^t - 1$.
- The **net present value capital budgeting rule** states that you should accept projects with a positive NPV and reject projects with a negative NPV.
- Taking positive NPV projects increases the value of the firm. Taking negative NPV projects decreases the value of the firm.
- NPV is definitively the best method for capital budgeting—the process by which you should accept or reject projects.

The NPV formula is so important that you must memorize it.

Let's work another NPV example. A project costs \$900 today, yields \$200/year for 2 years, then \$400/year for 2 years, and finally requires a cleanup expense of \$100. The prevailing interest rate is 5% per annum. These cash flows are summarized in Table 2.1. Should you take this project?

Let's work a project NPV example.

1. You need to determine the cost of capital for tying up money for 1 year, 2 years, 3 years, and so on. The compounding formula is

$$(1 + r_t) = (1 + r)^t = (1.05)^t = 1.05^t$$

   So for money right now, the cost of capital r_0 is $1.05^0 - 1 = 0$; for money in 1 year, r_1 is $1.05^1 - 1 = 5\%$; for money in 2 years, r_2 is $1.05^2 - 1 = 10.25\%$. And so on.

First, determine your multiyear costs of capital.

2. You need to translate the cost of capital into discount factors. Recall that these are 1 divided by 1 plus your cost of capital. A dollar in 1 year is worth $1/(1 + 5\%) = 1/1.05 \approx 0.9524$ dollars today. A dollar in 2 years is worth $1/(1 + 5\%)^2 = 1/1.05^2 \approx 0.9070$. And so on.
3. You can now translate the future cash flows into their present value equivalents by multiplying the payoffs by their appropriate discount factors. For example, the \$200 cash flow at time 1 is worth about $0.9524 \cdot \$200 \approx \$190.48$.

TABLE 2.1 HYPOTHETICAL PROJECT CASH FLOW TABLE

Time	Project Cash Flow	Interest Rate Annualized	Interest Rate Holding	Discount Factor	Present Value
t	C_t	r	r_t	$\frac{1}{(1+r)^t}$	$\text{PV}(C_t)$
Today	−$900	5.00%	0.00%	1.000	−$900.00
Year +1	+$200	5.00%	5.00%	0.9524	+$190.48
Year +2	+$200	5.00%	10.25%	0.9070	+$181.41
Year +3	+$400	5.00%	15.76%	0.8638	+$345.54
Year +4	+$400	5.00%	21.55%	0.8227	+$329.08
Year +5	−$100	5.00%	27.63%	0.7835	−$78.35
			Net Present Value (Sum):		$68.16

As a manager, you must estimate your project cash flows. The appropriate interest rate (also called cost of capital in this context) is provided to you by the opportunity cost of your investors—determined by the supply and demand for capital in the broader economy, where your investors can place their capital instead. The "Project Cash Flow" and the left interest rate column are the two input columns. The remaining columns are computed from these inputs. The goal is to calculate the final column.

4. Because present values are additive, you then sum up all the terms to compute the overall net present value. Make sure you include the original upfront cost as a negative.

Consequently, the project NPV is $68.16. Because this is a positive value, you should take this project.

If the upfront cost was higher, you should not take the project.

However, if the upfront expense was $1,000 instead of $900, the NPV would be negative (−$31.84), and you would be better off investing the money into the appropriate sequence of bonds from which the discount factors were computed. In this case, you should have rejected the project.

SOLVE NOW!

Q 2.35 Work out the present value of your tuition payments for the next 2 years. Assume that the tuition is $30,000 per year, payable at the start of the year. Your first tuition payment will occur in 6 months, and your second tuition payment will occur in 18 months. You can borrow capital at an interest rate of 6% per annum.

Q 2.36 Write down the NPV formula from memory.

Q 2.37 What is the NPV capital budgeting rule?

Q 2.38 Determine the NPV of the project in Table 2.1, if the per-period interest rate were 8% per year, not 5%. Should you take this project?

Q 2.39 You are considering a 3-year lease for a building, where you have to make one payment now, one in a year, and a final one in 2 years.

(a) Would you rather pay $1,000,000 up front, then $500,000 each in the following two years; or would you rather pay $700,000 each year?

(b) If the interest rate is 10%, what equal payment amount (rather than $700,000) would leave you indifferent? (This is also called the equivalent annual cost (EAC).)

➤ Section 3.4, "Projects With Different Lives and Rental Equivalents," p. 60

Q 2.40 Use a spreadsheet to answer the following question: Car dealer A offers a car for $2,200 up front (first payment), followed by $200 lease payments over the next 23 months. Car dealer B offers the same lease at a flat $300 per month (i.e., your first upfront payment is $300). Which lease do you prefer if the interest rate is 0.5% per month?

2.6A APPLICATION: ARE FASTER-GROWING FIRMS BETTER BARGAINS?

The firm's price should incorporate the firm's attributes.

Let's work another NPV problem applied to companies overall. Would it make more sense to invest in companies that grow quickly rather than slowly? If you wish, you can think of this question loosely as asking whether you should buy stocks in a fast-growing company like Google or in a slow-growing company like Procter & Gamble. The answer will be that this choice does not matter in a perfect market. Whether a company is growing quickly or slowly is already incorporated in the firm's price today, which is just the present value of the firm's cash flows that will accrue to the owners. Therefore, neither is the better deal.

Should you invest in a fast-grower or a slow-grower?

For example, consider company "Grow" (G) that will produce over the next 3 years

$$G_1 = \$100 \qquad G_2 = \$150 \qquad G_3 = \$250$$

and company "Shrink" (S) that will produce

$$S_1 = \$100 \qquad S_2 = \$90 \qquad S_3 = \$80$$

Is G not a better company to buy than S?

Let's find out: Compute the values.

There is no uncertainty involved, and both firms face the same cost of capital of 10% per annum. The price of G today is

$$\text{PV}(G) = \frac{\$100}{1.1^1} + \frac{\$150}{1.1^2} + \frac{\$250}{1.1^3} \approx \$402.70 \tag{2.3}$$

and the price of S today is

$$\text{PV}(S) = \frac{\$100}{1.1^1} + \frac{\$90}{1.1^2} + \frac{\$80}{1.1^3} \approx \$225.39$$

Your investment dollar grows at the same 10% rate. Your investment's growth rate is disconnected from the cash flow growth rate.

If you invest in G, then next year you will have $100 cash and own a company with $150 and $250 cash flows coming up. G's value at time 1 (so PV now has subscript 1) will thus be

$$\text{PV}_1(G) = \$100 + \frac{\$150}{1.1^1} + \frac{\$250}{1.1^2} \approx \$442.98$$

Your investment will have earned a rate of return of $442.98/$402.70 − 1 ≈ 10%. If you instead invest in S, then next year you will receive $100 cash and own a company with "only" \$90 and \$80 cash flows coming up. S's value will thus be

$$\text{PV}_1(S) = \$100 + \frac{\$90}{1.1^1} + \frac{\$80}{1.1^2} \approx \$247.93$$

Your investment will have earned a rate of return of \$247.93/\$225.39 − 1 ≈ 10%. In either case, you will earn the fair rate of return of 10%. Whether cash flows are growing at a rate of +50%, −10%, +237.5%, or −92% is irrelevant: *The firms' market prices today already reflect their future growth rates.* There is no necessary connection between the growth rate of the underlying project cash flows or earnings and the growth rate of your investment money (i.e., your expected rate of return).

Any sudden wealth gains would accrue to existing shareholders, not to new investors.

Make sure you understand the thought experiment here: This statement that higher-growth firms do not necessarily earn a higher rate of return does not mean that a firm in which managers succeed in increasing the future cash flows at no extra investment cost will not be worth more. Such firms will indeed be worth more, and the current owners will benefit from the rise in future cash flows, but this will also be reflected immediately in the price at which you can purchase this firm. This is an important corollary worth repeating. If General Electric has just won a large defense contract (like the equivalent of a lottery), shouldn't you purchase GE stock to participate in the windfall? Or if Wal-Mart managers do a great job and have put together a great firm, shouldn't you purchase Wal-Mart stock to participate in this windfall? The answer is that you cannot. The old shareholders of Wal-Mart are no dummies. They know the capabilities of Wal-Mart and how it will translate into cash flows. Why should they give you, a potential new shareholder, a special bargain for something to which you contributed nothing? Just providing more investment funds is not a big contribution—after all, there are millions of other investors equally willing to provide funds at the appropriately higher price. It is competition—among investors for providing funds and among firms for obtaining funds—that determines the expected rate of return that investors receive and the cost of capital that firms pay. There is actually a more general lesson here. Economics tells you that you must have a scarce resource if you want to earn above-normal profits. Whatever is abundant and/or provided by many will not be tremendously profitable.

SOLVE NOW!

Q 2.41 Assume that company G pays no interim dividends, so you receive \$536 at the end of the project. What is G's market value at time 1, 2, and 3? What is your rate of return in each year? Assume that the cost of capital is still 10%.

Q 2.42 Assume that company G pays out the full cash flows (refer to the text example) in earnings each period. What is G's market value at time 1, 2, and 3? What is your rate of return in each year?

Q 2.43 One month ago, a firm suffered a large court award against it that will force it to pay compensatory damages of \$100 million next January 1. Are shares in this firm a bad buy until January 2?

SUMMARY

This chapter covered the following major points:

- A perfect market assumes no taxes, no transaction costs, no opinion differences, and the presence of many buyers and sellers.
- A bond is a claim that promises to pay an amount of money in the future. Buying a bond is extending a loan. Issuing a bond is borrowing. Bond values are determined by their future payoffs.
- One hundred basis points are equal to 1%.
- The time value of money means that 1 dollar today is worth more than 1 dollar tomorrow, because of the interest that it can earn.
- Returns must not be averaged, but compounded over time.
- Interest rate quotes are *not* interest rates. For example, stated annual rates are usually not the effective annual rates that your money will earn in the bank. If in doubt, ask!
- The discounted present value (PV) translates future cash values into present cash values. The net present value (NPV) is the sum of all present values of a project, including the investment cost (usually, a negative upfront cash flow today).
- The values of bonds and interest rates move in opposite directions. A sudden increase in the prevailing economy-wide interest rate decreases the present value of a bond's future payouts and therefore decreases today's price of the bond. Conversely, a sudden decrease in the prevailing economy-wide interest rate increases the present value of a bond's future payouts and therefore increases today's price of the bond.
- The NPV formula can be written as

$$\begin{aligned} \text{NPV} &= C_0 + \frac{C_1}{1+r_1} + \frac{C_2}{1+r_2} + \cdots \\ &= C_0 + \frac{C_1}{1+r} + \frac{C_2}{(1+r)^2} + \cdots \end{aligned}$$

  In this context, r is called the discount rate or cost of capital, and $1/(1+r)$ is called the discount factor.

- The net present value capital budgeting rule states that you should accept projects with a positive NPV and reject projects with a negative NPV.
- In a perfect market, firms are worth the present value of their assets. Whether firms grow quickly or slowly does not make them more or less attractive investments in a perfect market because their prices always already reflect the present value of future cash flows.
- In a perfect market, the gains from sudden surprises accrue to old owners, not new capital providers, because old owners have no reason to want to share the spoils.

KEY TERMS

SOLVE NOW! SOLUTIONS

Q 2.1 The four perfect market assumptions are no taxes, no transaction costs, no differences in opinions, and no large buyers or sellers.

Q 2.2 A savings deposit is an investment in a series of short-term bonds.

Q 2.3 $r = (\$1{,}050 - \$1{,}000)/\$1{,}000 = 5\%$

Q 2.4 $r = \frac{\$25}{\$1{,}000} = 2.5\%$

Q 2.5 Yes, $10 = 1{,}000\%$.

Q 2.6 The dividend yield would be $\$1/\$40 = 2.5\%$, the capital gain would be $\$45 - \$40 = \$5$, so that its capital gain yield would be $\$5/\$40 = 12.5\%$, and the total rate of return would be $(\$46 - \$40)/\$40 = 15\%$.

Q 2.7 $1\% = 100$ basis points, so an increase of 3% is 300 basis points.

Q 2.8 20 basis points are 0.2%, so the interest rate declined from 10.0% to 9.8%.

Q 2.9 $r = 30\% = (x - \$250)/\$250 \quad \Longrightarrow x = 1.3 \cdot \$250 = \$325$

Q 2.10 $1.20^5 - 1 \approx 148.83\%$

Q 2.11 $\$2{,}000 \cdot 1.25^{15} \approx \$56{,}843.42$

Q 2.12 The total holding rate of return is $1.05^{20} - 1 \approx 165.33\%$, so you would end up with $\$200 \cdot (1 + 165.33\%) \approx \$530.66$.

Q 2.13 Losing one-third is a rate of return of -33%. To find the holding rate of return, compute $[1 + (-1/3)]^5 - 1 \approx -86.83\%$. About $(1 - 86.83\%) \cdot \$20{,}000 \approx \$2{,}633.74$ remains.

Q 2.14 $(1 + 100\%)^{1/5} - 1 \approx 14.87\%$

Q 2.15 $(1 + r_{0.25})^4 = (1 + r_1)$. Thus, $r_{0.25} = \sqrt[4]{1 + r_1} - 1 = 1.5^{1/4} - 1 \approx 10.67\%$.

Q 2.16 $r_2 = (1 + r_{0,1}) \cdot (1 + r_{1,2}) - 1 = 1.05 \cdot 1.05 - 1 = 10.25\%$

Q 2.17 $r_{10} = (1 + r_1)^{10} - 1 = 1.05^{10} - 1 \approx 62.89\%$

Q 2.18 $r_{100} = (1 + r_1)^{100} - 1 = 1.05^{100} - 1 = 130.5 \approx 13{,}050\%$. In words, this is about 130 times the initial investment, and substantially more than 500% (5 times the initial investment).

Q 2.19 Tripling is equivalent to earning a rate of return of 200%. Therefore, solve $(1 + 6\%)^x = (1 + 200\%)$, or $x \cdot \log(1.06) = \log(3.00)$ or $x = \log(3.00)/\log(1.06) \approx 18.85$ years.

Q 2.20 $(1 + r)^{365} = 1.12$. Therefore, $1.12^{(1/365)} - 1 \approx 0.00031054 = 0.031054\% \approx 3.1$ bp/day.

Q 2.21 The bank means to collect $12\%/365 \approx 3.288$ bp/day.

Q 2.22 The true daily interest rate, assuming 365 days, is $1.12^{1/365} - 1 \approx 0.031054\%$. To compute your true rate of return, compound this over 7 days: $(1 + 0.03105\%)^7 = 1.00031054^7 \approx 1.0021758$. (You could also compute the rate of return differently: There are 52.15 weeks in 365 days. Therefore, $r = (1 + 12\%)^{(1/52.15)} - 1 \approx 1.0021758$.) Your \$100,000 will grow into \$100,217.58. You would have earned \$217.58 in interest.

Q 2.23 With 12% in nominal APR interest *quoted*, you earn $12\%/365 \approx 0.032877\%$ per day. Therefore, the weekly rate of return is $(1 + 0.032877\%)^7 - 1 \approx 0.23036\%$. Your \$100,000 will grow into \$100,230.36. Note that you end up with more money from the 12% quoted rate than from the 12% effective rate.

Q 2.24 With 12% in nominal APR interest *quoted*, you earn $12\%/365 \approx 0.032877\%$ per day. Therefore, the annual rate of return is $(1 + 0.032877\%)^{365} - 1 \approx 12.747462\%$. Your \$100,000 will grow into \$112,747.46.

Q 2.25 The bank quote of 6% means that it will pay an interest rate of $6\%/365 \approx 0.0164384\%$ per day. This earns an actual interest rate of $(1 + 0.0164384\%)^{365} - 1 \approx 6.18\%$ per annum. Therefore, each invested \$100 grows to \$106.18, thus earning \$6.18 over the year.

Q 2.26 The bank quote of 8% means that you will have to pay an interest rate of $8\%/12 \approx 0.667\%$ per month. This earns an actual interest rate of $(1 + 0.667\%)^{12} - 1 \approx 8.30\%$ per annum. You will have to pay \$108.30 in repayment for every \$100 you borrowed.

Q 2.27 $r = 30\% = (\$250 - x)/x$. Thus, $x = \$250/1.30 \approx \$192.31$.

Q 2.28 $\$150/(1.05) \approx \$142.86$

Q 2.29 $\$150/[1 + (5\%/365)]^{365} \approx \$142.68$

Q 2.30 $1/[(1.05) \cdot (1.05)] \approx 0.9070$

Q 2.31 It is today's value in dollars for 1 future dollar, that is, at a specific point in time in the future.

Q 2.32 The rate of return and additional factors are unit-less. The latter two are in dollars (though the former is dollars in the future, while the latter is dollars today).

Q 2.33 Good. Your future payments would be worth less in today's money.

Q 2.34 The original interest rate is $\$100/\$95 - 1 \approx 5.26\%$. Increasing the interest rate by 150 basis points is 6.76%. This means that the price should be $\$100/(1.0676) \approx \$93.67$. A price change from \$95 to \$93.67 is a rate of return of $\$93.67/\$95 - 1 \approx -1.40\%$.

Q 2.35 The first tuition payment is worth $\$30{,}000/(1.06)^{1/2} \approx \$29{,}139$. The second tuition payment is worth $\$30{,}000/(1.06)^{3/2} \approx \$27{,}489$. Thus, the total present value is \$56,628.

Q 2.36 If you cannot write down the NPV formula by heart, do not go on until you have it memorized.

Q 2.37 Accept if NPV is positive. Reject if NPV is negative.

Q 2.38 $-\$900 + \$200/(1.08)^1 + \$200/(1.08)^2 + \$400/(1.08)^3 + \$400/(1.08)^4 - \$100/(1.08)^5 \approx \$0.14$. The NPV is positive. Therefore this is a worthwhile project that you should accept.

Q 2.39 For the 3-year building leases:

(a) Your preference depends on the interest rate. If the interest rate is zero, then you would prefer the $2 million sum-total payment to the $2.1 million rent. If the prevailing interest rate is less than 21.5%, it is better to lease. If it is more than 21.5%, you prefer the rent. For example, if it is 40%, the net present cost of the lease is $1.612 million, while the net present cost of the rent is $1.557 million.

(b) At a 10% interest rate, the total net present cost of the lease is $\$1 + \$0.5/1.1 + \$0.5/1.1^2 \approx \$1.868$ million. An equivalent rent contract must solve

$$x + \frac{x}{1.1} + \frac{x}{1.1^2} = \$1.868$$

Multiply by $1.1^2 = 1.21$

$$1.21 \cdot x + 1.1 \cdot x + x = \$1.868 \cdot 1.21$$

$$\Leftrightarrow x \cdot (1.21 + 1.1 + 1) = \$2{,}260.28$$

Therefore, the equivalent rental cost would be $x \approx \$682.864$.

Q 2.40 Lease A has an NPV of −$6,535. Lease B has an NPV of −$6,803. Therefore, lease A is cheaper.

Q 2.41 For easier naming, call 2000 your year 0. The firm's present value in 2000 is $\$536/1.10^3 \approx \$402.70$—but you already knew this. If you purchase this company, its value in 2001 depends on a cash flow stream that is $0 in 2001, $0 in year 2002, and $536 in year 2003. It will be worth $\$536/1.10^2 \approx \$442.98$ in 2001. In 2002, your firm will be worth $\$536/1.10 \approx \$487.27$. Finally, in 2003, it will be worth $536. Each year, you expect to earn 10%, which you can compute from the four firm values.

Q 2.42 Again, call 2000 your year 0. The firm's present value in 2000 is based on dividends of $100, $150, and $250 in the next three years. The firm value in 2000 is the $402.70 from page 33. The firm value in 2001 was also worked out to be $442.98, but you immediately receive $100 in cash, so the firm is worth only $\$442.98 - \$100 = \$342.98$. As an investor, you would have earned a rate of return of $\$442.98/\$402.70 - 1 \approx 10\%$. The firm value in 2002 is $PV_2(G) = \$250/1.1 \approx \$227.27$, but you will also receive $150 in cash, for a total firm-related wealth of $377.27. In addition, you will have the $100 from 2001, which would have grown to $110—for a total wealth of $487.27. Thus, starting with wealth of $442.98 and ending up with wealth of $487.27, you would have earned a rate of return of $\$487.27/\$442.98 - 1 \approx 10\%$. A similar computation shows that you will earn 10% from 2002 ($487.27) to 2003 ($536.00).

Q 2.43 No! The market will already have adjusted the price.

PROBLEMS

The ▬ indicates problems available in myfinancelab

Q 2.44 What is a perfect market? What were the assumptions made in this chapter that were not part of the perfect market scenario?

Q 2.45 What is the difference between a bond and a loan?

Q 2.46 In the text, I assumed you received the dividend at the end of the period. In the real world, if you received the dividend at the beginning of the period instead of the end of the period, could this change your effective rate of return? Why?

Q 2.47 Your stock costs $100 today, pays $5 in dividends at the end of the period, and then sells for $98. What is your rate of return?

Q 2.48 The interest rate has just increased from 6% to 8%. How many basis points is this?

Q 2.49 Assume an interest rate of 10% per year. How much would you lose over 5 years if you had to give up interest on the interest—that is, if you received 50% instead of compounded interest?

Q 2.50 Over 20 years, would you prefer 10% per annum, with interest compounding, or 15% per annum but without interest compounding? (That is, you receive the interest, but it is put into an account that earns no interest, which is what we call simple interest.)

Q 2.51 A project returned +30%, then −30%. Thus, its arithmetic average rate of return was 0%. If you invested $25,000, how much did you end up with? Is your rate of return positive or negative? How would your overall rate of return have been different if you first earned −30% and then +30%?

Q 2.52 A project returned +50%, then −40%. Thus, its arithmetic average rate of return was +5%. Is your rate of return positive or negative?

Q 2.53 An investment for $50,000 earns a rate of return of 1% in each month of a full year. How much money will you have at year's end?

Q 2.54 There is always disagreement about what stocks are good purchases. The typical degree of disagreement is whether a particular stock is likely to offer, say, a 10% (pessimistic) or a 20% (optimistic) annualized rate of return. For a $30 stock today, what does the difference in belief between these two opinions mean for the expected stock price from today to tomorrow? (Assume that there are 365 days in the year. Reflect on your answer for a moment, and recognize that a $30 stock typically moves about ±$1 on a typical day. This unexplainable up-and-down volatility is often called noise.)

Q 2.55 If the interest rate is 5% per annum, how long will it take to double your money? How long will it take to triple it?

Q 2.56 If the interest rate is 8% per annum, how long will it take to double your money?

Q 2.57 From Fibonacci's *Liber Abaci*, written in the year 1202: "A certain man gave 1 denaro at interest so that in 5 years he must receive double the denari, and in another 5, he must have double 2 of the denari and thus forever. How many denari from this 1 denaro must he have in 100 years?"

Q 2.58 A bank quotes you a loan interest rate of 14% on your credit card. If you charge $15,000 at the beginning of the year, how much will you have to repay at the end of the year?

Q 2.59 Go to the website of a bank of your choice. What kind of quote does your bank post for a CD, and what kind of quote does your bank post for a mortgage? Why?

Q 2.60 What is the 1-year discount factor if the interest rate is 33.33%?

Q 2.61 You can choose between the following rent payments:

(a) A lump sum cash payment of $100,000;
(b) 10 annual payments of $12,000 each, the first occurring immediately;
(c) 120 monthly payments of $1,200 each, the first occurring immediately. (Friendly suggestion: This is a lot easier to calculate on a computer spreadsheet.)
(d) Which rental payment scheme would you choose if the interest rate was an effective 5% per year?
(e) Spreadsheet question: At what interest rate would you be indifferent between the first and the second choice above? (Hint: Graph the NPV of the second project as a function of the interest rate.)

Q 2.62 A project has cash flows of $15,000, $10,000, and $5,000 in 1, 2, and 3 years, respectively. If the prevailing interest rate is 15%, would you buy the project if it costs $25,000?

Q 2.63 Consider the same project that costs $25,000 with cash flows of $15,000, $10,000, and $5,000. At what prevailing interest rate would this project be profitable? Try different interest rates, and plot the NPV on the y-axis, and the interest rate on the x-axis.

Q 2.64 On April 12, 2006, Microsoft stock traded for $27.11 and claimed to pay an annual dividend of $0.36. Assume that the first dividend will be paid in 1 year, and that it then grows by 5% each year for the next 5 years. Further, assume that the prevailing interest rate is 6% per year. At what price would you have to sell Microsoft stock in 5 years in order to break even?

Q 2.65 Assume you are 25 years old. The IAW insurance company is offering you the following retirement contract (called an *annuity*): Contribute $2,000 per year for the next 40 years.

When you reach 65 years of age, you will receive \$30,000 per year for as long as you live. Assume that you believe that the chance that you will die is 10% per year after you will have reached 65 years of age. In other words, you will receive the first payment with probability 90%, the second payment with probability 81%, and so on. Assume the prevailing interest rate is 5% per year, all payments occur at year-end, and it is January 1 now. Is this annuity a good deal? (Use a spreadsheet.)

Q 2.66 A project has the following cash flows in periods 1 through 4: −\$200, +\$200, −\$200, +\$200. If the prevailing interest rate is 3%, would you accept this project if you were offered an upfront payment of \$10 to do so?

Q 2.67 Assume you are a real estate broker with an exclusive contract—the condo association rules state that everyone selling their condominiums must go through you or a broker designated by you. A typical condo costs \$500,000 today and sells again every 5 years. This will last for 50 years, and then all bets are off. Your commission will be 3%. Condos appreciate in value at a rate of 2% per year. The interest rate is 10% per annum.

(a) What is the value of this exclusivity rule? In other words, at what price should you be willing to sell the privilege of exclusive condo representation to another broker?

(b) If free Internet advertising was equally effective and if it could replace all real estate brokers so that buyers' and sellers' agents would no longer earn the traditional 6% (3% each), what would happen to the value gain of the condo?

Q 2.68 If the interest rate is 5% per annum, what would be the equivalent annual cost (see Question 2.39) of a \$2,000 lease payment up front, followed by \$800 for three more years?

Q 2.69 The prevailing discount rate is 15% per annum. Firm *F*'s cash flows start with \$500 in year 1 and grow at 20% per annum for 3 years. Firm *S*'s cash flows also start with \$500 in year 1 but shrink at 20% per annum for 3 years. What are the prices of these two firms? Which one is the better "buy"?

Stock and Bond Valuation: Annuities and Perpetuities

IMPORTANT SHORTCUT FORMULAS

The present value formula is the main workhorse for valuing investments of all types, including stocks and bonds. But these rarely have just two or three future payments. Stocks may pay dividends forever. The most common mortgage bond has 30 years of monthly payments—360 of them. It would be possible but tedious to work with NPV formulas containing 360 terms.

Fortunately, there are some shortcut formulas that can speed up your PVcomputations if your projects have a particular set of cash flow patterns and the opportunity cost of capital is constant. The two most prominent such formulas are for projects called perpetuities (that have payments lasting forever) and annuities (that have payments lasting for a limited amount of years). Of course, no firm lasts forever, but the perpetuity formula is often a useful "quick-and-dirty" tool for a good approximation. In any case, the formulas you will learn in this chapter are in wide use, and they can even help you to understand the economics of corporate growth.

3.1 PERPETUITIES

A simple **perpetuity** is a project that has a stream of constant cash flows that repeats forever. If the cost of capital (i.e., the appropriate discount rate) is constant and the amount of money remains the same or grows at a constant rate, perpetuities lend themselves to fast present value solutions—very useful when you need to come up with quick rule-of-thumb estimates. Though the formulas may seem a bit intimidating at first, using them will quickly become second nature to you.

"Perpetuities" are projects with special kinds of cash flows, which permit the use of shortcut formulas.

3.1A THE SIMPLE PERPETUITY FORMULA

At a constant interest rate of 10%, how much money do you need to invest today to receive the same dollar amount of interest of $2 each year, starting next year, forever? Table 3.1 shows the present values of all future payments for a perpetuity paying $2

Here is an example of a perpetuity that pays $2 forever.

TABLE 3.1 PERPETUITY STREAM OF \$2 WITH INTEREST RATE $r = 10\%$

Time	Cash Flow	Discount Factor	Present Value	Cumulative
0		Nothing! You have no cash flow here!		
1	\$2	$1/(1+10\%)^1 \approx 0.909$	\$1.82	\$1.82
2	\$2	$1/(1+10\%)^2 \approx 0.826$	\$1.65	\$3.47
3	\$2	$1/(1+10\%)^3 \approx 0.751$	\$1.50	\$4.97
⋮				
50	\$2	$1/(1+10\%)^{50} \approx 0.0085$	\$0.02	\$19.83
⋮				
			Net Present Value (Sum):	\$20.00

forever, if the interest rate is 10% per annum. Note how there is no payment at time 0, and that the individual payment terms become smaller and smaller the further out we go.

The shortcut perpetuity formula.

To confirm the table's last row, which gives the perpetuity's net present value as \$20, you can spend from here to eternity to add up the infinite number of terms. But if you use a spreadsheet to compute and add up the first 50 terms, you will get a PV of \$19.83. If you add up the first 100 terms, you will get a PV of \$19.9986. Mathematically, the sum eventually converges to \$20 sharp. This is because there is a nice shortcut to computing the net present value of the perpetuity if the cost of capital is constant:

$$\text{Perpetuity PV} = \frac{\$2}{10\%} = \frac{\$2}{0.1} = \$20$$

$$\text{PV} = \frac{C_1}{r}$$

The "1" time subscript in the formula is to remind you that the first cash flow occurs not now, but next year—the cash flows themselves will remain the same amount next year, the year after, and so on.

IMPORTANT: A stream of constant cash flows (C dollars each period and forever) beginning *next* period (i.e., time 1), which is discounted at the same per-period cost of capital r forever, is a special perpetuity worth

$$\text{PV} = \frac{C_1}{r},$$

which is a shortcut for

$$\text{PV} = \frac{C_1}{1+r} + \frac{C_2}{(1+r)^2} + \frac{C_3}{(1+r)^3} + \cdots + \frac{C_T}{(1+r)^T} + \cdots$$

ANECDOTE The Oldest Institutions and Perpetuities

Perpetuities assume that projects last forever. But nothing really lasts forever. The oldest Western institution today may well be the Roman Catholic Church, which is about 2,000 years old. The oldest existing corporation in the United States is the Collegiate Reformed Protestant Dutch Church of the City of New York, formed in 1628 and granted a corporate charter by King William in 1696. The Canadian Hudson's Bay Company was founded in 1670 and claims to be the oldest continuously incorporated company in the world.

Guantanamo Naval Base was leased from Cuba in 1903 as a perpetuity by the United States in exchange for 2,000 pesos per annum in U.S. gold, equivalent to $4,085. In a speech, Fidel Castro has redefined time as "whatever is indefinite lasts 100 years." In any case, the Cuban government no longer recognizes the agreement and does not accept the annual payments—but has also wisely not yet tried to expel the Americans.

The easiest way for you to get comfortable with perpetuities is to solve some problems.

SOLVE NOW!

Q 3.1 From memory, write down the perpetuity formula. Be explicit on when the first cash flow occurs.

Q 3.2 What is the PV of a perpetuity paying $5 each month, beginning *next* month, if the monthly interest rate is a constant 0.5%/month?

Q 3.3 What is the PV of a perpetuity paying $15 each month, beginning *next* month, if the *effective* annual interest rate is a constant 12.68% per year?

Q 3.4 Under what interest rates would you prefer a perpetuity that pays $2 million per year beginning next year to a one-time payment of $40 million?

Q 3.5 In Britain, there are **Consol** bonds that are perpetuity bonds. (In the United States, the IRS does not allow companies to deduct the interest payments on perpetual bonds, so U.S. corporations do not issue Consol bonds.) What is the value of a Consol bond that promises to pay $2,000 per year if the prevailing interest rate is 4%?

3.1B THE GROWING PERPETUITY FORMULA

What if, instead of the same amount of cash every period, the cash flows increase over time? The **growing perpetuity** formula allows for a constant rate g per period, provided it is less than the interest rate. Table 3.2 shows a growing perpetuity that pays $2 next year, grows at a rate of 5%, and faces a cost of capital of 10%. The present value of the first 30 terms adds up to $30.09. The first 100 terms add up to $39.64. The first 200 terms add up to $39.98. Eventually, the sum approaches the formula

A growing perpetuity assumes that cash flows grow by a constant rate g forever.

$$\text{PV of Growing Perpetuity} = \frac{\$2}{10\% - 5\%} = \$40$$

$$\text{PV} = \frac{C_1}{r - g} \qquad (3.1)$$

TABLE 3.2 PERPETUITY STREAM WITH $C_1 = \$2$, GROWTH RATE $g = 5\%$, AND INTEREST RATE $r = 10\%$

Time	Cash Flow	Discount Rate	Discount Factor	Present Value	Cumulative
0	Nothing! You have no cash flow here!				
1	$(1 + 5\%)^0 \cdot \$2 = \$2.000$	$(1 + 10\%)^1$	0.909	\$1.818	\$1.82
2	$(1 + 5\%)^1 \cdot \$2 = \$2.100$	$(1 + 10\%)^2$	0.826	\$1.736	\$3.56
3	$(1 + 5\%)^2 \cdot \$2 = \$2.205$	$(1 + 10\%)^3$	0.751	\$1.657	\$5.22
⋮					
30	$(1 + 5\%)^{29} \cdot \$2 \approx \$8.232$	$(1 + 10\%)^{30}$	0.057	\$0.472	\$30.09
⋮					
			Net Present Value (Sum):		\$40.00

As before, the "1" subscript indicates that cash flows begin next period, not this period, but here it is necessary because future cash flows will be different. The interest rate is r and it is reduced by g, the growth rate of your cash flows. Note how the table shows that the first application of the growth factor g occurs 1 period after the first application of the discount factor. For example, the cash flow at time 30 is discounted by $(1 + r)^{30}$, but its cash flow is C multiplied by a growth factor of $(1 + g)^{29}$. You will later encounter many applications of the growing perpetuity formula. For example, it is common to assume that cash flows grow by the rate of inflation. You will also later use this formula to obtain so-called terminal values in a chapter of this book, in which you design so-called pro formas.

➤ Terminal value, Section 20.2, p. 736

IMPORTANT: A stream of cash flows growing at a rate of g each period and discounted at a constant interest rate r is worth

$$PV = \frac{C_1}{r - g}$$

The first cash flow, C_1, occurs next period (time 1), the second cash flow of $C_2 = C_1 \cdot (1 + g)$ occurs in 2 periods, and so forth, *forever*. For the formula to work, g can be negative, but r must be greater than g.

The growing perpetuity formula is worth memorizing.

Although a subscript on C makes this seem more painful, it is a good reminder here.

Be careful to use the cash flow next year in the numerator in the formula. The subscript "1" is there to remind you. For example, if you want to use this formula on your firm, and it earned \$100 million this year, and you expect it to grow at a 5% rate forever, then the correct cash flow in the numerator is $C_1 = \$105$ million, not \$100 million!

The formula is nonsensical when $r < g$.

What would happen if the cash flows grew faster than the interest rate ($g > r$)? Wouldn't the formula indicate a negative PV? Yes, but this is because the entire scenario would be nonsense. The present value in the perpetuities formulas is only less than infinity, because *in today's dollars*, each term in the sum is a little less than the term in the previous period. If g were greater than r, however, the cash flow 1 period later would be worth more even in today's dollars. For example, take our earlier example with a discount rate of 10%, but make the growth rate of cash flows $g = 15\%$. The first cash flow would be $\$2 \cdot 1.15 = \$2.30$, which discounts to \$2.09 today. The second cash flow would be $\$2 \cdot 1.15^2 = \$2.645$, which discounts to \$2.186 today. The present value of each cash flow is higher than that preceding it. Taking a sum over an infinite number of such increasing terms would yield infinity as the value. A value of infinity is clearly not sensible, as nothing in this world is worth an infinite amount of money. Therefore, the growing perpetuity formula yields a nonsensical negative value if $g \geq r$—as it should!

SOLVE NOW!

Q 3.6 From memory, write down the growing perpetuity formula.

Q 3.7 What is the PV of a perpetuity paying \$5 each month, beginning *this* month (in 1 second), if the monthly interest rate is a constant 0.5%/month (6.2%/year) and the cash flows will grow at a rate of 0.1%/month (1.2%/year)?

Q 3.8 What is the PV of a perpetuity paying \$8 each month, beginning *this* month (in 1 second), if the monthly interest rate is a constant 0.5%/month (6.2%/year) and the cash flows will grow at a rate of 0.8%/month (10%/year)?

Q 3.9 Here is an example of the most common use of the growing perpetuity model (called a pro forma). Your firm just finished the year, in which it had cash earnings of \$100 million. You forecast your firm to have a quick growth phase for 3 years, in which it grows at a rate of 20% per annum. Your firm's growth then slows down to 10% per annum for the next 3 years. Finally, beginning in year 7, you expect it to settle into its long-term growth rate of 5% per annum. You also expect your cost of capital to be 10% over the first 3 years, then 9% over the next 3 years, and 8% thereafter. What do you think your firm is worth today?

Q 3.10 An eternal patent contract states that the patentee will pay the patentor a fee of \$1.5 million next year. The contract terms state a fee growth with the inflation rate, which runs at 2% per annum. The appropriate cost of capital is 14%. What is the value of this patenting contract?

Q 3.11 How would the patent contract value change if the first payment did not occur next year, but tonight?

3.1C PERPETUITY APPLICATION: STOCK VALUATION WITH A GORDON GROWTH MODEL

Perpetuities are imperfect approximations, but often give a useful upper bound.

With their fixed interest and growth rates and eternal payment requirements, perpetuities are rarely exactly correct. But they can be very helpful for quick back-of-the-envelope estimates. For example, consider a mature and stable business with profits of \$1 million next year. Because it is stable, its profits are likely to grow at the inflation rate of, say, 2% per annum. This means it will earn \$1,020,000 in 2 years, \$1,040,400 in 3 years, and so on. The firm faces a cost of capital of 8%. The growing perpetuity formula indicates that this firm should probably be worth no more than

$$\text{Business Value} = \frac{\$1{,}000{,}000}{8\% - 2\%} \approx \$16{,}666{,}667$$

$$\text{Business Value} = \frac{C_1}{r - g}$$

because in reality, the firm will almost surely not exist forever. Of course, in real life, there are often even more significant uncertainties: Next year's profit may be different, the firm may grow at a different rate (or may grow at a different rate for a while) or face a different cost of capital for 1-year loans than it does for 30-year loans. Thus, \$16.7 million should be considered a quick-and-dirty useful approximation, perhaps for an upper limit, and not an exact number.

The Gordon growth model: constant eternal dividend growth.

The growing perpetuity model is sometimes directly applied to the stock market. For example, if you believe that a stock's dividends will grow by $g = 5\%$ forever, and if you believe that the appropriate rate of return is $r = 10\%$, and you expect the stock to earn and/or pay dividends of $D = \$10$ *next year*, then you would feel that a stock price today of

$$\text{Stock Price } P \text{ Today} = \frac{\$10}{10\% - 5\%} = \$200$$

$$\text{Stock Price } P \text{ Today} = \frac{\text{Dividends } D \text{ Next Year}}{r - g} \quad (3.2)$$

would be appropriate. In this context, the growing perpetuity model is often called the **Gordon growth model**, after its inventor, Myron Gordon.

You could estimate the cost of capital for GE, based on its dividend yield and its expected dividend growth rate.

Let us explore the Gordon growth model a bit more. In October 2004, Yahoo! *Finance* listed General Electric (GE) with a dividend yield of 2.43%. This is the analysts' consensus forecast of next year's dividends divided by the stock price, D/P. This is called the **dividend yield**. Rearrange Formula 3.2:

$$\frac{\text{Dividends Next Year}}{\text{Stock Price Today}} = r - g = 2.43\%$$

Therefore, you can infer that the market believes that the appropriate cost of capital (r) for General Electric exceeds its growth rate of dividends (g) by about 2.4%. Yahoo! *Finance* further links to a summary of GE's cash flow statement, which indicates that GE paid \$7.643 billion in dividends in 2003, and \$6.358 billion in 2001. Over these 2 years, the growth rate of dividends was about 9.6% per annum ($\$6.358 \cdot 1.096^2 \approx \$7.643$). Therefore, if you believe 9.6%/year is also a fair representation of the eternal future growth rate of GE's dividends, then the financial markets valued GE as if it had a per-annum cost of capital of about

$$r = \frac{\text{Dividends Next Year}}{\text{Stock Price Today}} + g \approx 2.4\% + 9.6\% = 12\%$$

Let's play another game that is prominent in the financial world. Earnings are, loosely speaking, cousins of the cash flows that corporate stockholders are receiving. You can then think of the value of the stock today as the value of the earnings stream that the stock will produce. After all, recall from Chapter 1 that owners receive all dividends and all cash flows (earnings), presumably the former being paid out from the latter. (In Chapter 13, I will explain a lot of this in more detail as well as why earnings are only approximately but not exactly cash flows.)

Let's presume that the formula also applied to earnings.

It is furthermore common to assume that stock market values are capitalized as if corporate earnings were eternal cash flows that are growing at a constant rate g applicable to earnings (which is not necessarily the same as the growth rate applicable to dividends). This means that you would assume that the value of the firm is

You could also estimate the cost of capital for GE based on its price/earnings ratio and its earnings growth rate.

$$\text{Stock Price } P \text{ Today} = \frac{\text{Earnings } E \text{ Next Year}}{r - g}$$

Thus, to determine the rate of return that investors require (the cost of capital), all you need is a forecast of earnings, the current stock price, and the eternal growth rate of earnings. Again, Yahoo! *Finance* gives you all the information you need. In October 2004, it listed GE's "trailing P/E" ratio—calculated as the current stock price divided by historical earnings—as 21. More interestingly, it listed the "forward P/E" ratio—calculated as the price divided by analysts' expectations of *next* year's earnings—as 18.5. The growing perpetuity formula wants the earnings *next* year, so the latter is closer to what you need. Yahoo! *Finance* further tells you that GE's earnings growth rate was 6.3%—the g in the formula if you are willing to assume that the current earnings growth rate is the long-term growth rate. Therefore, all you have to do is rearrange the growing perpetuity formula, and out comes an appropriate rate of return:

$$r = \frac{\text{Earnings Next Year}}{\text{Stock Price Today}} + g = \frac{1}{P/E} + g \approx \frac{1}{18.5} + 6.3\% \approx 11.7\%$$

Given GE's price/earnings ratio and growth rate of earnings, investors are expecting a rate of return of about 12% per annum.

It is important that you recognize these are just approximations that you should not take too seriously in terms of accuracy. GE will not last forever, earnings are not the cash flows you need, the discount rate is not eternally constant, earnings will not grow forever at 6.3%, and so on. However, the numbers are not uninteresting and may not even be too far off, either. GE is a very stable company that is likely to be around for a long time, and you could do a lot worse than assuming that the cost of capital (for investing in projects that are similar to GE stock ownership) is somewhere around 12% per annum—say, somewhere between 10% to 14% per annum.

Keep perspective! The model provides only a quick approximation.

➤ Price-earnings ratio, Section 14.2, p. 496

SOLVE NOW!

Q 3.12 A stock is paying a quarterly dividend of $5 in 1 month. The dividend is expected to increase every quarter by the inflation rate of 0.5% per quarter—so it will be $5.025 in the next quarter (i.e., paid out in 4 months). The prevailing cost of capital for this kind of stock is 9% per annum. What should this stock be worth?

Q 3.13 If a \$100 stock has earnings that are \$5 per year, and the appropriate cost of capital for this stock is 12% per year, what does the market expect the firm's "as-if-eternal dividends" to grow at?

3.2 ANNUITIES

An annuity pays the same amount for T years.

The second type of cash flow stream that lends itself to a quick formula is an **annuity**, which is a stream of equal cash flows for a given number of periods. Unlike a perpetuity, payments stop after T periods. For example, if the interest rate is 10% per period, what is the value of an annuity that pays \$5 per period for 3 periods?

Let us first do this the slow way. You can hand-compute the net present value to be

$$\text{PV} = \frac{\$5}{1.10} + \frac{\$5}{1.10^2} + \frac{\$5}{1.10^3} \approx \$12.4343$$

$$\text{PV} = \frac{C_1}{(1+r_1)} + \frac{C_2}{(1+r_2)} + \frac{C_3}{(1+r_3)}$$

$$= \frac{C_1}{(1+r)} + \frac{C_2}{(1+r)^2} + \frac{C_3}{(1+r)^3}$$

The annuity formula makes short work of this NPV calculation,

$$\text{PV} = \$5 \cdot \left\{\frac{1 - [1/(1+10\%)]^3}{10\%}\right\} \approx \$12.4343$$

$$\text{PV} = C_1 \cdot \left\{\frac{1 - [1/(1+r)]^T}{r}\right\} = \text{PV}$$

Is this really a shortcut? Maybe not for 3 periods, but try a 360-period annuity—which method do you prefer? Either works.

IMPORTANT: A stream of constant equal cash flows, beginning next period (time 1) and lasting for T periods, and discounted at a constant interest rate r, is worth

$$\text{PV} = \frac{C_1}{r} \cdot \left[1 - \frac{1}{(1+r)^T}\right]$$

SOLVE NOW!

Q 3.14 How many years does it take for an annuity to reach three-quarters the value of a perpetuity if the interest rate is 5%? If the interest rate is r? To reach fraction f of the value?

Q 3.15 Recall from memory the annuity formula.

Q 3.16 What is the PV of a 360-month annuity paying \$5 per month, beginning at \$5 next month (time 1), if the monthly interest rate is a constant 0.5%/month (6.2%/year)?

Q 3.17 Solve Fibonacci's annuity problem given in the Anecdote: Compare the PV of a stream of quarterly cash flows of 75 bezants versus the PV of a stream of annual cash flows of 300 bezants. Payments are always at period-end. The interest rate is 2% per month. What is the relative value of the two streams? Compute the difference for a 1-year investment first.

Q 3.18 In *L'Arithmetique*, written in 1558, Jean Trenchant posed the following question: "In the year 1555, King Henry, to conduct the war, took money from bankers at the rate of 4% per fair [quarter]. That is better terms for them than 16% per year. In this same year before the fair of Toussaints, he received by the hands of certain bankers the sum of 3,945,941 ecus and more, which they called 'Le Grand Party' on the condition that he will pay interest at 5% per fair for 41 fairs after which he will be finished. Which of these conditions is better for the bankers?" Translated, the question is whether a perpetuity at 4% per quarter is better or worse than a 41-quarter annuity at 5%.

ANECDOTE Fibonacci and the Invention of Net Present Value

William Goetzmann argues that Leonardo of Pisa, commonly called Fibonacci, may have invented not only the famous "Fibonacci series" but also the concept of net present value.

Fibonacci's family were merchants in the Mediterranean in the thirteenth century, with trade relations to Arab merchants in Northern Africa. Fibonacci wrote about mathematics primarily as a tool to solve merchants' problems—in effect, to understand the pricing of goods and currencies relative to one another. Think about how rich you could get if you could determine faster than your competition which goods were worth more in relation to others! In fact, you should think of Fibonacci and other Pisan merchants as the "financial engineers" of the thirteenth century.

Fibonacci wrote his most famous treatise, *Liber Abaci,* at age 30, publishing it in 1202. We still are solving the same kinds of problems today that Fibonacci explained. One of them—which you solve in Q3.17—is called "On a Soldier Receiving 300 Bezants for His Fief":

> A soldier is granted an annuity by the king of 300 bezants per year, paid in quarterly installments of 75 bezants. The king alters the payment schedule to an annual year-end payment of 300. The soldier is able to earn 2 bezants on 100 per month (over each quarter) on his investment. How much is his effective compensation after the terms of the annuity changed?

To solve this problem, you must know how to value payments at different points in the future—you must understand the time value of money. What is the value of 75 bezants in 1 quarter, 2 quarters, and so forth? What is the value of 300 bezants in 1 year, 2 years, and so on? Yes, money sooner is usually worth more than money later—but you need to determine by exactly how much in order to determine how good or bad the change is for the king and the soldier. To answer, you must use the interest rate Fibonacci gives and then compare the two different cash flow streams—the original payment schedule and the revised payment schedule—in terms of a common denominator. This common denominator will be the two streams' present values.

3.2A ANNUITY APPLICATION: FIXED-RATE MORTGAGE PAYMENTS

Mortgages and other loans are annuities, so the annuity formula is in common use.

Most mortgages are **fixed-rate mortgage loans**, and they are basically annuities. They promise a specified stream of equal cash payments each month to a lender. A 30-year mortgage with monthly payments is really a 360-payment annuity. (The "annu-ity" formula should really be called a "month-ity" formula in this case.) What would be your monthly payment if you took out a 30-year mortgage loan for $500,000 at a quoted interest rate of 7.5% per annum?

Lenders quote interest rates using the same convention as banks.

Before you can proceed further, you need to know one more bit of institutional knowledge here: Mortgage providers—like banks—quote interest by just dividing the mortgage quote by 12, so the true monthly interest rate is 7.5%/12 = 0.625%. (They do not compound; if they did, the monthly interest rate would be $(1 + 7.5\%)^{1/12} - 1 \approx 0.605\%$.)

The mortgage payment can be determined by solving the annuity formula.

A 30-year mortgage is an annuity with 360 equal payments with a discount rate of 0.625% per month. Its PV of $500,000 is the amount that you are borrowing. You want to determine the fixed monthly cash flow that gives the annuity this value:

$$\$500{,}000 = \frac{C_1}{0.625\%} \cdot \left[1 - \frac{1}{(1 + 0.625\%)^{360}}\right] \approx C_1 \cdot 143.018$$

$$\text{PV} = \frac{C_1}{r} \cdot \left[1 - \frac{1}{(1 + r)^T}\right]$$

Solving for the cash flow tells you that the monthly payment on your $500,000 mortgage will be $500,000/143.018 ≈ $3,496.07 for 360 months, beginning next month (time 1).

SIDE NOTE: Uncle Sam allows mortgage borrowers to deduct the interest, but not the principal, from their tax bills. The IRS imputes interest on the above mortgage as follows: In the first month, Uncle Sam proclaims 0.625% · $500,000 = $3,125 to be the tax-deductible mortgage interest payment. Therefore, the principal repayment is $3,496.07 − $3,125 = $371.07 and the remaining principal is $499,628.93. The following month, Uncle Sam proclaims 0.625% · $499,628.93 ≈ $3,122.68 to be the tax-deductible interest payment, $3,496.07 − $3,122.68 = $373.39 to be the principal repayment, and $499,255.54 as the remaining principal. And so on.

SOLVE NOW!

Q 3.19 Rental agreements are not much different from mortgages. For example, what would your rate of return be if you rented your $500,000 warehouse for 10 years at a monthly lease payment of $5,000? If you can earn 5% per annum elsewhere, would you rent out your warehouse?

Q 3.20 What is the monthly payment on a 15-year mortgage for every $1,000 of mortgage at an effective interest rate of 6.168% per year (here, 0.5% per month)?

3.2B ANNUITY APPLICATION: A LEVEL-COUPON BOND

Let us exercise your newfound knowledge in a more elaborate example—this time with bonds. Recall that a bond is a financial claim sold by a firm or government. Bonds come in many different varieties, but one useful classification is into coupon bonds and zero-bonds (short for **zero coupon bonds**). A **coupon bond** pays its holder cash at many different points in time, whereas a **zero-bond** pays only a single lump sum at the maturity of the bond with no interim coupon. Many coupon bonds promise to pay a regular coupon similar to the interest rate prevailing at the time of the bond's original sale, and then return a "principal amount" plus a final coupon at the end of the bond.

Unlike zer- bonds, coupon bonds pay not only at the final time.

For example, think of a coupon bond that will pay $1,500 each half-year (semiannual payment is very common) for 5 years, plus an additional $100,000 in 5 years. This payment pattern is so common that it has specially named features: A bond with coupon payments that remain the same for the life of the bond is called a **level-coupon bond.** (In fact, these types of bonds are by far the most common among all bonds in the wild.) The $100,000 here would be called the **principal**, in contrast to the $1,500 semiannual coupon. Level bonds are commonly named by just adding up all the coupon payments over 1 year (here, $3,000) and dividing this sum of annual coupon payments by the principal. Thus, this particular bond would be called a "3% semiannual coupon bond" ($3,000 coupon per year divided by the principal of $100,000). Now, the "3% coupon bond" is just a naming convention for the bond with these specific cash flow patterns—it is not the interest rate that you would expect if you bought this bond. In Section 2.4B, we called such name designations interest *quotes*, as distinct from interest *rates*. Of course, even if the bond were to cost $100,000 today (and you shall see below that it usually does not), the interest rate would not be 3% per annum, but $1.015^2 - 1 \approx 3.02\%$ per annum.

Bond naming conventions specify their promised payout patterns.

➤ Section 2.4B, "Compounding and Future Value," p. 19

What should this $100,000, 3% semiannual level-coupon bond sell for today? First, you should write down the payment structure for a 3% semiannual coupon bond. This comes from its defined promised payout pattern:

Step 1: Write down the bond's payment stream.

Year	Due Date	Bond Payment	Year	Due Date	Bond Payment
0.5	Nov 2002	$1,500	3.0	May 2005	$1,500
1.0	May 2003	$1,500	3.5	Nov 2005	$1,500
1.5	Nov 2003	$1,500	4.0	May 2006	$1,500
2.0	May 2004	$1,500	4.5	Nov 2006	$1,500
2.5	Nov 2004	$1,500	5.0	May 2007	$101,500

Second, you need to determine the appropriate rates of return that apply to these cash flows. In this example, assume that the prevailing interest rate is 5% per annum. This translates into 2.47% for 6 months, 10.25% for 2 years, and so on.

Step 2: Find the appropriate cost of capital for each payment.

Maturity	Discount Rate	Maturity	Discount Rate
6 Months	2.47%	36 Months	15.76%
12 Months	5.00%	42 Months	18.62%

18 Months	7.59%	48 Months	21.55%
24 Months	10.25%	54 Months	24.55%
30 Months	12.97%	60 Months	27.63%

Step 3: Compute the discount factor—it is $1/(1 + r_t)$.

Third, compute the discount factors, which are just $1/(1 + r_t) = 1/(1 + r)^t$, and multiply each future payment by its discount factor. This will give you the present value (PV) of each bond payment. From there, you can compute the bond's overall value:

Year	Due Date	Bond Payment	Rate of Return	Discount Factor	Present Value
0.5	Nov 2002	$1,500	2.47%	0.9759	$1,463.85
1.0	May 2003	$1,500	5.00%	0.9524	$1,428.57
1.5	Nov 2003	$1,500	7.59%	0.9294	$1,394.14
2.0	May 2004	$1,500	10.25%	0.9070	$1,360.54
2.5	Nov 2004	$1,500	12.97%	0.8852	$1,327.76
3.0	May 2005	$1,500	15.76%	0.8638	$1,295.76
3.5	Nov 2005	$1,500	18.62%	0.8430	$1,264.53
4.0	May 2006	$1,500	21.55%	0.8277	$1,234.05
4.5	Nov 2006	$1,500	24.55%	0.8029	$1,204.31
5.0	May 2007	$101,500	27.63%	0.7835	$79,527.91
				Sum:	$91,501.42

Discount and premium bonds.

You now know that you would expect this 3% semiannual level-coupon bond to be trading for $91,501.42 today in a perfect market. Because the current price of the bond is below its named final principal payment of $100,000, this bond would be said to trade at a **discount**. (The opposite would be a bond trading at a **premium**.)

Using the annuity formula to speed your calculations.

The bond's value can be calculated more quickly via the annuity formula. Let's work in half-year periods. You have 10 coupon cash flows, each $1,500, at a per-period interest rate of 2.47%. According to the formula, these 10 coupon payments are worth

$$PV = C_1 \cdot \left\{ \frac{1 - [1/(1+r)]^T}{r} \right\} = \$1{,}500 \cdot \left\{ \frac{1 - [1/(1.0247)]^{10}}{2.47\%} \right\} \approx \$13{,}148.81$$

In addition, you have the $100,000 repayment of principal, which will occur in year 5 and is therefore worth

$$PV = \frac{\$100{,}000}{(1+5\%)^5} \approx \frac{\$100{,}000}{1+27.63\%} \approx \$78{,}352.62$$

$$PV = \frac{C_5}{(1+r)^5} = \frac{C_5}{(1+r_5)}$$

Together, the present values of the bond's cash flows again add up to $91,501.42.

The coupon rate is *not* the interest rate.

Important Reminder of Quotes versus Returns: Never confuse a bond designation with the interest it pays. The "3% semiannual coupon bond" is just a designation for the bond's payout pattern. The bond will not give you coupon payments equal to 1.5% of your $91,501.42 investment (which would be $1,372.52). The prevailing interest rate (cost of capital) has nothing to do with the quoted interest rate on the coupon bond. You could just as well determine the value of a 0% coupon bond, or a 10% coupon bond, given the prevailing 5% economy-wide interest rate. Having said all this, in the real world, many corporations choose coupon rates similar to the prevailing interest rate, so that at the moment of inception, the bond will be trading at neither a premium nor a discount. At least for this one brief at-issue instant, the coupon rate and the economy-wide interest rate may actually be fairly close. However, soon after issuance, market interest rates will move around, while the bond's payments remain fixed, as designated by the bond's coupon name.

SOLVE NOW!

Q 3.21 You already learned that the value of one fixed future payment and the interest rate move in opposite directions (page 28). What happens to the bond price of $91,501.42 in the level-coupon bond example if the economy-wide interest rates were to suddenly move from 5% per annum to 6% per annum?

Q 3.22 Assume that the 3% level-coupon bond discussed in this chapter has not just 5 years with 10 payments, but 20 years with 40 payments. Also, assume that the interest rate is not 5% per annum, but 10.25% per annum. What are the bond payment patterns and the bond's value?

Q 3.23 Check that the rates of return in the coupon bond valuation example on page 52 are correct.

3.3 THE FOUR FORMULAS SUMMARIZED

The growing annuity formula—it is used only rarely.

I am not a fan of memorization, but you must remember the growing perpetuity formula. It would likely be useful if you could also remember the annuity formula. These formulas are used in many different contexts. There is also a fourth formula, the **growing annuity** formula, which nobody remembers, but which you should know to look up if you need it. It is

$$\text{PV} = \frac{C_1}{r-g} \cdot \left[1 - \frac{(1+g)^T}{(1+r)^T}\right]$$

It is sometimes used in the context of pension cash flows, which tend to grow for a fixed number of time periods (T in the formula above) and then stop. However, even then it is not a necessary device. It is often more convenient and flexible to just work with the cash flows themselves within a spreadsheet.

A full summary.

Figure 3.1 summarizes the four special cash flows. The top graph shows the pattern of cash flows. For perpetuities, they go on forever. For annuities, they eventually stop. The bottom graph shows the present value of these cash flows. Naturally, these bars are shorter than those of their cash flows, which just means that there is a time value of money. Below the graphs are the applicable formulas.

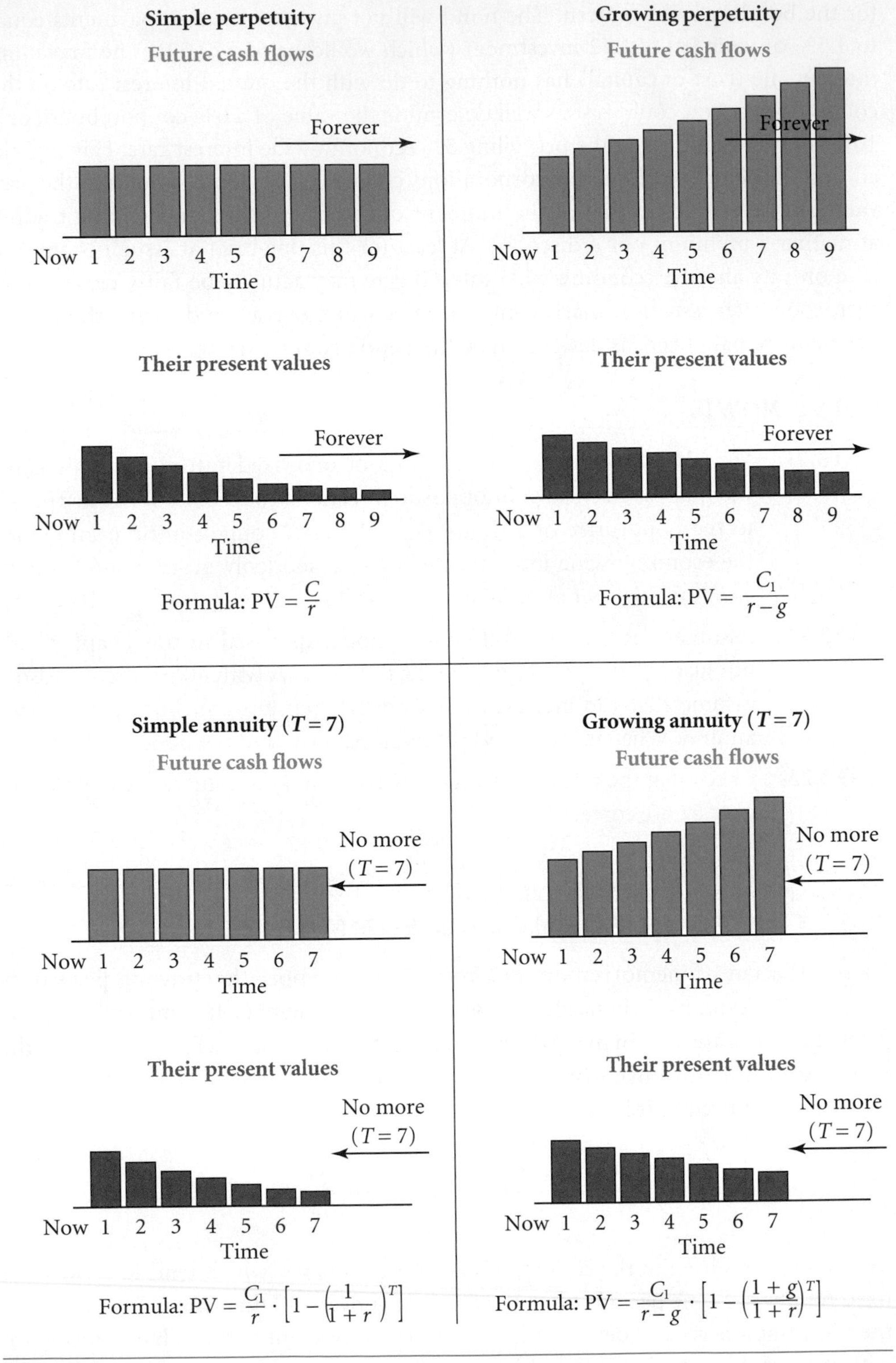

FIGURE 3.1 The Four Payoff Streams and Their Present Values

SOLVE NOW!

Q 3.24 In many defined-contribution pension plans, the employer provides a fixed-percentage contribution to the employee's retirement. Assume that you must contribute \$4,000 per annum beginning next year (time 1), growing annually with the inflation rate of 2% per year. What is the pension cost of hiring a 25-year-old who will stay with the company for 35 years? Assume a discount rate of 8% per year. Note: You need the growing annuity formula from page 53, which you should look up.

SUMMARY

This chapter covered the following major points:

- Figure 3.1 summarizes the four special cash flows and their quick valuation formulas.
- The PV of a simple perpetuity, which is a stream of constant cash flows that begin next period and that are to be discounted at the same annual cost of capital forever, is

$$PV = \frac{C_1}{r}$$

- The PV of a growing perpetuity—with constant growth g, cash flows C beginning next year (time 1), and constant per-period interest rate r—is

$$PV = \frac{C_1}{r - g}$$

- Stocks are often valued through an application of the growing perpetuity formula, called the Gordon dividend growth model.
- The PV of an annuity—T periods of constant C cash flows (beginning next year) and constant per-period interest rate r—is

$$PV = C_1 \cdot \left\{ \frac{1 - [1/(1+r)]^T}{r} \right\}$$

- Fixed-rate mortgages are annuities. The quoted interest rate on such bonds are those that come out of an application of the annuity formula.

KEY TERMS

annuity, 48
Consol, 43
coupon bond, 51
discount, 52
dividend yield, 46
fixed-rate mortgage loan, 50
Gordon growth model, 46
growing annuity, 53
growing perpetuity, 43
level-coupon bond, 51
perpetuity, 41
premium, 52
principal, 51
zero-bond, 51
zero coupon bond, 51

SOLVE NOW! SOLUTIONS

Q 3.1 C_1/r. The first cash flow occurs next period, not this period.

Q 3.2 $\text{PV} = C_1/r = \$5/0.005 = \$1{,}000$

Q 3.3 The interest rate is $1.1268^{(1/12)} - 1 \approx 1\%$ per month. Thus, $\text{PV} = C_1/r \approx \$15/0.01 \approx \$1{,}500$.

Q 3.4 Rearrange $P = C_1/r$ into $r = C_1/P = \$2/\$40 = 5\%$. At a 5% interest rate you are indifferent. If the interest rate is above 5%, the immediate one-time payment is better, because future cash flows are less valuable. If the interest rate is below 5%, the perpetuity payment is better, because future cash flows are more valuable.

Q 3.5 $\text{PV} = \$2{,}000/4\% = \$50{,}000$

Q 3.6 $C_1/(r - g)$.

Q 3.7 You get $C_0 = \$5$ today, and next month you will receive a payment of $C_1 = (1 + g) \cdot C_0 = 1.001 \cdot \$5 = \$5.005$. The growing perpetuity is worth $\text{PV} = C_1/(r - g) = \$5.005/(0.5\% - 0.1\%) = \$1{,}251.25$. The total value is \$1,256.25.

Q 3.8 This is a nonsensical question, because the value would be infinite if $g \geq r$.

Q 3.9 Your earnings will be as follows:

Pro Forma	Ended	Year 1	Year 2	Year 3	Year 4	Year 5	Year 6	Year 7	Year 8	. . .
Year's Rate		10%	10%	10%	9%	9%	9%	8%	8%	. . .
Discount Rate (compounded)		10%	21%	33.1%	45.1%	58.1%	72.4%	86.2%	101.1%	. . .
Growth Rate		20%	20%	20%	10%	10%	10%	5%	5%	. . .
Earnings (million \$)	(\$100)	\$120.00	\$144.00	\$172.80	\$190.08	\$209.09	\$230.00	\$241.50	\$253.57	
Terminal Value (million \$)						$\$253.57/(8\% - 5\%) \approx \$8{,}452.33$				
Present Value (million \$)		\$109.09	\$119.01	\$129.83	\$131.02	\$132.22	\$133.43	\$129.73		
Present Value (million \$)								\$4,540.41		

Therefore, the PV is \$884 million from cash flows that you computed explicitly, plus \$4,540 million from the cash flows that is the terminal value stand-in for all cash flows from year 8 to infinity. This terminal value was computed as \$8.452 billion in year 8, using the growing perpetuity formula. Together, the firm's present value is therefore around \$5.42 billion. Note: You could also calculate a terminal value in year 6 (for years 7 and beyond), and reach the same answer.

Q 3.10 $\$1.5 \text{ million}/(14\% - 2\%) = \$12.5 \text{ million}$.

Q 3.11 The immediate dividend would be worth \$1.5 million. In addition, you now have a growing perpetuity that starts with a payment of \$1.530 million. Therefore, the PV would be $\$1.500 + \$1.530/12\% = \$14.250$ million. Alternatively, you could multiply the \$12.5 million from your answer to Question 3.10 by $(1 + 14\%)$.

Q 3.12 First work out what the value would be if you stood at 1 month. The interest rate is $(1 + 9\%)^{1/12} - 1 \approx 0.7207\%$ per month, and $1.007207^3 - 1 \approx 2.1778\%$ per quarter. Thus, in 1 month, you will be entitled to a dividend stream of $\$5.025/(2.1778\% - 0.5\%) \approx \$299.50$. In addition, you get the \$5 for a total of \$304.50. Because this is your value in 1 month, discount \$304.50 at a 0.7207% interest rate to \$302.32 today.

Q 3.13 $g = r - E/P = 12\% - \$5/\$100 = 7\%$ per annum

Q 3.14 Compare the annuity and perpetuity formulas. The difference between them is the $1 - 1/(1 + r)^t$ term. To be three-quarters of the value, this term has to be 3/4. So you must solve $1 - 1/(1 + r)^t = 3/4$, or $1/(1 + r)^t = 1 - 3/4 = 1/4$ or $(1 + r)^t = 4$. Taking logs, $t = \log(4)/\log(1 + r)$. In the main question, r was 5%, so $t = \log(4)/\log(1.05) \approx 28.41$ years. More generally, to reach a given fraction f of value, $t = \log[1/(1 - f)]/\log(1 + r)$. Think of this number of years as helping you judge the quality of the infinite-period approximation in the real world. If it is more realistic that you have fewer than 30 years of cash flows instead of an infinite stream, then the perpetuity formula may not be a great approximation of value when the interest rate is 5%.

Q 3.15 The annuity formula is $C_1 \cdot (\{1 - [1/(1 + r)]^T\}/r)$.

Q 3.16 Your 360-month annuity is worth

$$C_1 \cdot \left\{\frac{1 - [1/(1+r)]^T}{r}\right\} = \$5 \cdot \left\{\frac{1 - [1/(1+0.005)]^{360}}{0.005}\right\}$$

$$\approx \$5 \cdot \left\{\frac{1 - 0.166}{0.005}\right\} \approx \$833.96$$

Q 3.17 For 1 year, the 300 bezants paid once at year-end are worth $300b/1.02^{12} \approx 236.55$ bezants today. Now for the quarterly payment schedule: The quarterly interest rate is $1.02^3 - 1 \approx 6.12\%$. Therefore, the 4-"quartity" is worth $75b/0.0612 \cdot [1 - 1/1.0612^4] \approx 75b/1.0612^1 + 75b/1.0612^2 + 75b/1.0612^3 + 75b/1.0612^4 \approx 259.17$ bezants. The soldier would have lost 22.62 bezants in present value, which is 8.73% of what he was promised. (The same loss of $236.55/259.17 - 1 \approx 8.73\%$ would apply to longer periods.)

Q 3.18 For each ecu (e), the perpetuity is worth $1e/0.04 = 25e$. The annuity is worth $1e/0.05 \cdot (1 - 1/1.05^{41}) \approx 17.29e$. Therefore, the perpetuity is better.

Q 3.19 To find the implicit cost of capital of the lease, you need to solve

$$\$500{,}000 = \frac{\$5{,}000}{r} \cdot \left[1 - \frac{1}{(1+r)^{120}}\right]$$

The solution is $r \approx 0.31142\%$ per month, or 3.8% per annum. This is the implied rate of return if you purchase the warehouse and then rent it out. You would be better off earning 5% elsewhere.

Q 3.20 For \$1,000 of mortgage, solve for C_1 in

$$\text{PV} = C_1 \cdot \left\{ \frac{1 - [1/(1+r)]^T}{r} \right\}$$

$$\$1{,}000 = C_1 \cdot \left\{ \frac{1 - [1/(1.005)]^{15 \cdot 12 = 180}}{0.005} \right\} \approx C_1 \cdot 118.504 \iff C_1 \approx \$8.44$$

In other words, for every \$1,000 of loan, you have to pay \$8.44 per month. For other loan amounts, just rescale the amounts.

Q 3.21 The semiannual interest rate would now increase from 2.47% to

$$r = \sqrt[2]{1 + 6\%} - 1 = \sqrt{1.06} - 1 \approx 2.9563\%$$

To get the bond's new present value, reuse the annuity formula

$$\begin{aligned} \text{PV} = \quad & C_1 \cdot \left\{ \frac{1 - [1/(1+r)]^T}{r} \right\} & + \quad & \frac{C_T}{1 + r_T} \\ \approx \$1{,}500 \cdot & \left\{ \frac{1 - [1/(1 + 2.9563\%)]^{10}}{2.9563\%} \right\} & + \quad & \frac{\$100{,}000}{(1 + 2.9563\%)^{10}} \\ \approx \quad & \$12{,}823.89 & + \quad & \$74{,}725.82 \quad \approx \$87{,}549.70 \end{aligned}$$

This bond would have lost \$3,951.72, or 4.3% of the original investment.

Q 3.22 The interest rate is 5% per half-year. Be my guest if you want to add 40 terms. I prefer the annuity method. The coupons are worth

$$\begin{aligned} \text{PV(Coupons)} &= C_1 \cdot \left\{ \frac{1 - [1/(1+r)]^T}{r} \right\} \\ &= \$1{,}500 \cdot \left\{ \frac{1 - [1/(1.05)]^{40}}{0.05} \right\} \approx \$25{,}738.63 \end{aligned}$$

The final payment is worth PV(Principal Repayment) $= \frac{\$100{,}000}{(1.05)^{40}} \approx \$14{,}204.57$. Therefore, the bond is worth about \$39,943.20 today.

Q 3.23 For 6 months, $(1 + 2.47\%)^2 - 1 \approx 5\%$. Now, define 6 months to be 1 period. Then, for t 6-month periods, you can simply compute an interest rate of $(1 + 2.47\%)^t - 1$. For example, the 30 months interest rate is $1.0247^5 - 1 \approx 12.97\%$.

Q 3.24 The solution is $\$4{,}000/(0.08 - 0.02) \cdot \left[1 - \frac{1.02^{35}}{1.08^{35}}\right] \approx \$57{,}649.23$.

PROBLEMS

The indicates problems available in myfinancelab

Q 3.25 A tall Starbucks coffee costs \$1.65 a day. If the bank's quoted interest rate is 6% per annum, compounded daily, and if the Starbucks price never changed, what would an endless, inheritable free subscription to one Starbucks coffee per day be worth today?

Q 3.26 If you could pay for your mortgage forever, how much would you have to pay per month for a \$1,000,000 mortgage, at a 6.5% annual interest rate? Work out the answer (a) if the 6.5% is a bank APR quote and (b) if the 6.5% is a true effective annual rate of return.

Q 3.27 What is the PV of a perpetuity paying $30 each month, beginning *next* month, if the annual interest rate is a constant effective 12.68% per year?

Q 3.28 What is the prevailing interest rate if a perpetual bond were to pay $100,000 per year *beginning next year* and costs $1,000,000 today?

Q 3.29 What is the prevailing interest rate if a perpetual bond were to pay $100,000 per year *beginning next year* (time 1) and payments grow with the inflation rate at about 2% per year, assuming the bond costs $1,000,000 today?

Q 3.30 A tall Starbucks coffee costs $1.65 a day. If the bank's quoted interest rate is 6% per annum and coffee prices increased at a 3% annual rate of inflation, what would an endless, inheritable free subscription to one Starbucks coffee per day be worth today?

Q 3.31 Economically, why does the growth rate of cash flows have to be less than the discount rate?

Q 3.32 Your firm just finished the year, in which it had cash earnings of $400 (thousand). You forecast your firm to have a quick growth phase from year 0 to year 5, in which it grows at a rate of 40% per annum. Your firm's growth then slows down to 20% per annum, from year 5 to year 10. Finally, beginning in year 11, you expect the firm to settle into its long-term growth rate of 2% per annum. You also expect your cost of capital to be 15% over the first 5 years, then 10% over the next 5 years, and 8% thereafter. What do you think your firm is worth today? (Note: This problem is easiest to work in a computer spreadsheet.)

Q 3.33 A stock pays an annual dividend of $2. The dividend is expected to increase by 2% per year (roughly the inflation rate) forever. The price of the stock is $40 per share. At what cost of capital is this stock priced?

Q 3.34 A tall Starbucks coffee costs $1.65 a day. If the bank's quoted interest rate is 6% per annum, compounded daily, and if the Starbucks price never changed, what would a lifetime free subscription to one Starbucks coffee per day be worth today, assuming you will live for 50 more years? What should it be worth to you to be able to bequeath or sell it upon your departure?

Q 3.35 What maximum price would you pay for a standard 8% level-coupon bond (with semiannual payments and a face value of $1,000) that has 10 years to maturity if the prevailing discount rate (your cost of capital) is an effective 10% per annum?

Q 3.36 If you have to pay off an effective 6.5% loan within the standard 30 years, then what are the per-month payments for the $1,000,000 mortgage? As in Question 3.26, consider both an effective 6.5% interest rate per year, and a bank quote of 6.5% (APR) per year.

Q 3.37 Structure a mortgage bond for $150,000 so that its monthly payments are $1,000. The prevailing interest rate is quoted at 6% (APR) per year.

Q 3.38 ADVANCED: You are valuing a firm with a "pro forma" (i.e., with your forward projection of what the cash flows will be). The firm had cash flows of $1,000,000 today, and is growing by a rate of 20% per annum this year. That is, in year 1, it will have a cash flow of $1.2 million. In each of the following years, the difference between the growth rate and the inflation rate of 2% (forever) halves. Thus, from year 1 to year 2, the growth rate is 20%, then 2% + (20% − 2%)/2 = 11%, then 2% + (11% − 2%)/2 = 6.5%, and so on. Assume that the appropriate discount rate for a firm of this riskiness is 12%. (It applies to the $1.2 million cash flow.) What do you believe the value of this firm to be? (Hint: It is common in pro formas to project forward for a given number of years, say, 5–10 years, and then to assume that the firm will be sold for a terminal value, assuming that it has steady growth.)

CHAPTER 3 APPENDIX

Advanced Material

3.4 PROJECTS WITH DIFFERENT LIVES AND RENTAL EQUIVALENTS

➤ Question 2.39, p. 32

You have already met the concept of an equivalent annual cost in Question 2.39. This concept becomes more useful if you know how to work with annuities.

Comparing Annual Payments to Multiyear Contracts

Let's work out a first example. Assume that the prevailing interest rate is 10% per annum. Would you rather sign a lease contract that obliges you to pay \$1,000, \$650, and \$650 in consecutive years, or would you rather pay rent of \$780 every year?

The present value of the lease payments is

$$\$1{,}000 + \frac{\$650}{1.1} + \frac{\$650}{1.1^2} \approx \$2{,}128.10$$

The proposed alternative rent would be

$$\$780 + \frac{\$780}{1.1} + \frac{\$780}{1.1^2} \approx \$2{,}133.72$$

The 3-year lease is cheaper for you—of course, assuming that you really want to use the building for 3 years. If you really needed the building for only 1 year, then a 1-year rental contract could be much better.

Can you work out at what annual rent you would be indifferent between leasing and renting? This is called the **equivalent annual cost** (EAC). Easy:

$$\text{EAC} + \frac{\text{EAC}}{1.1} + \frac{\text{EAC}}{1.1^2} = \$2{,}128.10 \Rightarrow \text{EAC} \approx \$777.95$$

This tells you that you are indifferent between the (\$1,000, \$650, \$650) 3-year lease and an annual payment of \$777.95, first payment due immediately. Another version of this calculation has you pay the rent at the end of the year. In this case,

$$\frac{\text{EAC}}{1.1} + \frac{\text{EAC}}{1.1^2} + \frac{\text{EAC}}{1.1^3} = \$2{,}128.10 \Rightarrow \text{EAC} \approx \$855.74 \qquad (3.3)$$

You would therefore also be indifferent between the 3-year lease, and paying \$855.74 for 3 years with rent payments occurring at year-end, not at year-start. Of course, you could have simply multiplied \$777.95 by 1.1 to arrive at \$855.74.

IMPORTANT: To work out the equivalent annual cost of a contract, use a two-step procedure:

1. Determine the present value of the cost of the contract.
2. Use an annuity calculation to translate this cost into regular and equal flows.

Now stare at Formula 3.3. The left-hand side is an annuity.

$$\frac{\text{EAC}}{10\%} \cdot \left[1 - \left(\frac{1}{1.1}\right)^3\right] = \$2{,}128.10 \quad \Rightarrow \text{EAC} \approx \frac{\$2{,}128.10}{2.48685} \approx \$855.74$$

$$\text{Annuity}(\text{EAC, 3 years}, r = 10\%) = \text{Contract Present Value}$$

If you prefer the version where the first payment occurs immediately, simply discount this by 10%:

$$\frac{\$855.74}{1.10} \approx \$777.95$$

$$\text{EAC}_{\text{“discount the beginning payments next year”}} = \frac{\text{EAC}_{\text{“beginning payments immediately”}}}{1 + r}$$

Don't get too worked up over this. For 3 years, you don't need to use the annuity formula if you prefer working with the long Formula 3.3 instead. However, if you have many payments, the annuity formula quickly becomes more convenient.

For practice, let us work another lease example. A 5-year lease requires a one-time upfront payment of \$1,600, followed by four payments of \$500. The prevailing interest rate is 10%. What is the equivalent annual cost of this lease? First, work out the present value of the lease payments. This is

$$\text{PV} = \$1{,}600 + \$500/1.1 + \$500/1.1^2 + \$500/1.1^3 + \$500/1.1^4 \approx \$3{,}184.93$$

Now you must solve

$$\text{EAC} + \text{EAC}/1.1 + \text{EAC}/1.1^2 + \text{EAC}/1.1^3 + \text{EAC}/1.1^4 = \$3{,}184.93$$

which is

$$\text{EAC} \cdot (1 + 0.9091 + 0.8264 + 0.7513 + 0.6830) \approx \$3{,}184.93$$

$$\Rightarrow \text{EAC} \approx \$3{,}184.93/4.1699 \approx \$763.80$$

Put differently, you would be indifferent between this 5-year lease and payment of \$763.80 per month, first payment immediately. Using the annuity formula,

$$\frac{\text{EAC}}{10\%} \cdot \left[1 - \left(\frac{1}{1.1}\right)^5\right] = \$3{,}184.93 \quad \Rightarrow \text{EAC} \approx \frac{\$3{,}184.93}{3.7908} \approx \$840.17$$

$$\text{Annuity}(\text{EAC, 5 years}, r = 10\%) = \text{Contract Present Value}$$

with the first payment at the end of the year.

Ready to move on to a real-world example? My car lease quoted \$1,500 due at signing, followed by \$500 per month for 35 months. What would be the EAC for this contract, assuming the prevailing interest rate was 0.5% per month? The present value cost of this contract was

$$\$1{,}500 + \frac{\$500}{0.005} \cdot \left[1 - \left(\frac{1}{1.005}\right)^{35}\right] \approx \$1{,}500 + \$16{,}018 = \$17{,}518$$

The equivalent annual cost, that is, what a rental without an upfront payment would have been, is therefore

$$\frac{\text{EAC}}{0.005} \cdot \left[1 - \left(\frac{1}{1.005}\right)^{36}\right] \approx \$17{,}518 \Rightarrow \text{EAC} = \frac{\$17{,}518}{32.8710} \approx \$532.93 \quad (3.4)$$

payable only at the end of each month.

Comparing Different Multiyear Contracts

Let's now compare two multiyear leases, instead of a multiyear lease versus an annual rent. For example, compare the 3-year lease from the previous section to the 5-year lease. First, note that before you even ask this question, you should consider your use of the building. If you need it for only 3 years, you should obviously choose the 3-year lease. If you need it for exactly 5 years, you would have to figure out how much it would cost you to obtain leases for 2 more years if you went with the 3-year lease. However, we shall make our lives simple. The particular question that we are interested in assumes that you do not care about whether you sign a 3-year or a 5-year lease. You only care about lowest cost.

On to the substance. The 3-year lease costs \$2,128.10. The 5-year lease costs \$3,184.93. Obviously, the 3-year lease is cheaper. Does this mean that the 3-year lease is better? Obviously not—the 5-year lease gives you 5 years of access, not just 3 years. This is why a 5-year lease is more expensive. So, how can you compare these two leases?

You have two methods, which always come to the same answer:

1. **Repeated lease:** You can repeat both leases until they end up with the same number of years. For example, to compare a 3-year lease with a 5-year lease, you would work out what 15 years worth of leases would cost. That is, you would compare the cost of 5 consecutive 3-year leases with the cost of 3 consecutive 5-year leases.

   We already worked out that a single 3-year lease beginning now would cost \$2,128.10. Thus, the first 3-year lease would cost \$2,128.10 in year 0. You would have to repeat it in year 3, when it would cost you another \$2,128.10 *then*. Repeat this in year 6, in year 9, and in year 12. Your present value cost of a 15-year lease is therefore

$$\$2{,}128.10 + \frac{\$2{,}128.10}{1.1^3} + \frac{\$2{,}128.10}{1.1^6} + \frac{\$2{,}128.10}{1.1^9} + \frac{\$2{,}128.10}{1.1^{12}} \approx \$6{,}509$$

   Your alternative 5-year lease would cost \$3,184.93 in year 0, \$3,184.93 in year 5, and \$3,184.93 in year 10. Therefore, your cost would be

$$\$3{,}184.93 + \frac{\$3{,}184.93}{1.1^5} + \frac{\$3{,}184.93}{1.1^{10}} \approx \$6{,}390$$

   Consequently, the 5-year lease is cheaper.

   This method works, but it is quite tedious. If you had to compare four different leases, say, a 3-year, 5-year, 7-year, and 11-year lease, you would have to work out what these leases cost over a 1,155-year period.

2. **Work out the equivalent annual costs:** Instead of comparing leases to one another, work out what their equivalent annual rents would be, and compare these. Well, you have already worked this out for these two leases. The 3-year lease has an EAC of $777.95; the 5-year lease has an EAC of $763.80. Therefore, the 5-year contract is cheaper on a per-annum basis. (If you used the year-end payment EAC, the cost of both would be 10% higher, so the 5-year lease would still be cheaper.)

   Moreover, you can use this to compare any number of contracts easily. There is no more need to work out the total cost for thousands of years!

Similar rental equivalent value problems also often arise when you compare different technologies—for example, you can purchase a machine that is likely to last for 18 years, and you must compare it against another machine that is likely to last for 22 years. The method for solving these problems is exactly the same, so try it in the next question.

SOLVE NOW!

Q 3.39 The car dealer also quoted me a 48-month lease in which the first installment was $2,000 and the other 47 monthly payments were only $450. The prevailing interest rate is 0.5%/month. What does the privilege of switching to a new car after 36 months cost me per month? (Recall from Formula 3.4 the EAC for the 36-month lease was $532.93.)

Q 3.40 Machine A costs $10,000 up front, and lasts for 18 years. It has annual maintenance costs of $1,000 per year. Machine B costs $15,000 up front, lasts for 22 years, and has annual maintenance costs of $800 per year. Both machines produce the same product. The interest rate is 12% per annum.

(a) What is the PV of the cost of each machine?

(b) What is the rental equivalent of each machine?

(c) Which machine is the better purchase if you assume no value to flexibility and do not expect different machine costs or contracting conditions in the future?

3.5 PERPETUITY AND ANNUITY DERIVATIONS

A perpetuity: The formula is

$$\frac{C}{1+r} + \frac{C}{(1+r)^2} + \cdots \frac{C}{(1+r)^t} + \cdots = \frac{C}{r}$$

You want to show that this is a true statement. Divide by C,

$$\frac{1}{1+r} + \frac{1}{(1+r)^2} + \cdots + \frac{1}{(1+r)^t} + \cdots = \frac{1}{r} \tag{3.5}$$

Multiply (3.5) by $(1+r)$,

$$1 + \frac{1}{(1+r)} + \cdots + \frac{1}{(1+r)^{t-1}} + \cdots = \frac{(1+r)}{r} \tag{3.6}$$

Subtract (3.5) from (3.6),

$$1 = \frac{(1+r)}{r} - \frac{1}{r}$$

The RHS simplifies into r/r, which makes this a true statement.

A growing perpetuity: You know from the simple perpetuity formula that

$$\sum_{t=1}^{\infty} \frac{C}{(1+r)^t} = \frac{C}{r} \Leftrightarrow \sum_{t=1}^{\infty} \frac{C}{f^t} = \frac{C}{f-1}$$

Return to the definition of a growing perpetuity, and pull out one $(1+g)$ factor from its cash flows,

$$\sum_{t=1}^{\infty} \frac{C \cdot (1+g)^{t-1}}{(1+r)^t} = \left(\frac{1}{1+g}\right) \cdot \sum_{t=1}^{\infty} \frac{C \cdot (1+g)^t}{(1+r)^t} = \left(\frac{1}{1+g}\right) \cdot \sum_{t=1}^{\infty} \frac{C}{\left[\frac{1+r}{1+g}\right]^t}$$

Let $\left[\frac{1+r}{1+g}\right]$ be f, and use the first formula. Then

$$\left(\frac{1}{1+g}\right) \cdot \left\{\sum_{t=1}^{\infty} \frac{C}{\left[\frac{1+r}{1+g}\right]^t}\right\} = \left(\frac{1}{1+g}\right) \cdot \left\{\frac{C}{\left[\frac{1+r}{1+g}\right] - 1}\right\}$$

and simplify this,

$$= \left(\frac{1}{1+g}\right) \cdot \left\{\frac{C}{\left[\frac{(1+r)-(1+g)}{1+g}\right]}\right\} = \left(\frac{1}{1+g}\right) \cdot \left\{\frac{C \cdot (1+g)}{[r-g]}\right\} = \frac{C}{r-g}$$

An annuity: Consider one perpetuity that pays \$10 forever, beginning in year 1. Consider another perpetuity that begins in 5 years and also pays \$10, beginning in year 6, forever. If you purchase the first annuity and sell the second annuity, you will receive \$10 each year for 5 years, and \$0 in every year thereafter.

	0	1	2	3	4	5	6	7	8	. . .
Perpetuity 1		+\$10	+\$10	+\$10	+\$10	+\$10	+\$10	+\$10	+\$10	. . .
equivalent to	+\$10/r									
Perpetuity 2							−\$10	−\$10	−\$10	. . .
equivalent to						−\$10/r				
Net Pattern		+\$10	+\$10	+\$10	+\$10	+\$10				
equivalent to	+\$10/r					−\$10/r				
Discount Factor		$\frac{1}{(1+r)^1}$	$\frac{1}{(1+r)^2}$	$\frac{1}{(1+r)^3}$	$\frac{1}{(1+r)^4}$	$\frac{1}{(1+r)^5}$				

This shows that \$10, beginning next year and ending in year 5, should be worth

$$\text{PV} = \frac{\$10}{r} - \frac{1}{(1+r)^5} \cdot \frac{\$10}{r}$$

$$= \frac{C}{r} - \frac{1}{(1+r)^5} \cdot \frac{C}{r} = \left(\frac{C}{r}\right) \cdot \left[1 - \frac{1}{(1+r)^T}\right]$$

which is just the annuity formula.

KEY TERMS

EAC, 60

equivalent annual cost, 60

SOLVE NOW! SOLUTIONS

Q 3.39 This contract costs \$2,000 plus $\$450/0.005 \cdot (1 - 1/1.005^{47}) \approx \$18{,}807$ for a total of \$20,807. The EAC is therefore \$488.65, payable at the end of every month. The difference is \$532.93 − \$488.65 − \$44.28 per month.

Q 3.40 (a) Machine A is

$$\text{PV(Cost)} = \$10{,}000 + \text{Annuity}(\$1{,}000,\ 18 \text{ years},\ 12\%)$$

$$= \$10{,}000 + \frac{\$1{,}000}{12\%} \cdot \left[1 - \frac{1}{1.12^{18}}\right] \approx \$17{,}249.67$$

Machine B is

$$\text{PV(Cost)} = \$15{,}000 + \text{Annuity}(\$800,\ 22 \text{ years},\ 12\%)$$

$$= \$15{,}000 + \frac{\$1{,}000}{12\%} \cdot \left[1 - \frac{1}{1.12^{22}}\right] \approx \$22{,}644.65$$

(b) The equivalent rental values are

$$\text{Annuity}(x,\ 18 \text{ years}) \equiv \frac{x}{0.12} \cdot \left(1 - \frac{1}{1.12^{18}}\right) \approx \$17{,}249.67 \Leftrightarrow x \approx \frac{\$17{,}249.67}{7.24967}$$

$$\approx \$2{,}379.37 \text{ for machine A}$$

$$\text{Annuity}(x,\ 22 \text{ years}) \equiv \frac{x}{0.12} \cdot \left(1 - \frac{1}{1.12^{22}}\right) \approx \$22{,}694.65 \Leftrightarrow x \approx \frac{\$22{,}644.65}{7.6446}$$

$$\approx \$2{,}962.16 \text{ for machine B}$$

(c) The 18-year machine has the lower rental cost, so it is the better deal—of course, under all the appropriate assumptions such as same ongoing need.

PROBLEMS

The ▭ *indicates problems available in* myfinancelab

Q 3.41 You can sell your building for \$200,000. Alternatively, you can lease out your building. The lessee will pay you \$2,000 per month. You will have to budget \$700 per month for upkeep, attention, and so on. At the end of the 20-year lease, you expect the building to be worthless, but the land to have a residual value of \$150,000. Your cost of capital is 0.5% per month. Should you sell or lease your building?

Q 3.42 The discount rate is 12.68% per annum. Your competitor offers a 5-year airplane lease for an upfront cost of \$30,000. The lessee will have to pay \$3,000 per year in insurance (each year in advance) and service costs, and \$3,000 per month lease fees.

(a) What is the customer's equivalent monthly cost of leasing an airplane?

(b) Your boss believes that customers would prefer a 4-year lease to a 5-year lease if it saves on lease payments. Assume insurance (of \$3,000 per year) and upfront lease payment (of \$30,000) stay the same. What would be the monthly lease payment to remain even?

(Assume that your customers can compute net present values and that airplanes do not age.)

A First Encounter with Capital Budgeting Rules

THE INTERNAL RATE OF RETURN, AND MORE

This chapter elaborates on the ideas presented in the previous chapter. We still remain in a world of constant interest rates, perfect foresight, and perfect markets. Let's look a little more closely at capital budgeting—the possible decision rules that can tell you whether to accept or reject projects. You already know the answer to the mystery, though: NPV is best. Still, there is one very important alternative to NPV: the internal rate of return, which generalizes the rate of return concept, and which often gives you good recommendations, too. You will see how it all fits together.

One caveat—although you already know the concept of NPV, and although you will learn more about capital budgeting rules in this chapter, most of the interesting and difficult issues in its application are delayed until Chapter 12 (i.e., after we have covered uncertainty and imperfect markets).

4.1 NET PRESENT VALUE

Recap: NPV is the most important building block in finance. You must be able to compute it in your sleep.

You have already learned how to use NPV in our perfect world. You first translate cash flows at different points in time into the same units—dollars today—before they can be compared or added. This translation between future values and present values—and its variant, net present value—may well be the most essential concept in finance.

A "free money" interpretation of NPV.

But why is NPV the right rule to use? The reason is that, at least in our perfect world with perfect information, a positive-NPV project is the equivalent of free money. For example, if you can borrow or lend money at 8% anywhere today and you have an investment opportunity that costs $1 and yields $1.09, you can immediately contract to receive $0.01 next year *for free*. (If you wish, discount it back to today, so you can consume it today.) Rejecting this project would make no sense. Similarly, if you can sell someone an investment opportunity for $1, which yields only $1.07 next year, you can again earn $0.01 *for free*. Again, rejecting this project would make no sense. (Remember that in our perfect world, you can buy or sell projects at will.) Only zero-NPV projects ($1 cost for $1.08 payoff) do not allow you to get free money. Of course, I am using this argument not to show you how to get rich but to convince you that the NPV rule makes sense and that any rule that comes to any conclusions other than those attained by NPV would not make sense.

IMPORTANT: In a perfect world, if you have all the right inputs to NPV, no other rule can make better decisions. Thus, it is the appropriate decision benchmark—and no other rule can beat it. This also means that information other than the NPV is redundant.

Positive-NPV projects are scarce.

In our perfect world with no uncertainty, logic dictates that positive-NPV projects must be scarce. If they were not scarce, they would be practically like free money. Everyone with access would want to take on cartloads of them. In such a scenario, the "run" on positive-NPV projects would continue until the economy-wide appropriate rate of return (cost of capital) has been bid up to the level where there would no longer be any positive-NPV projects.

In the real world, NPV is very important, but other measures can provide useful information, too.

As you will find out in later chapters, despite its conceptual simplicity, the application of NPV in the real world is often surprisingly difficult. The primary reason is that you rarely know cash flows and discount factors perfectly. This means that you must estimate them. The secondary reason is that the world is rarely 100% perfect—it is rare that there are absolutely zero taxes, no transaction costs, no disagreements, and infinitely many buyers and sellers. Nevertheless, even in an imperfect market, NPV remains the most important benchmark, but other rules may provide you with some additional useful information and potentially modified project choices.

4.1A SEPARATING INVESTMENT DECISIONS AND CONSUMPTION CHOICES: DOES PROJECT VALUE DEPEND ON WHEN YOU NEED CASH?

Who owns a project is not important in a perfect capital market.

In our perfect world, when you choose between NPV projects, should you let your preferences about the timing of cash flows influence your decisions? Perhaps you don't want to incur an upfront expense; perhaps you want money today; perhaps you want to defer your consumption and save for the future. Aren't these important factors in making your decision as to which project to choose? The answer is no—the value of any project is its net present value, regardless of your preferences.

The capital markets allow you to shift money across time periods—better than your investment projects can.

In a perfect market, how much cash the owner has also does not matter. Let me explain why. You already know about the time value of money, the fact that cash today is worth more than cash tomorrow. If you do not agree—that is, if you value money tomorrow more than you value money today—then just give it to me until you need it back. I can deposit it in my bank account to earn interest in the interim. In a perfect capital market, you can, of course, do better: You can always shift money between time periods at an "exchange rate" that reflects the time value of money.

It is this shifting-at-will that explains why ownership does not matter. Assume that you have \$150 cash on hand and that you have exclusive access to a project that costs \$100, and returns \$200 next year. The appropriate interest rate (cost of capital) is 10%—but you *really* want to live it up today. How much can you consume? And, would you take the project? Here is the NPV prescription in a perfect market:

Example: Even an "eager" consumer should take the positive-NPV project.

- Sell the project in the competitive market for its NPV:

$$-\$100 + \left(\frac{\$200}{1 + 10\%}\right) = -\$100 + \left(\frac{\$200}{1.10}\right) \approx \$81.82$$

- Spend the \$150 + (\$181.82 − \$100) ≈ \$231.82 today. You will be better off taking the project than consuming just your \$150 cash at hand.

Now, assume that you are Austin Powers, the frozen secret agent, who cannot consume this year. How much will you be able to consume next year? And, would you take the project? The NPV answer is:

A "sleeper" consumer should also take the positive-NPV project.

- Sell the project in the competitive market for

$$-\$100 + \frac{\$200}{1 + 10\%} \approx \$81.82$$

- Put the \$81.82 into the bank for 10% today. Get \$90 next year.
- Also put your \$150 into the bank at 10% interest to receive \$165 next year.
- Next year, consume \$90 + \$165 = \$255.

Of course, an equally simple solution would be to take the project and just put your remaining \$50 into a bank account.

The point of this argument is simple: Regardless of when you need or want cash (your consumption decision), you are better off taking all positive-NPV projects (your investment decision), and then using the capital markets to shift consumption to when you want it. It makes no sense to let your *consumption decisions* influence your *investment decisions*. This is called the **separation of decisions**: You can make investment decisions without concern for your consumption preferences. (However, this separation of investment and consumption decisions does not always hold in imperfect markets, in which you can face different borrowing and lending interest rates. You might take more projects if you have more cash.)

The moral of the story: Consumption and investment decisions can be separated in a perfect capital market.

➤ Imperfect markets, lack of separation, Section 10.1C, p. 308

Here is a simple application of our simple insight. After they have lost their clients' money, many brokers like to muddle the consumption/investment truth by claiming that they invested their clients' money for the long term, and not for the short term. This excuse presumes that long-term investments do worse in the short run than short-term investments. This makes little sense, because if this were the case, your broker should purchase the short-term investment and sell it when it is worth relatively more than the long-term investment in order to purchase relatively more of the (then relatively cheaper) long-term investment. The fact is that no matter whether an investor needs money sooner or later, the broker should always purchase the highest NPV investments. This gives clients the most wealth today—if you care about future consumption, you can always save the extra cash from finding the highest NPV investments today.

How Bad Are Mistakes?

ERRORS IN CASH FLOWS VERSUS ERRORS IN THE COST OF CAPITAL

In the real world, it is often impossible to get the NPV inputs perfectly correct.

Although it would be better to get everything perfect, it is often impossible to come up with perfect cash flow forecasts and appropriate interest rate estimates. Everyone makes errors when outcomes in the world are uncertain. How bad are estimation mistakes? Is it worse to commit an error in estimating cash flows or in estimating the cost of capital? To answer these questions, we will do a simple form of **scenario analysis**, in which we consider a very simple project to learn how changes in our estimates matter to the ultimate present value. Scenario analysis is also essential for managers, who need to learn how sensitive their estimated value is to reasonable alternative possible outcomes. Therefore, this method is also called a **sensitivity analysis**. (It becomes even more important when you work with real options in Chapter 12.)

The benchmark case: A short-term project, correctly valued.

Short-term projects: Assume that your project will pay off $200 next year, and the proper interest rate for such projects is 8%. Thus, the correct project present value is

$$\text{PV}_{\text{correct}} = \frac{\$200}{1 + 8\%} \approx \$185.19$$

Committing an error in cash flow estimation.

If you make a 10% error in your cash flow, mistakenly believing it to return $220, you will compute the present value to be

$$\text{PV}_{\text{CF error}} = \frac{\$220}{1 + 8\%} \approx \$203.70$$

The difference between $203.70 and $185.19 is a 10% error in your present value.

Committing an error in interest rate estimation.

In contrast, if you make a 10% error in your cost of capital (interest rate), mistakenly believing it to require a cost of capital (expected interest rate) of 8.8% rather than 8%, you will compute the present value to be

$$\text{PV}_{r\text{ error}} = \frac{\$200}{1 + 8.8\%} \approx \$183.82$$

The difference between $183.82 and $185.19 is less than $2, which is an error of about 1%.

A long-term project, correctly valued and incorrectly valued.

Long-term projects: Now take the same example but assume the cash flow will occur in 30 years. The correct present value is now

$$\text{PV}_{\text{correct}} = \frac{\$200}{(1 + 8\%)^{30}} = \frac{\$200}{1.08^{30}} \approx \$19.88$$

The 10% "cash flow error" present value is

$$PV_{CF\ error} = \frac{\$220}{(1+8\%)^{30}} = \frac{\$220}{1.08^{30}} \approx \$21.86$$

and the 10% "interest rate error" present value is

$$PV_{r\ error} = \frac{\$200}{(1+8.8\%)^{30}} = \frac{\$200}{(1.088\%)^{30}} \approx \$15.93$$

This calculation shows that cash flow estimation errors and interest rate estimation errors are now both important. For longer-term projects, estimating the correct interest rate becomes relatively more important. Yet, though correct, this argument may be misleading. Estimating cash flows 30 years into the future seems often more like voodoo than science. Your uncertainty usually explodes over longer horizons. In contrast, your uncertainty about the long-term cost of capital tends to grow very little with horizon—you might even be able to ask your investors today what they demand as an appropriate cost of capital! Of course, as difficult as cash flow estimation may be, you have no alternative. You simply must try to do your best at forecasting.

Both cash flow errors and cost of capital errors are important for long-term projects.

IMPORTANT:

- For short-term projects, errors in estimating correct interest rates are less problematic in computing NPV than are errors in estimating future cash flows.
- For long-term projects, errors in estimating correct interest rates and errors in estimating future cash flows are both problematic in computing NPV. Nevertheless, in reality, you will tend to find it more difficult to estimate far-away future cash flows (and thus you will face more errors) than you will find it to estimate the appropriate discount rate demanded by investors today for far-away cash flows.

SOLVE NOW!

Q 4.1 What is the main assumption that allows you to independently consider investment (project) choices without regard to when you need wealth (or how much money you currently have at hand)?

Q 4.2 You have $500 and really, really want to go to the Superbowl tonight (which will consume all your funds). You cannot wait until your project completes: The project costs $400 and offers a rate of return of 15%, although equivalent interest rates are only 10%. What should you do?

4.2 THE INTERNAL RATE OF RETURN (IRR)

There is another common capital budgeting method, which often leads to the same recommendations as the NPV rule. This method is useful because it does so through a different route and often provides good intuition about the project.

Our new captial budgeting method compares the project's rate of return to the prevailing rate of return.

Let's assume that you have a project with cash flows that translate into a rate of return of 20% (e.g., \$100 investment, \$120 payoff), and the prevailing discount rate is 10%. Because your project's rate of return of 20% is greater than the prevailing discount rate of 10%, you should intuitively realize that it is a good one. It is also a positive-NPV project—in the example, $-\$100 + \$120/1.1 \approx \$9.10$.

We need a "sort-of average rate of return" that is implicit in future cash flows. The IRR is this characteristic that describes multiple cash flows.

There is only one problem: How would you compute the rate of return on a project or bond that has many different payments? For example, say the investment costs \$100,000 and pays off \$5,000 in 1 year, \$10,000 in 2 years, and \$120,000 in 3 years. What is the rate of return of this project? Think about it. The rate of return formula works only if you have exactly one inflow and one outflow. This is not the case here. What you need now is a "kind-of" rate of return (a "statistic") that can take many inflows and outflows and provide something similar to a rate of return. Such a measure exists. It is called the **internal rate of return (IRR)**. The word "internal" is an indicator that the rate is intrinsic to your project, depending only on its cash flows.

IMPORTANT:

- The **internal rate of return** is the quantity **IRR**, which, given a complete set of cash flows, is the equation that solves the NPV formula set to zero,

$$0 = C_0 + \frac{C_1}{1 + \text{IRR}} + \frac{C_2}{(1 + \text{IRR})^2} + \frac{C_3}{(1 + \text{IRR})^3} + \cdots \qquad (4.1)$$

- If there are only two cash flows, the IRR is the rate of return. Thus, the IRR generalizes the concept of rate of return to multiple cash flows. Every rate of return is an IRR, but the reverse is not the case.
- The IRR itself is best thought of as a characteristic of project cash flows.

YTM is the same as IRR.

The internal rate of return is such a common statistic in the context of bonds that it has acquired a second name: the **yield-to-maturity (YTM)**. There is no difference between the IRR and the YTM.

IRR generalizes rates of return: A simple project's rate of return is its IRR.

Let's illustrate the IRR. First, if there is only one inflow and one outflow, the IRR is the simple rate of return. For example, if a simple project costs \$100 today and pays \$130 next year, the IRR is obtained by solving

$$-\$100 + \frac{\$130}{1 + \text{IRR}} = 0 \Leftrightarrow \text{IRR} = \frac{\$130 - \$100}{\$100} = 30\%$$

$$C_0 + \frac{C_1}{1 + \text{IRR}} = 0 \Leftrightarrow \text{IRR} = \frac{C_1 - C_0}{C_0}$$

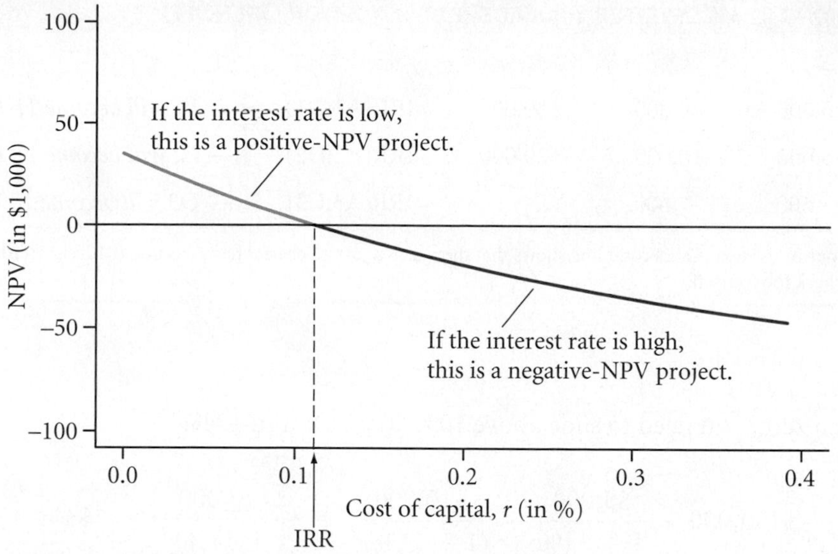

This figure draws the NPV for a project that costs $100,000 and pays $5,000, $10,000, and $120,000 in consecutive years. The IRR is the x-coordinate where the NPV function intersects the horizontal axis at 0.

FIGURE 4.1 NPV as a Function of the Interest Rate

Here is an iteration method that shows how you can solve the IRR equation yourself.

Now consider an example where a simple rate of return won't work: What number would best characterize the implied rate of return for a project that costs $100,000 today and that will yield $5,000, $10,000, and $120,000? You cannot compute a simple rate of return with four cash flows. Figure 4.1 shows you the NPV of this project as a function of the prevailing interest rate. If the discount rate is very low, then the NPV is positive. IRR is the interest rate that makes the NPV exactly equal to zero. In this case, this means that you should solve

$$0 = -\$100{,}000 + \frac{\$5{,}000}{1 + \text{IRR}} + \frac{\$10{,}000}{(1 + \text{IRR})^2} + \frac{\$120{,}000}{(1 + \text{IRR})^3}$$

$$0 = C_0 + \frac{C_1}{1 + \text{IRR}} + \frac{C_2}{(1 + \text{IRR})^2} + \frac{C_3}{(1 + \text{IRR})^3}$$

What is the discount rate that sets the NPV equation to zero? If you do not want to draw the full figure to find out where your NPV function crosses the zero axis, then you can try to solve such equations by trial and error. Start with two values, say, 5% and 10%.

$$-\$100{,}000 + \frac{\$5{,}000}{1 + 5\%} + \frac{\$10{,}000}{(1 + 5\%)^2} + \frac{\$120{,}000}{(1 + 5\%)^3} \approx \$17{,}493$$

$$-\$100{,}000 + \frac{\$5{,}000}{1 + 10\%} + \frac{\$10{,}000}{(1 + 10\%)^2} + \frac{\$120{,}000}{(1 + 10\%)^3} \approx \$2{,}968$$

TABLE 4.1 IRR CALCULATIONS IN A COMPUTER SPREADSHEET (EXCEL OR OPENOFFICE)

	A	B	C	D	E	
1	−100,000	5,000	10,000	120,000	=IRR(A1:D1)	← *E1 will become 11.14252%*
2	100,000	−5,000	−10,000	−120,000	=IRR(A2:D2)	← *E2 will become 11.14252%*
3	−1,000	600	600		=IRR(A3:C3)	← *D3 will become 13%*

The first line is the project worked out in the text. The second line shows that the negative of the project has the same IRR. The third line is just another example that you can check for yourself.

To reach zero, you need to slide above 10%. Try 11% and 12%,

$$-\$100{,}000 + \frac{\$5{,}000}{1+11\%} + \frac{\$10{,}000}{(1+11\%)^2} + \frac{\$120{,}000}{(1+11\%)^3} \approx \$364$$

$$-\$100{,}000 + \frac{\$5{,}000}{1+12\%} + \frac{\$10{,}000}{(1+12\%)^2} + \frac{\$120{,}000}{(1+12\%)^3} \approx -\$2{,}150$$

Okay, the solution is closer to 11%. Some more trial and error reveals

$$-\$100{,}000 + \frac{\$5{,}000}{1+11.14252\%} + \frac{\$10{,}000}{(1+11.14252\%)^2} + \frac{\$120{,}000}{(1+11.14252\%)^3} \approx 0$$

Therefore, the answer is that this project has an IRR of about 11.14%. You can think of the internal rate of return as a sort-of average rate of return embedded in the project's cash flows.

Spreadsheets make it easy to find the IRR fast.

There is no easy general formula to compute the IRR if you are dealing with more than three cash flows. However, an automated trial-and-error function to compute an IRR is built into modern computer spreadsheets and usually precludes the need to solve algebraic equations. Table 4.1 (row 1) shows how you would find the IRR for this project in a spreadsheet.

Multiplying all cash flows by the same factor does not change the IRR.

Note that the negative cash flow pattern in row 2 of Table 4.1 has the same IRR. That is, receiving an inflow of $100,000 followed by *payments* of $5,000, $10,000, and $120,000 also has an 11.14252% internal rate of return. You can see that this must be the case if you look back at the IRR formula. Any multiplicative factor simply cancels out and therefore has no impact on the solution.

$$0 = \text{Factor} \cdot C_0 + \frac{\text{Factor} \cdot C_1}{1+\text{IRR}} + \frac{\text{Factor} \cdot C_2}{(1+\text{IRR})^2} + \frac{\text{Factor} \cdot C_3}{(1+\text{IRR})^3} + \cdots$$

$$= \text{Factor} \cdot \left[C_0 + \frac{C_1}{1+\text{IRR}} + \frac{C_2}{(1+\text{IRR})^2} + \frac{C_3}{(1+\text{IRR})^3} + \cdots \right]$$

$$= C_0 + \frac{C_1}{1+\text{IRR}} + \frac{C_2}{(1+\text{IRR})^2} + \frac{C_3}{(1+\text{IRR})^3} + \cdots$$

SOLVE NOW!

Q 4.3 From memory, write down the equation that defines IRR.

Q 4.4 What is the IRR of a project that costs \$1,000 now and produces \$1,000 next year?

Q 4.5 What is the IRR of a project that costs \$1,000 now and produces \$500 next year and \$500 the year after?

Q 4.6 What is the IRR of a project that costs \$1,000 now and produces \$600 next year and \$600 the year after?

Q 4.7 What is the IRR of a project that costs \$1,000 now and produces \$900 next year and \$900 the year after?

Q 4.8 A project has cash flows of −\$100, \$55, and \$70 in consecutive years. Use a spreadsheet to find the IRR.

Q 4.9 What is the YTM of an x% annual level-coupon bond whose price is equal to the principal paid at maturity? For example, take a 5-year bond that costs \$1,000 today, pays 5% coupon (\$50 per year) for 4 years, and finally repays \$1,050 in principal and interest in year 5.

Q 4.10 What is the YTM of a 5-year zero-bond that costs \$1,000 today and promises to pay \$1,611?

Q 4.11 Compute the yield-to-maturity of a two-year bond that costs \$25,000 today and pays \$1,000 at the end of each of the 2 years. At the end of the second year, it also repays \$25,000. What is the bond's YTM?

4.2A PROJECTS WITH MULTIPLE OR NO IRRS

Here is an example of a project with two IRRs.

When projects have many positive and many negative cash flows, they can often have multiple internal rates of return. For example, take a project that costs \$100,000, pays \$205,000, and has cleanup costs of \$102,000. Figure 4.2 shows that this project has two internal rates of return: $r = -15\%$ and $r = 20\%$. Confirm this:

$$-\$100{,}000 + \frac{\$205{,}000}{1 + (-15\%)} - \frac{\$102{,}000}{[1 + (-15\%)]^2} = 0$$

$$-\$100{,}000 + \frac{\$205{,}000}{1 + 20\%} - \frac{\$102{,}000}{(1 + 20\%)^2} = 0$$

Huh? So does this project have an internal rate of return of −15% or an internal rate of return of 20%? The answer is both—the fact is that both IRRs are valid according to the definition. And don't think the number of possible solutions is limited to two—with other cash flows, there could be dozens. What do computer spreadsheets do if there are multiple IRRs? You may never know. They usually just pick one for you. They don't even give you a warning.

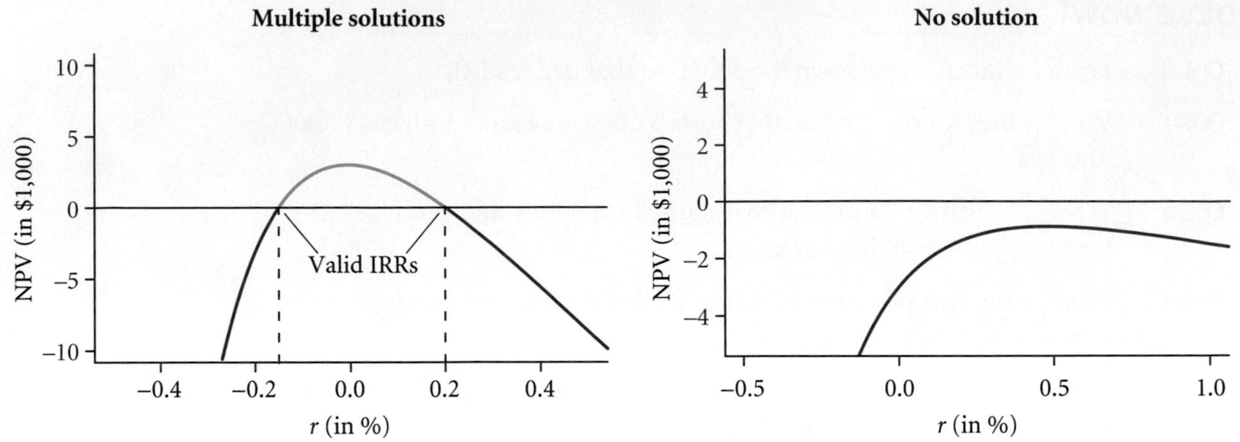

The left figure draws the NPV for a project that costs \$100,000, pays \$205,000, and then has cleanup costs of \$102,000. The right figure draws the NPV for a project that costs \$10,000, pays \$27,000, and then requires a \$20,000 cleanup cost.

FIGURE 4.2 Multiple and No IRR Solutions

Projects that have all negative or all positive cash flows have no IRRs—but so do some other projects.

While some projects have multiple IRRs, other projects have none. For example, what is the internal rate of return of a project that yields \$10 today and \$20 tomorrow (that is, it never demands an investment)? Such a project has no internal rate of return. The NPV formula is never zero, regardless of what the prevailing interest rate is. This makes sense, and the fact that there is no IRR is pretty obvious from the cash flows. After all, they both have the same sign. But what is the IRR of a project that has cash flows of \$10,000, pays \$27,000, and then requires a cleanup cost of \$20,000? Figure 4.2 shows that this project also has no rate of return at which its NPV would turn positive. Therefore, it has no IRR. What do computer spreadsheets do if there are no IRRs? Thankfully, most of the time, they give an error message that will alert you to the problem.

The most common types of investment projects have a unique IRR, because they have one outflow followed only by inflows (or vice versa).

Can you ever be sure that your project has one unique internal rate of return? Yes. It turns out that if you have one negative cash flow followed only by positive cash flows—which happens to be far and away the most common investment pattern—then your project has one and only one IRR. (Projects with cash flows with many different positive and negative signs can still have only one IRR, but it's not guaranteed.) Partly because bonds have such cash flow patterns, YTM is even more popular than IRR. Obviously, you also have a unique IRR if a project has the opposite cash flow pattern—that is, a positive cash inflow followed only by negative cash flows.

SOLVE NOW!

Q 4.12 Give an example of a problem that has multiple IRR solutions.

Q 4.13 Give an example of a project that has no IRR.

Q 4.14 For the following projects, plot the NPVs as a function of the prevailing interest rate and determine the appropriate IRRs.

Project	Year 0	1	2	3	4
(A)	+\$1,000	−\$5,000	+\$9,350	−\$7,750	+\$2,402.4
(B)	+\$50,000	−\$250,000	+\$467,500	−\$387,500	\$120,120
(C)	+\$100,000	−\$250,000	+\$200,000		
(D)	−\$100	+\$300	−\$400	+\$400	
(E)	+\$100	−\$300	+\$400	−\$400	
(F)	+\$200	−\$600	+\$800	−\$800	
(G)	−\$100	+\$300	−\$200		

4.2B IRR AS A CAPITAL BUDGETING RULE

One important reason why IRR is so useful is that it can often substitute for NPV as an investment criterion.

IMPORTANT:

- The IRR capital budgeting rule states that if and only if an investment project's IRR (a characteristic of project cash flows) is above its appropriate discount rate (cost of capital), it should be taken. In this context, the cost of capital is often called the **hurdle rate**.

In many cases, the IRR capital budgeting rule gives the same correct answer as the NPV capital budgeting rule. However, there are some delicate situations in which this is not the case. This will be explained below.

Let me illustrate this. Return to our project that costs \$100,000 and yields \$5,000, \$10,000, and \$120,000 with its IRR of 11.14%. The IRR capital budgeting rule states that if the prevailing cost of capital in the economy (i.e., the hurdle rate) to finance our project is 11.20%, then you should not take this project. If it is 11.10%, then you should take this project. Does NPV offer the same recommendation? Try it:

Confirm that the IRR and NPV capital budgeting rules give the same recommendation.

$$\text{NPV at } 11.10\% = -\$100{,}000 + \frac{\$5{,}000}{1+11.10\%} + \frac{\$10{,}000}{(1+11.10\%)^2} + \frac{\$120{,}000}{(1+11.10\%)^3} \approx +\$108$$

$$\text{NPV at } 11.20\% = -\$100{,}000 + \frac{\$5{,}000}{1+11.20\%} + \frac{\$10{,}000}{(1+11.20\%)^2} + \frac{\$120{,}000}{(1+11.20\%)^3} \approx -\$146$$

Indeed, you get the same recommendation.

If the cash flow is negative, the IRR stays the same, but the take-it-or-leave-it rule reverses.

If the cash flows are the exact opposite—that is, if you receive \$100,000 up front and pay out \$5,000, \$10,000, and \$120,000—then this would not really be an investment project, but more like investment financing. You would now want to take this financing alternative if and only if the prevailing interest rate is *above* 11.14%. Be careful about whether you want your IRR to be above or below the hurdle rate! (My advice to avoid such errors is to always work out the NPV, too—it will never mislead you.)

IRR can be computed before the cost of capital is known.

IRR is a characteristic of a project's cash flows. (It is not an interest rate.)

Why use the IRR instead of the NPV investment criterion? The answer is that the former is often quite intuitive and convenient, provided that the project's cash flow stream implies one unique IRR. In this case, IRR is convenient because you can compute it without having looked at financial markets, interest rates, or costs of capital. This is IRR's most important advantage over NPV: *It can be calculated before you know what the appropriate interest rate (cost of capital) is.* Moreover, IRR can give you useful project information in and of itself. It is also helpful in judging project profitability and thereby allows you to judge the performance of a manager—it is often easier to hold her to her earlier promise of delivering an IRR of 20% than it is to argue with her about what the appropriate cost of capital for her project should be.

SOLVE NOW!

Q 4.15 A project has cash flows of −\$1,000, −\$2,000, +\$3,000, and +\$4,000 in consecutive years. Your cost of capital is 30% per annum. Use the IRR rule to determine whether you should take this project. Does the NPV rule recommend the same action?

Q 4.16 A project has cash flows of −\$1,000, −\$2,000, −\$3,000, +\$4,000, and +\$5,000 in consecutive years. Your cost of capital is 20% per annum. Use the IRR rule to determine whether you should take this project. Confirm your recommendation using the NPV rule.

Q 4.17 A project has cash flows of +\$200, −\$180, −\$40 in consecutive years. The prevailing interest rate is 5%. Should you take this project?

Q 4.18 You can invest in a project with diminishing returns. Specifically, the formula relating next year's payoff to your investment today is $C_1 = \sqrt{-C_0}$, where C_0 and C_1 are measured in million dollars. For example, if you invest \$100,000 in the project today, it will return $\sqrt{\$0.1} \approx \$0.316$ million next year. The prevailing interest rate is 5% per annum. Use a spreadsheet to answer the following two questions:

(a) What is the IRR-maximizing investment choice? What is the NPV at this choice?

(b) What is the NPV-maximizing investment choice? What is the IRR at this choice?

4.2C PROBLEMS WITH IRR AS A CAPITAL BUDGETING RULE

IRR is safe to use when there is only one positive or only one negative cash flow.

If you use IRR *correctly* and in the right circumstances, it can give you the same answer as the NPV rule. (Of course, you cannot do any better than by doing right, so it is always safer to use the NPV rule than the IRR rule.) When does the IRR capital budgeting rule work well? If there is only one unique IRR, it is also often an elegant method. Of course, as just noted, you still have to make sure that you get the sign right. If your project requires an upfront outlay followed by inflows, you want to take the project if its IRR is *above* your cost of capital. If the project is financing (like debt, which has an upfront inflow followed by outflows), you want to take this project if its IRR is *below* your cost of capital. My advice is to use NPV as a check of your IRR calculations in any case.

IRR often fails in nonobvious ways when there are multiple negative or positive cash flows.

Unfortunately, if the IRR is not unique (and recall that there are projects with multiple IRRs or no IRR), then the IRR criterion becomes outright painful. For example, if your prevailing cost of capital is 9% and your project has IRRs of 6%, 8%, and 10%, should you take this project or avoid it? The answer is not obvious. In this case, to make an investment decision, you ultimately have to fall back to drawing a part of the NPV graph in one form or another. Thus, if you have a project with multiple IRRs, please take my advice: Just avoid IRR and fall back to using NPV. (Yes, it is possible to figure out how to use IRR, depending on whether the NPV function crosses the 0-axis from above or below, but working with IRR under such circumstances only begs for trouble, i.e., mistakes. There is also a "modified IRR" [the so-called MIRR] measure that can sometimes eliminate multiple solutions. It is not worth the bother.) If you have a project without any IRR, you again have to fall back to NPV, but doing so is simple here. Just work out whether the NPV function is above or below the 0-axis for any arbitrary discount rate, and use this to decide whether to take or to reject your project.

Two more problems: (1) IRR has no concept of scale; (2) there may not be an obvious hurdle rate to compare it to.

There are two more problems when using IRR that you need to be aware of:

1. **Project comparisons and scale:** The IRR criterion can mislead when projects are mutually exclusive. For example, if you had to choose, would you always prefer a project with a 100% IRR to a project with a 10% IRR? Think about it.

   What if the first project is an investment opportunity of $5 (returning $10), and the second project is an investment opportunity of $1,000 (returning $1,100)? Take the case where the prevailing discount rate is 5% per annum. Then,

Project	Year 0	Year 1	IRR	NPV @5%
A	−$5	+$10	100%	+$4.52
B	−$1,000	+$1,100	10%	+$47.62

   If you can only take one project, then you should take project B, even though its IRR is much lower than that of project A.

2. **Cost of capital comparison:** The next chapter explains that long-term interest rates are often higher than short-term interest rates. For example, in mid-2002, a 1-year Treasury bond offered a rate of return of 2%, while a 20-year bond offered a rate of return of 6%. Let's assume that your project is risk-free, too. Should you take a project if it has an IRR of 4%? There is no clear answer.

These two problems may seem obvious when highlighted in isolation. But in the context of complex, real-world, multiple-project analyses, they are surprisingly often overlooked.

SOLVE NOW!

Q 4.19 What are the problems with the IRR computation and criterion?

Q 4.20 The prevailing interest rate is 25%. If the following two projects are mutually exclusive, which should you take?

	Year				
Project	0	1	2	3	4
A	+\$50,000	−\$250,000	+\$467,500	−\$387,500	+\$120,120
B	−\$50,000	+\$250,000	−\$467,500	+\$387,500	−\$120,120

What does the NPV rule recommend? What does the IRR rule recommend?

Q 4.21 The prevailing interest rate is 25%. If the following two projects are mutually exclusive, which should you take?

	Year			
Project	0	1	2	3
A	+\$500,000	−\$200,000	−\$200,000	−\$200,000
B	+\$50,000	+\$25,000		

What does the NPV rule recommend? What does the IRR rule recommend?

Q 4.22 The prevailing interest rate is 10%. If the following three projects are mutually exclusive, which should you take?

	Year		
Project	0	1	2
1	−\$500	+\$300	+\$300
2	−\$50	+\$30	+\$30
3	−\$50	+\$35	+\$35

What does the NPV rule recommend? What does the IRR rule recommend?

Q 4.23 The prevailing interest rate is 5% over the first year and 10% over the second year. That is, over 2 years, your interest rate is $(1 + 5\%) \cdot (1 + 10\%) - 1 = 15.5\%$. Your project costs \$1,000 and will pay \$600 in the first year and \$500 in the second year. What does the IRR rule recommend? What does the NPV rule recommend?

4.3 THE PROFITABILITY INDEX

How the probability index is computed.

A less prominent measure that is sometimes used in capital budgeting is the **profitability index**. It divides the present value of future cash flows by the project cost (the negative of the first cash flow). For example, if you have a project with cash flows

Time	0	1	2	3	PV 1 to 3
Project A Cash Flow	−\$100	\$70	\$60	\$50	\$128.94

and the interest rate is 20% per annum, you would first compute the present value of future cash flows as

$$PV = \frac{\$70}{1.2} + \frac{\$60}{1.2^2} + \frac{\$50}{1.2^3} \approx \$128.94$$
$$= PV(C_1) + PV(C_2) + PV(C_3)$$

Subtract the \$100 upfront cost, and the NPV is \$28.94. The profitability index is

$$\text{Profitability Index} = \frac{\$128.94}{-(-\$100)} \approx 1.29$$

$$\text{Profitability Index} = \frac{\text{PV(Future Cash Flows)}}{\text{Original Cost}}$$

A positive-NPV project usually has a profitability index above 1—"usually" because the profitability index is meaningful only if the first cash flow is a cash outflow. When this is the case, you can use either NPV or the profitability index for a simple "accept/reject" decision: The statements "NPV > 0" and "profitability index > 1" are the same. That is, like IRR, the profitability index can give the correct answer in the most common situation of one negative cash flow up front followed by all positive cash flows thereafter.

A profitability index–based capital budgeting rule can give the same answer as IRR (and NPV).

Some managers like the fact that the profitability index gives information about relative performance and use of capital. For example,

Here it works nicely, and may even convey some information above and beyond IRR.

Time	0	1	2	3	PV 1 to 3
Project B Cash Flow	−\$10.00	\$21.14	\$18.12	\$15.10	\$38.94

has the same NPV of \$28.94 as the original project, but a profitability index higher than 1.29 because it requires less capital up front.

$$\text{Profitability Index} = \frac{\$38.94}{-(-\$10)} \approx 3.89$$

$$\text{Profitability Index} = \frac{\text{PV(Future Cash Flows)}}{\text{Original Cost}}$$

The reason is that the profitability index values the scale of the project differently. It is intuitively apparent that you would prefer the second project, even though it has the same NPV, because it requires less capital. It may even be less risky, but this can be deceiving, because we have not specified the risk of the future cash flows.

Unfortunately, this feature that you just considered an advantage can also be a disadvantage. You cannot use the profitability index to choose among different projects. For example, assume that your first project returns twice as much in cash flow in all future periods, so it is clearly the better project now.

But here is where the profitability index can go wrong: Like IRR, it has no concept of scale.

	Cash Flows in Year				Measures		
Time	0	1	2	3	$PV(C_1, C_2, C_3)$	NPV	PI
B	−\$10	\$21.14	\$18.12	\$15.10	\$38.94	\$28.94	$\frac{\$38.94}{-(-\$10)} \approx 3.89$
C	−\$100	\$140	\$120	\$100	\$257.87	\$157.87	$\frac{\$257.87}{-(-\$100)} \approx 2.58$

Note that the profitability index of project C is less than that of project B. The reason is that, when compared to NPV, the profitability index *really* "likes" lower-upfront investment projects. It can therefore indicate higher index values even when the NPV is lower. This is really the same scale problem that popped up when we tried to use IRR for comparing mutually exclusive projects. Both look at relative "percentage" performance, not at the dollar gain like NPV does. You should really consider the profitability index in choosing among projects only if the NPVs of the two projects are equal (or at least very similar).

SOLVE NOW!

Q 4.24 The prevailing interest rate is 10%. If the following three projects are mutually exclusive, which should you take?

	Year		
Project	0	1	2
1	−\$500	+\$300	+\$300
2	−\$50	+\$30	+\$30
3	−\$50	+\$35	+\$35

You have already worked out the recommendations of the NPV and the IRR rule. What does the profitability rule recommend?

4.4 THE PAYBACK CAPITAL BUDGETING RULE

The most common aberrant capital budgeting rule in the real world is the payback rule.

What if you want something more "practical" than the egghead "theoretical" capital budgeting methods? Aren't there easier methods that can help you make investment decisions? Yes, they exist—and they usually result in bad choices. Indeed, after IRR and NPV, the most commonly used capital budgeting rule is a "practical" one, the **payback rule**. You need to know why you should not fall for it.

Here is why choosing projects based solely on payback speed is dumb.

Under the payback rule, projects are assumed to be better if you can recover their original investment faster. For the most part, this is a stupid idea. Consider the following three projects:

Project	Year 1	Year 2	Year 3	Year 4	Payback Period
A	−\$5	+\$8			1 year
B	−\$5	+\$4	\$100		2 years
C	−\$5	+\$4	\$0	\$100,000	3 years

Project A has the shortest (best) payback period, but it is the worst of the three projects (assuming common discounting rates). Project B has the next shortest payback period, but it is the second-worst of the three projects (assuming reasonable interest rates). Project C has the longest (worst) payback period, but is the best project. There is also a version of payback in which future paybacks are discounted. This measure asks not how long it takes you to get your money back, but how long it takes you to get the present value of your money back. It is still a bad idea.

To be fair, payback can be an interesting number.

In fairness, the speed of payback can be an interesting statistic.

1. There is a beautiful simplicity to payback. It is easier for managers not trained in finance to understand "you will get your money back within 5 years" than it is to understand "the NPV is $50 million."
2. Payback's emphasis on earlier cash flows helps firms set criteria when they don't trust their managers. For instance, if your department manager claims that you will get your money back within 1 year, and 3 years have already passed without your having seen a penny, then something is probably wrong and you may need a better manager.
3. Payback can also help if you are an entrepeneur with limited capital, faced with an imperfect capital market. In such cases, your cost of capital can be very high and getting your money back in a short amount of time is paramount. The payback information can help you assess your future "liquidity."
4. Finally, in many ordinary situations, in which the choice is a pretty clear-cut yes or no, the results of the payback rule do not lead to severe mistakes (as would a rule that would ignore all time value of money). If you have a project in which you get your money back within 1 month, chances are that it's not a bad one, even from an NPV perspective. If you have a project in which it takes 50 years to get your money back, chances are that it has a negative NPV.

➤ Entrepreneurial finance, Section 10.5, p. 328

Having said all this, if you use payback to make decisions, it can easily lead you to take the wrong projects and ruin your company. Why take a chance when you know better capital budgeting methods? My view is that it is not a bad idea to work out the payback period and use it as "interesting side information," but you should never base project choices on it—and you should certainly never compare projects primarily on the basis of payback.

It is best to avoid payback as a primary decision rule.

4.5 HOW DO CHIEF FINANCIAL OFFICERS (CFOs) DECIDE?

So what do managers really use for capital budgeting? In a survey in 2001, Graham and Harvey (from Duke University) surveyed 392 managers, primarily **chief financial officers (CFOs)**, asking them what techniques they use when deciding on projects or acquisitions. The results are listed in Table 4.2. The two most prominent measures are also the correct ones: They are the "internal rate of return" and the "net present value" methods. Alas, the troublesome "payback period" method and its cousin, the "discounted payback period," still remain surprisingly common.

A survey asked CFOs what they use. It found the good methods (NPV and IRR) are most important.

Of course, this is your first encounter with capital budgeting rules, and there will be a lot more details and complications to come (especially for NPV). But let me

The two unexplained methods (P/E and accounting rate of return) in the table are based on accounting numbers.

TABLE 4.2 CFO VALUATION TECHNIQUES

Method	CFO Usage	Yields Correct Answer	Main Explanation
Internal Rate of Return (IRR)	(76%)	Often	Chapter 4
Net Present Value (NPV)	(75%)	(Almost) Always	Chapter 2
Payback Period	(57%)	Rarely	Chapter 4
Earning Multiples (P/E Ratios)	(39%)	With Caution	Chapter 14
Discounted Payback	(30%)	Rarely	Chapter 4
Accounting Rate of Return	(20%)	Rarely	Chapter 14
Profitability Index	(12%)	Often	Chapter 4

Rarely means "usually no—often used incorrectly in the real world." NPV works *if correctly applied*, which is why I added the qualifier "almost" to always. Of course, if you are considering an extremely good or an extremely bad project, almost any evaluation criterion is likely to give you the same recommendation. (Even a stopped clock gives you the right answer twice a day.)
Source: Campbell and Harvey, 2001.

briefly explain the two methods mentioned in the table that you do not know yet. They are the "earnings multiples" and the "accounting rate of return" methods. They will be explained in great detail in Chapters 13 and 14. In a nutshell, the "earnings multiples" method tries to compare your project's earnings directly to the earnings of other firms in the market. If your project costs less and earns more than these alternative opportunities, then the multiples approach usually suggests you take it. It can often be useful, but considerable caution is warranted. The "accounting rate of return" method uses an accounting "net income" and divides it by the "book value of equity." This is rarely a good idea—financial accounting is not designed to accurately reflect firm value. (Accounting statements are relatively better in measuring flows [like earnings] than they are in measuring stocks [like book value].)

➤ ROE=Accounting rate of return, p. 529

The survey unfortunately did not ask managers whether they select projects primarily to increase earnings—a pity.

Graham and Harvey did not allow respondents to select a third measure for project choice: a desire to maximize reported earnings. Managers care about earnings, especially in the short run and just before they are up for a performance evaluation or retirement. Thus, they may sometimes pass up good projects for which the payoff is far in the future.

Accounting-based rules are problematic.

As you will learn, rules that are based on accounting conventions and not on economics are generally not advisable. I recommend against using them. I have no idea what kind of projects you will end up with if you were to follow their recommendations—except that in many cases, if the measures are huge (e.g., if your accounting rate of return is 190% per annum), then chances are that the project is also positive NPV.

The real-life choice of projects to undertake is not only about mathematical rules, although they are often the right weapons in the fight to convince others to fund projects!

One view, perhaps cynical, is that all the capital budgeting methods that you have now learned give you not only the tools to choose the best projects but also the language necessary for you to argue intelligently and in a professional manner as to which of your favorite projects should be funded. In many corporations, it is "power" that rules. The most influential managers get disproportionally large funding for their projects. This is of course not a quantitative, objective, value-maximization method for choosing projects.

SUMMARY

This chapter covered the following major points:

- If the market is perfect and you have the correct inputs, then net present value is the undisputed correct method to use.
- In a perfect market, projects are worth their net present values. This value does not depend on who the owner is or when the owner needs cash. Any owner can always take the highest NPV projects and use the capital markets to shift cash into periods in which it is needed. Therefore, consumption and investment decisions can be made independently.
- The internal rate of return, IRR, is computed from a project's cash flows by setting the NPV formula equal to zero.
- The internal rate of return does not depend on the prevailing cost of capital. It is a project-specific measure. It can be interpreted as a "sort-of-average" rate of return implicit in many project cash flows. Unlike a simple rate of return, it can be computed when a project has more than one inflow and outflow.
- Projects can have multiple IRR solutions or no IRR solutions.
- Investment projects with IRRs above their costs of capital often, but not always, have positive net present values (NPV), and vice versa. Investment projects with IRRs below their costs of capital often, but not always, have negative net present values (NPV), and vice versa. If the project is a financing method rather than an ordinary investment project, these rules reverse.
- IRR suffers from comparison problems because it does not adjust for project scale. IRR can also be difficult to use if the cost of capital depends on the project cash flow timing.
- The profitability index is often acceptable, too. It rearranges the NPV formula. If used by itself, it often provides the same capital budgeting advice as NPV. But, like IRR, the profitability index can make projects with lower upfront costs and scale appear relatively more desirable.
- The payback measure is in common use. It suggests taking the projects that return the original investment most quickly. It discriminates against projects providing very large payments in the future. It sometimes provides useful information, but it is best avoided as a primary decision rule.
- The information that many other capital budgeting measures provide can sometimes be "interesting." However, they often provide results that are not sensible and therefore should generally be avoided—or at least consumed with great caution.
- NPV and IRR are the methods most popular with CFOs. This makes sense. It remains a minor mystery as to why the payback method enjoys the popularity that it does.

KEY TERMS

SOLVE NOW! SOLUTIONS

Q 4.1 The fact that you can use capital markets to shift money back and forth without costs allows you to consider investment and consumption choices independently.

Q 4.2 If you invest \$400, the project will give $\$400 \cdot 1.15 = \$460$ next period. The capital markets will value the project at $\$460/1.10 \approx \$418.18$. You should take the project and immediately sell it for \$418.18. Thereby, you will end up being able to consume $\$500 - \$400 + \$418.18 = \$518.18$.

Q 4.3 The equation that defines IRR is Formula 4.1 on page 72.

Q 4.4 $-\$1{,}000 + \$1{,}000/(1 + \text{IRR}) = 0 \quad \Longrightarrow \quad \text{IRR} = 0\%$

Q 4.5 $-\$1{,}000 + \$500/(1 + \text{IRR}) + \$500/(1 + \text{IRR})^2 = 0 \quad \Longrightarrow \quad \text{IRR} = 0\%$

Q 4.6 $-\$1{,}000 + \$600/(1 + \text{IRR}) + \$600/(1 + \text{IRR})^2 = 0 \quad \Longrightarrow \quad \text{IRR} \approx 13.07\%$

Q 4.7 $-\$1{,}000 + \$900/(1 + \text{IRR}) + \$900/(1 + \text{IRR})^2 = 0 \quad \Longrightarrow \quad \text{IRR} = 50\%$

Q 4.8 The spreadsheet function is called IRR(). The answer pops out as 15.5696%. Check: $-\$100 + \$55/1.16 + \$70/1.16^2 \approx 0$.

Q 4.9 The coupon bond's YTM is 5%, because $-\$1{,}000 + \frac{\$50}{1.05} + \frac{\$50}{1.05^2} + \frac{\$50}{1.05^3} + \frac{\$50}{1.05^4} + \frac{\$1{,}050}{1.05^5} = 0$. The YTM of such a bond (annual coupons) is equal to the coupon rate when a bond is selling for its face value.

Q 4.10 The YTM is 10%, because $\$1{,}000 + \$1{,}611/1.10^5 \approx 0$.

Q 4.11 You are seeking the solution to $-\$25{,}000 + \frac{\$1{,}000}{(1+\text{YTM})^1} + \frac{\$1{,}000}{(1+\text{YTM})^2} + \frac{\$25{,}000}{(1+\text{YTM})^2} = 0$. It is YTM = 4%.

Q 4.12 For example, $C_0 = -\$100$, $C_1 = +\$120$, $C_2 = -\$140$, $C_3 = +\$160$, $C_4 = -\$20$. (The solutions are IRR $\approx -85.96\%$ and IRR $\approx +9.96\%$. The important aspect is that your example has multiple inflows and multiple outflows.)

Q 4.13 For example, $C_0 = -\$100$, $C_1 = -\$200$, $C_2 = -\$50$. No interest rate can make their present value equal to zero, because all cash flows are negative. This project should never be taken, regardless of cost of capital.

Q 4.14 For projects (A) and (B), the valid IRRs are 10%, 20%, 30%, and 40%. The plot for (A) follows. The figure for (B) has a y-scale that is 50 times larger. For project (C), there is no IRR, also shown in the plot below.

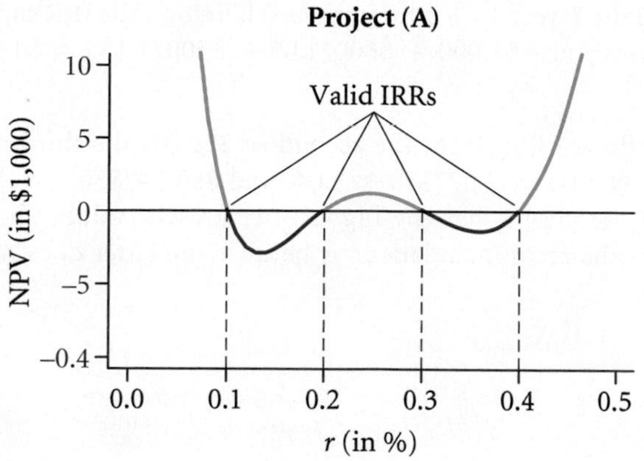

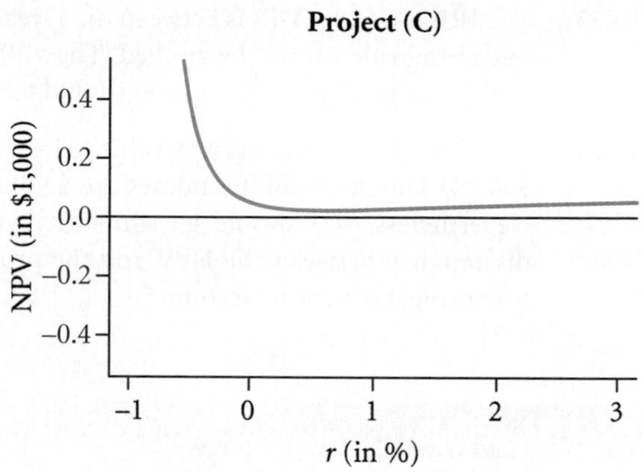

For projects (D), (E), and (F), the IRR is 100%. For project (G), the IRRs are 0% and 100%.

Q 4.15 The (unique) IRR is 56.16%. This is higher than your 30% cost of capital, so you should take this project. The NPV is +\$1,057.35. Because this is positive, it gives the same recommendation—accept.

Q 4.16 The IRR is 19.73%. This is lower than your 20% cost of capital, so you should not take this project. The NPV is −\$23.92. IRR and NPV agree on the reject recommendation.

Q 4.17 The IRR is 8.44%. This is above the prevailing interest rate. However, the cash flows are like that of a financing project. This means that it is a negative NPV project of −\$7.71. You should not take it.

Q 4.18 (a) The IRR-maximizing investment choice of C_0 is an epsilon. The IRR is then close to infinity. The NPV is 0. (b) The NPV-maximizing (and best) choice is an investment of \$226,757. This also happens to be the project's NPV. The IRR is 110%.

Q 4.19 The problems are (a) you need to get the sign right to determine whether you should accept the project above or below its hurdle rate; (b) you need to make sure you have only one unique IRR (or work with a more complicated version of IRR, which we have not done); (c) you cannot use it to compare different projects that have different scales; and (d) you must know your cost of capital.

Q 4.20 The first project has a positive NPV of

$$\text{NPV} = \$50{,}000 + \frac{-\$250{,}000}{1.25} + \frac{\$467{,}500}{1.25^2} + \frac{-\$387{,}500}{1.25^3} + \frac{\$120{,}120}{1.25^4} \approx \$1.15$$

The second project has an NPV of −\$1.15. You should take project A, but not B. If you plot the NPV as a function of the interest, you will see that there are multiple IRRs for these projects, specifically at 10%, 20%, 30%, and 40%. With a cost of capital of 25%, you cannot easily determine which of these two projects you should take. Make your life easy, and just use NPV instead.

Q 4.21 Project A has an NPV of

$$+\$500{,}000 + \frac{-\$200{,}000}{1.25} + \frac{-\$200{,}000}{(1.25)^2} + \frac{-\$200{,}000}{(1.25)^3} = \$109{,}600$$

It has an IRR of 9.70%. Project B has an NPV of \$70,000, and no IRR (it is always positive). Therefore, even though the second project should be taken for any interest rate—which is not the case for the first—the first project is better. Take project A.

Q 4.22 The first project has an NPV of \$20.66 and an IRR of 13.07%. The second project has an NPV of \$2.07 and the same IRR of 13.07%. The third project has an NPV of \$10.74 and an IRR of 25.69%. Still, you should take project 1.

Q 4.23 The IRR is 6.81%. This is between the 1-year 5% and the 2-year 10% interest rates. Therefore, the IRR capital budgeting rule cannot be applied. The NPV rule gives you $-\$1{,}000 + \$600/1.05 + \$500/1.155 \approx \$4.33$, so this is a good project that you should take.

Q 4.24 The first project has present values of future cash flows of \$520.66; the second of \$52.07; the third of \$60.74. The profitability indexes are $\$520.66/\$500 \approx 1.04$, $\$52.07/\$50 \approx 1.04$, and $\$60.74/\$50 \approx 1.21$. Nevertheless, you should go with the first project, because it has the highest net present value. The discrepancy between the NPV and the profitability rule recommendations is because the latter does not take project scale into account.

PROBLEMS

The ▬ *indicates problems available in* myfinancelab

Q 4.25 Given the same NPV, would you be willing to pay extra for a project that bears fruit during your lifetime rather than after you are gone?

Q 4.26 How bad a mistake is it to misestimate the cost of capital in a short-term project? Please illustrate.

Q 4.27 How bad a mistake is it to misestimate the cost of capital in a long-term project? Please illustrate.

Q 4.28 What is the difference between YTM and IRR?

Q 4.29 A project has cash flows of −\$1,000, +\$600, and +\$300 in consecutive years. What is the IRR?

Q 4.30 What is the YTM of a standard 6% level semiannual 10-year coupon bond that sells for its principal amount today (i.e., at par = \$100)?

Q 4.31 A coupon bond costs \$100, then pays \$10 interest each year for 10 years, and pays back its \$100 principal in 10 years. What is the bond's YTM?

Q 4.32 A project has cash flows −\$100, +\$55, and +\$60.50 in consecutive years. How can you characterize the "rate of return" (loosely speaking) embedded in its cash flows?

Q 4.33 Under what circumstances is an IRR a rate of return? Under what circumstances is a rate of return an IRR?

Q 4.34 Give an example of a problem that has multiple IRR solutions.

Q 4.35 Your project has cash flows of −\$1,000 in year 0, +\$3,550 in year 1, −\$4,185 in year 2, and +\$1,638 in year 3. What is its IRR?

Q 4.36 Your project has cash flows of −\$1,000 in year 0, +\$3,550 in year 1, −\$4,185 in year 2, and −\$1,638 in year 3. What is its IRR?

Q 4.37 A project has cash flows of +\$400, −\$300, and −\$300 in consecutive years. The prevailing interest rate is 5%. Should you take this project?

Q 4.38 A project has cash flows of −\$100, +\$55, and +\$60.50 in consecutive years. If the hurdle rate is 10%, should you accept the project?

Q 4.39 If a project has a cash inflow of \$1,000 followed by cash outflows of \$600 in two consecutive years, then under what discount rate scenario should you accept this project?

Q 4.40 You can invest in a project with returns that depend on the amount of your investment. Specifically, the formula relating next year's payoff (cash flow) to your investment today is $C_1 = \sqrt{-C_0} - \$0.1$, where C_0 and C_1 are measured in million dollars. For example, if you invest \$500,000 in the project today, it will return $\sqrt{\$0.5} - \$0.1 \approx \$0.632$ million next year. The prevailing interest rate is 6% per annum. Use a spreadsheet to answer the following two questions:

(a) What is the IRR-maximizing investment choice of C_0? What is the NPV at this level?

(b) What is the NPV-maximizing investment choice of C_0? What is the IRR at this level?

Q 4.41 The prevailing interest rate is 10%. If the following three projects are mutually exclusive, which should you take?

	Cash Flow in Year		
Project	0	1	2
A	+$500	−$300	−$300
B	+$50	−$30	−$30
C	+$50	−$35	−$35

What does the NPV rule recommend? What does the IRR rule recommend?

Q 4.42 What are the profitability indexes and the NPVs of the following two projects: project A that requires an investment of $5 and gives $20 per year for 3 years, and project B that requires an investment of $9 and gives $25 per year for 3 years? The interest rate is 10%. If you can invest in only one of the projects, which would you choose?

Q 4.43 Consider the following project:

Year	0	1	2	3	4	5	6
Cash Flow	−$10	$5	$8	$3	$3	$3	−$6

(a) What is the IRR?
(b) What is the payback time?
(c) What is the profitability index?

Q 4.44 Consider the following project:

Year	0	1	2	3	4	5	6	7
Cash Flow	$0	−$100	$50	$80	$30	$30	$30	−$60

(a) What is the IRR?
(b) What is the payback time?
(c) What is the profitability index?

Q 4.45 The prevailing cost of capital is 9% per annum. What would various capital budgeting rules recommend for the following projects?

	Cash Flow in Year				
Project	0	1	2	3	4
A	–$1,000	$300	$400	$500	$600
B	–$1,000	$150	$200	$1,000	$1,200
C	–$2,000	$1,900	$200		
D	–$200	$300			
E	–$200	$300	$0	–$100	

Q 4.46 What are the most prominent methods for capital budgeting in the real world? Which make sense?

Time-Varying Rates of Return and the Yield Curve

WHEN RATES OF RETURN ARE DIFFERENT

In this chapter, we make the world a little more complex and a lot more realistic, although we are still assuming perfect foresight and perfect markets. In the previous chapters, the interest rate was the same every period—if a 30-year bond offered an interest rate of 5.6% per annum, so did a 1-year bond. But this is not the case in the real world. Rates of return can and do vary with the length of time of an investment. This is why they are often called "time dependent" or "horizon dependent." For example, in December 2004, a 20-year U.S. Treasury bond offered an interest rate of 4.85% per year, while a 1-year U.S. Treasury bond offered an interest rate of only 2.23% per year.

Time-dependent interest rates are important not only for specialized bond traders, but for almost all investors. In fact, if you have ever walked by a bank that offers 6-month CDs for 3% and 5-year CDs for 5%, have you not wondered whether the 5-year CD is a better deal than the 6-month CD? And have you not wondered what role inflation plays in setting these interest rates?

And it is not only investors who need to worry about time-varying interest rates, but also corporate CEOs. If you are a CEO, you must be able to compare short-term and long-term projects and to compare short-term and long-term financing costs. After all, if your investors can earn higher rates of return in long-term Treasury bonds than in short-term Treasury bills, then they will likely also demand higher rates of return if you ask them to finance your long-term projects rather than your short-term projects. Conversely, if your corporation wants to finance projects by borrowing, you will likely have to pay a higher rate of return if you borrow long term.

In this chapter, you will learn how to work with time-dependent rates of return and inflation. In addition, this chapter contains an optional section, which explains many finer details about bonds.

5.1 WORKING WITH TIME-VARYING RATES OF RETURN

In the real world, rates of return usually differ depending on when the payments are made. For example, the interest rate next year could be higher or lower than it is this year. Moreover, it is often the case that long-term bonds offer different interest rates than short-term bonds. You must be able to work in such an environment, so let me give you the tools.

5.1A COMPOUNDING DIFFERENT RATES OF RETURN

A compounding example with time-dependent rates of return.

Fortunately, when working with time-varying interest rates, all the tools you have learned in previous chapters remain applicable (as promised). In particular, compounding still works exactly the same way. For example, what is the 2-year holding rate of return if the rate of return is 20% in the first year and 30% in the second year? (The latter is sometimes called the **reinvestment rate**.) You can determine the 2-year holding rate of return from the two 1-year rates of return using the same compounding formula as before:

$$(1 + r_{0,2}) = (1 + 20\%) \cdot (1 + 30\%) = (1 + 56\%)$$

$$(1 + r_{0,1}) \cdot (1 + r_{1,2}) = (1 + r_{0,2})$$

Subtract 1, and the answer is a total 2-year holding rate of return of 56%. If you prefer it shorter,

$$r_{0,2} = 1.20 \cdot 1.30 - 1 = 1.56 - 1 = 56\%$$

More notation—ugggh!

The calculation is not conceptually more difficult, but the notation is. You have to have subscripts not just for interest rates that begin now, but also for interest rates that begin in the future. Therefore, most of the examples in this chapter must use two subscripts: one for the time when the money is deposited, and one for the time when the money is returned. Thus, $r_{1,2}$ describes an interest rate from time 1 to time 2. Aside from this extra notation, the compounding formula is still the very same multiplicative "one-plus formula" for each interest rate (subtracting 1 at the end).

The general formula for compounding over many periods.

You can also compound to determine holding rates of return in the future. For example, if the 1-year rate of return is 30% from year 1 to year 2, 40% from year 2 to year 3, and 50% from year 3 to year 4, then what is your holding rate of return for investing beginning next year for 3 years? It is

$$\text{Given:} \quad r_{1,2} = 30\% \quad r_{2,3} = 40\% \quad r_{3,4} = 50\%$$

$$(1 + r_{1,4}) = (1 + 30\%) \cdot (1 + 40\%) \cdot (1 + 50\%) = (1 + 173\%)$$

$$(1 + r_{1,2}) \cdot (1 + r_{2,3}) \cdot (1 + r_{3,4}) = (1 + r_{1,4})$$

Subtracting 1, you see that the 3-year holding rate of return for an investment that takes money *next* year (not today!) and returns money in 4 years (appropriately called $r_{1,4}$) is 173%. Let's be clear about the timing. For example, say it was midnight of December 31, 2008, right now. This would be time 0. Time 1 would be midnight

December 31, 2009, and this is when you would invest your \$1. Three years later, on midnight December 31, 2012 (time 4), you would receive your original dollar plus an additional \$1.73, for a total return of \$2.73. Interest rates that begin right now—where the first subscript would be 0—are usually called **spot rates.** Interest rates that begin in the future are usually called **forward rates.**

SOLVE NOW!

Q 5.1 If the first-year interest rate is 2% and the second year interest is 3%, what is the 2-year total interest rate?

Q 5.2 Although a 2-year project had returned 22% in its first year, overall it lost half of its value. What was the project's rate of return after the first year?

Q 5.3 From 1991 to 2002, the stock market (specifically, the S&P 500) had the following annual rates of return:

Year	$\tilde{r}_{S\&P\ 500}$	Year	$\tilde{r}_{S\&P\ 500}$	Year	$\tilde{r}_{S\&P\ 500}$
1991	+0.2631	1995	+0.3411	1999	+0.1953
1992	+0.0446	1996	+0.2026	2000	−0.1014
1993	+0.0706	1997	+0.3101	2001	−0.1304
1994	−0.0154	1998	+0.2700	2002	−0.2337

What was the rate of return over the first 6 years, and what was it over the second 6 years? What was the rate of return over the whole 12 years?

Q 5.4 A project lost one-third of its value the first year, then gained fifty percent of its value, then lost two-thirds of its value, and finally doubled in value. What was the overall rate of return?

5.1B ANNUALIZED RATES OF RETURN

Per-unit standard measures are statistics that are conceptual aids.

Time-varying rates of return create a new complication that is best explained by an analogy. Is a car that travels 163,680 yards in 93 minutes fast or slow? It is not easy to say, because you are used to thinking in "miles per sixty minutes," not in "yards per ninety-three minutes." It makes sense to translate speeds into miles per hour for the purpose of comparing them. You can even do this for sprinters, who run for only 10 seconds. Speeds are just a standard measure of the rate of accumulation of distance per unit of time.

A per-unit standard for rates of return: annualized rates.

The same issue applies to rates of return: A rate of return of 58.6% over 8.32 years is not as easy to compare to other rates of return as a rate of return per year. Therefore, most rates of return are quoted as **annualized rates.** The average annualized rate of return is just a convenient unit of measurement for the rate at which money accumulates—a "sort-of-average" measure of performance. Of course, when you compute such an annualized rate of return, you do not mean that the investment earned the same annualized rate of return of, say, 5.7% each year—just as the car need not have traveled at 60 mph (163,680 yards in 93 minutes) each instant.

If you were earning a total 3-year holding rate of return of 173% over the 3-year period, what would your *annualized* rate of return be? The answer is not the **average rate of return** of $173\%/3 \approx 57.7\%$, because if you earned 57.7% per year, you would have ended up with $1.577^3 - 1 \approx 292\%$, not 173%. This incorrect answer of 57.7% ignores the *compounded interest on the interest* that you would earn after the first year and second year. Instead, to compute the annualized rate of return, you need to find a single hypothetical annual rate of return that, if you received it each and every year, would give you a 3-year holding rate of return of 173%.

Return to our example: You want to annualize our 3-year total holding rate of return.

How can you compute this? Call this hypothetical annual rate that you would have to earn each year for 3 years $r_{\bar{3}}$ (note the bar above the 3) in order to end up with a holding rate of return of 173%. To find $r_{\bar{3}}$, solve the equation

To find the t-year annualized interest rate, take the tth root of the total return (t is number of years).

$$(1 + r_{\bar{3}}) \cdot (1 + r_{\bar{3}}) \cdot (1 + r_{\bar{3}}) = (1 + 173\%)$$
$$(1 + r_{\bar{3}}) \cdot (1 + r_{\bar{3}}) \cdot (1 + r_{\bar{3}}) = (1 + r_{0,3})$$

or, for short,

$$(1 + r_{\bar{3}})^3 = (1 + 173\%)$$
$$(1 + r_{\bar{t}})^t = (1 + r_{0,t}) \tag{5.1}$$

In our example, the holding rate of return $r_{0,3}$ is known (173%) and the annualized rate of return $r_{\bar{3}}$ is unknown. Earning the same rate ($r_{\bar{3}}$) 3 years in a row should result in a holding rate of return of 173%. It is a "smoothed-out" rate of return of the 3 years' rates of return. Think of it as a hypothetical, single, constant-speed rate at which your money would have ended up as quickly at 173% as it did with the 30%, 40%, and 50% individual annual rates of return. The correct solution for $r_{\bar{3}}$ is obtained by computing the third root of 1 plus the total holding rate of return:

➤ Appendix A, "Background," p. A-1

$$(1 + r_{\bar{3}}) = (1 + 173\%)^{(1/3)} = \sqrt[3]{1 + 173\%} \approx 1 + 39.76\%$$
$$(1 + r_{0,t})^{(1/t)} = \sqrt[t]{1 + r_{0,t}} = (1 + r_{\bar{t}})$$

Confirm with your calculator that $r_{\bar{3}} \approx 39.76\%$,

$$1.3976 \cdot 1.3976 \cdot 1.3976 \approx (1 + 173\%)$$
$$(1 + r_{\bar{3}}) \cdot (1 + r_{\bar{3}}) \cdot (1 + r_{\bar{3}}) = (1 + r_{0,3})$$

In sum, if you invested money at a rate of 39.76% per annum for 3 years, you would end up with a total 3-year holding rate of return of 173%. As is the case here, for very long periods, the order of magnitude of the annualized rate will often be so different from the holding rate that you will intuitively immediately register whether the quantity $r_{0,3}$ or $r_{\bar{3}}$ is meant. In the real world very few rates of return, especially over long horizons, are quoted as holding rates of return. Most are quoted in annualized terms instead.

IMPORTANT: The total holding rate of return over t years, called $r_{0,t}$, is translated into an annualized rate of return , called $r_{\bar{t}}$, by taking the tth root:

$$(1 + r_{\bar{t}}) = \sqrt[t]{1 + r_{0,t}} = (1 + r_{0,t})^{1/t}$$

Compounding the annualized rate of return over t years yields the total holding rate of return.

Translating long-term dollar returns into annualized rates of return.

You also will often need to compute annualized rates of return from payoffs yourself. For example, what annualized rate of return would you expect from a \$100 investment today that promises a return of \$240 in 30 years? The first step is computing the total holding rate of return. Take the ending value (\$240) minus your beginning value (\$100), and divide by the beginning value. Thus, the total 30-year holding rate of return is

$$r_{0,30} = \frac{\$240 - \$100}{\$100} = 140\%$$

$$r_{0,30} = \frac{C_{30} - C_0}{C_0}$$

The annualized rate of return is the rate $r_{\overline{30}}$, which, if compounded for 30 years, offers a 140% rate of return,

$$(1 + r_{\overline{30}})^{30} = (1 + 140\%)$$

$$(1 + r_{\bar{t}})^t = (1 + r_{0,t})$$

Solve this equation by taking the 30th root,

$$(1 + r_{\overline{30}}) = (1 + 140\%)^{1/30} = \sqrt[30]{1 + 140\%} \approx 1 + 2.96\%$$

$$(1 + r_{\overline{30}}) = (1 + r_{0,30})^{1/30} = \sqrt[30]{1 + r_{0,30}}$$

Subtracting 1, you see that a return of \$240 in 30 years for an initial \$100 investment is equivalent to a 2.96% annualized rate of return.

Compounding $\approx$ adding. Annualizing $\approx$ averaging.

In the context of rates of return, compounding is similar to adding, while annualizing is similar to averaging. If you earn 1% twice, your compounded rate is 2.01%, similar to the rates themselves added (2%). Your annualized rate of return is 1%, similar to the average rate of return of 2.01%/2 = 1.005%. The difference is the interest on the interest.

Averaging can lead to surprising results—returns that are much higher than what you earned per year.

Now assume that you have an investment that doubles in value in the first year and then falls back to its original value. What would its average rate of return be? Doubling from, say, \$100 to \$200 is a rate of return of +100%. Falling back to \$100 is a rate of return of (\$100 − \$200)/\$200 = −50%. Therefore, the average rate of return would be [+100% + (−50%)]/2 = +25%. *But you have not made any money!* You started with \$100 and ended up with \$100. If you compound the returns, you get the answer of 0% that you were intuitively expecting:

$$(1 + 100\%) \cdot (1 - 50\%) = 1 + 0\% \Rightarrow r_{0,2} = 0\%$$

$$(1 + r_{0,1}) \cdot (1 + r_{1,2}) = (1 + r_{0,2})$$

It follows that the annualized rate of return $r_{\overline{2}}$ is also 0%. Conversely, an investment that produces +20% followed by −20% has an average rate of return of 0% but leaves you with a loss:

$$(1 + 20\%) \cdot (1 - 20\%) = (1 - 4\%) \Rightarrow r_{0,2} = -4\%$$

$$(1 + r_{0,1}) \cdot (1 + r_{1,2}) = (1 + r_{0,2})$$

For every \$100 of your original investment, you now have only \$96. The average rate of return of 0% does not reflect this loss. Both the compounded and therefore the annualized rates of return do tell you that you had a loss:

$$1 + r_{\overline{2}} = \sqrt{(1 + r_{0,2})} = \sqrt{1 - 4\%} = 1 - 2.02\% \Rightarrow r_{\overline{2}} \approx -2.02\%$$

If you were an investment advisor and quoting your historical performance, would you rather quote your average historical rate of return or your annualized rate of return? (Hint: The industry standard is to quote the average rate of return, not the annualized rate of return!)

Make sure to solve the following questions to gain more experience with compounding and annualizing over different time horizons.

SOLVE NOW!

Q 5.5 If you earn a rate of return of 5% over 4 months, what is the annualized rate of return?

Q 5.6 Assume that the 2-year holding rate of return is 40%. The average (arithmetic) rate of return is therefore 20% per year. What is the annualized (geometric) rate of return? Is the annualized rate the same as the average rate?

Q 5.7 Is the compounded rate of return higher or lower than the sum of the individual rates of return? Is the annualized rate of return higher or lower than the average of the individual rates of return? Why?

Q 5.8 Return to Question 5.3. What was the annualized rate of return on the S&P 500 over these 12 years?

Q 5.9 If the total holding interest rate is 50% for a 5-year investment, what is the annualized rate of return?

Q 5.10 If the per-year interest rate is 10% for each of the next 5 years, what is the annualized 5-year rate of return?

5.1C PRESENT VALUES WITH TIME-VARYING INTEREST RATES

The PV formula still looks very similar.

Let's proceed now to net present value with time-varying interest rates. What do you need to learn about the role of time-varying interest rates when computing NPV? The answer is essentially nothing new. You already know everything you need to know here. The net present value formula is still

$$
\begin{aligned}
\text{NPV} &= \text{PV}(C_0) + \text{PV}(C_1) + \text{PV}(C_2) + \text{PV}(C_3) + \cdots \\
&= C_0 + \frac{C_1}{1 + r_{0,1}} + \frac{C_2}{1 + r_{0,2}} + \frac{C_3}{1 + r_{0,3}} + \cdots \\
&= C_0 + \frac{C_1}{1 + r_{\bar{1}}} + \frac{C_2}{(1 + r_{\bar{2}})^2} + \frac{C_3}{(1 + r_{\bar{3}})^3} + \cdots \\
&= C_0 + \frac{C_1}{1 + r_{0,1}} + \frac{C_2}{(1 + r_{0,1}) \cdot (1 + r_{1,2})} + \frac{C_3}{(1 + r_{0,1}) \cdot (1 + r_{1,2}) \cdot (1 + r_{2,3})} + \cdots
\end{aligned}
$$

The only novelty is that you need to be more careful with your subscripts. You cannot simply assume that the multiyear holding returns (e.g., $1 + r_{0,2}$) are the squared 1-year rates of return ($(1 + r_{0,1})^2$). Instead, you must work with time-dependent costs of capital (interest rates). That's it.

Present values are still alike and thus can be added, subtracted, compared, and so on.

For example, say you have a project with an initial investment of \$12 that pays \$10 in 1 year and \$8 in 5 years. Assume that the 1-year interest rate is 5% and the 5-year annualized interest rate is 6% per annum. In this case,

$$
\text{PV}(\$10 \text{ in 1 year}) = \frac{\$10}{1.05} \approx \$9.52
$$

$$
\text{PV}(\$8 \text{ in 5 years}) = \frac{\$8}{1.06^5} \approx \$5.98
$$

It follows that the project's total value *today* (time 0) is \$15.50. If the project costs \$12, its net present value is

$$
\text{NPV} = -\$12 + \frac{\$10}{1.05} + \frac{\$8}{1.06^5} \approx \$3.50
$$

$$
\text{NPV} = C_0 + \frac{C_1}{1 + r_{0,1}} + \frac{C_5}{1 + r_{0,5}} = \text{NPV}
$$

Here is a typical NPV example.

➤ Table 2.1, p. 32

You can also rework a more involved project, equivalent to that in Table 2.1, which had the following cash flows:

Time	0	1	2	3	4	5
Project	−\$900	+\$200	+\$200	+\$400	+\$400	−\$100

To make it more interesting, let's now use a hypothetical current term structure of interest rates that is upward sloping. Assume this project requires an appropriate discount rate of 5% over 1 year, and 0.5% more for every subsequent year, so that the cost of capital reaches 7% annualized in the 5th year. The valuation method works the same way as it did in Table 2.1—you only have to be a little more careful with the interest rate subscripts. The correct solution is

Time	Project Cash Flow	Interest Rate In Year	Interest Rate Compounded	Discount Factor	Present Value
t	C_t	$r_{\bar{t}}$	$r_{0,t}$	$\frac{1}{1+r_{0,t}}$	$PV(C_t)$
Today	−$900	any	0.0%	1.0000	−$900.00
Year 1	+$200	5.0%	5.0%	0.9524	$190.48
Year 2	+$200	5.5%	11.3%	0.8985	$179.69
Year 3	+$400	6.0%	19.1%	0.8396	$335.85
Year 4	+$400	6.5%	28.6%	0.7773	$311.04
Year 5	−$100	7.0%	40.3%	0.7130	−$71.33
			Net Present Value (Sum):		$45.73

SOLVE NOW!

Q 5.11 A project costs $200 and will provide cash flows of +$100, +$300, and +$500 in consecutive years. The annualized interest rate is 3% per annum over 1 year, 4% per annum over 2 years, and 4.5% per annum over 3 years. What is this project's NPV?

5.2 INFLATION

Inflation is the increase in the price of the same good.

Let's make our world a little more realistic—and complex—by working out the effects of inflation. **Inflation** is the process by which goods cost more in the future than they cost today. When there is inflation, the price level is rising and money is losing its value. For example, if inflation is 100%, an apple that costs $0.50 today will cost $1 next year, a banana that costs $2 today will cost $4, and bread that costs $1 today will cost $2.

Inflation matters when contracts are not written to adjust for it.

Inflation may or may not matter, depending on how contracts are written. If you ignore inflation and write a contract that promises to deliver bread for the price of $1 next year, it is said to be in **nominal terms**—and you may have made a big mistake. The money you will be paid will be worth only half as much. You will only be able to buy one apple for each loaf of bread that you had agreed to sell for $1, not the two apples that anyone else will enjoy. On the other hand, you could write your contract in **real terms** (or **inflation-indexed terms**) today, in which case the inflationary price change would not matter. That is, you could build into your promised banana delivery price the inflation rate from today to next year. An example would be a contract that promises to deliver bananas at the rate of four apples per banana. If a contract is indexed to inflation, then inflation does not matter. However, in the United States inflation often does matter, because most contracts are in nominal terms and not inflation indexed. Therefore, you have to learn how to work with inflation.

ANECDOTE The German Hyperinflation of 1922

The most famous episode of **hyperinflation** occurred in Germany from August 1922 to November 1923. Prices more than quadrupled every month. The price for goods was higher in the evening than in the morning! Stamps had to be overprinted by the day, and shoppers went out in the morning with bags of money that were worthless by the end of the day. By the time Germany printed 1,000 billion Mark Bank Notes, no one trusted the currency anymore. This hyperinflation was stopped only by a drastic currency and financial system reform. But high inflation is not just a historic artifact. For example, many Latin American countries experienced annual doubling of prices in the early 1980s.

The opposite of inflation is **deflation** (negative inflation), a process in which the price level falls. Though much rarer, it happens. In fact, *Business Week* reported in November 2002 that an ongoing recession and low demand continued to force an ongoing decline in Japanese prices.

Many economists now believe that a modest inflation rate between 1% and 3% per year is a healthy number.

What effect, then, does inflation have on returns? On (net) present values? This is our next subject.

5.2A MEASURING THE INFLATION RATE

The CPI is the most common inflation measure.

The first important question is how you should define the inflation rate. Is the rate of change of the price of apples the best measure of inflation? What if apples (the fruit) become more expensive, but Apples (the computers) become less expensive? Defining inflation is actually rather tricky. To solve this problem, economists have invented *baskets* or *bundles* of goods and services that are deemed to be representative. Economists then measure an average price change for these items. The official source of most inflation measures is the **Bureau of Labor Statistics (BLS)**, which determines the compositions of a number of prominent bundles (indexes) and publishes the average total price of these bundles on a monthly basis. The most prominent such inflation measure is a hypothetical bundle of average household consumption, called the **Consumer Price Index (CPI)**. (The CPI components are roughly: housing 40%, food 20%, transportation 15%, medical care 10%, clothing 5%, entertainment 5%, others 5%.) The BLS offers inflation data at http://www.bls.gov/cpi/, and the *Wall Street Journal* prints the percent change in the CPI at the end of its regular column "Money Rates." (To give you an idea of the typical order of magnitude: In December 2004, for example, the Consumer Price Index showed a rate of price change of 3.3%/year—much higher than the inflation rate of 1.9% in December 2003, but a little lower than the 3.4% in December 2005.) A number of other indexes are also in common use as inflation measures, such as the **Producer Price Index (PPI)** or the broader **GDP Deflator**. They typically move fairly similarly to the CPI. There are also more specialized bundles, such as computer inflation indexes (the price of equivalent computer power does not inflate, but deflate, so the rate is usually negative), or indexes for prices of goods purchased in a particular region.

The CPI matters—even if it is calculated incorrectly.

The official inflation rate is not just a number—it is important in itself, because many contracts are specifically indexed to a particular inflation definition. For example, even if actual true inflation is zero, if the officially reported CPI rate is positive, the government must pay out more to Social Security recipients. The lower the official inflation rate, the less the government has to pay. You would therefore think that the government has the incentive to understate inflation. But, strangely, this has not been the case. On the contrary, there are strong political interest groups that hinder the BLS from even fixing mistakes that everyone knows overstate the CPI—that is, corrections that would result in *lower* official inflation numbers. In 1996, the Boskin Commission, consisting of a number of eminent economists, found that the CPI overstates inflation by about 74 basis points per annum—a huge difference. The main reasons were and continue to be that the BLS has been tardy in recognizing the growing importance of such factors as effective price declines in computer and telecommunication and the role of superstores such as Wal-Mart and Target.

Before we get moving, a final warning:

IMPORTANT: The common statement "in today's dollars" is ambiguous. Some people mean "inflation adjusted." Other people mean present values (i.e., "compared to an investment in risk-free bonds"). When in doubt, ask!

SOLVE NOW!

Q 5.12 Read the Bureau of Labor Statistics' website descriptions of the CPI and the PPI. How does the CPI differ conceptually from the PPI? Are the two different right now?

5.2B REAL AND NOMINAL INTEREST RATES

Nominal returns are what is normally quoted. *Real* returns are adjusted for inflation. They are what you want to know if you want to consume.

To work with inflation and to learn how you would properly index a contract for inflation, you first need to learn the difference between a **nominal return** and a **real return**. The nominal rate is what is usually quoted—a return that has not been adjusted for inflation. In contrast, the real rate of return "somehow takes out" inflation from the nominal rate in order to calculate a return "as if" there had been no price inflation to begin with. It is the real return that reflects the fact that, in the presence of inflation, a dollar in the future will have less purchasing power than a dollar today. It is the real rate of return that measures your trade-off between present and future consumption, taking into account the change in prices.

An extreme 100% inflation rate example: Prices double every year.

Start with a simple exaggerated scenario: Assume that the inflation rate is 100% per year and you can buy a bond that promises a *nominal* interest rate of 700%. What is your *real* rate of return? To find out, assume that \$1 buys one apple today. With an inflation rate of 100%, you need \$2 next year to buy the same apple. Your investment return will be \$1 · (1 + 700%) = \$8 for today's \$1 of investment. But this \$8 now applies to apples costing \$2 each. Your \$8 will buy 4 apples, not 8 apples. Your real rate of return (1 apple yields 4 apples) is therefore

$$r_{\text{real}} = \frac{(4 \text{ Apples for } \$8) - (1 \text{ Apple at } \$2)}{(1 \text{ Apple at } \$2)} = 300\%$$

For each dollar invested today, you will be able to purchase only 300% more apples next year (not 700% more) than you could purchase today. This is because inflation will reduce the purchasing power of your dollar by half.

Here is the correct conversion formula from nominal to real rates.

The correct formula to adjust for the inflation rate (π) is again a "one-plus" type formula. In our example, it is

$$(1 + 700\%) = (1 + 300\%) \cdot (1 + 100\%)$$
$$(1 + r_{\text{nominal}}) = (1 + r_{\text{real}}) \cdot (1 + \pi)$$

Turning this formula around gives you the real rate of return,

$$(1 + r_{\text{real}}) = \frac{1 + 700\%}{1 + 100\%} = 1 + 300\%$$
$$(1 + r_{\text{real}}) = \frac{(1 + r_{\text{nominal}})}{(1 + \pi)}$$

In plain English, a nominal interest rate of 700% is the same as a real interest rate of 300%, given an inflation rate of 100%.

IMPORTANT: The relation between nominal rates of return (r_{nominal}), real rates of return (r_{real}), and inflation (π) is

$$(1 + r_{\text{nominal}}) = (1 + r_{\text{real}}) \cdot (1 + \pi) \qquad (5.2)$$

For small rates, adding/subtracting is an okay approximation.

➤ Bills, notes, and bonds, Section 5.3, p. 102

As with compounding, if both are small, the mistake of just subtracting the inflation rate from the nominal interest rate to obtain the real interest rate is not too grave. For example, a 10-year U.S. Treasury note offered a yield of 4.10% in December 2004, and the current inflation rate was standing at 3.3%. If the inflation rate were to remain, then your real rate of return would have been

$$(1 + 4.10\%) \approx (1 + 0.77\%) \cdot (1 + 3.3\%) \approx 1 + 3.3\% + 0.77\% + 0.0254\%$$
$$(1 + r_{\text{nominal}}) = (1 + r_{\text{real}}) \cdot (1 + \pi) = 1 + \pi + r_{\text{real}} + \underbrace{r_{\text{real}} \cdot \pi}_{\text{cross-term}}$$

or, if you prefer it short,

$$r_{\text{real}} = \frac{1.0410}{1.033} - 1 \approx 0.77\%$$

➤ Adding or Compounding Interest Rates, and the cross-term, Section2.4A, p. 22

The last term in the first form is the mistake you would make by not using the one-plus formula and is sometimes called the cross-term. The cross-term difference of 2.5 basis points is easily swamped by your uncertainty about the 10-year future inflation rate. However, when inflation and interest rates are high—as they were, for example, in the late 1970s—then the cross-term can be important.

Real interest rates can be negative.

A positive time value of money—the fact that money tomorrow is worth more than money today—is only true for nominal quantities, not for real quantities. Only nominal interest rates are never negative. In the presence of inflation, real interest rates not only *can* be negative, but often *have* been negative. In fact, this was the case in December 2004 for some other bonds. For example, a 1-year U.S. Treasury note offered 2.58% and the inflation rate was 3.3%, which means that your real interest rate was −0.7% per annum. Every dollar you kept in such U.S. Treasuries was worth less in real purchasing power 1 year later. You would have ended up with more cash—but also with *less* purchasing power. Of course, if there are goods or projects that appreciate with inflation (inflation hedges, such as real estate or gold), and to the extent that these goods are both storable and traded in a perfect market, you would not expect to see negative real rates of return. After all, you could buy these projects today and sell them next year, and thereby earn a real rate of return that is positive. Many investors also reasonably believe that, unlike bonds that promise to pay fixed nominal amounts in the future, stocks are good insurance against inflation. They should appreciate in value when the price level increases because they are claims on real underlying projects, which presumably will similarly experience a price increase.

SOLVE NOW!

Q 5.13 From memory, write down the relationship between nominal rates of return (r_{nominal}), real rates of return (r_{real}), and the inflation rate (π).

Q 5.14 The nominal interest rate is 20%. Inflation is 5%. What is the real interest rate?

5.2C INFLATION IN NET PRESENT VALUES

The most fundamental rule is never to mix apples and oranges. Nominal cash flows must be discounted with nominal interest rates.

When it comes to inflation and net present value, there is a simple rule: Never mix apples and oranges. The beauty of NPV is that every project's cash flows are translated into the same units: today's dollars. Keep everything in the same units in the presence of inflation, so that this NPV advantage is not lost. When you use the NPV formula, always discount nominal cash flows with nominal discount rates, and real (inflation-adjusted) cash flows with real (inflation-adjusted) discount rates.

Our example discounted both in real and nominal terms.

Let's return to our "apple" example. With 700% nominal interest rates and 100% inflation, the real interest rate is (1 + 700%)/(1 + 100%) − 1 = 300%. What is the value of a project that gives 12 apples next year, given that apples cost $1 each today and $2 each next year?

There are two methods you can use:

Discount nominal cash flows with nominal rates. Discount real cash flows with real rates.

1. Discount the nominal cash flow of 12 apples next year ($2 · 12 = $24) with the nominal interest rate. Thus, the 12 future apples are worth

$$\frac{\text{Nominal Cash Flow}}{1 + \text{Nominal Rate}} = \frac{\$24}{1 + 700\%} = \$3$$

2. Discount the real cash flows of 12 apples next year with the real interest rate. Thus, the 12 future apples are worth

$$\frac{\text{Real Cash Flow}}{1 + \text{Real Rate}} = \frac{12 \text{ Apples}}{1 + 300\%} = 3 \text{ Apples}$$

in today's apples. Because an apple costs $1 today, the 12 apples next year are worth $3 today.

Both the real and the nominal methods arrive at the same NPV result. The opportunity cost of capital is that if you invest one apple today, you can quadruple your apple holdings by next year. Thus, a 12-apple harvest next year is worth 3 apples to you today. The higher nominal interest rates already reflect the fact that nominal cash flows next year are worth less than they are this year. As simple as this may sound, I have seen corporations first work out the real value of their goods in the future, and then discount this with standard nominal interest rates. Just don't!

IMPORTANT:

- Discount nominal cash flows with nominal interest rates.
- Discount real cash flows with real interest rates.

Either works. Never discount nominal cash flows with real interest rates, or vice versa.

Usually, it is best to work only with nominal quantities.

If you want to see this in algebra, the reason that the two methods come to the same result is that the inflation rate cancels out,

$$\text{PV} = \frac{\$24}{1 + 700\%} = \frac{12A}{1 + 300\%} = \frac{12A \cdot (1 + 100\%)}{(1 + 300\%) \cdot (1 + 100\%)}$$

$$= \frac{N}{1 + r_{\text{nominal}}} = \frac{R}{1 + r_{\text{real}}} = \frac{R \cdot (1 + \pi)}{(1 + r_{\text{real}}) \cdot (1 + \pi)}$$

where N is the nominal cash flow, R is the real cash flow, and π is the inflation rate. Most of the time, it is easier to work in nominal quantities. Nominal interest rates are far more common than real interest rates, and you can simply use published inflation rates to adjust the future price of goods to obtain future expected nominal cash flows.

SOLVE NOW!

Q 5.15 If the real interest is 3% per annum and the inflation rate is 8% per annum, then what is the present value of a $500,000 nominal payment next year?

5.3 TIME-VARYING INTEREST RATES: U.S. TREASURIES AND THE YIELD CURVE

The simplest and most important benchmark bonds nowadays are Treasuries. They have known and certain payouts.

It is now time to talk in more detail about the most important financial market in the world today: the market for bonds issued by the U.S. government. These bonds are called Treasuries and are perhaps the simplest projects around. This is because Treasuries cannot fail to pay. They promise to pay U.S. dollars, and the United States has the right to print more U.S. dollars if it were ever to run out. Thus, there is absolutely no uncertainty about repayment for Treasuries.

U.S. Treasury bills, notes, and bonds have different maturities.

The shorthand "Treasury" comes from the fact that the debt itself is issued by the U.S. Treasury Department. There are three main types:

1. **Treasury bills** (often abbreviated as **T-bills**) have maturities of less than 1 year.

2. **Treasury notes** have maturities between 1 and 10 years.
3. **Treasury bonds** have maturities greater than 10 years.

The 30-year bond is often called the **long bond**. Together the three are usually just called **Treasuries**. Conceptually, there is really no difference among them. All are really just bonds issued by the U.S. Treasury. Indeed, there can be Treasury bonds today that are due in 3 months—such as a 10-year Treasury note that was issued 9 years and 9 months ago. This is really the same obligation as a 3-month Treasury bill if just issued. Thus, we shall be casual with name distinctions.

The Treasuries market is one of the most important financial markets in the world.

As of October 2004, the United States owed over \$7.4 trillion in Treasury obligations, roughly \$25,000 per citizen. After Treasuries are sold by the government, they are then actively traded in what is one of the most important financial markets in the world today. It would not be uncommon for a dedicated bond trader to buy \$100 million of a Treasury note originally issued 10 years ago that has 5 years remaining, and 10 seconds later sell \$120 million of a 3-year Treasury note issued 6 years ago. Large buyers and sellers of Treasuries are easily found, and transaction costs are very low. Trading volume is huge: In 2004, it was about \$500 billion per trading day. Therefore, the annual trading volume in U.S. Treasuries—about $255 \cdot \$500$ billion $\approx \$130$ trillion—totaled over 10 times the U.S. economy's gross domestic product (GDP) of \$11 trillion. By 2006, trading volume had increased to \$530 billion per trading day.

The yield curve shows the annualized interest rate as a function of bond maturity.

It turns out that at any given moment in time, the interest rates on Treasuries usually differ, depending on what their maturity terms are. Fortunately, you already know how to handle time-varying rates of return, so we can now put your knowledge to the test. The principal tool for working with Treasury bonds is the **yield curve** (or **term structure of interest rates**). It is a graphical representation, where the time to maturity is on the x-axis and the annualized interest rates are on the y-axis. There are also yield curves on non-Treasury bonds, but the Treasury yield curve is so prominent that unless clarified further, the yield curve should be assumed to mean investments in U.S. Treasuries. The more precise name would be the **U.S. Treasuries yield curve**. This yield curve is so important that most other debt in the market, like mortgage rates or bank lending rates, are "benchmarked" relative to the Treasury yield curve. For example, if your firm wants to issue a 5-year bond, your creditors will want to compare your interest rate to that offered by equivalent Treasuries, and often will even describe your bond as offering "x basis points above the equivalent Treasury."

SOLVE NOW!

Q 5.16 What are the three types of Treasuries? How do they differ?

5.3A YIELD CURVE SHAPES

Yield curves are often but not always upward sloping.

Figure 5.1 shows some historical yield curves. They are commonly classified into four basic shapes:

1. Flat: There is little or no difference between annualized short-term and long-term rates. A flat yield curve is basically the scenario that was the subject of the previous chapter. It means you can simplify $(1 + r_{0,t}) \approx (1 + r)^t$.

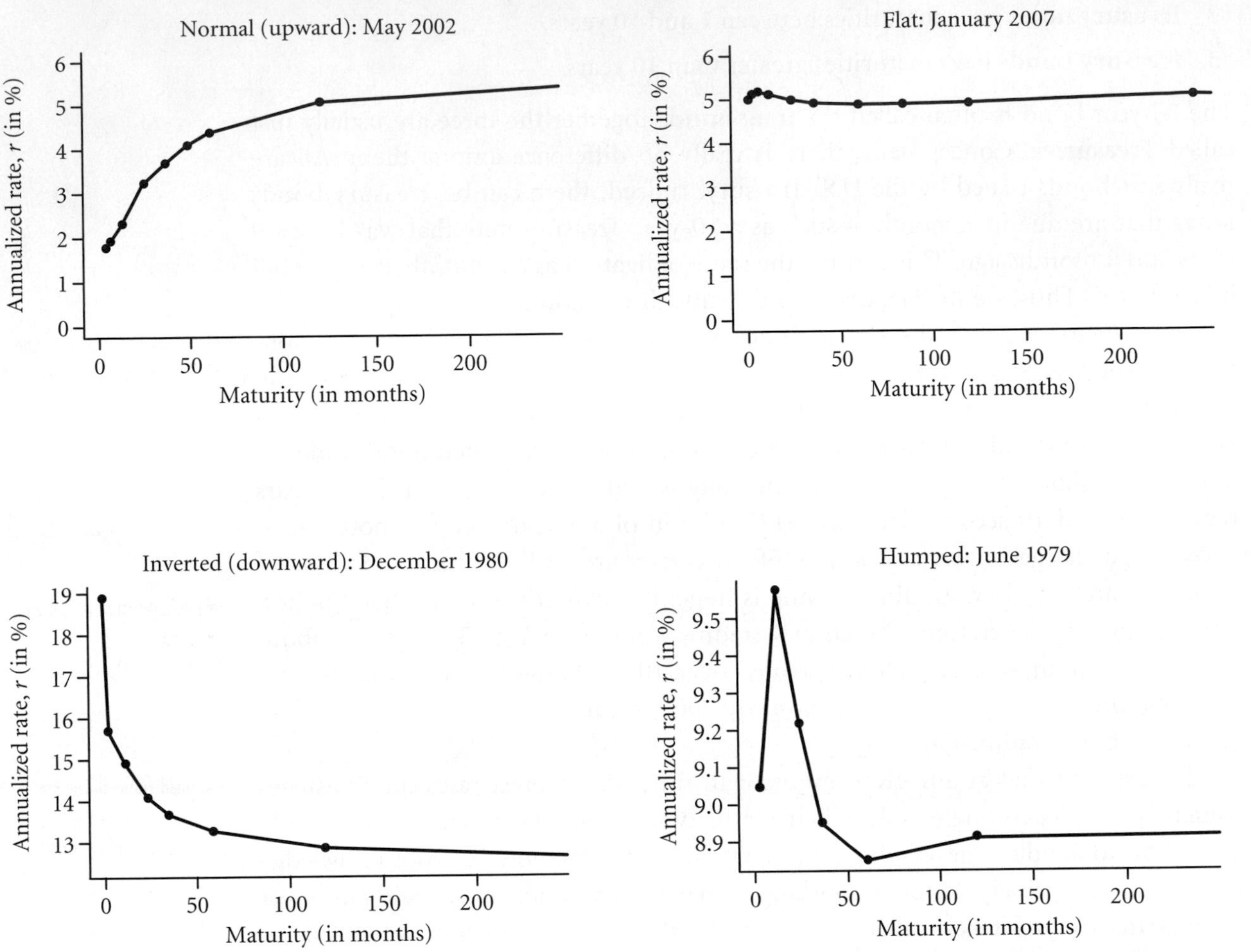

FIGURE 5.1 History: Some Yield Curves

2. Upward sloping ("normal"): Short-term rates are lower than long-term rates. This is the most common shape. It means that longer-term interest rates are higher than shorter-term interest rates. Since 1934, the steepest yield curve (the biggest difference between the long-term and the short-term Treasury rates) occurred in October 1992, when the long-term interest rate was 7.3% and the short-term interest rate was 2.9%—just as the economy pulled out of the recession of 1991.
3. Downward sloping ("inverted"): Short-term rates are higher than long-term rates.
4. Humped: Short-term rates and long-term rates are lower than medium-term rates.

Inverted and humped yield curves are relatively rare.

Common data sources for interest rates.

If you want to undertake your own research, you can find historical interest rates at the St. Louis Federal Reserve Bank at http://research.stlouisfed.org/fred. There are also the Treasury Management Pages at http://www.tmpages.com/. Or you can look at SmartMoney.com for historical yield curves. PiperJaffray.com has the current yield curve—as do many other financial sites and newspapers. Finance.yahoo.com/bonds

ANECDOTE Macroeconomic Implications of Different Yield Curve Shapes

Economists and pundits have long wondered what they can learn from the shape of the yield curve about the future of the economy. It appears that the yield curve shape is a useful—though unreliable and noisy—signal of where the economy is heading. Steep yield curves often signal emergence from a recession. Inverted yield curves often signal an impending recession. But can't the Federal Reserve Bank control the yield curve and thereby control the economy? It is true that the Fed can influence the yield curve. But ultimately the Fed does not control it—instead, it is the broader demand and supply for savings and credit in the economy. Economic research has shown that the Federal Reserve Bank has a good deal of influence on the short end of the Treasury curve—by expanding and contracting the supply of money and short-term loans in the economy—but not much influence on the long end of the Treasury curve.

provides not only the Treasury yield curve but also yield curves for many other types of bonds.

5.3B AN EXAMPLE: THE YIELD CURVE ON DECEMBER 31, 2004

Let's focus on working with one particular yield curve. Figure 5.2 shows the Treasury yields on December 31, 2004. This yield curve had the most common shape—it was an upward-sloping function. The curve tells you that if you had purchased a 3-month Treasury at the end of the day on December 31, 2004, your annualized interest rate would have been 1.63% per annum. (A \$100 investment would turn into $\$100 \cdot (1 + 1.63\%)^{1/4} \approx \$100 \cdot 1.0041 = \$100.41$ on March 31, 2004.) If you had purchased a 20-year bond, your annualized interest rate would have been 4.85% per annum.

We will analyze the Treasury yield curve at the end of December 2004.

DIGGING DEEPER

There are some small inaccuracies in my description of yield curve computations. My main simplification is that U.S. yield curves are based on semiannually-compounded coupon bonds in real life, whereas the text pretends that the yield is an annualized return. In corporate finance, the yield difference between annual compounding and semi-annual compounding is almost always inconsequential. However, realize that if you want to become a fixed-income trader, you should not take my description literally. Consult a dedicated fixed-income text instead.

Sometimes it is necessary to determine an interest rate for a bond that is not listed. This is usually done by interpolation. For example, if you had wanted to find the yield for a 9-month bond, a good guess would have been an interest rate halfway between the 6-month bond and the 12-month bond. In December 2004, this would have been an annualized yield of $(2.05\% + 2.23\%)/2 \approx 2.14\%$.

You can interpolate annualized interest rates on the yield curve.

As notation for the annualized horizon-dependent interest rates, we continue using our earlier method. We call the 2-year annualized interest rate $r_{\overline{2}}$ (here, 2.58%), the 3-year annualized interest rate $r_{\overline{3}}$ (here, 2.85%), and so on. It is always these overlined-subscript yields that are graphed in yield curves. Let's work with this particular yield curve, assuming it is based exclusively on zero-bonds, so you don't have to worry about interim payments.

The December 2004 yield curve was upward sloping: Annualized interest rates were higher for longer maturities.

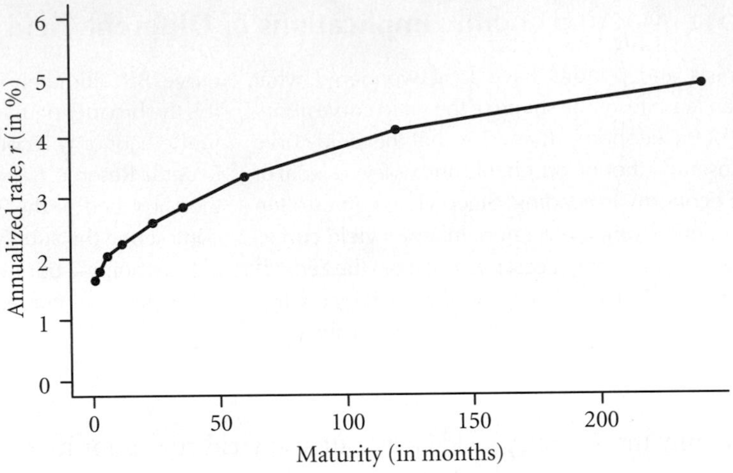

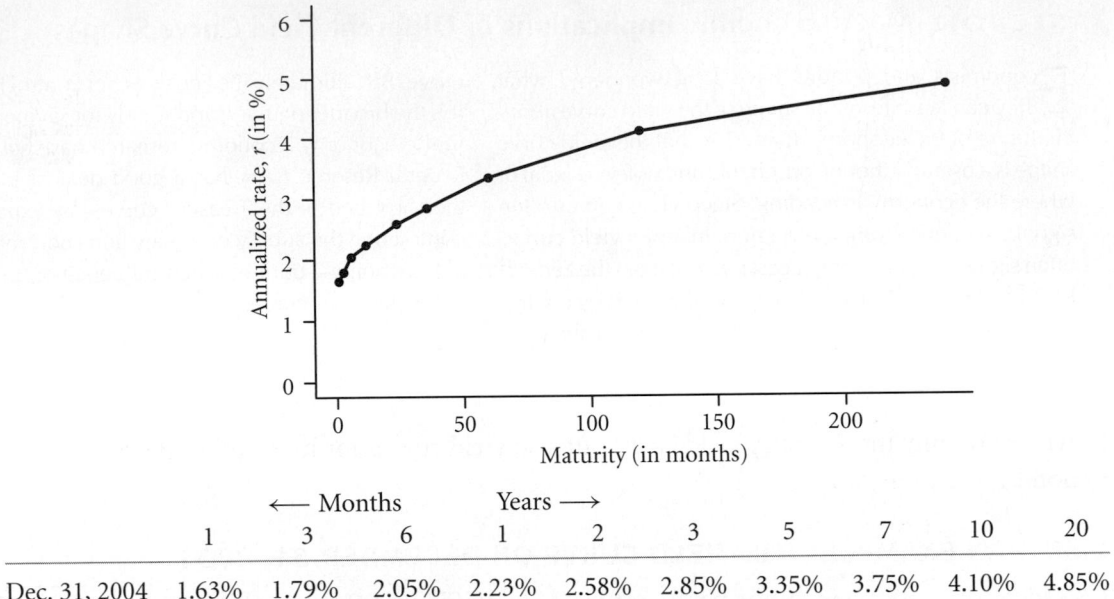

	← Months			Years →						
	1	3	6	1	2	3	5	7	10	20
Dec. 31, 2004	1.63%	1.79%	2.05%	2.23%	2.58%	2.85%	3.35%	3.75%	4.10%	4.85%

These rates are calculated from Treasury prices and are their annualized yields-to-maturity (internal rates of return). When using Treasury zero-bonds, they are just the standard discount rates computed from the final payment and today's price. Similar data can be found on the U.S. Treasury website at www.ustreas.gov or in the *Wall Street Journal*. The yield curve changes every day—although day-to-day changes are usually small. We shall work only with the December 2004 yield curve. (Note: In 2004, the U.S. Treasury did not issue 30-year bonds.)
Source: Federal Reserve, http://www.federalreserve.gov/releases/h15/data.htm

FIGURE 5.2 The Treasury Yield Curve on December 31, 2004

Computing the holding rate of return for 2-year Treasuries.

Holding rates of return First, let's figure out how much money you will have at maturity. That is, how much money did an investment of \$500,000 into U.S. 2-year notes (i.e., a loan to the U.S. government of \$500,000) on December 31, 2004, return on December 31, 2006? Use the data in Figure 5.2. Because the yield curve prints annualized rates of return, the total 2-year holding rate of return (as in Formula 5.1) is the twice compounded annualized rate of return,

➤ Formula 5.1, p. 93

$$r_{0,2} = 1.0258 \cdot 1.0258 - 1 \approx 5.23\%$$

$$r_{0,2} = (1 + r_{\overline{2}}) \cdot (1 + r_{\overline{2}}) - 1$$

so your \$500,000 will turn into

$$C_2 \approx (1 + 5.23\%) \cdot \$500{,}000 \approx \$526{,}150$$

$$C_2 = (1 + r_{0,2}) \cdot C_0$$

on December 31, 2006. (In the real world, you might have to pay a commission to arrange this transaction, so you would end up with a little less.) What if you had invested \$500,000 into 20-year Treasuries? Your 20-year holding rate of return would have been

Computing the holding rate of return for 20-year bonds.

$$r_{0,20} = 1.0485^{20} - 1 \approx 2.5785 - 1 \approx 157.85\%$$

$$r_{0,20} = (1 + r_{\overline{20}})^{20} - 1$$

Thus, an investment of $C_0 = \$500{,}000$ in December 2004 will turn into cash of $C_{20} \approx \$1.29$ million in December 2024.

Forward rates of return Second, let's figure out what the yield curve in December 31, 2004, implied about the 1-year interest rate from December 31, *2005*, to December 31, 2006. This would be best named $r_{1,2}$. It is an interest rate that begins in 1 year and ends in 2 years. This is called a **forward rate.**

Let's work out one forward rate implied by the December 2005 yield curve.

Our yield curve tells you that the 1-year annualized interest rate is $r_{\bar{1}} = 2.23\%$, and that the 2-year annualized rate of return is $r_{\bar{2}} = 2.58\%$. You already know that you can work out the two holding rates of return, $r_{0,1} = 2.23\%$ and $r_{0,2} = (1 + r_{\bar{2}})^2 - 1 \approx 5.23\%$. You only need to use the compounding formula to determine $r_{1,2}$:

$$(1 + 5.23\%) = (1 + 2.23\%) \cdot (1 + r_{1,2}) \Rightarrow r_{1,2} \approx 2.93\%$$

$$(1 + r_{0,2}) \quad = \quad (1 + r_{0,1}) \quad \cdot (1 + r_{1,2})$$

This is higher than both $r_{\bar{1}}$ and $r_{\bar{2}}$ from which you computed $r_{1,2}$.

Table 5.1 summarizes our 2-year calculations, and extends them by another year. (This allows you to check your results in an exercise below.) One question that you should ask yourself is whether I use so many subscripts in the notation just because I enjoy torturing you. The answer is an emphatic no: The subscripts are there for good reason. When you look at Table 5.1, for example, you have to distinguish between the following:

Is the proliferation of subscripts torture or necessity?

➤ Step-by-step computation of forward interest rates, Section 5.6, p. 121

- the three holding rates of return, $r_{0,t}$ (2.23%, 5.23%, and 8.80%)
- the three annualized rates of return, $r_{\bar{t}}$ (2.23%, 2.58%, and 2.85%)
- the three individual annual rates of return $r_{t-1,t}$ (2.23%, 2.93%, and 3.39%), where the second and third begin at different points in the future.

In real life, you have not just 3 yearly Treasuries, but many Treasuries between 1 day and 30 years. Anyone dealing with Treasuries (or CDs or any other fixed-income investment) that can have different maturities or that can start in the future must be prepared to deal with double subscripts.

TABLE 5.1 RELATION BETWEEN HOLDING RETURNS, ANNUALIZED RETURNS, AND YEAR-BY-YEAR RETURNS ON DECEMBER 31, 2004, BY FORMULA

	Rates of Return		
Maturity	Total Holding	Annualized	Compounded Rates
1 Year	$(1 + 2.23\%)$	$= (1 + 2.23\%)^1$	$= (1 + 2.23\%)$
	$(1 + r_{0,1})$	$= (1 + r_{\bar{1}})^1$	$= (1 + r_{0,1})$
2 Years	$(1 + 5.23\%)$	$\approx (1 + 2.58\%)^2$	$\approx (1 + 2.23\%) \cdot (1 + 2.93\%)$
	$(1 + r_{0,2})$	$= (1 + r_{\bar{2}})^2$	$= (1 + r_{0,1}) \cdot (1 + r_{1,2})$
3 Years	$(1 + 8.80\%)$	$\approx (1 + 2.85\%)^3$	$\approx (1 + 2.23\%) \cdot (1 + 2.93\%) \cdot (1 + 3.39\%)$
	$(1 + r_{0,3})$	$= (1 + r_{\bar{3}})^3$	$= (1 + r_{0,1}) \cdot (1 + r_{1,2}) \cdot (1 + r_{2,3})$

The individually compounded rates are the future interest rates. They are implied by the annualized rates quoted in the middle column. The text worked out the 2-year case. You will work out the 3-year case in Question 5.17. This computation will be repeated more slowly in Section 5.6.

Yes, corporate projects have double subscripts, too!

If Treasuries offer different annualized rates of return over different horizons, do corporate projects have to do so, too? Almost surely yes. If nothing else, they compete with Treasury bonds for investors' money. And just like Treasury bonds, many corporate projects do not begin immediately, but may take a year or more to prepare. Such project rates of return are essentially forward rates of return. Double subscripts—sometimes there is no way out in the real world!

SOLVE NOW!

Q 5.17 Compute the 3-year holding rate of return on December 31, 2004. Then, using the 2-year holding rate of return on December 31, 2004, of 5.23% and your calculated 3-year holding rate of return, compute the forward interest rate for a 1-year investment beginning on December 31, *2006*, and ending on December 31, 2007. Are these the numbers in Table 5.1?

Q 5.18 Repeat the calculation with the 5-year annualized rate of return of 3.35%. That is, what is the 5-year holding rate of return, and how can you compute the forward interest rate for a 2-year investment beginning on December 31, *2007*, and ending on December 31, 2009?

5.3C BOND PAYOFFS AND YOUR INVESTMENT HORIZON

Your investment horizon has no link to the time patterns of bond payoffs you invest in. You can always sell long-term bonds to get money quickly, if need be.

Should there be a link between your personal investment horizon and the kinds of bonds you may be holding? Let's say that you want to purchase a 3-year zero-coupon bond because it offers 2.85%, which is more than the 2.23% that a 1-year zero-coupon bond offers—but you also want to consume in 1 year. Can you still buy the longer-term bond? There is good news and bad news. The good news is that the answer is yes: There is no link whatsoever between your desire to get your money back and the point in time when the 3-year bond pays off. You can always buy a 3-year bond today, and sell it next year when it will have become a 2-year bond. The bad news is that in our perfect and certain market, this investment strategy will still only get you the 2.23% that the 1-year bond offers. If you purchase \$100 of the 3-year bond for $P = \$100/1.0285^3 \approx \$91.92$ today, next year it will be a 2-year bond with an interest rate of 2.93% in the first year and 3.39% in the second year (both worked out in Table 5.1). You can sell this bond next year for

$$P = \frac{\$100}{1 + r_{1,3}} = \frac{\$100}{(1 + r_{1,2}) \cdot (1 + r_{2,3})} = \frac{\$100}{1.0293 \cdot 1.0339} \approx \$93.97$$

Your 1-year holding rate of return would therefore be only (\$93.97 − \$91.92)/\$91.92 ≈ 2.23%—the same rate of return you would have received if you had purchased a 1-year bond.

5.3D THE EFFECT OF INTEREST RATE CHANGES ON SHORT-TERM AND LONG-TERM BONDS

Treasuries pay what they promise. They have no default risk. They do have the risk of interim interest rate changes.

Are 20-year bonds riskier than 1-year bonds? Of course, recall that repayment is no less certain with 20-year Treasury bonds than 1-year Treasury notes. (This would be an issue of concern if you were to evaluate corporate projects that can go bankrupt.

Long-term corporate bonds are often riskier than short-term corporate bonds—most firms are unlikely to go bankrupt this week, but more likely to go bankrupt over a multidecade time horizon.) So, for Treasury bonds, there is no uncertainty as far as payment uncertainty is concerned. But there may still be some interim risk, and even though we have not yet fully covered it, you can still intuitively figure out why this is so. Ask yourself how economy-wide bond prices (interest rates) can change in the interim (before maturity). What are the effects of sudden interest rate changes before maturity on bond values? It turns out that an equal-sized interest rate movement can be much more dramatic for long-term bonds than for short-term bonds. Let me try to illustrate why.

First, the effect of a 10bp change on the price of a 20-year bond.

The 20-year bond: Work out the value of a \$1,000 20-year zero-bond at the 4.85% interest rate prevailing in December 2004. It costs $\$1{,}000/1.0485^{20} \approx \$387.82$. You already know that when prevailing interest rates go up, the prices of outstanding bonds drop and you will lose money. For example, if interest rates increase by 10 basis points to 4.95%, the bond value decreases to $\$1{,}000/1.0495^{20} \approx \$380.50$. If interest rates decrease by 10 basis points to 4.75%, the bond value increases to $\$1{,}000/1.0475^{20} \approx \$395.29$. Thus, the effect of a 10-basis-point change in the prevailing 20-year yield induces an immediate percent change (an instant rate of return) in the value V of your bond of

$$\text{Up 10bp:} \quad r = \frac{V(r_{\overline{20}} = 4.95\%) - V(r_{\overline{20}} = 4.85\%)}{V(r_{\overline{20}} = 4.85\%)} = \frac{\$380.50 - \$387.82}{\$387.82} \approx -1.89\%$$

$$\text{Down 10bp:} \quad r = \frac{V(r_{\overline{20}} = 4.75\%) - V(r_{\overline{20}} = 4.85\%)}{V(r_{\overline{20}} = 4.85\%)} = \frac{\$395.29 - \$387.82}{\$387.82} \approx +1.93\%$$

So for every \$1 million you invest in 20-year bonds, you expose yourself to about \$19,000 in instant risk for every 10-basis-point yield change in the economy.

Second, the effect of a 10bp point change on the price of a 1-year note.

The 1-year Note: To keep the example identical, let's now assume that the 1-year note also has an interest rate of 4.85% and consider the same 10-basis-point change in the prevailing interest rate. In this case, the equivalent computations for the value of a 1-year note are \$954.65 at 4.75%, \$953.74 at 4.85%, and \$952.83 at 4.95%. Therefore, the equivalent instant rates of return are

$$\text{Up 10bp:} \quad r = \frac{V(r_{\overline{1}} = 4.95\%) - V(r_{\overline{1}} = 4.85\%)}{V(r_{\overline{1}} = 4.85\%)} = \frac{\$952.83 - \$953.74}{\$953.74} \approx -0.095\%$$

$$\text{Down 10bp:} \quad r = \frac{V(r_{\overline{1}} = 4.75\%) - V(r_{\overline{20}} = 4.85\%)}{V(r_{\overline{1}} = 4.85\%)} = \frac{\$954.65 - \$953.74}{\$953.74} \approx +0.095\%$$

For every $1 million you invest in 1-year notes, you expose yourself to a $950 risk for a 10-basis-point yield change in the economy.

An equal interest rate move affects longer-term bonds more strongly.

It follows that the value effect of an equal-sized change in prevailing interest rates is more severe for longer-term bonds. In turn, it follows that if the bond is due tomorrow, there is very little havoc that an interest rate change can wreak. You will be able to reinvest tomorrow at whatever the new rate will be. A long-term bond, on the other hand, may lose (or gain) a lot of value.

Again, in the interim, T-bonds are *not* risk-free!

In sum, you should always remember that Treasury bonds are risk-free in the sense that they cannot default (fail to return the promised payments), but they are risky in the sense that interim interest changes can change their values. Only the most short-term Treasury bills (say, due overnight) can truly be considered risk-free—virtually everything else is risky.

IMPORTANT: Though "fixed income," even Treasuries do not guarantee a "fixed rate of return" over horizons shorter than their maturities. Day to day, long-term Treasury bonds are generally riskier investments than short-term Treasury bills.

For the sake of illustration, I have not told you about two issues. The important one is that long-term rates are not as volatile as short-term rates. Nevertheless, in the real world, longer-term Treasuries are riskier.

Confession time: I have pulled two tricks on you. First, in the real world, it could be that short-term, economy-wide interest rates typically experience yield shifts of plus or minus 100 basis points, while long-term, economy-wide interest rates rarely budge. If this were true, long-term bonds could even be safer. The empirical evidence suggests that even though the volatility of prevailing interest rates in 20-year bonds is smaller than that of 1-year notes, it is not *that much* smaller. As a consequence, the typical annual variability in the rate of return of an investment in 20-year Treasury bonds was higher historically (around 10%) than the typical variability in the rate of return of an investment in 1-year Treasury notes (around 5%). Long-term Treasury securities are indeed riskier. Second, when I quoted you value losses of $950 (for the 1-year note) and $19,000 (for the 20-year bond), I ignored that between today and tomorrow, you would also earn 1 day's interest. On a $1,000,000 investment, this would be about $130. If you had invested the money in 1-year Treasury notes at 2.23% instead of in 20-year bonds at 4.85%, you would have only received about $60. Strictly speaking, this favors the long-term bond and thus $70 should be added to the long-term bond investment strategy—but $70 on $1 million is only about 1 basis point, and so for a quick-and-dirty calculation such as ours, ignoring it was reasonable.

SOLVE NOW!

Q 5.19 A 10-year and a 1-year zero-bond both offer an interest rate of 8% per annum.

(a) How does an increase of 1 basis point in the prevailing interest rate change the value of the 1-year bond? (Use 5 decimals in your calculation.)

(b) How does an increase of 1 basis point in the prevailing interest rate change the value of the 10-year bond?

(c) What is the ratio of the value change over the interest change? In calculus, this would be called the derivative of the value with respect to interest rate changes. Which derivative is larger?

How Bad Are Mistakes?

PAPER LOSSES

If you really need cash from a bond investment in 20 years, doesn't a prevailing interest rate increase cause only an interim **paper loss**? This is a cardinal logical error many investors commit. Say that a 10-basis-point increase happened overnight, and you had invested $1 million yesterday. You would have lost $19,000 of your net worth in 1 day! Put differently, waiting 1 day would have saved you $19,000 or allowed you to buy the same item for $19,000 less. Paper money is actual wealth. Thinking paper losses are any different from actual losses is a common but capital error. (The only exception to this rule is that realized gains and losses have different tax implications than unrealized gains and losses.)

"Only" a paper loss: A cardinal error!

➤ Tax treatment of realized and unrealized capital gains, Section 10.4, p. 321

IMPORTANT: "Paper losses" are actual losses.

5.4 WHY IS THE (NOMINAL) YIELD CURVE USUALLY UPWARD SLOPING?

Aren't you already wondering *why* the yield curve is not usually flat? Take our sample yield curve from December 2004. Why did the 20-year Treasury bonds in December 2004 pay 4.85% per year, while the 3-month Treasury bills paid only 1.63% per year? And why is an upward slope the most common shape?

But why? why? why?

Let's work with a simpler 2-year example. Let's say that the yield curve tells you that the 1-year rate is $r_{\bar{1}} = 5\%$ and the 2-year rate is $r_{\bar{2}} = 10\%$. You can work out that this means that the 1-year forward rate is $r_{1,2} \approx 15.24\%$. There are really only two possible explanations:

The two possible explanations are (1) higher future interest rates and/or (2) compensation for risk.

1. The 1-year interest rate next year will be higher than the 5% that it is today. Indeed, maybe next year's 1-year interest rate will be the 15.24% that it would be in a perfect world with perfect certainty.

2. Investors tend to earn higher rates of return holding long-term bonds than they do holding short-term bonds. For example, if the yield curve were to remain at exactly the same shape next year, then a $100 investment in consecutive 1-year bonds would give you interest of only about $10.25, while the same investment in 2-year bonds would give you (on average) $21.

In other words, the question is whether higher long-term interest rates today predict higher interest rates in the future, or whether they offer extra compensation for investors willing to hold longer-term bonds. Let's consider two possible variants of each of these two possibilities.

5.4A DOES IT PREDICT HIGHER FUTURE INFLATION?

If inflation is high, investors (typically) demand higher interest rates.

In general, when inflation is higher, you would expect investors to demand higher nominal interest rates. Consequently, you would expect nominal rates to go up when inflation rate expectations are going up. Similarly, you would expect nominal rates to go down when inflation rate expectations are going down. Of course, demand and supply do not mean that real rates of return need to be positive—indeed, the real rate of return is often negative, but the alternative of storing money under the mattress is even worse.

Are higher future inflation rates the cause of higher future interest rates?

Therefore, our first potential explanation for an upward-sloping yield curve is that investors believe that cash will be worth progressively less in the more distant future. That is, even though you will be able to earn higher interest rates over the long run, you may also believe that the inflation rate will increase from today's rate. Because inflation erodes the value of higher interest rates, interest rates should then be higher in the future just to compensate you for the lesser value of money in the future. Of course, this argument would apply only to a yield curve computed from Treasury debt that pays off in nominal terms. It should not apply to any bond payoffs that are inflation indexed.

TIPS are inflation-indexed Treasury bonds. They are not affected by inflation.

Fortunately, since 1997 the Treasury has been selling bonds that are inflation indexed. These bond contracts are written so that they pay out the promised interest rate plus the CPI inflation rate. They are called Treasury Inflation Protected Securities (**TIPS**, or sometimes just **CPI bonds**). By definition, they should not be affected by inflation in a perfect market. If the nominal yield curve is upward sloping because of higher future inflation rates, then a TIPS-based real yield curve should not be upward sloping.

You can compute an inflation-adjusted yield curve and compare it to the nominal yield curve—in December 2004, future inflation expectations were not the main driver of the upward-sloping yield curve.

In December 2004, the Treasury had issued four kinds of TIPS. Their interest rates (to which the CPI would be added) and the corresponding standard Treasury interest rates were

Maturity	5-year	7-year	10-year	20-year
TIPS Interest Rate	0.97%	1.35%	1.73%	2.13%
Ordinary Treasury Bonds	3.35%	3.75%	4.10%	4.85%

Obviously, the TIPS yield curve is also upward sloping. This suggests that higher future expected inflation rates are not the sole reason for the upward-sloping yield

ANECDOTE Inflation-Neutral Bonds

As it turns out, inflation-adjusted bonds had already been invented once before! The world's first known inflation-indexed bonds were issued by the Commonwealth of Massachusetts in 1780 during the Revolutionary War. These bonds were invented to deal with severe wartime inflation and discontent among soldiers in the U.S. Army with the decline in purchasing power of their pay. Although the bonds were successful, the concept of indexed bonds was abandoned after the immediate extreme inflationary environment passed, and largely forgotten. In 1780, the bonds were viewed as at best only an irregular expedient, since there was no formulated economic theory to justify indexation.

Source: Robert Shiller, "The Invention of Inflation-Indexed Bonds in Early America," October 2003.

curve. If you work out the implied inflation rates from these real and nominal interest rates using Formula 5.2, you find

➤ Formula 5.2, p. 100

Maturity	5-year	7-year	10-year	20-year
Implied Inflation Rate	2.36%	2.37%	2.33%	2.66%

So, standing in December 2004, about a 3 basispoint slope could be attributed to higher inflation expectations from 2014 to 2024, but that was about it. Most of the 150-basis-point difference between the 5-year and 20-year Treasury bond must have been due to something else. Of course, this was the case in December 2004—there is no guarantee that higher inflationary expectations won't play a bigger role in the future. Check back regularly.

SOLVE NOW!

Q 5.20 On May 31, 2002, the *Wall Street Journal* reported on page C10 that a 30-year inflation-adjusted bond offered a real yield of about 3.375% per year. The current inflation rate was only 1.6% per year, and a normal 30-year Treasury bond (not inflation adjusted) offered a nominal yield of 5.600% per year. In what scenario would you be better off buying one or the other?

5.4B DOES IT PREDICT HIGHER FUTURE INTEREST RATES?

Does a high forward interest rate predict a high future interest rate?

A closely related possibility is that the yield curve is typically upward sloping because short-term interest rates will be higher in the future. This is more generic than the previous explanation—higher future interest rates need not be caused by higher future inflation expectations. Maybe the 20-year yield of 4.85% was much higher than the 1-year yield of 2.23% because investors expected the 1-year interest rate in 2024 to be above 5% (the forward rate, $r_{20,21}$). This does not tell you *why* investors would expect interest rates to be so much higher in 2024 than in 2004—maybe capital will be more scarce then and investment opportunities will be better—but the precise reason is not important.

Alas, the historical data tells us "probably not much."

Unfortunately, we do not have a direct estimate of future interest rates the way we had a direct estimate of future inflation rates (from TIPS). Therefore, investigating this hypothesis requires looking at many years of evidence to learn whether future interest rates were well predicted by prevailing forward rates. The details are beyond our scope. However, I can tell you the punchline: Expectations of higher future rates of return ain't the reason why the yield curve is typically upward sloping (except maybe at the very short end of the yield curve, say, for interest rates that are for cash investments for less than 1 month).

5.4C DOES IT MEAN BARGAINS ON THE LONG END?

It must be either higher future interest rates or higher compensation for long-term bond investors.

If it is not the case that future interest rates are higher when forward rates are higher, it means that we are dealing with the second possible reason: On average, it must have been the case that investors earned more investing in long-term bonds than they did investing in short-term bonds that they would have had to keep rolling over. You would have ended up with more money if you had purchased 20-year bonds than if you had purchased 1-month bonds every month for 20 years. The empirical data confirms this.

Free money? Not in a perfect market.

But why were long-term bonds better investments than short-term bonds? Maybe the yield curve was upward sloping because investors were stupid. In this case, you might conclude that the 20-year bond offering 4.85% was a much better deal than the 1-year bond offering 2.23%. Alas, investor stupidity seems highly unlikely as a good explanation. The market for Treasury bond investments is close to perfect in the sense that we have used the definition. It is very competitive. If there was a great deal to be had, thousands of traders would have immediately jumped on it. More likely, the interest rate differential does not overthrow the old tried-and-true axiom, *You get what you pay for*. It is just a fact of life that investments for which the interest payments are tied down for 20 years must offer higher interest rates now in order to entice investors—for some good reason yet to be identified. It is important that you recognize that your cash itself is *not* tied down if you invest in a 20-year bond, because you can, of course, sell your 20-year bond tomorrow to another investor if you so desire.

5.4D DOES IT COMPENSATE INVESTORS FOR RISK?

The answer is probably compensation for risk.

➤ Section 5.3D, "The Effect of Interest Rate Changes on Short-Term and Long-Term Bonds," p. 108

If it isn't market stupidity that allows you to earn more money in long-term bonds than in rolled-over short-term bonds, then what else could it be? The empirical evidence suggests that it is most likely the phenomenon explained in Section 5.3D: Interim changes in prevailing interest rates have much more impact on long-term bonds than they have on short-term bonds. Recall that rolling over short-term bonds insulates you from the risk that interest rates will change in the future. If you hold a 1-day bond and interest rates double by tomorrow, you can just purchase more bonds tomorrow that will offer you twice the interest rate. In contrast, if you hold a long-term bond, you could lose your shirt. With long-term bonds being riskier than short-term bonds, investors only seem to want to buy them if they get some extra rate of return. Thus, long-term bonds need to offer investors more return on average.

5.5 CORPORATE INSIGHTS ABOUT TIME-VARYING COSTS OF CAPITAL FROM THE YIELD CURVE

Now that you understand that the yield curve is usually upward sloping for a good reason, you should recognize the family resemblance: Corporate projects are offering cash flows, just like Treasury bonds. Thus, it should not surprise you that longer-term projects often have to offer higher rates of return than shorter-term projects. And just because a longer-term project offers a higher expected rate of return does not necessarily mean that it has a higher NPV. Conversely, just because shorter-term borrowing allows firms to pay a lower expected rate of return does not necessarily mean that this creates value. (The U.S. Treasury does not rely exclusively on short-term borrowing, either.) A higher expected rate of return required for longer-term payments is (usually) a fact of life.

Extend this insight to corporations: Longer-term projects, even if they are not more likely to default, often face a higher cost of capital, and therefore should have to deliver higher returns.

IMPORTANT: Even in a perfect market without uncertainty:

- The appropriate cost of capital (rate of return) should usually depend on how long term the project is.
- Short-term corporate projects usually have lower costs of capital than long-term projects.
- Conversely, corporations usually face lower costs of capital (expected rates of return offered to creditors) if they borrow short term rather than long term.

SUMMARY

This chapter covered the following major points:

- Different horizon investments can offer different rates of return. This phenomenon is often called time-varying rates of return.
- The general formula for compounding works just as well for time-varying rates of return as it does for time-constant rates of return. You only lose the ability to exponentiate (one plus the 1-year rate of return) when you want to compute multiyear rates of return.
- A holding rate of return can be annualized for easier interpretation.
- The graph of annualized interest rates as a function of maturity is called the "term structure of interest rates" or the "yield curve."
- The yield curve is usually upward sloping. However, no law of finance is violated if it is downward sloping (inverted), humped, or flat.
- Net present value also works just as well for time-varying interest rates. You merely need to use the appropriate rate of return as the opportunity cost of capital in the denominator.
- An important side observation: "Paper losses" are no different from real losses.

- Inflation is the process by which money buys fewer goods in the future than it buys today. If contracts are inflation indexed in a perfect market, inflation is irrelevant. This is rarely the case.
- The relationship between nominal interest rates, real interest rates, and inflation rates is

$$(1 + r_{\text{nominal}}) = (1 + r_{\text{real}}) \cdot (1 + \text{Inflation Rate})$$

- Unlike nominal interest rates, real interest rates can—and often have been—negative.
- In NPV, you can either discount real cash flows with real interest rates, or discount nominal cash flows with nominal interest rates. The latter is usually more convenient.
- TIPS are Treasury bonds whose payments are indexed to future inflation rates, which therefore offer protection against future inflation. Short-term bond buyers are also less exposed to inflation rate changes than long-term bond buyers.
- Higher long-term interest rates could be either due to expectations of higher future interest rates or due to extra required compensation for investors willing to hold longer-term bonds. The empirical evidence suggests that historically the latter has been the more important factor.
- Corporations should realize that corporate project cash flows need to be discounted with specific costs of capital that may depend on the time at which the cash flows come due. It is not unusual that cash flows in the more distant future should require higher discount rates.

KEY TERMS

annualized rate, 92
average rate of return, 93
BLS, 98
Bureau of Labor Statistics, 98
Consumer Price Index, 98
CPI, 98
CPI bond, 112
deflation, 98
forward rate, 92, 107
GDP Deflator, 98
hyperinflation, 98
inflation, 97
inflation-indexed terms, 97
long bond, 103
nominal return, 99
nominal terms, 97
paper loss, 111
PPI, 98
Producer Price Index, 98
real return, 99
real terms, 97
reinvestment rate, 91
spot rate, 92
T-bill, 102
term structure of interest rates, 103
TIPS, 112
Treasuries, 103
Treasury bill, 102
Treasury bond, 103
Treasury note, 103
U.S. Treasuries yield curve, 103
yield curve, 103

SOLVE NOW! SOLUTIONS

Q 5.1 $r_{0,2} = (1 + r_{0,1}) \cdot (1 + r_{1,2}) - 1 = 1.02 \cdot 1.03 - 1 = 5.06\%$

Q 5.2 Solve $(1 + x) \cdot (1 + 22\%) = (1 - 50\%)$, so the project had a rate of return of -59.00%.

Q 5.3 Compounding, the returns were $(1.2631 - 1) = 26.31\%$ for the first year, $(1.2631 \cdot 1.0446) - 1 \approx 31.94\%$ for the second year, and so on. The sequence compounds further into 41.26%, 39.08%, 86.52%, 124.31%. Thus, over the first 6 years, the rate of return was 124.31%. If you continue compounding, you get 193.87%, 273.22%, 346.11%, 300.87%, 248.60%, 167.13%. Thus, over the entire 12 years, the holding rate of return was 167.13%. Your second 6-year rate of return can be computed as $1.3101 \cdot 1.2700 \cdot 1.1953 \cdot (1 - 0.1014) \cdot (1 - 0.1304) \cdot (1 - 0.2337) \approx 19.10\%$. You could have also computed it from $(1 + r_{0,12}) = (1 + r_{0,6}) \cdot (1 + r_{6,12})$, which solves into $r_{6,12} = (1 + r_{0,12})/(1 + r_{0,6}) - 1 = (1 + 167.13\%)/(1 + 124.31\%) \approx 19.09\%$. Actually, none of these numbers are entirely correct, because the reported returns themselves also suffer from small rounding errors. In real life, the rate of return was 166.4%.

Q 5.4 The returns were (−33%, +50%, −67%, +100%), so the overall rate of return was −33.33%.

Q 5.5 $1.05^{12/4} \approx 15.76\%$

Q 5.6 The annualized rate of return is $\sqrt{1.4} - 1 \approx 18.32\%$. It is therefore lower than the 20% average rate of return.

Q 5.7 The compounded rate of return is always higher than the sum, because you earn interest on interest. The annualized rate of return is lower than the average rate of return, again because you earn interest on the interest. For example, an investment of \$100 that turns into an investment of \$200 in 2 years has a total holding rate of return of 100%—which is an average rate of return of $100\%/2 = 50\%$ and an annualized rate of return of $\sqrt{(1 + 100\%)} - 1 \approx 41.42\%$. Investing \$100 at 41% per annum would yield \$200, which is higher than 50% per annum.

Q 5.8 $r_{\overline{12}} = \sqrt[12]{1 + 167.1\%} - 1 \approx 8.53\%$

Q 5.9 $r_{0,5} = 50\% \qquad (1 + r_{\overline{5}})^5 = 1.50 \qquad \Longrightarrow \qquad r_{\overline{5}} = 1.50^{1/5} - 1 \approx 8.45\%.$

Q 5.10 The annualized 5-year rate of return is the same 10%.

Q 5.11 This project is worth

$$-\$200 + \frac{\$100}{1.03} + \frac{\$300}{1.04^2} + \frac{\$500}{1.045^3} \approx \$612.60$$

Q 5.12 The CPI is the average price change to the consumer for a specific basket of goods. The PPI measures the price that producers are paying. Taxes, distribution costs, government subsidies, and basket composition drive a wedge between these two inflation measures.

Q 5.13 $(1 + r_{\text{nominal}}) = (1 + r_{\text{real}}) \cdot (1 + \pi)$

Q 5.14 $1.20/1.05 \approx 1.1429$. The real interest rate is 14.29%.

Q 5.15 The nominal interest rate is $1.03 \cdot 1.08 - 1 = 11.24\%$. Therefore, the cash flow is worth about $\$500{,}000/1.1124 \approx \$449{,}479$.

Q 5.16 Bills, notes, and bonds. T-bills have maturities of less than 1 year. T-notes have maturities from 1 to 10 years. T-bonds have maturities greater than 10 years.

Q 5.17 Yes. The answers are right in the table. The 3-year rate of return is $1.0285^3 - 1 \approx 8.80\%$. The forward rate is $1.088/1.0523 \approx 3.39\%$.

Q 5.18 $r_{0,5} = 1.0335^5 - 1 \approx 17.91\%$. Therefore, $1 + r_{3,5} = 1.0335^5/1.0285^3 - 1 \approx 8.38\%$, which is $\sqrt{1.0838} - 1 \approx 4.10\%$ in annualized terms.

Q 5.19
(a) For the 1-year bond, the value of a \$100 bond changes from $\$100/1.0800 \approx \$92.59259$ to $\$100/1.0801 \approx \$92.58402$. This is about a –0.009% change.
(b) For the 10-year bond, the value of a \$100 bond changes from $\$100/1.08^{10} \approx \$46.31935$ to $\$100/1.0801^{10} \approx \$46.27648$. This is a –0.09% change—ten times that of the 1-year bond.

(c) The derivative of the 1-year bond is $-0.009/0.01 \approx -1$. The derivative of the 10-year bond is $-0.09/0.01 \approx -9$. The derivative of the 10-year bond is nine times more negative.

Q 5.20 If inflation were to remain at 1.6% per year, the plain Treasury bond would offer a higher real rate of return because $1.056/1.016 - 1 \approx 3.9\%$ per year. But if inflation were to rise in the future, the inflation-adjusted TIPS bond could end up offering the higher rate of return.

PROBLEMS

The ▮ *indicates problems available in* myfinancelab

Q 5.21 Are you better off if a project first returns −10% followed by +30%, or if it first returns +30% followed by −10%?

Q 5.22 Compare two stocks. Both have earned on average 8% per year. However, stock A has oscillated between 6% and 10%. Stock B has oscillated between 3% and 13%. (For simplicity, say that they alternated.) If you had purchased $500 in each stock, how much would you have had 10 years later?

Q 5.23 Stock A alternates between +20% and −10% with equal probability. Stock B earns 4.5% per annum.

(a) What is the average rate of return for stock A?

(b) What is the average rate of return for stock B?

(c) How much would each dollar invested today in stock A earn in 10 years?

(d) How much would each dollar invested today in stock B earn in 10 years?

(e) What would a risk-neutral investor prefer on a one-shot basis versus on a multiyear basis?

(f) What is the main reason for what is going on here?

Q 5.24 Return to Question 5.3. What were the compounded and the annualized rates of return on the S&P 500 over the first 6 years (i.e., from 1991 to 1996 inclusive)?

Q 5.25 The following were the daily values of an investment in January 2001:

2-Jan	3-Jan	4-Jan
$1,283.27	$1,347.56	$1,333.34
5-Jan	**8-Jan**	**9-Jan**
$1,298.35	$1,295.86	$1,300.80

If returns had accumulated at the same rate over the entire 255 days of 2001, what would a $100 investment in 2001 have turned into? (Use 7 decimal places in this problem.)

Q 5.26 If the annualized 5-year rate of return is 10%, what is the total 5-year holding rate of return?

Q 5.27 If the annualized 5-year rate of return is 10%, and if the first year's rate of return is 15%, and if the returns in all other years are equal, what are they?

Q 5.28 The annual interest rate from year t to year $t+1$ is $r_{t,t+1} = 5\% + 0.3\% \cdot t$ (e.g., the rate of return from year 5 to year 6 is $5\% + 0.3\% \cdot 5 = 6.5\%$).

(a) What is the holding rate of return of a 10-year investment today?

(b) What is the annualized interest rate of this investment?

Q 5.29 A project has cash flows of +$100 (now at time 0), and −$100, +$100, and −$100 at the end of consecutive years. The interest rate is 6% per annum.

(a) What is the project's NPV?

(b) How does the value change if all cash flows will occur 1 year later?

(c) Repeat these two questions, but assume that the 1-year (annualized) interest rate is 5%, the 2-year is 6%, the 3-year is 7%, the 4-year is 8%, and so on.

Q 5.30 Using information from a current newspaper or a financial website, find out the current inflation rate.

Q 5.31 Using information from a current newspaper or a financial website, find the annualized current nominal interest rate on 30-day U.S. Treasury bills.

Q 5.32 Using the information from Questions 5.30 and 5.31, compute the annualized current real interest rate on 30-day Treasuries.

Q 5.33 If the nominal interest rate is 7% per year and the inflation rate is 2% per year, what is the exact real rate of return?

Q 5.34 The inflation rate is 1.5% per year. The real rate of return is 2.0% per year. A perpetuity project that paid $100 this year will provide income that grows by the inflation rate. Show what this project is truly worth. Do this in both nominal and real terms. (Be clear on what *never* to do.)

Q 5.35 If the annualized rate of return on insured tax-exempt municipal bonds will be 3% per annum and the inflation rate remains at 2% per annum, then what will be their real rate of return over 30 years?

Q 5.36 If the real interest rate is −1% per annum and the inflation rate is 3% per annum, then what is the present value of a $1,000,000 nominal payment next year?

Q 5.37 Inflation is 2% per year; the interest rate is 8% per year. Your perpetuity project has cash flows that grow at 1% faster than inflation forever, starting with $20 next year.

(a) What is the real interest rate, both accurate and approximate?
(b) What is the correct project PV?
(c) What would you get if you grew a perpetuity project of $20 by the real growth rate of 1%, and then discounted it at the nominal cost of capital?
(d) What would you get if you grew a perpetuity project of $20 by the nominal growth rate of 3%, and then discounted it at the real cost of capital?

Performing either of the latter two calculations is not an uncommon mistake in practice.

Q 5.38 You must value a perpetual lease. It will cost $100,000 each year *in real terms*—that is, its proceeds will not grow in real terms, but just contractually keep pace with inflation. The prevailing interest rate is 8% per year, and the inflation rate is 2% per year forever. The first cash flow of your project *next year* is $100,000 *quoted in today's real dollars*. What is the PV of the project? (Warning: Watch the timing and amount of your first payment.)

Q 5.39 If the real rate of return has been about 1% per month for long-term bonds, what would be the value of an investment that costs $100 today and returned $200 in 10 years?

Q 5.40 At your own personal bank, what is the prevailing savings account interest rate?

Q 5.41 Look up today's yield curve on a financial website. What is the 1-year rate of return on a risk-free Treasury? What is the 10-year rate of return on a risk-free Treasury? What is the 30-year rate of return on a risk-free Treasury?

Q 5.42 At today's prevailing Treasury rates, how much money would you receive from an investment of $100 in 1 year, 10 years, and 30 years? What are their annualized rates of return? What are their total holding rates of return?

Q 5.43 The 1-year forward interest rates are as follows:

Year	1	2	3	4	5	6
Interest rate	3%	4%	5%	6%	6%	6%
Year	**7**	**8**	**9**	**10**	**11**	**12**
Interest rate	7%	7%	7%	6%	5%	4%

(a) Draw the yield curve.
(b) Compute the 12 n-year compounded holding rates of return from now to year n.
(c) Compute the 12 annualized rates of return.
(d) Is there anything wrong in this example?

Q 5.44 The *annualized* interest rates are as follows:

Year	1	2	3	4	5	6
Interest rate	3%	4%	5%	6%	6%	6%
Year	**7**	**8**	**9**	**10**	**11**	**12**
Interest rate	7%	7%	7%	6%	5%	4%

(a) Draw the yield curve.
(b) Compute the 12 n-year compounded holding rates of return from now to year n.
(c) Compute the 12 1-year forward rates of return.
(d) Is there anything wrong in this example?

Q 5.45 Do long-term bonds pay more than short-term bonds because you only get money after a long time—money that you could need earlier?

Q 5.46 A 5-year, zero-coupon bond offers an interest rate of 8% per annum.

(a) How does a 1-basis-point increase in the prevailing interest rate change the value of this bond?
(b) What is the ratio of the value change over the interest change? In calculus, this would be called the derivative of the value with respect to interest rate changes.
(c) How does the derivative of wealth with respect to the interest rate vary with the length of the bond?

Q 5.47 Look at this week's interest rate on ordinary T-bonds and on TIPS. (You should be able to find this information, e.g., in the *Wall Street Journal* or through a fund on the Vanguard website.) What is the implied inflation rate at various time horizons?

Q 5.48 The yield curve is usually upward sloping. What does this mean?

(a) Investors earn a higher annualized rate of return from long-term T-bonds than short-term T-bills.
(b) Long-term T-bonds are better investments than short-term T-bills.
(c) Investors are expecting higher inflation in the future than they are today.
(d) Investors who are willing to take the risk of investing in long-term bonds on average earn a higher rate of return because they are taking more risk (that in the interim bond prices fall / interest rates rise).

Evaluate and discuss.

Q 5.49 Does the evidence suggest that long-term bonds tend to earn higher average rates of return than short-term bonds? If yes, why is this the case? If no, why is this not possible?

CHAPTER 5 APPENDIX

The Finer Points of Bonds

There are many other finer details to bonds and especially Treasury bonds. Although they are not necessary to follow the material in the remainder of this book, they are important. After all, U.S. Treasuries make up the most important homogeneous financial market in the world. Borrowing is also critically important in most corporate contexts. Any CFO who wants to finance projects by issuing corporate bonds will inevitably run into the issues discussed next.

5.6 EXTRACTING FORWARD INTEREST RATES

We will work out the forward rates step by step from the December 2004 yield curve.

➤ Forward rates in December 2004, Table 5.1, p. 107

Let's first revisit the forward rate computation from Table 5.1, but let's do it a little slower and more systematically. First, write down the generic relationships:

	Rates of Return		
Maturity	Total Holding	Annualized	Individually Compounded
1 Year	$(1 + r_{0,1})$	$= (1 + r_{\bar{1}})^1$	$= (1 + r_{0,1})$
2 Years	$(1 + r_{0,2})$	$= (1 + r_{\bar{2}})^2$	$= (1 + r_{0,1}) \cdot (1 + r_{1,2})$
3 Years	$(1 + r_{0,3})$	$= (1 + r_{\bar{3}})^3$	$= (1 + r_{0,1}) \cdot (1 + r_{1,2}) \cdot (1 + r_{2,3})$

Start by entering the rates that you can read off the yield curve, the third column. In December 2004, these interest rates were as follows:

	Rates of Return		
Maturity	Total Holding	Annualized	Individually Compounded
1 Year	$(1 + r_{0,1})$	$= (1 + 2.23\%)^1$	$= (1 + r_{0,1})$
2 Years	$(1 + r_{0,2})$	$\approx (1 + 2.58\%)^2$	$\approx (1 + r_{0,1}) \cdot (1 + r_{1,2})$
3 Years	$(1 + r_{0,3})$	$\approx (1 + 2.85\%)^3$	$\approx (1 + r_{0,1}) \cdot (1 + r_{1,2}) \cdot (1 + r_{2,3})$

This is what you always start with—the yield curve. To work out the remaining interest rates requires you to systematically (1) work out all holding rates of return; and then (2) work out individually compounded rates of return, going down the table, using the holding rates of return and the individually compounded rates of return that you just computed earlier.

The first step is to compute the holding rates of return in the second column:

	Rates of Return		
Maturity	Total Holding	Annualized	Individually Compounded
1 Year	$(1 + 2.23\%)$	$= (1 + 2.23\%)^1$	$= (1 + r_{0,1})$
2 Years	$(1 + 5.23\%)$	$\approx (1 + 2.58\%)^2$	$= (1 + r_{0,1}) \cdot (1 + r_{1,2})$
3 Years	$(1 + 8.80\%)$	$\approx (1 + 2.85\%)^3$	$= (1 + r_{0,1}) \cdot (1 + r_{1,2}) \cdot (1 + r_{2,3})$

Ultimately, you want to know what the implied future interest rates are. Work your way down. The first row is easy: You know that $r_{0,1}$ is 2.23%. You can also substitute this return into the other rows:

Maturity	Total Holding	Rates of Return Annualized	Individually Compounded
1 Year	$(1 + 2.23\%)$	$= (1 + 2.23\%)^1$	$= (1{+}2.23\%)$
2 Years	$(1 + 5.23\%)$	$\approx (1 + 2.58\%)^2$	$\approx (1{+}2.23\%) \cdot (1 + r_{1,2})$
3 Years	$(1 + 8.80\%)$	$\approx (1 + 2.85\%)^3$	$\approx (1{+}2.23\%) \cdot (1 + r_{1,2}) \cdot (1 + r_{2,3})$

Now you have to work on the 2-year row to determine $r_{1,2}$: You have one equation and one unknown in the 2-year row, so you can determine the interest to be

$$(1 + 5.23\%) = (1 + 2.23\%) \cdot (1 + r_{1,2})$$

$$\Longrightarrow (1 + r_{1,2}) = \left(\frac{1 + 5.23\%}{1 + 2.23\%}\right) \approx 1 + 2.93\%$$

Substitute this solution back into the table:

Maturity	Total Holding	Rates of Return Annualized	Individually Compounded
1 Year	$(1 + 2.23\%)$	$= (1 + 2.23\%)^1$	$= (1{+}2.23\%)$
2 Years	$(1 + 5.23\%)$	$\approx (1 + 2.58\%)^2$	$\approx (1{+}2.23\%) \cdot (1{+}2.93\%)$
3 Years	$(1 + 8.80\%)$	$\approx (1 + 2.85\%)^3$	$\approx (1{+}2.23\%) \cdot (1{+}2.93\%) \cdot (1 + r_{2,3})$

Now work on row 3. Again, you have one equation and one unknown in the 3-year row, so you can determine the interest to be

$$(1 + 8.80\%) = (1 + 2.23\%) \cdot (1 + 2.93\%) \cdot (1 + r_{2,3})$$

$$\Longrightarrow (1 + r_{2,3}) = \frac{1 + 8.80\%}{(1 + 2.23\%) \cdot (1 + 2.93\%)} \approx 1 + 3.39\%$$

Maturity	Total Holding	Rates of Return Annualized	Individually Compounded
1 Year	$(1 + 2.23\%)$	$= (1 + 2.23\%)^1$	$= (1{+}2.23\%)$
2 Years	$(1 + 5.23\%)$	$\approx (1 + 2.58\%)^2$	$\approx (1{+}2.23\%) \cdot (1{+}2.93\%)$
3 Years	$(1 + 8.80\%)$	$\approx (1 + 2.85\%)^3$	$\approx (1{+}2.23\%) \cdot (1{+}2.93\%) \cdot (1{+}3.39\%)$

Given the annualized rates of return in the yield curve, you can determine the whole set of implied forward interest rates. For example, the implied interest rate from year 2 to year 3 is 3.39%.

Think of the annualized interest rate as a sort-of-average interest rate.

Behind this arithmetic lies a pretty simple intuition: An annualized 2-year interest rate is "really sort of" an "average" interest rate over the interest rates from the first year and the second year. (In fact, the annualized rate is called the **geometric average**.) If you know that the average interest rate is 2.58%, and you know that the first half of this average is 2.23%, it must be that the second half of the average must be a number around 2.9% in order to average out to 2.58%. And, indeed, you worked out that the forward 1-year interest rate was 2.93%. It is not exact—due to compounding and cross-product terms—but it is fairly close.

SOLVE NOW!

Q 5.50 Continuing the yield curve example in the text, compute the 1-year forward interest rate $r_{3,4}$ from year 3 to year 4 if the 4-year annualized interest rate was 3.10%.

5.7 SHORTING AND LOCKING IN FORWARD INTEREST RATES

You will now learn how to lock in a future interest rate by trading current bonds.

One important reason for dwelling on forward rates is that you can lock them in! That is, you can use the yield curve to contract today for a 1-year interest rate for a loan that will begin in, say, 2 years. When would you want to do this? For example, you may have a corporate project that will require cash outlays in 2 years and pays off cash the year after. You may want to finance it today with money coming in when you need it, and money going out when you have it. Thus, you may want to lock in the forward rate that is determined by the yield curve today. This particular transaction is called a **forward transaction**. Incidentally, this particular type of forward transaction is so popular that an entire financial market on **interest forwards** has developed that allows speculators to do it all in one transaction. How these contracts are priced is now explained.

Forward interest rates are implied by today's yield curve. They will not be the actual future interest rates in a world of uncertainty.

Computing and locking rates are rarely important to ordinary small retail investors, but it can be very important for CFOs and paramount for bond traders. The forward interest rate applies to cash invested in the future. You have already used forward rates: We called them, for example $r_{2,3}$, the 1-year interest rate beginning in 2 years. Still, to be clear, I now want to rename this rate $f_{2,3}$, both for better memorization and for the real world, where you sometimes need to distinguish this forward interest rate that you know today from the 1-year interest rate that will actually come about in 2 years, which is an interest rate that you cannot know today. (It is only in our artificial world of perfect certainty that the forward interest rate and the future actual interest rate must be identical.)

Frictionless borrowing and lending of Treasury bonds allow investors to lock in future interest rates.

You need to learn how to buy and sell (short) Treasury bonds cleverly, so you can bet on future interest rates embedded in the yield curve. Working with and speculating on forward rates is the "bread-and-butter" not only for bond traders but also for many corporate treasurers. To learn the mechanism, assume that you can buy and sell Treasury bonds, even if you do not own them. In effect, we assume that you can borrow Treasury securities, sell them to third parties, receive the cash, buy back the bonds later in the market, and return them to the lender of the Treasury securities. This is called a **short sale** (the opposite—buying securities—is said to be a long position). Exhibit on page 124 explains the basic idea behind shorting. In effect, for Treasury bonds, short-selling enables you to do what the government does—"issue" a security, take in money, and return it to the lender with interest. For example, you may sell

How bond shorting works.

EXHIBIT THE MECHANICS OF AN APPLE SHORT SALE

Three Parties: Apple Lender, You, The Apple Market.

Today:

1. You borrow 1 apple from the lender in exchange for your safe promise to the lender to return this 1 apple next year. (You also pay the lender an extra 1 cent lending fee.)
2. You sell 1 apple into the apple market at the currently prevailing apple price. Say 1 apple costs $5 today. You now have $5 cash, which you can invest. Say you buy bonds that earn you a 1% interest rate.

Next Year:

1. You owe the lender 1 apple. Therefore, you must purchase 1 apple from the apple market.
   - If apples now cost $6, you must purchase 1 apple from the market at $6. You return the apple to the lender. Your net return on the apple is thus −$1, plus the $0.05 interest on $5, minus the 1 cent fee to the lender. You therefore lost 96 cents.
   - If apples now cost $4, you must purchase 1 apple from the market at $4. You return the apple to the lender. Your net return on the apple is thus +$1, plus the $0.05 interest on $5, minus the 1 cent fee to the lender. You therefore gained $1.04.

Net Effects:

- The apple lender has really continued to own the apple throughout and can sell the apple in year 1. There is no advantage for the lender to keep the apple in his own apple cellar rather than to lend it to you. In addition, the lender earns 1 cent by lending.
- The apple market buyer purchased an apple from you today and will never know where it came from (i.e., from a short sale).
- The apple market seller next year will never know what you do with the apple (i.e., that you will use it to make good on your previous year's apple loan).
- You speculated that the price of an apple would decline.
- Note that you did earn the interest rate along the way. Except for the fee you paid to the lender, you could sell the apple in the apple market today and use the proceeds to earn interest, just as an apple grower could have.

In the real world, short-selling is arranged so that you cannot sell the apple short, receive the $5, and then skip town. As a short-seller, you must assure the lender that you will be able to return the apple next year. As the short-seller, you must also pay the lender for all interim benefits that the apple would provide—though few apples pay dividends or coupons the way stocks and bonds often do.

short \$91,915.15 of a 3-year, zero-coupon Treasury note today with a 2.85% rate of interest. This will give you \$91,915.15 cash today but require you to come up with \$100,000 for repayment in 3 years. In effect, selling a Treasury short is a way of borrowing money. Physically, short transactions in the real world are often arranged by a broker, who finds someone who owns the 3-year Treasury note and who is willing to lend it to you (for a small fee). You will have to return this Treasury note to this lender the instant before the Treasury pays off the \$100,000. In the real world, for professional bond traders who can prove that they have enough funds to make good on *any* possible losses, this is easily possible and can be executed with extremely small transaction costs, perhaps 1–2 basis points. Thus, assuming no transaction costs is a reasonable assumption.

Shorting is the opposite of buying: It speculates that the value will decline.

Holding a security (i.e., being long) speculates that the value will go up, so selling a financial instrument (i.e., being short) speculates that the value will go down. If the price of the note tomorrow were to go down to \$50,000 (an annualized interest rate of $(\$100{,}000/\$50{,}000)^{1/3} - 1 \approx 26\%$), you could then purchase the Treasury note for \$50,000 to cover the \$100,000 commitment you have made for \$91,915.15, a profit of \$41,915.15. In fact, you could just return the Treasury to your lender right away. But if the price of the note tomorrow were to go to \$99,000 (an annualized interest rate of 0.33%), you would lose \$7,084.85.

Future cash flows from the "long leg" and the "short leg" of our investment strategy.

Now assume that you are able to buy a 2-year, zero-coupon Treasury note at an annualized interest rate of 2.58%, and able to sell (short) a 3-year note at an annualized interest rate of 2.85%, and do so without transaction costs. For the 3-year note, you would have to promise to pay back $\$100 \cdot 1.0880 \approx \$108.80$ in 3 years (cash outflow to you) for each \$100 you are borrowing today (cash inflow to you). For the 2-year note, you would invest these \$100 (cash outflow to you) and receive $\$100 \cdot 1.0523 \approx \$105.23$ in 2 years (cash inflow to you).

Now compute the rate of return of our strategy given known inflows and outflows.

Looking at Table 5.2, from your perspective, the simultaneous transaction in the two bonds results in an inflow of \$105.23 in year 2 followed by a cash outflow of \$108.80 in year 3. Effectively, you have committed to borrowing \$105.23 in year 2 and paying back \$108.80 in year 3. The interest rate for this loan is

$$f_{2,3} \approx \frac{\$108.80 - \$105.23}{\$105.23} \approx 3.39\%$$

$$f_{2,3} = \frac{C_0 \cdot (1 + r_{0,3}) - C_0 \cdot (1 + r_{0,2})}{C_0 \cdot (1 + r_{0,2})}$$

which is exactly the forward interest rate in Table 5.1.

➤ Table 5.1, p. 107

If you want, you could also design your investment strategy this way.

There are many ways to skin a cat. Here is an alternative way to work this, which you may or may not find easier. Start with the amount that you want to borrow/lend in a future period. For example, say you want to lend \$500 in year 2 and repay however much you need to in year 3. Lending \$500 in year 2 requires an outflow, which you can only accomplish with an inflow today. (Therefore, the first "leg" of your transaction is that you borrow, i.e., short the 2-year note.) Specifically, your inflow today is $\$500/1.0258^2 \approx \$475.17$. Now, invest the entire \$475.17 into the 3-year note, so that you have zero net cash flow today. (This second "leg" of your transaction is that you lend, i.e., purchase the 3-year note.) Done. What do these two transactions

TABLE 5.2 LOCKING IN A FUTURE INTEREST RATE VIA THE LONG-SHORT FORWARD INTEREST RATE SPREAD

Time	Purchased 2-Year Note Cash Flows		Shorted 3-Year Note Cash Flows		Net Cash Flow	
Today	−$100.00	(outflow)	+$100.00	(inflow)	$0.00	
Year 1	$0.00		$0.00		$0.00	
Year 2	+$105.23	(inflow)	$0.00		+$105.23	(inflow)
Year 3	$0.00		−$108.80	(outflow)	−$108.80	(outflow)

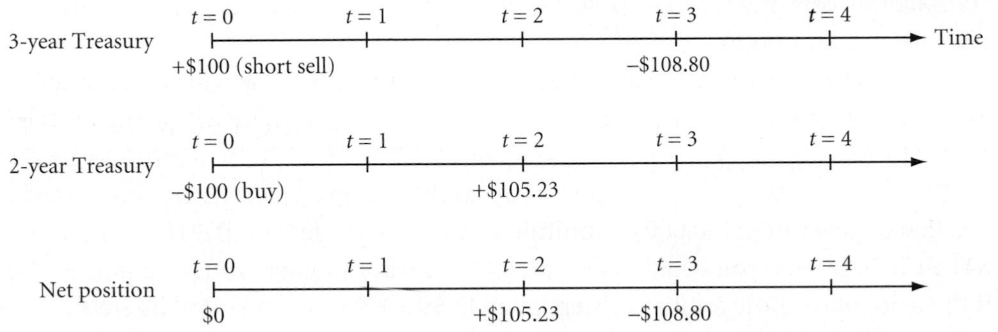

do? You will earn an inflow of $\$475.17 \cdot 1.0285^3 \approx \$516.97$ in 3 years. In total, your financial transactions have committed you to an outflow of $500 in year 2 in exchange for an inflow of $516.97 in year 3—otherwise known as 1-year lending in year 2 at a precommitted interest rate of 3.39%.

You get what you pay for: Your locked speculation can end up better or worse.

Should you engage in this transaction? If the 1-year interest rate in 2 years is higher than 3.39% using the forward lock-in strategy, you will be able to borrow at a lower interest rate than what will be prevailing then. Of course, if the interest rate is lower than 3.39%, you will have committed to borrow at an interest rate that is higher than what you could have gotten. In real life, the 1-year Treasury rate in December 2006 was 4.94%. Thus, this transaction would have been great.

SOLVE NOW!

Q 5.51 If you want to commit to saving at an interest rate of $f_{3,4}$ in December 2004, what would you have to do? (Assume any amount of investment you wish, and work from there.)

Q 5.52 If you want to commit to saving $500,000 in 3 years (i.e., you will deposit $500,000) at an interest rate of $f_{3,4} \approx 3.85\%$ (i.e., you will receive about $519,250), given $r_{\bar{3}} = 2.85\%$ and $r_{\bar{4}} = 3.10\%$, what would you have to do?

5.8 BOND DURATION

Maturity ignores all interim payments.

➤ Yield to maturity (YTM), Section 4.2, p. 72

In Section 4.2, you learned that you can summarize or characterize the multiple cash flows promised by a bond with the YTM. But how can you characterize the "term length" of a bond? The final payment, that is, the maturity, is flawed: Zero-bonds and coupon bonds may have the same maturity, but a high coupon bond could pay out a good amount of money early on. For example, a coupon bond could pay a $99 coupon the first month and leave $1 for one payment in 30 years. It would count as a 30-year bond—the same as a zero-bond that pays $100 in 30 years.

To measure the payout pattern of a bond, investors often rely on both maturity and **duration**—a measure of the *effective* time-length of a project. The simplest duration measure computes the time-weighted average of bond payouts, divided by the sum of all payments. For example, a 5-year coupon bond that pays $250 for 4 years and $1,250 in the fifth year, has a duration of 3.89 years, because

Duration is an "average" payout date.

$$\text{Plain Duration} = \frac{\$250 \cdot 1 + \$250 \cdot 2 + \$250 \cdot 3 + \$250 \cdot 4 + \$1{,}250 \cdot 5}{\$250 + \$250 + \$250 + \$250 + \$1{,}250} \approx 3.89$$

$$\frac{\text{Payment at Time 1} \cdot 1 + \text{Payment at Time 2} \cdot 2 + \cdots + \text{Payment at Time } T \cdot T}{\text{Payment at Time 1} + \text{Payment at Time 2} + \cdots + \text{Payment at Time } T}$$

(You can think of this as the "payment-weighted" payout year.) The idea is that you now consider this 5-year coupon bond to be shorter-term than a 5-year zero-bond (which has a 5-year duration)—and perhaps more similar to a 3.9-year zero-bond.

Duration is sometimes illustrated through the physical analog in Figure 5.3: If all payments were weights hanging from a (time) line, the duration is the point where the weights balance out, so that the line tilts neither right nor left.

Duration is like the "balancing point."

Macaulay duration alters plain duration by using the present value of payouts, not just nominal payouts. Thus, unlike plain duration, which merely characterizes

Macaulay duration uses the PV of payments and is usually a little bit less than plain duration.

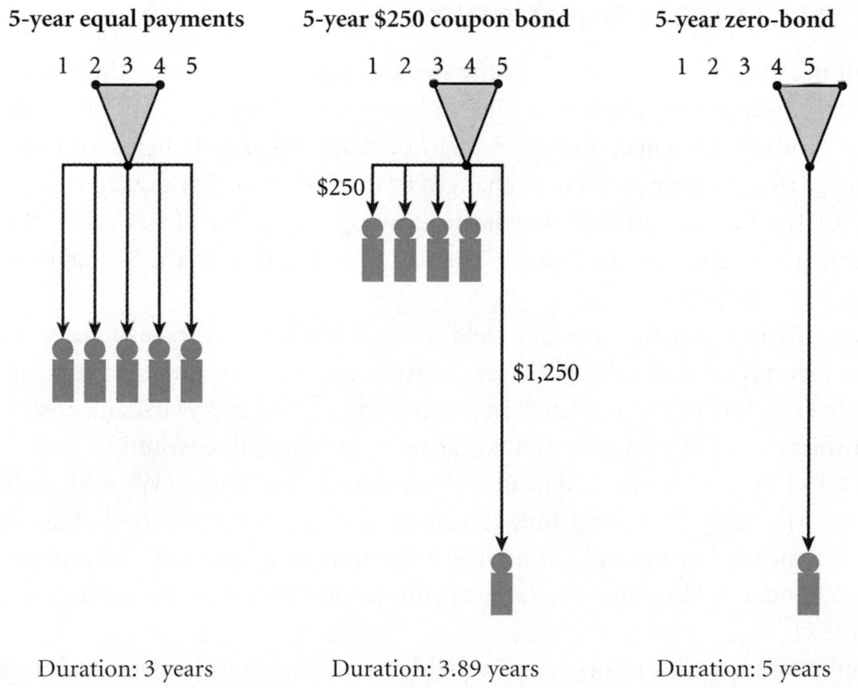

FIGURE 5.3 Physics Analogy Illustrating Plain Duration

bond cash flows regardless of economy-wide interest rates, Macaulay duration also depends on the prevailing yield curve. If the interest rate on all horizons is 5%, the Macaulay duration for your coupon bond is

$$\text{Macaulay Duration} = \frac{\$250/1.05 \cdot 1 + \$250/1.05^2 \cdot 2 + \$250/1.05^3 \cdot 3 + \$250/1.05^4 \cdot 4 + \$1{,}250/1.05^5 \cdot 5}{\$250/1.05 + \$250/1.05^2 + \$250/1.05^3 + \$250/1.05^4 + \$1{,}250/1.05^5}$$

$$= \frac{\$238 \cdot 1 + \$227 \cdot 2 + \$216 \cdot 3 + \$206 \cdot 4 + \$979 \cdot 5}{\$238 + \$227 + \$216 + \$206 + \$979} \approx 3.78$$

$$\frac{\text{PV(Payment at Time 1)} \cdot 1 + \text{PV(Payment at Time 2)} \cdot 2 + \cdots + \text{PV(Payment at Time } T) \cdot T}{\text{PV(Payment at Time 1)} + \text{PV(Payment at Time 2)} + \cdots + \text{PV(Payment at Time } T)}$$

It is this Macaulay duration measure that is most common in the real world.

SOLVE NOW!

Q 5.53 A 2-year bond costs $25,000 today. It pays $1,000 interest at the end of the first year and $1,000 interest at the end of the second year. At the end of the second year, it also repays the principal of $25,000. (Use 4 decimal places of accuracy when computing durations.)
(a) What is its plain duration?
(b) If the yield curve is a flat 0%, what is its Macaulay duration?
(c) If the yield curve is a flat 3%, what is its Macaulay duration?
(d) If the yield curve is a flat 10%, what is its Macaulay duration?

5.9 DURATION SIMILARITY

Duration is often used as an interest exposure measure.

Duration can also be used as a measure for the "term" of projects other than bonds. However, duration only works if all incoming cash flows are positive—otherwise, it may produce nonsense. Duration is important, because it helps you judge the exposure (risk) of your projects to changes in interest rates. For example, if you have a project (or bond portfolio) that has an average duration of 6.9 years, then it is probably more similar to the 7-year, Treasury zero note than to the 5-year, or 10-year, Treasury zero notes.

A concrete project example—a 3-year project that is more similar to a 2-year, zero note than a 3-year, zero note.

Now assume that the Treasury yield curve is 5% for 1-year, zero notes; 10% for 2-year, zero notes; and 15% for 3-year, zero notes. You can purchase a project that will deliver $1,000 in 1 year, $1,000 in 2 years, and $1,500 in 3 years, and costs $2,500. This project would be a good deal, because its present value would be $2,765.10. It has a YTM of 17.5% and a Macaulay duration of 2.01 years. (We shall only work with the Macaulay duration.) But, let's assume you are also worried about interest rate movements. For example, if interest rates were to quadruple, the project would not be a good one. How does the value of your project change as the yield curve moves around?

The effect of a constant shift of the yield curve. A project with a duration of x years behaves like a Treasury zero-bond with x years to maturity.

Let's work out how changes in the yield curve affect your projects and pure zero-notes, each promising $1,000 at maturity. First, your project. Assume that the entire yield curve shifts upward by 1%—the 5% zero note yield becomes a 6% yield, the 10%

becomes 11%, and the 15% becomes 16%. Your project value would now be

$$PV = \frac{\$1{,}000}{1.06} + \frac{\$1{,}000}{1.11^2} + \frac{\$1{,}500}{1.16^3} \approx \$2{,}716.01$$

This is an instant rate of return of $(\$2{,}716.01 - \$2{,}765.10)/\$2{,}765.10 \approx -1.776\%$.

Present Value of the Project	
Base Case	\$2,765.10
Entire yield curve shifts upward by 1%	\$2,716.01
Rate of Return	−1.78%

Is this more similar to how the 1-year, zero note changed; how the 2-year, zero note changed, or how the 3-year, zero note would have changed? Of course, zero notes are only affected by their specific interest rates, so you can work out the percent change one at a time or all simultaneously, and you would get the same answer.

Yield Curve

	Present Value of Treasuries with \$1,000 Face Value			
	Yield Change	Base Case	1% Shift Up	Rate of Return
1-Year note	5%→6%	\$952.38	\$943.40	−0.94%
2-Year note	10%→11%	\$826.45	\$811.62	−1.79%
3-Year note	15%→16%	\$657.52	\$640.66	−2.56%

The answer is that your project's value change is most similar to the 2-year, zero note value change. This is what your project's duration of 2.01 years told you—your project behaves most similarly to the 2-year note as far as its interest rate sensitivity is concerned.

5.10 DURATION HEDGING

A hedge matches assets and liabilities to reduce risk.

Now you know how your project would suffer from a change in the interest rate, but what can you do about it? The idea is to **hedge** your risk: You try to own the same assets long and short—you are matching liabilities and assets—so that you are insured against adverse changes. For example, it would be a perfect hedge if you purchased the project (the long position) and also shorted \$1,000 in the 1-year note, \$1,000 in the 2-year note, and \$1,500 in the 3-year note. You would be totally uninterested in where interest rates would be moving—your wealth would not be affected. (This is the "law of one price" in action. In fact, there is absolutely no risk of losing money.)

Why perfect hedges are rare.

In the real world, perfect hedges, whereby you can match all project cash flows perfectly, are rarely possible. First, the usual scenario is that you know only roughly what cash flows your project will return. Fortunately, it is often easier to guess your project's duration than all its individual cash flows. Second, it may also be difficult for smaller companies to short, say, 137 different Treasury zero-notes to match all project cash flows—the transaction costs would simply be too high. Third, you may not do any active matching, but you would still like to know what kind of exposure you are carrying. After all, you may not only have this project as an asset, but you may have liabilities (e.g., debt payments) that have a duration of 2.4 years—and you want to know how matched or mismatched your assets and liabilities are. Or you may use the newfound duration knowledge to choose among bank or mortgage loans with different durations, so that your assets and liabilities roughly match up in terms of their durations.

You can reduce your interest rate risk by matching the durations of your assets and liabilities.

For example, you know your project assets have a duration of 2 years—what kind of loan would you prefer? One that has a 1-year duration, a 2-year duration, or a 3-year duration? If you want to minimize your interest rate risk, you would prefer to borrow \$2,716 of a 2-year note—though the bank loan, too, may not be a zero note, but just some sort of loan with a 2-year duration. Would you be comfortable that the interest rate would not affect your wealth very much if you were to short the 2-year note and long the project? Yes and no—you would be comfortable that wholesale shifts of the yield curve would not affect you. You would, however, be exposed to changes in the shape of the yield curve—if only one of the interest rates were to shift, your project would be impacted differently than your 2-year note. In this case, your project's value would move less than the value of your 2-year note. In the real world, over short horizons, duration matching often works very well. Over longer horizons, however, you will have to constantly watch and rearrange assets and liabilities to prevent the gap from enlarging too much.

5.11 CONTINUOUS COMPOUNDING

Continuously compounded interest rates are "as if interest is paid every instant."

Progressively more frequently paid interest payments converge to the continuously compounded interest rate.

A subject of some interest to Wall Street traders, that is, the people who trade bonds or options for a living, is the concept of a **continuously compounded interest rate**. This is easiest to explain by example.

Assume that you receive \$120 next year for an investment of \$100 today. You already know that this represents a simple rate of return of 20%. What would the interest be if it were paid twice per year, the interest rate remained constant, and the \$100 would still come out to be \$120 at the end of the year? You have done this before:

$$(1 + r_{\text{semiannual}}) \cdot (1 + r_{\text{semiannual}}) = (1 + 20\%) \quad \Longrightarrow \quad r \approx 9.54\%$$

If you multiply this semiannual interest rate by 2, you get 19.08%. What if you received interest 12 times a year?

$$(1 + r_{\text{monthly}})^{12} = (1 + 20\%) \quad \Longrightarrow \quad r \approx 1.53\%$$

Multiply this monthly interest rate by 12 and you get 18.36%. What if you received interest 365 times a year?

$$(1 + r_{\text{daily}})^{365} = (1 + 20\%) \quad \Longrightarrow \quad r \approx 0.05\%$$

➤ Effective annual rate, Section 2.4C, p. 23

The 20% was called an "effective annual rate" in Section 2.4C. Multiply this daily interest rate by 365 and you get 18.25% (the annual quote). Now, what would this number be if you were to receive interest every single moment in time—the annual rate, compounded every instant?

The answer is, you guessed it, the continuously compounded interest rate, and it can be computed by taking the natural logarithm (abbreviated "ln" on your calculator and below) of 1 plus the simple interest rate

The limit: Use logs and exponents to translate between simple interest rates and continuously compounded interest rates.

➤ Appendix A, "Background," p. A-1

$$r_{\text{continuously compounded}} = \ln(1 + 20\%) \approx 18.23\%$$

$$r_{\text{continuously compounded}} = \ln(1 + r_{\text{simple}})$$

You must *never* directly apply a continuously compounded interest rate to a cash flow to compute your return. In this example, investing \$100 would not leave you with \$118.23 after 1 year. Indeed, if someone quoted you a continuously compounded interest rate, to determine how much money you will end up with, you would first have to convert the continuously compounded return into a simple interest rate

Warning: Never ever apply continuously compounded rates of return to cash flows!

$$r_{\text{simple}} = e^{r_{\text{continuously compounded}}} - 1 = e^{18.23\%} - 1 \approx 20\%$$

and then apply this interest rate to the cash flow. Alternatively, you can multiply the cash flow not by 1 plus the simple interest rate, but by $e^{r_{\text{continuously compounded}}}$.

Continuously compounded rates have two nice features: First, if the continuously compounded rate in period 1 is 10% and in period 2 is 20%, then the total 2-period continuously compounded rate is 30%—yes, continuously compounded interest rates can be added, so no more multiplying one-pluses! (This additivity is not a big advantage, though.) Second, they are more "symmetric." See, an ordinary rate of return lies between −100% and +∞, while the continuously compounded rate of return lies between −∞ and +∞. (This can be an advantage in statistical work, as can be the fact that the logarithm helps "pull in" large outliers.) However, the main need for continuously compounded interest rates arises in other formulas (such as the Black-Scholes option formula).

To calculate multiperiod interest returns, continuously compounded interest rates are never compounded, but added instead.

➤ Section 26.3A, "The Black-Scholes Formula," p. 993

SOLVE NOW!

Q 5.54 A bond pays \$150 for every \$100 invested. What is its continuously compounded interest rate?

Q 5.55 Confirm my claim that you can add continuously compounded interest rates. That is, a bond pays a continuously compounded interest rate of 10%. Upon maturity, the money can be reinvested at a continuously compounded interest rate of 20%. If you invest \$100 today, how much money will you end up with? What is the simple and continuously compounded interest rate over the 2 periods?

5.12 INSTITUTIONAL KNOWLEDGE: COMPOUNDING, PRICE QUOTES, AND STRIPS

Before I can relieve you of the "Treasury bonds" subject, you should know about two more issues, which up to now I have swept under the rug.

Small cheats on my part.

1. **Most Treasuries are not zero-bonds:** This whole chapter was based on the fiction that the yield curve was based on the discount rate of zero-bonds. This is not

ANECDOTE Stripping

The term "bond coupon" comes from an era when bond buyers took possession of a physical document that promised payment. To receive interest, the bond owner would clip a coupon off the paper (much like a supermarket coupon), mail it in, and then receive cash in return.

Beginning in the 1970s, some bond buyers (especially large investment banks) would clip at least some of the coupons from the bond and resell them separately. Someone would purchase coupon bonds, put them into separate escrow accounts, and sell them individually. This practice was called **stripping**. By the early 1980s, this practice had become more extreme—it was the original method by which zero-coupon bonds were created. That is, coupon bonds had turned into many zero-bonds, one for each coupon, plus one zero-bond for the principal. Indeed they were so common that they themselves became routinely traded.

Nowadays, Treasury bond owners no longer take physical possession of their bonds. Instead, since 1982, possession only means a record in a computer at the Treasury. Still, the names "coupon" and "stripping" have stuck. In 1985, the Treasury created its own coupon stripping program, and cleverly called it—**STRIPS**. This time, it is an acronym for **Separate Trading of Registered Interest and Principal of Securities**. Under the STRIPS program, the U.S. government issues with maturities of 10 years or more are eligible for transfer over Fedwire. The process involves wiring Treasury notes and bonds to the Federal Reserve Bank of New York and receiving separated computer entries representing its components in return. This has reduced the legal and insurance costs associated with the process of stripping a security prior to 1982. In May 1987, the Treasury began to allow the reconstitution of stripped securities. Nowadays, financial services companies can divide payments at will, with the Treasury acting as a reliable administrative agent.

The original advantage for zero-coupon bonds was—what else?—the tax code. The United States largely caught up with the new situation in 1982, although tax-exempt accounts still get some small advantages from them. But the main reason for U.S. bond stripping today are tax loopholes in Japan and other countries.

Source: New York Federal Reserve Bank.

➤ My earlier inaccuracy warning explained, Section 5.3B, p. 105

really true. In the United States, Treasuries actually pay interest twice per year. In Europe, government bonds pay interest once a year. The yield curves that you will usually find therefore quote the yields-to-maturity on coupon bonds, not the yields-to-maturity on zero-bonds.

This means that the duration of, say, the 5-year note may really only be 4.9 years, not 5.0 years. If the yield curve is flat, this makes no difference. Even if the yield curve is steep, it may cause a discrepancy of only a couple of basis points. For example, in the yield curve in our example, the difference was about 4 basis points for a 10-year, zero note versus a 10-year, coupon note.

To be clear—if you are a bond trader, these are differences that are of vital importance. But if you are a corporation or individual, this is almost never an issue worth wasting a lot of thought over.

As a bond trader, it is not too difficult to convert level-coupon bonds into zero-bonds. You can think of a semiannual 30-year, level-coupon bond as a project consisting of 59 relatively small zero notes, each maturing half a year after the other, and one big zero-bond, maturing in 30 years. If you feel like it, the next question will lead you step by step through the process of converting level-coupon bonds into what are called **STRIPS**.

2. **How the real world quotes Treasuries:** There are intricate calculations required to translate quotes into yields-to-maturity. If you need them, they are explained in detail at "Estimating Yields on Treasury Securities" at www.newyorkfed.org/

aboutthefed/fedpoint/fed28.html. Fortunately, nowadays, most publications already do the translation into YTM for you.

SOLVE NOW!

Q 5.56 ADVANCED: Let me lead you along in working out how you can "STRIP" a Treasury coupon bond. Assume the 12-month Treasury note costs \$10,065.22 and pays a coupon of \$150 in 6 months, and interest plus coupon of \$10,150 in 12 months. (Its payment patterns indicate that it was originally issued as a "3% semiannual, level-coupon note.") Now assume the 6-month Treasury bill costs \$10,103.96 and has only one remaining coupon-plus-principal payment of \$10,200. (It was originally issued [and perhaps many years ago] as a "4% semiannual, level-coupon bill.")

(a) What is the YTM of these two Treasuries?
(b) Graph a yield curve based on the maturity of these two Treasuries.
(c) What would be the price of a 1-year *zero* note?
(d) Graph a yield curve based on zero notes.
(e) Do the yield differences between the 1-year zero note and the 1-year coupon note seem large to you?

SUMMARY

This appendix covered the following major points:

- The information in the set of annualized rates of return, individual holding rates of return, and total holding rates of return is identical. Therefore, you can translate them into one another. For example, you can extract all forward interest rates from the prevailing yield curve.
- It explains how shorting transactions work.
- If you can both buy and short bonds, then you can lock in forward interest rates today.
- Bond duration is a characterization of *when* bond payments typically come in.
- The continuously compounded interest rate is $\ln(1 + r)$, where r is the simple interest rate.

KEY TERMS

continuously compounded interest rate, 130
duration, 127
forward transaction, 123
geometric average, 122
hedge, 129
interest forward, 123
Macaulay duration, 127
Separate Trading of Registered Interest and Principal of Securities, 132
short sale, 123
stripping, 132
STRIPS, 132

SOLVE NOW! SOLUTIONS

Q 5.50 $r_{0,3}$ was computed in the text as 8.80%. The 4-year holding rate of return is $r_{0,4} \approx 1.031^4 \approx 12.99\%$. Therefore, the 1-year forward rate from year 3 to year 4 is $r_{3,4} = (1 + r_{0,4})/(1 + r_{0,3}) - 1 \approx (1 + 12.99\%)/(1 + 8.80\%) - 1 \approx 3.85\%$.

Q 5.51 The 3-year rate is 2.85%. The 5-year rate is 3.35%. First, interpolate the 4-year interest rate: $r_{\bar{4}} = (2.85\% + 3.35\%)/2 = 3.10\%$. Buy \$1,000 of the 4-year, zero note and short \$1,000 of the 3-year, zero note (2.85%/year). Today, you receive and pay \$1,000, so the transaction does not cost you anything. In 3-years, you need to pay the 3-year note—that is, you need to pay $\$1{,}000 \cdot 1.0285^3 \approx \$1{,}087.96$. In 4 years, you receive from the 4-year note $\$1{,}000 \cdot 1.031^4 \approx \$1{,}129.89$. This is the equivalent of saving at an interest rate $r_{3,4}$ of 3.85%. A visual representation follows:

	t = 0	t = 1	t = 2	t = 3	t = 4
4-year Treasury	–\$1,000 (buy)				+\$1,129.89
3-year Treasury	+\$1,000 (short-sell)			–\$1,087.96	
Net position	\$0			–\$1,087.96	+\$1,129.89

Q 5.52 To commit to saving in year 3, you would need a cash outflow of \$500,000 in year 3. To get this, you need a cash inflow of $\$500{,}000/1.0285^3 \approx \$459{,}575.76$. Buy 4-year Treasuries for this amount today. Finance them by short-selling simultaneously 3-year Treasuries for the same amount. A visual representation is shown below.

	t = 0	t = 1	t = 2	t = 3	t = 4
4-year Treasury	–\$459,576 (buy)				+\$519,250
3-year Treasury	+\$459,576 (short-sell)			–\$500,000	
Net position	\$0			–\$500,000	+\$519,250

Q 5.53 For the bond with cash flows of \$25,000, –\$1,000, and –\$26,000, the durations (all quoted in units of years, because we quote the multiplication factors "1" and "2" in years) are as follows:
(a) The plain duration is

$$\text{Plain Duration} = \frac{\left(\sum_{t=1}^{2} \$1{,}000 \cdot t\right) + \$26{,}000 \cdot 2}{\left(\sum_{t=1}^{2} \$1{,}000\right) + \$26{,}000} = \frac{53{,}000}{27{,}000} \approx 1.96296$$

(b) If the yield curve is a flat 0%, plain and Macauley durations are the same. Thus, it is 1.96296 years.

(c) This Macauley duration is

$$\text{Macaulay Duration at 3\%} = \frac{\left(\sum_{t=1}^{2} \frac{\$1{,}000 \cdot t}{1.03^t}\right) + \frac{\$26{,}000 \cdot 2}{1.03^2}}{\left(\sum_{t=1}^{2} \frac{\$1{,}000}{1.03^t}\right) + \frac{\$26{,}000}{1.03^2}} = \frac{\frac{\$1{,}000 \cdot 1}{1.03^1} + \frac{\$1{,}000 \cdot 2}{1.03^2} + \frac{\$25{,}000 \cdot 2}{1.03^2}}{\frac{\$1{,}000}{1.03^1} + \frac{\$1{,}000}{1.03^2} + \frac{\$25{,}000}{1.03^2}}$$

$$\approx \frac{49{,}985.86}{25{,}478.37} \approx 1.96189$$

(d) This Macauley duration is

$$\text{Macaulay Duration at 10\%} = \frac{\left(\sum_{t=1}^{2} \frac{\$1{,}000 \cdot t}{1.10^t}\right) + \frac{\$25{,}000 \cdot 2}{1.10^2}}{\left(\sum_{t=1}^{2} \frac{\$1{,}000}{1.10^t}\right) + \frac{\$25{,}000}{1.10^2}} = \frac{\frac{\$1{,}000 \cdot 1}{1.10^1} + \frac{\$1{,}000 \cdot 2}{1.10^2} + \frac{\$25{,}000 \cdot 2}{1.10^2}}{\frac{\$1{,}000}{1.10^1} + \frac{\$1{,}000}{1.10^2} + \frac{\$25{,}000}{1.10^2}}$$

$$\approx \frac{43{,}884.30}{22{,}396.69} \approx 1.95941$$

Q 5.54 The simple interest rate is 50%. The continuously compounded interest rate is $\ln(1 + 50\%) \approx 40.55\%$.

Q 5.55 A 10% continuously compounded interest rate is a simple interest rate of $r_{0,1} = e^{0.10} - 1 \approx 10.52\%$, so you would have \$110.52 after 1 year. A 20% cc interest rate is a simple interest rate of $f_{1,2} = e^{0.20} - 1 \approx 22.14\%$. This means that your \$110.52 investment would turn into $1.02214 \cdot \$110.52 \approx \$134.99$. This means that the simple interest rate is $r_{0,2} \approx 34.99\%$. Thus, the cc interest rate is $\ln(1 + r_{0,2}) \approx \ln(1.3499) \approx 30\%$. Of course, you could have computed this faster: $V_t = e^{0.10} \cdot e^{0.20} \cdot V_0 = e^{0.10+0.20} \cdot V_0 = e^{0.30} \cdot \$100 \approx 1.3499 \cdot \$100 \approx \$134.99$.

Q 5.56 (a) To compute the YTM for the 12-month note:

$$-\$10{,}065.22 + \frac{\$150}{(1 + \text{YTM})^{0.5}} + \frac{\$10{,}150}{(1 + \text{YTM})^1} = 0$$

which solves to YTM $\approx$ 2.35%. To compute the YTM of the 6-month bill:

$$-\$10{,}103.96 + \frac{\$10{,}200}{(1 + \text{YTM})^{0.5}} = 0$$

which solves to YTM $\approx$ 1.91%.

(b) Do it.

(c) The \$150 coupon is worth $\$150/1.0191^{0.5} \approx \$148.59$. Therefore, the 1-year, zero note with one payment of \$10,150 due in 1 year costs $\$10{,}065.22 - \$148.59 = \$9{,}916.63$. This means that the 1-year, zero note with payoff of \$10,150 has a YTM of $\$10{,}150/\$9{,}916.63 - 1 \approx 2.35\%$.

(d) Do it.

(e) The difference between the YTM of the coupon note (1.91%) and the zero note (235%) is only 0.44 basis points—very small, even though the yield curve here is fairly steep. The reason is that the early 6-month coupon (earning a lower interest rate) makes little difference because the coupon payment is only \$150, and most of the YTM comes from the final payment. The coupon effect can become larger on very long horizons when the yield curve is steep, but it is very rarely more than 10–20 basis points.

PROBLEMS

The ▭ *indicates problems available in* myfinancelab

Q 5.57 Explain the difference between shorting in the real world, and shorting in a perfect world.

Q 5.58 The annualized interest rates are as follows:

Year	1	2	3	4	5	6
Interest Rate	3%	4%	5%	6%	6%	6%

Year	7	8	9	10	11	12
Interest Rate	7%	7%	7%	6%	5%	4%

(a) Compute the full set of forward rates.
(b) Plot the forward rates into the yield curve graph. Is there an intuitive relation between the forward rate curve and the yield curve?
(c) If you wanted to lock in an interest rate for savings of $100,000 from year 3 to year 4 (a 1-year investment), how exactly would you do it using existing bonds?

Q 5.59 At today's prevailing 1-year and 2-year Treasury rates,
(a) What is the 1-year forward interest rate on Treasuries?
(b) How would you commit today to borrowing $100,000 next year at this forward rate?

Q 5.60 A coupon bond costs $100, pays $10 interest each year, and in 10 years pays back $100 principal (ceasing to exist). What is the coupon bond's plain duration?

Q 5.61 A 10-year zero-bond has a YTM of 10%. What is its plain duration? What is its Macaulay duration?

Q 5.62 A 25-year bond costs $25,000 today and will pay $1,000 at year-end for the following 25 years. In the final year ($T = 25$), it also repays $25,000 in principal. (Use 4 decimal places of accuracy when computing durations.)
(a) What is its YTM?
(b) What is its plain duration?
(c) If the yield curve is a flat 3%, what is its Macaulay duration?
(d) If the yield curve is a flat 10%, what is its Macaulay duration?

Q 5.63 If the continuously compounded interest rate is 10% per annum in the first year and 20% the following year, what is your total continuously compounded interest rate over the 2 years? How much will you earn over these 2 years for $1 of investment?

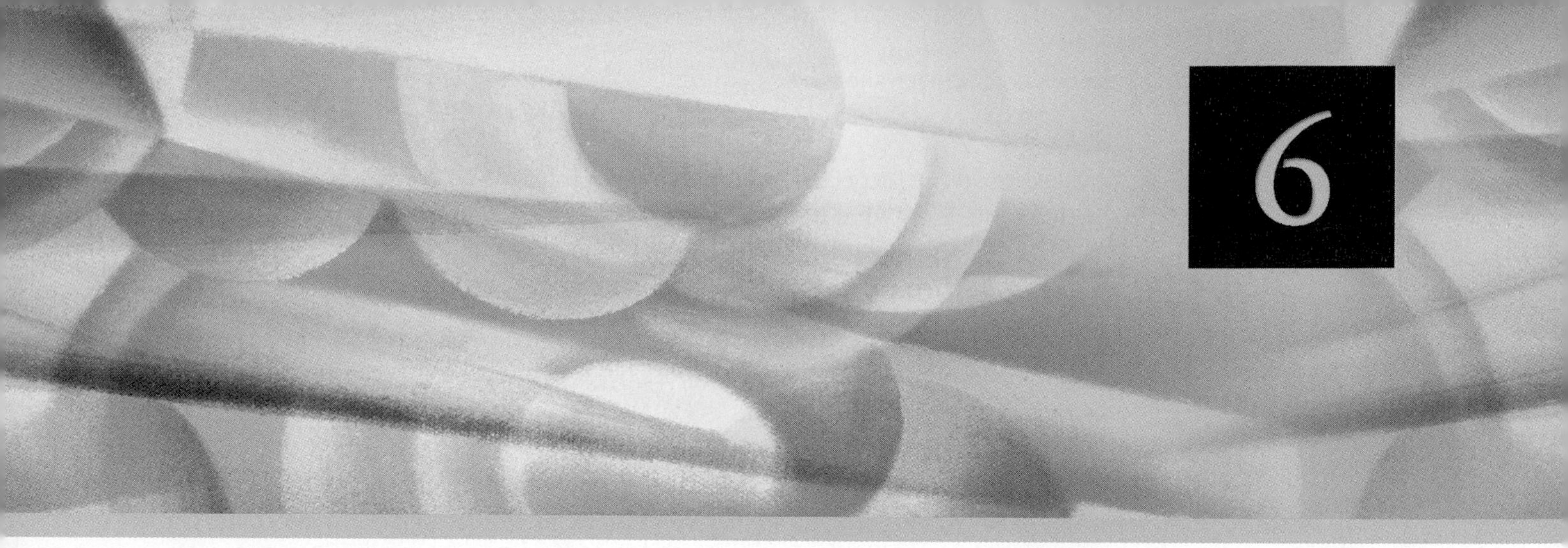

6

Uncertainty, Default, and Risk

PROMISED VERSUS EXPECTED RETURNS AND DEBT VERSUS EQUITY IN A RISK-NEUTRAL WORLD

You are now entering the world of uncertainty and abandoning the idea that you have perfect foresight. We shall still pretend that you live in a perfect market with no taxes, no transaction costs, no differences of opinion, and infinitely many investors and firms. The presence of uncertainty makes for enough additional complexity and realism.

Net present value still rules supreme, but you will now have to face the sad fact that it is no longer easy to use. It is not the NPV concept that is difficult. Instead, it is the inputs—the expected cash flows and appropriate costs of capital—that can be so very difficult to estimate in the real world.

In a world of uncertainty, there are scenarios in which you will get more cash than you expected and scenarios in which you will get less. The single most important insight is that you must therefore always draw a sharp distinction between *promised* (or *quoted* or *stated*) returns and *expected* returns. Because firms can default on payments or go bankrupt in the future, expected returns are lower than promised returns.

After setting forth the necessary statistical background, this chapter will cover two important finance topics: First, you get to determine how much lenders should charge borrowers if there is the possibility of default. Second, you learn how to work with the two important building blocks of financing—namely, debt and equity.

6.1 AN INTRODUCTION TO STATISTICS

Statistics is about characterizing an uncertain world.

Statistics has the reputation of being the most painful of the foundation sciences for finance—but you absolutely need to understand it to describe an uncertain future. Yes, it can be a difficult subject, but if you have ever placed a bet in the past, chances are that you already have a good intuitive grasp of what you need. In fact, I had already sneaked the term "expected" into previous chapters, even though it is only now that you learn precisely what it means.

6.1A RANDOM VARIABLES AND EXPECTED VALUES

The "expected value" is the average outcome if the random draw is repeated infinitely often.

The most important statistical concept is that of the **expected value**, which is the probability-weighted average of all possible outcomes. It is very similar to a **mean** or **average**. The difference is that the latter two names are used if you work with *past* outcomes, while the expected value applies if you work with *future* outcomes. For example, say you toss a coin, which can come up either heads or tails with equal probability. You receive \$1 if the coin comes up heads and \$2 if the coin comes up tails. Because you know that there is a 50% chance of \$1 and a 50% chance of \$2, the expected value of each coin toss is \$1.50. If you repeated this infinitely often, and if you recorded the series of **realizations** (actual outcomes), the mean would converge to exactly \$1.50. Of course, in any one throw, \$1.50 can never come up—the expected value does not need to be a possible realization of a single coin toss.

An expected value may not be a possible realization.

IMPORTANT: The expected value is just a mean (or average) if you repeat the random draws infinitely often.

A random variable is a number whose realization is not yet known.

To make it easier to work with uncertainty, statisticians have invented the concept of the **random variable**. It is a variable whose outcome has not yet been determined. In the coin toss example, you can define a random variable named c (for "coin toss outcome") that takes the value \$1 with 50% probability and the value \$2 with 50% probability. The expected value of c is \$1.50. To distinguish a random variable from an ordinary nonrandom variable, use a tilde (˜) over the variable. To denote the expected value, use the notation $\mathcal{E}$. In this bet,

$$\mathcal{E}(\tilde{c}) = 50\% \cdot \$1 + 50\% \cdot \$2 = \$1.50$$

$$\text{Expected Value(of Coin Toss)} = \mathcal{P}rob(\text{Heads}) \cdot \$1 + \mathcal{P}rob(\text{Tails}) \cdot \$2$$

After the coin has been tossed, the actual outcome c could, for example, be

$$c = \$2$$

After the toss, c is no longer a random variable, so there is no more tilde. Also, if you are certain about the outcome, perhaps because there is only one possible outcome, then the actual realization and the expected value are the same. The random variable is then the same as an ordinary nonrandom variable. Is the expected outcome of the coin toss a random variable? No: You know the expected outcome is \$1.50 even before the toss of the coin. The expected value is known; the uncertain outcome is not. The expected value is an ordinary nonrandom variable; the possible outcome is a random variable. Is the outcome of the coin throw *after* it has come down heads a random

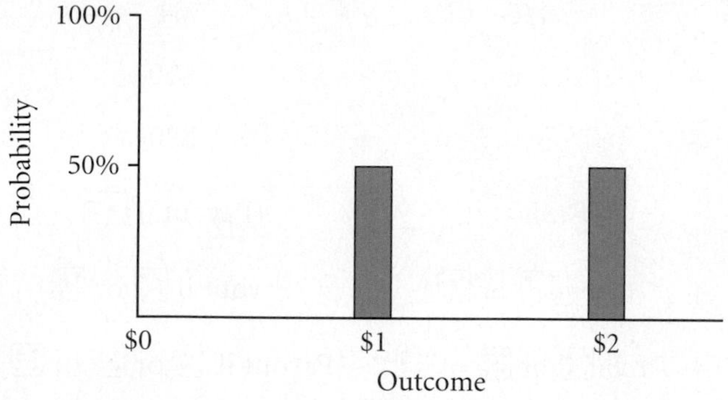

FIGURE 6.1 A Histogram for a Random Variable with Two Equally Likely Outcomes, $1 and $2

variable? No: It is an actual outcome and you know what it is (heads), so it is no longer a random variable.

A random variable is a statistical distribution.

A random variable is defined by the **probability distribution** of its possible outcomes. The coin throw distribution is simple: the value $1 with 50% probability and the value $2 with 50% probability. This is sometimes graphed in a **histogram**, which is a graph that has the possible outcomes on the x-axis and the frequency (or probability) on the y-axis. Figure 6.1 shows the histogram for the coin throw. In fact, you can think of a random variable (the tilde) as a placeholder for a histogram.

A final note—perfect markets.

One final clarification: In this chapter, we are eliminating our certainty assumption. But we are *not* (yet) eliminating our perfect market assumption. You may wonder what this means about the assumption that there is no disagreement. It means that we all must agree what the probabilities of all possible outcomes are. An example of an imperfect market would be if you believed that there was a 51% probability of an outcome of $1, and I believed there was a 50% probability of $1.

FAIR BETS

An example with three possible outcomes.

A **fair bet** is a bet that costs its expected value. If repeated infinitely often, both the person offering the bet and the person taking the bet would expect to end up even. For example, call D your payoff based on the following structure:

- There is a 1/6 chance that you will be paid $4;
- a 2/6 chance that you will be paid $10;
- and a 3/6 chance that you will be paid $20.

You can simulate this payoff structure by throwing a die and getting $4 if it comes up ⚀, $10 if it comes up ⚁ or ⚂, and $20 if it comes up ⚃, ⚄, or ⚅. What would be a fair price for this die bet? The uncertain payoff is a random variable, so you should call it $\tilde{D}$. First, you must determine $\mathcal{E}(\tilde{D})$. It is

$$
\begin{aligned}
\mathcal{E}(\tilde{D}) = \quad & 1/6 \cdot \$4 \\
+ \quad & 2/6 \cdot \$10 \\
+ \quad & 3/6 \cdot \$20 = \$14
\end{aligned}
$$

$$
\begin{aligned}
\mathcal{E}(\tilde{D}) = \quad & \mathcal{P}rob(⚀) \cdot (\text{Payout if ⚀}) \\
+ \quad & \mathcal{P}rob(⚁ \text{ or } ⚂) \cdot (\text{Payout if ⚁ or ⚂}) \\
+ \quad & \mathcal{P}rob(⚃ \text{ or } ⚄ \text{ or } ⚅) \cdot (\text{Payout if ⚃ or ⚄ or ⚅})
\end{aligned}
$$

If you repeat this bet a zillion times, you would expect to earn \$14 zillion. On average, each bet would earn \$14, although some sampling variation in actual trials would make this a little more or a little less. If it costs \$14 to buy a single bet, it would be fair.

The expected value is the probability-weighted sum of all possible outcomes.

Generally, the procedure to compute expected values is always the same: Multiply each outcome by its probability and add up all these products.

$$
\begin{aligned}
\mathcal{E}(\tilde{X}) = \quad & \mathcal{P}rob(\text{First Possible Outcome}) \cdot \text{Value of First Possible Outcome} \\
+ \quad & \mathcal{P}rob(\text{Second Possible Outcome}) \cdot \text{Value of Second Possible Outcome} \\
+ \quad & \vdots \\
+ \quad & \mathcal{P}rob(\text{Last Possible Outcome}) \cdot \text{Value of Last Possible Outcome}
\end{aligned}
$$

This is the formula that you used above,

$$
\begin{aligned}
\mathcal{E}(\tilde{D}) &= 1/6 \cdot \$4 + 2/6 \cdot \$10 + 3/6 \cdot \$20 = \$14 \\
&= \text{Sum of } [\mathcal{P}rob(\text{Each Outcome}) \times \text{Each Outcome}]
\end{aligned}
$$

Note that the formula is general. It works even with outcomes that are impossible. You would just assign probabilities of zero to them.

IMPORTANT: You must understand the following:

1. The difference between an ordinary variable and a random variable
2. The difference between a realization and an expectation
3. How to compute an expected value, given probabilities and outcomes
4. What a fair bet is

SOLVE NOW!

Q 6.1 Is the expected outcome (value) of a die throw a random variable?

Q 6.2 Could it be that the expected value of a bet is a random variable?

Q 6.3 An ordinary die throw came up with a ⚅ yesterday. What was its expected outcome before the throw? What was its realization?

Q 6.4 A stock that has the following probability distribution (outcome P_{+1}) costs $50. Is an investment in this stock a fair bet?

Prob	P_{+1}	*Prob*	P_{+1}	*Prob*	P_{+1}	*Prob*	P_{+1}
5%	$41	20%	$45	20%	$58	5%	$75
10%	$42	30%	$48	10%	$70		

6.1B VARIANCE AND STANDARD DEVIATION

In finance, we often need to measure the (average) **reward** that you expect to receive from making an investment. Usually, we use the expected value of the investment as our measure. We also often need to measure a second characteristic of investments, namely, **risk**. Thus, we also need summary measures of how spread out the possible outcomes are. These two concepts will play starring roles in the next few chapters, where you will explore them in great detail. For now, if you are curious, think of risk as a measure of the variability of outcomes around your expected mean. The most common measure of risk is the standard deviation, which takes the square root of the sum of squared deviations from the mean—a mouthful. Let's just do it once for our roll-of-the-dice problem. First, work out each squared deviation from the mean:

We will measure the "reward" as the expected value. Looking ahead, the standard deviation is the most common measure of "risk" (spread).

(Computing the variance can be a demeaning task.)

The first outcome is \$4. The mean is \$14, so the deviation from the mean is \$4 − \$14 = −\$10. You need the squared deviation from the mean, which is $(-\$10)^2 = +\$\$100$. The units are strange—dollars squared—and impossible to interpret intuitively. Don't even try.

The second outcome is \$10, so the deviation from the mean is \$10 − \$14 = −\$4. You need the squared deviation from the mean, which is $(-\$4)^2 = +\$\$16$.

The third outcome is \$20, so the deviation from the mean is \$20 − \$14 = +\$6. You need the squared deviation from the mean, which is $(\$6)^2 = +\$\$36$.

Now compute the expected value of these squared deviations, which is sometimes called the **variance**:

$$\mathcal{V}ar(\text{Dice}) = 1/6 \cdot (\$\$100) + 2/6 \cdot (\$\$16) + 3/6 \cdot \$\$36 = \$\$40$$

The **standard deviation** is

$$\mathcal{S}dv(\text{Dice}) = \sqrt{\$\$40} \approx \$6.32$$

There you have it—our mouthful: The standard deviation is the square root of the average squared deviation from the mean. Unlike the variance, the standard deviation has sensible units. Together, the mean and the standard deviation allow you to characterize your bet. It is common phrasing, though a bit loose, to state that you expect to earn \$14 (the expected value) from a single die throw, plus or minus \$6.32 (the standard deviation).

SOLVE NOW!

Q 6.5 Reconsider the stock investment from Question 6.4. What is its risk, that is, the standard deviation of its outcome P_{+1}?

6.1C RISK NEUTRALITY (AND PREVIEW OF RISK AVERSION)

Choosing investments only on the basis of expected values is assuming risk neutrality.

Fortunately, the expected value is all that you need to learn about statistics for this chapter. This is because we are assuming—only for learning purposes—that everyone is **risk neutral**. Essentially, this means that investors are willing to write or take any fair bet. For example, if you are risk neutral, you would be indifferent between getting $1 for sure and getting either $0 or $2, each with 50% probability. And you would be indifferent between earning 10% from a risk-free bond and earning either 0% or 20%, again with fifty-fifty probability, from a risky bond. You have no preference between investments with equal expected values, no matter how safe or uncertain these investments may be.

Risk aversion means you would prefer the safe project. Put differently, you would demand an extra "kicker" to take the riskier project instead.

If, instead, you are risk averse, you would not want to invest in the more risky alternative if both the risky and safe alternatives offered the same expected rate of return. You would prefer the safe $1 to the unsafe $0 or $2 investment. You would prefer the 10% risk-free Treasury bond to the unsafe corporate bond that would pay either 0% or 20%. In this case, if I wanted to sell you a risky project or a risky bond, I would have to offer you a higher expected rate of return as risk compensation. I might have to pay you, say, 5 cents to get you to be willing to accept the project that pays off $0 or $2 if you can instead earn $1 elsewhere. Alternatively, I would have to lower the price of my corporate bond so that it offers you a higher expected rate of return, say, 1% or 21% instead of 0% or 20%.

For a given investor, bigger bets usually require more compensation for risk.

It is true that if you are risk averse, you should not accept fair bets. (You can think of this as the definition of risk aversion.) But would you really worry about a bet for either +$1 or −$1? Probably not. For small bets, you are probably close to risk neutral—I may not have to pay you even 1 cent extra to induce you to take this bet. But what about a bet for plus or minus $100? Or for plus or minus $10,000? My guess is that you would be fairly reluctant to accept the latter bet without getting extra compensation for risk bearing. For most investors, the larger the bet, the more risk averse you are likely to be. To take the plus or minus $10,000 bet, I would probably have to offer you several hundred dollars extra.

Financial markets can spread risk and thereby lower the aggregate risk aversion.

However, your own personal risk aversion is not what matters in financial markets. Instead, the financial markets price investments in line with the market's aggregate risk aversion. The reason is risk sharing. For example, if you could share the $10,000 bet with 10,000 other students in your class, your own part of the bet would be only plus or minus $1. And some of your colleagues may be willing to accept even more risk for relatively less extra risk compensation—they may have healthier bank accounts or wealthier parents. Therefore, when you can lay bets across many investors, the effective risk aversion of the group will be lower than that of any of its members. And this is exactly how financial markets work: Their aggregate risk absorption capabilities are considerably higher than those of their individual investors. In effect, the financial markets are less risk averse than individual investors.

The tools you learn now will remain applicable under risk aversion.

You will study risk aversion in the next chapters. In this chapter, we will focus on pricing under risk neutrality. But, as always, all tools you learn in this simpler scenario will remain applicable in the more complex scenario in which investors are risk averse. Moreover, in the real world, the differences between promised and expected returns that are discussed in this chapter are often more important (in terms of value) than the extra compensation for risk aversion that is ignored in this chapter.

ANECDOTE The Ruin of the First Financial System

The earliest known example of widespread financial default occurred in the year 1788 B.C.E., when King Rim-Sin of Uruk (Mesopotamia) repealed *all* loan repayments. The royal edict effectively destroyed a system of flourishing commerce and finance, which was already many thousands of years old! It is not known why Rim-Sin did so.

SOLVE NOW!

Q 6.6 Are investors more risk averse for small bets or for large bets? Should "small" be defined relative to investor wealth?

Q 6.7 Are individual investors or investors in the aggregate more risk averse?

6.2 INTEREST RATES AND CREDIT RISK (DEFAULT RISK)

Most loans in the real world are not risk free, because the borrower may not fully pay back what was promised. How do you compute appropriate expected rates of return for risky bonds?

6.2A RISK-NEUTRAL INVESTORS DEMAND HIGHER PROMISED RATES

Put yourself into the position of a banker. Assume that a 1-year Treasury note offers a safe annual rate of return of 10%. Your immediate problem is that you are contemplating making a 1-year loan of $1 million to me. What interest rate should you charge me on the loan? If you are 100% certain that I will fully pay the agreed-upon amount, you can just charge me 10%. You earn just as much from me as from the Treasury note. Both will pay back $1,100,000.

If I will repay for sure, you should be okay if I promise you the same interest rate that the U.S. Treasury offers.

However, in the real world, there are few borrowers for whom you can be 100% certain that they will fully repay a loan. For example, assume you believe there is only a 50% chance that I will pay back the principal plus interest. (If I do pay it back, I will be called **solvent**). There is also a 50% chance that I will **default** (fail to pay all that I have promised). This is often informally called bankruptcy. In this case, I may only be able to pay back $750,000—all that I have got. If, as the bank, you were to charge me a 10% interest rate, your expected payout would be

If you quote me the same interest rate, you would expect to earn a lower interest rate if there is a chance of default.

$$\underset{\mathcal{P}rob(\text{Default})}{50\%} \cdot \underset{\text{Payment if Default}}{\$750{,}000} + \underset{\mathcal{P}rob(\text{Solvent})}{50\%} \cdot \underset{\text{Payment if Solvent}}{\$1{,}100{,}000} = \$925{,}000$$

Your *expected* return would not be $1,100,000, but only $925,000. Your *expected* rate of return would not be +10%, but only $925,000/$1,000,000 − 1 = −7.5%. Extending such a loan would not be—pardon the pun—in your best interest: You can do better by investing your $1,000,000 into government Treasury notes.

You should conclude that you must demand a higher interest rate from risky borrowers as a banker, even if you just want to "break even" (i.e., expect to earn the

You must ask for a higher promised interest—received only in good times—in order to make up for my default risk.

ANECDOTE A Short History of Bankruptcy

The framers of the United States Constitution had the English bankruptcy system in mind when they included the power to enact "uniform laws on the subject of bankruptcies" in Article I (powers of the legislative branch). The first United States bankruptcy law, passed in 1800, virtually copied the existing English law. United States bankruptcy laws thus have their conceptual origins in English bankruptcy law prior to 1800. On both sides of the Atlantic, however, much has changed since then.

Early English law had a distinctly pro-creditor orientation and was noteworthy for its harsh treatment of defaulting debtors. Imprisonment for debt was the order of the day, from the time of the Statute of Merchants in 1285 until Dickens's time in the mid-nineteenth century. The common law *Writs of Capias* authorized "body execution," that is, seizure of the body of the debtor, to be held until payment of the debt.

English law was not unique in its lack of solicitude for debtors. History's annals are replete with tales of harsh treatment of debtors. Punishments inflicted upon debtors included forfeiture of all property, relinquishment of the consortium of a spouse, imprisonment, and death. In Rome, creditors were apparently authorized to carve up the body of the debtor. However, scholars debate the extent to which the letter of that law was actually enforced.

Direct Source: Charles Jordan Tabb, 1995, "The History of the Bankruptcy Laws in the United States." www.bankruptcyfinder.com/historyofbkinusa.html. (The original article contains many more juicy historical tidbits.)

same \$1,100,000 that you could earn in Treasury notes). If you solve

$$\underbrace{50\%}_{Prob} \cdot \underbrace{\$750{,}000}_{\text{Payment if Default}} + \underbrace{50\%}_{Prob} \cdot \underbrace{\text{(Promised Repayment)}}_{\text{Payment if Solvent}} = \underbrace{\$1{,}100{,}000}_{\text{Treasury Payment}}$$

for the desired promised repayment, you will find that you must ask me for \$1,450,000. The promised interest rate is therefore \$1,450,000/\$1,000,000 − 1 = 45%. Of this 45%, 10% is the **time premium** that the Treasury pays. Therefore, you can call the remaining 35% the **default premium**—the difference between the promised rate and the expected rate that you, the lender, would have to demand just to break even. It is very important that you realize that the default premium is not extra compensation for your taking on more risk, say, relative to holding Treasuries. You don't receive any such extra compensation in a risk-neutral world. The default premium just fills the gap between the expected return and the promised return.

You are always quoted promised returns, and not expected returns. The risk is called "credit risk."

➤ Section 4.2, "The Internal Rate of Return (IRR)," p. 72

You rarely observe expected rates of return directly. Newspaper and financial documents almost always provide only the **promised interest rate**, which is therefore also called the **quoted interest rate** or the **stated interest rate**. When you read a published yield-to-maturity, it is also usually only a promised rate, not an expected rate—that is, the published yield is an internal rate of return that is calculated from promised payments, not from expected payments. Of course, you should never make capital budgeting decisions based on promised IRRs. You almost always want to use an expected IRR (YTM). But you usually have easy access only to the promised rate, not the expected rate. On Wall Street, the default premium is often called the **credit premium**, and **default risk** is often called **credit risk**.

SOLVE NOW!

Q 6.8 For what kind of bonds are expected interest rates and promised interest rates the same?

6.2B A MORE ELABORATE EXAMPLE WITH PROBABILITY RANGES

This distinction between expected and promised rates is so important that it is worthwhile to work another more involved example. Assume again that I ask you to lend me money. You believe that I will pay you what I promise with 98% probability; that I will repay half of what I borrowed with 1% probability; and that I will repay nothing with 1% probability. I want to borrow \$200 from you, which you could alternatively invest into a government bond promising \$210 (i.e., a 5% interest rate). What interest rate would you ask of me?

Again, I sometimes may not be able to repay.

If you ask me for a 5% interest rate, next year (time 1), your \$200 investment today (time 0) will produce the following:

If you ask me to pay the risk-free interest rate, you will on average earn less than the risk-free interest rate.

Payoff	Rate of Return	Frequency
C_1	$\tilde{r}$	$\mathcal{P}rob$
\$210	+5.0%	98% of the time
\$100	−50.0%	1% of the time
\$0	−100.0%	1% of the time

Therefore, your expected payoff is

$$\mathcal{E}(\tilde{C}_1) = 98\% \cdot \$210 + 1\% \cdot \$100 + 1\% \cdot \$0 = \$206.80$$

$$\mathcal{E}(\tilde{C}_1) = \mathcal{P}rob\ (C_1 \text{ will be Case 1}) \cdot C_1 \text{ Cash Flow in Case 1} + \mathcal{P}rob\ (C_1 \text{ will be Case 2}) \cdot C_1 \text{ Cash Flow in Case 2} + \mathcal{P}rob\ (C_1 \text{ will be Case 3}) \cdot C_1 \text{ Cash Flow in Case 3}$$

Your expected return of \$206.80 is less than the \$210 that the government promises. Put differently, if I *promise* you a rate of return of 5%,

$$\text{Promised}(\tilde{r}) = \frac{\$210 - \$200}{\$200} = 5.00\%$$

$$\text{Promised}(\tilde{r}) = \frac{\text{Promised}(\tilde{C}_1) - C_0}{C_0}$$

then your expected rate of return would only be

$$\mathcal{E}(\tilde{r}) = \frac{\$206.80 - \$200}{\$200} = 3.40\%$$

$$\mathcal{E}(\tilde{r}) = \frac{\mathcal{E}(\tilde{C}_1) - C_0}{C_0}$$

This is less than the 5% interest rate that Uncle Sam promises—and surely delivers.

Let's determine how much more interest promise you need to break even.

You need to determine how much I have to promise you just to break even. You want to expect to end up with the same \$210 that you could receive from Uncle Sam. The expected loan payoff is the probability-weighted average payoff. You want this payoff to be not \$206.80 but the \$210 that you can earn if you invest your \$200 into government bonds. You need to solve for an amount x that you receive if I have money,

$$\begin{aligned} \mathcal{E}(\tilde{C}_1) = {} & 98\% \cdot x \\ + {} & 1\% \cdot \$100 \\ + {} & 1\% \cdot \$0 = \$210.00 \end{aligned}$$

$$\begin{aligned} \mathcal{E}(\tilde{C}_1) = {} & \mathcal{P}rob\ (C_1 \text{ will be Case 1}) \cdot C_1 \text{ Cash Flow in Case 1} \\ & + \mathcal{P}rob\ (C_1 \text{ will be Case 2}) \cdot C_1 \text{ Cash Flow in Case 2} \\ & + \mathcal{P}rob\ (C_1 \text{ will be Case 3}) \cdot C_1 \text{ Cash Flow in Case 3} \end{aligned}$$

The solution is that if I promise you $x \approx \$213.27$, you will expect to earn the same 5% interest rate that you can earn in Treasury notes. This \$213.27 for a cash investment of \$200 is a *promised* interest rate of

$$\text{Promised}(\tilde{r}) \approx \frac{\$213.27 - \$200}{\$200} \approx 6.64\%$$

$$\text{Promised}(\tilde{r}) = \frac{\text{Promised}(\tilde{C}_1) - C_0}{C_0}$$

Such a promise provides the following:

Payoff C_1	Rate of Return $\tilde{r}$	Frequency $\mathcal{P}rob$
\$213.27	+6.64%	98% of the time
\$100.00	−50.00%	1% of the time
\$0.00	−100.00%	1% of the time

This comes to an *expected* interest rate of

$$\mathcal{E}(\tilde{r}) \approx 98\% \cdot (+6.64\%) + 1\% \cdot (-50\%) + 1\% \cdot (-100\%) \approx 5\%$$

SOLVE NOW!

Q 6.9 Recompute the example from the text, but assume now that the probability of receiving full payment in 1 year on a \$200 investment of \$210 is only 95%, the probability of receiving \$100 is 1%, and the probability of receiving absolutely no payment is 4%.

(a) At the promised interest rate of 5%, what is the expected interest rate?

(b) What interest rate is required as a promise to ensure an expected interest rate of 5%?

6.2C DECONSTRUCTING QUOTED RATES OF RETURN—TIME AND DEFAULT PREMIUMS

The difference of 1.63% between the promised (or quoted) interest rate of 6.63% and the expected interest rate of 5% is the default premium—it is the extra interest rate that is caused by the default risk. Of course, you only receive this 6.63% *if* everything goes perfectly. In our perfect market with risk-neutral investors,

The difference between the promised and expected interest rate in a risk-neutral perfect world is the default premium.

$$\begin{array}{ccccc} 6.63\% & = & 5\% & + & 1.63\% \\ \text{"Promised Interest Rate"} & = & \text{"Time Premium"} & + & \text{"Default Premium"} \end{array}$$

IMPORTANT: Except for 100%-safe bonds (Treasuries), the promised (or quoted) rate of return is higher than the expected rate of return. Never confuse the promised rate with the (lower) expected rate.

Financial securities and information providers rarely, if ever, provide expected rates of return. They almost always provide only quoted rates of return.

On average, the expected rate of return is the expected time premium plus the expected default premium. Because the *expected* default premium is zero *on average*,

In a perfect risk-neutral world, all securities have the same expected rate of return.

$$\begin{aligned} \mathcal{E}(\text{Rate of Return}) &= \mathcal{E}(\text{Time Premium}) + 0 \\ &= \mathcal{E}(\text{Time Premium}) + \mathcal{E}(\text{Realized Default Premium}) \end{aligned}$$

If you want to work this out, you can compute the expected realized default premium as follows: You will receive $6.63\% - 5\% = 1.63\%$ in 98% of all cases; $-50\% - 5\% = -55\%$ in 1% of all cases (note that you lose the time premium); and $-100\% - 5\% = -105\%$ in the remaining 1% of all cases (i.e., you lose not only all your money, but also the time premium). Therefore,

$$\begin{aligned} \mathcal{E}(\text{Realized Default Premium}) &\approx 98\% \cdot (+1.63\%) + 1\% \cdot (-55\%) \\ &\quad + 1\% \cdot (-105\%) \approx 0\% \end{aligned}$$

In addition to the 5% time premium and the 1.63% default premium, in the real world, there are also other premiums:

Warning: Additional premiums will follow later.

Risk premiums that compensate you with higher expected rates of return for your willingness to take on risk. They will be the subject of Chapter 9.

Imperfect market premiums (e.g., liquidity premiums) that compensate you for future difficulties in finding buyers for your bonds. They will be the subject of Chapter 10.

These premiums are typically much lower than time premiums and default premiums in a bond context (though they are not unimportant).

SOLVE NOW!

Q 6.10 Is the expected default premium positive?

TABLE 6.1 RATING CATEGORIES USED BY MOODY'S AND STANDARD & POOR'S

Investment Grade	Moody's	Standard & Poor's
Exceptional	Aaa, Aaa1, Aaa2, Aaa3	AAA, AAA-, AA+
Excellent	Aa, Aa1, Aa2, Aa3	AA, AA-, A+
Good	A, A1, A2, A3	A, A-, BBB+
Adequate	Baa, Baa1, Baa2, Baa3	BBB, BBB-
Speculative Grade ("Junk")	**Moody's**	**Standard & Poor's**
Questionable	Ba, Ba1, Ba2, Ba3	BB+, BB, BB-, B+
Poor	B, B1, B2, B3	B, B-, CCC+
Very Poor	Caa, Caa1, Caa2, Caa3	CCC, CCC-, CC+
Extremely Poor	Ca, Ca1, Ca2, Ca3	CC,CC-, C+
Lowest (Often Defaulted)	C	C

6.2D CREDIT RATINGS AND DEFAULT RATES

Bond rating agencies: The most important are Moody's and Standard & Poor's.

To make it easier for lenders to judge the probability of default, a number of data vendors for credit ratings have appeared. For individuals, Experian and Dun & Bradstreet provide credit ratings—you should request one for yourself if you have never seen one. For corporations, the two biggest credit rating agencies are **Moody's** and **Standard & Poor's (S&P)**. (There are also others, like *Duff and Phelps* and *Fitch*.) For a fee, these agencies rate the probability that the issuer's bonds will default. This fee depends on a number of factors, such as the identity of the issuer, the desired detail in the agencies' investigations and descriptions, and the features of the bond (e.g., a bond that will pay off within 1 year is usually less likely to default before maturity than a bond that will pay off in 30 years; thus, the former is easier to grade).

The most important grade distinction is "junk" versus "investment grade."

The credit rating agencies ultimately do not provide a whole set of default probabilities (e.g., 1% chance of 100% loss, 1.2% chance of 99% loss, etc.), but just an overall rating grade. Table 6.1 shows the categories for Moody's and Standard & Poor's. It is then up to the lender to translate the rating into an appropriate compensation for default risk. The top rating grades are called **investment grade**, while the bottom grades are called **speculative grade** (or **junk grade**).

EMPIRICAL EVIDENCE ON DEFAULT

Here are historical probabilities of bond defaults by credit ratings.

Ed Altman (from New York University) collected corporate bond statistics from 1971 to 2003. Figure 6.2 gives a sketch of how likely default (defined as missing at least one coupon payment) was for a given credit rating:

High-quality borrowers: Very few investment-grade bonds default—and especially right after issue when they still carry the original credit rating. The probability of default is less than 3% in total over a 10-year horizon (0.3% per annum).

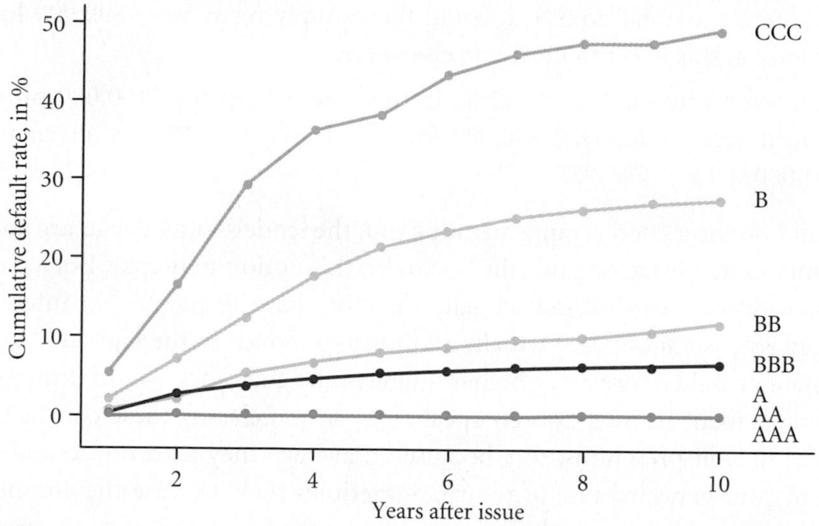

This figure shows the probability of default within *x* years after issue. For example, at some point during the first 7 years of their issue, 25% of all bonds originally issued as B (poor) had not delivered on at least one promised bond payment.

Source: Edward Altman and Gonzalo Fanjul, New York University, February 2004. Moody's also offers similar reports and publishes an interesting monthly report on credit risk, including corporate bond default forecasts (which change with the business cycle).

FIGURE 6.2 Cumulative Probability of Default by Original Rating

Low-quality borrowers: In an average year, about 3.5% to 5.5% of speculative-grade corporate bonds defaulted. But the default rate was time-varying. In recessions, the default rate was 10% per year; in booms, only 1.5% per year.

To estimate the expected loss, you need not only the probability of default, but also how much you receive in case of default. You cannot see it in the figure, but it turns out that an AAA or AA bond price was worth about 75 cents on the dollar upon default; an A bond price was worth about 50 cents on the dollar. In contrast, speculative-grade bonds returned much less in case of default. Their average value after default was only about 30–40 cents on the dollar, and it was again lower in recessions (25 cents) than in booms (50 cents).

The average amount of loss in case of default.

BOND CONTRACT OPTION FEATURES

Before I show you how bonds are priced, I need to let you know that bonds in the real world differ from one another not just in credit risk. Most bonds have additional contract features that may also influence their quoted rates of return. For example, many corporate bonds allow the issuer to repay the loan early. (The same applies to almost all domestic mortgages.) If the interest rates in the future fall, this can be a good thing for the borrower and a bad thing for the lender. The borrower would pay off the loan and borrow more cheaply elsewhere. If the interest rates in the future rise, the borrower gets to pay just the earlier low interest rate. For example, assume that the interest rate is 10% today and you are lending me $90,909 in exchange for my promise to pay you $100,000 next year. One second after you extend the loan, one of two scenarios can happen:

Before I show you real-world quoted returns, I must explain that they can contain contract premiums.

1. The interest may fall to 5%. I would then simply repay your \$90,909 loan and refinance at this lower interest rate elsewhere.
2. The interest rate may rise to 15%. In this case, I keep my \$100,000 promise to pay next year—I received \$90,909 for a loan that should have given me only $\$100,000/1.15 \approx \$86,957$.

This would not be a good arrangement for you, the lender—unless you are appropriately compensated for giving me, the borrower, this option to prepay. Borrowers who want the right to repay without penalty therefore have to pay higher interest rates when they issue such bonds. Virtually all mortgage bonds in the United States allow prepayment and therefore carry higher interest rates than they would if they did not have a prepayment feature. Loosely speaking, you can classify these contract option features as default premiums, too, because on average they tend not to add or subtract from your expected rate of return. Sometimes they increase the amount paid, and sometimes they decrease the amount paid by the lender—just as a solvent bond would pay more to the lender and an insolvent bond would pay less to the lender.

SOLVE NOW!

Q 6.11 Does the historical evidence show that lower-grade borrowers default more often or that they pay less upon default?

6.2E DIFFERENCES IN QUOTED BOND RETURNS IN 2002

Historical rates of return: Riskier bonds indeed have higher stated rates of return.

So how do real-world bond credit ratings translate into differences in promised (quoted) bond yields? Table 6.2 lists the borrowing rates of various issuers in May 2002. (Many other current interest rates can be found at www.bloomberg.com and bonds.yahoo.com.) The data look broadly consistent with our theory—bonds that have higher default risk have to offer higher promised rates of return. Bonds with higher (better) credit ratings can find lenders at lower interest rates (higher bond prices).

Expected rates of return were more similar to one another than Table 6.2 suggests.

Do lenders to creditors with higher risk end up with about the same average rate of return as lenders to creditors with lower risk? This would be the case in a perfect market in which lenders and borrowers are risk neutral. The evidence suggests that this is not exactly true, but it is also not too far from reality. The overwhelming majority of the relative spreads above the Treasury simply make the lender come out even. If I had to guess, I would say that of the 100-basis-point difference between medium- and high-quality long-term bonds in Table 6.2, about 80 basis points are due to credit risk; about 10 basis points are due to a mismatch between the maturity of the corporate bonds and the quoted interest rate off the yield curve or due to contract features; and about 10 basis points are extra compensation that creditors of low-quality corporations earn relative to creditors of high-quality corporations. Thus, my guess is that about 90% of the difference in stated bond yields is not premia that allow creditors to earn a higher expected rate of return for taking on riskier and more obscure bonds.

TABLE 6.2 PROMISED INTEREST RATES FOR SOME LOANS IN MAY 2002

Security (Bond)	Rating	Quoted Yield	Similar U.S. Treasury	Approximate Difference
FNMA May 2003	AAA	2.36%	2.22%	10bp
FNMA March 2031	AAA	6.29%	5.60%	70bp
United Airlines 11.21s14	B+	14.40%	4.82%	1,000bp
Boston Celtics 6s38	NR	9.40%	5.60%	400bp
Corporate High-Quality 1–10 years	AAA-AA (AAA-A+)	4.89%	≈ 3%–4%	100bp
Corporate Medium-Quality 1–10 years	A-BBB (A-Baa)	6.24%	≈ 3%–4%	250bp
Corporate High-Quality 10+ years	AAA-AA (AAA-A+)	6.76%	≈ 4%–5%	200bp
Corporate Medium-Quality 10+ years	A-BBB (A-Baa)	7.65%	≈ 4%–5%	300bp
High-Yield (Junk Bond) Corporates	BB- (Ba-)	11.36%	?	?

Source: Wall Street Journal, page C13. FNMA (page 1399) is a quasi-governmental agency that underwrites home mortgages. United was downgraded to B in June, CCC in August, CCC- in November, and defaulted in December. All yields are reported in annualized form.

6.2F CREDIT DEFAULT SWAPS

A large new market: credit default swaps.

The financial world is always changing and innovating. The components of bond returns described above used to be primarily a conceptual curiosity—firms would borrow money from their lenders, paying one interest rate that just contained all premiums. But then, with the introduction of **credit default swaps** (often abbreviated **credit swaps** or **CDS**), some premium components suddenly became themselves tradeable.

A CDS example: The swap seller insures the swap buyer.

Here is an example of a CDS: A large pension fund that holds a $15 million bond issued by HCA Inc. may decide to purchase a $10 million credit swap from a hedge fund that wants to bet that HCA will not go bankrupt. (The *Wall Street Journal* reported that this CDS contract cost about $130,000 in June 2006, but rose to over $400,000 in July because of a potential buyout deal that would increase the risk of future default.) If HCA goes bankrupt, the hedge fund owes the pension fund $10 million. In this case, purchasing the CDS in June was a lucky deal for the pension fund and an unlucky deal for the hedge fund—HCA indeed went bankrupt. The best way to think of such credit swaps is as an insurance contract, in which the swap seller (the hedge fund) is the insurance provider. The buyer of the credit swap pays the seller an upfront premium in exchange for a payment if a credit event (e.g., a failed payment or bankruptcy) occurs for a particular bond within a given number of years. The payment itself can be formula-determined, or it can be a guarantee by the CDS seller to buy the bond at a predetermined price. Another way of thinking of the upfront cost (the $130,000 that increased to $400,000) is as the default premium.

In effect, credit swaps allow investors to hold different premium components.

Credit swaps allow different funds to hold different premiums of a bond. In our example, the pension fund decided to earn primarily the time premium component of HCA's bonds, divesting itself of the credit risk and other components. The hedge fund took over the credit premium. It decided to speculate that HCA would not go bankrupt, and it could do so without having to take a large cash position in HCA's bonds.

The CDS market size is huge, and can shift risk into opaque corners.

➤ Over-the-counter, Section 7.2B, p. 193

Credit swaps are typically traded in lots of $5 million and last for 5 years (but 3 to 10 years is not unusual, either). This market is **over-the-counter (OTC)**—that is, negotiated one-to-one between two parties. This market is also very big: In 1997, there were "only" about $180 billion of credit swaps outstanding, but as of 2006, there were more than $17 trillion! No one knows for sure anymore who is really holding most of the credit risk in the economy nowadays. (Here is an example: In 2007, to the surprise of everyone, the German bank IKB collapsed because it held too many financial securities that were tied to U.S. mortgages.)

6.3 UNCERTAINTY IN CAPITAL BUDGETING

Next you learn about payoff diagrams, to characterize the main future contingencies.

Let's now return to the basic tasks of capital budgeting: selecting projects under uncertainty. Your task is to compute present values with imperfect knowledge about future outcomes. The principal tool in this task will be the **payoff table** (or **state table**), which assigns probabilities to the project value in each possible future value-relevant scenario. For example, a hard disk factory may depend on computer sales (say, low, medium, or high), whether hard disks have become obsolete (yes or no), whether the economy is in a recession or expansion, and what the oil price (a major transportation cost factor) turns out to be. It is the manager's task to create the appropriate "state" table, which specifies what variables and scenarios are most value-relevant and how the business will perform in each of them. Clearly, it is not an easy task even to understand what the key factors are, much less to determine the probabilities under which these factors will take on one or another value. Assessing how your own project will respond to them is an even harder task—but it is an inevitable one. If you want to understand the value of your project, you must understand what your project's key value drivers are and how your project will respond to these value drivers. Fortunately, for many projects, it is usually not necessary to describe all possible outcomes in the most minute detail—just a dozen or so scenarios are often enough to cover the most important possibilities.

6.3A PRESENT VALUE WITH STATE-CONTINGENT PAYOFF TABLES

Our example of this section: A building in Tornado Alley can end up with one of two possible future values.

We begin with the hypothetical purchase of a building for which the future value is uncertain. This building is peculiar, though: It lasts only until next year (time 1), and you must determine its value today (time 0). It has a 20% chance that it will be destroyed next year, say, by a tornado. In this case, its only value will be the land—say, $20,000. Otherwise, with 80% probability, the building will be worth $100,000. Naturally, the $100,000 market value next year would itself be the result of many factors—it could include any products that have been produced inside the building and any real-estate value appreciation, as well as a capitalized value that takes into account that a tornado might strike in subsequent years.

THE BUILDING'S EXPECTED VALUE

If you own the full building, your payoff table is as follows:

Event	Probability	Value
Tornado	20%	\$20,000
Sunshine	80%	\$100,000
⟹ Expected Future Value		\$84,000

The expected future building value of \$84,000 was computed as

To obtain the expected future cash value of the building, multiply each possible outcome by its probability.

$$\begin{aligned}\mathcal{E}(\text{Value at Time 1}) &= 20\% \cdot \$20{,}000 \\ &+ 80\% \cdot \$100{,}000 = \$84{,}000 \\ &= \mathcal{Prob}(\text{Tornado}) \cdot (\text{Value if Tornado Occurs}) \\ &+ \mathcal{Prob}(\text{Sunshine}) \cdot (\text{Value if Sunshine Occurs})\end{aligned}$$

Now, assume that the appropriate expected rate of return for a project of type "building" with this type of riskiness and with 1-year maturity is 10%. (This 10% discount rate is provided by demand and supply in the financial markets, and it is assumed to be known by you, the manager.) Your goal is to determine the present value—the appropriate price—for the building *today*.

Then discount back the expected cash value using the appropriate cost of capital.

There are two methods to arrive at the present value of the building—and they are almost identical to what you have done earlier. You only need to replace the known value with the expected value, and the known future rate of return with an expected rate of return. The first PV method is to compute the expected value of the building next period and to discount it at the cost of capital, here 10%:

Under uncertainty, you can use the net present value formula with expected (rather than actual, known) cash flows and with appropriate expected (rather than actual, known) rates of return.

$$\begin{aligned}\text{PV} &= \frac{\$84{,}000}{1 + 10\%} \approx \$76{,}363.64 \\ &= \frac{\mathcal{E}(\text{Value at Time 1})}{1 + \mathcal{E}(\tilde{r})}\end{aligned}$$

The second method is to compute the discounted state-contingent value of the building, and then take expected values. To do this, augment the earlier table:

Taking expectations and discounting can be done in any order.

Event	Probability	Value	Discount Factor	⇒	PV
Tornado	20%	\$20,000	1/1.10	⇒	\$18,181.82
Sunshine	80%	\$100,000	1/1.10	⇒	\$90,909.09

If the tornado strikes, the present value is \$18,181.82. *If* the sun shines, the present value is \$90,909.09. Thus, the expected value of the building can also be computed as

$$\begin{aligned}\text{PV} &\approx 20\% \cdot \$18{,}181.82 \\ &+ 80\% \cdot \$90{,}909.09 \approx \$76{,}363.64 \\ &= \mathcal{Prob}(\text{Tornado}) \cdot (\text{PV of Building if Tornado}) \\ &+ \mathcal{Prob}(\text{Sunshine}) \cdot (\text{PV of Building if Sunshine})\end{aligned}$$

Both methods lead to the same result: You can either first compute the expected value next year (20% · \$20,000 + 80% · \$100,000 = \$84,000) and then discount this expected value of \$84,000 to \$76,363.64, or you can first discount all possible future outcomes (\$20,000 to \$18,181.82, and \$100,000 to \$90,909.09) and then compute the expected value of the discounted values (20% · \$18,181.82 + 80% · \$90,909.09 ≈ \$76,363.64.)

IMPORTANT: Under uncertainty, in the NPV formula,

- known future cash flows are replaced by expected discounted cash flows, and
- known appropriate rates of return are replaced by appropriate expected rates of return.

You can first do the discounting and then take expectations, or vice versa. The order does not matter.

The State-Dependent Rates of Return

The state-contingent *rates* of return can also be probability-weighted to arrive at the average (expected) *rate* of return.

What would the rates of return be in the two states, and what would your overall expected rate of return be? If you have bought the building for \$76,363.64 and no tornado strikes, your actual rate of return will be

$$\text{If Sunshine:} \qquad r \approx \frac{\$100{,}000 - \$76{,}363.64}{\$76{,}363.64} \approx +30.95\%$$

If the tornado does strike, your rate of return will be

$$\text{If Tornado:} \qquad r \approx \frac{\$20{,}000 - \$76{,}363.64}{\$76{,}363.64} \approx -73.81\%$$

Therefore, your expected rate of return is

$$\mathcal{E}(\tilde{r}) \approx \quad 20\% \quad \cdot \quad (-73.81\%) \quad + \quad 80\% \quad \cdot \quad (+30.95\%) \quad \approx 10.00\%$$

$$\mathcal{E}(\tilde{r}) = \mathcal{P}rob(\text{Tornado}) \cdot (r \text{ if Tornado}) + \mathcal{P}rob(\text{Sunshine}) \cdot (r \text{ if Sunshine})$$

The probability state-weighted rates of return add up to the expected overall rate of return. This is as it should be: After all, you derived the proper price of the building today using a 10% expected rate of return.

SOLVE NOW!

Q 6.12 What changes have to be made to the NPV formula to handle an uncertain future?

Q 6.13 A factory can be worth \$500,000 or \$1,000,000 in 2 years, depending on product demand, each with equal probability. The appropriate cost of capital is 6% per year. What is the present value of the factory?

Q 6.14 A new product may be a dud (20% probability), an average seller (70% probability), or dynamite (10% probability). If it is a dud, the payoff will be $20,000; if it is an average seller, the payoff will be $40,000; and if it is dynamite, the payoff will be $80,000.

(a) What is the expected payoff of the project?

(b) The appropriate expected rate of return for such payoffs is 8%. What is the PV of the payoff?

(c) If the project is purchased for the appropriate present value, what will be the rates of return in each of the three outcomes?

(d) Confirm the expected rate of return when computed from the individual outcome-specific rates of return.

6.4 SPLITTING UNCERTAIN PROJECT PAYOFFS INTO DEBT AND EQUITY

Most projects are financed with a mix of debt and equity.

The most important reason for you to learn about state payoff tables is that they will help you understand cash flow rights. This leads to one of the most important concepts in finance: the difference between a **loan** (also called **debt**) and **levered ownership** (also called **levered equity**). Almost all companies and projects are financed with both debt and levered equity. You already know in principle what debt is. Levered equity is simply what accrues to the business owner *after* the debt is paid off. We leave it to later chapters to make a distinction between financial debt and other obligations—for example, tax obligations—and to cover the control rights that flow from securities—for example, how debt can force borrowers to pay up and how equity can replace poorly performing managers.

Other projects are financed the same way.

You probably already have an intuitive understanding about the distinction between debt and equity. If you own a house with a mortgage, you really own the house only after you have made all debt payments. If you have student loans, you *yourself* are the levered owner of your future income stream. That is, you get to consume "your" residual income only *after* your liabilities (including your nonfinancial debt) are paid back. But what will the levered owner and the lender get if the company's projects fail, if the house collapses, or if your career takes a turn toward the prison on Rikers Island? What is the appropriate compensation for the lender and the levered owner? The split of net present value streams into loans (debt) and levered equity lies at the heart of finance.

State-contingent claims have payoffs that depend on future states of nature.

You now know how to compute the present value of state-contingent payoffs—your building paid off differently in the two states of nature. Thus, your building was a state-contingent claim—its payoff depended on the outcome. But it is just one of many possible state-contingent claims. Another might promise to pay $1 if the sun shines and $25 if a tornado strikes. Using payoff tables, you can work out the value of *any* state-contingent claim and, in particular, the value of our two most important state-contingent claims, debt and equity.

6.4A THE LOAN

Assume the building is funded by a mortgagor and a residual, levered building owner.

Let's assume you want to finance the building purchase of $76,363.64 with a mortgage of $25,000. In effect, the single project "building" is being turned into two different projects, each of which can be owned by a different party. The first project is the

ANECDOTE Limited Liability

Limited liability was invented after the Renaissance, but it only became common in the nineteenth and twentieth centuries. Ultimately, it is this legal construction that allowed corporations to evolve into entities distinct from their owners. Thus, in 1911, the President of Columbia University wrote: "The limited liability corporation is the greatest single discovery of modern times. . . . Even steam and electricity are less important."

project "Mortgage Lending." The second project is the project "Residual Building Ownership," that is, ownership of the building but bundled with the obligation to repay the mortgage. This "Residual Building Ownership" investor will not receive a dime until *after* the debt has been satisfied. Such residual ownership is called **levered equity**, or just **equity** (or even **stock**) in the building, in order to avoid calling it "what's-left-over-after-the-loans-have-been-paid-off."

The first goal is to determine the appropriate promised interest rate on a "$25,000 value today" mortgage loan on the building.

What sort of interest rate would the creditor demand? To answer this question, you need to know what will happen if the building were to be condemned, because the mortgage value ($25,000 today) will be larger than the value of the building if the tornado strikes ($20,000 next year). We are assuming that the owner could walk away from it, and the creditor could repossess the building but not any of the borrower's other assets. Such a mortgage loan is called a **no-recourse loan**. There is no recourse other than taking possession of the asset itself. This arrangement is called **limited liability**. The building owner cannot lose more than the money that he originally puts in. Limited liability is the mainstay of many financial securities: For example, if you purchase stock in a company in the stock market, you cannot be held liable for more than your investment, regardless of how badly the company performs. (For home mortgages, some U.S. states do not limit the owner's liability; others do.)

Assume limited liability (true only in some U.S. states).

Start with the payoff table, and write down payoffs to project "Mortgage Lending."

➤ Section 6.2, "Interest Rates and Credit Risk(Default Risk)," p. 143

To compute the present value for the project "Mortgage Lending," return to the problem of setting an appropriate interest rate, given credit risk (from Section 6.2). Start with the following payoff table:

Event	*Prob*	Value	Discount Factor
Tornado	20%	$20,000	1/1.10
Sunshine	80%	Promised	1/1.10

The creditor receives the property worth $20,000 if the tornado strikes, or the full promised amount (to be determined) if the sun shines. To break even, the creditor must solve for the payoff to be received if the sun shines in exchange for lending $25,000 today. This is the "quoted" or "promised" payoff:

$$\$25{,}000 = 20\% \cdot \left(\frac{\$20{,}000}{1+10\%}\right) + 80\% \cdot \left(\frac{\text{Promise}}{1+10\%}\right)$$

$$\text{Loan Value at Time 0} = \mathcal{P}rob(\text{Tornado}) \cdot (\text{Loan PV if Tornado}) + \mathcal{P}rob(\text{Sunshine}) \cdot (\text{Loan PV if Sunshine})$$

You can solve this equation for the necessary promise, which is

$$\text{Promise} = \frac{(1+10\%)\cdot \$25{,}000 - 20\% \cdot \$20{,}000}{80\%} = \$29{,}375$$

$$= \frac{[1+\mathcal{E}(\tilde{r})]\cdot \text{Loan Value at Time 0} - \mathcal{P}rob(\text{Tornado}) \cdot \text{Value if Tornado}}{\mathcal{P}rob(\text{Sunshine})}$$

in repayment, paid by the borrower only if the sun shines.

With this promised payoff of $29,375 (if the sun shines), the lender's rate of return will be the **promised rate of return**:

The state-contingent rates of return in the tornado ("default") state and in the sunshine ("solvent") state can be probability-weighted to arrive at the expected rate of return.

$$\text{If Sunshine:} \quad r = \frac{\$29{,}375 - \$25{,}000}{\$25{,}000} = +17.50\%$$

The lender would not provide the mortgage at any lower promised interest rate. If the tornado strikes, the owner walks away, and the lender's rate of return will be

$$\text{If Tornado:} \quad r = \frac{\$20{,}000 - \$25{,}000}{\$25{,}000} = -20.00\%$$

Therefore, the lender's *expected* rate of return is

$$\mathcal{E}(\tilde{r}) = 20\% \cdot (-20.00\%) + 80\% \cdot (+17.50\%) = 10.00\%$$

$$\mathcal{E}(\tilde{r}) = \mathcal{P}rob(\text{Tornado}) \cdot (r \text{ if Tornado}) + \mathcal{P}rob(\text{Sunshine}) \cdot (r \text{ if Sunshine})$$

The stated rate of return is 17.5%; the expected rate of return is 10%. After all, in our risk-neutral perfect market, anyone investing for 1 year expects to earn an expected rate of return of 10%.

6.4B THE LEVERED EQUITY

Now compute the payoffs of the post-mortgage (i.e., levered) ownership of the building. The method is exactly the same.

As the residual building owner, what rate of return would you expect as proper compensation? You already know the building is worth $76,363.64 today. Thus, after the loan of $25,000, you need to pay in $51,363.64—presumably from your personal savings. Of course, you must compensate your lender: To contribute the $25,000 to the building purchase today, you must promise to pay the lender $29,375 next year. If the tornado strikes, the lender will confiscate your house, and all your invested personal savings will be lost. However, if the sun shines, the building will be worth $100,000 minus the promised $29,375, or $70,625. Your payoff table as the levered equity building owner is as follows:

Event	*Prob*	Value	Discount Factor
Tornado	20%	$0	1/1.10
Sunshine	80%	$70,625	1/1.10

It allows you to determine that the *expected* future levered building ownership payoff is $20\% \cdot \$0 + 80\% \cdot \$70{,}625 = \$56{,}500$. Therefore, the present value of levered building ownership is

$$\text{PV} = 20\% \cdot \left(\frac{\$0}{1+10\%}\right) + 80\% \cdot \left(\frac{\$70{,}625}{1+10\%}\right) \approx \$51{,}363.64$$

$$= \mathcal{P}rob(\text{Tornado}) \cdot (\text{PV if Tornado}) + \mathcal{P}rob(\text{Sunshine}) \cdot (\text{PV if Sunshine})$$

Again, knowing the state-contingent cash flows permits computation of state-contingent rates of return and the expected rate of return.

If the sun shines, your rate of return will be

$$\text{If Sunshine:} \quad r \approx \frac{\$70{,}625 - \$51{,}363.64}{\$51{,}363.64} \approx +37.50\%$$

If the tornado strikes, your rate of return will be

$$\text{If Tornado:} \quad r \approx \frac{\$0 - \$51{,}363.64}{\$51{,}363.64} = -100.00\%$$

The expected rate of return of levered equity ownership, that is, the building with the bundled mortgage obligation, is

$$\mathcal{E}(\tilde{r}) = 20\% \cdot (-100.00\%) + 80\% \cdot (+37.50\%) = 10.00\%$$

$$\mathcal{E}(\tilde{r}) = \mathcal{P}rob(\text{Tornado}) \cdot (r \text{ if Tornado}) + \mathcal{P}rob(\text{Sunshine}) \cdot (r \text{ if Sunshine})$$

6.4C REFLECTIONS ON THE EXAMPLE: PAYOFF TABLES

Payoff tables are fundamental tools to help you think about projects and financial claims. Admittedly, they can sometimes be tedious, especially if there are many different possible states. (There may even be infinitely many states, as in a bell-shaped, normally-distributed project outcome—but you can usually approximate even the most continuous and complex outcomes fairly well with no more than 10 discrete possible outcomes.)

There are three possible investment opportunities here. The bank is just another investor, with particular payoff patterns.

Table 6.3 shows how elegant such a table can be. It describes everything you need in a very concise manner: the state-contingent payoffs, expected payoffs, net present value, and expected rates of return for your house scenario. Because owning the mortgage and the levered equity is the same as owning the full building, the last two columns must add up to the values in the "Building Value" column. You could decide to be any kind of investor: a creditor (bank) who is loaning money in exchange for promised payment; a levered building owner who is taking a "piece left over after a loan"; or an unlevered building owner who is investing money into an unlevered project (i.e., taking the whole piece). All three investments are just state-contingent claims.

IMPORTANT: Whenever possible, in the presence of uncertainty, write down a payoff table to describe the probabilities of each possible event ("state") with its state-contingent payoff.

SOLVE NOW!

Q 6.15 In the example, the building was worth \$76,364, the mortgage was worth \$25,000, and the equity was worth \$51,364. The mortgage thus

TABLE 6.3 PAYOFF TABLE AND OVERALL VALUES AND RETURNS

Event	*Prob*	Building Value	Mortgage Value	Levered Ownership
Tornado	20%	$20,000	$20,000	$0
Sunshine	80%	$100,000	$29,375	$70,625
Expected Value at Time 1		$84,000	$27,500	$56,500
Present Value at Time 0		$76,364	$25,000	$51,364
From Time 0 to Time 1, $\mathcal{E}(\tilde{r})$		10%	10%	10%

In this example, the project is financed with $25,000 in mortgage promising $29,375 in payment.

financed 32.74% of the cost of the building, and the equity financed $67.26%. Is the arrangement identical to one in which two partners purchase the building together—one puts in $25,000 and owns 32.74%, and the other puts in $51,364 and owns 67.26%?

Q 6.16 Buildings are frequently financed with a mortgage that pays 80% of the price, not just 32.7% ($25,000 of $76,364). Produce a table similar to Table 6.3 for this case.

Q 6.17 ADVANCED: For illustration, we assumed that the sample building was not occupied. It consisted purely of capital amounts. But in the real world, part of the return earned by a building owner is rent. Now assume that rent of $11,000 is paid strictly at year-end and that both the state of nature (tornado or sun) and the mortgage loan payment happen only after the rent has been safely collected. The new building has a resale value of $120,000 if the sun shines, and a resale value of $20,000 if the tornado strikes. Again, assume a 10% discount rate.

(a) What is the value of the building today?
(b) What is the promised interest rate for a lender providing $25,000 in capital today?
(c) What is the value of residual ownership today?
(d) Conceptual question: What is the value of the building if the owner chooses to live in the building?

6.4D REFLECTIONS ON THE EXAMPLE: DEBT AND EQUITY RISK

We have only briefly mentioned risk. It was just not necessary to illustrate the main insights. In a risk-neutral world, all that matters is the expected rate of return, not the uncertainty about what you will receive. Of course, you can assess the risk even in our risk-neutral world where risk earns no extra compensation (a risk premium). So, which investment is most risky: full ownership, loan ownership, or levered ownership?

Evaluate the risk of the three types of projects, even if riskier projects do not earn higher expected rates of return.

Figure 6.3 plots the histograms of the rates of return for each of the three types of investments. For example, the equity loses everything with a 20% probability and earns 37.5% with 80% probability. As the visuals show, the loan is least risky, followed by the full ownership, followed by the levered ownership. There is an interesting intuition here. By taking the mortgage, the medium-risk project "building" has been split

Leveraging (mortgaging) a project splits it into a safer loan and a riskier levered ownership.

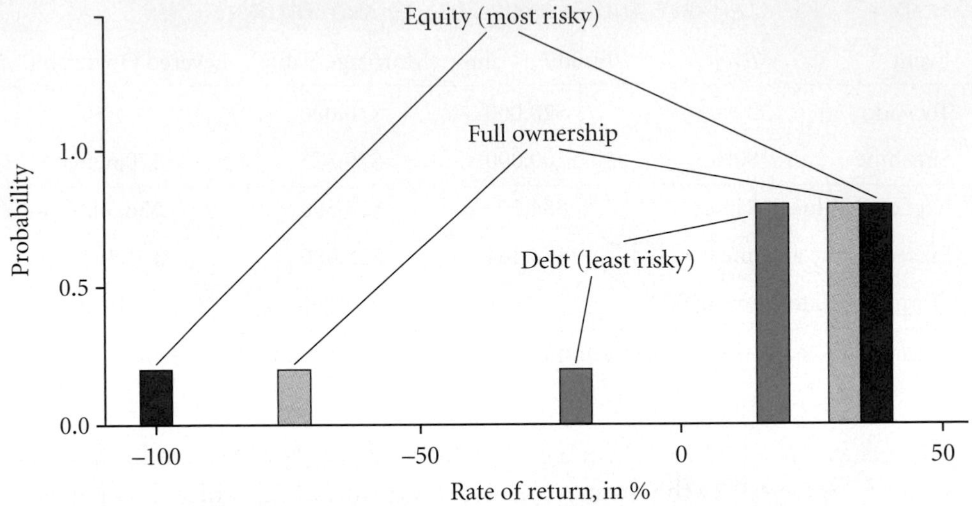

This figure graphs the two possible rates of return in the building example from Table 6.3. Note how equity payoffs are more spread out (risky) than full ownership payoffs, which in turn are more spread out than debt.

FIGURE 6.3 Three Probability Histograms for Project Rates of Return

into one more risky project "levered building" and one less risky project "mortgage." The combined "full building ownership" project therefore has an average risk.

If everyone is risk neutral, everyone should expect to earn 10%.

Of course, regardless of leverage, all investment projects in our risk-neutral world expect to earn a 10% rate of return. After all, 10% is the universal time premium here for investing money. (The default premium is a component only of promised interest rates, not of expected interest rates; see Section 6.2C). By assuming that investors are risk neutral, we have assumed that the risk premium is zero. Investors are willing to take any investment that offers an expected rate of return of 10%, regardless of risk. (If investors were risk averse, debt would offer a lower expected rate of return than the project, which would offer a lower expected rate of return than equity.)

➤ Section 6.2C, "Deconstructing Quoted Rates of Return—Time and Default Premiums," p. 147

Unrealistic, maybe! But ultimately, this is the basis for more realistic examples, and illustrative of the most important concepts.

Although our example has been a little sterile because we assumed away risk preferences, it is nevertheless very useful. Almost all projects in the real world are financed with loans extended by one party and levered ownership held by another party. Understanding debt and equity is as important to corporations as it is to building owners. After all, stocks in corporations are basically levered ownership claims that provide money only *after* the corporation has paid back its liabilities. The building example has given you the skills to compute state-contingent, promised, and expected payoffs, as well as state-contingent, promised, and expected rates of return. These are the necessary tools to work with debt, equity, or any other state-contingent claim. And really, all that will happen later when we introduce risk aversion is that you will add a few extra basis points of required compensation—more to equity (the riskiest claim), fewer to the project (the medium-risk claim), and still fewer to debt (the safest claim).

SOLVE NOW!

Q 6.18 Assume now that the loan does not *provide* \$25,000, but rather *promises* to pay off \$25,000.

(a) Repeat the table in the text that summarizes all the information.
(b) How much money do you get for this promise?
(c) What is the promised rate of return?
(d) How does the riskiness of the project "Full Building Ownership" compare to the riskiness of the project "Levered Building Ownership"?

Q 6.19 Repeat the example if the loan promises to pay off $20,000. Such a loan is risk free. How does the riskiness of the project "Full Building Ownership" compare to the riskiness of the project "Levered Building Ownership"?

6.4E WHAT "LEVERAGE" REALLY MEANS—FINANCIAL AND OPERATIONAL LEVERAGE

Leverage "amplifies" the equity stake.

Debt is often called **leverage**. We have already used the standard name "levered equity." Let me now explain why. A lever is a mechanical device that can amplify effects. In finance, a lever is something that allows a smaller equity investment to still control the firm and be more exposed to the underlying firm's gain or loss than unlevered ownership. That is, with leverage, a small change in the underlying project value translates into a larger change in value for levered equity, both up and down. You have seen this in our house example above, and specifically in Figure 6.3. Ordinary ownership would have cost you $76,364. But with leverage, you could take control of the house with cash of only $51,364. In addition, it also meant that if the sun shone, you would earn 37.5%, not just 30.95%; but if the tornado struck, you would lose *everything* rather than just 73.81%. Leverage amplified your stake.

The leverage concept can encompass more than just financial debt.

➤ Caculating leverage, Section 22.1, p. 821

Financial debt is a lever—but it is not the only one. Leverage can be and often is calculated using all corporate liabilities (which may include, e.g., accounts payable and pension obligations). More importantly, because leverage is a general concept rather than an accounting term, you should think of it in even broader terms. The idea of leverage is always that a smaller equity investment can control the firm and is more sensitive to firm value changes. Table 6.4 illustrates some different types of levers. In this table, you can pay $475 for machine and labor, and receive either $200 or $1,000 in product revenues, plus $150 as resale value for the machine. In the bad state, you lose 26%; in the good state, you earn 142%. The next line shows that financial leverage can magnify these rates of return into −100% or +540%. But instead of taking on financial debt, you could also lease the machine, which costs you $250, and pay for labor of $75. In this case, you have effectively levered up, increasing your risk to −38% and +208% but without taking on any financial leverage. It is the lease that has now become your leverage! And you can also combine real and financial leverage. Finally, there can even be differences in the degree to which the production technologies themselves are levered. The final example shows a different method of production, which is intrinsically more levered.

6.4F WORKING WITH MORE THAN TWO POSSIBLE OUTCOMES

Multiple outcomes will cause multiple breakpoints in the relation from promised to expected payoffs.

How does the two-scenario example generalize to multiple possible outcomes? For example, assume that the building could be worth $20,000, $40,000, $60,000, $80,000,

TABLE 6.4 FINANCIAL AND REAL LEVERAGE

Example Assumptions:

- Machine costs $400 and can be resold for $150.
- Labor costs are $75.
- Product produces $200 ("Bad") or $1,000 ("Good").
- Assume prevailing interest rate is 0.

			Dollars		Percent		
Leverage	Investment	You Pay	Bad	Good	Bad	Good	FLR
None	Pay for everything.	$475	$350	$1,150	−26%	+142%	0%
Financial	Borrow $350.	$125	$0	$800	−100%	+540%	74%
Real	Lease machine (payment = $250).	$325	$200	$1,000	−38%	+208%	0%
Real+Financial	Lease machine. Borrow $200.	$125	$0	$800	−100%	+540%	38%
Different Technology—Labor costs $40, different machine costs $400, has residual value of $115.							
Technology	Pay for everything.	$440	$315	$1,115	−28%	+153%	0%

FLR is financial leverage, which is defined as the fraction of financial debt divided by the sum of debt and equity.

or $100,000 with equal probability and that the appropriate expected interest rate is 10%. It follows that the building has a PV of $60,000/1.10 ≈ $54,545.45. If a loan promised $20,000, how much would you expect to receive? The full $20,000, of course:

$$\mathcal{E}(\text{Payoff}(\text{Loan Promise} = \$20{,}000)) = \$20{,}000$$

$$\mathcal{E}\begin{pmatrix} \text{Payoff of Loan} \\ \text{if } \$20{,}000 \le \text{ Loan Promise } \le \$20{,}000 \end{pmatrix} = \text{Loan}$$

If a loan promised $20,001, how much would you expect to receive? You would expect $20,000 for sure, plus the extra "marginal" $1 with 80% probability. In fact, you would expect only 80 cents for each dollar promised between $20,000 and $40,000. So, if a loan promised $40,000, you would expect to receive

$$\begin{aligned} \mathcal{E}(\text{ Payoff(Loan Promise} = \$40{,}000\text{))} &= \$20{,}000 + 80\% \cdot (\$40{,}000 - \$20{,}000) \\ &= \$36{,}000 \end{aligned}$$

$$\mathcal{E}\begin{pmatrix} \text{Payoff of Loan} \\ \text{if } \$20{,}000 \le \text{ Loan Promise } \le \$40{,}000 \end{pmatrix} = \$20{,}000 + 80\% \cdot (\text{Loan} - \$20{,}000)$$

If a loan promised you $40,001, how much would you expect to receive? You would get $20,000 for sure, plus another $20,000 with 80% probability (which is an expected $16,000), plus the marginal $1 with only 60% probability. Thus,

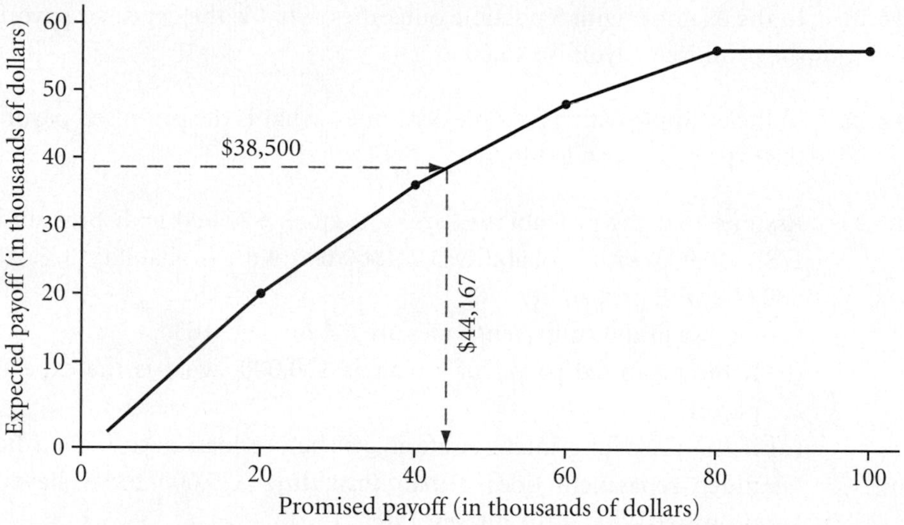

The firm will be worth $20,000, $40,000, $60,000, $80,000, or $100,000, each with equal probability. To borrow $35,000 today, the firm must offer an expected payoff of $38,500 next year. Following the arrow from the y-axis at $38,500 to the function and then down to the x-axis shows that this requires a promised payoff of $44,167.

FIGURE 6.4 Promised versus Expected Payoff for a Loan on the Project with Five Possible Payoffs

$$\mathcal{E}(\text{Payoff(Loan Promise} = \$40{,}001)) = \$20{,}000 + 80\% \cdot (\$40{,}000 - \$20{,}000) + 60\% \cdot \$41{,}001 - \$40{,}000)$$

$$= \$36{,}000.60$$

$$\mathcal{E}\left(\begin{array}{c}\text{Payoff of Loan} \\ \text{if } \$40{,}000 \leq \text{ Loan Promise } \leq \$60{,}000\end{array}\right) = \$20{,}000 + 80\% \cdot (\$40{,}000 - \$20{,}000) + 60\% \cdot (\text{Loan} - \$40{,}000) \tag{6.1}$$

And so on.

Figure 6.4 plots these expected payoffs as a function of the promised payoffs. With this figure, mortgage valuation becomes easy. For example, how much would the loan have to promise to provide $35,000 today? The expected payoff would have to be $(1 + 10\%) \cdot \$35{,}000 = \$38{,}500$. Figure 6.4 shows that an expected payoff of $38,500 corresponds to around $44,000 in promise. (The exact number can be worked out to be $44,167.) Of course, you cannot borrow more than $54,545.45—the project's present value. So, you can forget about the idea of obtaining a $55,000 mortgage.

You can now read off the appropriate promised value from the graph for any mortgage.

SOLVE NOW!

Q 6.20 If there were infinitely many possible outcomes (e.g., if the building value followed a statistical normal distribution), what would the graph of expected payoffs of the loan as a function of promised payoffs look like?

Q 6.21 In the example with 5 possible outcomes, what is the expected payoff if the promised payoff is $45,000?

Q 6.22 In the example with 5 possible outcomes, what is the promised payoff if the expected payoff is $45,000?

Q 6.23 Assume that the probabilities are not equal: $20,000 with probability 1/8, $40,000 with probability 3/8, $60,000 with probability 3/8, and $80,000 with probability 1/8.

(a) Draw a graph equivalent to Figure 6.4 on page 163.

(b) If the promised payoff of a loan is $50,000, what is the expected payoff?

(c) If the prevailing interest rate is 5% before loan payoff, then how much repayment does a loan providing $25,000 today have to promise? What is the interest rate?

You do not need to calculate these values if you can read them off your graph.

Q 6.24 A new product may be a dud (20% probability), an average seller (70% probability), or dynamite (10% probability). If it is a dud, the payoff will be $20,000; if it is an average seller, the payoff will be $40,000; if it is dynamite, the payoff will be $80,000. The appropriate expected rate of return is 6% per year. If a loan promises to pay off $40,000, what are the promised and expected rates of return?

Q 6.25 ADVANCED: What is the formula equivalent to Formula 6.1 on page 163 for promised payoffs between $60,000 and $80,000?

Q 6.26 ADVANCED: Can you work out the exact required promised payoff for the $45,000 loan for which a creditor would expect a payoff of $38,500?

How Bad Are Mistakes?

DISCOUNTING PROMISED CASH FLOWS WITH THE PROMISED COST OF CAPITAL

Two wrongs do not make one right: Do not think two errors cancel.

Sadly, it is not an uncommon mistake to believe that you can easily adjust the cash flows and the discount rates in order to paint over the need to estimate expected values. The most common version of this error is to discount promised cash flows with promised discount rates. After all, both numbers reflect default risk. The two default issues might cancel out one another, and you might end up with the correct value. *Or they might not cancel out, in which case you will end up with a nonsensical present value!*

To illustrate, say the appropriate expected rate of return is 10%. A suggested bond investment may promise \$16,000 for a \$100,000 investment, but with a default risk on the interest of 50% (the principal is insured). Your benchmark promised opportunity cost of capital may rely on risky bonds that have default premiums of 2%. Your project NPV is neither $-\$100{,}000 + \$116{,}000/1.12 \approx +\$3{,}571$ nor $-\$100{,}000 + \$100{,}000/1.10 + \$16{,}000/1.12 \approx +\$5{,}195$. Instead, you must work with expected values.

$$\text{Correct PV} = -\$100{,}000 + \frac{\$100{,}000}{1 + 10\%} + \frac{\$8{,}000}{1 + 10\%} \approx -\$1{,}818$$

This bond would be a bad investment.

SOLVE NOW!

Q 6.27 What is the relative importance of cash flow and cost of capital errors for a 10-year project?

Q 6.28 What is the relative importance of cash flow and cost of capital errors for a 100-year project?

Q 6.29 Is discount rate uncertainty relatively more problematic for long-term or for short-term projects?

SUMMARY

This chapter covered the following major points:

- Uncertainty means that a project may not return its promised amount.
- A random variable is one whose outcome has not yet been determined. It is characterized by its distribution of possible future outcomes.
- The "expected value" is the probability-weighted sum of all possible outcomes. It is the "average" or "mean," but it is applied to the future instead of to a historical data series. It is a measure of "reward."
- Risk neutrality means indifference between a safe bet and a risky bet if their expected rates of return are the same.
- The possibility of future default causes promised (quoted) interest rates to be higher than expected interest rates. Default risk is also often called credit risk.
- Most of the difference between promised and expected interest rates is due to default. Extra compensation for bearing more risk—the risk premium—and other premiums are typically smaller than the default premium for bonds.
- Credit ratings can help judge the probability of potential losses in default. Moody's and S&P are the two most prominent vendors of ratings for corporate bonds.

- The key tool for thinking about uncertainty is the payoff table. Each row represents one possible outcome, which contains the probability that the state will come about, the total project value that can be distributed, and the allocation of this total project value to different state-contingent claims. The state-contingent claims "carve up" the possible project payoffs.
- Most real-world projects are financed with the two most common state-contingent claims—debt and equity. Their payoff rights are best thought of in terms of payoff tables.
- Debt and equity are methods to parcel out total firm risk into one component that is safer than the overall firm (debt) and one that is riskier than the overall firm (equity).
- The presence of debt "levers up" equity investments. That is, a smaller upfront cash investment becomes more exposed to swings in the value of the underlying firm. However, there are also other leverage mechanisms that firms can choose (e.g., leasing or technology).
- If debt promises to pay more than the project can deliver in the worst state of nature, then the debt is risky and requires a promised interest rate in excess of its expected interest rate.
- NPV is robust to modest errors in the expected interest rate (the discount rate) for near-term cash flows. However, NPV is not necessarily robust with respect to modest errors in either expected cash flows or discount rates for distant cash flows.
- NPV suggests discounting expected cash flows with expected rates of return. If you instead discount promised cash flows with promised rates of return, there is no telling what your result will mean.

KEY TERMS

SOLVE NOW! SOLUTIONS

Q 6.1 No! The expected outcome (value) is assumed to be known—at least for an untampered die throw. The following is almost philosophy and beyond what you are supposed to know or answer here: It might, however, be that the expected value of an investment is not really known. In this case, it, too, could be a random variable in one sense—although you are assumed to be able to form an expectation (opinion) over anything, so in this sense, it would not be a random variable, either.

Q 6.2 If you do not know the exact bet, you may not know the expected value, which means that even the expected value is unknown. This may be the case for stocks, where you are often forced to guess what the expected rate of return will be (unlike for a die, for which you know the underlying physical process, which assures an expected value of 3.5). However, almost all finance theories assume you know the expected value. Fortunately, even if you do not know the expected value, finance theories hope you still often have a pretty good idea.

Q 6.3 If the random variable is the number of dots on the die, then the expected outcome is $1/6 \cdot (1) + 1/6 \cdot (2) + 1/6 \cdot (3) + 1/6 \cdot (4) + 1/6 \cdot (5) + 1/6 \cdot (6) = 3.5$. The realization was 6.

Q 6.4 The expected value of the stock investment is $5\% \cdot (\$41) + 10\% \cdot (\$42) + 20\% \cdot (\$45) + 30\% \cdot (\$48) + 20\% \cdot (\$58) + 10\% \cdot (\$70) + 5\% \cdot (\$75) = \$52$. Therefore, purchasing the stock at $50 is not a fair bet, but it is a good bet.

Q 6.5 The variance of the P_{+1} stock investment is $\mathcal{V}ar = 5\% \cdot (\$41 - \$52)^2 + 10\% \cdot (\$42 - \$52)^2 + 20\% \cdot (\$45 - \$52)^2 + 30\% \cdot (\$48 - \$52)^2 + 20\% \cdot (\$58 - \$52)^2 + 10\% \cdot (\$70 - \$52)^2 + 5\% \cdot (\$75 - \$52)^2 = 5\% \cdot \$\$121 + 10\% \cdot \$\$100 + 20\% \cdot \$\$49 + 30\% \cdot \$\$16 + 20\% \cdot \$\$36 + 10\% \cdot \$\$324 + 5\% \cdot \$\$529 = \$\$96.70$. Therefore, the standard deviation (risk) is $\sqrt{\$\$96.70} \approx \$9.83$.

Q 6.6 Investors are more risk averse for large bets relative to their wealth.

Q 6.7 Individual investors are more risk averse than investors in the aggregate.

Q 6.8 Expected and promised rates are the same only for government bonds. Most other bonds have some kind of default risk.

Q 6.9 With the revised probabilities:
(a) The expected payoff is now $95\% \cdot \$210 + 1\% \cdot \$100 + 4\% \cdot \$0 = \$200.50$. Therefore, the expected rate of return is $\$200.50/\$200 = 0.25\%$.
(b) You require an expected payoff of \$210 to expect to end up with 5%. Therefore, you must solve for a promised payment $95\% \cdot P + 1\% \cdot \$100 + 4\% \cdot \$0 = \$210 \Rightarrow P = \$209/0.95 = \$220$. On a loan of \$200, this is a 10% promised interest rate.

Q 6.10 No, the expected default premium is zero by definition.

Q 6.11 Both. The historical evidence is that lower-grade borrowers both default more often and pay less upon default.

Q 6.12 The actual cash flow is replaced by the expected cash flow, and the actual rate of return is replaced by the expected rate of return.

Q 6.13 The factory's expected value is $\mathcal{E}(\text{Value at Time 2}) = [0.5 \cdot \$500{,}000 + 0.5 \cdot \$1{,}000{,}000] = \$750{,}000$. Its present value is therefore $\$750{,}000/1.06^2 \approx \$667{,}497.33$.

Q 6.14 For the dynamite/dud project:
(a) The expected payoff is $\mathcal{E}(P) = 20\% \cdot \$20{,}000 + 70\% \cdot \$40{,}000 + 10\% \cdot \$80{,}000 = \$40{,}000$.
(b) The present value of the expected payoff is $\$40{,}000/1.08 \approx \$37{,}037$.
(c) The three rate of return outcomes are $\$20{,}000/\$37{,}037 - 1 \approx -46\%$, $\$40{,}000/\$37{,}037 - 1 \approx +8\%$, $\$80{,}000/\$37{,}037 - 1 \approx +116\%$.

(d) The expected rate of return is 20% · (−46%) + 70% · (+8%) + 10% · (+116%) = −9.2% + 5.6% + 11.6% = 8%.

Q 6.15 No! Partners would share payoffs proportionally, not according to "debt comes first." For example, in the tornado state, the 32.74% partner would receive only about \$6,500, not the entire \$20,000 that the debt owner receives.

Q 6.16 The 80% mortgage would finance 0.8 · \$76,363.64 ≈ \$61,090.91 today.

Event	*Prob*	Building Value	Mortgage Value	Levered Ownership
Tornado	20%	\$20,000	\$20,000	\$0
Sunshine	80%	\$100,000	\$79,000[a]	\$21,000
Expected Value at Time 1		\$84,000	\$67,200[b]	\$16,800
Present Value at Time 0		\$76,364	\$61,091	\$15,273
From Time 0 to Time 1, $\mathcal{E}(\tilde{r})$		10%	10%	10%

a. The necessary mortgage promise is (1.10 · \$61,091 − 0.2 · \$20,000)/0.8 ≈ \$79,000.
b. The expected mortgage payoff is 0.2 · \$20,000 + 0.8 · \$79,000 = \$67,200.

Q 6.17 Taking rent into account:
(a) In the sun state, the value is \$120,000 + \$11,000 = \$131,000. In the tornado state, the value is \$11,000 + \$20,000 = \$31,000. Therefore, the expected building value is \$111,000. The discounted building value today is \$111,000/1.10 ≈ \$100,909.09.
(b) Still the same as in the text: The lender's \$25,000 loan can still only get \$20,000, so it is a promise for \$29,375. The quoted interest rate is still 17.50%.
(c) \$100,909.09 − \$25,000 = \$75,909.09.
(d) Still \$100,909.09, assuming that the owner values living in the building as much as a tenant would. Owner-consumed rent is the equivalent of corporate dividends paid out to levered equity. Note: You can repeat this example assuming that the rent is an annuity of \$1,000 each month, and tornadoes strike mid-year.

Q 6.18 For the loan that promises to pay off \$25,000 (instead of providing it): In the tornado state, the creditor gets all \$20,000. In the sunshine state, the creditor receives the promise of \$25,000. Therefore, the creditor's expected payoff is 20% · \$20,000 + 80% · \$25,000 = \$24,000. To offer an expected rate of return of 10%, you can get \$24,000/1.1 ≈ \$21,818 from the creditor today.
(a) Repeating the table:

Event	*Prob*	Building Value	Mortgage Value	Levered Ownership
Tornado	20%	\$20,000	\$20,000	\$0
Sunshine	80%	\$100,000	\$25,000	\$75,000
Expected Value at Time 1		\$84,000	\$24,000	\$60,000
Present Value at Time 0		\$76,364	\$21,818	\$54,546
From Time 0 to Time 1, $\mathcal{E}(\tilde{r})$		10%	10%	10%

(b) The loan pays \$21,818 today.
(c) The promised rate of return is therefore \$25,000/\$21,818 − 1 ≈ 14.58%.
(d) The levered building ownership is riskier than the full building ownership.

Q 6.19 This risk-free loan pays off \$20,000 for certain. The levered ownership pays either \$0 or \$80,000, and costs \$64,000/1.10 ≈ \$58,182. Therefore, the rate of return is either −100% or +37.50%. You have already worked out full ownership in the text: It pays either \$20,000 or \$100,000, costs \$76,364, and offers either −73.81% or +30.95%. By inspection, the levered equity project is riskier. In effect, building ownership has become riskier, because the owner has chosen to sell off the risk-free component and retain only the risky component.

Event	*Prob*	Building Value	Mortgage Value	Levered Ownership
Tornado	20%	\$20,000	\$20,000	\$0
Sunshine	80%	\$100,000	\$20,000	\$80,000
Expected Value at Time 1		\$84,000	\$20,000	\$64,000
Present Value at Time 0		\$76,364	\$18,182	\$58,182
From Time 0 to Time 1, $\mathcal{E}(\tilde{r})$		10%	10%	10%

Q 6.20 With infinitely many possible outcomes, the function of expected payoffs would be a smooth increasing function. For the mathematical nitpickers: [a] We really should not allow a normal distribution, because the value of the building cannot be negative; [b] The function would increase monotonically, but it would asymptote to an upper bound.

Q 6.21 Visually, from the graph, for a promised payoff of \$45,000, the expected payoff is around \$40,000. The correct value can be obtained by plugging into Formula 6.1 on page 163:

$$\begin{aligned}\mathcal{E}(\text{Payoff(Loan Promise} = \$45{,}000)) &= \$20{,}000 + 80\% \cdot (\$40{,}000 - \$20{,}000) \\ &\quad + 60\% \cdot (\$45{,}000 - \$40{,}000) \\ &= \$39{,}000\end{aligned}$$

Q 6.22 Visually, from the graph, if the expected payoff is \$45,000, the promised payoff is around \$55,000. The correct value can be obtained by setting Formula 6.1 on page 163 equal to \$45,000 and solving for "Loan."

$$\begin{aligned}\mathcal{E}(\text{Payoff(Loan Promise} = x)) &= \$20{,}000 + 80\% \cdot (\$40{,}000 - \$20{,}000) \\ &\quad + 60\% \cdot (x - \$40{,}000) = \$45{,}000\end{aligned}$$

which simplifies to $0.6 \cdot (x - \$40{,}000) = \$9{,}000$. The solution is indeed \$55,000.

Q 6.23 Given the now unequal probabilities,
(a)

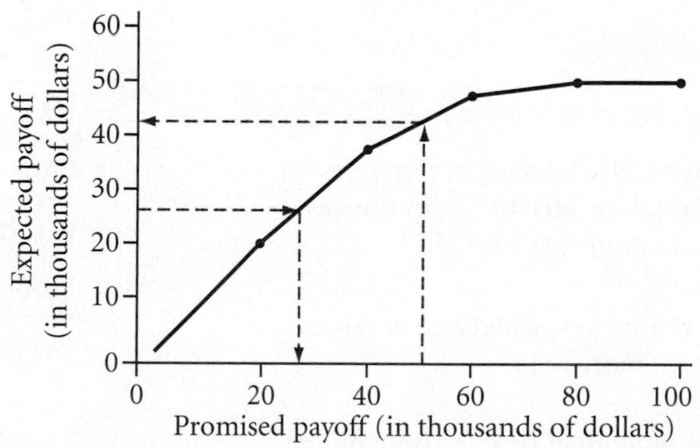

(b) The exact expected payoff is $1/8 \cdot \$20{,}000 + 3/8 \cdot \$40{,}000 + 1/2 \cdot \$50{,}000 = \$42{,}500$. The 1/2 is the probability that you will receive the \$50,000 that you have been promised, which occurs if the project ends up worth at least as much as your promised \$50,000. This means that it is the total probability that it will be worth \$60,000 or \$80,000.

(c) The loan must expect to pay off $(1 + 5\%) \cdot \$25{,}000 = \$26{,}250$. Therefore, solve $1/8 \cdot \$20{,}000 + 7/8 \cdot x = \$26{,}250$, so the exact promised payoff must be $x \approx \$27{,}142.86$.

Q 6.24 With 20% probability, the loan will pay off \$20,000; with 80% probability, the loan will pay off the full promised \$40,000. Therefore, the loan's expected payoff is $20\% \cdot \$20{,}000 + 80\% \cdot \$40{,}000 = \$36{,}000$. The loan's price is $\$36{,}000/1.06 \approx \$33{,}962$. Therefore, the promised rate of return is $\$40{,}000/\$33{,}962 - 1 \approx 17.8\%$. The expected rate of return was given: 6%.

Q 6.25 For promised payoffs between \$60,000 and \$80,000, solve $\mathcal{E}(\text{Payoff of Loan if } \$60{,}000 \leq \text{Loan Promise} \leq \$80{,}000) = \$20{,}000 + 80\% \cdot \$20{,}000 + 60\% \cdot \$20{,}000 + 40\% \cdot (\text{Loan} - \$60{,}000)$.

Q 6.26 Once you reach above $\$20{,}000 + 0.8 \cdot \$20{,}000 = \$36{,}000$ in expected value, you fall into the third piece of the function, where you receive only 60% on the dollar. Thus, you can set Formula 6.1 on page 163 equal to \$38,500 and solve for "Loan":

$$\mathcal{E}(\text{Payoff Given Loan Promise} = \$45{,}000) =$$

$$\$38{,}500 = \$20{,}000 + 80\% \cdot (\$40{,}000 - \$20{,}000) + 60\% \cdot (x - \$40{,}000)$$

The correct answer is indeed $x \approx \$44{,}166.67$.

Q 6.27 To assess relative error importance, consider a project that earns \$100 in 10 years and where the correct interest rate is 10%.

- The correct PV is $\$100/1.10^{10} \approx \$38.55$.
- If the cash flow is incorrectly estimated to be 10% higher, the incorrect PV is $\$110/1.10^{10} \approx \$42.41$. (This is 10% higher than the correct value.)
- If the interest rate is incorrectly estimated to be 10% lower, the incorrect PV is $\$100/1.09^{10} \approx \$42.24$. (This is 9.6% higher than the correct value.)

The misvaluation effects are reasonably similar at 10% interest rates. Naturally, percent valuation mistakes in interest rates are higher if the interest rate is higher (and lower if the interest rate is lower).

Q 6.28 Although the relative importance depends on the exact interest rate, here 100 years is so long that cost of capital errors almost surely matter for any reasonable interest rates now. Cash flow errors still matter and more so when uncertainty about future cash flows increases with the horizon, as most real-world cash flow uncertainty would.

Q 6.29 Discount rate uncertainty is relatively more problematic for long-term projects. For short-term projects, the exponents limit the damage.

PROBLEMS

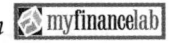

The ▮ *indicates problems available in* myfinancelab

Q 6.30 Is this morning's CNN forecast of tomorrow's temperature a random variable? Is tomorrow's temperature a random variable?

Q 6.31 Does a higher reward (expected rate of return) always come with more risk?

Q 6.32 Would a single individual be effectively more, equally, or less risk averse than a pool of such investors?

Q 6.33 A financial instrument will pay off as follows:

Probability	50%	25%	12.5%
Payoff	\$100	\$110	\$130
Probability	6.25%	3.125%	3.125%
Payoff	\$170	\$250	\$500

(a) What price today would make this a fair bet?

(b) What is the maximum price that a risk-averse investor would be willing to pay?

Q 6.34 Now assume that the financial instrument from Q6.33 costs $100.

(a) What is its expected rate of return?

(b) If the prevailing interest rate on time-equivalent Treasuries is 10%, and if financial default happens either completely (i.e., no repayment) or not at all (i.e., full promised payment), then what is the probability p that the security will pay off? In other words, assume that full repayment occurs with probability p and that zero repayment occurs with probability $1 - p$. What is the p that makes the expected rate of return equal to 10%?

Q 6.35 A bond will pay off $100 with probability 99% and will pay off nothing with probability 1%. The equivalent risk-free rate of return is 5%. What is an appropriate promised yield on this bond?

Q 6.36 An L.A. Lakers bond promises an investment rate of return of 9%. Time-equivalent Treasuries offer 6%. Is this necessarily a good investment? Explain.

Q 6.37 A Disney bond promises an investment rate of return of 7%. Time-equivalent Treasuries offer 7%. Is the Disney bond necessarily a bad investment? Explain.

Q 6.38 Go to the Vanguard website. Look at funds by asset class, and answer this question for different bond fund durations.

(a) What is the current yield-to-maturity of a taxable Vanguard bond fund invested in Treasury bonds?

(b) What is the current yield-to-maturity of a taxable Vanguard bond fund invested in investment-grade bonds?

(c) What is the current yield-to-maturity of a taxable Vanguard bond fund invested in high-yield bonds?

Q 6.39 Return to the example on page 146, but assume that the probability of receiving full payment of $210 in 1 year is only 95%, the probability of receiving $100 is 4%, and the probability of receiving absolutely no payment is 1%. If the bond quotes a rate of return of 12%, what is the time premium, the default premium, and the risk premium?

Q 6.40 Using information from a current newspaper or the WWW, what is the annualized yield on corporate bonds (high-quality, medium-quality, high-yield) today?

Q 6.41 What are the main bond rating agencies and categories? Roughly, what are the 10-year default rate differences between them?

Q 6.42 An IBM bond promising to pay $100,000 costs $90,090. Time-equivalent Treasuries offer 8%.

(a) Setting aside the risk neutrality and perfect markets assumption for this question only, what can you say about the risk premium, the default premium, and the liquidity premium?

(b) Returning to our assumption that markets are risk neutral, but still setting aside the perfect markets assumption for this question, what can you say about the risk premium, the default premium, and the liquidity premium?

(c) Assuming that the liquidity premium is 0.5%, what can you say about the risk premium, the default premium, and the liquidity premium?

Q 6.43 How is a credit swap like an insurance contract? Who is the insurer in a credit swap? Why would anyone want to buy such insurance?

Q 6.44 A bond promises to pay $12,000 and costs $10,000. The promised discount on equivalent bonds is 25% per annum. Is this bond a good deal?

Q 6.45 A project costs $19,000 and promises the following cash flows:

Year	1	2	3
Cash Flows	$12,500	$6,000	$3,000

The appropriate discount rate is 15% per annum. Should you invest in this project?

Q 6.46 Assume that the probability that the Patriots will win the Superbowl is 55%. A souvenir shop outside the stadium will earn net profits of $1.5 million if the Patriots win and $1.0 million if they lose. You are the loan officer of the bank to whom the shop applied for a loan. You can assume that your bank is risk neutral and that the bank can invest in safe projects that offer an expected rate of return of 10%.

(a) What interest rate would you quote if the owner asked you for a loan for $900,000 today?

(b) What interest rate would you quote if the owner asked you for a loan for $1,000,000 today?

(These questions require that you compute the amount that you would demand for repayment.)

Q 6.47 A new project has the following success probabilities:

	Failure	Success	Buyout
Prob	10%	85%	5%
Payoff (in millions)	$50	$200	$400

Assume risk neutrality. If a $100 bond collateralized by this project promises an interest rate of 8%, then what is the prevailing cost of capital, and what do shareholders receive if the buyout materializes?

Q 6.48 Debt is usually safer than equity. Does the risk of the rate of return on equity go up if the firm takes on more debt, *provided* the debt is low enough to remain risk free? Illustrate with an example that you make up.

Q 6.49 Under risk neutrality, a factory can be worth $500,000 or $1,000,000 in *2* years, depending on product demand, each with equal probability. The appropriate cost of capital is 6% per year. The factory can be financed with proceeds of $500,000 from loans today. What are the promised and expected cash flows and rates of return for the factory (without a loan), for the loan, and for a hypothetical factory owner who has to repay the loan first?

Q 6.50 Assume that the correct future cash flow is $100 and the correct discount rate is 10%. Consider the value effect of a 5% error in cash flows and the effect of a 5% error in discount rates.

(a) Graph the value effect (both in absolute values and in percent of the correct upfront present value) as a function of the number of years from 1 year to 20 years.

(b) Is this an accurate real-world representation of how your uncertainty about your own calculations should look?

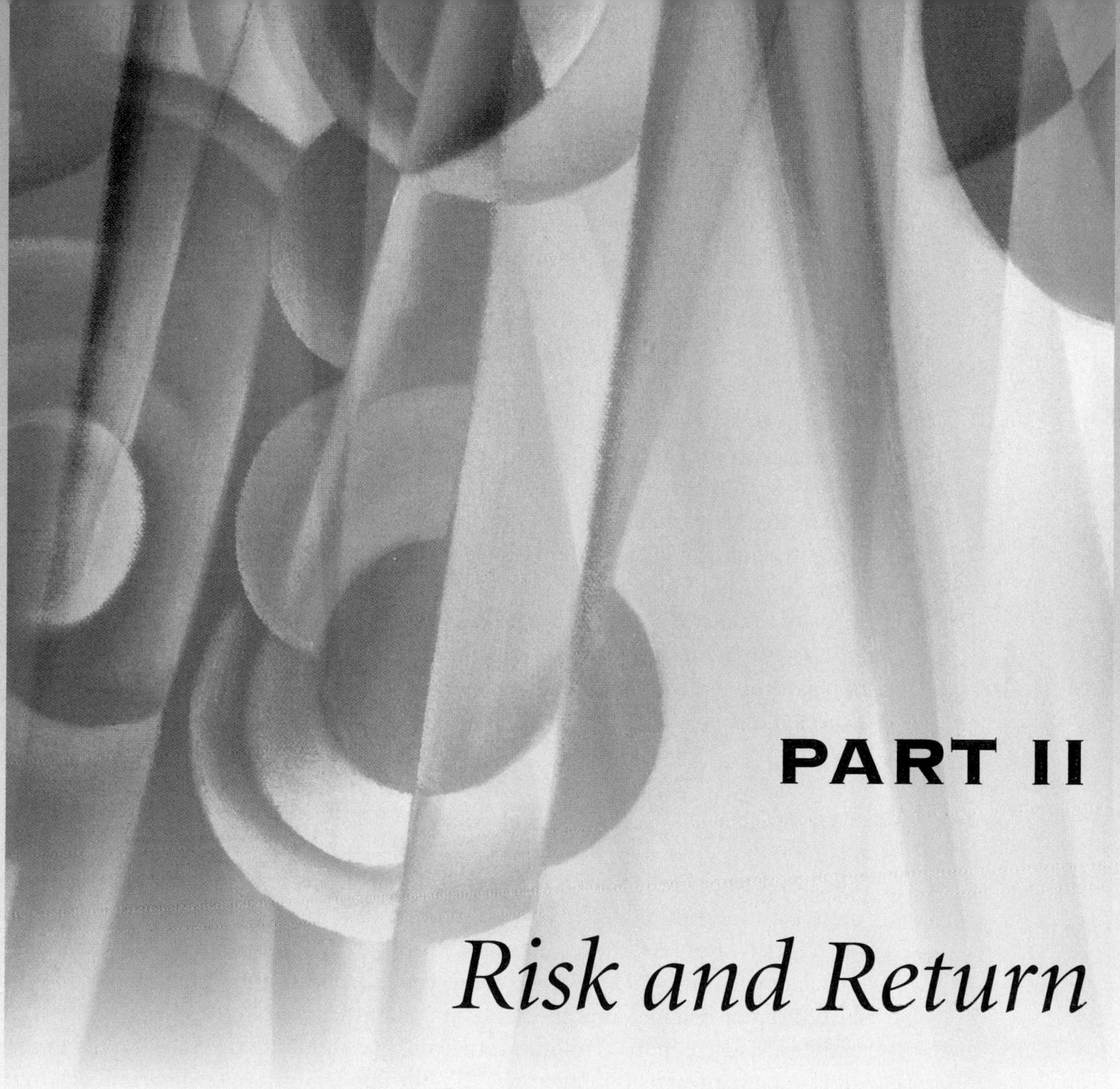

PART II

Risk and Return

IN A PERFECT MARKET UNDER RISK AVERSION

We are now moving on to the next step in complexity. We shall still (cowardly) maintain that financial markets are perfect: no information differences, no transaction costs, no taxes, and many buyers and sellers. But we are now abandoning the assumption that investors are risk neutral—that they are indifferent between receiving \$1 million for sure, and receiving \$500,000 or \$1,500,000 with equal probability. An investor who is risk averse prefers the safe \$1 million.

Risk aversion creates one huge novel complication: Under risk aversion, projects can influence one another from an "overall risk" perspective. If one project's return is always high (say, +20%) when the other project's return is low (say, −20%), and vice versa, then it can even be possible that the overall risk cancels out completely! This simple insight means that determining the best investment choices, selected from the large universe of available investment projects, becomes a much more difficult task for corporate investors and consequently, for their corporations' managers. Projects are no longer self-contained islands.

As a corporate manager, it now becomes a question of how your corporate projects work together with your other projects (for internal corporate risk management) or even with your investors' projects elsewhere. This also means that you need to first understand your investors' problems before you can answer what projects they would like you to undertake. So, who are your investors, what do they like and dislike, and how should you evaluate your project relative to what you believe your investors' alternatives are? What exactly *are* your investors' alternatives? How do your projects interact with your investors' other projects? This is a wide and deep subject, which is why we require an unprecedented three chapters: It requires a larger expedition into the world of uncertainty.

Although the details of how to invest now become more difficult, fortunately, all the important questions and tasks still remain the same—and, fortunately, so do many of the answers. As a corporate executive, you must still understand how to work with rates of return and how to decide whether to accept or reject investment projects. You can still use the net present value method. You still need knowledge of projects' expected cash flows, $\mathcal{E}(\widetilde{C})$, and of the cost of capital, $\mathcal{E}(\tilde{r})$,

$$\text{NPV} = C_0 + \frac{\mathcal{E}(\widetilde{C}_1)}{1 + \mathcal{E}(\tilde{r}_1)} + \frac{\mathcal{E}(\widetilde{C}_2)}{1 + \mathcal{E}(\tilde{r}_2)} + \cdots$$

The novel complication arises in the denominator. Investors' risk aversion influences the NPV (only) through $\mathcal{E}(\tilde{r})$. Still, it continues to be best to think of it as the opportunity cost of capital. As a manager, the difficulty is only that you must somehow calculate what it should be on behalf of your corporation's owners (investors). The cost of capital still measures the same thing: whether your investors have better alternatives elsewhere in the economy. If they do, you should return their capital to them and let them invest their money there. It is the opportunities elsewhere that determine your corporation's cost of capital, which in turn determines what projects you should take.

WHAT YOU WANT TO LEARN IN THIS PART

In sum, we now assume that investors are risk averse—as they truly are in the real world. Then what is the correct $\mathcal{E}(\tilde{r})$, the opportunity cost of capital, in the NPV formula? As in earlier chapters, great opportunities elsewhere in the economy still manifest themselves as a high cost of capital $\mathcal{E}(\tilde{r})$ that you should apply to your projects. But in this part of the book, you must judge all opportunities not only by their rewards, but also by their risks.

- Chapter 7 gives you a short tour of historical rates of return on various asset classes to whet your appetite, and explains some of the institutional setups of equity markets.

  Typical questions: Did stocks, bonds, or cash perform better over the last 30 years? How safe were stocks compared to bonds or cash? What are the roles of brokers and exchanges? How do stocks appear and disappear?

- Chapter 8 considers choices if investors like more reward and less risk. It takes the perspective of an investor. It explains how you should measure risk and reward, and how diversification reduces risk. It draws a strong distinction between a security's own risk and a security's contribution to an investor's overall portfolio risk.

  Typical questions: What is the standard deviation of the rate of return on my portfolio? What is IBM's market beta, and what does it mean for my portfolio? What is IBM's own risk, and should I care? What is the average market beta of my portfolio?

- Chapter 9 takes the perspective of a corporate CFO. It explains how you should measure investors' opportunity costs of capital, $\mathcal{E}(\tilde{r})$, given that your own corporate investment projects can help or hurt your investors in their overall risk-reward trade-off. This is the domain of the "capital asset pricing model" (CAPM).

  Typical questions: What characteristics should influence the appropriate expected rate of return that your investors care about? What should be the appropriate expected rate of return for any one particular project? Where do you find all the necessary inputs to use the CAPM? Can you trust it?

Looking ahead, Part III will explain what happens when financial markets or decision rules are not perfect.

You can find an intuitive explanation of investments, based on the proverb not to put all your eggs into one basket, at the book website, www.prenhall.com/welch.

7

A First Look at Investments

HISTORICAL RATES OF RETURN BACKGROUND AND MARKET INSTITUTIONS

The subject of investments is so interesting that I first want to give you a quick tour, instead of laying all the foundations first and showing you the evidence later. I will give you a glimpse of the world of historical returns on the three main asset classes of stocks, bonds, and "cash," so that you can visualize the main patterns that matter—patterns of risk, reward, and covariation. This chapter also describes a number of important institutions that allow investors to trade equities.

7.1 STOCKS, BONDS, AND CASH, 1970–2007

Cash, bonds, and stocks are the most commonly studied asset classes.

Financial investment opportunities are often classified into just a few broad **asset classes**. The three most prominent such classes are cash, bonds, and stocks.

Cash: The name *cash* here is actually a misnomer because it does not designate physical dollar bills under your mattress. Instead, it means debt securities that are very liquid, very low-risk, and very short-term. Other investments that are part of this generic asset class may be certificate of deposits (CDs), savings deposits, or commercial paper. (These are briefly explained in Appendix A.) Another common designation for cash is **money market**. To make our life easy, we will just join the club and also use the term "cash."

Bonds: These are debt instruments that are of longer maturity than cash. You already know much about bonds and their many different varieties. I find it easiest to think of this class as representing primarily long-term Treasury bonds. You could also broaden this class to include bonds of other varieties, such as corporate bonds, municipal bonds, foreign bonds, or even more exotic debt instruments.

Stocks: Stocks are sometimes all lumped together, and they are sometimes themselves further categorized into different asset classes. The most common subclassification for U.S. domestic stocks is as follows:

- There are a few hundred stocks issued by the largest firms that are quite visible and trade very frequently. Though not exact, you can think of the largest 500 firms as the constituents of the popular **S&P 500** stock market index. This asset class is also often called **large-cap stocks**. (Cap is an abbreviation for capitalization.) Our chapter will focus only on these large-cap S&P 500 stocks and call them "stocks."
- There are a few thousand other stocks. They are also sometimes put into multiple categories, such as "mid-cap" or "small-cap." Inevitably, these stocks tend to trade less often, and some seem outright neglected.

There are also other stock-related subclasses, such as industry stock portfolios, or a classification of stocks into "value firms" and "growth firms," and so on. We shall ignore everything except the large-cap stock portfolio.

These asset classes are only broadly representative of similar individual investments. We are omitting many other important asset classes.

Do not take these categories too literally. They may not be representative for all assets that would seem to fit the designation. For example, most long-term bonds in the economy behave like our bond asset class, but some long-term corporate bonds behave more like stocks. Analogously, a particular firm may own a lot of bonds, and its rates of return would look like those on bonds and not like those on stocks. It would also be perfectly reasonable to include more or fewer investments in these three asset classes. (We would hope that such modifications would alter our insights only a little bit.) More importantly, there are also many other important asset classes that we do not even have time to consider, such as real estate, hedge funds, financial derivatives, foreign investments, or art. Nevertheless, cash, bonds, and stocks (or subclasses thereof) are the three most studied financial asset classes, so we will begin our examination of investments by looking at their historical performances.

7.1A GRAPHICAL REPRESENTATIONS OF HISTORICAL RETURNS FOR THE S&P 500

All rates of return data are in the time-series diagram.

Start with Figure 7.1. It shows the year-by-year rates of return (with dividends) of the S&P 500. The table and the plot give the same data: You would have earned 3.5% in 1970, 13.8% in 1971, and so on. The average rate of return over all 38 years was 11.9% per annum—also marked by the red triangle on the left side and the dot-dashed line.

The histogram (statistical distribution) shows how spread out returns are.

Figures 7.2 and 7.3 take the same data as Figure 7.1 but present it differently. Figure 7.2 shows a histogram that is based on the number of returns that fall within a range. This makes it easier to see how spread out returns were—how common it was for the S&P 500 to perform really badly, perform just about okay, or perform really well. For example, the table in Figure 7.1 shows that 8 years (1971, 1972, 1979, 1982, 1986, 1988, 2004, and 2006) had rates of return between 10% and 20%. In our 38 years, the most frequent return range was between 0% and 10%. Yet there were also other years that had rates of return below 10%—and even 2 years in which you would have lost more than 20% of your money (1974 and 2002). Again, the red triangle indicates that the average rate of return was 11.9%.

The compound rate of return graph shows how long-run investments would have fared.

The compound rate of return graph in Figure 7.3 offers yet another perspective. It plots the compounded annual returns (on a logarithmic scale). For example, by the

Decade	Year 0	1	2	3	4	5	6	7	8	9
1970	3.5%	13.8%	18.3%	−13.9%	−24.4%	35.6%	23.0%	−6.5%	6.4%	17.6%
1980	30.4%	−4.3%	19.7%	21.6%	5.9%	30.1%	18.0%	5.5%	15.9%	30.4%
1990	−2.9%	29.2%	7.3%	9.8%	1.3%	36.3%	22.3%	32.6%	28.0%	20.7%
2000	−8.9%	−11.7%	−21.5%	27.9%	10.6%	4.8%	15.8%	5.5%		

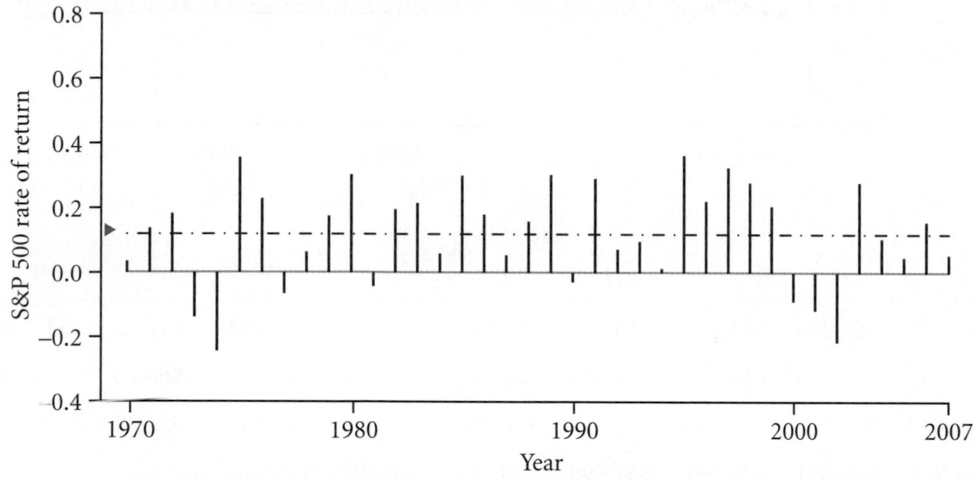

The time-series graph is a representation of the rates of return of the S&P 500 index (including dividends), as shown in the table above. The average rate of return was 11.9% (indicated by the red triangle and the dot-dashed line); the standard deviation was 15.9%.

FIGURE 7.1 The Time Series of Rates of Return on the S&P 500, 1970–2007

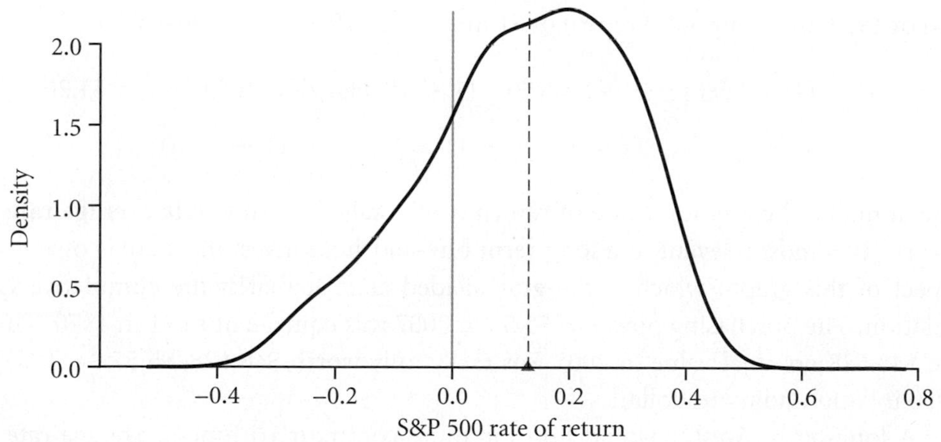

Return range	< −20%	−20% to −10%	−10% to 0%	0% to 10%	10% to 20%	20% to 30%	30% to 40%	> 40%
Number of years	2	2	4	9	8	7	6	

The graph and table are just different representations of the data in Figure 7.1. Formally, this type of graph is called a density function. It is really just a smoothed histogram.

FIGURE 7.2 The Statistical Distribution Function of S&P 500 Rates of Return, 1970–2007

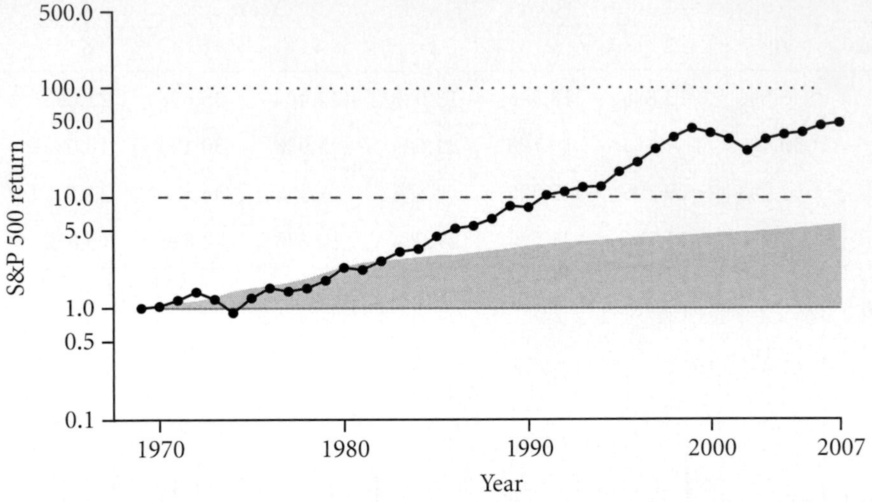

	Year									
Decade	0	1	2	3	4	5	6	7	8	9
1970	\$1.035	\$1.178	\$1.393	\$1.200	\$0.907	\$1.230	\$1.512	\$1.413	\$1.503	\$1.768
1980	\$2.305	\$2.205	\$2.639	\$3.209	\$3.399	\$4.421	\$5.219	\$5.505	\$6.380	\$8.319
1990	\$8.078	\$10.439	\$11.201	\$12.294	\$12.457	\$16.986	\$20.769	\$27.541	\$35.249	\$42.532
2000	\$38.744	\$34.221	\$26.851	\$34.354	\$37.994	\$39.811	\$46.097	\$48.628		

This graph and table are again just different representations of the same data in Figure 7.1. The gray area underneath the figure is the cumulative inflation-caused loss of purchasing power.

FIGURE 7.3 Compound Rates of Return for the S&P 500, 1970–2007

end of 1973, the compound return of \$1 invested in 1970 would have been

$$\begin{array}{ccccccccc} \$1 & \cdot & (1+3.5\%) & \cdot & (1+13.8\%) & \cdot & (1+18.3\%) & \cdot & (1-13.9\%) \approx \$1.20 \\ I_{1970} & \cdot & (1+r_{1970}) & \cdot & (1+r_{1971}) & \cdot & (1+r_{1972}) & \cdot & (1+r_{1973}) \end{array}$$

The annualized compound rate of return is also called a **geometric average rate of return.** It is most relevant to a long-term buy-and-hold investor. There is one novel aspect of this graph, which is the gray shaded area. It marks the cumulative CPI inflation. The purchasing power of \$5.57 in 2007 was equivalent to \$1 in 1970. Thus, the \$48.628 nominal value in 2007 was really only worth \$48.628/\$5.57 ≈ \$8.73 in 1970 inflation-adjusted dollars.

➤ Section 5.2, "Inflation," p. 97

Watch out whether you are being quoted average or annualized returns. The former is always higher, which is sometimes misleading.

A long-term investor would find the more common arithmetic average rate of return—commonly just called the mean or average—outright misleading. For example, a rate of return of −50% (you lose half) followed by +100% (you double) has the intuitively correct geometric net return of zero. However, the average rate of these two returns is a positive (−50% + 100%)/2 = +25%. Yikes. Unfortunately, there is no way to convert an arithmetic rate of return into a geometric rate of return (or an annualized rate of return). You will later even see a real-world example in which the geometric rate of return was −100% and the average rate of return was positive.

You can also see the discrepancy between the arithmetic and geometric rates of return in our S&P 500 data. The annualized rate of return from 1970–2007 (38 years) was

Geometric returns were 1.1% lower for our S&P 500 market index, too.

$$\$1 \cdot (1 + r)^{38} \approx \$48.63 \Leftrightarrow r \approx \sqrt[38]{48.63} - 1 \approx 10.8\%$$

The arithmetic rate of return of 11.9% was 1.1% higher. (And, of course, none of these figures take taxes into account.)

➤ Section 10.4A, "The Basics of (Federal) Income Taxes," p. 321

IMPORTANT: The annualized holding rate of return cannot be inferred from the average annual rate of return, and vice versa. The two are identical only if all rates of return are the same (i.e., when there is no risk). Otherwise, the geometric rate of return is always less than the arithmetic rate of return. (And the more risk, the bigger the difference.)

SOLVE NOW!

Q 7.1 What can you see in a time-series graph that is lost in a histogram?

Q 7.2 What can you see in a histogram that is more difficult to see in the time-series graph?

Q 7.3 What can you see in a compound return graph that is difficult to see in the time-series graph?

Q 7.4 What is the annualized holding rate of return and the average rate of return for each of the following?
(a) An asset that returns 5% each year.
(b) An asset that returns 0% and 10% in alternate years.
(c) An asset that returns −10% and 20% in alternate years.
Is the distance between the two returns larger when there is more risk?

7.1B HISTORICAL PERFORMANCE FOR A NUMBER OF INVESTMENTS

What does history tell you about rate of return patterns on the three major investment categories—stocks, bonds, and cash? You can find out by plotting exactly the same graphs as those in Figures 7.1, 7.2, and 7.3. Table 7.1 repeats them for a set of historical investment choices *all on the same scale*. You have already seen the third row—the performance of an investment in the S&P 500 stocks. I only changed the scale to make it easier to make direct comparisons to the other investments in the graphs below. These mini-graphs display a lot of information about the performance of these investments. Do not expect to understand everything at first glance: You need to meditate over Table 7.1 for a while to comprehend it. Each element tells its own story.

Explore the large comparative Table 7.1.

So let's compare the first three rows:

The first three rows show historical returns for the three asset classes.

Cash in the first row is the overnight Federal Funds interest rate. Note how tight the distribution of cash returns was around its 6.6% mean. You would never have lost money (in nominal terms), but you would rarely have earned much more than its

The first row is "cash."

TABLE 7.1 COMPARATIVE INVESTMENT PERFORMANCE, 1970–2007

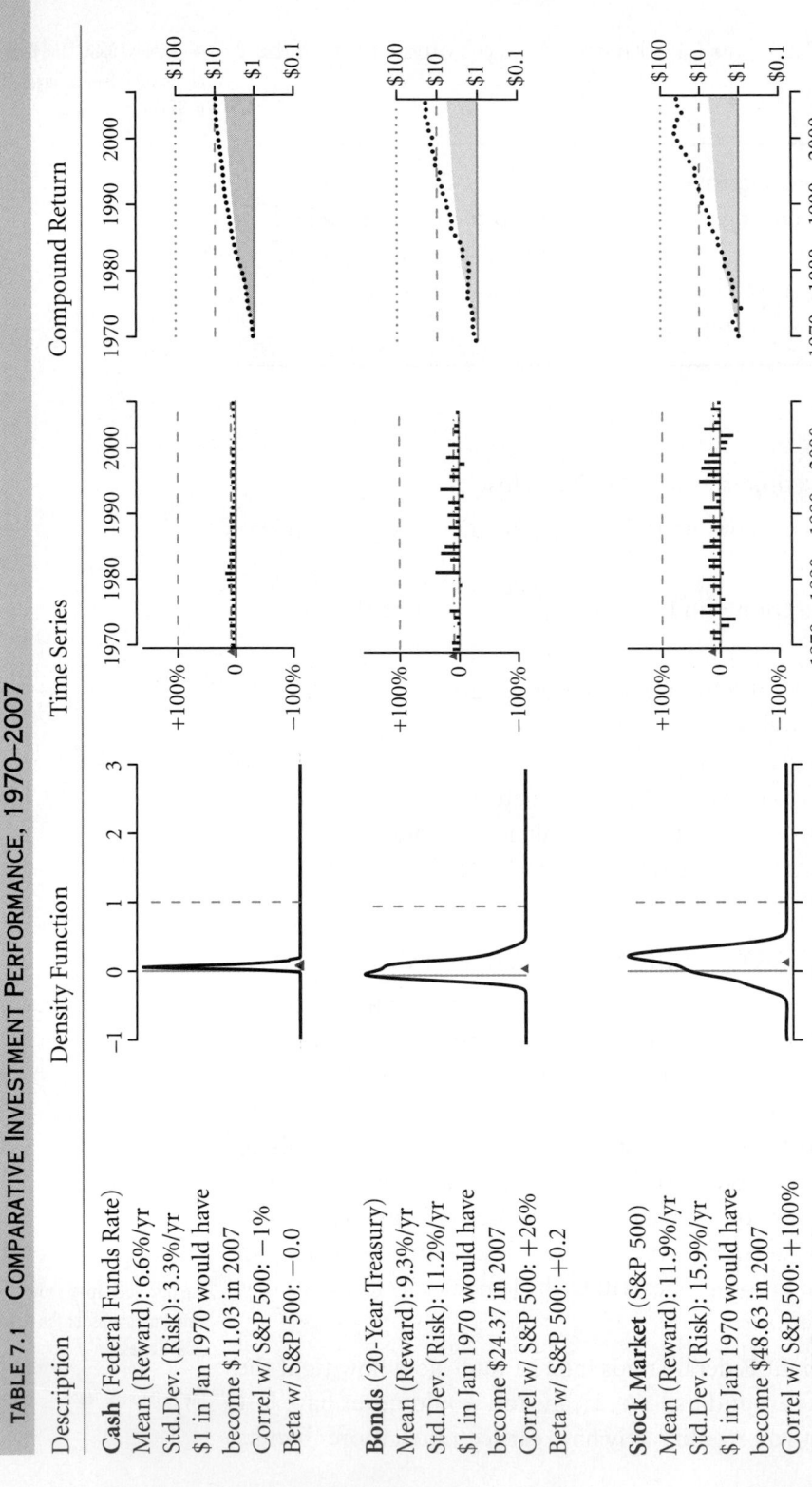

Description	Density Function	Time Series	Compound Return
Cash (Federal Funds Rate) Mean (Reward): 6.6%/yr Std.Dev. (Risk): 3.3%/yr $1 in Jan 1970 would have become $11.03 in 2007 Correl w/ S&P 500: −1% Beta w/ S&P 500: −0.0			
Bonds (20-Year Treasury) Mean (Reward): 9.3%/yr Std.Dev. (Risk): 11.2%/yr $1 in Jan 1970 would have become $24.37 in 2007 Correl w/ S&P 500: +26% Beta w/ S&P 500: +0.2			
Stock Market (S&P 500) Mean (Reward): 11.9%/yr Std.Dev. (Risk): 15.9%/yr $1 in Jan 1970 would have become $48.63 in 2007 Correl w/ S&P 500: +100% Beta w/ S&P 500: +1.0			

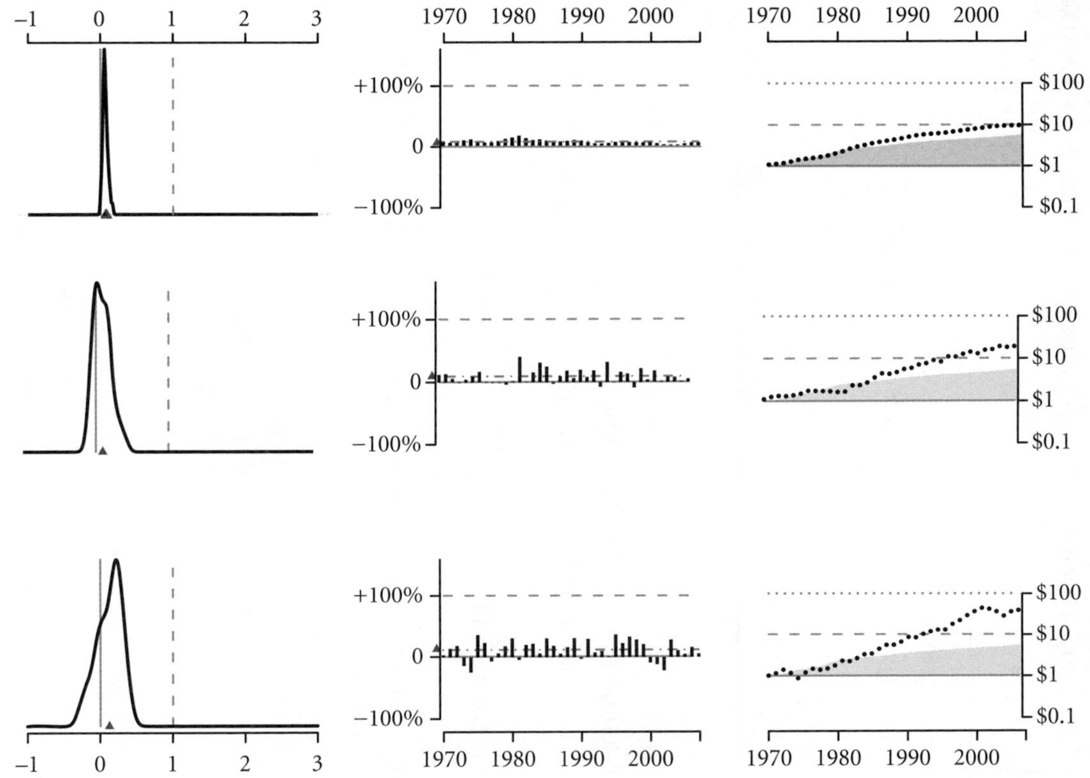

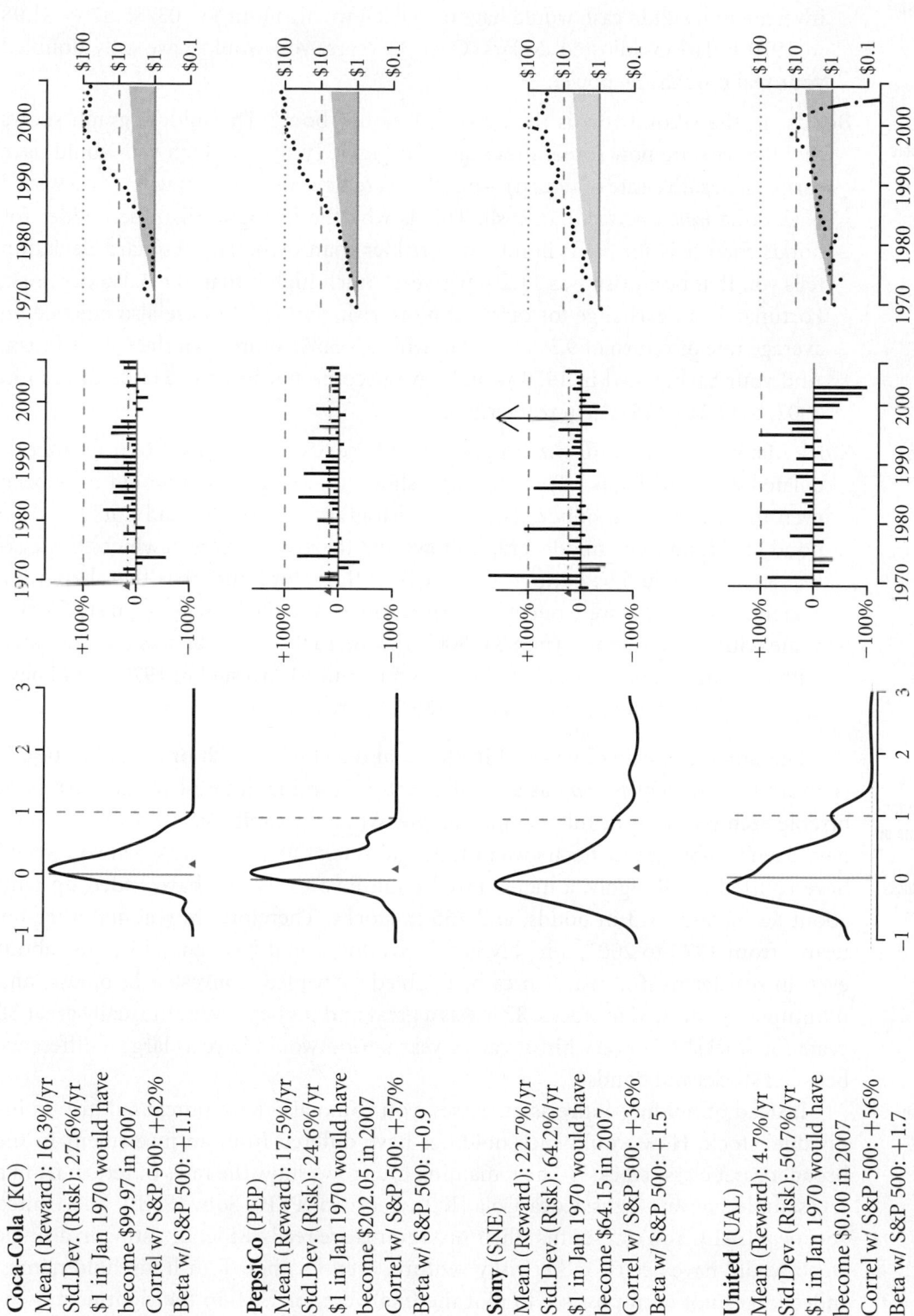

Coca-Cola (KO)
Mean (Reward): 16.3%/yr
Std.Dev. (Risk): 27.6%/yr
$1 in Jan 1970 would have become $99.97 in 2007
Correl w/ S&P 500: +62%
Beta w/ S&P 500: +1.1

PepsiCo (PEP)
Mean (Reward): 17.5%/yr
Std.Dev. (Risk): 24.6%/yr
$1 in Jan 1970 would have become $202.05 in 2007
Correl w/ S&P 500: +57%
Beta w/ S&P 500: +0.9

Sony (SNE)
Mean (Reward): 22.7%/yr
Std.Dev. (Risk): 64.2%/yr
$1 in Jan 1970 would have become $64.15 in 2007
Correl w/ S&P 500: +36%
Beta w/ S&P 500: +1.5

United (UAL)
Mean (Reward): 4.7%/yr
Std.Dev. (Risk): 50.7%/yr
$1 in Jan 1970 would have become $0.00 in 2007
Correl w/ S&P 500: +56%
Beta w/ S&P 500: +1.7

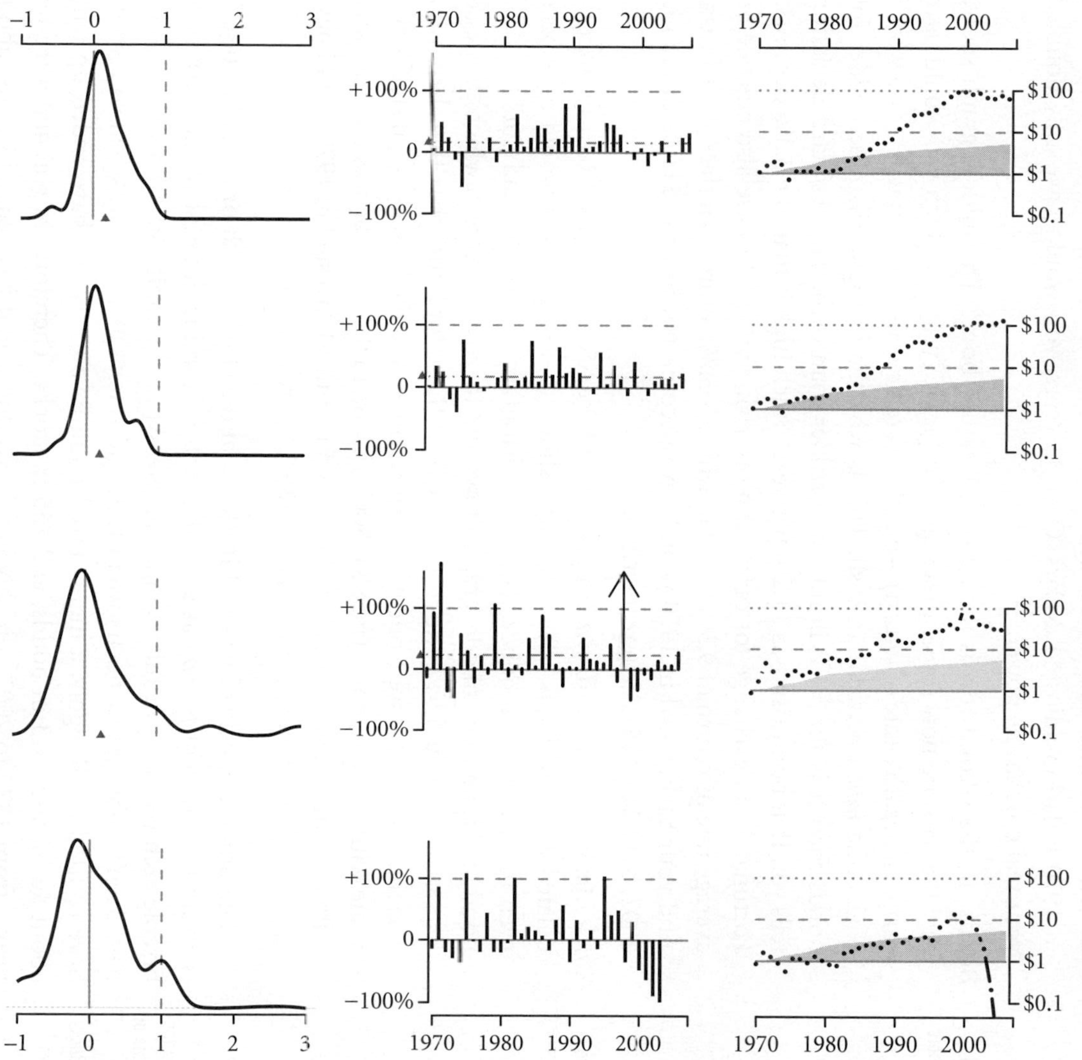

mean. The value of your total investment portfolio would have steadily marched upward—although pretty slowly. Each dollar invested in January 1970 would have become $11.03 at the end of 2007.

How much extra real inflation-adjusted value were these nominal returns really worth?

Of course, inflation would have eroded the value of each dollar. In purchasing power, your $1 in 1970 was equivalent to $5.57 in 2007. Therefore, the $11.03 investment result in cash would have only been worth about $11.03/$5.57 ≈ $1.98 in 1970 inflation-adjusted dollars. Over 38 years, you would have only doubled your real purchasing power.

Long-term bonds offered more reward, but were more variable, too.

➤ Section 6.1B, "Variance and Standard Deviation," p. 141

Bonds in the second row is the 20-year Treasury bond. The middle graph shows that the bars are now sometimes slightly negative (years in which you would have earned a negative rate of return)—but there are now also years in which you would have done *much* better than cash. This is why the histogram is much wider for bonds than it is for cash: Bonds were riskier than cash. The standard deviation tells you that bond risk was 11.2% per year, much higher than the 3.3% cash risk. Fortunately, in exchange for carrying more risk, you would have also enjoyed an average rate of return of 9.3% per year, which is 3.3% more than the 6.6% of cash. And your $1 invested in 1970 would have become not just the $11.03 of cash in 2007, but $24.37 ($4.38 in real terms).

Stocks offered even more reward, but were even more variable.

Stock Market in the third row is a portfolio of the S&P 500 firms. (Returns are calculated with dividends.) The left graph shows that large stocks would have been even more risky than bonds. The stock histogram is more "spread out" than the bond histogram. The middle graph shows that there were years in which the negatives of stocks could be quite a bit worse than those for bonds, but that there were also many years that were outright terrific. And again, the higher risk of stocks also came with more reward. The S&P 500's risk of 15.9% per year was compensated with a mean rate of return of 11.9% per year. Your $1 invested in 1970 would have ended up being worth $48.63 in 2007 ($8.73 in real terms).

Fixed-income investments performed relatively worse for taxable investors than the graphs in Table 7.1 indicate at first glance.

➤ Section 10.4A, "The Basics of (Federal) Income Taxes," p. 321

The difference between $48.63 in stocks and $11.03 in cash or $24.37 in bonds is an understatement *for you* as a retail investor. Nominal interest would have been taxable each year at your full income tax rate, while the capital gain on stocks would have been taxable at the much lower capital gains tax rate (and only when you would have realized it). Roughly, a highly taxed retail investor would have ended up with about $6 in cash, $13 in bonds, and $35 in stocks. Therefore, in real *and* after-tax terms, from 1970 to 2007, a highly taxed investor would have ended up just about even in real terms if invested in cash, doubled or tripled if invested in bonds, and quintupled if invested in stocks. This was a great and perhaps even unusually great 38 years for stocks! Not every historical 38-year period would have as large a difference between stocks and bonds.

Individual stocks can offer more reward and be even more risky.

Instead of holding entire asset classes, you could also have purchased just an individual stock. How would such holdings have differed from an investment in the broader asset class "stocks"? The remaining four rows show the rates of return from a few sample stalwart firms: Coca-Cola [KO], PepsiCo [PEP], Sony [SNE], and United Airlines [UAL]. You can see that their histograms are really wide: Investing in a single stock would have been a rather risky venture, even for these four household names. Indeed, it is not even possible to plot the final year for UAL in the rightmost compound return graph, because UAL stock investors lost *all* invested money in the 2003 bankruptcy, which on the logarithmic scale would have been minus infinity. And UAL illustrates another important issue: Despite losing all the money, it still had a positive average rate of return. (You already know why: This was the difference between geometric and arithmetic averages explained on page 180.)

SIDE NOTE: The following numbers are the major asset classes' returns according to Morningstar, a prominent financial data provider. All numbers are in percent per annum. Geometric averages are annualized; arithmetic averages are simple annual means. The 1970–2007 period is similar to the 1970–2007 period from Table 7.1, and thus gives a good comparison.

	1926–2007			1970–2007		
	"Reward"		Risk	"Reward"		Risk
Asset Class	Geo	Ari	SDV	Geo	Ari	SDV
Large-Firm (S&P 500) Stocks	10.4	12.3	20.0	11.1	12.4	16.6
Small-Firm Stocks	12.5	17.1	32.6	13.4	15.6	22.6
Long-Term Corporate Bonds	5.9	6.2	8.4	8.9	9.4	10.5
Long-Term Government Bonds	5.5	5.8	9.2	8.9	9.4	11.2
Intermediate Government Bonds	5.3	5.5	5.7	8.2	8.4	6.6
30-Day Treasuries	3.7	3.8	3.1	6.0	6.0	2.9
U.S. Inflation	3.0	3.1	4.2	4.6	4.7	3.1

Source: Ibbotson Stocks, Bonds, Bills and Inflation®, SBBI® Valuation Yearbook, © Morningstar 2008. Used with permission.

SOLVE NOW!

Q 7.5 Rank the following asset categories in terms of risk and reward: cash (money market), long-term bonds, the stock market, and a typical individual stock.

Q 7.6 Is the average individual stock safer or riskier than the stock market?

Q 7.7 Is it possible for an investment to have a positive average rate of return, but still lose you every penny?

7.1C COMOVEMENT, MARKET BETA, AND CORRELATION

Now we look at the correlation with the market, mentioned also in the leftmost column of Table 7.1.

Figure 7.4 highlights the rates of return on the S&P 500 and one specific stock, PepsiCo (PEP). The left column redraws the time-series graphs for these two investments from the third column in Table 7.1. Do you notice a correlation between these two series of rates of return? Are the years in which one is positive (or above its mean) more likely also to see the other be positive (or above its mean), and vice versa? It does seem that way. For example, the worst rates of return for both are 1974. Similarly, 1973 and 2002 were bad years for investors in either the S&P 500 or PepsiCo. In contrast, 1975,

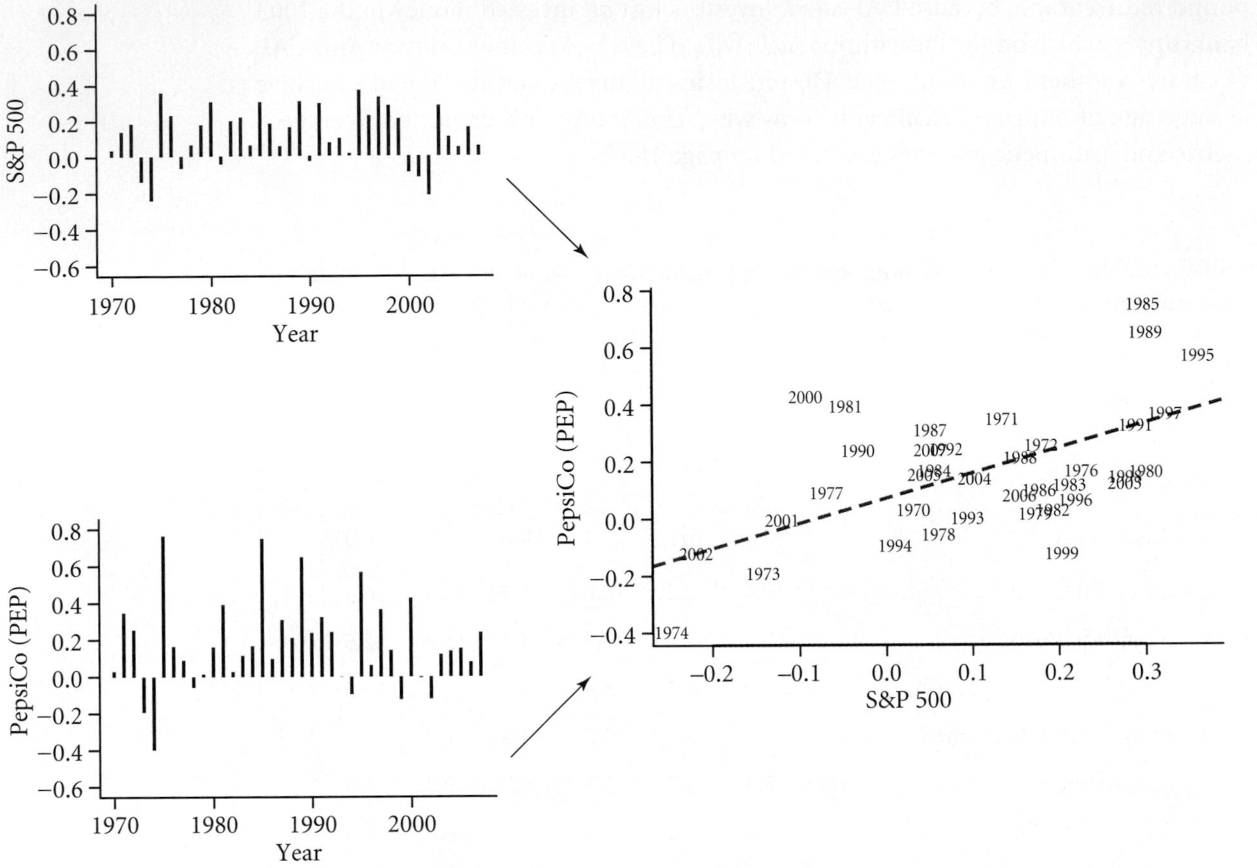

The top graph plots the annual rate of return on the S&P 500; the bottom graph plots the annual rate of return on PepsiCo. The graph on the right combines the information from the two graphs on the left. The stock market rate of return is on the *x*-axis, the PepsiCo rate of return is on the *y*-axis. The figure shows that in years when the stock market did well, PepsiCo tended to do well, too, and vice versa. This can be seen in the slope of the best-fitting line, which is called the market beta of PepsiCo. The market beta will play an important role in investments.

Reality Check: In practice, it is better to compute a market beta from the most recent 3 years of daily stock return data, and not from 38 years of annual stock return data.

FIGURE 7.4 Rates of Return on the S&P 500 and PepsiCo (PEP), 1970–2007

1985, 1989, and 1995 were good years for both. The correlation is not perfect: In 1999, the S&P 500 had a good year, but PepsiCo had a bad one; and in 2000, the market had a bad year, but PepsiCo had a good one. It is very common for all sorts of investments in the economy to move together with the stock market: In years of malaise, almost everything tends to be in malaise. In years of exuberance, almost everything tends to be exuberant. This tendency is called comovement.

Why do you care about comovement? Because you want assets that do well when everything else does poorly.

The comovement of investments is very important if you do not like risk. An investment that increases in value whenever the rest of your portfolio decreases in value is practically like "insurance" that pays off when you need it most. You might buy into such an investment even if it offers only a very low expected rate of return. In contrast, you might not like an investment that does very badly whenever the rest of your portfolio also does badly. To be included in your portfolio, such an investment would have to offer a very high expected rate of return.

How can you measure the extent to which securities covary with others? For example, how does PepsiCo covary with the S&P 500 (our stand-in for the market portfolio)? Did PepsiCo also go down when the market went down (making a bad situation worse), or did it go up (thereby serving as useful insurance)? How can you quantify such comovement?

Quantifying comovement.

You can answer this graphically. Plot the two return series against one another, as is done in the rightmost plot in Figure 7.4. Then find the line that best fits between the two series. (You will learn later how to compute it.) The slope of this line is called the **market beta** of a stock, and it is a measure of comovement between the rate of return on the stock with the rate of return on the market. It tells an investor whether this stock moved with or against the market. It carries great importance in financial economics.

Market beta is the slope of the best-fitting line (with the market's rate of return on the x-axis and the firm's rate of return on the y-axis).

- If the best-fitting line has a slope that is steeper than the 45° diagonal (well, if the x- and y-axes are drawn with the same scale), then the market beta is greater than 1. Such a line would imply that when the stock market did better (the x-axis), on average your stock did *a lot better* (the y-axis). For example, if a stock has a very steep positive slope—say, +3—then (assuming you hold the market portfolio) if the market dropped by an additional 10%, this stock would have been expected to drop by an additional 30%. If you primarily held the market portfolio, this new stock would have made your bad situation worse.
- If the slope is less than 1 (or even 0, a plain horizontal line), it means that, on average, your stock did not move as much (or not at all) with the stock market.
- If a stock has a very negative slope—say, −2—this investment would likely have "rescued" you when the market dropped by 10%. On average, it would have earned a positive 20% rate of return. Adding such a stock to your market portfolio would be like buying insurance.

PepsiCo's particular line had a slope of 0.9. That is, it was a little less steep than the diagonal line. In effect, this means that if you had held the stock market, PepsiCo would have been neither great insurance nor a great additional hazard for you. A 1% performance above (below) normal for the S&P would have meant you would have earned 0.9% above (below) normal in your PepsiCo holdings.

Instead of beta, you could measure comovement with another statistic that you may already have come across: the so-called **correlation**. Correlation and beta are related. The correlation has a feature that beta does not. A correlation of 100% indicates that two variables always perfectly move together; a correlation of 0% indicates that two variables move about independently; and a correlation of −100% indicates that two variables always perfectly move in opposite directions. (A correlation can never exceed +100% or −100%.) In PepsiCo's case, one can work out that the correlation is +58%. The correlation's limited range from −1 to +1 is both an advantage and a disadvantage. On the positive side, the correlation is a number that is often easier to judge than beta. On the negative side, the correlation has no concept of scale. It can be 100% even if the y variable moves only very, very mildly with x (e.g., if every $y = 0.0001 \cdot x$, the correlation is still a positive 100%). In contrast, beta can be anything from minus infinity to plus infinity.

Market beta is a cousin of correlation.

The sign of the correlation and beta are always the same.

A positive correlation always implies a positive beta, and vice versa. Of course, beta and correlation are only measures of *average* comovement: Even for investments with positive betas, there are individual years in which the investment and stock market do not move together (recall 1999 and 2000 for PepsiCo and the S&P 500). Stocks with negative betas, for which a negative market rate of return *on average* associates with a positive stock return (and vice versa), are rare. There are only a very few investment categories that are generally thought to be negatively correlated with the market—principally gold and other precious metals.

SOLVE NOW!

Q 7.8 How do you graph a "market beta"? What should be on the x-axis, and what should be on the y-axis? What is an individual data point?

Q 7.9 What is the market beta of the market?

7.1D THE BIG PICTURE TAKE-AWAYS

The main empirical regularities.

What can you learn from these graphs? Actually, almost everything that there is to learn about investments! I will explain these facts in much more detail soon. In the meantime, here are the most important points that the graphs show:

- History tells us that stocks offered higher average rates of return than bonds, which in turn offered higher average rates of return than cash. However, keep in mind that this was only *on average*. In any given year, the relationship might have been reversed. For example, stock investors lost 22% of their wealth in 2002, while cash investors gained about 1.7%.
- Although stocks did well (on average), you could have lost your shirt investing in them, especially if you had bet on just one individual stock. For example, if you had invested in United Airlines in 1970, you would have lost all your money.
- Cash was the safest investment—its distribution is tightly centered around its mean, so there were no years with negative returns. Bonds were riskier. Stocks were riskier yet. (Sometimes, stocks are called "noisy," because it is really difficult to predict how they will perform.)
- There seems to be a relationship between risk and reward: The riskier investments tended to have higher average rates of return. (However, you will learn in the next chapters that the risk has to be looked at in context. Thus, please do not overread the simple relationship between the mean and the standard deviation here.)
- Large portfolios consisting of many stocks tended to have less risk than individual stocks. The S&P 500 stocks had a risk of 16%, which was less than the risk of most individual stocks (e.g., PepsiCo had a risk of about 25%). This is due to the phenomenon of diversification.

➤ Section 8.2, "Portfolios, Diversification, and Investor Preferences," p. 205

- The average rate of return is always larger than the geometric (compound) rate of return. A positive average rate of return usually, but not always, translates into a positive compound holding rate of return. For example, United Airlines had a positive average rate of return, despite having lost all its investors' money.

- Stocks tend to move together. For example, if you look at 2001 and 2002, not only did the S&P 500 go down, but all the individual stocks tended to go down, too. In 1998, on the other hand, most stocks tended to go up (or at least not down much). The mid-1990s were good to all stocks. In contrast, money market returns had little to do with the stock market. Long-term bonds were in between.
- On an annual frequency, the correlation between cash and the stock market (the S&P 500) was about zero; the correlation between long-term bond returns and the stock market was around 25%; and the correlation between individual stocks and the stock market was around 30% to 70%. The fact that investment rates of return tend to move together is important. It is the foundation for the market beta, a measure of risk that we have touched on and that will be explained in detail in Chapter 8.

7.1E WILL HISTORY REPEAT ITSELF?

History is only useful over long horizons, not over just a few years.

As a financier, you are not interested in history for its own sake. Instead, you really want to know more about the future. History is useful only because it is your best available indicator of the future. But which history? One year? Thirty years? One hundred years? I can tell you that if you had drawn the graphs beginning in 1926 instead of 1970, the big conclusions would have remained the same. However, if you had started in 2001, things would have been different. What would you have seen? Two awful years for stock investors. You should know intuitively that this would not have been a representative sample period. To make any sensible inferences about what is going on in the financial markets, you need many years of history, not just one, two, or three—and certainly not the 6-week investment performance touted by some funds or friends (who also often display remarkable selective memory!). The flip side of this argument is that you cannot reliably say what the rate of return will be over your next year. It is easier to forecast the *average* annual rate of return over 5 to 10 years than over 1 year. Your investment outcome over any single year will be very noisy.

Even over long horizons, history can sometimes be misleading. The Nikkei-225 stock index is a good example.

Instead of relying on just 1 year, relying on statistics computed over many years is much better. However, although 20 to 30 years of performance is the minimum number necessary to learn something about return patterns, this is still not sufficient for you to be very confident. Again, you are really interested in what will happen in the next 5 to 10 years, not what did happen in the last 5 to 10 years. Yes, the historical performance can help you judge, but you should not trust it blindly. For example, an investor in UAL in 2000 might have guessed that the average rate of return for UAL would have been positive—and would have been sorely disappointed. Investors in the Japanese stock market in 1986 saw the Nikkei-225 stock market index rise from 10,000 to 40,000 by 1990—a 40% rate of return per year. If they had believed that history was a good guide, they would have expected $40{,}000 \cdot 1.40^{13} \approx 3.2$ million by the end of 2002. Instead, the Nikkei had fallen below 8,000 in April 2003 and has only recently recovered to 15,307 by December 2007. History would have been a terrible guide.

But you do not have much choice other than to rely on history.

Nevertheless, despite the intrinsic hazards in using historical information to forecast future returns, having historical data is a great advantage. It is a rich source of forecasting power, so like everyone else, you will have to use historical statistics. But please be careful not to rely too much on them. For example, if you look at an investment that had extremely high or low past historical rates of return, you may not want to believe that this is likely to continue.

Historical standard deviations and variances are good estimators of their future equivalents. This is not the case for historical average rates of return.

In relative terms, what historical information can you trust more and what historical information should you trust less?

Historical risk: Standard deviations and correlations (how stock movements tend to be related or unrelated) tend to be fairly stable, especially for large asset classes and diversified portfolios. That is, for 2008 to 2010, you can reasonably expect PepsiCo to have a risk of about 25% per year, a correlation of about 60%, and a market beta of about 1.

Historical mean reward: Historical average rates of return are not very reliable predictors of future expected rates of return. That is, you should not necessarily believe that PepsiCo will continue to earn an expected rate of return of 18% per year over the long run.

Realizations: You should definitely not believe that past realizations are good predictors of future realizations. Just because PepsiCo had a rate of return of 24% in 2007 does not make it likely that it will have a rate of return of 24% in 2008.

A lottery analogy may help you understand the last two points better. If you have played the lottery many times, your historical average rate of return is unlikely to be predictive of your future expected rate of return—especially if you have won it big at least once. Yes, you could trust it if you had millions of historical realizations, but you inevitably do not have so many. Consequently, your average historical payoff is only a mediocre predictor of your next week's payoff. And you should definitely not trust your most recent realization to be indicative of the future. Just because "5, 10, 12, 33, 34, 38" won last week does not mean that it will likely win again.

To make life easier, most finance assumes that we know all the statistical distributions describing future *expected* rates of return. But remain mindful of this leap of faith.

Henceforth, like almost all of finance, we will just assume that we know the statistical distributions from which future investment returns will be drawn. For exposition, this makes our task a lot easier. When you want to use our techniques in the real world, you will usually collect historical data and pretend that the future distribution is the same as the historical distribution. (Some investors in the real world use some more sophisticated techniques, but ultimately these techniques are also just variations on this theme.) However, don't trust this blindly—historical data is only an imperfect guide to the future.

7.2 A BRIEF OVERVIEW OF EQUITY-RELATED MARKET INSTITUTIONS

Let's look into the institutional arrangements for equity trading. After all, from a corporate perspective, stocks are more interesting than many other financial instruments, such as foreign government bonds, even if there is more money in foreign government bonds than in corporate equity. It is the equity holders who finance most of the risks of corporate projects. Moreover, although there is more money in nonequity financial markets, the subject area of investments also tends to focus on equities (stocks) because retail investors find it easy to participate and the data on stocks is relatively easy to come by. So it makes sense to describe a few institutional details as to how investors and stocks "connect"—exchange cash for claims, and vice versa.

7.2A BROKERS

Retail brokers execute trades and keep track of portfolios. They also arrange shorts.

Most individuals place their orders to buy or sell stocks with a **retail broker**, such as *Ameritrade* (a "deep-discount" broker), *Charles Schwab* (a "discount" broker), or *Merrill Lynch* (a "full-service" broker). Discount brokers may charge only about $10 commission per trade, but they often receive "rebate" payments back from the market maker to which they route your order. This is called "payment for order flow." The market maker in turn recoups this payment to the broker by executing your trade at a price that is less favorable. Although the purpose of such an arrangement seems deceptive, the evidence suggests that discount brokers are still often cheaper in facilitating investor trades—especially small investor trades—even after taking this hidden payment into account. They just are not as (relatively) cheap as they want to make you believe. Investors can place either **market orders**, which ask for execution at the current price, or **limit orders**, which ask for execution if the price is above or below a limit that the investor can specify. (There are also many other modifications of orders, e.g., *stop-loss* orders [which instruct a broker to sell a security if it has lost a certain amount of money], *good-til-canceled* orders, and *fill-or-kill* orders.) The first function of retail brokers then is to handle the execution of trades. They usually do so by routing investors' orders to a centralized trading location (e.g., a particular stock exchange), the choice of which is typically at the retail broker's discretion, as is the particular agent (e.g., floor broker) engaged to execute the trade. The second function of retail brokers is to keep track of investors' holdings, to facilitate purchasing **on margin** (whereby investors can borrow money to purchase stock, allowing them to purchase more securities than they could afford on a pure cash basis), and to facilitate selling securities "short," which allows investors to speculate that a stock will go down.

➤ Market maker, Section 7.2B, p. 192

Prime brokers leave execution to the client investor.

Many large institutional investors separate the two functions: The investor employs its own traders, while the broker takes care only of the bookkeeping of the investor's portfolio, margin provisions, and shorting provisions. Such limited brokers are called **prime brokers**.

HOW SHORTING STOCKS WORKS

Shorting is like borrowing and then issuing securities. The interest on the proceeds may be earned by the broker or by the client (or be shared).

If you want to speculate that a stock will go down, you would want to short it. This shorting would be arranged by your broker. Shorting is important enough to deserve an extended explanation:

- You find an investor in the market who is willing to lend you the shares. In a perfect market, this does not cost a penny. In the real world, the broker has to find a willing lender. Both the broker and lender usually earn a few basis points per year for doing you the favor of facilitating your short sale.
- After you have borrowed the shares, you sell them into the market to someone else who wanted to buy the shares. In a perfect market, you would keep the proceeds and earn interest on them. In the real world, your broker may force you to put these

➤ Section 5.7, "Shorting and Locking in Forward Interest Rates," p. 123

proceeds into low-yield safe bonds. If you are a small retail investor, your brokerage firm may even keep the interest proceeds altogether.

- When you want to "unwind" your short, you repurchase the shares and return them to your lender.

For example, if you borrowed the shares when they were trading for $50, and the shares now sell for $30, you can repurchase them for $20 less than what you sold them into the market for. This $20 is your profit. In an ideal world, you can think of your role effectively as the same as that of the company—you can issue shares and use the $50 proceeds to fund your investments (e.g., to earn interest). In the real world, you have to take transaction costs into account. (Shorting has become so common that there are now exchange-traded futures on stocks that make this even easier.)

➤ Section 25.1B, "Currency Forwards and Interest Rate Parity," p. 945

SOLVE NOW!

Q 7.10 What are the two main functions of brokerage firms?

Q 7.11 How does a prime broker differ from a retail broker?

Q 7.12 Is your rate of return higher if you short a stock in the perfect world or in the real world? Why?

7.2B EXCHANGES AND NON-EXCHANGES

The two big stock exchanges are the NYSE and NASDAQ. The NYSE is a hybrid market. The NASDAQ is only electronic.

A retail broker would route your transaction to a centralized trading location. The most prominent are exchanges. An **exchange** is a centralized trading location where financial securities are traded. The two most important stock exchanges in the United States are the **New York Stock Exchange** (**NYSE**, also nicknamed the **Big Board**) and **NASDAQ** (originally an acronym for "National Association of Securities Dealers Automated Quotation System"). The NYSE used to be exclusively an **auction market**, in which one designated **specialist** (assigned for each stock) managed the auction process by trading with individual brokers on the floor of the exchange. This specialist was often a monopolist. However, even the NYSE now conducts much of its trading electronically. In contrast to the NYSE's hybrid human-electronic process primarily in one physical location on Wall Street, NASDAQ has always been a purely electronic exchange without specialists. (For security reasons, its location—well, the location of its computer systems—is secret.) For each NASDAQ stock, there is at least one **market maker**, a broker-dealer who has agreed to stand by continuously to offer to buy or sell shares, electronically of course, thereby creating a liquid and immediate market for the general public. Moreover, market makers are paid for providing liquidity: They receive additional rebates from the exchange when they post a bid or an ask that is executed. Most NASDAQ stocks have multiple market makers, drawn from a pool of about 500 trading firms (such as J.P. Morgan or E*Trade), which compete to offer the best price. Market makers have one advantage over the general public: They can see the **limit order book**, which contains as-yet-unexecuted orders from investors to purchase or sell if the stock price changes—giving them a good idea at which price a lot of buying or selling activity will occur. The NYSE is the older exchange, and for historical reasons, is the biggest exchange for trading most "blue chip" stocks. ("Blue chip" now means "well-established and serious." Ironically, the term itself came from poker, where the highest-denomination chips were blue.) In 2006, the NYSE listed just under 3,000 companies worth about $25 trillion. (This is about twice the annual U.S. GDP.) NASDAQ tends to trade smaller and high-technology firms, lists about as many firms, and has more trading activity than the NYSE. Some stocks are traded on both exchanges.

Auction markets, popular in other countries, have lower execution costs, but also slower execution speeds.

Continuous trading—trading at any moment an investor wants to execute—relies on the presence of the standby intermediaries (specialists or market makers), who are willing to absorb shares when no one else is available. This is risky business, and thus any intermediary must earn a good rate of return to be willing to do so. To avoid this cost, some countries have organized their exchanges into noncontinuous auction systems, which match buy and sell orders a couple of times each day. The disadvantage is that you cannot execute orders immediately but have to delay until a whole range of buy orders and sell orders have accumulated. The advantage is that this eliminates the risk that an (expensive) intermediary would otherwise have to bear. Thus, auctions generally offer lower trading costs but slower execution.

New alternative trading institutions: electronic communication networks (ECNs).

Even in the United States, innovation and change are everywhere. For example, **electronic communication networks** (**ECNs**) have recently made big inroads into the trading business, replacing exchanges, especially for large institutional trades. (They can trade the same stocks that exchanges are trading, and thus they compete with exchanges in terms of cost and speed of execution.) An ECN cuts out the specialist, allowing investors to post price-contingent orders themselves. ECNs may specialize in lower execution costs, higher broker kickbacks, or faster execution. The biggest ECNs are Archipelago and Instinet. In 2005, the NYSE merged with Archipelago, and NASDAQ purchased Instinet. (It is hard to keep track of the most recent trading arrangements. For example, in 2006, the NYSE also merged with ArcaEx, yet another electronic trading system, and merged with Euronext, a pan-European stock exchange based in Paris. As of this writing, it is now officially called **NYSE Euronext**. In addition, the NYSE converted from a mutual company owned by its traders into a publicly traded for-profit company itself.)

Crossing networks and more . . .

An even more interesting method to buy and trade stocks is that of **crossing systems**, such as ITG's POSIT. ITG focuses primarily on matching large institutional trades with one another in an auction-like manner. If no match on the other side is found, the order may simply not be executed. But if a match is made, by cutting out the specialist or market maker, the execution is a lot cheaper than it would have been on an exchange. Recently, even more novel trading places have sprung up. For example, **Liquidnet** uses peer-to-peer networking—like the original Napster—to match buyers and sellers in real time. ECNs and electronic limit order books are now the dominant trading systems for equities worldwide, with only the U.S. exchange floors as holdouts. Similar exchanges and computer programs are also used to trade futures, derivatives, currencies, and even some bonds.

There are also informal financial markets, especially OTC (over-the-counter).

There are many other financial markets, too. There are financial exchanges handling stock options, commodities, insurance contracts, and so on. A huge segment is the **over-the-counter** (**OTC**) markets. Over-the-counter means "call around, usually to a set of traders well known to trade in the asset, until you find someone willing to buy or sell at a price you like." Though undergoing rapid institutional change, most bond transactions are still over-the-counter. Although OTC markets handle significantly more bond trading in terms of transaction dollar amounts than bond exchanges, OTC transaction costs are prohibitively high for retail investors. If you call without knowing the market in great detail, the person on the other end of the line will be happy to quote you a shamelessly high price, hoping that you do not know any better. The **NASD** (National Association of Securities Dealers) also operates a semi-OTC market for the stocks of smaller firms, which are listed on the so-called **pink sheets**. Foreign securities trade on their local national exchanges, but the costs for U.S. retail investors are again often too high to make direct participation worthwhile.

SOLVE NOW!

Q 7.13 How does a crossing system differ from an electronic exchange?

Q 7.14 What is a specialist? What is a market maker? When trading, what advantage do the two have over you?

Q 7.15 Describe some alternatives to trading on the main stock exchanges.

7.2C INVESTMENT COMPANIES AND VEHICLES

The SEC regulates many investment vehicles that are active in the U.S. financial markets. Under the Investment Company Act of 1940, there are three types of **investment companies**: open-end funds, closed-end funds, and unit investment trusts (UITs).

The "open end" feature allows investors to redeem their shares. It forces the fund's shares to trade for close to the value of its holdings.

In the United States, open-end fund is a synonym for mutual fund. (Elsewhere, mutual funds can include other classes.) Being **open end** means that the fund can create shares at will. Investors can also redeem their fund shares at the end of each trading day in exchange for the **net asset value** (NAV), which must be posted daily. This gives investors little reason to sell their fund shares to other investors—thus, mutual funds do not trade on any exchanges. The redemption right gives the law of one price a lot of bite—fund shares are almost always worth nearly exactly what their underlying holdings are worth. If an open-end fund's share price were to fall much below the value of its holdings, an arbitrageur could buy up the fund shares, redeem them, and thereby earn free money. (One discrepancy is due to some odd tax complications: the fund's capital gains and losses are passed through to the fund investors at the end of every year, but they may not be what every investor experienced.) Interestingly, in the United States, there are now more mutual funds than there are stocks in the financial market.

Closed-end funds do not allow shares to be redeemed. This is useful for funds which are investing in illiquid assets.

In a **closed-end fund**, there is one big initial primary offering of fund shares, and investors cannot redeem their fund shares for the underlying value. The advantage of a closed-end fund is that it can itself invest in assets that are less liquid. After all, it may not be forced to sell its holdings on the whims of its own investors. Many closed-end funds are exchange traded, so that if a closed-end fund investor needs cash, she can resell her shares. The disadvantage of the closed-end scheme is that the law of one price has much less bite. On average, closed-end funds trade persistently below the value of their underlying holdings, roughly in line with the (often high) fees that the managers of many of these closed-end funds are charging.

Both mutual funds and closed-end fund managers are allowed to trade their fund holdings quite actively—and many do so. Although some funds specialize in imitating common stock market indexes, many more try to guess the markets or try to be more "boutique." Most funds are classified into a category based on their general trading motivation (such as "market timing," or "growth" or "value," or "income" or "capital appreciation").

Mutual funds are open-ended, actively traded investment vehicles.

A **unit investment trust** (UIT) is sort of closed end in its creation (usually through one big primary offering) and sort of open end in its redemption policies (usually accepting investor redemption requests on demand). Moreover, SEC rules forbid UITs to trade actively (although this is about to change), and UITs must have a fixed termination date (even if it is 50 years in the future). UITs can be listed on a stock exchange, which makes it easy for retail investors to buy and sell them. Some early **exchange-traded funds** (**ETFs**) were structured as UITs, although this required some additional legal contortions that allowed them to create more shares on demand. This is why ETFs are nowadays usually structured as open-end funds.

UITs are passive "basket" investment vehicles.

Some other investment vehicles are regulated by the SEC under different rules. The most prominent may be certain kinds of **American Depositary Receipt** (**ADR**). An ADR is a passive investment vehicle that usually owns the stock of only one foreign security, held in escrow at a U.S. bank (usually the Bank of New York). The advantage of an ADR is that it makes it easier for U.S. retail investors to trade in the foreign security without incurring large transaction costs. ADRs are redeemable, which gives the law of one price great bite.

ADRs are investment vehicles, too. Many ADRs (though not all) are regulated by the SEC under different rules.

There are also funds that are structured so that they do not need to register with the SEC. This means that they cannot openly advertise for new investors and are limited to fewer than 100 investors. This includes most **hedge funds**, **venture capital funds**, and other **private equity funds**. Many **offshore funds** are set up to allow foreign investors to hold U.S. stocks not only without SEC regulation, but also without ever having to tread into the domain of the U.S. IRS.

Other funds are entirely unregulated.

7.2D HOW SECURITIES APPEAR AND DISAPPEAR

INFLOWS

Most publicly traded equities appear on public exchanges, almost always NASDAQ, through **initial public offerings** (**IPOs**). This is an event in which a privately traded company first sells shares to ordinary retail and institutional investors. IPOs are usually executed by **underwriters** (investment bankers such as Goldman Sachs or Merrill Lynch), which are familiar with the complex legal and regulatory process and which have easy access to an investor client base to buy the newly issued shares. Shares in IPOs are typically sold at a fixed price—and for about 10% below the price at which they are likely to trade on the first day of after-market open trading. (Many IPO shares are allocated to the brokerage firm's favorite customers, and they can be an important source of profit.)

Firms first sell public shares in IPOs.

➤ Goldman Sachs, Section 23.1E, p. 860

Usually, about a third of the company is sold in the IPO, and the typical IPO offers shares worth between \$20 million and \$100 million, although some are much larger (e.g., privatizations, like British Telecom). About two-thirds of all such IPO

Money also flows into the financial markets through SEOs.

ANECDOTE Trading Volume in the Tech Bubble

During the tech bubble of 1999 and 2000, IPOs appreciated by 65% on their opening day *on average*. Getting an IPO share allocation was like getting free money. Of course, ordinary investors rarely received any such share allocations—only the underwriter's favorite clients did. This later sparked a number of lawsuits, one of which revealed that Credit Suisse First Boston (CSFB) allocated shares of IPOs to more than 100 customers who, in return for IPO allocations, funneled between 33% and 65% of their IPO profits back to CSFB in the form of excessive trading of other stocks (like Compaq and Disney) at inflated trading commissions.

How important was this "kickback" activity? In the aggregate, in 1999 and 2000, underwriters left about $66 billion on the table for their first-day IPO buyers. If investors rebated 20% back to underwriters in the form of extra commissions, this would amount to $13 billion in excessive underwriter profits. At an average commission of 10 cents per share, this would require 130 billion shares to be traded, or an average of 250 million shares per trading day. This figure suggests that kickback portfolio churning may have accounted for as much as 10% of all shares traded!

Source: Ritter-Welch (2002).

companies never amount to much or even die within a couple of years, but the remaining third soon thereafter offer more shares in **seasoned equity offerings (SEOs)**. These days, however, much expansion in the number of shares in publicly traded companies—especially for large companies—comes not from seasoned equity offerings but from employee stock option plans, which eventually become unrestricted publicly traded shares.

A reverse merger has become another common way to enter the public financial markets.

Because IPOs face complex legal regulations, the alternative of **reverse mergers** has recently become prominent. In a reverse merger, a large, privately-owned company that wants to go public merges with a small company that is already publicly traded. The owners of the big company receive newly issued shares in the combined entity. And, of course, any time a publicly traded company purchases assets, such as privately held companies, and issues more shares, capital is in effect being deployed from the private sector into the public markets.

Publicly traded companies must follow rules. For example, they must report their financials, and restrict insider trading.

In 1933/1934, Congress established the **Securities and Exchange Commission (SEC)** through the *Securities Exchange Acts*. It further regulated investment advisors through the *Investment Advisers Act of 1940*. (The details of these acts can be obtained at the SEC website.) Aside from regulating the IPO process, they also prescribe what publicly traded corporations must do. For example, publicly traded companies must regularly report their financials and other information to the SEC. Moreover, these acts prohibit **insider trading** on unreleased specific information, although more general trading by insiders is legal (and seems to be done fairly profitably). The SEC can only pursue civil fines. It is up to the states to pursue criminal sanctions, which they often do simultaneously. (Other regulations that publicly traded firms have to follow derive from some other federal laws, and, more importantly, state laws.)

OUTFLOWS

Money flows out from the financial markets via dividends and share repurchases.

Capital flows out of the financial markets in a number of ways. The most important venues are capital distributions such as dividends and share repurchases. Many companies pay some of their earnings in **dividends** to investors. Dividends, of course, do not fall like manna from heaven. For example, a firm worth $100,000 may pay $1,000, and would therefore be worth \$99,000 after the dividend distribution. If you own a share of \$100, you would own (roughly) \$99 in stock and \$1 in dividends after the payment—still \$100 in total, no better or worse. (If you have to pay some taxes on dividend receipts, you might come out for the worse.) Alternatively, firms may reduce their outstanding shares by paying out earnings in **share repurchases**. For example, the firm may dedicate the \$1,000 to share repurchases, and you could ask the firm to use \$100 thereof to repurchase your share. But even if you hold onto your share, you have not lost anything. Previously, you owned \$100/\$100,000 = 0.1% of a \$100,000 company, for a net of \$100. Now, you will own \$100/\$99,000 ≈ 1.0101% of a \$99,000 company—multiply this to find that your share is still worth \$100. In either case, the value of outstanding public equity in the firm has shrunk from \$100,000 to \$99,000. We will discuss dividends and share repurchases in Chapter 19.

➤ Dividend irrelevance, Section 19.2, p. 707

Firms can also exit the public financial markets entirely by delisting. Delistings usually occur either when a firm is purchased by another firm or when it runs into financial difficulties so bad that they fail to meet minimum listing requirements. Often, such financial difficulties lead to bankruptcy or liquidation. Some firms even voluntarily liquidate, determining that they can pay their shareholders more if they sell their assets and return the money to them. This is rare because managers usually like to keep their jobs—even if continuation of the company is not in the interest of shareholders. More commonly, firms make bad investments and fall in value to the point where they are delisted from the exchange and/or go into bankruptcy. Fortunately, investors enjoy **limited liability**, which means that they can at most lose their investments and do not have to pay further for any sins of management.

Shares can also shrink out of the financial markets in bankruptcies, liquidations, and delistings.

➤ Bankruptcy and managers, Section 25.3, p. 957

➤ Limited liability, Section 6.4B, p. 157

SOLVE NOW!

Q 7.16 What should happen if the holdings of an open-end fund are worth much more than what the shares of the fund are trading for? What should happen in a closed-end fund?

Q 7.17 What are the main mechanisms by which money flows from investors into firms?

Q 7.18 What are the institutional mechanisms by which funds disappear from the public financial markets back into the pockets of investors?

Q 7.19 How do shares disappear from the stock exchange?

SUMMARY

This chapter covered the following major points:

- Table 7.1 showed an analysis of historical rate of return patterns of investments in cash, bonds, stock indexes, and individual stocks.
  - Stocks, on average, had higher average rates of return than bonds, which in turn had higher average rates of return than cash investments.
  - Individual stocks were most risky. Large stock market portfolios had lower risk than individual stock holdings. Bonds had lower risk yet, and cash was least risky.

- Stocks (and many other investments) tended to correlate positively: When the stock market overall had a good (bad) year, most stocks also had a good (bad) year.
- Most finance assumes that statistics are known. This is a leap of faith. In real life, historical data can help you in predicting the future, but it is not perfect. Historical risks and correlations are good predictors of their future equivalents; historical means may not be.
- Section 7.2 explained many institutional arrangements governing publicly traded equity securities. This includes the roles of retail and prime brokers, exchanges, and funds. It also described how stocks can be shorted, and how funds flow in and out of the financial markets.

KEY TERMS

SOLVE NOW! SOLUTIONS

Q 7.1 A time-series graph shows how individual years matter. This can no longer be seen in a histogram.

Q 7.2 A histogram makes it easier to see how frequent different types of outcomes are—and thus, where the distribution is centered and how spread out it is.

Q 7.3 A compound return graph shows how a time series of rates of return interacts to produce long-run returns. In other words, you can see whether a long-run investment would have made or lost money. This is difficult to see in a time-series graph.

Q 7.4 Note that because the returns in (b) and (c) alternate, you just need to work out the safe 2-year returns—thereafter, they will continue in their (unrealistic) patterns.

(a) 5% for both.
(b) Over 2 years, you earn $1.00 \cdot 1.10 - 1 = 10.00\%$. This means that the annualized rate of return is $\sqrt{1.1} - 1 \approx 4.88\%$. This is lower than the average rate of return, which is still 5%.
(c) Over 2 years, you earn $0.9 \cdot 1.20 - 1 = 8.00\%$. This means that the annualized rate of return is $\sqrt{1.08} - 1 \approx 3.92\%$. This is lower than the 5% average rate of return.

Yes. The difference between its annualized and its average rate of return is greater for a more volatile investment.

Q 7.5 The risk is usually increasing: lowest for cash, then bonds, then the stock market portfolio, and finally individual stocks. The average reward is increasing for the first three, but this is not necessarily true for an individual stock.

Q 7.6 Usually (but not always), individual stocks are riskier.

Q 7.7 Yes. For example, look at UAL in Table 7.1. It lost everything but still had a positive average arithmetic rate of return.

Q 7.8 To graph the market beta, the rate of return on the market (e.g., the S&P 500) should be on the x-axis, and the rate of return on the investment for which you want to determine the market beta should be on the y-axis. A data point is the two rates of return from the same given time period (e.g., over a year). The market beta is the slope of the best-fitting line.

Q 7.9 The market beta of the market is 1—you are plotting the rate of return on the market on both the x-axis and the y-axis, so the beta is the slope of this 45° diagonal line.

Q 7.10 Brokers execute orders and keep track of investors' portfolios. They also facilitate purchasing on margin.

Q 7.11 Prime brokers are usually used by larger investors. Prime brokers allow investors to employ their own traders to execute trades. (Like retail brokers, prime brokers provide portfolio accounting, margin, and securities borrowing.)

Q 7.12 Your rate of return is higher if you short a stock in the perfect world because you earn interest on the proceeds. In the real world, your broker may help himself to this interest.

Q 7.13 A crossing system does not execute trades unless there is a counterparty. It also tries to cross orders a few times a day.

Q 7.14 The specialist is often a monopolist who makes the market on the NYSE. The specialist buys and sells from his own inventory of a stock, thereby "making a market." Market makers are the equivalent on NASDAQ, but there are usually many and they compete with one another. Unlike ordinary investors, both specialists and market makers can see the limit orders placed by other investors.

Q 7.15 The alternatives are often electronic, and they often rely on matching trades—thus, they may not execute trades that they cannot match. Electronic communication networks are the dominant example of these. Another alternative is to execute the trade in the over-the-counter (OTC) market, which is a network of geographically dispersed dealers who are making markets in various securities.

Q 7.16 In an open-end fund, you should purchase fund shares and request redemption. (You could short the underlying holdings during the time you wait for the redemption in order not to suffer price risk.) In a closed-end fund, you would have to oust the management to allow you to redeem your shares.

Q 7.17 The main mechanisms by which money flows from investors into firms are first IPOs and SEOs, and second reverse mergers, which are then sold off to investors.

Q 7.18 Funds disappear from the public financial markets back into the pockets of investors through dividends and share repurchases.

Q 7.19 Shares can disappear in a delisting or a repurchase.

PROBLEMS

The ▆ *indicates problems available in* myfinancelab

Q 7.20 Using the information in Table 7.1 on page 182, compute the discrepancy between arithmetic and geometric rates of return for cash and stocks. Which one is lower? Why?

Q 7.21 Broadly speaking, what was the average rate of return on cash, bonds, and stocks? What time period are your numbers from?

Q 7.22 Broadly speaking, what was the average risk of cash, bonds, and stocks? What time period are your numbers from?

Q 7.23 How good are historical statistics as indicators of future statistics? Which kinds of statistics are better? Which kinds are worse?

Q 7.24 Does the market beta of stocks in the market average out to zero?

Q 7.25 Give an example in which a stock had a positive average rate of return, even though it lost its investors' money.

Q 7.26 Looking at the figures in this chapter, did 20-year bonds move with or against the U.S. stock market? Did bonds move more or less with the U.S. stock market than the foreign stock, Sony?

Q 7.27 Do individual stocks tend to move together? How could this be measured?

Q 7.28 Explain the differences between a market order and a limit order.

Q 7.29 What extra function do retail brokers handle that prime brokers do not?

Q 7.30 Describe the differences between the NYSE and NASDAQ.

Q 7.31 Roughly, how many firms are listed on the NYSE? How many are listed on NASDAQ? Then use a financial website to find an estimate of the current number.

Q 7.32 Is NASDAQ a crossing market?

Q 7.33 What are the two main mechanisms by which a privately held company can go public?

Q 7.34 When and under what circumstance was the SEC founded?

Q 7.35 Insider trading is a criminal offense. Does the SEC prosecute these charges?

Q 7.36 What is the OTC market?

Q 7.37 What are the three main types of investment companies as defined by the SEC? Which is the best deal in a perfect market?

Q 7.38 If a firm repurchases 1% of its shares, does this change the capitalization of the stock market on which it lists? If a firm pays 1% of its value in dividends, does this change the capitalization of the stock market on which it lists?

8 Investor Choice: Risk and Reward

We are still after the same prize: a good estimate of the corporate cost of capital ($\mathcal{E}(\tilde{r})$) in the NPV formula. But before you can understand the opportunity costs of capital for your firm's own projects, you have to understand the other opportunities that your investors have. This means that you must understand better what investors like (reward) and what they dislike (risk), how they are likely to measure their risks and rewards, how diversification works, what portfolios smart investors are likely to hold, and why "market beta" is a good measure of the contribution of an investment asset to the market portfolio's risk.

8.1 MEASURING RISK AND REWARD

We work with five assets that have four equally likely outcomes.

Put yourself into the shoes of an investor and start with the most basic questions: How should you measure the risk and reward of your portfolio? As always, we first cook up a simple example and then generalize our insights into a broader real-world context. Let's follow four risky assets (securities), named A through D, plus a risk-free asset named F. These assets could even be portfolios, themselves consisting of many individual portfolios, assets, and so on. (This is essentially what a mutual fund is.)

Historical samples can be viewed as scenarios.

There are four equally likely scenarios, named S1 through S4, as in Table 8.1. (If you find it easier to think in terms of historical outcomes, you can pretend that scenario S1 happened at time 1, S2 at time 2, and so forth, and you are now analyzing this historical data. This is not entirely correct, but often a helpful metaphor.) Which investment strategies do you deem better or worse, safer or riskier? It is the goal of this section to analyze the assets and scenarios in Table 8.1 to sharpen your understanding of the concepts and trade-offs of risk and reward.

➤ Why this is not entirely correct, Section 8.5A, p. 223

In a histogram, bars to the right mean higher returns. Bars that are more spread out indicate higher risk.

Visuals always help, so Figure 8.1 graphs the returns in Table 8.1. Each scenario is equally likely (the histogram bars are all equally tall), so you can just indicate where each outcome lies on the x-axis. In this histogram plot, you prefer assets that have scenario outcomes farther to the right (they have higher rates of return), outcomes

TABLE 8.1 RATES OF RETURN ON FIVE INVESTMENT ASSETS

Future	Assets' Rates of Return r: Pfio A (M)	Pfio B	Pfio C	Pfio D	Pfio F
In Scenario S1 ♣	−1.0%	+2.0%	−2.0%	+14.0%	+1.0%
In Scenario S2 ♦	+2.0%	+11.0%	+3.0%	+6.0%	+1.0%
In Scenario S3 ♥	+4.0%	−1.0%	+7.0%	0.0%	+1.0%
In Scenario S4 ♠	+11.0%	+4.0%	+12.0%	−12.0%	+1.0%
"Reward" ($\mathcal{E}(\tilde{r})$)	4.0%	4.0%	5.0%	2.0%	1.0%
"Variance" $\mathcal{V}ar(\tilde{r})$	19.5%%	19.5%%	26.5%%	90.0%%	0.0%%
"Risk" ($\mathcal{S}dv(\tilde{r})$)	4.42%	4.42%	5.15%	9.49%	0.00%

We use *pfio* as an abbreviation for *portfolio*. Variance ($\mathcal{V}ar$) and standard deviation ($\mathcal{S}dv$) were explained in Section 6.1B. The four scenarios are "stand-ins" for a much larger and exhaustive set of possible outcomes that could occur. For illustration, we assume that they are the only possible outcomes and that it is perfectly known that they occur with equal probability.

➤ Random variables *are* histograms, Section 6.1A, p. 138

that are *on average* farther to the right (they have higher *expected* rates of return), and outcomes that are more bunched together (they have less risk). Visual inspection shows that investment F has outcomes perfectly bunched at the same spot, so it is not only least risky but also risk-free. It is followed by the risky A and B, then C, and finally, the most risky, D.

8.1A MEASURING REWARD: THE EXPECTED RATE OF RETURN

Measure reward with the expected rate of return.

Although graphical measures are helpful, we also need algebraic formulas with associated numerical measures. A good measure for the **reward** is easy: You can use the **expected rate of return**, which is the probability-weighted average of all possible returns. For example, the mean rate of return for asset A is

$$\mathcal{E}(\tilde{r}_A) = (1/4)\cdot(-1\%) + (1/4)\cdot(+2\%) + (1/4)\cdot(+4\%) + (1/4)\cdot(+11\%)$$
$$= +4\%$$
$$\mathcal{E}(\tilde{r}_A) = \mathcal{P}rob(S1)\cdot(\tilde{r}_{S1}) + \mathcal{P}rob(S2)\cdot(\tilde{r}_{S2}) + \mathcal{P}rob(S3)\cdot(\tilde{r}_{S3}) + \mathcal{P}rob(S4)\cdot(\tilde{r}_{S4})$$

If you invest in A, you would expect to earn a rate of return of 4%. Because each outcome is equally likely, you can compute this faster as a simple average:

$$\mathcal{E}(\tilde{r}_A) = \frac{(-1\%) + (+2\%) + (+4\%) + (+11\%)}{4} = 4\%$$

8.1B MEASURING RISK: THE STANDARD DEVIATION OF THE RATE OF RETURN

Measure risk with the standard deviation of the rate of return.

➤ Measures of risk (standard deviation), Section 6.1B, p. 141

A good measure of risk is less obvious than a good measure of reward. You already got a good peek at the most common risk measures in Section 6.1B, but let's do it again in the context of our specific set of securities. Figure 8.1 shows that A is more spread out than F (i.e., A is more risky than F) and less spread out than D (i.e., A is less risky than

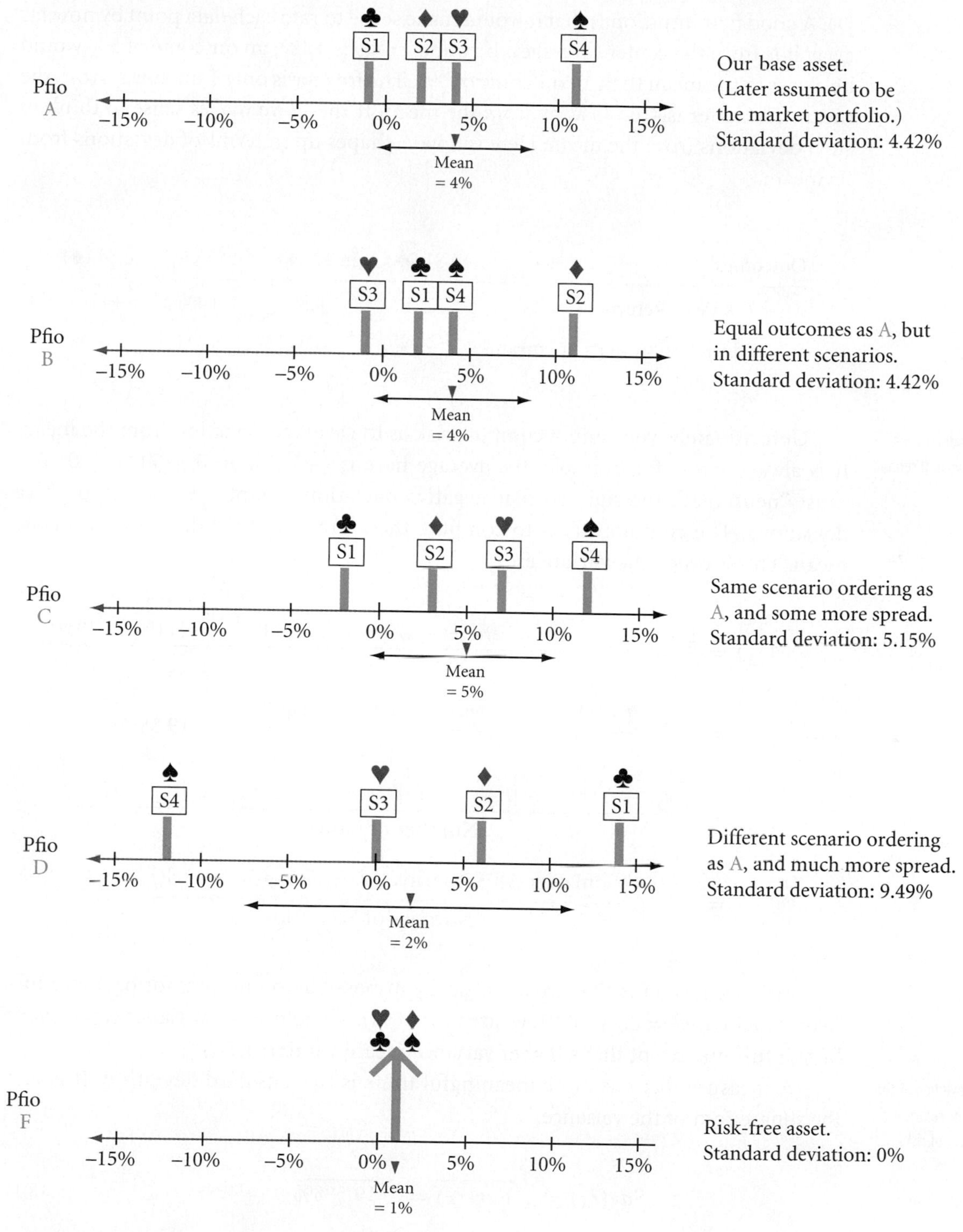

FIGURE 8.1 Graphical Perspectives on Performance

The graphs are standard histograms. Each outcome is equally likely, so each bar is 25% tall—with the exception of the bar in the final graph for the risk-free security, which is 100% tall. ♣ is the rate of return outcome in scenario S1, the ♦ in scenario S2, the ♥ in scenario S3, and the ♠ in scenario S4. The left-right arrows below the axes indicate the standard deviations.

D). A good first intuition is that it would make sense to rate each data point by how far away it is from the center (average). If your average is +4%, an outcome of 3% would be closer to the mean than an outcome of 0%. The former is only 1 unit away from the mean. The latter is 4 units away from the mean. It therefore makes sense to think in such deviations from the mean. Here is how A shapes up in terms of deviations from its mean:

Outcomes	In S1 (♣)	In S2 (♦)	In S3 (♥)	In S4 (♠)
Asset A Rate of Return	−1%	+2%	+4%	+11%
. . . in deviation from its 4% mean	−5%	−2%	0%	+7%

The average deviation from the mean is always 0. It cannot measure risk.

Unfortunately, you cannot compute risk as the average deviation from the mean. It is always zero—for example, the average here is $(-5 - 2 + 0 + 7)/4 = 0$. You must "neutralize" the sign, so that negative deviations count the same as positive deviations. The common fix is to compute the average *squared* deviation from the mean. This is called the **variance**:

$$\mathcal{V}ar(\tilde{r}_A) = \frac{(-1\% - 4\%)^2 + (2\% - 4\%)^2 + (4\% - 4\%)^2 + (11\% - 4\%)^2}{4}$$

$$= \frac{(-5\%)^2 + (-2\%)^2 + (0\%)^2 + (+7\%)^2}{4} = 19.5\%\%$$

$$= \frac{[r_{S1} - \mathcal{E}(\tilde{r})]^2 + [r_{S2} - \mathcal{E}(\tilde{r})]^2 + [r_{S3} - \mathcal{E}(\tilde{r})]^2 + [r_{S4} - \mathcal{E}(\tilde{r})]^2}{\text{Number of Outcomes}}$$

$$= \frac{\text{Sum over All Scenarios } \left[\tilde{r}_S \text{ in Scenario } S - \mathcal{E}(\tilde{r})\right]^2}{\text{Number of Scenarios}}$$

The variance has units that are intrinsically impossible to interpret for ordinary humans (% *squared* = $0.01 \cdot 0.01$, written as $x\%\%$). Therefore, the variance carries very little intuition, except that a higher variance means more risk.

The standard deviation of the portfolio's rate of return is a common measure of risk.

A measure that has more meaningful units is the **standard deviation**. It is just the square root of the variance,

$$\mathcal{S}dv(\tilde{r}_A) = \sqrt{\mathcal{V}ar(\tilde{r}_A)} = \sqrt{19.5\%\%} \approx 4.42\% \qquad (8.1)$$

The standard deviation of the portfolio's rate of return is the most common measure of overall ***portfolio risk***. Looking at Figure 8.1, you can see that this standard deviation of 4.42% seems like a reasonable measure of how far the typical outcome of A is away from the mean of A. The last row in Table 8.1 also lists the standard deviations of B–F. In Figure 8.1, you can see their visual representations: F is risk-free; A and B are equally risky at 4.42%; C is a little more risky at 5.15%; and D is most risky at 9.49%.

IMPORTANT:

- You can measure investment portfolio reward by the expected rate of return on the *overall* portfolio.
- You can measure investment portfolio risk by the standard deviation of the rate of return on the *overall* portfolio.

(Warning: You will not measure the investment risk *contributions* of individual assets inside the portfolio via their standard deviations. This will be explained in Section 8.3B.)

At this point, you should begin to wonder how risk and reward are related in a reasonable world. This will be the subject of much of the next chapter. The brief answer for now is that you can speculate in dumb ways that give you high investment risk with low reward—as anyone who has gambled knows. However, if you are smart, after eliminating all investment mistakes (the low-hanging fruit), you have no choice but to take on more risk if you want to earn higher rewards.

A preview: Smart investors eliminate unnecessary risk. After they have done so, more reward requires taking more risk.

SOLVE NOW!

Q 8.1 What happens if you compute the average deviation from the mean, rather than the average squared deviation from the mean?

Q 8.2 Asset A from Table 8.1 offers −1%, +2%, +4%, and +11% with equal probabilities. Now add 5% to each of these returns. This new asset offers +4%, +7%, +9%, and +16%. Compute the expected rate of return, the variance, and the standard deviation of this new asset. How does it compare to A?

Q 8.3 Compute the risk and reward of C from Table 8.1.

8.2 PORTFOLIOS, DIVERSIFICATION, AND INVESTOR PREFERENCES

In the real world, you are usually not constrained to purchase assets in isolation—you can purchase a little of each. This has the important consequence of reducing your overall portfolio risk. Let's see why.

Start again with investment assets A and B, which offer the same rates of return, but in different future scenarios. If you purchase $100 in either A or B, you would expect to earn $4 with a risk of $4.42. But what if you purchase $50 in A and $50 in B? Call this your investment portfolio P. In this case, your $100 investment would look like this:

Portfolios are bundles of multiple assets. Their returns can be averaged.

Scenario Outcome	S1 (♣)	S2 (♦)	S3 (♥)	S4 (♠)	Average
Return on $50 in A:	$49.50	$51.00	$52.00	$55.50	$52.00
Return on $50 in B:	$51.00	$55.50	$49.50	$52.00	$52.00
⇒ Total return in P:	$100.50	$106.50	$101.50	$107.50	$104.00
Cost = $100 ⇒ Rate of return in P:	0.5%	6.5%	1.5%	7.5%	4.0%

You can do this more quickly by using the returns on A and B themselves. In this case, your portfolio P invests portfolio weight $w_A = 50\%$ into A and $w_B = 50\%$ in B. For example, to obtain the 6.5% in scenario S2, you could have computed the portfolio rate of return from A's 2% rate of return and B's 11% rate as

$$\tilde{r}_P = \tilde{r}_{50\% \text{ in A}, 50\% \text{ in B}} \text{ (in S2)} = 50\% \cdot 2\% \quad + \quad 50\% \cdot 11\% = 6.5\%$$

$$\tilde{r}_{P=(w_1, w_2, \ldots, w_N)} \quad = \quad w_1 \cdot \tilde{r}_1 \quad + \cdots + \quad w_N \cdot \tilde{r}_N$$

Thus, you could have computed P's four scenario rates of return as follows:

$$\text{In S1 ♣:} \quad r_{P=(50\% \text{ in A}, 50\% \text{ in B}) \text{ in S1}} = 50\% \cdot (-1\%) + 50\% \cdot (+2.0\%) = 0.5\%$$

$$\text{In S2 ♦:} \quad r_{P=(50\% \text{ in A}, 50\% \text{ in B}) \text{ in S2}} = 50\% \cdot (+2\%) + 50\% \cdot (+11.0\%) = 6.5\%$$

$$\text{In S3 ♥:} \quad r_{P=(50\% \text{ in A}, 50\% \text{ in B}) \text{ in S3}} = 50\% \cdot (+4\%) + 50\% \cdot (-1.0\%) = 1.5\%$$

$$\text{In S4 ♠:} \quad r_{P=(50\% \text{ in A}, 50\% \text{ in B}) \text{ in S4}} = 50\% \cdot (+11\%) + 50\% \cdot (+4.0\%) = 7.5\%$$

$$r_{P \text{ in S}} \quad = \quad w_A \cdot r_{A \text{ in S}} \quad + \quad w_B \cdot r_{B \text{ in S}}$$

Visually, the A and B combination portfolio called P has lower variability (risk and range) than either A or B.

Now look at these three possible investment portfolios: A, B, and P. The four outcomes are plotted sequentially on the x-axis in Figure 8.2, as if they had occurred in different months. (As noted, this is not a bad way to think about scenarios.) Each box has the name of its portfolio in it. The gray and magenta areas from -1% to $+11\%$ are the outcome ranges for single investments in either A or B. However, the investment of half in A and half in B has a much smaller range of outcomes (from 0.5% to 7.5%), as shown by the blue area. This portfolio P simply has less variability and range than either of its two components.

Algebraically, the combination portfolio also has lower risk.

Can you use the algebraic measures to back up your visual perception? The average (expected) rate of return of the combination portfolio P is the same 4% as that of A and B. The risk of the combination portfolio P is lower, however, than the risk of either A or B. In fact, it is

$$\mathcal{V}ar_{\substack{50\% \text{ in A} \\ 50\% \text{ in B}}} = \frac{(0.5\% - 4\%)^2 + (6.5\% - 4\%)^2 + (1.5\% - 4\%)^2 + (7.5 - 4\%)^2}{4}$$

$$= 9.25\%\%$$

$$= \frac{[r_{S1} - \mathcal{E}(\tilde{r})]^2 + [r_{S2} - \mathcal{E}(\tilde{r})]^2 + [r_{S3} - \mathcal{E}(\tilde{r})]^2 + [r_{S4} - \mathcal{E}(\tilde{r})]^2}{N}$$

$$\Longrightarrow \quad \mathcal{S}dv_{50\% \text{ in A}, \ 50\% \text{ in B}} = \sqrt{\mathcal{V}ar} = \sqrt{9.25\%\%} \approx 3.04\%$$

An investment in either A or B has a risk of 4.42%. But an investment in half of A and half of B has a risk of only 3.04%! Why?

This is caused by diversification.

The reason is **diversification**—the mixing of different investments within a portfolio that reduces the impact of each one on the overall portfolio performance. More simply put, diversification means that not all of your eggs are in the same basket. If one investment component goes down, the other investment component sometimes

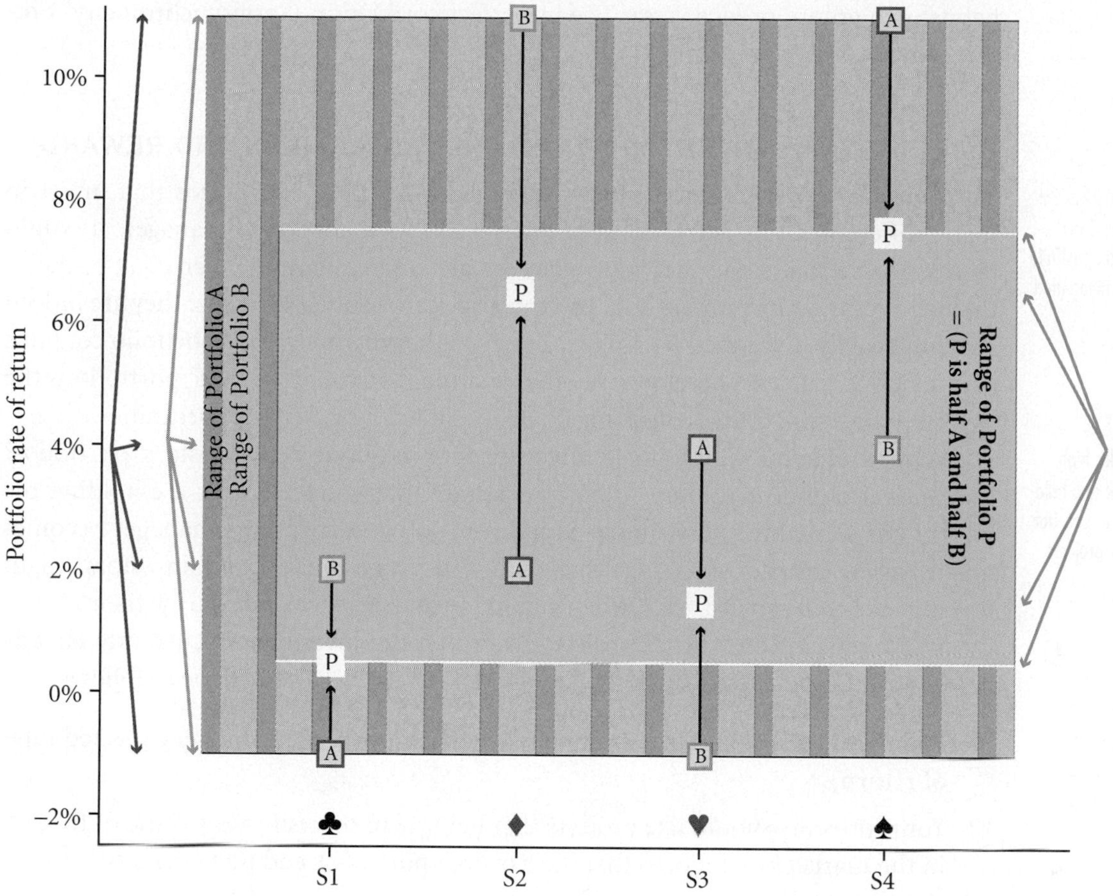

Future	Pfio A	Pfio B	Pfio P = AB
	Portfolio Rates of Return, r		
In Scenario S1 ♣	−1.0%	+2.0%	+0.5%
In Scenario S2 ♦	+2.0%	+11.0%	+6.5%
In Scenario S3 ♥	+4.0%	−1.0%	+1.5%
In Scenario S4 ♠	+11.0%	+4.0%	+7.5%
"Reward" ($\mathcal{E}(\tilde{r})$)	4.0%	4.0%	4.0%
"Risk" ($\mathcal{S}dv(\tilde{r})$)	4.42%	4.42%	**3.04%**
"Range" (see figure)	12%	12%	7%

Portfolio P is half A, half B. Because each half-A/half-B point is halfway between A and B, P has lower spread (risk) than either of its components, A and B, by itself. (The risks of A and B were computed as 4.42% in Formula 8.1 on page 204.) Returns on the single-asset portfolios A and B range from −1% to +11%, i.e., 12%. Returns on the combination-asset portfolio P range from +0.5% to +7.5%, i.e., 7%. This is color-coded as blue in the figure. The "spread arrows" on the left and the right also point to the possible outcomes of the three portfolios, indicating the variability visually. The combination portfolio has less spread.

FIGURE 8.2 Rate of Return Outcomes for A, B, and the 50%-50% Combination Portfolio P

happens to go up, or vice versa. The imperfect correlation ("nonsynchronicity") reduces the overall portfolio risk.

8.2A ASSUME INVESTORS CARE ONLY ABOUT RISK AND REWARD

Investors love diversification: the more the better. They could like the market portfolio because it is highly diversified.

This intuition suggests that heavily diversified portfolios—portfolios that invest in many different assets—tend to have lower risk. As a corporate manager, it would be reasonable to assume that your investors are smart. Because diversification helps them reduce their investment risk, you can also reasonably believe that they are indeed holding heavily diversified portfolios. The most heavily diversified portfolio contains a little of every asset. Therefore, we often assume that your investors' portfolio is the overall **market portfolio**, consisting of all available investment opportunities.

If your investors like high reward and low risk and hold the market portfolio, you can work out how your projects affect them.

Why would you want to make any assumptions about your investors' portfolios? The answer is that if you are willing to assume that your investors are holding the market (or something very similar to it), your job as a corporate manager becomes much easier. Instead of asking what each and every one of your investors might possibly like, you can just ask, "When would my investors want to give me their money for investment into my firm's project, given that my investors are currently already holding the broad overall stock market portfolio?" The answer will be as follows:

1. Your investors should like projects that offer more reward (higher expected rates of return).
2. Your investors should like projects that help them diversify away some of the risk in the market portfolio, so that their overall portfolios end up being less risky.

In sum, your corporate managerial task is to take those projects that your investors would like to add to their current (market) portfolios. You should therefore search for projects that have high expected rates of return and high diversification benefits with respect to the market. Let's now turn toward measuring this second characteristic: How can your projects aid your investors' diversification, and how should you measure how good this diversification is?

IMPORTANT:

- Diversification is based on imperfect correlation, or "nonsynchronicity," among investments. It helps smart investors reduce the overall portfolio risk.
- Therefore, as a corporate manager, absent other intelligence, you should believe that your investors tend to hold diversified portfolios. They could even hold portfolios as heavily diversified as the "entire market portfolio."
- As a corporate manager, your task is to think about how a little of your project can aid your investors in terms of its contribution to the risk and reward of their heavily diversified overall portfolios. (You should not think about how risky your project is in itself.)

SOLVE NOW!

Q 8.4 A combination portfolio named AB invests 90% in A and 10% in B.
(a) Compute its risk and reward.
(b) In a bar plot similar to those in Figure 8.1, would this new AB portfolio look less spread out than the P(50%, 50%) portfolio that was worked out in the table in Figure 8.2?

8.3 HOW TO MEASURE RISK CONTRIBUTION

If we are willing to assume that our smart investors are holding all assets in the market, then what projects offer them the best diversification?

8.3A AN ASSET'S OWN RISK IS NOT A GOOD MEASURE FOR ITS RISK CONTRIBUTION TO A PORTFOLIO

Comovement determines risk contribution.

Obviously, diversification does *not* help if two investment opportunities always move in the same direction. For example, if you try to diversify one $50 investment in A with another $50 investment in A (which always has the same outcomes), then your risk does not decrease. On the other hand, if two investment opportunities always move in *opposite* directions, then diversification works extremely well: One is a buffer for the other.

Pretend A is the market, now called M. Is C or D a better addition?

Let's formalize this intuition. For explanation's sake, assume that the stock market portfolio held by your investors is A from Table 8.1, so rename it M (for "market"). Assume that C and D are two projects that your firm could invest in, but you cannot choose both. C offers not only a higher expected rate of return than D (5% versus 2%) but also lower risk (5.15% versus 9.49%). As a manager, acting on behalf of your investors, would you therefore assume that project C is automatically better for them than D?

The combination MC has almost the same risk as M.

The answer is no. Let's assume that your investors start out with the market portfolio. Figure 8.3 shows what happens if they sell half of their M portfolio to invest in either C or D. You can call these two 50-50 portfolios MC and MD, respectively. Start with MC. If your investors reallocate half their money from M into C, their portfolios would have the following rates of return:

Scenario Outcome	$1 (♣)	S2 (♦)	S3 (♥)	S4 (♠)	Reward	Risk
MC	−1.5%	+2.5%	+5.5%	+11.5%	4.5%	4.74%

The left graph in Figure 8.3 plots the MC rates of return, plus the rates of return for both M and C by themselves. The magenta area is the range of portfolio C, the gray area is the range of portfolio A (i.e., M), and the blue area is the range of the combination portfolio. There is not much change in the risk of your portfolio in moving from a pure M portfolio to the MC portfolio. The risk actually increases from 4.42% to 4.74%.

The combination MD has much lower risk than M.

Now consider the combination of MD, which is the right graph in Figure 8.3. The pink area shows that, by itself, D is a very risky investment. However, if your investors

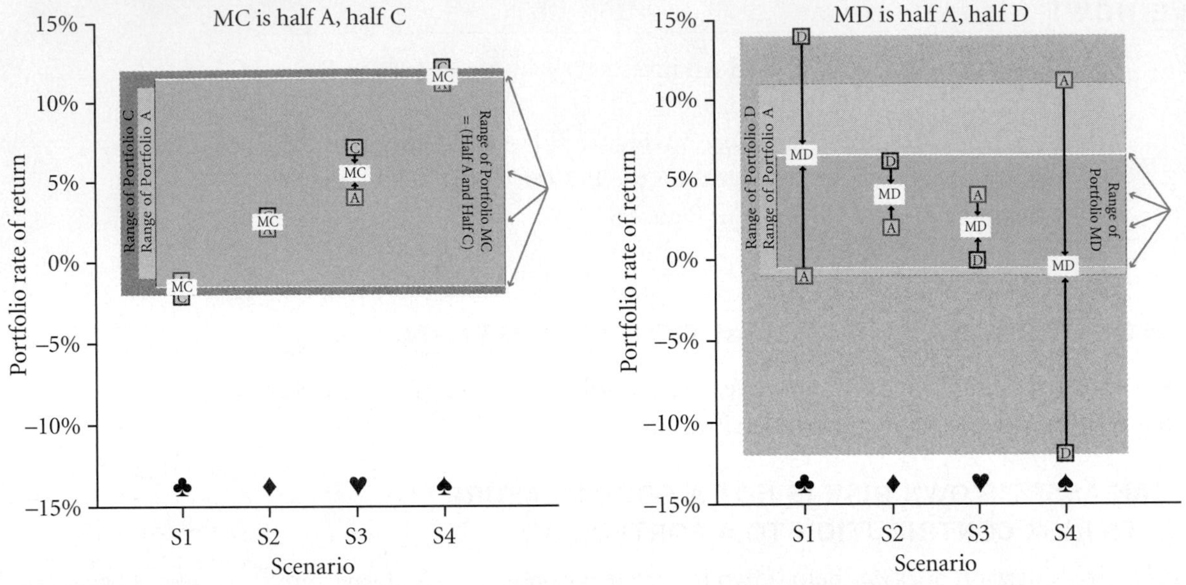

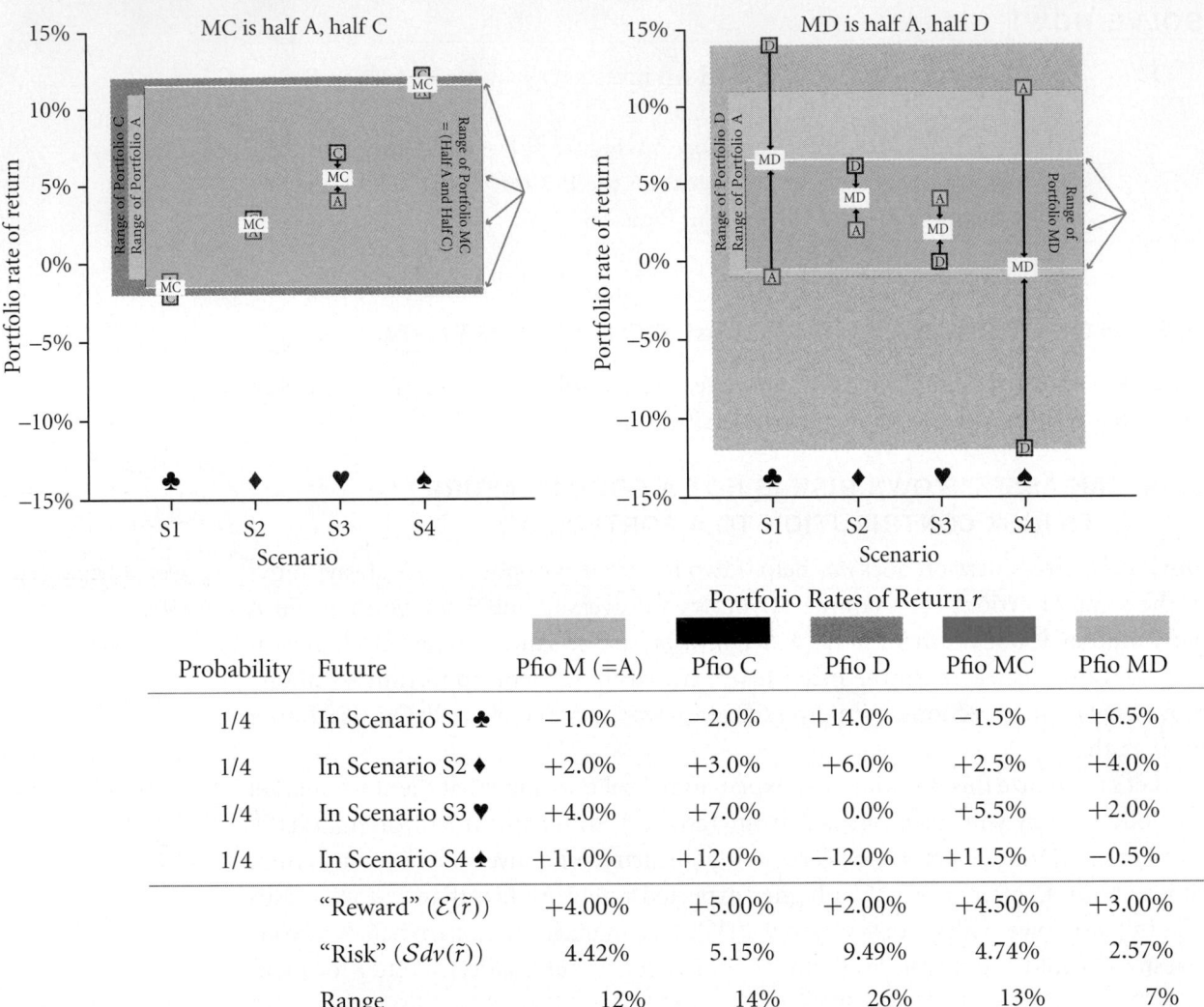

		Portfolio Rates of Return *r*				
Probability	Future	Pfio M (=A)	Pfio C	Pfio D	Pfio MC	Pfio MD
1/4	In Scenario S1 ♣	−1.0%	−2.0%	+14.0%	−1.5%	+6.5%
1/4	In Scenario S2 ♦	+2.0%	+3.0%	+6.0%	+2.5%	+4.0%
1/4	In Scenario S3 ♥	+4.0%	+7.0%	0.0%	+5.5%	+2.0%
1/4	In Scenario S4 ♠	+11.0%	+12.0%	−12.0%	+11.5%	−0.5%
	"Reward" ($\mathcal{E}(\tilde{r})$)	+4.00%	+5.00%	+2.00%	+4.50%	+3.00%
	"Risk" ($\mathcal{S}dv(\tilde{r})$)	4.42%	5.15%	9.49%	4.74%	2.57%
	Range	12%	14%	26%	13%	7%

Although the single-asset portfolio D is much riskier than the single-asset portfolio C, D is much better than C in reducing the risk of the market portfolio. This is because D tends to move opposite to the market. This can also be seen by looking at the color-coded ranges. The magenta range of C in the left figure is smaller than the pink range of D in the right figure. C is simply less risky an investment *in itself* than D. However, the blue range in the MC portfolio on the left is much bigger than the blue range in the MD portfolio on the right. As a portfolio component combined with the market portfolio, D adds much less risk than C. The arrows on the right of each figure also point to the possible outcomes of the combination portfolios, and help indicate their spreads.

FIGURE 8.3 Combining M with either C or D

instead reallocate half of their wealth from M into D, their overall portfolio would have the following rates of return:

Scenario Outcome	S1 (♣)	S2 (♦)	S3 (♥)	S4 (♠)	Reward	Risk
MD	+6.5%	+4.0%	+2.0%	−0.5%	3.0%	2.57%

This is much lower than the range of outcomes on the left (with portfolio C). The MD combination portfolio is simply much safer—even though D by itself is much riskier. If you compare the MC spread with the MD spread, the latter is much smaller. The algebraic risk measure, the standard deviation, confirms this: Even though D by itself is the riskiest choice, adding it to the M portfolio has reduced your investors' risk from 4.42% to 2.57%. In sum:

Portfolio	Reward	Risk	Note
M (=A) alone	4.00%	4.42%	The market portfolio that your investors were holding.
C alone	5.00%	5.15%	C is less risky than D, if purchased by itself.
D alone	2.00%	9.49%	
MC: half M, half C	4.50%	4.74%	If C is added to M, portfolio risk barely goes down,
MD: half M, half D	3.00%	2.57%	**but if D is added to M, portfolio risk goes down a lot!**

You now know that D's own higher standard deviation (9.49%) compared to C's (5.15%) is not a good indication of whether D helps your investors reduce portfolio risk more or less than C. If your investors are primarily holding M, then a very risky project like D can allow them to build lower-risk portfolios. However, if your investors are not holding any assets other than D, they would not care about D's diversification benefits and only about D's own risk. Thus, as a manager, you cannot determine whether your investors would prefer you to invest in C or D unless you know their entire portfolios. (Moreover, it could also depend on how your investors would like you to trade off more overall reward against more overall risk.)

The implication for your project choices as a corporate manager: Everything else equal, D could better reduce portfolio risk for your investors despite its higher own risk.

IMPORTANT: A project's (own) standard deviation is not necessarily a good measure of how it effects the risk of your investors' portfolios. Indeed, it is possible that a project with a very high standard deviation by itself may actually help lower an investor's overall portfolio risk.

SOLVE NOW!

Q 8.5 Confirm the risk and reward calculations for the MC and MD portfolios in the table under Figure 8.3.

8.3B BETA IS A GOOD MEASURE FOR AN ASSET'S RISK CONTRIBUTION TO A PORTFOLIO

Can you guess why portfolio D is so much better than portfolio C in reducing the overall risk when held in combination with the M portfolio? The reason is that D tends to go up when M tends to go down, and vice versa. The same cannot be said for C—it tends to move together with M. You could call this "synchronicity" or "comovement." It is why C does not help investors who are heavily invested in the overall market in their quests to reduce their portfolio risks. Figure 8.4 shows the comovement graphically. If you draw the best-fitting line between M and C, the line slopes up. (It is the same kind of line that you already saw in Section 7.1C.) This means that C tends to be higher when M is higher. If you draw the best-fitting line between M and D, the line slopes down. This means that D tends to be higher when M is lower, and vice versa.

D reduces M's risk because it tends to move in the opposite direction. Comovement can be measured by the slope of a line.

➤ Market beta of PepsiCo, Section 7.1C, p. 185

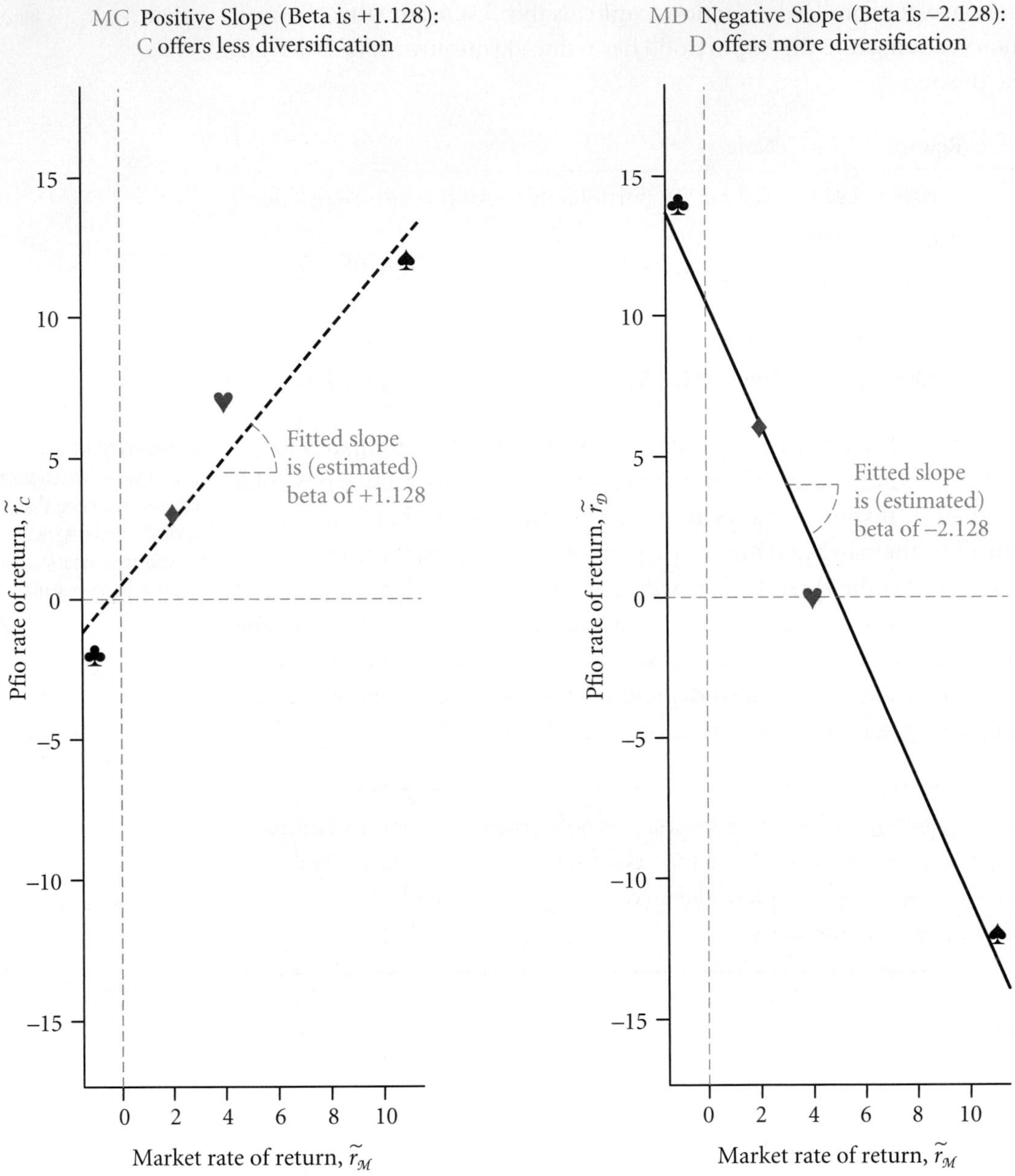

The four data points in each plot are taken from Table 8.1 on page 202. They are the rates of return on the portfolios M, C, and D. These rates of return are quoted in percentages. In the example, you know that these are the four true possible outcomes. In the real world, if the four points were not the true known outcomes, but just the historical outcomes (sample points), then the slope would not be the true unknown beta, but only the "estimated" beta.

FIGURE 8.4 Possible Outcomes: Rates of Return versus Market Rate of Return

This slope is a common measure of expected comovement or countermovement—how much diversification benefit an investor can obtain from adding a particular new project. A higher slope means more comovement and less diversification; a lower, or even negative, slope means less comovement and more diversification.

The slope of a line is generally called a **beta** because it is common to write the formula for a line as

The line's slope is called beta.

$$y = \alpha + \beta \cdot x \tag{8.2}$$

A beta of 1 is a 45° diagonal line; a beta of 0 is a horizontal line. A positive beta slopes up; a negative beta slopes down; and a beta of infinity is a vertical line. The particular line we care about in finance is the **market beta**. It matters if you can posit that your smart investors are primarily holding the market portfolio. If so, you want to know how the rate of return on your own project comoves with that of the market. This is exactly what the market beta of your project tells you. To find it, draw the rate of return on M on the x-axis (hence the prefix "market" in market beta) and the rate of return on your project (here, either C or D) on the y-axis. Then take a ruler and try to draw the best line between the four points. You will find that the market beta of C is positive (your best line is upward sloping), whereas the market beta of D is negative (your best line is downward sloping). In statistics, you should have learned that you can find the beta by running a linear regression. If you don't remember, no worries: In Section 8.3B, I will show you again how to compute them exactly. For now, take my word that the two best lines are

We want the beta of the asset's rate of return on the y-axis and the market's rate of return on the x-axis.

$$\begin{aligned} \tilde{r}_{C} &\approx 0.49\% + (+1.128) \cdot \tilde{r}_{M} \\ \tilde{r}_{D} &\approx 10.51\% + (-2.128) \cdot \tilde{r}_{M} \\ \tilde{r}_{i} &= \alpha_{i,M} + \beta_{i,M} \cdot \tilde{r}_{M} \end{aligned} \tag{8.3}$$

The subscripts on the betas remind you what the variables on the x-axis and the y-axis are. The first subscript is on the y-axis, the second is on the x-axis, so $\beta_{C,M} \approx 1.128$ and $\beta_{D,M} \approx -2.128$. In fact, market beta plays such an important role in finance that the name "beta" has itself become synonymous for "market beta," and the second subscript is usually omitted. Formula 8.3 is sometimes called the **market model**.

IMPORTANT:

- Diversification works better if the new investment project tends to move in the opposite direction of the rest of the portfolio than if it tends to move in the same direction.
- It is often reasonable to assume that smart investors are already holding the market portfolio and are now considering investing into just a little of one additional asset—your firm's new project.
- If this new investment asset has a negative beta with respect to the market (its "market beta"), it means that it tends to go down when the market goes up, and vice versa. If this new investment asset has a positive beta with respect to the market, it means that it tends to move together with the market. If this new investment asset has a zero beta with respect to the market, it means that it moves independently of the market for all practical purposes.

- The market beta is a good measure of an investment asset's risk contribution for an investor who holds the market portfolio. The lower (or negative) the market beta, the more this investment helps reduce your investor's risk.
- The market beta of an asset can be interpreted as a line slope, where the rate of return on the market is on the x-axis and the rate of return on the new asset is on the y-axis. The line states how you expect the new asset to perform as a function of how the market will perform.
- You can think of market beta as a measure for "toxicity." In a reasonable equilibrium, holding everything else constant, risk-averse investors who are holding the market portfolio would agree to pay more for assets that have lower market betas. They would pay less for assets with higher market betas.

Warning: All of this beta-related risk measuring is interesting only if your investors are holding (portfolios close to) the overall market.

Before we conclude, some caveats are in order. From your perspective as the manager of a company, perhaps a publicly traded one, it is reasonable to assume that your investors are holding the market portfolio. It is also reasonable to assume that your new project is just a tiny new additional component of your investors' overall portfolios. We will staunchly maintain these assumptions, but you should be aware that they may not always be appropriate. If your investors are *not* holding something close to the market portfolio, then your project's market beta would *not* be a good measure of your projects' risk contributions. In the extreme, if your investors are holding *only* your project, market beta would not measure the project's risk contribution at all. This is often the case for entrepreneurs. They often have no choice but to put all their money into one egg in one basket. Such investors care only about the project's standard deviation, not the project's market beta.

Alpha has meaning, too, even though you won't use it just yet.

Although we shall not use it further in this book, the alpha intercept in Formula 8.3 also plays an important role. Together, alpha and beta help determine how attractive an investment is. For example, if the rate of return on the market is 10%, Formula 8.3 tells you that you would expect the rate of return on D to be

$$\mathcal{E}\left[(\tilde{r}_{\text{D}})|\text{ if }\tilde{r}_{\text{M}} = 10\%\right] \approx 10.51\% + (-2.128)\cdot 10\% \approx -10.77\%$$

The higher the alpha, the better the average performance of your investment given any particular rate of return on the market. Just as investment professionals often call the market beta just beta, they often call this specific intercept (here 10.51%) just alpha. (There is one small complication: They usually subtract the risk-free interest rate first from both $\tilde{r}_{\text{D}}$ and $\tilde{r}_{\text{M}}$ in their regressions.)

Computing Market Betas from Historical Rates of Return

You can compute the best-fit beta via a 4-step procedure.

➤ Table 8.1, p. 202

Now that you understand what beta means, how can you actually compute it? Let me show you. Let's return to the assets in Table 8.1. What is the market beta of asset C? I have already told you that this slope is +1.128. To calculate it, I followed a tedious, but not mysterious, recipe. Here is what you have to do:

1. Just as you did for your variance calculations, first translate all returns into deviations from the mean. That is, for M, C, and D, subtract their own means from every realization.

First, de-mean each rate of return.
➤ Variance calculations, Section 6.1B, p. 141

	Original Rates of Return			Net-of-Mean Rates of Return		
Future	Pfio M	Pfio C	Pfio D	Pfio M	Pfio C	Pfio D
In Scenario S1 ♣	−1.0%	−2.0%	+14.0%	−5.0%	−7.0%	+12.0%
In Scenario S2 ♦	+2.0%	+3.0%	+6.0%	−2.0%	−2.0%	+4.0%
In Scenario S3 ♥	+4.0%	+7.0%	0.0%	0.0%	+2.0%	−2.0%
In Scenario S4 ♠	+11.0%	+12.0%	−12.0%	+7.0%	+7.0%	−14.0%
"Reward" ($\mathcal{E}(\tilde{r})$)	4.00%	5.00%	2.00%	0.00%	0.00%	0.00%

(How demeaning!)

2. Compute the variance of the series on the x-axis. This is the variance of the rates of return on M. With the net-of-mean M returns, this is easy:

Take squares and then average. This is the variance.

$$\mathcal{V}ar(\tilde{r}_M) = \frac{(-5\%)^2 + (-2\%)^2 + (0)^2 + (7\%)^2}{4} = 19.5\%\%$$

$$= \frac{\text{Sum over All Scenarios } S\text{: } [\tilde{r}_M \text{ in Scenario } S - \text{Average } \mathcal{E}(\tilde{r}_M)]^2}{N}$$

Because 1% is "multiply by 0.01," 19.5%% could be rewritten as 0.195% or 0.00195. (Note also that you do not need to compute the variances of either C or D to obtain their market betas.)

3. Compute the average product of the net-of-mean variables. In this case, you want to compute the market beta for C, so you work with the rates of return on M and C.

For covariances, multiply net-of-mean returns, then average.

$$\mathcal{C}ov(\tilde{r}_M, \tilde{r}_C) = \frac{(-5\%)\cdot(-7\%) + (-2\%)\cdot(-2\%) + (0)\cdot(2\%) + (7\%)\cdot(7\%)}{4}$$

$$= 22\%\% = 0.22\% \qquad (8.4)$$

$$= \frac{\text{Sum over All Scenarios } S\text{: } [\tilde{r}_M \text{ in Scenario } S - \mathcal{E}(\tilde{r}_M)]\cdot[\tilde{r}_C \text{ in Scenario } S - \mathcal{E}(\tilde{r}_C)]}{N}$$

This statistic is called the **covariance** between the rates of return on M and C.

4. The beta of C with respect to the market M, formally $\beta_{C,M}$ but often abbreviated as β_C, is the ratio of these two quantities,

The beta is the covariance divided by the variance.

$$\beta_C = \beta_{C,M} = \frac{22\%\%}{19.5\%\%} \approx 1.128 \qquad (8.5)$$

$$= \frac{\mathcal{C}ov(\tilde{r}_M, \tilde{r}_C)}{\mathcal{V}ar(\tilde{r}_M)}$$

You can confirm our calculations using a spreadsheet.

This slope of 1.128 (a little more than a perfect 45° diagonal) is exactly the market beta we drew in Figure 8.4. Many spreadsheets and all statistical programs can compute it for you: They call the routine that does this a **linear regression**.

Think of market beta as the characteristic of an asset.

You should always think of the beta of an asset i with respect to a portfolio P as a characteristic measure of your asset i relative to an underlying base portfolio P. The rate of return on P is on the x-axis; the rate of return on i is on the y-axis. As we stated earlier, most often—but not always—the portfolio P is the market portfolio, M, so $\beta_{\text{i,M}}$ is often just called the market beta, or even just the beta (and the second subscript is omitted).

The average beta of the market (all stocks) is 1, not 0.

Now think for a moment. What should the average beta of a stock in the economy be? Equivalently, what is the beta of the market portfolio itself? Replace the C in Formula 8.5 with M:

$$\beta_{\text{M}} = \frac{Cov(\tilde{r}_{\text{M}}, \tilde{r}_{\text{M}})}{Var(\tilde{r}_{\text{M}})}$$

If you look at the definition of covariance, you can see that the covariance of a variable with itself *is* the variance. (The covariance is a generalization of the variance concept from one variable to two variables.) Therefore, $Cov(\tilde{r}_{\text{M}}, \tilde{r}_{\text{M}}) = Var(\tilde{r}_{\text{M}})$, and the market beta of the market itself is 1. Graphically, if both the x-axis and the y-axis are graphing the same values, every point must lie on the diagonal. Economically, this should not be surprising, either: the market goes up one-to-one with the market.

Why torture you with computations? So you can play with scenarios.

Now that you know how to compute betas and covariances, you can consider scenarios for your project. For example, you might have a new project for which you would guess that it will have a rate of return of −5% if the market returns −10%; a rate of return of +5% if the market returns +5%; and a rate of return of 30% if the market returns 10%. Knowing how to compute a market beta therefore makes it useful to think of such scenarios. (You can also use this technique to explore the relationship between your projects and some other factors. For example, you could determine how your projects covary with the price of oil to learn about your project's oil risk exposure.)

➤ An oil-price beta, Section 9.8A, p. 292

Practical advice to help you estimate market beta in the real world: Use 3–5 years of daily observations and then adjust.

In the real world, you will sometimes think in terms of such scenarios, but more often you have to compute a market beta from historical rates of return for the overall stock market and for your project (or similar projects). Fortunately, as we noted up front, the beta computations themselves are exactly the same. In effect, when you use historical data, you simply assume that each time period was one representative scenario and proceed from there. Nevertheless, there are some real-world complications you should think about:

1. Should you use daily, weekly, monthly, or annual rates of return? The answer is that the best market beta estimates come from daily or weekly data. Annual data should be avoided (except in a textbook in which space is limited). Monthly data can be used if need be.
2. How much data should you use? Most researchers tend to use 3–5 years of historical rate of return data. This reflects a trade-off between having enough data and not going too far back into ancient history, which may be less relevant. If you have daily data, 3 years works quite well.

3. Is the historical beta a good estimate of the future beta? It turns out that history can sometimes be deceptive, especially if your estimated historical beta is far away from the market's beta average of 1. Fortunately, there are at least two methods to help adjust historical betas so that you get better estimates of future betas:
   (A) **Averaging:** You could rely not just on the historical beta computed from your own project's returns. Instead, you could use the average historical betas for many other projects that are similar to your own (for example, projects from the same industry or in the same size class). Such averages are usually less noisy.
   (B) **Shrinking:** You could "shrink" your historical beta toward the overall market beta of 1. For example, in the simplest such shrinker, you would simply compute an average of the overall market beta of 1 and your historical market beta estimate. If you computed a historical market beta of 4 for your project, you would work with a prediction of future market beta of about $(4 + 1)/2 = 2.5$ for your project.

   Many smart executives start with a statistical beta estimated from historical data and then use their intuitive judgment to adjust it.

SOLVE NOW!

Q 8.6 Return to your computation of market beta of 1.128 in Formula 8.5. We called it $\beta_{C,M}$, or β_C for short. Is the order of the subscripts important? That is, please compute $\beta_{M,C}$ and see whether it is also 1.128.

8.3C WHY NOT CORRELATION OR COVARIANCE?

Covariance and beta (and correlation) always have the same sign.

There is a close family relationship between covariance, beta, and correlation. The beta is the covariance divided by one of the variances. The correlation is the covariance divided by both standard deviations. The denominators are always positive. Thus, if the covariance is positive, so are the beta and the correlation; if the covariance is negative, so are the beta and the correlation; and if the covariance is zero, so are the beta and the correlation. The nice thing about the correlation, which makes it useful in many contexts outside finance, is that it has no scale and is always between −100% and +100%:

- Two variables that always move perfectly in the same direction have a correlation of 100%.
- Two variables that always move perfectly in opposite directions have a correlation of −100%.
- Two variables that are independent have a correlation of 0%.

This makes correlations very easy to interpret. The not-so-nice thing about correlation is that it has no scale and is always between −100% and +100%. This means that two investments, the second being a million times bigger than the first (all project rates of return multiplied by a million), have the same correlation with the stock market. Yet, the second investment would go up or down with any slight tremor in the market by a million times more, which would of course mean that it would contribute

TABLE 8.2 SOME MARKET BETAS AND CAPITALIZATIONS ON MAY 10, 2008

Company	Ticker	Mkt-Cap[a]	Market Beta Yahoo	Market Beta AOL	Company	Ticker	Mkt-Cap[a]	Market Beta Yahoo	Market Beta AOL
AMD	AMD	4	1.96	2.67	Intel	INTC	124	1.73	1.85
Coca-Cola	KO	130	0.52	0.78	PepsiCo	PEP	107	0.24	0.22
Citigroup	C	124	1.71	1.31	J.P. Morgan	JPM	158	0.85	0.91
Goldman Sachs	GS	74	2.24	1.84	Morgan Stanley	MS	51	1.75	1.71
IBM	IBM	170	0.95	0.94	Hewlett-Packard	HPQ	121	1.09	1.46
Dell	DELL	39	1.53	1.36	Sun	JAVA	10	1.01	2.13
Apple Inc	AAPL	162	2.86	2.57	Sony	SNE	45	0.97	1.08
Google	GOOG	180	2.60	2.17	Yahoo	YHOO	36	0.39	1.03
Ford	F	16	2.11	2.13	General Motors	GM	12	1.50	1.64
American Airlines	AMR	2	1.71	2.69	Southwest	LUV	9.5	−0.12	0.13
Exxon Mobil	XOM	469	1.14	1.04	Barrick Gold	ABX	34	−0.20	0.49
Philip Morris	PM	109	0.00	NA	Procter & Gamble	PG	199	0.63	0.57
Textron	TXT	15	1.46	1.81	Boeing	BA	63	1.08	1.22

a. "Mkt-Cap" is the equity market value in billions of dollars. Yahoo explained its betas as follows:

> The Beta is beta of equity. Beta is the monthly price change of a particular company relative to the monthly price change of the S&P 500. The time period for Beta is 5 years when available, and not less than 2.5 years. This value is updated monthly.

Note that Yahoo! *Finance* seems to ignore dividends, but this usually makes little difference. I could not find an explanation for the market betas provided by AOL. Google's market betas were the same as AOL's, but there was no explanation for them, either.

much more risk. The correlation ignores this, which disqualifies it as a serious candidate for a project risk measure. Fortunately, beta takes care of scale—indeed, the beta for the second project would be a million times larger. This is why we prefer beta over correlation as a measure of risk contribution to a portfolio.

8.3D INTERPRETING TYPICAL STOCK MARKET BETAS

Market beta works well when investors are holding the market and adding only a little of your project.

The market beta is the best measure of "diversification help" for an investor who holds the stock market portfolio and considers adding *just a little* of your firm's project. From your perspective as a manager seeking to attract investors, this is not a perfect, necessarily true assumption—but it is a reasonable one. Recall that we assume that investors are smart, so presumably they are holding highly diversified portfolios. To convince your market investors to like your \$10 million project, you just need the average investor to want to buy \$10 million divided by about \$20 trillion (the stock market capitalization), which is 1/2,000,000 of their portfolios. For your investors, your corporate projects are just tiny additions to their market portfolios.

Most financial websites publish market beta estimates.

You can look up the market betas of publicly traded stocks on many financial websites. Table 8.2 lists the betas of some randomly chosen companies in May 2008 from Yahoo! *Finance* and from AOL's finance site. Most company betas are in the range of around 0 to about 2.5. A beta above 1 is considered risk-increasing for an investor holding the overall stock market (it is riskier than the stock market itself), while a beta below 1 is considered risk-reducing. Betas that are negative are quite rare—in Table 8.2, there happen to be only two such stocks, Southwest and Barrick Gold, according to the Yahoo betas, and none according to the AOL betas.

Beta can be viewed as the marginal change of your project with respect to the market.

Market beta has yet another nice intuitive interpretation: It is the degree to which the firm's value tends to change if the stock market changes. For example, Apple's market beta of approximately 2.7 (somewhere between 2.57 and 2.86) says that if the stock market will return an extra 5% next year (above and beyond its expectations), Apple will return an extra $2.7 \cdot 5\% = 13.5\%$ (above and beyond Apple's expectations). Of course, market beta is not a measure of how good an investment Apple is. (This measure is the alpha [which can be interpreted as an expected rate of return]. In the next section, you will learn a model that relates market beta to the expected rate of return. For now let's assume for illustration that there is no reasonable relationship.) Let's make the absurd assumption that Apple's expected rate of return is -30% and the more reasonable assumption that the market's expected rate of return is 10%. All that Apple's market beta then tells you is that when the market does 1% better than expected (i.e., $(10\% + 1\% = 11\%)$), then Apple would do 2.7% better than expected (i.e., $(-30\% + 2.7 \cdot 1\% = -27.3\%)$). If the market does 0% (i.e., 10% worse than expected), Apple would be expected to do -57% (i.e., 27% worse than expected). And so on. Apple's high market beta is useful because it informs you that if you hold the stock market, adding Apple stock would not help you diversify your market risk very much. Holding Apple stock would amplify any market swings, not reduce them. In any case, Apple's market beta does not tell you whether Apple is priced so high that it is an investment with a negative expected rate of return that you should avoid in the first place.

SOLVE NOW!

Q 8.7 You estimate your project x to return -5% if the stock market returns -10%, and $+5\%$ if the stock market returns $+10\%$. What would you use as the market beta estimate for your project?

Q 8.8 You estimate your project to return $+5\%$ if the stock market returns -10%, and -5% if the stock market returns $+10\%$. What would you use as the market beta estimate for your project?

8.4 EXPECTED RATES OF RETURN AND MARKET BETAS FOR (WEIGHTED) PORTFOLIOS AND FIRMS

Portfolios consist of multiple assets (or of other portfolios). Value-weighted and equal-weighted portfolios are defined.

Let's go back to your managerial perspective of figuring out the risk and return of your corporate projects. Many small projects are bundled together, so it is very common for managers to consider multiple projects already packaged together as one portfolio. For example, you can think of your firm as a collection of divisions that have been packaged together. If division C is worth \$1 million and division D is worth \$2 million, then a firm consisting of C and D is worth \$3 million. C constitutes 1/3 of the portfolio

"Firm" and D constitutes 2/3 of the portfolio "Firm." This kind of portfolio is called a **value-weighted portfolio** because the weights correspond to the market values of the components. (A portfolio that invests \$100 in C and \$200 in D would also be value-weighted. A portfolio that invests equal amounts in the constituents (for example, \$500 in each) is called an **equal-weighted portfolio**.)

What are the expected rate of return and market beta of a portfolio?

Thus, as a manager, you have to know how to work with a portfolio (firm) when you have all the information about all of its underlying component stocks (projects). If I tell you what the expected rate of return on each project is, and what the market beta of each project is, can you tell me what the firm's overall expected rate of return and overall market beta are? Let's try it. Use the C and D stocks from Table 8.1 on page 202, and call CDD the portfolio (or firm) that consists of 1/3 investment in division C and 2/3 investment in division D.

You can average *actual* rates of return.

Actually you already know that individual portfolio rates of return can be averaged. For example, in scenario S4 (♠), investment C has a rate of return of +12%, and investment D has a rate of return of −12%. Consequently, the overall investment CDD has a rate of return of

$$r_{\text{CDD, in S4 }(\spadesuit)} = 1/3 \cdot (+12\%) + 2/3 \cdot (-12\%) = -4\%$$
$$= w_{\text{C}} \cdot r_{\text{C, in S4}} + w_{\text{D}} \cdot r_{\text{D, in S4}}$$

Let us verify this: Put \$100 into C and \$200 into D. C turns into 1.12 · \$100 = \$112. D turns into (1 − 12%) · \$200 = \$176. The total portfolio turns into \$288, which is a rate of return of \$288/\$300 − 1 = −4% on a \$300 investment.

You can average *expected* rates of return.

It is also intuitive that *expected* rates of return can be averaged. In our example, C has an *expected* rate of return of 5%, and D has an *expected* rate of return of 2%. Consequently, your overall firm CDD has an expected rate of return of

$$\mathcal{E}(\tilde{r}_{\text{CDD}}) = 1/3 \cdot (+5\%) + 2/3 \cdot (+2\%) = 3\%$$
$$= w_{\text{C}} \cdot \mathcal{E}(\tilde{r}_{\text{C}}) + w_{\text{D}} \cdot \mathcal{E}(\tilde{r}_{\text{D}})$$

Let us verify this, too. There are four possible outcomes: In S1, your actual rate of return is 8.67%; in S2, it is 5%; in S3, it is 2.33%; and in S4, it is −4%. The average of these four outcomes is indeed 3%.

News flash: You can also average market betas.

➤ Market betas of C and D, Formula 8.3, p. 213

But here is a remarkable and less intuitive fact: Market betas—that is, the projects' risk contributions to your investors' market portfolios—can be averaged, too. That is, I claim that the beta of CDD is the weighted average of the betas of C and D. You already computed the latter in Formula 8.3 as +1.128 and −2.128, respectively. Their value-weighted average is

$$\beta_{\text{CDD}} = 1/3 \cdot (+1.128) + 2/3 \cdot (-2.128) \approx -1.043 \qquad (8.6)$$
$$= w_{\text{C}} \cdot \beta_{\text{C}} + w_{\text{D}} \cdot \beta_{\text{D}}$$

(*But* you cannot average variances or standard deviations!)

You will be asked in Q 8.9 to confirm this. However, do not think for a moment that you can compute value-weighted averages for all statistics. For example, variances and standard deviations cannot be averaged.

IMPORTANT:

- You can think of the firm as a weighted investment portfolio of components, such as individual divisions or projects. For example, if a firm named ab consists only of two divisions, a and b, then its rate of return is always

$$\tilde{r}_{ab} = w_a \cdot \tilde{r}_a + w_b \cdot \tilde{r}_b$$

where the weights are the relative values of the two divisions. (You can also think of this one firm as a "subportfolio" within a larger overall portfolio, such as the market portfolio.)

- The expected rate of return ("reward") of a portfolio is the weighted average expected rate of return of its components,

$$\mathcal{E}(\tilde{r}_{ab}) = w_a \cdot \mathcal{E}(\tilde{r}_a) + w_b \cdot \mathcal{E}(\tilde{r}_b)$$

Therefore, the expected rate of return of a firm is the weighted average rate of return of its divisions.

- Like expected rates of return, betas can be weighted and averaged. The beta of a firm—i.e., the firm's "risk contribution" to the overall market portfolio—is the weighted average of the betas of its components,

$$\beta_{ab} = w_a \cdot \beta_a + w_b \cdot \beta_b$$

Therefore, the market beta of a firm is the weighted average market beta of its divisions.

- You cannot do analogous weighted averaging with variances or standard deviations.

A firm is a portfolio of debt and equity. Thus, the portfolio formulas apply to the firm (with debt and equity as its components), too!

You can think of the firm not only as consisting of divisions, but also as consisting of debt and equity. For example, say your $400 million firm is financed with debt worth $100 million and equity worth $300 million. If you own all debt and equity, you own the firm. What is the market beta of your firm's assets? Well, the beta of your overall firm must be the weighted average beta of its debt and equity. If your $100 million in debt has a market beta of, say, 0.4 and your $300 million of equity has a market beta of, say, 2.0, then your firm has a market beta of

$$1/4 \cdot (0.4) \quad + \quad 3/4 \cdot (2.0) \quad = 1.6$$

$$\beta_{\text{Firm}} = \left(\frac{\text{Debt value}}{\text{Firm value}}\right) \cdot \beta_{\text{Debt}} + \left(\frac{\text{Equity value}}{\text{Firm value}}\right) \cdot \beta_{\text{Equity}} \qquad (8.7)$$

This 1.6 is called the **asset beta** to distinguish it from the **equity beta** of 2.0 that financial websites report. Put differently, if your firm refinances itself to 100% equity (i.e., $400 million worth), then the reported market beta of your equity on Yahoo!

Finance would fall to 1.6. The asset beta is the measure of your firm's projects' risk contribution to the portfolio of your investors. It is the relevant measure that will determine the cost of capital that you should use as the hurdle rate for projects that are like the average project in your firm.

SOLVE NOW!

Q 8.9 Let's check that the beta combination formula (Formula 8.6 on page 220) is correct. Let me lead you along:

(a) Write down a table with the rate of return on the market and on portfolio CDD in each of the four possible states. (Hint: In scenario S1 [♣], the rate of return on CDD is 8.67%.) Then forget about C and D altogether. (In this question, you will work only with the market and CDD.)

(b) Compute the average rate of return on the market and on CDD.

(c) Write down a table with the de-meaned market rate of return and CDD rate of return in each of the four possible states. (The mean of the de-meaned returns must be zero.)

(d) Multiply the de-meaned rates of return in each scenario. This gives you four cross-products, each having units of %%. (Hint: In scenario S1 [♣], it is about −28.35%%.)

(e) Compute the average of these cross-products. This is the covariance between CDD and M.

(f) Divide the covariance between CDD and M by the variance of the market. Is it equal to the −1.04 from Formula 8.6?

(g) Which is faster—this route or Formula 8.6?

Q 8.10 Let's confirm that you cannot take a value-weighted average of component variances (and thus of standard deviations) the same way that you can take value-weighted average expected rates of return and value-weighted average market betas.

(a) What would the value-weighted average variance of CDD be?

(b) What is the actual variance of CDD?

Q 8.11 Consider an investment of 2/3 in C and 1/3 in D. Call this new portfolio CCD. Compute the variance, standard deviation, and market beta of CCD. Do this two ways: first from the four individual scenario rates of return of CCD, and then from the statistical properties of C and D itself.

Q 8.12 Assume that a firm will always have enough money to pay off its bonds, so the beta of its bonds is 0. (Being risk free, the rate of return on the bonds is obviously independent of the rate of return on the stock market.) Assume that the beta of the underlying assets is 2. What would financial websites report for the beta of the firm's equity if it changes its current capital structure from all equity to half debt and half equity? To 90% debt and 10% equity?

8.5 SPREADSHEET CALCULATIONS FOR RISK AND REWARD

Doing all these calculations by hand is tedious. We computed these statistics within the context of just four scenarios, so that you would understand their meanings better. However, you can do this faster in the real world. Usually, you would download reams of real historical rates of return data into a computer spreadsheet, like Excel or OpenOffice. Spreadsheets have all the functionality you need already built in—and you now understand what their functions actually calculate. In practice, you would use the following functions:

In real life, you can do calculations faster with a spreadsheet.

- **average**(*range*) computes the average (rate of return).
- **varp**(*range*) computes the (population) variance. If you worked with historical data instead of known scenarios, you would instead use the **var**(*range*) formula. (The latter divides by $N - 1$ rather than by N, which I will explain in a moment.)
- **stdevp**(*range*) computes the (population) standard deviation. If you used historical data instead of known scenarios, you would instead use the **stdev**(*range*) formula.
- **covar**(*range-1,range-2*) computes the population covariance between two series. If Excel was consistent, this function should be called covarp rather than covar.
- **correl**(*range-1,range-2*) computes the correlation between two series.
- **slope**(*range-Y,range-X*) computes a beta. If *range-Y* contains the rates of return of an investment and *range-X* contains the rates of return on the market, then this formula computes the market beta.

Table 8.3 shows a computer spreadsheet that computes everything that you did in this chapter.

8.5A STATISTICAL NUANCES

In this chapter, we have continued to presume (just as we did in Section 7.1E) that historical data gives us an unbiased guide to the future when it comes to means, variances, covariances, and betas. Of course, this is a simplification—and remember that it can be a problematic one. I already noted that this is less of a problem for covariances, variances, and betas than it is for means. Rely on historical means as predictors of future expected rates of return only at your own risk!

➤ Will history repeat itself?, Section 7.1E, p. 189

There is a second, smaller statistical issue that you should be aware of. Statisticians often use a covariance formula that divides by $N - 1$, not N. Strictly speaking, dividing by $N - 1$ is appropriate if you work with historical data. These are just sample draws and not the full population of possible outcomes. With a sample, you do not really know the true mean when you de-mean your observations. The division by a smaller number, $N - 1$, gives a larger but unbiased covariance estimate. It is also often called the *sample covariance*. In contrast, dividing by N is appropriate if you work with "scenarios" that you know to be true and equally likely. In this case, the statistic is often called the *population covariance*. The difference rarely matters in finance, where you usually have a lot of observations—except in our book examples where you have only four scenarios. (For example, dividing by $N = 1{,}000$ and by $N = 1{,}001$ gives almost the same number.)

When working with a *sample*, the (co)variance formula divides by $N-1$. When working with the *population*, the (co)variance formula divides by N.

TABLE 8.3 THE COMPUTER SPREADSHEET

	A	B	C	D	E	F	G	H	I	J	K	L	M	
1	Investor Choice, Sample Spreadsheet								Combinations with A (M)					
2									MB	MC	MD			
3		Base Portfolios							w_B	w_C	w_D		w_{CDD}	
4		A (M)	B	C	D		F		= 1/2	= 1/2	= 1/2		= (1/3, 2/3)	
5	**S1**	−1.0%	2.0%	−2.0%	14.0%		1.0%		= 0.5%	= −1.5%	= 6.5%		= 8.7%	
6	**S2**	2.0%	11.0%	3.0%	6.0%		1.0%		= 6.5%	= 2.5%	= 4.0%		= 5.0%	
7	**S3**	4.0%	−1.0%	7.0%	0.0%		1.0%		= 1.5%	= 5.5%	= 2.0%		= 2.3%	
8	**S4**	11.0%	4.0%	12.0%	−12.0%		1.0%		= 7.5%	= 11.5%	= −0.5%		= −4.0%	
9														
10														Formula
11	**Average**	= 4.0%	= 4.0%	= 5.0%	= 2.0%		= 1.0%		= 4.0%	= 4.5%	= 3.0%		= 3.0%	←=average(×5:×8)
12	**Variance**	= 0.1950%	= 0.1950%	= 0.2650%	= 0.9000%		= 0.0000%		= 0.093%	= 0.225%	= 0.066%		= 0.214%	←=varp(×5:×8)
13	**Risk**	= 4.42%	= 4.42%	= 5.15%	= 9.49%		= 0.000%		= 3.041%	= 4.743%	= 2.574%		= 4.625%	←=stdevp(×5:×8)
14														
15														
16	**Market Beta**	= 1.000	= −0.051	= 1.128	= −2.128		= 0.000		= 0.474	= 1.064	= −0.564		= −1.043	←=slope(×5:×8,B5:B8)
17														
18	**Alpha**	= 0.00%	= 4.21%	= 0.49%	= 10.51%		= 1.00%		= 2.10%	= 0.24%	= 5.26%		= 7.17%	←=intercept(×5:×8,B5:B8)
19	**Correlation**	= 100.0%	= −5.1%	= 96.8%	= −99.1%		= #DIV/0!		= 68.9%	= 99.1%	= −96.8%		= −99.6%	←=correl(×5:×8,B5:B8)
20	**Covariance**	= 0.20%	= −0.01%	= 0.22%	= −0.42%		= 0.00%		= 0.09%	= 0.21%	= −0.11%		= −0.20%	←=covar(×5:×8,B5:B8)

This spreadsheet (also available on the book website) demonstrates the main statistical calculations that are performed in this chapter. Please note that we are using the population variance and population standard deviation formulas, not the sample variance and sample standard deviation formulas. Spreadsheet cells that are formulas contain an '='. In rows 5–8, columns I–K are equal combinations of M (column B) and one other portfolio (B–D), which are in columns C–E, respectively. Column M is a weighted average of columns J and K. Formulas in rows 11–20 are given on the right side.

The only reason why you even needed to know this is that if you use a program that has a built-in variance or standard deviation function, you should not be surprised if you get numbers different from those you have computed in this chapter. In some programs, you can get both functions. In Excel, you can use the *varp* and *stdevp* population statistical functions to get the population statistics, not the *var* and *stdev* functions that would give you the sample statistics.

This is important to keep in mind if you use a spreadsheet to check your work.

Beta is not affected by whether you divide the variance/covariance by N or $N-1$, because both numerator (covariance) and denominator (variance) are divided by the same number.

For market beta, the divisor cancels out and does not matter.

Furthermore, statisticians distinguish between underlying unknown statistics and statistics estimated from the data. For example, they might call the unknown true mean μ and the sample mean m (or $\bar{x}$). They might call the unknown true beta β^T and the estimated sample beta a beta with a little hat ($\hat{\beta}$). And so on. Our book is casual about the difference for lack of space, but keep in mind that whenever you work with historical data, you are really just working with sample estimates.

My fault: Our notation should have distinguished between true population and estimated sample statistics.

SUMMARY

This chapter covered the following major points:

- The expected rate of return is a measure of expected reward.

$$\mathcal{E}(\tilde{r}_P) = \frac{\text{Sum over All Scenarios: [Return of Pfio P in Each Scenario]}}{N}$$

- The variance is (roughly) the average squared deviation from the mean.

$$\mathcal{V}ar(\tilde{r}_P) = \frac{\text{Sum over All Scenarios: [Return of Pfio P in Each Scenario} - \mathcal{E}(\tilde{r}_P)]^2}{N-1}$$

  Sometimes, you may divide by N instead of $N-1$. (With a lot of data, this makes no difference.) The variance is an intermediate input to the more interesting statistic, the standard deviation.

- The standard deviation is the square root of the variance. The standard deviation of the rate of return of a portfolio is commonly used as the measure of its risk.

$$\mathcal{S}dv(\tilde{r}_P) = \sqrt{\mathcal{V}ar(\tilde{r}_P)}$$

- Diversification reduces the risk of a portfolio.
- We assume that investors are smart enough to hold widely diversified portfolios, which resemble the overall market portfolio. Diversified portfolios offer higher expected rates of return at lower risks compared to undiversified portfolios.
- An individual asset's own risk is not a good measure of its risk contribution to a portfolio.
- Market beta is a good measure of the risk contribution of an individual asset for an investor who holds the market portfolio.

- Market betas for typical stocks range between 0 and 2.5.
- It is a straightforward application of formulas to compute beta, correlation, and covariance. They are closely related and always share the same sign.
- Like expected rates of return, betas can be averaged (using proper weighting). However, variances or standard deviations cannot be averaged.

KEY TERMS

asset beta, 221
beta, 213
covariance, 215
diversification, 206
equal-weighted portfolio, 220
equity beta, 221
expected rate of return, 202
linear regression, 216
market beta, 213
market model, 213
market portfolio, 208
portfolio risk, 204
reward, 202
standard deviation, 204
value-weighted portfolio, 220
variance, 204

SOLVE NOW! SOLUTIONS

Q 8.1 The average deviation from the mean is always 0.

Q 8.2 The mean of portfolio A was 4%. Adding 5% to each return will give you a mean of 9%, which is 5% higher. The variance and standard deviation remain at the same level, the latter being 4.42%. If you think of 5% as a constant c, you have just shown that $\mathcal{E}(\tilde{r} + c) = \mathcal{E}(\tilde{r}) + c$ and $\mathcal{S}dv(\tilde{r} + c) = \mathcal{S}dv(\tilde{r})$.

Q 8.3 The reward of portfolio C is its expected rate of return. This is simply $[(-2\%) + 3\% + 7\% + 12\%]/4 = 5\%$. (We just divide by 4, rather than multiply each term by 1/4, because all outcomes are equally likely.) The variance of C is $[(-7\%)^2 + (-2\%)^2 + (2\%)^2 + (7\%)^2]/4 = 26.5\%\%$. The standard deviation, which is our measure of risk, is $\sqrt{26.5\%\%} \approx 5.15\%$.

Q 8.4 For the combination portfolio of 90% in A and 10% in B:

(a) The reward, that is, the expected rate of return, is $0.9 \cdot 4\% + 0.1 \cdot 4\% = 4\%$. To work out the variance, first compute the rates of return in the four states:

$$S1: \; 0.9 \cdot (-1\%) + 0.1 \cdot (2\%) = -0.7\%$$

$$S2: \; 0.9 \cdot (2\%) + 0.1 \cdot (11\%) = 2.9\%$$

$$S3: \; 0.9 \cdot (4\%) + 0.1 \cdot (-1\%) = 3.5\%$$

$$S4: \; 0.9 \cdot (11\%) + 0.1 \cdot (4\%) = 10.3\%$$

The variance is

$$\frac{(-0.7\% - 4\%)^2 + (2.9\% - 4\%)^2 + (3.5\% - 4\%)^2 + (10.3\% - 4\%)^2}{4}$$

$$\approx \frac{22.09\%\% + 1.21\%\% + 0.25\%\% + +39.69\%\%}{4} = 15.81\%\%$$

The standard deviation is $\sqrt{15.81\%\%} \approx 3.98\%$.

(b) Figure 8.2 on page 207 showed that the risk (standard deviation) of the 50%-50% portfolio was 3.04%. The risk (standard deviation) of the 90%-10% portfolio is 3.98%. Thus, the latter portfolio looks more spread out in a bar plot.

Q 8.5 For the MC portfolio, the portfolio combination rates of return in the four scenarios were on the right side of the table in Figure 8.3 on page 210. Let's confirm them first:

$$\text{In S1:}\quad 0.5 \cdot (-1\%) + 0.5 \cdot (-2\%) = -1.5\%$$

$$\text{In S2:}\quad 0.5 \cdot (2\%) + 0.5 \cdot (3\%) = 2.5\%$$

$$\text{In S3:}\quad 0.5 \cdot (4\%) + 0.5 \cdot (7\%) = 5.5\%$$

$$\text{In S4:}\quad 0.5 \cdot (11\%) + 0.5 \cdot (12\%) = 11.5\%$$

The expected rate of return is

$$\mathcal{E}(\tilde{r}_{MC}) = \frac{-1.5\% + 2.5\% + 5.5\% + 11.5\%}{4} = 4.5\%$$

The variance of this portfolio is

$$\mathcal{V}ar_{MC} = \frac{(-1.5\% - 4.5\%)^2 + (2.5\% - 4.5\%)^2 + (5.5\% - 4.5\%)^2 + (11.5\% - 4.5\%)^2}{4} = 22.5\%\%$$

Therefore, $\mathcal{S}dv_{MC} = \sqrt{22.5\%\%} \approx 4.74\%$.
For the MD portfolio,

$$\text{In S1:}\quad 0.5 \cdot (-1\%) + 0.5 \cdot (14\%) = 6.5\%$$

$$\text{In S2:}\quad 0.5 \cdot (2\%) + 0.5 \cdot (6\%) = 4.0\%$$

$$\text{In S3:}\quad 0.5 \cdot (4\%) + 0.5 \cdot (0\%) = 2.0\%$$

$$\text{In S4:}\quad 0.5 \cdot (11\%) + 0.5 \cdot (-12\%) = -0.5\%$$

The expected rate of return is

$$\mathcal{E}(\tilde{r}_{MD}) = \frac{6.5\% + 4.0\% + 2.0\% - 0.5\%}{4} = 3\%$$

The variance is $\mathcal{V}ar_{MD} = [(6.5\% - 3\%)^2 + (4.0\% - 3\%)^2 + (2.0\% - 3\%)^2 + (-0.5\% - 3\%)^2]/4 =$ 6.625%%. Therefore, $\mathcal{S}dv_{MD} = \sqrt{6.625\%\%} \approx 2.57\%$.

Q 8.6 The order of subscripts on market beta is important. Algebraically, $\beta_{C,M} = [\text{cov}(\tilde{r}_C, \tilde{r}_M)]/[\text{var}(\tilde{r}_M)]$, while $\beta_{MC} = [\text{cov}(\tilde{r}_C, \tilde{r}_M)]/[\text{var}(\tilde{r}_C)]$. The denominator is different. The easiest way to compute the latter is to pick off the standard deviation of 5.15% from Table 8.1 and square it (26.52%% = 0.2652%). Therefore, the beta is

$$\beta_{M,C} = \frac{\mathcal{C}ov(\tilde{r}_M, \tilde{r}_C)}{\mathcal{V}ar(\tilde{r}_C)} \approx \frac{0.22\%}{0.2652\%} \approx 0.83$$

This is not the same as $\beta_{C,M} \approx 1.128$. Fortunately, you will never ever need to compute $\beta_{M,C}$. I only asked you to do this computation so that you realize that the subscript order is important.

Q 8.7 The market beta of this project is

$$\beta_{x,M} = \frac{\tilde{r}_{x,2} - \tilde{r}_{x,1}}{\tilde{r}_{M,2} - \tilde{r}_{M,1}} = \frac{(-5\%) - (+5\%)}{(-10\%) - (+10\%)} = +0.5$$

(This is not "half as volatile" because market beta is not a measure of volatility.)

Q 8.8 Using the same formula, the market beta is $[(+5\%) - (-5\%)]/[(-10\% - (+10\%)] = -0.5$.

Q 8.9 To check that Formula 8.6 on page 220 is correct, you must compute the market beta for CDD from the rates of return for the entire firm CDD.

(a) The second and third columns in the following table show the rates of return on the market and on CDD in each of the four states:

	Original Base Rates		Net-of-Mean Rates		
Scenario	$\tilde{r}_M$	$\tilde{r}_{CDD}$	$\tilde{r}_M$	$\tilde{r}_{CDD}$	Cross-product
In S1 (♣)	−1%	8.67%	−5%	5.67%	−28.35%%
In S2 (♦)	2%	5.00%	−2%	2.00%	−4.00%%
In S3 (♥)	4%	2.33%	0%	−0.67%	0.00%%
In S4 (♠)	11%	−4.00%	7%	−7.00%	−49.00%%
Mean	4%	3%	0%	0%	−20.33%%

(b) The average rates of return are in the last row of the table.
(c) The de-meaned rates of return are in the fourth and fifth columns.
(d) The cross-products are in the sixth column.
(e) The average cross-product is in the last row of the sixth column.
(f) Using Formula 8.6, the beta of investment CDD is

$$\beta_{CDD} \approx \frac{Cov(\tilde{r}_M, \tilde{r}_C)}{Var(\tilde{r}_M)} = \frac{-0.2033\%}{0.195\%} \approx -1.04$$

(g) Formula 8.6 is a bit easier than this route. The advantage would be even more obvious if you had a few hundred securities and a few thousand trading days, and you already knew the market beta for each of them individually.

In any case, you have now confirmed that Formula 8.6 yielded the same result. You did not catch me in a lie.

Q 8.10 To confirm that you cannot value-weight variances (and thus standard deviations):

(a) The variance of $\tilde{r}_C$ was 26.5%%. The variance of $\tilde{r}_D$ was 90.0%%. The value-weighted average of one part variance of C and two parts variance of D is $w_C \cdot \tilde{r}_C + w_D \cdot \tilde{r}_D = 1/3 \cdot 26.5\%\% + 2/3 \cdot 90.0\%\% \approx 68.83\%$.

(b) The actual variance of CDD is $Var(\tilde{r}_{CDD}) \approx [(5.67\%)^2 + (2\%)^2 + (-0.67\%)^2 + (-7\%)^2]/4 \approx 85.6\%\%/4 \approx 21.4\%\%$.

Q 8.11 The CCD portfolio has rates of return of 3.3333%, 4.00%, 4.6667%, and 4.00% in the four states. De-meaned, this is −0.6667%, 0%, 0.6667%, and 0%. Therefore, the variance of CCD is $[(-0.6667\%)^2 + (0\%)^2 + (0.6667\%)^2 + (0\%)^2]/4 \approx 0.224\%\%$, and its standard deviation is 0.47%. The de-meaned rates of return on M are −5%, −2%, 0, and 7%. The cross-products of the de-meaned CCD rates of return with the de-meaned M rates of return are therefore 3.3333%%, 0, 0, and 0. Therefore, the covariance of CCD and M is $(3.3333\%\% + 0 \cdot 3)/4 \approx 0.8333\%\%$. The variance of the market is 19.5%%. Therefore, the market beta of CCD is $0.833/19.5 \approx 0.0427$. This was the first method. Now the second method: $\beta_{CCD} = w_C \cdot \beta_C + w_D \cdot \beta_D \approx 2/3 \cdot (+1.128) + 1/3 \cdot (-2.128) \approx 0.0427$.

Q 8.12 For a firm whose debt is risk free, the overall firm beta is $\beta_{Firm} = 0.5 \cdot \beta_{Equity} + 0.5 \cdot \beta_{Debt}$. Thus, $0.5 \cdot \beta_{Equity} + 0.5 \cdot 0 = 2$. Solve for $\beta_{Equity} = \beta_{Firm}/0.5 = 4$. For the (90%, 10%) case, the equity beta jumps to $\beta_{Equity} = 2/0.1 = 20$.

PROBLEMS

The [ ] indicates problems available in myfinancelab

When not otherwise specified in these problems, questions refer to the named portfolios A through F from Table 8.1.

Q 8.13 Multiply each rate of return for A by 2.0. This portfolio offers −2%, +4%, +8%, and +22%. Compute the expected rate of return and standard deviation of this new portfolio. How do they compare to those of the original portfolio A?

Q 8.14 The following were the closing year-end prices of the Japanese stock market index, the Nikkei-225:

1984	11,474	1992	16,925	2000	13,786
1985	13,011	1993	17,417	2001	10,335
1986	18,821	1994	19,723	2002	8,579
1987	22,957	1995	19,868	2003	10,677
1988	29,698	1996	19,361	2004	11,489
1989	38,916	1997	15,259	2005	16,111
1990	24,120	1998	13,842	2006	17,225
1991	22,984	1999	18,934	2007	15,308

Assume that each historical rate of return was exactly one representative scenario (independent sample draw) that you can use to estimate the future. If a Japanese investor had purchased a mutual fund that imitated the Nikkei-225, what would her annual rates of return, compounded rate of return (from the end of 1984 to the end of 2007), average rate of return, and risk have been?

Q 8.15 Compute the value-weighted average of 1/3 of the standard deviation of C and 2/3 of the standard deviation of D. Is it the same as the standard deviation of a CDD portfolio of 1/3 C and 2/3 D, in which your investment rate of return would be $1/3 \cdot \tilde{r}_C + 2/3 \cdot \tilde{r}_D$?

Q 8.16 What are the risk and reward of a combination portfolio that invests 40% in A and 60% in B?

Q 8.17 Consider the following five assets, which have rates of return in six equally likely possible scenarios:

	Scenarios					
	Awful	Poor	Med.	Okay	Good	Great
Asset P1	−2%	0%	2%	4%	6%	10%
Asset P2	−1%	2%	2%	2%	3%	3%
Asset P3	−6%	2%	2%	3%	3%	1%
Asset P4	−4%	2%	2%	2%	2%	20%
Asset P5	10%	6%	4%	2%	0%	−2%

(a) Assume you can only purchase one of these assets. What are their risks and rewards?
(b) Supplement your previous risk-reward rankings of assets P1–P5 with those of combination portfolios that consist of half P1 and half of each of the other 4 portfolios, P2–P5. What are the risks and rewards of these four portfolios?
(c) Assume that P1 is the market. Plot the rates of return for P1 on the *x*-axis and the return for each of the other stocks on their own *y*-axes. Then draw lines that you think best fit the points. Do not try to compute the beta—just use the force (and your eyes), Luke. If you had to buy just a little bit of one of these P2–P5 assets, and you wanted to lower your risk, which would be best?

Q 8.18 Assume you have invested half of your wealth in a risk-free asset and half in a risky portfolio P. Is it theoretically possible to lower your portfolio risk if you move your risk-free asset holdings into another risky portfolio Q? In other words, can you ever reduce your risk more by buying a risky security than by buying a risk-free asset?

Q 8.19 Why is it so common to use historical financial data to estimate future market betas?

Q 8.20 Is it wise to rely on historical statistical distributions as our guide to the future?

Q 8.21 Look up the market betas of the companies in Table 8.2. Have they changed dramatically since May 2008, or have they remained reasonably stable?

Q 8.22 You estimate your project to return −20% if the stock market returns −10%, and +5% if the stock market returns +10%. What would you use as the market beta estimate for your project?

Q 8.23 Go to Yahoo! *Finance*. Obtain 2 years' worth of weekly rates of return for PepsiCo and for the S&P 500 index. Use a spreadsheet to compute PepsiCo's market beta.

Q 8.24 Consider the following assets:

	Scenario		
	Bad	Okay	Good
Market M	−5%	5%	15%
Asset X	−2%	−3%	25%
Asset Y	−4%	−6%	30%

(a) Compute the market betas for assets X and Y.
(b) Compute the correlations of assets X and Y with M.
(c) Assume you were holding only M. You now are selling off 10% of your M portfolio to replace it with 10% of either X or Y. Would an MX portfolio or an MY portfolio be riskier?
(d) Is the correlation indicative of which of these two portfolios ended up riskier? Is the market beta indicative?

Q 8.25 Compute the expected rates of return and the portfolio betas for many possible portfolio combinations (i.e., different weights) of C and D from Table 8.1 on page 202. (Your weight in D is 1 minus your weight in C.) Plot the two against one another. What does your plot look like?

Q 8.26 The following represents the probability distribution for the rates of return for next month:

Probability	Pfio P	Market M
1/6	−20%	−5%
2/6	−5%	+5%
2/6	+10%	0%
1/6	+50%	+10%

Compute by hand (and show your work) for all the following questions.
(a) What are the risks and rewards of P and M?
(b) What is the correlation of M and P?
(c) What is the market beta of P?
(d) If you were to hold 1/3 of your portfolio in the risk-free asset, and 2/3 in portfolio P, what would its market beta be?

Q 8.27 Download the historical prices for the S&P 500 index (~spx or ~gspc) and for VPACX (the *Vanguard Pacific Stock Index* mutual fund) from Yahoo! *Finance*, beginning January 1, 2004, and ending December 31 of last year. Load them into a spreadsheet and position them next to one another. Compute the historical rates of return. Compute the risk and reward. Compute VPACX's market beta with respect to the S&P 500 index. How do your estimates compare to the Fund Risk as noted by Yahoo! *Finance*?

Q 8.28 Download 5 years of historical monthly (dividend-adjusted) prices for Coca-Cola (KO) and the S&P 500 from Yahoo! *Finance*.
(a) Compute the monthly rates of return.
(b) Compute the average rate of return and risk of portfolios that combine KO and the S&P 500 in the following proportions: (0.0, 1.0), (0.2, 0.8), (0.4, 0.6), (0.6, 0.4), (0.8, 0.2), (1.0, 0.0). Then plot them against one another. What does the plot look like?
(c) Compute the market beta of Coca-Cola.

Q 8.29 Are historical covariances or means more trustworthy as estimators of the future?

Q 8.30 Why do some statistical packages estimate covariances differently (and different from those we computed in this chapter)? Does the same problem also apply to expected rates of return (means) and betas?

CHAPTER 8 APPENDIX

Trade-Off between Risk and Return

8.6 AN INVESTOR'S SPECIFIC TRADE-OFF BETWEEN RISK AND REWARD

This appendix develops the trade-off between risk and return. Although this is not central to the subject of corporate finance, it is central to the subject of investments. So, where are we and where are we going?

What is the optimal portfolio of assets? (A portfolio is a complete set of weights on all possible assets.)

- You already know that diversification reduces risk.
- Therefore, you know that you like diversification.
- You know that assets that covary negatively with the rest of your portfolio are particularly desirable from a diversification perspective.
- The beta of an asset with respect to a portfolio is its measure of "toxicity" in the context of the portfolio.

The question that you cannot yet answer is

- Exactly how much of each asset should you purchase?

For example, is it better to purchase 25% in A and 75% in B, or 50% in each? How do you determine good investment weights? What is your optimal investment portfolio?

Let's make up two new base assets, H and I. (If you wish, you can think of these assets as themselves being portfolios containing many different stocks.) How do you find the best combination portfolio of H and I? Table 8.4 shows some of the portfolios you could put together. Let's confirm the numbers for at least one of these. Portfolio K invests $w_H = 1/3$ in H and $w_I = 2/3$ in I, which means it has the following possible outcomes:

Table 8.4 computes different combinations of two assets to get various portfolio risk-reward characteristics.

$$\text{In Scenario S1} \clubsuit \; \tilde{r}_K = 1/3 \cdot (-6\%) + 2/3 \cdot (-12\%) = -10\%$$

$$\text{In Scenario S2} \blacklozenge \; \tilde{r}_K = 1/3 \cdot (+12\%) + 2/3 \cdot (+18\%) = +16\%$$

$$\text{In Scenario S3} \heartsuit \; \tilde{r}_K = 1/3 \cdot (0\%) + 2/3 \cdot (+24\%) = +16\%$$

$$\text{In Scenario S4} \spadesuit \; \tilde{r}_K = 1/3 \cdot (+18\%) + 2/3 \cdot (+6\%) = +10\%$$

$$\tilde{r}_K = w_H \cdot (\tilde{r}_H) + w_I \cdot (\tilde{r}_I)$$

The expected rate of return of this portfolio, given all possible future scenarios, is then

$$\mathcal{E}(\tilde{r}_K) = 1/4 \cdot (-10\%) + 1/4 \cdot (+16\%) + 1/4 \cdot (+16\%) + 1/4 \cdot (+10\%) = 8\%$$

$$\mathcal{E}(\tilde{r}) = \text{Sum over All Scenarios } S\text{: } \mathcal{P}rob(\text{Scenario } S) \cdot \text{Outcome in Scenario } S$$

To compute the variance of K, you follow the procedure laid out in Section 6.1B: First, take out the mean from the rates of return:

➤ Standard deviation, Section 6.1B, p. 141

$$\begin{aligned}
&\text{In Scenario S1} \clubsuit \; -10\% - 8\% = -18\% \\
&\text{In Scenario S2} \blacklozenge \; +16\% - 8\% = +8\% \\
&\text{In Scenario S3} \heartsuit \; +16\% - 8\% = +8\% \\
&\text{In Scenario S4} \spadesuit \; +10\% - 8\% = +2\% \\
&\qquad \tilde{r}_K - \mathcal{E}(\tilde{r}_K)
\end{aligned}$$

Second, square them and compute the average:

$$\mathcal{V}ar(\tilde{r}_K) = \frac{(-18\%)^2 + (+8\%)^2 + (+8\%)^2 + (+2\%)^2}{4} = 114\%\% \qquad (8.8)$$

The risk is therefore $\mathcal{S}dv(\tilde{r}_J) = \sqrt{\mathcal{V}ar(\tilde{r}_K)} = \sqrt{114\%\%} \approx 10.68\%$. You have now confirmed the three statistics for portfolio K in Table 8.4: the 8% expected rate of return (reward), 114%% variance, and 10.68% standard deviation (risk).

Do you care about your portfolio's beta or your portfolio's standard deviation? Make sure you understand the answer to this question.

IMPORTANT:

- As an investor, you usually care only about your portfolio's standard deviation (risk). (You rarely ever care about the overall market beta of your asset holdings.)
- If you are the CFO of a firm that wants to get into the market portfolio, so that investors willingly buy your shares, then you do care about your single firm's market beta. You should not care primarily about your firm's own standard deviation (idiosyncratic risk), because your investors do not care about it. They can diversify away your firm's idiosyncratic risk.

TABLE 8.4 PORTFOLIOS USED TO ILLUSTRATE MEAN-VARIANCE COMBINATIONS

	Base Assets		Combination Portfolios				
	100% in Pfio H	100% in Pfio I	1/4 in H 3/4 in I	1/3 in H 2/3 in I	1/2 in H 1/2 in I	2/3 in H 1/3 in I	3/4 in H 1/4 in I
Pfio Name	H	I	J	K	L	M	N
In Scenario S1 ♣	−6.0%	−12.0%	−10.50%	−10.00%	−9.00%	−8.00%	−7.50%
In Scenario S2 ♦	+12.0%	+18.0%	+16.50%	+16.00%	+15.00%	+14.00%	+13.50%
In Scenario S3 ♥	0.0%	+24.0%	+18.00%	+16.00%	+12.00%	+8.00%	+6.00%
In Scenario S4 ♠	+18.0%	+6.0%	+9.00%	+10.00%	+12.00%	+14.00%	+15.00%
"Reward" ($\mathcal{E}(\tilde{r})$)	6.00%	9.00%	8.25%	8.00%	7.50%	7.00%	6.75%
"Variance" ($\mathcal{V}ar(\tilde{r})$)	90.0%%	189.0%%	128.8%%	114.0%%	92.2%%	81.0%%	79.3%%
"Risk" ($\mathcal{S}dv(\tilde{r})$)	9.49%	13.75%	11.35%	10.68%	9.60%	9.00%	8.91%

These are the two base assets (and their combinations) used to illustrate the mean-variance efficient frontier in Section 8.8.

SOLVE NOW!

Q 8.31 Confirm the portfolio variance and standard deviation if you invest in portfolio M ($w_H = 2/3$) in Table 8.4.

Q 8.32 Confirm the portfolio variance and standard deviation if you invest in portfolio N ($w_H = 3/4$) in Table 8.4.

8.7 A SHORTCUT FORMULA FOR THE RISK OF A PORTFOLIO

There is a shortcut formula that can make portfolio variance computations faster. This shortcut allows you to compute the variance of a portfolio as a function of the weights in each constituent asset. To use it, you need to know the covariances between all assets. The formula also avoids having to first work out the rate of return of the combination portfolio in each and every scenario—not a big deal when there are four scenarios, but a very big deal if you have a thousand daily observations, each of which can count as a scenario, and you want to consider many portfolios with various weights.

We want to write the portfolio variance as a function of the component investment weights. This is a common shortcut formula.

For our two assets, you need only one extra number for the new variance shortcut formula: You have to compute the covariance between your two base portfolios, here H and I. You have already worked with the covariance in Section 8.3B. It is defined as the average product of the two net-of-mean returns. Subtract the mean (6% for H and 9% for I) from each scenario's realization:

Example: We still need the covariance between H and I.

➤ Covariance computation, Section 8.3B, p. 214

	Portfolio H		Portfolio I	
In Scenario S1 ♣	$\tilde{r}_H - \mathcal{E}(\tilde{r}_H)$	$= -12\%$	$\tilde{r}_I - \mathcal{E}(\tilde{r}_I)$	$= -21\%$
In Scenario S2 ♦	$\tilde{r}_H - \mathcal{E}(\tilde{r}_H)$	$= +6\%$	$\tilde{r}_I - \mathcal{E}(\tilde{r}_I)$	$= +9\%$
In Scenario S3 ♥	$\tilde{r}_H - \mathcal{E}(\tilde{r}_H)$	$= -6\%$	$\tilde{r}_I - \mathcal{E}(\tilde{r}_I)$	$= +15\%$
In Scenario S4 ♠	$\tilde{r}_H - \mathcal{E}(\tilde{r}_H)$	$= +12\%$	$\tilde{r}_I - \mathcal{E}(\tilde{r}_I)$	$= -3\%$

Therefore,

$$Cov(\tilde{r}_H, \tilde{r}_I) = \frac{(-12\%) \cdot (-21\%) + (+6\%) \cdot (+9\%) + (-6\%) \cdot (+15\%) + (+12\%) \cdot (-3\%)}{4} = +45\%\%$$

$$Cov(\tilde{r}_H, \tilde{r}_I) = \frac{\text{Sum over All Scenarios (or Observations) } S\text{: } [\tilde{r}_{H,S} - \mathcal{E}(\tilde{r}_H)] \cdot [\tilde{r}_{I,S} - \mathcal{E}(\tilde{r}_I)]}{N} \quad (8.9)$$

H and I are positively correlated—these investments tend to move together. Intuitively, this means, for example, that if the rate of return on portfolio H exceeds its 6% mean, portfolio I will also tend to exceed its own 9% mean.

Without further ado, the box that follows gives the shortcut formula for two assets.

IMPORTANT: The variance of a portfolio P that consists only of A and B, that is, with returns of $\tilde{r}_P = w_A \cdot \tilde{r}_A + w_B \cdot \tilde{r}_B$, where w_A is the portfolio weight in component A, and w_B is the portfolio weight in component B, is

$$\mathcal{V}ar(\tilde{r}_P) = w_A^2 \cdot \mathcal{V}ar(\tilde{r}_A) + w_B^2 \cdot \mathcal{V}ar(\tilde{r}_B) + 2 \cdot w_A \cdot w_B \cdot \mathcal{C}ov(\tilde{r}_A, \tilde{r}_B) \quad (8.10)$$

Check whether this is correct. Try it out on portfolio K, which invests 1/3 in H and 2/3 in I:

$$\begin{aligned}\mathcal{V}ar(\tilde{r}_K) &= (1/3)^2 \cdot \mathcal{V}ar(\tilde{r}_H) + (2/3)^2 \cdot \mathcal{V}ar(\tilde{r}_I) + 2 \cdot (1/3) \cdot (2/3) \cdot \mathcal{C}ov(\tilde{r}_H, \tilde{r}_I) \\ &= (1/3)^2 \cdot 90\%\% + (2/3)^2 \cdot 189\%\% + 2 \cdot (1/3) \cdot (2/3) \cdot (+45\%\%) \\ &= 114\%\%\end{aligned}$$

This is the same result as we computed in Formula 8.8, so the shortcut indeed gives the correct answer.

The general formula comes with a good memorization aid.

One way to remember this formula—and the more general version with more than two securities—is to create a matrix of all your assets. It's simple. Write all your assets' names on both edges, their weights next to them, and write into each cell what is on the edges as well as a covariance between what's on the edges:

		A w_A	B w_B	C w_C	...
A	w_A	$w_A \cdot w_A \cdot \mathcal{C}ov(\tilde{r}_A, \tilde{r}_A)$	$w_A \cdot w_B \cdot \mathcal{C}ov(\tilde{r}_A, \tilde{r}_B)$	$w_A \cdot w_C \cdot \mathcal{C}ov(\tilde{r}_A, \tilde{r}_C)$	
B	w_B	$w_B \cdot w_A \cdot \mathcal{C}ov(\tilde{r}_B, \tilde{r}_A)$	$w_B \cdot w_B \cdot \mathcal{C}ov(\tilde{r}_B, \tilde{r}_B)$	$w_B \cdot w_C \cdot \mathcal{C}ov(\tilde{r}_B, \tilde{r}_C)$	
C	w_C	$w_C \cdot w_A \cdot \mathcal{C}ov(\tilde{r}_C, \tilde{r}_A)$	$w_C \cdot w_B \cdot \mathcal{C}ov(\tilde{r}_C, \tilde{r}_B)$	$w_C \cdot w_C \cdot \mathcal{C}ov(\tilde{r}_C, \tilde{r}_C)$	
⋮					⋱

That's it. By the way, did you notice that if you have m securities, there are only m variance terms in this matrix (on the diagonal), but $m^2 - m$ covariance terms? For 500 assets, you have 500 variance cells and 249,500 covariance cells. Adding the next security to the portfolio would add 1 variance term and 500 covariance terms. It should suggest to you that it need not be far-fetched to believe that the covariance of assets—how they fit together—can be more important than their own variances.

Apply the formula to compute the variance of K again.

Now substitute our specific investment weights for portfolio K, which are $w_H = 1/3$, $w_I = 2/3$. Let me also show you that investments that you do not own (call a sample one J) just drop out of the formula:

		H 1/3	I 2/3	J 0	...
H	1/3	$1/3 \cdot 1/3 \cdot \mathcal{C}ov(\tilde{r}_H, \tilde{r}_H)$	$1/3 \cdot 2/3 \cdot \mathcal{C}ov(\tilde{r}_H, \tilde{r}_I)$	$1/3 \cdot 0 \cdot \mathcal{C}ov(\tilde{r}_H, \tilde{r}_J)$	
I	2/3	$2/3 \cdot 1/3 \cdot \mathcal{C}ov(\tilde{r}_I, \tilde{r}_H)$	$2/3 \cdot 2/3 \cdot \mathcal{C}ov(\tilde{r}_I, \tilde{r}_I)$	$2/3 \cdot 0 \cdot \mathcal{C}ov(\tilde{r}_I, \tilde{r}_J)$	
J	0	$0 \cdot 1/3 \cdot \mathcal{C}ov(\tilde{r}_J, \tilde{r}_H)$	$0 \cdot 2/3 \cdot \mathcal{C}ov(\tilde{r}_J, \tilde{r}_I)$	$2/3 \cdot 0 \cdot \mathcal{C}ov(\tilde{r}_J, \tilde{r}_J)$	
⋮					⋱

All cells with J just multiply everything with a zero, so they can be omitted. Next, use the fact that, by definition, the covariance of something with itself is its variance. So, the matrix is

		H	I
		1/3	2/3
H	1/3	1/3 · 1/3 · 90%%	1/3 · 2/3 · 45%%
I	2/3	2/3 · 1/3 · 45%%	2/3 · 2/3 · 189%%

Add up all the cells, and you have the variance of portfolio K.

$$\mathcal{V}ar(\tilde{r}_K) = 1/3 \cdot 1/3 \cdot 90\%\% + \ 1/3 \cdot 2/3 \cdot 45\%\%$$
$$2/3 \cdot 1/3 \cdot 45\%\% + 2/3 \cdot 2/3 \cdot 189\%\% = 114\%\%$$

Again, this is the correct answer that you already knew.

This formula is useful if you want to try thousands of different portfolios (investment weights).

For H and I, this formula is not any more convenient than computing the scenario or historical time series of portfolio returns first and then computing the variance of this one series. However, the formula is a lot more convenient if you have to compute the portfolio variance of thousands of different combinations of H and I and there are hundreds of scenarios. And it is precisely this process—recomputing the overall portfolio variance many times—that is at the heart of determining the best portfolio: You want to know how different portfolio weights change your portfolio risk. Your alternative to the shortcut would be to recompute the returns for each of the hundreds of possible portfolio weight combinations—which would quickly become very painful.

SOLVE NOW!

Q 8.33 Show that the shortcut Formula 8.10 works for portfolio M, in which H is 2/3. That is, does it give the same 81.0%% noted in Table 8.4 on page 232?

Q 8.34 Show that the shortcut Formula 8.10 works for portfolio N, in which H is 3/4. That is, does it give the same 79.3%% noted in Table 8.4?

Q 8.35 (This question is very important. Please do not pass over it.) Let's consider a stock market index, such as the S&P 500. It had a historical average rate of return of about 12% per annum, and a historical standard deviation of about 20% per annum. Assume for the moment:

(a) **Known statistical distributions:** You know the expected reward and risk. In our example, we assume that they are the historical averages and risks. This is convenient.

(b) **Independent stock returns:** Stock returns are (mostly) uncorrelated over time periods. This is reasonable because if this were not so, you could earn money purchasing stocks based on their prior performance in a perfect market. (This will be the subject of Chapter 11.)

(c) **No compounding:** The rate of return over X years is the simple sum of X annual rates of return. (That is, we ignore the cross-product terms that are rates of return on rates of return.) This is problematic over decades, but not over just a few months or even years.

Our goal is to work out how asset risk grows with time under these assumptions. The variance shortcut formula will help us.

(a) Write down the formula for the total rate of return over 2 years.
(b) What is the expected total rate of return over 2 years?
(c) Write down the formula for the variance over 2 years.
(d) What is the specific risk here (variance and standard deviation) over 2 years?
(e) The **Sharpe ratio** is a common (though flawed) measure of portfolio performance. It is usually computed as the expected rate of return above the risk-free rate, then divided by the standard deviation. Assume that the risk-free rate is 6%. Thus, the 1-year Sharpe ratio is $(12\% - 6\%)/20\% \approx 0.3$. What is the 2-year Sharpe ratio?
(f) What are the expected rate of return and risk (variance and standard deviation) over 4 years? What is the 4-year Sharpe ratio?
(g) What are the expected rate of return and risk (variance and standard deviation) over 16 years? What is the 16-year Sharpe ratio?
(h) What are the expected rate of return and risk (variance and standard deviation) over T years? What is the T-year Sharpe ratio?
(i) What are the expected rate of return and risk (variance and standard deviation) over 1 month? What is the 1-month Sharpe ratio?
(j) What are the expected rate of return and risk (variance and standard deviation) over 1 trading day? What is the 1-day Sharpe ratio? Assume 250 trading days per year.

8.8 GRAPHING THE MEAN-VARIANCE EFFICIENT FRONTIER

Graphing the trade-off between risk and reward . . .

Let's now graph the portfolio risk on the x-axis and the portfolio reward on the y-axis for each portfolio from Table 8.4 on page 232. Figure 8.5 does it for you. Can you see a pattern? To make it easier, I have taken the liberty of adding a few more portfolios. (You can confirm that I have computed the risk and reward of one of these portfolios in Q 8.36.)

. . . is called the mean-variance efficient frontier.

If you picked many more portfolios with portfolio weights on H between 0 and 100%, you would eventually end up with Figure 8.6. The curve is called the **mean-variance efficient frontier** (**MVE frontier**), and it is the region where the best risk-reward portfolios lie. There must not be any portfolios to the northwest of this frontier—they would have a higher expected rate of return for a given risk, or lower risk for a given expected rate of return. If these existed, they would themselves be the MVE frontier. (The shape of the mean-variance efficient frontier is a so-called hyperbola when the x-axis is the standard deviation.)

The minimum-variance portfolio is the west-most portfolio.

The west-most portfolio on the efficient frontier is called the **minimum-variance portfolio** because you cannot create a portfolio with lower risk. You need a lot of algebra to find it, so I have worked this out for you. In our example, the minimum-variance portfolio has a weight of 76.191% on H and 23.809% on I, and it achieves

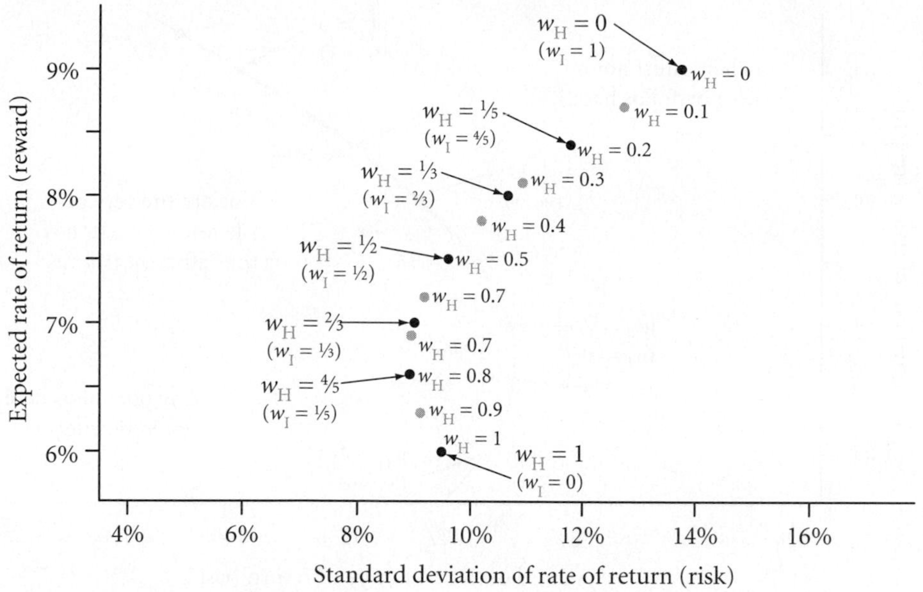

These are the portfolios from Table 8.4, and then some more in gray that I computed—a hobby.

FIGURE 8.5 The Risk-Reward Trade-Off between H and I: More Portfolios

as low a risk as 8.9%. Although the graph's scale is too small for you to check this graphically, you can compute the risk of this minimum-variance portfolio that I gave you and compare it to the risk of two portfolios that invest either a little more or a little less into H.

$$w_H = 76.0\% : \mathcal{S}dv(\tilde{r}_P) \approx 8.9042911\%$$

$$w_H = 76.2\% : \mathcal{S}dv(\tilde{r}_P) \approx 8.9042526\% \quad \longleftarrow \text{ I claimed lowest risk} \qquad (8.11)$$

$$w_H = 76.4\% : \mathcal{S}dv(\tilde{r}_P) \approx 8.9042992\%$$

$$\mathcal{S}dv(\tilde{r}_P) = \sqrt{\mathcal{V}ar(\tilde{r}_P) = \mathcal{V}ar[w_H \cdot \tilde{r}_H + (1 - w_H) \cdot \tilde{r}_I]} \qquad (8.12)$$

If there are assets that can be combined to construct a risk-free asset, then the minimum-variance portfolio will touch the y-axis at 0. If there are only two assets, this means their correlation would have to be -1. More commonly, the minimum-variance portfolio does not touch the y-axis and still has positive risk.

There is one feature of a more general mean-variance graph that this particular graph cannot illustrate. If you had started with more than two base portfolios H and I, you could have found many combination portfolios that would have been outright inferior. They would have been a cloud of points inside and southeast of the efficient frontier. However, the efficient frontier itself would still look very similar to what is in Figure 8.6—a hyperbola on the upper northwest frontier.

One feature is not visible in this figure, because there are only two portfolios: With more assets, many portfolio combinations lie in the interior—a cloud of points.

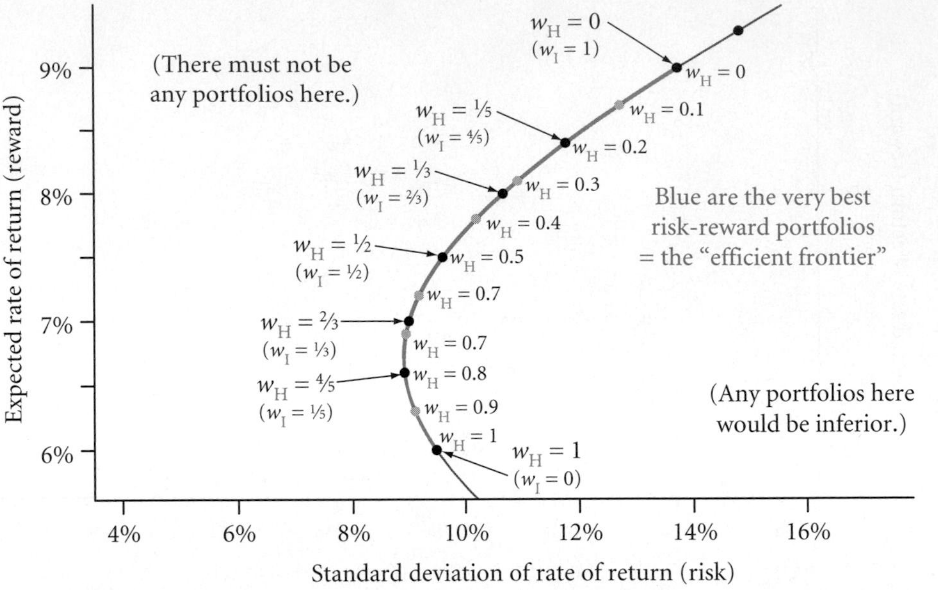

This connects the points on the efficient frontier to Figure 8.5. Additionally, it completes the efficient frontier beyond interior portfolios, that is, allowing for portfolios that short one or the other portfolio (in magenta).

FIGURE 8.6 The Risk-Reward Trade-Off between H and I: Sets

ALLOWING SHORTED POSITIONS

Extending the MVEF to allow for short positions extends the graph.

Each point on the mean-variance frontier represents one set of investment weights. Interestingly, the relevant formulas work just as well with negative weights as they do with positive weights. For example, if $w_H = (-0.1)$ and $w_I = 1.1$, then the sum of your individual investments is still 100%, and

$$\mathcal{E}(\tilde{r}_P) = (-0.1) \cdot 6\% + (1.1) \cdot 9\% = 9.3\%$$

$$\mathcal{E}(\tilde{r}_P) = w_H \cdot \mathcal{E}(\tilde{r}_H) + w_I \cdot \mathcal{E}(\tilde{r}_I)$$

and

$$\mathcal{S}dv(\tilde{r}_P) = \sqrt{(-0.1)^2 \cdot 90\%\% + (1.1)^2 \cdot 189\%\% + 2 \cdot (-0.1) \cdot (1.1) \cdot 45\%\%} \approx 14.82\%$$

$$\mathcal{S}dv(\tilde{r}_P) = \sqrt{w_H^2 \cdot \mathcal{V}ar(\tilde{r}_H) + w_I^2 \cdot \mathcal{V}ar(\tilde{r}_I) + 2 \cdot w_H \cdot w_I \cdot \mathcal{C}ov(\tilde{r}_I, \tilde{r}_H)}$$

(If you wish, you can first confirm this: This portfolio would return −12.6% (♣), 18.6% (♦), 26.4% (♥), or 4.8% (♠). Therefore, the expected rate of return is 9.3%, and the standard deviation is 14.82%.) This portfolio is marked at the top in Figure 8.6. It is on the continuation of the hyperbola. Actually, I have done more, drawing the rest of the hyperbola in magenta. These are portfolios that contain shorted assets.

The economic meaning of shorting reexplained.

➤ Shorting stocks, Section 7.2A, p. 191

But what is the meaning of an investment with negative weight? It was explained in Section 7.2A: It is shorting a stock. In brief, perfect shorting works as follows: If you short a security, you promise to provide the appropriate returns, rather than earn them. For example, say you want to go short $200 in H and I want to go long $200 in H. I would purchase H from you. This would work as follows:

- I must give you \$200 today. (If you want, you can invest this to earn interest.)
- Next year, you must give me exactly what I would get if I had purchased H, not from you, but from someone else who really would have given me the security. That is, if ♣ comes about, you must pay me \$188; if ♦ comes about, you must pay me \$224; if ♥ comes about, you must pay me \$200; and if ♠ comes about, you must pay me \$236.

In other words, I won't notice whether you sold me the security or someone else (who had it) sold me the security. This is simple ownership—a 100% investment ownership. Your own rate of return is the exact opposite of my return. For example, if I earn −6%, you would gain +6%. After all, you received \$200 from me (at time 0) and are only returning \$188 to me (at time 1). What would your return be if you sold \$200 of H to me, thereby going short, and then used the \$200 to purchase H from someone else in the market? It would always be zero—going long and short by the same amount cancels out perfectly. In a perfect market, you would not earn any money or lose any money.

SOLVE NOW!

Q 8.36 Compute the risk and reward of the portfolio $w_H = 0.1$, $w_I = 0.9$, as in Table 8.4 on page 232. Confirm that this portfolio is drawn correctly in Figure 8.5.

Q 8.37 If there are two risky portfolios that have a correlation of −1 with positive investment weights, what would the expected rate of return on this portfolio be?

Q 8.38 If H and I were more correlated, what would the efficient frontier between them look like? If H and I were less (or more negatively) correlated, what would the efficient frontier between them look like? (Hint: Think about the variance of the combination portfolio that invests half in each.)

Q 8.39 Draw the efficient frontier for the following two base assets, H and Z:

	In Scenario			
Base Portfolio	S1 ♣	S2 ♦	S3 ♥	S4 ♠
H	−6%	+12%	0%	+18%
Z	−12%	+18%	+15%	+15%

Also, compute the covariance between H and Z. Is it higher or lower than what you computed in the text for H and I? How does the efficient frontier compare to what you have drawn in this chapter?

8.9 ADDING A RISK-FREE ASSET

A special case: The risk and reward of combinations of portfolios with the risk-free asset are both simple linear functions.

In the real world, you usually have access to a risk-free Treasury. It turns out that the presence of a risk-free asset plays an important role, not only in the model of the next chapter (the CAPM), but also in these mean-variance graphs. So let us now add a risk-free rate ("F") of 4%. Start with the following three basis portfolios:

Future	H	I	F
In Scenario S1 ♣	−6.0%	−12.0%	4.00%
In Scenario S2 ♦	+12.0%	+18.0%	4.00%
In Scenario S3 ♥	0.0%	+24.0%	4.00%
In Scenario S4 ♠	+18.0%	+6.0%	4.00%
"Reward" ($\mathcal{E}(R)$)	6.00%	9.00%	4.00%
"Variance" ($\mathcal{V}ar(R)$)	90.0%%	189.0%%	0.0%%
"Risk" ($\mathcal{S}dv(R)$)	9.49%	13.75%	0.00%

Begin by determining the risk and reward of a portfolio S that invests 1/2 in H and 1/2 in F: Its rate of return is defined as $\tilde{r}_S = w_H \cdot \tilde{r}_H + w_F \cdot \tilde{r}_F = 1/2 \cdot \tilde{r}_H + 1/2 \cdot 4\%$. The expected reward of this portfolio is

$$\mathcal{E}(\tilde{r}_S) = 1/2 \cdot 6\% + (1 - 1/2) \cdot 4\% = 5\%$$
$$\mathcal{E}(\tilde{r}_S) = w_H \cdot \mathcal{E}(\tilde{r}_H) + (1 - w_H) \cdot r_F \quad (8.13)$$

➤ Portfolio variance, Formula 8.10, p. 234

For the risk component, use Formula 8.10. A risk-free rate, such as the 4% Treasury rate, has neither a variance nor a covariance with anything else. (Makes sense that a fixed constant number that is always the same has no variance, doesn't it?) For portfolio S, use $(1 - w_H) = w_F$ and you get

$$\mathcal{V}ar(\tilde{r}_S) = (1/2)^2 \cdot 90\%\% + (1 - 1/2)^2 \cdot 0\% + 2 \cdot 1/2 \cdot (1 - 1/2) \cdot 0\% = 1/4 \cdot 90\%\%$$
$$\mathcal{V}ar(\tilde{r}_S) = w_H^2 \cdot \mathcal{V}ar(\tilde{r}_H) + w_F^2 \cdot \mathcal{V}ar(r_F) + 2 \cdot w_H \cdot w_F \cdot \mathcal{C}ov(\tilde{r}_H, r_F) = (w_H)^2 \cdot \mathcal{V}ar(\tilde{r}_H)$$

This formula is a lot simpler than the typical variance formula, with its second variance term and its covariance term. It also means that we can compute the standard deviation more easily:

$$\mathcal{S}dv(\tilde{r}_S) = \sqrt{(1/2)^2 \cdot 90\%\%} = 1/2 \cdot \sqrt{90\%\%} \approx 1/2 \cdot 9.49\% \approx 4.74\%$$
$$\mathcal{S}dv(\tilde{r}_S) = \sqrt{(w_H)^2 \cdot \mathcal{V}ar(\tilde{r}_H)} = w_H \cdot \sqrt{\mathcal{V}ar(\tilde{r}_H)} = w_H \cdot \mathcal{S}dv(\tilde{r}_H) \quad (8.14)$$

This states that the risk of your overall portfolio is proportional to the risk of your investment in asset H, with your investment weight being the proportionality factor.

Combining different weights of any risky portfolio with the risk-free asset yields a straight line.

You can repeat this for many different portfolio weights:

Weight w_H	0.0	0.2	0.4	0.6	0.8	1.0
Expected Return	4.0%	4.4%	4.8%	5.2%	5.6%	6.0%
Standard Deviation	0.000%	1.898%	3.796%	5.694%	7.592%	9.490%

The algebra that shows that the relation between the risk and reward of a risky portfolio and the risk-free asset is a line.

If you plot these points into the figure, you will immediately notice that the relationship between risk and reward is now a line. Figure 8.7 does it for you.

You can also show this algebraically. Rearrange Formula 8.14 into $w_H = \mathcal{S}dv(\tilde{r}_S)/\mathcal{S}dv(\tilde{r}_H) = \mathcal{S}dv(\tilde{r}_S)/9.49\%$. Then use this to substitute out w_H in Formula 8.13:

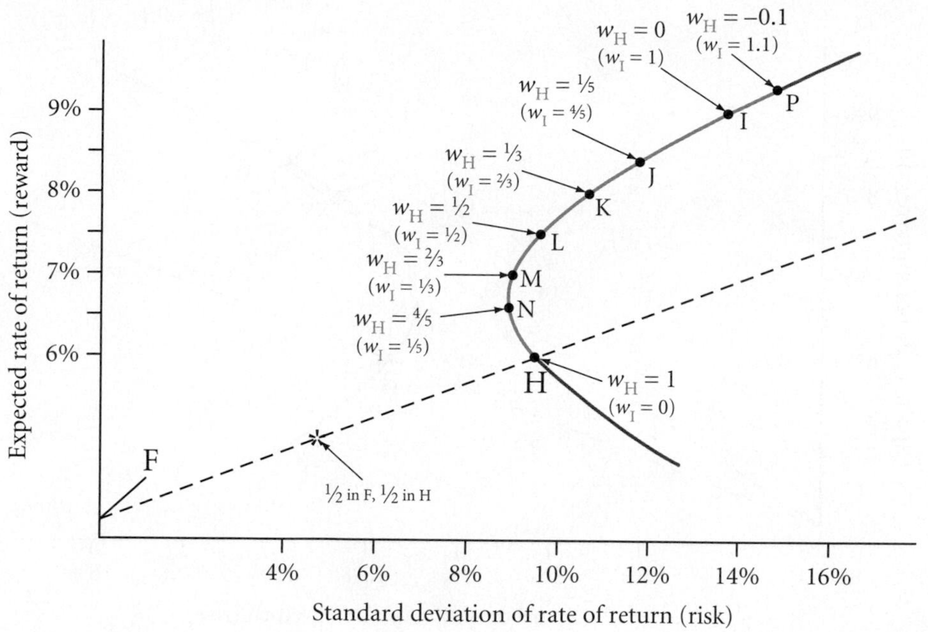

This adds a risk-free rate of 4% to Figure 8.5. The line represents risks and rewards for portfolios that combine portfolio H and the risk-free rate F. Please note that this line is *not* the security markets line (the CAPM). Here, the x-axis is the standard deviation (of the overall portfolio rate of return). In the security market line (SML) explained in chapter 9, the x-axis is the market beta (of individual assets).

FIGURE 8.7 The Risk-Reward Trade-Off between H and F

$$\begin{aligned}
\mathcal{E}(\tilde{r}_S) &= w_H \cdot 6\% + (1 - w_H) \cdot 4\% = w_H \cdot (6\% - 4\%) + 4\% \\
&= \left[\frac{Sdv(\tilde{r}_S)}{9.49\%}\right] \cdot (6\% - 4\%) + 4\% = 4\% + 0.21 \cdot Sdv(\tilde{r}_S)
\end{aligned}$$

$$\begin{aligned}
\mathcal{E}(\tilde{r}_S) &= w_H \cdot \mathcal{E}(\tilde{r}_H) + (1 - w_H) \cdot r_F = w_H \cdot (\mathcal{E}(\tilde{r}_H) - r_F) + r_F \\
&= \left[\frac{Sdv(\tilde{r}_S)}{Sdv(\tilde{r}_H)}\right] \cdot [\mathcal{E}(\tilde{r}_H) - r_F] + r_F = r_F + \left[\frac{\mathcal{E}(\tilde{r}_H) - r_F}{Sdv(\tilde{r}_H)}\right] \cdot Sdv(\tilde{r}_S)
\end{aligned}$$

This is the formula for a line: r_F is the intercept and $\left[(\mathcal{E}(\tilde{r}_H) - r_F)/(Sdv(\tilde{r}_H))\right]$ is the slope.

IMPORTANT: When you plot the portfolio mean versus the portfolio standard deviation for combination portfolios of a risk-free asset F with any risky portfolio P, they lie on the straight line between F and P.

But would you really want to purchase such a combination of H and F? Could you purchase a different portfolio in combination with F that would do better? Would the combination of L and F not perform better?

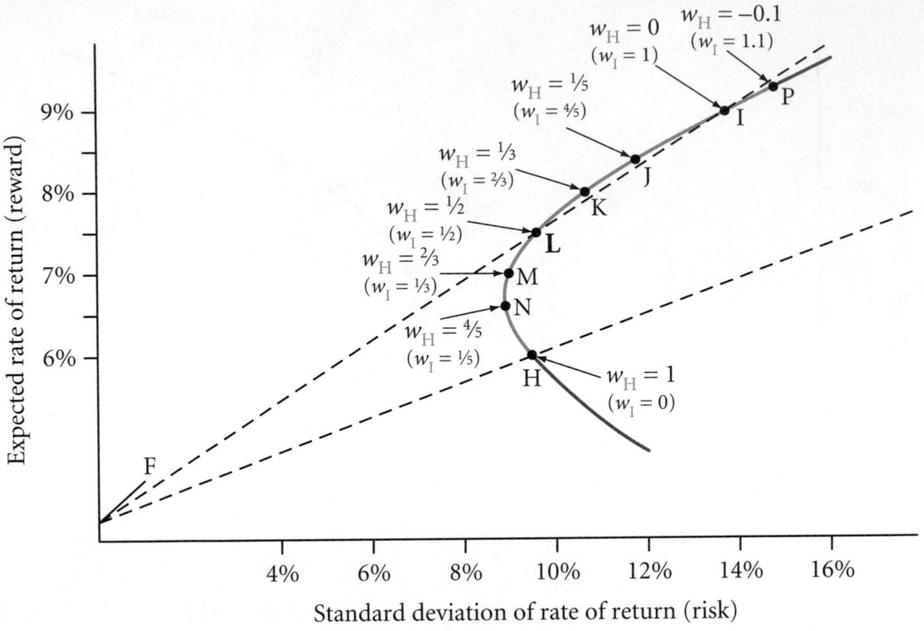

Adding to Figure 8.7, the new line represents risks and rewards for portfolios that combine portfolio L and the risk-free asset F.

FIGURE 8.8 The Risk-Reward Trade-Off between L and F

Figure 8.8 draws combinations of the risk-free asset and portfolio L. This combination of F and L indeed does a lot better—but you can do even better yet. Can you guess what portfolio you would purchase?

With a risk-free asset, the best portfolio is the line that is tangent to the efficient frontier of risky assets.

The answer is drawn in Figure 8.9—you would purchase a combination portfolio of the risk-free asset and whatever portfolio on the previous efficient frontier would be *tangent*—you tilt the line up until it just touches the mean-variance frontier among the risky assets. This line is called the **capital market line**. Here, the exact investment proportions in the risky assets are difficult to see, but if you could blow up the figure, you would see that this is the portfolio that invests about 30% in H and 70% in I. Let's call it T, for tangency portfolio.

Do all smart investors make the same portfolio decision in the presence of a risk-free asset? Yes and no.

Who would want to purchase a portfolio combination that invests more or less than 30% in H and 70% in I? Nobody! Each and every smart investor would purchase only a combination of F and T, regardless of risk aversion. (This is called the **two-fund separation theorem**.) Different risk tolerances would lead them to allocate different sums to the tangency portfolio and the risk-free asset, but no investor would purchase a risky portfolio with investment weights different from those in the tangency portfolio T.

IMPORTANT: In the presence of a risk-free asset, all smart investors purchase combinations of the tangency portfolio and the risk-free asset.

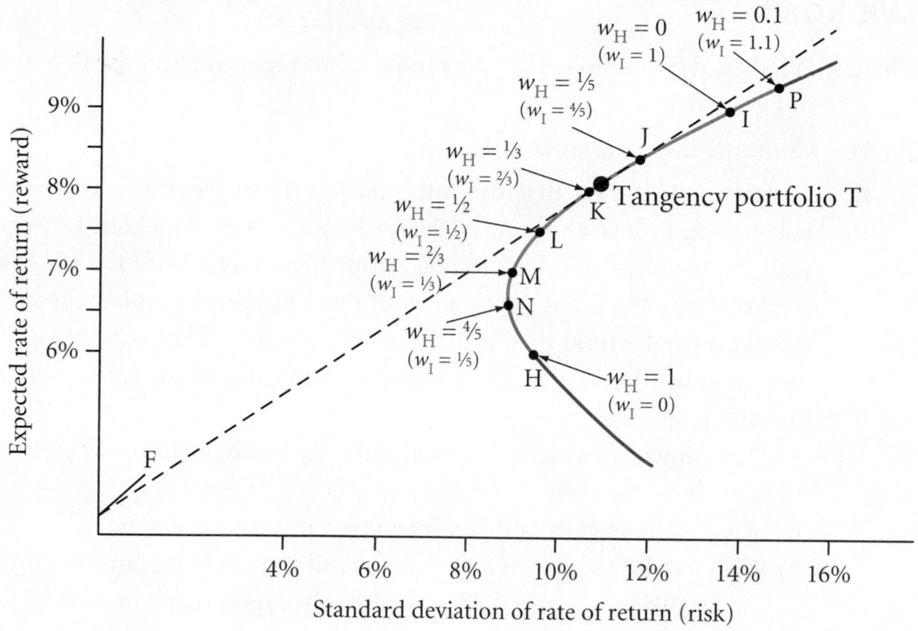

The capital market line represents risks and rewards for portfolios that combine the tangency portfolio T and the risk-free rate F. It represents the best opportunities available.

FIGURE 8.9 The Risk-Reward Trade-Off between T and F

CAPM Preview

Chapter 9 explains the most common model of security pricing, the CAPM. In brief, it states that the market portfolio is mean-variance efficient—and nothing else. How can this happen? Well, if *every* investor is smart and all the various CAPM assumptions and conditions are satisfied (explained soon), then each investor holds only a combination of T and the risk-free asset. Math dictates that this means that the value-weighted market portfolio of all investors' holdings is therefore also a combination of T and the risk-free asset. Therefore, it is also mean-variance efficient.

In equilibrium, if all investors buy combinations of the risk-free asset and the tangency portfolio, the market portfolio is on the efficient frontier.

IMPORTANT: In the CAPM, the market portfolio of risky claims is the tangency portfolio.

(Of course, conversely, if some investors do not hold the market tangency portfolio, then the overall market portfolio [could but] need not be the tangency portfolio.)

If the CAPM holds, that is, if T is the market portfolio, then portfolio optimization is beautifully easy for any investor—just purchase a combination of the market portfolio and the risk-free asset. You never even need to compute an efficient frontier. Of course, in the real world, the market portfolio may not be the tangency portfolio—but then, this is the same as stating that the CAPM does not hold. *In fact, the CAPM is nothing more and nothing less than the statement that the market portfolio is the tangency portfolio.*

The CAPM can make investing really easy—no computer program necessary!

SOLVE NOW!

Q 8.40 What kind of portfolios are the points to the right of H on the line itself in Figure 8.7?

Q 8.41 Compute the covariance of H and F.

Q 8.42 Formula 8.11 noted that the minimum-variance portfolio without a risk-free asset invests about 76.2% in H and about 24.8% in I. (Work with the rounded numbers to make your life easier.) With the risk-free asset offering 4%, what portfolio would you purchase that has the same risk, and what would its improvement in reward be? First think about how to solve this. However, this is a difficult question, so we will go through it step by step.

(a) Copy down the risk of this minimum-variance portfolio when there is no risk-free asset.

(b) What is the reward of this minimum-variance portfolio?

(c) With a risk-free rate of 4%, it turns out that the tangency portfolio invests 30% in H and 70% in I. What are its returns in each of the four scenarios?

(d) What is its reward? (Check this visually in the graph!)

(e) What is its risk? (Check this visually in the graph!)

(f) Using the analog of Formula 8.14, what investment weight w_T in T would give you the same risk as the minimum-variance portfolio? (If you had \$100, how much would you put into T, and how much would you put into a risk-free savings account?)

(g) Given this weight w_T, what is the reward of this combination portfolio? How much better is this than the situation where no risk-free asset was available?

Q 8.43 Would the tangency portfolio invest in more or less H if the risk-free rate were 3% instead of 4%? (Hint: Think visually.)

KEY TERMS

capital market line, 242
on margin, 246
mean-variance efficient frontier, 236
minimum-variance portfolio, 236
MVE frontier, 236
sharpe ratio, 236
two-fund separation theorem, 242

SOLVE NOW! SOLUTIONS

Q 8.31 The rates of return of portfolio M in Table 8.4 are −8% (♣), +14% (♦), 8% (♥), and 14% (♠). The deviations from the mean are −15%, 7%, 1%, and 7%. When squared, they are 225%%, 49%%, 1%%, and 49%%. The sum is 324%%; the average is 81%%. Thus, the standard deviation is indeed 9%.

Q 8.32 The portfolio variance of portfolio N in Table 8.4 is

$$\mathcal{S}dv(\tilde{r}_H) = \sqrt{\mathcal{V}ar(\tilde{r}_H)} = \sqrt{\frac{(-7.5\% - 6.75\%)^2 + (13.5\% - 6.75\%)^2 + (6\% - 6.75\%)^2 + (15\% - 6.75\%)^2}{4}}$$

$$= \sqrt{\frac{203.0625\%\% + 45.5625\%\% + 0.5625\%\% + 68.0625\%\%}{4}}$$

$$\approx \sqrt{79.31\%\%} \approx 8.91\%$$

Q 8.33 For M, the covariance between H and I was computed as 45%% in Formula 8.9. The variance of H is 90%% (from Table 8.4 on page 232), the variance of I is 189%% (from the same figure). Therefore, using the shortcut Formula 8.10, $\mathcal{V}ar(\tilde{r}_M) = (2/3)^2 \cdot 90\%\% + (1/3)^2 \cdot 189\%\% + 2 \cdot (2/3) \cdot (1/3) \cdot 45\%\% = 81\%\%$.

Q 8.34 The covariance between H and I is 45%% (Formula 8.9). The variance of H is 90%%, the variance of I is 189%% (Table 8.4). Therefore, the shortcut Formula 8.10 gives

$$\mathcal{V}ar(\tilde{r}_M) = (3/4)^2 \cdot 90\%\% + (1/4)^2 \cdot 189\%\% + 2 \cdot (3/4) \cdot (1/4) \cdot 45\%\% = 79.3125\%\%$$

Q 8.35 This is an important question. In fact, you should memorize Formula 8.15 that describes how risk grows over time. The assumption that there is no compounding (that you can ignore the cross-product) and that risk is roughly constant per period is reasonable over periods that are not more than a few years long.

(a) If we can ignore the cross-products, then we are using a simple weighted-average formula with weights of 1 on each term: $\tilde{r}_{0,2} \approx 1 \cdot \tilde{r}_{0,1} + 1 \cdot \tilde{r}_{1,2}$. (The exact formula would have been $\tilde{r}_{0,2} = \tilde{r}_{0,1} + \tilde{r}_{1,2} + \tilde{r}_{0,1} \cdot \tilde{r}_{1,2}$.)

(b) The expected rate of return over 2 years is $\mathcal{E}(\tilde{r}_{0,2}) \approx \mathcal{E}(\tilde{r}_{0,1}) + \mathcal{E}(\tilde{r}_{1,2}) = 12\% + 12\% = 24\%$.

(c) The variance of the rate of return over 2 years is $\mathcal{V}ar(\tilde{r}_{0,2}) \approx 1 \cdot \mathcal{V}ar(\tilde{r}_{0,1}) + 1 \cdot \mathcal{V}ar(\tilde{r}_{1,2}) + 2 \cdot 1 \cdot 1 \cdot \mathcal{C}ov(\tilde{r}_{0,1}, \tilde{r}_{0,2})$. In a perfect market, the last term should be approximately zero.

(d) The variance over 2 years for our specific example is

$$\mathcal{V}ar(\tilde{r}_{0,2}) \approx 1 \cdot \mathcal{V}ar(\tilde{r}_{0,1}) + 1 \cdot \mathcal{V}ar(\tilde{r}_{1,2}) + \quad 0$$

$$= \quad (20\%)^2 \quad + \quad (20\%)^2 \quad = 2 \cdot (20\%)^2 = 800\%\%$$

Therefore, the standard deviation is $\sqrt{2} \cdot 20\% \approx 28\%$.

(e) The Sharpe ratio is $2 \cdot (12\% - 6\%)/28\% \approx 0.43$.

(f) The variance is $4 \cdot (20\%)^2 = 1600\%\%$. The standard deviation is $20\% \cdot \sqrt{4} = 40\%$. The Sharpe ratio is $(6\% \cdot 4)/(20\% \cdot \sqrt{4}) = 0.3 \cdot \sqrt{4} = 0.6$.

(g) The variance is $16 \cdot (20\%)^2 = 6400\%$. The standard deviation is $20\% \cdot \sqrt{16} = 80\%$. The Sharpe ratio is $0.3 \cdot \sqrt{16} \approx 1.2$.

(h) The variance is $T \cdot (20\%)^2$. The standard deviation is $20\% \cdot \sqrt{T}$. In other words, the standard deviation grows with the square root of the number of time periods:

IMPORTANT: How asset risk grows with time: $$\mathcal{S}dv(\tilde{r}_{0,T}) \approx \sqrt{T} \cdot \mathcal{S}dv(\tilde{r}_{0,1}) \qquad (8.15)$$

If the rates of return on an asset are approximately uncorrelated over time (a perfect market consequence), if the risk in different time periods remains constant, and ignoring all cross-product terms. The Sharpe ratio is $0.3 \cdot \sqrt{T}$.

(i) The formulas also work with fractions. The variance is therefore $1/12 \cdot (20\%)^2 \approx 33.3\%\%$. The standard deviation is therefore $\sqrt{1/12} \cdot 20\% \approx 5.8\%$. The monthly Sharpe ratio is $\sqrt{1/12} \cdot 30\% \approx 0.09$.

(j) The variance is $1/250 \cdot (20\%)^2 = 1.6\%\%$. The standard deviation is $\sqrt{1/250} \cdot 20\% \approx 1.3\%$. The daily Sharpe ratio is about 0.019.

Q 8.36 The mean rate of return for portfolio ($w_H = 0.1$, $w_I = 0.9$) is $0.1 \cdot 6\% + 0.9 \cdot 9\% = 8.7\%$. You can also compute this from the rates of return in the 4 states -11.4%, 17.4%, 21.6%, and 7.2%. De-meaned, these returns are -20.1%, 8.7%, 12.9%, and -1.5%. The variance is therefore $(404.01\%\% + 75.69\%\% + 166.41\%\% + 2.25\%\%)/4 = 162.09\%\% = 0.016209$. Therefore, the standard deviation (risk) is $\sqrt{162.09\%\%} \approx 12.7\%$.

Q 8.37 Two risky portfolios with a correlation of -1 can be combined into an asset that has no risk. Thus, its expected rate of return has to be the same as that on the risk-free asset—or you could get rich in a perfect market.

Q 8.38 If the correlation was higher, diversification would help less, so the risk would be higher. Therefore, the efficient frontier would not bend as far toward the west (a risk of 0). An easy way to check this is to rearrange the returns so that they correlate more positively, as you will do in the next question. If the correlation was lower, diversification would help more, so the risk would be lower. Therefore, the efficient frontier would bend closer toward the west (a risk of 0).

Q 8.39 The covariance between H and Z is 85.5%%, which is much higher than the 45%% covariance between H and I from Formula 8.9 on page 233. This means that the correlation between H and Z shoots up to 74% (from 35% for the correlation between H and I). This means that the efficient frontier is less dented toward the west. Put differently, the minimum-variance portfolio moves toward the east.

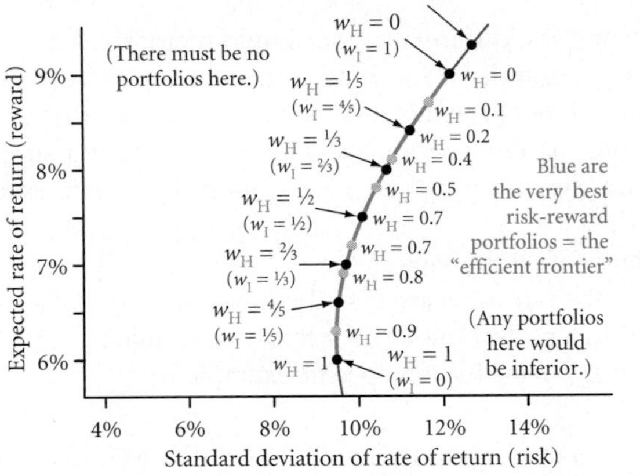

Q 8.40 Portfolios to the right of H on the line have a negative weight in F and a weight above 1 in H. (The portfolio weights must add to 100%!) This means that they would borrow money at a 4% annual interest rate to purchase more of portfolio H. (Purchasing stocks with money borrowed at an interest rate is called **on margin**.)

Q 8.41 Because the net-of-mean F is always 0, so is its coproduct with anything else. This means that the covariance of the risk-free asset with any risky asset is zero, too.

Q 8.42 This question asks you to show how much better off you are with this particular risk-free asset for a particular risk choice.

(a) In Formula 8.12 on page 237, we showed that this no-risk-free minimum-variance portfolio with an investment weight of 76.2% in H and 24.8% in I has a risk of about 8.90%.

(b) The reward of this no-risk-free-asset-available, minimum-variance portfolio is $\mathcal{E}(\tilde{r}) = 76.2\% \cdot 6\% + 24.8\% \cdot 9\% \approx 6.8\%$.

(c) With a weight of 30% in H and 70% in I, the rates of return in the four scenarios for the tangency portfolio T are as follows:

In Scenario ♣: $0.3 \cdot (-6\%) + 0.7 \cdot (-12\%) = -10.2\%$

In Scenario ♦: $0.3 \cdot (12\%) + 0.7 \cdot (18\%) = +16.2\%$

In Scenario ♥: $0.3 \cdot (0\%) + 0.7 \cdot (24\%) = +16.8\%$

In Scenario ♠: $0.3 \cdot (18\%) + 0.7 \cdot (6\%) = +9.6\%$

(These calculations will reappear later in Table 9.2 on page 290.)

(d) The reward of the tangency portfolio is $\mathcal{E}(\tilde{r}_T) = (-10.2\% + 16.2\% + 16.8\% + 9.6\%)/4 = 8.1\%$.

(e) Its risk is $Sdv(\tilde{r}_T) = \sqrt{[(-18.3\%)^2 + (8.1\%)^2 + (8.7\%)^2 + (1.5\%)^2]/4} \approx 10.94\%$.

(f) You want the expected rate of return of a portfolio that uses the risk-free asset and that has a risk of 10.94% (i.e., the same that the no-risk minimum-variance portfolio had). Solve

$$8.9\% = w_T \cdot 10.94\%$$

$$Sdv(\tilde{r}) = w_T \cdot Sdv(\tilde{r}_T)$$

Therefore, $w_T \approx 81.35\%$. In words, a portfolio of 81.35% in the tangency portfolio T and 18.65% in the risk-free asset F has the same risk of 10.94%.

(g) You now want to know the expected rate of return on the portfolio $(w_T, w_F) = (81.35\%, 18.65\%)$:

$$\mathcal{E}(\tilde{r}) \approx 81.35\% \cdot 8.1\% + 18.65\% \cdot 4\% \approx 7.33\%$$

$$\mathcal{E}(\tilde{r}) = w_T \cdot \mathcal{E}(\tilde{r}_T) + w_F \cdot r_F$$

You therefore would expect to receive a 7.33% − 6.71% ≈ 62 basis points higher expected rate of return if you have access to this risk-free rate.

Q 8.43 If the risk-free rate were lower, then the tangency line would become steeper. The tangency portfolio would shift from around K to around L. Therefore, it would involve more H.

PROBLEMS

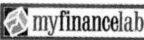

The [ ] indicates problems available in myfinancelab

Q 8.44 Recompute the portfolio variance if you invest in a portfolio O with $w_H = 90\%$ and $w_I = 10\%$ in Table 8.4.

(a) Compute the rates of return on the portfolio in each scenario, and then treat the resulting portfolio as one asset. What is portfolio O's risk and reward?

(b) Compute the same variance with the shortcut Formula 8.10 on page 234.

Q 8.45 An asset has an annual mean of 12% and standard deviation of 30% per year. What would you expect its monthly mean and standard deviation to be?

Q 8.46 Mathematically and based on Figure 8.6 on page 238, the risk and reward of the portfolio $w_H = -0.2$, $w_I = -1.2$.

Q 8.47 In the absence of a risk-free asset, would anyone buy the portfolio $w_H = 110\%$, $w_I = -10\%$?

Q 8.48 The Vanguard European stock fund, Pacific stock fund, and Exxon Mobil reported the following historical dividend-adjusted prices:

Year	1991	1992	1993	1994	1995	1996
VEURX	6.53	7.15	6.91	9.34	9.03	11.17
VPACX	7.18	7.41	6.30	9.52	9.08	9.97
XOM	9.57	10.07	10.88	10.97	15.29	19.18

Year	1997	1998	1999	2000	2001
VEURX	13.50	17.45	21.42	23.38	23.13
VPACX	8.39	7.17	7.01	10.41	8.10
XOM	24.63	30.14	33.94	37.42	34.57

Year	2002	2003	2004	2005	2006
VEURX	17.50	14.42	21.22	24.87	29.53
VPACX	5.64	5.42	7.94	9.08	11.93
XOM	31.50	38.01	48.67	54.41	75.67

(a) Compute the means and covariances of the rates of return on these three assets.

(b) Draw the efficient frontier if you can only invest in VEURX and VPACX.

(c) Now add Exxon Mobil. Use Excel to draw 1,000 random numbers in two columns, called wE and wP. (Create one formula, and copy it into all of the cells.) Each of these 2,000 cells should use the formula 'rand()*3-1'. Create a new column that is 1.0 minus wE and wP, and call it wX. Now consider these random numbers as investment weights in VEURX, VPACX, and XOM. Compute the risk and reward for each of these portfolios (one portfolio is three numbers: one wE, one wP, and one wX), using the standard deviation and expected rate of return formulas. Finally, create an *x-y* plot that shows, for each of your wE, wP, and wX portfolios, the risk-reward combinations. What does the plot look like?

(d) If the risk-free rate stood at 5% per annum, what would be the tangency portfolio?

Q 8.49 Return to the example with a risk-free asset in Formula 8.14 on page 240. What are the risk and reward of a portfolio that invests $w_H = 150\%$? (This means that if you have \$100, you would borrow \$50 at the 4% annual interest rate to purchase \$150 of H—more than your portfolio wealth itself.)

9

The Capital Asset Pricing Model

Knowing how risk (market beta) and reward (expected rate of return) are measured, you are now ready to proceed to the punchline: a formula that relates the appropriate reward of investment projects to their risks. This means that if you can judge the risk of new corporate investment projects, then you can determine their appropriate costs of capital in the NPV formula. Alas, like NPV, the formula may be simple, but the application is hard. The devil is in the details.

We will first review what you already know. Then you will learn all about this new model—the CAPM. Finally, you will get to apply it.

One apology in advance: In this chapter, I do not fully explain where all formulas come from. This is because it really takes a full investments course to derive them. (The appendix goes into more detail, but if you really want to learn about investments, you need a full course on the subject.)

9.1 WHAT YOU ALREADY KNOW AND WHAT YOU WANT TO KNOW

You are still after an estimate for your opportunity cost of capital.

First, you already know the right train of thought for capital budgeting purposes: As a corporate manager, your task is to determine whether you should accept a project or reject it. You make this decision with the NPV formula. To determine the discount factor in the NPV formula, you need to estimate an appropriate cost of capital—or, more precisely, the *opportunity* cost of capital for your investors. This means that you need to judge what a fair expected rate of return, $\mathcal{E}(\tilde{r})$, for your project is, given your project's risk characteristics. If your project offers a lower expected return than what your investors can earn elsewhere in similarly risky projects, then you should not put your investors' money into your project but instead return it to them. If your project offers more expected return, then you should go ahead and invest their money into your project. Put differently, your goal is to learn what your investors, if asked, would have wanted you to invest in on their behalves.

Assume perfect markets, that investors dislike risk and like reward, and more.

Second, to proceed, the perfect market assumptions are not enough. We now assume that investors like overall portfolio reward (expected return) and dislike overall portfolio risk (variance or standard deviation of return). We assume that investors are smart. Presumably, this means that they diversify appropriately, hopefully holding something reasonably close to the market portfolio. We assume that investors all have access to exactly the same set of assets. (This means we are ignoring investments in people's own houses or education, for example.) And finally, mostly for convenience, we assume that they want to maximize their wealth in the stock market for only one period.

This allows you to figure out how they—and how you should—measure project risk and reward.

Third, for investors with these preferences, you can follow their trains of thought. You can infer how your investors view the risk and reward of your individual projects. The reward of your project is its expected rate of return. The risk of your project is *not* your project's own risk by itself, but the contribution of your project to your investors' overall portfolio risk. This can be measured by the market beta of your project—a measure of its "toxicity." A project that decreases in value when the market decreases in value, and increases when the market increases, has a positive market beta. A project that increases in value when the market decreases in value, and vice versa, has a negative market beta. A project with a low market beta helps an investor who holds a portfolio similar to the market portfolio to reduce the overall investment risk.

This gives you a trade-off between risk and reward "in equilibrium."

You can also draw some additional conclusions without any math. In our assumed perfect world, you can guess that investors will have already snatched up the best projects—those that have low risk and high expected rates of return. In fact, anyone selling projects with lower risk contribution can ask for a higher price, which in turn immediately drives down their expected rates of return. Consequently, what is available for purchase in the real world must be subject to some trade-off: Projects that have more market risk contribution must offer a higher expected rate of return if their sellers want to convince investors to purchase them. But what *exactly* does this relationship between risk and reward look like? This is the subject of this chapter—it is the domain of the capital asset pricing model, the CAPM.

SOLVE NOW!

Q 9.1 What are the assumptions underlying the CAPM? Are the perfect market assumptions among them? Are there more?

9.2 THE CAPITAL ASSET PRICING MODEL (CAPM)—A COOKBOOK RECIPE APPROACH

The CAPM gives you the cost of capital if you give it the risk-free rate, the expected rate of return on the market, and your project's market beta.

The **capital asset pricing model** (CAPM) is a model that gives you an appropriate expected rate of return (cost of capital) for each project if you give it the project's relevant risk characteristics. The model states that an investment's cost of capital is lower when it offers better diversification benefits for an investor who holds the overall stock market portfolio—less required reward for less risk contribution. Market beta is its measure. Projects contributing more risk (market beta) require a higher expected rate of return for you to want them; projects contributing less risk require a lower expected rate of return for you to want them. This is the precise relationship that the CAPM gives you.

IMPORTANT: To estimate the required expected rate of return for a project or firm—that is, the cost of capital—according to the CAPM, you need three inputs:

1. The risk-free rate of return, r_F
2. The expected rate of return on the overall stock market, $\mathcal{E}(\tilde{r}_M)$
3. A firm's or project's beta with respect to the market, β_i

The CAPM formula is

$$\mathcal{E}(\tilde{r}_i) = r_F + \left[\mathcal{E}(\tilde{r}_M) - r_F\right] \cdot \beta_i \qquad (9.1)$$

where i is the name of your project and $\mathcal{E}(\tilde{r}_i)$ is your project's expected rate of return (the tilde indicates that the return is unknown).

The difference between the expected rate of return on the risky stock market and the risk-free investment, $\left[\mathcal{E}(\tilde{r}_M) - r_F\right]$, is called the **equity premium** or **market risk premium**, discussed in more detail later.

You need to memorize the CAPM formula.

A first quick use of the CAPM formula.

Let's use the formula. If you believe that the risk-free rate is 3% and the expected rate of return on the stock market is 7%, then the CAPM states that

$$\mathcal{E}(\tilde{r}_i) = 3\% + (7\% - 3\%) \cdot \beta_i = 3\% + 4\% \cdot \beta_i$$

$$\mathcal{E}(\tilde{r}_i) = r_F + \left[\mathcal{E}(\tilde{r}_M) - r_F\right] \cdot \beta_i$$

Therefore, a project with a beta of 0.5 should have a cost of capital of $3\% + 4\% \cdot 0.5 = 5\%$, and a project with a beta of 2.0 should have a cost of capital of $3\% + 4\% \cdot 2.0 = 11\%$. The CAPM gives an opportunity cost for your investors' capital: If the project with the beta of 2.0 cannot earn a rate of return of 11%, you should not take this project and instead return the money to your investors. Your project would add too much risk for its reward. Your investors have better opportunities elsewhere.

It is easier to work in required returns than in prices.

The CAPM is called an **asset pricing model**, even though it is most often expressed in terms of a required expected rate of return rather than in terms of an appropriate project price. If the project's price is its fair market value in a perfect market, then you can always work the CAPM return first, and discount the expected cash flow into an appropriate price second. (Otherwise, you will have to take two aspirins and work with a more difficult version of the CAPM formula that is called certainty equivalence. It is explained in the chapter appendix.)

➤ Price form of the CAPM, Section 9.6, p. 281

The CAPM formula tells you what investors care about: comovement with the market.

The CAPM specifically ignores the standard deviation of individual projects' rates of return. That is, the model posits that investors do not care about it, because they are smart enough to diversify such idiosyncratic risk away. It further posits that investors do care about the project market betas, because these measure the risk components that investors holding the market portfolio cannot diversify away.

The CAPM has three inputs. We will cover them in detail.

➤ Will history repeat itself?, Section 7.1E, p. 189

For the three CAPM inputs, as always, you are really interested in the future: the future expected rate of return on the market and the future beta of your firm/project with respect to the market, not the past average rates of return or the past market betas. And, as usual, you have no choice other than to rely on estimates that are based at least partly on historical data. In Section 9.4, you will learn how you can estimate each CAPM input. But let's explore the model itself first, assuming that you know all the inputs.

9.2A THE SECURITY MARKET LINE (SML)

Examples of CAPM rates of return that individual securities should offer.

Let's apply the CAPM in a specific example. Assume that the risk-free rate is 3% per year and that the stock market offers an expected rate of return of 8% per year. The CAPM formula then states that a stock with a beta of 1 should offer an expected rate of return of $3\% + (8\% - 3\%) \cdot 1 = 8\%$ per year; that a stock with a beta of 0 should offer an expected rate of return of $3\% + (8\% - 3\%) \cdot 0 = 3\%$ per year; that a stock with a beta of 1/2 should offer an expected rate of return of $3\% + (8\% - 3\%) \cdot 0.5 = 5.5\%$ per year; that a stock with a beta of 2 should offer an expected rate of return of $3\% + (8\% - 3\%) \cdot 2 = 13\%$ per year; and so on.

The SML is just a graphical representation of the CAPM formula.

The CAPM formula is often graphed as the **security market line (SML)**, which shows the relationship between the expected rate of return of a project and its beta. Figure 9.1 draws a first security market line for seven assets. Each stock (or project) is a

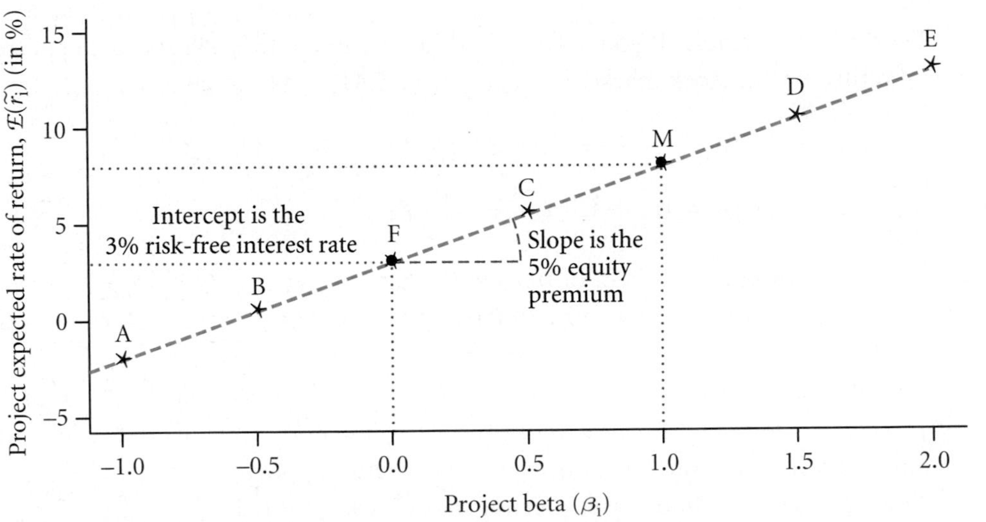

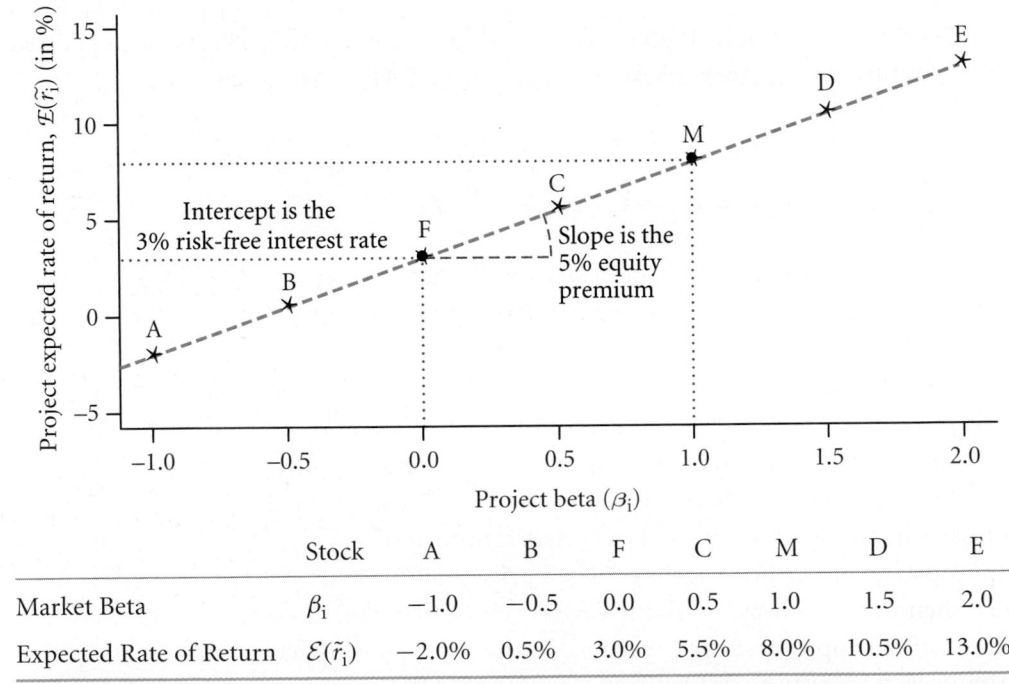

Stock		A	B	F	C	M	D	E
Market Beta	β_i	−1.0	−0.5	0.0	0.5	1.0	1.5	2.0
Expected Rate of Return	$\mathcal{E}(\tilde{r}_i)$	−2.0%	0.5%	3.0%	5.5%	8.0%	10.5%	13.0%

This graph plots the CAPM relation $\mathcal{E}(\tilde{r}_i) = r_F + [\mathcal{E}(\tilde{r}_M) - r_F] \cdot \beta_i = 3\% + (8\% - 3\%) \cdot \beta_i$, where β_i is the beta of an individual asset with respect to the market. In this graph, we assume that the risk-free rate is 3% and the equity premium is 5%. Each point is one asset (such as a stock, a project, or a mutual fund). The point M in this graph could also be any other security with a $\beta_i = 1$. F could be the risk-free asset or any other security with a $\beta_i = 0$.

FIGURE 9.1 The Security Market Line

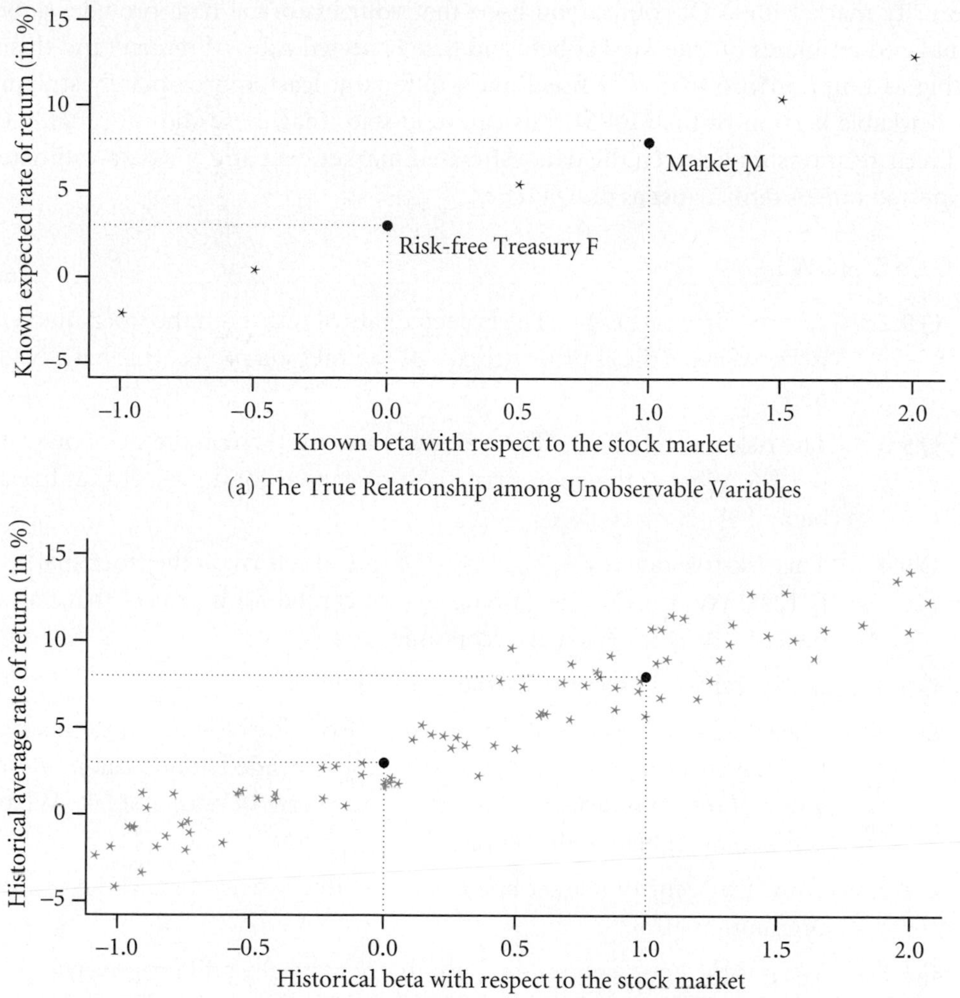

(a) The True Relationship among Unobservable Variables

(b) The Estimable Relationship among Observable Variables

The lower panel shows what we are usually confronted with: Historical average returns and historical betas are just estimates from the data. We hope they are representative of the true underlying mean returns and true betas, which in turn would mean that they will also be indicative of the future mean returns and betas.

FIGURE 9.2 The Security Market Line in an Ideal CAPM World

point in this coordinate system. Because all assets properly follow the CAPM formula in our example, they must lie on a straight line. In other words, the SML is just a graphical representation of the CAPM formula. The slope of this line is the equity premium, $\mathcal{E}(\tilde{r}_M) - r_F$, and the intercept is the risk-free rate, r_F.

If you know the inputs, the SML is a sharp line; if you estimate them, it is a scatterplot.

Alas, in the real world, even if the CAPM holds, you would not have the data to draw Figure 9.1. The reason is that you do not know true expected returns and true market betas. Figure 9.2 plots two graphs in a perfect CAPM world. The top graph repeats Figure 9.1 and assumes you know CAPM inputs—the true market betas and true expected rates of return—although in truth you really cannot observe them. This line is perfectly straight. In the bottom graph, you have to rely only on observables—estimates of expected returns and betas, presumably based mostly on historical data averages. Now you can only fit an “estimated security market line,” not the “true security market line." Of course, you hope that your historical data provides good, unbiased estimates of true market beta and true expected rates of return (and this is a big assumption), so that your fitted line will look at least approximately straight. A workable version of the CAPM thus can only state that there should roughly be a linear relationship between the data-estimated market beta and the data-estimated expected rate of return, just as drawn here.

SOLVE NOW!

Q 9.2 The risk-free rate is 4%. The expected rate of return on the stock market is 7%. What is the appropriate cost of capital for a project that has a beta of 3?

Q 9.3 The risk-free rate is 4%. The expected rate of return on the stock market is 12%. What is the appropriate cost of capital for a project that has a beta of 3?

Q 9.4 The risk-free rate is 4%. The expected rate of return on the stock market is 12%. What is the appropriate cost of capital for a project that has a beta of −3? Does this make economic sense?

Q 9.5 Is the real-world security market line a line?

Q 9.6 The risk-free rate is 4%. The expected rate of return on the stock market is 7%. A corporation intends to issue publicly traded bonds that *promise* a rate of return of 6% and offer an *expected* rate of return of 5%. What is the implicit beta of the bonds?

Q 9.7 Draw the security market line if the risk-free rate is 5% and the equity premium is 10%.

Q 9.8 What is the equity premium, both mathematically and intuitively?

9.3 THE CAPM COST OF CAPITAL IN THE PRESENT VALUE FORMULA

We usually use the CAPM output, the expected rate of return, as our discount rate.

For a corporate manager, the most important need for the CAPM arises in the denominator of the NPV formula:

$$\text{NPV} = C_0 + \frac{\mathcal{E}(\tilde{C}_1)}{1 + \mathcal{E}(\tilde{r}_1)} + \frac{\mathcal{E}(\tilde{C}_2)}{1 + \mathcal{E}(\tilde{r}_2)} + \cdots$$

The CAPM gives you an estimate for the opportunity cost of capital, $\mathcal{E}(\tilde{r})$. Together, the CAPM and the NPV formulas tell you again that cash flows that correlate more with the overall market are of less value to your investors and therefore require higher expected rates of return ($\mathcal{E}(\tilde{r})$) in order to pass muster (well, the hurdle rate).

9.3A DECONSTRUCTING QUOTED RATES OF RETURN—RISK PREMIUMS

Reminder: Stated bond yields contain time and default premiums.

Let me return to the subject of Section 6.2C. You learned that in a perfect and risk-neutral world, stated rates of return consist of a time premium and a default premium.

On average, the default premium is zero, so the expected rate of return is just the time premium.

➤ Time and default premiums, Section 6.2C, p. 147

The CAPM extends the expected rate of return to a world in which investors are risk averse. It gives you an expected rate of return that adds a **risk premium** (as a reward for your willingness to absorb risk) to the time premium.

The CAPM gives you the time and risk premiums.

$$\text{Promised Rate of Return} = \text{Time Premium} + \text{Default Premium} + \text{Risk Premium}$$

$$\text{Actual Earned Rate} = \text{Time Premium} + \text{Default Realization} + \text{Risk Premium}$$

$$\underbrace{\text{Expected Rate of Return}}_{\text{provided by the CAPM}} = \text{Time Premium} + \text{Expected Risk Premium}$$

In the risk-neutral perfect world, there were no differences in *expected* rates of return across assets. There were only differences in *stated* rates of return. The CAPM changes all this—different assets can now also have different *expected* rates of return.

However, the CAPM does *not* take default risk into account, much less give you an appropriate stated rate of return. You should therefore wonder: How do you find the appropriate quoted rate of return in the real world? After all, it is this stated rate of return that is usually publicly posted, not the expected rate of return. Put differently, how do you put the default risk and CAPM risk into one valuation?

Important: *The CAPM totally ignores default risk and, thus, does not provide a default premium. You must take care of it yourself!*

Here is an example. Say you want to determine the PV of a corporate zero-bond that has a beta of 0.25 and promises to deliver \$200 next year. This bond pays off 95% of the time, and 5% of the time it totally defaults. Assume that the risk-free rate of return is 6% per annum and that the expected rate of return on the market is 10%. Therefore, the CAPM states that the expected rate of return on your bond must be

A specific bond example: First compute the price necessary to make you "even" relative to the Treasury if you are risk-neutral. This price is based on the time premium and the default premium.

$$\begin{aligned}\mathcal{E}(\tilde{r}_{\text{Bond}}) &= 6\% + \quad 4\% \quad \cdot 0.25 = 7\% \\ &= r_F + [\mathcal{E}(\tilde{r}_M) - r_F] \cdot \beta_{\text{Bond}}\end{aligned}$$

This takes care of the time and risk premiums. To take the bond's default risk into account, you must still find the numerator. You cannot use the promised payment. You must adjust it for the probability of default. You expect to receive not \$200, but

$$\begin{aligned}\mathcal{E}(\tilde{C}_{\text{Bond}}) &= \quad 95\% \quad \cdot \$200 + \quad 5\% \quad \cdot \quad 0 \quad = \$190 \\ &= \mathcal{P}rob(\text{No Default}) \cdot \text{Promise} + \mathcal{P}rob(\text{Default}) \cdot \text{Nothing}\end{aligned}$$

Therefore, the present value formula states that the value of the bond is

$$\text{PV}_{\text{Bond}} = \frac{\mathcal{E}(\tilde{C}_{\text{Bond}})}{1 + \mathcal{E}(\tilde{r}_{\text{Bond}})} = \frac{\$190}{1 + 7\%} \approx \$177.57$$

Given this price, you can now compute the promised (or quoted) rate of return on this bond:

$$\text{Promised Rate of Return} = \frac{\$200 - \$177.57}{\$177.57} \approx 12.6\%$$

$$= \frac{\text{Promised Cash Flow} - \text{PV}}{\text{PV}}$$

The risk premium is above and beyond the time and default premiums. On average, risky investments earn more than risk-free investments now.

You can now quantify the three components in this example. For this bond, the time premium of money is 6% per annum—it is the rate of return that an equivalent-term Treasury offers. The time premium plus the risk premium is provided by the CAPM, and it is 7% per annum. Therefore, 1% per annum is your "average" compensation for your willingness to hold this risky bond instead of the risk-free Treasury. The remaining 12.6% − 7% = 5.6% per annum is the default premium: You do not expect to earn money from this default premium "on average." You only earn it if the bond does not default.

$$\begin{array}{ccccccc} 12.6\% & = & 6\% & + & 5.6\% & + & 1\% \\ \text{Promised Interest Rate} & = & \text{Time Premium} & + & \text{Default Premium} & + & \text{Risk Premium} \end{array}$$

In the real world, most bonds have fairly small market betas (often much smaller than 0.25) and thus fairly low risk premiums. Instead, most of the premium that ordinary corporate bonds quote above equivalent risk-free Treasury rates is not due to the risk premium, but due to the default premium (and some imperfect market premiums that you will learn in Chapter 10). For corporate projects and equity, however, the risk premium can loom quite large.

In sum, in this section you learned the following:

IMPORTANT:

- The CAPM provides an expected rate of return.
- This return is not a stated (promised, quoted) rate of return, because it does not include a default premium.
- The probability of default must be handled in the NPV numerator (through the expected cash flow), and not in the NPV denominator (through the expected rate of return).

SOLVE NOW!

Q 9.9 A corporate bond with a beta of 0.2 will pay off next year with 99% probability. The risk-free rate is 3% per annum, and the equity premium is 5% per annum.
(a) What is the price of this bond?
(b) What is its promised rate of return?
(c) Decompose the bond's quoted rate of return into its components.

Q 9.10 Going to your school has total additional and opportunity costs of $30,000 *this year and up front*. With 90% probability, you are likely to graduate from your school. If you do not graduate, you have lost the entire sum. Graduating from the school will increase your 40-year lifetime annual salary by roughly $5,000 per year, but more so when the stock market rate of return is high than when it is low. For argument's sake, assume that your extra-income beta is 1.5. Assume the risk-free rate is 3%, and the equity premium is 5%. What is the value of your education?

9.4 ESTIMATING THE CAPM INPUTS

How can you obtain reasonable estimates of the three inputs into the CAPM formula $\mathcal{E}(\tilde{r}_i) = r_F + [\mathcal{E}(\tilde{r}_M) - r_F] \cdot \beta_i$?

9.4A THE EQUITY PREMIUM

You must provide the CAPM with the equity premium. Good luck!

The input that is most difficult to estimate is the equity premium. It measures the extra expected rate of return that risky projects are offering above and beyond what risk-free projects are offering. Worse: Not only is the equity premium difficult to estimate, but the value you choose can also have a tremendous influence over your estimated cost of capital. Of course, the theoretical CAPM model assumes that you know the *expected* rate of return on the market perfectly, not that you have to estimate it. Yet, in real life, the equity premium is not posted anywhere, and *no one really knows the correct number*. There are a number of methods to guesstimate it—but, unfortunately, they do not tend to agree with one another. This leaves me with two choices: Either I can throw you one estimate and pretend it is the only one, or I can tell you about the different methods that lead to different estimates. I prefer the latter, if only because the former would eventually leave you startled to discover that your boss has used another number and has therefore come up with another cost-of-capital estimate. I will explain the intuition behind five different methods and describe the estimates that their respective intuitions suggest. In this way, you can make up your own mind as to what you deem to be an appropriate equity premium estimate.

Method 1: Historical averages.

1. **Historical averages I:** The first course of action is to assume that whatever the equity premium was in the past will continue in the future. In this case, you can rely on historical average equity premiums as good indicators of future risk premiums.

   ➤ Morningstar sidenote, p. 185

   ➤ Geometric versus arithmetic averages, Section 7.1A, p. 180

   As of 2007, Morningstar reported the arithmetic average equity premium to be 12.3 − 3.8% = **8.5%** per annum if you start the data in 1926 and 12.4 − 6.0% = **6.4%** per annum if you start in 1970. (The buy-and-hold geometric equivalent averages were **6.5%** and **4.9%**.) However, if you start computing the average in 1869, even the arithmetic equity premium estimate drops to around **6.0%**. Maybe you should start in 1771? Or 1980? Which is the best estimation period? And is the United States the right country to consider, or should you take a more global and long-term perspective? (A recent paper suggests that over many countries and more than 100 years, the average equity premium was more like **4.0%**. The United States may have had a lucky streak, not indicative of the future.) No one really knows what the right start date and set of countries should be for judging future U.S. performance. If you choose too few years, your sample average could be unreliable. For example, what happened over the last 20 or 30 years might just have been happenstance and not representative of the statistical process driving returns. Such an estimate would carry a lot of uncertainty. Although your estimate can be more reliable if you use more years, you are then leaning more heavily on a brave assumption that the world has not changed. That is, if you choose too many years, the data in the earlier part of your sample period may be so different from today that it is no longer relevant. Do you really want to argue that the experience of 1880 still has relevance today?

Method 2: Inverse historical averages.

2. **Historical averages II:** The second estimation method looks at historical equity premiums in the opposite light. If stocks become more desirable, perhaps because investors have become less risk averse, then more investors compete to own them, drive up the price, and thereby lower the future expected rates of return. High historical rates of return would then be indicative of low future expected rates of return.

   An even more extreme version of this argument suggests that high past equity returns could have been not just due to high ex-ante equity premiums, but due to historical **bubbles** in the stock market. The proponents of the bubble view usually cannot quantify the appropriate equity premium, but they do argue that it is lower after recent market run-ups—exactly the opposite of what proponents of the historical averages I method argue.

SIDE NOTE: A **bubble** is a runaway market, in which rationality has temporarily disappeared. There is a lot of debate as to whether bubbles in the stock market ever occurred. A strong case can be made that technology stocks experienced a bubble from around 1998 to 2000. It is often called the **dot-com bubble**, the **internet bubble**, or simply the **tech bubble**. There is no convincing explanation based on fundamentals that can explain *both* why the NASDAQ Index climbed from 2,280 in March 1999 to 5,000 by March 2000, *and* why it then dropped back to 1,640 by April 2001.

Method 3: Dividend or earnings yields.

3. **Current predictive ratios:** The third method tries to predict the stock market rate of return actively with historical dividend yields (i.e., the dividend payments received by stockholders). Higher dividend yields should make stocks more attractive and therefore predict higher future equity premiums. The equity premium estimation is usually done in two steps: First, you must estimate a statistical regression that predicts next year's equity premium with this year's dividend yield; then, you substitute the currently prevailing dividend yield into your estimated regression to get a prediction. Unfortunately, as of 2008, current dividend yields were so low that the predicted equity premium was negative—which would make no sense. Variations of this method have used interest rates or earnings yields, typically with similar results. In any case, the empirical evidence suggests that this method would have yielded poor predictions—for example, it predicted low equity premiums in the 1990s, which was a period of superb stock market performance.

Method 4: Introspection and philosophy.

4. **Philosophical prediction:** The fourth method wonders how much rate of return is required to entice reasonable investors to switch from bonds into stocks. Even with an equity premium as low as 3%, over 25 years, an equity investor would end up with more than twice the money of a bond investor. Naturally, in a perfect

market, nothing should come for free, and the reward for risk-taking should be just about fair. Therefore, equity premiums of 6–8% just seem too high for the amount of risk observed in the stock market. This philosophical method generally suggests equity premiums of about **1%** to **3%**.

5. **Consensus survey:** The fifth method just asks investors or experts (or people who don't know either) what they deem reasonable. The ranges can vary widely, and they seem to correlate with very recent stock market returns. For example, in late 2000, right after a huge run-up in the stock market, surveys by *Fortune* or *Gallup/Paine Webber* had investors expecting equity premiums as high as 15% per year. (They were acutely disappointed: The stock market dropped by as much as 30% over the following two years. Maybe they just got the sign wrong?!) The consulting firm McKinsey uses a standard of around 5% to 6%. The Social Security Administration settled on a standard of around 4%. A joint poll by Graham and Harvey (from Duke) and *CFO Magazine* found that the 2005 average equity premium estimate of CFOs was around 3% per annum. And in a survey of finance professors in late 2007, the most common equity premium estimate was **5%** for a 1-year horizon and **6%** for a 30-year horizon.

Method 5: Just ask!

What to choose? Welcome to the club! No one knows the true equity premium. On Monday, February 28, 2005, the *Wall Street Journal* reported the following average after-inflation forecasts from then to 2050 (per annum):

Analysts' estimates are all over the map, too. Estimates between 2% and 6% per annum seem reasonable.

		Inflation Adjusted			
Name	Organization	Stocks	Government Bonds	Corp. Bonds	Forecast Equity Premium
William Dudley	Goldman Sachs	5.0%	2.0%	2.5%	3.0%
Jeremy Siegel	Wharton	6.0%	1.8%	2.3%	4.2%
David Rosenberg	Merrill Lynch	4.0%	3.0%	4.0%	1.0%
Ethan Harris	Lehman Brothers	4.0%	3.5%	2.5%	0.5%
Robert Shiller	Yale	4.6%	2.2%	2.7%	2.4%
Robert LaVorgna	Deutsche Bank	6.5%	4.0%	5.0%	2.5%
Parul Jain	Nomura	4.5%	3.5%	4.0%	1.0%
John Lonski	Moody's	4.0%	2.0%	3.0%	2.0%
David Malpass	Bear Stearns	5.5%	3.5%	4.3%	2.0%
Jim Glassman	JP Morgan	4.0%	2.5%	3.5%	1.5%
				Average	2.0%

It does not matter that these numbers are inflation adjusted. Because the equity premium is a difference, inflation cancels out. However, it matters whether you quote the equity premium with respect to a short-term or a long-term interest rate. It is more common to use a short rate, because short-term bonds are typically safer and therefore closer to the risk-free asset that is in the spirit of the CAPM. This is why you may want to add another 1% to the equity premium estimates calculated in this table—the long-term government bonds used in the table usually carry higher interest rates than

ANECDOTE Was the 20th Century Really the "American Century?"

The compound rate of return in the United States was about 8% per year from 1920 to 1995. Adjusted for inflation, it was about 6%. In contrast, an investor who had invested in Romania in 1937 experienced not only the German invasion and Soviet domination, but also a real annual capital appreciation of about −27% per annum over its 4 years of stock market existence (1937–1941). Similar fates befell many other Eastern European countries, but even countries not experiencing political disasters often proved to be less than stellar investments. For example, Argentina had a stock market from 1947 to 1965, even though its only function seems to have been to wipe out its investors. Peru tried three times: From 1941 to 1953 and from 1957 to 1977, its stock market investors lost *all* their money. But the third time was the charm: From 1988 to 1995, its investors earned a whopping 63% real rate of return. India's stock market started in 1940 and offered its investors a real rate of return of just about −1% per annum. Pakistan started in 1960 and offered about −0.1% per annum.

Even European countries with long stock market histories and no political trouble did not perform as well as the United States. For example, Switzerland and Denmark earned nominal rates of return of about 5% per annum from 1920 to 1995, while the United States earned about 8% per annum.

The United States stock market was indeed an unusual above-average performer in the twentieth century. Will the twenty-first century be the Chinese century? Or do Chinese steel prices already reflect this?

Source: Mosley Goetzmann and Jorion, 1999.

➤ Duration, Section 5.8, p. 126

➤ Geometric versus arithmetic averages, Section 7.1A, p. 180

their short-term counterparts. On the other hand, if your project is longer term, you may want to adopt a risk-free bond whose duration is more similar to that of your project. You would then even prefer the equity premium estimates in this table. In addition, these are arithmetic rates of return. You already know that they are higher than geometric rates of return. (A +20% rate of return followed by a −20% rate of return gives you a 0% arithmetic average, but leaves you with a 2-year loss of 4%.) Thus, if your project is long term, don't expect your project to offer geometric returns that can be compared to arithmetic returns on the market. It would be an unfair benchmark.

Remain consistent: Don't use different equity premium estimates for different projects.

You now know that no one can tell you the authoritative number for the equity premium. It does not exist. Everyone is guessing, but there is no way around it—you have to take a stance on the equity premium. I cannot insulate you from this problem. I could give you the arguments that you should contemplate when you are picking *your* number. Now I can also give you my own take: First, I have my doubts that equity premiums will return to the historical levels of 8% anytime soon. (The twentieth century was the "American Century" for a good reason: There were a lot of positive surprises for American investors.) I personally prefer equity premium estimates between **2%** and **4%**. (Incidentally, it is my impression that there is relatively less disagreement about equity premium forecasts today than there was just 5 to 10 years ago.) But realize that reasonable individuals can choose equity premium estimates as low as 1% or as high as 8%. Of course, I personally find their estimates less believable the farther they are from my own personal range. And I find anything outside this 1% to 8% range just too tough to swallow. Second, whatever equity premium you do choose, *be consistent*. Do not use 3% for investing in one project and 8% for investing in another. Being consistent can sometimes reduce your relative mistakes in choosing one project over another.

The equity premium is an extremely important number, even absent the CAPM.

Yes, the equity premium may be difficult to estimate, but there is really no way around taking a stance. Even if you had never heard of the CAPM, you would still consider the equity premium to be one of the two most important number in finance (together with the risk-free rate, the other CAPM input). If you believe that the equity premium is high, you would want to allocate a lot of your personal assets to stocks. Otherwise, you would allocate more to bonds. You really do need it for basic investing purposes, too—no escape possible.

The CAPM is about relative pricing, not absolute pricing.

In a corporate context, like every other corporate manager, you cannot let your limited knowledge of the equity premium stop you from making investment decisions. In order to use the CAPM, you do need to judge the appropriate reward for risky projects relative to risk-free projects. Indeed, you can think of the CAPM as telling you the *relative* expected rate of return for projects, not the *absolute* expected rate of return. Given *your* estimate of how much risky projects should earn relative to safe projects, the CAPM can tell you the costs of capital for projects of riskiness "beta." But the basic judgment of the appropriate spread between risky and safe projects is left up to you.

No way around it: You must guesstimate the equity premium.

Finally, I have been deliberately vague about the "market." In CAPM theory, the market should be all investable assets in the economy, including real estate, art, risky bonds, and so on. In practice, we typically use only a stock market index. And among stock market indexes, it often does not matter too much which index is used—whether it is the value-weighted stock market index, the **Dow Jones 30** (another popular market index consisting of 30 large stocks in different industries), or the S&P 500. The S&P 500 is perhaps the most often used stand-in for the stock market, because its performance is posted everywhere, and because historical returns are readily downloadable. From the perspective of a corporate executive, it is a reasonable simplification to use the S&P 500 as the market.

The S&P 500 is usually used as an approximation for the market.

SOLVE NOW!

Q 9.11 What are appropriate equity premium estimates? What are not? What kind of reasoning are you relying on?

9.4B THE RISK-FREE RATE AND MULTIYEAR CONSIDERATIONS

Which risk-free rate?

The second input into the CAPM formula is the risk-free rate of return. It is relatively easily obtained from Treasuries. There is one small issue, though—which Treasury? What if the yield curve is upward sloping and Treasuries yield 2% per year over 1 year, 4% per year over 10 years, and 5% per year over 30 years? How would you use the CAPM? Which interest rate should you pick in a multiyear context?

➤ Section 5.3, "Time-Varying Interest Rates: U.S. Treasuries and the Yield Curve," p. 102

Advice: Pick the interest rate for a Treasury that is "most similar" to your project.

Actually, the CAPM offers no guidance, because it has no concept of more than one single time period or a yield curve. However, from a practical perspective, it makes sense to match projects and Treasuries:

To estimate one benchmark required expected rate of return (e.g., for benchmarking your project's one IRR), you should probably use the yield on Treasuries that seem to take similar time to come to fruition as your own project. A good rule of thumb is to pick the risk-free rate closest by some measure (e.g., maturity or duration) to your project. For example, to value a machine that operates for 3 years, it could make sense to use an average of the 1-year, 2-year, and 3-year risk-free zero interest rates—perhaps 2.5% per annum. On the other hand, if you have a 10-year project, you would probably use the 10-year Treasury rate of 4% as your risk-free rate of return. You may think this is a pretty loose method to handle an important question (and it is), but it is also a very reasonable one. Think about the opportunity cost of capital for an investment with a beta of 0. If you are willing to commit your money for 10 years, you could earn the 10-year Treasury rate of return. It would be your opportunity cost of capital. If you are willing to commit your money only for 3 months, you could earn only the 3-month Treasury rate—usually a lower opportunity cost for your capital.

To estimate multiple required expected rates of return (e.g., for an NPV analysis with cash flows occurring at many different times), you should probably use different zero-bond rates, each corresponding to the timing of the cash flow in the numerator.

There is universal agreement that you should use a risk-free rate that is similar to the duration of your project in the first part of the CAPM formula (where it appears by itself). Thus, if your project has a beta of 0, you should expect to offer the same rate of return as the duration-equivalent risk-free Treasury. If your project takes longer to complete, and if the yield curve is upward sloping, then your project would have to offer a higher expected rate of return.

A philosophical question of practical importance: Is the equity premium horizon-dependent?

But should you also use a different risk-free rate in the second part of the formula (where the risk-free rate is part of the equity premium)? Your answer must depend on whether you believe that the expected rate of return on the stock market is higher for longer-term investments. This would be a reasonable conjecture—after all, if risk-averse Treasury investors can expect a higher rate of return if they buy longer-term claims, why would risk-averse equity investors not also expect a higher rate of return if they buy longer-term claims? If the expected rate of return on the stock market is higher for longer-term projects, too, then any premium for longer-term investments could cancel out in the equity premium, and you could use the same equity premium regardless of how long term your project is. Unfortunately, no one knows the answer. (After all, we don't know with great confidence even the short-term expected rate of return on the stock market.) My personal preference is to use the same (geometric) equity premium estimate, regardless of the duration of the project. Other CAPM users may come to a different conclusion.

SOLVE NOW!

Q 9.12 What is today's risk-free rate for a 1-year project? For a 10-year project?

Q 9.13 If you can use only one Treasury, which risk-free rate should you use for a project that will yield $5 million each year for 10 years?

9.4C INVESTMENT PROJECTS' MARKET BETAS

Unlike the risk-free rate and the equity premium, beta is specific to each project.

Finally, you must estimate your project's **market beta**. It measures how the rate of return of your project fluctuates with that of the overall market. Unlike the previous two inputs, which are the same for every project/stock in the economy, the beta input depends on your specific project characteristics: Different investments have different betas.

The Implications of Beta for a Project's Risk and Reward

You already understand the role of market beta in determining the expected rate of return for an asset. This is the security market line—that is, the CAPM formula itself is an upward-sloping line when the expected rate of return is plotted against beta. But market beta also has implications for the standard deviation of an asset. Assets that have a zero beta are not exposed to market risk. Therefore, everything else equal, these assets tend to have less risk than other assets. Assets that have very high or very negative market betas are more subject to the ups and downs of the stock market overall. For example, in a CAPM world with a risk-free rate of 3% and an equity premium of 5%, a stock with a market beta of zero would be expected to earn about 3% on average, regardless whether the stock market went up or down by 20% this month. In contrast, a stock with a market beta of −3 would be expected to earn $3\% + (20\% - 3\%) \cdot (-3) = -48\%$ if the stock market went up by 20%, and $3\% + (-20\% - 3\%) \cdot (-3) = 72\%$ if the stock market went down by 20%. This cofluctuation induces extra standard deviation in addition to whatever the firm's own risk may have been. The left graph in Figure 9.3 illustrates this.

Projects with higher betas have more market risk, so their own idiosyncratic variances tend to be higher, too.

The right graph in Figure 9.3 shows conditional rates of return. It changes the x-axis to the actually experienced future rate of return on the stock market. Note that the y-axis is not the actual rate of return on a stock, but still just its expected rate of return. (The actual rate of return will be some number centered around the graphed expected rate of return.) Assets with positive betas have higher expected rates of return when the market does better. Assets with negative betas have higher expected rates of return when the market does worse. If the stock market turns in the same rate of return as the risk-free asset, beta does not matter. The graph also shows that stocks with negative betas tend to offer lower expected rates of return than stocks with positive betas. After all, low-beta stocks effectively serve as insurance against overall market movements. (A lower expected rate of return is also synonymous with a higher price today.)

Beta also influences conditional expected rates of return.

Beta Estimation

How do you find good beta estimates? Depending on the project, this can be easy or difficult.

Market betas for publicly traded firms: For publicly traded stocks, finding a market beta for its equity is usually easy. Almost every financial website publishes them.

If publicly traded, it's easy: Look it up or run regressions.

Market betas from a regression: You could also run the market model regression yourself. There is no mystery: The betas published on financial websites are really just estimated from historical time-series regressions, too. They do exactly what we did in Section 8.3B: They compute the covariance, divide it by the market variance, and perhaps do a little bit of shrinking.

➤ Estimating betas from historical data, Section 8.3B, p. 214

Market betas from comparables: One problem with the simple regression method is that individual betas are often very noisy. (Shrinking helps a little, though.) For example, think of a pharmaceutical company whose product happened to be rejected by the FDA. This would cause a large negative rate of return in one particular month. This month would now become a "statistical outlier." If the market happened to go up (down) this particular month, the company would likely end up having a negative (positive) market beta estimate—and this beta

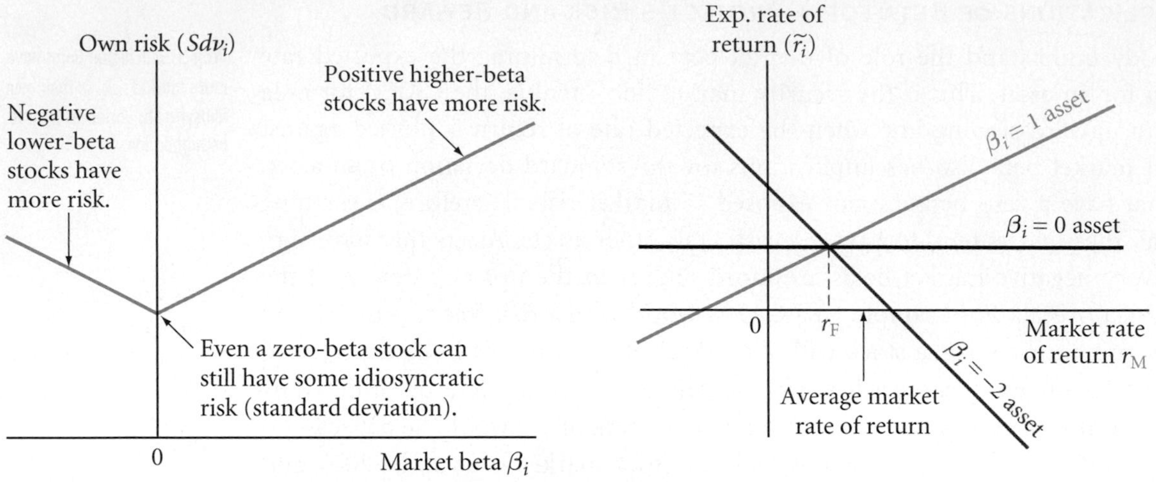

The left graph shows that *everything else equal*, a zero market beta stock has the lowest standard deviation. This is because market volatility would not transmit into such assets' own rates of return (through their market betas). The right graph shows that assets with a positive market beta do better when the market rate of return is high, while assets with a negative market beta do better when the market rate of return is low. If the market performs as well as the risk-free rate, all assets should do about the same in a CAPM world. (On average, positive beta stocks need to offer higher expected rates of return because outcomes to the right of the risk-free rate are more likely than outcomes to the left of the risk-free rate.)

FIGURE 9.3 More Perspectives on Beta

estimate would likely be unrepresentative of the future market beta. In the long run, such announcements would appear randomly, so beta would still be the right estimate—but by the time the long run happens, you may already be dead. To reduce estimation noise in practice, it is common to estimate not just the beta of the firm in question but also the beta of a couple of similar firms (comparables similar in size and industry, perhaps), and then to use a beta that reflects some sort of average among them.

For private firms, use comparable, publicly traded stocks.

If your project has no historical rate of return experience—perhaps because it is only a division of a publicly traded company or because the company is not publicly traded—you may have no choice other than this method of estimating a beta from comparable firms. (However, recall that the CAPM is only meaningful to begin with if your investors hold most of their wealth in the market portfolio.) For example, if you believe your new soda company project is similar to PepsiCo, you could adopt the asset beta of PepsiCo and use it to compute the CAPM expected rate of return. Realizing that firms that are smaller than PepsiCo, such as your own, tend to have higher betas, you might increase your beta estimate.

Market betas based on economic intuition: If you really cannot think of a good publicly traded firm that you trust to be a good comparable, you may have to rely more heavily on your judgment. Think about how the rate of return of your project is likely to covary with the stock market. If you can make such a judgment, you can rearrange the CAPM formula to obtain a beta estimate:

$$\mathcal{E}(\tilde{r}_i) = r_F + \left[\mathcal{E}(\tilde{r}_M) - r_F\right] \cdot \beta_i \iff \beta_i = \frac{\mathcal{E}(\tilde{r}_i) - r_F}{\mathcal{E}(\tilde{r}_M) - r_F}$$

The right side of this formula helps translate your intuition into a beta estimate. You can ask such questions as "What rate of return (above the risk-free rate) will your project have if the stock market were to have +10% or −10% rate of return (above the risk-free rate)?" Clearly, such guesswork is difficult and error-prone—but it can provide a beta estimate when no other is available.

EQUITY AND ASSET BETAS REVISITED

Don't use the equity beta to estimate your project's hurdle rate. Use the asset beta instead.

➤ Asset and equity betas, Formula 8.7, p. 221

It is important that you always distinguish between asset betas and equity betas. Let me remind you with an example. Assume that the risk-free rate is 4% and the equity premium is 5%. You own a $100 million project with an asset beta of 2.0 that you can finance with $20 million of risk-free debt. By definition, risk-free debt has a beta of 0. To find your equity beta, write down the formula for your asset beta (firm beta):

$$20\% \cdot (0) + 80\% \cdot (\beta_{\text{Equity}}) = 2.0$$

$$\beta_{\text{Firm}} = \left(\frac{\text{Debt value}}{\text{Firm value}}\right) \cdot \beta_{\text{Debt}} + \left(\frac{\text{Equity value}}{\text{Firm value}}\right) \cdot \beta_{\text{Equity}}$$

Solve this to find that your equity beta is 2.5. This is what you would find on Yahoo! *Finance*. You would not want to base the hurdle rate of your typical average project on it: Such a mistake would recommend you use a hurdle rate of $\mathcal{E}(\tilde{r}_{\text{i}}) = r_{\text{F}} + \left[\mathcal{E}(\tilde{r}_{\text{M}}) - r_{\text{F}}\right] \cdot \beta_{\text{i}} = 4\% + 5\% \cdot 2.5 = 16.5\%$. This would be too high. Instead, you should require your project to return $\mathcal{E}(\tilde{r}_{\text{i}}) = 4\% + 5\% \cdot 2.0 = 14\%$.

➤ Typical, average, and marginal betas, Section 12.3, p. 393

If you use comparables, first unlever them.

Conversely, if your project is private, you may have to find its hurdle rate by looking at public comparables. Let's presume you find a similarly sized firm with a similar business that Yahoo! *Finance* lists with a beta of 4. Remember that financial websites always list only the equity beta. The CAPM tells you that the expected rate of return on the equity is $4\% + 5\% \cdot 4 = 24\%$. However, this is not necessarily the hurdle rate for your project. When you look further on Yahoo! *Finance*, you see that your comparable is financed with 90% debt and 10% equity. (If the comparable had very little debt, a debt beta of 0 might have been a good assumption, but, unfortunately, in this case it is not.) Corporate debt rarely has good historical return data that would allow you to estimate a debt beta. Consequently, practitioners often estimate the expected rate of return on debt via debt comparables based on the credit rating. Say your comparable's debt is rated BB and say that BB bonds have offered *expected* rates of return of 100 basis points above the Treasury. (This might be 200 basis points *quoted* above the Treasury). With the Treasury standing at 4%, you would estimate the comparable's cost of capital on debt to be 5%. The rest is easy. The expected rate of return on your project should be

➤ Credit ratings, Section 6.2D, p. 148

$$\mathcal{E}(\tilde{r}_{\text{Project}}) = 90\% \cdot 5\% + 10\% \cdot 24\% = 6.9\%$$

$$= w_{\text{Debt}} \cdot \mathcal{E}(\tilde{r}_{\text{Debt}}) + w_{\text{Equity}} \cdot \mathcal{E}(\tilde{r}_{\text{Equity}})$$

This would make a good hurdle rate estimate for your project.

SOLVE NOW!

Q 9.14 According to the CAPM formula, a zero-beta asset should have the same expected rate of return as the risk-free rate. Can a zero-beta asset still have a positive standard deviation? Does it make sense that such a risky asset would not offer a higher rate of return than a risk-free asset in a world in which investors are risk averse?

Q 9.15 A comparable firm (with comparable size and in a comparable business) has a Yahoo! *Finance*–listed equity beta of 2.5 and a debt/asset ratio of 2/3. Assume the debt is risk free.

(a) Estimate the beta for your firm if your projects have similar betas, but your firm will carry a debt/asset ratio of 1/3.

(b) If the risk-free rate is 3% and the equity premium is 2%, then what should you use as your firm's hurdle rate?

(c) What do investors demand as the expected rate of return on the comparable firm's equity and on your own equity?

Q 9.16 You own a stock market portfolio that has a market beta of 2.4, but you are getting married to someone who has a portfolio with a market beta of0.4. You are three times as wealthy as your future significant other. What is the beta of your joint portfolio?

9.5 EMPIRICAL EVIDENCE: IS THE CAPM THE RIGHT MODEL?

Now you know how securities should be priced in a perfect CAPM world. What evidence would lead you to conclude that the CAPM is *not* an accurate description of reality? And does the CAPM seem to hold or not?

9.5A THE SML IF THE CAPM DOES NOT WORK

Q: What happens if a stock offers too much or too little expected rate of return? A: Investor stampedes.

What would happen from the CAPM's perspective if a stock offered more than its appropriate expected rate of return? Investors in the economy would want to buy more of the stock than would be available: Its price would be too low. It would be too good a deal. Investors would immediately flock to it, and because there would not be enough of this stock, investors would bid up its price and thereby lower its expected rate of return. The price of the stock would settle at the correct CAPM expected rate of return. Conversely, what would happen if a stock offered less than its due expected rate of return? Investors would not be willing to hold enough of the stock: The stock's price would be too high, and its price would fall.

Assets not priced according to the CAPM do not allow you to make money for nothing. However, it could imply good deals.

Neither situation should happen in the real world—investors are just too smart. However, you must realize that if a stock were not to follow the CAPM formula, buying it would still be risky. Yes, such a stock would offer too high or too low an expected rate of return and thus be a good or a bad deal, attracting too many or too few investors chasing a limited amount of project—but it would still remain a risky investment, and no investor could earn risk-free profit.

Some security market lines if the CAPM does not hold.

Under what circumstances would you lose faith in the CAPM? Figure 9.4 shows what security market relations could look like if the CAPM did not work. In plot (a),

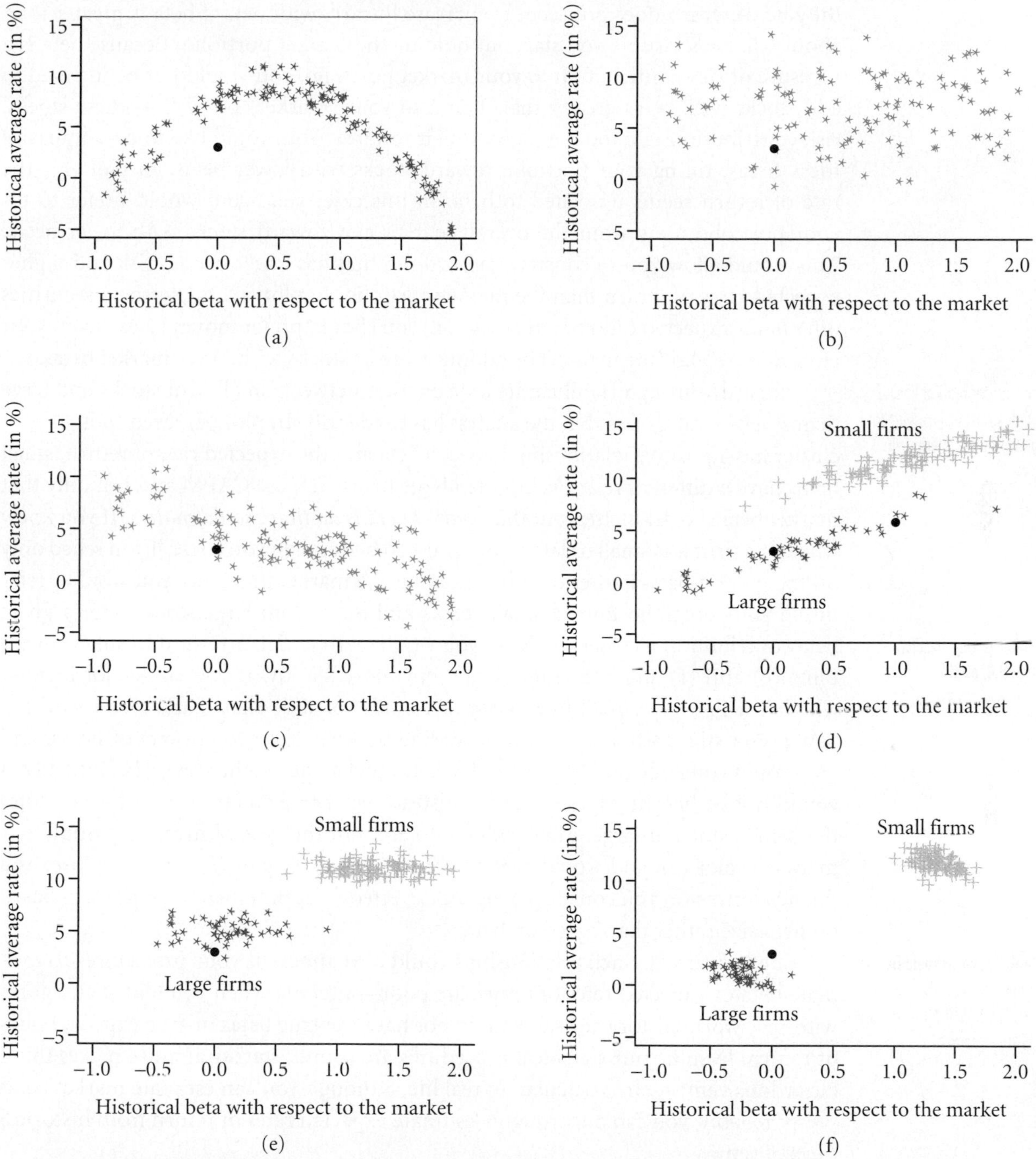

Each point is the historical beta and historical average rate of return on one asset. (The risk-free rates is noted with a fat dot.) In plots (d) through (f), small firms tend to have both higher market betas and rates of return. In these figures, the security market line does not appear to be one upward-sloping line that depends only on market beta—as the CAPM suggests. Therefore, if these patterns are not just statistical mirages, you should be able to invest better than just in the market: From the CAPM perspective, you can find "great deal" stocks that offer too much expected return given their risk contributions to your (market) portfolio, which you would therefore want to overemphasize; and "poor deal" stocks that offer too little expected return, given their risk contributions, which you would therefore want to underemphasize.

FIGURE 9.4 The Security Market Line in Non-CAPM Worlds

the rate of return does not seem to increase linearly with beta if beta is greater than about 0.5. Let's assume you start out holding the market portfolio. Because beta is a measure of risk contribution to your market portfolio, you would not be inclined to add stocks with betas greater than 1 or 2 to your (market) portfolio—these stocks' risk contributions are too high, given their rewards. You would like to de-emphasize these firms, tilting your portfolio toward stocks with lower betas. In plot (b), the rate of return seems unrelated to beta. In this case, you again would prefer to tilt your portfolio away from the overall market and toward stocks with lower betas. This would allow you to construct a portfolio that has lower overall risk and higher expected rates of return than the market portfolio. In plot (c), higher-beta securities offer *lower* expected rates of return. Again, you should prefer moving away from your current portfolio (the market) by adding more of stocks with lower market betas.

More security market lines if the CAPM fails with respect to a specific better alternative.

Plots (d) through (f) illustrate a distinction between small firm stocks and large firm stocks—categories that the analyst has to identify. In plot (d), even though each cluster has a positive relationship between beta and the expected rate of return, small firms have a different relationship than large firms. Yet, the CAPM says not only that market beta should matter, but that *market beta is all that should matter*. If you knew whether a firm was small or large, you could do better than you could if you relied only on the market beta. Rather than just holding the market portfolio, you would prefer tilting your portfolio toward small stocks and away from large stocks—for a given beta contribution to your portfolio, you would earn a higher reward in small stocks. Plots (e) and (f) show the same issue, but more starkly. If you could not identify whether a firm was small or large, you would conclude that market beta works—you would still draw a straight positive line between the two clusters of firms, and you would conclude that higher market beta stocks offer higher rewards. But truly, it would not be beta at all that matters. Instead, what truly matters would be whether the firm is small or large. After taking into account the type of firm, beta would not matter in plot (e), and would even matter *negatively* in plot (f). In either case, as a financial investor, you could earn higher expected rates of return buying stocks based on firm size rather than based on beta.

➤ Other pricing factors, Section 9.8, p. 292

Historical patterns could be spurious.

But be warned: Such relationships could also appear if your procedures to estimate beta or expected rates of return are poor—after all, when you plot such figures with real-world historical data, you do not have the true betas or true expected rates of return. Even if your statistical procedures are sound, statistical noise makes this a hazardous venture. In particular, in real life, although you can estimate market betas pretty reliably, you can only roughly estimate expected rates of return from historical rates of return.

9.5B THE HISTORICAL ESTIMATED SML

A model is a model—it ain't always perfect.

Before I let you in on the truth, please realize that a model is just a model—models are never perfect descriptions of reality. They can be useful within a certain domain, even if on closer examination they are rejected. For example, we do not live in a world of Newtonian gravity. Einstein's model of relativity is a better model—though it, too, is not capable of explaining everything. Yet no one would use Einstein's model to calculate how quickly objects fall. The Newtonian model is entirely appropriate and much easier to use. Similarly, planetary scientists use Einstein's model, even though we know it, too, fails to account for quantum effects—but it does well enough for the purposes at hand and there are as yet no better alternatives (even though string theory is trying hard).

The dark but open secret is that this latter situation is pretty much the situation in which corporations find themselves—the CAPM is not really correct. However, we have no good all-around alternatives that are clearly better.

The Empirical Evidence: Where It Works

This empirical relation looks reasonably linear and upward sloping: good for the CAPM.

But let me first explain where the CAPM works and where it fails. What does the security market line look like in real life? Figure 9.5 plots the relationships from 1970 to 2003. The typical stock with a beta of 0 earned a rate of return of about 0.6% per month (8% per annum), while the typical stock with a beta of 1 (e.g., the stock market itself) earned a rate of return of about 1.4% per month (18% per annum). Not drawn in the figure, the average stock with a beta of 2 earned about 2.2% per month (30% per annum), and the average stock with a beta of 3 earned about 3.5% per month (50% per annum). (These annual returns are arithmetic averages—the geometric annual rates of return would have been lower.) You can see that these 34 years were a very

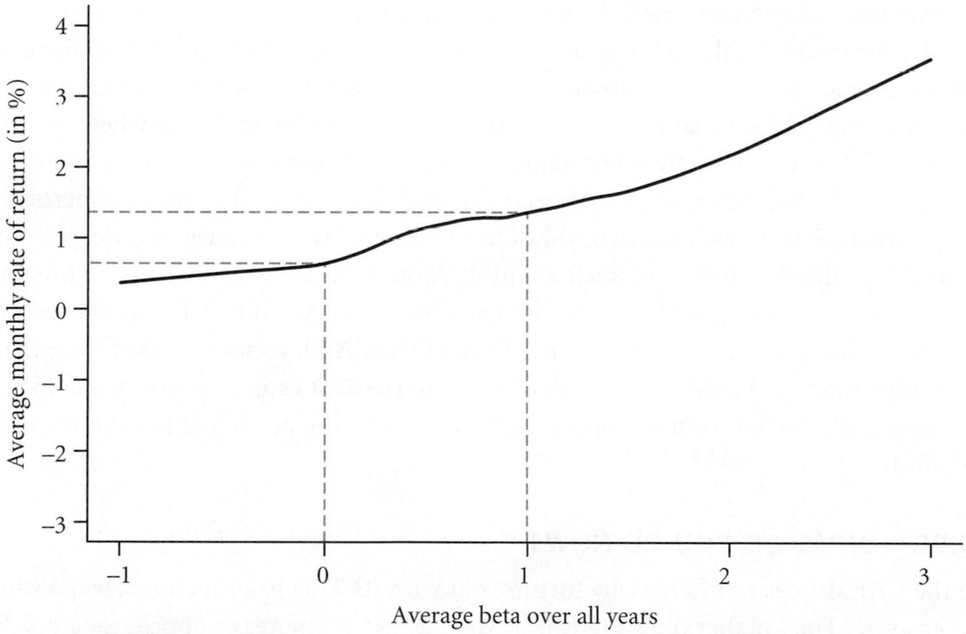

This is the real empirical relationship between monthly betas and monthly average rates of return from 1970 to 2003. (The latter are not annualized.) The betas are with respect to the value-weighted stock market. Extreme observations were truncated at −1 and +3 for beta, and at −3% and +4% for monthly returns. The black line is "smoothed" to fit points locally, allowing it to show nonlinearities. The dashed blue line indicates that this smoothed line suggests that "beta = 0" securities had approximate rates of return of 64 basis points per month, or about 8% per annum. The typical "beta = 1" securities had approximate rates of return of 136 basis points per month, or about 18% per annum. (Because these are arithmetic averages, you would have earned less than this in a buy-and-hold strategy.)

FIGURE 9.5 Average Historical Rates of Return against Historical Market Betas, 1970–2003.

good period for risky financial investments! Most important, from the perspective of the CAPM, the historical relationship between average rates of return and betas seems to have been reasonably close to linear, just as the CAPM suggests. If we stopped now, I would have advised you to conclude that the CAPM is a pretty good model.

The Empirical Evidence: Where It Fails

But this is deceptive: The CAPM fails against specific better alternatives.

But look back at Figure 9.4. The empirical evidence—that is, hundreds of academic papers—shows that the CAPM may or may not fail in the sense of the first three plots. (There is some dispute.) But the evidence is clear that, the CAPM fails more in the sense of the last three plots: There are better alternative classifications of stocks. Although you cannot see this in Figure 9.5, the CAPM fails when stocks are split into groups based on other characteristics. The empirical reality is therefore closer to the latter three figures than it is to the idealized CAPM world.

Clusters of firms on the northwest contain value firms; clusters on the southeast contain growth firms.

The most damaging evidence may well be that firms that are classified as exciting "growth firms" (they have low sales and accounting values but high market values—the Googles of this world) generally underperform boring "value firms" (the opposite—the PepsiCos of this world). Figure 9.6 illustrates roughly where these types of stocks tended to cluster in the plot of betas versus expected rates of return. The plot also notes two other stock characteristics (big versus small firms and recent winners versus losers) that could predict which firms had high average returns and which firms had low average returns. Moreover, if we take into account these other characteristics, market beta no longer seems to be too important, at all.

➤ Other stock characteristics, Section 9.8, p. 292

What now?

Unfortunately, although we can rationalize after the fact why these specific firm characteristics mattered for subsequent returns, we really know of no great reasons why they should have mattered in the first place. We also do not know whether these characteristics are themselves just stand-ins for something else that we have not yet found, or whether they matter in themselves. And not only do we finance experts not know for sure what characteristics should matter and why, but we also don't know how CFOs should operate in such a world. Should we advise managers to pretend that their firms are growth firms—because investors like this claim so much that they are willing to pay a lot for shares of such firms? And, as soon as they have their investors' money, should we then advise them to invest it as if they were value firms? No one really knows. (On the plus side, it keeps ongoing academic finance research interesting.)

9.5C WHAT DO YOU DO NOW?

If the CAPM does not hold, why torture you with it? This is a much easier question to answer. (The tougher question is how you can get estimates of appropriate hurdle rates for your projects in this case.)

Reasonable cost-of-capital estimates (often): Even though the CAPM is rejected, market beta is still often a useful cost-of-capital measure for a corporate finance manager.

Beta can also work as a proxy for firm size.

Why? Look again at the last three plots in Figure 9.4. Let's presume it was just firm size that mattered to expected rates of return. If you have a beta of around

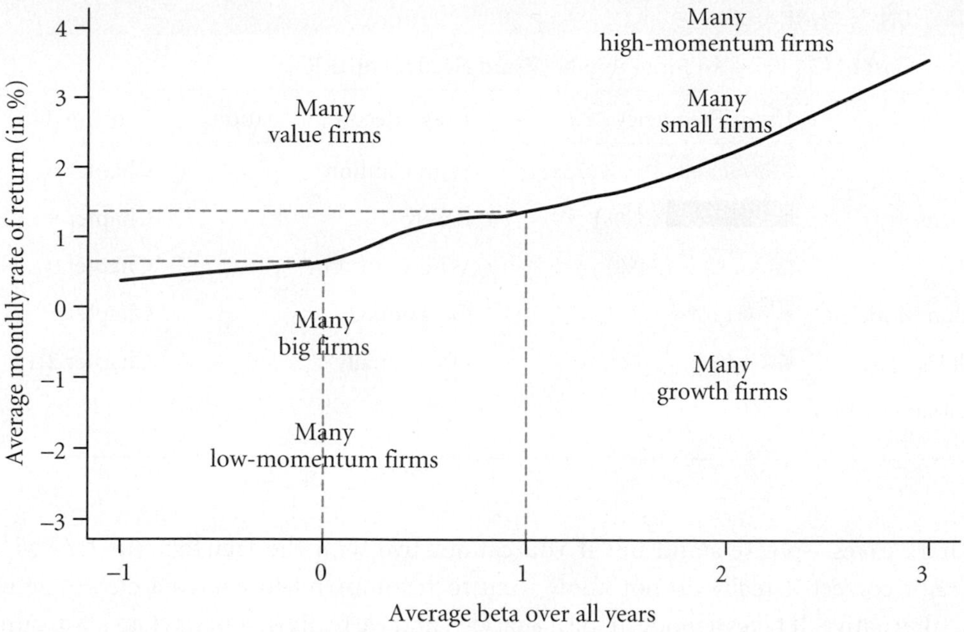

Stocks with positive (negative) momentum have experienced unusually good (bad) returns over the last 34 years (winners/losers). Small firms and big firms are self-explanatory. Value firms are "boring" firms with high sales and accounting values, but low market values—such as Procter & Gamble or RJR Nabisco. Growth firms are "exciting" firms with low sales, but high market values—such as Google or Apple.

FIGURE 9.6 Historical Firm Types Locations in Plot of Rates of Return against Historical Market Beta, 1970–2003.

1.5, you are more than likely a small firm with an expected rate of return of 10% to 15%; if you have a beta of around 0, you are more than likely a big firm with an expected rate of return of 3% to 7%. Thus, beta would still provide you with a decent cost-of-capital estimate, even though it was not market beta itself that mattered, but whether your firm was large or small. (Market beta helped by indicating to you whether your firm was a big or a small firm.) Admittedly, using an incorrect model is not an ideal situation, but the cost-of-capital estimates are often reasonable enough that corporate managers generally can live with them for purposes of finding a hurdle rate.

This logic does not apply to extreme value and growth firms: Value firms with higher expected rates of return do not have higher betas. Thus, you should not use the CAPM as a proxy to compute expected rates of return for projects (stocks) that are extreme value or growth firms—for such firms, the CAPM cost-of-capital estimates could be far off. Don't rely on them.

However, please avoid the CAPM for extreme growth or value firms.

Good intuition: The CAPM has impeccable intuition. It is a model that shines through its simplicity and focuses on what *should* matter—diversification. It thereby often helps you to sharpen your thinking about what your corporate projects should offer your investors.

The CAPM is based on the important concept of diversification.

And let's not forget—the CAPM is easy to use, at least relative to the potential alternatives that you can learn about in Section 9.8.

➤ CAPM alternatives, Section 9.8, p. 292

TABLE 9.1 CFO VALUATION TECHNIQUES

Cost of Capital—An Input into NPV and Needed for IRR

Method	Usage Frequency	Usage Recommendation	Explained in
CAPM	(73%)	With Caution	Chapter 9
Historical Average Returns	(39%)	Rarely	Chapter 8
Modified CAPM	(34%)	With Caution	Chapter 9
Backed Out from Gordon Model	(16%)	Occasionally	Chapter 3
Whatever Investors Tell Us	(14%)	Occasionally	Chapter 2

Rarely means "usually no, and often used incorrectly."
Source: Campbell and Harvey, 2001.

There really is no better alternative to the CAPM.

Alternatives—please stand up: If you cannot live with the fact that the CAPM is not correct, I really do not know what to recommend to you as a clearly better alternative. It takes a model to beat a model, and we really do not have an all-around good replacement for the CAPM. This is why we stick to the CAPM.

For example, one alternative model is to use the size and value/growth firm characteristics that I just mentioned as proxies for appropriate expected rates of return. But it is not even clear whether the higher returns for value firms reflect appropriate rewards for risk-taking that investors require (and which therefore should flow into a hurdle rate), or whether these firms earned superior returns because the stock market was not perfect (and which therefore need not flow into a hurdle rate). Imperfect markets are the subject of our next chapters.

Important: Everyone expects you to know the CAPM!

Everyone uses it: Table 9.1 shows that we are not alone: 73% of the CFOs reported that they always or almost always use the CAPM. (And CAPM use was even more common among large firms and among CFOs with an MBA.) No alternative method was used very often. Consequently, you have no choice but to understand the CAPM model well—*if you will work for a corporation, then the CAPM is the benchmark model that your future employer will likely use—and will expect you to understand well*. The CAPM is simply *the* standard. The CAPM is also used as a benchmark by many investors rating their (investment) managers, by government regulatory commissions, by courts in tort cases, and so on. It is literally the dominant, if not the only, universal model for the cost of capital.

My personal opinion: Use the CAPM with caution in a corporate finance context for capital budgeting.

Let me infuse a bit more of my personal opinion now. Different academics draw different conclusions from the empirical evidence. Some recommend outright against using the CAPM, but most professors recommend "use with caution." I am among them. I would suggest that, as a student, your concern should be about the domain within which you should reasonably use the CAPM. Think about whether it is useful for your own cost-of-capital estimates, or whether the CAPM errors would likely be too large to be useful.

Here is what I would definitely warn against:

Don't expect accuracy and don't use it for financial investing.

Accuracy: The CAPM is a poor model if precision is of the essence. If you believe that CAPM expected rates of return should be calculated with any digits after the decimal point, then you are deluded. Please realize that, at best, the CAPM can only offer expected rates of return that are of the "right order of magnitude," plus or minus a few percentage points perhaps.

Actually, if accuracy and precision are important, you are thoroughly in trouble. We do not have *any* models that offer great accuracy. (Fortunately, it is often more important that you estimate value *better* than your competitors than that you estimate value very accurately. And always remember that valuation is as much an art as it is a science.)

Investment purposes: If you are not a corporate CFO looking for a project hurdle rate, but a financial investor looking for good investments from the universe of financial instruments, please don't use the CAPM. Although the CAPM offers the correct intuition that wide diversification needs to be an important part of *any* good investment strategy, there *are* still better investment strategies than just investing in the market index. Some are explained in Section 9.8; more will be discussed in an advanced investments course.

Avoid using the CAPM for financial investment purposes.

And also please do not confuse the CAPM with the mean-variance framework discussed in the previous chapter. Mean-variance optimization is an asset-selection technique for your individual portfolio, and it works, regardless of whether the CAPM works or not.

➤ Mean-variance optimization, Section 8.8, p. 236

IMPORTANT:

- Be aware of the strengths and weaknesses of the CAPM.
- The empirical evidence suggests that the CAPM is not a great model for predicting expected rates of return. This is especially so for extreme-value and extreme-growth firms, or firms having experienced very high or very low rates of return recently.
- The CAPM is still the benchmark model in the real world. Every corporation uses it—and every corporation expects you to know it.
- The CAPM offers reasonably good estimates for the cost of capital (hurdle rate) in many, but not all, corporate settings.
- The CAPM never offers great accuracy.
- The CAPM may be a decent model for corporate capital budgeting, but it is not a good model for a financial market investor. The CAPM speculates that the market portfolio is mean-variance efficient. In real life, you can optimize your portfolio and choose portfolios closer to the mean-variance frontier.
- Mean-variance optimization works even if the CAPM does not.

SOLVE NOW!

Q 9.17 Does the empirical evidence suggest that the CAPM is correct?

Q 9.18 If the CAPM is wrong, why do you need to learn it?

How Bad Are Mistakes?

HOW ROBUST IS THE CAPM?

Where will we go wrong?

By now, you should realize that you will never perfectly know the required inputs for the CAPM. You can only make educated guesses. And even *after* the fact, you will never be sure—you observe only realized rates of return, never expected rates of return. Exactly how robust are CAPM estimates with respect to errors in its inputs? Well, it depends on the inputs.

Errors in the risk-free rate tend to be small.

The risk-free rate: Errors in the risk-free rate (r_F) are likely to be modest. The risk-free rate can be considered to be almost known for practical purposes. Just make sure to use Treasuries that match the timing of your project cash flows.

Errors in beta estimates are meaningful but still tend to be modest.

Market beta: Reasonable beta estimates typically have some uncertainty, but good comparables can often be found in the public market. If due care is exercised, a typical range of uncertainty about beta might be about plus or minus 0.4. For example, if the equity premium is 3% and if you believe your beta is 2, but it is really 1.6 instead, then you would overestimate the appropriate expected rate of return by $2 \cdot 3\% - 1.6 \cdot 3\% = 1.2\%$. Although this level of uncertainty is not insignificant, it is often tolerable in corporate practice.

Disagreement about the equity premium tends to be large—and this can make a big difference.

Equity premium estimates: Reasonable equity premium estimates can range from about 1% per year to about 8% per year—a large range. *To date, there is no universally accepted method to estimate the expected rate of return on the market, so this disagreement cannot be easily settled with data and academic studies.* Unfortunately, reasonable differences of opinion in estimating the expected rate of return on the market can have a large influence on expected rate of return estimates. For example, assume the risk-free rate is 3%, and take a project with a beta of 2. The CAPM might advise this corporation that potential investors demand either an expected rate of return of 5% per year (equity premium estimate of 1%) or an expected rate of return of 19% per year (equity premium estimate of 8%), or anything in between. This is—to put it bluntly—a miserably large range of possible cost-of-capital estimates. (And this range does not even consider the fact that *actual* future project rates of return will necessarily differ from *expected rates of return*!) Of course, in the real world, managers who want to take a project will argue that the expected rate of return on the market is low. This means that their own project looks relatively more attractive. Potential buyers of projects will argue that the expected rate of return on the market is high. This means that they claim they have great opportunities elsewhere, so that they can justify a lower price offer for this project.

I repeat: *Use the CAPM as guidance, not as gospel.*

Model errors: What about the CAPM as a model itself? This error is difficult to assess. Perhaps a reasonable approach is to use the CAPM in a corporate context unless the firm is unusual—an extreme value or growth or small firm, for example. Just remain aware that the model use itself introduces errors.

ANECDOTE "Cost of Capital" Expert Witnessing

When Congress tried to force the "Baby Bells" (the split-up parts of the original AT&T) to open up their local telephone lines to competition, it decreed that the Baby Bells were entitled to a fair return on their infrastructure investment—with fair return to be measured by the CAPM. (The CAPM is either the de facto or legislated standard for measuring the cost of capital in many other regulated industries, too.) The estimated value of the telecommunication infrastructure in the United States is about \$10 to \$15 billion. A difference in the estimated equity premium of 1% may sound small, but even in as small an industry as local telecommunications, it meant about \$100 to \$150 million a year—enough to hire hordes of lawyers and valuation consultants opining in court on the appropriate equity premium. Some of my colleagues bought nice houses with the legal fees.

I did not get the call. I lack the ability to keep a straight face while stating that "the equity premium is exactly *x* point *y* percent," which was an important qualification for being such an expert. In an unrelated case in which I did testify, the opposing expert witness even explicitly criticized my statement that my cost-of-capital estimate was an imprecise range—unlike me, he could provide an exact estimate!

You will often use the CAPM expected rate of return as your cost of capital in an NPV calculation. Here, you combine errors and uncertainty about expected cash flows with your errors and uncertainty in CAPM estimates. What should you worry about? Recall that in Section 4.1A, you learned the relative importance of correct inputs into the NPV formula. The basic conclusion was that for short-term projects, getting the cash flows right is more important than getting the expected rates of return right; for long-term projects, getting both right is important. We just discussed the relative importance of getting the equity premium and the project beta right. Now recall that your basic conclusion was that the CAPM formula is first and foremost exposed to errors in the market risk premium (equity premium), though it is also somewhat exposed to beta estimates. Putting these two insights together suggests that for short-term projects, worrying about exact beta estimates is less important than worrying about estimating cash flows first and the appropriate equity premium second. For long-term projects, the order of importance remains the same, but having good equity premium estimates now becomes relatively more important. In contrast, in most cases, honest mistakes in beta, *given reasonable care*, are relatively less problematic.

When you put NPV and the CAPM together, watch first for cash flow errors and then for equity premium errors.

➤ Errors in cash flows and discount rates, Section 4.1A, p. 70

SOLVE NOW!

Q 9.19 Is the CAPM likely to be more accurate for a project where the beta is very high, one where it is very low, or one where it is zero?

Q 9.20 To value an ordinarily risky project, that is, a project with a beta in the vicinity of about 1, what is the relative contribution of your personal uncertainty (lack of knowledge) in (a) the risk-free rate, (b) the equity premium, (c) the beta, and (d) the expected cash flows? Consider both long-term and short-term investments. Where are the trouble spots?

SUMMARY

This chapter covered the following major points:

- The CAPM provides an "opportunity cost of capital" for investors, which corporations can use as the cost of capital in the NPV formula. The CAPM formula is

$$\mathcal{E}(\tilde{r}_i) = r_F + \left[\mathcal{E}(\tilde{r}_M) - r_F\right] \cdot \beta_i$$

  Thus, there are three inputs: the risk-free rate of return (r_F), the expected rate of return on the stock market ($\mathcal{E}(\tilde{r}_M)$), and the project's or firm's market beta (β_i). Only the latter is project-specific.

- The line plotting expected rates of return against market beta is called the security market line (SML).
- The CAPM provides an expected rate of return, consisting of the time premium and the risk premium. It ignores the default premium. In the NPV formula, the default risk and default premium work through the expected cash flow in the numerator, not through the expected rate of return (cost of capital) in the denominator.
- The expected rate of return on the market is often a critical CAPM input, especially if market beta is high—but it is difficult to guess. There are at least five different common guesstimation methods, but no one really knows which one is best. Reasonable estimates for the equity premium ($\mathcal{E}(\tilde{r}_M) - r_F$) range from about 1% to 8% per annum. (The author likes 2% to 4%.)
- For r_F, you should use risk-free Treasuries that match the timing of your project's cash flows.
- There are a number of methods to estimate market beta. For publicly traded firms, it can be obtained from commercial data vendors (or self-computed). For private firms or projects, a similar publicly traded firm can often be found. Finally, managerial scenarios can be used to estimate market betas.
- The empirical SML from 1970 to 2003 has a reasonably CAPM-consistent upward slope, even though this is only true if other characteristics (such as growth/value) are not controlled for. Therefore, the CAPM is not a good model for investing purposes, although it often remains a reasonable model for capital budgeting purposes.
- The chapter appendix discusses certainty equivalence and CAPM alternatives (such as the APT and the Fama-French-Momentum model). You must use the certainty equivalence form of the CAPM when projects are purchased or sold for prices other than their fair market values. It is also often the only method if only underlying cash flows rather than value estimates are available.

KEY TERMS

SOLVE NOW! SOLUTIONS

Q 9.1 Yes, the perfect market is an assumption underlying the CAPM. In addition,
(a) Investors are rational utility maximizers.
(b) Investors care only about overall portfolio mean rate of return and risk at one given point in time.
(c) All parameters are known (not discussed until later in the chapter).
(d) All assets are traded. Every investor can purchase every asset.

Q 9.2 With $r_F = 4\%$ and $\mathcal{E}(\tilde{r}_M) = 7\%$, the cost of capital for a project with a beta of 3 is $\mathcal{E}(\tilde{r}) = r_F + [\mathcal{E}(\tilde{r}_M) - r_F] \cdot \beta_i = 4\% + (7\% - 4\%) \cdot 3 = 13\%$.

Q 9.3 With $r_F = 4\%$ and $\mathcal{E}(\tilde{r}_M) = 12\%$, the cost of capital for a project with a beta of 3 is $\mathcal{E}(\tilde{r}) = r_F + [\mathcal{E}(\tilde{r}_M) - r_F] \cdot \beta_i = 4\% + (12\% - 4\%) \cdot 3 = 28\%$.

Q 9.4 With $r_F = 4\%$ and $\mathcal{E}(\tilde{r}_M) = 12\%$, the cost of capital for a project with a beta of -3 is $\mathcal{E}(\tilde{r}) = r_F + [\mathcal{E}(\tilde{r}_M) - r_F] \cdot \beta_i = 4\% + (12\% - 4\%) \cdot (-3) = -20\%$. Yes, it does make sense that a project can offer a negative expected rate of return. Such projects are such great investments that you would be willing to expect losses on them, just because of the great insurance that they are offering.

Q 9.5 No—the real-world SML is based on historical data and not true expectations. It would be a scatterplot of historical risk and reward points. If the CAPM holds, a straight, upward-sloping line would fit them best.

Q 9.6 Write down the CAPM formula and solve $\mathcal{E}(\tilde{r}_i) = r_F + [\mathcal{E}(\tilde{r}_M) - r_F] \cdot \beta_i = 4\% + (7\% - 4\%) \cdot \beta_i = 5\%$. Therefore, $\beta_i = 1/3$. Note that we are ignoring the promised rate of return.

Q 9.7

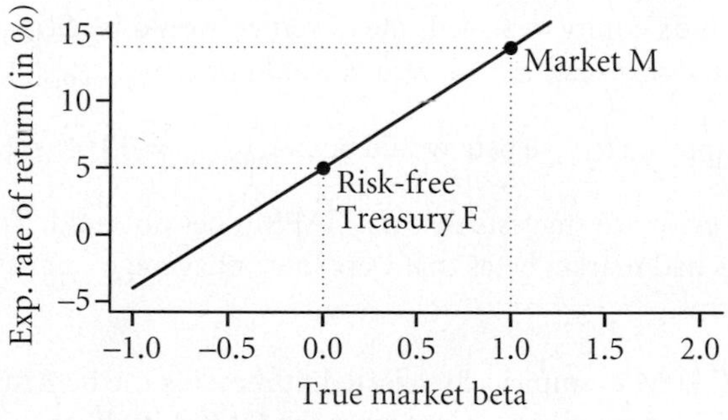

Q 9.8 The equity premium, $\mathcal{E}(\tilde{r}_M) - r_F$, is the premium that the stock market expects to offer on the risky market above and beyond what it offers on Treasuries.

Q 9.9 It does not matter what you choose as the per-unit payoff of the bond. If you choose \$100, you expect it to return \$99.
(a) Thus, the price of the bond is PV $= \$99/(1 + [3\% + 5\% \cdot 0.2]) \approx \$95.19$.
(b) Therefore, the promised rate of return on the bond is $\$100/\$95.19 - 1 \approx 5.05\%$.

(c) The risk-free rate is 3%, so this is the time premium (which contains any inflation premium). The (expected) risk premium is 1%. The remaining 1.05% is the default premium.

Q 9.10 The cost needs to be discounted with the current interest rate. Since payment is up front, this cost is \$30,000 now! The appropriate expected rate of return for cash flows (of your earnings) is $3\% + 5\% \cdot 1.5 = 10.5\%$. You can now use the annuity formula to determine the PV if you graduate:

$$\frac{\$5{,}000}{10.5\%} \cdot \left[1 - \left(\frac{1}{1 + 10.5\%}\right)^{40}\right] \approx \$47{,}619 \cdot 98.2\% \approx \$46{,}741.46$$

With 90% probability, you will do so, which means that the appropriate risk-adjusted and discounted cash flow is about \$42,067.32. The NPV of your education is therefore about \$12,067.32.

Q 9.11 An estimate between 1% and 8% per year is reasonable. Anything below 0% and above 10% would seem unreasonable to me. For reasoning, please see the different methods in the chapter.

Q 9.12 Use the 1-year Treasury rate for the 1-year project, especially if the 1-year project produces most of its cash flows at the end of the year. If it produces constant cash flows throughout the year, a 6-month Treasury rate might be more appropriate. Because the 10-year project could have a duration of cash flows much shorter than 10 years, depending on use, you might choose a risk-free Treasury rate that is between 5 and 10 years. Of course, it would be even better if you match the individual project cash flows with individual Treasuries.

Q 9.13 The duration of this cash flow is around, or a little under, 5 years. Thus, a 5-year zero Treasury would be a reasonably good guess. You should not be using a 30-day, a 30-year, or even a 10-year Treasury. The 10-year Treasury would have too much of its payments as principal repayment at the end of its 10-year term.

Q 9.14 Yes, a zero-beta asset can still have its own idiosyncratic risk. And, yes, it is perfectly kosher for a zero-beta asset to offer the same expected rate of return as the risk-free asset. The reason is that investors hold gazillions of assets, so the idiosyncratic risk of the zero-beta asset will just diversify away.

Q 9.15 This is an asset beta versus equity beta question. Because the debt is almost risk free, we can use $\beta_{\text{Debt}} \approx 0$.

(a) First compute an unlevered asset beta for your comparable with its debt-to-asset ratio of 2 to 3. This is $\beta_{\text{Asset}} = w_{\text{Debt}} \cdot \beta_{\text{Debt}} + w_{\text{Equity}} \cdot \beta_{\text{Equity}} = (2/3) \cdot 0 + (1/3) \cdot 2.5 \approx 0.833$. Next, assume that your project has the same asset beta, but a smaller debt-to-asset ratio of 1 to 3, and compute your own equity beta: $\beta_{\text{Asset}} = w_{\text{Debt}} \cdot \beta_{\text{Debt}} + w_{\text{Equity}} \cdot \beta_{\text{Equity}} \Rightarrow 0.833 \approx (1/3) \cdot 0 + (2/3) \cdot \beta_{\text{Equity}} \Rightarrow \beta_{\text{Equity}} = 1.25$.

(b) With an asset beta of 0.83, your firm's asset hurdle rate should be $\mathcal{E}(\tilde{r}_i) = 3\% + 2\% \cdot 0.83 \approx 4.7\%$.

(c) Your comparable's equity expected rate of return would be $\mathcal{E}(\tilde{r}_{\text{Comps Equity}}) = 3\% + 2\% \cdot 2.5 = 8\%$. Your own equity's expected rate of return would be $\mathcal{E}(\tilde{r}_{\text{Your Equity}}) = 3\% + 2\% \cdot 1.25 = 5.5\%$

Q 9.16 Your combined happy-marriage beta would be $\beta_{\text{Combined}} = (3/4) \cdot 2.4 + (1/4) \cdot 0.4 = 1.9$.

Q 9.17 No, the empirical evidence suggests that the CAPM does not hold. The most important violation seems to be that value firms had market betas that were low, yet average returns that were high. The opposite was the case for growth firms.

Q 9.18 Even though the CAPM is empirically rejected, it remains the benchmark model that everyone uses in the real world. Moreover, even if you do not trust the CAPM itself, at the very least it suggests that covariance with the market could be an important factor.

Q 9.19 The CAPM should work very well if beta is about 0. The reason is that you do not even need to guess the equity premium if this is so.

Q 9.20 For short-term investments, the expected cash flows are most critical to estimate well (see Section 4.1A on page 70). In this case, the trouble spot (d) is really all that matters. For long-term projects, the cost of capital becomes relatively more important to get right, too. The market betas and risk-free rates are usually relatively low maintenance (though not trouble free), having only modest degrees of uncertainty. The equity premium will be the most important problem factor in the cost-of-capital estimation. Thus, the trouble spots for long-term projects are (b) and (d).

PROBLEMS

The ▮ *indicates problems available in* myfinancelab

Q 9.21 What are the assumptions underlying the CAPM? Are the perfect market assumptions among them? Are there more?

Q 9.22 If the CAPM holds, then what should you do as the manager if you cannot find projects that meet the hurdle rate suggested by the CAPM?

Q 9.23 In a perfect world and in the absence of externalities, should you take only the projects with the highest NPV?

Q 9.24 Write down the CAPM formula. Which are economy-wide inputs, and which are project-specific inputs?

Q 9.25 The risk-free rate is 6%. The expected rate of return on the stock market is 8%. What is the appropriate cost of capital for a project that has a beta of 2?

Q 9.26 The risk-free rate is 6%. The expected rate of return on the stock market is 10%. What is the appropriate cost of capital for a project that has a beta of −2? Does this make economic sense?

Q 9.27 Draw the SML if the true expected rate of return on the market is 6% per annum and the risk-free rate is 2% per annum. How would the figure look if you were not sure about the expected rate of return on the market?

Q 9.28 A junk bond with a beta of 0.4 will default with 20% probability. If it does, investors receive only 60% of what is due to them. The risk-free rate is 3% per annum and the risk premium is 5% per annum. What is the price of this bond, its promised rate of return, and its expected rate of return?

Q 9.29 What would it take for a bond to have a larger risk premium than default premium?

Q 9.30 A corporate zero-bond promises 7% in 1 year. Its market beta is 0.3. The equity premium is 4%; the equivalent Treasury rate is 3%. What is the appropriate bond price today?

Q 9.31 Explain the basic schools of thought when it comes to equity premium estimation.

Q 9.32 If you do not want to estimate the equity premium, what are your alternatives to finding a cost-of-capital estimate?

Q 9.33 Explain in 200 words or less: What are reasonable guesstimates for the market risk premium and why?

Q 9.34 Should you use the same risk-free rate of return both as the CAPM formula intercept and in the equity premium calculation, or should you assume an equity premium that is independent of investment horizon?

Q 9.35 Should a negative-beta asset offer a higher or a lower expected rate of return than the risk-free asset? Does this make sense?

Q 9.36 An unlevered firm has an asset market beta of 1.5. The risk-free rate is 3%. The equity premium is 4%.

(a) What is the firm's cost of capital?
(b) The firm refinances itself. It repurchases half of its stock with debt that it issues. Assume that this debt is risk free. What is the equity beta of the levered firm?
(c) According to the CAPM, what rate of return does the firm have to offer to its *creditors*?
(d) According to the CAPM, what rate of return does the firm have to offer to its *levered equity holders*?
(e) Has the firm's weighted average cost of capital improved?

Q 9.37 Consider the following historical rate of return series:

Year	S&P 500	IBM	Year	S&P 500	IBM
1991	+0.2631	−0.2124	2000	−0.1014	−0.2120
1992	+0.0446	−0.4336	2001	−0.1304	+0.4231

Year	S&P 500	IBM	Year	S&P 500	IBM
1993	+0.0706	+0.1208	2002	−0.2337	−0.3570
1994	−0.0154	+0.3012	2003	+0.2638	+0.2049
1995	+0.3411	+0.2430	2004	+0.0899	+0.0719
1996	+0.2026	+0.6584	2005	+0.0300	−0.1583
1997	+0.3101	+0.3811	2006	+0.1362	+0.1977
1998	+0.2700	+0.7624	2007	+0.0353	+0.1284
1999	+0.1953	+0.1701			

(a) What was IBM's equity beta over this sample period?
(b) If IBM had a debt/equity ratio of 70%, what was its asset beta? (Hint: To determine a D/A ratio, make up an example in which a firm has a 70% D/E ratio.)
(c) How important is the 1992 observation to your beta estimate?
(d) If HP is similar to IBM in its business but has a debt/equity ratio of 10%, what would you expect HP's levered equity beta to be? (Hint: Use the same leverage conversion trick.)

Q 9.38 Look up betas on Yahoo! *Finance* today, and compare them to those in Table 8.2 on page 218.
(a) How does the beta of Intel today compare to its earlier estimate from May 2008? Was its beta stable (over time)?
(b) How does the beta of AMD today compare to its earlier estimate from May 2008? Was its beta stable?
(c) AMD is a much smaller firm than Intel. How do their betas compare?

Q 9.39 A comparable firm (in a comparable business) has an equity beta of 2.5 and a debt/equity ratio of 2. The debt is almost risk free. Estimate the beta for your equity if projects have constant betas, but your firm will carry a debt/equity ratio of 1/2. (Hint: To translate a debt-to-equity ratio into a debt-to-asset ratio, make up an example.)

Q 9.40 A Fortune 100 firm is financed with $15 billion in debt and $5 billion in equity. Its historical levered equity beta has been 2. If the firm were to increase its leverage from $15 billion to $18 billion and use the cash to repurchase shares, what would you expect its levered equity beta to be?

Q 9.41 The prevailing risk-free rate is 5% per annum. A competitor to your own firm, though publicly traded, has been using an overall project cost of capital of 12% per annum. The competitor is financed by 1/3 debt and 2/3 equity. This firm has had an estimated levered beta of 1.5. What is it using as its equity premium estimate?

Q 9.42 Apply the CAPM. Assume the risk-free rate of return is the current yield on 5-year bonds. Assume that the market's expected rate of return is 3% per year above this. Download 5 years of daily rate of return data on four funds: NAESX, VLACX, VUVLX, and VWUSX.
- What were the historical average rates of return?
- What were the historical market betas?
- What were the historical market betas, adjusted (shrunk) toward 1 by averaging with 1?
- How do these estimates compare to the market beta estimates of the financial website from which you downloaded the data?
- Does it appear as if these funds followed a CAPM-like relationship?

Q 9.43 Draw some possible security markets relations that would not be consistent with the CAPM.

Q 9.44 Does the empirical evidence suggest that the CAPM is correct?

Q 9.45 Why do you need to understand the CAPM?

Q 9.46 Under what circumstances is the CAPM a good model to use? What are the main arguments in favor of using it? When is it not a good model?

Q 9.47 Explain the kinds of projects for which it is important to get accurate equity premium estimates.

CHAPTER 9 APPENDIX

Certainty Equivalence, CAPM Theory and Background, and CAPM Alternatives

9.6 APPLICATION: CERTAINTY EQUIVALENCE

How can you value a project if you do not know the efficient price today?

As I noted earlier, the CAPM is called an asset pricing model—but then it is presented in terms of rates of return, not prices. What if you wanted to know the value of an investment asset with an uncertain rate of return? Put differently, if I asked you how much in cash you would be willing to pay for an asset, you would find it difficult to use the CAPM to tell me your "certain price" today that would leave you indifferent. This price is called the **certainty equivalent**.

The fact that you don't yet know how to answer this question turns out to have one perplexing consequence, which leaves you with one important and difficult conceptual issue best illustrated with a brainteaser: What is today's value of a gift expected to return $100 next year?

9.6A VALUING GOODS NOT PRICED AT FAIR VALUE

At a price of zero, is the appropriate cost of capital in the CAPM formula infinite? No!

Start with this puzzle: How do you even compute the beta of the gift's rate of return with the rate of return on the stock market? The price is $0 today, which means that your actual rate of return will be infinite! But you clearly should be able to put a value on this gift. Indeed, your intuition should tell you that this cash flow is most likely worth a little less than $100, the specifics depending on how the gift's cash flow covaries with the stock market. But, how do you compute this value? The solution to this puzzle is that the *price* of the gift may be $0 today, but its *present value* today (PV) is not—and it is the latter (i.e., the fair value) that is used to compute returns and betas in the CAPM, not the former. (For the rest of this section, assume that all expectations and covariances are from time 0 to time 1.)

IMPORTANT:

- The CAPM works only with expected rates of return that are computed from the *true* perfect market asset values today and the true perfect market expected value tomorrow.
- If either the price today or the value next period is not fair, then you cannot compute an expected rate of return and assume that it should satisfy the standard CAPM formula, $\mathcal{E}(\tilde{r}_i) = r_F + [\mathcal{E}(\tilde{r}_M) - r_F] \cdot \beta_i$.

The CAPM works only on fair prices in perfect markets.

Of course, in a perfect and efficient market, what you get is what you pay for ($P = \text{PV}$), so this issue would never arise. But, if you buy an asset at a better or worse deal ($P < \text{PV}$ or $P > \text{PV}$), for example, from a benevolent or malevolent friend, then you can absolutely not use such a price to compute the expected rate of return in the CAPM formula. The same applies to $\mathcal{E}(\tilde{P})$: The expected value tomorrow must be the true expected value, not a sweetheart deal value at which you may let go of the asset, nor an excessive price at which you can find a desperate buyer. If it is, you cannot use the CAPM formula.

Here is how to rearrange the CAPM formula into the certainty equivalence (CEV) formula.

Now, return to the question of how to value a gift. The specific computational problem is tricky: If you knew the present value today, you could compute a rate of return for the cash flow. Then, from the rate of return, you could compute the project beta, which you could use to find the discount rate to translate the expected cash flow back into the present value (supposedly the price) today. Alas, you do not know the price, so you cannot compute a rate of return. To solve this dilemma, you must use an alternative form of the CAPM formula.

IMPORTANT: It's **certainty equivalence form** rearranges the CAPM formula into

$$\text{PV} = \frac{\mathcal{E}(\tilde{P}) - \lambda \cdot Cov(\tilde{P}, \tilde{r}_M)}{1 + r_F} \quad \text{where } \lambda = \frac{\mathcal{E}(\tilde{r}_M - r_F)}{Var(\tilde{r}_M)} \tag{9.2}$$

where PV is the price today and $\tilde{P}$ is the price next period.

It gives the price (not the rate of return) today.

If there is only one future cash flow at time 1, then $\tilde{P}$ is this cash flow, and the rates of return are from time 0 to time 1. As before, we need the risk-free rate and an estimate of the equity premium. Let's work with a risk-free rate of 3% and an expected equity premium of 5%. In addition, we need the volatility of the stock market. Let's assume for our example's sake that the standard deviation is 20%. This means that the variance is 20% · 20% = 0.04, and therefore that lambda is 0.05/0.04 = 1.25. You could now value projects as:

$$\text{PV} = \frac{\mathcal{E}(\tilde{P}) - 1.25 \cdot Cov(\tilde{P}, \tilde{r}_M)}{1 + 3\%} = \underbrace{\frac{\mathcal{E}(\tilde{P})}{1 + 3\%}}_{\text{as-if-risk-free}} - \underbrace{\left(\frac{1.25}{1 + 3\%}\right) \cdot Cov(\tilde{P}, \tilde{r}_M)}_{\text{risk discount}} \tag{9.3}$$

The name "certainty equivalence" is apt. The first form in Formula 9.2 shows that, after you have reduced the expected value of the future cash flow ($\mathcal{E}(\tilde{P})$) by some number that relates to the cash flow's covariance with the market, you can then treat this reduced value as if it were a perfectly certain future cash flow and discount it with the risk-free rate. The second form in Formula 9.3 shows that you can decompose the price (present value) today into an "as-if-risk-free" value that is discounted only by the time premium (with the risk-free rate), and an additional risk premium (discount) that adjusts for any covariance risk with the stock market.

Watch out: The covariance here is related to—but not exactly equal to—the market beta.

The covariance between the future value $\tilde{P}$ and the rate of return on the market is related—but not identical to—the project's market beta. It is *not* the covariance of the project's *rate* of return with the market rate of return, either. It is the covariance of the project's *cash flow* with the market rate of return, instead.

Example: Find the gift's price if the covariance is 0.

With the certainty equivalence formula, you can now begin thinking about how to value your $100 expected gift. Assuming that the risk-free rate is 3% per annum, and that the lambda is the aforementioned 1.25,

$$\text{PV} = \frac{\$100 - 1.25 \cdot Cov(\tilde{P}, \tilde{r}_M)}{1 + 3\%}$$

$$\text{PV} = \frac{\mathcal{E}(\tilde{P}) - \lambda \cdot Cov(\tilde{P}, \tilde{r}_M)}{1 + r_F}$$

If you believe that the gift's payout does not covary with the rate of return on the market, then $Cov(\tilde{P}, \tilde{r}_M) = 0$, and

$$\text{PV} = \frac{\$100 - 1.25 \cdot 0}{1 + 3\%} = \frac{\$100}{1 + 3\%} \approx \$97.09$$

$$\text{PV} = \frac{\mathcal{E}(\tilde{P}) - \lambda \cdot Cov(\tilde{P}, \tilde{r}_M)}{1 + r_F}$$

Example: Find the gift's price if the covariance is positive.

Now let's see what the value is if you believe that your windfall does covary with the market. How can you estimate your cash flows' covariance with the rate of return of the stock market? You need to write down some scenarios and then compute the covariance. This is easiest to understand in an example. Let's assume that you believe that if the market goes up by 28%, your gift will be $200; if the market goes down by 12%, your gift will be $0. Further, you also believe these two outcomes are equally likely.

Prob:	1/2 Bad	1/2 Good	Mean	*Var*	*Sdv*
Stock Market	−12%	+28%	8%	400%%	20%
Our Windfall	$0	$200	$100	$$10,000	$100

I have chosen the stock market characteristics to match the example above. That is, the expected rate of return on the market is 8%, and its variance is $[(28\% - 8\%)^2 + (-12\% - 8\%)^2]/2 = 0.04$. Now you can use the covariance formula to compute the average product of deviations from the means. This is

➤ Covariance computation, Formula 8.4, p. 215

$$Cov(\tilde{P}, \tilde{r}_M) = \frac{(\$200 - \$100) \cdot (28\% - 8\%) + (\$0 - \$100) \cdot (-12\% - 8\%)}{2} = \$20$$

$$= \frac{\text{Sum of all } [\tilde{P}_{\text{outcome j}} - \mathcal{E}(\tilde{P}_{\text{outcome j}})] \cdot [\tilde{r}_{\text{M, outcome j}} - \mathcal{E}(\tilde{r}_M)]}{N}$$

Lambda is still 1.25, and you can now use the certainty equivalence formula to value your expected windfall of $100 next year. The gift is worth

$$\text{PV} = \frac{\$100 - 1.25 \cdot \$20}{1 + 3\%} = \frac{\$75}{1 + 3\%} \approx \$72.82$$

$$\text{PV} = \frac{\mathcal{E}(\tilde{P}) - \lambda \cdot Cov(\tilde{P}, \tilde{r}_M)}{1 + r_F}$$

This is a lot less than the $97.09 it would be worth if it did not covary with the market.

An alternative way to write the CEV formula.

There are two more ways to rearrange the certainty equivalence formula. The first changes the cash flow covariance into a cash flow regression beta. You can do this by using the formula

$$b_{\tilde{P},\tilde{r}_M} = \frac{\$20}{0.04} = \$500$$
$$= \frac{Cov(P_1, \tilde{r}_M)}{Var(\tilde{r}_M)}$$

This $b_{\tilde{P},\tilde{r}_M}$ is the slope of a regression line in which the future cash value (not the rate of return) is the dependent variable. You can now use a third certainty equivalence form, which gives the same result:

$$PV = \frac{\$100}{1+3\%} - \left[\frac{5\%}{1+3\%}\right] \cdot \$500 \approx \$72.82$$
$$PV = \frac{\mathcal{E}(\tilde{P})}{1+r_F} - \left[\frac{\mathcal{E}(\tilde{r}_M) - r_F}{1+r_F}\right] \cdot b_{\tilde{P},\tilde{r}_M}$$

A final form is really more like the original CAPM. It translates the cash flow regression beta back into the ordinary CAPM beta, which we all love. To do this, use the formula

$$\beta_P \approx \frac{\$500}{\$72.82} \approx 6.867 \quad (9.4)$$
$$\beta_P = \frac{b_{\tilde{P},\tilde{r}_M}}{PV}$$

Of course, you usually do not know the \$72.82 price to begin with, which is why this is a less useful form (though you might start with a beta from comparables). You can now compute the value as

$$PV = \frac{\$100/1.03}{1 + \left(\frac{8\%-3\%}{1.03}\right) \cdot 6.867} \approx \$72.82$$
$$PV = \frac{P_1/(1+r_F)}{1 + \left[\frac{\mathcal{E}(\tilde{r}_M)-r_F}{1+r_F}\right] \cdot \beta_i}$$

I find this CAPM form rather useful. It says that after you have discounted the project by the risk-free rate, you discount it a second time using $\left[\frac{\mathcal{E}(\tilde{r}_M)-r_F}{1+r_F}\right] \cdot \beta_i$ as your second interest rate. If you can find a good comparable market-beta, you are home free!

DIGGING DEEPER

Knowing the fair price of \$72.8155, you can check that you have really just worked with the CAPM formula. The project will either provide a rate of return of $\$200/\$72.8155 - 1 \approx 174.67\%$, or a rate of return of -100%, for an expected rate of return of **37.33%**. Let's confirm this:

Ordinary market beta: The market beta computed with rates of return is

$$\beta_i = \beta_{i,M} = \frac{Cov(\tilde{r}_i, \tilde{r}_M)}{Var(\tilde{r}_M)} \approx \frac{\frac{(+174.67\%-37.33\%)\cdot(+28\%-8\%)+(-100\%-37.33\%)\cdot(-12\%-8\%)}{2}}{\frac{(+28\%-8\%)^2+(-12\%-8\%)^2}{2}} \approx \frac{0.274667}{0.04} \approx 6.867$$

Ordinary CAPM expected rate of return: The CAPM formula states that the expected rate of return, given this beta of 6.867, should be

$$\mathcal{E}(\tilde{r}_i) = r_F + [\mathcal{E}(\tilde{r}_M) - r_F] \cdot \beta_i \approx 0.03 + (0.08 - 0.03) \cdot 6.867 \approx 0.3733$$

which is indeed what we computed as our average between 174.67% and -100%.

SOLVE NOW!

Q 9.48 Although you are a millionaire, keeping all your money in the market, you have managed to secure a great deal: If you promise to go to school (which costs you a net disutility worth \$10,000 today), then your even richer Uncle Vinny will buy you a Ferrari (expected to be worth \$200,000), provided his business can afford it. He is an undertaker by profession, so his business will have the money if the stock market drops, but not if it increases. For simplicity, assume that the stock market drops in 1 year out of every 4 years. When it does, it goes down by -10%; when it does not, it goes up by 18%. (Write it out as four separate possible state outcomes to make your life simpler.) The risk-free rate is 6%. What is your uncle's deal worth to you?

9.6B APPLICATION: THE CAPM HURDLE RATE FOR A PROJECT WITH CASH FLOW HISTORY ONLY

Here is your first professional consulting assignment: You are asked to advise a privately held firm on its appropriate cost of capital. The owners of this firm are very wealthy and widely diversified, so that their remaining portfolio is similar to the market portfolio. (Otherwise, our investor's opportunity cost of capital may not be well represented by the CAPM—the calculations here are not relevant for a typical, cash-strapped entrepreneur, whose portfolio would *not* be similar to the market portfolio.) To make this a more realistic and difficult task, assume this firm is either privately held or only a division of a publicly held firm, so that you cannot find historical public market values and so that there are no obvious publicly traded comparable firms. Instead, the firm hands you its historical annual cash flows:

Your task: Find the opportunity cost of capital of a privately held corporation.

Year:	1999	2000	2001	2002	2003	2004	Average
S&P 500	+21.4%	−5.7%	−12.8%	−21.9%	+26.4%	+9.0%	+2.7%
Cash flows	\$8,794	\$5,373	\$8,397	\$6,314	\$9,430	\$9,838	\$8,024

In an ideal world, this is an easy problem: You could compute the value of this firm every year, then compute the beta of the firm's rate of return with respect to the market rate of return, and plug this into the CAPM formula. Alas, assessing annual firm value changes from annual cash flows is beyond my capability. You can also not assume that percent changes in the firm's cash flows are percent changes in the firm's value—just consider what would happen to your estimates if the firm had earned zero in one year. All this does not let you off the hook: What cost of capital are you recommending? Having only a time series of historical cash flows (and no rates of return) is a very applied, and not simply an obscure, theoretical problem. You might first want to reflect on how difficult it is to solve this problem without the certainty equivalence formula.

We are assuming independent cash flows. In real life, be careful. Be very careful.

First, we have to make our usual assumption that our historical cash flows and market rates of return are representative of the future. However, here we have to make a much bigger assumption. It could be that your cash flows in one year are not a draw from the same distribution of cash flows, but that they also say a lot about your future cash flows. For example, a lousy year could induce the firm to make changes to raise cash flows. Or a great year could signal the beginning of more great years in the future. If either is the case, our naive application of the CEV method fails. (Instead of using a cash flow, you would have to use the expected value of the firm next year—a very difficult task in itself.) Let me repeat this:

> **Big Warning:** In the way we are now using our CEV approach on historical cash flow data, we are assuming that historical cash flows are independent draws that inform you about the distribution of future cash flows. This means that there should be no autocorrelation—any year's cash flow should not be any more indicative of next year's cash flow than any others. More sophisticated techniques could remedy this shortcoming, but we do not have the space to cover them.

Here is a heroic attempt to value this private firm.

Under this cash flow assumption, we begin by computing the beta of the firm's cash flows with respect to the S&P 500. This is easier if we work with differences from the mean:

Year:	1999	2000	2001	2002	2003	2004	Average
De-meaned S&P 500	+18.7%	−8.4%	−15.5%	−24.6%	+23.7%	+6.3%	0%
De-meaned Cash Flows	+\$770	−\$2,651	+\$373	−\$1,710	+\$1,406	+\$1,814	\$0

To compute the covariance of the S&P 500 returns with our cash flows, we multiply these and take the average (well, we divide by $N-1$, because this is a sample, not the population, but it won't matter much in the end),

$$Cov_{\text{CF},\tilde{r}_{\text{M}}} = \frac{(+18.7\%) \cdot (+\$770) + (-8.4\%) \cdot (-\$2{,}651) + \cdots + (+6.3\%) \cdot (+\$1{,}814)}{5} \approx \$235.4$$

and compute the variance of the S&P 500 returns

$$\mathcal{V}ar(\tilde{r}_M) = \frac{(+18.7\%)^2 + (-8.4\%)^2 + \cdots + (6.3\%)^2}{5} \approx 0.0374$$

The cash flow beta is the ratio of these,

$$b_{CF,M} = \frac{\mathcal{C}ov_{CF,\tilde{r}_M}}{\mathcal{V}ar(\tilde{r}_M)} = \frac{\$235.4}{0.03734} \approx \$6{,}304$$

The historical mean cash flow was \$8,024. We still need an assumption of a suitable equity premium and a suitable risk-free rate. Let's adopt 4% and 3%, respectively. In this case, the value of our firm would be

Now substitute the inputs into the CEV formula.

$$\text{PV} = \frac{\$8{,}024}{1 + 3\%} - \left[\frac{4\%}{1 + 3\%}\right] \cdot \$6{,}304 \approx \$7{,}790 - \$245 \approx \$7{,}545$$

$$= \frac{\mathcal{E}(\tilde{CF})}{1 + r_F} - \left[\frac{\mathcal{E}(\tilde{r}_M) - r_F}{1 + r_F}\right] \cdot b_{\tilde{CF},\tilde{r}_M}$$

The certainty equivalence formula tells us that because our firm's cash flows are correlated with the market, we shall impute an additional risk discount of \$245. We can translate this into a cost-of-capital estimate—at what discount rate would we arrive at a value of \$7,545?

$$\$7{,}545 = \frac{\$8{,}024}{1 + \mathcal{E}(\tilde{r})} \Rightarrow \mathcal{E}(\tilde{r}) \approx 6.3\%$$

$$\text{PV} = \frac{\mathcal{E}(\text{CF})}{1 + \mathcal{E}(\tilde{r})}$$

We now have an estimate of the cost of capital for our cash flow for next year. We can also translate this into an equivalent returns-based market beta, which is

$$3\% + 4\% \cdot \beta_{i,M} = 6.3\% \Rightarrow \beta \approx 0.8$$

$$r_F + [\mathcal{E}(\tilde{r}_M) - r_F] \cdot \beta_{i,M}$$

Of course, you could have used Formula 9.4 instead: With a present value of \$7,545, the cash flow beta of \$6,304 divided by \$7,545 would have yielded the same ordinary beta estimate of 0.8.

➤ Translation to standard market beta, Formula 9.4, p. 284

Are we close?

Now I can reveal who the firm in this example really was—it was IBM. Because it is publicly traded, we can see how our own estimate of IBM's cost of capital and market beta would have come out if we had computed it from IBM's annual market values. Its rates of return were as follows:

Year:	1999	2000	2001	2002	2003	2004	Average
IBM's Rate of Return	+17.5%	−20.8%	+43.0%	−35.5%	+20.5%	+7.2%	+5.3%

If you compute the market beta of these annual returns, you will find an estimate of 0.7—very close to the estimate we obtained from our cash flow series. (For IBM, this is a fairly low estimate. If we used monthly cash flows or monthly stock returns, we would obtain a higher market beta estimate.)

SOLVE NOW!

Q 9.49 A firm reported the following cash flows:

Year:	1999	2000	2001	2002	2003	2004	Average
S&P 500	+21.4%	−5.7%	−12.8%	−21.9%	+26.4%	+9.0%	+2.7%
Cash Flows	+$2,864	+$1,666	−$1,040	+$52	+$1,478	−$962	+$676

(Note that the cash flows are close to nothing in 2002 and even negative in 2004, the latter preventing you from computing percent changes in cash flows.) Still assuming an equity premium of 4% and a risk-free rate of 3%, what cost of capital would you recommend for 1 year of this firm's cash flows?

9.7 THEORY: THE CAPM BASIS

This chapter has given you only a cookbook approach to the CAPM. There is usually not enough time to cover the art and science of investments in a corporate finance course. This appendix sketches some of the plumbing that goes into putting the CAPM together.

9.7A MATH: PORTFOLIO SEPARATION

A portfolio consisting only of MVE portfolios is itself MVE.

➤ Two-fund separation, Section 8.9, p. 239

In our world of risk-free assets, the combination of two mean-variance efficient (MVE) portfolios is itself MVE. It may almost seem silly to emphasize this simple math fact, but it is extremely important to the CAPM derivation. If a risk-free asset is available (and, de facto, it is), the proof is simple. Every MVE portfolio is a simple combination of the tangency portfolio and the risk-free asset. There are no other assets that any other investor might hold instead. So, adding the next investor can add only more tangency portfolio and more risk-free asset to the market portfolio. And, therefore, if the two investors marry, their portfolio is still MVE.

IMPORTANT: Mathematics dictates that combining MVE portfolios yields an MVE portfolio.

The reverse does not hold. That is, combining portfolios that are not MVE could still yield an MVE portfolio—if only by accident. Incidentally, even if there is no risk-free asset, this still holds. That is, the combination of two MVE portfolios is itself MVE. This is not easy to see, but trust me that it can be proven.

No economics or behavior was involved in this mathematical proof. It is true no matter how investors behave. Later, we will add some economics: If all investors hold MVE portfolios, then portfolio separation will imply that the overall value-weighted stock market portfolio is also MVE. In turn, this means the market portfolio must be on the tangency line itself. Because there is only one risky portfolio that qualifies, the market portfolio of risky assets must be the tangency portfolio itself.

9.7B MATH: THE MEAN-VARIANCE EFFICIENT FRONTIER AND CAPM-TYPE FORMULAS

Now let's connect the mean-variance efficient frontier and the CAPM formula, $\mathcal{E}(\tilde{r}_i) = r_F + [\mathcal{E}(\tilde{r}_M) - r_F] \cdot \beta_i$. This formula must hold for each and every security in the market. You can think of it as a relationship that relates the reward of *each component* of the market portfolio to its risk contribution. But why does the efficient frontier, which graphs only the *overall* portfolio risk (standard deviation) and reward, relate to a formula about each and every one of the portfolio's many individual constituents and their market betas? At first glance, the two do not even seem to play in the same ballpark. But there is a good connection. Intuitively, the CAPM formula states that in the portfolios on the MVE frontier, no component can offer too little or too much reward for its portfolio risk contribution. If it did, you could form a better portfolio by buying more or less of it, and therefore your overall original portfolio would not have been on the MVE frontier to begin with!

Every component in an MVE portfolio must follow a fair risk contribution versus reward relationship—or you could do better.

➤ Efficient frontier, Section 8.8, p. 236

Here is my claim: If even a single stock does not follow the CAPM formula, then I can form a portfolio that has higher reward with lower risk. (Put differently, the stock market portfolio would not have been the efficient tangency portfolio.) Let me show you how this works. We recycle the portfolios from Section 8.9. Take portfolio N, also in Table 9.2. It has 75% investment in H and 25% investment in I. It is not MVE if a risk-free security offers a 4% rate of return. Relative to the tangency portfolio T, N has too much H and too little I in it. (Recall that portfolio T invests about 30% in H and 70% in I.) Put differently, if you owned only N, then security H would be relatively too expensive and unattractive, and security I would be relatively too cheap and attractive. You could perform better than N if you sold some of the expensive H and bought more of the cheap I. In contrast, this logic should not apply for your tangency portfolio T. If you own T, you should not be able to do better. All securities should seem appropriately priced to you. This is the logic underlying the CAPM formula. It gives each security an appropriate reward, given this security's risk contribution (measured by beta with respect to the overall portfolio).

Intuition: In portfolio N, you have too much H and too little I. H is really too expensive *for you* given your portfolio N. I is really too cheap *for you*.

Let's confirm that the CAPM formula holds only for the tangency portfolio T, and not for portfolio N.

Example: The CAPM formula works (only) for the tangency portfolio.

The risk-reward relationship in the tangency portfolio: Do we get a CAPM-type relationship between securities' expected rate of return and their betas if the efficient T is the market portfolio? Let's check. The CAPM-type relationship would be:

T is MVE, so all its constituents follow a CAPM formula.

$$\mathcal{E}(\tilde{r}_i) = r_F + [\mathcal{E}(\tilde{r}_T) - r_F] \cdot \beta_{i,T}$$

The beta of security i with respect to portfolio T ($\beta_{i,T}$) is your measure of the risk contribution of security i to portfolio T. You need to compute these betas (with respect to the overall portfolio T) for both securities H and I. This is the covariance of H and T, divided by the variance of T. I have worked this out for you, so trust me that this number is $\beta_{H,T} \approx 0.49$. Similarly, $\beta_{I,T} \approx 1.22$. Substitute these two betas into the relationship, and you find

TABLE 9.2 EFFICIENT AND INEFFICIENT PORTFOLIOS

	Base Portfolios		Risk Free	Inefficient	Tangency
Future	H	I	F	N	T
In Scenario S1 ♣	−6.0%	−12.0%	4.00%	−7.50%	−10.2%
In Scenario S2 ♦	+12.0%	+18.0%	4.00%	+13.50%	+16.2%
In Scenario S3 ♥	0.0%	+24.0%	4.00%	+6.00%	+16.8%
In Scenario S4 ♠	+18.0%	+6.0%	4.00%	+15.00%	+9.6%
"Reward" ($\mathcal{E}(\tilde{r})$)	6.00%	9.00%	4.00%	6.75%	8.10%
"Variance" ($\mathcal{V}ar(r)$)	90.0%%	189.0%%	0.0%%	79.3%%	119.6%%
"Risk" ($\mathcal{S}dv(\tilde{r})$)	9.49%	13.75%	0.00%	8.91%	10.94%

H and I are the two base assets that form the mean-variance efficient frontier of risky assets. F is the risk-free asset. N and T are combinations of the H and I assets that are used to illustrate the mean-variance frontier with a risk-free asset. The portfolio N appeared in Table 8.4 on page 232 and invests 75% in H, 25% in I. It is not mean-variance efficient. Portfolio T invests about 30% in H, 70% in I. These assets are graphed in Figure 8.9 on page 243.

$$\mathcal{E}(\tilde{r}_{\text{H}}) \approx 4\% + [8.1\% - 4\%] \cdot 0.49 \approx 6\%$$
$$\mathcal{E}(\tilde{r}_{\text{I}}) \approx 4\% + [8.1\% - 4\%] \cdot 1.22 \approx 9\%$$
$$\mathcal{E}(\tilde{r}_{\text{i}}) = r_{\text{F}} + [\mathcal{E}(\tilde{r}_{\text{T}}) - r_{\text{F}}] \cdot \beta_{\text{i,T}}$$

If you look at Table 9.2, you will see that this is exactly what these two securities offer, which is exactly as CAPM suggests: There is a linear relationship between each security's expected rate of return and beta with respect to the market. You cannot do better by either selling or buying more of H or I. You are already holding them in the best proportions. And, therefore, T is indeed mean-variance efficient.

If N were MVE, its constituents should follow a CAPM formula. Here they do not follow the CAPM formula.

The risk-reward relationship in any other portfolio: Is this also the case for another portfolio that is not mean-variance efficient (i.e., on the mean-variance efficient frontier)? Could we get a CAPM-like relationship between securities' expected rate of return and their betas if the inefficient N is the market portfolio? Let's check. The CAPM-type relationship would be

$$\mathcal{E}(\tilde{r}_{\text{i}}) = r_{\text{F}} + [\mathcal{E}(\tilde{r}_{\text{N}}) - r_{\text{F}}] \cdot \beta_{\text{i,N}}$$

The beta of security i with respect to portfolio N ($\beta_{\text{i,N}}$) is your measure of the risk contribution of security i to portfolio N. Trust me again that $\beta_{\text{H,N}} \approx 0.99$ and $\beta_{\text{I,N}} \approx 1.02$. Substitute these two betas in, and you find

$$\mathcal{E}(\tilde{r}_{\text{H}}) \approx 4\% + [8.1\% - 4\%] \cdot 0.99 \approx 8.07\%$$
$$\mathcal{E}(\tilde{r}_{\text{I}}) \approx 4\% + [8.1\% - 4\%] \cdot 1.02 \approx 8.19\%$$
$$\mathcal{E}(\tilde{r}_{\text{i}}) = r_{\text{F}} + [\mathcal{E}(\tilde{r}_{\text{N}}) - r_{\text{F}}] \cdot \beta_{\text{i,N}}$$

But if you look at Table 9.2, you will see that portfolio H offers a reward of only 6% while portfolio I offers a reward of 9%. In this portfolio N, H is too expensive and I is too cheap. You would do better to get rid of some H and buy more I. Therefore, you have now confirmed that if the inefficient N were the market portfolio, a CAPM-type formula would not hold! H would be too expensive in the market, and I would be too cheap in the market. Therefore, N would not be a mean-variance efficient portfolio.

IMPORTANT: Mathematics dictates that if and only if a portfolio T is MVE, all assets must follow the linear relation,

$$\tilde{r}_i = r_F + [\mathcal{E}(\tilde{r}_T) - r_F] \cdot \beta_{i,T}$$

Therefore, if the market portfolio is MVE,

$$\tilde{r}_i = r_F + [\mathcal{E}(\tilde{r}_M) - r_F] \cdot \beta_i$$

Again, no economics was involved. The formulas are correct no matter how investors behave.

SOLVE NOW!

Q 9.50 This question asks you to confirm the beta computations. Work with the data from Table 9.2.
(a) Compute the covariance between H and N.
(b) Compute the covariance between I and N.
(c) Compute the variance of N.
(d) Compute the beta of H with respect to N.
(e) Compute the beta of I with respect to N.
Repeat this for portfolio T as the reference portfolio instead of N. (Recall that T holds 30% in H and 70% in I.)

Q 9.51 Confirm that the portfolio H is not mean-variance efficient if the risk-free rate of return is 4%.

9.7C ECONOMICS: THE CAPM AND ITS LOGIC

Actually, you probably already understand how the previous chapter and this chapter fit together to produce the CAPM.

The CAPM is the statement that the market portfolio is the MVE tangency portfolio.

- The mean-variance efficient frontier plots the achievable combinations of overall portfolio risk and reward.

➤ From, Section 8.8, p. 236

- With a risk-free security, the real efficient frontier becomes the line connecting the risk-free rate with the tangency portfolio from the efficient frontier, using only the risky securities.

➤ From, Section 8.9, p. 239

➤ From, Section 8.9, p. 239

- An investor who wishes to be on the mean-variance efficient frontier will purchase a combination of the tangency portfolio and the risk-free rate.

➤ From, Section 9.7B, p. 289

- Portfolios on the efficient frontier do not underinvest or overinvest in individual securities. Therefore, for portfolios on the efficient frontier, individual securities must follow the CAPM security market line (SML). If one security were to offer too much or too little reward (measured by expected rate of return) for its risk contribution (measured by portfolio beta), then this original portfolio could be improved upon by buying more or less of this one security—and therefore it would not have been mean-variance efficient to begin with.

You learned about the CAPM in this chapter. It gives you an appropriate hurdle rate (cost of capital) for corporate and other projects. But where does the CAPM and its formula really come from? Put it all together:

- Mathematics: If all investors in the market buy a combination of the tangency portfolio and the risk-free rate, then their combined portfolio is also a combination of the tangency portfolio and the risk-free rate. (Duh!)
- Economics: The CAPM is only one economic statement: The market portfolio lies on the efficient frontier. If all investors buy mean-variance efficient portfolios, this is necessarily true. Indeed, the tangency portfolio must be the overall market portfolio. If it were not, it would make no sense: Investors would jointly seek to own more or less of some security than there would be available for purchase.
- Mathematics: The rest (the CAPM formula) is just a mathematical consequence. The previous subsection gave you a taste of the proof—that all securities in efficient frontier portfolios must follow a CAPM-type formula, that is, a security market line:

$$\mathcal{E}(\tilde{r}_{\mathrm{i}}) = r_{\mathrm{F}} + [\mathcal{E}(\tilde{r}_{\mathrm{M}}) - r_{\mathrm{F}}] \cdot \beta_{\mathrm{i}}$$

9.8 THEORY: CAPM ALTERNATIVES!?

In a survey in 2007, about 75% of all finance professors recommended the CAPM for use in a corporate capital budgeting context. About 5% recommended the so-called APT. And 10% recommended the so-called Fama-French factors. Not surprisingly, these two alternative models have not only some advantages but also big disadvantages relative to the CAPM from a capital budgeting perspective—if it were otherwise, we would have deserted the CAPM. (Forms of these models clearly work better for financial investment purposes, though.) It is impossible to explain these models fully in a first corporate finance course, but I want to give you at least a sketch.

9.8A THE ARBITRAGE PRICING THEORY (APT) AND INTERTEMPORAL CAPM (ICAPM)

For understanding the analogy later, first recap the CAPM.

The first alternative is an extension of the ordinary CAPM, called the **intertemporal CAPM (ICAPM)**. The second is called the **arbitrage pricing theory (APT)**. In practical use, the two are almost indistinguishable, so I will just treat them as one and the same model here. Let's think back as to how you would apply the CAPM:

1. The CAPM asks you to measure how each stock's rate of return moves together with the overall stock market rate of return. This is its market beta.
2. The model's intuition is that investors dislike stocks that move together with the stock market and like stocks that move against the stock market.
3. The CAPM tells you the exact formula by which you should receive a higher average rate of return for firms that expose you to a lot of covariation with the stock market. It may be

$$\mathcal{E}(\tilde{r}_i) = 4\% + 5\% \cdot \beta_{i,\mathrm{M}}$$

where the second subscript reminds you that this beta measures a stock's sensitivity with respect to the market.

You might care about economy-wide factors other than the rate of return on the stock market (e.g., oil prices).

Now let's assume that stocks differ not only in how they move with or against the stock market, but also in how they move with or against other economic factors, say, the oil price. You might care about oil price changes because your business may do poorly if energy costs rise. Therefore, if you can find a stock that increases in value when oil prices rise, you would consider this stock to be good insurance against bad business—just as you consider a stock that goes up when the market goes down to be good insurance against market downturns in the CAPM framework. (If you are in this situation, chances are that you would really like to hold stocks like Exxon or Chevron.)

Different stocks can have different exposures to other economy-wide factors.

How can you measure whether a stock goes up or down with the oil price? Simple—you get this measure the same way that you get a measure of whether a stock goes up or down with the stock market. For each stock, you run a time-series regression, in which the independent variable is not the rate of return on the stock market but the oil price change:

$$\tilde{r}_i = a + \beta_{i,\text{Oil Price Change}} \cdot (\text{Oil Price Change})$$

This gives you a beta for each stock that measures how its rate of return moves with oil price changes. A stock that has a very large $\beta_{i,\text{oil price change}}$ (say, 5) would go up a lot if the oil price increases—think Exxon. A stock that has a negative $\beta_{i,\text{oil price change}}$ (say, −3) would go down when the oil price increases—think United Parcel Service (which has to pay more for gas when the oil price increases).

And here is the analogy: Assets with higher exposures (betas) to these factors have to offer higher or lower expected rates of return.

Would you be willing to pay more for a stock that acts as an insurance against oil price increases? If your livelihood is adversely affected by oil price changes, then the answer is probably yes. The more important question is whether this is also the attitude of most investors in the market. If it is, then a stock like Exxon, which has a high $\beta_{i,\text{oil price change}}$, would be more desirable. Such a stock would not have to offer as high a rate of return as another stock that has a low $\beta_{i,\text{oil price change}}$. The APT then gives you a formula that relates the oil-price-change beta (and other betas like it) to the expected rate of return on a stock—something like

$$\mathcal{E}(\tilde{r}_i) = 4\% + 5\% \cdot \beta_{i,\mathrm{M}} - 3\% \cdot \beta_{i,\text{Oil Price Change}}$$

You can now use the formula the same way you used the CAPM formula. To recap, the APT works like the CAPM but allows more than just one beta (and just one risk premium):

1. The APT asks you to measure for each stock how it moves with respect to factors (like the oil price) that you decide on. This gives you, for each stock, a set of market betas—one exposure for each factor.
2. The intuition is that investors like stocks that have high or low betas with respect to these factors. (The sign depends on investors' preferences.)
3. The APT tells you the exact formula by which you should receive a higher average rate of return for firms that expose you to bad covariation with respect to the factors that matter.

What Are the APT Factors?

Common APT models use as factors interest rate changes, GDP changes, bankruptcy risk, the returns of growth stocks, and the returns of small firms. Each stock then has a beta with respect to these factors. And an APT formula relates the average rate of return to these betas.

APT flexibility is both good and bad.

Unfortunately, the APT is even harder to use than the CAPM. The good news is that it allows you to specify that investors care about factors other than the overall stock market. You then use the beta of your project with respect to the market to determine the appropriate expected rate of return. The bad news is that it allows you to specify that investors care about factors other than the overall stock market. The problem is that the APT does not give you any guidance on what these factors should be. What factors do academics recommend? Sorry, there is no consensus of what the best APT factors are. So the APT's flexibility is both a blessing and a curse.

Canned usage is easy *if* you pay for it. However, estimates can vary widely.

Most commonly, corporations rely on third-party vendors who have developed such APT models. This way, they get at least a second opinion on their average cost of capital. (This is rarely done for individual projects, even though we know that costs of capital should be computed project by project.) The APT vendor reports APT factors (the market beta and the oil price change in our example) and the "premiums" (4%, 5%, −3% in our example) and then estimates your firm's betas with respect to these premiums. You can then multiply the factors with the premiums to obtain an alternative measure for the cost of capital. Alas, there is no guarantee that any one particular APT model is the right model. In fact, two APT vendors can easily derive completely different cost-of-capital estimates. You have to judge which one is better. In other words, use the APT at your own risk.

SOLVE NOW!

Q 9.52 Explain how the APT model is similar to, but more general than, the CAPM.

9.8B THE FAMA-FRENCH-MOMENTUM (-AND-MORE) MODEL

The Fama-French factors plus momentum.

While the ICAPM and APT developed out of a tradition of theoretical models with empirical applications, another set of models has come out of a tradition of empirical research. The most prominent empirical regularities right now seem to be the following:

1. **Momentum:** Stocks tend to perform better if they have had high stock returns over the previous 12 months, not including the most recent month. (Omitting this last month is very important.) The firm's own momentum is a very robust positive predictor, except in January (where it reverses).
2. **Value:** Stocks tend to perform better if they have high accounting book value of equity divided by the market value of equity. Firms that fit this criterion are called **value firms**, while firms that have higher market values than accounting book values are called **growth firms**. A typical value firm is "boring," like the diaper vendor Procter & Gamble. A typical growth firm is "exciting," like Google or Apple. In the long run, the superior stock return performance of value firms relative to growth firms has been a very robust relationship, too—even though there were some periods when it did not hold—first and foremost during the dot com bubble of late 1990s.
3. **Size:** There is some evidence that smaller firms perform better than larger firms. The role of firm size is not as strong and robust as the two preceding effects.

➤ Book value of equity, Chapter 13, p. 445

➤ Bubbles, Section 9.4A, p. 257

The latter two regularities are usually called the **Fama-French factors** because it was Eugene Fama and Ken French who investigated them most thoroughly. The first regularity was suggested as an addition by Mark Carhart. Please don't think that these three empirical regularities are the only ones. There are literally dozens more (accounting accruals and net issuing activity are particularly noteworthy). However, these three factors are perhaps the most prominent. (For more determinants of average rates of return, you really have to read an investments textbook.)

Use of the Model in a Corporate Context

How can you use this model in a corporate context? Let me sketch how one version would work. Ken French posts the historical rates of return for the equity premium (which he calls XMKT) and the three other factors on his website at Dartmouth. Here they are.

Finding exposures—like APT exposures.

XMKT: The equity premium is the average rate of return on the stock market net of the risk-free rate. The average rate of return on XMKT (from 1927 to 2006) was about 8.5%.

UMD (up-minus-down): The momentum net portfolio is the average rate of return on firms having done well over the last 12 months ("winners") minus the average rate of return on firms having done poorly ("loosers"). It is logged to omit the last month. The average rate of return on this portfolio was about 8.9%.

HML (high-minus-low): The high "value" portfolio is the average rate of return on stocks with high accounting book value relative to market value. The "low" portfolio is the same for stocks with the opposite characteristics (i.e., "growth"). The average rate of return on the net portfolio was about 4.6%.

SMB (small-minus-big): The "small firm" portfolio is the average rate of return on stocks of small firms. The "big firm" portfolio is the same for large firms. The average rate of return on the net portfolio was about 3.8%.

You would first run a time-series regression of your own project's (i) historical rates of return *net of the risk-free rate* on the four time-series:

$$\tilde{r}_i - r_F = a_i + b_i \cdot \text{XMKT} + c_i \cdot \text{UMD} + d_i \cdot \text{HML} + e_i \cdot \text{SMB} + \text{noise}$$

Note that the abnormal return of 3% should *not* repeat.

Now let's say that your regression package estimated your project's coefficients to be $a = 3\%$, $b = 2$, $c = 0$, $d = 0$, and $e = 0$. Well, then your particular stock behaves almost like a CAPM stock with a market beta of 2, because your model would reduce to

$$\mathcal{E}(\tilde{r}_i) - r_F = 3\% + 2 \cdot \mathcal{E}(\text{XMKT}) = 3\% + 2 \cdot [\mathcal{E}(\tilde{r}_M) - r_F] \quad (9.5)$$

Note that the risk-free rate intercept is already on the left-hand side, so your 3% estimated intercept would be an excess rate of return that your stock has earned historically, above and beyond what the model would have suggested. You would therefore also not expect this extra 3% rate of return to repeat.

Here is how you would use the model to find a hurdle rate for one particular project.

What would be a good hurdle rate for your project? If you believe the future equity premium to be 5% and the Treasury risk-free rate to be 4%, then you would expect your stock's rate of return to be

$$\mathcal{E}(\tilde{r}_i) - 4\% = 2 \cdot 5\%$$

$$\mathcal{E}(\tilde{r}_i) - r_F = \beta_{i,\text{XMKT}} \cdot \mathcal{E}(\text{XMKT})$$

The model suggests an expected rate of return of $\mathcal{E}(\tilde{r}_i) = 4\% + 2 \cdot 5\% = 14\%$ for your project. Note how the application omits the 3% from Formula 9.5 here—the reason, as just noted, is that the 3% was an unusual rate of return that you would not expect to repeat. Note that instead of using your 5% guess about the future equity premium, you could have used the historical average rate of return on XMKT. From 1927 to 2006, it was 8.5%. In this case, you would have required your project to earn a rate of return of $4\% + 2 \cdot 8.5\% \approx 21\%$.

Okay, here comes a useful application of the model. The above project was just for practice.

Now let's choose another project. Let's say you estimate coefficients $a = 3\%$, $b = 0.5$, $c = -1$, $d = 2$, and $e = -2$ for this one. Again, you would need some estimates of the future average rate of return for the four factors, just as you needed an estimate for the future average rate of return for the equity premium. Remember how we agonized about the equity premium? You really should agonize equally about all four risk premium estimates now. However, for lack of a good source and great intuition, most people just use the historical average rates of return, mentioned above. If you buy into the hypothesis that the historical averages are good predictors of the future premiums, you would then estimate your project's appropriate expected rate of return to be

$$\begin{aligned}\mathcal{E}(\tilde{r}_i) - r_F &= 0.5 \cdot \mathcal{E}(\text{XMKT}) + (-1) \cdot \mathcal{E}(\text{UMD}) + 2 \cdot \mathcal{E}(\text{HML}) + (-2) \cdot \mathcal{E}(\text{SMB}) \\ &= 0.5 \cdot 8.5\% + (-1) \cdot 8.9\% + 2 \cdot 4.6\% + (-2) \cdot 3.8\% \\ &= -3.05\%\end{aligned}$$

With a risk-free rate of return of 5%, you would set your project hurdle rate to be about 5% − 3% = 2%.

Practical notes, especially with respect to momentum.

Some final notes: Often, one would use only a two factor model—based on value/growth and either beta or size—for capital budgeting. Firm size and firm market beta are sufficiently highly correlated that in most practical capital budgeting applications, you can ignore firm size and rely on market beta alone (or the opposite). Moreover, momentum is such a short-term phenomenon that it is usually irrelevant for long-term capital budgeting purposes. Relying on 1-year momentum for cost-of-capital estimates for 10-year investments in a corporate context does not make sense. This is why UMD is often excluded from this model in a corporate context. Moreover, this form of the model does not do justice, especially to momentum, which is more of an idiosyncratic effect than a factor exposure to UMD. A better model would work with firms' own momentum rather than these factor betas. (In an APT context, one could then view these characteristics of stocks as picking up firms' betas to some factors. Of course, other researchers believe that these are not really betas, but more a reflection of market inefficiencies, the subject of Chapter 11.) This is all too telegraphic, of course. You should really consult an investments text to learn how to do this better.

SOLVE NOW!

Q 9.53 Assume that you ran a time-series regression with your project on the Fama-French factors and found the following:

$$\mathcal{E}(\tilde{r}_i) - r_F = (-2\%) + (1.3) \cdot \text{XMKT} + (0.1) \cdot \text{UMD} + (-1) \cdot \text{HML} + (-0.1) \cdot \text{SMB}$$

What would the Fama-French-Momentum model suggest you use as the hurdle rate for this project? Recall that $\mathcal{E}(\text{XMKT}) \approx 8.5\%$, $\mathcal{E}(\text{UMD}) \approx 8.9\%$, $\mathcal{E}(\text{HML}) \approx 4.6\%$, and $\mathcal{E}(\text{SMB}) \approx 3.8\%$. Assume that the prevailing risk-free Treasury offers 3%.

KEY TERMS

APT, 292
arbitrage pricing theory, 292
certainty equivalence form, 282
certainty equivalent, 281
Fama-French factors, 295
growth firms, 295
ICAPM, 292
intertemporal CAPM, 292
value firms, 295

SOLVE NOW! SOLUTIONS

Q 9.48 This is a certainty equivalence question. Although it is not a gift per se, you cannot assume that \$10,000 is a fair market value, so that you can compute a rate of return of 1,900%—after all, it is your uncle trying to do something nice for you. There are four outcomes:

Prob:	1/4 Drop	1/4 No-Drop	1/4 No-Drop	1/4 No-Drop	Mean
Stock Market	−10%	+18%	+18%	+18%	11%
Ferrari	$200,000	$0	$0	$0	$50,000

Plug this into the formula and find $Cov(\tilde{P}, \tilde{r}_M) = 1/4 \cdot [\$150{,}000 \cdot (-21\%) + (-\$50{,}000) \cdot (7\%) + (-\$50{,}000) \cdot (7\%) + (-\$50{,}000) \cdot (7\%)] = -\$10{,}500$. We also need to determine the variance of the market. It is $Cov(\tilde{r}_M, \tilde{r}_M) = [(-21\%)^2 + (7\%)^2 + (7\%)^2 + (7\%)^2]/4 = 147\%\%$ (which incidentally comes to a standard deviation of 12% per annum—a bit low.) With the risk-free rate of 6%, lambda (λ) in Formula 9.2 is $(11\% - 6\%)/147\%\% \approx 3.4$. You can now use the certainty equivalence formula: The expected value of the Ferrari gift is $50,000. If it were a safe payoff, it would be worth $\$50{,}000/1.06 \approx \$47{,}169.81$. Because you get more if the rest of your portfolio goes down, the Ferrari gift is actually great insurance for you. You value it $3.4 \cdot (\$10{,}500)/1.06 \approx \$33{,}679.25$ above its risk-free equivalent of $47,169.81: This Ferrari is therefore worth $80,849.06. You have to pay $10,000 today, of course, so you have managed to secure a deal that is worth $70,849.06.

Q 9.49 First, compute the de-meaned cash flows:

Year	1999	2000	2001	2002	2003	2004	Average	Variance
S&P 500	+21.4%	−5.7%	−12.8%	−21.9%	+26.4%	+9.0%	+2.7%	373.4%%*
Cash Flows	+$2,864	+$1,666	−$1,040	+$52	+$1,478	−$962	+$676	
De-meaned S&P 500	+18.7%	−8.4%	−15.5%	−24.6%	+23.7%	+6.3%	0%	
De-meaned Cash Flows	+$2,188	+$990	−$1,716	+$624	+$802	−$1,638	$0	
Cross-Product	$408.36	−$83.46	$266.60	$153.79	$189.73	−$102.67	$166.47*	

The asterisk reminds you that I divided both the average cross-product and the variance by 5 rather than 6 to reflect the fact that this is a sample and not the population. The cash flow beta is about $\$166.47/373.4\%\% \approx \$4{,}458.19$. We now have the inputs to use our formula:

$$\text{PV} \approx \frac{\$676}{1+3\%} - \left[\frac{4\%}{1+3\%}\right] \cdot \$4{,}458.19 \approx \$657 - \$173 \approx \$484$$

$$= \frac{\mathcal{E}(\tilde{P})}{1+r_F} - \left[\frac{\mathcal{E}(\tilde{r}_M) - r_F}{1+r_F}\right] \cdot b_{\tilde{P},\tilde{r}_M}$$

This suggests a cost of capital of about $\mathcal{E}(C_{1\text{ year}})/P_0 - 1 \approx \$676/\$484 - 1 \approx 40\%$. It turns out that this firm was Sony. This cost-of-capital estimate seems far too high. This is probably because the cash flow beta of Sony was way too high in relation to the ordinary CAPM market beta of Sony. Our CEV calculations did not do well in assessing value, probably because Sony's cash flows were far more volatile than its value.

Q 9.50 Working off Table 9.2:

(a) The covariance between H and N is 78.75%%.
(b) The covariance between I and N is 81%%.
(c) The variance of N is 79.31%%. Actually, this number was in the table itself.
(d) The beta is the covariance divided by the variance: $\beta_{H,N} = 78.75\%\%/79.31\%\% \approx 0.993$.
(e) This is $\beta_{I,N} = 81\%\%/79.31\%\% \approx 1.021$.

Repeating the exercise for portfolio T instead of N: The covariance of T and H is 58.5%%, between T and I is 145.8%%, and between T and itself is 119.6%% (the variance). Thus, the beta of H with respect to T is $\beta_{H,T} = 58.5\%\%/119.6\%\% \approx 0.49$. The beta of I with respect to T is $\beta_{I,T} = 145.8\%\%/119.6\%\% \approx 1.22$. This confirms the market betas I claimed in the text.

Q 9.51 Recall the data from Table 9.2:

	♣	♦	♥	♠	Mean	Var
I	−6%	+12%	0%	18%	6%	90%%
H	−12%	+18%	+24%	+6%	9%	189%%

Now compute the beta of H and I with respect to portfolio H. The beta of H with respect to itself is 1. The beta of I with respect to H is $\beta_{I,H} = 45\%\%/90\%\% = 0.5$. For a CAPM formula to hold, you need $\mathcal{E}(\tilde{r}_H) = r_F + [\mathcal{E}(\tilde{r}_H) - r_F] \cdot \beta_{H,H} = 4\% + 5\% \cdot 1 = 9\%$. For H, the CAPM formula is okay. Now work I: $\mathcal{E}(\tilde{r}_I) = r_F + [\mathcal{E}(\tilde{r}_H) - r_F] \cdot \beta_{I,H} = 4\% + 5\% \cdot 0.5 = 6.5\%$. Aha! The CAPM-type relationship is violated for I. It should offer 6.5%, but it offers 6% in real life. Therefore, you should purchase less of it.

Q 9.52 The APT is almost like a multifactor version of the CAPM. Whereas in the CAPM, everything depends on one factor (that is, the rate of return on the stock market), in the APT there can be multiple factors (such as the rate of return on the stock market, the rate of return from investing in oil, and so on). Both models then say that assets that are more exposed to these risks have to offer higher expected rates of return. Unlike the CAPM, the APT does not necessarily assume that the rate of return on the stock market is one factor. It also does not assume that there is an optimal market portfolio, in which all investors should invest.

Q 9.53 The Fama-French-Momentum model suggests

$$\begin{aligned}\mathcal{E}(\tilde{r}_i) - r_F &= (1.3) \cdot \mathcal{E}(\text{XMKT}) + (0.1) \cdot \mathcal{E}(\text{UMD}) + (-1) \cdot \mathcal{E}(\text{HML}) + (-0.1) \cdot \mathcal{E}(\text{SMB}) \\ &\approx (1.3) \cdot 8.5\% + (0.1) \cdot 8.9\% + (-1) \cdot 4.6\% + (-0.1) \cdot 3.8\% \\ &\approx 6.96\% \approx 7\%\end{aligned}$$

This is a rate quoted *above* the risk-free rate. Thus, your appropriate cost of capital (hurdle rate) would be 3% + 7% = 10%.

PROBLEMS

The ▒▒ *indicates problems available in* myfinancelab

Q 9.54 Although you are a millionaire, keeping all your money in the market, you have managed to secure a great deal: If you give your even richer Uncle Vinny $20,000 today, he will help you buy a house, expected to be worth $1,000,000—if his business can afford it. He is a stockbroker by profession, so his business will have the money if the stock market increases, but not if it drops. For simplicity, assume that the stock market drops in 1 year out of every 4 years. When it does, it goes down by −10%; when it does not, it goes up by 18%. (Write it out as four separate possible state outcomes to make your life simpler.) The risk-free rate is 5%. What is your uncle's promise worth at market value?

Q 9.55 Your corporate division had the following net cash flows:

Year:	1999	2000	2001	2002
S&P 500	+21.4%	−5.7%	−12.8%	−21.9%
Cash Flows	+$2,000	$0	$0	$0

Year:	2003	2004	2005
S&P 500	+26.4%	+9.0%	+3.0%
Cash Flows	+$2,500	+$1,000	+$500

Assume that the risk-free rate is 1% per annum and the equity premium is 3%. Use the certainty equivalence concept to answer the following questions:

- What should be a reasonable value approximation for this corporate division?
- What should be the cost of capital for this corporate division?

Q 9.56 Confirm that the portfolio L that invests 50% in H and 50% in I is not mean-variance efficient. If the risk-free rate of return is 4%, confirm that the CAPM relationship does not hold for L.

Q 9.57 Outline the logic that leads to the CAPM. What is mathematics? What is economics?

Q 9.58 What are the APT factors?

Q 9.59 What are the Fama-French-Momentum factors?

Q 9.60 Assume that you ran a time-series regression with your project on the Fama-French factors and found the following:

$$\mathcal{E}(\tilde{r}_i) - r_F = (12\%) + (0.3) \cdot \text{XMKT} + (0.3) \cdot \text{UMD} + (-0.5) \cdot \text{HML} + (-0.5) \cdot \text{SMB}$$

If the risk-free rate is 4%, what would the Fama-French-Momentum model suggest you use as the hurdle rate for this project?

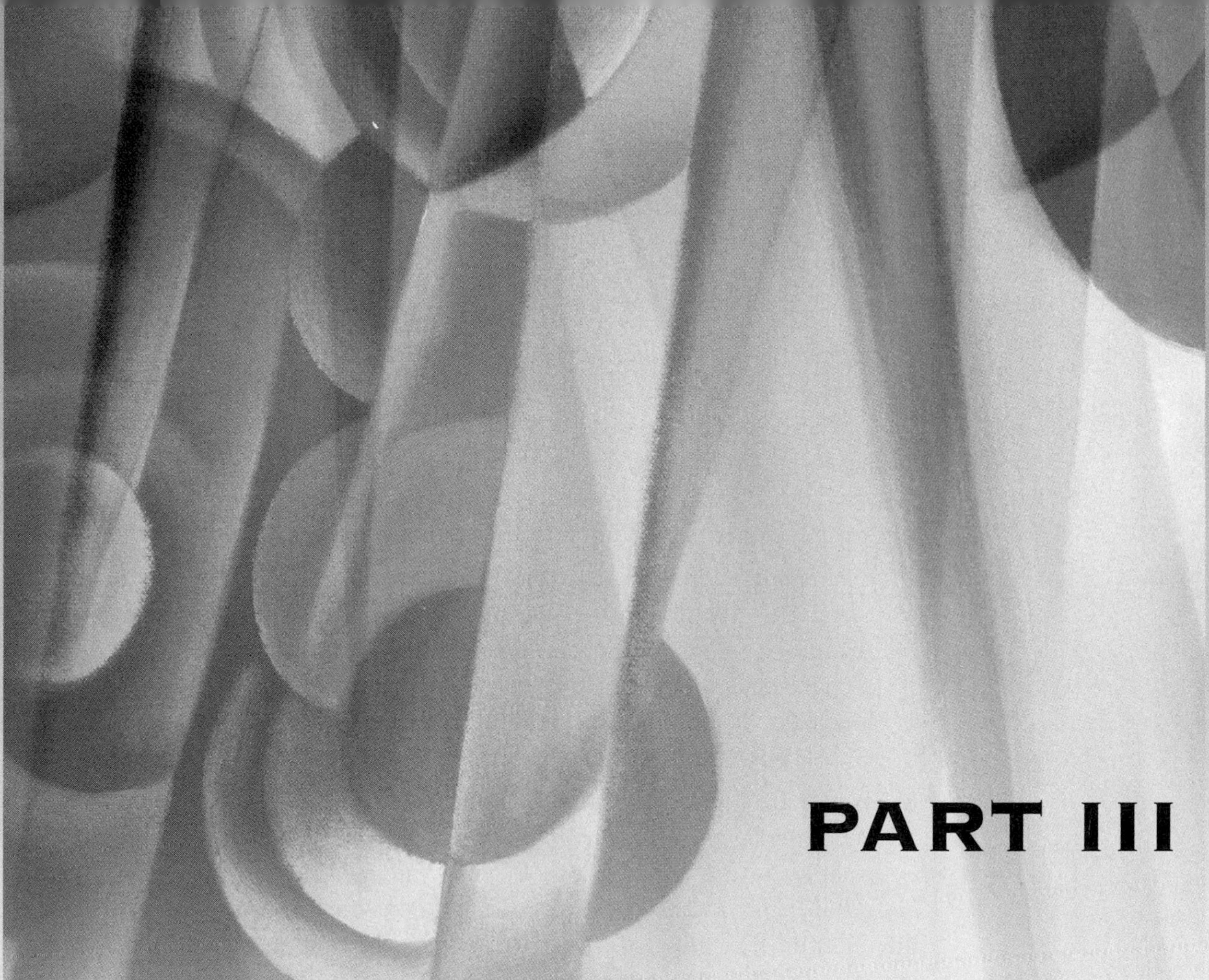

PART III

Value and Market Efficiency in an Imperfect Market

You now understand the theory of finance in perfect markets. It is precisely the four perfect market assumptions that have allowed modern finance to become the "science" that it is today. Every important concept of finance has been derived in this perfect markets context first. In fact, with only a few exceptions, most finance formulas used in the real world today are still based on the (false) assumption that the world is perfect!

Fortunately, many financial markets are close to perfect, so the distance between theory and practice in finance is often small. However, it is almost never zero. The real world is definitely dirtier than our perfect one, and you can't just close your eyes and wish you were still in Kansas. Thus, the chapters in this part explain how you can navigate the troubled waters of the real world.

WHAT YOU WANT TO LEARN IN THIS PART

- In Chapter 10, you will learn not only why the four perfect market assumptions are too good to be true, but also why they are so important. You will learn to think about what happens when individuals have different information, when financial markets are noncompetitive, and when investors or firms have to pay transaction costs and taxes. Sometimes you can adjust the perfect markets formulas explicitly to take market imperfections into account; sometimes you can only do so intuitively.

  Typical questions: What are typical transaction costs, and how do you work with them? How do taxes work? Why are capital gains better than ordinary income? If you have to pay 40% income taxes on interest receipts, the inflation rate is 2% per annum, and your investment promises 5% per annum, how much can you buy in goods tomorrow? Should you take this investment if you can earn 5% in taxable bonds and 3% in tax-exempt municipal bonds?

- In Chapter 11, you will learn about a concept that is not as strict as that of a perfect market: an efficient market. A market is said to be efficient if it uses all available information in the price setting. *All perfect markets are efficient (in equilibrium), but not all efficient markets are perfect.* Whether financial markets are efficient is the question that lies at the heart of "behavioral finance," a field of finance that asks whether individual investor irrationality—doubtlessly present—can be strong enough to influence financial market prices.

  Typical questions: Could it be that market efficiency is not absolute but comes in different degrees? What exactly are the disagreements between classical finance and behavioral finance? What processes can stock prices reasonably follow? Do stock prices follow random walks? What is the signal-to-noise ratio in the context of financial markets? What is an arbitrage? What should you think of market gurus? What can you learn from stock price reactions to events?

10

Market Imperfections

INFORMATION/OPINIONS, MARKET DEPTH, TRANSACTION COSTS, AND TAXES

So far, we have assumed no differences in opinions (and thus information), no transaction costs, no taxes, and a large market with many sellers and buyers—a "perfect market." Even when we covered uncertainty, risk, and the CAPM, we were still in the perfect market framework. In fact, most formulas in finance used in the real world today rely on the perfect markets assumptions. Without them, depending on the situation, they might be outright wrong.

Why is it that these perfect markets assumptions are so important? You will learn that it is because of what they have done for us: They have given us one unique, appropriate, expected rate of return—whether you want to borrow someone else's money to finance your projects or lend your money to someone else undertaking projects. Breaking these assumptions causes havoc in our models: Without a unique expected rate of return, project prices are no longer unique. Instead, they depend on the cash position of their owners. Without a unique price, what does "value" even mean in the first place?

Still, as wonderful as perfect markets are, they do not exist. They are conceptual, not real—although some financial markets come very close. You now have to leave this frictionless, utopian world and learn how to think about financial questions in "imperfect markets." Fortunately, many of your tools (and specifically NPV) will still work. But you need to apply them with a lot more caution and realize their limits.

10.1 CAUSES AND CONSEQUENCES OF IMPERFECT MARKETS

Without perfect markets, borrowing and lending rates are not equal.

So far, we have not distinguished between the cost of capital at which you can borrow money to finance your projects and the rate of return at which you can save money. In "perfect markets," these two rates are the same. Remarkably, the purpose of all four perfect markets assumptions is only to accomplish this one fact. It is the one fact on which everything else rests:

Perfect markets create an equality between borrowing and lending rates.

Without equal borrowing and lending rates, project market value is not unique.

The implications of what happens when this is not the case are far-reaching. If these rates are not equal, then you cannot move in and out of an investment as often as you like. More fundamentally, even the value of a project stops being unique. Instead, a project may be worth any number in a whole range of possible values. Indeed, the whole concept of one project value may become meaningless. Value might depend on who owns the project, what the tastes of the individuals' relatives are, or even what time of day it is. We cannot even claim any longer that the value of a project is its PV. But let's take this one step at a time.

SOLVE NOW!

Q 10.1 What does the assumption of a perfect market buy you that would not be satisfied in an imperfect market?

10.1A JUDGING MARKET PERFECTION FOR PEPSICO SHARES AND HOUSES

For PepsiCo shares, the perfect market assumptions are not perfectly true, but they are not too far from the truth.

Start by contemplating the four perfect markets assumptions for a stock like PepsiCo:

1. **No differences in opinion:** Recall that this assumption does not mean that there is no uncertainty, but that investors do not disagree about the uncertainty. Objective, rational traders with access to the same kind of information should come to similar conclusions about PepsiCo's value. They should agree on the distribution of prices that PepsiCo shares will likely sell at tomorrow, which in turn defines share value today. For the most part, it is unlikely that rational traders would have great disagreement about the value of PepsiCo shares—they should realize that it is not very likely that they can predict the price of PepsiCo much better than the market. Any disagreements would likely be minor. Of course, if some traders have insider information, then they could predict tomorrow's price better, and the perfect market would be no more—but trading on inside information is illegal.
2. **Infinitely many investors and firms:** On a normal single day in 2006, around $250 million worth of PepsiCo shares changed hands. This is a lot of buyers and sellers. Thus, PepsiCo shares appear to trade in a competitive market, in which no single buyer or seller influences the price. There are lots of potential buyers willing to purchase the shares for the same price (or maybe just a tiny bit less), and lots of potential sellers willing to sell the shares for the same price (or maybe just a tiny bit more).
3. **No transaction costs:** Trading PepsiCo shares does incur transaction costs, but these are modest. A typical total round-trip transaction cost spread for PepsiCo is about 5 cents on a $50 share price—10 basis points. An institutional trader may even be able to beat this. There are no searching costs for finding out the proper price of PepsiCo shares (it is posted by the NYSE), and there are very low costs to locating a buyer or seller.

4. **No taxes:** This may be the most problematic perfect market assumption in this context. Fortunately, we need this assumption of no taxes primarily for one purpose: The return to a seller owning PepsiCo shares should not be different from the same rate of return to a buyer. Here is what I mean.

   Consider an extreme example in which PepsiCo starts out at \$20 per share and happens to end up at \$80 per share 2 years later. Assume the capital gains tax rate is 20% and the risk-free discount rate is 5%. How much value is saved if you hold shares for 2 years versus if you sell them to me midway? If you keep the shares, the taxable capital gains would be on \$80 − \$20 = \$60. At a 20% capital gains tax rate, Uncle Sam would collect \$12. If you instead trade them to me at \$50 after the first year, the capital gains consequences would be on \$30 first for you (20% · \$30 = \$6), and then on \$30 at the end for me (\$6 again). This violates the perfect market assumption, because if you hold the shares for 2 years, the present value of the tax obligation at $\$12/1.05^2 \approx \$10.88$. If you sell them to me, it is $\$6/1.05 + \$6/1.05^2 \approx \$11.16$. Thus, shares are worth more if you hold them than if you trade them.

   But the difference in how we value shares is really only in regard to the interest on the interim taxation. It is only 28 cents on a gain of \$60. Moreover, this example is extreme not only in the 300% rate of return, but also in assuming a worst-case taxation scenario. This chapter later explains that many capital gains can be offset by capital losses and that investor tax timing discretion can further lower taxes. Furthermore, most shares are now held by institutions. Many of these are pension funds, which are entirely tax-exempt and therefore face no tax implications when trading.

In sum, the market for PepsiCo shares may indeed be reasonably close to perfect to allow you to use this as a first working assumption.

For real estate, the market is not perfect. Thus, there may not be a unique value.

Unfortunately, not every good is traded in a perfect market. For example, think about selling your house—a pertinent question for many in the real estate slump of 2008. What is its value? What if your house is in a very remote part of the country, if potential buyers are sporadic, if alternative houses with the same characteristics are rare, or if the government imposes much higher property taxes on new owners (as, e.g., California does)? Intuitively, the value of your house could now depend on the luck of the draw (how many potential buyers are in the vicinity and see the ad, whether a potential buyer wants to live in exactly this kind of house, and so on); your urgency to sell (depending perhaps on whether you have the luxury to turn down a lowball first offer); or whether you need to sell at all (as current owner, you may be better off enjoying low property taxes, so your house may be worth a lot more to you than to a potential buyer). The value of such a house can be difficult to determine because the market can be far from perfect—and the house value may not even be one unique number.

Use your judgment about market imperfections. Neither buyers nor sellers are assured of a fair price.

The range in which possible values lie depends on the degree to which you believe the market is not perfect. For example, if you know that taxes or transaction costs can represent at most 2–3% of the value of a project, then you know that even if value is not absolutely unique, it is pretty close to unique—possible values sit in a fairly tight range. On the other hand, if you believe that there are few potential buyers for your house, but that some of these potential buyers would purchase the house at much higher prices than others, then it depends on your financial situation as to whether you should accept or decline a buyer's lowball offer.

Many financial markets are not perfect, either.

Not all financial markets are close to perfect, either. Information differences, the unique power of large buyers or sellers in the market, transaction costs, or special taxes can sometimes play a role. For example, many corporate bonds are traded primarily over-the-counter. Just a small number of financial firms may make a market in them. If you want to buy or sell such a corporate bond, you must call their designated in-house desk trader. These traders are often your only market venue, and they will definitely try to gauge your expertise when negotiating a price with you. You could easily end up paying a lot more for a bond than what you could then sell it back for just 1 minute later.

➤ Over-the-counter, Section 7.2B, p. 192

To repeat—no market, financial or otherwise, is ever "perfectly perfect." For some financial instruments, it is very close, though.

IMPORTANT: For many financial securities—for example, for large publicly traded stocks—the assumption that the market is perfect is reasonable. For other financial securities and many nonfinancial goods, this assumption is less accurate.

SOLVE NOW!

Q 10.2 What is the difference between a perfect market and a competitive market?

Q 10.3 Does a perfect capital market exist in the real world? What is the use of the perfect markets concept?

10.1B PERFECT MARKET ASSUMPTIONS AND VIOLATIONS

The four perfect market assumptions, and how their failures can drive wedges between borrowing and lending rates.

Now think more rigorously about what happens when each of the perfect market assumptions is violated:

1. **No differences in opinion (information):** This assumption means that everyone interprets all uncertainty in the same way in a perfect market. How could this assumption be violated? Here is an example. If your bank believes that there is a 50% chance that you will go bankrupt and default, and you believe that there is only a 10% chance, then your bank will lend you money only if you pay a much higher interest rate than what you will think appropriate. You will consider your borrowing rate to be too high. Of course, this also breaks the equality of one fair rate at which you can borrow and lend. Your expected rate of return is now lower when you lend than when you borrow.

   To avoid this, our perfect markets assumptions include one that posits *everyone has the same information and agrees on what it means.*

2. **Infinitely many investors and firms:** This really means that the market is very "deep." By itself, the assumption of the presence of many buyers and sellers defines a **competitive market**—one in which no buyer or seller has any market power. If

buyers or sellers are heterogeneous, then this assumption must be slightly modified. It must be that you can easily find many of the most eager types of buyers and sellers. For example, if a project is worth more if it is owned or financed by a particular type—e.g., if a golf range is owned by a golf pro—then these golf pros would be the most eager potential buyers. This assumption then says that there must be a large number of golf pros.

How could this assumption be violated? If there is only one bank that you can do business with, then this bank will want to exploit its monopoly power. It will charge you a higher interest rate if you want to borrow money than it will pay you if you want to deposit money—and you will have no good alternative.

To avoid this, our perfect markets assumptions include one that posits *there are infinitely many buyers and sellers.*

3. **No transaction costs:** Transaction costs here are defined in a very broad sense, and they include indirect costs, such as your time and money to search for the best deal. In a perfect market, you can buy and sell without paying *any* such costs.

   How could this assumption be violated? If it costs $1,000 to process the paperwork involved in a loan, you will incur this cost only if you need to borrow, but not if you want to save. Similarly, if it costs you 3 days of work to find the appropriate lender, it means that you will effectively have to pay more than just the borrowing rate. You will have to factor in your 3 days as a cost. Any such transaction costs make your effective borrowing interest rate higher than your effective savings interest rate.

   To avoid this, our perfect markets assumptions include one that posits *there are zero transaction costs.*

4. **No taxes:** More accurately, this means that there is no distorting government interference (such as government regulation), and that there are no tax advantages or disadvantages to buying or selling securities. Specifically, neither trading of the good nor its possession by one particular owner should change the total tax consequences.

   How could this assumption be violated? If you have to pay taxes on interest earned, but cannot deduct taxes on interest paid, your de facto savings rate will be lower than your borrowing rate. Similarly, if the total taxes paid are higher when shares one traded, they could be worth more if they were never traded to begin with. Another violation could be a government regulation requiring you to file lengthy legal documents with the SEC every time you have to sneeze—well, every time you have to execute some transaction.

   To avoid this, our perfect markets assumptions include one that posits *there are no taxes.*

These four assumptions are actually "overkill," but if they hold, you are safe. Thinking about them helps you judge how close to perfect a given market actually is. However, the real usefulness of the perfect market is *not* that you should believe that it exists in the real world. Instead, its usefulness is that it gives you some simple first-order methods and tools that help you value goods. If these assumptions do not hold, borrowing and lending rates may or may not be similar enough to allow us to still use perfect market tools or variations thereon. (Almost all common finance formulas hope this is the case.)

Let's hope the imperfections are not extreme—if they are too extreme, the entire market may even disappear.

If these assumptions are far from the situation in the real world, nothing will work anymore. In fact, markets may cease to function entirely. For example, if you fear that other parties you would be transacting with are *much* better informed than you are, you could only lose—the other party would take full advantage of you, selling to you only if the price is too high. If you can avoid it, you should never trade. Such a market collapse may have happened in the market for corporate bonds *for retail investors*. These bonds are traded over-the-counter, which means that the Wall Street trader on the other side of the phone tries to gauge how much an ordinary retail investor actually knows about the correct value of these bonds. As a result, retail investors are so systematically disadvantaged that it makes no sense for them to buy corporate bonds directly. Instead, they are better off buying bond funds, where someone else who does not suffer a knowledge disadvantage (a bond mutual fund) buys and sells corporate bonds on their behalves. Similarly, if transaction costs are extremely high, there may be no market in which anyone could profitably buy or sell. Fortunately, such total market collapses tend to occur only if the perfect market violations are large. With modest violations, the benefits of transacting tend to outweigh the costs to buyers and sellers, and so markets can still function. This is the kind of situation this chapter considers.

SOLVE NOW!

Q 10.4 Without looking back, what are the perfect market assumptions?

10.1C AMBIGUOUS VALUE IN IMPERFECT MARKETS

If savings and investment interest rates differ, the project's value (NPV) can depend on how wealthy the owner is—more generally, on *who* the owner is.

➤ Investment consumption separation, Section 4.1A, p. 68

Why is an inequality between borrowing and lending rates so problematic? It is because it breaks the "unique value aspect" of projects. In a perfect market, project value depends *only* on the project, and not on you personally or on your cash position. You can think of this as a clean separation between the concepts of ownership and value. It also leads to the "separation of investments and financing decisions." Project owners can make investment choices based on the quality of the projects themselves, not based on their personal wealth or financing options. Indeed, the NPV formula does not have an input for your identity or current wealth—its only inputs are the project's cash flows and the rate of return on alternative investments.

An example of how project value can depend on your wealth. Consequently, a project's value may no longer be a single dollar figure, but any figure within a dollar range.

For example, assume that you can lend (invest cash) and borrow money at the same 4% in a perfect market. What is the net present value of a project that invests \$1,000 today and returns \$1,050 next period? It is \$9.62. It does not depend on whether you have money or not. If you do not have the \$1,000 today, you borrow \$1,009.62, invest \$1,000, and hand the \$1,050 to the lender next year. But if the financial market is imperfect and the borrowing and lending rates are *not* the same, then the value of the project does depend on you, because it depends on your cash holdings. For example, assume that you can lend money (invest cash) at 3% and borrow money (receive cash) at 7%. What is the net present value of a project that invests \$1,000 today and returns \$1,050 next period?

- If you have \$1,000 and your alternative is to invest your money in the bank, you will only get \$1,030 from the bank. You should take the project rather than invest in the bank so that you can earn \$20 more.
- If you do not have the \$1,000, you will have to borrow \$1,000 from the bank to receive \$1,050 from the project. But because you will have to pay the bank \$1,070, you will lose \$20 net. You should not take the project.

The value of the project and your best decision whether to take the project or not now depends on how much cash you have. Consequently, the separation between your project choice and your financial position breaks down. Having to take your current cash holdings into account when making investment choices makes capital budgeting decisions more difficult. In this example, it is fairly easy: If you have a lot of wealth, you should take the project. If you have no cash, you should not take it. But think about projects that have cash inflows and outflows in the future and how your decisions could interact with your own wealth positions in the future. This can become vexingly difficult. You can also see that the project value is no longer unique in imperfect markets. In our example, it could be anything between +\$19.42 (\$1,050 discounted at 3%) and −\$18.69 (\$1,050 discounted at 7%). The same ambiguity applies to ownership. Your capital budgeting decision can be different when you already own the project versus when you are just contemplating purchasing it. Again, your identity matters to the value of the project.

IMPORTANT: If the market is not perfect, the separation of ownership and value breaks down. Therefore, project value is no longer unique. It can depend on who owns the project.

Do You Always Get What You Pay For?

Reflect a little on the insight that projects may not have unique values. You surely have heard the saying that "it's only worth what people are willing to pay for it" and the claim that some item "is worth much more than it is being sold for." Which is correct? Are there any good deals? The answer is that both are correct and neither is correct. The first claim is really meaningful only to the extent that markets are *perfect*: If a market is perfect, items are indeed worth exactly what buyers are willing to pay for them. The second claim is meaningful only to the extent that markets are *imperfect*: If a market is imperfect, items have no unique value. Different people can place different values on the item, and some third party may consider an item worth much more than what it was sold for.

Are there any good deals? Maybe—but how would one even define a good deal in an imperfect market?

In sum, when someone claims that a stock or firm is really worth more than he or she is selling it for, there are only a small number of explanations:

Salespeople may distort the truth and claim great deals.

1. There may be pure kindheartedness toward any buyer, or a desire by a seller to lose wealth. Not very likely.
2. The seller may not have access to a perfect market to sell the goods. This may make the seller accept a low amount of money for the good, so depending on how you look at it, the good may be sold for more or less than the seller thinks it is worth.

3. The market is perfect and the seller may be committing a conceptual mistake. The good is worth neither more nor less than what it is being sold for—it is worth exactly how much it is being sold for.
4. The seller may be lying and is using this claim as a sales tactic.

SOLVE NOW!

Q 10.5 Your borrowing rate is 10% per year. Your lending rate is 4% per year. Your project costs $1,000 and will have a rate of return of 8%. Assume you have $900 to invest.

(a) Should you take the project?

(b) You can think of the $900 as the amount of money that you are not consuming. Say your wealth is $2,000, but in the previous question, you wanted to consume $1,100. Could you still consume this much and take the project? How much could you consume and still want to take the project?

10.1D SOCIAL VALUE AND SURPLUS

Buyers get what they pay for in a perfect market. They can "trust" market prices.

Perfect markets are not just privately useful but are also socially useful. If a market is perfect, buyers and sellers need not worry that one deal is better than another—that buying is better than selling, or vice versa. For example, consider gasoline and imagine that you do not yet know when and where on your road trip you will need to pump more gas. Unlike shares of stock, gas is not the same good everywhere: Gas in one location can be more valuable than gas in another location (as anyone who has ever run out of gas can testify). But in populated areas, the market for gasoline is pretty competitive and close to perfect—there are many buyers (drivers) and sellers (gas stations). This makes it very likely that the first gas station you see will have a reasonably fair price. If you drive by the first gas station and it advertises a price of $3 per gallon, it is unlikely that you will find another gas station offering the same gas for $2 per gallon or $4 per gallon within a couple of miles. Chances are that "the price is fair," or this particular gas station would probably have disappeared by now. (The same applies, of course, in many financial markets, such as those for large company stocks, Treasury bonds, or certain types of mortgages.) As long as the market is very competitive—or better yet, perfect—most deals are likely to be fair deals.

Perfect markets do not mean most buyers and sellers don't care: Perfect markets offer (maximum) surplus for average buyers and sellers.

There is an important conceptual twist here: If you are paying what an item is worth, it does not necessarily mean that you are paying what you *personally* value the good at. For example, if you are running out of gas and you are bad at pushing a 2-ton vehicle, you might very well be willing to pay $10 per gallon—but fortunately, all you need to pay in a competitive market is the market price. The difference between what you personally value a good for and what you pay for it is called your "surplus." Although everyone is paying what the good is worth in a perfect market, most buyers and sellers can come away being better off—only the marginal buyer and seller are indifferent.

SOLVE NOW!

Q 10.6 Evaluate the following statement: "In a perfect market, no one is getting a good deal. Thus, it would not matter from a social perspective if this market were not available."

10.2 OPINIONS, DISAGREEMENTS, AND INSIDER INFORMATION

The rest of this chapter will hone in on the four individual imperfections.

You are now ready to learn how to handle violations of each perfect market assumption, one by one. You need to learn both how to judge the degree to which markets are imperfect and how to deal with them as a real-world investor or manager. (Even if there is no unique value, you can still learn how to think about maximizing your own wealth.) The remainder of the chapter thus explores the extent of market imperfections, what can mitigate them, and how you should work with them.

Information (opinions) is first.

We begin with the effects of disagreements, the violation of the first perfect market assumption that everyone has the same opinion. Like the other assumptions, this works well in some situations and poorly in others.

10.2A EXPECTED RETURN DIFFERENCES OR PROMISED RETURN DIFFERENCES?

Different opinions can lead to disagreements about what the project will pay.

The assumption of no disagreement is only relevant in a world of uncertainty—it would be absurd to believe that differences in opinion could exist if there were no uncertainty. So what happens if the lender and borrower have different information or different judgments about the same information? Most prominently, they could disagree about the default risk. For example, if you have no credit history, then a lender who does not know you might be especially afraid of not receiving promised repayments from you—from the perspective of such a lender, you would be extremely high-risk. Your lender might estimate your appropriate default probability to be 30% and thus may demand an appropriate default premium from you of, say, 10%—an interest rate similar to what credit card vendors are charging. On the other hand, *you* may know that you will indeed return the lender's money, because you know that you will work hard and that you will have the money for sure. In your opinion, a fair and appropriate default premium should therefore be 0%.

Expected rates of return for borrowing and lending now become different.

When your potential lender and you have different opinions, you will face different expected interest rates depending on whether you want to save or borrow. You can use your knowledge from Chapter 6 to work an example to understand the difference between a perfect and an imperfect market scenario.

Do not confuse different *promised* borrowing/lending rates in perfect markets . . .

Perfect Markets: Assume that the bank and you agree that you have a 20% probability of default, in which case you will not repay anything. For simplicity, assume risk neutrality and that the appropriate interest rate is 5%. Solving $80\% \cdot r + 20\% \cdot (-100\%) = 5\%$ for the interest rate that you would have to promise yields $r = 31.25\%$. This gives the bank an expected rate of return of 5%. In contrast, the bank is government insured, so if you deposit your money with it, it would be default free.

	Promised	Expected
Your Savings Rate	5%	5%
Your Borrowing Rate	31.25%	5%

➤ Credit spreads, Section 6.2C, p. 147

Although your quoted interest rate is higher by the credit spread, if you want to borrow your cost of capital is still the same 5% either way.

. . . with different *expected* borrowing/lending rates in imperfect markets.

Imperfect Markets: Now assume that the bank and you disagree about your default probability. The bank believes that it is 30%—it could be that it has experienced such a default rate for borrowers who seemed to look similar from the perspective of your bank. In contrast, you believe that your default probability is 10%. The bank will therefore quote you an interest rate of $70\% \cdot r + 30\% \cdot (-100\%) = 5\% \Longrightarrow r = 50\%$. Alas, you believe that the expected rate of return at the 50% quoted interest rate is $90\% \cdot 50\% + 10\% \cdot (-100\%) = 35\%$.

	Promised	Expected
Your Savings Rate	5%	5%
Your Borrowing Rate	50% from the bank's perspective	5%
Your Borrowing Rate	50% from your perspective	35%

The disagreements (information differences) are now causing differences in *expected* returns. The borrowing and lending *expected* rates of return are no longer the same. If the bank is wrong, your cost of capital now depends on whether you want to borrow or lend. And even if the bank is right, from your wrong perspective, you are still facing different borrowing and lending rates.

IMPORTANT:

- The fact that credit spreads reflect a default premium—a difference between the *promised* rate of return and the *expected* rate of return—is not a market imperfection.
- The fact that credit spreads reflect differences in opinion between borrower and lender—a difference about the two assessed *expected* rates of return—is a market imperfection.

SOLVE NOW!

Q 10.7 Can there be a difference in the borrowing and lending rates quoted by the bank in perfect markets?

Q 10.8 "If the world is risk neutral and the market is perfect, then the promised and expected rates of return may be different, but the expected rate of return on all loans should be equal." Evaluate.

Q 10.9 A bond will pay off \$100 with probability 99%, and nothing with probability 1% next year. The equivalent appropriate expected rate of return for risk-free bonds is 5%.

(a) What is an appropriate promised yield on this bond today?
(b) The borrower believes the probability of payoff is 100%. How much money does he believe he has to overpay today?

10.2B COVENANTS, COLLATERAL, AND CREDIT RATING AGENCIES

Even when borrowers would love to convince their lenders, they may not be able to.

If you are an entrepreneur who wants to start a company, what can you do to reduce your cost of capital? The answer is that it is in your interest to disclose to the lender all the information you can—provided you are the type of entrepreneur who is likely to pay back the loan. You want to reduce the lender's doubt about future repayment. Unfortunately, this can be very difficult. The lender can neither peer into your brain nor give you a good lie detector test. Even after you have done everything possible to reduce the lender's doubts about you (provided your credit history, collateral, and so on), there will still be some residual information differences—they are just a fact of life. To the extent that you can reduce such information differences, your firm will be able to enjoy lower costs of capital. Also, if you as a borrower fail to give your best to convince the lender of your quality, then the lender should assume that you are not an average company but instead the very worst—or else you would have tried to communicate as much as possible.

Good borrowers want to convey credibly to the lender how good they are.

There are at least three important mechanisms that have evolved to alleviate such information differences. The first mechanism is **covenants**, which are contractual agreements that specify up front what a debtor must do to maintain credit. They can include such requirements as the maintenance of insurance or a minimum corporate value. The second mechanism is **collateral**, which are assets that the creditor can repossess if payments are not made—anything that inflicts pain on the debtor will do. For example, if defaulting debtors were thrown into debtors' prison (as they often were until the nineteenth century), the promise to repay would be more credible and lenders would be more inclined to provide funding at lower rates. Of course, for the unlucky few who just happened to suffer incredibly bad luck ex-post, debtors' prison had some definite drawbacks.

Credit rating agencies help lenders estimate the probability of borrower default.

The third mechanism to alleviate repayment uncertainty is a credit rating, which is a history of past payments to help assess the probability of future default. This is why you need to give your Social Security number if you want to take out a substantial personal loan—the lender will check up on you. The same is true for large corporations. It may be easier to judge corporate default risk for large companies than personal default risk, but it is still not easy and it costs both time and money. You already learned about these credit ratings in Section 6.2D.

➤ Credit ratings, Section 6.2D, p. 148

ANECDOTE Sumerian Debt Contracts

Among the earliest known collateralized debt contracts is a tablet from Sumeria (Mesopotamia), which promised delivery of silver and gave as security the son of the borrower. (The tablet can be viewed at www.museumofmoney.org/babylon/index.html.) Such contracts are illegal today, but de facto "debt slavery" for debts not repaid is still common in many countries, according to the September 2003 issue of *National Geographic*.

Incidentally, bond credit ratings have been historically useless for stock trading strategies.

Unfortunately, although bond rating agencies update their ratings if the condition of the firm changes, the empirical evidence suggests that these bond ratings are not very good in helping an investor earn superior rates of return. In fact, the ratings seem to respond more to drops in the value of the underlying bonds than vice versa. The bond rating agencies seem to be more reactive than proactive. (The low quality of debt ratings has also played a role in the credit crisis of 2008. Not surprisingly, it has become an important political issue how one might induce the ratings' providers to improve their products.)

Let me close with a philosophical observation: Financial markets are truly amazing. People who would never lend their neighbors a few thousand dollars (fearing that they would not pay it back) have no second thoughts about lending total strangers in anonymous markets their entire lives' savings. It is the combination of the governance of repayments and risk-spreading that has allowed financial markets to develop even in the presence of great uncertainty.

SOLVE NOW!

Q 10.10 What mechanisms can borrowers use to assure lenders? If providing this information is not legally required, will they still volunteer to do so?

10.3 MARKET DEPTH AND TRANSACTION COSTS

The assumption "no market power" is straightforward.

Our second perfect market assumption states that markets are very deep, consisting of many buyers and sellers. If there is only one lender, this lender will have market power over you. Of course, she will exploit her power by charging you a higher borrowing rate and offering you a lower deposit interest rate. Such an extreme form of market power is called a monopoly, but there are many milder forms of such power, too. For example, if you are already shopping in a grocery store, this store has a degree of market power over you. Even if the milk is 3 cents more expensive than in another store, you will still buy the milk where you are. Or say there is only one ATM close to you. In principle, you could get capital from any number of banks, but locally there is really only this one provider. Fortunately, such uniqueness of capital provision is rarely an important issue in the United States for corporations, especially large ones.

Transaction costs are this section's main topic.

So let's move on to the third perfect markets assumption: the role of transaction costs. Transaction costs drive a wedge between borrowing and lending rates. For example, if it is difficult and costly to administer loans, an investor must charge you a higher borrowing rate than deposit rate just to break even. This is the subject of this section, in which you will learn how corporations and individuals should handle transaction costs.

10.3A TYPICAL COSTS WHEN TRADING REAL GOODS—REAL ESTATE

Real estate is an important market in itself. How perfect is it?

When you engage in transactions—that is, purchases or sales—you face costs to facilitate them. One way to think about the magnitude of transaction costs is to compute how much is lost if you decided that you have made a mistake the instant after a purchase, which you now want to undo by reselling. Real estate—most people's biggest asset—is a perfect example to illustrate transaction costs. What does selling or buying a house really cost?

ANECDOTE Real Estate Agents: Who Works for Whom?

Real estate agents are conflicted. If they sell sooner, they can spend their time focusing on other properties. Thus, the typical seller's agent will try to get the seller to reduce the price in order to make a quicker sale. Similarly, the buyer's agent will try to get the buyer to increase the offer. In a financial sense, the buyer's agent is working on behalf of the seller, and the seller's agent is working on behalf of the buyer. Interestingly, Steve Levitt of *Freakonomics* fame found that when agents sell their own houses, their homes tend to stay on the market for about 10 days longer and sell for about 2% more. *Source:* Steve Levitt, University of Chicago.

Direct transaction costs: a transfer of money.

Direct costs such as brokerage commissions: Housing transaction costs are so high and so important that they are worth a digression. In the United States, if a house is sold, the seller's broker typically receives 6% of the value of the house as commission (and splits this commission with the buyer's agent). Thus, if a real estate agent sells your house for $300,000, her commission is $18,000. Put differently, without an agent, the buyer and seller could have split the $18,000 between themselves.

Think of transactions in "round-trip" form.

Although only the seller pays the broker's cost, it makes sense to think of transaction costs in terms of **round-trip costs**—how much worse off you are if you buy and then immediately sell. You would be mistaken if you thought that when you buy a house, you have not incurred any transaction costs because the seller had to pay them—you have incurred an implicit transaction cost in the future when you need to resell your investment. Of course, you usually do not immediately sell assets, so you should not forget about the timing of your future selling transaction costs in your NPV calculations.

House transaction costs are calculated based on the whole house, not based on your levered slice.

If you borrow to finance the investment, transaction costs may be higher than you think. The real estate agent earns 6% of the value of the house, not 6% of the amount of money you put into the house. On a house purchase of $500,000, the typical loan is 80% of the purchase price, or $400,000, leaving you to put in $100,000 in equity. Selling the house the day after the purchase reduces your wealth of $100,000 by the commission of $30,000—for an investment rate of return of −30%. This is not a risk component; it is a pure and certain transaction cost.

Let's add some price volatility.

How good is your purchase if the house price decreases or increases by 10%? If house prices decline by 10% (or if you overpaid by 10%), the house can only be resold for $450,000, which leaves $423,000 after agent commissions. As the house owner, you are left with $23,000 on a $100,000 investment. A 10% decline in real estate values has reduced your net worth by 77%! In comparison, a 10% increase in real estate values increases the value of the house to $550,000, which means that $517,000 is left after real estate commissions. Your rate of return for the same up movement would thus be only 17%. If a 10% increase and a 10% decrease are equally likely, your instant expected loss is 30%!

Other direct costs.

In addition to direct agent commissions, there are also many other direct transaction costs. These can range from advertising, to insurance company payments, to house inspectors, to the local land registry, to postage—all of which cost the parties money.

Indirect transaction costs are the loss of other opportunities.

Indirect costs such as opportunity costs: Then there is the seller's and buyer's time required to learn as much as possible about the value of the house, and the effort involved to help the agent sell the house. These may be significant costs, even if they involve no cash outlay. If the house cannot be sold immediately but stays empty for a while, the forgone rent is part of the transaction costs. The implicit cost of not having the house put to its best alternative use is called an **opportunity cost**—the cost of forgoing the next-best choice. Opportunity costs are just as real as direct cash costs.

10.3B TYPICAL COSTS WHEN TRADING FINANCIAL GOODS—STOCKS

Stock transactions also incur direct and indirect costs.

Transactions in financial markets also incur transaction costs. If an investor wants to buy or sell shares, the broker charges a fee, as does the stock exchange that facilitates the transaction. In addition, investors have to consider their time to communicate with the broker to initiate the purchase or sale of a stock as an opportunity cost.

The typical direct transaction costs for stocks are much, much lower.

Direct costs such as brokerage and market maker commissions: Still, the transaction costs for selling financial instruments are much lower than they are for most other goods. Let's look at a few reasons why. First, even if you want to buy (or sell) $1 million worth of stock, some Internet brokers now charge as little as $10 per transaction. Your round-trip transaction, which is a buy and a sale, costs only $20 in broker's commission. In addition, you have to pay the **spread** (the difference between the bid price and the ask price) to the stock exchange. For example, a large company stock like PepsiCo may have a publicly posted price of $50 per share. But you can neither buy nor sell at $50. Instead, the $50 is really just the average of two prices: the **bid price** of $49.92, at which another investor or the exchange's market maker is currently willing to buy shares and the **ask price** of $50.08, at which another investor or the exchange's market maker is currently willing to sell shares. Therefore, you can (probably) purchase shares at $50.08 and sell them at $49.92, a loss of "only" 16 cents, which amounts to round-trip transaction costs of $(\$49.92 - \$50.08)/\$50.08 \approx -0.32\%$. (Typical market spreads for PepsiCo shares are even lower.) You can compute the total costs of buying and selling 20,000 shares ($1,000,000 worth) of PepsiCo stock as follows:

Financial Round-Trip Transaction

Purchase 20,000 Shares	Pay $\$50.08 \cdot 20{,}000 = \$1{,}001{,}600$	
Add Broker Commission	+ $10	= $1,001,610
Sell 20,000 Shares	Receive $\$49.92 \cdot 20{,}000 = \$998{,}400$	
Subtract Broker Commission	− $10	= $998,390
	Net Round-Trip Transaction Costs	$3,220

This is not *exactly* correct, though, because the bid and ask prices that the stock exchanges post are only valid for 100 shares. Moreover, some transactions can occur inside the bid-ask spread, but for most large round-trip orders, chances are that you may have to pay more than $50.08 or receive less than $49.92. So 0.32% is probably a bit too small. (In fact, if your trade is large enough, you may even move the publicly posted exchange price away from $50!) Your buy order may have to pay $50.20, and your sell may only get you $49.85. In real life, the true round-trip transaction cost on a $1 million position in PepsiCo shares may be on the order of magnitude of 50 basis points.

An example of how stunningly low stock transaction costs can be.

An example of how low transaction costs in stock can be is illustrated by an extremely large trade in a very liquid security that occurred on Thursday, November 30, 2006, at 12:12pm. Kirk Kerkorian, a billionaire investor, sold 5% of GM (a block of

TABLE 10.1 COMPARISON OF TRANSACTION COSTS ON STOCKS AND REAL ESTATE

Cost Type	Explanation	Real Estate (House)	Financial Security (Stock)
Direct	Typical round-trip commission, etc.	≥6%	0–1%
Search/Research	Time to determine fair price	High	Zero
Search/Liquidity	Time waiting to find buyer	Variable	Zero

28 million shares) at $29.25 per share (or about $820 million)—almost to the penny for the price that GM shares were trading at on the NYSE. Upon receiving the news, the GM stock price dropped to $28.49—but within 1 hour, it had recovered and even reached $29.50. Don't you find it remarkable how the sale of even very large blocks of shares seems to barely move the stock price?

The typical indirect transaction costs (opportunity costs) for stocks are also very low.

Indirect costs such as opportunity costs: Investors do not need to spend a lot of time to find out the latest price of the stock: It is instantly available from many sources (e.g., from Yahoo! *Finance*). The information research costs are very low: Unlike a house, the value of a stock is immediately known. Finally, upon demand, a buyer can be found practically instantaneously, so search and waiting costs are also very low. In contrast, recall the often multimonth waiting periods if you want to sell your house.

COMPARING STOCK TRANSACTION COSTS TO HOUSING TRANSACTION COSTS

Compared to other economic assets . . .

Let's compare the transaction costs in buying and selling financial securities to those of a house. Aside from the direct real estate broker fees of 6% (for the $100,000 equity investment in the $500,000 house, this comes to $30,000 for a round-trip transaction), you must add the other fees and waiting time. Chances are that you will be in for other transaction costs—say, another $10,000. And houses are just one example: Many transactions of physical goods or labor services (but not all) can incur similarly high transaction costs.

. . . financial securities have such low transaction costs that they can be assumed to be almost zero for buy-and-hold investors.

In contrast, if you want to buy or sell 100 shares in, say, Microsoft stock, your transaction costs are relatively low. Because there are many buyers and many sellers, financial transaction costs are comparably tiny. Even for a $100,000 equity investment in a medium-sized firm's stock, the transaction costs are typically only about $300–$500. Assuming a perfect market for trading large stocks may not be a perfectly correct assumption, but it is not far off. It certainly is convenient to assume that financial transaction costs are zero. For an individual buying and selling ordinary stocks only rarely (a **buy-and-hold** investor), a zero-transaction-cost assumption is often quite reasonable. But if you are a **day trader**—someone who buys and sells stocks daily—our perfect market assumption would be inappropriate.

SOLVE NOW!

Q 10.11 What would you guess the transaction costs to be for a round-trip transaction of $10,000 worth of shares in Dell Computer? Describe in percentage and in absolute terms.

Q 10.12 List important transaction cost components, both direct and indirect.

10.3C TRANSACTION COSTS IN RETURNS AND NET PRESENT VALUES

As an investor, you usually care about rates of return *after* all transaction costs have been taken into account, not about pre-transaction-cost rates of return from quoted prices. Let's work out how you should take these transaction costs on both sides (buy and sell) into account.

Rates of return: Work with after-transaction-cost rates.

Return to our housing example. If you purchase a house for \$1,000,000 and you sell it to the next buyer at \$1,100,000 through a broker, your rate of return is not 10%. At selling time, the broker charges you a 6% commission. There are also some other costs that reduce the amount of money you receive, not to mention your many opportunity costs. Say these costs amount to \$70,000 in total. In addition, even when you purchased the house, you most likely had to pay some extra costs (such as an escrow transfer fee) above and beyond the \$1,000,000—say, \$5,000. Your rate of return would therefore not be \$1,100,000/\$1,000,000 − 1 = 10%, but only

$$r = \frac{(\$1{,}100{,}000 - \$70{,}000) - (\$1{,}000{,}000 + \$5{,}000)}{(\$1{,}000{,}000 + \$5{,}000)} \approx 2.5\%$$

$$\text{Rate of Return} = \frac{\begin{matrix}\text{Dollars Returned} \\ \text{after Transaction Costs}\end{matrix} - \begin{matrix}\text{Dollars Invested} \\ \text{after Transaction Costs}\end{matrix}}{\text{Dollars Invested after Transaction Costs}}$$

Note how the \$5,000 must be added to, not subtracted from, the price you originally paid. The price you paid was ultimately higher than \$1,000,000. The \$5,000 works against you. (Incidentally, in order to make their returns look more appealing, many professional fund managers quote their investors' rates of return before taking their own fees (transaction costs) into account. They add a footnote at the bottom that satisfies the lawyers so that you cannot sue the fund for having been misled—you are supposed to know how to adjust the returns to take these transaction costs into account.)

Net present value: Work with after-transaction-cost cash flows *and* with after-transaction opportunity costs of capital.

How do you take care of transaction costs in present value calculations? This is relatively straightforward. In the example, you put in \$1,005,000 and receive \$1,030,000—say, after 1 year:

$$\text{NPV} = -\$1{,}005{,}000 + \frac{\$1{,}030{,}000}{1 + \text{ Opportunity Cost of Capital}}$$

The only thing you must still take care of is to quote your opportunity cost of capital also in after-transaction cost terms. You may not be able to get a 10% rate of return in comparable investments either, because you may also be required to pay a transaction cost on them. In this case, assume that your alternative investment with equal characteristics in the financial markets (not the housing markets) would earn an 8% per year rate of return, but with a 50-basis-point transaction cost. Your project would then have an appropriate NPV of

$$\text{NPV} = -\$1{,}005{,}000 + \frac{\$1{,}030{,}000}{1.075} \approx -\$46{,}860$$

SOLVE NOW!

Q 10.13 Compute your after-transaction-costs rate of return on purchasing a house for $1,000,000 if you have to pay 0.5% transaction fees up front and pay a 6% broker's commission (plus 2% in waiting costs) at the end of 1 year. Assume a $4,000/month effective dividend of enjoying living in the house. Assume that your opportunity cost of capital (not the bank quoted interest rate) is 7% per year. At what rate of capital appreciation would the NPV be zero if you resold the house after 1 year?

10.3D THE VALUE OF LIQUIDITY

Anticipating future transaction costs, buyers demand a higher rate of return for more illiquid investments.

When *future* transaction costs influence your up front willingness to purchase an asset, proper pricing gets even more interesting and complex. You might not want to purchase a house even if you *expect* to recoup your transaction costs, because you dislike the fact that you do not know whether it will be easy or hard to resell. After all, if you purchase a stock or bond instead, you know you can resell without much transaction cost whenever you want.

"Liquidity" is a common analogy that finance has borrowed from physics.

What would make you want to take the risk of sitting on a house for months without being able to sell it? To get you to purchase a house would require the seller to compensate you. The seller would have to offer you a **liquidity premium**—an extra expected rate of return to compensate you for your willingness to hold an asset that you will find difficult to convert into cash if a need were to arise. The liquidity analogy comes from physics. The same way that physical movement is impeded by physical friction, economic transactions are impeded by transaction costs.

Liquidity (or lack thereof) is super-important in most markets, but we do not fully understand it yet.

Housing may be an extreme example, but liquidity effects appear to be important everywhere, even in financial markets with their low transaction costs. (Some financial markets are generally considered low-friction, or even close to frictionless.) Even finance professors and the best fund managers do not yet fully understand liquidity premiums, but we do know that they can be very important. Let us look at some examples of where liquidity premiums seem to play important roles.

TREASURY BONDS

Even Treasuries have differences in liquidity: on-the-run and off-the-run bonds.

Believe it or not, even Treasuries have differences in liquidity. The most recently issued Treasury of a particular maturity is called **on-the-run**. Every bond trader who wants to trade a bond with roughly this maturity (and the financial press) focuses on this particular bond. This makes it easier to buy and sell the on-the-run bond than a similar, but not identical, **off-the-run** bond. For example, in November 2000, the 10-year on-the-run Treasury bond traded for a yield-to-maturity of 5.6% per annum, while a bond that was just a couple of days off in terms of its maturity (and thus practically identical) traded at 5.75% per annum. In other words, you would have been able to purchase the off-the-run bond at a much lower price than the on-the-run bond.

The reason why you might want to purchase the on-the-run bond, even though it had a higher price, would be that you could resell it much more quickly and easily than the equivalent off-the-run bond. Of course, as the date approaches when this

10-year bond is about to lose its on-the-run designation and another bond is about to become the on-the-run 10-year bond, the old on-the-run bond drops in value.

Investors prefer on-the-run bonds because of their immediate liquidity.

In a perfect world, there should be no difference between these two types of bonds. Yet, when a 2-year bond is on-the-run, its bid-ask spread is on average about 1 basis point lower, and it offers on average 0.6 basis points less in yield. For a 10-year bond, both the bid-ask spread and the yield difference between the on-the-run and off-the-run Treasury are usually about 3 basis points. This can only be explained by an investor preference for the immediate liquidity of the current on-the-run bond.

Liquidity Provision As a Business: Market Making

You can think of a market maker on an exchange as someone who is providing liquidity. As a retail investor, you can sell your securities to the market maker in an instant, and it is up to the market maker to find some other investor who wants to hold it long term. To provide this liquidity, the market maker earns the bid-ask spread—a part of the liquidity premium.

Liquidity provision is a common business.

The provision of liquidity in markets of any kind is a common business. For example, you can think of antique stores or used car dealerships as liquidity providers that try to buy cheap (being a standby buyer) and sell expensive (being a standby seller). Being a liquidity provider can require big risks and capital outlays. If it were easy, everyone could do it—and then there would be no more money in liquidity provision!

Liquidity Runs

Liquidity crises are extremely interesting.

The most remarkable empirical regularity about liquidity, however, is that every few years, investors in all markets suddenly seem to prefer only the most liquid securities. This is called a **flight to quality** or **run on liquidity**. In such situations, the spreads on almost all bonds—regardless of whether they are Latin American, European, corporate, mortgage related, and so on—relative to Treasuries tend to widen all at the same time.

How the liquidity run in 2008 spread.

In early 2008, the U.S. economy was facing just such a run on liquidity. It started in the mortgage sector, then spread to many other bonds. Every fund and bank was afraid that its investors would pull their lines of credit. Thus, they themselves were pulling lines of credit that they had extended to their clients (often other banks and funds). Many were selling even highly rated securities for low prices (sometimes fire-sale prices), just to avoid being caught themselves in an even worse liquidity run. There were many extremely curious pricing oddities during the 2008 liquidity run, but they were difficult to exploit by arbitrageurs (because no one would trust lending them the money to execute these arbitrages). For example, 2-year bonds issued by a federal government agency, GNMA, and thus fully backed by the federal government, traded at a full 200 basis points higher than the equivalent Treasuries.

If you are liquid in a liquidity crisis, you can earn a lot of money.

Selling liquidity in order to collect the liquidity premium is also a very common method for Wall Street firms and hedge funds to make money—perhaps even *the* most common. If you know you will not need liquidity at sudden notice or that you want to hold bonds to maturity, it can make sense to purchase less liquid securities to earn the liquidity premium. A sample strategy might be to buy illiquid corporate bonds, financed with cheaper borrowed money. Most of the time, this strategy makes modest amounts of money consistently—except when a flight to liquidity occurs and liquidity spreads widen. Exactly such a situation led to the collapse of a well-known hedge fund named Long-Term Capital Management (LTCM) in 1998. After Russia defaulted on its debt, the spreads on almost every bond increased from wide to wider—the average corporate bond spread in the United States rose from about 4% to about 8% in one week! LTCM simply could not find any buyers for its large holdings of non-Treasury bonds. On the other hand, those funds that could hold onto their positions throughout the crisis or who provided extra liquidity (buying securities that were now very cheap) did extremely well when liquidity returned to normal and their illiquid securities went back up in price. The same fate probably befell Bear Stearns in 2008. If it could have held onto its illiquid investments, or unwound them slowly it probably would not have met its early demise.

SOLVE NOW!

Q 10.14 What is the difference between a liquidity premium and a transaction cost?

10.4 TAXES

> The art of taxation consists in so plucking the goose as to get the most feathers with the least hissing.
> —*Jean-Baptiste Colbert*

> Certainty? In this world nothing is certain but death and taxes.
> —*Benjamin Franklin*

Our fourth violation of market perfection is taxes. They are pervasive and are often an economically large component of project returns. The actual tax code itself is very complex, and its details change every year, but the basics have remained in place for a long time and are similar in most countries. Let me summarize briefly what you shall need to know for this book.

10.4A THE BASICS OF (FEDERAL) INCOME TAXES

The tax code basics have been simple and stable, but the details are complex and ever changing.

The **Internal Revenue Service** (**IRS**) taxes individuals and corporations similarly. (There are some differences, but we don't have the space to discuss them.) Gross income is adjusted by a set of allowable deductions into taxable income, and a (progressive) tax rate is applied. **Before-tax expenses** (deductions) are better for taxpayers than **after-tax expenses**. For example, if you earn $100,000 and there was only one 40% bracket, a $50,000 before-tax expense would leave you

$$(\$100{,}000 - \$50{,}000) \cdot (1 - 40\%) = \$30{,}000$$

$$\text{Before-Tax Net Return} \cdot (1 - \text{Tax Rate}) = \text{After-Tax Net Return}$$

while the same $50,000 as an after-tax expense would leave you with only

$$\$100{,}000 \cdot (1 - 40\%) - \$50{,}000 = \$10{,}000$$

➤ Other tax shelters, Section 17.6F, p. 633

Perhaps the most important deductible items for both corporations and individuals are interest payments, although individuals can deduct them only for mortgages. In addition, there are some other deductions such as pension contributions. There are also some nonprofit investors (such as pension funds) that are entirely tax-exempt.

Among the four tax classes of income, dividends receipts and capital gains are the two best.

The tax code categorizes income into four different classes: ordinary income, interest income, dividend income, and capital gains. The tax rates on these classes differ, as does the ability to apply deductions on them to reduce the income tax burden.

Ordinary income applies to most income that is not derived from financial investments (such as wages). Individuals are allowed only very few deductions thereon, and the tax rate is the highest. The highest marginal ordinary federal income tax rate was about 35% in 2008.

Interest income is basically treated like ordinary income.

Dividend income from qualifying U.S. corporations is taxed at a significantly lower rate, often less than half that of ordinary income.

Capital gains on assets owned for 1 year or more (under the 2008 tax code) are also taxed at low rates similar to those at which dividends are taxed. (Assets held for less than 1 year are taxed essentially at the same rate as ordinary income.) In addition, unlike other income, which is taxed every year, both short-term and long-term capital gains are taxed only when realized, and losses can easily be deducted against gains.

From the perspective of an investor, capital gains are mildly preferable to dividend income, and both are greatly preferable to interest income.

The difference between marginal and average tax rates.

The **average tax rate** (the ratio of paid taxes to taxable income) is lower than the **marginal tax rate** (the rate on the last dollar of income), because lower marginal tax rates are applied to your first few dollars of income in the progressive U.S. tax system. For example, in 2008, the first \$8,025 were taxed at 10%, the next \$24,525 at 15%. Thus, ignoring a variety of subsequent adjustments, if you earned \$20,000, you would have paid taxes of

$$\text{Tax} = 10\% \cdot \$8{,}025 + 15\% \cdot (\$20{,}000 - \$8{,}025) = \$2{,}598.75$$

Therefore, your marginal tax rate—the one applicable to your last dollar of income—was 15%, while your average tax rate was about 13.0%. Economists almost always work only with marginal tax rates, because they are relevant to your earning 1 dollar more or less. For large corporations, the distinction is often minor, because beginning at around \$75,000 of income, the federal tax rate is about 34% (as of 2008). A corporation that earns or loses \$10 million has an average tax rate that is for all practical purposes the same as its marginal tax rate.

The tax picture here is rather incomplete.

Of course, there are also other important taxes, such as state income taxes, Social Security and Medicare taxes, property taxes, sales taxes, and so on. In recent years, an alternative tax system, the **alternative minimum tax** (AMT), has become as important as the standard federal income tax system. Because the AMT categorizes most income the same way, we won't distinguish between the standard income tax and the alternative minimum tax. If you have to file in multiple states or even in multiple countries—although there are rules that try to avoid double taxation—the details can be hair-raisingly complex. (Professional athletes have to pay taxes in every state in which they have played a game, for example.) If you find yourself in such a situation, may the Force be with you!

IMPORTANT:

- Remember that there are some tax-exempt investors, such as pension funds.
- You must understand how income taxes are computed (the principles, not the details), how to find the marginal tax rate, how to compute the average tax rate, and why the average tax rate is usually lower than the marginal tax rate.
- Expenses that can be paid from before-tax income are better than expenses that must be paid from after-tax income. Specifically, interest expenses are tax-deductible and thus better for the taxpayer.
- Capital gains (and secondarily dividend) income enjoys preferential tax treatment for the recipient, relative to interest and ordinary income.

SOLVE NOW!

Q 10.15 Is it better for the taxpayer to have a before-tax or an after-tax expense? Why?

Q 10.16 What types of income do taxpayers prefer? Why?

Q 10.17 Why is the marginal tax rate usually lower than the average tax rate?

10.4B THE EFFECT OF TAXES ON RATES OF RETURN

Taxes are on profits, not on values or sales. Nevertheless, they are often much larger than transaction costs.

How does finance work if there are income taxes? Mechanically, taxes are similar to transaction costs—they take a "cut," which makes investments less profitable. One difference between them is that income taxes are higher on more profitable transactions, whereas plain transaction costs are the same whether you made money or lost money. And, of course, taxes often have many more nuances. A second and perhaps more important difference is that taxes are often orders of magnitude bigger and thus more important than ordinary transaction costs—except in illustrative textbook examples. For many investors and corporations, tax planning is an issue of first-order importance.

Taxable investors (unlike tax-exempt investors) care about *after*-tax inflows and outflows.

In the end, all investors should care about is after-tax returns, not before-tax returns. It should not matter whether you receive \$100 that has to be taxed at 50% or whether you receive \$50 that does not have to be taxed. This leads to a recommendation analogous to that for transaction costs—*work only in after-tax money*. For example, say you invest \$100,000 in after-tax money to earn a return of \$160,000. Your marginal tax rate is 25%. Taxes are on the net return of \$60,000, so your after-tax net return is

$$75\% \cdot \$60{,}000 = \$45{,}000$$

$$(1 - \tau) \cdot \text{Before-Tax Net Return} = \text{After-Tax Net Return}$$

(The tax rate is commonly abbreviated with the Greek letter τ, tau.) In addition, you will receive your original investment back, so your after-tax rate of return is

$$r_{\text{after tax}} = \frac{\$145{,}000 - \$100{,}000}{\$100{,}000} = 45\%$$

Tax-Exempt Bonds and the Marginal Investor

State and municipal bonds' interest payments are legally exempt from (federal) income taxes.

In the United States, interest paid on bonds issued by smaller governmental entities is legally tax-exempt. (The constitution's writers did not want to have the federal government burden states' or local governments' efforts to raise money.) If you own one of these bonds, you do not need to declare the interest on your federal income tax forms, and sometimes not even on your state's income tax form, either. (The arrangement differs from bond to bond.) The most prominent tax-exempt bonds are often just called **municipal bonds**, **muni bonds**, or even **munis** for short. As their name suggests, many are issued by municipalities such as the City of Los Angeles (CA) or the City of Canton (OH). State bonds are also categorized as muni bonds, because they are also exempt from federal income tax. Unfortunately, unlike the U.S. Treasury, municipalities can and have gone bankrupt, so their bonds may not fully repay. For example, Orange County (CA) prominently defaulted in December 1994.) Still, many muni bonds are fairly safe AAA credit. Tax-exempt bonds are often best compared to taxable corporate bonds with similar bond ratings. The difference between the prevailing interest rates on equally risky taxable and tax-exempt bonds allows us to determine the effective tax rate in the economy.

In March 2008, taxable bonds offered 133 basis points per annum above munis. An investor in the 35% tax bracket should have preferred the tax-exempt muni bond.

For example, on March 28, 2008, Bloomberg reported that tax-exempt AAA-rated 10-year muni bonds traded at a yield of 4.05%. Corporate 10-year AAA bonds traded at 5.38%. Which one would be a better investment *for you*? Well, it depends. If you invested \$100 into munis at a 4.05% interest rate, you would receive \$4.05 at year's end. Uncle Sam would get none of it. If you invested \$100 in corporate bonds at a 5.38% interest rate, you would receive \$5.38 at year's end. If your federal income tax rate is 0%, you would clearly prefer the \$5.38 to the \$4.05. However, if your marginal tax rate is 35%, Uncle Sam would collect $\$5.38 \cdot 35\% \approx \$1.88$ and leave you with \$3.50. In terms of after-tax rate of return, this is

$$r_{\text{after tax}} = (1 - 35\%) \cdot 5.38\% \approx 3.50\%$$

$$r_{\text{after tax}} = (1 - \tau) \cdot r_{\text{before tax}}$$

With a 35% marginal federal income tax rate, you should prefer the 4.05% tax-exempt bond to the 5.38% taxable bond.

Investors above a critical tax rate should prefer the muni bond.

In economics, almost everything that is important is "on the margin." Thus, economists like to think about a hypothetical marginal investor. This is an investor whose marginal income tax rate is such that she would be exactly indifferent between buying the tax-exempt bond and the taxable bond. Using the previous formula, the marginal investor has a tax rate of

$$4.05\% = (1 - \tau_{\text{marginal}}) \cdot 5.38\% \Leftrightarrow \tau_{\text{marginal}} = 1 - \frac{4.05\%}{5.38\%} \approx 24.7\%$$

$$r_{\text{after tax}} = (1 - \tau_{\text{marginal}}) \cdot r_{\text{before tax}} \Leftrightarrow \tau_{\text{marginal}} = 1 - \frac{r_{\text{after tax}}}{r_{\text{before tax}}}$$

Any investor with a marginal income tax rate above 24.7% (such as a high-income retail investor) should prefer the tax-exempt bond. Any investor with a marginal income tax rate below 24.7% (such as a tax-exempt pension fund) should prefer the taxable bond. When economists think more generally about how assets are priced, they also use this tax rate as the effective economy-wide one.

SOLVE NOW!

Q 10.18 If your tax rate is 20%, what interest rate do you earn in after-tax terms if the before-tax interest rate is 6%?

Q 10.19 If the marginal investor's tax rate is 30% and taxable bonds offer a rate of return of 6%, what rate of return do equivalent muni bonds offer?

Q 10.20 On March 28, 2008, tax-exempt AAA-rated 5-year muni bonds traded at a yield of 3.04%. Corporate 5-year AAA bonds traded at 4.14%. What was the marginal investor's tax rate?

10.4C TAXES IN NET PRESENT VALUES

You should only care about your own after-tax cash flows.

Again, as with transaction costs, you should take care to work only with cash in the same units—here, this means cash that you can use for consumption. Again, it should not matter whether you receive \$100 that has to be taxed at 50% or whether you receive \$50 that does not have to be taxed. As far as NPV is concerned, you should compute everything in after-tax dollars. This includes all cash flows, whether they occur today or tomorrow, and whether they are inflows or outflows.

> **IMPORTANT:** Do all NPV calculations in *after-tax* money. This applies both to the expected cash flows and to the opportunity cost of capital.

You must compute the after-tax opportunity cost of capital.

Unfortunately, you cannot simply discount before-tax cash flows with the before-tax cost of capital (wrong!) and expect to come up with the same result as when you discount after-tax cash flows with after-tax costs of capital (right!).

Your opportunity cost of capital depends on your own tax rate.

For example, consider a project that costs \$10,000 and returns \$13,000 next year. Your tax rate is 40%, and 1-year equivalently risky bonds return 25% if their income is taxable and 10% if their income is not taxable. First, you must decide what your opportunity cost of capital is. Section 10.4B showed that if you invest \$100 into taxables, you will receive \$125 but the IRS will confiscate (\$125 − \$100) · 40% = \$10. You will thus own \$115 in after-tax wealth. Tax-exempts grow only to \$110, so you prefer the taxable bond—it is the taxable equally risky bond that determines your opportunity cost of capital. Your equivalent after-tax rate of return is therefore 15%.

This 15% is your after-tax "opportunity" cost of capital—it is your best alternative use of capital elsewhere.

You must discount your after-tax expected cash flows with your after-tax opportunity cost of capital.

Return to your \$10,000 project now. You know that your taxable project returns 30% taxable (\$3,000), while taxable bonds return 25% (\$2,500), so NPV should tell you to take this project. Uncle Sam will confiscate 40% · \$3,000 = \$1,200, leaving you with \$11,800. Therefore, the NPV of your project is

$$\text{NPV} = -\$10{,}000 + \frac{\$11{,}800}{1 + 15\%} \approx \$260.87 \qquad \frac{\text{after-tax cash flows}}{\text{after-tax cost of capital}}$$

$$\text{NPV} = C_0 + \frac{\mathcal{E}(\widetilde{C}_1)}{1 + \mathcal{E}(\tilde{r}_1)}$$

Here are incorrect shortcut attempts, working with before-tax cash flows and/or before-tax costs of capital.

It makes intuitive sense: If you had invested money into the bonds, you would have ended up with \$11,500. Instead, you will end up with \$11,800, the \$300 difference occurring next year. Discounted, the \$261 seems intuitively correct. Of course, there are an infinite number of ways of getting *incorrect* solutions, but recognize that none of the following calculations that use the before-tax expected cash flows (and try different discount rates) give the same correct result:

$$\text{NPV} \neq -\$10{,}000 + \frac{\$13{,}000}{1 + 25\%} = \$400 \qquad \frac{\text{taxable cash flows}}{\text{taxable bond cost of capital}}$$

$$\text{NPV} \neq -\$10{,}000 + \frac{\$13{,}000}{1 + 15\%} \approx \$1{,}304.35 \qquad \frac{\text{taxable cash flows}}{\text{after-tax cost of capital}}$$

$$\text{NPV} \neq -\$10{,}000 + \frac{\$13{,}000}{1 + 10\%} \approx \$1{,}818.18 \qquad \frac{\text{taxable cash flows}}{\text{muni cost of capital}}$$

You have no choice: *You cannot work with before-tax expected cash flows.* Instead, you need to go through the exercise of carefully computing after-tax cash flows and discounting with your after-tax opportunity cost of capital.

In some, but not all, situations, you can compare two projects based on their before-tax NPVs.

You know that computing after-tax cash flows is a pain. Can you at least compare two *equally* taxable projects in terms of their before-tax NPV? If one project is better than the other in before-tax terms, is it also better in after-tax terms? If yes, then you could at least do relative capital budgeting with before-tax project cash flows. This may or may not work, and here is why. Compare project SAFE, which costs \$1,000 and will provide \$1,500 this evening; and project UNSAFE, which costs \$1,000 and will provide either \$500 or \$2,500 this evening with equal probability. The expected payout is the same, and the cost of capital is practically 0% for 1 day. If you are in the 20% marginal tax bracket, project SAFE will leave you with \$500 in *taxable* earnings. The IRS will collect 20% · (\$1,500 − \$1,000) = \$100, leaving you with +\$400 in after-tax net return. Project UNSAFE will either give you \$1,500 or −\$500 in *taxable* earnings.

- If the project succeeds, you would send \$1,500 · 20% = \$300 to the IRS. If the project fails, and if you can use the losses to offset gains from projects elsewhere, you would send \$500 · 20% = \$100 *less* to the IRS (because your taxable profits elsewhere would be reduced). In this case, projects SAFE and UNSAFE would have the same expected tax costs and after-tax cash flows: 1/2 · \$300 + 1/2 · (−\$100) = \$100.

- If you drop into a different tax bracket, say, 25%, when your (additional) net income is $1,000 higher, then project UNSAFE becomes less desirable than project SAFE. For the $1,500 income, the first $500 would still cost you $100 in tax, but the remaining $1,000 would cost you $250. Thus, your project's marginal tax obligation would be either $350 or −$100, for an expected tax burden of $125. (The same logic applies if your losses would make you fall into a lower tax bracket—the UNSAFE project would become less desirable, because the tax reduction would be worth less.)
- If you have no capital gains elsewhere that you can reduce with the UNSAFE project capital loss, then the UNSAFE project would again be worth less. Corporations can ask for a tax refund on old gains, so the unrealized tax loss factor is less binding than it is for individuals, who may have to carry the capital loss forward until they have sufficient income again to use it—if ever.

Thus, whether you can compare projects on a before-tax basis depends on whether you have perfect symmetry in the applicable marginal tax rates across projects. If you do, then the project that is more profitable in after-tax terms is also more profitable in before-tax terms. This would allow you to simply compare projects by their before-tax NPVs. If gains and losses face different taxation—either because of tax bracket changes or because of your inability to use the tax losses elsewhere—then you cannot simply choose the project with the higher before-tax NPV. You will have to go through the entire after-tax NPV calculations and compare them.

IMPORTANT: You can only compare projects on a before-tax NPV basis if the tax treatment is absolutely symmetric. This requires consideration of your overall tax situation.

Two more tax-adjusting corporate valuation methods, WACC and APV, unfortunately have to wait.

You now know how to discount projects in the presence of income taxes. However, you do not yet know how to compute the proper discount rate for projects that are financed by debt and equity, because debt and equity face different tax consequences. Unfortunately, you will have to wait until Chapter 17 before we can do a good job discussing the two suitable methods—called APV and WACC—to handle differential taxation for different corporate securities.

SOLVE NOW!

Q 10.21 You have a project that costs $50,000 and will return $80,000 in 3 years. Your marginal capital gains tax rate on the $30,000 gain will be 37.5%. Treasuries pay a rate of return of 8% per year; munis pay a rate of return of 3% per year. What is the NPV of your project?

Q 10.22 You are in the 33.3% tax bracket. A project will return $14,000 in 1 year for a $12,000 investment—a $2,000 net return. The equivalent tax-exempt bond yields 15%, and the equivalent taxable bond yields 20%. What is the NPV of this project?

Q 10.23 It is not uncommon for individuals to forget about taxes, especially when investments are small and payoffs are large but rare. Say you are in the 30% tax bracket. Is the NPV of a $1 lottery ticket that pays off taxable winnings of $10 million with a chance of 1 in 9 million positive or negative? How would it change if you could purchase the lottery ticket with before-tax money?

10.4D TAX TIMING

It is often better if you are taxed only at the very end, rather than in the interim.

In many situations, the IRS does not allow reinvestment of funds generated by a project without an interim tax penalty. This can be important when you compare one long-term investment to multiple short-term investments that are otherwise identical. For example, consider a farmer in the 40% tax bracket who purchases grain (seed) that costs $300 and that triples its value every year.

- If the IRS considers this farm to be *one long-term 2-year project*, the farmer can use the first harvest to reseed, so $300 seed turns into $900 in 1 year and then into a $2,700 harvest in 2 years. Uncle Sam considers the profit to be $2,400 and so collects taxes of $960. The farmer is left with an after-tax cash flow of $2,700 − $960 = $1,740.
- If the IRS considers this production to be *two consecutive 1-year projects*, then the farmer's after-tax profits are lower. He ends up with $900 at the end of the first year. Uncle Sam collects 40% · ($900 − $300) = $240, leaving the farmer with $660. Replanted, the $660 grows to $1,980, of which the IRS collects another 40% · ($1,980 − $660) = $528. The farmer is left with an after-tax cash flow of $1,980 − $528 = $1,452.

The discrepancy between $1,740 and $1,452 is due to the fact that the long-term project can avoid the interim taxation. Similar issues arise whenever an expense can be reclassified from "reinvested profits" (taxed, if not with some credit at reinvestment time) into "necessary maintenance."

SOLVE NOW!

Q 10.24 Assume your marginal tax rate is 25%. Assume that the IRS would tax payments only when made. (Sorry, in real life, the IRS nowadays does tax zero-bonds even when they do not yet pay out anything.)

(a) What is the future value of a 10-year zero-bond priced at a YTM of 10%? How much does the IRS get to keep?

(b) What is the future value of a 10-year annual level-coupon bond priced at a YTM of 10%, assuming that coupons are immediately reinvested at the same 10%?

(c) What would it be worth to you today to be taxed only at the end (via the zero-bond) and not in the interim (via the coupon bond)? Which is better?

10.5 ENTREPRENEURIAL FINANCE

For large companies, a perfect market assumption with equal borrowing and lending rates is reasonable.

Now that you understand how to work with market imperfections, for what types of firms do they matter most? Market imperfections are probably just mild for large, publicly traded corporations. These types of firms typically face only modest interest rate spreads between their (risky) borrowing and lending rates. Of course, their *promised* borrowing interest rates are a little higher than what they can receive investing their money in Treasury bonds. Yet, given that they still have some possibility of going bankrupt, large firms' required *expected* borrowing costs of capital are probably fairly close to the *expected* rates of return they could earn if they invested in bonds with characteristics similar to the bonds that they themselves have issued. Thus, large public corporations can often pretend to live in a reasonably perfect market. This also means that they have the luxury of separating their project choices from their financial needs.

➤ Altman study of bond default rates, Section 6.2D, p. 148

For entrepreneurs, a perfect market assumption is problematic.

In the world of individuals, entrepreneurs, and small companies, however, it is quite plausible that the costs of capital are often higher than equivalent expected savings interest rates. In fact, the most important difference between "ordinary corporate finance" and "entrepreneurial finance" are the degree to which their capital markets are perfect. Almost all entrepreneurs find it very difficult to convey credibly their intent and ability to pay back loans. And any credit that entrepreneurs receive is usually also very illiquid: Lenders cannot easily convert it into cash, should the need arise. Therefore, they demand a high liquidity spread, too. Many entrepreneurs even end up having to resort to financing projects with credit cards, which may charge 1,000 basis points or more above Treasury.

The *expected* costs of capital are often very high for entrepreneurs needing capital.

In sum, small firms often face extraordinarily high differentials between expected borrowing and lending rates. Entrepreneurs' high borrowing costs can thus prevent them from taking many projects that they would have undertaken if they had the money already on hand. Cash-on-hand can become a prime determinant of all their decisions. More established firms or wealthier entrepreneurs should optimally take more projects than poorer entrepreneurs. Yes, the world is not fair.

Be careful: Don't believe entrepreneurial claims! Often, high borrowing rates are just promised, not expected.

However, be careful in the real world before you believe the claims of entrepreneurs. Entrepreneurs also tend to have notoriously overoptimistic views of their prospects. Even venture capitalists, the financing vehicle for many high-tech entrepreneurial ventures, which advertise rates of return of 30% per year or more, seem to have managed to return only a couple of percentage points above the risk-free rate over the last 30 years. Adjusting for the correct default rates may actually mean that entrepreneurs face only high *promised* borrowing costs, not high *expected* borrowing costs. Thus, the large quoted spread between entrepreneurs' borrowing and lending rates, which is really all that you can easily observe, likely has a large component that is due not to information disagreements but simply to credit risk.

The courts apply an ad hoc discount to the values of entrepreneurial companies based on their limited access to capital.

This issue of how to deal with market imperfections for small firms also arises frequently in the courts, where a cost-of-capital estimate is necessary to compute the value for an entrepreneurial enterprise—for example, for purposes of assessing the inheritance tax or resolving disputes among former business partners. (Such valuation services are an important revenue business for many finance professors and consulting firms.) It has become customary and legally acceptable to compute first the value of an equivalent publicly traded business or company as if it faced a perfect market, and then to apply a "private discount" of around 10% to 30% of firm value in order to reflect the limited access to capital. The amount of this discount is ad hoc, but it is better than no attempt at all.

SOLVE NOW!

Q 10.25 What are the two possible reasons why entrepreneurs often have to finance their projects with credit cards, which can charge interest rates as high as 1,000 basis points above Treasury?

10.6 DECONSTRUCTING QUOTED RATES OF RETURN—LIQUIDITY AND TAX PREMIUMS

➤ Section 6.2C, "Deconstructing Quoted Rates of Return—Time and Default Premiums," p. 147

➤ Section 9.3A, "Deconstructing Quoted Rates of Return—Risk Premiums," p. 254

In Sections 6.2C and 9.3A, you learned that you could decompose quoted rates of return into a time premium, a default premium, and a risk premium. Market imperfections can create additional premiums.

$$\text{Promised Rate of Return} = \text{Time Premium} + \text{Default Premium} + \text{Risk Premium} + \text{Imperfect Market Premiums}$$

$$\text{Expected Rate of Return} = \underbrace{\text{Time Premium} + \text{Risk Premium}}_{\text{provided by the CAPM}} + \text{Imperfect Market Premiums}$$

Quantifying imperfect market premiums is not easy, but we will try anyway. Unfortunately, there is not much that can be said about one of the imperfect market premiums—the premium compensating for differences in opinions. The nature of information disagreements is that they are idiosyncratic. This does not mean that they are unimportant. As noted earlier they can be so large, even in financial markets, that they may destroy a financial market's viability. Fortunately, the other three imperfections—taxes, transaction costs, and shallow markets—create premiums that are often a little easier to quantify than the premium associated with information disagreements.

Tax premiums are usually "investment class" similar.

Tax differences are often modest across assets in the *same* class. However, when there are assets that are treated differently from a tax perspective, the one with the worse treatment has to offer a higher rate of return. For example, municipal bonds are excluded from federal taxation. Therefore, non-municipal bonds have to offer a higher rate of return relative to these tax-exempt bonds. Similarly, unlike federal Treasury bonds, the holders of corporate bonds are subject to state income taxes. This means that corporate bonds need to pay a premium relative to Treasuries—a **tax premium**.

Let me expand the imperfect market premium into its component premiums.

Transaction costs and deep markets also play important roles. The resulting premiums are often lumped under the general term "liquidity premiums." The idea is that, given a choice between a very liquid security that you can resell in an instant to many different investors in case you need money and a very illiquid security, you will demand an extra rate of return to buy the less liquid one. We can thus extend our earlier premiums analysis to the following:

$$\text{Promised Rate of Return} = \text{Time Premium} + \text{Default Premium} + \text{Risk Premium} + \text{Liquidity Premium} + \text{Tax Premium}$$

$$\text{Actual Earned Rate} = \text{Time Premium} + \text{Default Realization} + \text{Risk Premium} + \text{Liquidity Premium} + \text{Tax Premium}$$

$$\text{Expected Rate of Return} = \text{Time Premium} + \text{Expected Risk Premium} + \text{Liquidity Premium} + \text{Tax Premium}$$

Again, there could be other premiums that should go into this formula, such as information premiums or bond contract feature premiums. I omit them because I don't have empirical evidence to show you. In addition, our concept of a clean decomposition is a little problematic in itself, because these premiums overlap. For example, it is quite possible that there are covariance-risk aspects to liquidity. (In other words, it could be that liquidity spreads increase when the market goes down, which would mean that they have a positive market beta.) Thus, a part of the quoted spread could be considered either as a risk premium or as a liquidity premium. Nevertheless, the basic decomposition in the above formulas is useful.

Corporate bonds: CAPM-type market covariance risk may matter for junk bonds, but it would be trivial for AAA-grade bonds.

➤ Section 6.2D, "Credit Ratings and Default Rates," p. 148

Let's go back to corporate bonds. You already learned in Section 6.2D that many corporate bonds have significant default risk, which means that they have to offer a default premium (relative to Treasuries, of course). Let me now tell you that, depending on credit rating, they have market betas between about 0.1 (investment-grade bonds) and 0.5 (junk bonds). This means that junk bonds may have to offer a meaningfully large premium to compensate investors for market risk, but for investment-grade bonds, any beta premium would be trivial.

Liquidity premiums could be high for all types of risky bonds. Tax premiums are probably similar among all taxable bonds.

However, many corporate bonds are difficult to resell quickly—most have to be traded over-the-counter, and not on an organized exchange. Therefore, they have to offer their buyers a liquidity premium. Finally, corporate bonds are subject to state income taxes. This means that they have to offer a tax premium.

Differences in expected rates of return by credit rating suggest that riskier and less liquid bonds earn more than safer bonds—but not as much more as they seem to promise.

In the Ed Altman study you first saw in Section 6.2D, the historical average rates of return on corporate bonds from 1971 to 2003 were as follows:

The typical investment-grade bond promised about 200 basis points above the equivalent Treasury bond. However, investors ended up with only about 20–40 basis points above the Treasury. Thus, about 170 basis points was the default premium.

The typical junk bond promised a spread of about 500 basis points per annum above the 10-year Treasury bond. However, investors ended up with a spread of "only" about 220 basis points. The default premium was therefore about 280 basis points.

This suggests that the default premium is the most important premium in stated corporate bond yields. Only about 20–40 basis points for investment-grade and about 220 basis points for junk bonds still remain to be explained by the sum of the risk, liquidity, and other premiums.

Figure 10.1 decomposes *expected* rates of return into market risk, liquidity premiums, and tax premiums.

Frank de Jong, a professor at the University of Amsterdam, produced a similar study on bonds from 1985 to 2003. Unlike Altman, he decomposed the *average* (expected) rates of return into a liquidity risk premium, a market risk premium, and a tax premium. Figure 10.1 shows that about 40 basis points for AAA and 250 basis

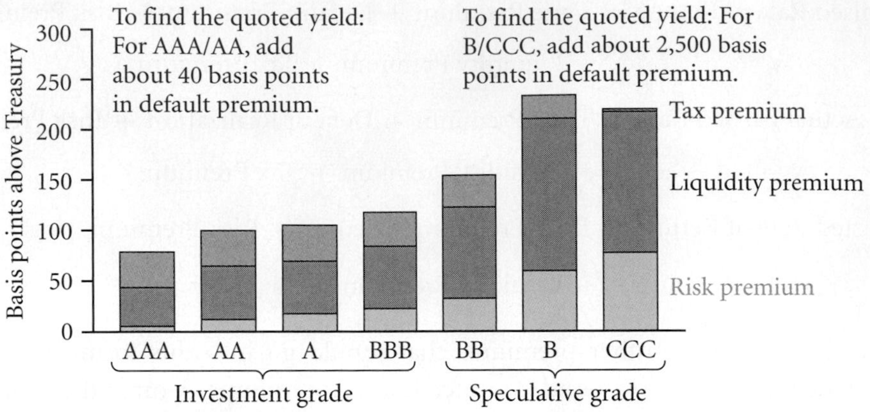

These are estimates of *expected* yield premiums for long-term corporate bonds. For highly rated bonds, the liquidity and tax premiums are much larger than the risk premium. For very low-rated bonds, the liquidity premium becomes relatively more important, followed by the risk premium and then the tax premium.
To obtain stated (quoted) bond yields, you would have to add the default premium. The time premium has been taken out because all spreads are relative to the prevailing time-equivalent Treasury yield. For example, the average AAA bond would have quoted 7.2% when the average Treasury bond yielded 6%. The default premium would have added about 40 basis points, with the remaining 80 basis points having been compensation for risk, liquidity, and taxes. *Source:* De Jong and Driessen, 2005. Reprinted with permission of the authors.

FIGURE 10.1 The Components of Expected Rates of Return in Corporate Bonds, 1985–2003

points for CCC bonds were pure default premiums that you would not have earned on average. With betas of around 0.1, the market risk premium was negligibly small for AAA and AA bonds, but then was higher for CCC-rated bonds, accounting for as much as 1% yield per year. The liquidity premium was about 50 basis points for highly rated bonds, and 100–150 basis points for junk bonds. Incidentally, many institutional investors are only allowed to hold investment-grade bonds. Thus, dropping from investment grade to speculative grade incurs a large liquidity penalty. You can see this in the sudden and unusually steep rise in yield for BB and B bonds. Finally, the state income tax premium was about 20–30 basis points for all bonds, except for the CCC bonds (which may simply be a data glitch).

SOLVE NOW!

Q 10.26 How important are the various premiums for investment-grade bonds and junk bonds? (Omit the time premium.)

10.7 MULTIPLE EFFECTS: HOW TO WORK NOVEL PROBLEMS

Life is tough—it does not always offer simple solutions.

➤ Inflation, Section 5.2, p. 97

Of course, in the messy real world, you can suffer many problems (such as inflation, transaction costs, disagreements, sole potential buyers, and taxes) all at once, not just in isolation. In fact, there are so many possible real-world problems that no one can possibly give you a formula for each one. Thus, it is important that you approach the real world keeping a multitude of issues in mind.

1. Ask yourself in a given situation whether the assumption of a perfect market is reasonably appropriate. For example, in the case of large and possibly tax-exempt companies, you may consider it reasonable to get away with assuming a perfect market, and just work out the "perfect market" answer—a simple NPV, for example. Then think about the direction in which market imperfections would push you, judge the magnitude, and make an intuitive adjustment. You can thereby often work out a good answer without the enormous complications that the perfectly correct answer would require.

If you get lucky, you may get good estimates ignoring market inefficiencies altogether. Adjust a little maybe just intuitively.

2. If you conclude that you are a long way from home (i.e., from a perfect market), then you must first determine which market imperfections are most important. Then you must work out a good solution by yourself. If you had hoped for the one magic bullet that tells you how to solve every different kind of problem you might encounter, I have to disappoint you. There are just too many possibilities, and the task is often hard. Probably the best way to answer such new and thorny questions is to internalize the method of "thinking by numerical example." You really need to become able to work out formulas for yourself when you need them.

You must learn how to think for yourself. I can now only teach you the method, not the solution.

10.7A SOLVING A PROBLEM WITH INFLATION AND TAXES

For example, let's see how you could approach a situation with both taxes and inflation. Always start by making up some numbers you find easy to work with. Let's say you are considering an investment of $100. Further, assume you will earn a 10% rate of return on your $100 investment and Uncle Sam will take $\tau = 40\%$ (or $4 on your $10 return). Therefore, you get $110 before taxes but end up with only $106 in nominal terms. What you have just calculated is

Now work an example of how both taxes and inflation could interact.

$$\$100 \cdot [1 + 10\% \cdot (1 - 40\%)] = \$106$$

$$C_0 \cdot \left[1 + r_{\text{nominal, before tax}} \cdot (1 - \tau)\right] = C_1$$

Now you need to determine what your $106 is really worth, so you must introduce inflation. Pick some round number, say, a rate of $\pi = 5\%$ per annum. Consequently, in purchasing power, the $106 is worth:

$$\frac{\$106}{1 + 5\%} \approx \$100.95$$

$$\frac{C_1}{1 + \pi} = P_0$$

Your after-tax, post-inflation, real rate of return is $100.95/$100 − 1 = 0.95%. Knowing the numerical result, you need to translate your numbers into a formula. You computed

$$r_{\text{after tax, real}} = \frac{\$100.95 - \$100}{\$100} = \frac{\frac{\$100\cdot[1+10\%\cdot(1-40\%)]}{1+5\%} - \$100}{\$100}$$

$$= \frac{10\% \cdot (1-40\%) - 5\%}{1+5\%} \approx 0.95\%$$

$$r_{\text{after tax, real}} = \frac{P_0 - C_0}{C_0} = \frac{\frac{C_0\cdot[1+r_{\text{nominal, before tax}}\cdot(1-\tau)]}{1+\pi} - C_0}{C_0}$$

$$= \frac{r_{\text{nominal, before tax}} \cdot (1-\tau) - \pi}{1+\pi} \qquad (10.1)$$

This is, of course, not a formula that anyone remembers. However, it is a useful illustration of how you should approach and simplify complex questions—numerical example first, formula second.

Taxes on Nominal Returns?

If the real interest rate stays constant, does inflation hurt an investor? Yes, because taxes are assessed on *nominal* returns.

Here is an interesting question: If the real rate of return remains constant, does it help or hurt an investor if inflation goes up? Let's assume that the real rate of return is a constant 20%. If inflation is 50%, then the nominal rate of return is 80% (because $(1 + 50\%) \cdot (1 + 20\%) = 1 + 80\%$): You get \$180 for a \$100 investment. Now add income taxes to the tune of 40%. The IRS sees \$80 in interest, taxes \$32, and leaves you with \$48. Your \$148 will thus be worth $\$148/(1 + 50\%) \approx \$98.67$ in real value. Instead of a 20% increase in real purchasing power when you save money, you now suffer a $\$98.67/\$100 - 1 \approx -1.3\%$ change in real purchasing power. Despite a high real interest rate, Uncle Sam ended up with more, and you ended up with less purchasing power than you started with. The reason is that although Uncle Sam claims to tax only interest gains, you can actually lose in *real* terms because the interest tax is on *nominal* interest payments. Contrast this with the same scenario without inflation. In this case, if the real rate of return were still 20%, you would have earned \$20, Uncle Sam would have taxed you \$8, and you could have kept \$112 in real value.

IMPORTANT: If real before-tax interest rates remain constant, because the IRS taxes nominal returns, not real returns, you get the following results:

- Higher inflation and interest rates hurt *taxable* savers.
- Higher inflation and interest rates help *taxable* borrowers.

(Economic forces of demand and supply for capital may therefore have to adjust, so that real rates of return increase when inflation increases.)

For much of postwar U.S. history, real rates of return on short-term government bonds have indeed been *negative* for taxed investors.

SOLVE NOW!

Q 10.27 Assume you have both taxes and inflation. You are in the 20% tax bracket, and the inflation rate is 5% per year. A 1-year project offers you $3,000 return for a $20,000 investment. Taxable bonds offer a rate of return of 10% per year. What is the NPV of this project? Extra credit if you can derive the formula yourself!

Q 10.28 ADVANCED: Assume the inflation rate is 100% per year and the nominal rate of interest is 700% per year. (This was also our apples example from Section 5.2.) Now, assume that there is also a 25% default rate. That is, 1 in 4 apples are returned with worms inside and will therefore not be sellable (and be worth $0). What is your real rate of return? What is the formula?

Q 10.29 REALLY ADVANCED: Assume there is a 10% nominal rate of return, a tax rate of 40%, and an inflation rate of 5%. (In the taxes-and-inflation example from Formula 10.1 we worked out that the post-inflation, after-tax rate of return was 0.95%.) Now, add a default rate, d, of 2%, where all money is lost (−100% return). What is the real, post-inflation, after-tax, post-default ratc of return? (Hint: Losses are tax-deductible, too. Assume that the default rate reduces the nominal rate of return (on which taxes are charged) because you do not just take 1 such loan, but 1 million, which practically assures you of the exact default rate without any sampling variation.)

Q 10.30 If the private sector is a net saver (e.g., leaving the public sector as a net borrower), does Uncle Sam have an incentive to reduce or increase inflation?

SUMMARY

This chapter covered the following major points:

- If markets are perfect, everyone has the same information and there are infinitely many buyers and sellers, no transaction costs, and no taxes.
- In perfect markets, *promised* borrowing and lending rates can be different, but *expected* borrowing and lending rates cannot. In imperfect markets, even *expected* borrowing and lending rates can be different.
- If markets are not perfect, capital budgeting decisions can then depend on the cash position of the project owner. NPV and interest rate computations can still be used, although you have to exert special care in working with correct and meaningful inputs (especially for the cost of capital). This is usually best done by thinking in terms of concrete examples first, then translating them into formulas later.

- Transaction costs can be direct (such as commissions) or indirect (such as search or waiting costs). It is often useful to think of round-trip transaction costs.
- Financial assets' transaction costs tend to be very low, so that it is reasonable in many (but not all) circumstances just to ignore them.
- In the real world, buyers often prefer more liquid investments. To induce them to purchase a less liquid investment may require offering them some additional expected rate of return.
- Many financial markets have such low transaction costs and are often so liquid that they are believed to be close to perfect—there are so many buyers and so many sellers that it is unlikely that you would pay too much or too little for an asset. Such assets are likely to be worth what you pay for them.
- The tax code is complex. For the most part, individuals and corporations are taxed similarly. You must understand the following:
  - How income taxes are computed (the principles, not the details)
  - The fact that expenses that can be paid from before-tax income are better than expenses that must be paid from after-tax income
  - How to compute the average tax rate
  - How to obtain the marginal tax rate
  - That capital gains enjoy preferential tax treatment
  - Why the average and marginal tax rates differ, and why the marginal tax rate is usually higher than the average tax rate
- Taxable interest rates can be converted into equivalent tax-exempt interest rates, given the appropriate marginal tax rate.
- Tax-exempt bonds are usually advantageous for investors in high-income tax brackets. You can compute the critical tax rate for the investor who is indifferent between the two.
- You should do all NPV calculations with after-transaction-cost and after-tax cash flows and costs of capital.
- Long-term projects often suffer less interim taxation than short-term projects.
- Entrepreneurial finance can be viewed as the finance of imperfect markets.
- Quoted rates of return on financial instruments contain a time premium, a default premium, a risk premium, and different imperfect market premiums. For many bonds, the imperfect market premiums are larger than the (CAPM-style) risk premium (compensating for covariance with the market).
- The IRS taxes nominal returns, not real returns. This means that higher inflation rates are bad for savers and good for borrowers.

KEY TERMS

after-tax expense, 321
alternative minimum tax, 322
AMT, 322
ask price, 316
average tax rate, 322
before-tax expense, 321
bid price, 316
buy-and-hold, 317
collateral, 313
competitive market, 306
covenants, 313
day trader, 317
flight to quality, 320
Internal Revenue Service, 321
IRS, 321
liquidity premium, 319
marginal tax rate, 322
muni, 324
muni bonds, 324
municipal bond, 324
off-the-run, 319
on-the-run, 319
opportunity cost, 316
round-trip costs, 315
run on liquidity, 320
spread, 316
tax premium, 330

SOLVE NOW! SOLUTIONS

Q 10.1 In a perfect market, borrowing and lending rates are identical. An important implication of equal borrowing and lending rates is that there is a unique price for which a product would be selling (which we can then call its value).

Q 10.2 A competitive market is only one of the four conditions of a perfect market.

Q 10.3 There is no perfect capital market in this world. However, the concept of a perfect market helps you evaluate what departures from a perfect market really mean—and even what kind of departures you should be thinking about.

Q 10.4 The perfect market assumptions are: (a) no differences in information, (b) no market power, (c) no transaction costs, and (d) no taxes.

Q 10.5 For the \$1,000 cost project:

(a) You would have to borrow \$100 at an interest rate of 10% in order to take the project. If you take the project, you will therefore have $\$1{,}000 \cdot 1.08 - \$110 = \$970$ next period. If instead you invest \$900 at the 4% savings rate, you will receive only \$936. You should definitely take the project.

(b) There is a trade-off between investing a smaller sum in the bank and a larger sum in the project now. Say you invest I. If you put it into the bank, you receive $I \cdot (1 + 4\%) = I \cdot 1.04$. If you put I into the project, you receive $\$1{,}000 \cdot 1.08$ from the project, borrow $(\$1{,}000 - I)$ at an interest rate of 10%. Therefore, you must solve

$$I \cdot 1.04 = \$1{,}000 \cdot 1.08 - (\$1{,}000 - I) \cdot 1.1$$

The solution is $I \approx \$333.33$, which means that if you want to consume more than \$1,666.67, you should not take the project. Check: [1] If you consume \$1,700, you have a remaining \$300 to invest. The bank would pay \$312 next year. The project would pay off \$1,080, but you would have to borrow \$700 and pay back \$770, for a net of \$310. You should not take the project. [2] If you consume \$1,600, you have a remaining \$400 to invest. The bank would pay \$416 next year. The project would pay off \$1,080, but you would have to borrow \$600 and pay back \$660, for a net of \$420. You should take the project.

Q 10.6 False. A perfect market is still socially valuable, because sellers and buyers receive surpluses. The buyer surplus is the difference between the value that the good has to a particular buyer and the price at which this buyer can acquire it. (A similar argument applies to the seller—the nonmarginal producer can sell the good for a higher dollar amount than it costs to provide the good.) It is only the "marginal" buyer and seller that get no surplus. All inframarginal buyers and sellers are better off.

Q 10.7 Yes, banks can quote different borrowing and lending rates even in a perfect market! Stated interest rates include a default premium. A perfect market is about equality of *expected* rates, not about equality of *promised* rates.

Q 10.8 True. In a perfect and risk-neutral market, the default rates may be quite different, but the expected rates of return on all investments should be the same.

Q 10.9 (a) The expected payoff is \$99. The discounted expected payoff is $\$99/1.05 \approx \$94.286$. The promised yield is therefore $\$100/\$94.286 - 1 \approx 6.06\%$.
(b) This borrower would believe the value to be $\$100/1.05 \approx \$95.238$. Therefore, the borrower believes he has to overpay by about 95 cents.

Q 10.10 Covenants, collateral, and credit ratings are all common mechanisms to aid the lender in determining the probability of default. Even if disclosure is not required, good borrowers would still want to do so. Therefore, no bank would trust a borrower who is not disclosing as much information as possible. To get credit, it is in the interest of the borrower to volunteer information.

Q 10.11 Dell is a large stock, just like PepsiCo. Therefore, a round-trip transaction would probably cost a bid-ask spread of between 0.1% and 0.3%. On a \$10,000 investment, the bid-ask cost would be around \$20, and broker fees would probably be around \$10 to \$30 with a discount broker. Thus, \$50 (or 0.5%) is a reasonable estimate.

Q 10.12 Direct transaction cost components: broker costs, market maker or exchange costs (bid-ask spread), and other cash expenses (e.g., advertising costs and postage). Indirect transaction cost components: time taken to do research and/or searching for a buyer or seller, opportunity costs, anxiety, and so on.

Q 10.13 For this house transaction cost question, you first need to assume a proper discount rate for the \$4,000/month rent. At a 7% effective interest rate per year, your true monthly rate is $1.07^{1/12} - 1 \approx 0.5654\%$ per month). A reasonable assumption to value the rent stream is as a 1-year annuity, whose value is $\$4{,}000/r \cdot [1 - 1/(1+r)^{12}] \approx \$46{,}281$ today. Therefore,

$$-(\$1{,}000{,}000 + \$5{,}000) + \$46{,}281 + \frac{x \cdot (1 - 8\%)}{1.07} = 0$$

Solve this to $x \approx \$1{,}115{,}031$, so your capital appreciation must be 11.5% per annum for this project to be zero NPV for you.

Q 10.14 A liquidity premium is an up front lower price to compensate you for transaction costs later on. This can allow you to earn a higher expected rate of return on the investment.

Q 10.15 A taxpayer prefers to have a before-tax expense, because it reduces the amount that Uncle Sam considers as income, which Uncle Sam would then want to tax.

Q 10.16 The first preference of taxpayers is to receive income in the form of capital gains (especially as long-term capital gains, which is usually under the control of the taxpayer). Their second preference is to receive income in the form of dividends. Both are much better forms of income than interest income or ordinary income. They are both taxed at lower rates under the U.S. tax code. (In 2008, their rates were about 15%, compared to 30% or more for interest and ordinary income). In addition, capital gains can most easily be offset by capital losses elsewhere, and there is no interim taxation before the capital gains realization.

Q 10.17 The marginal tax rate is usually *not* lower but higher. The average tax rate is usually lower, because the first few dollars of income are taxed at lower tax rates.

Q 10.18 For every \$100, you receive \$6. Uncle Sam takes 20% of \$6, or \$1.20. Your after-tax rate of return is \$4.80/\$100 = 4.8%. You could have also computed $(1 - 20\%) \cdot 6\% = 4.8\%$ directly.

Q 10.19 If the marginal investor's tax rate is 30% and taxable bonds offer a rate of return of 6%, then munis should offer $r = 70\% \cdot 6\% = 4.2\%$ to earn the marginal investor the same after-tax income.

Q 10.20 On March 28, 2008, 5-year AAA munis were offering $3.04\%/4.14\% \approx 73.43\%$ of the 5-year corporate AAA yields. Therefore, $(1 - \tau) \approx 0.7343$, which means that the marginal investor's tax rate was $\tau \approx 26.57\%$.

Q 10.21 First, you need to compute your best opportunity cost of capital if you do not take your project.

- The Treasury will pay \$108 before tax. You could therefore earn \$108 − 0.375 · \$8 = \$105 after taxes. This is an after-tax rate of return of 5%.
- The muni will pay only \$103 after taxes. This is an after-tax rate of return of 3%.

Comparing the two, your opportunity cost of capital—that is, your best investment opportunity elsewhere—is 5% *in after-tax terms*. Now, move on to your project. It will have to pay taxes on \$30,000, so you will have \$18,750 net return left after taxes, which comes to an after-tax amount of \$80,000 − \$18,750 = \$61,250. Your project NPV is therefore $-\$50{,}000 + \$61{,}250/1.05^3 \approx +\$2{,}910$. This is a great project!

Q 10.22 Your opportunity cost of capital is determined by the tax-exempt bond, because $66.67\% \cdot 20\% < 15\%$. Your project's \$2,000 will turn into $66.67\% \cdot \$2{,}000 \approx \$1{,}334$ after-tax earnings, or \$13,334 after-tax cash flow. Therefore, your NPV is $-\$12{,}000 + \$13{,}334/(1 + 15\%) \approx -\$405.22$. Check: The after-tax rate of return of the project's cash flow is $\$13{,}334/\$12{,}000 - 1 \approx 11.11\%$. This is less than 15%. You are better off investing in tax-exempt bonds.

Q 10.23 The \$1 is paid from after-tax income, so leave it as is. The \$10 million is taxed, so you will only receive \$7 million. With a 1 in 9 million chance of winning, the expected payoff is $\$7{,}000{,}000 \cdot 1/9{,}000{,}000 + \$0 \cdot 8{,}999{,}999/9{,}000{,}000 \approx 78$ cents. Therefore, the NPV is negative for any cost of capital. If you could pay with before-tax money, the ticket would cost you only 70 cents in terms of after-tax money, so for interest rates below $\$0.7778/\$0.70 - 1 \approx 11.1\%$ or so, the lottery would be a positive-NPV investment. (This assumes that you are risk neutral, on average, for such a small idiosyncratic investment.)

Q 10.24 For comparing the zero- and coupon bonds, assume you start with \$1,000 of money:

(a) The 10% zero-bond would have a single before-tax payout of $\$1{,}000 \cdot 1.10^{10} \approx \$2{,}593.74$, for which the IRS would collect $\$1{,}593.74 \cdot 25\% \approx \$398.44$ in year 10. This means that you would keep an after-tax zero-bond payout of \$2,195.30.

(b) The 10% coupon bond has an after-tax rate of return of 7.5% per annum, because it is always taxed at 25% in the very same year. Reinvestment yields an after-tax rate of return of 7.5% (\$75 in the first year on \$1,000). After 10 years, you are left with $\$1{,}000 \cdot 1.075^{10} \approx \$2{,}061.03$.

(c) The tax savings on the zero-bond are \$134 in 10 years. Therefore, the zero-bond is better.

Q 10.25 Entrepreneurs pay interest rates as high as 1,000 basis points for one of two reasons: First, default rates are high. (This is not necessarily a difference in expected rates of return.) Second, market imperfections (especially information differences about default probabilities and liquidity premiums) are high. Banks cannot easily determine which entrepreneurs are for real and which ones will go bankrupt and take the bank's money with them. The entrepreneurs may or may not be better at knowing whether their inventions will work. (This can be a market imperfection.)

Q 10.26 From Altman's evidence: The default premium seems more important than the other non-time premiums. From de Jong's evidence, ranking the remaining premiums: For investment-grade bonds, the liquidity and tax premiums seem to explain most of the return above the Treasury. Risk premiums are very small. For junk bonds, liquidity and risk premiums can become large. The risk premium is typically still lower than the liquidity premium. The tax premium becomes relatively small.

Q 10.27 What is your after-tax rate of return on taxable bonds? \$100 will grow to \$110 at a 10% interest rate before tax, minus the 20% that Uncle Sam collects. Uncle Sam takes $1.1 \cdot \$100 = \$110$, subtracts \$100, and then leaves you with only 80% thereof:

$$r_{\text{after tax}} = \frac{80\% \cdot (\$110 - \$100)}{\$100} = 8\%$$

$$r_{\text{after tax}} = \frac{(1-\tau)\cdot(C_1 - C_0)}{C_0}$$

where τ is your tax rate of 20%. $(C_1 - C_0)/C_0$ is the before-tax rate of return, so this is just

$$r_{\text{after tax}} = 80\% \cdot 10\% = 8\%$$
$$= (1-\tau)\cdot r_{\text{before tax}}$$

Now, in before-tax terms, your project offers a 15% rate of return. In after-tax terms, the project offers 80% · \$3,000 = \$2,400 net return. On your investment of \$20,000, this is a 12% after-tax rate of return. (On the same \$20,000, the taxable bond would offer only 80% · (\$22,000 − \$20,000) = \$1,600 net return (8%). So, you know that the NPV should be positive.) Therefore, the project NPV is

$$\text{NPV} = -\$20{,}000 + \frac{\$20{,}000 + 80\% \cdot (\$23{,}000 - \$20{,}000)}{1 + 8\%} \approx \$740.74$$

$$\text{NPV} = C_0 + \frac{C_0 + (1-\tau)\cdot(C_1 - C_0)}{1 + r_{\text{after tax}}}$$

You can now easily substitute any other cash flows or interest rates into these formulas to obtain the NPV. Note that everything is computed in nominal dollars, so you do not need the information about the inflation rate! (And you needed it in nominal, because taxes are computed based on nominal gains, not real gains.)

Q 10.28 First, a simple version of the answer: Your one real apple becomes eight nominal pseudoapples (at 700%), which is four real apples after 100% inflation. One goes bad, so you are left with three apples, i.e., a rate of return of 200%.

Now, the more complete version: Your numeraire is one apple ($1a$) that costs \$1. You will get \$8 in nominal terms, next year ($a \cdot (1 + r_{\text{nominal, before tax}}) = a \cdot (1 + 700\%) = 8 \cdot a$). This will purchase apples that cost \$2 each ($(1+\pi) = (1 + 100\%) = \$2$), that is, four apples ($a \cdot (1 + r_{\text{nominal, before tax}})/(1+\pi) = 1a \cdot (1+700\%)/(1+100\%) = 4a$). However, one of the apples ($d = 25\%$) is bad, so you will get only three apples ($a_1 = a_0 \cdot (1 + r_{\text{nominal, before tax}})/(1+\pi)\cdot(1-d) = 1 \cdot a_0 \cdot (1+700\%)/(1+100\%)\cdot 75\% = 3 \cdot a_0$). Therefore, the real rate of return is $(a_1 - a_0)/a_0$, or

$$r_{\text{real, after tax, post default}} = \frac{(1a \cdot \frac{1+700\%}{1+100\%} \cdot 75\%) - 1a}{1a} = 300\% - 1 = 200\%$$

$$r_{\text{real, after tax, post default}} = \frac{[1a \cdot \frac{1+r_{\text{nominal, before tax}}}{1+\pi} \cdot (1-d)] - 1a}{1a}$$

The "$1a$" of course cancels, because the formula applies to any number of apples or other goods.

Q 10.29 Instead of 10%, you earn only 98% · 10% + 2% · (−100%) = 7.8%. Translated into a formula, this is $(1-d)\cdot r_{\text{nominal, before tax}} + d \cdot (-100\%) = r_{\text{nominal, before tax}} - d \cdot (1 + r_{\text{nominal, before tax}}) = 10\% - 2\% \cdot (1 + 10\%) = 7.8\%$. Now, using the formula from page 334,

$$r_{\text{after tax, real, post default}} = \frac{V_0 - C_0}{C_0} = \frac{\frac{C_0 \cdot [1 + r_{\text{nominal, before tax}} \cdot (1-\tau)]}{1+\pi} - C_0}{C_0}$$

$$= \frac{r_{\text{nominal, before tax}} \cdot (1 - \tau) - \pi}{1 + \pi}$$

replace the nominal interest rate $r_{\text{nominal, before tax}}$ with the default reduced nominal rate $r_{\text{nominal, before tax}} - d \cdot (1 + r_{\text{nominal, before tax}})$, so the new formula is

$$r_{\text{post default, after tax, real}} = \frac{V_0 - C_0}{C_0}$$

$$= \frac{\frac{C_0 \cdot [1 + (r_{\text{nominal, before tax}} - d \cdot (1 + r_{\text{nominal, before tax}})) \cdot (1-\tau)]}{1+\pi} - C_0}{C_0}$$

$$= \frac{(r_{\text{nominal, before tax}} - d \cdot (1 + r_{\text{nominal, before tax}})) \cdot (1 - \tau) - \pi}{1 + \pi}$$

$$= \frac{7.8\% \cdot (1 - 40\%) - 5\%}{1 + 5\%} \approx -0.30\%$$

Q 10.30 Uncle Sam would benefit from an increase in inflation, because he taxes nominal rates of return, not real rates of return. In the real world, interest rates would also have to rise to compensate private savers for this extra "tax" on money.

PROBLEMS

The ▇ *indicates problems available in* myfinancelab

Q 10.31 Evaluate whether supermarkets operate in perfect markets.

Q 10.32 What are the perfect market assumptions?

Q 10.33 Your borrowing rate is 15% per year. Your lending rate is 10% per year. The project costs \$5,000 and has a rate of return of 12%.

(a) Should you take the project if you have \$2,000 to invest?

(b) If you have \$3,000 to invest?

(c) If you have \$4,000 to invest?

Q 10.34 "If the world is risk neutral, then the promised and expected rates of return may be different but the expected rates of return on all loans should be equal." Evaluate.

Q 10.35 An entrepreneur is quoted a loan rate of 12% at the local bank, while the bank pays depositors 6% per annum.

(a) If in bankruptcy the entrepreneur will not pay back anything, but otherwise everything will be repaid, then what does the bank believe the probability of failure to be?

(b) What is the quoted default premium?

(c) Compute the expected default premium.

Q 10.36 Go to Edgar on the SEC's website. Look up the *El Torito* company (also *Real Mex Restaurants, Inc*) S-4 filing on 2004-06-09. Describe the covenants and requirements to which El Torito is obligated. (Note: This may take a while, but reading this S-4 will introduce you to how these agreements look in the real world.)

Q 10.37 The bid quote on a corporate bond is \$212; the ask is \$215. You expect this bond to return its promised 15% per annum for sure. In contrast, T-bonds offer only 6% per annum but have no spread. If you have to liquidate your position in 1 month, what would a $1 million investment be worth in either instrument? Which instrument should you purchase?

Q 10.38 Look up on a financial website what the cost of a round-trip transaction on $10,000 worth of shares in Dell would cost you today.

Q 10.39 You have discovered an investment strategy that can beat the market by 300 basis points per year. Assume the stock market is expected to return 9% per annum. Unfortunately, to implement your strategy, you will have to turn over your portfolio three times a year. Think of this as rebalancing (selling and purchasing) 25% of your portfolio every month. You have very good traders, who can execute trades at a cost of only 7.5 cents per transaction (15 cents round-trip) on a $30 stock. Does this strategy make sense?

Q 10.40 A day trader has $10 million in assets. She buys and sells 30% of her portfolio every day. Assume this day trader is very good and incurs single round-trip transaction costs of only 10 cents on a $30 stock. Roughly, by how much does this day trader's strategy have to beat the benchmark in order to make this a profitable activity? Assume that the trader could earn $200,000 in an equivalent alternative employment and that there are 255 trading days per year.

Q 10.41 Search online for the current federal income tax rates on the four different types of income for individual taxpayers and corporate taxpayers.

(a) What are these rates?
(b) Assume that a corporation has just earned $2 million in ordinary income, $1 million in interest income, and $3 million in realized long-term capital gains (net). Focusing only on the basics and ignoring deductions, what is its tax obligation? What are its marginal tax rates? What is its average tax rate?
(c) Assume that you (an individual) have just earned $2 million in ordinary income, $1 million in interest income, and $3 million in realized long-term capital gains (net). Focusing only on the basics and ignoring deductions, what is your income tax obligation? What is your marginal tax rate? What is your average tax rate?
(d) How much would your state income tax, Social Security, and Medicare add to your tax bill? Is your state income tax payment a before-tax or an after-tax expense?

Q 10.42 If your tax rate is 40%, what interest rate do you earn in after-tax terms if the before-tax interest rate is 6%?

Q 10.43 On September 28, 2007, tax-exempt AAA rated 10-year muni bonds traded at a yield of 3.99%. Corporate 10-year AAA bonds traded at 5.70%. What was the marginal investor's tax rate?

Q 10.44 Go to the Vanguard website and look up VWITX and VBIIX.

(a) What is the current yield of a tax-exempt Vanguard bond fund?
(b) What is your state income tax treatment?
(c) How does it compare to the most similar Vanguard taxable bond fund?
(d) What tax rate would an investor have to suffer in order to be indifferent between the two bond funds?

Q 10.45 Consider a real estate project. It costs $1,000,000. Thereafter, it will produce $60,000 in taxable ordinary income before depreciation every year. Favorable tax treatment means that the project will produce $100,000 in tax depreciation write-offs each year for 10 years (nothing thereafter). For example, if you had $500,000 in ordinary income in year 2 without this project, you would now only have $400,000 in ordinary income instead. At the end of 10 years, you can sell this project for $800,000. All of this $800,000 will be fully taxable as write-up at your capital gains tax rate of 20%. If your ordinary income tax is 33% per annum, if taxable bonds offer a rate of return of 8% per annum, and tax-exempt munis offer a rate of 6% per annum, what would be the NPV of this project?

Q 10.46 You are in the 25% tax bracket. A project will return $20,000 next year for a $17,000 investment—a $3,000 net return. The equivalent tax-exempt bond yields 14%, and the equivalent taxable bond yields 20%. What is the NPV of this project?

Q 10.47 The lottery gives you a 1 in 14 million chance of winning the jackpot. It promises \$20 million to the lucky winner. A ticket costs \$1. Alas, the lottery forgot to mention that winnings are paid over 20 years (with the first \$1 million payment occurring immediately), that inflation is 2% per year, and that winnings are taxable. Is the lottery a good investment? (Assume that you are in a 40% marginal income tax bracket and that the appropriate nominal discount rate is 10% per year.)

11

Perfect and Efficient Markets, and Classical and Behavioral Finance

HOW TRUSTWORTHY ARE MARKET PRICES?

This chapter explains the concept of an efficient market, which is closely linked to that of a perfect market. A market is said to be efficient if it does not ignore available information. To illuminate perfect and efficient markets, this chapter also explains arbitrage, an essential concept of finance, without which no study of finance would be complete. We then discuss the consequences of the concepts: What do efficient and/or perfect markets mean for predicting stock performance? How should you interpret the success of famous investors? And how can you use the concept of efficient markets to run an event study to help assess the valuation impact of big corporate events?

11.1 MARKET EFFICIENCY

Market efficiency means the market uses all available information in setting the price.

A perfect market sets up stiff competition among many investors. This forces them to use all available information as well as they possibly can. This is called **market efficiency**: a situation in which prices reflect *all* available information. In a fully efficient market, you should not be able to use any available information to predict future returns better than the market can.

➤ Mean-variance efficiency, Section 8.8, p. 236

> **IMPORTANT:** A price is called **efficient** if the market has set the price correctly using *all* available information.
>
> Warning: Market efficiency is a different concept from mean-variance efficiency, which was used in the context of portfolio optimization. Economists love the word "efficiency" and thus use it in many contexts.

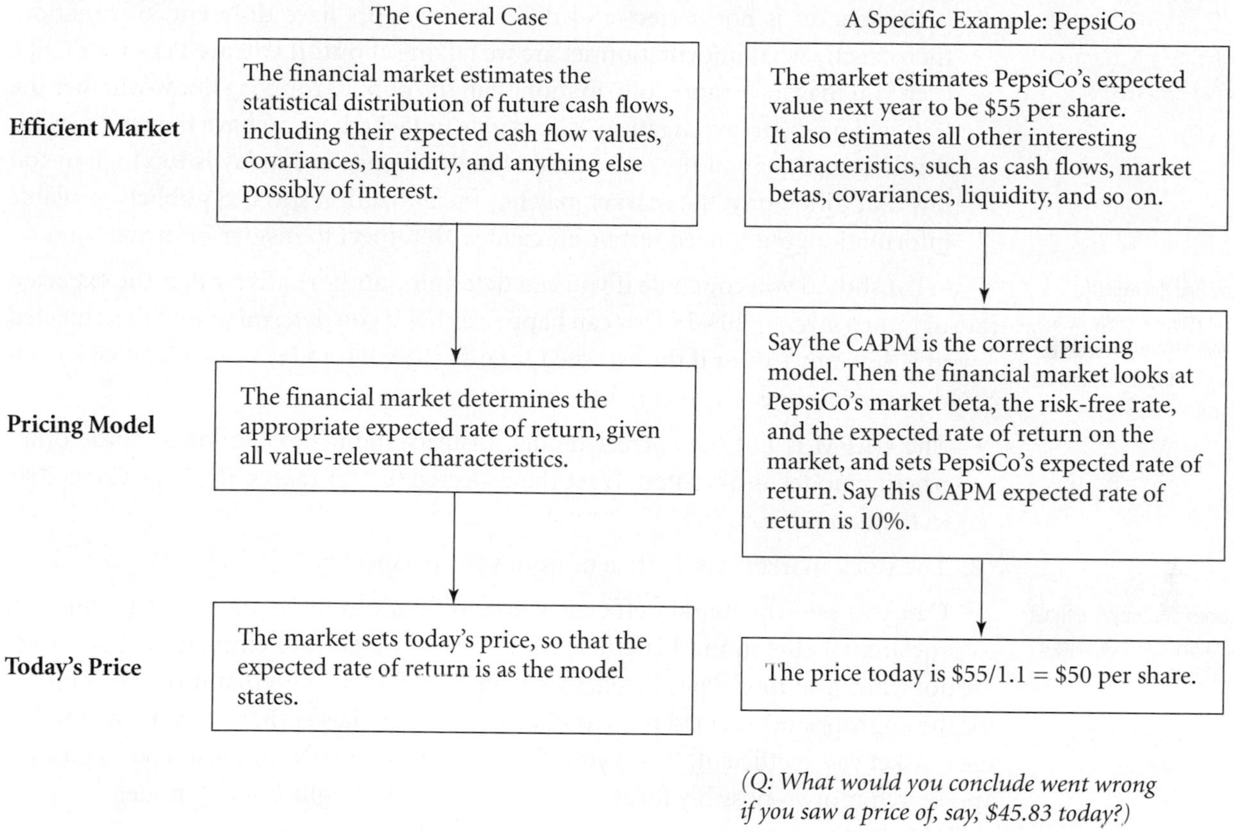
The General Case
A Specific Example: PepsiCo
Efficient Market
The financial market estimates the statistical distribution of future cash flows, including their expected cash flow values, covariances, liquidity, and anything else possibly of interest.
The market estimates PepsiCo's expected value next year to be $55 per share. It also estimates all other interesting characteristics, such as cash flows, market betas, covariances, liquidity, and so on.
Pricing Model
The financial market determines the appropriate expected rate of return, given all value-relevant characteristics.
Say the CAPM is the correct pricing model. Then the financial market looks at PepsiCo's market beta, the risk-free rate, and the expected rate of return on the market, and sets PepsiCo's expected rate of return. Say this CAPM expected rate of return is 10%.
Today's Price
The market sets today's price, so that the expected rate of return is as the model states.
The price today is $55/1.1 = $50 per share.
(Q: What would you conclude went wrong if you saw a price of, say, $45.83 today?)

FIGURE 11.1 Market Efficiency and Pricing Model

Figure 11.1 illustrates an efficient market. Suppose the market considers an expected rate of return of 10% on PepsiCo stock to be a fair rate of return, given PepsiCo's characteristics. This figure of 10% could come, for instance, from the CAPM. Market efficiency then pins down the relation between the best estimate of the price next year and the price today. In our example, if the market expects PepsiCo to trade for $55 next year, it should set the price today at $50. The market would not be efficient if it set today's price at $49 or $51. You can turn this around, too. You should not be able to locate information that tells you today when/if/that the true expected value tomorrow is really $60 (for an expected rate of return of 20%) or $50 next year (for an expected rate of return of 0%). If you could find information that tells you authoritatively that a better estimate of next year's price is $60 (or $50), then PepsiCo's stock would be mispriced. A market that has overlooked your information would not be efficient.

An example: PepsiCo's price today is based on the best estimate of future characteristics, obtained from a model like the CAPM.

The practical use of the "efficient markets" concept begs two questions:

What is the model? What is the information set?

1. Where does the figure of 10% come from? It has to come from some model that tells you what rate of return PepsiCo should have to offer given its characteristics, such as risk, liquidity, and so on. The CAPM is such a model (though only a modestly successful one). Without a good model of what you should expect the rate of return to be, market efficiency is too vague a concept to be meaningful.

2. If the market is not perfect and different investors have different information, then exactly what information set are we talking about? If you are PepsiCo's CEO, then you may have more information than the public. You may know whether the SEC will open an investigation against you and whether you have the next new hit drink in the lab right now. You could know whether $50 today is too high or too low. Put differently, the market may be efficient with respect to publicly available information, but it need not be efficient with respect to insider information.

If you find the expected rate of return is really 20%: (a) Your 10% model could be wrong; (b) the market was not efficient.

What should you conclude if you can determine authoritatively that the expected rate of return is really 20%? (This can happen either if you determine that the expected payoff is $60, not $55, or if the expected payoff is $55, but today's price is $45.83.) You could now draw one of two conclusions:

1. The CAPM is not the correct model. Instead, the market followed some other pricing model and wanted to set the expected rate of return for PepsiCo at 20% in the first place.
2. The stock market is not efficient from your perspective.

Is market efficiency so difficult to disprove that it becomes a "faith"?

Can you see why market efficiency is so difficult to prove or reject? If you wish to proclaim a belief in market efficiency, and if you then find empirically that prices are not what your model predicted, you would simply proclaim that it was your model for the appropriate expected returns in your financial market that was wrong, not that the market was inefficient. It was your fault, not the market's. You just have to go back and search more—possibly forever—until you find the right pricing model.

SOLVE NOW!

Q 11.1 What does it mean for a market to be efficient?

Q 11.2 As a believer in efficient markets, what would you likely answer when heretics claim that they can reject market efficiency because they have found assets that pay too much for their risk?

11.1A SHORT-TERM VERSUS LONG-TERM MARKET EFFICIENCY

Practically useful? Rarely over very long horizons—efficiency is more a matter of faith.

Over long horizons (say, 1 year or longer), market efficiency is extremely difficult to disprove. The reason is that no one knows exactly what the correct model of pricing is—the CAPM may often be a reasonable model, but it is not infallible and its estimates are rarely accurate in practice. We are not sure whether a stock like PepsiCo should earn 10%, 20%, or 30% a year. This renders market efficiency a concept that in practice often evades empirical testing. It is also why market efficiency is sometimes (unfairly) disparaged as being more religion than science. Based on the existing long-run evidence, some reasonable analysts conclude that financial markets are generally efficient (and our [CAPM] pricing model is wrong); and other reasonable analysts conclude that financial markets are generally not efficient.

Okay, let me qualify this for long horizons.

Of course, in extreme circumstances, market efficiency can be a useful claim even on such long horizons. We know that no reasonable model of financial markets should give investors great bets like "+$1 million with 99% probability" and "−$1 with 1% probability." Expected returns this high would be way out of line with *any* reasonable pricing model. Even expected rates of return of 100% per year would surely be unreasonable for stocks such as PepsiCo. Of course, few people doubt that the stock market is, to such a first approximation, efficient—we all know that you just can't earn that much. But there is a large gray zone where it is difficult to distinguish between model error and market inefficiency. Because no one knows for sure what the correct model of expected stock returns is, no one can tell you affirmatively whether the stock market set the price of PepsiCo stock so as to offer investors an expected rate of return on PepsiCo of, say, 10% a year or 12% a year.

Practically useful? Definitely yes over short horizons.

However, over short horizons (say, a day or so), market efficiency is a surprisingly useful concept. The reason is that over a single day it does not matter as much whether you believe the expected rate of return on PepsiCo is 0%, 10%, or 20% per annum. Even on the high-end of 20% per annum, the expected rate of return is still only about 5 basis points per day. Roughly speaking, regardless of whether you believe in the CAPM or not, you should expect day-to-day returns to be just a tiny bit above 0%. You should attribute most daily price movement to random fluctuations, presumably caused by unpredictable news of changes in the economic environment. However, if you can predict day-to-day stock movements (and you have thousands of days of historical stock returns to work with), then chances are that you would not blame the pricing model. Instead, you would probably conclude that the market is not efficient.

IMPORTANT:

- Over short time intervals (say, hours or days), market efficiency is a very powerful concept. The expected rate of return should be tiny. If it is different, the market is probably inefficient.
- Over long time intervals (say, months or years), it is difficult to pin down what the appropriate expected rate of return is. This makes it difficult to disentangle errors in the pricing model from market inefficiency.

SOLVE NOW!

Q 11.3 Is market efficiency a more powerful concept over long horizons or short horizons?

11.1B RELATION TO PERFECT MARKET

Perfect market $\Rightarrow$ efficient market.

Although the efficient market concept is different from the perfect market concept the two are intimately linked—in fact, so much so that they are often confused. The reason is that if a market is perfect, economic forces drive it instantly toward market efficiency. Put differently, if a market were perfect but inefficient, everyone would want to earn great returns and trade the same way. It would be too easy to become rich. Market prices would instantly adjust to prevent this. Therefore, if a market is perfect, it is inevitably also efficient.

Efficient market $\not\Rightarrow$ perfect market.

The converse is not true, however. It is quite possible for an imperfect market—for example, one in which there are taxes or different opinions—to be efficient. You could even (crudely) think of market efficiency as the result of the trades of many investors with many different information sets (opinions). The market price is the outcome at which investors no longer wish to trade further. Appropriately weighted, one half believes the market price is too low; the other half believes it is too high. Of course, efficiency should be contemplated market by market. It is not only possible but even likely that some financial markets are efficient, while other markets are not. The closer to perfect a market is, the more likely it is also efficient.

Transaction costs are often culprits in keeping prices from their efficient levels.

Perhaps the most important perfect market assumption driving prices toward efficiency is the absence of transaction costs. Without transaction costs, it would be easy for you and other investors to trade on any information that the market has not yet incorporated in the stock price—and thereby earn an unusually good expected rate of return. However, the no-free-lunch axiom applies here, too. High transaction costs would make it more likely that you could expect to find violations of efficient markets. But if it is very expensive to trade and if the market is therefore not efficient and does not respond to news immediately, it would also be very difficult for you to take advantage of such inefficiencies.

Investor competition pushes markets toward efficiency.

Here is a practical example of how any market inefficiency would disappear quickly in a perfect market: What would you do if you learned that the market always goes down on rainy days and up on sunny days? It is unlikely that the average investor requires extra return to hold stocks on sunny days—and, even if the average investor does, it is enough for you if you are not among them. You would never buy stocks when the weather forecast predicts that rain is coming. Instead, you would only buy stocks when the weather forecast predicts that the sun will shine. Investors like yourself—and there are of course many such investors in perfect markets—would rapidly bid up the prices before the sun shone, so that the prices would no longer systematically go up on sunny days. The end result is that if markets are efficient, then you should not be able to earn abnormally good sunny-day returns—at least not this easily. In a reasonable world, to earn higher expected rates of return, you must be willing to take on something that other investors are reluctant to take on—such as higher portfolio risk. Today's weather alone should not do it. (Actually, there is academic disagreement now whether the weather in New York City has a (small) influence on stock returns. Some papers claim it does, so that the market is inefficient. Other papers dispute this, claiming the historical correlation is spurious and disappears if the statistical tests are done correctly.)

Prices should be generally efficient even in a nonperfect financial market. Who would be willing to hold overpriced stuff?

Conversely, it is easier to believe that markets are *not* (or less) efficient if transaction costs are high. But even if the market is not perfect, market inefficiencies should still raise eyebrows. For example, let's say that the appropriate rate of return on PepsiCo was still 10% for an expected future price of \$55—but when you look, you find that the current price today is already \$58. (The true rate of return is thus −5.2%.) In a perfect market, many investors would immediately want to exploit this by selling PepsiCo short. This may not be possible if the market is so imperfect that the costs of going short are too high. However, this leaves the question of why investors who already own PepsiCo shares would not sell them ASAP. They would not incur the shorting transaction costs and would avoid the lower-than-appropriate rate of return. (Maybe they are asleep!?) Such "economic self-interested behavior" adds to the "third-party investor pressure" in driving markets toward efficient pricing, even in a market that is imperfect.

➤ Shorting stocks, Section 8.8, p. 238

IMPORTANT:

- If a market is perfect, market forces should drive it strongly and quickly toward efficiency.
- If a market is not perfect, self-interested individual behavior should still drive it toward efficiency. But this force is much weaker, and third-party traders may not be able to aid in the process.

SOLVE NOW!

Q 11.4 How does an efficient market differ from a perfect market?

Q 11.5 Is it more or less likely for a financial market to be efficient when transaction costs are low?

11.1C MARKET EFFICIENCY IN MODERN FINANCIAL MARKETS

You can reasonably assume that markets are efficient for large corporate stocks.

In the United States, the financial markets for Treasuries, for large corporate stocks, index mutual funds, currencies, and others, seem reasonably close to perfect and thus efficient. They are definitely very competitive. There are millions of buyers and sellers, thousands of tax-exempt investors, modest transaction costs, and it seems unlikely that some investors have real inside information. It is difficult to believe that you or I could outsmart the prices in such markets. After all, thousands of other traders are likely equally as smart. They would flock to good bargains and avoid bad bargains along with us. Of course, the smaller the firm, the less perfect and the less efficient the market in its stock is likely to be. Many small stocks on the NASDAQ exchange trade only rarely, and they can have large transaction costs:

➤ Bid-ask spread, Section 10.3B, p. 316

- The bid-ask spread is often high.
- The posted bid-ask spread is only guaranteed for 100 shares—if you want to trade more shares, the price is likely to move against you.
- Commissions can be high.
- Shorting small stocks can be very costly when compared to the ideal of a perfect world in which you have full access to the proceeds (e.g., to earn interest).

In a round-trip transaction, you will face the first three issues once when you buy and once when you sell. Thus, it is unlikely that small stocks will immediately and fully reflect all information appropriately. The historical prices you see posted may be "stale" and may not even reflect the price that would have applied if you had wanted to trade. Market efficiency is never white or black, but always a shade of gray—just as it is for perfect markets. Large, liquid S&P 100 stocks are pretty close to efficient; small NASDAQ stocks may not be.

The advantage of an efficient market: Prices can be trusted.

The fact that large-firm stock markets are pretty efficient means that, by and large, you can trust these financial markets to get asset values about right—at least within the limits of the typical transaction costs—and to get it right *immediately*. As an investor, would you not rather face an inefficient market? If it were inefficient, you might be able to find some good bets (opportunities that earn unusually high expected rates of return). But it would not all be gravy. In an inefficient market, you

➤ Great bets, Section 11.4, p. 360

ANECDOTE "Trading Places" and Citrus Futures

The 1983 hit comedy *Trading Places*, starring Dan Akroyd and Eddie Murphy, centers around the trading of orange juice frozen concentrate **futures contracts** on the **New York Futures Exchange**. (A future is a contract that specifies terms to buy or sell a commodity in the future—in this case, oranges.) If it is going to rain or if there is a frost, oranges will be scarcer and the futures price will rise. You can learn more about futures contracts at the website of the **New York Mercantile Exchange** at www.nymex.com.

In a 1984 paper in the *American Economic Review*, Richard Roll found that these citrus futures contracts predict whether the U.S. Weather Service's forecast for central Florida temperatures is too high or too low. It is a great example of how financial markets help aggregate information better than the best nonfinancial institution. This should not surprise you. After all, there is a lot of money at stake!

could not rely on market prices being fair—they could be inappropriately too high or too low. You would never really know whether you are overpaying or underpaying. Investing would be a very messy business. You might have to spend a lot of time and money to determine whether prices are fair. The advantage of efficient markets is that if you hold a portfolio of many large and liquid stocks, you do not have to spend a lot of time and money to perform **due diligence** in order to determine whether stocks are fairly priced. All you need to do is to make sure you are appropriately diversified to meet your risk-reward preference. And you can probably accomplish this goal by purchasing just a few large index-mimicking mutual funds.

SOLVE NOW!

Q 11.6 Would you expect the market for the dollar–euro exchange rate to be more or less perfect and efficient than the NYSE?

11.2 CLASSIFICATIONS OF MARKET EFFICIENCY BELIEFS AND BEHAVIORAL FINANCE

Classical versus behavioral finance.

A firm belief in efficient markets is what defines a school of thought known as **classical finance**, an outgrowth of the school of **rational economics**. Their belief is that the evidence supports the **efficient market hypothesis**, or **EMH**, which holds that all securities are priced efficiently. In contrast, another school of thought often dubbed **behavioral finance** posits that markets sometimes do *not* use all available information. Depending on how strong a believer in classical finance versus behavioral finance you are, you may believe that there are no especially good trading opportunities, few trading opportunities, or plenty of trading opportunities. Both camps agree, however, that market perfection plays a crucial role in determining whether a particular market is efficient or not.

Many large financial markets in the United States are probably close to efficient.

Almost all financial economists, regardless of camp, believe in basic market efficiency for large markets and liquid securities. No respectable economist believes that it is easy to get very rich trading on easily available information. Instead, the disagreement is, loosely, about whether stock markets are "99% efficient" or "97% efficient." Classical finance believes in the former, behavioral finance in the latter. Of course, you

ANECDOTE How to Get Squeezed and Lose Money Even When You Are Right

Even in cases where it is probable that the market mispriced stocks, such as technology stocks during the famous "Internet bubble" at the turn of the millennium, it was almost impossible for an individual investor to take advantage of the market inefficiency. Believe me, I know.

In 1998, I shorted Netscape. I believed that Netscape's browser was about to be taken to the cleaners by Microsoft's Internet Explorer. I was right on my prediction—but in February 1999, AOL paid a lot of money to acquire Netscape. Not satisfied with one mistake, I proceeded to my next mistake. I believed Yahoo (YHOO) was worth less than what it was trading for. I speculated that it would go down. After I had lost more than three times my original investment, I realized that I had to either close my bet or risk going bankrupt. Consequently, I terminated my bet. Yes, I would have been right in the end and made a lot of money if I had held on longer, but I simply could not afford the risk (and mental anguish) any longer. I learned from this episode—after 15 years as a financial economist—that even if the stock market is irrational and even if it overvalues a stock by three times, it can also be irrational enough to overvalue it by yet another three times.

Later on, I found out that I was not alone. The most reprinted article in the history of *Fortune* magazine was "Mr. Buffett on the Stock Market," from November 22, 1999, in which famed financier Warren Buffett warned about the overvaluations of tech stocks and Internet stocks. Like me, Buffett had suffered from years of poor performance (and from yet another quarter of misery to follow), as Internet stocks reached ever higher.

Not everyone believes there was a bubble. The book's website has an impromptu email conversation between myself and Eugene Fama (perhaps the most famous finance professor alive and a strong defender of market efficiency). This will give you an authentic impression of the ongoing dialogue among finance professors.

can trade millions of dollars in large-firm stocks or market indexes relatively easily and at low transaction costs. Thus, it does not require huge efficiency violations for behavioral finance economists to be right and for classical finance economists to be wrong. Exploiting just the tiny—say, 100% − 97% = 3%—violations from market efficiency could make you a star investor. (This is also not coincidentally why so many fund managers publicly proclaim their faith in behavioral finance.) However, don't take me too literally here—the 99% versus 97% is an analogy, and there is really a spectrum of beliefs in market efficiency among economists and fund managers. Now, although you should realize that any classification scheme really identifies just segments on a continuous line, you can still try to classify financial economists and investors by their faiths in efficiency. Let's look at some such classifications.

11.2A THE TRADITIONAL CLASSIFICATION

The traditional definition of market efficiency focuses on information. In the traditional classification, market efficiency comes in three strengths: weak, semistrong, and strong.

The traditional classification of market efficiency is about the type of information needed to beat the market.

Weak market efficiency says that all information in past prices is reflected in today's prices so that **technical analysis** (trading based solely on historical price patterns) cannot be used to beat the market. Put differently, the market is the best technical analyst.

Semistrong market efficiency says that all public information is reflected in today's stock prices, so that neither **fundamental trading** (based on underlying firm fundamentals, such as cash flows or discount rates) nor technical analysis can be used to beat the market. Put differently, the market is both the best technical and fundamental analyst.

Strong market efficiency says that all information, both public and private, is reflected in today's stock prices, so that nothing—not even private insider information—can be used to beat the market. Put differently, the market is the best analyst and cannot be beat.

Many finance professors no longer believe in *perfect* efficiency.

In this traditional classification, all finance professors nowadays believe that most financial markets are not strong-form efficient: Insider trading may be illegal, but it works. However, arguments rage on as to which markets are semistrong-form efficient or even weak-form efficient, and even for large and liquid financial markets (such as large firms traded on the NYSE or NASDAQ, or some options on the CBOE). Finance professors regularly publish papers that find new rules that would have outperformed reasonable average rates of return historically, often by large margins. Among them are some particular forms of momentum strategies (buying stocks that have gone up and selling stocks that have gone down over the last year) and value strategies (buying boring old-economy stocks, selling glamorous high-growth new-economy stocks). These strategies would have offered "excess returns" as high as 1–2% per month.

➤ Momentum and value trading, Section 9.8B, p. 294

Why do many trading strategies seem to have worked historically?

Market efficiency champions quickly point out that many of these strategies' returns were **spurious**: They disappeared almost as quickly as they were discovered, and they probably were never real to begin with. Also, many of these trading strategies would have required such high transaction costs that they would not have been profitable in the real world. That is, even if prices had not incorporated all information, thus leaving the market inefficient, they may have been well within the bounds of transaction costs. Yet, some trading strategies, such as momentum or value, do seem to have produced large historical excess returns even after transaction costs. One good question is whether they will continue to work. (Personally, I am not claiming that they will or will not work in the future.) A second good question raised by EMH proponents is what part of these strategy returns was appropriate compensation for risk (not captured by the CAPM) and thus not excessive to begin with.

➤ Value stocks, Section 9.8B, p. 294

The returns to collecting information must be in "balance" with their costs.

One conceptual question that vexed academics for a long time was how markets could be efficient to begin with. After all, if there is no money to be made, why would anyone bother collecting information on firms? And if no one bothers to collect information on firms, how can the market incorporate all information and thus be efficient? Eventually, a resolution to this puzzle was offered by Grossman and Stiglitz. They argued that markets can never be 100% efficient—they can only be, say, "99%" efficient. In equilibrium, good information collectors should earn just about enough trading profits to break even on their costs of information collecting. On the margin, the expected costs of learning and trading on more information are exactly equal to the expected trading profits. The informed investors earn this money trading against **noise traders**, who do not collect information and who may trade for idiosyncratic reasons (e.g., to pay for tuition).

SOLVE NOW!

Q 11.7 Which form of market efficiency do momentum trading strategies seem to violate?

11.2B THE FUNDAMENTALS-BASED CLASSIFICATION AND BEHAVIORAL FINANCE

I prefer an alternative classification of market efficiency, which grades economists based on their belief in whether prevailing market prices reflect underlying values:

My preferred taxonomy of market efficiency is based on how much prices deviate from value.

A true believer would argue that financial prices always reflect the best estimate of net present value of all future cash flows. This means that stock prices should change correctly if and only if news about fundamentals (cash flows or discount rates) appears.

A firm believer would argue that financial prices may sometimes deviate from the appropriate best estimate of future cash flows. However, transaction costs make it practically impossible for investors to find unusually good bets.

A mild believer would also argue that financial prices may sometimes deviate from the appropriate best estimate of future cash flows. However, unlike a firm believer, a mild believer would argue that there are occasions when it is possible to exploit this misvaluation. This would result in the occasional unusually good bet. Usually, the profitabilities of such bets should remain within economically reasonable magnitudes—a couple of percentage points a year on the high side. Mild believers thus think that smart fund managers can offer investors slightly better bets, but nothing more. There are no guarantees.

A nonbeliever would argue that financial prices regularly deviate from the appropriate value, and to an extent that allows investors to obtain great bets fairly routinely.

These classes are progressively weaker. For example, a firm believer need not be a true believer. Firm belief can be the right club to join if financial price changes are indeed unpredictable, but not because of news about fundamentals. There could be unrelated noise in stock price changes, especially in the short run. A mild believer need not be a firm believer: Transaction costs may be low enough to permit great trading strategies based on efficient markets violations. A nonbeliever need not be a mild believer: Financial markets may just beg to be exploited.

There is even some really weird but dramatic evidence against market efficiency.

Occasionally, there is evidence that refutes even the truest of believers—but this is rare. The most dramatic example occurred in 2000, when the network company 3COM spun off the PDA company Palm. Widely reported in the press at the time, 3COM retained 95% of Palm's stock—and announced that each shareholder of 3COM would soon receive 1.525 shares of Palm. After the IPO, Palm closed at \$95.06 per share. Therefore, 3COM should have been worth at least $1.525 \cdot \$95.06 \approx \$145$. Instead, 3COM shares closed at \$81.81. (It was impossible to exploit this discrepancy, because it was impossible to find Palm shares to short. Palm shares enjoyed an almost uninterrupted fall in price, down to less than \$2 per share by 2003.)

This evidence as a whole suggests that the financial markets are usually somewhere between mildly and firmly efficient.

Where do most finance professors sit in this classification of beliefs? Virtually no academic is a perpetual nonbeliever, and only a very few remain in the "true believer" camp. Instead, most finance professors are somewhere between the "mild believer" camp (the center of behavioral finance) and the "firm believer" camp (the center of classical finance). The debates between the two more extreme sides of these camps—the more "classical rational economists" and the more "behavioral economists"—are intellectually exciting. After all, bringing new evidence to bear on these disagreements is the process by which we learn more.

Buyer beware: Here is my own opinion.

Let me tell you my personal view. I sit right in the middle between the two schools of thought, somewhere in the firm-to-mild camp. In my view, most investors believe that they have more knowledge and control than they actually have. This is why I believe that trading in the stock market seems so (inexplicably) active. Many investors seem to believe that they can predict when stocks are going to go up or down. Some pundits like to call this "investor psychology." However, I also believe that an individual investor is unlikely to be able to find rate-of-return patterns in the stock market to earn high excess returns. A very few sophisticated funds may be able to earn systematically a few basis points extra per year. But these funds are scarce. Even after decades of academic research that has tried to identify better-performing funds, academics usually find that only about half of all funds outperform the market and half underperform the market—even before fund transaction costs.

SOLVE NOW!

Q 11.8 If you believe that market values do not always perfectly reflect underlying fundamental values, but that trading costs nevertheless prevent you from exploiting this profitably (in large scale), where would you classify yourself?

11.3 THE RANDOM WALK AND THE SIGNAL-TO-NOISE RATIO

The low signal-to-noise ratio allows our arguments about market efficiency to continue.

Why is the debate over market efficiency so tough to settle? It is the fact that the **signal-to-noise ratio** in financial returns is low. The signal-to-noise description draws on an analogy from physics—the **signal** (the appropriate expected price change) is small compared to the **noise** (the day-to-day price **volatility** that clouds our senses).

Let me illustrate the signal-to-noise ratio with a stock's rate of return on a particular day.

Let me explain. What are typical price change magnitudes? For example, October 4, 2007, was a fairly quiet and uneventful day on the financial markets. Ten-year Treasuries stood at 4.523%, down 2 basis points (−0.44%); 13-week T-bills traded at 3.84% (−0.13%); and 59% of NYSE stocks advanced, while 37% declined. The Dow Jones rose 6.26 (0.04%) to 13,974.31. The S&P 500 rose by +0.21%. On this day, the volume leaders (not the biggest price movers) were Level 3 Communications (+4.38%), Sun Microsystems (−1.56%), Cisco (−0.92%), and Ford Motor (+2.02%). (The 10 biggest price movers were smaller stocks, which gained between +116% and +20%.) Let me now pick two stocks randomly that had no big news on this day: PepsiCo gained 0.54% and IBM lost 0.61%. What can you learn from these magnitudes? Read on.

11.3A THE SIGNAL

Let's first put your statistical and financial expertise to good use: *In a perfect market, if the shares of a company cost \$50 today, what do you expect them to cost tomorrow?* What is a typical daily rate of return on a stock? Could you expect a reasonable model of market prices to predict that 1 day's stock price movement could be something on the order of ±1%? Think about it: If the expected rate of return on a stock were the same as the typical up or down movement of 1% per day, the rate of return on this stock over the 255 trading days in 1 year would be more than 1,000%. The \$50 stock would be worth over \$600 by next year. Who would want to sell such a stock? Who would not want to bid a lot more than \$50 for it right now? The same argument applies to a price decline of 1% per day. An investment strategy of holding onto such stocks would transform \$50 into less than \$5 by next year. Who would ever want to hold onto such stocks? The same logic would also apply to a signal that tells you on some days that one particular stock is expected to go up by 1% and on other days that some other particular stock is expected to go down by 1%. Each day, you would earn 1% by either going long or short in the relevant stock—according to your signal—and end up filthy rich. (The investors on the other side would end up poor.)

You cannot expect a real-world trading signal to be as strong as 1% per day: It would amount to over 1,000% per year.

So what kind of average daily returns can you expect from the U.S. stock market? Say a reasonable range of rates of return is between 0% and 40% per year. For 255 trading days, absent complications, this gives you daily rates of return of between 0 basis points and about 15 basis points. The majority of stocks should allow you to earn expected rates of return of between 5 and 10 basis points a day. One basis point of signal per day is 3% per year. Thus, when you test for market efficiency with a reasonable model of stock pricing, about 5 to 10 basis points per day is what you would expect to find for most stocks. If your signal allows you to earn 1 bp extra per day, then your strategy will be better by about 3% per year.

Let's make this into a formula. If your expected rate of return is a small constant m, that is, $\mathcal{E}(\tilde{r}) = [\mathcal{E}(\tilde{P}_1) - P_0]/P_0 = m$, then your best expectation of the price tomorrow ($\tilde{P}_1$) must be roughly the price today (P_0).

Over short intervals, the stock price should follow a mostly unpredictable random walk with practically no drift.

$$\text{Expected Price Tomorrow} = \text{Price Today} + \text{Tiny Drift}$$

$$\mathcal{E}(\tilde{P}_1) \quad = \quad P_0 \quad + \underbrace{m \cdot P_0}_{\text{Tiny Drift}} \tag{11.1}$$

This is customarily called a **random walk** with drift. As you just learned, depending on the stock, this tiny drift m may be around 5 to 10 basis points for most stocks. You should not be able to predict better than this drift, because this is your expected rate of return in an efficient perfect market.

Note that price behavior very close to a random walk is a necessary consequence of an efficient market, but you cannot conclude that a market is (truly) efficient just because stock prices follow roughly a random walk. For example, a market would be inefficient if you could find advance knowledge based on some other external signal—say, whether the sun is shining on a particular day—that would tell you whether the stock price will go up or down the following day. In this case, stock prices would still

Don't wag the tail: Market efficiency $\Rightarrow$ random walk. Random walk $\not\Rightarrow$ market efficiency.

ANECDOTE Great Mathematicians and Gambling: The Origin of the Random Walk

In the 1700s, it was not beneath mathematicians to study how to gamble in order to gamble better. Jacob Bernoulli (1654–1705) and Abraham DeMoivre (1667–1754) studied the random walk of a gambler's stake in fair games.

Later reinventions and applications of the random-walk concept abound: Jan Ingenhausz (1730–1799), a physician and plant physiologist, placed charcoal powder on an alcohol film and observed that the grains moved randomly. The botanist Robert Brown (1773–1858) reported erratic dancing of small particles in fluids at rest. Albert Einstein (1879–1955) considered such fluids to be composed of discrete molecules, whose many collisions with a "Brownian particle" caused the particle to jump in random directions—a random walk. Einstein's analysis not only explained **Brownian motion**, which has itself become a building block of high-tech finance nowadays, but also bolstered the case for the existence of atoms, which was not yet universally accepted. The first recorded use of the phrase "random walk" was by Lord Raleigh (1842–1919) in 1899. (Raleigh made a connection between diffusive heat flow and random scattering and showed that a one-dimensional random walk could provide an approximate solution to a parabolic differential equation.) The name is believed to have originated with the description of a drunk who stands on a ladder. The drunk can walk up or down and does so in a random fashion—just like stocks.

Fortunately, in 1900, Louis Bachelier introduced the random-walk theory of financial market fluctuations (although Karl Pearson (1857–1936) introduced the term "random walk" only later, in 1905), finding that bond prices could diffuse in the same manner as heat. Unfortunately, this has only pointed out the obvious: It is not easy for an investor to outperform the market. The first rigorous and published investigation of the random-walk hypothesis was done by Alfred Cowles, an eclectic investor and economist at Yale in the 1930s and 1940s.

Source: Mostly Michael F. Schlesinger, Office of Naval Research, *Scienceweek.com,* 2001.

follow a random walk, but your signal would allow you to outperform the EMH. The random walk only states that the known lagged price can't be this signal.

A Complication—Transaction Costs

Transaction costs destroy the profitability of many high turnover strategies.

➤ Transaction costs, Section 10.3, p. 314

The important point of perfect markets (and market efficiency) is that, given today's information, no signal can be very accurate. It should not be possible to predict stock price movements accurately enough to earn, say, 1% on a given day. Of course, in the real world, financial markets are not perfect and there are financial transaction costs that would also prevent you from really exploiting misvaluations, especially short-lived ones that require a lot of trading to exploit. You would have to pay money to your broker to buy the shares, and again to sell shares. (This is why financial markets are not exactly perfectly competitive, only approximately perfectly competitive.) Even small transaction costs can render trading strategies with very high turnover unprofitable. Even if the bid-ask spread is only 10 basis points, if incurred 255 trading days a year, you would only be left with $(1 - 0.1\%)^{255} = 0.999^{255} \approx 77\%$ of your original investment. For a *daily* trading strategy in which you have to pay the bid-ask spread every day, you need to have a signal that allows you to earn at least 23% per year before you break even—and few signals are that good.

It may be best to think of the EMH in terms of after-transaction costs.

In an imperfect market with transaction costs, you can view the efficient market hypothesis in one of two ways:

1. The EMH should hold if you work with post-transaction cost rates of return. 1% per day is still unreasonably large, because typical round-trip transaction costs

should not exceed 10 to 30 basis points, depending on the stock and the size of the trade. A daily rate of return of 0.7% is still way too large.

2. The EMH could hold if you realize that certain investors have lower transaction costs. For example, a signal may tell you to purchase a stock today and sell it tomorrow. You would have to pay transaction costs. But the investor who was considering selling the stock anyway only needs to wait another day to take advantage of the misvaluation before selling it. This investor really incurs no additional transaction costs.

So the EMH won't hold perfectly in an imperfect market, but it should be a fairly reasonable description of reality—at least it is one that you can use to compute back-of-the-envelope magnitudes and it is a hypothesis that can be tested.

SOLVE NOW!

Q 11.9 From memory, write down the formula for a random walk.

Q 11.10 What is the typical expected rate of return on a stock on an average trading day?

Q 11.11 What kind of rates of return does a strategy of trading stocks once a day have to offer in order for you to earn a positive rate of return? Assume typical real-world trading transaction costs are about 10 basis points.

11.3B THE NOISE

To put more emphasis on the noise, we can write our random walk with drift in terms of the stock prices that you will actually observe:

The daily noise in stock returns is much larger than the daily signal.

$$\text{Price Tomorrow} = \text{Price Today} + \text{Tiny Drift} + \text{Noise}$$

$$\tilde{P}_1 = P_0 + m \cdot P_0 + \tilde{\epsilon}$$

What do we know about reasonable typical standard deviations for the noise for U.S. stocks? There is no particular theoretical reason why the day-to-day standard deviation of a particular stock could not be 10%, 50%, or even 100%. So it is best for us simply to rely on the empirical data. Historical averages suggest the following:

- The typical day-to-day standard deviation of individual stocks in the market is around 2–3% per day, of course depending on the firm. For well-diversified portfolios, like stock market indexes, the standard deviation is usually lower—perhaps 1–2% per day.

October 4, 2007, was on the low side in terms of volatility, but the typical noise movement of 200 to 300 basis points for individual stocks was clearly much higher than the 5 to 10 basis points that you would expect them to earn.

IMPORTANT: In the financial market context, "random walk" refers to a process in which the *expected* value tomorrow is (almost) the same as the value today. Technically,

$$\mathcal{E}(\tilde{P}_1) = P_0 + \underbrace{m \cdot P_0}_{\text{Tiny Drift}} \Leftrightarrow \tilde{P}_1 = P_0 + \underbrace{m \cdot P_0}_{\text{Tiny Drift}} + \underbrace{\tilde{\epsilon}}_{\text{Noise}}$$

where m is a very small positive drift. (Another version of a random walk is $\mathcal{E}(\tilde{P}_1) = P_0 + m$; in practice, this version is almost indistinguishable from the one in the main formula.)

Naturally, *actual* values tomorrow will likely be different from their values today. The empirical stock price evidence is highly favorable. Stock prices indeed tend to follow roughly a random walk, at least in the short run. This means that you cannot get rich trading based on past prices.

SOLVE NOW!

Q 11.12 What is the typical movement of a stock on an average day?

Q 11.13 If stocks follow a random walk, can the price tomorrow be different from the price today?

11.3C DETECTING AN INTERESTING SIGNAL IN THE NOISE

Detecting signal in a lot of noise is difficult.

You now know that the tiny drift is typically around 5 to 10 basis points per day, and the noise is typically about 100 to 300 basis points per day for U.S. stocks and stock portfolios. How easy is it to determine whether you are facing a stock with 5 basis points' signal versus one with, say, 7 basis points' signal? Why 7 basis points? Because it is what you should be earning extra every day if you have a signal that allows you to earn an extra 5% per year in expected performance, above and beyond what your model of risk-adjusted returns says you should be earning. (A performance of 5% per year in risk-adjusted returns would be stellar for just about any fund.) Put differently, to determine whether your signal is real or illusory, you must be able to distinguish between an appropriate 5 basis points and an excessive 7 basis points for the average daily rate of return.

You cannot conclude anything from just 1 day of return

How easy is it to detect an extra signal of 2 basis points when hidden in noise of about 200 basis points? Obviously, 1 daily return is not going to do it. If I tell you that your investment pick happened to earn 50 basis points today, you could not reliably conclude that it was your signal. In fact, if anything, you should believe it was primarily noise. Recall from your statistics course that the T-statistic is defined as the mean divided by the standard deviation, $\mathcal{E}(\tilde{r})/\ \mathcal{S}dv(\tilde{r})$. If your strategy performs as expected, your 1-day T-statistic would be only $2\text{bp}/200\text{bp} = 0.01$. To have good statistical confidence, you would want a T-statistic of around 2. Your expected 0.01 is a long way off.

You cannot consider multiple returns from the same day as independent observations.

To draw reliable conclusions, you need a lot more independent daily observations. Unfortunately, you cannot use the returns from many stocks from the same day as independent signals. First, your signal may only be for some particular stocks and not for all stocks. Second, all stocks tend to move together on a given day and are therefore not independent observations. (If all 100 oil stocks go up, and your signal suggested holding oil stocks, you do not have 100 independent observations confirming your signal's ability to predict.)

Fortunately, you can regard returns from different days as independent observations. You can therefore use sequential days of investment performance to investigate the quality of your signal. How many daily returns would you need to expect to be able to reliably detect a signal of an extra 2 basis points hidden in noise of 200 basis points? Let's ignore compounding and pretend that rates of return over time are just the simple sum of daily rates of return. In this case, your expected rate of return over N days is N times the expected rate of return over 1 day. Recall from Question 8.35 that the standard deviation of your rate of return over N days is $\sqrt{N}$ times the standard deviation over 1 day. Your T-statistic over N days is therefore

You can use consecutive days as independent observations. Here is how mean, standard deviation, and T-statistic accumulate over time.

➤ Standard deviation of a sum, Question 8.35, p. 236

$$N\text{-day } T\text{-Statistic} = \frac{\text{Excess Mean}}{\text{Standard Deviation}} = \frac{N \cdot \mathcal{E}(\tilde{r})}{\sqrt{N} \cdot \mathcal{S}dv(\tilde{r})} = \sqrt{N} \cdot \text{1-day } T\text{-Statistic}$$

How many trading days (N) do you need in order to expect a T-statistic of 2 if your 1-day T-statistic is 0.01? You need $200^2 = 40{,}000$ days to have such confidence. This is about 157 years worth of data. This is if your strategy performs as expected—if the world is not changing and your signal's forecasting ability is not deteriorating. If your signal is not about individual stocks, but about large diversified portfolios, then the noise is lower than 200 basis points. If it is, say, noise of 100 basis points per day, which may be the case for highly diversified portfolios, then you only need about $100^2 = 10{,}000$ days (39 years) of data. There are many signals for such diversified trading strategies, which can therefore be examined with real-world data. (I already described some of these, principally momentum and book/market value, although it is not perfectly clear whether their high historical average returns were due to risk or due to market inefficiencies.) Still, with the world and the signal always changing (after all, there may be more and more investors trying to profit from historical signals), the historical evidence alone may not always be entirely convincing.

Only diversified strategies that perform well for many decades give us the chance to learn whether they are real.

➤ Momentum and book/market, Section 9.8B, p. 294

IMPORTANT:

- The quality of your inference about a strategy's performance increases roughly with the square root of time.
- On an average day, the typical stock may easily move up or down by about 20 to 50 times as much as it offers in expected rate of return. Therefore, it takes at least many decades, if not centuries, of data to reliably conclude whether a signal-based strategy picking individual stocks is real or illusory.

SOLVE NOW!

Q 11.14 To be a consistent superstar trader, by how many basis points should you be able to outperform the risk-adjusted financial market per typical day?

Q 11.15 Assume that the typical day-to-day noise (standard deviation) is about 100 basis points. Assume that you have the kind of stock-picking ability that earns you an extra 200 basis points per annum. Assume no transaction costs. Ignore compounding and assume that your rate of return is the sum of returns over trading days. Assume there are 255 trading days per year.

(a) With only 1-day performance, how much extra do you expect to earn per day?
(b) How bad is your noise over 1 day?
(c) What is your expected T-statistic (the excess mean divided by the standard deviation)?

Recall from your statistics course that a T-statistic of 1.96 gives you good statistical confidence above the 95% level. In Question 8.35, you learned that the standard deviation grows with the square root of time.

(d) With 255 trading days of performance, how much extra rate of return do you expect to earn per annum?
(e) How bad is your noise over 255 days?
(f) What is your expected T-statistic now?
(g) Work out how many years you would expect to wait before you would obtain reliable statistical evidence that you have a positive ability to pick stocks.

11.4 TRUE ARBITRAGE AND RISK(Y) ARBITRAGE

Measuring investment performance brushes on a closely related topic—what exactly is the financial concept of arbitrage? Intuitively, an arbitrage is a great investment opportunity, perhaps so great that you should not be able to find one. It is the desire of traders to exploit any arbitrage opportunity as soon as it appears that makes financial markets efficient. It is a matter of basic financial literacy for you to understand what arbitrage is.

11.4A THE DEFINITION OF ARBITRAGE

In a perfect market, the market will be efficient and the law of one price will hold.

➤ Law of one price, Section 1.1A, p. 2

First recall that the *law of one price* states that two identical items at the same time and location should have the same price. This is true in a perfect market, but even if the market is not perfect, it can be (and in fact usually is) still true. For example, even if all investors disagree about the future, even if there are taxes, even if there are transaction costs, and even if there is only one market maker, it should be, and usually still is, the case that one share of IBM costs the same as another. But in a perfect market, the law of one price does not just *usually* hold; it must *always* hold. If it were not to hold, you and the other infinitely many potential buyers could find arbitrage opportunities. The arbitrage concept is so important that you should understand it exactly, not just intuitively.

IMPORTANT:

A **true arbitrage** is a business transaction

- that offers positive net cash inflows in at least some scenarios,
- and under no circumstance—either today or in the future—has a negative net cash flow. This means that it is risk free.

An example: $5 for free.

A **risk(y) arbitrage** is a business transaction that may not be risk free but that still offers an excessive expected rate of return given its (risk and other) characteristics. A good way to think of a risk(y) arbitrage is as a **great bet**. Admittedly, the term "risk(y) arbitrage" is an oxymoron. However, Wall Street uses the term "risk arbitrage" for a particular type of trading (most often in the context of M&A transactions) that is similar to the sense in which we shall be using it. Thus, we shall commit the same sin.

An example: A chance to win $1,000,000 with 99% probability and to lose $1 with 1% probability.

Arbitrage is the "perpetual motion" of economics. It is defined in terms of (the possibility of) negative cash outlays.

Arbitrage is an ex-ante concept, not an ex-post concept—beforehand, not after the fact. For example, it does not mean that a lottery ticket that won was an arbitrage. Ex ante, a lottery ticket is not an arbitrage. Please also pay close attention to what the "no-negative-cash-flow" condition means in the definition of arbitrage:

➤ Ex-ante fair bet, Section 6.1A, p. 139

1. Arbitrage is not the same as "earning money without risk." After all, Treasuries do just that, and they are not arbitrage. The reason is that you have to lay out cash to buy Treasuries. This is a negative net cash flow today.
2. Arbitrage is also not the same as "receiving money today without a clear obligation to repay": If you are willing to accept risk, you can often receive cash today. For example, insurance companies take money in exchange for the possibility that they may have to pay up in the future.

"Risk(y)" arbitrage ≈ great bet. Unlike a true arbitrage, a risk(y) arbitrage could possibly lose a little money.

Now contemplate the difference between the examples of the true arbitrage and the risk(y) arbitrage in the definition. You can lose $1 with 1% probability in the risky arbitrage, so it is "just" a great bet and not a true arbitrage. One difference is conceptual: Every investor would want to take a true arbitrage opportunity, but an infinitely risk-averse investor would not take a risk(y) arbitrage. This does not mean that, given an either-or choice, a less risk-averse investor would necessarily prefer the small, true arbitrage opportunity. In our example, would you prefer the $5 true arbitrage, if it cannot be repeated, to the risk(y) arbitrage with an expected payout is close to $1 million? (If you could scale the true arbitrage opportunity to take it infinitely many times, the true arbitrage opportunity would dominate, of course.) Of course, this example of risk(y) arbitrage was extreme. More realistically, bets are never this great—"very good" is rare enough. And because there is still risk, you may not want to scale up good but risk(y) arbitrage bets in the same way you would always want to scale up true arbitrage bets as much as possible. Eventually, with enough investment in the risk(y) bet, your risk aversion would kick in and stop you from taking more of it.

There should be few arbitrages in competitive financial markets. Only this fact allows us to study and describe (sane) markets.

Most of all, unless financial markets are very imperfect, you should not expect to find many arbitrage opportunities of either type. If you agree with this assessment—basically that the world is sane and that money does not grow on trees—you can draw some surprisingly strong conclusions about how financial markets work. If you disagree, why are you still in this class? If you are right, you should be among the richest people in the world and there is little that this book can teach you.

SOLVE NOW!

Q 11.16 Is earning money without risk an arbitrage?

Q 11.17 Explain when and why you would prefer a true arbitrage to a risk(y) arbitrage opportunity.

11.4B MORE HYPOTHETICAL ARBITRAGE EXAMPLES

In a sense, positive-NPV projects *under certainty* are arbitrage.

Of course, it is difficult to find real-world examples of arbitrage. Arbitrage is principally a concept. What would a hypothetical arbitrage opportunity look like? For example, if you can purchase an item for $1, borrow at an interest rate of 9% (all costs, including your time), and sell the item tomorrow for $1.10 for sure, you earn 1 cent for certain today without any possible negative net cash flows in the future. If you ever stumble upon such an opportunity, please take it—it is a positive-NPV project! More than this, it is a true arbitrage because you cannot lose money in any scenario; it is riskless. Yet it is obviously not a very important arbitrage by itself. Searching for 1-cent arbitrage opportunities in financial markets is potentially more lucrative, because they often allow transactions to be scaled up. If you could repeat this 1-cent arbitrage 1 billion times, then you could earn $10 million. Unfortunately, although you may find an arbitrage that works once for 1 cent, it is unlikely that you can find such an arbitrage opportunity that works for 1 billion items. After all, you are not the only one searching in the financial markets! True arbitrage opportunities are difficult or outright impossible to find in the real world, especially in very competitive financial markets.

Small arbitrages matter only if they are scalable.

Arbitrage could conceivably occur between different financial markets.

Another hypothetical example of arbitrage would involve stock prices that are out of sync on different stock exchanges. If PEP shares are quoted for $51 on the Frankfurt Stock Exchange, and for $50 on the New York Stock Exchange, you could theoretically buy one share in New York for $50 and sell it in Frankfurt for $51. You then pocket $1 today. If you can do this with 20,000 PEP shares worth $1 million, you earn $20,000 without effort or risk.

But be skeptical. There are many complications to take into account.

But before you conclude that this is an arbitrage, you still have to make sure that you have not forgotten about costs or risks. The arbitrage may be a lot more limited than it seems—or may not even be present at all. Consider the following issues:

1. Could the price change in between the time you buy the shares in New York and the time you sell the shares in Frankfurt (even if it is only 3 seconds)? If such execution-timing risk exists, this is not pure arbitrage because there is a chance of a negative net cash flow. The real-world evidence suggests that price discrepancies between markets often disappear within a few seconds.

2. Did you account for the direct and indirect transaction costs? How much commission do you have to pay? Is $51 the Frankfurt bid price at which you can sell shares in a market, and $50 the NYSE ask price at which you can buy shares? Can you sell the share in Frankfurt and get it quickly enough from New York to Frankfurt to make the closing? Have you accounted for the value of your own time watching the screen for opportunities?

➤ Bid and ask prices, Section 10.3B, p. 316

3. Could the share prices move when you want to transact a significant amount of shares? Only the first 100 shares may be available for $50 for a net profit of $100. The next 900 shares may cost $50.50—perhaps still worthwhile, but less profitable. And purchasing the remaining 19,000 shares may cost you $51 or more.
4. Did you account for your fixed cost of setting up your business? If it costs you a million dollars to get offices and computers in order to "arbitrage" a few thousand dollars, it is obviously not a real arbitrage. So you must account for how expensive it is to set up your operations.

It may be that small arbitrage opportunities occur from time to time, but large financial firms are constantly running automated computer trading programs that search for even tiny arbitrage opportunities in order to exploit them as soon as they appear—and thereby make them disappear.

SOLVE NOW!

Q 11.18 Before you dedicate your life to exploiting a seeming arbitrage between financial markets, what questions should you ask?

11.5 INVESTMENT CONSEQUENCES

Is the past rate of return a good signal for the future rate of return?

How does the EMH matter to you if you are an investor? In an efficient market, there should be no obvious signals to outperform the risk-adjusted appropriate expected return to the tune of, say, 10 basis points a day above transaction costs. For sure, it should not be possible for you or anyone else to earn arbitrage returns. Let's consider two examples—technical analysis and investment fund management.

11.5A WEAK-FORM EFFICIENCY AND TECHNICAL ANALYSIS

Could there be "cycles" in the market?

The main point of the traditional classification of market efficiency, specifically the "weak" version, is the claim that you should not become rich by trading a strategy that relies only on historical prices. So let me start with some trick questions. Look at the various graphs in Figure 11.2. Do they show what stock market patterns could look like? Perhaps. Does it make sense to think that all these patterns can be representative of the future? Absolutely not! Graphs (a) and (b) display a strong regular cycling pattern. If they were representative of the future, you should quickly become a wealthy technical analyst! You would purchase the stock only when it has "bottomed out"—a pattern that you can reasonably detect if you see a multimonth period of losses followed by about a quarter of stable returns. It need not be the kind of regular cycles in the figure: Any good predictable patterns (such as "every time the price hits $22,

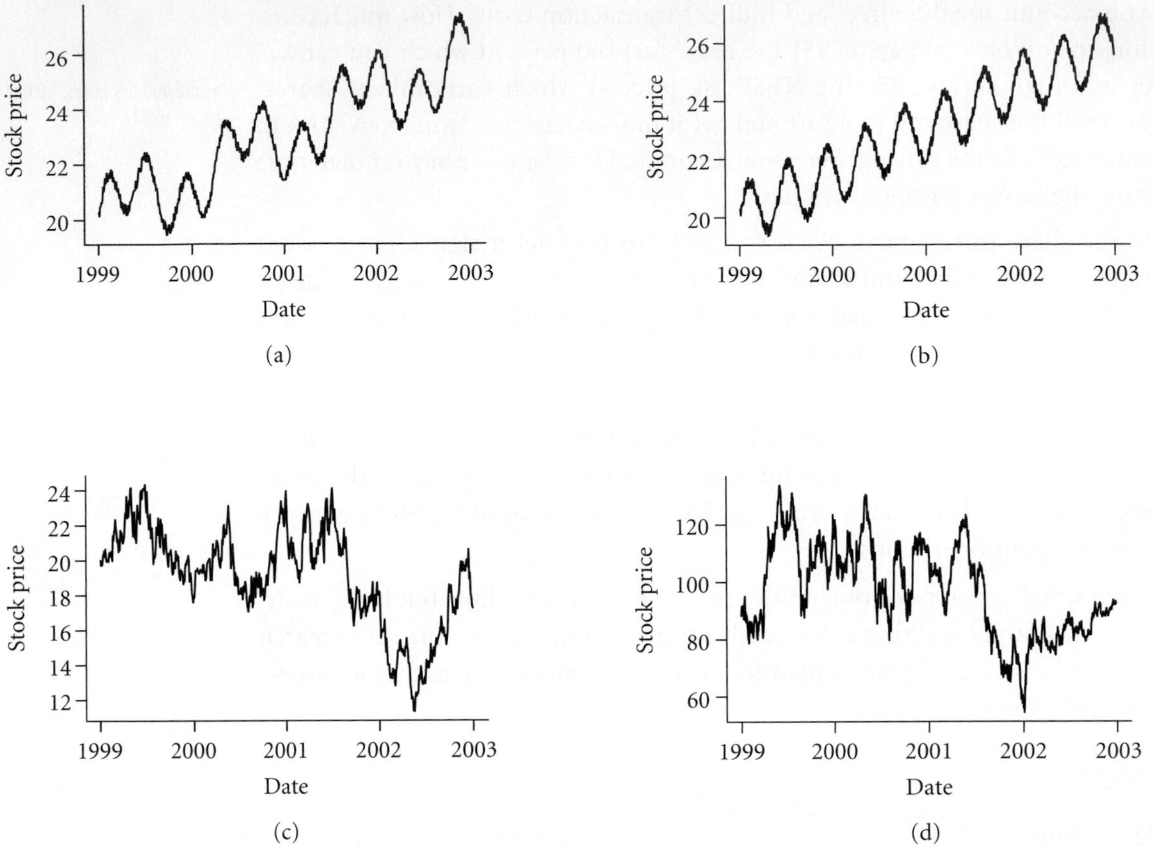

If these patterns were systematic, some of them should make you rich. Which ones? And which is the real series?

FIGURE 11.2 Potential Stock Price Patterns

it drops by $2") would allow you to get rich. Now, if you look hard enough, can you find some stocks in the real world that have historically behaved like these graphs? Yes—because with over 10,000 stocks currently trading, by pure chance, maybe one or two could show a pattern that would look remarkably similar to a cycle pattern. But, despite assurances from some stock analysts that you could have made money if you had just trusted their cycle patterns and that you should trust them henceforth, the patterns would *not* be representative of the future—they would just be historical coincidence.

Cycles are not reasonably likely—although there are ups and downs in the market, too.

On the other hand, graphs (c) and (d) could actually be representative. On average, each price in the next month is just a tiny bit higher than the previous (i.e., the expected rate of return on stocks is positive), but the important aspect of (c) and (d) is that there is a lot of *noise*, up or down. Noise is by definition unpredictable, and stock prices must largely be unpredictable, or you could outsmart the stock market. Incidentally, one of these graphs is a real stock price that I picked at random, while the other is a simulated random walk. Can you detect which one? I cannot! The real-world price series looks just like a simulation of patternless day-to-day random-walk changes. In fact, if you ever look at graphical representations of stock prices, most will

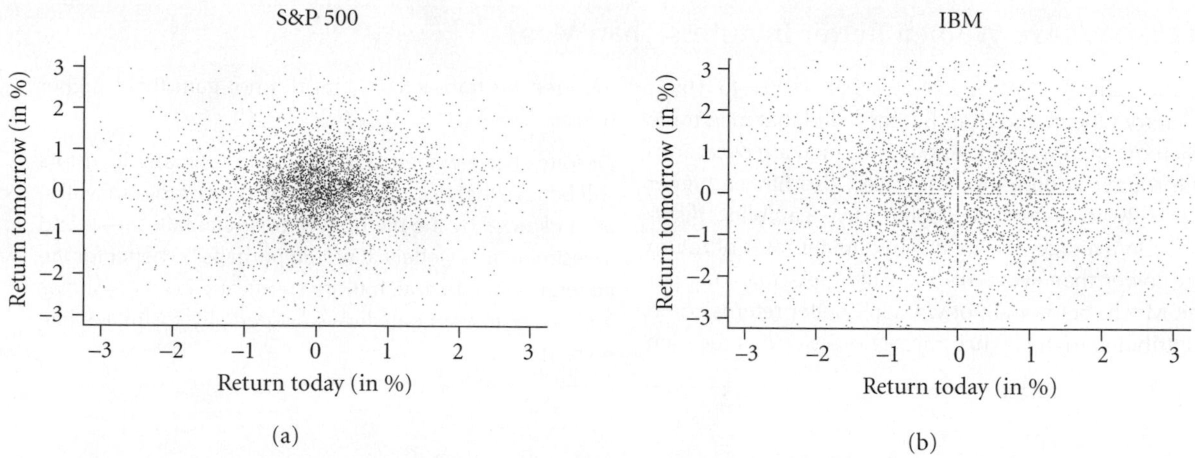

Note: The figures chop off some outliers, especially the crash of 1987 and mini-crash of 1989, but even if they are included, there is no apparent predictability.

FIGURE 11.3 The Relation between Lagged and Current Rates of Return

look very much like graphs (c) and (d) and very unlike graphs (a) and (b). (Solution: Graph (d) is an actual stock price series of IBM.)

The Empirical Evidence

Predicting with past rates of return mostly appears to fail.

Traders have been trying all sorts of strategies in their efforts to become rich. So how well does technical analysis—which tries to find patterns in historical stock prices—typically do? For example, one version has it that stocks that rise one day are more likely to fall back the next day. Figure 11.3 shows tomorrow's rate of return on the S&P 500 and on IBM as a function of today's rate of return (from 1985 to 2003). The graphs show no pattern that would allow you to get rich quickly. There is definitely not much juice in trying to predict how a stock will perform tomorrow, given how it performed today. (Although difficult to spot here, there is a small day-to-day reversal in this data—a tiny negative slope. This is caused by the **bid-ask bounce**: If a stock's closing price is a [higher] ask price, on average it will fall back the next day when it will close with either a bid or an ask price with roughly equal probability. If the stock's closing price is a [lower] bid price, on average it will gain the next day. This is a data illusion and not exploitable.) Similar conclusions apply if you extend your use of historical price information beyond yesterday. You can even try out your own technical analysis at a number of financial websites, such as Yahoo! *Finance*—look up any stock and choose "Charts," then "Technical Analysis"; it is fun, but unfortunately fairly useless.

Momentum: Firms that did well over the last year (with 1-month lag) continue to do well.

➤ Momentum, Section 9.8B, p. 294

However, over annual horizons, it appears as if stocks tend to continue their pattern just a little bit. This is the "momentum" effect mentioned earlier. It should be covered in more detail in an investments course. (Of course, as you already know from Section 11.1A, it is very difficult to determine whether an extra few percent is an appropriate rate of return to compensate investors for some risk, or whether it is a market inefficiency.)

ANECDOTE Are Women Better Investors Than Men?

Analyzing 35,000 households from 1991 to 1997, Terry Odean and Brad Barber found that men trade 45% more than women. Apparently, men are overconfident in their trading prowess. (Men also have a higher propensity to suffer from compulsive gambling disorders.) On average, the men's investment rates of return were lower than women's by a little less than 1% per year. Much, but not all, of women's better returns could be attributed to the higher transaction costs that the men incurred for transactions that did not gain them higher returns.

Despite strong evidence to the contrary, many investors still believe that stock prices do not follow random walks, as evidenced by the plethora of financial talk shows and investment newsletters. It would perhaps be better for the general public to watch more sports and cooking shows and fewer investment shows—especially for males like myself!

11.5B INVESTMENT MANAGER PERFORMANCE EVALUATION

What about celebrity investors?

What about all the televised stock analysts who explain which stocks are undervalued and which stocks are overvalued? And what about the aforementioned technical analysis, the art of seeing patterns (shoulders, price barriers, faces, etc.) in historical prices and using them to forecast future prices? And what about famous investors such as Warren Buffett, George Soros, and many others? Should you trust them?

What could you conclude from their stellar past performances? These are three possibilities.

First, recall that the low signal-to-noise ratio means it is difficult to determine why a particular trading strategy has earned high returns:

- Was it because it had a lucky outcome, which will not repeat (random luck)?
- Was it because it took on some risk that your appropriate return model forgot (your fault in measuring performance)?
- Or was it because the market was inefficient (you have a good signal, skill, and trading ability)?

This is not just a problem for academics. In fact, we finance professors are lucky: We can continue to write papers that argue one side or the other. The real conundrum is faced by every investor in the real world every day: How do you distinguish between a good and a bad signal—between skill and luck—when it comes to investing or to selecting a fund manager?

Here are possible objections to believing in their magical investment abilities (and in inefficient markets).

But the signal-to-noise ratio problem is not even the only problem that you need to consider when you pick an investment manager. If you believe that the market is inefficient so that your fund manager can make you money, consider the following:

Why would they tell anyone?

Evidence? Of course, maybe there are some investors who *can* pick stocks. Unfortunately, they would not want anyone to learn how they do it. In fact, they may want to do so secretly and privately, never eager to appear on anyone's radar screen. This can make it difficult to find investors with superior ability and thus impossible to confirm their abilities.

➤ Ascertaining superior performance, Section 11.3C, p. 359

Enough data? Recall our earlier conclusion that a strategy with great performance requires many decades before you can realistically conclude that it has worked. (This is assuming that the world is not changing.) Few strategies have such long track records.

Remarkably, the most common industry standard for evaluating funds is their most recent 3 years of investment performance. There is no disagreement that most of the 3-year performance of funds is noise. This means that many investors (and especially investors in hedge funds) shift their holdings often based on noise. Why? Either they do not understand how long it takes to determine reliably whether a strategy works (possible), or they do not care too much about reliability (more likely). If they believe that there are many other strategies that also have a close to 50-50 probability of success, then eliminating one strategy that had 3 bad years and therefore only a 49-51 probability of success may not be a costly choice.

The industry standard of 3 years' performance is not driven by the need to get solid statistical inference.

Monkeys on keyboards? There are about 10,000 mutual funds today that invest money on their investors' behalf. How many of them are likely to outperform the overall stock market next year (at least before they collect fees) if none of them has any superior investing ability? About 5,000. How many of these outperform the year thereafter? About 2,500. Even if there is absolutely no ability, pure randomness means that about 10 funds outperform the market every year for 10 years in a row. With enough candidates, some funds will inevitably produce consistently positive long-run track records.

Pure chance means that some investors succeed many years in a row.

➤ Mutual funds, Section 7.2C, p. 194

Who is still alive? What happens to the funds that have underperformed several years in a row? They disappear quietly. What happens to the funds that have outperformed several years in a row? They proudly announce their performances, advertise, boast, and collect more investments from outside investors. Their managers are supported by larger "research teams," appear better dressed and more "professional," and fly in executive jets. They are the ones that are most visible. Indeed, if you made money 10 years in a row in the stock market, would you not believe yourself that you have the ability to pick stocks?

Good past performers grow.

Now put yourself in the shoes of an investor looking at the universe of mutual funds offered today. First, you won't notice funds that have performed poorly. They have already disappeared. Second, you will notice that the larger funds seem to have done better. On average, it will seem that currently available funds indeed can make you money—even if in the real world there is absolutely no ability. This phenomenon is called **survivorship bias**, because it means that you cannot consider the historical performance of existing funds to be a fair projection of their future performance.

Why funds' average historical performance looks good to you as an investor *today*.

Who gets the rents from trading ability? Even if the financial markets were inefficient and even if some fund managers could in fact systematically outperform the market, in a reasonable market, these fund managers would charge appropriately high fees to capture all the advantages that they provide to investors. After all, it is the fund manager who would have the scarce skill (picking stocks) and not the typical investor. Investors with money would compete to place money with such managers and accept higher and higher fund fees. In the end, it would be highly unlikely that uninformed investors could earn excess returns by investing in some manager's actively trading fund.

If there was superior fund performance, the fund manager—not the investor—would profit the most.

In sum, if you are looking for future performance, past performance may be your best guide. But always remember that recent past performance is still a very poor guide.

ANECDOTE The Three Top Investment Books of 1996

The three best-selling investment books of spring 1996 were David and Tom Gardner's *Motley Fool Investment Guide*, based on a popular investment website; Matt Seto's *The Whiz Kid of Wall Street's Investment Guide* (Matt Seto was 17 years of age at the time); and the *Beardstown Ladies' Common-Sense Investment Guide*, authored by septuagenarians whose first book mixed cooking recipes with investment advice. All touted "common-sense methods" to beat the market, earning 30% per year or more. Not a week went by without dozens of prominent radio and TV shows featuring their advice. Why does anyone need a Ph.D in finance? It is difficult to argue with performance!

Naturally, best-selling books are a great business. However, the stock performance of these three experts was not.

1. From 1996 to 2002, the *Motley Fool* recommended a number of hypothetical portfolios (now discontinued!). In 1997, they launched a real-money portfolio, called DRIP. From July 28, 1997, to July 31, 2002, it lost about 10%, while the S&P 500 lost 2.5% and NASDAQ lost 15%. One should not judge a fund by just 5 years of performance (and certainly not without risk adjustment), but it does appear that the *Motley Fool* has not exactly found the Holy Grail of investment opportunities.
2. Matt Seto stopped publishing his stock picking performance and decided to pursue a career as a student.
3. The Beardstown Ladies, five books richer, were found to have miscalculated their returns: Their returns were not 30%, but 9%—significantly lower than the 15% turned in by the S&P 500 stock market index during their investment period.

How disappointing: On average, about one of them should have continued beating the market, one should have done about the same as the market, and one should have underperformed it.

Source: Time Magazine, March 1998.

Many hedge funds are compensated on the upside. This does not solve investors' problem, but the alternative is no better.

Obviously, picking the right investment manager is not an easy task. Many mutual funds earn fees regardless of whether they make you money or not. Would it be better to have them participate in the upside (as is the case for hedge funds)? Maybe, but consider this: I give you stock tips, and I ask for money only if you make money. In fact, I only want 10% of your winnings. "You have nothing to lose." I only get something if I help you make money. Sounds like a deal? Now, if I pick a stock randomly, I have a 50-50 chance of making money. If you gain, I get something. If you lose, I pay nothing. In effect, I am arbitraging you! Remember next time someone gives you a great stock tip to regard it with some skepticism: It probably has a 50-50 chance of being right. (Maybe I should give you the advice to buy a stock, and your neighbor the advice to sell it. This way, I will surely make money from one of you.) My only mistake is that I have told you my plan.

THE EMPIRICAL EVIDENCE

You must realize that even top investors can have at most mild predictive abilities.

So what is the empirical evidence? In general, it suggests that fund managers' luck is far more important than their ability. Whenever academics (or the *Wall Street Journal*) have searched for better performance among analysts or professional fund managers who have outperformed in the past, they have found little or no exceptional forward-looking performance. (If some managers were truly capable of systematically earning better rates of return by picking stocks, you would expect those managers who have picked better in the past to pick better in the future also.) The evidence is that about 54% of mutual funds that have outperformed their benchmarks over the last 1–3 years tend to outperform their benchmarks over the following 1–3 years. This is better than 50%, but not by much. And if you subtract fund fees, the average performance drops significantly below 50%. As fund prospectuses aptly note, and as the evidence suggests, *past performance is no predictor of future performance*.

There are, of course, other ways to make money: Warren Buffett's fund, **Berkshire Hathaway**, for example, runs many businesses (e.g., insurance and aircraft), too. These businesses make money. But it is money earned the old-fashioned way—through hard work, liquidity provision, and risk-taking. Writing insurance is risky business, and it deserves extra return. Warren Buffett himself would of course not attribute his own performance to luck, but to his ability. Still, even he acknowledges that the efficient markets hypothesis is the most natural benchmark. He is on record stating that "the professors who taught efficient market theory said that someone throwing darts at the stock tables could select stock portfolios having prospects just as good as ones selected by the brightest, most hard-working securities analyst. Observing correctly that the market was frequently efficient, they went on to conclude incorrectly that it was always efficient." Even Buffett is still a mild believer!

For the most part, it seems that old-fashioned work and insurance (or liquidity) provision work better in earning returns than stock picking.

➤ Liquidity provision as a business, Section 10.3D, p. 319

In sum, most finance professors nowadays would agree that when one particular investor earns an unusual amount of money, even over a few years, it is usually more likely due to luck than to ability. The burden of proof is with the side that is claiming superior signals and investing ability—and a number of former finance professors have taken up the challenge and started their own funds.

Where should the burden of proof be?

IMPORTANT: Even in an efficient market, in which no one can pick stocks better than anybody else, with a very large number of investors, many will beat the market. A small number of investors will beat the market again and again.

In the real world, there is little evidence that investors who did well picking stocks in the past are better at picking stocks in the future when compared to investors who did poorly.

SOLVE NOW!

Q 11.19 If you want to determine whether fund managers have an ability to outperform the stock market, given that many of them are likely to beat the market, does it make sense to look for these high-ability managers among the better historical performers?

Q 11.20 If a firm employs 10,000 analysts, how many of them are likely to issue forecasts that beat the market 10 years in a row *if* none of them has special any ability and there are no transaction costs?

Q 11.21 Explain what survivorship bias is and how it manifests itself in the mutual fund context.

11.6 CORPORATE CONSEQUENCES

When creating value for your firm, there are three different market scenarios to consider.

How does the EMH matter to you if you are a manager? Does it matter whether financial markets are perfect, efficient, or neither? Because a perfect market implies an efficient market, you need to think about three different cases:

1. The market is efficient and perfect.
2. The market is efficient but not perfect.
3. The market is neither efficient nor perfect.

These cases help you organize your thoughts about what it takes to create value—which is *the* most important question if you are the CFO. Can you add value by changing your capital structure? Can you create value by splitting your shares, so that every share becomes two shares? Can you create value by paying out dividends next year rather than this year? Can you create value by changing how you present your earnings to investors? Can you create value by taking over other companies because/when they are priced too low if you do not have anything unique to add?

11.6A IF THE FINANCIAL MARKET IS (CLOSE TO) PERFECT

In perfect markets, all that counts are the firm's underlying projects.

If the financial market is perfect, the answers to these questions are simple—they are always no. It does not matter how the firm communicates its earnings to investors, what its capital structure is, how many shares the firm has, how it pays out its dividends, and so on. In fact, you already know that the firm is worth the value of its underlying projects' present values. Everything else is irrelevant.

You cannot fool your investors by how you report your earnings.

➤ Do reported earnings matter?, Section 13.1, p. 445

Earnings reporting: For example, if you have previously reported your foreign division's earnings separately and now you consolidate them into your main earnings, you would indeed increase the firm's reported earnings. However, it would not create anything intrinsically valuable. Such a change should not add or subtract firm value. Your firm owned the subsidiaries' cash flows before and after its reporting change. Your investors can add or subtract the subsidiaries' numbers themselves, whether you include or exclude them in your overall report.

There must be no value to changing capital structure.

➤ Capital structure arbitrage, Section 16.3, p. 578

Capital structure: For example, say your firm is currently financed with equity only and worth \$100, but if you had a 50-50 debt-to-equity ratio it would be worth \$102. In this case, an arbitrageur could buy your firm, issue \$51 in debt and \$51 in equity, and pocket \$2. With legions of entrepreneurs competing to do this, your firm value would instantly adjust to \$102. Thus, a \$100 price for your firm would be absurd.

Stock splits must be irrelevant, too.

➤ Stock splits, Section 19.2, p. 707

Stock splits: In a stock split, each old share becomes multiple new shares. For example, if each share trading at \$80 were to become two shares, the new shares should trade for \$40 each in a perfect market. Nothing fundamental about your underlying projects would have changed. Splitting by itself cannot add value. If this were not the case—for example, if shares would be worth \$41 each after the split—arbitrageurs would purchase the old shares for \$80, and sell them an instant later for the equivalent of $2 \cdot \$41 = \$82$, pocketing \$2.

Still trying to fool investors, this time with dividends? Fugeddaboutit.

➤ Stock dividends, Section 19.2, p. 707

Dividends: The same argument applies to dividends. In a perfect market, a \$100 firm that pays \$10 in dividends should be worth \$90 thereafter—no value is magically created or destroyed. Keeping the money for another year in the marginal zero-

NPV investment (e.g., Treasuries) is as good as paying it out. Investors in a perfect market can borrow against this extra future money and use it today.

The lesson is simple: As a manager, you should forget about the smoke and mirrors and instead focus exclusively on finding and executing projects with positive net present values.

11.6B IF THE FINANCIAL MARKET IS NOT PERFECT BUT AT LEAST EFFICIENT

An efficient market means "the price is right." Thus, you can learn from your own market price.

If markets are not perfect but efficient, the implications are not as profound. However, it means that you can still obtain valuable market intelligence. Your market price is the aggregate assessment of many investors who have put their money where their mouths are. The market price aggregates a whole lot of information that you as a corporate manager may not learn as easily yourself. For instance, if your stock price seems very high relative to current fundamentals, it probably means that the market sees great opportunities ahead for your firm and expects that you will take them. Thus, you should consider growing the business. Naturally, a high firm value allows you to raise more funds from the financial markets at favorable rates. On the other hand, if the stock price is very low, it probably means that the financial market anticipates your business to go down or expects you to waste the remaining money. In this case, you should think carefully about whether you should reinvest investors' money into the business or into repurchasing the (relatively cheap) stock.

You can also learn from other market prices.

In addition to learning from your own company's market price, you can also learn from all sorts of other market prices. You can find out how good your competitors' opportunities are, and whether you should get into the fray. Commodity price information can also be very helpful. If the price of oil in the forward market is \$100/barrel, it probably does not make sense for you to plan ahead based on an oil price of \$70/barrel. The financial market price for oil forwards is very large and efficient. It makes no sense for you to plan your business around much lower or higher oil prices in 6 months, simply because if you really knew this better, you could get rich easily without needing any of your current businesses—just start trading oil futures. This may sound obvious, but it is sometimes easy to overlook the obvious in the heat of the battle. For instance, a large conglomerate oil company in the 1990s planned to explore for more oil, based on a working assumption of doubling oil prices within 2 years. This company could just have purchased oil in the market instead of drilling. Why explore for oil if you can buy oil cheaper in the market? If you are a farmer planting, the futures exchanges provide you with forward prices for corn and wheat, and you can use this free price information to help you decide which crop to plant.

Personal opinion alone (without synergies) is not a good argument for taking over other companies.

Let's consider a specific example of how you can learn from market prices in an efficient market. Put yourselves in the shoes of a smart and successful manager of an aircraft manufacturer. Every morning, you read the newspaper, and every morning you think that company X should really be worth a lot more. It makes no sense to you that X has annual earnings of \$10/share but its shares are trading at only \$50/share. X just seems undervalued. Should you go out and buy it? If the market is perfect, the answer is no. You would have no competitive advantage in owning X. The hordes of arbitrageurs could have accomplished it in an instant, and less expensively than you ever could. On the other hand, owning X would not do any harm either. But let's take away the perfect market assumption and leave only the efficient market assumption. This means that both your aircraft company's price and the price of X are correct. Buying X because you think that X is undervalued is likely to be wrong. After all, our working assumption is that the financial markets have used all available information to find the best possible price.

However, in an imperfect market, it is possible for an acquisition to add value . . .

However, in the absence of perfect markets, the efficient market does not mean that you should never be able to create value by buying other companies. You can indeed sometimes create value. The trick is that you must be able to do something that investors cannot do for themselves, because the market is imperfect. Most likely, this would be related to your business's real operations. For example, if X is a supersonic aircraft parts supplier, you may have better information about the supplier's product. You may know that you will reward it with a huge contract soon. Or, by owning the patents of this supplier, you may make it more difficult for other aircraft companies to compete with you. Or you may find cost savings by cutting out the middleman in purchasing these parts, or improving X's products through your own intellectual capital, or by increasing the scale of operations. All of these can add value to the firm—value that outside arbitrageurs cannot accomplish without you. (This violates the infinitely many potential buyers assumption of a perfect market.)

. . . as long as you have more than just an opinion that the market got prices wrong.

But be careful: Market efficiency means that you cannot create value for your shareholders simply by your personal view that X is undervalued. Yes, you may be smart, but the financial markets are just as smart and presumably could recognize just as well whether X is undervalued—in fact, chances are that the target was rightly valued to begin with and it was you who got the target value wrong. For example, if X manufactures diapers, it is highly unlikely that you would create value for your shareholders, even if the firm is trading for only 5 times earnings and this makes no sense to you.

In an imperfect market, you can also create value with financial transactions that reduce market imperfections.

The same argument applies to all sorts of other corporate actions. You may be able to create value by reducing perfect market barriers. For example, you may be able to create value by reducing the costs with which investors can trade your shares (e.g., by listing on an exchange). Or you may be able to reduce mistrust that your investors have in your creditworthiness by hiring a good auditor or by reporting your earnings in a transparent fashion. Indeed, there is evidence that there are many corporate activities that can create value by reducing the perfect market frictions, even in very efficient financial markets. For example, when firms split their shares 2-to-1, it is not necessarily the case that the two post-split shares are worth exactly half of the pre-split share of, say, \$80. Instead, they tend to be worth a little more, say, around \$40.20. The likely reason is that managers signal their confidence in the future by splitting shares today. This brings more information to the market.

➤ Splits as signals, Section 19.4B, p. 718

11.6C IF THE FINANCIAL MARKET IS NOT EVEN EFFICIENT

What should you do if markets are not efficient?

Loosely speaking, financial markets tend to be reasonably, but not always perfectly, efficient. Perfect market efficiency is almost surely *not* a good description of reality.

Even in a perfectly rational market, as an executive, you may know the firm value better than the market—for example, you may know that your company is about to sign a large contract, but this information cannot yet be disclosed. What should you do if you know that the stock price is not equal to the appropriate market value? The right way to conceptualize your problem is to consider what you would do if you were the sole owner of the firm. You would really care about firm value. (As its executive, you should want to maximize this value on behalf of the owners.)

➤ Strong market efficiency, Section 11.2A, p. 351

If your shares are undervalued, you should recognize that your cost of capital is effectively too high, given the true characteristics of your project. The reason is that you cannot raise risky capital at fair prices—especially equity capital. The CAPM clearly is no longer the right model for the cost of capital.

If you are undervalued, sometimes it is better to pass up positive-NPV projects . . .

For example, assume that you know that your current projects will return \$500 tomorrow. Also assume that you have no cash and that you can only raise financing through equity. Now assume you come across a new project that costs \$100 and will return a terrific \$200 tomorrow. The problem is that your investors do not believe that the firm will return \$700, falsely believing that the combined firm will only be worth, say, \$200. Thus, to raise \$100, you would have to sell 50% of your firm, and keep only 50% of the true \$700 return, for a true \$350 share of it. You would therefore be better off passing up this new project and just taking the \$500 from the old project. Put differently, the opportunity cost of new capital to fund this project is way too high for you.

➤ Separation of financing and investing decisions, Section 10.1C, p. 308

You would definitely not want to raise cash at these "high" prices. Instead, you would want to do the opposite. The best use of corporate cash may now be to repurchase your own cheap, underpriced shares, for example, from other investors. However, there is an intrinsic paradox here: As an executive, you are supposed to act on behalf of your shareholders. Therefore, repurchasing underpriced shares from them at bargain prices would not be what would make the selling shareholders better off. (It would, however, make your remaining shareholders better off.)

. . . and use your cash to repurchase your own shares.

➤ Share repurchases and value to remaining investors, Section 19.2, p. 707

If your shares are overvalued, your cost of capital would be very low. You should be tempted to take more projects. This is easiest to see if you again consider what you would do if you were the primary owner of this overpriced firm. You would want to sell more equity shares at higher prices and pay the money out in dividends to existing shareholders. (Alternatively, you can just invest in Treasury securities.) Here the paradox is, of course, that just one instant later, as CEO, you are now the representative of these new shareholders to whom you have just sold overpriced shares. They will not be happy campers. (Many researchers believe that this is exactly what happened when AOL purchased Time-Warner at the height of the Internet craze in the late 1990s. AOL used its overpriced shares to purchase Time-Warner's real assets.)

If you are overvalued, sometimes it is better just to issue more shares.

These are robust insights for CEO's who are not conflicted and wish to act on behalf of their existing shareholders.

IMPORTANT: When managers have superior information:

- If the firm is undervalued, CEOs should assume a relatively high cost of capital and consider repurchasing the firm's own shares.
- If the firm is overvalued, CEOs should assume a relatively low cost of capital and consider issuing more of the firm's own shares.

A good decision rule for managers is to take projects up to the point where the marginal costs and benefits of projects are the same as what they could obtain from repurchasing or issuing the firm's own shares.

➤ Overconfidence, Section 12.7, p. 418

(It can become a bit more complex if you see yourself as a representative of both new and old shareholders, though.) But be careful: Most executives are notorious for *always believing* that the financial markets do not fully reflect the value of their companies even if they have no inside information—as an executive, you should be wary of your own perceptions and biases!

SOLVE NOW!

Q 11.22 For convenience, assume a zero discount rate. You have no cash on hand and can only raise financing for new projects by issuing more equity. You know that your existing project will truly return $500 next year. Everyone knows that your second, newer project costs $200, but only you know that it will return only $180 next year. This newer project is the only one that investors think is in line with your current expertise—you cannot raise funds and deposit them elsewhere (or any new investors would smell a rat).

(a) Does your second, newer project have a positive or negative NPV?

(b) If your investors know both true projects' costs, but they also (incorrectly) believe that you have the magic touch and any of your expertise projects will earn a rate of return of 100%, what fraction of the firm would you have to sell to raise $200 to start the new project?

(c) If you act on behalf of your existing investors, should you take this new project?

11.6D COMPARISON AND SUMMARY

A summary of the two market concepts and their consequences.

Here is a summary of the two conceptual classifications of how markets work:

Efficient versus inefficient markets: If the market is efficient, you can learn from financial market prices, because they accurately incorporate the information of financial market participants. This means that you cannot create value by taking over other companies just because you think that these companies are worth more than they are trading for.

If the market is inefficient, you may be able to identify underpriced firms that you can take over, or even create value by working on how information about your own company comes to the market.

Perfect versus imperfect markets: If the market is perfect, you can focus exclusively on your projects' net present values. You can forget about most financial choices, such as what your capital structure should be, how you should report earnings, and so on.

If the market is imperfect, you can create value, often by reducing the market imperfections themselves. For example, you could signal what you know about your company's prospects by reporting earnings sooner. On occasion, this can even become a dilemma: For example, what should you do if you know that a project has a positive NPV but the financial market does not believe you? If you take it, your stock price may go down. Now you have to think about the lesser of two evils—passing up on the project, or passing up on a higher stock price.

Don't be too dogmatic: Nothing is perfectly perfect or perfectly imperfect.

In the real world, financial markets are definitely not 100% perfect. For large firms, they are very close to efficient, but this is not necessarily so for small firms. Still, the economic magnitudes of deviations should be fairly modest. As a real-world manager of a publicly traded corporation, it is generally better for you to focus on underlying value creation than on actions that investors can accomplish for themselves without you. It makes sense for you to believe that market prices are almost always informative, but not to believe too slavishly that they are also always fully efficient—you may have better information than the market. Use it wisely when you have it.

11.7 EVENT STUDIES CAN MEASURE INSTANT VALUE IMPACTS

Market reactions should be immediate and reflect all value changes.

The immediacy of price reactions in any efficient market offers a surprising application: In some cases, market price reactions can allow you to estimate value consequences more easily than traditional NPV techniques, using a technique called an event study. An **event study** is an empirical analysis of the effect of a set of events on the price of assets. The idea of an event study is that if the public market is valuing projects appropriately, and if the value of an unexpected event or action is \$1 million, then the stock price should increase by \$1 million the minute the event becomes publicly known. You can therefore (often) back out cash flow value changes from stock price changes. (I will soon explain when this works well, and when this does not work well.)

SOLVE NOW!

Q 11.23 In a perfect market, what kind of response ("unusual" stock price change and "unusual" rate of return) would you expect when your company announces that it has struck oil and plans to pay a special dividend next month? What reaction do you expect over this month? What reaction do you expect on the day that it pays the dividends?

11.7A AN EXAMPLE: THE CONGRESSIONAL MIDTERM ELECTION OF 2006

Our event study: the value consequences of the 2006 election in the United States.

Here is an example of a practical event study. In the congressional midterm election of 2006, the Democratic Party ran on a six-point platform. Two of these points concerned specific industries: energy ("energy independence") and health care ("a health care system that works for everyone"). Having been in power for many years, the Republican Party had aligned itself closely with the oil industry and the pharmaceutical industry. For example, the GOP had written into its Medicare drug plan that the government could not use its buying power to negotiate for lower drug prices. In contrast, the Democrats were expected to allow the government to negotiate prices with drug companies more aggressively, or even to institute price controls on some of the more expensive drug regimens.

Tell me: How much did the Democratic takeover of Congress in 2006 hurt publicly traded companies?

What if you were hired as a consultant to assess the value effect of a Democratic victory? Would there really be something that Democrats were likely to do differently that would harm companies in the oil and gas and health care sectors? You could do this the traditional way: Estimate what the Democrats would likely do, project how it would affect the earnings of drug companies, forecast how long the Democrats would stay in power, and so on. This is a very difficult task. However, if you are willing to accept that financial markets are efficient, and that the election was the only value-relevant event during the night of the election from Tuesday to Wednesday, then you can use the market stock price reaction to the election as your measure of the value effect of legislative branch control. Here is how.

The Resolution of Uncertainty during Election Night

How can you find the probability that either party would win?

Prior to the election on November 7, 2006, opinion polls had projected that the Democrats would win the House of Representatives but not the Senate. However, during the last few days before the election, the Republicans had seemed to narrow the gap. But exactly what was expected? Different forecasters published different polls, and they did not all agree. Where could you learn authoritative probabilities that either party would win?

Of course, the best source is a market—and there just happens to be one.

If you believe in reasonable market efficiency, the best information source would be a financial market, in which bettors place their money where their mouths are. Fortunately, such an "election market" indeed exists at the University of Iowa (and Thomas Rietz and Joyce Berg kindly shared their intraday data with me). In this market, investors could bet that either party would win. On election night, Tuesday, November 7, 2006, at the market closing time of 4 p.m. EST, speculators had placed the probabilities of wins (based on last trading quotes of the hour) as follows:

	House Republican	House Democrat	Total Senate
Senate Republican	12%	54%	66%
Senate Democrat	0%	34%	34%
Total House	12%	88%	

Thus, investors believed that the House would go Democrat (with 88% probability) and that the Senate would go Republican (with 66% probability). The probability that the Senate would be Republican and the House would be Democrat was around 54%.

By 11 a.m., the market had realized the outcome.

By the time the NYSE reopened (i.e., on Wednesday, November 8, at 9:30 a.m. EST), many but not all election results had been posted. The probabilities had thus adjusted as follows:

	House Republican	House Democrat	Total Senate
Senate Republican	0%	17%	17%
Senate Democrat	0%	82%	82%
Total House	0%	100%	

The middle column shows that the Democrat takeover of the House of Representatives was fully known by the opening of the stock exchange, and although votes were still being counted, it had also become clear that even the Senate may have gone Democrat. By 11 a.m., the probability had already reached 97%. The Democrats had won both chambers!

To assess the value effect of this Democratic win, we only need to determine how stocks were affected by the overnight probability change from 34% to 82% of a complete Democratic victory.

The Effect on the Overall Stock Market

As usual, our stock price information comes from Yahoo! *Finance*. The graph in Figure 11.4 shows that the S&P 500 had risen prior to the election but then dropped 35 basis points during election night.

The overall stock market rate of return during election night was negative.

How much money did the S&P 500 companies bleed? The S&P 500 represented about $12.6 trillion in market capitalization on election night. Thus, the 35 bp loss corresponded to a value loss of about $44 billion. It is important that you realize that this $44 billion is not the entire value loss that a Democratic Congress would inflict on the S&P 500 companies. The reason is that the $44 billion reflects only the shift in the probability that the House would go Democrat (from 88% to 100%) and the probability that the Senate would go Democrat (from 34% to 82%). In the extreme, if the S&P 500 investors had known the election outcome fully and with certainty on Tuesday afternoon, then the market should not have fallen at all. No new information would have been revealed by the actual election results. (This was obviously not the case here.)

On election night, the S&P 500 lost about 35 bp on $12.6 trillion in capitalization, i.e., about $44 billion.

How do we work with those partial probability changes? Let me make up a new example. Let's say the market was worth $200, and you knew that Republicans would transfer $100 to corporate America that Democrats would not. However, the day before the election, the market believed that Democrats would win with 98% probability. In this case, you would see the corporate sector be valued by investors at $98\% \cdot \$200 + 2\% \cdot \$300 = \$202$ just before the election. If the Democrats win, the market would be worth $200 after the election. It is not this $2 difference that is of interest to you, but the $100 difference number that you want to learn about.

What was the full value loss caused by the Democrats' win over the Republicans?

How can you infer the full $100 effect if all you see is the $2 change? You need to divide the stock value change of $2 by the change in probability from 2% to 0%:

Adjusting for the market's ex-ante beliefs just about doubles the 35-bp loss estimate.

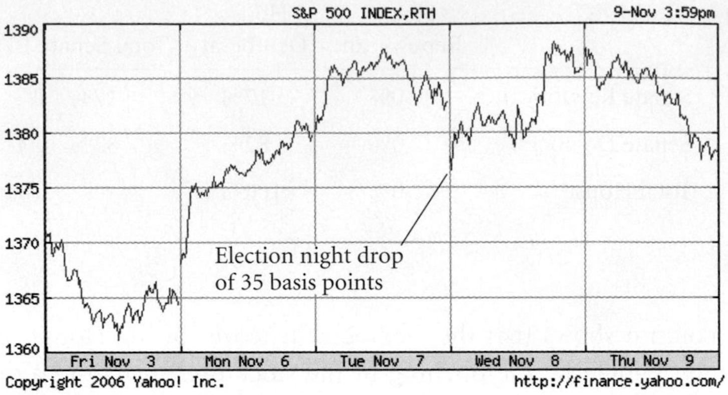

Most of the election results materialized into stock prices from the night of Tuesday, November 7, to Wednesday, November 8. The S&P 500 dropped from 1,383 to 1,378 (a 35 bp loss).

Source: Reproduced with permission of Yahoo! Inc. © 2008 by Yahoo! Inc. YAHOO! and the YAHOO! logo are trademarks of Yahoo! Inc.

FIGURE 11.4 Index Stock Price, Bond, and Gold Reactions around the 2006 Midterm Election

$$\$100 = \frac{\$2}{2\% - 0\%}$$

$$\frac{\text{Full Value if Event Takes Place}}{\text{versus Event Does Not Take Place}} = \frac{\text{Value if Probability is 2\%} - \text{Value if Probability is 0\%}}{\text{Probability 2\%} - \text{Probability 0\%}}$$

We need to use this insight to assess the full effect of the Democratic victory in the 2006 election. Let's assume that the important event was the joint loss of the House and Senate to the Democrats. Define the following event:

Event	Pre-Election	Post-Election	Change
Democrats win House and Senate	34%	82%	48%

Then apply the formula. The full corporate value loss to S&P 500 companies that was caused by the Democratic takeover of House and Senate was

$$\frac{\text{Full Value if Democrats Win Both Chambers}}{\text{versus They Do Not Win Both Chambers}} = \frac{35 \text{ bp}}{82\% - 34\%} \approx 73 \text{ bp}$$

Not surprisingly, with a probability change of about 50%, any value change just about doubles—here the 35-bp drop becomes 73 bp. Thus, if this probability change from 34% to 82% for a full Democratic victory was the value-relevant overnight event, then you can conclude that the full effect of the Democratic victory over the Republicans cost the corporate sector around 73 bp $\cdot$ \$12.6 trillion $\approx$ \$92 billion. Interestingly, if you repeat the same exercise for oil and gas firms and for health care firms, you will find that oil and gas companies were not affected by the electoral change, but health care plans, drugs, and hospital chains dropped significantly. The market considered the Democrats' claims that they would take on oil and gas as empty posturing (or preventable by the Republican administration), but believed the Democrats' platform claims about health care reform.

11.7B IMPORTANT EVENT STUDY LIMITATIONS

Event studies are not without drawbacks. There are usually three important problems that you have to deal with.

Event studies are not a panacea.

Event importance: Event studies work well only if the event is significant enough to influence the overall stock market valuation: If a $1 billion stock fluctuates on average by $10 million a day, it is practically impossible to use an event study to determine the value of a project worth $100,000. To use our physics analogy, the noise would drown out the signal. A reasonable rule of thumb is to take the ratio of the typical daily stock market value fluctuation (here, $10 million) divided by the order of magnitude of the value consequence (here, $100,000, so the ratio is $10,000,000/$100,000 = 100), and then require 50 times as many event observations (firms) as this ratio. For the example, this would require 5,000 event observations—which is likely too many to make such a study feasible for all but the most frequent events.

Big problem #1: You need to have enough big event occurrences.

In our November election event study, we knew we had a potentially important value-relevant event, especially for oil and gas and health care companies.

Event anticipation: Event studies rely on the fact that stock markets react only to news—that is, the unanticipated component of an information release. There must be a clear event date. But many events are anticipated, announced over a period of time, or never formally announced. For example, if a company was expected with 80% probability to win a contract worth $1,000,000, the stock price would have already reflected $800,000. The news that the company actually won the contract would raise the stock price by only $200,000, not by $1,000,000. The news that the company would not have won the contract would drop the stock price by $800,000, however. Isolating market expectations can be very difficult. More than likely, the analyst would not know after the fact how expected the event was by the market at the time. (And, worse: Insider trading before the event may have already moved the stock price to the $1,000,000 before the public announcement.) Therefore, in many cases, the event study technique is better at helping to determine whether an event is good or bad for a company than it is in helping to compute an exact value gain.

Problem #2: You need to know exactly when news comes out—you want only the unanticipated information.

I selected this particular election event study, because we knew both the prior probability and the posterior probability. This allowed us to compute the full-value effect of the election. Usually, we are not so lucky, which means it is much more difficult to translate stock price reactions into exact value figures. If you do not know the ex-ante probabilities, you can assume how anticipated an event was, or try to estimate an ex-ante probability from the data, or merely use the event study technique to determine whether an event is beneficial or detrimental.

Simultaneous events (contamination): The event study technique relies on the fact that the event can be precisely isolated from other events. If other events occur in the same time window, any value consequence may stem from these other events, and not from the event that is being examined. Unfortunately, many events occur at the same time. For example, at annual shareholders' meetings, there are often simultaneous announcements of dividend changes, corporate charter changes, institutional votes, information about successions, tough questions from shareholders, and so on.

Problem #3: There are often simultaneous events.

There is always the danger that what a study may attribute to dividend changes is due really to simultaneous announcements of, say, a corporate charter change instead. You can only hope that the content in these other simultaneous value events is nonsystematic, so that it only adds noise that will average out over many different firms.

In our November election event study, we knew that the election was the dominant event of the night. Few other value-relevant news stories came out.

Event studies work even if the CAPM does not.

In sum, event studies can be very powerful tools to measure the value effects of many changes. The usual problems of finding appropriate expected rates of return (or trusting the CAPM) matter little when it comes to 1- to 3-day events, because the average CAPM return is only around 5 basis points for a stock per day. Whether the true expected rate of return is closer to 4 or to 6 basis points is really irrelevant. Such small differences in mean expected returns are hopefully small compared with the signal that you expect from the event.

SOLVE NOW!

Q 11.24 Is the average value change on the announcement date a good measure of the average value consequence of an event?

Q 11.25 Are event studies better suited to events that occur on the same day for all companies, or better suited to events that occur on a different day for every single company?

Q 11.26 How sensitive are event study results to the use of the CAPM?

Q 11.27 What are the factors that make an event study more likely to be informative?

11.7C CAPITAL-STRUCTURE-RELATED AND OTHER EVENT STUDY RESULTS

Event studies have been used on many different events. In finance, they often tell us whether corporate actions are good news.

There have been event studies on all sorts of events, ranging from new legislation, to corporate name changes, to analysts' opinions, to corporate earnings, to stock splits, to corporate dividends, to corporate debt and equity issuance and retirement, to deaths of the founder, and so on. Here are some of the more important findings. (You will see some more evidence obtained from event studies again in later chapters, especially in the chapters on capital structure and payout policies.) On the day of the announcement, firm values *increase* on average:

- When firms announce increases in dividends, share repurchases, or stock splits (by about 0.1–1%; if you are interested, there is a longer explanation in Chapter 19)
- When firms are taken over by other firms (by about 10–30%)
- When firms announce earnings that significantly beat analysts' expectations
- When firms announce that the FDA has approved one of their drugs
- When the founding CEO dies (by about 3–4%)

Conversely, firm values *decrease* on average:

ANECDOTE The Effects of Sanctions on South Africa

South Africa's apartheid regime (1948–1994) rightly deserved to be overthrown. To accelerate its demise, the U.S. Congress imposed banking and tax-related sanctions on firms doing business with South Africa's apartheid regime.

We may all wish we could report success—that sanctions on South Africa's racist regime had been effective. Unfortunately, the event study evidence is clear that sanctions played no economic role. Upon the announcement of new sanctions or corporate divestments, neither prices of targeted U.S. companies nor of South African financial securities moved. One explanation is that there were too many loopholes and non-U.S. firms that were willing and able to evade the boycott.

Although we can conclude that, despite all its publicity, the boycott was largely ineffective in economic terms, sanctions may still be appropriate on moral grounds regardless of their economic effectiveness. Whether to boycott socially objectionable behavior is a decision that policymakers should make, not economists. The role of the financial economist is only to inform policymakers of the ultimate effectiveness of their actions.

Source: Teoh, Welch, Wazzan, *Journal of Business*, 1999.

- When firms announce new stock sales (by about 1–3%; if you are interested, there is a longer explanation in Chapter 22)
- When firms overpay for other firms in acquisitions
- When firms announce lower-than-expected earnings
- When firms fend off an acquirer who has made a bid
- When firms announce that the FDA has rejected one of their drugs

Unfortunately, because we do not know the markets' probability assessments prior to these announcements (unlike in our election event study, where we learned it from the Iowa market), these value estimates are conservative lower bounds. There is also a complete web chapter written only about the stock price announcement responses to capital structure changes and payouts. Not mentioned, event studies have also informed us whether certain government regulations had a positive or negative impact on firms. For example, we know which firms were helped and which firms were hurt when the telecommunications, trucking, and airline markets were deregulated.

SOLVE NOW!

Q 11.28 What kind of corporate events are greeted as good news by the financial markets? What events are greeted as bad news?

SUMMARY

This chapter covered the following major points:

- Market efficiency means that the market uses all available information in setting prices to offer "appropriate rates of return."
- In the short run, the appropriate expected rate of return on stocks must be small. Therefore, market efficiency prescribes that stocks roughly follow random walks.

- In the long run, it is rarely clear what this "appropriate rate of return" should be. Because noise makes it difficult to measure the average rate of return accurately, it is also difficult to test either models like the CAPM or long-run market efficiency.
- Beliefs in efficient markets come in different forms.
  - The standard efficient markets classification emphasizes what information it would take to beat the market: weak form (past stock price patterns are not enough to beat the market), semistrong form (other historical firm information is not enough to beat the market), and strong form (inside information is not enough to beat the market).
  - A more current efficient markets classification emphasizes the rationality of the stock market: true believer (stock prices always reflect underlying project NPVs), firm believer (small deviations between price and value, but difficult to take advantage of), mild believer (small deviations between price and value, and somewhat possible to take advantage of), or nonbeliever (arbitrage opportunities abound).
- The overall evidence suggests that it is not easy to become rich—a belief shared by most finance professors. The relative strength of their beliefs in market efficiency—the extent to which professors believe that market prices always reflect underlying value—separates finance professors into "rationalists" (or "classical" economists) and "behavioralists."
- In a perfect and efficient market, investors should not find arbitrage opportunities:
  - True arbitrage is a riskless bet with no negative net cash flows under any circumstances. Everyone would like to take all true arbitrage opportunities. When and if they appear, they are likely to be very small.
  - Risk(y) arbitrage is more like a great bet. An infinitely risk-averse investor would not want to take it, because there is a chance that risk(y) arbitrage will lose money.
  - Both true and risk(y) arbitrage opportunities should be very rare in the real world. An investor who is not too risk averse may or may not prefer taking one large, great bet to taking one tiny, true arbitrage.
- Given the millions of investors, many will beat the stock market by chance, and some investors will beat the stock market many years in a row. Market efficiency does not mean that there are not some investors who will beat the stock market 10 years in a row *ex-post*; rather, it means that any one particular investor is unlikely to beat the stock market *ex-ante* 10 years in a row.
- Managers can learn valuable information from market prices, both from their own share prices and from other prices. To improve corporate firm value, managers must create fundamental value—they must undertake positive-NPV projects. Simple activities such as purchasing a random firm to lower risk or splitting shares will not add value.
- Event studies allow you to ascertain the corporate value impact of sharp events, such as election results, legislative action (FDA rulings), or corporate events (dividend increases).

KEY TERMS

behavioral finance, 350
Berkshire Hathaway, 369
bid-ask bounce, 365
Brownian motion, 356
classical finance, 350
due diligence, 350
efficient, 344
efficient market hypothesis, 350
EMH, 350
event study, 375
fundamental trading, 351
futures contract, 350
great bet, 361
market efficiency, 344
New York Futures Exchange, 350
New York Mercantile Exchange, 350
noise, 354
noise trader, 352
random walk, 355
rational economics, 350
risk(y) arbitrage, 361
semistrong market efficiency, 351
signal, 354
signal-to-noise ratio, 354
spurious, 352
strong market efficiency, 352
survivorship bias, 367
technical analysis, 351
true arbitrage, 361
volatility, 354
weak market efficiency, 351

SOLVE NOW! SOLUTIONS

Q 11.1 The "efficient market" phrase is shorthand for "the market uses all available information in the setting of its price." There are further classifications as to the precise degree of market efficiency, which depend on what information counts as "available."

Q 11.2 As a believer in market efficiency, you would point out that the heretics are wrong in how they measure the risk-reward trade-off (the model for what expected rates of return should be). Your second line of defense would be to ask the provocative question why the heretics are not yet rich. (Of course, you would have to claim it was by pure chance if the heretic that you are talking to *is* rich.)

Q 11.3 Market efficiency is a much more powerful concept over short horizons, because the expected rate of return over a short horizon (say, a day) is very small (a few basis points) in virtually all reasonable models of market pricing.

Q 11.4 An efficient market is one in which the market uses all available information. In a perfect market, market pressures by arbitrageurs will make market efficiency come true, so a perfect market should be efficient. However, an efficient market need not be perfect. For example, stocks could be priced fairly even when there are taxes.

Q 11.5 Markets are more likely to be efficient when transaction costs are low, because this makes it easier for smart investors to compete away any unusual opportunities.

Q 11.6 The foreign currency market may well be the biggest market in the world, with the dollar and the euro both being the world's two main currencies. With so many smart investors trading on the exact same instrument, and with incredibly low transaction costs, we would expect arbitrageurs to take advantage of even the smallest inefficiency. Thus, it would seem likely that the foreign exchange market is much more efficient—and much closer to perfection.

Q 11.7 Momentum strategies seem to violate even weak-form market efficiency—unless you believe that their returns are just normal because they reflect some sort of normal compensation for risk.

Q 11.8 If you believe that market values do not always perfectly reflect underlying fundamental values, but that trading costs nevertheless prevent you from exploiting this profitably (in large scale), then you should classify yourself as a firm believer in market efficiency.

Q 11.9 The random-walk formula is on page 355. It states that the expected price tomorrow is the price today plus a drift. The drift can be a small constant or a very small fraction of the price today.

Q 11.10 If a stock has an expected rate of return of 20% per year—which is definitely on the high side for most firms—the daily rate of return would be $1.2^{1/255} - 1 \approx 7.15$ basis points. If you computed the non-compounding

$0.20/255 \approx 7.84$ basis points, or even used 365 calendar days instead of 255 trading days, it would have been okay for our purposes, too.

Q 11.11 A *daily* trading strategy would have to offer above 20% per annum in order to overcome typical transaction costs. The calculation in the text came to about 23% per annum.

Q 11.12 The typical movement (variation) of a stock is around plus or minus 2% to 3% a day. The average rate of return on a day is much lower. Thus, the signal-to-noise ratio is very low.

Q 11.13 Even if the stock price follows a random walk, its actual price can definitely—and most likely will be—different from today's price. Only the *expected* price is the same as the price today.

Q 11.14 If you want to be a superstar trader who outperforms by, say, about 4% per year, you would have to earn an extra $\sqrt[255]{1.04} - 1 \approx 1.54$ basis points per day.

Q 11.15 With 100 basis points per day of noise and 200 basis points per year of excess performance:
(a) With 1 day's performance, you would expect $200/255 \approx 0.7843$ basis points per day.
(b) The noise was given as 100 basis points per day.
(c) The expected T-statistic is about $0.7843/100 \approx 0.007843$.
(d) Over 255 days, the performance was given as 200 basis points.
(e) The noise would be $100 \cdot \sqrt{255} \approx 1{,}597$ basis points.
(f) The expected T-statistic would be about $200/1{,}597 \approx 0.125$.
(g) You need to solve $(0.78 \cdot N)/(100 \cdot \sqrt{N}) \geq 1.96$, or $0.0078 \cdot \sqrt{N} \geq 1.96$. The critical N is approximately 63,000 trading days—which is about 247 years.

Q 11.16 No! Treasuries earn money without risk, but they are not an arbitrage, because investing in them requires a negative net cash flow up front.

Q 11.17 If the true arbitrage opportunity can only be done once and gains \$10, it is probably worse than a risk(y) arbitrage that loses 1 cent with 1% probability, and gains \$1,000,000 with 99% probability.

Q 11.18 Good topics to consider when thinking about how plausible an arbitrage is include: time and execution risk, direct and indirect transaction costs, price impact of trades, and fixed costs.

Q 11.19 Yes, it makes sense to look for high-ability managers among historical high performers. However, many high-ability managers will have underperformed historically, and many low-ability managers will have outperformed historically.

Q 11.20 If each of the 10,000 analysts has a 50-50 chance to beat the market in any given year, then the answer is that $10{,}000/2^{10} \approx 10$ analysts beat the market 10 years in a row.

Q 11.21 Survivorship bias means that you, as an investor, will only see the funds that were ex-post successful. Most unsuccessful funds do not show up in the historical statistics of funds in existence today. Existing funds will therefore have had positive performances in the past.

Q 11.22 (a) This project has a negative NPV, $-\$200 + \$180 = -\$20$, at the zero interest rate. (A positive interest rate would make it even more negative.)
(b) If you do take this second newer project, all your investors would believe that your firm would be worth $(\$500 + \$200) \cdot (1 + 100\%) = \$1{,}400$. To raise \$200 in funding, you would therefore have to sell $\$200/\$1{,}400 \approx 14.286\%$ of your firm.
(c) The true value of your firm will be $(\$500 + \$180) = \$680$, and the 14.3% stake is worth only \$97.14. Put differently, your old investors have just sold a \$180 project for \$97.14, giving them a net profit of \$82.86. You can also compute this directly: Your old investors will therefore own $(1 - 14.286\%) \cdot \$680 \approx \$582.86$. This is \$82.86 more than the \$500 that they would own if you did not take the new project. You should take it if you are acting on behalf of the existing investors.

Q 11.23 The immediate share price response to the news that you have struck oil would be positive. Over the following month, you would not expect any unusual upward or downward drift: It should be about zero. Finally, when your firm pays out the special dividend, the rate of return should be zero on average, too, because the market would have known that the dividend would be paid. Of course, its share price will have to drop by the amount of the dividend paid to keep the return around zero. Chapter 19 explains how this may not be the case in the presence of market imperfections, especially personal income taxes on dividend payouts.

Q 11.24 No. The average value change on the announcement date is only a good measure of the *unexpected* average value consequence of an event.

Q 11.25 Event studies are better suited to studying events that occur on different days for different companies. This reduces the probability of "event contamination."
For example, let's presume that you are interested in the effect of a low inflation announcement on September 12, 2005. Your evidence shows that stock prices went up on this day. Therefore, you might be tempted to conclude that the inflation announcement had a positive stock price influence. However, this overlooks an important problem. On this day, a million other things may have happened: the President coughed, the Congress squabbled, the Fed grumbled, the FDA changed its mind on genetic engineering, investors grew colder on mining stocks and hotter on game stocks, OPEC met, the Europeans demonstrated against U.S. policy, and so on. Are you really sure that it was the inflation announcement that made stocks go up and none of the other events? In contrast, if the event day is different for every firm, sometimes these other events will positively influence the market, sometimes negatively. Net in net, this other-events contamination is more likely different on different days and thus it will more likely wash out.
Of course, if your event is on different days but still always on firms' annual meetings, then you have the different problem that there could be a lot of other value-relevant news that is being disclosed simultaneously. In this case, you are likely to have more noise, uncertainty, and contamination to deal with than in the case where event days occurred randomly for different firms.

Q 11.26 The CAPM is practically irrelevant. Over a 1-, 2-, or 3-day window, the expected rate of return does not matter much.

Q 11.27 An event study is likely to be more informative if the value impact of the event is big and unanticipated, and if you can study many companies that have had such events in the past.

Q 11.28 Good news: becoming an acquisition target; the announcement of new dividends, share repurchases, and stock splits; earnings significantly higher than analysts' projections; FDA approvals; and CEO deaths. Bad news: Acquiring other firms at too high a price; the issuance of new equity stock; earnings significantly lower than analysts' projections; declining an acquirer's bid; and FDA rejections.

PROBLEMS

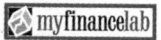

The ▬ *indicates problems available in* myfinancelab

Q 11.29 What kind of evidence would heretics against market efficiency ideally want to muster? If they fail to find this kind of evidence, does it mean that you should conclude that markets are efficient?

Q 11.30 Define "efficient market" and explain how it differs from a perfect market.

Q 11.31 Peter Lynch, a famous former fund manager for Fidelity, suggested that it is wise to invest in stocks based on "local knowledge"—you invest in the stock of your local supermarket if you notice that it does better than expected. In an efficient stock market, is this a wise recommendation?

Q 11.32 Evaluate the following statement: It does not matter what portfolio you are holding in a perfect and efficient stock market.

Q 11.33 A paper by Frieder and Zittrain looks at spam email touting a particular stock. Such distributions increased the trading volume and resulted in a 4–5% gain over the 2 days following the spam release. Is this evidence against market efficiency?

Q 11.34 What are the three main categories in the traditional market efficiency classification? Give an example of what each excludes.

Q 11.35 Comment on the following statement: "An efficient market seems like an impossible concept. In an efficient market, no one can earn excess returns. Therefore, no one collects information. Therefore, prices do not contain information, and collecting information should earn excess returns."

Q 11.36 Describe the fundamentals-based classification of the strength of belief in market efficiency. Explain how one individual can be at one level but not in the level above or below.

Q 11.37 Does a random walk imply that the expected rate of return on a stock is zero?

Q 11.38 Assume that the typical day-to-day noise (standard deviation) is about 100 basis points. Assume that you have the kind of stock-picking ability that earns you an extra 400 basis points per annum. Assume no transaction costs. Ignore compounding and assume that your rate of return is the sum of returns over trading days. Assume there are 255 trading days per year.

(a) With only 1 day of performance, how much extra do you expect to earn per day?
(b) How bad is your noise over 1 day?
(c) What is your expected T-statistic (the excess mean divided by the standard deviation)?
(d) With 255 trading days of performance, how much extra do you expect to earn per annum?
(e) How bad is your noise over 255 days?
(f) What is your expected T-statistic now?
(g) Work out how many years you would expect to wait before you would obtain reliable statistical evidence that you have a positive ability to pick stocks.

Q 11.39 Define arbitrage. How is it different from a great bet? Is one always better than the other?

Q 11.40 Would it make sense for a model of the financial world to assume that there is no arbitrage? Would it make sense for a model of the financial world to assume that there are no great bets?

Q 11.41 What kind of costs should you consider when evaluating whether an opportunity is an arbitrage?

Q 11.42 The typical hedge fund investor evaluates its fund based on the most recent 3 years of performance. What do you think of this practice?

Q 11.43 Why does the average mutual fund in the market today appear to have been a great performer? Does this evidence suggest that these funds will be good performers in the future, at least on average?

Q 11.44 Do you expect fund managers with high ability to prefer compensation that is more performance based? How good an "insurance" is this for fund investors?

Q 11.45 If a corporation acquires another firm, it can lower the firm's uncertainty. This should lower its cost of capital. This should create value. Is this correct?

Q 11.46 Give an example of how the cost of capital for taking a project can be too high if the market has undervalued your firm.

Q 11.47 For convenience, assume a zero discount rate. You know that your current projects cost \$400 today and will truly return \$500 next year—but your investors believe they will return only \$400. In addition, you have no cash on hand and can only raise financing for new projects by issuing more equity. A new project costs \$200 and will return \$220 next year. Your investors mistakenly believe that your firm will earn an internal rate of return of 0%, either with or without this new project. Acting on behalf of your existing investors, should you take this project? Does it have a positive NPV?

Q 11.48 At http://biz.yahoo.com/p/510mktd.html, Yahoo! *Finance* classifies "Drug Manufacturers—Major." Compute the average rate of return of 10 of these firms from the day before to the day after the 2006 election (November 7, 2006). How were your 10 stocks influenced by the Democratic election win?

Q 11.49 Which of the following are good candidates for ascertaining the value effects with an event study, and why?

(a) An acquirer wants to buy the firm.
(b) The CEO dies.
(c) The CEO ages.
(d) Positive earnings surprise at the annual meetings.
(e) Purchase of a new machine.
(f) A law is passed to force the company to reduce its emissions.
(g) An ad campaign.

Q 11.50 Use a financial website to conduct an event study of big corporate acquisitions over the last 12 months. How did their announcements impact the value of the acquirer and the value of the target? Was there a relationship between the announcement response and acquirer/target size?

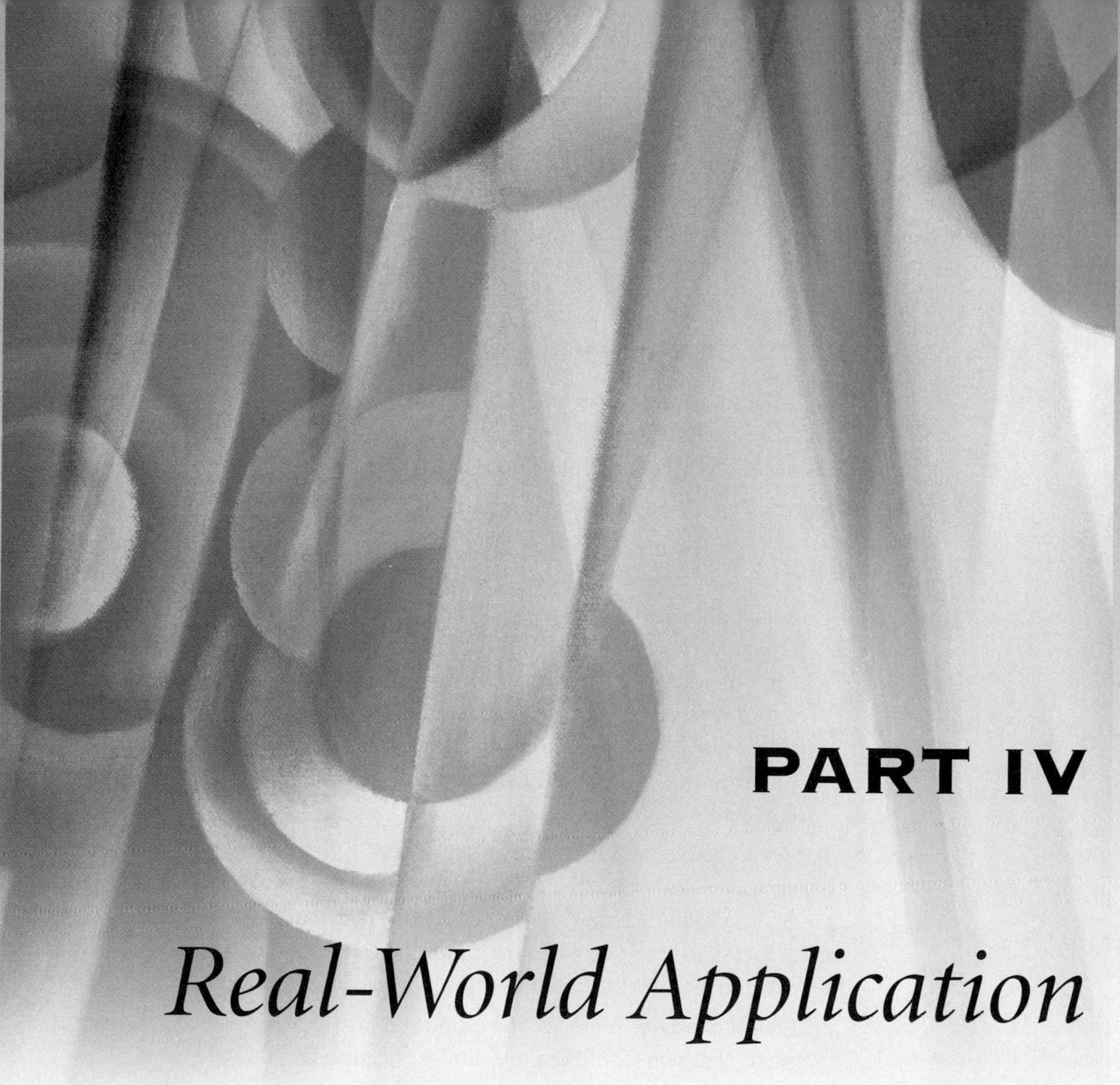

PART IV

Real-World Application

CAPITAL BUDGETING, FINANCIAL STATEMENTS AND VALUATION, AND COMPARABLES

You now know *all* the important cost of capital and present value concepts. But you cannot yet appreciate all the nuances and difficulties of their application in a corporate environment. In the real world, valuation can prove to be quite difficult because firms do not exist merely in order to provide clean and convenient illustrations of the theoretical constructs! Thus, the next issue on the agenda is for you to learn (better) how to apply what you have learned in previous chapters.

By necessity, this part consists of a variety of subjects. First, you will learn about the many difficulties in applying the seemingly-so-simple capital budgeting concepts. NPV and IRR can have sharp teeth! Chapter 12 covers the various pitfalls that you are likely to encounter when using net present value in practice. Next, you will learn how to read the financial information that publicly traded companies provide. Let me just state that the net income is not the cash flow that you need as your direct input into your NPV analysis. Finally, you will learn about an alternative (and distant cousin) to classical NPV analysis: comparables. Sometimes, they are better than NPV, sometimes they are worse. Comparables are dangerous, though: They are exceptionally easy to misuse.

WHAT YOU WANT TO LEARN IN THIS PART

The primary goal of this part is to show you the breadth of issues and problems that arise in the application of the concepts from the previous chapters, and especially in the application of net present values.

- Chapter 12 goes over many important issues that you should pay attention to when you have to make investment decisions.

  Typical questions: In valuing an acquisition target, should you use your own cost of capital or the target's cost of capital? How should you think of projects that have side effects—for example, projects that pollute the air? How should you think of sunk costs? What is a "real option"? How do you value contingencies and your own flexibility to change course in the future? How should your assessment of investment value change if you know that someone else had to estimate the cash flows? Do people generally tend to misestimate future cash flows in systematically erroneous ways?

- Chapter 13 explains how you can extract cash flow estimates for a present value analysis from corporate financial statements. This is easiest to understand in the context of a hypothetical firm for which you construct the financials yourself. This makes it easy to translate them back into the economic cash flows that you need. At the end, you also get to extract the cash flows from a real financial statement.

  Typical question: What are the economic cash flows in PepsiCo's financial statements that you would use to estimate the present value of PepsiCo?

- Chapter 14 shows how you can learn more information about your own firm, using publicly available information from comparable firms. It also explains a method of valuation that is both similar to, and different from, net present value.

  Typical questions: How does "comparables-based" valuation differ from PV-based valuation? When is the P/E (price/earnings) ratio a good number to look at? What should the P/E ratio of your project be? How and when can you average P/E ratios? What can you learn from other financial ratios?

12

Capital Budgeting Applications and Pitfalls

TIPS AND TRICKS!

Applying the concepts of NPV and IRR in the real world can be very difficult. This chapter explains many of the nuances and pitfalls in their application. It will help you avoid many kinds of common mistakes that many companies commit almost every day—mistakes that cost them value.

12.1 SO MANY RETURNS: THE INTERNAL RATE OF RETURN, THE COST OF CAPITAL, THE HURDLE RATE, AND THE EXPECTED RATE OF RETURN

Before we begin, let us just recap the four rates that are commonly used in finance: the *internal rate of return*, the *cost of capital*, the *expected rate of return*, and the *hurdle rate*.

In the real world, these four terms are often used casually and interchangeably.

Internal rate of return: The internal rate of return is a characteristic of project cash flows (hence "internal") and usually has nothing to do with capital markets (unless the project itself is a capital markets–related project). This is its big advantage—you can calculate it before you ever look at the capital markets. It is only later that you will compare the IRR to the prevailing rate of return in the economy. The IRR is the rate that is most different from the three rates below. Be careful, though: You should not use promised cash flows to compute it. IRR requires *expected* cash flows, which are much harder to come by.

➤ IRR, Section 4.2, p. 72

Cost of capital: Always think of it as the *opportunity* cost of capital. It is the rate of return your investors could expect to receive by investing in similar projects elsewhere. It is determined by the prevailing required rates of return for projects of your type. Therefore, it is driven by the demand and supply for capital in the economy—the expected rate of return that your investors demand in order to give you money willingly. In perfect capital markets, with many lenders and borrowers,

➤ Cost of capital, Section 2.5, p. 25

loans usually have zero net present values. (Otherwise the borrower or lender is giving away free money.) The cost of capital is sometimes called the "required expected rate of return." The CAPM is one perfect-markets model that provides an estimate of the cost of capital. Finally, realize that the cost of capital is itself an expected value concept—you do not need to write the "expected cost of capital."

Expected rate of return: The expected rate of return is a generic term. It could mean your project's expected rate of return, or the cost of capital (the lender's expected rate of return). In most cases, if your project's actual expected rate of return is above its required expected rate of return (the cost of capital), then it is a positive-NPV project. If management makes smart decisions, projects' expected rates of return are above their costs of capital. The very last marginal project often has an expected rate of return just about the same as the cost of capital.

➤ Expected rate of return, Section 8.1A, p. 202

Hurdle rate: The appropriate project hurdle rate is the expected rate of return above which management decides to accept and go forward with the project. It is set neither by the financial markets nor by the project, but by management. Bad management could choose any arbitrary, or even outright idiotic, hurdle rate. Good management should accept all projects that have positive net present values.

➤ Hurdle rate, Section 4.2B, p. 77

Usually, this means that good managers should set a project's hurdle rate to be equal to the project's cost of capital, and management should then determine whether the project's IRR exceeds this hurdle rate. If management makes smart decisions, taking all positive-NPV projects, the "hurdle rate," "cost of capital," and "required expected rate of return" are all the same.

Warning: The IRR should be an expected return concept, but it is often misapplied to promised returns.

➤ Agency issues, Section 12.8, p. 420

You already know that expected project returns are difficult to come by. Managers often incorrectly use promised rates of return. Because corporations are aware that claims based on expected project returns are regularly inflated, many of them have established hurdle rates high above a reasonable cost of capital for such projects. It is not uncommon to find corporations requiring projects to have hurdle rates of 15% or more, even when the cost of capital for such projects would seem to be on the order of only 10%. Venture capitalists even regularly employ project hurdle rates as high as 30%, knowing full well that this is far above the rate of return that their projects are *truly expected* to earn.

The differences are sometimes subtle, and the terms are often used interchangeably—which is okay in many, but not all, situations.

SOLVE NOW!

Q 12.1 Can you compare a project's internal rate of return to its hurdle rate?

Q 12.2 Can you compare a project's cost of capital to its hurdle rate in a perfect market?

12.2 PROMISED, EXPECTED, TYPICAL, OR MOST LIKELY?

The simplest error—confusing promised and expected returns—is perhaps the worst.

By now, you know that you must distinguish between promised and expected numbers. In particular, the CAPM is a model of expected rates of return and simply does not tell you anything about credit risk. When you want to apply the present value formula, you must use the *expected* cash flows in the numerator (adjusted for credit risk), not the *promised* cash flows. Never discount promised cash flows with CAPM costs of capital!

12.2A PROMISED AND EXPECTED RETURNS

Here is how users get it wrong most of the time.

Let's recap this. Say you have a B-rated corporate zero-bond that promises \$1,000 next year and has a beta of 0.2. Assuming you believe that the risk-free rate is 5% and the equity premium is 3%, you can still not compute the bond price as

$$\text{PV} \neq \frac{\$1{,}000}{1 + 5\% + 3\% \cdot 0.2} \approx \$946.97$$

$$\text{PV} \neq \frac{\text{Promised Cash Flow}}{1 + r_F + [\mathcal{E}(\tilde{r}_M) - r_F] \cdot \beta_i}$$

Yes, in a perfect CAPM world, the expected rate of return on this bond should be $5\% + 3\% \cdot 0.2 = 5.6\%$. (In an imperfect world, you would have to add the liquidity and tax premiums.) Yet, to determine the price, it is not enough for you to know the *promised* bond cash flow. You need the *expected* cash flow, a number that is always less than \$1,000. The same problem arises, of course, not only in the context of bonds but also in the context of corporate projects. You cannot simply discount the "good-scenario" cash flows. You must discount the project's expected cash flows!

➤ Imperfect market premiums, Section 10.6, p. 330

For capital budgeting (comparison to the cost of capital), an IRR must be computed from the project's expected (and not promised) cash flows.

The same mistake appears sometimes in another form when managers use the IRR capital budgeting rule. This rule says "accept the project if its IRR is above the hurdle rate." The common mistake here is that the cash flows from which the IRR must be computed are not the promised cash flows, but the expected cash flows. You can of course compute a number from the promised cash flows, but you should probably call it the "promised IRR" to distinguish it clearly from the "expected IRR"—and you should never compare the promised IRR to a hurdle rate based on the expected rates of return of other projects in the economy when you want to determine whether you should accept the project or not. In fact, the promised IRR should not be used for capital budgeting purposes.

SOLVE NOW!

Q 12.3 An Amazon.com bond quotes an internal rate of return of 8% per annum. Assuming the market is perfect, is this its cost of capital?

12.2B EXPECTED, TYPICAL, AND MOST LIKELY SCENARIOS

The NPV formula requires expected cash flows, not typical cash flows. (Do not ignore low-probability events.)

Managers often commit a related (but milder) error in applying NPV. They tend to confuse expected values with "typical" or "most likely." (Statistically speaking, this means that they confuse the mean with the median or the mode of a distribution.) If you do this, you will fail to consider low-probability events appropriately: a plane crash, a legal suit, an especially severe recession, or a terrific new client.

An example: The statistical distribution has a left tail.

For example, your business may have the following payoffs:

Event	Probability	Value
Good Business	46%	\$1,200,000
Normal Business	44%	\$1,000,000
Lawyers Sue for Punitive Damages	10%	−\$10,000,000

The most likely payoff is \$1,200,000. The median payoff is \$1,000,000. The expected payoff, however, is only

$$\mathcal{E}(\text{Payoff}) = 46\% \cdot \$1{,}200{,}000 + 44\% \cdot \$1{,}000{,}000 + 10\% \cdot (-\$10{,}000{,}000)$$
$$= -\$8{,}000$$

It is the latter that is required in an NPV analysis. If you run this business 100 times, you would receive \$1.2 million 46 times, \$1 million 44 times, and lose \$10 million 10 times. Fortunately, if the statistical distribution is symmetric—as it is in the case of the normal bell-shaped distribution—then the center of the distribution is all three: mean, median, and mode. Unfortunately, few businesses are immune to low-probability shocks, often negative, so you need to think about whether the distinction between mean, median, and mode is applicable to your business.

SOLVE NOW!

Q 12.4 A zero-bond promises \$100,000 and has a beta of 0.3. If the risk-free rate is 5%, and the equity premium is 3%, and the CAPM holds, then what is the bond's price?

Q 12.5 A machine that costs \$900,000 is likely to break irreparably with 10% probability at the end of each year (assuming it worked the previous year). (Many electric devices without moving parts have such breakdown characteristics.) However, the regulatory agency has phased out this machine, and so will neither allow you to replace it nor use it for more than 5 years. The machine can produce \$300,000 in profit every year. The discount rate is 12% per annum. (This means that the machine will produce some value between $\$0.3/1.12 \approx \$0.268$ million [if it breaks down immediately] and \$1.081 million [if it lasts for all 5 years] in present value.)

(a) What is the most likely operating time? If this comes true, what is the value?

(b) How long do you expect this machine to operate? (Hint: First work this out case by case for a 2-year machine, then for a 3-year machine. Think "D," "WD," "WWD," "WWWD," and "WWWWD," where W means working and D means dead.) If it were to last exactly as long as its expected lifetime, what would be the present value?

(c) What is the correct present value of this project?

12.3 BADLY BLENDED COSTS OF CAPITAL

Do you remember that you learned as one of your first lessons about NPVs that you can add them if projects are independent? Yet, believe it or not, although most managers know that it is impossible to add value by merely combining independent projects, in practice they often make exactly this mistake. This mistake arises most commonly in contexts in which costs of capital need to be blended across multiple projects. As always, the concept is straightforward, but the devil is in the details. It is easy to overlook the forest in the trees. Let's make sure you do not commit this mistake.

Independent projects should be considered based on their own costs of capital.

12.3A DOES RISK REDUCTION CREATE VALUE?

In the 1960s and 1970s, many firms became **conglomerates**, that is, companies with widely diversified and often unrelated holdings. Can firms add value through such diversification? The answer is "usually no." Diversification indeed reduces the standard deviation of the rate of return of the company—so diversified companies are less risky—but in a perfect market, your investors can just as well diversify risk for themselves. They don't need the firm to do it for them.

Diversification reduces risk, but does not create value.

For example, if your \$900 million firm ABC (e.g., with a beta of 2 and a risk of 20%) is planning to take over the \$100 million firm DEF (e.g., with a beta of 1 and also a risk of 20%), the resulting firm is worth \$1 billion. ABC + DEF indeed has an idiosyncratic risk lower than 20% if the two firms are not perfectly correlated, but your investors (or a mutual fund) could just purchase 90% of ABC and 10% of DEF and thereby achieve the very same diversification benefits. If anything, you have robbed investors of a degree of freedom here: They no longer have the ability to purchase, say, 50% in ABC and 50% in DEF. (In a CAPM world, this does not matter.) The CAPM makes it explicit that the cost of capital does not change unduly. Say both firms follow the CAPM pricing formula, and say that the risk-free rate is 3% and the equity premium is 5%,

A specific diversification example worked out for you, in which projects are priced fairly, and diversification neither creates nor destroys value.

$$\mathcal{E}(\tilde{r}_{\text{ABC}}) = 3\% + \quad 5\% \quad \cdot \quad 2 \quad = 13\%$$
$$\mathcal{E}(\tilde{r}_{\text{ABC}}) = r_{\text{F}} + \left[\mathcal{E}(\tilde{r}_{\text{M}}) - r_{\text{F}}\right] \cdot \beta_{\text{ABC}}$$

and

$$\mathcal{E}(\tilde{r}_{\text{DEF}}) = 3\% + \quad 5\% \quad \cdot \quad 1 \quad = 8\%$$
$$\mathcal{E}(\tilde{r}_{\text{DEF}}) = r_{\text{F}} + \left[\mathcal{E}(\tilde{r}_{\text{M}}) - r_{\text{F}}\right] \cdot \beta_{\text{DEF}}$$

The newly formed company will have an expected rate of return (cost of capital) of

➤ Value-weighted portfolios, Section 8.4, p. 219

$$\mathcal{E}(\tilde{r}_{\text{ABC+DEF}}) = 90\% \cdot \quad 13\% \quad + 10\% \cdot \quad 8\% \quad = 12.5\%$$
$$\mathcal{E}(\tilde{r}_{\text{ABC+DEF}}) = w_{\text{ABC}} \cdot \mathcal{E}(\tilde{r}_{\text{ABC}}) + w_{\text{DEF}} \cdot \mathcal{E}(\tilde{r}_{\text{DEF}})$$

ANECDOTE Risk and Conglomeration

In the 1970s, a lot of firms diversified to become conglomerates. Management argued that conglomerates tended to have lower risk, which created value for shareholders. This argument was, of course, total nonsense: Investors could diversify for themselves. It was the managers who liked lower risk, with less chance of losing their jobs and higher compensation packages that came from running a bigger company. Worse, because conglomerates often operated less efficiently than individual stand-alone, focused companies, diversification actually often destroyed firm value. In the 1980s, there were many "bust-up buyouts," which created value by purchasing conglomerates to sell off the pieces.

A good example of such a conglomerate was Gulf and Western. It was simultaneously involved in oil, movies (Paramount), recording (Stax), rocket engines, stereo components, finance, publishing (Simon and Schuster), auto parts, cigars, and on and on. It promptly crashed and split up in the 1980s. A more current example is Tyco, which has over 260,000 employees in 50 separate business lines, including electronics, undersea fiber optic cables, health care, adhesives, plastics, and alarm systems. (Its former executive, Dennis Kozlowski, became famous for his extravagant looting of Tyco's assets. With so many business lines, no wonder no one noticed for years!) The most interesting conglomerate, however, may be General Electric. It has hundreds of business lines, but unlike most other conglomerates, GE appears to have been running most of its divisions quite well.

and a market beta of

$$\beta_{\text{ABC+DEF}} = 90\% \cdot 2 + 10\% \cdot 1 = 1.9$$
$$\beta_{\text{ABC+DEF}} = w_{\text{ABC}} \cdot \beta_{\text{ABC}} + w_{\text{DEF}} \cdot \beta_{\text{DEF}}$$

The merged company will still follow the CAPM,

$$\mathcal{E}(\tilde{r}_{\text{ABC+DEF}}) = 3\% + 5\% \cdot 1.9 = 12.5\%$$
$$\mathcal{E}(\tilde{r}_{\text{ABC+DEF}}) = r_F + [\mathcal{E}(\tilde{r}_M) - r_F] \cdot \beta_{\text{ABC+DEF}}$$

Its cost of capital has not unduly increased or declined. In an ideal CAPM world, no value has been added or destroyed—even though ABC + DEF has a risk lower than the 20% per annum that its two constituents had.

Synergies determine M&A value for shareholders; lower risk (diversification) does not. Managers, however, are conflicted: They like lower risk.

Of course, some mergers can add value due to synergies, which will be discussed in the next section. But these synergies are not a result of the plain diversification effect. Many researchers believe that the most common but unspoken rationale for mergers are not synergies but the fact that managers like to take over other firms. They prefer the reduced idiosyncratic firm uncertainty and higher salaries guaranteed by larger firms to the higher risk and lower salaries in sharply focused, smaller firms. To justify a merger, managers will want to argue for a lower cost of capital for the target any way they can—including incorrectly using the acquirer's cost of capital. (This is an example of an agency conflict, which will be explained later in this chapter.) There is also good evidence that in the real world, diversified firms often do not operate as efficiently as stand-alone firms (e.g., due to limited attention span of management or more bureaucratization). Many mergers actually *destroy* firm value.

Does Corporate Risk Management Create Value?

Although risk management is discussed in more detail in Chapter 26, let me give you a brief preview. Firms can reduce their own overall risk by **hedging**. A hedge is an arrangement that reduces the firm's volatility. For example, a refinery could purchase crude oil today in order not to suffer if the future oil price were to increase.

Hedging is a form of risk management.

➤ Risk management and hedging, Section 26.5C, p. 1005

Remarkably, a firm with a high market beta could even transform itself into a firm with a low market beta! (Hedge funds often do this.) The firm can hedge away market risk by selling the stock market itself. S&P 500 futures contracts make shorting the stock market exceptionally easy. Whenever the stock market goes up, the futures contract goes up in value. Being the seller, the hedging firm's side of the futures contract goes down in value. Put differently, the firm's hedge contract has a negative market beta. The hedged firm is now a bundle, consisting of the unhedged firm plus this contract. Therefore, the market beta of the hedged firm would be lower than the market beta of the unhedged firm. If it wanted, the firm could even make its own market beta zero or negative. Usually, being hedged against market risk would also reduce the overall idiosyncratic risk of the firm. Many firms hedge against other risks. For example, Southwest Airlines purchases jet fuel far in advance (through futures contracts), which reduces its exposure to subsequent rises in the price of jet fuel.

Hedging against stock market risk can lower the market beta and risk of the firm. Hedging against jet fuel price increases can reduce risk exposure.

➤ Shorting stocks, Section 7.2A, p. 191

But would this hedging contract create firm value in a perfect market? No. The firm has not given its investors a new positive-NPV project. If investors had wanted less exposure to the overall stock market, *they could have shorted the stock market themselves*. Alternatively, investors can simply undo a firm's hedging—they can buy the financial markets contracts that the firm has sold. This undoes any corporate hedge from the investors' perspectives. So, in itself, in a perfect market, trading fairly priced hedging contracts neither adds nor subtracts value. It is only if the market is imperfect that a hedge may allow a firm to operate more efficiently. For example, the extra cash from a hedge contract could help the firm to avoid running into a liquidity crunch in situations in which more funding would be difficult to raise. Or the firm may have inside information concerning what the future will hold and thus whether the hedged good is underpriced. In this case, risk management could add value.

Does hedging create value? Only in an imperfect market.

Summary

IMPORTANT: In a perfect market, the following holds:

- If two firms are independent, then combining them into a conglomerate usually reduces the overall firm risk, but does not create value for investors. Investors can easily diversify risk themselves.
- Adding independent projects to the firm cannot create value if these projects are not positive-NPV in themselves.

In an imperfect market, the value effects of hedging are complex. Hedges could indeed add (or subtract) value.

SOLVE NOW!

Q 12.6 When two unrelated firms with uncorrelated rates of return merge, is the resulting conglomerate riskier or safer? Does this add value?

12.3B HOW TO MISUSE THE CAPM

A common misuse of CAPM is to use a uniform cost of capital for all projects.

This brings us to the most common abuse of the CAPM and NPV: managers forgetting that NPVs of independent projects are additive. Sounds obvious, but here is how it gets lost in the details: NPVs are only additive if you use the individual projects' own costs of capital. You cannot use the firm's overall cost of capital for its individual projects.

WHEN ACQUIRING ANOTHER COMPANY

Assume the firm uses the same overall cost of capital for all projects.

Assume the risk-free rate of return is 3% and the equity premium is 4%. Your old firm, cleverly named *old*, is worth \$100 and has a market beta of 0.5. An acquisition target (or just a new project), cleverly named *new*, costs \$10 and is expected to pay off \$11 next year. (Its rate of return is therefore 10%.) The beta of this new project is 3.

Here is a negative-NPV project. No sane firm should take it.

The simplest method to compute the value of acquiring project *new* relies on the fact that the NPVs of independent projects are additive. You can value the new project using its own expected cash flows and its own cost of capital. *Who* owns *new* should matter little: The project is worth what it is worth. Therefore, *new* should offer an expected rate of return of

$$\text{Correct Cost of Capital: } \mathcal{E}(\tilde{r}_{new}) = 3\% + \quad 4\% \quad \cdot \ 3 \ = 15\%$$
$$\mathcal{E}(\tilde{r}_{new}) = r_F + [\mathcal{E}(\tilde{r}_M) - r_F] \cdot \beta_{new}$$

and the true NPV of project *new* is

$$\text{NPV}_{new} = -\$10 + \frac{\$11}{1 + 15\%} \approx -\$0.43$$

Therefore, if firm *old* adopts project *new*, *new*'s owners would be 43 cents poorer than they would be if their managers did not adopt it (i.e., \$100 versus \$99.57).

Bad company policy: Using its own cost of capital on this project, the firm would mistakenly take it.

Unfortunately, in many firms, it is standard policy to evaluate *all* projects by the firm's overall cost of capital. Would such a firm take the *new* project now? Evaluated with a market beta of 0.5, the hurdle rate for the project would be

$$\text{Incorrect Cost of Capital: } \mathcal{E}(\tilde{r}_{old}) = 3\% + \quad 4\% \quad \cdot \ 0.5 = 5\%$$
$$\mathcal{E}(\tilde{r}_{old}) = r_F + \left[\mathcal{E}(\tilde{r}_M) - r_F\right] \cdot \beta_{old}$$

With its internal rate of return of \$11/\$10 − 1 = 10%, which is greater than the 5% incorrect cost of capital, a (bad) manager would indeed take this project.

The loss if the firm takes this project is exactly the negative NPV of the project.

If the *old* firm did take project *new*, how would its value change? With a beta of 0.5, the old firm had an expected rate of return of 3% + 4% · 0.5 = 5%. Its expected value next year would be $105. Using PV, we see that the present value of the combined firm would be

$$PV_{\text{combined}} = \frac{\$105}{1 + 5\%} + \frac{\$11}{1 + 15\%} \approx \$109.57$$

$$PV_{\text{combined}} = PV_{old} + PV_{new}$$

This is 43 cents less than the original value of $100 plus the $10 acquisition cost of the new project. Taking the project has made the *old* owners 43 cents poorer.

Real-world exception: If the capital market for the target is inefficient, the act of acquisition can create value.

Of course, not all mergers are driven by such mistakes. Contrary to the perfect CAPM world, it is not always true in the real world that mergers *never* add value on the cost-of-capital side. If capital markets are not as efficient for small firms as they are for large firms, it would be possible for a large acquirer to create value. For example, if a target previously had no access to a perfect capital market, then the cost of capital to the target can change when it is acquired. The correct cost of capital for valuing the acquisition (the target), however, is still *neither* the cost of capital of the acquirer *nor* the blended post-acquisition cost of capital of the firm. Instead, the correct cost of capital then is that rate that is appropriate for the target's projects, given the "now ordinary" access to capital markets. For example, if an entrepreneur inventor of holographic displays previously had faced a cost of capital of, say, 303%, primarily due to access only to personal credit card and credit shark financing, and if this inventor's business is purchased by IBM with its cost of capital of 6.5% (market beta of 1.5), the proper cost of capital is neither IBM's (market beta–based) cost nor a blended average between 303% and 6.5%. Instead, if part of IBM, the holographic project division should be evaluated at a cost of capital that is appropriate for projects of the market beta risk class "holographic display projects." This can add value relative to the 303% earlier cost of capital. (Of course, there are also many examples of large corporations that have destroyed all innovativeness and thereby all value in small companies that they had taken over.)

➤ Entrepreneurial finance, Section 10.5, p. 328

When Acquiring Another Project

Projects must be discounted by their own market betas.

It is important that you realize that not only firms to be acquired, but also smaller projects themselves, consist of components with different market betas, which therefore have different costs of capital. For example, when firms keep cash on hand in Treasuries, such investments have a zero market beta, which is lower than the beta for the firms' other projects. These bonds should not need to earn the same expected rate of return as investments in the firm's risky projects. (The presence of this cash in the firm lowers the average beta of the firm and thus the average cost of capital for the firm by the just-appropriate amount.)

A project can have components that require one cost of capital, and other components (even contingent ones) that require another cost of capital.

Here is another application, which shows how you can decompose projects into categories with different costs of capital: Assume that you consider purchasing a rocket to launch a telecom satellite next year. It would take you 1 year to build the rocket, at which point you would have to pay $80 million. Then you launch it. If the rocket fails (50% chance), then your investment will be lost. If the rocket succeeds, the satellite will produce a revenue stream with an appropriate beta of 2, beginning immediately (telecom revenues tend to have a high covariance with the market.) The telecom's expected cash flows will be \$20 million *forever*. Assume that the risk-free rate is 3% per year and the market equity premium is 5%.

The solution to this multi-cost-of-capital problem.

The correct solution is to think of the rocket as one project and of the telecom revenues as another project. The rocket project has only idiosyncratic risk; therefore, its beta is close to zero, and its discount factor is just about the risk-free rate of return of 3%. The rocket value (in millions of dollars today) is

$$\text{PV}_{\text{rocket}} = \frac{-\$80}{1 + 3\%} \approx -\$77.7$$

You can think of this as the cost of storing the \$80 million in Treasuries until you are ready to proceed to your second project. The telecom revenues, however, are a risky perpetuity. With a beta of 2, their cash flows should be discounted at $3\% + 5\% \cdot 2 = 13\%$—and these flows appear with a 50-50 probability only. Therefore,

$$\text{PV}_{\text{telecom}} = \frac{\mathcal{E}(\text{Telecom Cash Flows})}{\mathcal{E}(\tilde{r}_{\text{telecom discount rate}})} = \frac{50\% \cdot \$20}{13\%} \approx \$76.9$$

Consequently, the combined project has an NPV of about $-\$1$ million. If you had mistakenly discounted the rocket's \$80 million cost by the same 13%, you would have mistakenly valued it at $-\$80/1.13 + \$76.9 \approx +\$6.1$ million.

SOLVE NOW!

Q 12.7 Some companies believe they can use the blended post-acquisition cost of capital as the appropriate discount rate. However, this also leads to incorrect decisions. Let's explore this in the context of the example in the text: The risk-free rate is 3%, the equity premium is 4%, and the old firm is worth \$100 and has a market beta of 0.5. The new project costs \$10, is expected to pay off \$11 next year, and has a beta of 3.

(a) What is the value of the new project, discounted at its true cost of capital, 15%?
(b) What is the weight of the new project in the firm? (Assume that the combined firm value is around \$109.48.)
(c) What is the beta of the overall (combined) firm?
(d) Use this beta to compute the combined cost of capital.
(e) Will the firm take this project? (Use an IRR analysis.)
(f) If the firm takes the project, what will the firm's value be?

12.3C DIFFERENTIAL COSTS OF CAPITAL—THEORY AND PRACTICE

In practice, a good number of firms do not use project-specific costs of capital.

It is indisputably the case that projects must be discounted by their project-specific costs of capital. Yet Graham and Harvey found in their 2001 survey that just about half of surveyed CFOs *always*—and *incorrectly*—used the firm's overall cost of capital rather than the project-specific cost of capital! And even fewer CFOs correctly discounted cash flows of different riskiness within projects. The easy conclusion is that CFOs are ignorant—and many CFOs may indeed use a uniform cost of capital simply because they are ignorant.

➤ 2001 CFO survey, Section 4.5, p. 83

However, even some intelligent CFOs use the same discount rate quite deliberately on many different types of projects. Why? You already know that it can be difficult to estimate the appropriate cost of capital correctly. In theory, the CAPM works perfectly. In practice, it does not. In theory, you know the expected equity premium input. In practice, you are just guessing. In theory, you know the market beta of all your projects. In practice, you may not.

A possible reason: Finding project costs of capital may just be too difficult. Intuitive methods anchoring on the firm's cost of capital may work better than formal methods.

➤ CAPM accuracy?, Section 9.5B, p. 268

1. Even the historical betas of publicly traded corporations are not entirely reliable and indicative of the future. Different estimation methods can come up with different numbers. This is why you may want to use the average market betas of similar, publicly traded companies or the market beta of an entire industry. But many of your projects may be so idiosyncratic, so unusual, or in such far-away locales, that no comparable may seem particularly suitable.
2. You could try to estimate your own market beta. To do so, you would need a time series of historical project values, not just historical project cash flows. This is because you cannot rely on historical cash flow variation as a substitute for historical value variation. You already know that the market values themselves are the present discounted values of *all* future cash flows, not just the present discounted value of just one period's cash flow.

   Here is an example of how this can go awry. Consider a firm whose cash flows are perfectly known. Therefore, its appropriate true discount rate would be close to the risk-free rate. However, if its cash flows occur only every other month ($200, $0, $200, . . .), this firm would have infinite monthly cash flow volatility (−100% followed by +∞%). Its percent changes in cash flows would not be indicative of its value-based rates of return. Plus, almost surely, it would have an extreme market beta estimate, indicating a wrong cost of capital. In order to estimate your market beta, you would need to somehow obtain a time series of estimated market values from the known time series of cash flows. Of course, you already know that it is difficult to estimate one market value for your firm—but estimating a time series of how this market value changes every month is entirely beyond anyone's capability. (When only cash flows [but not market values] are known, your estimates must necessarily be less accurate. The best way to estimate an appropriate cost of capital relies on the certainty equivalence formula explained in Section 9.6.)

➤ Certainty equivalence, Section 9.6, p. 281

3. Many firms may not have *any* historical experience that you can use, not just for market values, but even for cash flows. There would be nothing you could verifiably and credibly use to estimate in the first place.

In addition, you have not even yet considered such issues as the influence of liquidity and tax premiums on your cost of capital. Quite simply, you must be aware of the painful reality that our methods for estimating the cost of capital are usually just not as robust as we would like them to be.

➤ Imperfect markets premiums, Section 10.6, p. 330

Together, your uncertainties distort not only your overall corporate cost-of-capital estimates, but also your relative cost of capital estimates across different projects. Consequently, the problem with assigning different costs of capital to different projects may now become one of disagreement. Division managers can argue endlessly about why their projects should be assigned a lower cost of capital. Is this how you want your division managers to spend their time? And do you want your

Flexible costs of capital can cause endless debate and worsen agency conflicts.

managers to play revenue games? Managers could even shift revenues from weeks in which the stock market performed well into weeks in which the stock market performed poorly in order to produce a lower market beta. The cost-of-capital estimate itself then becomes a pawn in the game of agency conflict and response—all managers would like to convince themselves and others that a low cost of capital for their own divisions is best. What the overall corporation would like to have in order to suppress such "gaming of the system" would be immutable good estimates of the cost of capital *for each division and potential project* that no one can argue about. In the reality of corporate politics, however, it may be easier to commit to one-and-the-same immutable cost of capital *for all projects* than it would be to have different costs of capital for each division and project. This is not to argue that this one cost of capital is necessarily a good system, but just that there are cases in which having *one* systemwide cost of capital may be a necessary evil.

How Bad Are Mistakes?

DO PROJECTS REALLY NEED THEIR OWN COSTS OF CAPITAL?

You will never get the cost of capital perfectly right. Get it right where it matters!

Does every project really need its own cost of capital? Let's not miss the forest here. Yes, in theory, each component must be discounted at its own discount rate if you want to get the value (and incentives) right. However, in practice, if you want to value each paper clip by its own cost of capital, you will never come up with a reasonable firm value—you will lose the forest among the trees. You need to keep your perspective as to what reasonable errors are and what unreasonable errors are. The question is one of magnitude: If you are acquiring a totally different company or project, with a vastly different cost of capital, and this project will be a significant fraction of the firm, then the choice of cost of capital matters and you should differentiate. However, if you are valuing a project that is uncertain, the project is relatively small, and its cost of capital is reasonably similar to your overall cost of capital, you can probably live with some error. It all depends—your mileage may vary!

IMPORTANT:

- Theoretically, all projects must be discounted by their own costs of capital, and not by the firm's overall cost of capital.
- Practically, the effort involved and the "gaming" by division managers prevent you from discounting every project—every paper clip—by its own cost of capital.

It is up to you to determine when it is important to work with different costs of capital and when it is better to use just one cost of capital.

12.4 THE ECONOMICS OF PROJECT INTERACTIONS

If projects are independent, you have the luxury to consider them in isolation. You can compute separately the costs and benefits necessary to make a decision whether to accept or reject each project. However, in the real world, projects are not always independent. To focus on the issue at hand, assume a zero interest rate (so you do not have to discount at all). Let's consider managing an aquarium, where you can add a large shark to the exhibition tank at a cost of $50,000 for projected additional ticket receipts of $120,000. Or you can add a large octopus at a cost of $75,000 for projected additional ticket receipts of $200,000.

An example of projects whose cash flows are not independent. In fact, they "interact" (in the same aquarium).

	Ticket Receipts	−	Creature Cost	=	Net Profit
Shark	$120,000	−	$50,000	=	$70,000
Octopus	$200,000	−	$75,000	=	$125,000

Regrettably, adding both the shark and the octopus would not increase project value by $195,000, because octopuses are known to have negative effects on similarly-sized sharks—they eat them. Thus, the best achievable project value is only $125,000 (skip the shark!). Stocking the aquarium with an octopus plus some lobsters would cost only $75,000 plus some minimum outlay for the lobsters—necessary to allow the octopus to remain alive. If you do not add the lobsters, you would end up with a starved and expiring octopus, and thus not many ticket sales. So you should either want to add the octopus and the lobsters together, or neither. The question in this section is how you should deal with projects that can influence one another. To use our metaphor, how should you stock the aquarium?

12.4A THE ULTIMATE PROJECT SELECTION RULE

IMPORTANT: The ultimate project selection rule: Consider all possible project combinations and select the combination of projects that gives the highest overall NPV.

Optimal project selection is easier said than done. It is easy for two projects at a time, because there are only four options to consider: take neither, take one, take the other, or take both. But the complexity quickly explodes when there are more projects. For three projects, there are eight options. For four projects, there are 16 options. For 10 projects, there are about a thousand options. For 20 projects, there are over a million options. And so on. Even the simplest corporate projects can easily involve hundreds of decisions that have to be made. For your small aquarium, you may want to consider about 54,000 different fish species—and each may interact with many others. Furthermore, you should consider what fish you may want to add in the future and how many of each. Mathematically, it is an impossible task to find the perfect combination.

There are too many possible action choices in the real world to evaluate (to compute NPV for). You need rules and heuristics!

To help you determine which projects to take, you need to find some rules that help you make a decision. Such rules of thumb are called **heuristics**–that is, rules that simplify your decisions even if they are not always correct. One common heuristic algorithm is to consider project combinations, one at a time. Start with the project

The "greedy" heuristic: Always take the next most profitable project.

combination that would give you the highest NPV if you were only allowed to take two projects (one pair from a set of many different projects). For example, start with your two favorite fish. Then take this pair as fixed, that is, treat it as a single project. Now see which project (next fish) adds the most value to your existing pair. Continue until adding the best remaining project no longer increases value. Computer scientists call this the greedy algorithm. It is a good heuristic, because it drastically cuts down the possible project combinations to consider and usually gives a pretty good set of projects. There are many possible enhancements to this algorithm, such as forward and backward iterations, in which one considers replacing one project at a time with every other option. Full-fledged algorithms and combinatorial enhancements that guarantee optimal choice are really the domain of computer science and operations research, not of finance. Yet many of these algorithms have been shown to require more time than the duration of the universe, unless you make simplifications that distort the business problem so much that the results are likely no longer trustworthy. Fortunately, finance is in the domain of economics, and economics can help simplify the project selection problem.

12.4B PROJECT PAIRS

Project combinations can be classified into positive, zero, and negative interaction combinations.

Considering projects in pairs not only is common practice, but also clarifies many economic issues. With two projects, you can decompose the total net present value into three terms:

$$\text{Overall NPV} = \text{NPV Project 1} + \text{NPV Project 2} + \text{NPV Interactions}$$

For example, if you were to stock both the shark and the octopus, you would get ticket receipts of $200,000 (octopus) but pay $125,000 (octopus and shark), for a net of $75,000. Therefore, net receipts are

$$\underset{\text{NPV Aquarium with Both}}{\$75{,}000} = \underset{\text{NPV Shark}}{\$70{,}000} + \underset{\text{NPV Octopus}}{\$125{,}000} + \underset{\substack{\text{NPV Octopus Eats Shark,}\\ \text{So No More Shark Ticket Receipts}}}{(-\$120{,}000)}$$

The final term reflects the interaction of the two projects. It suggests that you can classify project combinations into one of three different categories:

1. Projects with zero interactions
2. Projects with positive interactions
3. Projects with negative interactions

Interactions are also sometimes called **externalities** in economics, because one project has external influences on other projects—sometimes imposing external costs, and sometimes providing external benefits. Let's consider these three cases separately.

ZERO PROJECT INTERACTIONS

Project independence is the most common case. It allows the simplest decision making.

Most projects in this world are **independent**—they have no mutual interactions. For example, a mall in Maine probably has no effect on a mall in Oregon. It neither steals customers from Oregon nor attracts extra customers. Independent project payoffs permit the separate evaluation of each project. This makes decision making very easy:

- Taking any positive-NPV project increases firm value.
- Taking a zero-NPV project leaves firm value unchanged.
- Taking any negative-NPV project decreases firm value.

If projects are independent, then the project interaction term is zero, and project NPVs are additive. Project independence makes decisions a lot easier: For 20 projects, only 20 independent decisions (accept or reject) have to be made, not a million.

IMPORTANT: You can evaluate zero-interaction projects independently. In this case, you can simply add project NPVs.

POSITIVE PROJECT INTERACTIONS

Positive interactions mean that the sum of the parts is worth more than the parts individually. If one project has a positive influence on the NPV of another project, you cannot value it without taking into account this positive influence. For example, think of a new product as one project and of an advertising campaign as another project. The advertising campaign project is of lesser use without the product, and the product is of lesser use without the advertising campaign. You must consider creating a product and an advertising campaign together. Such positive externalities are even more plentiful in smaller decisions. For example, a computer keyboard is less useful without a computer, and a computer is less useful without a keyboard. In fact, some projects or products only make sense if purchased together. In this case, producers may bundle them together and/or purchasers may only buy them as bundles.

In many cases, what makes a project a project in the firm's mind is often the indivisibility of its components.

In the corporate context, investment in *infrastructure* is another classical example of positive project interactions. For example, building a road, hiring a security firm, or laying a fast Internet connection could enhance the values of many divisions simultaneously. The firm should factor in the increase in value to *all* divisions when deciding on how much infrastructure to add.

Infrastructure can benefit many different projects.

Don't take positive externalities too lightly: On a philosophical basis, positive project interactions are the reason why firms exist in the first place. If there were no cost savings to having all resources combined in the firm, all of us could work as individuals and dispense with firms altogether.

Positive externalities are why firms exist to begin with.

IMPORTANT: When deciding whether to take a project, you must credit all positive interactions to the project. The overall NPV is higher than the individual project NPVs alone.

Internal conflict and cost allocation procedures (discussed further as "agency conflicts" below) often hinder corporations from taking advantage of many positive externalities. For example, in real life, your division managers might argue that they should not be charged for the Internet connection, because they did not request it and therefore do not really need it (even if it were to increase their divisions' values). After

Agency issues often prevent properly crediting projects with all their contributions.

all, division managers would prefer getting the Internet for free from the company instead of paying for it out of their own divisional budgets.

Another name for positive externalities: synergies.

➤ Mergers and acquisitions, Section 23.3A, p. 879

Nowadays, managers who want to acquire other companies usually claim the presence of large positive externalities. **Synergies** are the managerial term for positive externalities between an acquirer and a potential acquisition target. It has become an important managerial buzzword. For example, in the 2001 acquisition of Compaq by Hewlett-Packard, HP touted synergies of $2.5 billion—most from cutting employees. Of course, whether enough synergies are ever realized to outweigh the acquisition costs is always another question.

NEGATIVE PROJECT INTERACTIONS

Negative interactions exist when taking one project decreases the value of another project.

Negative interactions mean that the sum of the parts is worth less than the parts individually. In this case, projects have negative influences on one another and thereby decrease one another's value. Economists sometimes call negative externalities **diseconomies of scale**. Here are a few examples.

Pollution and congestion: Think of an airline company with two divisions, but only one maintenance facility. One division handles cargo; the other handles passengers. If the cargo division wants to expand, it will use more of the maintenance capacity. This will leave the passenger division with longer service waiting times. In the extreme, the extra delays may cost the passenger division more than the extra profits that the expanded cargo operation adds.

Cannibalization: If a new Apple computer can produce $100,000 in NPV compared to an older Windows machine that only produces $70,000 in NPV, how should you credit the Apple machine? The answer is that the Apple would eliminate the positive cash flows produced by the existing Windows machine, so the cash flow of the project "replace Windows with Apple" is only $30,000: the $100,000 minus the $70,000 that the now-unused Windows machine would have produced. Be careful what you consider cannibalization, though. For example, in the 1970s, IBM did not produce personal computers, fearful of cannibalizing its mainframe computer business. IBM's mistake was that it did not realize that other computer manufacturers were able to step in and eat much of IBM's mainframe business for themselves. Put differently, IBM had not realized that the present value of its mainframe business's future cash flows had already changed with the advent of new technology in the competitive market that it was in.

Bureaucratization and internal conflict: If more projects are adopted, project management may find it increasingly difficult to make good decisions in a reasonable time frame. This may require more cumbersome bureaucracy and reduce cash flows for all other divisions. A good example of bureaucratic destruction of projects can be found on Moishe Lettvin's blog (Google is your friend). A programmer who worked for Microsoft for 7 years, he describes how it took between 24 and 43 people, separated by six layers of management, over a year just to talk about the Windows boot menu—and no one really knew who had the power to make the final decision.

Resource exhaustion: Perhaps the most common source of negative externalities—and one that is often underestimated—is **limited attention span**. Management can

> pay only so much attention to so many different issues. An extra project distracts from the attention previously received by existing projects. There are many anecdotal examples of overstretched attention spans. The most recent example of failed attention management may be the 2007 credit collapse, which left many investment banks with huge losses, and which ultimately cost the CEOs of Merrill Lynch, Citigroup, and others their jobs. Most of these CEOs did not even know what their firms' holdings and exposures were. They had to correct their own estimates multiple times, as they themselves learned only after the fact what their firms had actually invested in.

Although costs always include opportunity costs, in the case of negative project externalities these opportunity costs are more obvious. If your project cannibalizes another project or requires more attention, it's clearly an opportunity cost.

IMPORTANT: When deciding whether to take a project, charge all negative interactions to the project. Because of these negative interactions, the overall NPV will be lower than the individual project NPVs alone.

Again, as in the case of positive externalities, agency issues and cost allocation systems often prevent proper accounting for negative externalities in the real world. Whatever division created the negative externality will argue that it is not its problem and that the complaining division overstates the problem. Clearly, companies that are better at overcoming these issues will end up being more profitable.

Again, agency issues often prevent properly crediting projects for all their detractions.

SOLVE NOW!

Q 12.8 Why are zero externalities so convenient for a valuation problem?

Q 12.9 A company must decide if it should move division A to a new location. If division A moves, it will be housed in a new building that reduces its operating costs by $10,000 per year forever. The new building costs $120,000. Moving division A allows division B to expand within the old factory. This enables B to increase its profitability by $3,000 per year forever. If the discount rate is 10%, should division A move?

Q 12.10 A firm can purchase a new punch press for $10,000. The new press will allow the firm to enter the widget industry, thereby earning $2,000 per year in profits forever. However, the punch press will displace several screw machines that produce $1,500 per year in profits. If the interest rate is 10%, should the new punch press be purchased?

12.5 EVALUATING PROJECTS INCREMENTALLY

Usually, managers do not make the decision for all interacting projects simultaneously. Instead, many projects are already in place. Although existing projects should also constantly be evaluated in an ideal world, the manager often has to make a decision about adding or not adding a single new project (or project complex) in the

Capital budgeting rule for a scenario in which you can either take or not take one extra project. The rest stays in place.

real world. For practical purposes, the old projects are often present, given, and unalterable. The new project may have positive or negative externalities on other existing projects, and the question is how best to decide whether to take it or not. This simplifies the decision even further: The question is now only whether the new project adds or subtracts value from the total. In this case, economists use the concept of decision **on the margin**—holding the existing project structure as is, what is the *additional* contribution of the new project?

The aquarium haunts us (you): You can come to the right decision by using the marginal method, too.

Return to the aquarium example. Let's work it via the method of contributions on the margin. Naturally, we should arrive at the same conclusion:

- If you already have the octopus in the tank (with its NPV of \$125,000), should you add the shark? If you do, you pay an additional (**incremental** or **marginal**) \$50,000 and get nothing—because the shark will become octopus food, which generates no additional ticket sales. Thus, the marginal benefit of adding the shark is −\$50,000. Therefore, you should not add the shark.
- If you already have the shark in the tank with its NPV of \$70,000, should you add the octopus? Your marginal cost to add the octopus is \$75,000 for the beast itself. In ticket sales, you would lose the \$120,000 in shark receipts but gain \$200,000 in octopus receipts. Your net benefit would therefore be \$200,000 − \$120,000 − \$75,000 = +\$5,000. Consequently, you should add the octopus, even though you know that your shark will become pet food!

Of course, if you can sell the shark or put it into its own aquarium, your calculations would change—though you would then also have to consider the marginal cost of selling the shark or getting a new aquarium. (In the real world, chances are that your octopus's animal keeper would not want to see his influence reduced and would probably come up with a thousand reasons why this is not feasible and why you should use your money to buy more octopuses instead.)

IMPORTANT:

- The decision on whether to take one additional project should be made based on the following rule:

$$\text{Accept New Project If:} \quad \text{Total Firm NPV with New Project} > \text{Total Firm NPV without New Project}$$

- This means that the single new project should be credited with any value increase or value decrease that it confers on other projects.
- When considering a project on the margin (i.e., extra), credit/charge to this project all externalities that this project conveys onto the existing firm.
- Everything else equal, projects with positive externalities on the rest of the firm have higher marginal benefits than do projects with negative externalities.

The big advantage of the marginal method is its solvability when there are many, many choices—possibly infinitely many.

Although the marginal perspective on costs and benefits has also worked for our discrete "yes or no" projects, it becomes a lot more useful when you consider projects of which you can take a little more or a little less. (In fact, enumerating all possible combinations is no longer feasible.) Marginal thinking also helps you to understand economies of scale, sunk costs, overhead allocation, and space capacity. The marginal perspective on costs and benefits is particularly useful when it comes to projects that are not just "yes or no" but are projects of which you can take a varying amount—more or less of the project. With rare exceptions, the incremental way of thinking is the only way to make sense out of the real-world complexity of the problem.

SOLVE NOW!

Q 12.11 A notebook computer costs \$2,500; a desktop computer costs \$1,500. If you buy either the notebook or the desktop, you can increase your productivity to \$9,000. If you buy both, you can increase your productivity to \$11,000. (There is no time-value dimension to your choice.) Assume there is no computer resale market or alternative use for a computer.

(a) If you do not own either, should you buy the notebook, the desktop, both, or neither?

(b) If you own the notebook, should you buy the desktop? What are the marginal costs and benefits?

(c) If you own the desktop, should you buy the notebook? What are the marginal costs and benefits?

12.5A ECONOMIES OF SCALE

Consider an example in which there are **economies of scale**—the more airplanes you build, the lower your average per-airplane production cost will be (in millions):

An example in which your production function is continuous and exhibits economies of scale.

$$\text{Average Cost per Airplane} = \$4 + \frac{\$10}{\text{Number of Airplanes} + 1}$$

This states that it costs $\$4 + \$10/(1 + 1) = \$9$ million to produce 1 airplane. Producing 100 airplanes costs you $\$4 + \$10/(100 + 1) \approx \$4.10$ million per airplane. Again, let's assume that the interest rate is zero, so you do not need to discount.

Now say that you are currently selling 4 airplanes domestically, each for a price of \$8 million. Your firm's net value is

Should you expand production?

$$\text{Total Net Value @ 4 Airplanes} = 4 \cdot \$8 - 4 \cdot \left[\$4 + \frac{\$10}{4+1}\right] \tag{12.1}$$
$$= \$32 - \$24 = \$8$$

Your big decision now is whether you should expand internationally. It would cost you \$16 million to open a foreign sales office, but doing so would sell another 5 airplanes at the same \$8 million per-airplane price. Should you expand?

With 9 airplanes in production, your average cost would fall to $\$4 + \$10/10 = \$5$ million per airplane. This means that 5 airplanes would cost only \$25 million to build now, and bring in $5 \cdot \$8 = \$40$ million. The value of your foreign office would therefore be

An average cost calculation tells you not to expand.

$$\begin{array}{lcccccccc} \text{Value of Foreign Office} & = & 5 \cdot \$8 & - & 5 \cdot \$5 & - & \$16 & = & -\$1 \\ \text{Value} & = & \text{Gross Sales} & - & \text{Average Cost} & - & \text{Start-Up Cost} & & \end{array}$$

This calculation suggests that you should not expand internationally.

Wrong! The reason is that the foreign sales office also lowers the cost of domestic production!

Unfortunately, this calculation is wrong. To see this, compute your *total* net value if you open the foreign office. Your 9 airplanes generate sales of \$72 million. Subtract your production costs of 9 · \$5 = \$45 million and your opening costs of \$16 million. This means that your firm would be worth

$$\text{Total Net Value @ 9 Airplanes} = 9 \cdot \$8 - 9 \cdot \$5 - \$16 = \$11 \qquad (12.2)$$

This is more than the \$8 million that you earned without the foreign office. This is the correct calculation. It tells you that you should expand internationally, because this expansion will increase your net value by \$3 million.

You must credit the foreign office with any domestic cost reductions.

The difference between the right calculation and the wrong calculation is that your foreign office has one additional marginal benefit that the first calculation overlooked: Foreign sales also reduce the average production cost of your domestic production. This cost reduction is a positive externality that you must credit to your foreign office. If you do not, you are throwing away \$3 million.

Thinking in terms of marginal costs exposes the economies of scale.

It is often more intuitive to think of projects such as airplanes in terms of marginal costs and benefits. The extra marginal cost of each airplane changes airplane by airplane—it is the difference in total costs of all airplanes:

Airplanes	Average	Total	Marginal	Airplanes	Average	Total	Marginal
1	\$9.00	\$ 9.00	\$9.000	6	\$5.43	\$32.57	\$4.238
2	\$7.33	\$14.67	\$5.667	7	\$5.25	\$36.75	\$4.179
3	\$6.50	\$19.50	\$4.833	8	\$5.11	\$40.89	\$4.139
4	\$6.00	\$24.00	\$4.500	9	\$5.00	\$45.00	\$4.111
5	\$5.67	\$28.33	\$4.333	10	\$4.91	\$49.09	\$4.091

If you go from 4 airplanes to 9 airplanes, your production creates extra marginal costs of \$4.333 + \$4.238 + \$4.179 + \$4.139 + \$4.111 = \$21 (million). There is an additional marginal cost of \$16 million to open the foreign office. The total marginal cost is therefore \$37 million. The marginal benefit of 5 extra airplanes is \$40 million. Therefore, your foreign sales office creates marginal value of \$40 − \$37 = \$3 million. This is exactly the difference between \$8 million from Formula 12.1 and \$11 million from Formula 12.2. Thinking in terms of marginal costs and benefits is just a different and sometimes more convenient way to compare overall project values.

Economies of scale are often responsible for the big corporate success stories of our time.

Economies of scale (decreasing marginal costs) are often responsible for the biggest corporate success stories. For example, Wal-Mart and Dell have managed not only to use their scales to negotiate considerable supplier discounts, but they have also created inventory and distribution systems that allow them to spread their fixed costs very efficiently over the large quantities of goods they sell. They have the lowest costs and highest industry inventory turnover rates—two factors that allow them to benefit tremendously from their economies of scale. Similarly, Microsoft enjoys economies of scale—with a large fixed cost and almost zero variable cost, Microsoft can swamp the planet with copies of Windows. No commercial alternative can compete—Microsoft can always drop its price low enough to drive its competitor out of business. The socially optimal number of operating-systems software companies is very small and may even be just one—it is what economists call a **natural monopoly**. If you think of the economy as one big firm, you would not want to incur the same huge fixed software-development cost twice. The same applies to utilities: You would not want two types of cable strung to everyone's house, two types of telephone lines, and two types of power lines. But companies with monopolies can also hurt the economy: They will want to charge higher prices to exploit their monopoly powers. Society has therefore often found it advantageous to regulate monopolists. Unfortunately, the regulatory agencies are themselves often "captured" by the companies that they are supposed to regulate, which can sometimes hurt the economy even more than the monopolies themselves. There are no easy and obvious solutions.

Of course, there are also plenty of examples in which marginal costs are not decreasing, but increasing, with the number of items produced. In such cases, you must charge the diseconomies of scale to the new division you are adding. If you do not, you will be inclined to overexpand and thereby reduce your firm's overall value.

Negative economies of scale work alike.

SOLVE NOW!

Q 12.12 The average production cost per good is estimated at $\$5 + \$15/(x+1)$. The firm can currently sell 10 units at \$20 per unit.

(a) What is the current total profit of the firm?

(b) How much should the firm value the opportunity to sell one extra good to a new vendor? In other words, what is the marginal cost of selling one extra good?

(c) A new vendor offers to pay \$19 for one unit. However, your other existing vendors would find out and demand the same price. What is the marginal cost and benefit of signing up this new vendor now? Should you sign up this new vendor?

Q 12.13 A firm faces diseconomies of scale in both production and sales. It can produce goods for an average per-unit cost of $\$5 + (Q \cdot \$1 + \$20)/100$, where Q is the number of units. For example, to produce 10 goods would cost $10 \cdot (\$5 + \$30/100) = \$53$. The market price per good is $\$7 - Q \cdot \$1/100$. So, sales of 10 goods would generate $10 \cdot (\$7 - \$10/100) = \$69$ in gross revenues. Use a spreadsheet to answer the following questions.

(a) How many items should the firm produce?

(b) What are the average per-unit gross sales at this point?

(c) What is the average per-unit production cost at this point?

(d) What are the average per-unit net sales (gross minus cost) at this point?

(e) What are the marginal per-unit sales at this point?

(f) What is the marginal per-unit cost at this point?
(g) What is the marginal per-unit net change at this point?
(h) If your average per unit net change at this point is positive, should you expand production? Why?

12.5B SUNK COSTS

Sunk costs cannot be altered or reversed and thus should not enter into your current decisions.

Sunk costs are, in a sense, the opposite of marginal costs. A **sunk cost** is an incurred cost that cannot be altered or reversed. It is a done deal and therefore should not enter into your decisions today. It is what it is.

An example of how first the capital investment becomes sunk, and then how the produced goods themselves become sunk.

For example, consider circuit board production—a very competitive industry. If you have just completed a circuit board factory for $1 billion, it is a sunk cost. What matters now is *not* that you spent $1 billion, but how much the production of each circuit board costs. Having invested $1 billion is irrelevant. What remains relevant is that the presence of the factory makes the marginal cost of production of circuit boards very cheap. It is only this marginal cost that matters when you decide whether or not to produce circuit boards. If the marginal board production cost is $100 each, but you can only sell them for $90 each, then you should not build boards, regardless of how much you spent on the factory. Though tempting, the logic of "we have spent $1 billion, so we may as well put it to use" is just plain wrong. Now, assume that the market price for boards is $180, so you go ahead and manufacture 1 million boards at a cost of $100 each. Alas, your production run has just finished, and the price of boards—contrary to everyone's best expectations—has dropped from $180 each to $10 each. At this point, the board production cost is sunk, too. Whether the boards cost you $100 to manufacture or $1 to manufacture is irrelevant. The cost of the production run is sunk. If boards now sell at $10 each, assuming you cannot store them, you should sell them for $10 each. Virtually all supply costs eventually become sunk costs, and all that matters when you want to sell a completed product is the demand for the product.

Sunk costs are everywhere!

Sunk costs are everywhere. With the passage of time, virtually all decisions at some point become irrevocable and thus sunk. The examples are so abundant that you can even find whole books about them. Allan Teger's book *Too Much Invested to Quit* describes investments such as the continuing Concorde airplane development even after it had already become clear that it would never become profitable.

Time is a good proxy for what is sunk, but it may not be the deciding factor.

One more note—time itself often, but not always, decides on what is sunk or not. Contracts may allow you to undo things that happened in the past (thereby converting a sunk cost into a cost about which you still can make decisions), or they may bind you irrevocably to things that will happen in the future.

IMPORTANT: A sunk cost has no cost contribution on the margin. It should therefore be ignored.

Exasperation—letting sunk costs frustrate you and misinterpret your marginal costs and benefits.

The flip side of not ignoring sunk costs and refusing to throw in the towel is "exasperation"—though it can come about through compartmentalization (explained in Section 12.7). It can occur when you think that you have already put too much money into the project, and rather than spend any more, you throw in the towel. You just consider your budget to be exhausted and you abandon the project, rather than doing the right thing (which would be to finish it).

12.5C OVERHEAD ALLOCATION

A closely related mistake is to forget that "overhead" is often a sunk cost. By definition, overhead is not a marginal cost but something that has been incurred already and is allocated to departments. For example, assume your firm has spent $500,000 on a computer that is currently idle half the time. It serves only one division. Assume that another division can take an additional project that produces $60,000 in net present value but will consume 20% of the computer's time. Should your firm take this project? If 20% of the cost of the computer is allocated to this new project (i.e., 20% · $500,000 = $100,000), the net present value of the new project would appear to be −$40,000. But the correct decision process is not to allocate the existing overhead as a cost to divisions. The $500,000 on overhead has already been spent. The computer is a sunk cost—assuming that it really would sit idle otherwise and find no better purpose. It may seem unfair to have charged only the original division for the computer and exempt the other opportunistic divisions. Yet taking this additional project will produce $60,000 in profits without any additional cost—clearly, a good thing. Everyone who has worked in a corporation can recite plenty of examples in which overhead allocation has killed otherwise profitable projects.

Allocating already existing overhead budget to a project (i.e., adding it to the new project's cost) is a common real-world example of bad project valuation and decision making.

REAL-WORLD DILEMMAS IN ALLOCATING SPARE CAPACITY

Limited capacity is a subject that is closely related to overhead allocation. For example, consider building or buying corporate car garages that can park 300 cars for $1.5 million per garage. As CEO, you have to make choices about how many garages you want to have and how you should charge your corporate divisions for parking spots. Of course, having a garage makes owning corporate cars more profitable, because they will not deteriorate as much. A new garage offers a positive externality on the project "corporate cars."

If capacity is otherwise unusable, it should have a zero price.

Here is a bad solution to your problem: Charge users the average cost of building the garage. For example, you may calculate that about 150 cars from your corporate divisions would volunteer to use it, then divide the cost of $1.5 million by 150, and allow these divisions to buy spots at $10,000 each (which may be equivalent to, say, $60 rent per month). First, you may run into the standard overhead allocation problem. You may find that 75 of the 150 cars may not even take you up on the offer, and you may have to increase the rate to $120 per month. At this rate, more may jump ship, and you may end up with no cars wanting to go in. Second, even if you get all 150 cars to sign up, you still end up with another 150 empty spots—spots that could be used to park other, older corporate cars. You would never have built a garage just for them, but it would make sense to put them into the existing garage if it is otherwise empty. The marginal cost of adding one more old car would be zero. Is this how you should price parking spots?

Average cost allocation—an empty parking spot problem.

If you charge zero to the division for older cars, how would your other divisions with newer cars, who are still paying for their parking spots, feel? Should these divisions be charged then? After all, the marginal cost of their new cars, given that

Should you charge your new division? Should you charge anyone?

the garage is already built, is also zero. These are internal cost allocation issues that inevitably bring out the worst in discussions among corporate division managers. Everyone will claim that it should be the other party that should pay more of the cost.

Often you do not have easy, smooth margins. And you face more questions—these are difficult real-world dilemmas.

One reason why this is so difficult is that you can only add capacity in discrete chunks. And there is a time dimension, too. Should you really charge zero for parking corporate cars if you suspect that the unused capacity will not remain unused forever? What if another division comes along that wants to rent the 150 currently unused garage spaces in the future? Do you then kick out all the older cars that you gave spots to for free (or a very low price)? How should you charge this new division if it wants to rent 160 spaces? Should you give it the 150 remaining unused parking spots for free and build a new garage for the extra 10 cars? Presuming that garages can only be built in increments of 300 parking spots each, should you build another 300-car garage? Should this new division pay for the new garage, or should the divisions that held the original 150 spots pay a part of this or relinquish some of their original spots? If you ask the new division to pay, should it get a refund if some of the 290 spots are eventually rented out? Should you charge parking fees for these 290 spots? Tough questions.

Here is how to think about the parking allocation in terms of margins.

Usually, you should think in terms of the relevant marginal benefits and costs. But this does not work well if capacity can only be added in large discrete chunks. In that case, the extra cost of just one more parking spot is either zero or \$1.5 million. If you charge marginal cost, demand also may not be marginal. At an internal price of zero, you will likely have a large number of users—more than the garage can accommodate. At a price of \$1.5 million, no user will want to pay for the garage. You can think of less extreme schemes, but the basic problem is intrinsically the discreteness of capacity.

Advice: Use a market-pricing system if you can, to push the decision down to the divisions themselves. But do not try to maximize garage profits.

Remarkably, there are clear answers as to how you should solve your two dilemmas:

1. **Pricing of existing capacity:** You should use the magic of the market-price system to allocate your existing capacity. You should set the internal price of each parking spot so that those users who would value the garage the most will want to reserve exactly the 300 spots that are available. Do not set the parking spot price so that the garage generates maximum profits. (If you do, you may find yourself with parking rates that are too high, and cars that are parked on the street while the garage has some unfilled spots.) If there are more existing spots than cars that could benefit from a spot, then you should even set the parking spot price to zero. From an overall corporate perspective, it does not matter how or who you charge—just as long as you get the optimal capacity utilization. To the extent that cost allocation distorts optimal marginal decision making (i.e., that cars that should be in the garage end up not using the garage), it should be avoided.
2. **Building more capacity:** You should build more capacity when the marginal cost of adding the garage of \$1.5 million is less than the marginal benefit of parking cars indoors. In principle, this is easy. In practice, this is difficult, because you need to forecast future parking needs.

Note that neither of these two decision rules requires the garage to generate profits by itself. In fact, your goal is to maximize the overall profit of the firm, which is achieved through optimal capacity allocation. It is irrelevant whether this increase comes about through a profitable garage or through more profitable divisions.

MANAGERIAL GAMING

Unfortunately, real life is not always so simple. Return to the earlier example of an Internet connection that has a positive influence on all divisions. You know that divisional managers will not want to pay for it if they can enjoy it for free—you cannot rely on them telling you correctly how much they will benefit. Would it solve your problem to charge only divisions that are voluntarily signing up for the Internet connection, and to forcibly exclude those that do not? If you do this, then you could solve the problem of everyone claiming that they do not need the Internet connection. However, you are then stuck with the problem that you may have a lot of unused network capacity that sits around, has zero marginal cost, and could be handed to the nonrequesters at zero cost. This would create more profit for the firm. Of course, if you do this, or even if it is suspected that you will do this, then no division would claim that they need the Internet to begin with, so that they will ultimately get it for free. In sum, what makes these problems so difficult in the real world is that as the boss, you often do not know the true marginal benefits and marginal costs, and you end up having to "play games" with your divisional managers to try to make the right decision. Such is real life! And in real life, more often than not, headquarters just mandates Internet usage and charges divisions for it, whether they like it or not. Hopefully, this is also the correct choice from a firmwide value-maximization perspective.

It becomes much harder if you do not know the right outcome, so you have to "play games" with your subordinate managers.

➤ Internet connection example, Section 12.4B, p. 403

SOLVE NOW!

Q 12.14 A company rents 40,000 square feet of space and is using 30,000 square feet for its present operations. It wishes to add a new division that will use the remaining 10,000 square feet. If it adds the division, equipment will cost \$210,000 once, and the operations will generate \$50,000 in profits every year. Presently, the office staff costs \$160,000 per year. However, the expansion requires a larger staff, bringing costs up to \$180,000 per year. If the cost of capital $r = 10\%$, should the firm expand?

12.6 REAL OPTIONS

There is another valuation issue that you have to consider. It can be even more important than externalities—and more difficult to work out. It is the fact that your ability to change course in the future, depending on the prevailing economic environment in the future, can itself create value. Such flexibility is called a **real option** (or sometimes a **strategic option**). In principle, the valuation of a real option is just a complex variant of the NPV problem. You have to assess all expected cash flows and their costs of capital correctly. In practice, the resulting complications can be so difficult that entire books have been written on this subject. Let me give you a taste of what real options are and how to value them.

A real option is the value of the flexibility to change course in the future.

12.6A A SPECIFIC REAL OPTIONS EXAMPLE

An example of a factory.

A factory costs \$3 million to build. It can transform \$2 million worth of inputs into 1 million gadgets. If demand is strong, gadgets will sell for \$9 each. If demand is weak, gadgets will sell for \$1 each. The discount rate is 10%. The expected value of the factory is therefore (in millions)

$$\text{NPV} = -\$3 + \frac{50\% \cdot (\$1 - \$2) + 50\% \cdot (\$9 - \$2)}{1.1} \approx -\$0.273$$

$$\text{NPV} = \text{Factory Cost} + \text{Present Value of Net Sales}$$

You should not undertake this project. Or should you?

Without the real option, you could have calculated the NPV using just the most likely (expected) pricing path.

Take a look at Figure 12.1. Without considering real options, there are two possible outcomes:

1. **Weak demand:** The running factory will yield −\$1 million in net sales, which turns into −\$3.909 million in total net present value.
2. **Strong demand:** The running factory will yield \$7 million in net sales, which turns into +\$3.364 million in total net present value.

Because both outcomes are equally likely, your loss is the \$0.273 million already calculated.

With the real option, you can shut down the factory if there is no demand.

However, if you can shut down the factory when demand is weak, then your factory is worth more. You still get the upside (a full \$3.364 million in present value), but you no longer suffer the full −\$3.909 million downside. That is, you would still be out the upfront \$3 million cost of the factory, but you would at least not produce an extra future loss of \$1 million by running it. *With* the real option to shut down when demand is weak, your factory is worth about $50\% \cdot (-\$3) + 50\% \cdot (\$3.364) = +\$0.182$ million.

Uncertainty usually makes real options more valuable!

Remarkably, real options are an instance in finance where you actually like uncertainty in the underlying economic environment. For example, how would you value the project if you could change the sales from the +\$1 and +\$9 million to \$0 and +\$10 million? In the bad state, it would not make a difference to you. You would still just shut down the factory and lose \$3 million. However, in the good state, you would now earn \$8 million next year, not \$7 million. Your NPV would therefore go from \$0.182 million to $50\% \cdot (-\$3) + 50\% \cdot (\$4.273) \approx +\$0.637$ million.

Family resemblance: This particular real option is like limited liability.

➤ Limited liability, Section 6.4, p. 155

This firm with its real option is a little similar to a contingent equity claim: *As owner, you can still get the upside but you don't suffer the full downside.* However, it is not the limited liability that has created this payoff pattern. Instead, it is your managerial flexibility that increases the factory's expected cash flow. Your flexibility means that this factory is well worth building.

SOLVE NOW!

Q 12.15 Your factory can stamp 150,000 CDs at a cost of \$5 per CD, or 500,000 CDs at a cost of \$8 per CD. If your CD has a hit song, you can can sell it to retailers for \$10 per CD. Otherwise, you can only charge \$6 per CD. There is a 1-in-10 chance that your CD will be a hit. You will not find out whether you have a hit until next year, but fortunately this will be before you have to stamp CDs. Your cost of capital is 10% per year. You only have the lease of the factory for next year. There is no production this year.

(a) What is the expected selling price per CD?

(b) How many CDs should you produce at the expected selling price—that is, if you had to gear the factory for a particular production quantity today?

(c) What is the value of your factory if you can decide next year?

(d) What is the value of flexibility in this example?

Prob	Component	Ignore Real Option Always Run Factory (Dumb NPV)	Recognize Real Option Shut Down if Optimal (Smart NPV)
50% Demand is Weak	Factory, Time 0	−$3 million	−$3 million
	Inputs, Time 1	−$2 million	$0 million
	Sales, Time 1	+$1 million	$0 million
	Net, Time 1	= −$1 million	= $0 million
	⇒ NPV at 10%, Time 0	−$3.909 million	−$3 million
50% Demand is Strong	Factory, Time 0	−$3 million	−$3 million
	Inputs, Time 1	−$2 million	−$2 million
	Sales, Time 1	+$9 million	+$9 million
	Net, Time 1	= $7 million	= $7 million
	⇒ NPV at 10%, Time 0	+$3.364 million	+$3.364 million
	Total Net Present Value	−$0.273 million	+$0.182 million

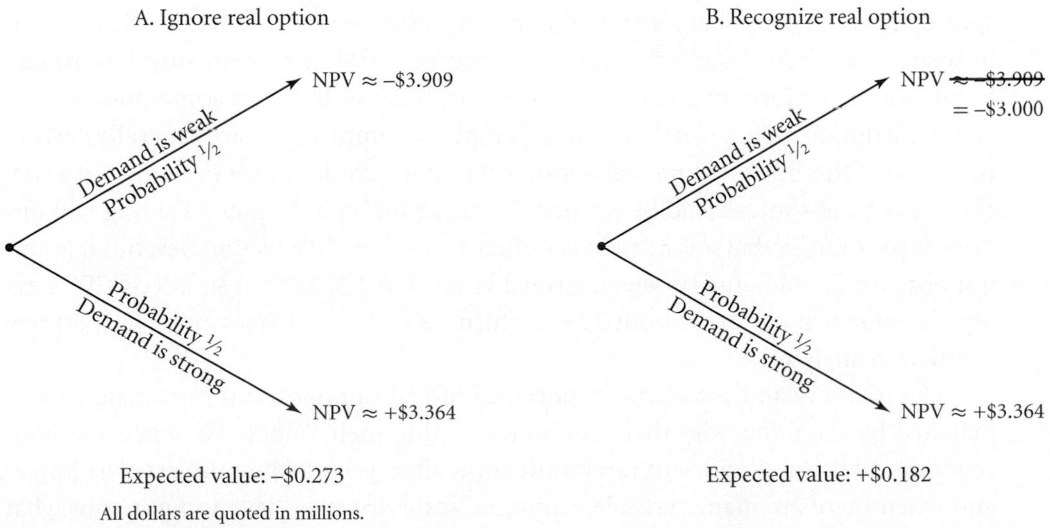

All dollars are quoted in millions.

FIGURE 12.1 A State-Contingent Payoff Table for the Factory

12.6B IMPORTANCE AND DIFFICULTY

You cannot work out the project value based on the expected input and output costs. You must work out a scenario analysis in a decision tree.

The reason why real options are so difficult to value is that you get the wrong answer if you are working out the value at the expected (or most likely) inputs. In our example, the expected gross sales were $(50\% \cdot \$9 + 50\% \cdot \$1) = \$5$ million. This was more than the \$2 million cost of inputs. Thus, you would operate, which would give you \$3 million in expected net sales *next year*. This is not enough to cover the \$3 million in upfront factory costs *today*. You would therefore conclude that you should not undertake the factory—a mistake. In effect, in our example, working with the expected inputs is the same as assuming that you would always act the same way in the future, regardless of demand. Instead, the correct way to value a real option is first to consider all possible future demand scenarios, then to determine your own optimal behavior and the resulting cash flows in each scenario, and only finally to compute expectations over all possible scenarios. This is almost always easiest to do in a decision tree, like the one at the bottom of Figure 12.1. In management-speak, it is called **scenario analysis**.

IMPORTANT:

- The expected value of a project is not the value of the project at its expected value or its expected inputs.
- This means that you cannot value a real option by computing project value in the expected (or most likely) scenario.
- Instead, you must first determine all possible scenarios, then figure out your own behavior and the cash flow this earns in each scenario, and only finally compute the expected net present values over all scenarios.

Here is what real-world managers tell us they do.

➤ Sensitivity analysis, Section 4.1A, p. 70

➤ CFO valuation method survey, Section 4.5, p. 83

Sensitivity analysis is a close relative of scenario analysis. It means trying out different assumptions to see how sensitive the NPV is, and is usually done in a valuation spreadsheet. If it considers different managerial responses, it becomes in effect a form of scenario analysis. **Simulation analysis** (also called **Monte Carlo simulation**) can be an automated form of sensitivity or scenario analysis. It, too, is sometimes used to value real options. These methods can be simple or complex, and are generally beyond the scope of this book. (More real option valuation techniques are explained in a web chapter, which—you should be warned—is also a difficult chapter.) Valuing real options is so complex that it is not used as often as simpler NPV techniques, but it is also not obscure. In the same survey described in Section 4.5, 27% of surveyed CFOs explicitly value real options. About 52% perform sensitivity analyses and 14% perform simulation analyses.

Real options are tough to value. If the optimal decision depends on the past history (and not just the current environment), then this problem becomes even harder.

The ubiquity and economic importance of real options are unfortunately often matched by the difficulties that arise in estimating their values. They become both economically more important (and more difficult to value) when projects last longer and when there are many possible economic scenarios. You have to figure out what you would do in every possible *future* scenario. Sometimes, this is feasible. If there is only one variable that determines your optimal action, such as one prevailing product price, then the problem can often be broken down in a way that simplifies it. Sometimes, this is infeasible. If your decisions cannot be made based on just one variable, but instead depend in turn on the future or the past, then the complexities become vexing. For example, if it costs money to close and reopen your plant, then your decision to close the plant must also depend on your assessment of how quickly the product price can recover. If there is a good chance of recovery soon and if closing/reopening a factory is expensive, you may take your chances and continue operating your factory even if you incur a small loss. In turn, this means that you may find yourself with an operating or nonoperating plant, depending on the history of past demand, and this can influence what you decide to do in this period, too. With history dependence, even your optimal decision rule itself can be very difficult to work out. In any case, the current product price is no longer the only decision variable that you have to take into consideration, and this makes it a complex problem.

A final complication that I have avoided here is that the presence of a real option can have an influence not only on the expected cash flows but also on the cost of capital. For example, if this real option helps you to avoid losses when the stock market goes down, then your market beta, and with it, your cost of capital are lower, too. You already know that the cost of capital can have a strong value influence, especially for long-lived projects.

There are also cost-of-capital implications, but we have mostly ignored them.

➤ Cost-of-capital errors, Section 4.1A, p. 70

12.6C EMBEDDED REAL OPTIONS

Most corporate projects teem with embedded real options. For example:

Here are some other examples of real options.

Expansion or contractions: If the future turns out better (or worse) than expected, firms can expand (or contract). In the extreme, firms may outright abandon a project.

Acceleration and delay: If the future turns out better (or worse) than expected, firms can speed up (or slow down) projects. This can often be done by hiring (or firing) additional consultants and contractors.

Switching: Different technologies may be best in different future scenarios—and some projects may be more amenable to multiple technology alternatives.

Spinoffs: If a technology makes a serendipitous discovery, firms can start entirely new businesses.

Section 12.10 values some examples of these options.

➤ Real options, Section 12.10, p. 433

In fact, many projects are nothing but real options: For example, the value of unused land around cities is essentially the option that the city might expand enough to make building on the land economically worthwhile. Research and development often have no immediate usefulness, or even usefulness in the most likely scenario—but there is a chance that it might yield a highly profitable discovery. You have to consider this real option value in your expected cash flow computation, or you will underestimate your project's value.

Many projects are nothing except real options.

Different projects contain different types of real options.

Real options become even more tantalizing when you consider not just the real options for one particular project but the fact that different projects come with different types of real options. For example, replacing workers with expensive, high-fixed-cost robots may be cheaper in the most likely scenario, but it effectively gives up on the real option to lay off workers if the future turns out worse than expected. Have you properly valued the project that has more real options?

It is most important to recognize the real options that you have.

Obviously, it would be best if you knew perfectly the types and exact values of all your real options. In practice, this is usually impossible. You should therefore focus on the most important real options. Strange as it may sound, the most common mistake that many managers commit when it comes to real options is that they just do not recognize that the real options are there. Once you recognize real options, even if you cannot fully value them, at least you can try to find an "intuitive" value adjustment. Fortunately, you have one further bit of knowledge that may help you here: The presence of a real option can only increase project value, because it is the value of *your* flexibility.

DIGGING DEEPER

This chapter's appendix escalates the depth of explanations for real options. The Real Options web chapter escalates it even further.

12.7 BEHAVIORAL BIASES

Model inputs are usually not what they should be.

One issue that we have ignored so far is that you need accurate inputs and that you need to use them rationally if you want to make good decisions. But most cash flow and cost-of-capital estimates rely on human judgment, which is prone to errors of all sorts. We know that our brains tend to commit systematic decision errors. Managers who do not recognize these biases will systematically make poor decisions.

Innate human decision biases cause predictable valuation mistakes.

There are literally dozens of well-known behavioral errors, but limited space allows us to highlight just three: **overconfidence**, **relativism**, and **compartmentalization.**

1. **Overconfidence** is the tendency of people to believe that their own assessments are more accurate than they really are. In lab experiments, ordinary people are found to be dramatically overconfident. When asked to provide a 90% confidence interval—which is just a range within which they are confident that their true value will lie in 9 out of 10 times—most people end up being correct only 5 out of 10 times.

   It is difficult to document overconfidence empirically—after all, if it were easy, managers would recognize it themselves and avoid it. However, there is empirical evidence that many managers who are already heavily invested in their own company tend to throw caution overboard and voluntarily invest much of their own money into the corporation—even in companies in rather shaky financial shape. There is also good empirical evidence that those of us who are most opti-

ANECDOTE Small Business Failures

In New York City, two out of every five new restaurants close within 1 year. Nationwide, the best estimates suggest that about 90% of all restaurants close within 2 years. If successful, the average restaurant earns a return of about 10% per year. Owners seem to lose money on average. So, why open yet another restaurant? I mentioned earlier that restaurateurs may just enjoy owning restaurants. But a more likely explanation is that restaurateurs are overly optimistic and just do not realize how tough it is to run a restaurant profitably.

More generally, a Small Business Administration study of small business failures from 1989 to 1992 found that 33% of businesses failed within 2 years, 50% within 4 years, and 66% within 6 years. Yet in a survey of about 3,000 entrepreneurs, 81% of entrepreneurs believed that their chances of success were at least 70%, and 33% believed that they had zero chance of failure!

mistic in overestimating our own life expectancy disproportionately will become entrepreneurs. Even if optimism is a disease, it seems to be a necessary one for entrepreneurs!

To understand overconfidence better, please fill out the self-testing questionnaire at the book website. Taking it will make you realize the issue better than reading long paragraphs of commentary in this book ever could. Incidentally, the only population segments who are known not to be systematically overconfident are weather forecasters and clinically depressed patients.

www.prenhall.com/welch

2. **Relativism** is the tendency of people to consider issues of relative scale when they should not. For example, most people are willing to drive 15 minutes to a store farther away to save \$40 on the purchase of \$80 worth of groceries, but they would not be willing to drive the 15 minutes to a car dealer farther away to save \$100 on the purchase of a new \$20,000 car. The savings appear to be less important in the context of the car purchase (0.5%) than in the context of a grocery purchase (50%). But this is flawed logic, similar to comparing IRRs while ignoring project scale. The marginal cost is driving 15 minutes extra, and the marginal benefit is a higher \$100 in the context of the car than the \$40 in the context of the groceries. Put differently, the problem is that humans tend to think in terms of percentages. The smaller the amount of money at stake, the more severe this problem often becomes. When a gas station advertises a price of \$2 per gallon rather than \$2.10, some customers drive for miles and wait in long lines—all to fill a 20-gallon gas tank at a total savings that amounts to a mere \$2.

3. **Compartmentalization** is the tendency of people to categorize decisions. Most people are more inclined to spend more when the same category has produced an unexpected windfall earlier. For example, winning a lottery prize while attending a baseball game often makes winners more likely to purchase more baseball tickets, even though the project "baseball game" has not changed in profitability. Similarly, an unexpected loss may stop people from an otherwise profitable investment that they should make. For example, say an individual likes to attend a particular baseball game. If she loses her baseball game ticket, she is less likely to purchase a replacement, even though the cost and benefit of purchasing the ticket

are the same as they were when the original ticket was purchased. Compartmentalization can sometimes be the opposite of the sunk cost mistake. For example, Federal Express went through three venture capital funding rounds in the 1970s, the first two leading to rather disappointing operating profits. The investors that then compartmentalized—refusing to throw "good money after bad money"—lost everything. Only investors in the final venture capital round got rich.

Know thyself to avoid these errors!

SOLVE NOW!

Q 12.16 Is relativism a bigger problem when evaluating small projects or large projects?

Q 12.17 Describe common mental decision biases, and how they are likely to bias NPV calculations.

Q 12.18 Take the overconfidence quiz at www.prenhall.com/welch.

12.8 INCENTIVE (AGENCY) BIASES

Incentive problems arise when the information provider has incentives that are different from those of the project owner.

Mental biases are not the only source of bad choices. Another kind of bias arises when one person is acting on behalf of another. This is called an **agency** problem—a situation in which the owner of a project has to rely on information from someone else, who has divergent interests. An example may be shareholders who rely on corporate management to undertake projects on their behalf, or a division manager who has to rely on department managers for information about how profitable their proposed projects really are. A cynical synopsis of agency biases would be that "all people act and lie in their own self-interests." Now, although everyone does have incentives to lie—or at least to color the truth—organizations are especially rife with such agency distortions. Of course, few people sit down and contemplate how to best and intentionally lie. Instead, they convince themselves that what is in their best interest is indeed the best route to take. Thus, mental biases often reinforce incentive problems: "Wishful thinking" is a disease from which we all suffer.

Conflict-of-interest dilemmas are pervasive and important in organizations.

You can take the fact that we have already had to mention agency issues repeatedly in this chapter as an indication of how important and pervasive they are. But, again, lack of space forces us to highlight just a few issues with some examples:

1. **Competition for capital:** Managers often compete for scarce resources. For example, division managers may want to obtain capital for their projects. A less optimistic but more accurate estimate of the project cash flows may induce headquarters to allocate capital to another division instead. Thus, division managers often end up in a race to make their potential projects appear in the most favorable and profitable lights.
2. **Employment concerns:** Managers and employees do not want to lose their jobs. For example, scientists may tend to highlight the potential and downplay the drawbacks of their areas of research. After all, not doing so may cut the project and thereby cost them their funding and then their jobs.

3. **Perks:** Managers do not like to give up perks. For example, division managers may like to have their own secretaries or even request private airplanes. Thus, they are likely to overstate the usefulness of the project "administrative assistance" or "private plane transportation."
4. **Power:** Managers typically love to build their own little "empires." For example, they may want to grow and control their departments because bigger departments convey more prestige and because they are a stepping stone to further promotion, either internally or externally. For the same reason, managers often prefer not to maximize profits, but instead focus on maximizing sales.
5. **Hidden slack:** Managers like the ability to be able to cover up problems that may arise in the future. For example, division managers may want to hide the profitability of their divisions, fearing that headquarters may siphon off "their" profits into other divisions. They may prefer to hide the generated value (through legal accounting maneuvers discussed in the next chapter) in the belief that the cash they produced in good times "belongs" to them and that they are entitled to use it in bad times.
6. **Reluctance to take risk:** Managers may hesitate to take on risk. For example, they may not want to take a positive-NPV project because they may get fired if it fails—and may not be rewarded enough if it succeeds. A popular saying once was that "no one was ever fired for buying IBM," although these days Microsoft has taken over IBM's role.
7. **Direct theft:** Managers and employees have even been known to steal outright from the company. For example, a night club manager may not ring sales into the cash register. Or a sales agent may "forget" to charge her cousins. In some cases, this can be a fine line. Is taking a pad of paper from your company or answering a personal email on company computers really theft? In other cases, the theft is blatant. In September 2002, Dennis Kozlowski, former CEO of Tyco, was charged with looting $600 million. His primary defense was that he did so in broad daylight—with approval from the corporate board that he had helped put in place. (Dennis is now indisposed for the next 25 years.)

We do know where agency problems play bigger roles and where they play lesser roles:

Agency problems are worse in certain (known) situations.

1. **Scale and owner engagement:** In a small company with one owner and one employee, agency conflicts are less important than they are in big corporations with their many layers of management and disengaged owners.

   Do you believe that professionally run companies really make the best decisions on behalf of their public shareholders? Remember that agency issues do not just arise between shareholders and management—they start with the lowest-level employee and bubble all the way up to the top-level CEO. Decision making is often based on a chain of miscommunications or even deceptions. It is a testament to the importance of sharing risks among many investors that large, publicly traded companies still manage to net-in-net create shareholder value!
2. **Project duration:** If the project is short term and/or comes with good interim progress points, it is easier to reward managers appropriately for success and

punish them for failure than it is for longer-term projects. For example, think how you would judge and reward a manager who is (supposedly) working on an R&D project that is not likely to have visible results for decades. This is a difficult task. Agency problems for large and very-long-term projects may be so intrinsically high that they cannot be undertaken.

3. **External noise:** If good luck is an integral and important part of the project, it becomes more difficult to judge managerial performance, which in turn aggravates agency issues. For example, it is relatively easy to measure the productivity of a line worker in a factory; you know whether he works or slacks off. Therefore, agency problems matter less. In contrast, it is more difficult to determine if your sales agent worked hard but the customer just did not bite, or if your sales agent was to blame. Similarly, your nightwatch security guard may or may not be working hard, and it could take years before you could learn (probably the hard way) whether she regularly stayed awake or just dozed off.
4. **Opaqueness:** If information is very difficult for outsiders to come by, agency problems will be worse. For example, if only your manager sees what projects are available, he can present only those that he would like to undertake. He can also not mention those that have higher NPVs but require skills he may not have or that require work he finds unpleasant.

There are mechanisms that can help control agency problems.

We also know that there are a number of mechanisms that can help alleviate agency problems.

1. **Audits:** If the company runs independent assessments or audits, managers can make decisions based on better information, even if their employees are unwilling to provide it. However, many consultants suffer from the same disease as employees: They know that they are most likely to be rehired if they tell the manager what she wants to hear.
2. **Truth-telling incentives:** If managers can be rewarded for telling the truth, agency conflicts will become less important. For example, if your company has a research scientist who has expertise in alpha-proteins and works on an alpha-protein project, your goal as manager should be to allow this scientist to say, without suffering any negative consequences, "Do not waste your money putting any more research dollars into alpha-proteins." This means that the scientist's salary and promotion chances must remain the same regardless of the research outcome—even if this means that she no longer has a good alternative use for her time and effort. You might even offer a reward for any scientists who voluntarily cancel their projects due to unviability.

   Would you really be willing to carry through on such a promise? Would your research scientists believe you?

   Some companies also undertake **postaudits**, which are designed to evaluate not only the quality of the financial numbers (like a usual audit) but also the quality of managers' upfront forecasts. Knowing that such postaudits will be held will strengthen the incentives of managers to give accurate forecasts to begin with.
3. **Contingent compensation:** If managers are rewarded more if a project succeeds and punished if a project fails, agency conflicts will become less important. This

is the carrot-and-stick approach. For example, if you pay your managers bonuses only when their projects succeed (or fire them when their projects fail), then your managers will work harder and choose projects that they believe are more likely to succeed.

Of course, like any other mechanism to control agency problems, this control strategy has its costs, too. Managers have to feed their families, and you may not be able to attract the best managers if you force them to take on so much risk. (The capital markets are probably better at taking risk than individual families!) And such managers may also be more reluctant to take good risks on behalf of the company—risks that they *should* take in the interest of shareholders—if they are themselves risk averse and compensated by outcome.

4. **Reputation:** If managers can build a reputation for truth-telling and capable management, they are less likely to undertake bad projects. For example, agency concerns are likely to be a worse problem when it comes to secret one-shot projects, where your managers cannot build a track record that will help them with future projects. On the other hand, sometimes reputational considerations can themselves become the problem. Witness the many dysfunctional but beautifully artistic office buildings that are primarily monuments to some famous architectural firms.
5. **Capital rationing:** If nothing helps to restrain your managers from wasting money when they get it, just don't give it to them. Or give them only enough money to satisfy their most urgent needs, hoping that these needs will then more likely be positive-NPV projects.
6. **Selecting managers:** There are people out there who are more inclined to be honest and others who are not. If you can hire managers of high integrity, they may not abuse the firm, even when it is in their own self-interest.

Some losses due to conflict of interest are unavoidable. The best "solution" is ample skepticism and common sense.

There are no obvious solutions to these decision-bias problems. You would not want to spend a million dollars in audit fees and complex control mechanisms to save a hundred dollars in theft. You would not want to hire a manager of the highest integrity who is utterly incompetent over another manager who may steal a small amount but will otherwise generate enormous value for shareholders. In the real world, you have to realize that all firms suffer from the fact that their employees act in their own—but not necessarily in the firm's—best interest. All you can do is to try to limit this intelligently. As a manager or principal, remain skeptical of your employees' estimates and judgments and take the biases and incentives of each information provider into account. My last word: Again, do not believe that just because you have spent only a few pages on agency issues that they are not important—they are everywhere. (Later in this book, in Chapter 24, you will learn more about "corporate governance," which is all about agency conflicts.)

SOLVE NOW!

Q 12.19 Describe common agency problems and explain how they are likely to bias corporate NPV calculations.

ANECDOTE Fiduciary Responsibility, or the Fox Guarding the Henhouse

On Wednesday, December 29, 2004, the *Wall Street Journal* reported on page 1:

> In the biggest U.S. merger this year, JP Morgan Chase & Co. announced last January it would acquire Bank One Corp. To assure investors it was paying fair price, JP Morgan told them in a proxy filing it had obtained an opinion from one of "the top five financial advisors in the world."
>
> Itself.
>
> The in-house bankers at JP Morgan endorsed the $56.9 billion price—negotiated by their boss—as "fair."

Next to it was a sidebar called "Passing Muster," which explained:

> A 'fairness' opinion tells a company's board that a deal's terms are fair to shareholders.
>
> **Purpose:** Legal protection from an investor claim that a deal was done without due care.
>
> **Cost:** A few hundred thousand dollars to a few million.
>
> **Potential Conflicts**
>
> - Bankers may have incentives to call a deal fair because most of their advisory fee is paid only if the deal closes.
> - Bankers' fee is tied to the deal price.
> - Bankers may support a deal where executives will personally profit, in hopes of securing future work.
> - Bankers use financial data supplied by a client that wants the deal to go through.
> - When the deal maker is a bank, its own bankers often write the fairness opinion.

Remember that everyone—in-house bankers, management, and corporate boards—are employed by the shareholders, to whom they owe fiduciary responsibility and whose interests they are supposed to represent. It is a clear agency conflict for an employee to provide a fairness opinion. But it would also be difficult for management to have these in-house bankers fired for doing them a personal favor—another agency conflict.

And there is also the original agency conflict: the incentive of acquiring managers to pay too high a price or of target managers to accept too low a price. Here is how the WSJ story continues:

> But during the negotiations, Bank One Chief Jamie Dimon had suggested selling his bank for billions of dollars less if, among other conditions, he immediately became chief of the merged firm, according to a person familiar with the talks. That suggestion wasn't accepted by JP Morgan.

Obviously, Jamie Dimon did not offer to pay his own personal billions for the privilege of becoming CEO, but Bank One's shareholders' billions. Obviously, the JP Morgan management did not decline the billions on behalf of their own pockets, but on behalf of JP Morgan shareholders' pockets.

Still, there are of course the corporate boards that could have fired either the in-house bankers or their management teams. Neither happened. Instead, Jamie Dimon took over as head of JP Morgan, as scheduled, on December 31, 2005.

12.9 AN NPV CHECKLIST

If you think academics like to make easy things difficult, you have it totally wrong. It is academics who try to avoid the difficult problems.

After reading this chapter, you probably understand now why professors think "theory is easy." The complications of real life make theory look like a child's game. Yes, the principles of capital budgeting theory are easy—only their application is hard. It is usually very difficult to estimate future cash flows (and even their appropriate interest rates), especially for far-in-the-future returns. It is usually more important and more difficult to avoid errors for the expected cash flow (the NPV numerator) than it is for the cost of capital (the NPV denominator). The NPV formula is less robust to cash flow errors than it is to cost-of-capital errors, and it is "easier" to commit dramatic errors in the cash flow estimation than in the cost-of-capital estimation.

Here is an abbreviated list of issues to worry about when using NPV.

Here is an abbreviated checklist of items to consider when working out NPV estimates.

- ✓ **Appropriate (after-tax) dollars** (pages 97, 101):
  - ✓ Have you quoted all relevant inputs and outputs in relevant-to-you after-tax dollars? This applies to both expected cash flows and to appropriate discount rates. (Corporate income taxes will be covered in more detail in Chapter 17.)
  - ✓ Have you properly included inflation? Preferably, have you performed all computations using nominal expected future cash flows and nominal costs of capital, with inflation used only to gross up nominal cash flows appropriately?

- ✓ **Interactions** (pages 396, 401):
  - ✓ Have you credited all projects with their contributions, positive or negative, to the values of other projects (externalities)?
  - ✓ Have you judged all projects "on the margin," that is, without charging them for unalterable or previously made choices, such as sunk costs, overhead, and so on?
  - ✓ Have you used the cost of capital applicable to each project component, respectively, and not the (incorrect) overall average cost of capital? (Note: Some errors and simplifications here are unavoidable in the real world, because it is impossible to put different costs of capital on each paper clip.)

- ✓ **Real options and flexibility** (page 413, Section 12.10, Chapter 26, Real Options web chapter):
  - ✓ Have you considered all possible future options (using scenario analyses) in order to find the correct *expected* cash flows, such as,
    - ✓ your ability to extend a product into different markets,
    - ✓ your ability to find product spinoffs,
    - ✓ your ability to learn about future products,
    - ✓ your ability to stop the project if conditions are bad,
    - ✓ your ability to delay the project if conditions are bad,
    - ✓ your ability to mothball the project if conditions are bad and to restart the project if conditions improve,
    - ✓ your ability to accelerate the project if conditions are good,
    - ✓ your ability to expand the project if conditions are good,

    and so on?

- ✓ **Accuracy** (pages 70, 274, 418, 420):
  - ✓ How accurate are your estimated project cash flows?
  - ✓ If project success and project cash flows were estimated by someone else, what are the motives of the estimator? How tainted can these estimates be? Does the estimator want the project accepted or rejected?
  - ✓ Is it possible to get another independent evaluation/audit of the project estimates?
  - ✓ Can your cash flow estimates be improved by doing more research?
  - ✓ Given unavoidable simplifications, assumptions, and errors, how sensitive/robust are your NPV calculations to changes therein?

- ✓ **Correct inputs** (page 391):
  - ✓ Are your cash flows *expected* rather than *promised*? Are your interest rates *expected* rather than *promised*? (Recall: Expected interest rates are below promised interest rates due to default premiums, not just due to risk premiums.)
  - ✓ Are your expected cash flows the "average outcome" (correct), and not the "most likely outcome" (incorrect)?
  - ✓ Do your expected cash flow estimates include the correct weighted probabilities of low-probability events, especially for negative outcomes?
  - ✓ If you need to borrow money to execute the project, have you used the expected (not the promised) borrowing rate as your cost of capital? If capital is already available, are you using your expected lending (investments) rate as the appropriate cost of capital?
- ✓ **Corporate income taxes** (page 612):

➤ WACC and APV, Section 17.2, p. 612

  - ✓ For use of WACC and APV, is the numerator in your NPV calculation the expected cash flow "as if all equity financed"? (This means that the company bears the full brunt of its corporate income tax load.)
  - ✓ In the weighted cost of capital, is your debt cost of capital the *expected* (not the promised) interest rate on debt? Is your numerator the *expected* cash flow, not the *promised* cash flow?

A final warning: Although many of these issues seem obvious in isolation, they are much harder to spot and take care of in complex real-world situations than in our highlighted expositions. Watch out! Another warning against the most common error is worth its own box:

IMPORTANT: The most common NPV method is to estimate cash flows for the numerator, and to use an expected rate of return (cost of capital) from the CAPM formula (see Chapter 9).

- ✓ The default risk is handled only in the numerator, that is, in the computation of expected cash flows.
- ✓ The time premium and risk premium are handled only in the denominator. The CAPM formula provides an expected rate of return, which contains only these two components.
- ✓ Do not try to adjust the numerator for the time premium or the risk premium. Do not try to add a default premium to the rate of return in the denominator. (This would yield a promised, not an expected, rate of return on capital.) Do not believe that by using the CAPM expected rate of return you have taken default risk into consideration.

SOLVE NOW!

Q 12.20 The CEO projects earnings of $100 million next year. List three reasons why this might not be a good input into an NPV valuation.

SUMMARY

This chapter covered the following major points:

- You should never confuse promised and expected cash flows in the numerator, or promised and expected rates of return in the denominator. The *expected* cash flows are often not the *most likely* cash flows, either.
- Corporations can reduce their risk by diversification—but if investors can do so themselves as easily, diversification per se does not create value. As a manager, you can create value only by increasing cash flows or decreasing market beta (the cost of capital). Diversification for the sake of diversification does not add value.
- You should not use the cost of capital (and the market beta) applicable to the entire firm, but rather the cost of capital (and the market beta) applicable to this new project. However, because the effort involved can be enormous, it is reasonable to use individual, project-specific costs of capital only when it really makes a difference.
- When selecting projects, consider all possible project combinations and choose the combination that gives you the highest overall NPV.
- You should attribute to each project's NPV its influence on other projects, either positive or negative. If a project is independent from other projects, you can consider its NPV in isolation, and add it to the total.
- You should think about how you can take advantage of, or create, positive externalities among projects. If you cannot, there is no reason for the firm to exist in the first place.
- You should think "on the margin"—take all projects that contribute more marginal benefits than they create marginal costs.
- You should consider economies of scale, which can reduce average production costs and thus add to project value.
- You should ignore sunk costs.
- You should take real options into account. These are the value of your ability to change course depending on future conditions. They include your flexibility to delay or accelerate projects, and to expand or shut down projects.
- You should be aware of your own biases, such as overconfidence, relativism, compartmentalization, and others.
- You should realize that real-world implementation problems—which range from differences in short-term marginal costs and long-term marginal costs to political reasons and agency considerations inside corporations—often make taking the best set of projects difficult.
- You should design your operations so as to reduce agency conflicts when it is marginally profitable to do so.
- To make your task a little easier, refer to the NPV checklist in Section 12.9.

No doubt about it: Good capital budgeting is a difficult problem. Each subsection covered in this chapter can easily be expanded into a full chapter, or even a full book. There are pitfalls everywhere. In the end, capital budgeting is as much an art as it is a science. You have to rely as much on common sense and intuition as on the mechanics of valuation. The best analysis combines both.

KEY TERMS

agency, 420
audits, 422
compartmentalization, 418
conglomerates, 393
diseconomies of scale, 404
economies of scale, 407
externalities, 402
hedging, 395
heuristic, 401
incremental, 406
independent, 402
interaction, 402
limited attention span, 404
limited capacity, 411
on the margin, 406
marginal, 406
Monte Carlo simulation, 416
natural monopoly, 409
negative interaction, 404
overconfidence, 418
positive interaction, 403
postaudit, 422
real option, 413
relativism, 418
scenario analysis, 416
simulation analysis, 416
strategic option, 413
sunk cost, 410
synergy, 404

SOLVE NOW! SOLUTIONS

Q 12.1 Yes, it makes sense to compare the project's IRR to a hurdle rate. Indeed, if the hurdle rate is the cost of capital, the IRR rule tells you what you should do.

Q 12.2 Comparing a project's cost of capital to its hurdle rate would be silly, because your hurdle rate is just another name for your cost of capital in a perfect market.

Q 12.3 The Amazon.com bond's stated 8% is a promised rate of return. It is not the expected rate of return. Therefore, it is not the cost of capital.

Q 12.4 You cannot determine this, because you do not know the expected bond payoff.

Q 12.5 For the $900,000 machine, the probabilities of different outcomes are as follows:

Scenario	D	WD	WWD	WWWD	WWWWD	Exp Val
Probability	10%	$90\% \cdot 10\%$	$90\%^2 \cdot 10\%$	$90\%^3 \cdot 10\%$	$1 -$ rest	
	$= 0.10$	$= 0.09$	$= 0.081$	$= 0.0729$	$= 0.6561$	
Lifetime (years)	1	2	3	4	5	4.095
PV	$267,857	$507,015	$720,549	$911,205	$1,081,433	$906,737

(a) The single most likely outcome (with 65.6% probability) is that the machine will operate for all 5 years (because there is only a 10% breakage probability each year). At this most likely outcome, the present value would be $\text{PV} = (\$300{,}000/0.12) \cdot (1 - 1/1.12^5) \approx \$1{,}081{,}433$. The NPV would be $181,433.
(b) The expected lifetime of the machine is about 4.1 years. If the machine lasted for 4 years, the present value would be $911,205.
(c) The true expected value is $906,737.

Q 12.6 The merged firm has a lower standard deviation (it is safer), but this adds no value.

Q 12.7 (a) The new project's value is $11/1.15 ≈ $9.57. At a cost of $10, the net present value is −$0.43.
(b) The value today of the new project is $11/1.15 ≈ $9.57. Therefore, the weight of the new project is $w_{new} = \text{PV}_{new}/\text{PV}_{\text{combined}} \approx \$9.57/\$109.48 \approx 8.74\%$.
(c) The beta of the combined firm is $\beta_{\text{combined}} = w_{old} \cdot \beta_{old} + w_{new} \cdot \beta_{\text{new}} \approx 91.26\% \cdot 0.5 + 8.74\% \cdot 3 \approx 0.719$.
(d) The combined cost of capital according to the CAPM is $\mathcal{E}(\tilde{r}_{\text{combined}}) \approx 3\% + 4\% \cdot 0.719 = 5.876\%$.
(e) Yes! The IRR of *new* is 10%. (For IRR, see Chapter 5, page 90.) 10% is above the blended cost of capital of 5.876%.
(f) The firm value would be

$$\text{PV} = \frac{\mathcal{E}(C_{new}) + \mathcal{E}(C_{old})}{1 + \mathcal{E}(\tilde{r}_{\text{combined}})} \approx \frac{\$105 + \$11}{1 + 5.876\%} \approx \$109.57$$

Again, you conclude that the firm has destroyed $0.43.

Q 12.8 Zero externalities are convenient for valuation, because they allow you to add up NPVs. If there are nonzero externalities, the total NPV is larger or smaller than the sum of its part.

Q 12.9 Without taking the externality into account, the NPV of division A's move would be negative. The $120,000 of costs would be higher than the benefit of $10,000/10% = $100,000. However, the correct answer is "Yes, division A should move." Moving saves $10,000/10% = $100,000 in division A costs and $3,000/10%=$30,000 in division B costs. The total savings is therefore $130,000, which is $10,000 greater than the cost of the building.

Q 12.10 The firm should not purchase the press, because it earns $2,000/10% = $20,000. But the press costs $10,000 to purchase and eliminates $1,500/10% = $15,000 of profits from the screw machines. The total cost of the press, including the $15,000 in opportunity costs, is $25,000. The project's net present value is $20,000 − $25,000 = −$5,000.

Q 12.11 (a) Either purchasing the desktop or the notebook would be a positive-NPV project. However, you should purchase the desktop, because it is cheaper (more bang for the buck).
(b) You should still purchase the desktop. The marginal cost is $1,500. The marginal benefit is $11,000 − $9,000 = $2,000.
(c) You should not purchase the notebook. The marginal cost is $2,500. The marginal benefit is $2,000.

Q 12.12 (a) The profit of the firm is $\text{Profit}(x = 10) = 10 \cdot [\$20 - \$5 - \$15/(10 + 1)] \approx \$136.36$.
(b) With 11 goods, the cost to produce is $5 + $15/(11 + 1) = $6.25. With 10 goods, it was $5 + $15/(10 + 1) ≈ $6.36. The marginal production cost is $6.25 · 11 − $6.36 · 10 = $5.15.
(c) The marginal cost would now be an additional $1 times 10 in rebates. It would therefore cost the firm $5.15 plus $10, or $15.15. Thus, because the marginal revenue of $19 exceeds the marginal cost of $15.15, the firm should still sign everyone up.

Q 12.13

Units	Sales Price $7 - Q/100$	Total Production Cost $5 + (Q + 20)/100$	Net Sales
1	$6.99	$5.21	$1.78
2	$13.96	$10.44	$3.52
⋮			
43	$282.51	$242.09	$40.42
44	$288.64	$248.16	$40.48
45	$294.75	$254.25	$40.50
46	$300.84	$260.36	$40.48
47	$306.91	$266.49	$40.42
⋮			

(a) The table shows that the optimal production is 45 units.
(b) The average per-unit gross sales at $Q = 45$ is \$294.75/45 = \$6.55.
(c) The average per-unit production cost at $Q = 45$ is \$254.25/45 = \$5.65.
(d) The net sales at $Q = 45$ are \$40.50/45 = \$0.90.
(e) From 44 to 45, the marginal per-unit sales is \$294.75 − \$288.64 = \$6.11. From 45 to 46, it is \$6.09.
(f) From 44 to 45, the marginal per-unit cost is \$254.25 − \$248.16 = \$6.09. From 45 to 46, it is \$6.11.
(g) It is just about \$0. (If you move from 44 to 45 units, or from 46 to 45 units, you gain 2 cents.) This is what it means to be at the optimal production level.
(h) Your average per-unit net change at $Q = 45$ is still positive, but you should *not* expand production. If you do, you are ignoring the negative effects that unit number 46 would have on all your earlier units. This means that you would earn less money in total, not more.

Q 12.14 Yes, the firm should expand. The PV of the division's profits will be \$50,000/10% = \$500,000. The division costs are \$210,000 for new equipment and \$20,000 per year in increased overhead. The PV of the increased overhead is \$20,000/10% = \$200,000. The total PV cost of the new division is \$210,000 + \$200,000 = \$410,000, and the PV of the benefits is \$500,000. Thus, bringing in the new division represents a project with an NPV of +\$90,000.

Q 12.15 (a) The expected per-CD selling price is \$6 · 90% + \$10 · 10% = \$6.40.
(b) If \$6.40 was the price, you would gear your factory to produce 150,000 CDs. Without flexibility, your factory would be worth 150,000 · (\$6.40 − \$5) = \$210,000.
(c) You would expect to earn 0.9 · (150,000 · [\$6 − \$5]) + 0.1 · (500,000 · [\$12 − \$8]) = \$135,000 + \$200,000 = \$235,000.
(d) The value of flexibility is \$235,000 − \$210,000 = \$25,000.

Q 12.16 Relativism may induce you to make mistakes on both types of projects (and it is not clear which one is worse): For small projects, you may chase a large percentage increase too vigorously. For large projects, you may not realize that even a small rate of return can be a lot of money.

Q 12.17 Mental decision biases are the subject of Section 12.7. The text discussed overconfidence, relativism, and compartmentalization.

Q 12.18 The average student does not get one question wrong, but five questions wrong.

Q 12.19 Agency problems are the subject of Section 12.8. The text discussed eagerness for capital, employment concerns, desire for perks, desire for power, desire to work less, desire not to take risks, and direct theft. The effects can be manifold, often resulting is misvaluation of projects.

Q 12.20 First, the CEO's projected figures probably represent the most likely outcome, not the expected outcome. It is probably more likely that the firm will go bankrupt due to totally unforeseen circumstances than it is likely that the firm will have a windfall. Second, the CEO has an incentive to distort the truth and to report better projections than are most likely. This is an agency problem. Third, the CEO is probably subject to mental biases, too.

PROBLEMS

The ▬ *indicates problems available in* myfinancelab

Q 12.21 Can you compare a project's internal rate of return to its expected rate of return?

Q 12.22 Does it make sense to distinguish between a promised and an expected internal rate of return? What do issuers provide? What do you usually need?

Q 12.23 A zero-bond has a stated rate of return of 8%. Its price today is \$92,593. What is its expected payoff?

Q 12.24 A machine that costs \$2,000 is likely to break irreparably with 20% probability at the end of each year (assuming it worked the previous year). You can neither replace it nor use it for more than 5 years. (Many electric devices without moving parts have such breakdown characteristics.) The machine can produce $1,000 in profit every year. The discount rate is 12% per annum.

(a) What is the most likely operating time? If this comes true, what is the value?
(b) What is the expected operating time? If this comes true, what is the value?
(c) What is the true net present value of this machine? (Hint: First work this out case by case for a 2-year machine, then for a 3-year machine. Think "D," "WD," "WWD," "WWWD," and "WWWWD," where W means working and D means dead.)

Q 12.25 A $300 million firm has a beta of 2. The risk-free rate is 4%; the equity premium is 3%. Assume that the firm can easily tap a perfect capital market to obtain another $95 million. The firm can also easily tap the financial markets. So far, it has had a policy of only accepting projects with an IRR above the hurdle rate of 10%. Suddenly, one of its main suppliers (perhaps one facing credit constraints) has approached the firm for a 1-year loan. It is for sure that the loan is risk free for you—you hold more than enough sway over your supplier to ensure repayment. The supplier wants to borrow $100 million and pay back $106 million next year.

(a) Without the new loan, what is the firm expected to earn?
(b) What is the NPV of the loan?
(c) If the firm changes its policy and extends the loan, how would its value change?
(d) If the firm changes its policy and extends the loan, approximately how would its beta change?
(e) If the firm changes its policy and extends the loan, approximately how would its cost of capital change?
(f) If the firm changes its policy and extends the loan, can you compute the combined firm's NPV by dividing its expected cash flows (assets) by its combined cost of capital?
(g) Should the firm change its policy?

Q 12.26 Assume that the risk-free rate is 5% and the equity premium is 2%. A $1 billion firm with a beta of 2 has just sold one of its divisions for a fair price of $200 million. The CEO is concerned that investors expect the firm to earn 9%, and so believes keeping the money in short-term Treasuries that only pay 5% would be a bad idea. Is it really a bad idea?

Q 12.27 What are the arguments for and the arguments against discounting every project by its own cost of capital?

Q 12.28 As the CEO of an expanding airlines cargo division, would you acknowledge that an increase in your operations would be harmful to the passenger division? Should you be charged for the increased use of shared maintenance facilities?

Q 12.29 What are the main sources of positive externalities? What are the main sources of negative externalities?

Q 12.30 As a manufacturer, you have to decide how many regional distributors to sign up. Serving a distributor costs more the farther away it is from the factory, and different distributors have different demand. By region, gross revenues and costs are (in millions of dollars) as follows:

Distributor	A	B	C	D	E	F	G
Gross Revenue	$5	$4	$4	$3	$2	$7	$1
Cost	$2	$2	$3	$4	$4	$5	$6

There is no "time value of money" dimension in this problem.

(a) Is it feasible to work out all possible combinations of distributors you can service? Is it sensible?
(b) Which regions should you deliver to?
(c) What is the total profit for serving them?
(d) What is the marginal benefit and cost of serving the least profitable of your serviced distributors?
(e) What would be the marginal benefit and cost of serving one more distributor?
(f) Now assume that to get into this business, you would also have to set up the factory. This would cost you a one-time upfront expense of $5 million. You can think of this as spreading the cost across distributors. How would this change your decision?

Q 12.31 A firm can produce goods for an average per-unit cost of $\$5 + \$10/(Q \cdot \$1 + 2)$. For example, to produce 10 goods would cost

$10 \cdot (\$5 + \$10/12) \approx \$58.33$. The market price per good is $\$7 - Q \cdot \$1/10$. So, you can fetch $10 \cdot (\$7 - \$10/10) = \$60$ for selling 10 goods. Use a spreadsheet to answer the following questions.
(a) What is the break-even point where total gross revenues are equal to total cost?
(b) What is the gross profit (revenues minus costs) at the break-even point?
(c) What is the marginal gross profit at the break-even point?
(d) How many items should the firm produce?
(e) What is the average per-unit gross profit at this point?
(f) What is the marginal gross profit at this point?

Q 12.32 A perpetual firm's headquarters consumes \$1 million per year. It has six divisions of equal size, but not equal profitability. The annual profitabilities (in thousands of dollars) are as follows:

Project	A	B	C	D	E	F
Profitability	\$180	\$450	\$900	\$80	\$130	\$300

The cost of capital is $r = 10\%$.
(a) What is the firm's NPV?
(b) If the firm adopts a rule whereby each division has to carry its fair (size-based) share of the headquarter overhead, what is the firm's NPV?

Q 12.33 Comment on, "It is best to allocate costs only to divisions that request a resource."

Q 12.34 Comment on, "It is best to allocate costs to divisions that benefit from a resource."

Q 12.35 Your factory can stamp 150,000 CDs at a cost of \$5 per CD, or 500,000 CDs at a cost of \$8 per CD. If your CD has a hit song, you can sell it to retailers for \$10 per CD. If it is a moderate success, you can only charge \$6 per CD. If it is a complete bomb, you cannot sell it at all. There is a 1-in-10 chance that your CD will be a hit, and a 3-in-10 chance that it will be a bomb. You will not find out whether you have a hit until next year, but fortunately this will be before you have to stamp CDs. Your cost of capital is 10% per year. You only have the lease of the factory for next year. There is no production this year.
(a) What is the expected selling price per CD?
(b) How many CDs should you produce at the expected selling price—that is, if you had to gear the factory for a particular production quantity today?
(c) What is the value of your factory if you can decide next year?
(d) What is the value of flexibility in this example?

Q 12.36 What are the types of real options that firms need to take into account in their project valuations?

Q 12.37 You have to purchase \$600 worth of staples. You have just found out that the stationery store across from you charges \$300 more than the warehouse outlet 20 miles away. Would you spend the 40 minutes to drive to the warehouse? Now, assume you are buying a Porsche that costs \$100,000. You have just found out that the Porsche dealer 40 minutes away offers the Porsche for \$300 less. Assuming you can receive after-market service in both locations, would you drive 40 minutes to pay \$99,700? What should you do from an economic perspective? Is this what you would be tempted to do?

Q 12.38 Explain how you can exploit human biases in attracting signups for your new health club.

Q 12.39 Describe a manifestation of an agency problem, where it is worse, and what can be done to remedy it.

Q 12.40 Are agency problems worse in upstart firms? Discuss.

Q 12.41 Should you suppress all agency conflicts? Discuss.

Q 12.42 Contrast Google and Wal-Mart. Which agency conflicts are likely to inflict Google worse than Wal-Mart, and vice versa? Discuss.

Q 12.43 Recall as many items from the NPV checklist as you can remember. Which are you most likely to forget?

CHAPTER 12 APPENDIX

Valuing Some More Real Options

We ignore the problem of assigning different costs of capital to real options.

This appendix demonstrates how to work out the value of different types of real options. By assuming the world is risk neutral, it is ignoring the fact that discount rates can be higher when there are more real options. (Depending on the context, not fretting too much about the correct discount rate can be forgivable or deadly.) Real options are tough enough to value even without this added complication. This is not an easy appendix!

12.10 DECISION TREES: ONE SET OF PARAMETERS

A more involved two-level tree example.

Assume that you own a firm that can produce 150,000 units of a good at a cost of \$100/unit. The retail price of your good was \$500/unit recently, but you now expect it to go up or down by \$100/unit this year, that is, either to \$400/unit or \$600/unit. The year thereafter, you expect it to go up or down by \$200/unit. These price scenarios can be shown in a simple tree:

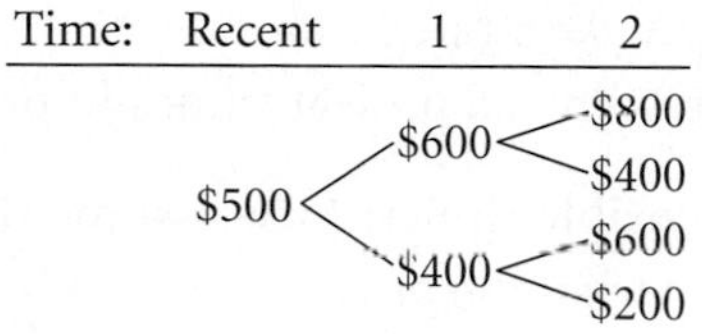

All price changes are equally likely. The fixed costs of running the plant are \$50 million, and rent (regardless of whether you run the plant or not) is \$10 million.

The cost of capital and timing assumptions.

The world is risk neutral and the prevailing interest rate is 10% per year, which applies to this coming year's cash flows and which will be twice compounded when applied to the following year's cash flows. Moreover, assume that you know at the beginning of each year what the price over the whole year will be, because you receive customer orders at this point. (To model intrayear uncertainty more realistically, you would have to deal with more periods—not any more difficult in concept but much more tedious.)

Here is an illustration of how the model works.

As an example, compute the firm value if you know that the price will go to \$600/unit and then to \$400/unit, and if you know that you will operate the plant this year but not the following year. The first year, you would earn revenues of 150,000 units $\cdot$ (\$600/unit $-$ \$100/unit) $=$ \$75 million, pay fixed costs of \$50 million, and rent of \$10 million. Your net profits would be \$15 million, which discounts to \$13.64 million at 10% if you use the present value formula. The second year, you would earn no revenues and pay no fixed costs, but you would still pay rent of \$10 million. This discounts to $\$10/1.1^2 \approx \$8.26$ million. In sum, under this price path and with this operating policy, your firm would have an NPV of $\$13.64 - \$8.26 = \$5.38$ million.

Your task is to work out value based on your ability to respond to the environment.

Let's take the same project and consider its value in a number of scenarios, which differ in the assumption of what you know and how you can respond to the prevailing environment.

No flexibility—all choices made up front: First, let's compute the value under inflexible behavior. This is one extreme benchmark. What is the value if you have to make your decision today of whether to operate or not in all future scenarios? That is, the firm would either have to operate or not operate in both future periods with the \$600/unit and \$400/unit scenarios.

- If you do not start the plant, you would simply value the firm at \$0.
- If you do start the plant, then you must make the calculations that the tree in Figure 12.2 shows. If the price increases to \$600, you earn \$75 − \$50 − \$10 = \$15 million. If it decreases to \$400, you earn \$45 − \$10 − \$50 = −\$15 million. Therefore, your expected revenues are \$0. The following year, you earn +\$45 million, −\$15 million, +\$15 million, or −\$45 million. This again comes to an expected \$0.

I rigged the example—the firm value is \$0 if you have no flexibility.

In this example, it really does not matter whether you start the plant or not—your firm value is always \$0.

Importantly, this \$0 is also the value if you work with expected outcomes instead of the tree. The expected price in both future years is \$500/unit. At the expected price, your \$100/unit production cost translates into expected revenues of \$60 million. You would still have to pay for rent and fixed costs, at \$60 million per year. Indeed, working with expected values is the same as assuming that you do not have the ability to make strategic choices in the future (discussed next)—a common source of underestimated project values in practice.

All real options—the fully flexible choice: Now assume the opposite extreme benchmark: You know each year what the price is and you have perfect flexibility to shut down and reopen the plant in response to market conditions. This option is called the "timing option." Here, if the retail price is above \$500/unit, you would operate. For example, if the retail price is \$600/unit, your marginal revenues are \$150,000 · (\$600/unit − \$100/unit) − \$50,000,000 = \$25,000,000. Subtract \$10 million in sunk rent cost, and you end up with revenues of \$15 million. If the retail price is \$400/unit, you earn \$45 million, which is not enough to cover the \$50 million fixed operating costs, so you are better off not operating and just paying the rent of \$10 million.

If you have perfect flexibility, you get "the max."

Figure 12.3 shows your valuation and optimal decision tree now. Again, the figure highlights important flexibility-related choices in blue. The heavy boxes indicate that you operate the plant; the other boxes indicate that you do not. You earn +\$15 million or −\$10 million in the first year. The expected value is \$2.5 million, which discounts to \$2.3 million (indicated at the bottom of the figure). The final year, you earn +\$45 million, −\$10 million, +\$15 million, or −\$10 million, which is an expected value of \$10 million and a discounted value of \$8.3 million. Therefore, this firm is worth about +\$10.5 million.

The value to having knowledge and the flexibility to act on it (knowledge without flexibility is useless!) has transformed this firm from a nothing into a gem. It is this value-through-flexibility that your "strategic option to respond" has created. Put differently, the value of your real option is +\$10.5 million.

The option to delay choice: Often, you do not have full flexibility. Instead, you have some real options, but not perfect flexibility. For example, what would happen

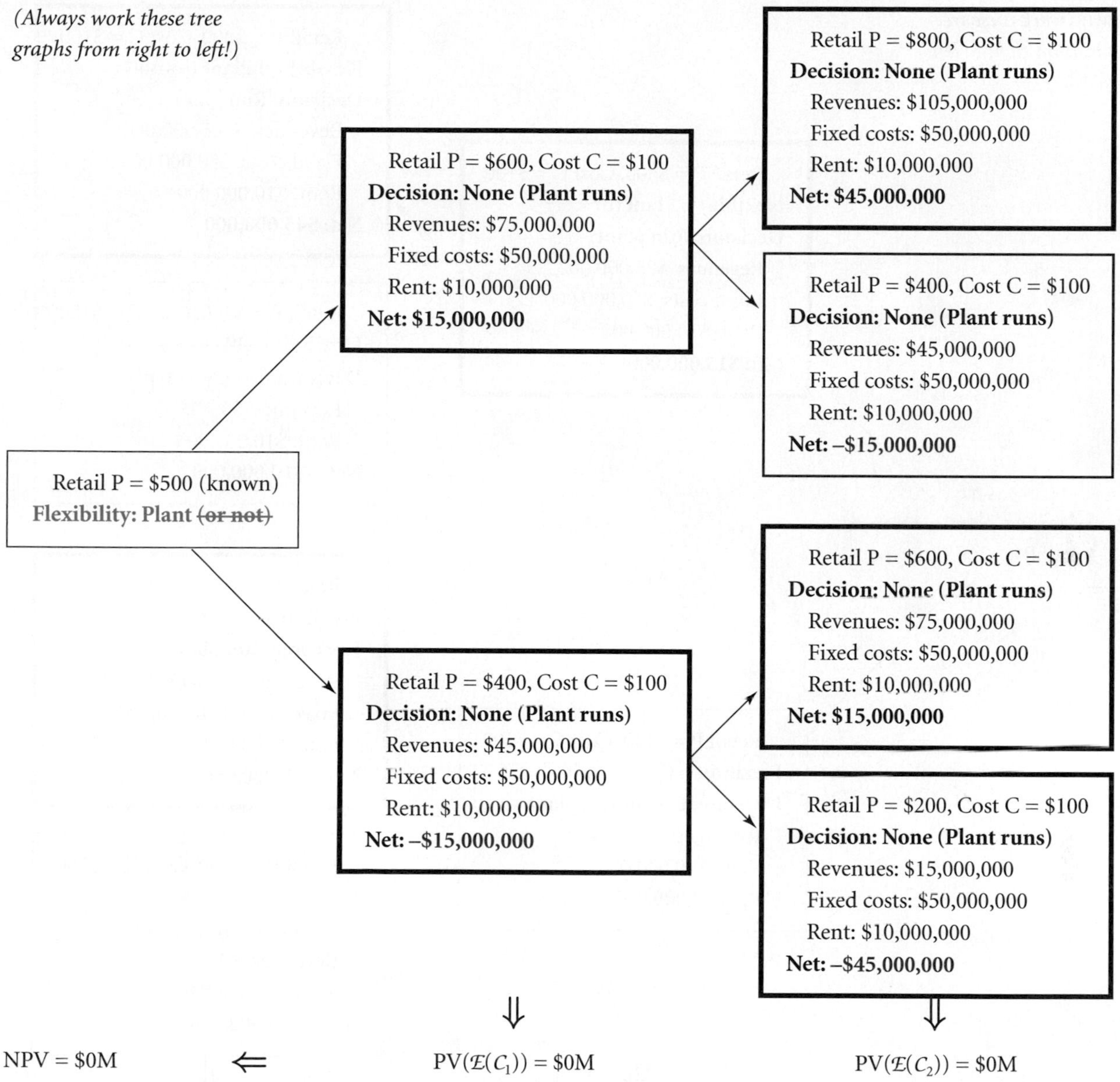

FIGURE 12.2 Value Under No Flexibility—Always Operate the Plant

if you had the option to delay your decision by 1 year, more specifically, to run the plant only if the price appreciates to \$600/unit, but not if it depreciates to \$400/unit? If you run the plant next year, you have to run it the following year. If you do not run the plant next year, you cannot run it the following year, either.

Figure 12.4 shows your revised decision tree. The average outcome is \$5 million divided by 2 in the first year, and \$10 million divided by 4 in the second year. Discount the first by 10% and the second by 21%, and you find the net of $\$2.5/1.1 + \$2.5/1.1^2 \approx \$4.3$ million. You can come to the same \$4.3 million solution by following your decisions in time:

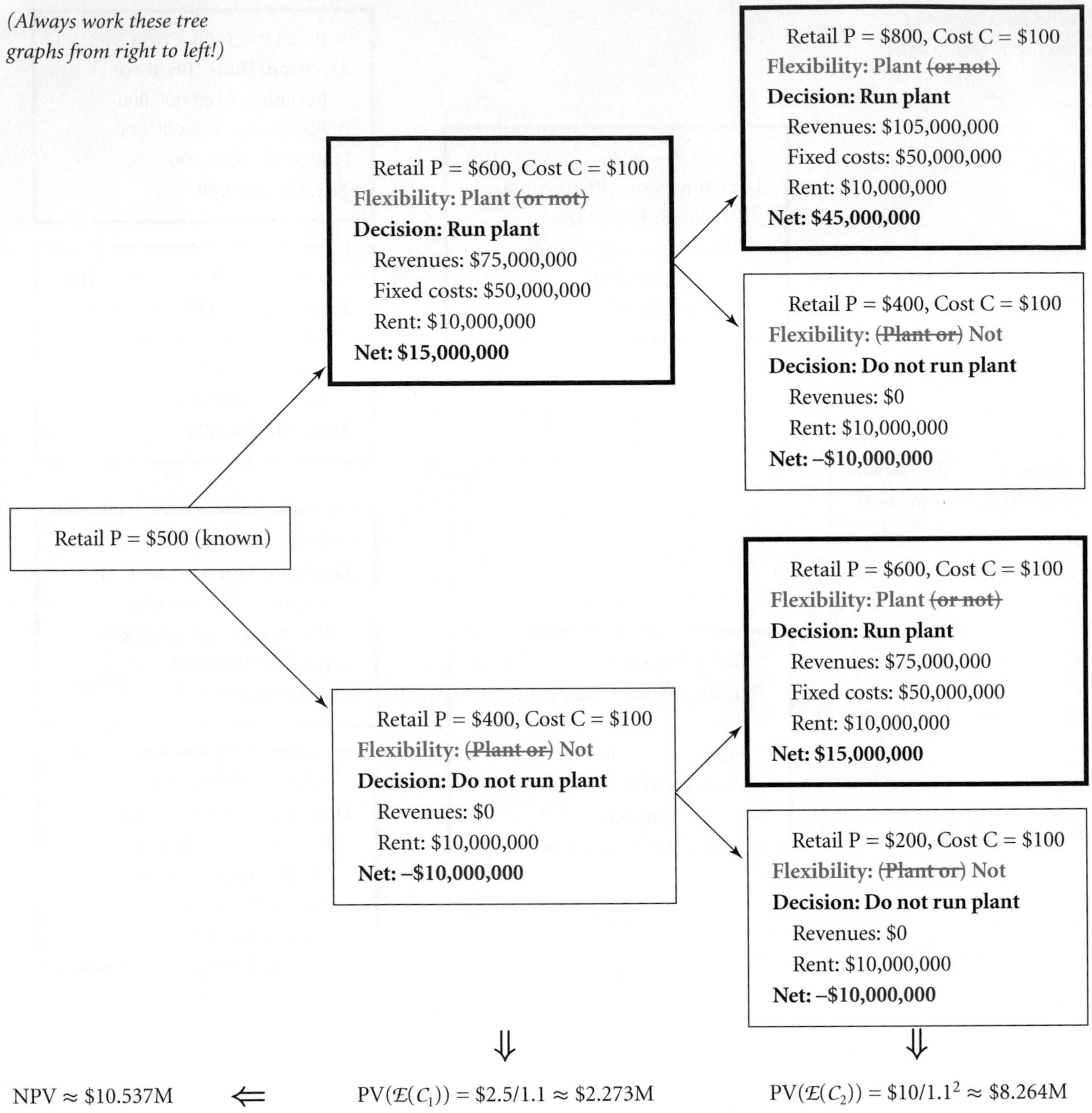

FIGURE 12.3 Value Under Perfect Flexibility—Full Knowledge and Choice

- If the retail price increases to $600/unit, your best decision is to operate the plant. You will earn $15 million in the first year, and either gain $45 million or lose $15 million the second year. Your net is $\$15/1.10 \approx \$13.6$ million plus $(0.5 \cdot \$45 + 0.5 \cdot [-\$15])/1.10^2 \approx \$12.4$ million. The total is $26 million in expected present value.
- If the retail price falls to $400, you commit to shuttering the plant. Your net is a sure loss of $10 million in each of the 2 years. In present value, this is $-\$9.1$

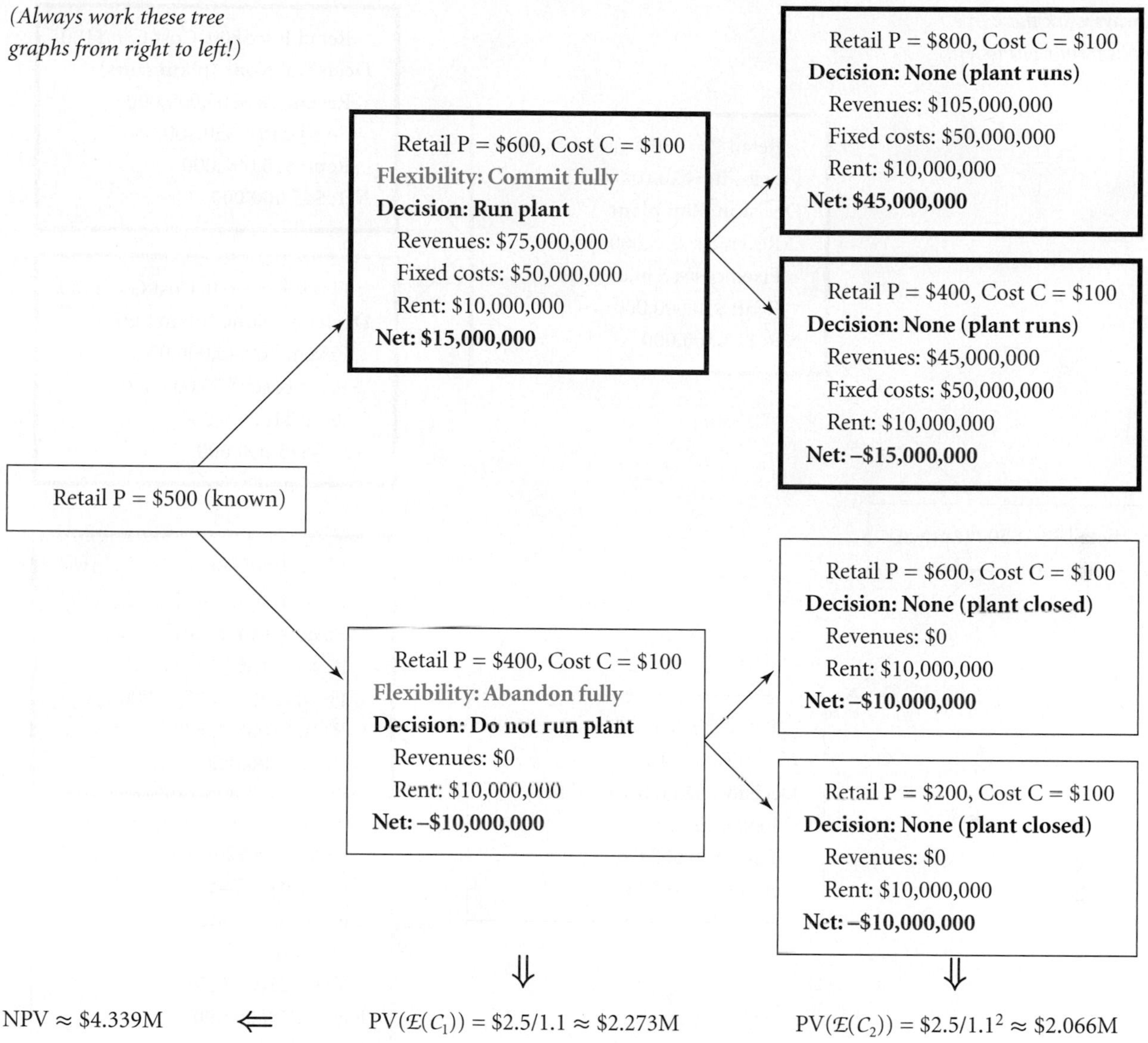

FIGURE 12.4 Value to 1-Year-Ahead Information (or Ability to Delay Choice until Year 1)

million followed by −$8.3 million. Your total is a loss of $17.4 million in expected present value.

Both price paths are equally likely, so the plant is worth about $0.5 \cdot (-\$17.4) + 0.5 \cdot \$26 \approx \$4.3$ million.

Intuitively, the reason why a plant with this more limited real option does not reach +$10.5 million under the full flexibility real option is that you would still have to operate the plant in the final period if the price is $400/unit (which you would rather not do), and you would fail to run the plant in the final period if the price is $600/unit (which you would rather do).

The option to start later: An alternative scenario would allow you to start the plant anytime you wish, but once you start the plant, you cannot stop it. Figure 12.5

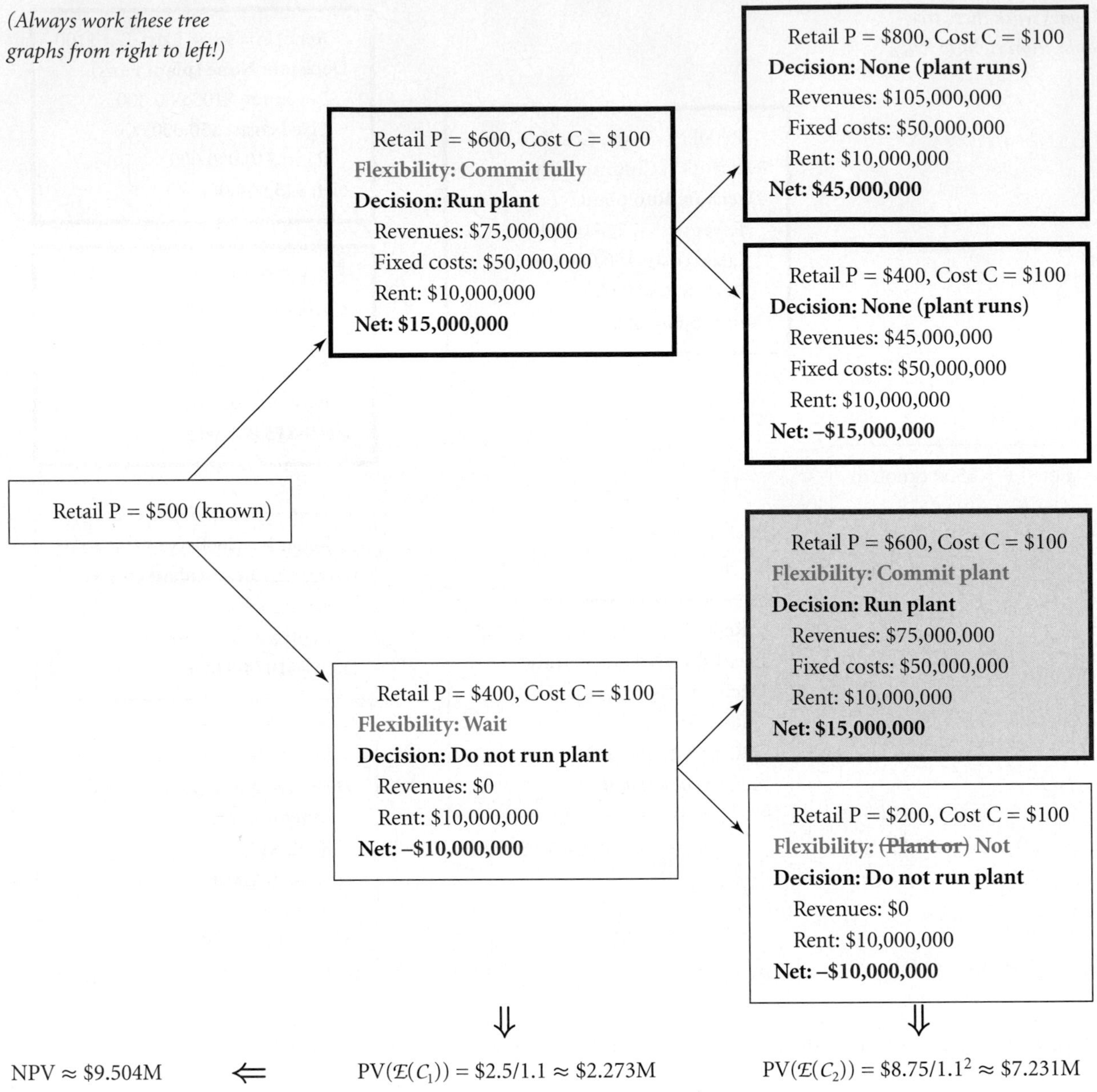

FIGURE 12.5 Value to Flexible Plant Starting (But Not Stopping)

shows the tree for this scenario—the plant value now comes to +$9.5 million. This is more than you get from the option to delay in this scenario, because there is one node (where the price hits $600/unit) where you now could make money where previously you had to have already committed yourself not to operate. (The relevant box that is different is the one with the red box.) But this is less than what you get under perfect flexibility, because you are still robbed of the option to shut down if the retail price is $400/unit in the final period.

The option to stop later: Yet another alternative scenario would force you to keep a once-closed plant stopped. That is, you cannot restart a plant once you have

(Always work these tree graphs from right to left!)

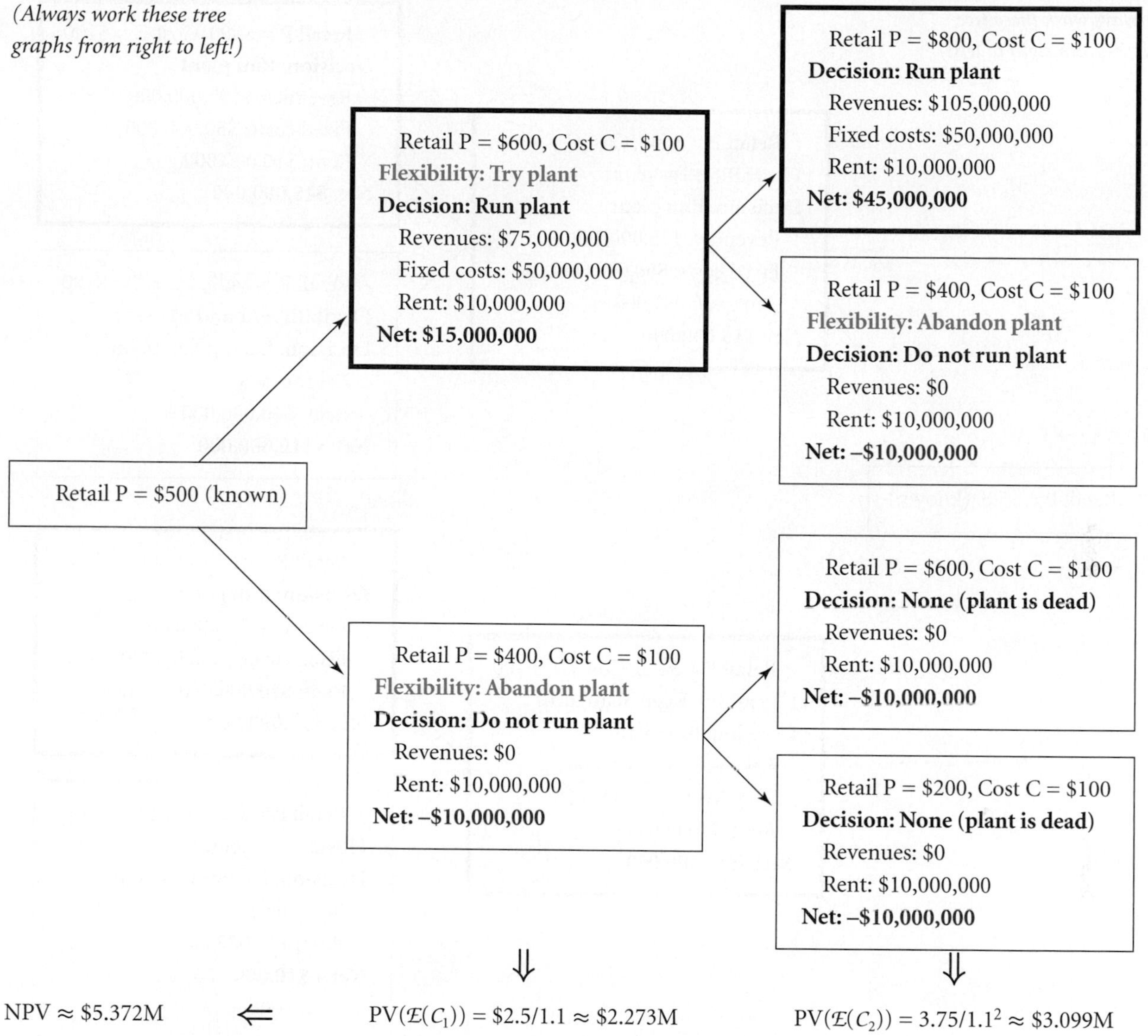

FIGURE 12.6 Value to Flexible Plant Stopping (But Not Starting)—Strategy 1: Close at $400

shut the burners off and allowed your skilled workers to leave. This is called the "abandonment option."

This case also illustrates that decision trees can become complex. If the price falls to $400/unit at first, should you run the plant or not? If you do not run the plant, you save money but you lose the real option to operate if the price then appreciates to $600/unit. Actually, you have no choice but to compute the best value both ways. Figure 12.6 and Figure 12.7 show the two decision trees. If you close the plant, your firm would be worth $5.4 million (Figure 12.6). If you keep the plant open—eating a loss of $15 million rather than just $10 million that first year—your firm would be worth $8.3M, because you keep the real option to operate if the retail price were to increase again to $600/unit. Therefore, keeping the plant open is the better strategy.

What should you do if the price falls to $400/unit at year 1?

(Always work these tree graphs from right to left!)

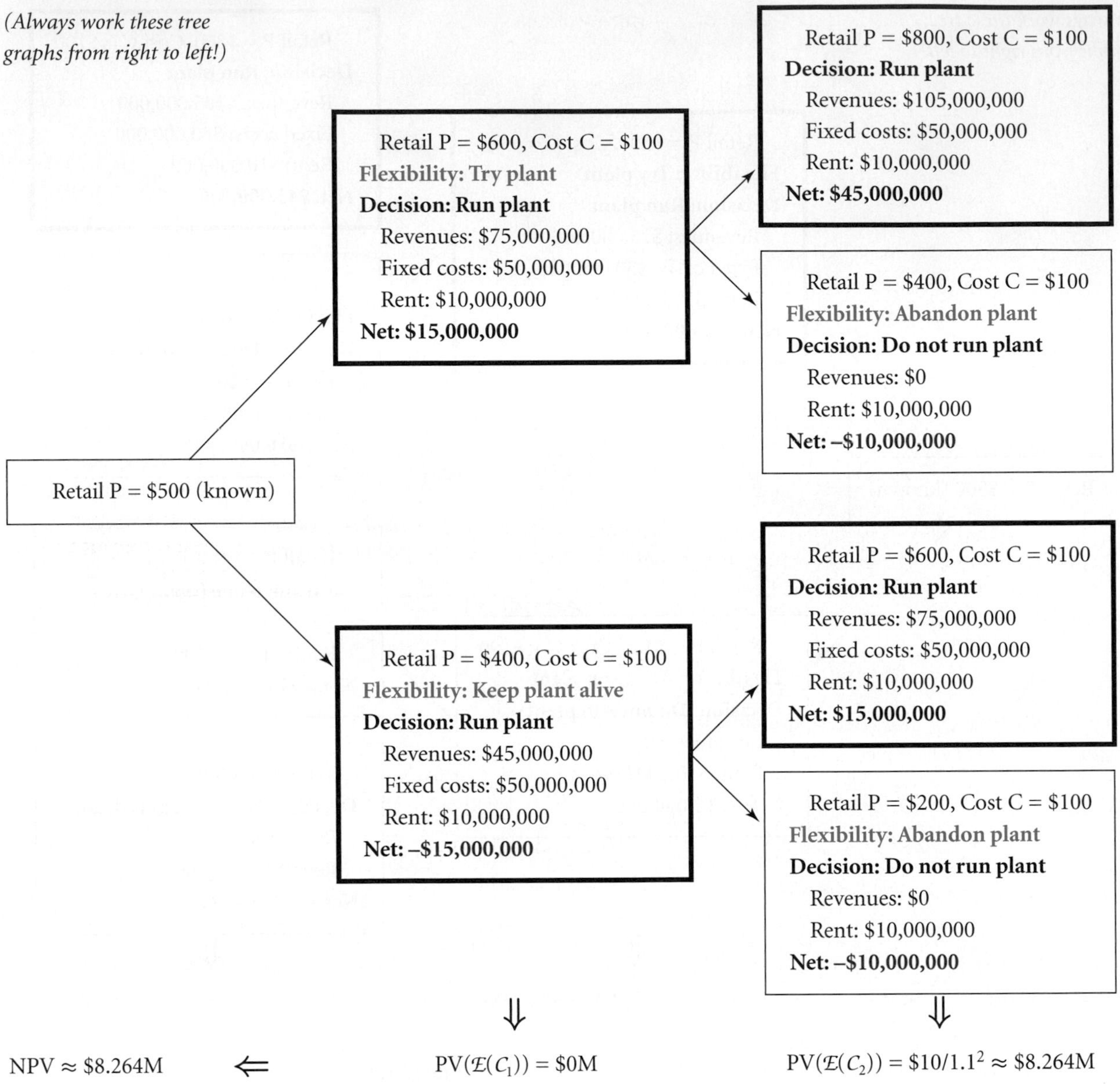

FIGURE 12.7 Value to Flexible Plant Stopping (But Not Starting)—Strategy 2: Run at $400

You really need to consider all possible future strategies in response to all possible future price paths.

Solving such trees is a difficult problem, because your optimal strategy next year does not just depend on that year but also on future years. In fact, in our previous examples, I have cheated in making it easy for you: I had told you the strategy at each node. Real option problems are difficult to value, precisely because your optimal strategy at any node can depend both on the current state of your firm and on all future possible scenarios.

The web chapter on real options explains how you can solve such problems more systematically. Decisions are often worked out "backwards": You start with the final year and work your way toward today. Another important tool is the aforementioned scenario analysis, which simply means trying out different input values—some more pessimistic—to see how they impact the estimated value of a project. (Scenario analysis and sensitivity analysis are very similar. The former is sometimes used as the name if more than one input value is changed; the latter if only one input value is changed.) Finally, also explained in the web chapter, there is a form of automated scenario analysis (called Monte Carlo simulation), in which you can specify a whole range of possible future scenarios. The spreadsheet itself can then compute the expected outcomes in many different scenarios using different decision-making strategies that you would specify.

12.11 PROJECTS WITH DIFFERENT PARAMETERS

This example was a little artificial, because it kept the same parameters throughout. This symmetry made it easy to explain and compare options. More commonly, the parameters themselves will change and determine the extent of your flexibility (and thus the value of your real option). This is best explained by example.

Consider how, in the real world, different projects have different parameters. Different projects are different bundles of real options.

Fixed versus flexible technology choice: Let's assume that you have a factory with a fully flexible technology, as illustrated in Figure 12.3. I am now offering you an alternative technology, which eliminates your fixed operating costs of $50 million per year but requires a one-time upfront $80 million investment. (You are installing robots that will replace expensive manpower.) At first blush, this seems like a great idea—you no longer have to spend $100 million, which discounts to $\$50/1.1 + \$50/1.1^2 \approx \$86.777$ million today. But is this really a savings of $6.777 million for you? No. It ignores the real option of flexibility that human workers have over robots: They can be hired and fired. Once purchased, robots cannot be laid off depending on demand. Figure 12.8 shows that with the robots you would have, you end up with $6.777 million, rather than $10.537 million. Robots, therefore, are not a great idea. Incidentally, it is often suggested that the value of smart employees is not their initial or even expected value, but the fact that smart people have the flexibility to attack novel problems for which they are not initially hired. Think about it—your value may be primarily that of a real option!

Adding plant capacity: Another interesting real option is the option to expand. You can view this as the choice to build currently unused capacity.

For example, say you can choose between two options:

- Your current fully flexible production technology that allows you to produce 150,000 units at $100/unit (as in Figure 12.3).
- Another production technology that builds the following extra capacity: You can still produce 150,000 units at $100/unit, but you can also double your production with 300,000 units at a cost of $200/unit, though with higher machine costs of $100,000.

Note that doubling increases the cost of *all* goods, not just the cost of the extra 150,000 units. It would cost you $60 million in variable production costs rather

(Always work these tree graphs from right to left!)

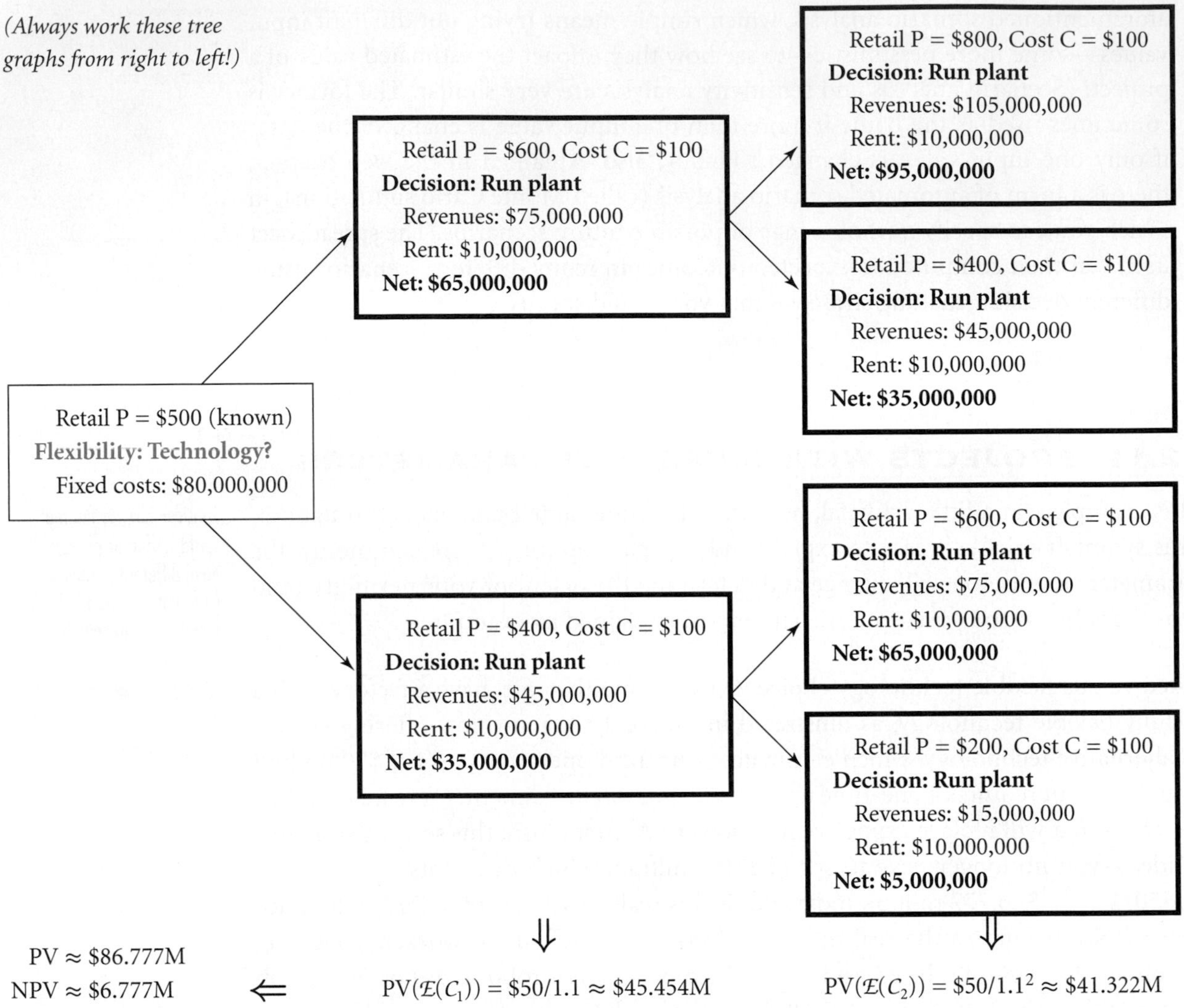

FIGURE 12.8 Value of a One-Time $80 Million Fixed-Cost Technology with Different Parameters (no more fixed costs per period, but a one-time upfront expense)

than just $15 million, and $100 million in fixed costs rather than just $50 million—that is, almost $95 million more if you ever wanted to use such extra capacity! Would you be willing to pay $3 million to upgrade your plant to such a technology?

Figure 12.9 shows you the firm value with the option to expand. If the retail price hits its all-time high of $800/unit, the unused capacity is worth a tremendous amount. Therefore, the value of the firm increases to $15.7 million from your earlier optimal value of $10.5 million, easily enough to justify a $3 million expenditure.

SOLVE NOW!

Q 12.44 A business produces 100,000 gadgets that cost $1 each to produce and sell for $1.80 each (last year and just now). To produce another 100,000

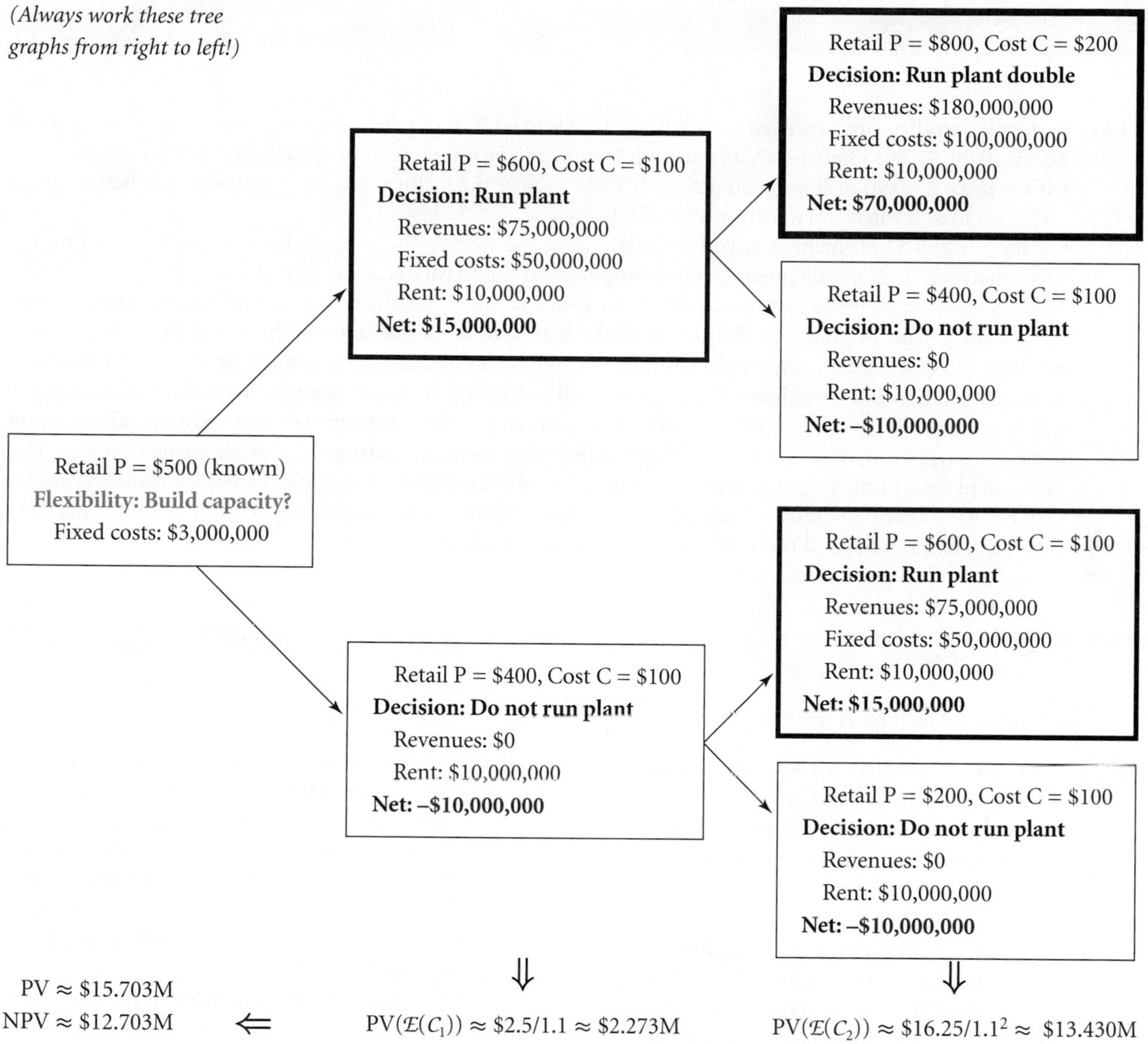

FIGURE 12.9 Value of an Expansion Technology with Different Parameters (relative to Figure 12.3)

gadgets requires running the machine at night, which increases production costs from $1 to $2. The business can last for up to 2 years (but think about how you would solve this for 5 years). In every year, with 10% probability, the output price doubles; with 10% probability, the output price halves; and with 80% probability, the price stays the same as in the previous year. Shutting down the factory for 1 year costs $9,000. Reopening it costs $10,000. The cost of capital is a constant 5% per year. What is the value of this factory? (This is a difficult problem, but unfortunately not an unrealistic one.)

SOLVE NOW! SOLUTIONS

Q 12.44 Tree problems like this one need to be solved "backwards." You can start in year 2 with a prevailing price of \$0.45, \$0.90, \$1.80, \$3.60, or \$7.20, and your factory can be either open or closed. In this final period:

- If the price is \$0.90 or lower, you definitely want to close the factory, because a \$9,000 loss is better than a \$10,000 loss. If the factory is already closed, lucky you.
- If the price is \$1.80 or higher, you definitely want the factory to be open, because an \$80,000 profit fortunately outweighs all opening and closing costs. If the factory is already open, lucky you.

Now consider what to do in year 1. If the price drops to \$0.90, you have a decision to make: Operate the factory for a year, hoping that the future will be better, or close the factory. Operating losses would be \$10,000. Closing immediately would cost only \$9,000. If you operate today, you incur an extra \$1,000 loss. In exchange, there is a 10% chance that the price will go back up, in which case you got lucky. In this case, you will have saved \$10,000 in reopening costs. Thus, you are exactly indifferent between closing and operating if the price has dropped. (Of course, if the price is higher today, operating today is the correct choice.) The problem of determining optimal choices as a function of environmental variables can get incredibly complex very easily. Scenario analysis (or just plain real-world experience and intuition) is really the only analysis method. This goes beyond the scope of an introductory textbook.

PROBLEMS

The ▬ *indicates problems available in* myfinancelab

Q 12.45 You own a plant that has \$90 of production costs. To close an open plant costs \$0. To open a closed plant costs \$0. The production can be sold for \$100 in year 0 (now). Next year, the selling value will be either 25% higher or 20% lower. (This is called a recombining tree, which makes computations easier. You will see what I mean.) These two cases happen with equal probability. For simplicity, assume a zero cost of capital, so dollars next year are just as valuable as dollars this year.

(a) What is the present value of this plant if it exists for 3 years?

(b) What is the present value of this plant if it exists for 4 years?

(c) What is the present value of this plant if it exists for 5 years?

Change the following two parameters: To close an open plant costs \$5. To open a closed plant costs \$20. (Hint: I want you to learn how the decisions in such trees can become more difficult when the plant can be in different states at each node. Therefore, consider putting each of the following phrases at each decision node: "if I come in already operating the plant, then . . . ," and "if I come in with a closed plant, then . . . ." Consider working the tree backward.)

(d) What is the present value of this plant if it exists for 3 years?

(e) What is the present value of this plant if it exists for 4 years?

(f) What is the present value of this plant if it exists for 5 years?

Note: This is a long question—and questions like it can easily become even more difficult. For example, it could be that the costs of closing or opening itself depend on what you did in the previous periods or what the price was in the previous period.

13

From Financial Statements to Economic Cash Flows

TRANSLATING ACCOUNTING INTO FINANCE (PRESENT VALUE CASH FLOWS)

Financial accounting is the "language of business." Although this book is not about financial statements, you must understand both their logic and their fundamentals. They contain information about the cash flows you need for an NPV analysis, as well as a lot of other useful information. Without understanding accounting, you also cannot understand corporate income taxes—a necessary NPV input.

This chapter begins with a simple hypothetical project. Its economics make computing NPV easy. The chapter then explains how accountants would describe the project in a financial statement. This makes it easy for you to see the correspondence between the finance and the accounting descriptions. Finally, the chapter applies the same analysis to the financial statements of a real corporation, PepsiCo (PEP).

This chapter also gently introduces some more details about corporate income taxes and capital structure. They will be explained in greater detail in Chapter 17.

13.1 FINANCIAL STATEMENTS

You already know that the value of a firm is determined by its underlying projects. These projects have cash flows that you use in an NPV analysis. Unfortunately, the accounting financials do not contain the kind of cash flows that you need for an NPV analysis. In addition to learning how to convert financials into cash flows, there are also many other good reasons why you should understand financial statements:

Isn't accounting just irrelevant numbers? Isn't what matters the project's actual cash flows, no matter how it is reported? (Yes and No.)

1. If you want to have an intelligent conversation about corporate finance and economics, you must understand the language of accounting. In particular, you must understand what earnings are—and what they are not.

2. Subsidiaries and corporations report financial statements, designed by accountants for accountants. It is true that they do not report the exact cash flows and cash flow projections that you need for PV discounting. But how can you make good decisions about which projects to take if you cannot understand the only information to which you may ever have access to?

3. Given that it may be all the information you ever get, you must be able to read what the company is willing to tell you if you want to get a glimpse of the operations of a publicly traded corporation or better understand its economics. If you want to acquire a company, the corporate financials may be your primary source of information.

4. The IRS levies corporate income tax. This tax is computed from a tax-specific variant of the corporate income statement. It relies on the same accounting logic as the published financials. (The reported public and unreported tax statements are constructed using the same accounting principles. But there are differences that are mandated by the respective regulatory agencies.) Because income taxes are definite costs, you must be able to understand and construct financial statements that properly subtract taxes from the projected cash flows when you want to compute NPV. And, if you become a tax guru, you may even learn how to structure projects so as to minimize the tax obligations, although most of this is beyond the scope of a first finance textbook.

5. Many contracts are written on the basis of financials. For example, a bond covenant may require the company to maintain a current ratio greater than 1.5. Even if a change in accounting rules should not matter theoretically, such contracts can influence the reported financials on your projects' cash flows.

6. There is no doubt that managers care about their financial statements, if only because executive compensation is often linked to the numbers reported in them. Moreover, managers can engage in many maneuvers to manipulate their earnings *legally.* For example, firms can often increase their reported earnings by changing their depreciation policies (explained below). Companies are also known to actively lobby the accounting standards boards at great expense. For example, in December 2004 the accounting standards board finally adopted a mandatory rule that companies must value employee stock options when they are granted. Until 2004, firms' financial statements could treat these option grants as if they cost nothing. This rule was adopted despite extremely vigorous opposition by corporate lobbies, which was aimed at the accounting standards board and Congress. The reason is that although this new rule did not ask firms to change projects, it drastically reduced the *reported* net income (earnings), especially of technology firms.

   Why should companies care about whether options costs have to be subtracted from reported earnings? After all, companies had disclosed enough information in the footnotes to allow investors to determine these costs themselves. This is a big question. Some behavioral finance researchers believe that the financial markets value companies *as if they do not fully understand corporate financials.* That is, not only do they share the common belief that firms "manage" their earnings, but they also believe that the market fails to see through even mechanical accounting computations.

Naturally, the presumption that the financial markets cannot understand accounting is a controversial hypothesis. If true, this could lead to all sorts of troublesome consequences. Value may no longer be just NPV, but instead be based partly on smoke and mirrors. For example, if the market cannot understand financials, you should realize that it could have real share-price consequences when managers (legally) manipulate their earnings. A firm would especially benefit from a higher share price when it wants to sell more of its shares to the public. In this case, managers could and should maneuver their financials (legally, of course) to increase their earnings just before the equity issue. There is good evidence that firms do this—and also that the financial markets are regularly disappointed by these firms' performances years after their equity issues.

Even more troublesome, there is also evidence that managers prefer not to take some positive-NPV projects if these projects would harm their earnings. Does this sound far-fetched? In fact, in a survey of 401 senior financial executives, Graham, Harvey, and Rajgopal found that 55% would delay starting a project and 80% would defer maintenance and research spending in order to meet earnings targets. Starting projects and doing maintenance and R&D are presumably the right kinds of (positive-NPV) projects, so not taking them decreases the underlying real value of the firm—even though it may increase the financial image of the firm's projects.

Our chapter's accounting perspective: how to extract economic cash flows.

It is of course impossible for an introductory finance textbook to explain all the nuances of accounting. Instead, we focus here on only one issue of importance to a financier: How can you obtain the cash flows that you need for an NPV analysis, and why can you not use earnings? Accounting has, of course, more to offer than just this—and, fortunately, you can learn more about its broader scope in your accounting course.

SOLVE NOW!

Q 13.1 Although accounting numbers are sometimes thought of as imaginary presentations, why is a firm not just a firm, and accounting numbers not just "funny numbers"? That is, what is the most important direct cash flow influence of accounting in most corporations?

13.1A THE CONTENTS OF FINANCIALS

Companies communicate their internal operations through standardized financial reports.

Publicly traded companies report their **financial results** (or **financials**) in **financial reports** to their shareholders and to the public. The standard rules that go into preparing the public financial statements are called **GAAP** (Generally Accepted Accounting Principles) and change rarely. They are set by a number of policymakers, most prominently **FASB** (Financial Accounting Standards Board). The most important financial report is the **annual report**, which is filed with the SEC in Form **10-K**. (There is also a much shorter required **quarterly report**, called a **10-Q**.) Almost all annual reports begin with a general description of the business and business developments, followed by the more formal presentation of the firm's financials. As a financier, you are most likely primarily interested in the financials. After all, you care more about *how much* money the firm makes than about *how* it makes it. Nevertheless, as much as you might like to keep the firm a black box, you rarely can: Knowledge of "how money is made" is usually necessary for good knowledge of "how much money is made" and "how more money can be made."

You must read some samples—please!

If you have not seen an annual report (with financial statements), please spend some time reading one. Most large corporations publish their financials on their websites, so access is easy. If you own shares of stock in a publicly traded company, the annual report is also automatically mailed to you. Moreover, the SEC runs **EDGAR**—a comprehensive electronic repository of corporate financials, including annual and quarterly reports.

13.1B PEPSICO'S FINANCIALS

We look at PepsiCo financials.

Tables 13.1–13.4 contain the financial statements that PepsiCo reported in its 2001 annual report. (The entire annual report is available at http://www.pepsico.com/PEP_Investors/AnnualReports/01/pepsico_annual2001.pdf.) If you are wondering why we are using such old statements, there is a good reason. It will allow us to track in Chapter 20 what actually happened to PepsiCo in subsequent years. In any case, nothing major has changed in the accounting rules since 2001, so every principle in these statements remains applicable today.

The financial statements: balance sheet, income statement, cash flow statement, and the relatively less important equity statement.

Every financial report has four main statements:

The balance sheet in Table 13.1 provides a snapshot of the firm's assets and liabilities at a fixed point in time. (It is a measure of "stock," not of "flow" over an interval.)

Some assets (mostly cash and securities, accounts receivable, and inventories) are classified as **current assets**. The idea is that these assets will convert into cash within one year or less. They are thus short term in nature and are used by the firm to fund its day-to-day operations. They are also often (but not always) fairly easy to liquidate in case of distress. Current assets contrast with other assets such as plants or brand reputation (an intangible asset), which are expected to generate cash over more than one year. Noncurrent assets are often much harder to convert into cold, hard cash if the firm needs money quickly.

As in finance, accounting forces the sum total of all assets to be owned by creditors and shareholders. And, as with assets, some creditors are owed money over the short term. These are called **current liabilities**. Noncurrent liabilities include other debt that is more long term. And then there are obligations to our "friend," the IRS. The remainder—whatever assets are not accounted for by debt owed to creditors—is called equity. Therefore,

$$\text{Assets} = \text{Liabilities} + \text{Shareholders' Equity}$$

If all assets and liabilities are properly valued, this accounting **book value** of shareholders' equity would be the market value, too. However, accounting rules and difficulties in valuing assets and liabilities often render the book value of shareholders' equity into more of a "plug-in" number that serves to equalize assets and liabilities than an intrinsically meaningful figure. *You have been warned!*

TABLE 13.1 CONSOLIDATED BALANCE SHEET, PEPSICO, INC. AND SUBSIDIARIES

December 29, 2001, and December 30, 2000

	(in millions except per share amounts)	2001	2000
	ASSETS		
	Current Assets		
1	Cash and cash equivalents	$683	$ 1,038
2	Short-term investments, at cost	966	467
3		1,649	1,505
4	Accounts and notes receivable, net	2,142	2,129
5	Inventories	1,310	1,192
6	Prepaid expenses and other current assets	752	791
7	**Total Current Assets**	5,853	5,617
8	**Property, Plant and Equipment, net**	6,876	6,558
9	**Intangible Assets, net**	4,841	4,714
10	**Investments in Unconsolidated Affiliates**	2,871	2,979
11	**Other Assets**	1,254	889
12	**Total Assets**	$21,695	$20,757
	LIABILITIES AND SHAREHOLDERS' EQUITY		
	Current Liabilities		
13	Short-term borrowings	$ 354	$ 202
14	Accounts payable and other current liabilities	4,461	4,529
15	Income taxes payable	183	64
16	**Total Current Liabilities**	4,998	4,795
17	**Long-Term Debt**	2,651	3,009
18	**Other Liabilities**	3,876	3,960
19	**Deferred Income Taxes**	1,496	1,367
20	**Preferred Stock, no par value**	26	49
21	**Deferred Compensation—Preferred**	—	(27)
	Common Shareholders' Equity		
22	Common stock, par value $1\frac{2}{3}$ c per share (issued 1,782 and 2,029 shares, respectively)	30	34
23	Capital in excess of par value	13	375
24	Deferred compensation	—	(21)
25	Retained earnings	11,519	16,510
26	Accumulated other comprehensive loss	(1,646)	(1,374)
27	Less: repurchased common stock, at cost (26 and 280 shares, respectively)	(1,268)	(7,920)
28	**Total Common Shareholders' Equity**	8,648	7,604
29	**Total Liabilities and Shareholders' Equity**	$21,695	$20,757

See accompanying notes to consolidated financial statements.

TABLE 13.2 CONSOLIDATED STATEMENT OF COMMON SHAREHOLDERS' EQUITY, PEPSICO, INC. AND SUBSIDIARIES

Fiscal years ended December 29, 2001, December 30, 2000, and December 25, 1999

	2001		2000		1999	
(in millions)	Shares	Amount	Shares	Amount	Shares	Amount
Common Stock						
Balance, beginning of year	2,029	$ 34	2,030	$ 34	2,037	34
Share repurchases	—	—	(9)	—	(13)	—
Stock option exercises	6	—	—	—	—	—
Quaker stock option exercises	3	—	8	—	6	—
Shares issued to effect merger	(256)	(4)	0	—	—	—
Balance, end of year	1,782	30	2,029	34	2,030	34
Capital in Excess of Par Value						
Balance, beginning of year		375		559		904
Share repurchases		—		(236)		(370)
Stock option exercises [a]		82		52		(21)
Reissued shares		150		—		—
Shares issued to effect merger		(595)		—		—
Other		1		—		46
Balance, end of year		13		375		559
Deferred Compensation						
Balance, beginning of year		(21)		(45)		(68)
Net activity		21		24		23
Balance, end of year		—		(21)		(45)
Retained Earnings						
Balance, beginning of year		16,510		14,921		13,356
Net income		2,662		2,543		2,505
Shares issued to effect merger		(6,644)		—		—
Cash dividends declared—common		(1,005)		(950)		(936)
Cash dividends declared—preferred		(4)		(4)		(4)
Balance, end of year		11,519		16,510		14,921
Accumulated Other Comprehensive Loss						
Balance, beginning of year		(1,374)		(1,085)		(1,139)
Currency translation adjustment (CTA)		(218)		(289)		(136)
CTA reclassification adjustment		—		—		175
Cash flow hedges, net of tax:						
Cumulative effect of accounting change		3		—		—
Derivative (losses)/gains, net		(21)		—		—
Minimum pension liability adjustment, net of tax		(38)		(2)		17
Other		2		2		(2)
Balance, end of year		(1,646)		(1,374)		(1,085)
Repurchased Common Stock						
Balance, beginning of year	(280)	(7,920)	(271)	(7,306)	(255)	(6,535)
Shares repurchased	(35)	(1,716)	(38)	(1,430)	(36)	(1,285)
Stock option exercises	20	751	29	816	20	514
Reissued shares	13	374	—	—	—	—
Shares issued to effect merger	256	7,243	—	—	—	—
Balance, end of year	(26)	(1,268)	(280)	(7,920)	(271)	(7,306)
Total Common Shareholders' Equity		$ 8,648		$ 7,604		$ 7,078

a. Includes total tax benefit of $212 in 2001, $177 in 2000 and $105 in 1999.

See accompanying notes to consolidated financial statements. These include a closing stock price of $49.05/share, which indicates a market capitalization of $87.4 billion.

TABLE 13.3 CONSOLIDATED STATEMENT OF INCOME, PEPSICO, INC. AND SUBSIDIARIES

Fiscal years ended December 29, 2001, December 30, 2000, and December 25, 1999

	(in millions except per share amounts)	2001	2000	1999
	NET SALES			
1	New PepsiCo	$26,935	$25,479	$22,970
2	Bottling operations	—	—	2,123
3	Total Net Sales	26,935	25,479	25,093
	COSTS AND EXPENSES			
4	Cost of sales	10,754	10,226	10,326
5	Selling, general and administrative expenses	11,608	11,104	11,018
6	Amortization of intangible assets	165	147	193
7	Merger-related costs	356	—	—
8	Other impairment and restructuring charges	31	184	73
9	Total Costs and Expenses	22,914	21,661	21,610
	OPERATING PROFIT			
10	New PepsiCo	$4,021	$3,818	$3,430
11	Bottling operations	—	—	2,123
12	Total Operating Profit	$4,021	$3,818	$3,483
13	Bottling equity income and transaction gains/(loss), net	160	130	1,083
14	Interest expense	(219)	(272)	(421)
15	Interest income	67	85	130
	(net interest income is sum of preceding three items)	= 8	= −57	= 792
16	**INCOME BEFORE INCOME TAXES**	4,029	3,761	4,275
17	**PROVISION FOR INCOME TAXES**	1,367	1,218	1,770
18	**NET INCOME**	$ 2,662	$ 2,543	$ 2,505
	NET INCOME PER COMMON SHARE			
19	Basic	$ 1.51	$ 1.45	$ 1.41
20	Diluted	$ 1.47	$ 1.42	$ 1.38

See accompanying notes to consolidated financial statements.

TABLE 13.4 CONSOLIDATED STATEMENT OF CASH FLOWS, PEPSICO, INC. AND SUBSIDIARIES

Fiscal years ended December 29, 2001, December 30, 2000, and December 25, 1999

	(in millions)	52 Weeks Ending 12/29/01	53 Weeks Ending 12/30/00	52 Weeks Ending 12/25/99
	Cash Flows—Operating Activities			
1	Net income	$2,662	$2,543	$2,505
	Adjustments to reconcile net income to net cash provided by operating activities			
2	Bottling equity income, net	(160)	(130)	(1,083)
3	Depreciation and amortization	1,082	1,093	1,156
4	Merger-related costs	356	—	—
5	Other impairment and restructuring charges	31	184	73
6	Cash payments for merger-related costs and restructuring charges	(273)	(38)	(98)
7	Deferred income taxes	162	33	73
8	Deferred compensation—ESOP	48	36	32
9	Other noncash charges and credits, net	209	303	368
	Changes in operating working capital, excluding effects of acquisitions and dispositions			
10	Accounts and notes receivable	7	(52)	(141)
11	Inventories	(75)	(51)	(202)
12	Prepaid expenses and other current assets	(6)	(35)	(209)
13	Accounts payable and other current liabilities	(236)	219	357
14	Income taxes payable	394	335	274
15	Net change in operating working capital	84	416	79
16	**Net Cash Provided by Operating Activities**	4,201	4,440	3,605
	Cash Flows—Investing Activities			
17	Capital spending	(1,324)	(1,352)	(1,341)
18	Acquisitions and investments in unconsolidated affiliates	(432)	(98)	(430)
19	Sales of businesses	—	33	513
20	Sales of property, plant & equipment	—	57	130
	Short-term investments. by original maturity			
21	More than three months—purchases	(2,537)	(4,950)	(2,209)
22	More than three months—payments	2,078	4,585	2,220
23	Three months or less, net	(41)	(9)	12
24	Other, net	(381)	(262)	(67)
25	**Net Cash Used for Investing Activities**	(2,637)	(1,996)	(1,172)

(Continued on the following page)

TABLE 13.4 (CONTINUED)

	(in millions)	52 Weeks Ending 12/29/01	53 Weeks Ending 12/30/00	52 Weeks Ending 12/25/99
	Cash Flows—Financing Activities			
26	Proceeds from issuances of long-term debt	324	130	3,480
27	Payments of long-term debt	(573)	(879)	(1,216)
	Short-term borrowings, by original maturity			
28	More than three months—proceeds	788	198	3,699
29	More than three months—payments	(483)	(155)	(2,758)
30	Three months or less, net—payments	(397)	1	(2,814)
31	Cash dividends paid	(994)	(949)	(935)
32	Share repurchases—common	(1,716)	(1,430)	(1,285)
33	Share repurchases—preferred	(10)	—	—
34	Quaker share repurchases	(5)	(254)	(382)
35	Proceeds from issuance of shares in connection with the Quaker merger	524	—	—
36	Proceeds from exercises of stock options	623	690	383
37	**Net Cash Used for Financing Activities**	(1,919)	(2,648)	(1,828)
38	Effect of Exchange Rate Changes on Cash and Cash Equivalents	—	(4)	3
39	**Net (Decrease)/Increase in Cash and Cash Equivalents**	(355)	(208)	(608)
40	**Cash and Cash Equivalents—Beginning of Year**	1,038	1,246	638
41	**Cash and Cash Equivalents—End of Period**	$683	$1,038	$1,246
	Supplemental Cash Flow Information			
42	Interest paid	$159	$226	$384
43	Income taxes paid	$857	$876	$689
44	Acquisitions			
45	Fair value of assets acquired	$604	$ 80	$717
46	Cash paid and debt issued	(432)	(98)	(438)
47	Liabilities assumed	$172	$(18)	$279

The owners' equity statement (or "shareholders' equity statement") in Table 13.2 explains the history of capital originally contributed to the firm, and of earnings that were retained (not paid out). We will not use this statement any further.

The income statement in Table 13.3 reports the revenues and expenses of the company, resulting in earnings (also called net income) over the year. (Thus, it reports measures of "flows," not of "stocks.")

In the above three statements, accountants seek to "smooth out" temporary hiccups—which you will learn about in a moment. It is only in the fourth statement that this is not attempted:

The cash flow statement in Table 13.4 reports the sources and uses of cash over the year. (It is a measure of "flow," not of "stock.")

You should stare at these four PepsiCo statements for a while. But however hard you look, you will not be able to find an item entitled "cash flow for an NPV analysis." And the cash flows on the cash flow statement look nothing like the earnings, which is what the world seems to consider important! Somehow, you must learn what these financials mean so that you can extract what you really need from them: a "cash flow for an NPV analysis" from the four financial statements.

The most important statements are the income and cash flow statements, not the two stock statements.

For the most part, GAAP rules focus more on the accuracy of the two flow statements than on the accuracy of the two stock statements. (The balance sheet does contain important information, but many of its entries are precarious.) Fortunately, this suits us well. We will be spending a lot of time explaining the income statement and cash flow statement. The upshot is that the cash flow statement comes closest to what you want. However, to understand why it is insufficient and where it comes from, you need to take a wider expedition into the logic of accounting (and, specifically, of net income), which is different from the logic of finance (and, specifically, of NPV cash flows). Your next step is to learn how to read, interpret, and transform financial statements into the cash flows that an NPV analysis demands. You also need this expedition to get a better understanding of earnings and financial statements in general.

13.1C WHY FINANCIERS AND ACCOUNTANTS THINK DIFFERENTLY

Earnings anticipate future costs and benefits (in some odd sense).

Financiers try to understand the firm value by working with the exact timing of hard cash inflows and outflows over the entire project's lifetime. Like financiers, accountants are interested in firm value. (However, this is an oversimplification, because accounting estimates are also subject to a number of considerations that can trump their desire for accuracy—first and foremost, an explicit desire to remain conservative. For example, entries on the balance sheet are recorded at the lower of cost or market value. Thus, even if an accountant knows that the value is higher than the cost, she may not want to use this information. We will mostly ignore conservatism, and focus on how we can use accounting information for our purposes.) Unlike financiers, accountants focus not just on economic cash flows but also on annual earnings (a flow variable). These earnings try to incorporate changes in the expected future immediately into the firm's net income today.

The difference between income and economic cash flows is "accruals."

The main difference between these two concepts of income and cash flows is **accruals**, which are economic transactions that have delayed cash implications. For example, if I owe your firm $10,000 and have committed to paying you tomorrow, the accountant would record your current firm value to be $10,000 (perhaps time- and credit-risk adjusted). In contrast, the financier would consider this to be a zero cash-flow today—until tomorrow, when the payment actually occurs. The contrast is that the accountant (by and large) wants the financial statements to be a good (though also conservative) representation of the economic value of the firm *today* (i.e., you already own my commitment to pay), instead of a representation of the exact timing of inflows and outflows. The financier needs the timing of cash flows for the NPV discounting instead.

Accruals can be classified into long-term accruals and short-term accruals. The primary **long-term accrual** is **depreciation**, which is the allocation of the cost of an asset over a period of time. For example, when a financier purchases a maintenance-free machine, he sees a machine that costs a lot of cash today and produces cash flows in the future. If the machine needs to be replaced every 20 years, then the financier sees a sharp spike in cash outflows every 20 years, followed by no further expenditures (but hopefully many cash inflows).

When financiers buy a machine, they see one big expense spike up front, followed by years of no further expenses.

The accountant, however, sees the machine as an asset that uses up a fraction of its value each year. An accountant would try to determine an amount by which the machine deteriorates in each year, and she would only consider this prorated deterioration to be the annual outflow (called an **expense**). The purchase of a $1 million machine would therefore not be an earnings reduction of $1 million in the first year, followed by $0 in the remaining 19 years. Instead, it would be an expense of, say, $50,000 in each of the 20 years. (This is a common method of depreciation and is called **straight-line depreciation**, here over 20 years. There are others.) Note also how neither the accounting nor the finance figure may be entirely accurate value-wise if you had to suddenly liquidate the machine after 1 year (e.g., if the firm went bankrupt). The machine could presumably be sold, but whether it could be sold for $950,000 or not at all would depend on the type of machine and prevailing market conditions.

For this machine, accountants see depreciation: only a little bit of use every year, but for many years.

To complicate matters further, accountants often use different standardized schedules over which particular assets are depreciated. These are called **impairment rules**, and you already know the straight-line rule. Residential investment properties (houses), for example, are commonly depreciated straight-line over 40 years (or 27.5 years for tax purposes)—often regardless of whether the house is constructed of straw or brick. The predetermined value schedule is usually not accurate. For example, if investors have recently developed a taste for old buildings, it could be that a building's value has doubled in line with prevailing real estate price increases, even though the financial statements might record this building to be worth nothing. (Even this is oversimplified. On occasion, accountants invoke procedures that allow them to adjust the value of an asset midway through its accounting life—but more often downward than upward.) Another common impairment rule is accelerated depreciation. (One form thereof is called MACRS, which is especially important in a tax context. But we are straying too far for the moment.)

This "little bit of use" cost comes from standardized impairment schedules.

If the machine happens to continue working after 20 years, the financials that have just treated the machine as a $50,000 expense in year 20 will now treat it as a

There is usually inconsistency at the point when the machine has been fully depreciated.

ANECDOTE Trashy Accounting at Waste Management

On December 14, 1998, Waste Management (WMX) settled a class action lawsuit by shareholders for $220 million, then the largest such settlement ever. The suit alleged that WMX had overstated its income by $1.32 billion over an 8-year period. From 1994 through 1997, about 47% of the company's reported income was fictitious. One of WMX's dubious practices was that it had changed the accounting life of its waste containers from 12 years to 18 years. Therefore, each year, it subtracted less depreciation, which increased its reported earnings by $1.7 billion. Of course, during that time, managers were handsomely rewarded for their superior earnings performance.

$0 expense in year 21. It remains worth $0 because it cannot depreciate any further—it has already been fully depreciated. The financier sees no difference between year 20 and year 21, just as long as the machine continues to work.

For short-term accruals, such as receivables, accounting logic relies on predicted future cash inflows.

Short-term accruals come in a variety of guises. To a financier, what matters is the timing of cash coming in and cash going out. A sale for credit is not cash *until* the company has collected the cash. To the accountant, if the firm sells $100 worth of goods on credit, the $100 is booked as revenue (which flows immediately into net income), even though no money has yet arrived. In the accounting view, the sale has been made. To reflect the delay in payment, accountants increase the **receivables** by $100. (Sometimes, firms simultaneously establish an allowance for estimated nonpayments [bad debts].)

The logic of finance relies exclusively on actual cash flows (or immediate values).

Another short-term accrual is **income tax**, which a financier considers to be an outflow only when it has to be paid—at least not until (the corporate equivalent of) April 15 of the following year. However, on the income statement, when a firm in the 40% corporate tax bracket makes $100 in profits, the income statement immediately subtracts the corporate income tax of $40 (which will eventually have to be paid on the $100 in profits) and therefore records net income of only $60. To reflect the fact that the full $100 cash is still around, $40 is recorded as **taxes payable**.

Both approaches have their own advantages and disadvantages.

In sum, for a financier, the machine costs a lot of cash today (so it is an immediate negative), the accounts receivable are not yet cash inflows (so they are not yet positives), and the corporate income tax is not yet a cash outflow (so it is not yet a negative). For an accountant, the machine costs a prorated amount over a period of years, the accounts receivable are immediate positive earnings, and the corporate income tax is an immediate cost. There is definite logic in the approaches of both accounting and finance: The accounting approach may be better in giving a snapshot impression of the firm's value; the finance approach is better in measuring the timing of the cash inflows and cash outflows for valuation purposes. Note that valuation leans much more heavily on the assumption that *all* future cash flows are fully considered. Today's cash flows alone would *not* usually make for a good snapshot of the firm's situation: The firm is not worth a negative amount just because it has recently purchased a machine that has caused a large negative cash flow this year.

SOLVE NOW!

Q 13.2 What is the main difference between the depiction of a project in accounting (net income) and in finance (economic cash flows)?

Q 13.3 Is the firm's lifetime sum of net income roughly equal to the firm's lifetime sum of cash flows?

13.2 A BOTTOM-UP EXAMPLE—LONG-TERM ACCRUALS (DEPRECIATION)

This hypothetical project will illustrate the difference between an accounting and a finance perspective for depreciation.

Rather than starting off trying to understand a creature as complex as the PepsiCo financials, let's begin with a simple firm for which you know the cash flows. Your firm is basically just one machine, described in Table 13.5. We shall construct hypothetical financials, and then we shall reverse-engineer them. The machine is rather unusual: It lasts 6 years; it has no maintenance costs; it requires capital expenditures not only in the first but also the second year; and it produces full output even in year 1. It produces net sales (after taking costs into account) of $60 per year, and customers pay cash immediately. Your corporate income tax rate is 40%, and your cost of capital is 12% per year. With $50 of debt at 10% interest, the firm's annual interest payments are $5. (The debt interest is lower than the firm's average cost of capital, because investors are risk averse.) In this section, all sales and all expenses are assumed to be cash transactions and not delayed.

➤ Risk aversion and cost of capital, Section 6.4D, p. 160

13.2A DOING ACCOUNTING

Depreciation schedules are not exact.

For the public financials, GAAP requests that firms use their discretion to match reported depreciation to true depreciation, *although conservatively so*. (There are exceptions.) In real life, matching actual life to accounting life is almost impossible to accomplish, if only because it is often unclear up front how long the assets will really last. (For this reason, many firms rely on standard depreciation schedules.) In contrast to the public statements, when it comes to tax accounting, the differences between actual and accounting life are even more pronounced. Depreciation rules for computing the corporate income tax are set by Congress. They are intentionally based on strict mechanical schedules, regardless of the true asset life, and change with tax laws—quite

TABLE 13.5 A HYPOTHETICAL PROJECT

Project			
Real Physical Lifespan	6 years		
Capital Expenditure	$75, year 1		
	$75, year 2	Available Financing—Executed	
Gross Output	$70/year	Debt Capacity	$50
– Input Costs (Cash)	$5/year	Debt Interest Rate	10%/year
– Selling Costs (Cash)	$5/year		(= $5/year)
= Net Output	$60/year		
Overall Cost of Capital	12%/year	Accounting Treatment	
Corporate Tax Rate (τ)	40%/year	Project Life	3 years

Note: This debt contract provides cash necessary in year 1, and requires a first interest payment in year 2. Both principal and interest are repaid in year 6.

TABLE 13.6 INCOME STATEMENT AND EXCERPT OF CASH FLOW STATEMENT OF HYPOTHETICAL MACHINE

Income Statement

	Year	1	2	3	4	5	6
	Sales (Revenues)	$70	$70	$70	$70	$70	$70
−	Cost of Goods Sold (COGS)	$5	$5	$5	$5	$5	$5
−	Selling, General & Administrative Expenses (SG&A)	$5	$5	$5	$5	$5	$5
=	EBITDA	$60	$60	$60	$60	$60	$60
−	Depreciation	$25	$50	$50	$25	$0	$0
=	EBIT (operating income)	$35	$10	$10	$35	$60	$60
−	Interest Expense	$0	$5	$5	$5	$5	$5
=	EAIBT (or EBT)	$35	$5	$5	$30	$55	$55
−	Corporate Income Tax (at 40%)	$14	$2	$2	$12	$22	$22
=	Net Income	$21	$3	$3	$18	$33	$33

Excerpts from the Cash Flow Statement

Year	1	2	3	4	5	6
Capital Expenditures[a]	−$75	−$75	—	—	—	—
Net Debt Issue	+$50	—	—	—	—	−$50
Depreciation	+$25	+$50	+$50	+$25	$0	$0

Although I have broken depreciation out in this income statement, it is usually part of other components, most likely COGS or SG&A. Fortunately, depreciation is always fully broken out in the cash flow statement. This is why you need to look it up in the latter.

a. *Sign Warning:* The accounting convention is to record capital expenditures as a negative number, i.e., as −$75, on the cash flow statement. But beware: The same capital expenditures would be recorded as a positive asset on the balance sheet.

often. (Even states can have their own rules.) Although GAAP and IRS schedules are almost always different, for now just assume that both GAAP and the IRS have decreed that this particular machine should be depreciated over 3 years, even though it lasts longer. Consequently, $75 generates $25 in depreciation, 3 years in a row, beginning in the year of the capital expenditure, and none after the third year. How does depreciation affect the reported financials?

A standard project's income statement.

The income statement for this project is shown in Table 13.6. In going down the leftmost column of any of these tables, you will notice that accounting has its own jargon, just like finance. **COGS** abbreviates **cost of goods sold. SG&A** abbreviates **selling, general & administrative expenses.** Both of these are expenditures that have to be subtracted from **sales** (or **revenues**) to arrive at **EBITDA** (**earnings before interest, taxes, depreciation, and amortization**). Next subtract out depreciation, which is a subject that deserves the long discussion below and that we will return to in a moment. Thus, you arrive at **operating income**, also called **EBIT** (**earnings before interest and taxes**). Finally, take out interest expense at a rate of 10% per year and corporate income tax (which you can compute from the firm's tax rate of 40%) and arrive at plain **earnings**, also called **net income.** Net income is often called the "bottom line," because of where it appears.

Compare the similarity of our income statement to PepsiCo's.

Note the similarity of this simple project's income statement to PepsiCo's income statement from Table 13.3. In 2001, PepsiCo had $26,935 million in sales. COGS and SG&A (which included some depreciation) added up to $10,754 + $11,608 = $22,362 million. Amortization (another form of depreciation explained below) subtracted $165 million. Other expenses amounted to $387 million, leaving you with EBIT of $26,935 − $22,362 − $165 − $356 − $31 = $4,021 million. In PepsiCo's case, the combination of bottling equity income and transaction gains, interest expenses, and interest income was determined to be its net interest income of $8 million, perhaps better called net investment income here. Uncle Sam demanded $1,367 million, leaving shareholders with net income of $2,662 million. Yes, PepsiCo has a few extra items, and changes some of the names around, but a broad similarity should be apparent.

Capital expenditures and debt issuing are recorded on the cash flow statement, not the income statement.

You have already reported almost all the information of your project on the income statement. The two exceptions are the capital expenditures and the net debt issue. These do not go onto the income statement. Instead, they are reported on the cash flow statement (also in Table 13.6). In this case, capital expenditures are $75 in year 1 and $75 in year 2, followed by $0 in all subsequent years. Net debt issuing is $50 in year 1, and the debt principal repayment of $50 occurs in year 6. (In addition, the cash flow statement also reports depreciation. I will soon explain why you should actually read depreciation off the cash flow statement—not off the income statement.)

Here is how capital expenditures enter the income statement: depreciation.

This is not to say that project capital expenditures and debt play no role in the income statement—they do, but not one-to-one. Specifically, capital expenditures reduce net income (in the income statement) only slowly through depreciation:

Year 1: The first $25 depreciation from the first year's $75 capital expenditures is accounted for.

Year 2: The second $25 depreciation from the first year's $75 capital expenditures is accounted for, plus the first $25 depreciation from the second year's $75 capital expenditures is accounted for. Thus, a total of $50 is depreciated.

Year 3: The third and final $25 remaining depreciation from the first year's $75 capital expenditures is accounted for, plus the second $25 depreciation from the second year's capital expenditures. Again, a total of $50 is depreciated.

Year 4: There is no more depreciation from the first year's capital expenditures. You only have the third installment of the second year's capital expenditures left. Thus, depreciation is $25.

You can visualize this as follows:

Year	1	2	3	4	5
Capital Expense	$75	$75			
Depreciation of First $75	$25	$25	$25		
Depreciation of Second $75		$25	$25	$25	
Sum Total Depreciation	$25	$50	$50	$25	$0

The principal on the loan, either its funding or its repayment, plays no role on the income statement. However, the interest paid on the loan does go onto the income statement.

13.2B DOING FINANCE

Here is the difference between full ownership and levered ownership.

Now, forget accounting for a moment and instead value the machine from a finance perspective. The firm consists of three components: the machine itself, the tax obligation, and the loan.

$$\text{NPV Project} = \text{NPV Machine} - \text{NPV Taxes}$$

$$\text{NPV Levered Ownership} = \text{NPV Machine} - \text{NPV Taxes} + \text{NPV Loan}$$

Full project ownership is equivalent to holding both the debt (including all liabilities) and equity (the machine), and earning the cash flows due to both creditors and shareholders. Levered equity ownership adds the project "loan" to the package. As full project owner (debt plus equity), in the first year, you must originally supply $50 more in capital than if you are just a levered equity owner, but in subsequent years, as full owner, you then do not need to worry about paying back a lender.

Look only at inflows and outflows of the first component of the firm—the machine's actual cash flows, without taxes and loan.

First work out the actual cash flows of the first component, the machine itself. Without the taxes and the loan, the machine produces the following:

$$\text{NPV}_{\text{machine}} = \frac{\$60 - \$75}{(1+12\%)^1} + \frac{\$60 - \$75}{(1+12\%)^2} + \frac{\$60}{(1+12\%)^3} + \frac{\$60}{(1+12\%)^4} + \frac{\$60}{(1+12\%)^5} + \frac{\$60}{(1+12\%)^6} \approx \$119.93$$

$$\text{NPV}_{\text{machine}} = \frac{C_1}{1+r_1} + \frac{C_2}{1+r_2} + \frac{C_3}{1+r_3} + \frac{C_4}{1+r_4} + \frac{C_5}{1+r_5} + \frac{C_6}{1+r_6}$$

The tax obligation is a negative-NPV project, which must be valued.

➤ Table 13.6, p. 458

➤ Discount factor on tax obligations, Section 17.7, p. 643

Unfortunately, corporate income tax—the second component—is an actual cost that cannot be ignored. Looking at Table 13.6, you see that Uncle Sam collects $14 in the first year, then $2 twice, then $12, and finally $22 twice. Assume that the stream of tax obligations has the same discount rate (12%) as that of the overall firm. (To value the future tax obligations, you need to know the appropriate discount factor. Unfortunately, we need to delay this issue until Chapter 17. It is both convenient and customary [if not exactly correct] to use the firm's overall cost of capital as the discount rate for its tax obligations.) With this cost-of-capital assumption, the net present cost of the tax liability is

$$\text{NPV}_{\text{tax liability}} = \frac{\$14}{1.12^1} + \frac{\$2}{1.12^2} + \frac{\$2}{1.12^3} + \frac{\$12}{1.12^4} + \frac{\$22}{1.12^5} + \frac{\$22}{1.12^6} \approx \$46.77$$

Put together,

Determine the project NPV.

$$\text{NPV}_{\text{project}} \approx \$119.93 - \$46.77 = \$73.16$$

$$\text{NPV Project} = \text{NPV Machine} - \text{NPV Taxes}$$

Now consider the third component—the loan. Assume that you are not the "full project owner," but only the "residual levered equity owner," so you do not extend the loan yourself. Instead, you would obtain a loan from a (hopefully) perfect capital market. Let us assume that your company "got what it paid for," a fair deal—a reasonable assumption for most large corporations. Your loan that provides \$50 and pays interest at a rate of 10% should thus be zero NPV. (This saves you the effort of having to compute the NPV of the loan.)

The loan usually is a "zero-NPV" project, unless you can get an unusually great deal or suffer an unusually bad deal on the loan.

$$\text{NPV}_{\text{loan}} = \$0$$

Be my guest, though, and make the effort:

$$\text{NPV}_{\text{loan}} = \frac{+\$50}{1.10^1} + \frac{-\$5}{1.10^2} + \frac{-\$5}{1.10^3} + \frac{-\$5}{1.10^4} + \frac{-\$5}{1.10^5} + \frac{(-\$50) + (-\$5)}{1.10^6} = \$0$$

Therefore, the project NPV with the loan, that is, levered equity ownership, is the same as the project NPV without the loan. This makes sense: You are not generating or destroying any value by borrowing from one bank rather than another. Therefore,

$$\text{NPV}_{\text{levered ownership}} = \$119.93 - \$46.77 + \$0 = \$73.16$$

$$\text{NPV}_{\text{levered ownership}} = \text{NPV Machine} - \text{NPV Taxes} + \text{NPV Loan}$$

Although the NPV remains the same, the cash flows to levered equity ownership are different from the cash flows to the project. The cash flows (and net income) are shown in Table 13.7. Note how different the cash flows and net income are. Net income is highest in years 5 and 6, but the levered cash flow in year 6 is negative. In contrast, in year 3—the year with the highest levered cash flow—net income is lowest.

Earnings and cash flows are often very different.

13.2C REVERSE-ENGINEERING ACCOUNTING INTO FINANCE

If you did not know about the details of this machine but saw only the financials, could you compute the correct firm value by discounting the net income? Discounting net income with a cost of capital of 12% would yield

Discounting the net income would *not* give you the true project NPV.

$$\begin{array}{l}\text{Incorrect}\\ \text{NPV}_{\text{via net income}}\end{array} = \frac{\$21}{1.12^1} + \frac{\$3}{1.12^2} + \frac{\$3}{1.12^3} + \frac{\$18}{1.12^4} + \frac{\$33}{1.12\%^5} + \frac{\$33}{1.12^6} \approx \$70.16$$

which is definitely not the correct answer of \$73.16. Neither would it be correct to discount the net income with a cost of capital of 10%,

$$\begin{array}{l}\text{Incorrect}\\ \text{NPV}_{\text{via net income}}\end{array} = \frac{\$21}{1.10^1} + \frac{\$3}{1.10^2} + \frac{\$3}{1.10^3} + \frac{\$18}{1.10^4} + \frac{\$33}{1.10^5} + \frac{\$33}{1.10^6} \approx \$75.24$$

TABLE 13.7 CASH FLOWS AND NET INCOME SUMMARY

	Year 1	2	3	4	5	6	Discount Rate	NPV
Cash Flow, Machine w/o Tax	−$15	−$15	+$60	+$60	+$60	+$60	12%	$119.93
Cash Flow, Uncle Sam	−$14	−$2	−$2	−$12	−$22	−$22	12%	−$46.77
Cash Flow, **Project, After Tax**	−$29	−$17	+$58	+$48	+$38	+$38	12%	$73.16
Cash Flow, Loan	+$50	−$5	−$5	−$5	−$5	−$55	10%	$0.00
Residual Cash Flow:								
Levered Ownership	+$21	−$22	+$53	+$43	+$33	−$17		$73.16
For Comparison:								
Net Income	$21	$3	$3	$18	$33	$33	N/A	N/A

Because investors are risk averse, the discount rate (also called the cost of capital or required expected rate of return) is higher for the machine than it is for the loan.

Instead, you must reverse-engineer the economic cash flows from the corporate financials.

How can you reverse-engineer the correct cash flows for the NPV analysis from the financials? You first need to translate the financials back into the cash flows that NPV analysis can use. You just need to retrace your steps. You have both the income statement and cash flow statement at your disposal. First, to obtain the machine cash flow, you can apply the formula

		Year 1	Year 2	
	EBIT	+$35	+$10	
+	Depreciation	+$25	+$50	
"+"	(−) Capital Expenditures	+(−$75)	+(−$75)	(13.1)
=	Cash Flow, Project, Before Tax	−$15	−$15	

➤ Table 13.6, p. 458

to the numbers from Table 13.6. You add back the depreciation, because it *was not* an actual cash outflow, and you subtract the capital expenditures, because they *were* actual cash flows. I find the formula most intuitive if I think of the "depreciation + capital expenditures" terms as undoing the accountants' smoothing of the cost of machines over multiple periods.

IMPORTANT: The main operation to take care of long-term accruals in the conversion from net income into cash flows is to undo the smoothing—add back the depreciation and subtract out the capital expense.

SIDE NOTE: The formula signs themselves seem ambiguous, because accountants use different sign conventions in different spots. For example, because capital expenditures are usually quoted as negative terms on the cash flow statement, in order to subtract capital expenditures, you just add the (negative) number. In the formula below, you want to subtract corporate income tax, which appears on the income statement (Table 13.6) as a positive. Therefore, you have to subtract the positive. Sigh . . . I try to clarify the meaning (and to warn you) with the quotes around the + in the formulas themselves.

Finish the reverse-engineering by subtracting off taxes.

Now you need to subtract corporate income taxes (and, again, look at the numbers themselves to clarify the signs in your mind; income tax is sometimes quoted as a negative, sometimes as a positive). This gives you the following after-tax project cash flow:

		Year 1	Year 2	
	EBIT	+\$35	+\$10	
+	Depreciation	+\$25	+\$50	
"+"	(−)Capital Expenditures	+(−\$75)	+(−\$75)	(13.2)
−	(+)Corporate Income Tax	−(+\$14)	−(+\$2)	
=	Cash Flow, Project, After Tax	−\$29	−\$17	

A different way to skin our cat—to reverse-engineer it.

There is an alternative equivalent method to get these numbers. Net income already has corporate income tax subtracted out, but it also has interest expense subtracted out. You get the same cash flow if you start with net income instead of EBIT but add back the interest expense:

		Year 1	Year 2
	Net Income	+\$21	+\$3
+	Depreciation	+\$25	+\$50
"+"	(−)Capital Expenditures	+(−\$75)	+(−\$75)
+	Interest Expense	+\$0	+\$5
=	Cash Flow, Project, After Tax	−\$29	−\$17

Investors (equity and debt together) must thus come up with \$29 in the first year and \$17 in the second year. (You can read the cash flows in later years from line 3 of Table 13.7.)

The cash flow to levered equity shareholders takes care of money coming in from and going out to creditors.

If the project is financed partly by borrowing, then what part of the \$29 and \$17 can be financed by creditors, and what residual part must be financed by you? In the first year, your creditors provide \$50; in the second year, creditors get back \$5. Therefore, levered equity actually receives a positive net cash flow of \$21 in the first year, and a negative cash flow of \$22 in the second year. Therefore, with the loan financed from the outside, you must add all loan inflows (principal proceeds) and

ANECDOTE Solid Financial Analysis

EBITDA was all the rage among consultants and Wall Street for many years, because it seems both closer to cash flows than EBIT and more impervious to managerial earnings manipulation through accruals. Sadly, discounting EBITDA can be worse than discounting EBIT *if* capital expenditures are not netted out—and they usually are not netted out. (Not subtracting capital expenditures, and not subtracting depreciation is equivalent to assuming that product falls like manna from heaven. EBIT may spread capital expenditures over time periods in a strange way, but at least it does not totally forget it!) Sometimes, a little bit of knowledge is more dangerous than no knowledge.

In June 2003, a Bear Stearns analyst valued American Italian Pasta, a small NYSE-listed pasta maker. Unfortunately, Herb Greenberg from TheStreet.com discovered that he forgot to subtract capital expenditures—instead, he had added them. This mistake had increased the value of American Italian Pasta from $19 to $58.49 per share (then trading at $43.65). Bear Stearns admitted the mistake and came up with a new valuation in which Bear Stearns boosted the estimate of the company's operating cash flows and dropped its estimate of the cost of capital. Presto! The NPV of this company was suddenly $68 per share. How fortunate that Bear Stearns' estimates were so robust to basic errors. Incidentally, American Italian Pasta traded at $30 in mid-2004, just above $20 by the end of 2004, and at around $10 by the end of 2005.

subtract all loan outflows (both principal and interest). Therefore, the cash flow for levered equity shareholders is as follows:

		Year 1	Year 2
	EBIT	+$35	+$10
+	Depreciation	+$25	+$50
"+"	(−)Capital Expenditures	+(−$75)	+(−$75)
−	Corporate Income Tax	−$14	−$2
=	Cash Flow, Project	−$29	−$17
+	Net Debt Issue	+$50	$0
−	Interest Expense	$0	−$5
=	Cash Flow, Levered Equity Ownership	+$21	−$22

A different way to skin our cat.

Again, net income already has both corporate income tax and interest expense subtracted out, so the same result comes out if you instead use the following formula:

		Year 1	Year 2
	Net Income	+$21	+$3
+	Depreciation	+$25	+$50
"+"	(−)Capital Expenditures	+(−$75)	+(−$75)
+	Net Debt Issue	+$50	$0
=	Cash Flow, Levered Equity Ownership	+$21	−$22

(13.3)

SOLVE NOW!

Q 13.4 Show that Formulas 13.1 through 13.3 yield the cash flows in years 3 through 6 in Table 13.7.

Q 13.5 Using the same cash flows as in the NPV analysis in Table 13.7, how would the project NPV change if you used a 10% cost of capital (instead of 12%) on the tax liability?

13.2D DEPRECIATION NUANCES

I mentioned earlier that you should read depreciation off the cash flow statement, not the income statement. I now want to explain a little more about real-world accounting for depreciation.

Why you need to get the depreciation number from the cash flow statement.

Depreciation can come in three different forms: **depreciation**, **depletion**, and **amortization**. They are all "allocated expenses" and not actual cash outflows. The name differences come from the asset types to which they apply.

Depreciation comes in different forms with different names.

Depreciation applies to **tangible assets**, such as factories.

Depletion applies to **natural resources**, such as mines.

Amortization applies to **intangible assets**, such as patents, copyrights, licenses, franchises, and so on. As late as the 1970s, average intangible assets for publicly traded U.S. firms were below 10%. Today, it is these intangible assets that have become the overwhelming majority of public firms' assets. (The exact amortization rules are laid down in FASB Rule 142; they are complex and much beyond our scope.)

Because depreciation, depletion, and amortization are conceptually the same thing, they are often lumped together under the catch-all phrase "depreciation," a convention that we are following.

The reason why you need to use the cash flow statement to learn about depreciation is that the income statement does not report an exact equivalent for the depreciation that we wrote down for the machine on our hypothetical income statement. Instead, on the income statement, corporations can break out the depreciation (as we did) or decide to roll it into either "cost of goods sold" or "selling, general & administrative expenses." (Doing so does not affect reported net income.) For a machine, chances are that a real firm would not have reported it separately, but would have rolled it into COGS. In PepsiCo's case, most—but not all—depreciation was actually lumped into SG&A. PepsiCo's amortization on the income statement contains only the depreciation of some nonphysical plant assets.

In real life, do not use the depreciation and amortization on the income statement to extract economic cash flows.

IMPORTANT:

- Do not use depreciation or amortization figures from the income statement to undo the accounting adjustments for capital expenses. These figures are incomplete. You must use the depreciation figures from the cash flow statement.
- The most common use of the memorized rule "add depreciation to net income" has many users read both net income and depreciation off the same income statement. This is wrong.

Therefore, the only complete picture of depreciation of all kinds, equivalent to our depreciation entries in our machine example, can be found on the cash flow statement. For PepsiCo, this is the $1,082 in line 3 of the cash flow statement in

Go to the cash flow statement for the depreciation number that is the equivalent of what we had in the machine example.

Table 13.4. It is this number that is the exact equivalent of the depreciation row ($25, $50, $50, $25, $0, $0) for the machine in Table 13.6, not the $165 million amortization that PepsiCo reports on line 6 of its income statement in Table 13.3.

SOLVE NOW!

Q 13.6 Rework the example (income statement, cash flow statement excerpts, cash flows, and NPV) with the following parameters:

Project		Available Financing—Executed	
Real Physical Lifespan	5 years	Debt Capacity	$100
Cost	$120, year 1	Debt Interest Rate	8%/year
Gross Output	$80/year	Accounting Treatment	
− Input Costs	$6/year	Depreciation Method	Linear
− Selling Costs	$8/year	Accounting Life	4 years
= Net Output	$66/year		
Overall Cost of Capital	8%/year		
Corporate Tax Rate (τ)	50%/year		

Debt does not require interest payment in year 1. The world is risk neutral, because the debt and the project require the same expected rate of return (cost of capital).

Q 13.7 For the machine example in the text, do both the financials and the cash flow analysis using monthly discounting. Assume that the loan is taken at the beginning of the year, and most expenses and income occur pro rata. (Warning: Use a computer spreadsheet. Do not work this question by hand!)

13.3 A BOTTOM-UP EXAMPLE—DEFERRED TAXES

The IRS depreciation schedules (and some other details) are not the same as those in the public financials.

Our next real-world complication to attack is the fact that GAAP and the IRS require different depreciation schedules. To extract the economic cash flows, you need to learn how to undo the accounting for what the firm reports on its public financials and what the firm actually pays to the IRS.

In an example, we have the IRS allow for faster depreciation.

Assume that the above example illustrated what GAAP requires the firm to disclose on its financial statements. The novelty is that we now assume that the IRS allows you to depreciate your plant in a different "accelerated fashion." Let's say the IRS depreciation schedule is not $25 each for 3 years (as reported in your public financials), but $60 in the first year and $15 in the second year.

Year	1	2	3	4
Capital Expense	$75	$75		
Depreciation of First $75	$60	$15		
Depreciation of Second $75		$60	$15	
Sum Total Depreciation	$60	$75	$15	$0

Consequently, although the accounting statement construction logic for the IRS is exactly the same as it is for your publicly reported financials, the numbers on your undisclosed IRS financials are necessarily different from those in your reported public financials:

IRS Income Statement (Not Disclosed)

	Year	1	2	3	4	5	6
	Sales	$70	$70	$70	$70	$70	$70
–	COGS	$5	$5	$5	$5	$5	$5
–	SG&A	$5	$5	$5	$5	$5	$5
=	EBITDA	$60	$60	$60	$60	$60	$60
–	IRS Depreciation	$60	$75	$15	$0	$0	$0
=	EBIT, IRS	$0	–$15	$45	$60	$60	$60
–	Interest Expense, IRS	$0	$5	$5	$5	$5	$5
=	EAIBT (or EBT), IRS	$0	–$20	$40	$55	$55	$55
–	**Corporate Income Tax (at 40%)**	**$0**	**–$8**	**$16**	**$22**	**$22**	**$22**

(The IRS is not interested in a net income figure, so there is no reason to compute it.) Now compare the actual true taxes on your IRS financials against the GAAP allocated income taxes in Table 13.6:

➤ Table 13.6, p. 458

	Year:	1	2	3	4	5	6
Public Reported Income Statement	Pretend Tax	$14	$2	$2	$12	$22	$22
Undisclosed IRS Calculation	Actual Tax	$0	–$8	$16	$22	$22	$22

Both lines contain $74 in total taxes, but your real IRS taxes are lower in the first 2 years and higher in the next 2 years. This is because the IRS permitted a faster depreciation schedule than GAAP did. (Good for you! The firm receives cash earlier.)

Unfortunately, firms do not disclose their IRS financials, so you cannot work with them. Fortunately, publicly traded firms are required to report the differences between "IRS real taxes" and "GAAP pretend taxes." This is done in a "coded" fashion on the balance sheet and called accumulated **deferred taxes**. It is the "cumulated differences between GAAP and IRS taxes." To understand this better, think of a hypothetical

The deferred tax account on the balance sheet allows you to learn the real taxes paid.

annual flow number that would be the amount by which you have overreported taxes on your financials:

Year:	1	2	3	4	5	6
"Deferred Tax" Annual Overreporting	$14	$10	−$14	−$10	$0	$0

This is still not reported. However, its cumulative sum is reported:

Year:	1	2	3	4	5	6
Reported "Deferred Tax" Account	$14	$24	$10	$0	$0	$0

This deferred tax is reported as a liability on the balance sheet. An intuitive way to think of this number is as the amount by which your reported financial statements have overstated your real income taxes (and thus understated your real income) to date. Our example firm had overreported on the disclosed financials the taxes that it had paid by $24 by the end of year 2 ($14 in year 1 and $10 in year 2).

Here is how you work your way back to uncover the actual taxes paid to the IRS.

Your task is again reverse-engineering—how can you undo the fake income tax term and replace it with a real income tax? Here is the procedure:

1. Compute the annual overreporting of deferred tax from the reported deferred tax account. To do this, compute the change in this deferred tax account every year:

Year:	1	2	3	4	5	6
Reported "Deferred Tax" Liability	$14	$24	$10	$0	$0	$0
Consecutive Annual Increase	$14	$10	−$14	−$10	$0	$0

2. To recover actual taxes paid, subtract the change from the GAAP-reported taxes paid:

	Year:	1	2	3	4	5	6
	Reported GAAP Taxes	$14	$2	$2	$12	$22	$22
−	Consecutive Annual Increase	$14	$10	−$14	−$10	$0	$0
=	Actual Taxes Paid to the IRS	$0	−$8	$16	$22	$22	$22

3. For financial figures that are before tax, subtract the actual taxes paid instead of the GAAP taxes paid. For example,

	Year:	1	2	3	4	5	6
	Cash Flow, Machine w/o Tax	−$15	−$15	$60	$60	$60	$60
−	True Taxes, IRS	$0	−$8	$16	$22	$22	$22
=	Cash Flow, **Project**	−$15	−$7	$44	$38	$38	$38

For financial figures that are after tax, such as after-tax cash flows, first add back the GAAP taxes that your after-tax figure had already subtracted. Then subtract the actual IRS taxes paid instead. Or, simpler, just add increases in deferred tax. For example, add these changes to the after-tax cash flows that you computed in Table 13.7 on page 462:

	Year:	1	2	3	4	5	6
	Earlier Formula, Cash Flow, **Project, After Tax**	−$29	−$17	$58	$48	$38	$38
+	Changes in Deferred Tax	$14	$10	−$14	−$10	$0	$0
=	Better Formula Cash Flows, **Project**	−$15	−$7	$44	$38	$38	$38

In sum, the new and improved formula to extract cash flows from financial statements is

Reverse-engineering: Add changes in deferred taxes to the cash flows from the earlier formula.

		Year 1	Year 2
	EBIT	+$35	+$10
+	Depreciation	+$25	+$50
"+"	(−)Capital Expenditures	+(−$75)	+(−$75)
−	(+)Corporate Income Tax	−(+$14)	−(+$2)
=	Cash Flow, Project, After Tax, GAAP Taxes	−$29	−$17
+	Changes in Deferred Taxes	+$14	+$10
=	Cash Flows, Project, After Tax, Real	−$15	−$7

That's it. You are done with taking care of the differences between the GAAP and IRS taxes.

SOLVE NOW!

Q 13.8 What are "deferred taxes"? On which of the four financial statements do they appear?

Q 13.9 Assume a firm reports the following information:

	2007	2006	2005
Deferred Tax Liability	$110	$332	$223

You have calculated the after-tax cash flows for a project based on GAAP to be $300 in 2007 and −$100 in 2006. What are the actual after-tax cash flows for the project?

13.4 A BOTTOM-UP EXAMPLE—SHORT-TERM ACCRUALS AND WORKING CAPITAL

More accruals are hidden in working capital.

In addition to long-term accruals and deferred taxes, you also need to learn how to undo short-term accruals. To run a business day to day requires cash. Firms must put money into cash registers (to make change), into inventories (to have something to sell), and into extending credit to buyers (to get them to bite). This is called **working capital** or current assets. Current assets are **cash**, **accounts receivable**, and **inventories**. We will mostly work with **net working capital**, which are current assets minus current liabilities, often just called working capital (without the "net" qualification).

TABLE 13.8 MULTIYEAR WORKING CAPITAL

	Year	0	1	2	3
Finance	1. Sales (Net Income) Made, Payment Later	$0	$100	$300	$0
	2. Actual Cash Receipts (for NPV Cash Flow)	$0	$0	$100	$300
Accounting	3. Reported Net Income	$0	$100	$300	$0
	4. Reported Accounts Receivable	$0	$100	$300	$0

I have made up the sales number in line 1. The actual cash receipts in line 2 arise because customers always pay 1 year later. Lines 3 and 4 show how accountants book these sales and payment patterns. (Ultimately, your task will be to translate accounting numbers back into cash receipts numbers.)

Current liabilities are **accounts payable**, **bank overdrafts**, **taxes payable**, and other soon-due bills.

$$\text{Net Working Capital} = (\text{Current Assets}) - (\text{Current Liabilities})$$
$$= (\text{Cash} + \text{Accounts Receivable} + \text{Inventories})$$
$$- (\text{Accounts Payable} + \text{Bank Overdrafts} + \text{Taxes Payable})$$

Net income books cash before it comes in, so accounts receivable need to be taken out.

The cash flow effects of working capital changes are best explained with an example. Say that a firm sells $100 of goods on credit at year 1. The firm books $100 as net income. But because the $100 is not yet available, the firm also books $100 into accounts receivable. To compute actual cash flows, recognize that the cash has not yet materialized: You need to subtract the $100 accounts receivable from the $100 net income.

These differences between cash flows and net income are year-to-year *changes* in working capital.

This becomes more interesting if you consider multiple years. For example, the firm in Table 13.8 always sells on credit and is always paid by its customers the following year. An NPV analysis requires the firm's actual cash receipts in line 2, but accountants have provided only the information in lines 3 and 4. How do you get back the information in line 2? Year 1 has already been discussed: You subtracted accounts receivable from net income to obtain the actual cash inflows of $0. Year 2 is more interesting: The firm previously had accounts receivable of $100, but now has accounts receivable of $300. It is the +$200 (= $300 − $100) *change* in accounts receivable that needs to be subtracted from the $300 in net income in order to infer the actual cash receipts of $100. In year 3, the firm no longer grows and is liquidated, so the remaining receivable turn into cash that can be recaptured from the business. Again, the formula to obtain the NPV cash flow (line 2) subtracts the change in working capital (accounts receivable) of $0 − $300 = −$300 from the $0 net income to conclude that you got a +$300 cash inflow. Table 13.9 shows these calculations. (Incidentally, recall how you started this subsection with the year 1 computation: You subtracted $100 in accounts receivable from the $100 net income. This worked only because the accounts receivable was the same as the *change* in accounts receivable, because the original accounts receivable was zero.)

TABLE 13.9 MULTIYEAR WORKING CAPITAL

	Year	0	1	2	3
Finance	1. Sales (Net Income) Made, Payment Later	\$0	\$100	\$300	\$0
	2. Actual Cash Receipts (for NPV Cash Flow)	\$0	\$0	\$100	\$300
Accounting	3. Reported Net Income	\$0	\$100	\$300	\$0
	4. Reported Accounts Receivable	\$0	\$100	\$300	\$0
	Your Computations				
5. Change in Accounts Receivable		*\$0*	*+\$100*	*+\$200*	*−\$300*
6. Net Income (line 3) − Change in Accounts Receivable (line 5)		*\$0*	*\$0*	*+\$100*	*+\$300*

Line 6 recovers line 2 from the financials.

ANECDOTE Working Capital Management

Entrepreneurs usually fail for one of two reasons, and both are common: The first is that the business is just not a good idea to begin with. There is not much you can do about this. The second is that the business is too good of an idea and the entrepreneur is not equipped to handle the success. The growth in sales consumes so much cash for increases in working capital that the firm fails to pay back its own loans: The cash is tied up in production, or in inventory, or in credit extended to customers (payment to be received), when instead it is needed to flow back to the bank. For growing firms, proper working capital management is an issue of first-order importance.

Working capital already contains other delayed payments, making our lives easier.

Other short-term accruals that are components of working capital work similarly. For example, although corporate income tax is deducted on the income statement for the year in which the earnings have occurred, firms do not have to immediately pay these taxes. Instead, they can often defer them—at least until (the corporate equivalent of) April 15 of the following year. To the extent that more taxes can be delayed, more cash is available than is suggested by net income. Therefore, delayed taxes must be added back to net income when computing finance cash flows. Of course, at some point in the future, these taxes payable will have to be paid, and they will then have to be counted as a cash outflow of the firm. But, for now, the permitted delay in payment is like a government loan at zero interest—and one that the accounting item net income ignores.

IMPORTANT: The main operation to take care of short-term accruals in the conversion from net income into cash flows is to undo the smoothing—subtract *changes* in net working capital. (Equivalently, you can add *decreases* in net working capital.)

SIDE NOTE: Alas, as with capital expenditures, the cash flow statement has its sign conventions. The change in cash, accounts receivable, and inventories is recorded as a negative. But accounts payable do not have the opposite sign from accounts receivable, though they are already an outflow (negative); they are left as is. As a result, to compute the firm's net working capital from its line items (accounts receivable, accounts payable, etc.), you do not subtract current liabilities (e.g., accounts payable) from current assets (e.g., accounts receivable), but add them together.

Here is an example of the accounting sign conventions. Table 13.4 (PepsiCo's cash flows) listed PepsiCo's changes in working capital as 84, 416, and 79 (in million dollars) for the years 2001, 2000, and 1999:

Cash Flow Statement	December		
	2001	2000	1999
Current Assets			
Accounts Receivable	+7	−52	−141
Inventories	−75	−51	−202
Prepaid Expenses, Etc.	−6	−35	−209
Current Liabilities			
Accounts Payable, Etc.	−236	+219	+357
Corporate Income Tax, Payable	+394	+335	+274
Adjustments for Change in Operating Working Capital	+84	+416	+79

This excludes the effects of acquisitions and dispositions. All figures are in millions of dollars.

Because these figures come from the cash flow statement, to obtain the adjustments for change in operating working capital, all figures are simply added up, not netted out! (The sign of current liabilities has already been reversed for you.) If you stumble onto the fact that these numbers cannot be inferred from other parts of the financial statements, this is because these numbers exclude the effects of acquisitions and dispositions, as well as nonoperating working capital (a catch-all category for a number of items).

Where would you find changes in cash (in the register) itself? These are *not* in the changes of working capital. Instead, they are what you find at the bottom of the cash flow statement. In other words, the very purpose of the cash flow statement is to tell you by how much the cash account on the balance sheet is changing year to year.

Expand our valuation formula for another source of cash.

You can now expand our formulas to include changes in working capital:

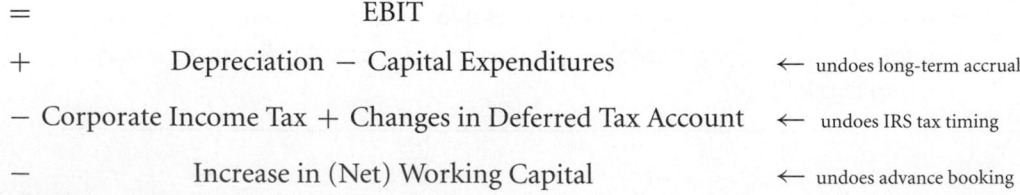

	Project Economic Cash Flow	
=	EBIT	
+	Depreciation − Capital Expenditures	← undoes long-term accruals
−	Corporate Income Tax + Changes in Deferred Tax Account	← undoes IRS tax timing
−	Increase in (Net) Working Capital	← undoes advance booking

(In this formula, I am quoting the purchasing of assets in capital expenditures as a positive number. If you are using the negative number from the cash flow statement, don't subtract it, but add it.)

SOLVE NOW!

Q 13.10 A firm reports the following financials.

Year	0	1	2	3	4	5	6
Reported Sales (=Net Income)	\$0	\$100	\$100	\$300	\$300	\$100	\$0
Reported Accounts Receivable	\$0	\$100	\$120	\$340	\$320	\$120	\$0

Can you describe the firm's customer payment patterns? Extract the cash flows.

Q 13.11 Construct the financials for a firm that has quarterly sales and net income of \$100, \$200, \$300, \$200, and \$100. Half of all customers pay immediately, while the other half always pay *two* quarters after purchase.

Q 13.12 ADVANCED: Amazonia can pay suppliers after it has sold to customers. Amazonia has 25% margins and is reporting the following

Month	Jan	Feb	Mar	Apr	May
Reported Sales	\$0	\$100	\$100	\$400	\$0
Reported Net Income	\$0	\$25	\$25	\$100	\$0
Reported Accounts Payable	\$0	\$75	\$75	\$300	\$0

What are Amazonia's actual cash flows?

13.5 EARNINGS MANAGEMENT

There is considerable discretion in financial reporting.

Even though the United States has the tightest accounting regulations of any country, managers still have a lot of discretion when it comes to financials. There is also no clear line where accounting judgments become unethical or even criminal. The border zone between ethical and unethical behavior is a ramp of gray—it may be easy to make a judgment when one is in the clean white zone or in the clean black zone, but in between it is often a slippery slope.

Not only earnings—but also cash flows—can be managed.

You already know that managers must make many judgments when it comes to accrual accounting. For example, managers can judge overoptimistically how many products customers will return, how much debt will not be repaid, how much inventory will spoil, how long equipment will last, whether a payment is an expense (fully subtracted from earnings) or an investment (an asset that is depreciated over time), or how much of an expense is "unusual." However, manipulation is possible not only for earnings and accruals but also for cash flows—though doing so may be more difficult and costly. For example, if a firm designates some of its short-term securities as "trading instruments," their sale can then create extra cash—what was not cash before now counts as cash! Similarly, you already know that firms can reduce inventory, delay payments to suppliers, and lean on customers to accelerate payment—all of which will generate immediate cash, but doing so will also possibly anger suppliers and customers so much that it will hurt the business in the long run. Firms can also sell off their receivables at a discount, which may raise the immediate cash at hand but reduce the profit that the firm will ultimately receive. A particularly interesting form of earnings management occurs when a firm aggressively sells products on credit. The sales could be immediately booked as earnings, with the loans counting as investments. Of course, if the customers default, all the company has accomplished is giving away its product for free.

Comparing (short-term) accruals to those of similar firms (industry, size, and growth rate) can sometimes give you good warning signs.

One quick measure of comparing how aggressive or conservative financials are is to compare the firm to other similar firms on the basis of the ratio of its short-term accruals divided by its sales. It is important that "similar" here means firms that are not only in the same industry but also growing at roughly the same rate. The reason is that growing firms usually consume a lot of cash—an established firm will show higher cash flows than a growing firm. If the firm is unusual in having much higher accruals—especially short-term accruals—than comparable firms, it is a warning sign that this firm deserves more scrutiny. Managers who decide to manipulate their numbers to jack up their earnings more than likely will try to manage their accruals aggressively in order to create higher earnings, too. Of course, this does not mean that all managers who manage their accruals aggressively do so to deceive the market and will therefore underperform later on. A manager who is very optimistic about the future may treat accruals aggressively—believing in few returns, great sales, and a better future all around. Indeed, as noted earlier, the slope from managerial optimism to illegal earnings manipulation is slippery. Finally, another earnings warning sign for the wary investor is when a firm changes its fiscal year—this is sometimes done in order to make it more difficult to compare financials to past performance or to financials of other firms in the same industry.

SOLVE NOW!

Q 13.13 Are short-term accruals or long-term accruals easier to manipulate?

Q 13.14 Give some examples of how a firm can depress the earnings that it currently reports in order to report higher earnings later.

13.6 EXTRACTING ECONOMIC CASH FLOWS FROM PEPSICO'S FINANCIALS

The PepsiCo cash flow statement looks very much like our construction.

Now, if you take another look at the complete PepsiCo cash flow statement in Table 13.4 (remember that all numbers are in millions), you can immediately see the procedures that we have just discussed—starting with net income of $2,662 (line 1), adding back depreciation of $1,082 (line 3), subtracting capital spending of $1,324 (line 17), adding (changes in) deferred income taxes of $162 (line 7), and adding the decrease in net working capital of $84 (line 15).

Now "wing it" for PepsiCo—each firm does it a little differently.

There are also some other items that have not been explained, so let's tie up these loose ends. There are two pieces of good news here. First, you now understand the main logic of what is going on. Second, you can now rely on the accountants to do most of the hard work for you. The logic of how to handle the remaining items in the cash flow statement is either similar to what we have already discussed and/or obvious from the name. For instance, you hopefully won't need an explanation from me for "bottling equity income, net" on line 2 in Table 13.4, which is just below "net income." It is probably just another form of net income—even if I knew its meaning better than you, it would not help if I explained it to you, because every company has its own unique collection of named items in their financial statements. Like me, you will have to "wing it"—or, better, seek to understand the specific company you are analyzing.

Here are two more potentially important items: goodwill and miscellani.

There are two more common items on cash flow statements, which we have not discussed, however. One is called **investment in goodwill**. I have no idea who came up with this name, because it is a total misnomer. It actually has to do with cash laid out when our firm has acquired other firms. PepsiCo apparently had not made any large recent acquisitions, so it did not report goodwill. The other is miscellaneous increases in net other assets. They consolidate a number of other items on the cash flow statement, for which I do not have a better category.

Using our semi-complete cash flow formula to assess PepsiCo's project cash flows.

Putting short-term and long-term accruals and other sources/uses of cash together yields the complete formula in Table 13.10. You can use it to estimate the cash flows for an NPV analysis from financial statements. Not surprisingly, when you take both long-term and short-term accruals into account, as well as a slew of other items, the formula begins to look almost like PepsiCo's own cash flow statement, though rearranged. It starts with income before taxes and after interest of \$4,029 (from the income statement). To make this income before taxes and before interest, add back the interest expense. PepsiCo actually earned net interest of \$8, so this becomes \$4,021. This is EBIT. Now we really get started. Subtract reported income taxes of \$1,367. This gets you to net income after taxes before interest expense, an amount of \$2,654 that is called "net operating profit." Now adjust for when taxes were really paid rather than accounted for, adding back deferred taxes of \$162. Now undo the accruals. For long-term accruals, add back depreciation of \$1,082 and subtract capital expenditures of \$1,324. For short-term accruals, add the \$84 decrease in working capital. Next, there are a number of miscellaneous operating items, which differ from firm to firm: bottling equity of −\$160, merger-related charges of \$83 (\$356 − \$273), deferred ESOP compensation of \$48, and other charges of \$31 + \$209. Together, these were a cash inflow of \$211 (double negative). This left PepsiCo with \$2,869 of cash from operations. Of this amount, \$432 was used for net acquisitions, \$500 went into more short-term investments (which are actually almost like cash), and \$381 disappeared through other channels. This left PepsiCo's financial claimants—debt and equity together—with \$1,556.

Now apportioning the PepsiCo cash flows to creditors and shareholders.

With \$1,556 cash flows generated by PepsiCo's projects, all that is left is to apportion them between creditors and shareholders. Shareholders receive inflows from new debt issued, and pay interest and principal. New debt plus principal repayment is called "net issuance of debt." For PepsiCo, this amounted to −\$341, which means that PepsiCo actually paid down debt. This left shareholders with \$1,215. Shareholders also have to pay interest. In PepsiCo's case, shareholders actually earned \$8 in interest. This left them with \$1,223.

TABLE 13.10 A Formula to Compute Cash Flows for a Present Value Analysis

			PepsiCo, 2001	Financial Statement Source
		Earnings after Interest before Taxes	$4,029	Income Statement (IS), L16
	+	Interest Expense (and Bottling Equity Income)	+ ($8)	IS, L13 + L14 + L15
=		Earnings before Interest and Taxes (EBIT)	= $4,021	IS, L10
	–	Corporate Income Tax	– $1,367	IS, L17
=		Net Operating Profit	= $2,654	(also Net Income Minus Interest Expense)
	+	Changes in Deferred Taxes	+ $162	Cash Flow Statement (CFS), L7
	+	Depreciation	+ $1,082	CFS, L3
=		Gross Cash Flow	= $3,898	
	–	Capital Expenditures	– $1,324	CFS, L17
	–	Changes in Working Capital (incl. Taxes Payable, etc.)	– ($84)	CFS, L15
	–	Investment in Goodwill		(usually CFS; PepsiCo reported none.)
	–	Miscellaneous Increases in Net Other Assets	– ($211)	CFS, L2 + L4 + L5 + L6 + L8 + L9
=		Free Cash Flow from Operations	= $2,869	
	–	Acquisitions and Divestitures	– $432	CFS, L18 + L19 + L20
	–	Short-Term Investments	– $500	CFS, L21 + L22 + L23
	–	Miscellaneous Investing	– $381	CFS, L24
=		Total Project Firm Cash Flow to Financial Debt and Equity	= $1,556	(also CFS L16 + L25 – (IS L13 + L14 + L15))
	+	Net Issuance of Debt	+ ($341)	CFS, L26 + L27 + L28 + L29 + L30
	–	Interest Expense	– ($8)	IS, L13 + L14 + L15
=		Total Cash Flow to Levered Equity	= $1,223	

This table follows the accounting convention of reporting negative numbers in parentheses. Be careful—subtracting negative numbers yields positives. Keeping signs correct is often the most difficult aspect of this task.

Please do not consider our cash flow formula to be the perfect, end-all formula to compute NPV cash flows. No formula can cover *all* items in *all* companies. Even for PepsiCo, we had to lump together some items and ignore others (such as foreign exchange effects). Again, every business operates and reports differently. Still, the formula in Table 13.10 is a good start for estimating realized cash flows for an NPV analysis for most firms in the real world, and for understanding the link between earnings and cash flows.

We have a suggestive cash flow formula, not a perfect catch-all one.

IMPORTANT: The easiest way to extract economic cash flows for a present value analysis is to rely on the accounting cash flow statement. We only need to take care of the fact that accountants consider interest a cost of doing business, whereas financiers consider it a payout to capital providers.

Project cash flows (CF) are due to financial creditors and shareholders together and are computed as

$$\begin{aligned}\text{Project Cash Flow} &= \text{Cash Flow from Operating Activity}\\ &\quad + \text{Cash Flow from Investing Activity}\\ &\quad + \text{Interest Expense} \qquad (13.4)\end{aligned}$$

Net income, a component of cash flow from operating activity, has had interest expense subtracted out. But interest expense is cash that is being returned to (debt) investors. Thus, to obtain the total amount of cash flows generated by the project and available (paid out to) the sum total of both creditors and shareholders, the interest expense (from the income statement) must be added back.

Equity cash flows (CF) are available only to levered equity shareholders:

$$\begin{aligned}\text{Equity Cash Flow} &= \text{Cash Flow from Operating Activity}\\ &\quad + \text{Cash Flow from Investing Activity}\\ &\quad + \text{Net Issuance of Debt}\\ &= \text{Project Cash Flow} \qquad (13.5)\\ &\quad + \text{Net Issuance of Debt} - \text{Interest Expense}\end{aligned}$$

On Wall Street, analysts also call the cash flow to financial debt and equity **free cash flow**. Sometimes, they work with an abbreviated formula:

A common shortcut formula: "free cash flow."

$$\begin{aligned}\text{Free Cash Flow} = &\quad \text{EBIT} - \text{Taxes}\\ &+ \text{Depletion \& Depreciation \& Amortization}\\ &- \text{Capital Expenditures} - \text{Increases in Working Capital}\end{aligned}$$

The idea is to determine the following: If you were to take over the company, seize activities like acquisitions, and (to make your computation simpler) ignore items that are often not as large (like deferred taxes), how much cash could you wring out of the firm? For PepsiCo, this would have been $4,021 − $1,367 + $1,082 − $1,324 − (−$84) = $2,496.

Here is a much easier and foolproof method *if* you have the cash flow statement.

Fortunately, you can often avoid having to construct the cash flow with this long formula yourself. For a firm that has reported full financials, you can rely on the corporate **cash flow statement** itself. After all, it tries to construct most of the information for you. Its big categories, including some for which we just had a vague miscellaneous designation in our long formula, are cash flows from operating activity and cash flows from investing activity. You can use this sum instead of fiddling with the components. There is only one difference between what accountants consider cash flows and what financiers consider cash flows—it is interest payments. Accountants consider interest payments an expense necessary to run the business. Financiers consider them a distribution to the firm's financiers. If you take care of this detail, you can then rely on our accounting friends.

PepsiCo's cash flow, the easy way.

Will these formulas give you the same result? Apply them to PepsiCo. Adding **total operating activity** of +$4,201 and **total investing activity** of −$2,637 gives $1,564 in **operating activity net of investing activity**. Finally, you need to add back any interest expense that was taken out from net income. (After all, the project generated these funds and they were paid out, just as dividends are paid out.) In PepsiCo's case, it is not an interest expense, but net interest income, so the cash flow that you would use in an NPV analysis of the business of PepsiCo for 2001 is

$$\text{Project Cash Flow} = \$4{,}201 + (-\$2{,}637) + (-\$8) = \$1{,}556$$
$$\text{Project Cash Flow} = \text{Operating} + \text{Investing} + \text{Interest Expense}$$

(PepsiCo is the rare company that did not pay interest income, but rather earned interest income in 2001!) These are the cash flows accruing to all claimants together, debt and equity. You are still interested in the cash flow that is earned by PepsiCo's levered equity (without the creditors). You need to add cash obtained from **net issuance of debt** (the difference of debt principal that was raised and debt principal that was repaid, which you can read from the cash flow statement), and you need to subtract interest that was paid:

$$\text{Equity Cash Flows} = \$1{,}556 + (-\$341) - (-\$8) = \$1{,}223$$
$$\text{Equity Cash Flows} = \text{Project Cash} + \text{Net Issuance of Debt} - \text{Interest Expense}$$

Both numbers are identical to those in Table 13.10. It must be noted that you might sometimes need the longer formula with its individual components, because the individual line items may need to be discounted by different interest rates. You will see more of this later.

How much did PepsiCo's earnings and cash flows differ?

PepsiCo showed an increase in net income from 1999 to 2001. Did it also have an increase in cash flows? The answer is no. In 1999, PepsiCo had NPV cash flows of $3,605 − $1,172 − $792 = $1,641; in 2000, it had cash flows of $4,440 − $1,996 + $57 = $2,501; and in 2001, it had NPV cash flows of $4,201 − $2,637 − $8 = $1,556. Yet, even in 2000, managers used **changes in working capital** to prevent PepsiCo's cash flows from dropping even further. It may be that PepsiCo did not show a stellar 3-year improvement, after all. On the other hand, the cash was not discarded, but used. Naturally, judging whether these were profitable investment uses is a difficult matter.

What PepsiCo did with the money.

The cash flow statement in Table 13.4 also continues where we stopped. It proceeds to tell you what PepsiCo did with its projects' (post-interest) cash flows (all dollar figures are in millions):

Dividends: It used \$994 to pay dividends.

Equity: It repurchased \$1,716 in common stock plus \$10 in preferred stock, and \$5 of Quaker stock. It also received \$524 and \$623 as payment in exchange for shares. The net was a cash use of \$584.

Debt: It issued \$324 and paid off \$573 in long-term debt, issued \$788 in short-term debt, and repurchased \$483 and \$397. The net was a cash use of \$341.

In sum, PepsiCo had total capital market payout activities of \$1,919. In fact, this means it paid out more than it made in 2001 to the tune of \$1,919 − (\$1,556 + \$8) = \$355. (Presumably, PepsiCo still had cash lying around. Of course, this cash, too, was not generated in 1999, as PepsiCo also bled cash in 2000. It was in 1999 that PepsiCo produced the cash it consumed in 2000 and 2001.)

The task is done!

Your task is done—you can now look at a financial statement and obtain an estimate of the information it contains about cash flows that matter to your NPV analysis.

SOLVE NOW!

Q 13.15 From memory, can you recall the main components of economic cash flows that are used in an NPV analysis? Do you understand the logic?

Q 13.16 A new firm reports the following financials (in million dollars):

	Income Statement	December 2001	2000	1999
=	Revenue	200	162	150
	COGS	60	58	57
	+ SG&A	20	19	18
=	**Operating Income**	120	85	75
–	Net Interest Income (Gains & Losses)	35	35	35
=	**Income before Tax**	85	50	40
–	Corporate Income Tax (at 40%)	34	20	16
=	**Income after Tax**	51	30	24
–	Extraordinary Items	0	0	0
=	**Net Income**	51	30	24

The firm also reports:

Source	Item	2001	2000	1999
Cash Flow Statement	Capital Expenditures	0	30	200
Cash Flow Statement	Depreciation	25	23	20
Balance Sheet	Deferred Taxes	20	16	0
Balance Sheet	Accumulated Depreciation	68	43	20
Balance Sheet	Working Capital	35	25	20

(You will need to compute changes in deferred taxes, which are \$20 − \$16 = \$4 in 2001, as well as changes in working capital.) Can you compute an estimate of cash flows produced by this firm in these three years?

Q 13.17 What are the cash flows produced by PepsiCo's projects in 1999, 2000, and 2001? What are the cash flows available to residual equity shareholders in 1999, 2000, and 2001?

Q 13.18 Do a financial analysis for Microsoft. Obtain the past financial statements from a website of your choice (e.g., Yahoo! *Finance* or Microsoft's own website). Compute the cash flows that you would use for an NPV analysis of the value of the firm and the value of the equity, beginning in 2003 and ending in 2005.

SUMMARY

This chapter covered the following major points:

- There are four required financial statements: the balance sheet, the income statement, the shareholders' equity statement, and the cash flow statement. Although every company reports its numbers a little differently, the major elements of these statements are fairly standard.
- Financial statements also serve more purposes than just NPV calculations, and are well worth studying in more detail—elsewhere.
- Earnings (net income) are *not* the cash flow inputs required in an NPV analysis.
- Accountants use "accruals" in their net income (earnings) computation, which you need to undo in order to extract actual cash flows.
- The primary long-term accrual is "depreciation," an allocation of capital expenditures. The prime operation to undo this is to add back depreciation and subtract out capital expenditures.
- Deferred taxes adjust for differences in the depreciation schedules that GAAP and the IRS prescribe.
- The primary short-term accrual is "changes in working capital," an allocation of soon-expected but not-yet-executed cash inflows and cash outflows. Examples are accounts payable, accounts receivable, and taxes payable. The prime operation to undo them is to subtract changes in working capital.

- If a cash flow statement is available, it conveniently handles most of the difficulties in undoing accruals for the NPV analysis. However, accountants believe interest expense to be a cost of operations, whereas financiers believe it to be a payout to financiers. Thus, interest expense requires special handling.
- Formula 13.4 shows how to compute cash flows that accrue to project financiers (the "owners," which, in the sense it is used here, are debt holders plus equity holders). It is cash flow from operating activity, plus cash flow from investing equity, plus interest expense.
- Formula 13.5 shows how to compute cash flows that accrue to levered equity owners (equity only). It is the cash flow that accrues to project owners, plus net issuance of debt, minus interest expense.

A final observation: One common source of (avoidable) errors when analyzing financial statements is getting the accounting convention signs wrong.

KEY TERMS

SOLVE NOW! SOLUTIONS

Q 13.1 There are many reasons. For example, Uncle Sam uses accounting methods to compute corporate income taxes. Secondary influences come from the fact that many contracts are contingent on accounting numbers (e.g., debt covenants).

Q 13.2 The main difference between how accountants see income and how financiers see cash flows is accruals. Examples are the treatment of depreciation (versus capital expenses) and the delayed payments/receipts.

Q 13.3 Basically yes: The lifetime sum of net income should be approximately equal to the firm's lifetime cash flows. Cash flows just have different timing. For example, a firm's capital expenditures are not booked immediately, but the sum of all lifetime depreciation should add up to the sum of all lifetime capital expenditures. This abstracts away from some discounting that accountants are doing, and many specific accounting cases that we have not covered, but the intent of earnings is that it should come out alike.

Q 13.4 Completing the calculations in Table 13.7 beyond years 1 and 2 (which are illustrated in the chapter text), years 3 through 6 are as follows:

	Years			
Formula 13.1:	3	4	5	6
EBIT	\$10	\$35	\$60	\$60
+ Depreciation	\$50	\$25	\$0	\$0
– Capital Expenditures	\$0	\$0	\$0	\$0
= Cash Flow, Project, Before Tax	\$60	\$60	\$60	\$60
Formula 13.2:				
– Corporate Income Tax	\$2	\$12	\$22	\$22
= Cash Flow, Project, After Tax	\$58	\$48	\$38	\$38
Formula 13.3:				
+ Net Debt Issue	\$0	\$0	\$0	–\$50
– Interest Expense	\$5	\$5	\$5	\$5
= Cash Flow, Levered Equity Ownership	\$53	\$43	\$33	–\$17

Alternatively,

	Years			
	3	4	5	6
Net Income	\$3	\$18	\$33	\$33
+ Depreciation	\$50	\$25	\$0	\$0
– Capital Expenditures	0	0	0	0
+ Net Debt Issue	\$0	\$0	\$0	–\$50
= Cash Flow, Levered Equity Ownership	\$53	\$43	\$33	–\$17

Q 13.5 Analogous to the cash flows in Table 13.7, a 10% instead of a 12% cost of capital on the tax liability would increase the NPV of the tax obligation from \$46.77 to

$$\text{NPV}_{\text{tax liability}} = \frac{\$14}{1.1} + \frac{\$2}{1.1^2} + \frac{\$2}{1.1^3} + \frac{\$12}{1.1^4} + \frac{\$22}{1.1^5} + \frac{\$22}{1.1^6} \approx \$50.16$$

Therefore, the project value would decrease by \$3.39.

Q 13.6 The income statement is now as follows:

	Year	1	2	3	4	5
	Sales (Revenues)	\$80	\$80	\$80	\$80	\$80
–	Cost of Goods Sold (COGS)	\$6	\$6	\$6	\$6	\$6
–	Selling, General & Administrative Expenses (SG&A)	\$8	\$8	\$8	\$8	\$8

=	EBITDA	$66	$66	$66	$66	$66
−	Depreciation	$30	$30	$30	$30	$0
=	EBIT (Operating Income)	$36	$36	$36	$36	$66
−	Interest Expense	$0	$8	$8	$8	$8
=	EAIBT (or EBT)	$36	$28	$28	$28	$58
−	Corporate Income Tax (at 50%)	$18	$14	$14	$14	$29
=	Net Income	$18	$14	$14	$14	$29

The cash flow statement excerpt is now as follows:

Year	1	2	3	4	5
Capital Expenditures	−$120	—	—	—	—
Net Debt Issue	+$100	—	—	—	−$100
Depreciation	$30	$30	$30	$30	$0

The cash flow formula is EBIT plus depreciation (or use EBITDA instead) minus capital expenditures, minus corporate income tax. For year 1, this is: $36 + $30 − $120 − $18 = −$72. The first levered equity cash flows are −$72 + $100 = +$28.

Cash Flow	Discount Rate	1	2	3	4	5	NPV
Machine	8%	−$54	$66	$66	$66	$66	$152.41
Uncle Sam	8%	−$18	−$14	−$14	−$14	−$29	−$69.81
Project	8%	−$72	+$52	+$52	+$52	+$37	$82.60
Loan	8%	+$100	−$8	−$8	−$8	−$108	$0
Levered Ownership	8%	+$28	+$44	+$44	+$44	−$71	$82.60

Q 13.7 The (summarized) cash flows using monthly discounting are as follows:

Month	1	2 to 12	13	14 to 36	37 to 48	49 to 71	72	PV
EBIT	$2.92	$2.92	$0.83	$0.83	$2.92	$5.00	$5.00	
Depreciation	$2.08	$2.08	$4.17	$4.17	$2.08	0	0	
Cap. Exp.	−$75	0	−$75	0	0	0	0	
Project CF, Before Tax	−$70.00	$5.00	−$70.00	$5.00	$5.00	$5.00	$5.00	$115.59
Tax	$1.00	$1.00	$0.16	$0.16	$1.00	$1.83	$1.83	$46.25
Project CF, After Tax	−$71.00	$4.00	−$70.16	$4.84	$4.00	$3.17	$3.17	$69.34
Loan	$50	−$0.42	−$0.42	−$0.42	−$0.42	−$0.42	−$50.42	$0.00
Levered Cash Flow	−$21.00	$3.58	−$70.58	$4.42	$3.58	$2.75	−$47.25	$69.34

Tax is calculated as 40% · (EBIT − Depreciation − Interest Expense). For discounting, this uses a 1% monthly rate for project cash flows and taxes, and an 0.83% rate for the loan.

Q 13.8 Deferred taxes is an account that represents the cumulated difference between taxes indicated on the firm's income statement and the (lower) amount of taxes that the firm has actually paid. They are the results of different accounting procedures that are used for reporting to shareholders and for reporting to Uncle Sam. (Note: Deferred taxes are *not* adjusted for the fact that taxes are typically paid the year after the income is earned.) They are reported on the balance sheet.

Q 13.9 The deferred tax account increased \$109 from 2005 to 2006. This means that the cash outflow was not as large as the income statement would have you believe. Thus, we add that back to the GAAP cash flows. The 2006 real after-tax cash flow was −\$100 + \$109 = \$9. The deferred tax account decreased \$222 from 2006 to 2007. This means that the firm paid out more than what the taxes on the income statement indicated, so this reduces the project cash flow. The 2007 real after-tax cash flow was \$300 − \$222 = \$78.

Q 13.10 To find the cash flows, work out the change in accounts receivable each year. Then subtract these changes from the net income.

Year	1	2	3	4	5	6
Reported Net Income	\$100	\$100	\$300	\$300	\$100	\$0
Reported Accounts Receivable	\$100	\$120	\$340	\$320	\$120	\$0
Change in Accounts Receivable	\$100	\$20	\$220	−\$20	−\$200	−\$120
Cash Flows	\$0	\$80	\$80	\$320	\$300	\$120

The firm's customers did not all pay the next period. Therefore, the cash flows were delayed.

Q 13.11 The cash flows are as follows:

	Quarter	1	2	3	4	5	6	7
	Reported Net Income	\$100	\$200	\$300	\$200	\$100	\$0	\$0
	Immediate Cash Flows	\$50	\$100	\$150	\$100	\$50	\$0	\$0
	+ Delayed Cash Flows			+\$50	+\$100	+\$150	+\$100	+\$50
⇒	= Cash Flows	=\$50	=\$100	=\$200	=\$200	=\$200	=\$100	=\$50
⇒	Change in A/R	\$50	\$100	\$100	\$0	−\$100	−\$100	−\$50
⇒	Accounts Receivable	\$50	\$150	\$250	\$250	\$150	\$50	\$0

It is easier to obtain the change in A/R first: You know that net income minus the change in A/R must add up to cash flows (change in A/R = net income − cash flows). And, knowing the change in A/R, calculating accounts receivable requires simple addition.

Q 13.12 In February, Amazonia has cash inflows of \$100 (\$25 net income plus \$75 change in accounts payable). In March, Amazonia has another \$100 in sales, but payables stay the same. (It has to pay its old suppliers \$75, even though it gets to keep \$75 from its new suppliers.) Amazonia gets cash inflows of \$25 only. In April, Amazonia gets net income cash inflows of \$100, plus the \$225 change in payables, for cash inflows of \$325. Finally, in May, Amazonia has cash outflows of \$300. The pattern is as follows:

Month	Jan	Feb	Mar	Apr	May
Cash Flows	\$0	\$100	\$25	\$325	−\$300

Note that Amazonia has total 5-month cash flows of \$150, just as it has total 5-month net income of \$150. The working capital has only influenced the timing attribution.

Q 13.13 Short-term accruals are easier to manipulate. To manipulate long-term accruals, you would have to manipulate the depreciation schedule, and though this may be possible a few times, if it is done often, it will most surely raise eyebrows.

Q 13.14 If a firm assumes that fewer of its customers will actually pay their bills in the future (i.e., more will default), then its earnings are (too) conservative. There are also many other ways in which a firm can do this that have not been discussed. For example, a firm can take out a reserve against a judgment in a pending lawsuit.

Q 13.15 The main components for a cash flow analysis are in Table 13.10. Start with EBIT. Then undo accruals for taxes: Subtract off corporate income tax and add changes in deferred taxes. Then undo long-term accruals: Subtract off capital expenditures and add back depreciation. Then take care of the other components, changes in working capital first. Don't forget goodwill and other miscellani—they are quite big in some firms.

Q 13.16 To compute the cash flows (in millions) produced by the firm (project), use the long formula in Table 13.10:

			2001	2000	1999
	Earnings before Interest and Taxes (EBIT)		$120	$85	$75
−	Corporate Income Tax	−	$34	$20	$16
+	Changes in Deferred Taxes	+	$4 [a]	$16 [a]	N/A
=	Net Operating Profit	=	$90	$81	N/A
+	Depreciation	+	$25	$23	$20 [b]
=	Gross Cash Flow	=	$115	$104	N/A
−	Changes in Working Capital	−	$10 [a]	$5 [a]	N/A
−	Capital Expenditures	−	$0	$30	$200
=	Free Cash Flow from Operations	=	$105	$69	N/A

a. Note that the balance sheet gave the level of deferred taxes and the level of working capital, not the *changes* in these variables. You had to compute the differences yourself.
b. Depreciation is only available from the cash flow statement, not from the balance sheet.

Q 13.17 The easiest ways to compute cash flows to residual equity shareholders are Formulas 13.4 and 13.5. PepsiCo's project cash flows, available for satisfaction of both creditors and shareholders, are as follows (in millions):

		2001	2000	1999
	Cash Flow from Operating Activity	$4,201	$4,440	$3,605
+	Cash Flow from Investing Activity	−$2,637	−$1,996	−$1,172
+	Interest Expense	−$8	$57	−$792
=	Cash Flow from Projects	$1,556	$2,501	$1,641

PepsiCo's shareholder cash flows are as follows (in millions):

		2001	2000	1999
	Cash Flow from Operating Activity	$4,201	$4,440	$3,605
+	Cash Flow from Investing Activity	−$2,637	−$1,996	−$1,172
+	Net Issuance of Debt	−$341	−$705	$391
=	Cash Flow to Equity	$1,223	$1,739	$2,824

Q 13.18 For Microsoft (http://www.microsoft.com/msft/reports/ar05/staticversion/10k_fr_cas.html), the underlying project cash flows would have been as follows:

		2005	2004	2003
	Operating Cash Flows	$16,605	$14,626	$15,797
+	Investing Cash Flows	$15,027	−$3,842	−$7,495
+	Interest Expense (Income Statement)	$0	$0	$0
=	Cash Flow to Project	$31,632	$11,284	$8,302

Microsoft has no debt, so all cash flows accrue to equity holders.

PROBLEMS

The *indicates problems available in* myfinancelab

Q 13.19 Which statements on the firm's financial reports are about flows, and which are about stocks?

Q 13.20 Use an appropriate website to find out how MACRS works. How would you depreciate $10,000 in computer equipment?

Q 13.21 What would be the most common accounting value of residential investment property that you purchased for $3 million in each of the next 50 years? (Hint: Use a straight line 40-year depreciation schedule.)

Q 13.22 What is an accrual? How do long-term and short-term accruals differ?

Q 13.23 Consider purchasing a $50,000 SUV that you expect to last for 10 years. The IRS uses an MACRS 5-year depreciation schedule on cars. It allows depreciating 20% in year 1, 32%, 19.2%, 11.52%, 11.52%, and 5.76% in the following years. You can finance this car yourself. You can produce income of $100,000 per year with it. Maintenance costs will be $5,000 per year. Your income tax rate is 30% per annum. Your cost of capital is 12% per annum.

(a) What are the income and cash flow statements for this car?

(b) What is the economic value of this car?

(c) Show how you can infer the economic value of the car from the financials.

Q 13.24 Repeat the previous question, but assume that you finance the entire car with a loan that charges 10% interest per annum.

Q 13.25 PepsiCo's balance sheet lists its deferred income taxes as $1,367 million in 2000 and $1,496 million in 2001. Its net income statement further listed income tax payments of $1,367 million in 2001. How much did PepsiCo actually pay in income taxes in 2001?

Q 13.26 Construct the financials for a firm that has quarterly sales and net income of $100, $200, $300, $200, $100. One-quarter of all customers pay immediately, while the other three-quarters always pay *two* quarters after purchase.

Q 13.27 Consider the following project:

Project	
Real Physical Lifespan	6 years
Cost	$150
Gross Output	$50 in year 1
	$80 in year 2
	$90 in year 3
	$50 in year 4
	$25 in year 5
	$0 in year 6
− Input Costs (cash)	$5/year
− Selling Costs (cash)	$5/year
Overall Cost of Capital	12%/year
Corporate Tax Rate (τ)	40%/year
Available Financing	
Debt Capacity	$50
Debt Interest Rate	10%/year
Accounting Treatment	
Accounting Life	3 years
Depreciation Method	Linear

Assume customers pay 1 year after delivery. Construct (the relevant items of) the balance sheet, the income statement, and the cash flow statement. Compute the value of this firm, both from finance principles and from the financial statements. (Please note that this is a time-intensive question—almost a mini-case.)

Q 13.28 PepsiCo reported the following information (in million dollars):

Income Statement

Year	1999	2000	2001
Net Income	$2,505	$2,543	$2,662

Balance Sheet

Year	1999	2000	2001
Accounts Receivable		$2,129	$2,142
Inventories		$1,192	$1,310
Prepaid Expenses		$791	$752
Accounts Payable		$4,529	$4,461
Corporate Income Tax, Payable		$64	$183

Ignoring all other accruals, how would you adjust PepsiCo's net income to be more cash-oriented, that is, reflective of short-term accruals?

Q 13.29 Coca-Cola reported the following information (in million dollars):

Income Statement

Year	2003	2004	2005
Net Income	$4,347	$4,847	$4,872

Balance Sheet

Year	2003	2004	2005
Accounts Receivable		$2,244	$2,281
Inventories		$1,420	$1,424
Prepaid Expenses		$1,849	$1,778
Accounts Payable		$4,403	$4,493
Loans Payable		$4,531	$4,518
Current Maturities of Long-Term Debt		$1,490	$28
Corporate Income Tax, Payable		$709	$797

Ignoring all other accruals, how would you adjust Coca-Cola's net income to be more cash-oriented, that is, reflective of short-term accruals?

Q 13.30 Give some examples of how a firm can depress the cash flows that it reports in order to report higher cash flows later.

Q 13.31 Explain why EBITDA is more difficult to manipulate than EBIT.

Q 13.32 Among PepsiCo's working capital items in 2001, which items allowed PepsiCo to pull cash out of the business, and which items forced PepsiCo to put more back into the business?

Q 13.33 Coca-Cola's financials are in the appendix.

(a) Put together a table equivalent to Table 13.10 for Coca-Cola for 2001.

(b) Explain how your table handles long-term and short-term accruals.

(c) Show how an abbreviated computation method can come to the same result.

Q 13.34 Preferably answer this question from memory: If you have access to a firm's cash flow statement and net income statement, how would you compute the economic cash flows that accrue to shareholders?

CHAPTER 13 APPENDIX

Supplementary Financials—Coca-Cola

The following two pages contain the financials for Coca-Cola from 1999–2001—the same three years that we are using in this chapter to analyze PepsiCo. Note that all of the financials in this chapter are a little dated. In Chapter 20, we will produce a pro-forma projection, which we can then begin in 2002. Because it is 2008 as I am writing this, we can then in turn compare our predicted pro-forma performance against actual outcomes. Are you missing anything important because the financials are dated? The answer is no, because their format has not changed at all since 2002. Everything you can learn from analyzing 2001 financials remains applicable as of 2008.

Now, in this appendix, I am showing you two versions of Coca-Cola's financials: a restated version in Table 13.11 and an original version in Table 13.12. When firms undergo dramatic changes, such as when they acquire another firm, it becomes impossible to compare the current financials to previous financials. You could learn very little if Coca-Cola reported $20 billion in sales in 2001, purchased PepsiCo in 2002, and reported $50 billion in sales in 2002. Did sales increase or decrease for the combined PepsiCo-Coca-Cola from 2001 and 2002? (In this case, you could piece it together yourself, but if the acquired company had been private, you could not.) To provide investors with this information, Coca-Cola would also report in 2002 what its sales would have been if PepsiCo had already been a part of it in 2001. This would be called "2001 (restated)." Of course, only the original, unrestated information would truly have been known by an investor in December 2001—unless this investor would have known in advance that Coca-Cola would purchase PepsiCo.

As far as the Coca-Cola in 2001 was concerned, it seems to have divested some assets during fiscal year 2001. It originally reported sales of $20,458 million for 2000, but later restated them to $19,889 million. If you want to learn more about what other firms Coca-Cola sold or purchased, you would have to read the entire financials.

TABLE 13.11 COCA-COLA'S FINANCIALS FROM EDGARSCAN, RESTATED (QUOTED IN MILLION DOLLARS)

	Income Statement	2001	December 2000	1999
=	Revenues	20,092	19,889	19,284
	COGS	6,044	6,204	6,009
	+ SG&A (incl. Depreciation)	8,696	8,551	8,480
	+ Other Expenses	0	1,443	813
−	= **Total Operating Expenses**	14,740	16,198	15,302
=	**Operating Income**	5,352	3,691	3,982
	+ Other Net Income	607	155	174
=	**EBIT**	5,959	3,846	4,156
+	Interest Expense	289	447	337
=	**Income before Tax**	5,670	3,399	3,819
−	Income Tax	1,691	1,222	1,388
=	**Income after Tax**	3,979	2,177	2,431
−	Extraordinary Items	10	0	0
=	**Net Income**	3,969	2,177	2,431

	Cash Flow Statement	2001	December 2000	1999
	Net Income	3,969	2,177	2,431
+	Depreciation and Depletion	803	773	792
+	Deferred Taxes	56	3	97
+	Noncash Items	−256	1,484	1,120
+	Changes in Working Capital	−462	−852	−557
=	**Total Operating Activity**	4,110	3,585	3,883
	Capital Expenditures	−769	−733	−1,069
+	Investments	−1	−218	−342
+	Other Investing	−418	−214	−2,010
=	**Total Investing Activity**	−1,188	−1,165	−3,421
	Dividends	−1,791	−1,685	−1,580
+	Net Issuance of Stock	−113	−198	−153
+	Net Issuance of Debt	−926	−585	+956
=	**Total Financing Activity**	−2,830	−2,072	−471
−	Foreign Exchange Effects	−45	−140	−28
=	**Net Change in Cash**	47	208	−37

Restated numbers alter past financials to reflect the composition of a firm as if its main divisions were the same in the past as they are today. Therefore, when a large division is sold, its contribution to past financials is removed; and when another firm is acquired, its contribution to past financials is merged as if the two firms had always been joined. Reprinted with permission. The next table shows the original financials for comparison.

TABLE 13.12 COCA-COLA FINANCIAL STATEMENTS FROM YAHOO! FINANCE, NOT RESTATED (QUOTED IN MILLION DOLLARS)

	Income Statement	2001	December 2000	1999
=	Revenues	20,092	20,458	19,805
	COGS	6,044	6,204	6,009
	+ SG&A	8,696	10,563	9,814
	+ Depreciation and Amortization			
	+ Unusual Expenses			
−	= **Total Operating Expenses**			
=	**Operating Income**	5,352	3,691	3,982
	+ Other Net Income	607	155	174
=	**EBIT**	5,959	3,846	4,156
−	Interest Expense	289	447	337
=	**Income before Tax**	5,670	3,399	3,819
−	Income Tax	1,691	1,222	1,388
=	**Income after Tax**	3,979	2,177	2,431
−	Extraordinary Items	10	0	0
=	**Net Income**	3,969	2,177	2,431

	Cash Flow Statement	2001	December 2000	1999
	Net Income	3,969	773	792
+	Depreciation and Depletion	803	773	792
+	Deferred Taxes			
+	Non-Cash Items			
+	Changes in Working Capital			
=	**Total Operating Activity**	4,110	3,585	3,883
	Capital Expenditures	−769	−733	−1,069
+	Investments	−1	−218	−518
+	Other Investing	−418	−214	−1,834
=	**Total Investing Activity**	−1,188	−1,165	−3,421
	Financing Cash Flow Items			
+	Dividends	−1,791	−1,685	−1,580
+	Net Issuance of Stock	−113	−198	−153
+	Net Issuance of Debt	−926	−585	+956
=	**Total Financing Activity**	−2,830	−2,072	−471
−	Foreign Exchange Effects	−45	−140	−28
=	**Net Change in Cash**	47	208	−37

Source: Reproduced with permission of Yahoo! Inc. © 2008 by Yahoo! Inc. YAHOO! and the YAHOO! logo are trademarks of Yahoo! Inc.

Valuation from Comparables and Some Financial Ratios

A PRACTICAL APPROACH

You now know how to read financial statements, how to obtain cash flows from financial statements, and how to value them. You also know that forecasting cash flows is a very difficult task. Are there any shortcuts? Are there any good alternatives to NPV? Is there anything else you can do with financial statements?

Surprisingly, the answer is yes. There is one alternative approach often resorted to by practitioners. It is called "valuation by comparables," or "comps" for short. Executed correctly, comps can give answers that are as good as those that you can obtain with a thorough NPV analysis. In practice, sometimes the method of NPV gives a better value estimate, and sometimes the method of comparables does.

The basic idea behind valuation by comparables is simple and best understood by analogy: Assume that you want to determine the value of five red marbles. If black marbles cost \$2 apiece, and if you are willing to make the assumption that red marbles are valued like black marbles, then you can compute that the value of your five red marbles should be \$10. It is not necessary to forecast what value marbles will have in the future or what discount factor applies: The market price of black marbles has already taken all this information into account.

Of course, the more similar black marbles are to red marbles, the better this method works. If they are not similar, you can go spectacularly wrong. If black marbles are made from coal and red marbles are made from rubies, then your value estimate can be orders of magnitude off.

In sum, the method of comparables relies on three assumptions:

1. You can identify projects that are close comparables. Here it is "other marbles."
2. You can identify a measure that is value-relevant. Here it is "being a marble," not "being of red color" (in which case cherries or Ferraris would make better comparables than black marbles).
3. The market values comparable projects similarly. This is the law of one price.

14.1 COMPARABLES AND NET PRESENT VALUE

An example application of comparables based on the P/E ratio.

Let us begin with a brief example of a common valuation task. You need to find a good market value for Gateway. By the method of comparables, you first have to find another company that you deem to be similar. Let's assume you choose Dell as your comparable. Second, you have to decide on a particular value-relevant attribute as your benchmark. Let's use earnings. The most common valuation comparable, then, is the price/earnings ratio (P/E). In early 2006, Dell had a market value of \$71.5 billion and earnings of \$3 billion, giving it a P/E ratio of 23.8. Each dollar of Dell earnings therefore translated into \$23.80 of equity value. Third, you must assume that the financial markets value firms like Dell and Gateway at the same P/E ratio. Then, because Gateway had earnings of \$49.6 million, the method of comparables suggests

$$\underbrace{\text{Value of Gateway Equity}}_{\text{Gateway Value}} \approx \underbrace{23.8}_{\text{Dell P/E}} \cdot \underbrace{\$49.6 \text{ million}}_{\text{Gateway Earnings (E)}} \approx \$1.2 \text{ billion}$$

In reality, Gateway was worth about \$925 million, so this comparables-based value estimate was too high by about 30%. This is neither particularly good nor bad, but a typical valuation error.

Comparables are seductively easy to compute.

The single biggest problem of comparables is that they are "seductive." They are so easy to compute that the temptation to use them badly is always there. Without good knowledge of the weaknesses of this method, you are getting only the dark side of the Force. But use comparables correctly, and you can get valuable information that is not easy to find by any other method.

14.1A THE LAW OF ONE PRICE

Ultimately, NPV and comparables-based valuation are both applications of the law of one price—first cousins.

Ultimately, the comparables method is really not that different from the "estimated NPV" method. Both methods seek to estimate a true net present value. Both methods want to do so by valuing your project *relative* to other projects. In an estimated NPV analysis, you compare your own project to a benchmark through the opportunity cost of capital (the discount rate). In comparables-based analysis, you compare your own project to a benchmark through a valuation ratio, such as P/E, for one or a number of similar firms. Although both estimated NPV and comparables are based on relative valuation, comparables lean more heavily on identification of immediately similar projects and on the assumption that the market has valued these particular projects correctly. NPV is a bit more forgiving, in that the opportunity cost of capital uses a broader swath of alternatives than just a couple of similar-looking firms in an industry. (Think of NPV as effectively allowing you to use all investment opportunities in the economy as your benchmark.) But conceptually, either financial valuation method works the same way: through the law of one price.

➤ Law of one price, Section 1.1A, p. 2

IMPORTANT: It is the *law of one price* that ultimately gives you a present value estimate. This law states that companies with the same attributes should have the same value in a perfect market. In reality, it means that companies with similar attributes should have similar values.

Let me expand upon this. To find the true net present value of a project, you must choose one or more attributes upon which to base your valuation.

Both methods work with "attributes" of firms. (NPV values an estimated statistic.)

- One attribute can be your NPV *estimate*. You cannot use the *true* NPV, simply because you do not know it. In fact, if you knew it, you would be done.
- Another attribute can be the earnings for similar firms from the same industry. (You would then work with price/earnings ratios.)

There are also many other possible value-relevant attributes (e.g., cash flows or sales). However, the estimated NPV and earnings are the most prominent. In real life, you might even use multiple attributes. But multidimensional graphs are tough to draw, so we shall consider only single-attribute valuation techniques. Let us call a valuation attribute simply an "attribute" or a "measure." If you draw your attribute on the x-axis and the true firm value on the y-axis, you would hope that the relationship is close and accurate.

An example of a law-of-one-price valuation in which firms with similar attributes have similar values.

For example, look at graph (a) in Figure 14.1. Here the law of one price works well. All firms line up nicely, like ducks in a row. This suggests that your measure is value relevant, although it does not prove it. (It could merely be a lucky coincidence.) Now assume that you want to value a firm whose attribute (measure) is 60, which is indicated by a vertical line. You can easily identify similar firms, some with higher and some with lower measures. Your valuation is now simple and accurate. And it matters little whether your measure is estimated NPV, earnings, sales, or something else.

Unfortunately, this is not how it usually is in reality. Usually, there is more noise.

Graph (b) shows the situation in which you will usually find yourself. The values of all companies are surrounded by a good deal of uncertainty relative to your attribute measure. This is usually the case even if you use estimated NPV. Although theory tells you that true NPV would make the perfect measure, the fact that you had to estimate your NPV inputs usually renders your graph more like (b) than (a).

Here are examples where the pricing method works poorly.

Graphs (c) and (d) illustrate two more problems that are common in the context of valuation by comparables. In (c), you have no comparables that have a similar measure as your firm. Your earnings may be 60, but all comparables from your industry have earnings of around 15 to 25. How should you extrapolate? The graph draws two possible lines, and they come up with rather different values for your firm. In this case, analysts sometimes expand the set of firms they look at, so that they also find some firms with higher P/E ratios. Unfortunately, P/E ratios may mean something very different for firms drawn from a broader set of industries. So you might find yourself with a better value estimate, or you might end up with what you see in (d)—a measure that has very little or no relation to value.

The main conceptual requirements for using the law of one price.

In sum, the following are important for valuation:

1. You need to have a good value-relevant attribute. "Estimated NPV" and "earnings" (which then works through the P/E ratio) are among them, but there can be others.
2. You need to find other publicly traded companies that are similar to your own firm, so that you can believe that their price-to-attribute ratios should be similar. Preferably, you would have many such firms, some with measures higher, others with measures lower than your own firm. Preferably, your measure is relevant and accurate so that all comparables' market valuations line up nicely.

The law of one price gives you an accurate valuation only if these conditions are met.

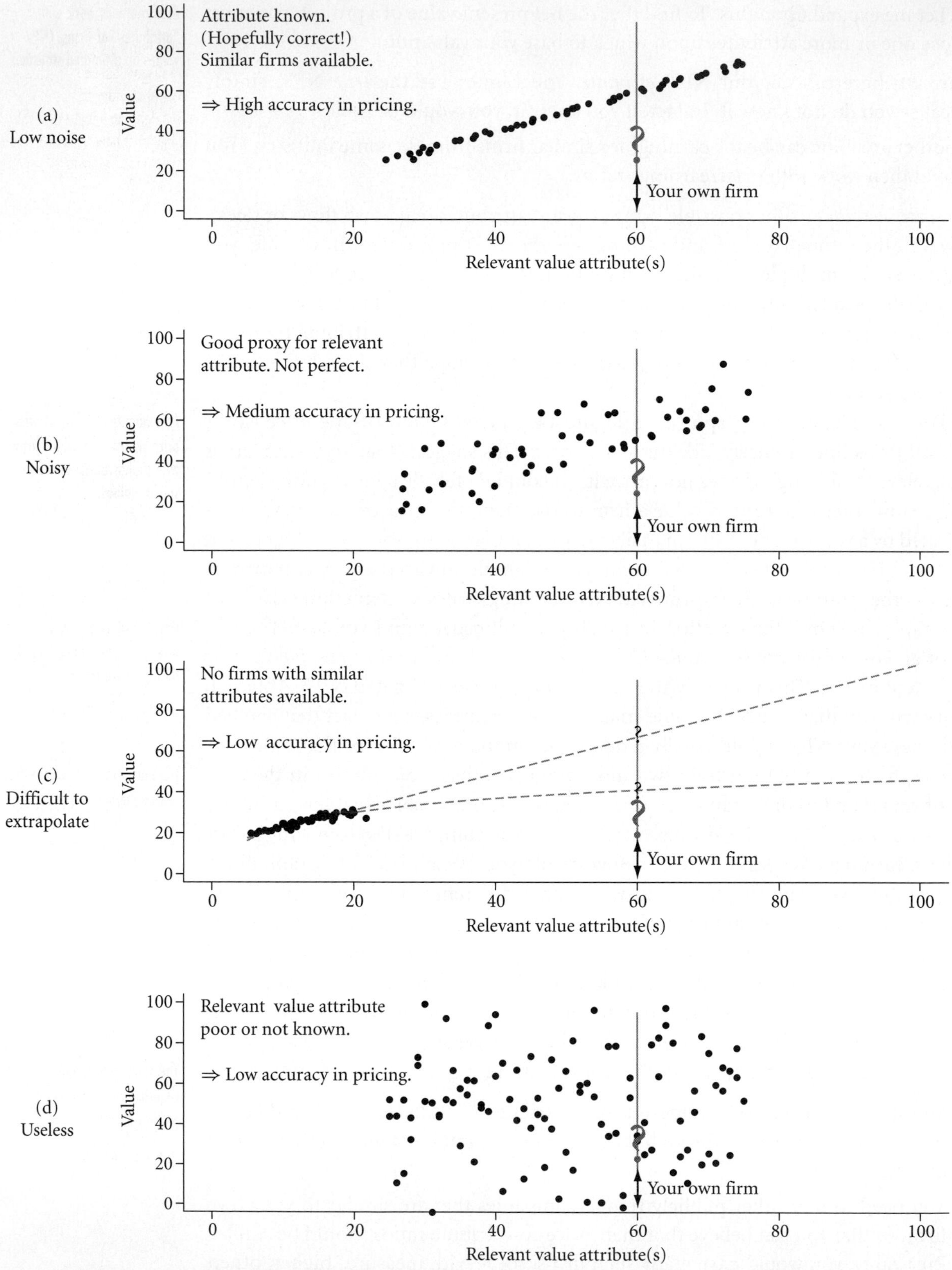

The goal is to value a firm with a value attribute of 60. Publicly traded firms' valuations are big dots. In graph (a), this seems to work almost perfectly. In graph (b), there is a lot of uncertainty, but there are firms with higher and lower value attributes. In graph (c), there are no firms that are similar, so it is difficult to extrapolate a value. In graph (d), the value attribute fails altogether.

FIGURE 14.1 Conceptual Valuation Issues

Which Is Better?

Now that you know that both estimated NPV and comparables are based on similar ideas, how do the two compare?

NPV has input estimation problems, but comparables are even more ad hoc in what the right input is. Comparables also often have a "no similar firms exist" problem.

Estimated NPV as a method has a lot of advantages. It has a beautiful theory ("true NPV") behind it. It identifies for you exactly what matters (the expected future cash flows) and how differently timed cash flows matter in different ways (through the discount rate). The theory even gives you the exact relationship between various estimated inputs and your final measures (the present value formula). To the extent that you can reach the ideals of the theory—finding good expected cash flow and discount rate estimates—you know that your valuation is accurate! (The theory even allows you to skip the time-consuming process of calibrating your measure to those of similar firms. If your inputs are accurate, then estimated NPV and true NPV have a one-to-one correspondence.) However, the estimated-NPV method also has two main disadvantages. First, your input estimates—especially your cash flow estimates—can be far off from the truth. Second, there is no objective standard for your estimates, and a third party cannot verify them. If you say the expected cash flows in 10 years will be $1 million, and I say that they will be $5 million, who is right?

Comparables as a method also has strengths and weaknesses. If there is a high correlation between the true NPV and your measure, then it can provide remarkably accurate value estimates. Its main disadvantage is that it is much more ad hoc: You have to make two important judgment calls. First, what is a good comparable firm? Second, what should you use as the appropriate valuation attribute? Again, earnings (through the P/E ratio) is a common measure, but it may not work well, and other attributes could fit better in your particular situation. Unlike estimated NPV, there is no one-to-one relationship between your measure and true NPV, so you must rely heavily on many firms in a graph such as those in Figure 14.1. Moreover, as with NPV, there are also numerous devils in the details, which you will soon learn more about. Yet one advantage of comparables is that the inputs can be more objective and verifiable than those for NPV. Earnings and prices are known, so analysts can agree on precise numbers. Nevertheless, subjectivity comes back into play because analysts rarely agree on what firms are appropriate comparables and what attribute fits best. Such disagreement can create dramatically different subjective estimates, too.

In sum, you trade off judgmental uncertainty about future expected cash flows and appropriate discount rates (in an NPV estimate) against judgmental uncertainty about how good your measure is and how similar your comparable firms are.

Examples in which one method is better than the other.

To be specific, consider an attempt to value an investment in PepsiCo shares. If your alternative is an investment in Treasury bonds, the method of comparables would fail miserably. T-bonds are so dissimilar that you should have no faith in any comps-based value estimate. You would prefer an NPV-based estimate. But if you have a close comparable, say, an investment in Coca-Cola, then you could easily end up preferring a comparables-based valuation. It probably approximates the true NPV better than any estimate of future expected cash flows you could ever come up with. You would in effect be better off free riding on the wonderfully accurate valuation (incorporating all the true expected future cash flows and appropriate discount rates) that has already been provided for you by the financial markets through Coca-Cola's market price.

SOLVE NOW!

Q 14.1 What is the law of one price?

Q 14.2 How do comparable projects enter the NPV formula?

14.2 THE PRICE/EARNINGS (P/E) RATIO

For valuation, price ratios (multiples) are most convenient.

Now that you understand the general concept, let's dive into the details. The kind of ratios that you would be most interested in have a value in the numerator and an attribute in the denominator. The reason is that if you have a good price-ratio estimate, you merely need to multiply it by your project's or firm's attribute, and out comes an estimate of price:

$$\underbrace{\left(\frac{\text{Price}}{\text{Attribute}}\right)}_{\text{from Comparables}} \cdot \text{Attribute of Your Project} = \text{Price Estimate for Your Project}$$

We will spend a lot of time on the P/E ratio, and discuss other ratios thereafter. It will then become clear to you why the P/E ratio is the most popular comparables measure.

14.2A DEFINITION

The price/earnings ratio is price divided by earnings. Dividing a stock by a flow is a bit odd.

The **price/earnings ratio** is commonly abbreviated as **P-E ratio**, **P/E ratio**, or **PE ratio**,

$$\underbrace{\left(\frac{\text{Price}}{\text{Earnings}}\right)}_{\text{from Comparables}} \cdot \text{Earnings of Your Project} = \text{Price Estimate for Your Project}$$

The price is a stock quantity (a snapshot), whereas the earnings, usually net income, is a flow measure (usually over a 1-year time period). This should raise one immediate caution that you should keep in the back of your mind: It is rare that apples divided by oranges gives you a meaningful number. In the case of the P/E ratio, the hope is that 1-year annual earnings are a good proxy for a stock value based on the entire set of all future discounted earnings flows. If 1-year earnings are not representative of many future earnings, the P/E ratio is most likely not a good measure.

It makes no difference whether you work with per-share or overall firmwide earnings.

It does not matter if you compute P/E firmwide or on a per-share basis. A firm worth \$100 million with earnings of \$5 million has a P/E ratio of 20. If it has 50 million shares outstanding, its price per share is \$2, its earnings per share is 10 cents, and its P/E ratio computed from these quantities is still 20. Its shares sell for 20 times earnings.

Earnings can be analysts' consensus forecast for next year, or current earnings. We keep the notation loose.

In the real world, price/earnings ratios are often, *but not always,* quoted as the current market price divided by the analysts' consensus estimate of *next* year's earnings. (This is an *expected* quantity, known today.) The advantage is that these expected earnings focus more on the future—and valuation is forward looking, not backward looking. Moreover, an informal variant of the growing perpetuity formula, $P = C/(r - g)$, is often used. This variant, $\text{Price}_t = (\text{Expected Earnings}_{t+1})/(\text{Cost of Capital} - \text{Expected Growth Rate of Earnings})$, relates today's price to next period's earnings. (In any case, this matters little: The intuition would remain the same if you used the most recently reported earnings instead.) This chapter keeps the notation on the perpetuity formula a bit loose—the underlying P/E theory is only an intuitive guide and not intended to be exact.

➤ Growing perpetuities, Formula 3.1, p. 43

After a whole chapter about why you cannot use earnings instead of cash flows for an NPV valuation, is it not a step back to revert to earnings? Actually, no. The reason is that current earnings are often better representatives of future cash flows than current cash flows. At first glance, this may seem odd to you. However, it makes sense. Cash flows are usually more "spiky" than earnings. When a firm makes a large capital expenditure or acquisition, it may have a large negative cash flow one year, followed by positive cash flows in the following years. This spikiness is not a problem in an NPV analysis, because the higher future cash flows also enter in the future terms. In contrast, earnings try to smooth inflows and outflows of large expenditures over many periods. It is a number that accountants have created for the very purpose you need here: a representative short-term stand-in for the long-term picture. For computing one representative ratio with just a single year's data, the current accounting earnings are usually more representative of the future than a current cash flow would be. On the negative side, earnings can vary tremendously from period to period, and managers can manipulate them more easily than they can manipulate cash flows.

Why use earnings and not cash flows in the ratio? Because accountants try to reflect more future in earnings.

Sometimes you may want to use the reciprocal of the P/E ratio, the earnings/price ratio, more commonly called the **earnings yield**:

The earnings yield, (E/P yield) is the inverse of the P/E ratio.

$$\text{Earnings Yield} = \frac{\text{Earnings}}{\text{Price}} = \frac{1}{\text{P/E Ratio}}$$

You can view the earnings yield as the percentage of price that is due to current earnings. The earnings yield has one big advantage over the price/earnings ratio. If the earnings are zero or negative, the price/earnings ratio is meaningless, and often indicated as not applicable (NA or N/A). If earnings are tiny, P/E ratios can be huge. In contrast, because a denominator price is always positive, the earnings yield is always meaningful, even if earnings are negative. If the earnings are positive, then a higher price/earnings ratio implies a lower earnings/price yield, and vice versa.

SOLVE NOW!

Q 14.3 Why is it more common to compute a price/earnings ratio than a price/cash flow ratio?

14.2B WHY P/E RATIOS DIFFER

One way to think of the P/E ratio is that it attaches an implicit overall value to each dollar of earnings. At a P/E ratio of 20, you might say that each extra dollar of earnings translates into an extra $20 worth of valuation—the shares sell for 20 times earnings.

The main question: What drives differences in firms' P/E ratios?

But where do price/earnings ratios come from? What do they mean? Why do they differ across firms and industries?

One reason is that P/E ratios use current earnings as a proxy for all future earnings.

The reason is that today's earnings can mean different things for the future for different firms. If you believe that today's earnings are the last that your firm will ever produce, then your value estimate per dollar of current earnings should be lower than if you believe that today's earnings are just a shadow of bigger earnings that will soon arrive.

IMPORTANT: All else equal, the price/earnings ratio is higher for firms with more future growth.

This is easiest to understand with an example using the perpetuity formula.

In the growing perpetuity formula from Chapter 3, the relation between next year's single earnings number and the stream of future earnings is captured by one parameter: the expected growth rate. (In case you are curious, in the growing perpetuity formula, it can also be the case that firms with lower costs of capital can have higher P/E ratios, but this is rarely the main channel. Thus, we focus mostly on the growth channel.) Let's think about this.

Illustration of Differences in Expected Earnings Growth Rates

Assume firms are growing perpetuities. Let's determine a sensible price/earnings ratio for a hypothetical firm.

Assume that your firm is expected to earn cash of \$100 next year and that its appropriate cost of capital is 15%. This firm is a perpetuity whose income will grow by 5% per year forever. Also, assume that earnings are representative of cash flows. Adopting a variant of the growing perpetuity, Formula 3.1 ($P = C/(r - g)$), assume that the value of this firm is

$$\text{Value} = \frac{\$100}{15\% - 5\%} = \$1{,}000$$

$$\text{Value} = \text{Price} = \frac{\text{Expected Earnings}}{\text{Appropriate Interest Rate} - \text{Expected Growth Rate of Earnings}} \tag{14.1}$$

With a price of \$1,000 and expected earnings of \$100, the firm's price divided by expected earnings is its P/E ratio,

$$\frac{\text{Price}}{\text{Expected Earnings}} = \frac{\$1{,}000}{\$100} = \frac{1}{15\% - 5\%} = 10$$

$$\frac{\text{Price}}{\text{Expected Earnings}} = \frac{\left(\frac{\text{Expected Earnings}}{\text{Appropriate Interest Rate} - \text{Expected Growth Rate of Earnings}}\right)}{\text{Expected Earnings}}$$

$$= \frac{1}{\text{Appropriate Interest Rate} - \text{Expected Growth Rate of Earnings}}$$

Faster-growing firms have higher price/earnings ratios.

What if this firm grew not by 5% but by 10% per year (forever)? Then its price/earnings ratio would be

$$\frac{\text{Price}}{\text{Expected Earnings}} = \frac{1}{15\% - 10\%} = 20$$

This shows that the P/E ratio of this firm is higher if it has more future earnings growth.

What if the market expected this firm to shrink by 5% each year? Such a firm would have a price/earnings ratio of only

Conversely, slower-growing firms have lower price/earnings ratios.

$$\frac{\text{Price}}{\text{Expected Earnings}} = \frac{1}{15\% - (-5\%)} = 5$$

Cigarette producers, for example, may suffer from negative annual growth rates and as a result have low price/earnings ratios. For example, in May 2002, RJR Nabisco and Philip Morris (now Altria) had P/E ratios of about 12. Contrast this with high-growth firms such as AMGEN (a high-tech pharmaceutical), which had a P/E ratio of about 40, and Microsoft, which had a P/E ratio of about 45.

In sum, you can conclude that high price/earnings ratios are at least partly a reflection of the market's expectations about how fast a firm's future earnings will grow (relative to its cost of capital).

A paradox: High growth rates for shrinking companies?

Despite everything I have just stated, you can also find some companies that have performed poorly and even shrunk, but which still have high P/E ratios. For example, in October 2005, Sun Microsystems had a P/E ratio of 45—three times as high as Microsoft's P/E ratio at the time of 16. Does this mean that the theory is wrong? On the contrary! P/E is a value ratio relative to current earnings. Sun was generally believed to have experienced tough times from 2001 to 2005. Presumably, the market did not expect Sun's low earnings to be representative of its more long-term earnings. Instead, it expected Sun's future earnings potential to be much higher than its distressed 2005 earnings. Relative to its 2005 earnings, Sun may indeed have been a growth company!

Remember that the growth rate of earnings is *not* the expected rate of return to investors.

➤ Section 2.6A, "Application: Are Faster-Growing Firms Better Bargains?," p. 33

Do you find it confusing that earnings can grow by only 5% but investors expect to receive a 15% rate of return? Shouldn't an investor's expected rate of return be the growth rate of earnings? No—not at all. (Indeed, the expected rate of return $[\mathcal{E}(\tilde{r})]$ cannot be equal to the growth rate of earnings $[\mathcal{E}(\tilde{g})]$, or the NPV would be infinite.) The reason is that *the price today already capitalizes all future earnings*. For example, take a firm whose appropriate cost of capital is 10% and that will produce \$100 next year, \$50 the next year, and \$0 thereafter. There is no uncertainty. Clearly, the cash flows/earnings of the firm are shrinking dramatically. But the value of the firm today is $\$100/1.1 + \$50/1.1^2 \approx \$132.23$. Next year, the investor will receive \$100 and hold a remaining project of $\$50/1.1^1 \approx \$45.45$, for a total wealth of \$145.45. The (expected) rate of return, that is, the cost of capital, is $\$145.45/\$132.23 - 1 \approx +10\%$, even though the growth rate of earnings is -50%.

THE PRESENT VALUE OF GROWTH OPPORTUNITIES (PVGO)

Practitioners often work with PVGO (present value of growth opportunities).

Another common way to express the same information—to give perspective to the meaning of the growth component in P/E ratios—comes from decomposing the cash flows of a firm into two components: the ratio of a different hypothetical firm that has the same projected earnings as our company but has stopped growing, and the ratio of another hypothetical firm that has zero earnings right now but consists exclusively of growth opportunities. The latter component has a specific name. It is called the

present value of growth opportunities (PVGO). You can split the market value of any company—regardless of its actual earnings—into these two components. You can label them the "steady" and "growth" components.

It comes from a hypothetical split of earnings into a "steady" part and a "growth" part.

For example, consider three eternal firms, all priced at \$150 and all with an appropriate cost of capital of 10%. The first (stable) firm has expected earnings of \$15, the second (growth) firm has expected earnings of \$12, and the third (shrinking) firm has expected earnings of \$20. What are their PVGOs? Decompose these firms' values into their two components:

1. **The stable firm** is worth

$$\$150 = \frac{\$15}{10\%} + \ ? = \$150 + ? \qquad (14.2)$$

$$\text{Price} = \frac{\text{Expected Earnings}}{\text{Cost of Capital}} + \text{PVGO}$$

To be an equality, the question mark must stand for \$0. The market has priced this firm exactly as if it had no expectation of any future growth. Thus, 100% of this firm's value comes from the "steady component," and 0% from the "growth component." Eventually, in the very long run, you would expect mature and stable companies to settle into this mode.

2. **The growing firm** is also trading at \$150, but it earns only a constant \$12 next year. Its constant steady component would only be worth \$120:

$$\$150 = \frac{\$12}{10\%} + \ ? = \$120 + ?$$

$$\text{Price} = \frac{\text{Expected Earnings}}{\text{Cost of Capital}} + \text{PVGO}$$

With this firm's "steady component" worth \$120, its growth opportunities must be worth PVGO = \$30. Taking this further, you would say that \$30/\$150 = 20% of the firm's value is due to future growth opportunities, and 80% is due to its steady business.

3. **The shrinking firm** should have been worth \$20/10% = \$200 today if the market had expected it to earn its constant \$20 forever. To justify its actual market value of \$150, it must have negative growth in the future:

$$\$150 = \frac{\$20}{10\%} + \ ? = \$200 + ?$$

$$\text{Price} = \frac{\text{Expected Earnings}}{\text{Cost of Capital}} + \text{PVGO}$$

Specifically, the subtractive part is PVGO = −\$50. This firm is not expected to be able to maintain its business.

So, PVGO is aptly named: Firms that are stable have zero PVGO, firms that are growing have positive PVGO, and firms that are shrinking have negative PVGO.

SOLVE NOW!

Q 14.4 Which is likely to have a higher price/earnings ratio: Google or PepsiCo?

Q 14.5 A firm has earnings of \$230 *this year*, grows by about 6% each year, and has a price/earnings ratio of 40. What would its price/earnings ratio be if it could grow by 7% each year instead? How much would its value increase?

Q 14.6 Rearrange Formula 14.2 into its price/earnings form. What does this say about the earnings/price yield for firms with no PVGO? About firms with positive PVGO? Negative PVGO?

Q 14.7 If PVGO is positive, is $\mathcal{E}(g)$ positive or negative?

Q 14.8 Consider a stable firm with a market value of \$1,000 that produces cash of \$100 per year forever. The prevailing cost of capital for the firm is 10%.

(a) Assume that the firm is financed with 100% equity. What is the P/E ratio?

(b) Assume that if the firm refinances to a capital structure where \$500 is financed with debt and \$500 is financed with equity, then its debt has a cost of capital of 7.5% and the equity has a cost of capital of 12.5%. (The numbers I chose make sense in a perfect market. The so-called weighted cost of capital ($\$500/\$1{,}000 \cdot 7.5\% + \$500/\$1{,}000 \cdot 12.5\%$) is still exactly 10%. The firm's cost of capital has not changed.) What is the firm's equity P/E ratio now?

(c) Has the increase in debt increased or decreased the firm's P/E ratio?

14.2C EMPIRICAL EVIDENCE

Let us now look at the empirical data. First, we shall explore the actual relationship between P/E ratios and earnings growth for many firms in a cross section (a snapshot) and then the relationship between the stock market's P/E ratio and expected earnings growth (a time series).

P/E RATIOS AND EARNINGS GROWTH RATES FOR SELECTED FIRMS IN NOVEMBER 2004

Here is a sample of firms to illustrate the usefulness of PVGO.

Table 14.1 presents PVGO calculations for a few real firms. Market capitalization, earnings, price-earnings, and market beta figures are readily downloadable from Yahoo! *Finance* and other data vendors. For inputs, I only had to estimate a cost of capital, which I did using a simple CAPM and reported in the table. Table 14.1 then uses Formula 14.2 to compute the PVGO, dividing it by the current market capitalization (in order to report it as a fraction of firm value). Apparently, in late 2004, the market believed that the future lay with Google (\$44 billion in market cap) and Pixar (\$5 billion), and not with U.S. Steel (\$5 billion) or Ford Motor (\$25 billion).

TABLE 14.1 VARIOUS P/E RATIOS IN EARLY NOVEMBER 2004

Company	P/E	$\mathcal{E}(\tilde{r})$	PVGO/Price	Company	P/E	$\mathcal{E}(\tilde{r})$	PVGO/Price
Google	50	10%	80%	Coca-Cola	20	6%	20%
Pixar	45	8%	72%	Exxon	15	7%	5%
Cisco	20	12%	60%	Procter & Gamble	19	5%	0%
PepsiCo	20	10%	50%	Altria	12	6%	−40%
Microsoft	21	8%	40%	GM	8	9%	−40%
Home Depot	17	9%	35%	U.S. Steel	6	11%	−50%
Boeing	20	7%	30%	Ford Motor	7	9%	−60%
Wal-Mart	21	7%	30%	RJR Nabisco	10	6%	−65%

The P/E inputs were downloaded from Yahoo! *Finance*. Their P/E ratios rely on forward-looking analysts' consensus estimates. I estimated the cost of capital as $\mathcal{E}(\tilde{r}) = 5\% + 3\% \cdot \beta$. Betas are from Yahoo! *Finance*, except for Google, whose beta I estimated. (Other data vendors could report other beta estimates.) I computed the ratio PVGO/Price from Formula 14.2:

$$\frac{\text{PVGO}}{\text{Price}} = 1 - \frac{1}{\mathcal{E}(\tilde{r}) \cdot \text{P/E ratio}}$$

I rounded PVGO/P intentionally rather starkly to remove the illusion of accuracy. I also made no attempt to adjust for corporate debt ratios, which will be explained in Section 14.3D. Altria is better known as Philip Morris.

P/E Ratios and Earnings Growth Rates for All Firms in December 2000

Do high-growth firms in the real world have higher P/E ratios (lower E/P yields)?

The P/E ratio theory works nicely on paper, and provides some useful numbers in Table 14.1—but does it hold water more broadly in the real world? Let's find out. Look again at Formula 14.1. It states that

$$\text{Price Now} = \frac{\text{Expected Earnings Next Year}}{\text{Cost of Capital} - \text{Eternal Earnings Growth Rate}}$$

Rearrange this into

$$\frac{\text{Expected Earnings Next Year}}{\text{Price Now}} = \text{Cost of Capital} - \text{Eternal Earnings Growth Rate}$$

This is the theory that we want to test with empirical evidence. Yahoo! *Finance* provides us with firms' prices today, their most recent earnings, and analysts' forecasts of next year's earnings. We "only" need the cost of capital and the eternal earnings growth rate. To estimate them, we need to make some assumptions:

Eternal earnings growth: Absent better methods, we shall assume that analysts' current earnings growth forecast (i.e., expected future earnings minus recent earnings, divided by recent earnings) also proxies well for the eternal growth rate. Our 1-year proxy is easy to compute (take the forecast of next year's earnings, subtract the most recent earnings, and divide by the most recent earnings)—unlike the eternal earnings growth estimate, which is a pain. This proxy assumption simplifies our theory into

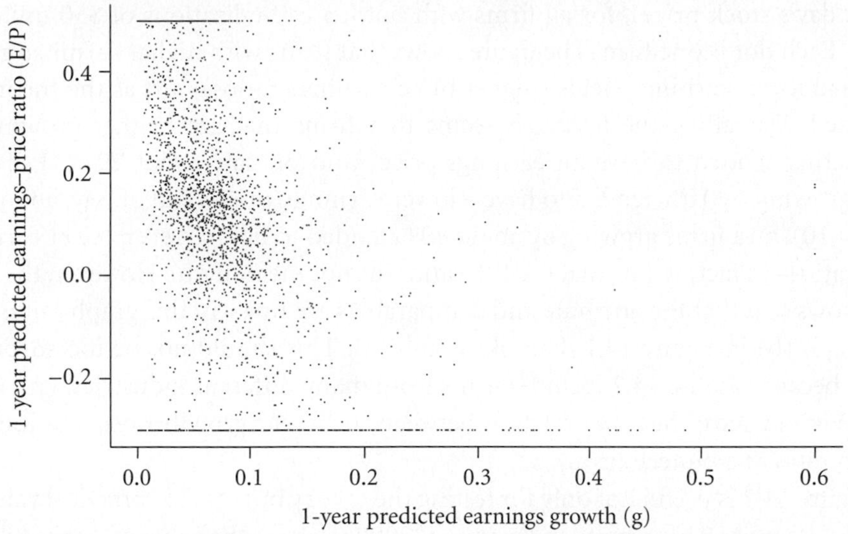

The theory predicts a negative relation between the earnings yield and earnings growth rates: Firms with higher earnings growth rates should have lower earnings/price ratios. The plot shows that this was indeed the case in December 2000.

(Details: In order to reduce the influence of outliers, values were winsorized (truncated) at a P/E ratio of 100%, and earnings growth rates of −30% and +50%. This is reasonable, both economically and statistically.)

Data Sources: The market values and analysts' consensus earnings forecasts (to compute the predicted earnings growth rate and the earnings yields) are from Yahoo! *Finance*. Yahoo! *Finance* obtains analysts' forecasts in turn from the prominent data vendor I/B/E/S.

Source: Reproduced with permission of Yahoo! Inc. © 2008 by Yahoo! Inc. YAHOO! and the YAHOO! logo are trademarks of Yahoo! Inc.

FIGURE 14.2 The Relationship between 1-Year Predicted Earnings Growth Rates and 1-Year Predicted Earnings Price Yields, in December 2000

$$\frac{\text{Expected Earnings Next Year}}{\text{Price Now}} = \text{Cost of Capital} - \text{Next Year's Earnings Growth Rate}$$

The cost of capital: We could estimate the appropriate expected rate of return via the CAPM, but I want to avoid relying on the CAPM when testing the P/E theory. Instead, let's remain vague. Stipulate that the cost of capital is

$$\text{Cost of Capital} = \text{Some Fraction} \cdot \text{Next Year's Earnings Growth Rate}$$

and that "some fraction" is a number less than 1. This says that the cost of capital can be a little higher for high-growth companies, but not too much higher. Substituting this cost-of-capital assumption into our theory, it simplifies to

$$\frac{\text{Expected Earnings Next Year}}{\text{Price Now}} = \underbrace{(\text{Some Fraction} - 1)}_{\text{A Negative Number}} \cdot \text{Next Year's Earnings Growth Rate}$$

Because "some fraction" is less than 1, the theory now predicts that *when you plot the expected earnings yield against the earnings growth rate, the relation should be negative*. This is exactly what we want to test in the data.

Figure 14.2 shows data as of December 2000. It plots the *predicted now-to-next-year earnings growth rate* against the *earnings yield* (the ratio of predicted earnings

The evidence supports the theory (with mild auxiliary assumptions): High-growth firms have lower E/P (and thus higher P/E) ratios.

over today's stock price), for all firms with market capitalizations of $50 million or more. Each dot is one firm. The figure shows that firms with higher earnings growth rates had lower earnings yields (higher price/earnings ratios), just as the theory had predicted. Eyeballing the figure, it seems that firms that are neither growing nor contracting tended to have an earnings/price ratio of, say, about 20% (P/E $\approx$ 5), firms growing by 10% tended to have a lower earnings/price ratio of, say, about 10% (P/E $\approx$ 10), and firms growing by about 40% tended to have an even lower earnings-price ratio—in fact, so low that the P/E ratio was not meaningful. However, the figure also shows you that the attribute and comparables are noisy in this graph—it is more like graph (b) in Figure 14.1 than like graph (a). This should not be too surprising, either, because Figure 14.2 includes firms from many different industries. (An airline firm may not have the same relation between its 1-year growth rates and long-run growth rates as a biotech firm.)

You could have used the figure to estimate a comparables-based firm value in December 2000.

Figure 14.2 is useful not only for testing the theory but also for practical valuation analysis. If you had been hired in December 2000 to assess the value of a privately held firm for which you only knew the earnings, Figure 14.2 would have been very useful. For example, if your firm had earnings of $10 million, and was expected to grow them to $11 million by December 2001, the figure indicates that your 10% earnings growth rate would have translated into likely E/P yields of between about 2% and 20%, with 10% being perhaps the best number. Therefore, reasonable value estimates for this company might have been somewhere between 50 · $11 million = $550 million and 5 · $11 million = $55 million, with 10 · $11 million = $110 million being a decent average estimate.

Unfortunately, the relation between earnings growth and price/earnings ratios (and thus the figure) changes over the business cycle, so you must use an up-to-date version for today's valuation.

Unfortunately, you cannot use this specific December 2000 figure to assess appropriate P/E ratios *today*. The reason is that during economic booms, earnings growth is high, and, although P/E ratios are high, too, they are not high enough for the eternal smooth-growth formula. After all, such earnings growth is unsustainable. Eventually, the boom must end. In contrast, during recessions, earnings growth can be negative. Yet P/E ratios remain relatively too high, because investors expect that earnings will eventually grow again. For example, in December 2000 corporate earnings grew at an average rate of +40%, which was clearly unsustainable. If you had relied on the growing perpetuity formulas, firms would have seemed to be undervalued. By December 2001, that is, post 9/11, the opposite had happened: The median earnings had fallen at a year-to-year rate of −40%. Investors would not have expected this malaise to last forever. If you had relied on the growing perpetuity formulas, firms would have appeared to be overvalued.

IMPORTANT: The relation between earnings growth and earnings/price yields, using only 1-year-ahead earnings forecasts, is not stable over the business cycle. Therefore, to value firms, you must first work out today's prevailing relation between earnings growth and earnings yields (the inverse of P/E ratios).

This says that you cannot therefore use Figure 14.2 to estimate a good P/E ratio from expected earnings growth *today*! Instead, if you need to value a firm based on its current growth rates *today*, you must recreate this graph based on current data.

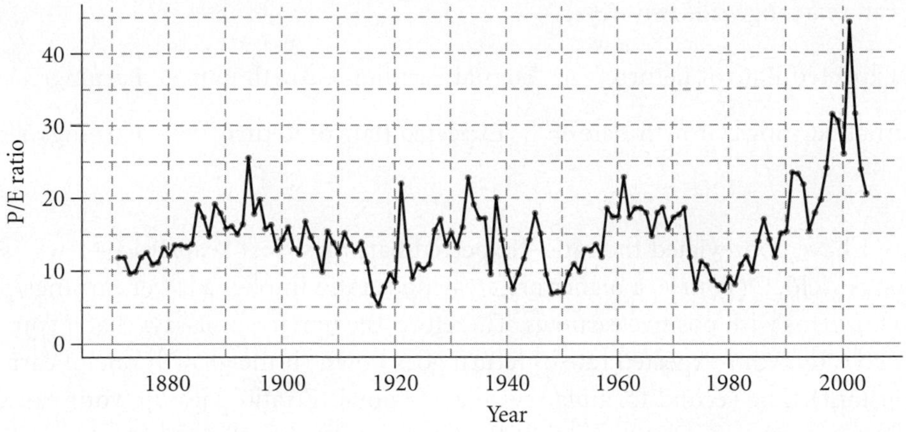

This shows the history of the price/earnings ratio for the S&P 500. It peaked in March 2002 at a value of 46.
Data Source: Robert Shiller's website, http://aida.econ.yale.edu/~shiller/. Reproduced by permission of Professor Robert J. Shiller, Robertshiller.com.

FIGURE 14.3 The P/E Ratio of the S&P 500

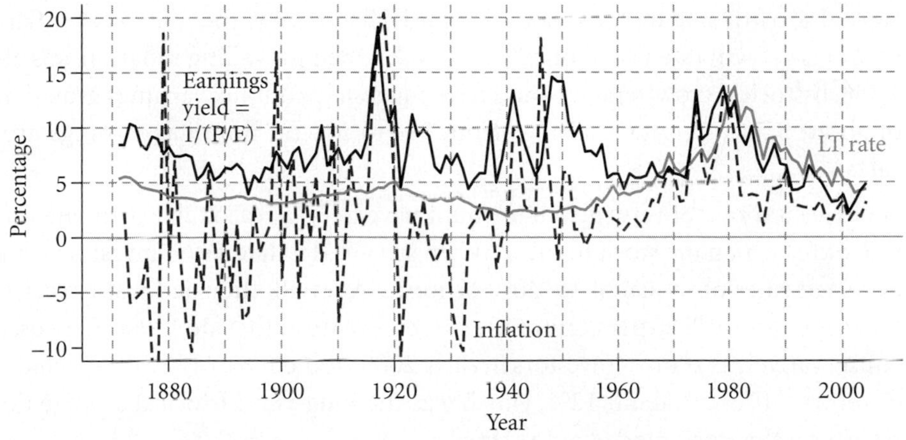

This graph shows the inverse (the E/P yield), plus the inflation rate and prevailing 20-year T-Bond rate.
Data Source: Robert Shiller's website, http://aida.econ.yale.edu/~shiller/. Reproduced by permission of Professor Robert J. Shiller, Robertshiller.com.

FIGURE 14.4 The Earnings Yield of the S&P 500

INTERPRETING (HISTORICAL) P/E RATIOS FOR THE S&P 500

Let's apply your insights about P/E ratios to the overall stock market. We shall use the S&P 500 as a stand-in. Figure 14.3 graphs the P/E ratio of the S&P 500. You should immediately notice the spike in 2000, when the P/E ratio exceeded 40. This meant that investors considered every $1 of corporate earnings to be the equivalent of $40 in value—much above historical standards. Figure 14.4 provides some more historical context: The earnings yield peaked in 1980, and has declined since.

Use the theory on the S&P 500: the historical P/E ratio.

How can you interpret the spike of 2000? Start with our theory,

The 2000 spike should have been due to some combination of earnings growth and expected rates of return on the market.

$$\text{Price Now} = \frac{\text{Expected Earnings Next Year}}{\text{Expected Rate of Return} - \text{Eternal Earnings Growth Rate}}$$

You can rearrange this two ways:

$$\text{Expected Rate of Return} = \text{Eternal Earnings Growth Rate} + \text{Earnings Yield}$$
$$\text{Eternal Earnings Growth Rate} = \text{Expected Rate of Return} - \text{Earnings Yield} \qquad (14.3)$$

where I have abbreviated the ratio "Expected Earnings Next Year/Price Now" as the earnings yield. Of course, a higher price/earnings ratio implies a lower earnings/price ratio for firms with positive earnings. Therefore, the first formula says that if your P/E ratio goes up, your expected rate of return goes down (if the growth rate of earnings is constant). The second formula says that if your P/E ratio goes up, your expected earnings growth rate also goes up (if the expected rate of return is constant). These are the only two possible explanations for high price/earnings ratios.

Do the numbers fit in 2000? Probably not. The P/E ratio was too high to justify high future stock returns, even given aggressive earnings growth.

Let's put ourselves into investors' shoes, and see how the numbers fit in 2000.

1. **The earnings yield:** At a P/E ratio of 40, the earnings yield was about 2.5%. No guesswork needed.
2. **The earnings growth rate:** What would have been a reasonable estimate for the eternal growth rate of corporate earnings? Historically, the real (post-inflation) earnings growth rate was about 2%. In 2000, when prevailing inflation was about 1.5%, historical growth rates would have suggested nominal earnings growth rates of about 3.5%. Entertain a range from 3% to 5% for nominal earnings growth rates.
3. **The expected rate of return:** What would have been a reasonable estimate for the rate of return on the stock market? When surveyed in late 1999, investors claimed expected rates of return of 15–20% or more. After all, they had just experienced returns of above 25% per annum over several years in the late 1990s. Let's assume conservatively that most investors in early 2000 would have claimed expected rates of return of "only" about 12%, which was the long-run historical average rate of return on the stock market at the time.
4. **Plug it all in:** Pick the lowest expected rate of return on the stock market (12%), the highest corporate earnings growth rate (5%), and the P/E ratio of 40. Plug in these estimates:

$$\underset{\text{Earnings Yield}}{2.5\%} \overset{?}{\neq} \underset{\text{Expected Rate of Return}}{12\%} - \underset{\text{Eternal Earnings Growth Rate}}{5\%}$$

It doesn't take a sophisticated financier to realize that these numbers do not add up. Something is wrong. Obviously, it isn't the P/E ratio. Thus, it must have been the case (a) that the expected rate of return was not 12%, but more like 7.5%; (b) that the expected growth rate of corporate earnings was not 5%, but more like 9.5%; or (c) some combination of the two.

We can actually narrow this down a little further. The highest *long-run* real growth rate of earnings (at the start of the Industrial Revolution) was no more than 4% per year. Add inflation, and you would estimate the nominal growth rate of earnings to be around 6%—and realize that this means that you would have predicted no less than the equivalent of a second industrial revolution. In fact, this was exactly what analysts at the time were touting to investors: It was the *new economy*, where old rules no longer applied. Even if you had bought into their argument, however, you should still have expected stock market returns of no more than 10% for the formula to add up. In fact, our earlier estimate in Section 9.4A was that a reasonable equity premium seems to be around 3–5%. To estimate the expected rate of return on the stock market, you must add back the Treasury bond yield, which stood at about 5% in 2000, for a reasonable range of 8–10%—just about right. Investors buying stocks with expectations of rates of return above 10% must simply have been overoptimistic. This argument was most forcefully advanced by Professor Robert Shiller's best seller, *Irrational Exuberance*. It was published just before the stock market peaked in 2000—good timing, which transformed Shiller into an instant market guru.

Your conclusion should be that expectations of future stock returns must have been low in 2000.

➤ Equity premium estimates, Section 9.4A, p. 257

SOLVE NOW!

Q 14.9 Confirm the PVGO/price ratio for Google that is reported in Table 14.1. (Use the formula below the table.)

Q 14.10 Is the relation between earnings multiples and earnings growth rates usually positive or negative? Is it always so? If not, why not?

Q 14.11 If the P/E ratio on the S&P 500 is 20, given historical earnings growth patterns, what would be a reasonable estimate of long-run future expected rates of return on the stock market?

14.3 PROBLEMS WITH PRICE/EARNINGS RATIOS

You are now ready to learn more details about how to value individual firms from comparables—and what the pitfalls are.

Table 14.2 reproduces entries from the *Wall Street Journal* stock price columns on May 31, 2002. It shows that the price/earnings ratio was 35 for Coca-Cola, 34 for PepsiCo, and 21 for Cadbury Schweppes. The (previous day's closing) price per share

Here is a set of real-world earnings numbers.

TABLE 14.2 EXCERPT FROM THE WALL STREET JOURNAL FINANCIALS, FOR MAY 30, 2002

YTD %CHG	52-Week HI	52-Week LO	STOCK (SYM)	DIV	YLD %	P/E	VOL 100s	CLOSE	NET CHG
13.5	31.91	23.55	Cadbury Schweppes (CSG)	0.70g	2.4	21	475	29.20	−0.20
15.4	57.91	42.59	Coca-Cola (KO)	0.80	1.5	35	47,565	54.39	0.24
4.6	53.50	43.08	PepsiCo (PEP)	0.60f	1.2	34	26,539	50.93	0.00

The *Wall Street Journal*'s explanation states that the P/E ratio is based on the closing price and on diluted per-share earnings ignoring extraordinary items, as available, for the most recent 4 quarters. Fully diluted earnings means that all common stock equivalents (convertible bonds, preferred stock, warrants, and rights) have been included. (Actually, the most convenient source of financial information on individual stocks may no longer be the newspaper. Websites like Yahoo! *Finance* make it even easier to find more comprehensive financial information.)

was \$54.39 for Coca-Cola, \$50.93 for PepsiCo and \$29.20 for Cadbury Schweppes. Using this information, you can back out Coca-Cola's earnings per share as

$$\frac{\$54.39}{\text{Earnings}_{\text{KO}}} = 35 \quad \Leftrightarrow \quad \text{Earnings}_{\text{KO}} = \left(\frac{\$54.39}{35}\right) \approx \$1.55$$

$$\left(\frac{\text{Price}_{\text{KO}}}{\text{Earnings}_{\text{KO}}}\right) = \left(\frac{\text{Price}}{\text{Earnings}}\right)_{\text{KO}} \quad \Leftrightarrow \quad \text{Earnings}_{\text{KO}} = \left(\frac{\text{Price}_{\text{KO}}}{\text{P/E}_{\text{KO}}}\right)$$

The task is to value PepsiCo based on Coca-Cola's P/E ratio.

Now do a valuation-by-comparables for PepsiCo. That is, pretend that you do not know PepsiCo's value but that you do know PepsiCo's internal financials (earnings). Your task is to value the shares of PepsiCo in light of the value of shares of Coca-Cola. To consider Coca-Cola to be a comparable company for PepsiCo requires making the heroic assumption that the two are similar firms, at least in terms of earnings multiples. If you are willing to do so, you can apply Coca-Cola's P/E ratio of 35 to PepsiCo earnings of $\$50.93/34 \approx \$1.50$ per share:

$$\frac{\text{Price}_{\text{PEP}}}{\$1.50} = 35 \quad \Leftrightarrow \quad \text{Price}_{\text{PEP}} = 35 \cdot \$1.50 = \$52.50$$

$$\left(\frac{\text{Price}_{\text{PEP}}}{\text{Earnings}_{\text{PEP}}}\right) = \left(\frac{\text{Price}}{\text{Earnings}}\right)_{\text{KO}} \quad \Leftrightarrow \quad \text{Price}_{\text{PEP}} = \left(\frac{\text{Price}}{\text{Earnings}}\right)_{\text{KO}} \cdot \text{Earnings}_{\text{PEP}}$$

In PepsiCo's case, valuation-by-comps against Coca-Cola works well.

The valuation-by-comps method suggests that PepsiCo should have been worth \$52.50. This was higher than the \$50.93 that PepsiCo shares were actually trading for, but a difference of less than \$2 (about 3%) is very small compared to your normal valuation uncertainty. Here the method of comparables has worked very well in predicting a correct market value for PepsiCo.

In Cadbury Schweppes's case, valuation-by-comps against Coca-Cola does not work well.

Now, assume that you instead owned Cadbury Schweppes (CSG), that it was not yet publicly traded, and that it had just earned \$1.39 per share (\$29.20/\$21). Applying the Coca-Cola P/E ratio of 35 to Cadbury Schweppes's earnings, you would have expected CSG to trade for

$$\frac{\text{Price}_{\text{CSG}}}{\$1.39} = 35 \quad \Leftrightarrow \quad \text{Price}_{\text{CSG}} = 35 \cdot \$1.39 = \$48.65$$

$$\left(\frac{\text{Price}_{\text{CSG}}}{\text{Earnings}_{\text{CSG}}}\right) = \left(\frac{\text{Price}}{\text{Earnings}}\right)_{\text{KO}} \quad \Leftrightarrow \quad \text{Price}_{\text{CSG}} = \left(\frac{\text{Price}}{\text{Earnings}}\right)_{\text{KO}} \cdot \text{Earnings}_{\text{CSG}}$$

You would have been far off! The P/E ratios were not comparable: The value of Cadbury Schweppes shares in the public markets was \$29.20 per share, not \$48.65 per share. The method of comparables would have misled you.

If comparables are dissimilar, either the market is wrong or the comparable is wrong. Usually, it is the latter.

What could have gone wrong in the Cadbury Schweppes comps-based valuation? There are basically two possible explanations. The first explanation is that the law of one price has failed. The stock market valuations—of CSG, KO, or both—were just plain wrong. This is unlikely. If the market values were systematically wrong, you could presumably get rich if you purchased undervalued firms. Thus, let's assume that market misvaluation is not the principal reason. The second explanation is that your assumption that the two firms were basically alike was incorrect. This is the more likely cause. There is a long litany of reasons why comparables are not really comparable, and why the technique failed you in valuing Cadbury Schweppes. Here is an outline of possible problems:

➤ Getting rich "easily", Section 11.5, p. 363

Problems in selecting comparable firms: Comparing businesses is almost always problematic. Every firm is a unique combination of many different projects. Cadbury Schweppes owns Dr. Pepper, 7-Up, A&W Root Beer, Canada Dry, Hawaiian Punch, Snapple, Mott's Apple products, Clamato juice, plus some confectionary brands. This may not be comparable to Coca-Cola, which owns Coca-Cola Bottling, Minute Maid, Odwalla, and some other drink companies. Each of these businesses has its own profitability, and each may deserve its own P/E ratio. Even for the cola business, as any soda connoisseur knows, not even Pepsi Cola and Coca-Cola are perfect substitutes. Different consumer tastes may cause different growth rates, especially in different countries.

Section 14.3A will examine the selection of comparable firms; and Section 14.3B will discuss the aggregation of multiple P/E ratios into one measure.

Problems in comparing the ratio (accounting numbers): Not all accounting statements are prepared the same way. Here are a few possible discrepancies in regard to the Cadbury Schweppes valuation:

- Maybe as a British firm, Cadbury Schweppes uses other accounting methods than Coca-Cola. Its earnings number could thus be calculated very differently.
- Maybe Cadbury Schweppes had an unusual year. If so, then today's earnings would not be expected to proxy for future earnings growth in a similar fashion as Coca-Cola.
- Maybe Cadbury Schweppes finished its annual statement 11 months before Coca-Cola, and comparing last year's Cadbury earnings to this year's earnings is not a good idea (or vice versa). Section 14.3C will explain how to adjust better for differences in the timing of reports.
- Maybe Cadbury Schweppes and Coca-Cola have different debt ratios. Section 14.3D will explain how debt can distort P/E ratios.
- Maybe extraordinary items (which I excluded above) should have been included to make these firms more comparable. Section 14.4 will discuss some other financial ratios.

Let's look at these problems in more detail.

14.3A SELECTION OF COMPARISON FIRMS

Finding good comparables: On what dimension should comparables be similar?

Normally, the single biggest problem with valuation by the method of comparables is finding good comparable projects. For instance, assume that you own a little soda producer, called *Your Beverage Corporation* (YBC), with earnings of $10 million. Which of the 10,000 or so publicly traded companies are most comparable to your firm (or project)? Are firms more similar if they are similar in assets, similar in their business products and services, similar in their geographical coverage, similar in their age, or similar in their size and scale? Do they have to be similar in all respects? If so, chances are that not a single of the 10,000 firms will qualify!

Which alternative firm is the best comparable?

Let us assume that after extensive research and much agonizing, you have identified the (same) three companies: KO, PEP, and CSG. Which one is most similar? You know that depending on which firm you select, your valuation could be \$210 million (Cadbury Schweppes, P/E = 21), \$340 million (PepsiCo, P/E = 34), or \$350 million (Coca-Cola, P/E = 35). Which shall it be?

Different conclusions about the value of the same firm: Analyst errors and biases can create wide variations in valuations.

Selecting comparables depends both on the judgment and on the motives of the analyst. In the YBC case, one analyst may consider all three firms (KO, PEP, and CSG) to be similar, but CSG to be most similar because it is the smallest comparison firm. She may determine that a good P/E ratio would be 20. Another analyst might consider Coca-Cola and PepsiCo to be better comparables, because they tend to serve the same market as YBC. He may determine that a good P/E ratio would be 30. The owner of YBC may want to sell out and try to find a buyer willing to pay as much as possible, so she might claim Coca-Cola to be the only true comparable, leading to a P/E ratio of 35. The potential buyer of YBC may instead claim Cadbury Schweppes to be the only comparable, and in fact attribute an extra discount to YBC: After all, YBC is a lot smaller than CSG, and the buyer may feel that YBC deserves only a P/E ratio of, say, only 10. There is no definitive right or wrong choice.

14.3B (NON-)AGGREGATION OF COMPARABLES

Betas and costs of capital combine nicely—you can take value-weighted averages. A merged company is worth the same as the sum of its parts. Is this true for P/E ratios? No!

Assume you are an analyst who relies on NPV for valuation. Your NPV analysis tells you that firm A is worth \$1,000 and firm B is worth \$5,000. If A and B merge and there are no synergies, what would your NPV analysis of the merged AB firm be? It would predict a \$6,000 value, of course. (This is because your cost-of-capital averages can be value-weighted, and present values can be added.) Would this also be the case if you are an analyst who relies on comparables methods instead of net present value for your valuation? The answer is no—based on your analysis of the merged AB firm's price/earnings ratio, you would claim that its value was different from \$6,000. Yikes!

You would want to average somehow. (Unfortunately, it has no underlying valid basis.)

The averaging property also has implications about how you value conglomerates and whether you can "average" P/E ratios for multiple comparable firms. You were probably tempted not to adopt either the CSG P/E ratio of 21 or the KO P/E ratio of 35 as your P/E ratio estimate for YBC, but rather to "split the difference." A reasonable P/E ratio that is better than either may thus be 28. With \$10 million in earnings, this might mean YBC valuations of around \$210 to \$350 million, with \$280 million a "golden" (or brassy) middle. Unfortunately, although some sort of averaging may be the easiest solution, it is not a correct solution. It is also hazardous. Here is why: Companies are collections of many projects. How would you like it if your valuation method gave you a \$1,000 estimate for A, a \$5,000 estimate for B, and, say, a \$12,750 estimate for a merged AB firm (even in the absence of synergies)? Probably not so much. So is the P/E ratio of a company the same as the weighted-average P/E ratio of its subsidiaries, so that you can seamlessly work with either individual subsidiary P/E ratios or with overall company P/E ratios? Unfortunately, the answer is no.

An example of why the average of individual P/E ratios is not the overall P/E ratio.

Consider two firms. Firm A has a 5% growth rate and earnings of \$100 (next year). Firm B has a 14% growth rate and earnings of \$50 (next year). Both have a 15% cost of capital. Their respective values should be

$$\text{Price}_{\text{A}} = \text{Value}_{\text{A}} = \frac{\$100}{15\% - 5\%} = \$1{,}000 \Longrightarrow \text{P/E} = 10$$

$$\text{Price}_{\text{B}} = \text{Value}_{\text{B}} = \frac{\$50}{15\% - 14\%} = \$5{,}000 \Longrightarrow \text{P/E} = 100$$

What would happen if these two firms merged into a single conglomerate, called AB? Assume AB does not operate any differently—the two firms would just report their financials jointly. AB must be worth \$6,000—after all, nothing has changed, and you know that NPVs are additive. It would have earnings of \$150. Thus, its P/E ratio would be \$6,000/\$150 = 40.

$$\text{Correct but Unknown AB P/E Ratio:} \quad \frac{\text{Price}_{\text{AB}}}{\text{Earnings}_{\text{AB}}} = 40 \Longrightarrow \text{Price}_{\text{AB}} = 40 \cdot \text{Earnings}_{\text{AB}}$$

Your goal is to value AB. Fortunately, you just happen to know a perfectly comparable firm for division A (trading at about P/E = 10), and a perfectly comparable firm for division B (trading at about P/E = 100). You even have a good idea of the relative size of the divisions inside AB (1 to 5). Knowing the combined earnings of AB of \$150, you want to estimate a value for AB, based on your two comparables. Unfortunately, neither the unweighted-average P/E ratio nor the weighted-average P/E ratio gives you the correct desired P/E ratio of 40:

$$\text{Unweighted P/E Average of A and B} \quad \left(\frac{1}{2}\right) \cdot \left(\frac{\text{Price}_{\text{A}}}{\text{Earnings}_{\text{A}}}\right) + \left(\frac{1}{2}\right) \cdot \left(\frac{\text{Price}_{\text{B}}}{\text{Earnings}_{\text{B}}}\right) = 55$$

$$\text{Weighted P/E Average of A and B} \quad \left(\frac{1}{6}\right) \cdot \left(\frac{\text{Price}_{\text{A}}}{\text{Earnings}_{\text{A}}}\right) + \left(\frac{5}{6}\right) \cdot \left(\frac{\text{Price}_{\text{B}}}{\text{Earnings}_{\text{B}}}\right) = 85$$

Applying either of these two P/E ratios to your \$150 in earnings would result in a price assessment for AB that would be too high. With a P/E ratio of 55, AB would be worth 55 · \$150 = \$8,250. With a P/E ratio of 85, AB would be worth 85 · \$150 = \$12,750.

IMPORTANT:

- Unlike market betas and costs of capital, price/earnings ratios cannot be value-weighted and averaged in the sense that it should not change the value conclusions.
- Mergers can change the P/E ratio even if they do not create value.
- However, in real life, analysts average anyway—not because it is a good way to do it, but because they have no better alternative.

Lack of sensible aggregation makes it difficult to value even well-defined firms, especially if the comparables are divisions inside of larger firms.

The inability to aggregate divisions' P/E ratios not only is an issue for the firm that is to be valued, but also makes it difficult to extract a single comparable ratio for a division from inside of a conglomerate firm. In our case, let's assume that you only wanted to value the U.S. Dr. Pepper division of CSG, and that the U.S. Minute Maid division of Coca-Cola is a perfect comparable for it. But how do you extract a P/E ratio for the Minute Maid division if all you know is the P/E ratio of the overall Coca-Cola company with its many components? You can't!

The consequences of the aggregation failure mean, strictly speaking, that only the most basic single-product firms should be compared.

There are no good methods to aggregate and disaggregate P/E ratios. Therefore, strictly speaking, you can only compare full firms that are similar. It also means that P/E ratios are likely to work well only for simple and well-defined companies, and not so well for complex conglomerates. In retrospect, it would have been a coincidence if the naïve attempts to apply the overall P/E ratio of Coca-Cola to Cadbury Schweppes's overall earnings would have worked. Indeed, in retrospect, it was an amazing coincidence that PepsiCo and Coca-Cola had such similar P/E ratios. You lived for a brief moment in blissful ignorance.

How Bad Are Mistakes?

AVERAGING P/E RATIOS AND THE 1/X DOMAIN PROBLEM

A P/E ratio in which E is small or negative is bad, bad, super-bad!

Unfortunately, averaging P/E ratios is not only formally wrong, it can also create huge problems by itself. The main problem is that ratios are not sensible if their denominator is tiny, zero, or negative. This is the case for the P/E ratio, because earnings can be (temporarily) zero or negative. This can totally mess up any P/E ratio analysis. The function 1/Earnings is both discontinuous and very steep when earnings are close to zero. For instance, if a firm with a price of $10 has projected earnings of 1 cent, it has a P/E ratio of 1,000; if its earnings fall by just one more cent, it has a P/E ratio that is undefined; if its earnings fall by yet another cent, its P/E ratio suddenly becomes −1,000. We shall call this the "1/*X* domain problem."

An example of how valuing one firm via comps from two similar firms yields obviously wrong results.

Consider the example where the choice of industry comparables for C is A.

	Value (Price)	Earnings (Earnings)		P/E Ratio	E/P Yield
Firm A	$20	−$5	⇒	−4	−25.0%
		Industry Average:		−4	−25.0%
Firm C	?	$2			

This would imply a negative value for Firm C,

$$\text{Value}_{\text{C}} = \text{Earnings}_{\text{C}} \cdot (\text{P/E ratio}_{\text{A}}) = \$2 \cdot (-4) = -\$8$$

A value of −$8 for a firm with positive earnings and limited liability is not sensible. Luckily, this comparables-derived valuation is so far out that no analyst would not notice it.

Unfortunately, this is not always the case. Averaging P/E ratios can look reasonable at first glance (as on p.513) . . .

Yet, this problem is sometimes overlooked when an analyst uses a P/E *industry* average. For example, assume the analyst has one more comparable firm:

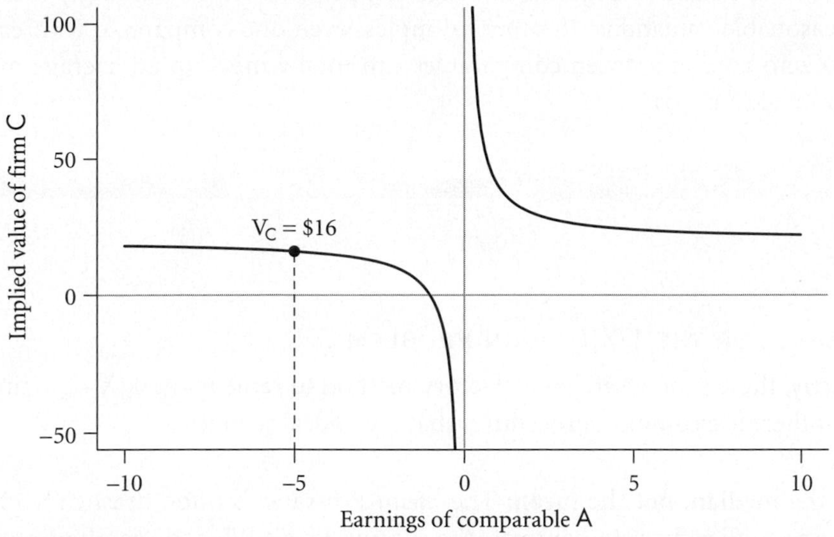

If the earnings of the comparable A are \$1, you get a sensible value for your firm C. If the earnings are a little bit lower, you get a nonsensically high number; if the earnings are a little bit lower, you get an impossibly low negative number; and if the earnings are yet a little bit lower, you can get a positive number that can appear at first glance to be of reasonable magnitude, but which is of course totally nonsensical.

FIGURE 14.5 Implied Value versus Earnings Changes of One Comparable

	Value (Price)	Earnings (Earnings)		P/E Ratio	E/P Yield
Firm A	\$20	−\$5	⇒	−4	−25.0%
Firm B	\$1,000	+\$50	⇒	20	5.0%
		Industry Average:		8	12.5%
Firm C	?	\$2			

The average industry P/E ratio would be $[20 + (-4)]/2 = 8$. This is a reasonable-looking P/E ratio average that might not raise a red flag. A thoughtless analyst could end the analysis with the conclusion that Firm C should be worth $\text{Value}_C = \text{Earnings}_C \cdot (P_{B+A}/E_{B+A}) = \$2 \cdot 8 = \$16$.

Yet Figure 14.5 makes the absurdity of this particular P/E ratio averaging clear. What happens to the implied value of C if A's earnings had been just a little different?

. . . but it is not correct.

- If firm A had a performance of −\$2 instead of −\$5, the average P/E ratio would have been $[20 + (-10)]/2 = 5$, and your implied value for C would still have been a seemingly reasonable \$10.
- If firm A had a performance of −\$1, the average P/E ratio would have been $[20 + (-20)]/2 = 0$. Given limited liability, how can our firm value be nothing?
- If firm A had a performance of −\$0.10, the average P/E ratio would have been $[20 + (-200)]/2 = (-90)$, and your implied value would now be −\$180. Huh?
- If firm A had a performance of +\$0.10, the average P/E ratio would have been $[20 + (200)]/2 = 110$, and your implied value would be a positive \$220. Yikes!

As you can see, small changes in earnings can produce either seemingly reasonable or unreasonable valuations. In other examples, even one comparable with earnings close to zero among a dozen comparables can totally mess up an average of many comparable P/E ratios.

REMEDIES FOR THE 1/X DOMAIN PROBLEM

Here is a set of ad hoc methods to improve the averaging of P/E ratios. None are perfect. All are ad hoc.

Ultimately, there is no entirely satisfactory method to remedy the $1/X$ domain problem, but there are common procedures that try to deal with it:

1. **Use the median, not the mean:** The *mean* P/E ratio is often drastically changed by one outlier firm. In contrast, the *median* firm's P/E ratio is often not based on one negative earnings firm. Unfortunately, it also ignores potentially useful information: the P/E ratios of all firms above or below those of the median firm.
2. **Ignore nonpositive earnings firms:** One common industry practice is to drop out firms with nonpositive earnings from P/E averages. Unfortunately, this is not necessarily a good solution. First, you want an accurate valuation, and the stock market did value firm A at \$20. You have no good reason to ignore firms with low earnings. Second, dropping out firms creates its own problem: A comparable firm could drop out of the P/E average if its earnings were −10 cents, but suddenly drop back in if its earnings were +10 cents—and then exert enormous influence. (Sometimes, analysts even exclude firms with positive but low earnings.) In our example, if A had earnings of −10 cents, you would value C at a P/E ratio of 20 (i.e., $\text{Value}_C = \$40$), but if A had earnings of just +10 cents, you would value C at a P/E ratio of 110 (i.e., $\text{Value}_C = \$220$).

   In sum, a small change in the earnings of just one comparable could still have a very large impact on your comparables valuation due to arbitrary inclusion/exclusion of comparables (rather than closeness of earnings to zero).
3. **Average E/P yields and invert:** The E/P yield is guaranteed to have a positive denominator. Therefore, it avoids the $1/X$ domain problem. In the example, the E/P yield of firm B is $\$50/\$1,000 = 5\%$; the E/P yield of firm A if it earned −\$0.10 is $-\$0.10/\$20 = -0.5\%$. The average E/P yield is thus $[5\% + (-0.5\%)]/2 = 2.25\%$. Inverting this back into a P/E ratio provides a halfway sensible value for the P/E ratio ($1/2.25\% \approx 44$).
4. **Work with sums:** Instead of averaging individual firms' P/E ratios, you can first add up all Ps and all Es before you divide them. In the example where A earned −\$0.10, the total industry earnings would be $\$50.00 - \$0.10 = \$49.90$, the entire industry market value would be $\$1,000 + \$20 = \$1,020$, and the average P/E ratio would be $\$1,020/\$49.90 \approx 20.441$. In this method, firms are effectively weighted by their relative market valuation. Large firms influence the outcome more than small firms. This may or may not be desirable. In the example, B would become the dominant determinant of your comparable valuation ratio.

ANECDOTE Which P/E Ratio to Believe?

Exchange-traded funds (ETFs) are baskets of securities, often put together to mimic an index. You can think of ETFs as firms for which you know the value—and price/earnings ratio—of each and every division (stock component).

On March 13, 2006, the *Wall Street Journal* reported that Barclays Global Investors calculated the P/E ratio of its iShares S&P 500 ETF as 16.4 and that of its iShares Russell 2000 ETF as 19.1. The Russell 2000 includes many midmarket firms. It garnered nearly $7.5 billion from investors and was one of the fastest-growing funds in 2006. Do these two funds look comparable in terms of their valuation ratios?

If you had computed the weighted sum of the market value of all stocks in the Russell 2000 index and divided that figure by the companies' total earnings, you would have found that this ETF had a P/E ratio of 41, not 19.1. Why the difference? It is because BGI excludes all loss-making companies in its iShares ETF when computing its P/E ratio—thus there were many Russell 2000 components excluded. Karl Cheng, an iShares portfolio manager, said that investors don't normally look at negative P/E ratios for companies, so they don't include them in their average. He suggested that investors should consider other measures. Thanks, Karl!

Source: Wall Street Journal, March 13, 2006 (page C3).

These methods can sometimes provide reasonable estimates if only a very few among many firms in the industry have negative earnings. If this is not the case, it is better not to use the P/E ratio in the first place.

IMPORTANT:

- Formally, neither P/E ratios nor E/P yields can be averaged across projects or firms.
- In real life, some sort of informal averaging is often called for. This is because it is often worse to rely on just one single comparable.
- Simple averaging can lead to nonsensible estimates. There are ways to do it better: using the median, dropping firms with low earnings, averaging E/P yields, or dividing only aggregate price by aggregate earnings.

Never take P/E ratio averages literally. Your goal is only to find an "intuitively good average P/E ratio equivalent" for your type of firm, derived from multiple comparables, not an exact number.

SOLVE NOW!

Q 14.12 Is the P/E ratio of a merged company with two divisions, A and B, the value-weighted or equal-weighted average of the P/E ratios of these divisions?

Q 14.13 A firm with a P/E ratio of 20 wants to take over a firm half its size with a P/E ratio of 50. What is the P/E ratio of the merged firm?

Q 14.14 Why can it be most hazardous to work with P/E ratio averages? What would you call this problem (and where does it come from)?

Q 14.15 What can you do if only one among a dozen industry comparables has a negative P/E ratio?

14.3C TRAILING 12-MONTH (TTM) FIGURES AND OTHER ADJUSTMENTS

When comparable firms report annual statements in different months, the intrayear change in economic climate can introduce another problem.

There is one "small" mechanical detail remaining: timing. First, is it meaningful to use annual earnings for a firm if the last annual report was from 11 months ago? Or should you use just the most recent quarter's numbers? Second, some firms report earnings in June, others in December. You may not want to compare financials that are timed too differently, especially if the economy has changed in the second half of the year. For example, consider the following reports:

	2001				2002		
	Q1 (Mar)	Q2 (Jun)	Q3 (Sep)	Q4 (Dec)	Q1 (Mar)	Q2 (Jun)	Q3 (Sep)
Comparable Firm	$1	$2	$3	$9	$5	$6	$7

⇒ 2001 Annual Earnings: $15

Your own firm has closed its financial year with annual earnings of $12 in October 2002. What are the relevant comparable earnings? Should you compare your own annual earnings of $12 to the dated annual earnings of $15 from December 2001?

Fortunately, this time difference can be relatively easily taken care of via "trailing 12-month" (TTM) figures.

You could try to work directly with quarterly earnings, but this is usually not a good idea, either. Most firms do more business in December, and December can be the first month in a quarter or the last month in a quarter. Not only are different quarters difficult to compare across firms, but the December quarter may be difficult to compare even to the other quarters of the same firm. Generally, the best method to adjust flows (such as earnings) into a "most recent annualized equivalent" is to use a **trailing 12-month (TTM)** adjustment. In the example, this means adding the earnings from Q4-2001 through Q3-2002:

$$\text{As if Annual in Sep. 2002} = \$9 + \$5 + \$6 + \$7 = \$27$$
$$\text{TTM Earnings} = \text{Q4-01} + \text{Q1-02} + \text{Q2-02} + \text{Q3-02}$$

Using the reported earnings, you can also compute this as follows:

$$\text{As if Annual} = \$15 + (\$5 - \$1) + (\$6 - \$2) + (\$7 - \$3) = \$27$$
$$\text{TTM Earnings} = \text{Ann-01} + (\text{Q1-02} - \text{Q1-01}) + (\text{Q2-02} - \text{Q2-01}) + (\text{Q3-02} - \text{Q3-01})$$

TTM only works for "flow" numbers (such as income), not for stock numbers (such as assets).

There are three final caveats: First, TTM adjusts only "flow" numbers (such as earnings or sales), never "stock" numbers (such as corporate assets or liabilities). Stock numbers are whatever they have been reported as most recently. Second, firms sometimes account for 52-week years or 53-week years, even making consecutive-year comparisons problematic. Third, firms can, and occasionally do, change their fiscal year. They often do so to make it intentionally more difficult to compare numbers. In this case, you must exercise extra care.

SOLVE NOW!

Q 14.16 The following are quarterly earnings and assets for Coca-Cola and PepsiCo (in millions of dollars) from 2002 financial reports, including restated figures for 2001 (for PepsiCo):

	KO				PEP			
Quarter Ending	Earnings Quarterly	Earnings Annual	Assets Quarterly	Assets Annual	Earnings Quarterly	Earnings Annual	Assets Quarterly	Assets Annual
6/2002	1,290		25,287		888		24,200	
3/2002	801 [a]		23,689		651		22,611	
12/2001	914	3,979	22,417	22,417	667	2,662	21,695	21,695
9/2001	1,074		22,665		627		23,036	
6/2001	1,118		22,387		798		N/A [b]	
3/2001	873		22,248		570		N/A [b]	
12/2000	242	2,177	20,834	20,834	698	2,543	20,757	20,757

a. A onetime cummultive accounting change dropped this to −125.
b. Because PepsiCo did not report quarterly assets when it restated its financials, these assets could not be found.

If it is now July 2002, what would be good comparable earnings and comparable assets for these two firms?

14.3D DEBT ADJUSTMENTS FOR P/E RATIOS

Does leverage influence P/E ratios?

As you already know, companies can be financed through a mix of debt and equity. Does the P/E ratio of a firm depend on this mix? If a firm with more debt in its capital structure has a different P/E ratio, then you cannot compare two otherwise identical companies, *because* they have different debt ratios. Put differently, your "just-perfect" comparable firm that does everything just like your own firm might have just evaporated, simply because it has a different capital structure.

Unfortunately, the answer is yes.

It turns out that debt indeed changes the P/E ratio, but not necessarily either positively or negatively. Roughly speaking:

- For growth companies (with a high earnings growth rate), more debt tends to increase the P/E ratio.
- For value companies (with a zero or negative earnings growth rate), more debt tends to decrease the P/E ratio.

You will get to see this for yourself in the problems at the end of the chapter.

Here are some sample inputs from Yahoo! *Finance*. We illustrate adjusting P/E ratios for different leverage ratios.

More importantly, how can you make your firms more comparable again? (If you don't, you should not compare them.) One sensible method to eliminate the influence of debt is to move from an equity-based P/E ratio to a firm-based P/E ratio, both for the firm to be valued and its benchmarks. To do this, you must add the earnings-equivalent payments to creditors (i.e., interest payments) to the denominator, and add (financial) debt to the value of equity. Let's try this. First gather the relevant information from Yahoo! *Finance* (all quoted dollars are in billions):

	Coca-Cola (KO)	PepsiCo (PEP)	Cadbury (CSG)
Interest Expense, Dec. 01	$0.244	$0.207	$0.155
Earnings, Dec. 01	$3.91	$2.74	$0.72
Equity Market Value, May 02	$136.85	$93.16	$15.12
Equity Book Value, Dec. 01	$11.37	$8.65	$4.12
Debt Book Value, Dec. 01	$5.12	$3.00	$2.00
Capital Book Value, Dec. 01	$16.48	$11.65	$6.12

It is easy to compute the standard, levered debt ratios. They are also reported on many financial websites:

	Coca Cola (KO)	PepsiCo (PEP)	Cadbury (CSG)
Levered Reported P/E, Market Value	35	34	21

Think about how the P/E ratios of levered firms would change if they were unlevered.

What would happen if each company unlevered itself?

1. All debt would become equity. We want to add the current market value (from May 2002) to the book value of debt from December 2001, simply because we do not have a market value of debt in December 2002.
2. All interest payments would become equity payments.

In a perfect market this information is enough to compute the unlevered P/E ratio. In an imperfect market, a change in leverage could also change the total amount of cash flows. For example, if a firm could save on corporate income taxes by having more debt, the total pie of payments to debt and equity could increase. Let's ignore this for now, and focus on the perfect market scenario. In this case,

	Coca-Cola (KO)	PepsiCo (PEP)	Cadbury (CSG)
Interest + Earnings, Dec. 01	$4.15	$2.95	$0.88
Capital Market Value, May 02	$142.0	$96.2	$17.1
Unlevered Computed P/E	34.2	32.6	19.4

Unfortunately, in this case, after proper adjustment for leverage, the P/E ratios have become no more similar. (Doing it right would make our valuation inference worse.)

Does it appear as if Cadbury Schweppes (the underlying unlevered company) is now a lot more like PepsiCo than levered Cadbury Schweppes shares were to levered PepsiCo shares? Unfortunately, the answer is no. The P/E ratio of Cadbury Schweppes is even more different from those of Coca-Cola and PepsiCo than it was before. You also have some more information to evaluate your earlier remarkable finding that PepsiCo could be accurately valued with the comparable of Coca-Cola. You chose Coca-Cola because you believed that the firm of Coca-Cola would be similar to PepsiCo, not because you believed that the equity shares of Coca-Cola would be similar to those of PepsiCo. But, in this case, the firms of Coca-Cola and PepsiCo are a little less similar than the equity shares of Coca-Cola and PepsiCo: Their unlevered P/E ratios are a little farther apart than their levered P/E ratios. If you had properly applied the valuation ratio of one firm to the other firm, you would have concluded that PepsiCo and Coca-Cola are not so similar after all. Nevertheless, unlevering in this case has not changed much, simply because these three firms did not have much debt (in market value). The unlevered KO and CSG were no more similar to the unlevered PEP than the levered KO and CSG were similar to the levered PEP. We did not get much mileage out of unlevering.

SOLVE NOW!

Q 14.17 A firm has a P/E ratio of 12 and a debt/equity ratio of 2:1 (66.7%). What would its unlevered P/E ratio (i.e., the P/E ratio of its underlying business) approximately be?

Q 14.18 On October 9, 2002, the seven auto manufacturers publicly traded in the United States were as follows:

Manufacturer	Market Cap	Earnings	Manufacturer	Market Cap	Earnings
Volvo (ADR)	$5.7	−$0.18	DaimlerChrysler	$32.3	$4.63
Ford	$14.1	−$5.30	Honda (ADR)	$37.7	$3.09
GM	$18.8	$1.83	Toyota (ADR)	$87.3	$4.51
Nissan (ADR)	$27.0	$2.55			

(All quoted dollars are in billions. Ignore debt. ADR means American Depositary Receipt, a method by which foreign companies can list on the New York Stock Exchange.) On the same day, Yahoo! Germany reported that Volkswagen AG had earnings of 3.8 billion euros. In terms of sales, Volkswagen was most similar to Volvo and Ford. What would you expect Volkswagen to be worth? What assumptions are you making?

14.4 OTHER FINANCIAL RATIOS

Let's look at financial ratios.

The P/E ratio is just one commonly used financial ratio. There are many others. Unfortunately, many users do not understand what these ratios really mean. As a result, they can lead to bad questions and wrong answers. However, properly used, they can be useful to understanding not only firm value but also other firm characteristics (such as risk or precariousness of the business). This section discusses two kinds of financial ratios. First, it covers other ratios that are primarily used for valuation. Second, it explains some ratios that measure profitability and debt burden. Their purpose is typically just to inform about the economics of the firm, not to advise you directly as to the appropriate value.

14.4A VALUATION RATIOS

A valuation ratio has price in the numerator and something else in the denominator.

A **valuation ratio** has price in its numerator and some measurable attribute in its denominator. The P/E ratio is the most common and typically best such ratio, although it is no magic bullet. Some other quantities regularly also appear as attributes in the denominator. Given a chosen valuation attribute, the analyst finds comparable firm(s) and multiplies the comparables' price/attribute ratios by the firm's own attribute to determine its value. This works well only if firms are similar enough. It is, of course, not possible to write down an exhaustive list of all other valuation ratios. Only the imagination limits the quantities that can be used in the denominator.

EARNINGS-BASED MULTIPLES

You can use different flavors of earnings.

Your ultimate goal is to find a measure that is proportional to value. This means that you may want to use a different form of earnings. Earnings can be defined in a variety of ways: with or without extraordinary items, diluted, and so on. There is no right or wrong way for valuation purposes: Your goal is to find a ratio that makes your comparable firm appear to be as similar as possible to your own firm. You already saw one common alternative measure of earnings in Chapter 13, EBITDA (earnings before interest, taxes, depreciation, and amortization). Its rationale is that accounting depreciation is so fictional that it should not be subtracted out. But EBITDA has problems, too. It does not consider capital expenditures at all. Thus, this measure could suggest the same price/earnings multiple for a firm that reinvests all of its current earnings into capital expenditures (to produce higher future earnings) versus a firm that reinvests none. This is not a good thing.

➤ EBITDA, solid financial analysis, Anecdote in Section 13.2C, p. 464

You can use cash flows, although they are more spiky.

In Chapter 13, you also learned that you can subtract off capital expenditures from EBITDA. This brings you close to a price/cash flow ratio. Yet such ratios can suffer from the shortcoming that cash flows can be very "lumpy" from year to year. (In a year when the firm makes a lot of fixed investments, the cash flows are often negative—and not reflective of the future.) This is why earnings-based multiples often (but not always) work better than cash flow–based multiples—and why the latter is therefore more common than the former.

The PEG ratio is a common real-world statistic. It has the right inputs but puts them together incorrectly.

➤ Formula 14.3, p. 506

You may also run across a **PEG ratio**, which is the P/E ratio divided by earnings growth. Interestingly, it uses basically the same ingredients as Formula 14.3. The idea behind both formulas is that firms with higher P/E ratios and lower growth rates of earnings are expensive and therefore will produce lower future returns. Unfortunately, the PEG ratio scrambles what it does with these inputs. For example, if the growth rate of earnings is very small, the PEG ratio pretty much produces nonsense. (Interestingly, empirically, low-growth firms are the firms that tend to produce higher average market rates of return, not lower rates of return.) My advice: Avoid the PEG ratio.

MULTIPLES BASED ON BOOK EQUITY: BEWARE!

Accounting is better at flow measures than stock measures.

➤ Flow versus stock financials' accuracy, Section 13.1B, p. 454

The valuation measures so far have divided a market-based snapshot (the stock value) by an accounting flow, either from the income or cash flow statements. Generally, financial accounting is geared toward producing relatively accurate flow values, not accurate stock values. Thus, if you choose a stock number from the balance sheet as your valuation attribute, you need to be especially suspicious.

The book value of equity is particularly tempting and problematic.

There is one particular balance sheet number that looks very attractive at first sight: the book value (BV) of equity. This could be a great attribute for the market value of equity, which you want. (For example, if all firms had a book value that is two-thirds of the market value, it would be a perfect valuation attribute. The ratio method would undo the two-thirds bias.) Unfortunately, you should treat the book value of equity as especially suspicious. After the accountants have completed all their bookkeeping, the book value of equity becomes what is required to equalize the left-hand side and right-hand side of the balance sheet. Put differently, it is a "placeholder" and can on occasion even be entirely meaningless. For example, it can be negative—not a sensible value for a claim with limited liability. (It also means that if the book value of equity is in the denominator, the market-to-book equity ratio suffers from the $1/X$ domain problem.) Because of the way that depreciation and other rules work, firms in the same industry can have very different equity book values if they are of different age. For older firms, the book value is often just a fraction of the true market value.

Sometimes, you may want to use the book value of debt or the book value of assets. Fortunately, unlike the book value of equity, the book value of debt is usually reasonably acceptable, especially if interest rates have not changed dramatically since the debt's issue. Besides, you rarely have an alternative, since the market value of debt (or of total liabilities) is usually not available. Unfortunately, the book value of assets remains troublesome. It is the sum of the book value of equity, financial debt, and nonfinancial liabilities. Because the book value of equity is not the market value of equity, the accounting construct "total assets" generally misstates (often understates) the true value of the firm. This means that ratios that divide by total book assets are (often) seemingly high.

Don't confuse my statement: The book value of debt is often reasonable; only the book value of equity or the book value of assets are not.

With all these caveats, I can now tell you about an alternative to price/earnings or price/cash flow ratios: the **market-equity-to-book-equity ratio**. Sometimes, the book value is interpreted as an estimate of physical replacement value. (Often, it is not a good estimate.) In this case, the market-to-book ratio is sometimes interpreted as a measure of what the firm as a sum adds to above and beyond its pieces. In any case, my advice is this: If you do use a multiple that relies on the book/equity attribute, hoping that similar firms have similar market-to-book ratios, be careful to compare only similarly sized and similarly aged firms. *Do not compare start-up firms to established publicly traded firms.*

The BV versus MV ratio. Older firms have different book value biases than young firms, so don't compare one to the other.

More Esoteric or Specialized Multiples

Sometimes you cannot use any of the above measures. You may have to value a firm that does not have positive earnings, equity, or even sales. This is the case for many research firms. They are primarily a bunch of real options.

Many biotech firms have neither earnings nor sales. What can you use?

➤ Real options, Section 12.6, p. 413

Price/sales (P/S) ratios: If the firm has negative earnings but positive sales, analysts often resort to a price/sales ratio. Because sales are never negative, it largely avoids the $1/X$ domain problem. The idea is that firms with higher sales should be worth more. This ratio also has the advantage that sales may be more difficult to manipulate than earnings, so it is sometimes used even for firms with positive earnings.

P/S has no "negative S" ($1/X$) domain problem. It may work when P/E fails. (Small sales could still be a problem.)

The P/S ratio was especially popular during the tech bubble of 1998 to 2000, when few Internet firms had positive earnings. At that time, many firms, such as Amazon, sold merchandise at a loss. Naturally, it is relatively easy to sell \$100 bills for \$99! Nevertheless, to compare Internet firms, most of which had negative earnings, many analysts indeed relied on a price/sales ratio. It followed then that the more Amazon sold, the more money it lost—and the more valuable it appeared to be. This was perplexing, to say the least.

Firms losing money can have great sales.

In sum, firms can increase sales and market share at the expense of profitability. If value is based on P/S, the implied firm value would be higher for a firm that pursues a pricing strategy that may be bad.

Rolls-Royce and Ford have similar valuation ratios based on P/E.

Problems with price/sales ratio comparisons are also common in normal times. Some firms have intrinsically low sales, but high profitability. Compare Ford and Rolls-Royce in 2005. Quoting all dollars in billions, we have

	Sales	Earnings	Debt	(MV) Equity	P/E Ratio
Rolls-Royce	\$12	\$0.64	\$14	\$6.5	10.2
Ford Motor	\$170	\$2.0	\$150	\$20	10.0

They do not have similar price/sales ratio.

If you value Rolls-Royce with Ford's P/E ratio, or vice versa, you would come up with a reasonable valuation. Unfortunately, the same cannot be said for the price/sales ratio. Each dollar of Rolls-Royce sales translated into about 50 cents of equity. Each dollar of Ford sales translated into about 10 cents of equity.

$$P/S_{\text{Rolls-Royce}} = \frac{\$6.5}{\$12} \approx 0.54$$

$$P/S_{\text{Ford}} = \frac{\$20}{\$170} \approx 0.12$$

Although both are in the same industry, Rolls-Royce specializes in low-volume, high-value-added niche products at high margins, while Ford follows the opposite strategy. If you mistakenly apply Rolls-Royce's P/S ratio of 0.54 to Ford, you would have overestimated Ford's value at $0.54 \cdot \$170 \approx \$92$ billion, which is off by a factor of four!

When firms do not have any sales yet, or when all firms' standard financials (earnings, sales, etc.) seem irrelevant to the eventual long-term profitability of the firm, analysts may use even stranger ratios. Here are a few:

Price/employees ratio: This ratio assumes that the employees at the comparable firm are as productive as the employees in the company to be valued. One problem is that this ratio induces firms to hire incompetent employees on the cheap in order to increase their valuations. After all, firms with more employees are presumably worth more.

Price/scientists ratio: As above.

Price/patent ratio: This ratio is another popular technology valuation ratio for scientific firms. Alas, one patent is not the same as another. U.S. Patent #174465 (March 1876) for the Bell telephone was worth a lot more than U.S. Patent #953212 (September 2004) for a "full body teleportation system: a pulsed gravitational wave wormhole generator system that teleports a human being through hyperspace from one location to another." Again, filing patents is cheap. Making meaningful discoveries is not.

Price/anything else: Your imagination is the limit.

If you can, avoid these ratios. Instead, it is better to think about the probability that the company will be successful and its potential cash flows if it is.

Most valuation ratios only make sense if you compute them for the entire value of the firm (that is, the value of all equity plus the value of all liabilities). The reason is that sales, employees, scientists, or patents are firmwide and independent of financing. However, the amount of equity is not. Here is what I mean: Let's assume that Rolls-Royce had been 100% equity financed, while Ford had remained as is. Rolls-Royce would have been worth about $14 + $6.5 ≈ $20.5 billion. Each dollar of sales would have translated into equity of $1.71. Applying this ratio directly to Ford's sales would have made you think that Ford's equity should have been worth 1.71 · $170 ≈ $290 billion, not $20 billion. *A price/sales ratio in which the price is equity is garbage.* If you decide that you want to use a price/sales ratio, make sure that you only work with a full-firm-value-to-sales ratio, not an equity-value-to-sales ratio. How does this situation compare with price/earnings ratios? Although P/E ratios also change with the debt ratio, the change is relatively mild. A simple sanity condition still applies: A firm with more debt financing has both a lower price of equity and lower earnings. Both the numerator and denominator change together.

Most other ratios cannot be used to value equity, only to value assets.

Firms with more debt have lower equity and lower earnings.

SOLVE NOW!

Q 14.19 When would you use a price/sales ratio? Why?

Q 14.20 Why are price/sales ratios problematic?

Q 14.21 On July 28, 2003 (all quoted dollars are in billions):

Firm	Cash	Sales	Dividends	Value	D/E
CSG	N/A	$9.2	$0.4	$12.2	153%
KO	$3.6	$20.3	$2.2	$110.8	43%
PEP	$1.8	$25.9	$1.1	$81.0	22%

Hansen Natural had $210,000 in cash, $9.22 million in sales, zero dividends, and a debt/equity ratio of 10%. What would a price/cash ratio predict its value to be? A price/sales ratio? A price/dividend ratio? Elaborate on some shortcomings.

14.4B NONVALUATION DIAGNOSTIC FINANCIAL RATIOS

Not all ratios are used to estimate firm value. Some ratios can help you assess a firm's financial health and profitability—or they can be merely interesting. They can help in the "art" of valuation if they can help you learn more about the economics of the firm. For example, a number of ratios are commonly used to judge proximity to bankruptcy and profitability. Like valuation multiples, many ratios are reasonably similar *within* industry, but not *across* industries. They also often vary over the business cycle. Thus, they should only be compared to similar firms at the same time. Nevertheless, on occasion, ratios can be so extreme that they can raise a good warning flag. For example, if you find that the firm has 10 times its earnings in interest due, you might become somewhat concerned about the possibility of bankruptcy, regardless of what is standard in the industry at the time.

Many other ratios are in common use for judging such factors as financial health and profitability.

Quick recap of the PepsiCo numbers.

First, a short recap of some important balance sheet numbers for PepsiCo:

	Book Value					Market Value
PepsiCo, 2001	Total Assets	Common Equity	Total Liabilities	Financial Debt	Financial Capital	Common Equity
In millions	$21,695	$8,648	$13,021	$3,005	$11,653	$87,407

➤ Preferred equity, Section 15.3, p. 552

Sometimes, analysts use not just common equity, but all equity (including preferred equity). These days, few large firms issue preferred equity, so this rarely makes much difference. PepsiCo also had almost no preferred equity, so we will just use common equity. **Financial debt** is usually defined as the sum of long-term debt ($2,651) and debt in current liabilities ($354), which adds up to $3,005. Total liabilities are $4,998 + $2,651 + $3,876 + $1,496 = $13,021; this can also be computed by subtracting equity from assets, $21,695 − $8,648 − $26 = $13,021. In addition to financial debt, total liabilities include such obligations as current liabilities, pension liabilities, and the like.

You can now compute ratios for PepsiCo.

➤ Section 13.1B, "PepsiCo's Financials," p. 448

Without further ado, here are some of the more interesting and common ratios. The sample calculations for PepsiCo in 2001 are based on the financials from Section 13.1B. Be aware that many of these ratios exist in various flavors. The ratios are sorted, so that the ones in the beginning tend to reflect financial health and liquidity, while the ones at the end tend to reflect profitability. (Investopedia.com offers a nice reference for many of these ratios.)

Measures of Leverage and Financial Precariousness

Debt-related (potentially distress-related) ratios.

We begin with ratios that reflect the firm's debt load. A firm that has high debt ratios (especially compared to its industry) must often be especially careful to manage its cash and inflows well, so as to avoid a credit crunch. Moreover, if it wants to borrow more money, then potential new creditors often use such ratios to judge whether the firm will default. They will often judge indebtedness relative to profitability, cash flow, and industry.

The debt/equity ratio and liabilities/equity ratio come in many variations. For example, the long-term debt-to-equity ratio, defined in terms of market value of equity, is

$$\text{PepsiCo, 2001: } \frac{\text{Long-Term Debt}}{\text{Market Value (MV) of Equity}} = \frac{\$2{,}651}{\$87{,}407} \approx 3.0\%$$

The broader financial debt-to-equity ratio is

$$\text{PepsiCo, 2001: } \frac{\text{Financial Debt}}{\text{Market Value (MV) of Equity}} = \frac{\$3{,}005}{\$87{,}407} \approx 3.4\%$$

Even broader,

$$\text{PepsiCo, 2001: } \frac{\text{All Liabilities}}{\text{Market Value (MV) of Equity}} = \frac{\$13{,}021}{\$87{,}407} \approx 15\%$$

Some analysts use the book value of equity, which you can find on PepsiCo's balance sheet. For example,

$$\text{PepsiCo, 2001: } \frac{\text{Financial Debt}}{\text{Book Value (BV) of Equity}} = \frac{\$3{,}005}{\$8{,}648} \approx 35\%$$

You can also immediately notice how much higher the book-based ratio makes PepsiCo's debt ratio appear. I have already explained why I cannot recommend book value–based equity ratios. But intuitively, too, it is difficult to think of PepsiCo, a firm with an equity market cap of almost \$90 billion, as having a 35% debt ratio, based on its (puny) \$3.0 billion debt.

Debt ratios add the value of debt to the denominator. Because market value of debt is rarely available, a common variant adds the book value of debt and the market value of equity. For example,

$$\text{PepsiCo, 2001: } \frac{\text{Long-Term Debt}}{\text{MV of Equity} + \text{BV of Debt}} = \frac{\$2{,}651}{\$87{,}407 + \$13{,}021} \approx 2.6\%$$

$$\text{PepsiCo, 2001: } \frac{\text{All Liabilities}}{\text{MV of Equity} + \text{BV of Debt}} = \frac{\$13{,}021}{\$87{,}407 + \$13{,}021} \approx 13\%$$

Some analysts divide by the book value of assets, which again tends to produce ratios that are too high. A better procedure is to subtract the book value of equity from the book value of assets and then add back the market value of equity.

You may also run into a definition for the firm's debt ratio that divides financial debt by total assets. (This is usually computed with book values. For PepsiCo, this would be $(\$2{,}651 + \$354)/\$21{,}695 \approx 14\%$.) The intent is to compare firms based on how solid they are leverage-wise. Unfortunately, this is often wrong. Consider two simple firms:

Please avoid debt divided by assets as a measure of leverage.

	Financial Debt	Nonfinancial Liabilities	Book Equity	Debt Ratio
Firm A	\$100	—	\$100	50%
Firm B	\$100	\$300	\$100	20%

Firm A has the same financial debt and equity as firm B. It is also clearly financially more solid and less indebted. Nevertheless, the financial-debt-to-asset ratio incorrectly shows a much *higher* debt ratio. (The underlying problem is that equity is not the opposite of financial liabilities; instead, equity and other financial liabilities together are the opposite.)

(Choosing the optimal leverage is the focus of the next part of the book. Thus, we will devote a whole section to the subject of measuring ratios in the special topics part.)

➤ Section 22.1, "How to Measure Leverage," p. 821

Times interest earned (TIE) is often used to gauge long-term solvency. It is computed as earnings before interest (usually also before taxes) divided by the firm's interest.

It is the inverse of interest coverage, so a lower number means the firm's debt burden is more precarious.

$$\text{PepsiCo, 2001:} \quad \frac{\text{Operating Income}}{\text{Interest Payments}} = \frac{\$4{,}021}{\$219} \approx 18$$

The definition of interest coverage can be ambiguous. The most common definition here is identical to TIE. (It is also occasionally defined as its inverse: the ratio of debt payments due, as a fraction of cash flows or EBIT.) Many variations exist: Debt payments can be only interest due, or include both principal and interest. Cash flows can be any of a number of choices. Popular choices are pure cash flows, operating cash flows, net income plus depreciation minus capital expenditures, and net income plus depreciation. Refer back to Table 13.10 for PepsiCo's cash flows to compute, for example,

➤ Table 13.10, p. 476

$$\text{PepsiCo, 2001:} \quad \frac{\text{Interest Expense} - \text{Interest Income}}{\text{Operating Cash Flow}} = \frac{\$219 - 67}{\$4{,}201} \approx 3.6\%$$

The commonly used current ratio is the ratio of **current assets** (cash, accounts receivable, inventory, marketable securities, etc.) over **current liabilities** (soon-due interest, accounts payable, short-term loans payable, etc.). It is a measure of short-term liquidity.

➤ PepsiCo's working capital, Section 13.4, p. 472

$$\text{PepsiCo, 2001:} \quad \frac{\text{Current Assets}}{\text{Current Liabilities}} = \frac{\$5{,}853}{\$4{,}998} \approx 1.2$$

The current ratio is often interpreted to be "healthy" if it is greater than 1.5. This means that each $1 of current liabilities is covered by $1.5 in current assets. Do not read too much into this ratio. PepsiCo is very healthy, even though its current ratio is low. (For PepsiCo, it probably means that it runs its operations very leanly. For another company, such a low ratio might be more precarious.)

The quick ratio (or acid ratio) is similar to the current ratio but deletes inventories from current assets. The idea is that a firm with a high quick ratio can cover immediate expenses with immediate income. Inventory is subtracted, because unlike the other components of working capital, it still needs to be sold to turn into cash quickly.

$$\text{PepsiCo, 2001:} \quad \frac{\text{Current Assets} - \text{Inventories}}{\text{Current Liabilities}} = \frac{\$5{,}853 - \$1{,}310}{\$4{,}998} \approx 0.9$$

The acid ratio is often considered "healthy" if it is greater than 1.0. Again, for PepsiCo, this ratio is fairly unimportant. The **cash ratio** further eliminates receivables from current assets.

Duration and maturity are not indebtedness ratios, but they can be helpful.

➤ Section 5.8, "Bond Duration," p. 126

Duration and maturity were explained in the bond context, but they can also be applied to projects and even to firms. They can measure whether the firm is making short-term or long-term investments. This is not an ordinary ratio, in that it requires projections of future cash flows.

Here are measures that are a little more profitability- and efficiency-based.

Many **turnover** ratios divide sales by another number, usually a component of net working capital. (A variant uses "cost of goods sold" instead of sales as the numerator.)

- **Inventory turnover** measures how often your inventories translate into sales.

$$\text{PepsiCo, 2001: } \frac{\text{Net Sales}}{\text{Inventories}} = \frac{\$26{,}935}{\$1{,}310} \approx 21 \text{ Times (per year)}$$

  A high ratio usually means efficient inventory management. Most financials also provide the components of inventories, so you could further decompose this. (Of course, firms can also manipulate this ratio not by improving efficiency, but by selling their inventories at a discount.)

- **Receivables turnover** measures how quickly your customers are paying you.

$$\text{PepsiCo, 2001: } \frac{\text{Net Sales}}{\text{Receivables}} = \frac{\$26{,}935}{\$2{,}142} \approx 13 \text{ Times (per year)}$$

- **Payables turnover** measures how quickly you are paying your suppliers.

$$\text{PepsiCo, 2001: } \frac{\text{Net Sales}}{\text{Payables}} = \frac{\$26{,}935}{\$4{,}461} \approx 6 \text{ Times (per year)}$$

These measures are sometimes inverted (1 divided by the ratio) and multiplied by 365 to obtain a "number of days" measure. For example,

- **Days of receivables outstanding** (DRO), also called **days of sales outstanding** (DSO) or **average collection period**. To compute DRO, divide accounts receivable by total sales on credit and multiply by the number of days per year.

$$\text{PepsiCo, 2001: } \frac{365 \text{ Days} \cdot \text{Receivables}}{\text{Net Sales}} = \frac{365 \text{ Days} \cdot \$2{,}142}{\$26{,}935} \approx 29 \text{ Days}$$

  PepsiCo collects its bills after about a month. A lengthening of this number often indicates that customers are running into financial difficulties. Such firms should probably reexamine their credit policies.

- **Days of inventories outstanding** is inventory divided by total sales on credit, times number of days outstanding.

$$\text{PepsiCo, 2001: } \frac{365 \text{ Days} \cdot \text{Inventories}}{\text{Net Sales}} = \frac{365 \text{ Days} \cdot \$1{,}310}{\$26{,}935} \approx 18 \text{ Days}$$

  PepsiCo turns over its inventory every 18 days.

- **Days of payables outstanding** (DPO) is accounts payable divided by total sales on credit, times number of days outstanding.

$$\text{PepsiCo, 2001: } \frac{365 \text{ Days} \cdot \text{Payables}}{\text{Net Sales}} = \frac{365 \text{ Days} \cdot \$4{,}461}{\$26{,}935} \approx 60 \text{ Days}$$

A lengthening of this number could mean that PepsiCo is having difficulties coming up with cash to meet its financial obligations—or that it found a way to pay bills more efficiently (more slowly in this case).

There are also combined versions, such as the **cash conversion cycle**, which is the sum of the inventory-processing period and the number of days needed to collect receivables, minus the number of days the firm takes to pay its suppliers. For PepsiCo, this would be 18 + 29 − 60, a negative number that is difficult to interpret intuitively.

Turnover ratios and their derivatives (below) are especially important for firms in the commodities and retail sectors, such as Wal-Mart. Good turnover control often allows firms to deploy economies of scale. In this sense, the above ratios measure corporate efficiency, which can help managers judge their own efficiency relative to that of their competition.

Measures of Profitability

Next are some accounting methods to compute margins or returns.

The **net profit margin** (NPM) or **return on sales** (ROS) is the net income divided by sales.

$$\text{PepsiCo, 2001: } \frac{\text{Net Income}}{\text{Sales}} = \frac{\$2{,}662}{\$26{,}935} \approx 10\%$$

PepsiCo could translate about 10 cents of every dollar sold into net income. Analysts also sometimes use other measures of income. For example, when they work with operating income instead of net income, the resulting measure would be called an **operating profit margin**. The gross profit margin uses gross income instead of net income.

Many growth firms have uninterpretable margins, because they may have practically no income and no sales.

The **return on (book) assets** (ROA) divides net income by the book value of assets.

$$\text{PepsiCo, 2001: } \frac{\text{Net Income}}{\text{BV of Assets}} = \frac{\$2{,}662}{\$21{,}695} \approx 12\%$$

A variant of this measure that adds back interest expense is better, because it recognizes that assets pay out cash to both shareholders and creditors. Nevertheless, both measures are dubious, because the book value of assets contains the book value of equity and is therefore unreliable. You can think of the E/P yield as a better, market-based ROA measure.

➤ Warning on book values, Section 14.4A, p. 520

The **return on (book) equity** (ROE) divides net income by the book value of equity. You also know by now that I *really* do not like book equity–based measures.

$$\text{PepsiCo, 2001: } \frac{\text{Net Income}}{\text{BV of Equity}} = \frac{\$2{,}662}{\$8{,}648} \approx 31\%$$

Total asset turnover (TAT) measures how much assets are required to produce sales. Again, with book value of assets in the denominator, this is not a reliable ratio.

$$\text{PepsiCo, 2001:} \ \frac{\text{Sales}}{\text{BV of Assets}} = \frac{\$26{,}935}{\$21{,}695} \approx 1.2$$

For ratios in which both the numerator and the denominator are flows, such as the ROS ratio, we use the same time period for both. But for ratios with one flow and one stock, such as ROA and ROE, you have a choice. You can divide ROA (or ROE) by the assets (or equity) at the start of the period, at the end of the period, or even by an average of the two.

The so-called **DuPont model** multiplies and divides a few more quantities into the definitions of ROA and ROE in an attempt to learn more about the drivers of value.

The DuPont model—it is in common use, but it explains something that is not very meaningful.

$$\text{ROE} = \frac{\text{Net Income}}{\text{BV of Equity}} = \underbrace{\frac{\text{Net Income}}{\text{Sales}}}_{\text{Profit Margin}} \cdot \underbrace{\frac{\text{Assets}}{\text{Book Equity}}}_{\text{BV of Multiplier}} \cdot \underbrace{\frac{\text{Sales}}{\text{Assets}}}_{\text{Asset Turnover}}$$

A similar operation can be applied to a variant of ROA:

$$\text{ROA} = \frac{\text{EBIAT}}{\text{Assets}} = \frac{\text{EBIAT}}{\text{Sales}} \cdot \frac{\text{Sales}}{\text{Assets}}$$

where EBIAT is earnings before interest after taxes. Your immediate question should be, "Why should you care about any decomposition of ROE or ROA in the first place?" Both measures are based on the book value of equity, which Section 14.4A pointed out as having severe problems. Your second question should be, "Can you trust the components of this decomposition, at least one of which also includes the book value of equity?" For both of these, hold your nose and hope that your comparable firms' book values of equity are bad in a similar direction as your own. In this case, the DuPont model may usefully inform you about what you can do to raise ROE or ROA. For example, everything else equal, if you can increase your asset turnover, it is likely that your ROE will increase. Your third question should be, "Why am I bothering you with this?" I can answer this one more easily: The individuals administering the CFA exam keep the DuPont model as one of their staples, and you may run into some corporate treasurers who still use it.

Measures Related to Stock Market Capitalization

Let us now proceed to measures that are more oriented toward the stock market.

Measures that are more oriented toward shareholders and the stock market.

The **book-equity-to-market-equity ratio** is the inverse of the book equity–based valuation multiple. If you get lucky (and don't count on it), the book value of assets is representative of how much the assets would cost to replace. (By the way, your chances are better if the firm is very young.) If you are indeed lucky, then the book-equity-to-market-equity ratio can be interpreted as a measure of how much market value the firm has created via its unique growth opportunities.

$$\text{PepsiCo, 2001: } \frac{\text{BV of Equity}}{\text{MV of Equity}} = \frac{\$8{,}648}{\$87{,}407} \approx 9.9\%$$

However, in PepsiCo's case, it is more likely that the book value of its equity is simply a number without much meaning. PepsiCo owns tangible and intangible assets—both accounted for by the accountants—that are worth far more than their book values.

The **dividend payout ratio** measures what percent of earnings is paid out as dividends. Holding everything else equal, the same firm that pays out more of its earnings today would pay out less in the future. (If it had retained earnings, it would have earned more cash for payout later.)

$$\text{PepsiCo, 2001: } \frac{\text{Dividends}}{\text{Net Income}} = \frac{\$994}{\$2{,}662} \approx 37\%$$

PepsiCo's dividends here were those paid both to common and preferred equity (explained soon). The dividends here included both common and preferred dividends, because PepsiCo paid only $4 million to preferred equity (all of which was held in its employee stock option plan [ESOP]). More commonly, this dividend-based ratio and the ones below would be computed only for dividends paid to common equity.

The **payout ratio** expands the payout from only dividends to include share repurchases, or even net repurchases (i.e., share repurchases net of share issues).

$$\text{PepsiCo, 2001: } \frac{\text{Dividends} + \text{Equity Repurchasing}}{\text{Net Income}} = \frac{\$2{,}725}{\$2{,}662} \approx 102\%$$

$$\text{PepsiCo, 2001: } \frac{\text{Dividends} + \text{Equity Repurchasing} - \text{Equity Issuing}}{\text{Net Income}} = \frac{\$2{,}201}{\$2{,}662} \approx 83\%$$

PepsiCo distributed most of its earnings to shareholders.

The **dividend yield** is the amount of dividends divided by the share price. Dividends are a flow measure, whereas the stock price is a stock measure. Consequently, dividends can be measured relative to the price at the beginning of the period or to the price at the end of the period. In the latter case, it is called the **dividend/price ratio.**

$$\text{PepsiCo, 2001: } \frac{\text{Dividends}}{\text{MV of Equity}} = \frac{\$994}{\$87{,}407} \approx 1.1\%$$

Equity repurchases are also payouts to shareholders, so you can enlarge this measure to a payout/price ratio,

$$\text{PepsiCo, 2001: } \frac{\text{Dividends} + \text{Equity Repurchasing}}{\text{MV of Equity}} = \frac{\$2{,}725}{\$87{,}407} \approx 3.1\%$$

Earnings retention ratios are changes in retained earnings (i.e., this year's earnings that were not paid out), divided either by sales, assets, or income. All else equal, a firm that retains more earnings today should pay out more in the future. After all, the retained earnings should be reinvested, so such firms should have higher expected earnings growth. Retention ratios are usually calculated as 1 minus the dividend payout ratio, 1 minus the sum of dividends and equity repurchases divided by net income, or 1 minus the sum of dividends and net equity repurchases divided by net income. For example, PepsiCo paid out $994 in dividends and $1,731 in share repurchases. Thus,

$$\text{PepsiCo, 2001: } \frac{\text{Net Income} - \text{Payout}}{\text{Net Income}} = \frac{\$2{,}662 - \$2{,}725}{\$2{,}662} \approx -2.4\%$$

PepsiCo also issued $524 of shares in connection with the Quaker merger, so

$$\text{PepsiCo, 2001: } \frac{\text{Net Income} - \text{Net Payout}}{\text{Net Income}} = \frac{\$2{,}662 - \$2{,}725 + \$524}{\$2{,}662} \approx 17.3\%$$

You can easily think of variations here, such as inclusion or exclusion of preferred stock payments, and so on.

How useful are these ratios? It depends on the situation, the industry, and the particular ratio for the particular firm—and what you expect to learn. If every firm in the industry has almost the same ratio—for example, days of receivables average somewhere between 25 and 32 days everywhere, but the firm in which you are considering investing reports 7 days—you should wonder about the economics of this shorter number. Is your firm better in obtaining money quickly? Does it do so by giving rebates to faster paying customers? Does it mostly work on a cash basis, while other firms in the industry work on credit? If so, why? Or is your firm simply cooking its books?

The ratios can be useful, but please don't live by them.

SOLVE NOW!

Q 14.22 How would you measure a financial-debt-to-equity ratio?

Q 14.23 What is the "current ratio"? Is a firm more or less precarious if this ratio is high?

Q 14.24 A firm has sales of $30,000 and receivables of $6,000. What is its receivables turnover? What is its DRO?

Q 14.25 What is the difference between the dividend/price ratio and the dividend payout ratio?

SUMMARY

Should you estimate value based on comparables or net present value? In practice, comparables enjoy great popularity, primarily because their minimal application does not require much thought. Anyone can look up another firm's P/E ratio and

Use both comparables and estimated-NPV valuation methods, and use common sense to decide what you believe.

multiply it by the earnings of the firm to be valued. In contrast, even a rough NPV analysis is quite involved. Of course, after reading this chapter, you should understand that both methods rely on inputs that you will almost surely never know perfectly. You will never have the perfect comparable, and you will never know the correct expected future cash flows. Fortunately, the cause of errors is different for these two methods. Therefore, if you use both, you can often get a better idea of where the true value lies. This does not mean that you should average the valuation estimates obtained from NPV and comparables. Instead, you should perform both analyses and then take a step back and make up your mind as to which combination of methods seems to make the most sense in your particular situation. Yes, valuation is as much an art as it is a science. It consists of the tools that you have learned *and* your ability to judge. If you can judge better than others, you will end up a rich person.

This chapter covered the following major points:

- Comparables can provide an alternative valuation of firms and projects. The comparables valuation techniques and estimated NPV have different weaknesses, which therefore often makes it worthwhile to contemplate both.

- A comparables analysis relies on three assumptions:
  (1) The identification of good value-relevant attribute(s)
  (2) The identification of good comparable firms with known market values
  (3) The law of one price

- The most common value attribute is earnings, making the P/E ratio the natural way to infer value. The P/E ratio divides the price of the firm by its earnings. This can be done with aggregate firm numbers or on a per-share basis.

  Often, earnings are not the current earnings but analysts' consensual earnings forecasts.

- All else equal, higher-growth firms have higher P/E ratios.

- Comparables suffer from a variety of problems, some of which cannot be corrected. These problems can usually be traced back to the difficulty in finding good comparables.

- Never mechanically average P/E ratios. The $1/X$ domain problem can be toxic. Use one of the suggested techniques (such as using the median, ignoring firms with nonpositive earnings, averaging E/P ratios, or working with sums) to reduce its influence. Of course, none of the remedies are very attractive, so you may be better off avoiding P/E ratios altogether.

- There are also many other ratios that can be used to judge the profitability and the financial health of a company. As far as valuation is concerned, their primary purpose is often only to provide useful background information.

KEY TERMS

SOLVE NOW! SOLUTIONS

Q 14.1 The law of one price states that items with similar attributes should be priced similarly.

Q 14.2 Comparable projects enter the NPV formula through the (opportunity) cost of capital, also called the discount rate, usually abbreviated $\mathcal{E}(r)$.

Q 14.3 It is more common to compute a price/earnings ratio than a price/cash flow ratio because the earnings measure incorporates some forward-looking information, and is therefore less "spiky."

Q 14.4 Google is growing faster than PepsiCo, so it would have a higher P/E ratio.

Q 14.5 $\text{E/P} = \mathcal{E}(\tilde{r}) - \mathcal{E}(\tilde{g}) \Rightarrow \mathcal{E}(\tilde{r}) = \text{E/P} + \mathcal{E}(\tilde{g}) = 1/40 + 6\% = 8.5\%$. Therefore, $\text{E/P} = 8.5\% - 7\% = 1.5\%$ and its P/E ratio would shoot from 40 to 66.7. The percentage change in value would therefore be $66.7/40 - 1 \approx 67\%$.

Q 14.6 Rearranging Formula 14.2,

$$\frac{\text{Price}}{\text{Expected Earnings}} = \frac{1}{\text{Cost of Capital}} + \frac{\text{PVGO}}{\text{Expected Earnings}}$$

It states that firms with zero PVGOs have E/P yields equal to their costs of capital. Firms that are growing have E/P yields below their costs of capital. Firms that are shrinking have E/P yields above their costs of capital.

Q 14.7 If PVGO is positive, $\mathcal{E}(g)$ is also positive.

Q 14.8 For the stable firm:

(a) The P/E ratio is \$1,000/\$100 = 10.
(b) The debt now has to receive \$500 · 7.5% = \$37.50 in interest every month. Therefore, there is \$62.50 available to the equity. Therefore, the P/E ratio is \$500/\$62.50 = 8.
(c) The increase in debt has decreased the firm's P/E ratio.

Q 14.9 Using the formula in Table 14.1,

$$\frac{\text{PVGO}}{\text{Price}} = 1 - \frac{1}{10\% \cdot 50} = 80\%$$

$$\frac{\text{PVGO}}{\text{Price}} = 1 - \frac{1}{\mathcal{E}(\tilde{r}) \cdot \text{P/E ratio}}$$

Q 14.10 The relation between earnings multiples and earnings growth rates is usually negative. It is not always so, because it is not stable over the business cycle. During recessions, cash cow firms may actually trade at higher multiples than (precarious) growth firms. In a sense, as indicated by the formulas, economic recessions can transform what were previously growth firms in growing markets into dying firms!

Q 14.11 With a P/E ratio of 20 on the S&P 500, its E/P yield would be around 5%. The real earnings growth rate has been around 2%. Thus, the real stock market rate of return would be around 7%. Add inflation, and you get an estimate of the nominal rate of return on the stock market.

Q 14.12 The P/E ratio of the merged A and B company is neither the equal-weighted nor the value-weighted average! See Section 14.3B.

Q 14.13 Let's do an example. The acquirer has value of \$100, so it needs to have earnings of \$5. The target has value of \$50, so it needs to have earnings of \$1. This means that the combined firm will have earnings of \$6 and value of \$150. Its P/E ratio will thus be 25.

Q 14.14 Averaging P/E ratios is very hazardous because it can easily lead to misleading estimates, as explained in Section 14.3B. We called it the "$1/X$ domain problem." The main problem is that earnings can be nonpositive or tiny.

Q 14.15 If only one among a dozen industry comps has a negative P/E ratio, you can ignore this firm with nonpositive earnings, you can use the median industry ratio, you can work with E/P yields and invert them, or you can work with sums of prices and sums of earnings—or all of the above.

Q 14.16 Earnings (in millions of dollars): The TTM earnings for KO is 3,979 + (801 − 873) + (1,290 − 1,118) = 4,079. The TTM earnings for PEP is 2,662 + (651 − 570) + (888 − 798) = 2,833. Assets (in millions of dollars): You would not compute a TTM, but instead use the most recent assets: 25,287 for Coca-Cola and 24,200 for PepsiCo, because these are "stock" numbers, not "flow" numbers.

Q 14.17 This question about the unlevered P/E ratio cannot be answered if you do not know the different costs of capital. For example, if the firm's cost of capital is equal to the debt cost of capital, the P/E ratio would not change at all!

Q 14.18 Yahoo! Germany reported an actual market value of \$10.52 billion euros and an earnings yield of 36.9% (P/E of 27). The easy part is supplementing the table:

Manufacturer	Market Cap	Earnings	P/E Ratio	E/P Yield
Volvo (ADR)	\$5.7	−\$0.18	−31.7	−3.2%
Ford	\$14.1	−\$5.30	−2.7	−37.6%
GM	\$18.8	\$1.83	10.3	9.7%
Nissan (ADR)	\$27.0	\$2.55	10.6	9.4%
DaimlerChrysler	\$32.3	\$4.63	7.0	14.3%

Honda (ADR)	$37.7	$3.09	12.2	8.2%
Toyota (ADR)	$87.3	$4.51	19.4	5.2%
Sum	$222.9	$11.13	25.1	6.0%
Average	$31.8	$1.59	3.6	0.9%

The hard part is deciding on a suitable P/E comparable. Our first method (average E/P yield, then invert) suggests adopting the astronomical ratio of $1/0.9\% \approx 111$, due to Ford's enormous loss in terms of market capitalization (Ford had $85 billion in sales and a positive EBITDA of $4.8 billion. But Ford also has ongoing depreciation on the order of $15 billion per year, but capital and other expenditures on the order of $18 [2001] to $37 billion [2000 and 1999].) Our second method (sum up Es and Ps first) suggests $\$222.9/\$11.13 \approx 20$, but it weighs the larger (and Japanese) firms more highly. Nevertheless, in this case, the second method came closer to the actual Volkswagen P/E multiple of 27.

Incidentally, by mid-2003, VW had introduced a couple of flops and its earnings had sagged to $2.5 billion, though its market capitalization had increased to $15 billion. This meant that Volkswagen's P/E multiple had shrunk from 27 to 6 in just 9 months! As to assumptions, they all fall into the category of "apples like apples." For example, you are assuming (hoping) that leverage ratios are similar, foreign earnings are comparable, timing is the same, and so on.

Q 14.19 You would use a price/sales ratio if earnings are negative and/or you believe that sales are more representative than earnings of the future value of the firm.

Q 14.20 Firms can increase sales at the expense of profitability. (Just sell goods for a very low price.) Moreover, you should never compute a P/S ratio for equity. You should only compute one for the entire firm.

Q 14.21 The price/cash ratio, price/sales ratio, and price/dividend ratio are usually calculated without debt adjustment—the equivalent of surgery without anesthesia. This is a huge problem, but it also makes this exercise relatively easy.

Firm	Value/Cash	Value/Sales	Value/Dividends
CSG	N/A	1.3	31
KO	30.8	5.5	50
PEP	45	3.1	74

- The cash-based ratio suggests a value between $6.5 million and $9.5 million. The cash-based ratio values all firms as if only current cash has any meaning, and the ongoing operations are irrelevant (except to the extent that they have influenced current cash).
- The sales-based ratio suggests a value between $12.0 million, $28.6 million, and $50.7 million. Because the smaller comparables have lower ratios, one might settle on a lower value. The sales-based ratio ignores that CSG's equity value is relatively low because more of its value is capitalized with debt than with equity.
- The dividend-based ratio suggests a zero value. Obviously, this is not a perfect estimate. Firms can choose different payout policies.

Hansen's actual value on this day was $51.4 million.

Q 14.22 A common financial-debt-to-equity ratio computes the sum of long-term debt plus debt in current liabilities, divided by the sum of the market value of the firm's equity.

Q 14.23 The current ratio is the ratio of current assets over current liabilities. A firm is less precarious if this ratio is high. (However, too high of a current ratio may mean that the firm is investing too much in short-term assets, which typically yield less.)

Q 14.24 Its receivables turnover is $\$30{,}000/\$6{,}000 = 5$ times per year. DRO is $365 \cdot \$6{,}000/\$30{,}000 = 73$ days.

Q 14.25 The dividend/price ratio divides dividends by price; the dividend payout divides dividends by net income.

PROBLEMS

The *indicates problems available in* myfinancelab

Q 14.26 What are the three main requirements for a comps-based valuation?

Q 14.27 When negotiating house prices, would you value your next residence by the method of comparables or by the method of NPV? If comparables, what kind of ratio might you use?

Q 14.28 Is it better to compute a price/earnings ratio on a per-share basis or on an aggregate (total value) basis?

Q 14.29 Is it better to use cash flows or earnings in your valuation multiple? Why?

Q 14.30 Which is likely to have a higher price/earnings ratio: Google or Exxon?

Q 14.31 Consider a growing firm that produces cash of \$10 million next year. The firm's cash flow growth rate is 15% per annum. The firm's cost of capital is 20%.

(a) What is the market value of this firm?

(b) What is the firm's P/E ratio if it has no debt?

(c) Now assume that the cost of capital for debt of \$100 million is 8%, while the cost of capital for the remaining levered equity is 32%. (Again, the weighted average cost of capital is $50\% \cdot 8\% + 50\% \cdot 32\% = 20\%$, so the firm's cost of capital has not changed.) Interest on the \$100 million debt is paid out. What is the equity's P/E ratio now?

(d) Has the increase in debt increased or decreased the firm's P/E ratio?

Q 14.32 Assume that the prevailing interest rate is 8% per year for value firms and 12% per year for growth firms. A growth firm with earnings of \$100,000 has a market value of \$100,000,000, while a value firm with earnings of \$1,000,000 has a market value of \$20,000,000.

(a) What are the implicit growth rates?

(b) What are the PVGOs?

Q 14.33 Pick 8 firms in the "department stores" sector. Using a financial website (e.g., Yahoo! *Finance*), graph next year's expected growth of earnings against the firms' earnings/price yield. Is there a relation?

Q 14.34 If the P/E ratio on the S&P 500 is 10, given historical earnings growth patterns, what would be a reasonable estimate of long-run future expected rates of return on the stock market? Assume a long-run inflation rate of 2.5% per annum.

Q 14.35 A firm has earnings of \$200, and a price/earnings ratio of 20. What is its implied growth rate, if its cost of capital is about 10%?

Q 14.36 Redo Shiller's value analysis today. Find the current P/E ratio of the S&P 500 on the Web. Assume that the expected real growth rate of GDP is 2.5% per annum. What does the stock market suggest is the S&P 500's expected rate of return these days?

Q 14.37 Use Ford's P/E ratio to value General Motors today. If Ford still has negative earnings, then use Google to value Microsoft.

Q 14.38 A firm with a P/E ratio of 10 wants to take over a firm half its size with a P/E ratio of 25. What will be the P/E ratio of the merged firm?

Q 14.39 Compute a TTM earnings number for Microsoft.

Q 14.40 What are the main problems of comparables? Give an example of each, preferably real-world or numeric examples.

Q 14.41 Is it reasonable to compare IBM's P/E ratio based on equity to that of Microsoft? Is it more or less reasonable to compare IBM's P/E ratio based on total firm value to that of Microsoft?

Q 14.42 Is there a problem with using a book value–based equity measure? If so, why, and when does it matter?

Q 14.43 How could you value a biotech start-up that has no sales or earnings?

Q 14.44 What is the "quick ratio"? Is a firm more or less precarious if this ratio is high?

Q 14.45 What ingredients are in the DuPont model? What are its problems?

PART V

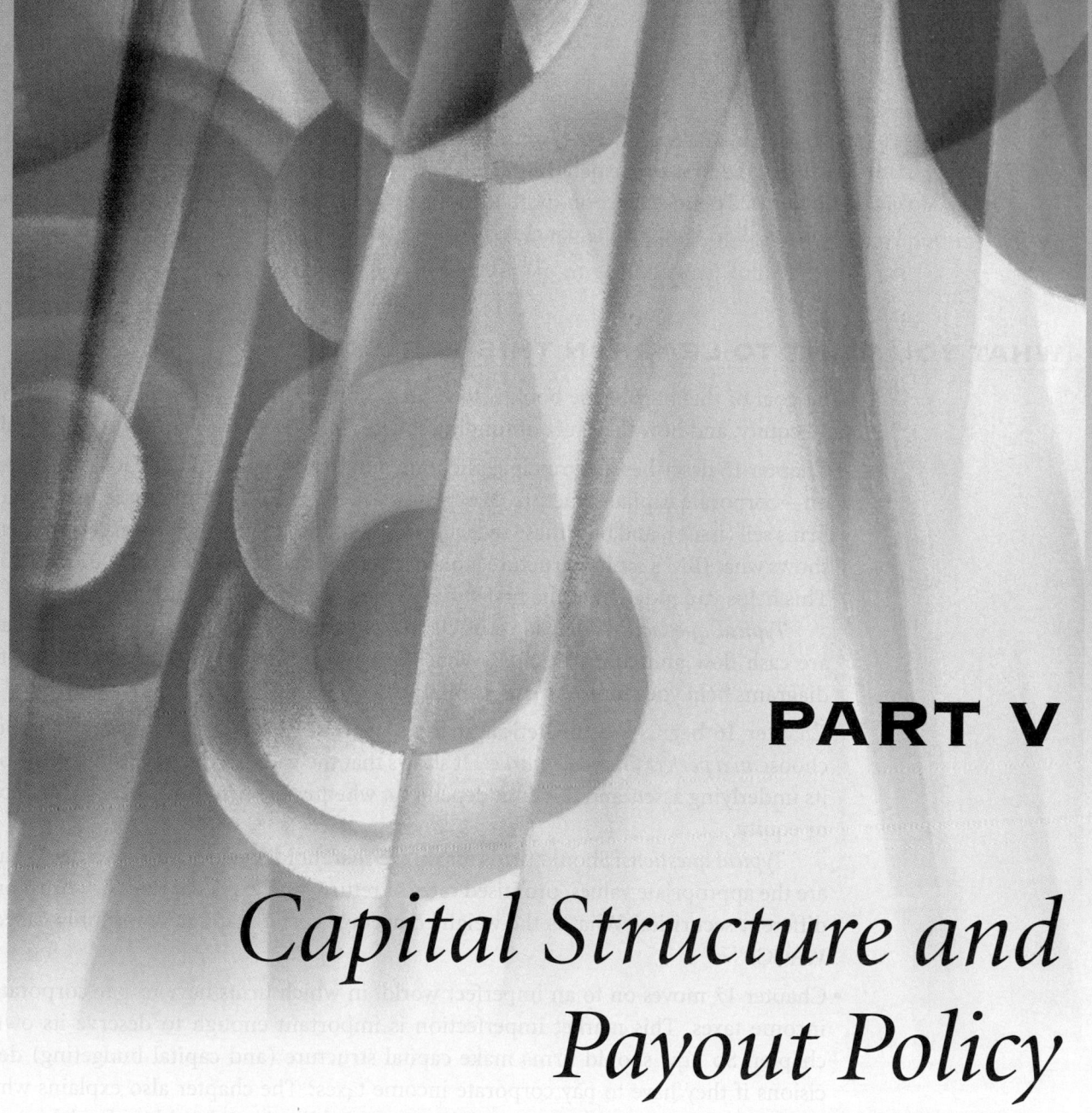

Capital Structure and Payout Policy

FINANCING PROJECTS

Although you now know how you should value projects and how you should think about your costs of capital, you do not yet know how firms can best get new investors to part with their cash. We just assumed that if you had a positive-NPV project, then the cash to start it would be there. However, in the real world, you must somehow get funds first. For example, you could use earnings that you do not pay out. Or you could borrow money. Or you could sell off your accounts receivable. Or you could issue more equity to new shareholders. In this part, we discuss both the types of claims that firms can sell to potential investors and the selling process itself.

- Chapter 19 describes equity payout strategies: dividends and share repurchases. *Typical questions:* Are dividend payments better or worse than share repurchases? Does it matter? How do firms decide to pay out money they earn?

Chapters 22–24 contain material that topically belong to this part but which few classes are likely to have the time to cover in the first course.

15

Corporate Claims

WHO OWNS WHAT?

How should projects be financed? You have already encountered the two basic financing choices that firms have: Current firm owners can accept new limited partners, which they can accomplish by issuing equity (stock). Or they can borrow money, which they can accomplish by issuing debt (bonds), either to public lenders or private lenders (such as banks). However, there are also many other financial claims that firm owners can sell, most of which are hybrids of these two basic choices, debt and equity. In addition, there are other claims that arise in the conduct of business, such as accounts payable, pension obligations, and income taxes due. The **capital structure** is the sum total of all claims on the assets of the firms. Together, the claims represent the rights that own all the firm's assets—they *are* the firm.

In the first part of this chapter, you will learn about the basic choices that corporations have. It explains that you should think of a claim as a bundle of cash flow rights and control rights. The cash flow rights describe how much money the claims holders are supposed to receive. The control rights describe what claims holders can and cannot do, especially when they do not receive the cash flows originally promised to them.

In the second part of this chapter, you will see how IBM's capital structure evolved from 2001 to 2003. It will show you how complex real-world capital structures can be.

15.1 THE BASIC BUILDING BLOCKS

The firm's charter sets up the governance of the firm.

The **corporate charter** is the document that lays down the basics of the firm. It specifies who formally holds decision power, how the firm can engage in further contracts, how the charter can be amended, and so on. The corporate charter also addresses how the firm may be governed in the future. Together with the legal and regulatory framework in which it operates—which is jurisdiction dependent—the charter facilitates the creation of financial and nonfinancial claims, each with its own cash flow rights and control rights. It is this nexus of implicit and explicit contracts that defines the firm broadly, and its financial structure specifically. Our interest in this chapter is this capital structure—which is the sum total of all the claims on the firm's assets. It should not surprise you when I tell you that you have already encountered many features of financial claims, given how important they are and given that we are already more than halfway through the book.

Even real estate owners do not fully own properties. They have to accept certain obligations.

➤ Mortgage and levered equity, Section 6.3A, p. 152

The most basic aspects of capital structure were first explained in the context of the example of a building from Chapter 6. If you finance your building with a mortgage, you own only the residual unmortgaged part as levered equity. This means that you really do not fully own the building. Although you can make a lot of decisions about the building, there are others you cannot make. For example, your mortgage covenants prevent you from demolishing the building or from selling it and keeping all the money. To do either, you must first repay the mortgage. And, of course, as a property owner, you also must satisfy other claims that do not arise financially but instead arise in the context of real ownership. For example, you must pay your county property tax obligation, or the county can repossess your building. And through legal ownership, you also have to accept other obligations. For example, you cannot simply convert your building into a liquor store without obtaining zoning permissions. In reality, any property owner is only part owner—the building is really owned by the (so-miscalled) property owner, plus the mortgage company, plus other claimants.

This is exactly how shareholders "own" corporations—only after other obligations are satisfied.

➤ Limited liability, Section 6.4, p. 155

This is exactly how things work in the corporate context. The firm's assets are owned by multiple claimants. The basic building blocks of the firm's financial structure are **liabilities** (often called **leverage**) and **equity** (often called **stock**), respectively. To use our metaphor, the shareholders are the equivalent of the levered property owner (although with assured limited liability). They are usually in charge, but there are clear limits to what they are allowed to do. Such limits come from covenants that the shareholders accepted earlier—covenants that the firm took on when it borrowed money or when it acquired or operated its assets. For example, most corporate bond covenants prevent firms from destroying or not maintaining their assets, or from selling the assets and paying out the cash to shareholders. The set of all claims on the firm's future payoffs is called its capital structure.

Firms are owned by financial claims (e.g., debt and equity) and nonfinancial claims (e.g., Uncle Sam, pension obligations, and vendor credit).

Claims are often classified into financial and nonfinancial ones:

- Financial claims are debt and equity. They are often loosely called **securities**, the name indicating registration with the **Securities and Exchange Commission** (**SEC**). However, the term has become so common that it is now used much more liberally. For example, neither foreign securities nor privately placed securities are necessarily registered with the SEC.
- Nonfinancial claims are such obligations as corporate income taxes due, pension obligations, and accounts payable.

By strict definition, to fully own the firm and be permitted to do whatever you wish, you must own *all claims* that the firm has issued. It is not enough for you to own only *all stock* or even all financial claims. In the most extreme perspective, you can never fully own any firm, because Uncle Sam always has some claim to future cash flows that you can never acquire.

Every meaningful claim has two important aspects:

Claims have two important features: cash flow rights and control rights.

Cash flow rights, which describe how firm-generated cash will be allocated.

Control rights, which allow the claim owners to enforce their cash flow rights. For example, creditors can force the firm into bankruptcy if the firm does not pay its obligations; and stockholders can appoint the corporate board, which in turn appoints management, which runs the firms.

SOLVE NOW!

Q 15.1 What is a control right? Give some examples.

Q 15.2 Is it ever possible for a private individual to fully own a firm?

15.1A CASH FLOW RIGHTS AS PAYOFF DIAGRAMS

Cash flow rights define payoff diagrams, which plot the claims' payoffs as a function of the underlying firm value at one fixed point in time.

➤ Contingent claims payoff, Table 6.3, p. 159

You have already learned the main tool for the analysis of *cash flow rights* in Chapter 6—payoff tables for contingent claims. Let's apply them in the corporate context. For example, consider a firm with a capital structure that consists of equity, a single bond that promises to pay $200 next year, and no other claims. The value of the corporation is the total value promised to bondholders and shareholders. How much each claims holder receives depends on the value of the firm. Figure 15.1 is a **payoff diagram**. It shows that if the firm is worth $100, bondholders receive $100 and shareholders receive nothing. If the firm is worth $200, bondholders receive $200 and shareholders receive nothing. If the firm is worth $300, bondholders receive $200 and shareholders receive $100. If the firm is worth $400, bondholders receive $200 and shareholders receive $200. And so on. This is the best way to think of the cash flow rights of bonds, stocks, and most other financial claims. Because you can call the future value of the firm (the base asset) the underlying **state**, debt and equity are often called **state-contingent claims**: Their future values depend on the future state of the firm.

In a perfect market, the "firm terminates" aspect of the payoff diagram is not important.

Note that if the market is perfect, it is not important to the analysis whether the firm continues to exist after the bond comes due. You could imagine that the firm is then sold to new owners for its fair value first. The proceeds are then distributed to stockholders and bondholders according to their claims. Of course, stockholders and bondholders could use these proceeds to repurchase the firm immediately if they so desire.

Nevertheless, payoff diagrams cannot illustrate time-varying aspects of claims. They only illustrate firm-value varying aspects of claims.

Although payoff diagrams are very useful as conceptual aids, they do not convey all the information about a claim's cash flow rights. They work best for contracts that have only one payment at one fixed point in time. Our example above showed how easy they make it to understand a zero-bond. Unfortunately, payoff diagrams are not good at illustrating features that are themselves a function of time or a function of many different points in time. It would be more difficult to use the payoff diagram to fully describe a coupon bond, because coupon bonds have many different payment dates. Payoff diagrams are even less useful to illustrate the value of a claim that receives randomly timed future payoffs. Nevertheless, even in such cases, there is usually a link between the value of the firm and the value of the financial claim—so thinking of

Firm Value	Bond Value	Stock Value
$0	$0	$0
$50	$50	$0
$100	$100	$0
$150	$150	$0
$200	$200	$0
$250	$200	$50
$300	$200	$100
$350	$200	$150
⋮		

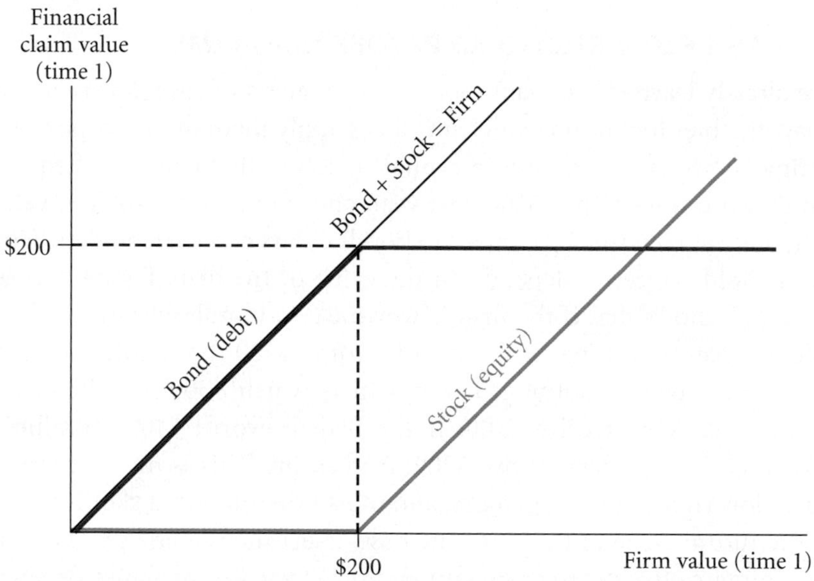

The bond in this example has a face value of $200. Thus, at maturity, if the firm is worth less than $200, the bond receives the entire firm. If the firm is worth more than $200, the bond receives $200 and the levered equity receives the rest. If you own both claims, you own the firm, which is the black diagonal line.

FIGURE 15.1 Sample Bond and Stock Payoff Table and Diagram (at Maturity)

financial claims as contingent claims in the context of payoff diagrams often remains a useful conceptual, if not entirely accurate, tool.

SOLVE NOW!

Q 15.3 Write down a payoff table for a stock and a zero-bond with a promised payoff of $300 million. What does the graph look like?

Q 15.4 Can you add payoff functions graphically in the payoff diagrams (if you own multiple claims), or do you first need to write down a revised payoff table? How? If so, what does the sum of all added claims look like?

Q 15.5 To gain some practice with payoff diagrams, assume your medical insurance pays 90% of your medical expenses, subject to a $500 deductible and an annual limit of \$10,000 payout. Write down your insurance payoff table and graph an insurance payoff diagram, as a function of your medical expenses. What is the slope of the line at each segment?

Q 15.6 Can you draw a payoff diagram for a semiannual coupon bond with 15 remaining 10% coupon payments until maturity?

15.2 LIABILITIES

Firms' total liabilities are often classified into financial and nonfinancial claims.

15.2A FINANCIAL CLAIMS (DEBT)

You have already worked extensively with financial liabilities, such as bonds of all varieties in Part I. Still, let us review the rights of debt in the corporate context.

Bonds are loans to companies with specified obligations.

➤ Various bond features, Section 6.2D, p. 148

Cash flow rights: Bonds are just loans that promise specific payoffs at specific times in the future. The borrower (or issuer) receives cash up front and contractually promises to pay cash in the future. The returned cash is commonly classified into interest payments (usually tax-deductible for the issuer) and repayment of principal. Most corporate bonds promise payments every 3 or 6 months and repay the remaining principal at **maturity**. In the event of liquidation, the law states that the **absolute priority rule** (APR) be applied. Bonds are senior securities, so their holders receive what they have been promised first, before more-junior claimants (such as equity) can receive anything. Different bonds from the same firm can themselves be classified into more- and less-senior claims, too. The more-senior bonds have first dibs when the firm's cash is distributed, and only after they are fully paid off do the junior bondholders receive anything.

Bondholders have no control rights, unless the firm fails to pay what it promised or a bond covenant is violated.

Control rights: Unless the firm violates a bond covenant or is near financial distress (in which case, the law imparts managers with fiduciary responsibilities toward bondholders, too), bondholders typically do not have the right to participate in the decisions of the firm or the selection of its management. *But* if the firm misses a payment or violates a covenant that it has taken on to obtain the bond financing, then the bondholders have the right to force the firm into bankruptcy.

The U.S. Constitution has made bankruptcy a federal issue. The current *Federal Bankruptcy Code* allows for either corporate reorganization under **Chapter 11** or corporate liquidation under **Chapter 7**, named for their respective chapters. Both are supervised by a federal bankruptcy trustee under the supervision of a federal bankruptcy court. Either creditors or the firm itself can petition to enter bankruptcy.

In theory, bankruptcy allows bondholders to take over and thereby either keep the entire firm, or force it to pay what they were contractually promised. In practice, this is not as easy in the United States as it is, for example, in many European countries—but it does happen frequently enough. After the creditors' obligations are satisfied, any residual cash left over is paid to the more junior securities. In any case, no managers survive Chapter 7 (the firm is gone!), and few managers survive Chapter 11 bankruptcy. Not surprisingly, managers generally try to avoid missing bond payments like the plague.

ANECDOTE Judge Lifland and Eastern Airlines' Creditors

The absolute priority rule is the theory. In practice, bankruptcy courts can and sometimes do violate the pre-agreed priority rules in the bankruptcy process. In turn, because corporate managers can choose where to file for bankruptcy, they usually do so in the court where they expect to fare best.

Bankruptcy Judge Burton Lifland, of the Southern District of New York, was so notorious for violating creditors' rights that he attracted not only Eastern Airlines' bankruptcy, but also those of Manville, Orion Pictures, and LTV. But it was Eastern Airlines that was Judge Lifland's crowning achievement: When it went bankrupt in March 1989, it was fully solvent. Unsecured creditors would have likely been satisfied in full. Instead, Judge Lifland allowed Eastern to continue operating for 2 more years, partially on the basis that closing it would have disrupted Christmas travel. Eastern's ongoing operation evaporated about $1.5 billion through operating losses and another $100 million through legal fees. In the end, unsecured creditors received practically nothing of their $2.3 billion claim.

Despite such occasional spectacular examples of drastic APR violations, more commonly they are mild. (They may even be necessary. After all, society would not want to see lawyers starve!) These days, creditors are aware of expected violations and accumulating legal fees, and they therefore take them into account when they purchase bonds and stocks in the first place. Thus, the cost of legal wrangling primarily worsens corporations' borrowing terms up front, and not the creditors' payoffs.

In addition to bonds' universal right of repayment (through control in default), many lenders grant their creditors additional control rights in the original lending agreement. These provisions are called **covenants**. For example, a loan agreement may specify that the firm must maintain a certain level of liquidity. If it does not, its loan can be declared to be in default and it becomes due. If the firm fails to repay, creditors can petition the courts to force the firm into bankruptcy.

Firms can contract any claim features they wish. Perfect markets offer fair pricing, but this does not mean that every bond feature is equally smart.

Bond features are not written in stone. Over time, firms have experimented and developed many variations and hybrids. Naturally, if any claim offers more features or protections that are of value to investors, then their buyers are willing to pay more for the claim up front. In a perfect market, companies receive and investors pay the appropriate fair share (price), regardless of the features chosen by corporations offering claims for sale. The features described in this chapter are among those that have survived, evolved, and thrived over the years—those that increase value. Of course, corporations could issue claims that do not maximize value, even if they are fairly priced. For example, a claim might offer its owner the right to become CEO if it were to rain in Los Angeles next April 21. When sold, this claim would fetch an appropriate efficient and fair price in the market, but it would probably significantly lower the overall value of the firm.

Par value is meaningless for equity. For bonds, par value helps to calculate the coupon payment schedule.

➤ Par value, Section 3.2B, p. 52

You may sometimes see the term **par value**. Although it is usually a vacuous concept when it comes to equity, it has meaning for bonds. However, it is not really a value, but only a way to quote coupon payment flow patterns. That is, coupon payout schedules at origination are described by the bond's par value. (Issues that are sold below par are discount bonds, issues that are sold above par are premium bonds.) Principal and par value, and/or interest and coupon payment need not be identical, not even at the time of issue, much less later. But never think of par value as a real value.

ANECDOTE Are Convertibles Debt or Equity?

In a 2002 survey in which CFOs were asked to describe why they issue convertible debt, the most frequent answers alluded to the fact that convertibles are "equity in disguise": 58% of the managers answered that it is an inexpensive way to issue "delayed" common stock; 50% answered that they did so because they considered their own stock currently undervalued, which again could be interpreted as managers thinking of convertibles as equity in disguise.

Source: Graham and Harvey, Duke, 2002.

CONVERTIBLE BONDS

A convertible bond is an example of how a bond can be more than plain vanilla. Convertible debt gives holders the right to convert this debt into equity at a predetermined price at predetermined dates. Thus, convertibles are hybrids with both debt and equity characteristics. Here is a simple example: A firm with 400 outstanding shares of equity has 200 outstanding convertible bonds that promise $10,000 each in January 2050. Each such bond can be converted, at the bondholder's discretion, into three new shares of stock. This means that if all bondholders convert, they will own 60% of the firm. The original shareholders will own only 40% *but without an obligation to repay the debt*. The cost to shareholders will therefore no longer be the money that the firm has to pay to creditors, but a loss in ownership. This lessening of ownership is called **dilution**.

Convertible bonds allow the bondholder to exchange the bond into something else, usually into equity.

If you own these 200 bonds, what would you do if the value of the firm's assets in January 2050 were $2 million or less? Your 200 bonds would own the entire $2 million that the firm is worth. It would not be in your interest to exchange your bonds for shares. But what would you do if the value were $1 billion? You would make the following calculation: If you take advantage of the convertibility feature and exchange your 200 bonds for 600 shares, there will be 1,000 shares in total. Your shares will therefore own 60% of the firm, or $600 million—a whole lot more than the $2 million that you would receive if you did not convert. Therefore, you will exercise your right to convert.

When a convertible comes due, its holders can decide whether they want to remain as such or become shareholders at the previously agreed-upon terms.

What is the firm value at which you would be indifferent between converting and not converting? It is where 60% of the firm would be equal to $2 million. This occurs when the firm value is equal to $\$2/0.6 \approx \$3.33$ million. To summarize:

Here is how to determine the firm value cutoff at which convertible bondholders prefer to convert.

- If the firm's value is below $2 million, the convertible bonds get everything.
- Between $2 and $3.3 million, the convertible bonds receive $2 million and the shareholders get the residual above $2 million.
- And above $3.3 million, both shareholders and bondholders benefit from higher values. The convertible bondholders own 60% of the firm's value; the shareholders own 40% of the firm's value.

The payoff diagram in Figure 15.2 shows the value of the claims.

Convertible bonds are popular, perhaps because they tend to align the interests of shareholders and bondholders. For example, if shareholders wanted to take a project that would help them but (accidentally or intentionally) hurt plain bondholders, the bondholders would usually try to fight the project. However, if the bonds were

Preview: Why is the conversion feature useful?

➤ Bondholder expropriation, Section 18.5, p. 676

Firm Value	Convertible Bond Value	Common Stock Value
$0	$0	$0
$1,000	$1,000	$0
$1,500	$1,500	$0
$2,000	$2,000	$0
$2,500	$2,000	$500
$3,000	$2,000	$1,000
$3,333	$2,000	$1,333
$3,500	$2,100	$1,400
$4,000	$2,400	$1,600
$4,500	$2,700	$1,800
⋮		

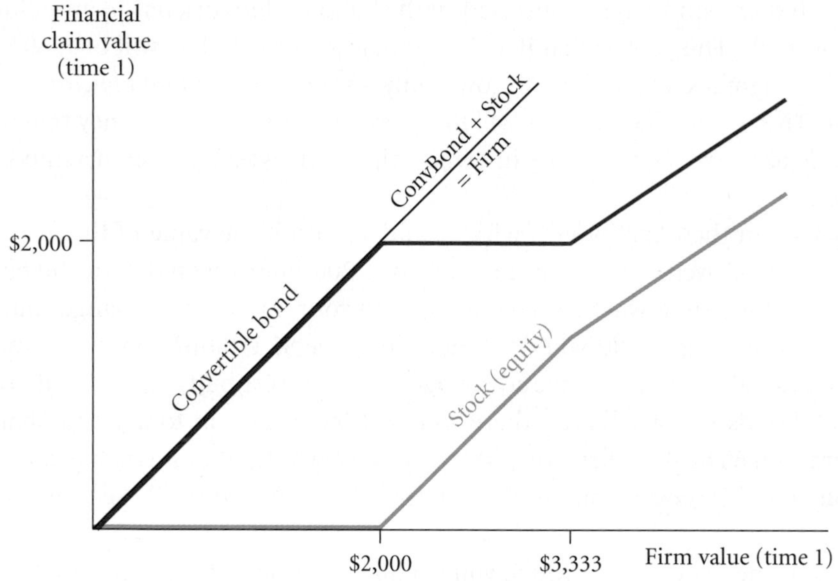

FIGURE 15.2 Sample Convertible Bond and Stock Payoff Table Diagram (at Maturity)

convertible, the bondholders could also profit from the resulting value increase and then not oppose such a project.

Firm owners are willing to give up the right to convert, because this feature increases the cash that creditors pay them up front.

One final question: Why would shareholders be willing to give bondholders this right to convert, which in effect deprives them of much upside? The answer must be that by doing so, bondholders are willing to pay more for the bond up front. This means that the shareholders can negotiate for a lower interest rate. And, indeed, you know that if financial markets are perfect, bondholders get what they pay for.

Bonds come in a thousand varieties—and then some. Here are some common features.

Other Corporate Bond Features

If the bond claim includes more rights, then its interest rate is usually lower (equivalently, the value of the bond is higher). The issuer can choose what specific rights to offer to buyers and what rights to reserve for the firm. Among the more common bond features are the following:

Bond covenants specify that the firm will keep certain promises, or else it will be forced to repurchase (**redeem**) the bond. Among the more common covenants are restrictions on what the firm can do with its assets, how much in dividends it may pay, how many and what kinds of other financial claims it may issue, what kinds of financial ratios (e.g., the debt-to-equity ratio) it needs to maintain, who the auditor is, what happens if the corporation defaults on any other bond, how much of its own bonds the firm will repurchase in each year, and so on. (This last feature is called a *sinking fund* provision and is common. See below.) Interestingly, the use of covenants varies over time. In good times, when plenty of credit is chasing investment opportunities, lenders are often less strict in their demands for specific covenants.

Bond seniority specifies exactly which bonds receive first dibs in case of bankruptcy and liquidation. A **senior bond** will have to be satisfied in full before a **subordinated bond** (or **junior bond**) may receive any money. In turn, equity receives its funds only after even the most junior bonds have been fully satisfied.

Collateral (or **security**) are specific corporate assets pledged to a specific bond in case of default. For example, mortgage bonds are collateralized by the value of the underlying real estate. If the issuer fails to pay, the bondholders may repossess the underlying real estate and use it to satisfy their claim. If the real estate is not enough to satisfy the claim of the **secured bond**, the remaining claim becomes an ordinary bond, waiting in line with other creditors for payment.

Convertibility, as you have seen, allows the bondholder to exchange the bond for shares.

Putability allows the bondholder to return the bond to the issuer, in exchange for a pre-agreed payment. This is like convertibility, except that the conversion is into cash, not into equity.

Callability allows the issuer (the firm) to "call in" the outstanding bond at a prespecified price. For example, a callable bond contract may state that the firm can redeem the bond by paying back principal plus 10% rate of interest in May 2020. Usually, callable bonds do not allow a call for the first 5 years of the life of the bond. Callability is often present with convertibility, so that the call can be used to force bondholders to convert: The corporation calls the bonds, and the holder of the bond finds that it is in her interest to convert the bond into equity rather than to accept repayment.

While a convertible bond gives bondholders extra rights, callable bonds give the firm extra rights. Therefore, when a bond contains a call feature, it is less valuable than an otherwise identical bond. This means that issuers of bonds receive less money when they include a call feature. Put differently, the corporation must pay a higher interest rate up front if it reserves a call feature. In effect, every mortgage in the United States is a callable bond, because the seller of the bond (the homeowner) can just pay back the remaining loan balance (the **principal**) and be absolved of all further obligations. Naturally, homeowners pay for this privilege with a higher interest rate up front.

The call feature is a good example of where payoff diagrams do not capture the whole situation. The value of the callable bond is often more a function of the prevailing interest rate than it is a function of the firm value. Corporations tend to call bonds when the economy-wide interest rate has dropped so that replacement bonds have become much cheaper. (Similarly, homeowners tend to repay their mortgages and refinance when the mortgage interest rate has dropped.) But because the interest rate is not a one-to-one function of the firm value in the future, the payoff diagram against the firm value at a fixed point in time would not tell the whole story.

A **sinking fund** is a provision that the firm will repurchase a specified fraction (no more and no less) of the principal before maturity. Unlike the call feature, there is no optionality here. Thus, in one sense, it helps the purchaser by assuring that the firm pays back the money along the way. In another sense, it helps the firm, because it allows the firm to call a part of the bond early, often at a discount.

CFOs must also make decisions on the following corporate bond features. You already learned about them in Part I, because these features are shared by noncorporate bonds:

Bond maturity is the time to final payback. Indeed, borrowing may be very short term (as short as overnight!), or very long term (as long as forever). Bonds of different maturities may have different names. For example, **commercial paper** is short-term debt, often guaranteed by a bank's credit line (see below), and therefore is almost risk free to the lender. (To participate in this market, firms must have an investment-grade credit rating.) On the corporate balance sheet, **funded debt** is the term for debt that has a maturity of less than 1 year. **Unfunded debt** has a maturity of more than 1 year.

Again, payoff diagrams do not do bond maturity full justice. The reason is that maturity can sometimes be like "super-seniority." That is, a subordinated bond may be repaid before the more senior bonds come due, and, once paid, the money paid to the subordinated bond can often not be reclaimed to satisfy the senior creditor's higher-priority claims.

➤ Duration, Section 5.8, p. 126

Bond duration is a measure of how soon payments are made.

➤ Zero and coupon bonds, Section 5.3D, p. 108

Coupon bonds versus **zero-bonds:** Zero-bonds pay a fixed amount of money only at a final date. Coupon bonds make (interest) payments on a regular schedule, typically (but not always) twice a year, and the principal is repaid as a **balloon payment** at the end.

➤ Units, Section 18.5C, p. 679

A **unit** is a bundle of multiple types of financial claims that are sold together. For example, one common type of unit bundles a bond with a warrant. (A **warrant** is a right to buy equity shares that the firm will then issue for a prespecified price at prespecified times in the future.) The purchaser can keep both types of claims or unbundle them and sell them separately.

➤ Prime rate and LIBOR, Bond Glossary, p. B-1

Fixed-rate debt versus **floating-rate debt:** Fixed-rate bonds usually promise to pay a predetermined interest rate over the life of the bond. Floating-rate bonds offer a spread relative to some other interest rate, usually to *LIBOR* or to the *prime rate*. Highly reputable companies can typically borrow at interest rates that are about LIBOR. More risky companies typically pay interest rates that are about

100–300 basis points (1–3%) above LIBOR. The interest rate on floating-rate debt is also often **capped** or **collared**—that is, the interest rate will never exceed a predetermined ceiling.

There is no limit to the imagination as far as bond features are concerned. For example, the Russian carmaker Avtovaz issued Lada bonds in 1994, which allowed the holders to convert their bonds into Lada cars. Other bonds have had payoffs linked to commodities (such as the price of oil), to other financial claims, or to exchange rates.

Here is an example of a less common bond feature.

CONCENTRATED BANK DEBT OR DIFFUSE PUBLIC BONDS?

Another important dimension along which loans differ is whether there is a relationship between the lender and the issuer. Firms can raise funds with a public debt issue, in which there is typically no relationship between the borrower and the many diffuse lenders, or with a private debt issue (e.g., a **bank loan**), in which there is often only one lender. The advantage of borrowing from the bank is that a single lender may get to know the firm, monitor it so that it acts appropriately in the future, and thereby grant better terms. The disadvantage is that there is less competition among banks for extending loans than there is among public bondholders. Bank loans can also take the form of a **credit line**. Credit lines are like instant debt, permitting borrowers to draw down money (and pay higher interest) only upon need. (Borrowers typically agree to pay a low interest rate even on the unused part of the credit line.) The opposite of a credit line is **negotiated debt**, in which both the bank and the firm commit to a fixed loan. Just as the lines between debt and equity are often blurry, so are the lines between bank loans, private debt, and public debt. There is now a large market for loans extended by syndicates of banks, in which multiple lenders can share the risk of a loan. It accounted for more than $1 trillion in new loans in 2006. On the other hand, many individual banks now routinely resell loans that they have made to firms. Then there are also vulture investors who purchase dispersed public debt in order to monitor the actions of the company, behaving much like a bank—as one fully coordinated lender. (And the liquidity crisis of 2008 has thrown these markets into general disarray, so it is not yet clear how they will look in years to come.)

A public bond is usually owned by many diffuse creditors. A bank loan is usually owned by one (or just a few) banks. A bank loan can take the form of a credit line or of negotiated debt.

SOLVE NOW!

Q 15.7 A firm is financed with a senior bond that promises to pay $100, a junior bond that promises to pay $200 (of lower seniority but of equal maturity to the senior bond), and equity. Write down the payoff table and then draw the payoff diagrams when the two bonds are due.

Q 15.8 A convertible zero-bond that promises $10,000 can be converted into 50 shares of equity at its maturity date. If there are 2,000 such bonds and 300,000 shares outstanding, what would the payoff table and diagram for both bondholders and equity holders look like?

Q 15.9 Write down the equity payoff table and draw the payoff diagram if the firm has the following capital structure:

- 1,000 senior bonds with promised payoffs for a total of $100 million, convertible into 50 million new equity shares

- 500 junior bonds with promised payoffs for a total of $50 million, convertible (at the bondholder's discretion) into 15 million new shares
- 100 million equity shares for the rest of the firm

It is easiest to work with aggregate figures, that is, consider the firm value in increments of $50 million. (Hint: At what equity value and at what firm value [the two are not the same] would the senior convert?)

Q 15.10 Write down all bond features (variations) that you remember.

15.2B NONFINANCIAL LIABILITIES

For nonfinancial liabilities, cash flow and control rights can be weak or strong.

Although our book's focus is primarily on financial claims, most of the discussion also applies to nonfinancial claims. However, nonfinancial liabilities can vary widely in terms of both cash flow and control rights. They can have rights that are weaker or stronger than those of financial claims.

A nonfinancial liability with strong control rights: income tax obligations.

For example, Uncle Sam has cash flow rights that are specified in the tax code (i.e., computed according to tax laws and IRS rules). By law, corporate income tax obligations have priority before any other claim. The control rights that enforce this claim are similarly very powerful and even include criminal sanctions. If you evade corporate taxes, you can go to jail.

A nonfinancial liability with weak control rights: a customer who purchased a warranty from the firm.

On the other hand, your suppliers have fairly weak cash flow rights. They are supposed to be paid for the goods they have delivered to you. However, the cost of legally enforcing modest financial claims in the United States often exceeds the value of the claims. Thus, the best control right of your suppliers may be the threat to stop doing business with your firm if you do not pay. The same poor control rights often apply to customers, who may have purchased your products with a warranty. The customers may or may not have legal rights, but the enforcement costs are so high that they may not be worth the paper they are written on.

15.3 EQUITY (STOCK)

Stock = Equity. Ordinary = Common.

➤ Levered equity, Section 6.4, p. 155

Stock is another name for equity, which you have already encountered in earlier chapters. If not further qualified, it refers to the most common flavor, which is called just this—**common** (or sometimes **ordinary**). **Common stock**, **ordinary equity**, and **common equity** are all the same thing. The terms **stockholders** or **shareholders** are just abbreviations for **stock shareholders**.

Shareholders usually have last dibs (i.e., money only after other obligations have been paid) but enjoy unlimited upside.

Cash flow rights: Stock receives whatever is left over *after* all liabilities have been honored. Thus, the bad news is that equity typically has the lowest priority in bankruptcy. If the firm does poorly, shareholders may get nothing. The good news is that the equity gets all the rest—potentially unlimited upside for the common equity. If shareholders are lucky, they receive dividend payments and capital appreciation.

Dividends have to be paid from *after-tax* earnings. Any paid-out dividends were thus taxed "at the source." Sometimes, other companies own these dividend-paying shares. The tax code intends to reduce a second round of tax for corporate owners on dividend income that was already taxed once at a source company. Thus, the **corporate dividend exclusion rule** has historically allowed corporations to pay a reduced tax rate on their dividend receipts. (However, this is subject to qualification—it can depend on whether the source firm was fully subject to income tax payments, on the type of firm paying the dividend, on the contractual ability of the issuer to call back the equity, and on the recipient's percent ownership.) In contrast to corporate investors, individual investors were historically subject to being taxed a second time at the full dividend personal income tax rate. This is called the **double taxation of dividends**, though it has been greatly reduced by the Bush tax cuts of 2003. (Similar arrangements have long been the norm in many other countries, such as in the United Kingdom.)

Control rights: Unlike creditors, shareholders cannot force the firm into bankruptcy if it refuses to pay dividends. Instead, shareholders' main control right is their right to elect the **corporate board**. The board is legally the principal of the firm and owns the control rights over the company itself. (The legal details to accomplish this delegation of power vary by corporate charter, by state, and by country.) The corporate board in turn appoints the managers, to whom they further delegate many, if not most, day-to-day control rights.

Shareholders elect the corporate board, which appoints and supervises management.

In addition to this contracted right, managers also have a legal **fiduciary responsibility** to shareholders, except if the firm is in financial distress, in which case this responsibility extends to both creditors and shareholders. There is some disagreement about whether dispersed shareholders in large, publicly traded corporations possess an effective control over the board (and in turn management) in real life, or whether it is more the other way around. The conflict between shareholders and managers is the focus of Chapter 24 on corporate governance.

Most companies have only one type of common equity. A few firms have different classes that differ in the number of votes each share carries. (Sometimes, they receive different amounts of dividends, too.) For example, when Rupert Murdoch purchased the Dow Jones company in 2007, he had to contend with the Bancroft founding family that owned only 24.7% of the total number of shares but controlled 64.2% of the votes. (Since the mid-1990s, the NYSE has refused to accept new firms that have such dual share classes.)

Nowadays in the United States, there is usually only one flavor of common equity.

In sum, although not perfectly correct, you can usually think of the equity holders as the corporate owners, though limited in power and protected by limited liability.

There are two other less common types of equity claims. They no longer play an important role in most large publicly traded firms, but they still have some use in small privately held companies. (Venture capitalists often use them.)

Preferred equity is a claim with both debt and equity characteristics. Unlike ordinary equity, where dividends are declared annually at the discretion of management, preferred equity's dividends are specified at issuance (for example, $2.25 per calendar quarter per share). The preferred dividends are also usually higher than common dividends. In addition, the preferred equity covenants usually state that their dividend payments have priority over any dividend payments to common stock.

Preferred equity has some equity and some debt characteristics.

As equity, preferred is junior to any liabilities. However, the preferred covenants usually specify a higher priority relative to common equity in case of bankruptcy. Preferred equity also lacks the ability of creditors to force the firm into bankruptcy if the firm fails to pay the preferred dividends.

Preferred equity is often retired on a fixed schedule—even though many preferred equities have no formal maturity. Many preferred shares are redeemable, and if this is the case, investors receiving these dividends must treat them as interest income for tax purposes. As with common stock, some preferred stock is traded on public stock exchanges.

Naturally, many other features can be explicitly added by covenant. Indeed, the only context in which preferred equity is still commonly used nowadays is as **convertible preferred** in the context of nonpublic venture capital financing. These claims typically have covenants that provide explicitly for voting rights. The holders of such claims are usually themselves corporations—venture capitalists—who can write off the claims if the firm fails, or convert them into common equity if the firm succeeds.

We don't have time to cover warrants and options in detail here.

Warrants and options give their owners the right to purchase stock in the future at a predetermined price. If it is a warrant, the shares that the firm will provide are newly issued (and thus dilutive). Options and warrants are usually even more junior than common equity. They are often of value only if the firm experiences extraordinarily good times. In publicly traded corporations, they rarely have control rights—except for the right of the owner to convert them into equity. For more information on warrants and options, refer to Chapter 26.

SOLVE NOW!

Q 15.11 Do shareholders enjoy limited liability?

Q 15.12 Did the Bush dividend tax cuts make corporate and individual holders of shares more similar or more dissimilar in terms of their dividend income tax treatments?

Q 15.13 In what sense is preferred equity like bonds? In what sense is preferred equity like stocks?

15.4 TRACKING IBM'S CAPITAL STRUCTURE FROM 2001 TO 2003

You will learn a lot about capital structure by following a sample company (IBM) from 2001 to 2003.

You now have the conceptual understanding of how you should think about different financial claims—their cash flow rights and control rights. In the real world, capital structure is highly complex. Perhaps the best way to understand what it *really* looks like is to examine the real-world capital structure of one company. We shall choose IBM, because it illustrates the many facets of capital structure quite nicely. And we'll look specifically at the period from 2001 to 2003, because this was a turbulent period at the end of the technology boom of the late 1990s. Table 15.1 shows IBM's balance sheets from 2001 to 2003—you can download IBM's complete historical financials from IBM's corporate website. (Some numbers were restated in 2003, and thus not reported in 2001 and 2002 as I report them.) I added the "change" lines to the table to make it easier to see quickly what was happening. The top part of the table shows how IBM's liabilities evolved; the bottom part shows how IBM's equity evolved.

TABLE 15.1 MAJOR COMPONENTS OF DEBT AND EQUITY FOR IBM, 2001–2003 (DOLLARS IN MILLIONS, EXCEPT SHARE DATA)

Liabilities		2001		2002 (revised)		2003	
Long-Term Debt	Change	$15,963	+$4,023	$19,986	−$3,000	$16,986	(see Table 15.2)
Short-Term Liabilities	Change	$35,119	−$569	$34,550 ($34,220)	+$3,350	$37,900	(see Table 15.3)
includes Short-Term Financial Debt of		*$11,188*	*−$5,157*	*$6,031*	*+$615*	*$6,646*	(see Table 15.3)
Pension Liabilities	Change	$10,308	+$2,907	$13,215	+$1,036	$14,251	
Other Liabilities	Change	$5,465	+$486	$5,951 ($6,281)	+$1,175	$7,456	(see Table 15.4)
Minority Interest		None		None		None	
Negative Goodwill		None		None		None	
Total Liabilities	Change	$66,855	+$6,847	$73,702	+$2,891	$76,593	
Financial Debt	Change	$27,151	−$1,134	$26,017	−$2,385	$23,632	

Equity		2001		2002		2003
Total Issued Shares				1920.96		1937.39
−Treasury Shares =				−198.59		−242.88
Number of Shares Outstanding	Change	1,723.19	−0.82	1,722.37	−27.86	1,694.51
Book Price/Share	Change	$13.61/s	−0.38/s	$13.23/s	+3.21/s	$16.44/s
Market Price/Share	Change	$120.96/s	−43.46/s	$77.50/s	+15.18/s	$92.68/s
Stockholder's Equity (Book Value)	Change	$23,448	−$666	$22,782	+$5,082	$27,864
Market Value of Equity	Change	$208,437	−$74,953	$133,484	+$23,563	$157,047

Source: Courtesy of IBM

15.4A IBM'S LIABILITIES

First look at the constituents of IBM's liabilities. A glance at Table 15.1 tells you that there are four main categories of IBM's liabilities: long-term debt, short-term (or current) liabilities, pension liabilities, and other liabilities. Other firms may have two more components: minority interest of the business owned by third parties (which is therefore almost like equity) and negative goodwill (related to an accounting discount

IBM had four nonzero liability components.

at which IBM might have purchased other companies). These two items rarely play large roles (except in companies that have been involved in large M&A activities), and they did not play any role in the case of IBM.

More detail about a firm's capital structure usually has to be teased out of the financial footnotes.

If you want to learn more details about what all these claims are, you have to dive into the **financial footnotes** accompanying IBM's financial statements. These footnotes usually explain what the liabilities really are—and they are usually much longer than the financial statements themselves. Let me show you what I learned. It is not important for you to understand every little detail—IBM is just one company, and every company looks a little different. Your goal is to learn the basics and to be able to look up and interpret information when you need it.

Long-Term Debt

IBM's long-term debt consisted of many different securities. From 2001 to 2003, long-term debt increased and then decreased, mostly driven by IBM's notes.

Table 15.2 shows *how* IBM's long-term debt first increased by $4 billion and then decreased by $3 billion. Like many other large Fortune 100 companies, IBM had a myriad of publicly traded long-term bonds outstanding. (Small firms tend to rely more on bank debt.)

Straight bonds: The top part of Table 15.2 shows IBM's straight long-term bonds (debentures). (Note that one of IBM's bonds has about 90 years remaining to maturity! We can guess that these bonds do not appear to have an active call feature, or IBM would surely have retired its 8.375% bond due in 2019, given that it had considerably lower borrowing costs in 2003.) We can also guess that these bonds did not have an active sinking fund provision, because in most of these, the outstanding principal remained constant from 2001 to 2003. The only bond on which IBM retired any principal was its 6.5% bond, due in 2028. As to new debt, you can find deep in the footnotes that IBM issued a 5.875% bond for $600 million at 97.65 on October 1, 2003. (Par is 100, so this issue was below par. This bond was a discount bond, which means that its IRR was above 5.875%.)

Net-in-net, Table 15.2 shows that IBM did not change its straight bond borrowing from 2001 to 2002, and increased it by only $219 million from 2002 to 2003.

➤ Treasury notes, Section 5.3, p. 102

Notes: There was more financing action in IBM's notes. **Notes** are in essence short-term bonds. They are also often callable. Together, these two features make it easy for a corporation to expand or contract debt, as needed.

IBM increased its medium-term notes by $3.5 billion from 2001 to 2002, and then decreased it by $2.4 billion from 2002 to 2003. (Relatively lower interest rates may help explain some of the shift from longer-term notes into medium-term notes in 2002, but not in 2003. In any case, the two do not exactly offset one another.)

Net-in-net, $3.5 billion of IBM's $4 billion increase in long-term borrowing in 2002 and $2.4 billion of IBM's $3 billion decrease came from its medium-term notes. Other notes were used to offset some of this, but, nevertheless, IBM seems to have mostly used its notes program to expand or contract its long-term borrowing needs.

Hybrid financing: Note also that IBM had one hybrid debt-equity instrument—a convertible 3.43% note. It was issued by IBM to the partners of Pricewaterhouse Coopers Consulting (PwCC), a firm that IBM acquired in late 2002.

TABLE 15.2 IBM'S LONG-TERM LIABILITIES (DOLLARS IN MILLIONS)

At Dec 31	Maturities	2001		2002		2003
U.S. Dollars:						
Debentures:						
5.875%	2032	—		—		$600
6.22%	2027	$500		$500		$500
6.5%	2028	$700		$700		**$319**
7.0%	2025	$600		$600		$600
7.0%	2045	$150		$150		$150
7.125%	2096	$850		$850		$850
7.5%	2013	$550		$550		$550
8.375%	2019	$750		$750		$750
Change		$4,100	±$0	$4,100	+$219	$4,319
Conv. Notes: 3.43% [a]	2007	—		$328		$309
Notes: 6%, 5.9% [b]	2003–32	$2,772		$2,130		$3,034
Med.-Term Notes: 4%, 3.7% [b] (Change)	2003–18	$3,620	+$3,493	$7,113	−$2,423	$4,690
Other: 4.9%, 4.0% [b]	2003–09	$828		$610		$508
Change		$11,320	+$2,961	$14,281	−$1,421	$12,860
Other Currencies [c]						
Euros (5.4%, 5.3%) [b]	2003–09	$3,042		$2,111		$1,174
Yen (1.0%, 1.1%) [b]	2003–15	$4,749		$4,976		$4,363
Canadian (5.8%, 5.8%) [b]	2003–11	$441		$445		$201
Swiss (4.0%, 4.0%) [b]	2003	$151		$180		–
Other (6.6%, 6.0%) [b]	2003–14	$726		$730		$770
Change		$20,429	+$2,294	$22,723	−$3,355	$19,368
Unamort. (Prem.)/Disc.		$47		−$1		$15
SFAS #133 Fair Value Adj. [c]		$396		$978		$806
Change		$20,778	+$2,924	$23,702	−$3,543	$20,159
Less Current Maturities		$4,815		$3,716		$3,173
Total (Change)		$15,963	+$4,023	$19,986	−$3,000	$16,986

a. These convertible notes were issued in the 2002 acquisition of PwCC to PwCC partners, and some began converting into equity in 2003.

b. The first interest rate is the average from 2001 to 2002, the second from 2002 to 2003.

c. This item "marks to market" the value of the debt instruments when interest rates change. The IBM footnotes detail this further as "*In accordance with the requirements of SFAS No. 133, the portion of the company's fixed rate debt obligations that is hedged is reflected in the Consolidated Statement of Financial Position as an amount equal to the sum of the debt's carrying value plus a SFAS No. 133 fair value adjustment representing changes recorded in the fair value of the hedged debt obligations attributable to movements in market interest rates and applicable foreign currency exchange rates.*"

Foreign borrowing: Over this time period, IBM repurchased a good deal of euro debt. The euro appreciated in value from about 1.1 €/$ in 2001 to about 0.9 €/$ by 2002, but the decline in the value of IBM's euro debt obligations was even steeper. IBM also reduced its Canadian debt, and eliminated its Swiss franc debt. In contrast, IBM continues to rely heavily on financing in yen. Nevertheless, you cannot interpret these changes as speculation on exchange rates, because IBM described elsewhere in its financials how it hedged some of its currency risk. Moreover, not only IBM's obligations but also many of its assets were overseas, so the net exposure of IBM to foreign currency is not easy to determine.

➤ Currency hedging, Section 25.4, p. 963

Fair value adjustment: Usually, long-term debt is carried at historical value, not market value. However, some of IBM's debt was hedged against yield curve movements, too—that is, IBM had financial contracts that would change opposite in value to those of some or all of its bonds. From 2001 to 2003, short-term interest rates fell, while long-term interest rates remained around 5%. The fair value adjustment reflects the change in value of the hedged bonds. (Somewhere on the asset side of IBM's balance sheet will be an opposite item—an asset measuring the value change experienced by the hedge instruments.)

Current maturities: Some of IBM's long-term debt became current (had less than 1 year left before coming due) and therefore was reclassified into short-term liabilities. This could account for about $1.1 billion less in long-term borrowing in 2002, and $543 million less in 2003.

In sum, there are many long-term financing instruments that can play a role. In IBM's case, the most important factor influencing changes in borrowing was the expansion and contraction of its medium-term notes program.

Current Liabilities

Note the many different short-term obligations—including many nonfinancial liabilities!

Table 15.3 breaks out current (i.e., short-term) liabilities, which are due to be paid within 1 year. The CFO has more immediate influence over new issuing of more short-term financial debt (commercial paper and short-term loan borrowing) than almost any other claim. Table 15.3 also shows you long-term debt (due in more than 1 year) that became short-term debt (with less than 1 year remaining) as the year went by. The remaining liabilities were not financial. They were incurred in the course of the firm's operations. IBM actively reduced its short-term borrowing from 2001 to 2002, and then expanded it from 2002 to 2003.

Other Liabilities

Table 15.4 shows other liabilities that had an impact on the amount of corporate debt. IBM's other liabilities drifted upward from 2001 to 2003. Only changes in restructuring actions really mattered in 2002. In 2003, however, both changes in IBM's deferred taxes and deferred income increased somewhat. Nevertheless, other liabilities were also generally small (at around $5 to $7 billion) compared to IBM's total liabilities of $65 to $75 billion.

TABLE 15.3 IBM'S CURRENT (SHORT-TERM) LIABILITIES (DOLLARS IN MILLIONS)

		2001		2002 (revised)		2003
Short-Term Debt	Change	$11,188	−$5,157	$6,031	+$615	$6,646
Commercial Paper	Change	*$4,809*	−$3,507	*$1,302*	+$1047	*$2,349*
+ Short-Term Loans	Change	*$1,564*	−$551	*$1,013*	+$111	*$1,124*
+ Long-Term Debt, Current	Change	*$4,815*	−$1,099	*$3,716*	−$543	*$3,173*
Taxes	Change	$4,644	+$832	$5,476	−$1	$5,475
Accounts Payable	Change	$7,047	+$583	$7,630	+$830	$8,460
Comp. and Benefits	Change	$3,796	−$72	$3,724	−$53	$3,671
Deferred Income	Change	$4,223	+$1,053	$5,276[a] ($4,946)	+$1,546	$6,492
Other Accrued Liabilities	Change	$4,221	+$2,192	$6,413	+$743	$7,156
Total Current	Change	$35,119	−$569	$34,550 ($34,220)	+$3,680	$37,900

a. This revision shifted $330 from deferred income into other liabilities, which can be seen in Table 15.4.

OTHER OBSERVATIONS AND DISCUSSION

Refer back to Table 15.1. Just under 20% of IBM's obligations in 2003 were pension obligations to its more than 300,000 current and former employees. For many older and personnel-intensive firms, such as IBM, pensions are important liabilities. (These firms often have so-called defined benefit pension plans, in which the firm agrees to pay employees a pension that is based on a formula.) Firms do not need to fund *all* their future pension obligations, and indeed many firms fail to do so. Some firms, however, are more conservative and may even overfund their plans. (In the past, some of these firms have then found themselves the target of an external takeover attempt, in which the acquirer attempted to gain control of the excess pension assets in order to finance the acquisition itself.) The financial aspects of pensions are complex, but the financial footnotes contain a wealth of information about them. (IBM, in particular, had spent many years in court trying to change its [overfunded] pension plan into a cash plan. You can read more about this on IBM's website.) Unfortunately, it is almost impossibly difficult to discuss pensions adequately in less than a chapter (or less than a full book)—and it would lead you far away from the main topic—so we shall not discuss pensions any further.

Pension obligations are very important for some firms with many employees—for IBM, they were almost as important as its long-term debt.

➤ Mergers and acquisitions, Section 23.3, p. 877

TABLE 15.4 IBM'S OTHER LIABILITIES (DOLLARS IN MILLIONS)

		2001		2002 (revised)		2003
Deferred Taxes		$1,485		$1,450		$1,834
	Change		−$35		+$384	
Deferred Income		$1,145		$1,079 ($1,409)[a]		$1,842
	Change		−$66		+$433	
Exec. Comp. Accruals		$868		$851		$1,036
	Change		−$17		+$185	
Restructuring Actions		$589		$1,024		$871
	Change		+$435		−$153	
Postemployment, Preretirement		$493		$573 ($572)		$579
	Change		+$80		+$7	
Disability Benefits		N/A		N/A ($304)[b]		$349
	Change		+$0		+$45	
Environmental Accruals		$215		$208		$214
	Change		−$7		+$6	
Other		$670		$766 ($463)[c]		$731
	Change		+$96		+$268	
Total		$5,465		$5,951 ($6,281)		$7,456
	Change		+$486		+$1,175	

a. This revision from $1,079 to $1,409 shifted $330 from deferred income into other liabilities, which can be seen in Table 15.3.
b. IBM broke out $304 million disability benefits in 2003, previously classified as "other."

The time dimension of IBM's obligations: IBM's debt became longer term from 2001 to 2003.

Did you notice that Table 15.1 shows that IBM shifted its obligations from short-term debt into medium- and long-term debt in 2002? You can see this by dividing long-term debt by the sum of long-term debt plus financial debt in short-term liabilities from Table 15.1:

$$\text{2001:} \quad \$15{,}963/(\$15{,}963 + \$11{,}188) \approx 59\%$$

$$\text{2002:} \quad \$19{,}986/(\$19{,}986 + \$6{,}031) \approx 77\%$$

$$\text{2003:} \quad \$16{,}986/(\$16{,}986 + \$6{,}646) \approx 72\%$$

$$\text{Year:} \quad \text{Long-Term Debt}/(\text{Long-Term Debt} + \text{Short-Term Debt})$$

Incidentally, you could also see the same directions in borrowing trends within IBM's long-term liabilities, that is, in its arrangement between long-term notes and medium-term notes (Table 15.2).

The prevailing yield curve.

The passing of time itself also made outstanding obligations shorter term, so you might like to know how IBM's financial obligations for each year developed. If you dig more deeply into the financial footnotes, you can discover this aspect of IBM's capital structure:

	Term Structure of IBM's Liabilities Coming Due								
	2001	2002	2003	2004	2005	2006	2007	2008	2009
As of 2001	$11,188	$5,186	$3,106	$1,501	$1,904	$2,261	$6,471	←	←
As of 2002		$6,031	$3,949	$3,613	$1,670	$2,705	$846+$9,940		←
As of 2003			$6,646	$4,072	$3,113	$2,760	$1,289+$225+$7,942		

This shows that IBM changed its capital structure dynamically. This was probably related to how economy-wide interest rates changed over this period:

	Maturity	2000	2001	2002	2003
Treasury, Short-Term	1 month	≈5%	2.47%	1.63%	1.02%
Treasury, Medium-Term	3 years	6.22%	4.09%	3.10%	2.10%
Treasury, Long-Term	20 years	6.23%	5.63%	5.43%	4.96%
Corporate, Short-Term	1 month	6.3%	3.8%	1.7%	1.1%
Aaa Bonds	Medium-Term	7.6%	7.1%	6.5%	5.7%

The footnotes further tell us about IBM's unused credit lines:

Credit lines can be an important source of credit.

	2001	2002	2003
Unused Credit Lines	$16,121	$16,934	$15,883

To put them into perspective, realize that the unused credit lines were of a similar order of magnitude as IBM's long-term debt!

The financial footnotes also tell a little bit about IBM's interest payments:

The 10-K also gives some interest rate information.

	2001	2002	2003
Interest Paid and Accrued	$1,235	$815	$663

Again, to add a little more perspective, in 2001, IBM earned $7.7 billion; in 2002, it earned $5.3 billion; and in 2003; it earned $7.6 billion. Somewhere, deep in the bowels of the 2003 financials, IBM also reported that its commercial paper (very, very short-term borrowing) had a weighted-average interest cost of 1%, while its short-term borrowings had a weighted-average interest cost of 2.5%. You could also try to estimate the average interest rate on all debt. With $663 million in interest on financial debt of $16,986 + $6,646 = $23,632 million, the average interest rate would have been around 2.8%.

15.4B IBM'S EQUITY

Common equity: IBM did not change its number of shares by very much.

Table 15.5 illustrates the evolution of IBM's equity. You can see that preferred equity disappeared completely in fiscal year 2002. (The background is that in 1995 the IBM board had decided to repurchase all its remaining 7.5% callable preferred stock, and this was ultimately completed on May 18, 2001. This is not unusual—as already noted, preferred equity has largely disappeared from large publicly traded corporations.) Moving on to common equity, about 1.9 billion shares of IBM were officially issued. Of these, IBM itself held about 190 and 199 million shares in 2001 and 2002,

TABLE 15.5 IBM'S EQUITY AND SOME OTHER INFORMATION (DOLLARS IN MILLIONS, EXCEPT SHARE DATA)

		2001		2002		2003
Preferred	Authorized	150,000,000		—		—
	Outstanding	2,546,011		—		—
Common	Authorized	4,687,500,000		4,687,500,000		4,687,500,000
	Issued	1,913,513,218		1,920,957,772		1,937,393,604
	Change		+7,444,554		+16,435,832	
	Treasury	190,319,489		198,590,876		242,884,969
	Change		+8,271,387		+44,294,093	
	Outstanding	1,723,193,729		1,722,366,896		1,694,508,635
	Change		−826,833		−27,858,261	
	Identifiable Changes					
	PwCC Acquisition Issue, Restricted		−3,677,213			
	To Pension Fund, from Treasury		−24,037,354			
	Repurchase I		+48,481,100		+49,994,514	
	Repurchase II ESOP		+189,797		+291,921	
	Issue to ESOP, from Treasury		−979,246		−2,120,293	
	PwCC Acquisition Issue[a]		−$254			
	Repurchase I		+$4,212		+$4,403	
	Repurchase II ESOP		+$18		+$24	
	To Pension Fund		−$1,871			
Retained Earnings		$30,142		$31,555		$37,525
Book Equity		$23,448		$22,782		$27,864
	Cash Dividends Paid		−$1,005		−$1,085	
	Common Stock Transactions		−$3,087		−$3,232	
	For Comparison: Interest Paid		−$831		−$853	
	For Perspective: Taxes Paid		−$1,707		−$1,841	
Common Price/Share		$120.96		$77.50		$92.68
⇒ Common Market Value		$208,437		$133,484		$157,047

a. An additional $30 million is recorded to be issued in the future.

respectively, and 243 million shares in 2003. (They are called **treasury shares.**) IBM therefore had 1.7 billion shares outstanding. If you had owned all of these 1.7 billion externally held shares, you would have owned all of IBM's common equity (although your ownership of the 200 million treasury shares would have been indirect through your ownership of the outstanding shares—after all, a firm cannot own itself). This number remained fairly constant, even though IBM actively repurchased its shares. Yet, although the dollar amount was large, it was only a small fraction of the company's outstanding stock. In addition, IBM then turned around and used these shares in other transactions, for example, to fund the PwCC acquisition or to fund its employee stock option plans (**ESOP**). Consequently, although repurchases and net stock transactions were larger than interest payments and dividend payments combined, the active issuing or repurchasing of shares ultimately did not play much of a role in changing IBM's capital structure.

However, IBM's stock price changed, which played a very large role in moving IBM's equity capitalization.

Instead, almost all the change in the value of equity came through one mechanism: changes in the price of each IBM share. From 2001 to 2002, shares dropped from $120.96 to $77.50, thereby losing about one-third of its market value. From 2002 to 2003, the market value bounced back again by about 20%. The effect was a drop in the equity value from $208 billion to $133 billion, followed by an increase back to $157 billion.

15.4C OBSERVATIONS ON THE EVOLUTION OF IBM'S CAPITAL STRUCTURE

Where did IBM's big capital structure changes come from?

You now understand how IBM's capital structure changed from 2001 to 2003. IBM's liabilities evolved fairly steadily. About one-quarter of its total liabilities consisted of pension and other unspecified liabilities. The pension obligations, in particular, marched upward fairly steadily. In terms of IBM's total liabilities increase of about $2.9 billion, the pension and other obligations accounted for one-half and three-quarters in 2002 and 2003, respectively. About another one-quarter of IBM's total liabilities (of about $70 billion) consisted of its long-term debt; the remaining one-half of total liabilities was short-term debt. In 2002, IBM ratcheted up its medium-term notes borrowing, accounting for a debt increase of $3.5 billion. In 2003, IBM mostly kept its borrowing at the same level, but shifted it from longer-term into shorter-term debt. These changes in the value of IBM's liabilities were dwarfed by the changes in the value of IBM's *equity*—and almost all of it came from changes in the per-share price, not from changes in the number of shares outstanding.

It is sometimes useful to think about the components of the capital structure as how easily they can be used as sources of funding.

This suggests that a useful perspective is to think about capital structure changes as being driven by three factors:

1. Claims that are for the most part outside the day-to-day control of the CFO—such as pension fund obligations.
2. Claims whose value is mostly determined by the performance of the company and the financial markets—such as common equity.
3. Claims that are for the most part under the day-to-day control of the CFO—such as the firm's financial claims. The obvious examples are (bank) debt and short-term notes. These are most interesting for us financiers, because they are often the primary source of marginal capital to fund new projects.

Total-liabilities-to-assets and financial-debt-to-capital are two good summary statistics that measure leverage.

We still need a summary measure to characterize a firm's indebtedness. There are two good common statistics:

1. **Total-liabilities-to-total-assets ratio:** In 2003, IBM had a ratio of the value of total liabilities to total assets of $76,593/$104,457 ≈ 74% when assets are measured in book value. However, though common, this measuring of the assets (through its equity component) in terms of book value is clearly not accurate. If measured in market value, instead, IBM's equity increases from $27,864 to $157,047 (i.e., by $129,183). This means that assets increase to $233,640. IBM's 2003 market-based liabilities-to-asset ratio was therefore $76,593/$233,640 ≈ 33%.
2. **Financial-debt-to-capital ratio:** Financial debt consists of two components: long-term debt and debt in current liabilities. IBM's financial debt was $23,632 in 2003. Capital consists of two components: financial debt and equity. (Capital therefore excludes the nonfinancial-liabilities component that is in assets). IBM's financial capital in 2003 was $23,632 + $27,864 = $51,496 in book value. Consequently, in book value, IBM's 2003 financial-debt-to-capital ratio was $23,632/$51,496 ≈ 46%. If we measure in market value, capital was a higher $23,632 + $157,047 = $180,679, instead. Consequently, in market value, the financial-debt-to-capital ratio was $23,632/$180,679 ≈ 13%.

➤ How to measure leverage, Section 22.1, p. 821

These are just summary statistics. No single statistic can convey a full picture of IBM's complex capital structure. Depending on the context, you may find one or the other (or both) measures to be more suitable for your needs. Section 22.1 has a more detailed discussion of these and other, better, measures of leverage. However, even without more detail, it seems pretty obvious that IBM was on solid financial footing and without fear of pending financial distress.

SOLVE NOW!

Q 15.14 List some of the bigger categories that can go into the firm's capital structure.

Q 15.15 To purchase all common equity in a firm, do you need to purchase all outstanding or all issued shares?

Q 15.16 From year to year, does the market value of debt or equity tend to move around more?

SUMMARY

This chapter covered the following major points:

- In the real world, firms are financed by a whole set of different financial claims. The same firm may have senior debt, junior debt (perhaps with a conversion feature), equity, and warrants. The right way to think about all these claims often involves the "magic" of the payoff table and the payoff diagram: If the firm ends up worth very little, only the senior debt is paid. If the firm is worth a little more, both the senior and the junior debt are paid. If the firm is worth even more, the equity becomes valuable and, finally, so do the warrant and/or the conversion feature.

- The two most basic building blocks of capital structure are debt and equity. These differ in their cash flow rights and in their control rights:
  - Debt has first rights to the distribution of cash flows. It is "senior." It can force the firm into bankruptcy if payments are not made.
  - Equity gets only what is leftover after debt has been satisfied. It is "junior." It is in control of the firm, unless the firm finds itself in financial distress.
- Payoff tables and payoff diagrams are often good ways to describe the cash flow rights of debt and equity. They are state-contingent claims, where the firm value is the state. But the plots are not perfect in summarizing all the important information about claims. They ignore factors that can influence security value other than the firm value at one point in time, such as the time pattern of multiple payouts, control rights, or economy-wide interest rates.
- Convertible bonds allow their owners to convert their bonds into shares. They can therefore often be considered as part debt, part equity.
- Preferred equity cannot force bankruptcy, but it receives its dividends before common equity does.
- Corporate borrowing comes in thousands of different varieties. For example, it can be plain, convertible, callable, fixed-rate or floating-rate, short-term or long-term, and so on. It can have detailed covenants of many kinds.
- The lines between different financial instruments are blurry. Issuers regularly introduce new kinds of securities that carry features that were traditionally associated only with either debt or equity. Nothing is written in stone. Debt and equity (or bank, private, and public debt) are nowadays better considered to be concepts rather than sharp categories.
- Equity is less colorful than debt. For many companies, it consists of only one class of common equity.

Looking at IBM in greater detail, you learned the following:

- Capital structure changes are influenced by factors under management's immediate control (primarily financial claims, such as debt issuing and share repurchasing), factors related to operations (primarily nonfinancial liabilities, such as pension obligations and working capital), and factors beyond management's immediate control (such as value changes, that is, stock returns).
- The big liability categories (for IBM) were long-term debt, short-term liabilities, pension liabilities (details of which depend on the company), and the catch-all category called other liabilities. (Minority interest and negative goodwill are usually less important.)
- Financial debt is the sum of long-term debt plus the financial debt component of short-term liabilities.

- The financial footnotes give more details about firms' liabilities. Financial debt can contain many different types of borrowing simultaneously—bonds, notes, foreign credit, hybrid securities, credit-line–related borrowing, bank debt, and so on. Short-term debt contains financial debt, tax obligations soon due, accounts payable, compensation-related liabilities, and other items. Nonfinancial liabilities contain accounts payable and (usually) a large amount of specified or unspecified other liabilities. These other liabilities can contain such items as deferred taxes and deferred income, executive compensation, retirement-related items, disability benefits, environmental liabilities, and the like.
- Firms can, and often do, take the term structure of interest rates into account when they issue or retire debt. This means that their current capital structures are often history (interest-rate) dependent.
- The total-liabilities-to-assets ratio and the financial-debt-to-financial-capital ratio are two reasonable summary measures of indebtedness. Their value can be quite different, not only from one another but also depending on whether the equity component is measured in book value or market value.

KEY TERMS

absolute priority rule, 545
APR, 545
balloon payment, 550
bank loan, 551
bond covenant, 549
bond duration, 550
bond maturity, 550
bond seniority, 549
callability, 549
capital structure, 541
capped, 551
Chapter 11, 545
Chapter 7, 545
collared, 551
collateral, 549
commercial paper, 550
common, 552
common equity, 552
common stock, 552
convertibility, 549
convertible preferred, 554
corporate board, 553
corporate charter, 541
corporate dividend exclusion rule, 552
coupon bond, 550
covenant, 546
credit line, 551
dilution, 547
double taxation of dividends, 553
equity, 542
ESOP, 563
fiduciary responsibility, 553
financial footnote, 556
fixed-rate debt, 550
floating-rate debt, 550
funded debt, 550
junior bond, 549
leverage, 542
liabilities, 542
maturity, 545
negotiated debt, 551
notes, 556
ordinary, 552
ordinary equity, 552
par value, 546
payoff diagram, 543
preferred equity, 553
principal, 549
putability, 549
redeem, 549
SEC, 542
secured bond, 549
securities, 542
Securities and Exchange Commission, 542
security, 549
senior bond, 549
shareholders, 552
sinking fund, 550
state, 543
state-contingent claim, 543
stock, 542
stockholder, 552
stock shareholder, 552
subordinated bond, 549
treasury shares, 563
unfunded debt, 550
unit, 550
warrant, 550
zero-bond, 550

SOLVE NOW! SOLUTIONS

Q 15.1 A control right is the right to influence decisions, specifically by changing management and/or the board.

Q 15.2 Individuals can never really own everything. The IRS and community have inalienable property rights over every firm in existence.

Q 15.3 The payoff table for the $300 million zero-bond is as follows (in million dollars):

Firm Value	Bond Value	Stock Value
$0	$0	$0
$100	$100	$0
$200	$200	$0
$300	$300	$0
$350	$300	$50
$400	$300	$100
⋮		

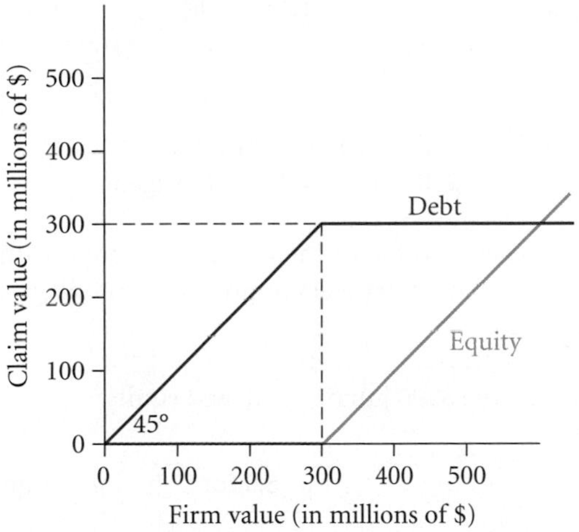

The bond is a diagonal line until firm value is $300, and then a horizontal line. The stock is a horizontal line at $0 until $300, and then a diagonal line.

Q 15.4 Yes, you can add up payoffs. It is basically stacking up lines. The sum total must be one diagonal line (i.e., slope of 1)—it is the value of the firm. Perhaps this is easiest to see if you draw it all, and then convince yourself that you can stack!

Q 15.5 For the medical insurance reimbursement example, consider an example. If you submit annual claims of $750, you first have to pay the deductible of $500 yourself. On the remaining $250, you get a reimbursement of 90%, that is, $90\% \cdot \$250 = \$225$. Doing this for more medical claims,

Medical Costs	Insurance Payout	Medical Costs	Insurance Payout
$0	$0	⋮	⋮
$250	$0	$11,500	$9,900

$500	$0	$11,600	$9,990
$750	$225	$11,611	$10,000
$1,000	$450	$11,700	$10,000
$2,000	$1,350	$12,000	$10,000
$3,000	$2,250	$13,000	$10,000
⋮		⋮	

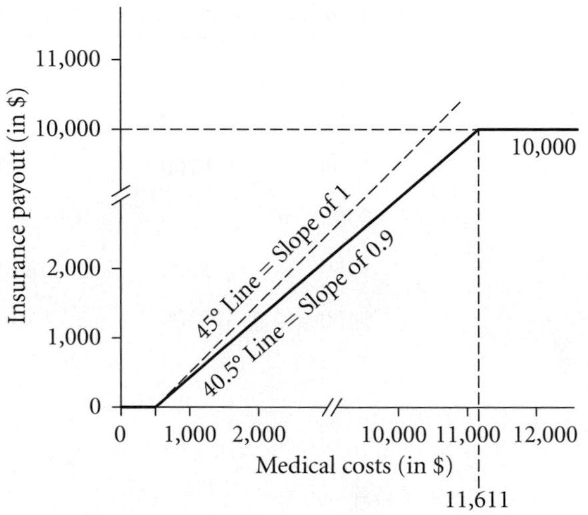

The "slope" is zero until $500 is reached, then 90% until $11,611.11 is reached (where the payout is [$11,611.11 − $500] · 0.9 = $10,000), and then zero again.

Q 15.6 No, you cannot draw a good payoff diagram for a coupon bond with so many remaining payments—at least not easily without making a lot of extra assumptions. Payoff diagrams only work well for a security's value at one given point in time.

Q 15.7 For the $100 senior bond, the $200 junior bond, and equity:

Firm	Senior	Junior	Equity
$0	$0	$0	$0
$50	$50	$0	$0
$100	$100	$0	$0
$150	$100	$50	$0
$200	$100	$100	$0
$250	$100	$150	$0
$300	$100	$200	$0
$350	$100	$200	$50
$400	$100	$200	$100
$450	$100	$200	$150
⋮			

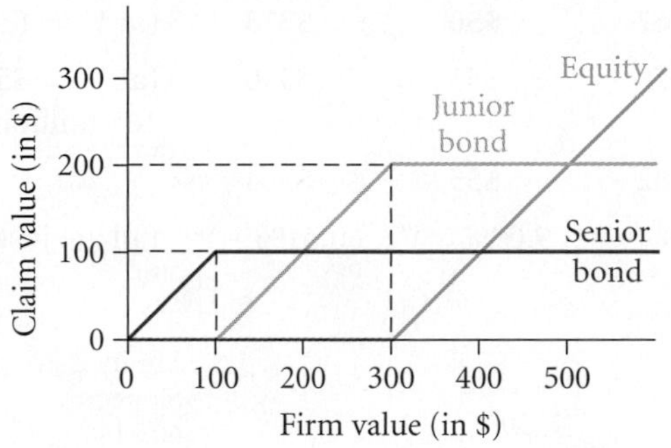

Q 15.8 For the 2,000 convertible $10,000 zero-bonds that can be converted into 50 shares of equity each (with 300,000 shares outstanding): If the firm is worth less than $2,000 \cdot \$10,000 = \$20$ million, the bondholders own the entire firm and shareholders receive nothing. If the bonds convert, they will be equivalent to one-quarter of all shares. At $80 million, bondholders are indifferent between converting and not converting, because $\$20,000,000/0.25 = \$80,000,000$. The payoff diagram for the debt is therefore a diagonal line (i.e., slope of 1) until $20 million, then a horizontal line until $80 million, and a line with a slope of 0.25 beyond $80 million. For equity, the line is horizontal until $20 million, then diagonal (i.e., slope of 1) until $80 million, and a line with a slope of 0.75 beyond $80 million.

Q 15.9 The question seems difficult, but it does become easy once you realize the following:

- If the junior does not convert, then the senior's 50 million in new equity shares would represent 50/150 or one-third of the equity (not the company!). Thus, the senior would convert if the value of the equity reaches $300 million. This occurs when the firm value reaches $350 million, because the junior creditors still would have their "$50 million first" claim.
- If the senior has converted, then the junior's 15 million in new equity shares if it converts would represent 15/165 of the firm. This is about 9.1% of the firm value. Therefore, at a firm value of $550 million (solve $x \cdot 15/165 = \$50$), the junior would be indifferent between exercising and not exercising.

These two insights make it easy to write down the payoff table (note my irregular value stepping when it is convenient for explanation), all in millions:

Firm Value	Senior Bond	Junior Bond	Equity	Remarks
$0	$0	$0	$0	
$50	$50	$0	$0	
$100	$100	$0	$0	
$150	$100	$50	$0	
$200	$100	$50	$50	
$250	$100	$50	$100	
$300	$100	$50	$150	
$350	**$100**	**$50**	**$200**	(at $V = \$350$, senior is indifferent to converting)
$353	$101	$50	$202	(at $V = \$353$, senior has converted; there are now 150 million shares worth $303 in equity)
$400	$117	$50	$233	
$450	$133	$50	$267	
$500	$150	$50	$300	

	\$550	**\$167**	**\$50**	**\$333**	(at $V = \$550$, junior is indifferent to converting)
	\$561	\$170	\$51	\$340	(at $V = \$561$, junior has converted; there are now 165 million shares in equity)
	\$600	\$182	\$55	\$364	
$\forall$ V > \$550	V	$30.30\% \cdot V$	$9.09\% \cdot V$	$60.61\% \cdot V$	(all are just fractional equity)

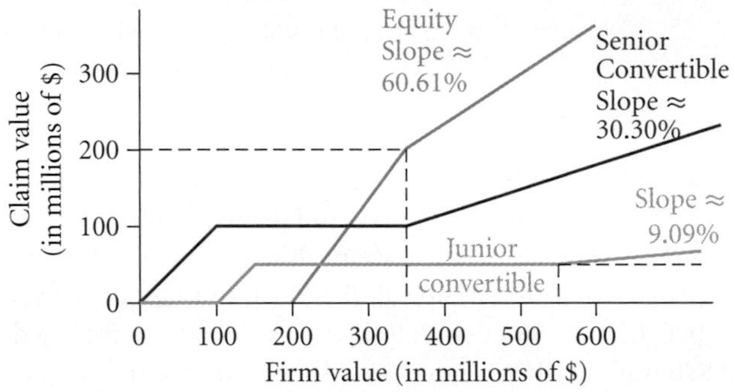

Q 15.10 The various bond features are fully described in Section 15.2A. Here is a short description: Most bonds make interest payments on a regular basis (e.g., semiannually or annually) and repay the principal of the bond at maturity. The interest rate (or coupon rate) may be either fixed or floating with some benchmark rate, (e.g., the prime rate). Bonds also come with covenants that are other requirements that a firm must abide by, such as a minimum level of liquidity, a maximum amount of debt, and/or a sinking fund requirement. Some bonds may be designated as senior to other bonds issued by the firm, which gives their holders a prior claim over the junior bond investors. Some bonds may also be collateralized, in which case the bond is backed by one or more of the firm's assets. In addition, a bond may be convertible, callable, or putable.

Q 15.11 Shareholders indeed enjoy limited liability, which is the fact that they can only lose their actual investment. They do not forfeit their personal possessions if the corporate managers act badly.

Q 15.12 The Bush dividend tax cuts reduced the double taxation of individuals. Because corporations always had some form thereof, they made corporations and individuals more similar.

Q 15.13 Preferred equity is like a bond in that it does not participate in the upside, and in that preferred equity is usually de facto senior to common equity. This applies both in bankruptcy and in respect to the dividends: Common shares do not get their dividends until preferred shareholders have received their dividends. Preferred equity is like a stock in that its payments are not tax deductible by the issuer, and in that preferred shareholders have no ability to force the firm into bankruptcy if their dividends are not paid.

Q 15.14 Liabilities consists of long-term debt (bonds and notes), short-term debt (financial, taxes, payables, etc.), pension debt, and other debt. Equity consists of common and preferred stock.

Q 15.15 You cannot purchase all issued shares, because the firm holds treasury shares, which are a component of all issued shares. Instead, you need to purchase all outstanding shares. This gives you indirect control over the treasury shares, which the firm already holds itself.

Q 15.16 The value of equity moves around a lot more, primarily because it is a "levered value," which is more sensitive to changes in the value of the underlying firm. In contrast, debt changes drastically primarily when a firm issues or retires debt.

PROBLEMS

The ▬ *indicates problems available in* myfinancelab

Q 15.17 What is a cash flow right? How does it differ from a control right?

Q 15.18 Write down the payoff table and graph the payoff diagram for an insurance contract with a deductible of $100,000, a coverage of 80% of the loss, and a maximum payout of $1,000,000.

Q 15.19 Draw a final payoff diagram for a stock and a bond, where the bond promises to pay off $500 in 1 year.

Q 15.20 What can payoff diagrams illustrate well? Where do they fail?

Q 15.21 What are the two uses of the abbreviation "APR"?

Q 15.22 What are the main mechanisms through which creditors can increase the likelihood of being repaid? Give some examples.

Q 15.23 A convertible zero-bond that promises $20,000 can be converted into 100 shares of equity at its maturity date. If there are 8,000 such bonds and 1,200,000 shares outstanding, what would the payoff table and diagram for both bondholders and stockholders look like?

Q 15.24 Write down all bond features (variations) that you remember.

Q 15.25 What is the main control mechanism through which shareholders increase the likelihood of ever receiving cash?

Q 15.26 What are the main control rights for common equity, preferred equity, and debt?

Q 15.27 Is common stock or preferred stock more common? Does the name "preferred" mean it is better to own preferred stock than common stock?

Q 15.28 What are financial notes?

Q 15.29 What are the main categories of long-term liabilities?

Q 15.30 What is commercial paper?

Q 15.31 What are the main categories of short-term liabilities?

Q 15.32 Explain how the capital structure of IBM changed from 2003 to 2005.

16

Capital Structure and Capital Budgeting in a Perfect Market

SHOULD A COMPANY ISSUE STOCKS OR BONDS?

How should entrepreneurs and managers think of the multitudes of instruments with which they can finance the firm? To understand how a firm should choose its capital structure, we start with the world that is easiest to understand and that you already know: the "perfect market" (no opinion differences, no transaction costs, no taxes, and no important buyers or sellers). This chapter shows (again) that the value of the firm's capital in a perfect market is determined by the present value of its projects, and not by whether the firm is financed with debt or equity. This is because in the perfect financial markets, someone would immediately step in to correct any mistakes managers could commit. As a result, the value of the firm's capital cannot depend on the claims a firm might choose to issue.

This chapter also explains the simplest version of the weighted average cost of capital formula (WACC). The next few chapters will then explain how financing in the real world differs from financing in this perfect-markets world.

There are some small subtleties, however, when it comes to nonfinancial claims. Product markets are often not perfect. In these cases, the firm's average and marginal costs of capital can be different. Nevertheless, if the financial claims exist in a perfect market, then it is often still the case that the firm's marginal cost of capital—which is what managers ultimately want to know—is that of its financial claims. The financial claims' weighted average cost of capital would then still be the firm's marginal cost of capital. (However, this cost of capital would *not* be the firm's average cost of capital.)

16.1 CONCEPTUAL BASICS—MAXIMIZATION OF EQUITY VALUE OR FIRM VALUE?

Now that you understand the claims that firms *can* and *do* issue, let's focus on what they *should* issue. The best way to conceptualize an optimal firm structure is as follows: You are the entrepreneur who owns all of the firm. You want to sell it for the highest possible price. Your goal is to design your firm—including your corporate charter and capital structure—in a way that maximizes its total market value *today*. This value is the price that new investors are willing to pay to buy the firm from you. If your firm's charter or its capital structure allows or even induces you or your managers to do bad things in the future, then who would want to buy your firm today? Thus, the better you design your firm today, the higher the price that you can get from outside investors. (The design of the firm will be an even more important subject in Chapter 24, in which we will discuss corporate governance.)

You should think about an optimal capital structure from the perspective of an all-owning entrepreneur.

Let's first talk about what management will want to do in the future. Who does management represent (other than themselves)? Who *should* management represent? Does it make a difference whether management is representing just the shareholders or all the claimants on the firm? A popular view in the press is that the goal of managers should be **shareholder wealth maximization**. In the presence of other claims—such as financial debt, pension obligations, and accounts payable—this is not as simple as it may seem.

Should our entrepreneur incentivize management to maximize shareholder value?

Shareholders elect the corporate board of directors. Legally, this board is the principal of the firm. In turn, the board appoints management, which has a primary legal **fiduciary duty** only to shareholders. This is eminently sensible—management should negotiate on behalf of the residual equity owners for good terms with its suppliers, creditors, and so on, and not willingly pay such other claimants more than the firm has to. However, the legal situation changes when decisions made by management can threaten insolvency. In this case, management's legal fiduciary responsibility extends to other claimants, too. Again, this makes sense, because if the firm is underwater, it may ultimately belong to the creditors. These responsibilities can be different in other countries. For example, in German joint stock companies, limited liability companies, and cooperatives with more than 500 employees, one-third of the members of the **supervisory board** must be employees. And in the case of companies in the iron, coal, and steel industry, shareholders and representatives of the workforce must be equally represented on the firm's supervisory board. German firms must also appoint one director who represents the employees and has a responsibility "for social affairs." In sum, German corporate boards are legally tasked with more than just shareholder wealth.

In the United States, managers primarily represent shareholders, although their duty may extend to creditors if the firm should go into distress.

In practice, U.S. managers see themselves primarily as representatives of shareholders and not as representatives of creditors. Yet even if managers seek to maximize shareholder wealth, it is not necessarily clear how they should think and what they should do. Let me illustrate this. When both bondholders and shareholders benefit from a manager's actions, there is no problem. But what if there are situations in which optimizing the value of the equity is the opposite of optimizing the overall firm's value? For example, assume it is possible for managers to increase the value of equity by \$1, but at a cost to the value of financial debt of \$3. (You will later learn

The dilemma—a situation in which shareholder maximization and firm value maximization are in conflict.

➤ Bondholder expropriation, Section 18.5, p. 676

how easy it is to do exactly this.) This "expropriative" transaction would destroy $2 in the net value of the firm. Even in our perfect world, this is the type of situation that can create a dilemma for management: Should management maximize firm value or shareholder value? Recall that it is shareholders who ultimately vote managers into office and allow them to stay there. When the time comes, managers may find it in their interest to execute this dubious transaction because doing so raises the equity value—and with it their executive bonuses. Whether this transaction hurts creditors or destroys value may not even enter their minds.

Rational bond buyers understand future conflicts of interest and assume the worst.

However, there is one hole in this logic. Put yourself in the shoes of the original entrepreneur today. You are trying to set up a corporate charter and capital structure that maximizes the value of your firm, that is, the price you could get if you sold it today. You want to find the best capital structure *today*. How can you attract new investors? How can you persuade them to part with their hard-earned cash? Clearly, any potential creditor contemplating purchasing your bonds will take into consideration what your managers may do to them in the future. If it looks as if managers will want to execute the aforementioned dubious transaction, your potential creditors would rationally demand much higher interest rates. If you cannot commit the firm today *not* to undertake the $3-for-$1 transaction in the future, your prospective bond buyers will realize today (before the fact, or **ex-ante**) that you or your management will have the incentive to execute it later (after the fact, or **ex-post**), no matter what you tell them today.

To secure financing at a low cost of capital, entrepreneurs want to commit not to expropriate bond buyers in the future.

If potential investors believe your firm will undertake this transaction in the future, what will your firm be worth today? The answer is "less than a firm that was committed not to destroy $2 of value in the future." Therefore, you have a choice:

- You can avoid debt altogether, although this may hamper you for other reasons explained later.
- You can find a way to commit yourself today not to exploit bondholders in the future.
- You can sell the firm today for a lower net present value. This takes into account your value destruction tomorrow—because everyone realizes that you will be irresistibly tempted to destroy $2 of firm value.

It should be clear to you that you should want to do everything in your power to commit yourself visibly today not to exploit bondholders in the future. Committing yourself can optimize the value of your firm in the future, which in turn maximizes the value of your firm today.

The conceptual basis of capital structure theory: Future behavior and events impact corporate value and costs of capital today.

This is one of the most important insights with respect to capital structure, and one worth repeating again and again: The cost of *ex-post* actions against claimants is not only borne by claimants tomorrow, but also internalized by the owners today. Thus, it is in owners' best interests today to commit themselves not to exploit future claimants tomorrow—especially if everyone knows that when the time comes, owners will want to change their minds. The advantage of a firm that is committed to maximizing firm value in the future is that it can obtain a better price for its claims (e.g., a lower interest rate for its bonds) today. Therefore, it is the firm itself that has the incentive to try to find ways to commit itself today (ex-ante) to treating claimants well in the future (ex-post).

From a financial perspective, the ex-ante capital structure that results in the highest firm value today is the optimal capital structure. This entire argument is based on the implication that *caveat emptor* ("buyer beware") works: Bond and stock purchasers are forward looking. Moreover, they can only be hurt to the extent that future opportunistic actions by management are unforeseen surprises.

The entrepreneur's goal is to design a capital structure that will maximize firm value today.

In a perfect capital market, what will happen if your current management team cannot commit to avoid such bad future \$3-for-\$1 exchanges? In this case, another management team that has the ability to restrain itself would value the firm more highly than the current management team. It would purchase the firm and make an immediate profit. The competition among many management teams with this capability would push the firm toward the best capital structure. At the risk of sounding repetitive, the most important point of this chapter is that firms that can commit to doing "the right thing" tomorrow (ex-post) are worth more today (ex-ante). *It is a direct consequence that entrepreneurs should maximize firm value and not just shareholder value.*

Competition among management teams could pressure firms to improve capital structures.

IMPORTANT:

- In deciding on an appropriate price to pay, the buyers of financial claims take into account what the firm is likely to do in the future.
- The basis of **optimal capital structure** theory is the insight that entrepreneurs want to maximize the value of the firm in an upfront sale today, and not necessarily the value of equity today or in the future.

In our theoretical perfect world, management should be committed to maximizing firm value, not shareholder value. In real life, even in existing companies, these two objectives differ only rarely (and usually only when firms are close to financial distress). Therefore the popular mantra of "shareholder value maximization" is most often synonymous with "total value maximization." The distinction then is useful more as a pedagogical tool: *The best capital structure is the one that maximizes overall value.* In the real world, however, managers are far less conflicted with respect to favoring shareholders at the expense of bondholders than they are conflicted with respect to their own welfare. (These are the agency conflicts that we first discussed in Section 12.8 and that we will take up again in great length in Chapter 24). In some cases, managers' own self-interests may even lead them to take projects that favor creditors over shareholders—a force that mitigates their incentives to expropriate creditors on behalf of the shareholders.

The conflict between shareholders and bondholders is usually dwarfed by the conflict between managers and owners.

➤ Agency conflicts, Section 12.8, p. 420

SOLVE NOW!

Q 16.1 Explain the difference between ex-ante and ex-post, especially in the capital structure context. Give an example where the two differ.

Q 16.2 Can an ex-post maximizing choice be bad from an ex-ante perspective? If you could, would you want to restrain yourself from acting in such a way later on?

Q 16.3 If a firm has just learned of a legal loophole that allows it to renege on its obligations to pay back its creditors, should it do so?

16.2 MODIGLIANI AND MILLER: THE INFORMAL WAY

A now-famous Miller presentation illustrates the main capital structure insights.

The famous **Modigliani-Miller (M&M)** propositions (honored with two Nobel Prizes) are a good start to understanding firms' capital structure decisions. Although the M&M theory involves some complex algebraic calculations, it is actually based on some surprisingly simple ideas—which the following anecdote explains not only in a funnier, but also better, way than any complex calculations. It is an excerpt from an acceptance speech by Merton Miller for an honorary doctorate at Louvain, Belgium, in 1986. (His coauthor, Franco Modigliani, had just won a Nobel Prize; Merton Miller would receive his own Nobel Prize a few years later.)

> How difficult it is to summarize briefly the contribution of these papers was brought home to me very clearly last October after Franco Modigliani was awarded the Nobel Prize in Economics in part—but, of course, only in part—for the work in finance. The television camera crews from our local stations in Chicago immediately descended upon me. "We understand," they said, "that you worked with Modigliani some years back in developing these M&M theorems and we wonder if you could explain them briefly to our television viewers." "How briefly?" I asked. "Oh, take 10 seconds," was the reply.
>
> Ten seconds to explain the work of a lifetime! Ten seconds to describe two carefully reasoned articles each running to more than 30 printed pages and each with 60 or so long footnotes! When they saw the look of dismay on my face, they said: "You don't have to go into details. Just give us the main points in simple, commonsense terms."
>
> The main point of the first or cost-of-capital article was, in principle at least, simple enough to make. It said that in an economist's ideal world of complete and perfect capital markets and with full and symmetric information among all market participants, the total market value of all the securities issued by a firm was governed by the earning power and risk of its underlying real assets and was independent of how the mix of securities issued to finance it was divided between debt instruments and equity capital. Some corporate treasurers might well think that they could enhance total value by increasing the proportion of debt instruments because yields on debt instruments, given their lower risk, are, by and large, substantially below those on equity capital. But, under the ideal conditions assumed, the added risk to the shareholders from issuing more debt will raise required yields on the equity by just enough to offset the seeming gain from use of low-cost debt.
>
> Such a summary would not only have been too long, but it relied on shorthand terms and concepts, like perfect capital markets, that are rich in connotations to economists, but hardly so to the general public. I thought, instead, of an analogy that we ourselves had invoked in the original paper. "Think of the firm," I said, "as a gigantic tub of whole milk. The farmer can sell the whole milk as is. Or he can separate out the cream and sell it at a considerably higher price

than the whole milk would bring. (Selling cream is the analog of a firm selling low-yield and hence high-priced debt securities.) But, of course, what the farmer would have left would be skim milk, with low butterfat content and that would sell for much less than whole milk. Skim milk corresponds to the levered equity. The M&M proposition says that if there were no costs of separation (and, of course, no government dairy support programs), the cream plus the skim milk would bring the same price as the whole milk."

The television people conferred among themselves for a while. They informed me that it was still too long, too complicated and too academic. "Don't you have you anything simpler?" they asked. I thought of another way that the M&M proposition is presented which emphasizes the notion of market completeness and stresses the role of securities as devices for "partitioning" a firm's payoffs in each possible state of the world among the group of its capital suppliers. "Think of the firm," I said, "as a gigantic pizza, divided into quarters. If now, you cut each quarter in half into eighths, the M&M proposition says that you will have more pieces, but not more pizza."

Again there was a whispered conference among the camera crew and the director came back and said: "Professor, we understand from the press release that there were two M&M propositions. Maybe we should try the other one."

He was referring, of course, to the dividend invariance proposition and I know from long experience that attempts at brief statements of that one always cause problems. The term "dividend" has acquired too great a halo of pleasant connotations for people to accept the notion that the more dividends the better might not always be true. Dividends, however, as we pointed out in our article, do not fall like manna from heaven. The funds to pay them have to come from somewhere—either from cutting back on real investments or from further sales (or reduced purchases) of financial instruments. The M&M dividend proposition offered no advice as to which source or how much to tap. It claimed, rather, that once the firm had made its real operating and investment decisions, its dividend policy would have no effect on shareholder value. Any seeming gain in wealth from raising the dividend and giving the shareholders more cash would be offset by the subtraction of that part of their interest in the firm sold off to provide the necessary funds. To convey that notion within my allotted 10 seconds I said: "The M&M dividend proposition amounts to saying that if you take money from your left-hand pocket and put it in your right-hand pocket, you are no better off."

Once again whispered conversation. This time, they shut the lights off. They folded up their equipment. They thanked me for my cooperation. They said they would get back to me. But I knew that I had somehow lost my chance to start a new career as a packager of economic wisdom for TV viewers in convenient 10-second sound bites. Some have the talent for it; and some just don't.

These simple, commonsense analogies certainly do less than full justice to the M&M propositions; crude caricatures or cartoons they may be but they do have some resemblance. So much, in fact, that looking back now after more than 25 years it is hard to understand why they were so strongly resisted at first. One writer—David Durand, the same critic who had so strongly attacked the Markowitz model—even checked out the prices for whole milk, skim milk and cream in his neighborhood supermarket. He found, of course, that the M&M propositions didn't hold exactly; but, of course, empirical relations never do.

SOLVE NOW!

Q 16.4 Explain the M&M argument to your 10-year-old sibling, using Merton Miller's analogies.

16.3 MODIGLIANI AND MILLER: THE FORMAL WAY

In a perfect financial market, no financial security adds or subtracts value.

The point that Modigliani and Miller argued is that under perfect conditions, the total value of all financial securities is the same, regardless of whether the firm is financed by equity or debt, or anything in between.

IMPORTANT: The Modigliani-Miller propositions state that in a perfect world, the value of a firm is independent of how it is financed. Instead, it is the underlying projects that determine the value of the firm.

Modigliani and Miller proved their argument by showing that there would be arbitrage opportunities if the value of the firm depended on how it is financed. Because there should be no arbitrage in real life, it follows that firms should be able to choose any mix of securities without impact on their values. This perfect world that M&M describe relies on the familiar perfect-market assumptions:

- There are no transaction costs. In this context, it excludes such frictions as deadweight losses before and in bankruptcy.
- Capital markets are perfectly competitive, with a large number of investors competing to buy and sell securities.
- There are no taxes.
- There are no differences in opinion and information.

➤ Imperfect capital markets, Section 10.1, p. 303

You already know that these assumptions are the basics of any study of finance, even though they do not hold *perfectly* in the wild. However, once you understand how the M&M argument works, it becomes easier to understand what happens when these assumptions are violated—and to understand how important such violations can be. Indeed, the next few chapters are all about what happens if the world is *not* perfect.

M&M view #1: This is simple if we assume a fixed investment policy for the moment.

How does the M&M proof work? For simplicity, take it as given that the firm has already decided on what projects to take. (M&M stated this as one of their necessary assumptions, but it turns out not to matter in a fully perfect market.) The firm now considers how to finance its projects. Because we all agree on all current and future projects' expected cash flows and proper discount rates, we agree on the present value of these projects today. Call the value of the projects under a hypothetical best capital structure "PV." (This is almost by definition the present value that the firm's projects can fetch in our perfect capital market, of course.) The M&M proposition says that the present value of the firm's projects must equal the present value of the firm's issued claims today. In other words, if the firm has no debt and issues 100% equity, the equity must sell for the PV of the projects. If the firm instead finances itself by 50% debt and 50% equity, the two together must sell for the same PV. If the firm issues x% debt and (1 − x%) equity, the two together must sell for PV. The capital structure cannot change the project PV.

M&M is old news to you.

➤ Splitting payoffs into debt and equity, Section 6.4, p. 155

Actually, this M&M argument should not come as a surprise to you. In Section 6.4, without calling it M&M, you already used it in the context of financing a building. You learned that neither the building value nor the weighted cost of capital were influenced by your debt versus equity mix: The building was worth what it was worth. This is M&M precisely. It is the very same argument.

M&M view #2: Additivity of projects and financing.

Another way is to think of M&M financing as a decision that can be made independent of the underlying projects. In this case, net present values are additive. Thus,

$$\text{Firm Value} = \text{Project Value} + \text{Financing Value} \qquad (16.1)$$

Perfect-market financing is zero NPV.

The M&M proposition states that any method of financing in a perfect market has an NPV of $0. Neither debt nor equity, nor any combination of debt and equity, can change the present value contribution of financing. Any type of financing is obtained from perfectly competitive investors. For the M&M proposition to break down, it would have to be the case that some kind of financing scheme could add or subtract net present value.

M&M proof: The argument with a little formality.

This is so important that it is worthwhile to put this general but verbal-only proof into a more concrete scenario analysis. To accomplish this as simply as possible, let's work with a firm worth $100. Assume that all claims have to offer the same expected rate of return of 10%, which also means that investors are risk neutral. (You will work an example in a risk-averse world in Section 16.4A. Risk neutrality is just for convenience, not because it makes any difference.) There are two ways to prove the proposition that it makes no difference as to whether the firm is financed with debt or equity:

Absence-of-arbitrage: You could get rich if there was a capital structure worth $1 more or $1 less than what the firm is worth under the current structure.

The full restructuring (takeover) argument: Assume that the managers could find—and actually did choose—a capital structure that makes the firm worth $1 less than its PV. For example, assume that the firm is worth PV= $100 under the optimal capital structure of 80% equity and 20% debt; and assume further that the firm is worth only $99 under the capital structure of 50% equity and 50% debt that the firm has actually chosen. Then, all you need to do to get rich is to purchase all old equity and all old debt, that is, the entire firm, for $99. Now issue claims duplicating the optimal capital structure (assumed to be 80% equity and 20% debt). These claims will sell for $100, and you pocket an instant arbitrage profit of $1.

Competition: Others would want to arbitrage, too—until the M&M proposition works.

Unfortunately, in a perfect market, you would not be the only one to notice this opportunity. After all, all opinions are universally shared. Other arbitrageurs would compete, too. The only price at which no one will overbid you for the right to purchase the firm's current claims is $100. But notice that this means that the value of the old claims is instantly bid up to be equal to the price that the firm is worth under the optimal capital structure. The logical conclusion is that regardless of the financial structure that managers choose, they can sell their claims for $100, that is, the present value of their projects.

TABLE 16.1 ILLUSTRATION OF THE M&M PROPOSITION WITH RISK-NEUTRAL INVESTORS

	Bad Luck	Good Luck	Future Expected Value	Today's Present Value
Prob:	1/2	1/2		
Firm	$60	$160	$110	$100
Capital Structure LD: Bond with Face Value = $55				
Debt	$55	$55	$55	$50
Equity	$5	$105	$55	$50
Capital Structure MD: Bond with Face Value = $94				
Debt	$60	$94	$77	$70
Equity	$0	$66	$33	$30

The cost of capital in this example is 10% for all claims. (This is equivalent to assuming the financial markets are risk neutral.) Later in this chapter, you will work an example in which the cost of capital is higher for riskier projects. The table shows how the value of the firm remains the same, regardless of how it is financed—whether it is 100% equity financed, 50% equity financed, or 30% equity financed. This is because the world is perfect.

Any capital structure would be bid up to the value of the hypothetically best capital structure.

Table 16.1 shows the only logical possibility for a firm whose project will be worth either $60 or $160. The expected future value is $110; the present value is $100. Under hypothetical capital structure LD ("less debt"), the firm issues debt with face value $55. Consequently, bondholders face no uncertainty, and they will pay $55/(1 + 10%) = $50. Equity holders will receive either $5 or $105, and they are thus prepared to pay $55/(1 + 10%) = $50. Simply adding the value of the firm's claims adds up to the same $100. Under hypothetical capital structure MD ("more debt"), the firm issues debt with face value $94. Consequently, bondholders will now receive either $60 or $94, and they are willing to pay $70 today. Equity holders will receive $0 or $66, and they are willing to pay $30 for this privilege. Again, the value of all claims adds to $100.

Ignoring control rights, here is a "partial purchase and sale" M&M proof.

The homemade restructuring argument: A more surprising proof relies on the fact that you can relever the claims yourself—you do not need to own the entire firm to do it. The idea is that you do not buy 100% of the firm, but only 1% of the firm. If you buy 1% of all the firm's claims, you receive 1% of the projects' payoffs. You can then repackage and sell claims that imitate the payoffs under the presumably better capital structure for 1% of the firm's higher value, receiving an arbitrage profit of 1% of the value difference.

For example, assume that the firm has chosen capital structure LD, but you and other investors would really, really like capital structure MD. Perhaps you would really, really like to own a claim that pays $0.60 in the bad state and $0.94 in the good state. This would cost you 1% of the bond's $70 price, or $0.70. How can you purchase the existing LD claims to give you the MD-equivalent claim that you prefer *without* any cooperation by the LD-type firm?

You could sell synthetic MD securities if you can purchase worse LD securities.

First, work out what your claims are if you purchase d bonds and e stocks in the LD firm. You will receive payoffs of $d \cdot \$55 + e \cdot \$5$ in the bad scenario, and $d \cdot \$55 + e \cdot \$105$ in the good scenario. You want to end up with $0.60 in the bad scenario, and \$0.94 in the good scenario—two equations, two unknowns:

$$\text{Bad Luck} \quad d \cdot \$55 + e \cdot \$5 = \$0.60 \quad d \approx 0.0106$$

$$\text{Good Luck} \quad d \cdot \$55 + e \cdot \$105 = \$0.94 \quad e \approx 0.0034$$

If you purchase 0.0106 LD bonds and 0.0034 of the LD equity, you will end up with \$0.60 in the bad state, \$0.94 in the good state—exactly the same as an MD firm would have given you! How much would you have to pay to get these payoffs? The cost today would be $d \cdot \$50 + e \cdot \$50 = 0.0106 \cdot \$50 + 0.0034 \cdot \$50 = \$0.70$, exactly the same as your desired payoffs would have cost you if the firm itself had chosen an MD capital structure.

In effect, you have manufactured the capital structure payoffs that you like without the cooperation of the firm itself. By repeating this exercise, you can replicate the payoffs of *any* financial claims in *any* kind of capital structure.

From here, it is an easy step to the M&M argument. If the value of the firm is higher under the MD capital structure than it is under the LD capital structure, you can yourself transform the lower-cost claims under the capital structure into the higher-value claims under a better capital structure. You could sell them, and thereby earn an arbitrage profit. This would contradict the conjecture that the firm value could depend on its capital structure—in a perfect world, this should not be possible.

However, there is an important caveat to this homemade restructuring proof: Homemade leverage only allows you to obtain the cash flow rights of claims under any different arbitrary, and presumably better, capital structure. *It does not give you the control rights!* It can fail, for example, if a better capital structure has more value *only* if you obtain majority voting control that allows you to fire the management and change policy to what the firm should really be doing.

Beware: This homemade restructuring argument ignores control rights.

Let me explain in more detail why the "full restructure" argument with control rights is more general. The "homemade restructuring" argument must assume the payoffs are not influenced by the capital structure. What happens if a firm finances itself with securities that are just bad—for example, with securities that have covenants requiring the firm to change management every week? How can a firm be worth as much under this awful capital structure as it would be if it had chosen more sensible securities? There are two ways to handle this issue.

There are two ways to take care of control rights.

1. You can avoid all control rights–related issues by assuming that the projects and cash flows of the firm are already fixed. Thus, it does not matter whether the management changes every week. Control rights are irrelevant. Even if the firm changed its capital structure, its projects would still generate the same cash flows. This is the path that the M&M 1957 paper took—as we did above, too.

Fixed projects means control rights cannot change project cash flows.

2. You can rely on the full restructuring (takeover) argument, discussed above. It leans more heavily on the perfect market assumption, because you must be able to freely buy and sell enough securities not just to restructure 1% of the firm's payoff promises, but enough securities to take full control of the firm. And this is also the real reason why the M&M argument worked: It assumes that if you own all the shares, you own all the control rights. This allows you to fire the old

Full market perfection with full control rights means that firms always take the best projects.

management and restructure the firm's capital structure in an optimal fashion. (It also assumes you can undo any damage this bad management may have begun to set into action.) Thus, a firm with the bad capital structure that requires changing management every week could simply not exist.

Again, you would not be the only one to recognize that this creates value. Therefore, in this perfect world, firms not only end up with the optimal capital structure but also with the optimal set of projects. They are always priced at exactly what they should be worth under the optimal operating and financing policy that they would indeed be pursuing.

The bad capital structures would not exist for longer than a short instant.

The M&M implications are sometimes misunderstood. Yes, they do state that capital structure cannot influence value. But you should now realize why even an awful capital structure would be worth as much as a good capital structure. It is because the former would instantly disappear—competitive markets would bid to purchase all the (badly aligned) securities and restructure them into something better. Therefore, it is more accurate to think of the M&M proposition as stating not only that all capital structures are worth the same (which is true), but that bad capital structures are immediately eliminated and thus never observed in real life.

IMPORTANT: In Modigliani and Miller's world of perfect capital markets, arbitrage restrictions force the value of the firm's financial claims to be the same regardless of the firm's mix of debt and equity. A consequence of the perfect financial market assumption is that:

- Managers can make their real operations choices first without paying any attention to their debt and equity choices.

This can suffice for an M&M proof, in which project cash flows are fixed at whatever these real operations will generate. More interestingly, if arbitrageurs can undo what bad managers would otherwise want to commit, then the following holds true:

- Bad *capital structures* would be instantly eliminated by arbitrageurs and are thus never observed.
- Bad *project choices* would be instantly eliminated by arbitrageurs and are thus never observed.

Of course, if the world is *not* perfect, capital structure could matter to the value of the firm.

Know what to care about and what not to care about!

To the extent that the M&M proposition has some degree of realism, it is both good news and bad news. It is good news that you now know where to focus your efforts. You should try to increase the value of your firm's underlying projects—by increasing their expected cash flows, by reducing their costs of capital, or by doing both. It is bad news that you now know that you cannot add too much value by fiddling around with how you finance your projects if your financial markets are reasonably close to perfect.

SOLVE NOW!

Q 16.5 Under what assumptions does capital structure not matter?

Q 16.6 What does the assumption of risk neutrality "buy" in the M&M proof?

Q 16.7 In the example from Table 16.1, how would you purchase the equivalent of 5% of the equity of a hypothetical MD firm if all that was traded were the claims of the LD firm?

Q 16.8 Is the "homemade leverage restructuring" a full proof of the M&M proposition that capital structure is irrelevant? If not, what is missing?

Q 16.9 Under M&M, if contracts cannot be renegotiated, could existing managers destroy shareholder value? Does this change the value of the firm?

16.4 THE WEIGHTED AVERAGE COST OF CAPITAL (WACC)

Revisit the contingent claims example under risk aversion. Equity now requires a higher expected rate of return.

➤ Splitting building payoffs into debt and equity, Section 6.4, p. 155

The value of the firm does not depend on the financing in a perfect market. This is equivalent to stating that the overall cost of capital to the firm does not depend on its debt ratio. To show that our example also works when the world is not risk neutral, let's repeat the building with mortgage example from Section 6.4. However, we now allow riskier claims to have higher expected rates of return. We can already draw on your knowledge of net present value, the capital asset pricing model, and capital structure concepts. Another reason why this example is important is that it reintroduces the concept of the "weighted average cost of capital" (WACC) in the corporate context. (The next chapter gives you a generalized WACC formula if corporations pay income tax.)

16.4A AN EXAMPLE IN A RISK-AVERSE WORLD IN WHICH RISKIER SECURITIES MUST OFFER HIGHER EXPECTED RATES OF RETURN

All tools learned in Section 6.4 still apply under risk aversion.

When investors are risk averse, riskier claims have to offer higher expected rates of return. Nevertheless, our basic tools remain exactly the same as those in Section 6.4: payoff tables, promised rates of return, and expected rates of return.

The payoff table example applies to firms just as it did to buildings.

From Chapter 15, you know that debt and equity are contingent claims on the underlying project. Although we continue calling this project a building (to keep correspondence with Section 6.4), we now extend the metaphor. Consider the corporation to be the same as an unlevered building, the mortgage the same as corporate debt, the levered building equity ownership the same as corporate equity, and the possibilities of sunshine and tornadoes as future good or bad scenarios that the firm might face. There are no conceptual differences. We do however take one shortcut: We ignore all nonfinancial liabilities and pretend that our firm is financed entirely by financial debt and equity.

Recap the example parameters.

The parameters of the problem are as follows:

- The probability of sunshine is 80%; the probability of a tornado is 20%.
- If the sun shines, the project is worth $100,000; if the tornado strikes, the project is worth only $20,000.

- The appropriate cost of capital (at which investors are willing to borrow or save) is 10% for the overall project. We retain this cost of capital for the overall project, though not for the debt and equity. You had also computed earlier that the building must then be worth \$76,363.64.

Risk aversion causes *expected* interest rates on debt to be lower than *expected* rates of return on the project.

The novelty is that we now assume that Treasuries pay a lower *expected* rate of return. This is equivalent to assuming that investors are risk averse. The debt on the building is not exactly risk free, either. Assume that a particular risky bond on this building that promises to pay \$28,125 requires a 6% *expected* rate of return. (This 6% expected rate of return must be higher than the true risk-free rate of return [e.g., 5.6%], and lower than the 10% required expected rate of return for projects that are of the riskiness of "unlevered building" ownership.) Your model inputs are as shown:

		Financing Scheme 1	Financing Scheme 2	
		100% Equity	Bond (promises \$28,125)	Levered Equity (after \$28,125 obligation)
$\mathcal{P}rob$(Sunshine) = 80%	\$100,000.00			
$\mathcal{P}rob$(Tornado) = 20%	\$20,000.00			
$\mathcal{E}$ Future Payoff				
Price P Today				
$\mathcal{E}$ Rate of Return ($\mathcal{E}(\tilde{r})$)		10%	6%	

Compute the state-contingent payoffs.

Your goal is to determine what the appropriate cost of capital for the levered equity is. You can do this step by step:

Step 1: Find out how much the owners receive if they own the entire building (scheme AE for "all equity") versus if they promise \$28,125 to bondholders and retain only the levered equity (scheme DE for "debt and equity"). Naturally, in each state, the bond and the levered equity together must own the entire building:

		Financing Scheme AE	Financing Scheme DE	
		100% Equity	Bond (promises \$28,125)	Levered Equity (after \$28,125 obligation)
$\mathcal{P}rob$(Sunshine) = 80%	\$100,000.00	\$100,000.00	\$28,125.00	\$71,875.00
$\mathcal{P}rob$(Tornado) = 20%	\$20,000.00	\$20,000.00	\$20,000.00	\$0.00
$\mathcal{E}$ Future Payoff				
Price P Today				
$\mathcal{E}$ Rate of Return ($\mathcal{E}(\tilde{r})$)		10%	6%	

Compute the expected payoffs.

Step 2: Compute the expected value of each claim, using the probabilities of sunshine versus tornado. Note that the expected payoffs of the bond and the levered stock together must add up to the expected payoff on the building (i.e., as if the building were 100% equity financed).

		Financing Scheme AE	Financing Scheme DE	
		100% Equity	Bond (promises \$28,125)	Levered Equity (after \$28,125 obligation)
$Prob$(Sunshine) = 80%	\$100,000.00	\$100,000.00	\$28,125.00	\$71,875.00
$Prob$(Tornado) = 20%	\$20,000.00	\$20,000.00	\$20,000.00	\$0.00
$\mathcal{E}$ Future Payoff		\$84,000.00	\$26,500.00	\$57,500.00
Price P Today				
$\mathcal{E}$ Rate of Return ($\mathcal{E}(\tilde{r})$)		10%	6%	

Step 3: Discount the expected cash flows by the appropriate cost of capital demanded by the capital providers:

Discount the expected payoffs on the overall project and on the debt.

		Financing Scheme AE	Financing Scheme DE	
		100% Equity	Bond (promises \$28,125)	Levered Equity (after \$28,125 obligation)
$Prob$(Sunshine) = 80%	\$100,000.00	\$100,000.00	\$28,125.00	\$71,875.00
$Prob$(Tornado) = 20%	\$20,000.00	\$20,000.00	\$20,000.00	\$0.00
$\mathcal{E}$ Future Payoff		\$84,000.00	\$26,500.00	\$57,500.00
Price P Today		\$76,363.64	\$25,000.00	
$\mathcal{E}$ Rate of Return ($\mathcal{E}(\tilde{r})$)		10%	6%	

Step 4: Invoke the perfect market assumptions. Everyone can buy or sell without transaction costs, taxes, or any other impediments. By "absence of arbitrage," the value of the building if financed by a bond plus levered equity must be the same as the value of the building if 100% equity financed. Put differently, if you own all of the bond and all of the levered equity ownership, you own the same thing as the building—and vice versa. Now use the arbitrage condition that the value of the levered equity plus the value of the bond should equal the total building value.

Determine the value of the levered equity.

		Financing Scheme AE	Financing Scheme DE	
		100% Equity	Bond (promises \$28,125)	Levered Equity (after \$28,125 obligation)
$Prob$(Sunshine) = 80%	\$100,000.00	\$100,000.00	\$28,125.00	\$71,875.00
$Prob$(Tornado) = 20%	\$20,000.00	\$20,000.00	\$20,000.00	\$0.00
$\mathcal{E}$ Future Payoff		\$84,000.00	\$26,500.00	\$57,500.00
Price P Today		\$76,363.64	\$25,000.00	\$51,363.64
$\mathcal{E}$ Rate of Return ($\mathcal{E}(\tilde{r})$)		10%	6%	

Compute the appropriate expected rate of return on the levered equity.

Step 5: Levered equity ownership, which sells for \$51,363.64 and expects to pay off \$57,500.00, offers an expected rate of return of \$57,500.00/\$51,363.64 − 1 ≈ 11.95%:

		Scheme AE	Scheme DE	
		100% Equity	Bond (promises \$28,125)	Levered Equity (after \$28,125 obligation)
$\mathcal{P}rob$(Sunshine) = 80%	\$100,000.00	\$100,000.00	\$28,125.00	\$71,875.00
$\mathcal{P}rob$(Tornado) = 20%	\$20,000.00	\$20,000.00	\$20,000.00	\$0.00
	$\mathcal{E}$ Future Payoff	\$84,000.00	\$26,500.00	\$57,500.00
	Price P Today	\$76,363.64	\$25,000.00	\$51,363.64
	$\mathcal{E}$ Rate of Return ($\mathcal{E}(\tilde{r})$)	10%	6%	11.95%

Compute the riskiness of a dollar investment in each financial instrument.

Given the prices of the two claims and their payoffs in each state, you can work out the rates of return as follows:

	Contingent Rate of Return		Expected Rate of Return
	Tornado	Sunshine	(Appropriate)
Unlevered Ownership (100% Equity)	$\frac{\$20{,}000}{\$76{,}364} - 1 \approx -73.81\%$	$\frac{\$100{,}000}{\$76{,}364} - 1 \approx +30.95\%$	$\frac{\$84{,}000}{\$76{,}364} - 1 \approx +10.00\%$
Loan Ownership (Bond)	$\frac{\$20{,}000}{\$25{,}000} - 1 = -20.00\%$	$\frac{\$28{,}125}{\$25{,}000} - 1 = +12.50\%$	$\frac{\$26{,}500}{\$25{,}000} - 1 = +6.00\%$
Levered Ownership (Levered Equity)	$\frac{\$0}{\$51{,}364} - 1 = -100.00\%$	$\frac{\$71{,}875}{\$51{,}364} - 1 \approx +39.93\%$	$\frac{\$57{,}500}{\$51{,}364} - 1 \approx +11.95\%$

You started knowing only the costs of capital for the firm (10%) and the firm's bond (6%), and you were able to determine the cost of capital on the firm's levered equity (11.95%).

Debt is less risky than unlevered ownership, which is less risky than levered equity ownership.

➤ Figure 6.3, p. 160

As was also the case in the example with risk-neutral investors in Figure 6.3, the rates of return to levered equity are more risky (−100% or +39.93%) than those to unlevered ownership (−73.81% or +30.95%), which in turn are more risky than those to the corporate loan (−20% or +12.50%). But whereas these risk differences did not affect the expected rates of return in the risk-neutral world, they do in a risk-averse world. The **cost of capital** (the expected rate of return at which you, the owner, can obtain financing) is now higher for levered equity ownership than it is for unlevered ownership, which in turn is higher than it is for loan ownership. Moreover, you could work out *exactly* how high this expected rate of return on levered equity ownership must be. You only needed the "absence of arbitrage" argument in the perfect M&M world: Given the expected rate of return on the building and on the bond, you could determine the expected rate of return on levered equity ownership. (Alternatively, if you had known the appropriate expected rate of return on levered equity ownership and the rate of return on the bond, you could have worked out the appropriate expected rate of return on unlevered ownership.) Of course, these differences in expected rates of return should ultimately also be governed by some model like the CAPM, which you will see in Section 16.4D.

SOLVE NOW!

Q 16.10 A firm can be worth \$50 million, \$150 million, or \$400 million, each with equal probabilities. The firm is financed with one bond, promising to pay \$100 million at an interest rate of 5%. If the firm's projects require an appropriate cost of capital of 10%, then what is the firm's equity cost of capital? What is the debt's promised rate of return?

Q 16.11 Work out the standard deviation of the rates of return—the standard measure of risk—for each of the three possible types of claims (full ownership, debt, and levered equity) in the building example in the text.

Q 16.12 Assume that you have access to a project worth \$100 that you cannot fully finance yourself. Moreover, you have only 20% of the project that you can finance and you need the money back next year, because you will have no other source of income. Can you fund the project?

16.4B THE WACC FORMULA (WITHOUT TAXES)

The WACC is independent of debt and equity distribution.

The above example provides a natural transition into the **weighted average cost of capital (WACC)**. It is the value-weighted average cost of capital of all the firm's claims. Because the value of the firm is determined by the value of its assets and is independent of the division between debt and equity, the same independence should hold true for the cost of capital. Let's check, then, that if the perfect-markets arbitrage condition holds—that is, if bonds and stocks together cost the same as the firm—then the cost of capital for the overall firm is the weighted cost of capital of stocks and bonds.

If you know any two costs of capital, you can deduce the third.

The constant WACC implies that the costs of capital of debt, equity, and the overall firm are directly linked. If you know the costs of capital for the debt and the equity, you can infer the cost of capital for the firm. Alternatively, if you know the cost of capital for the firm and the debt, you can infer the cost of capital for the equity. *If you know any two costs of capital, you can compute the third one.*

Here is a line-by-line derivation of the WACC formula.

Let's show this again to translate the numerical example into a formula for the WACC. No matter which state will come about, the debt and equity together own the firm:

$$\begin{array}{lrcrcr} \text{Sunshine (80\%):} & \$28{,}125 & + & \$71{,}875 & = & \$100{,}000 \\ \text{Tornado (20\%):} & \$20{,}000 & + & \$0 & = & \$20{,}000 \\ & \text{Debt}_{\text{Next Year}} & + & \text{Equity}_{\text{Next Year}} & = & \text{Firm}_{\text{Next Year}} \end{array}$$

Therefore, the expected value of debt and equity together must be equal to the expected value of the firm:

$$\begin{array}{ccccc} \$57{,}500 & + & \$26{,}500 & = & \$84{,}000 \\ \mathcal{E}(\text{Equity}_{\text{Next Year}}) & + & \mathcal{E}(\text{Debt}_{\text{Next Year}}) & = & \mathcal{E}(\text{Firm}_{\text{Next Year}}) \end{array}$$

You can rewrite this in terms of today's values and expected rates of return ($\mathcal{E}(\tilde{r})$) from time $t = 0$ to $t = 1$:

$$
\begin{aligned}
&\$57{,}500 &+\quad& \$26{,}500 &=\quad& \$84{,}000\\
\approx\ &\$51{,}363.64\cdot(1+11.95\%) &+\quad& \$25{,}000\cdot(1+6\%) &\approx\quad& \$76{,}363.64\cdot(1+10\%)\\
&\mathcal{E}(\text{Equity}_{\text{Next Year}}) &+\quad& \mathcal{E}(\text{Debt}_{\text{Next Year}}) &=\quad& \mathcal{E}(\text{Firm}_{\text{Next Year}})
\end{aligned}
$$

$$
= \text{Equity}_{\text{Today}}\cdot\left[1+\mathcal{E}(\tilde{r}_{\text{Equity}})\right] + \text{Debt}_{\text{Today}}\cdot\left[1+\mathcal{E}(\tilde{r}_{\text{Debt}})\right] = \text{Firm}_{\text{Today}}\cdot\left[1+\mathcal{E}(\tilde{r}_{\text{Firm}})\right]
$$

Omit the time subscripts on the expected rates of return to reduce clutter. (There is no risk of confusion because our examples use only two time periods.) Divide each term by the firm value today ($\text{Firm}_{\text{Today}}$) to express this formula in terms of percentages of firm value:

$$
\left(\frac{\$51{,}363.64}{\$76{,}363.64}\right)\cdot(1+11.95\%) + \left(\frac{\$25{,}000.00}{\$76{,}363.64}\right)\cdot(1+6\%) \approx 1+10\%
$$

$$
\left(\frac{\text{Equity}_{\text{Today}}}{\text{Firm}_{\text{Today}}}\right)\cdot\left[1+\mathcal{E}(\tilde{r}_{\text{Equity}})\right] + \left(\frac{\text{Debt}_{\text{Today}}}{\text{Firm}_{\text{Today}}}\right)\cdot\left[1+\mathcal{E}(\tilde{r}_{\text{Debt}})\right] = \left[1+\mathcal{E}(\tilde{r}_{\text{Firm}})\right]
$$

$\text{Equity}_{\text{Today}}/\text{Firm}_{\text{Today}}$ is the weight of equity in the firm's value today, so you can call it $w_{\text{Equity, Today}}$ or simply w_{Equity}, because it is common to just omit the time subscript if the time is now. Similarly, $\text{Debt}_{\text{Today}}/\text{Firm}_{\text{Today}}$ is w_{Debt}. Therefore, you can write this formula as

$$
67.26\%\cdot(1+11.95\%) + 32.74\%\cdot(1+6\%) \approx 1+10\%
$$

$$
w_{\text{Equity}}\cdot\left[1+\mathcal{E}(\tilde{r}_{\text{Equity}})\right] + w_{\text{Debt}}\cdot\left[1+\mathcal{E}(\tilde{r}_{\text{Debt}})\right] = \left[1+\mathcal{E}(\tilde{r}_{\text{Firm}})\right]
$$

Multiply the weight percentages into the brackets,

$$
67.26\% + 67.26\%\cdot 11.95\% + 32.74\% + 32.74\%\cdot 6\% \approx 1+10\%
$$

$$
w_{\text{Equity}} + w_{\text{Equity}}\cdot\mathcal{E}(\tilde{r}_{\text{Equity}}) + w_{\text{Debt}} + w_{\text{Debt}}\cdot\mathcal{E}(\tilde{r}_{\text{Debt}}) = 1+\mathcal{E}(\tilde{r}_{\text{Firm}})
$$

Because debt and equity own the firm, $w_{\text{Debt}} + w_{\text{Equity}} = 1$, which cancels the "1+" term on the right side. You have arrived at the weighted average cost of capital (WACC) formula:

$$
\text{WACC} \approx 67.26\%\cdot 11.95\% + 32.74\%\cdot 6\% \approx 10\%
$$

$$
\text{WACC} = w_{\text{Equity}}\cdot\mathcal{E}(\tilde{r}_{\text{Equity}}) + w_{\text{Debt}}\cdot\mathcal{E}(\tilde{r}_{\text{Debt}}) = \mathcal{E}(\tilde{r}_{\text{Firm}})
$$

Because a cost of capital is itself an *expected* rate of return, you do not need an expectation operator in front of the WACC—it is implied. The next two chapters will explain how WACC must be modified in the presence of corporate income taxes and other perfect-market distortions.

16.4C HOW THE COST OF CAPITAL AND QUOTED INTEREST RATES VARY WITH LEVERAGE

We want to consider different capital structures now.

You now understand how to compute costs of capital. But I want you to switch from "tree knowledge" to "forest knowledge"—how shifts in capital structures generally influence individual securities' costs of capital. So return now to the debt-and-equity-only numerical example. Everything included, we just worked out:

Medium leverage.

		Scheme AE	Scheme DE	
		100% Equity	Bond (promises $28,125)	Levered Equity (after $28,125 obligation)
$\mathcal{P}rob$(Sunshine) = 80%	$100,000.00	$100,000.00	$28,125.00	$71,875.00
$\mathcal{P}rob$(Tornado) = 20%	$20,000.00	$20,000.00	$20,000.00	$0.00
$\mathcal{E}$ Future Payoff		$84,000.00	$26,500.00	$57,500.00
$\mathcal{E}$ Rate of Return ($\mathcal{E}(\tilde{r})$)		10%	6%	11.95%
Price P Today		$76,363.64	$25,000.00	$51,363.64
Capital Structure Weight (Security Price/Firm Value)			32.74%	67.26%
Promised Rate of Return (Bond Promise/Bond Price − 1)			12.5%	

To generalize, I need to describe how the debt cost of capital varies with leverage.

How would the promised rate of return, the expected rate of return, and the debt/equity ratio change if the firm changed the amount it borrowed? For the sake of illustration, I want an example in which the corporate debt offers an expected rate of return of 6% if the debt promises $28,125. I can accomplish this if I fix the risk-free rate at 5.55% and linearly increase the cost of debt capital once the firm promises to pay more than $20,000 to its creditors, and at 10% if the debt promises the entire firm. To do so, I use the formula

$$\mathcal{E}(\tilde{r}_{\text{Debt}}) \approx 4.053\% + 5.947\% \cdot w_{\text{Debt}} \quad \text{only if} \quad w_{\text{Debt}} > 25\% \Leftrightarrow \mathcal{E}(\tilde{r}_{\text{Debt}}) \geq 5.55\%$$

This formula applies only if the computed rate exceeds the 5.55% risk-free rate (which is the case if $w_{\text{Debt}} > 25\%$). With this formula, we can now recompute the example for all possible capital structures under risk aversion.

Check the debt cost of capital formula.

First confirm that this formula works for the two structures you already know: At $w_{\text{Debt}} \approx 32.74\%$, the expected debt interest rate is $4.053\% + 5.947\% \cdot 32.74\% \approx 6\%$. This was our original example. The important numbers for us are as follows:

Debt Promises		Expected Rate of Return			Weight	
Payoff	Interest Rate	Debt	Equity	Firm	Debt	Equity
$28,125	12.5%	6%	11.95%	10%	32.74%	67.26%

You can also check what happens if the debt is 100% of the firm. At $w_{\text{Debt}} = 100\%$, the debt *is* the firm and its cost of capital must be 10%.

Debt Promises		Expected Rate of Return			Weight	
Payoff	Interest Rate	Debt	Equity	Firm	Debt	Equity
All	All	10%	N/A	10%	100%	0%

Low leverage.

Use the formula to work out two more examples. If the debt promises $10,000, then it is risk free and you would use $\mathcal{E}(\tilde{r}_{\text{Debt}}) \approx 5.55\%$.

		100% Equity	Bond (promises \$10,000)	Levered Equity (after \$10,000 obligation)
$\mathcal{P}rob$(Sunshine) = 80%	\$100,000.00	\$100,000.00	\$10,000.00	\$90,000.00
$\mathcal{P}rob$(Tornado) = 20%	\$20,000.00	\$20,000.00	\$10,000.00	\$10,000.00
$\mathcal{E}$ Future Payoff		\$84,000.00	\$10,000.00	\$74,000.00
$\mathcal{E}$ Rate of Return ($\mathcal{E}(\tilde{r})$)		10%	5.55%	10.64%
Price P Today		\$76,363.64	\$9,478.67	\$66,884.97
Capital Structure Weight (Security Price/Firm Value)			12.41%	87.59%
Promised Rate of Return (Bond Promise/Bond Price − 1)			5.55%	

High leverage.

If the debt promises \$50,000 and the debt is risky, then you would use $\mathcal{E}(\tilde{r}_{\text{Debt}}) \approx 7.25\%$ and the example becomes:

		100% Equity	Bond (promises \$50,000)	Levered Equity (after \$50,000 obligation)
$\mathcal{P}rob$(Sunshine) = 80%	\$100,000.00	\$100,000.00	\$50,000.00	\$50,000.00
$\mathcal{P}rob$(Tornado) = 20%	\$20,000.00	\$20,000.00	\$20,000.00	\$0.00
$\mathcal{E}$ Future Payoff		\$84,000.00	\$44,000.00	\$40,000.00
$\mathcal{E}$ Rate of Return ($\mathcal{E}(\tilde{r})$)		10%	7.25%	13.19%
Price P Today		\$76,363.64	\$41,025.64	\$35,338.00
Capital Structure Weight (Security Price/Firm Value)			53.72%	46.28%
Promised Rate of Return (Bond Promise/Bond Price − 1)			21.88%	

Many different leverages.

If you know how to work all the examples above, then you can confirm the following numbers:

Debt Promises		Expected Rate of Return			Weight	
Payoff	Interest Rate	Debt	Equity	Firm	Debt	Equity
\$10,000	5.55%	5.55%	10.64%	10%	12.41%	87.59%
\$28,125	12.50%	6.00%	11.95%	10%	32.74%	67.26%
\$50,000	21.88%	7.25%	13.19%	10%	53.72%	46.28%
\$75,000	27.31%	8.64%	14.59%	10%	77.14%	22.86%
∞	All	10.00%	—	10%	100.00%	0%

DIGGING DEEPER

If you had to solve rather than just confirm this, you would solve for two unknowns, w_{Debt} and $\mathcal{E}(\tilde{r}_{\text{Debt}})$:

$$w_{\text{Debt}} \approx \text{Bond Price}/\$76{,}363.64 \quad \text{where} \quad \text{Bond Price} = \frac{(80\% \cdot \text{Promise} + 20\% \cdot \$20{,}000)}{1 + \mathcal{E}(\tilde{r}_{\text{Debt}})}$$

$$\mathcal{E}(\tilde{r}_{\text{Debt}}) \approx 4.053\% + 0.05947 \cdot w_{\text{Debt}}$$

The solutions are

$$w_{\text{Debt}} \approx -8.7484 + 1.32725 \cdot f\,(\text{Promise})$$

$$\mathcal{E}(\tilde{r}_{\text{Debt}}) \approx -0.479735 + 0.0789317 \cdot f\,(\text{Promise})$$

where $f(\text{Promise}) = \left(\sqrt{439{,}458 + \text{Promise}}\right)/100$.

How Bad Are Mistakes?

IF ALL SECURITIES ARE RISKIER, IS THE FIRM RISKIER?

Does more debt increase the firm's cost of capital? Does it increase the debt cost of capital? Does it increase the equity cost of capital?

Many practitioners commit a serious logical mistake. They argue as follows:

1. If the firm takes on more debt, the debt becomes riskier and the cost of capital for the debt ($\mathcal{E}(\tilde{r}_{\text{Debt}})$) increases.
2. If the firm takes on more debt, the equity becomes riskier and the cost of capital for the equity ($\mathcal{E}(\tilde{r}_{\text{Equity}})$) increases.
3. Because the firm consists of only debt and equity, the firm also becomes riskier when the firm takes on more debt, which must mean that the firm's cost of capital ($\mathcal{E}(\tilde{r}_{\text{Firm}})$) increases. A financier may even want to reduce the firm's debt in order to avoid such increases in volatility of the firm.

The fact that both debt and equity become riskier as the firm takes on more debt does *not* mean that the overall firm becomes riskier.

The first two statements are correct. With more debt, the cost of capital on debt increases because it becomes riskier: In corporate default, the debt is less likely to receive what it was promised. The equity also becomes riskier: The cost of capital on equity rises, because in financial default, which is now more likely to occur, more cash goes to the creditors before equity holders receive anything. It is only the final conclusion—"the firm also becomes riskier"—that is wrong. The reason is that when the firm takes on more debt, the weight of the debt (w_{Debt}) increases and the weight of the equity ($w_{\text{Equity}} = 1 - w_{\text{Debt}}$) decreases. Because the cost of capital for debt ($\mathcal{E}(\tilde{r}_{\text{Debt}})$) is lower than the cost of capital for equity ($\mathcal{E}(\tilde{r}_{\text{Equity}})$), the weighted sum remains the same. Recall the following:

Low Debt	$12.41\% \cdot 5.55\% + 87.59\% \cdot 10.64\% \approx 10\%$
Medium Debt	$53.72\% \cdot 7.25\% + 46.28\% \cdot 13.19\% \approx 10\%$
High Debt	$77.14\% \cdot 8.64\% + 22.86\% \cdot 14.59\% \approx 10\%$
	$w_{\text{Debt}} \cdot \mathcal{E}(\tilde{r}_{\text{Debt}}) + w_{\text{Equity}} \cdot \mathcal{E}(\tilde{r}_{\text{Equity}}) = \mathcal{E}(\tilde{r}_{\text{Firm}})$

Check that statements 1 and 2 are correct and that statement 3 is incorrect: The costs of capital for both debt and equity are higher when the firm has more debt, but the overall cost of capital for the firm has not changed. In the perfect M&M world, the overall cost of capital is independent of the mix between debt and equity.

THE SUMMARY GRAPHS

The x-axis is the promise to creditors, the y-axis is the (expected) rate of return. There are 3 distinctly different regions.

I have done the calculations for many more debt ratios and graphed the rates of return in Figure 16.1. (This is the "forest" view I wanted to get to.) The graph shows that you can think of three cases:

A risk-free debt domain: In the region where the bond promises to pay no more than \$20,000, the debt is risk free and therefore enjoys a constant cost of capital of exactly

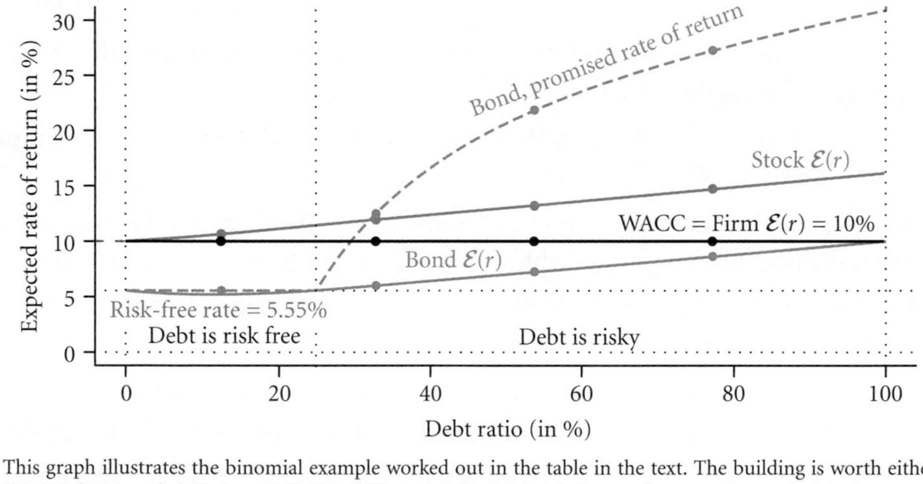

This graph illustrates the binomial example worked out in the table in the text. The building is worth either \$20,000 (20% probability) or \$100,000 (80% probability). The circles are the examples worked in the text or in the Solve Now! questions. For example, the dots where the debt ratio is 32.74% come from the problem in which the firm borrows \$25,000 and promises to pay \$28,125. Creditors are promised 12.5%, but they expect to receive only 6%. Equity receives an expected rate of return of 11.95%. If the firm's debt is less than \$20,000/1.0555 ≈ \$18,948.37, which is \$18,948.37/\$76,363.64 ≈ 24.8% of the firm's assets, it is risk free and both promises and pays 5.55%.

Further observations:

- Both the debt and equity have to offer higher expected rates of return when there is more debt in the capital structure.
- Nevertheless, the weighted average cost of capital remains at 10%.
- The quoted interest rate to the creditors rises very quickly when the debt is risky, and it exceeds not only the expected interest rate for creditors but also the expected rate of return for equity.

FIGURE 16.1 The Cost of Capital in a Perfect World—Binomial Payoffs

5.55%. Put differently, the same 5.55% cost of capital applies to loans between $1 and $18,948 (today).

Now, notice that the expected rate of return to equity is not constant in this region. Equity enjoys the 10% cost of capital equal to that of the firm only if there is exactly zero debt. As soon as the firm takes on *any* debt—even riskless debt—the expected rate of return to the equity has to increase. For example, if the firm takes on $15,000 in debt, the equity requires an expected rate of return of 11.0% to participate.

A risky debt domain in which debt and equity are both at risk: If the debt obligation is worth more than $18,948.37 today, then the debt becomes risky. In this domain, not only shareholders, but also bondholders, must earn a higher expected rate of return. Nevertheless, the weighted average cost of capital remains at 10%. The reason is that as the debt ratio increases, the share of the higher-return equity in the capital structure falls.

A domain in which debt owns the entire firm: If the firm promises $100,000 or more to creditors, equity owners never receive anything. Thus, they are unwilling to provide any capital, which is why the green line ends at $100,000. The bond now assumes the firm's cost of capital of 10%, and any promise to pay more than $100,000 is entirely irrelevant.

There is just one region where the x-axis is the debt ratio and the cash flows are normally distributed.

In the wild, the plot looks a little different from the graph in Figure 16.1. The reason is that the example was somewhat abnormal. It was "binomial" in that the firm could only end up with one of two possible outcomes. A more common situation is one in which a firm has, loosely speaking, normally (bell-shaped) distributed payoffs. Figure 16.2 illustrates such a project. It also has an expected payoff of $84,000 and a standard deviation of $32,000, identical to that in our binomial example. The calculations proceed the same way as those in the binomial case, except there are now many more cases than just payoffs of $20,000 and $100,000 to work out. The figure shows that the shape of the lines may have changed, but most of the intuition has not.

Here is what you should learn from Figure 16.2.

Because it is always possible that the firm will be worth nothing, it is now impossible for the firm to issue riskless bonds. Thus, there is no risk-free region anymore. Instead, the debt's required interest rate now rises smoothly with the weight of debt in the firm's capital structure everywhere. However, for low debt ratios, there is little difference between riskless and slightly risky debt for all practical purposes. In fact, until the debt ratio reaches about 40%, the probability that it will not pay off is so low that the cost of debt capital is practically indistinguishable from the risk-free rate without a magnifying glass. (Even the promised rate of return is only slightly higher.) Yet, once the debt ratio reaches a high level, say, 60% to 80% of the firm value, the corporate interest rate can be significantly higher than the risk-free rate. Another small difference from the earlier graph is that the cost of capital on equity increases more quickly. In highly levered companies, it can reach stratospheric levels—easily three times the cost of capital for the firm, or more. But, most importantly, we are still in a perfect world, so the expected cost of capital for the overall firm remains an unchanged 10%, regardless of capital structure.

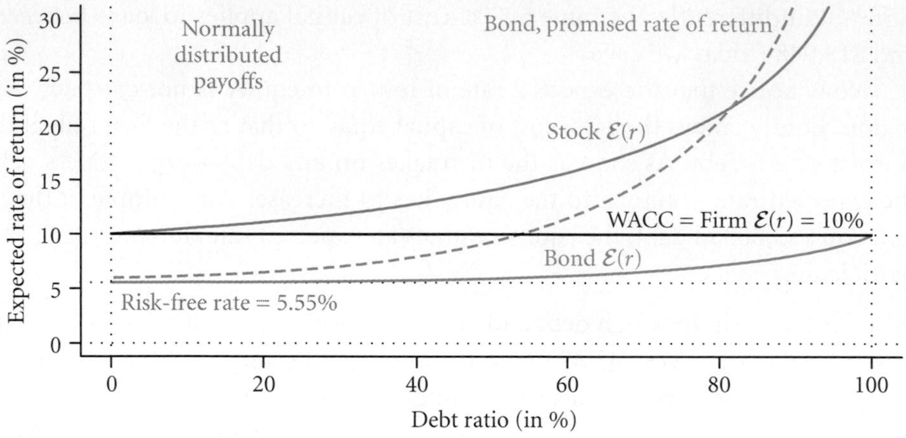

This is the equivalent of Figure 16.1, but payoffs are no longer binomially distributed. Instead, they are now normally distributed. The parameters in this figure were intentionally chosen to remain similar to those in the binomial example.

FIGURE 16.2 The Cost of Capital in a Perfect World—Normal Payoffs

How Bad Are Mistakes?

CAN THE EQUITY'S COST OF CAPITAL BE LOWER THAN THE RATE THAT THE FIRM IS PAYING TO ITS CREDITORS?

Promised rates of return to the lender can rise even more steeply, though.

You already know that the equity cost of capital is always higher than the debt cost of capital. So, can the equity's cost of capital be lower than the interest rate that the firm is paying on its debt? Careful—you must recognize what the interest rate is that creditors demand. Note how quickly the bond's *quoted* rate of return rises in Figure 16.2. With risky debt, the promised rate of return rises much faster than the bond's expected rate of return. In the real world, the financially naïve often fixate on this promised rate of return and do not focus enough on the expected rate of return. They then make a logical mistake of comparing the equity expected rate of return (e.g., from the CAPM) to the interest *quoted* by the bank. Even in our binomial example in Figure 16.1, the CAPM cost of capital of 11.95% for the equity is lower than the quoted interest rate of 12.5% that the firm has to pay to the bank. But it is the debt that has the lower cost of capital (only 6%), not the equity! In other words, there are many real-world situations in which the correct equity cost of capital is *lower* than the quoted interest rate on the debt.

SOLVE NOW!

Q 16.13 Confirm all the numbers in the contingent claims table on page 590. For example, you do not need to work out $w_{\text{Debt}} \approx 53.72\%$ independently, but you should confirm it.

Q 16.14 Work the example from page 589 if the debt promises \$75,000 and $\mathcal{E}(\tilde{r}_{\text{Debt}}) = 8.64\%$. Confirm that the weight of the debt in the capital structure is 77.14%.

Q 16.15 Compared to hypothetical firm B, hypothetical firm A has both a higher cost of capital for its debt and a higher cost of capital for its equity. Does this necessarily imply that firm A has a higher overall cost of capital than firm B?

16.4D THE CAPM, WACC, AND NPV—A SEAMLESS FIT

You should be suspicious: Does this argument really fit with our earlier models, like the CAPM?

Are you scratching your head? How can this all fit together so seamlessly? How can the expected rate of return on equity have been tied down by the expected rate of return on the projects and the expected rate of return on the debt? Should the expected rate of return on any project be determined by its risk (market beta), instead? Another interesting observation is that the 6% on debt and the 11.95% on levered equity must have been determined by the supply and demand of investors. Why did supply and demand meet at these points? This must come from a model such as the CAPM. In the end, the theories better fit one another, or else you could be in big trouble. One theory might give a different answer than the other.

Fortunately, all the models fit. NPV, WACC, and the CAPM are often all used together.

Fortunately, this is not the case. You can combine NPV, WACC, and the CAPM. They work well with one another. It is common to use the CAPM to provide appropriate expected rates of return on debt and equity, compute the weighted average to obtain a WACC, and then use this WACC as the denominator in the NPV formula. Let's see how this works. Switch to a different project so that we can start with the CAPM right off the bat. Consider a project that can be financed with low-risk debt with a market beta of 0.1, worth Debt = \$400 today; and with high-risk equity with a market beta of 2.5, worth Equity = \$250 today. The risk-free rate of return is 4%; the equity premium is 3%. What is the cost of capital of the overall project (Firm)?

The standard method is to compute first the appropriate expected rates of return for the debt and the equity. Use the CAPM to find the expected rates of return:

$$\mathcal{E}(\tilde{r}_{\text{Debt}}) = 4\% + 3\% \cdot 0.1 = 4.3\%$$

$$\mathcal{E}(\tilde{r}_{\text{Equity}}) = 4\% + 3\% \cdot 2.5 = 11.5\%$$

$$\mathcal{E}(\tilde{r}_{\text{i}}) = r_{\text{F}} + \left[\mathcal{E}(\tilde{r}_{\text{M}}) - r_{\text{F}}\right] \cdot \beta_{\text{i}}$$

Second, compute the weights of each claim in the capital structure:

$$w_{\text{Debt}} = \left(\frac{\$400}{\$400 + \$250}\right) \approx 61.5\%$$

$$w_{\text{Equity}} = \left(\frac{\$250}{\$400 + \$250}\right) \approx 38.5\%$$

Third, compute the weighted average cost of capital:

$$\begin{aligned} \text{WACC} &\approx 61.5\% \cdot 4.3\% + 38.5\% \cdot 11.5\% \approx 7.1\% \\ & w_{\text{Debt}} \cdot \mathcal{E}(\tilde{r}_{\text{Debt}}) + w_{\text{Equity}} \cdot \mathcal{E}(\tilde{r}_{\text{Equity}}) = \mathcal{E}(\tilde{r}_{\text{Firm}}) \end{aligned}$$

An alternative method relies on the weighted-average project beta,

$$\beta_{\text{Firm}} = \left(\frac{\$400}{\$400 + \$250}\right) \cdot 0.1 + \left(\frac{\$250}{\$400 + \$250}\right) \cdot 2.5 \approx 1.023$$

$$\beta_{\text{Firm}} = w_{\text{Debt}} \cdot \beta_{\text{Debt}} + w_{\text{Equity}} \cdot \beta_{\text{Equity}}$$

This means that the project's cost of capital is

$$\mathcal{E}(\tilde{r}_{\text{Firm}}) = 4\% + 3\% \cdot 1.023 \approx 7.1\%$$

$$\mathcal{E}(\tilde{r}_{\text{i}}) = r_{\text{F}} + \left[\mathcal{E}(\tilde{r}_{\text{M}}) - r_{\text{F}}\right] \cdot \beta_{\text{i}}$$

This is the same 7.1% as the cost-of-capital estimate you computed with the standard method.

You can now use this 7.1% cost-of-capital estimate as the hurdle rate for firm-type projects, or use it to discount the project's expected cash flows to obtain a present value estimate. For example, if the project earns \$800 with probability 48% and \$600 with probability 52%, then

$$\text{PV} = \frac{48\% \cdot \$800 + 52\% \cdot \$600}{1 + 7.1\%} \approx \$650$$

(Of course, I had to make up the expected cash flows so that the debt and equity indeed could add up to \$650.)

You cannot use the promised debt interest rate in the WACC formula. You must use the expected debt interest rate.

Is the WACC the weighted average of the interest rate that the firm pays to the bank and the expected rate of return on equity? Definitely not. The bank's quoted interest rate is the *promised* rate of return to debt. This is higher than the *expected* interest rate that goes into the WACC formula. (It is higher because of the default premium). How do you find the expected rate of return on the financial debt? Pretty much the same way as you find the expected rate of return on equity or other financial claims: Use a model like the CAPM, which provides the expected rates of return. Indeed, we just used it for this purpose above. (The CAPM cost of capital is the sum of the time premium and the systematic risk premium, and it appropriately ignores the debt's idiosyncratic risk and default premium.) You can estimate the beta from the debt's historical monthly rates of return, and then substitute it into the CAPM formula. Sometimes it can be even easier: If the debt is short-term and investment-grade, then the debt beta is likely very small. In this case, and only in this case, you can work with an $\mathcal{E}(\tilde{r}_{\text{Debt}})$ that is reasonably close to the risk-free rate (and/or the rate that the firm is paying to the bank).

DIGGING DEEPER

I can prove that the "debt ratio adjustment for beta" formula (Formula 9.2 on page 282), the WACC (Formula 16.2 on page 599), and the CAPM (Formula 9.1 on page 251) are mutually compatible in the perfect-markets scenario.

In this current chapter, we developed the basic WACC formula (the cost of capital for the overall "Firm"—not to be confused with F, the subscript for the risk-free security):

$$\mathcal{E}(\tilde{r}_{\text{Firm}}) = w_{\text{Debt}} \cdot \mathcal{E}(\tilde{r}_{\text{Debt}}) + w_{\text{Equity}} \cdot \mathcal{E}(\tilde{r}_{\text{Equity}})$$

Substitute the CAPM Formula 9.1 into the three expected rates of return in the WACC formula:

$$r_F + \left[\mathcal{E}(\tilde{r}_M) - r_F\right] \cdot \beta_{\text{Firm}} = w_{\text{Debt}} \cdot \left\{r_F + \left[\mathcal{E}(\tilde{r}_M) - r_F\right] \cdot \beta_{\text{Debt}}\right\} + w_{\text{Equity}} \cdot \left\{r_F + \left[\mathcal{E}(\tilde{r}_M) - r_F\right] \cdot \beta_{\text{Equity}}\right\}$$

Pull out the risk-free rates of return:

$$r_F + \left[\mathcal{E}(\tilde{r}_M) - r_F\right] \cdot \beta_{\text{Firm}}$$

$$= w_{\text{Debt}} \cdot r_F + w_{\text{Equity}} \cdot r_F + w_{\text{Debt}} \cdot \left\{\left[\mathcal{E}(\tilde{r}_M) - r_F\right] \cdot \beta_{\text{Debt}}\right\} + w_{\text{Equity}} \cdot \left\{\left[\mathcal{E}(\tilde{r}_M) - r_F\right] \cdot \beta_{\text{Equity}}\right\}$$

Recognize that $(w_{\text{Equity}} + w_{\text{Debt}}) = 1$, so $(w_{\text{Equity}} + w_{\text{Debt}}) \cdot r_F = r_F$:

$$\left[\mathcal{E}(\tilde{r}_M) - r_F\right] \cdot \beta_{\text{Firm}} = w_{\text{Debt}} \cdot \left[\mathcal{E}(\tilde{r}_M) - r_F\right] \cdot \beta_{\text{Debt}} + w_{\text{Equity}} \cdot \left[\mathcal{E}(\tilde{r}_M) - r_F\right] \cdot \beta_{\text{Equity}}$$

Divide by $\left[\mathcal{E}(\tilde{r}_M) - r_F\right]$:

$$\beta_{\text{Firm}} = w_{\text{Debt}} \cdot \beta_{\text{Debt}} + w_{\text{Equity}} \cdot \beta_{\text{Equity}}$$

This is exactly our relationship in Formula 9.2, which relates betas to one another! Indeed, all three formulas share the same intuition: Firms and claims with higher betas are riskier and thus have to offer higher expected rates of return.

SOLVE NOW!

Q 16.16 Assume the risk-free rate of return is 3% and the equity premium is 4%. A firm worth \$100 million has a market beta of 3. A new project that costs \$10 million appears. It is expected to pay off \$11 million next year. The beta of this new project is 0.5.

(a) If the firm does everything right, what is the NPV of the project? Should the firm take it?

(b) However, the firm evaluates all projects by its overall cost of capital. Would this firm take the project?

(c) What is the value of a firm that undertakes this new project?

(d) What fraction of the equity would the old shareholders have to give up from a combined firm in order to raise the \$10 million to undertake the project?

(e) What fraction of the firm value today would be the old projects, what fraction would be the new project?
(f) How would the beta of the firm change?
(g) How would the firm's average cost of capital change?

16.4E THE EFFECT OF DEBT ON EARNINGS PER SHARE AND PRICE/EARNINGS RATIOS

EPS is meaningless.

What is the effect of debt on earnings per share (EPS)? This is a meaningless question, because EPS depends not on the firm but on the number of shares. The same capital structure can exist under different numbers of shares. Equity can be worth $7 million with 1 million shares valued at $7/share (an expected EPS of $0.70/share) or with 100,000 shares valued at $70/share (an expected EPS of $7/share). Any EPS figure is possible.

P/E is a more sensible ratio. It can go up or down. Ultimately, P/E is not important, though—only value is.

➤ Debt adjustment for P/E ratios, Section 14.3D, p. 517

A more meaningful question is how leverage influences P/E ratios. I had already sneaked this into Section 14.3D, but you had to trust me blindly that debt offers a lower expected rate of return than equity. The examples in that section satisfied the M&M constant WACC—and showed that more debt can sometimes cause lower P/E ratios (especially in value firms) and sometimes cause higher P/E ratios (especially in high-growth firms).

16.5 THE BIG PICTURE: HOW TO THINK OF DEBT AND EQUITY

IMPORTANT:

In a perfect M&M world with only financial debt and equity:

The Value of Claims

- The value of the firm is independent of cash flow or control rights, because arbitrageurs can—and always will—rearrange claims into an optimal structure.
- An "absence of arbitrage" relationship ensures that this sum total of the values of all its claims is equal to the total underlying project value.
- Claims "partition" the firm's payoffs in future states of the world. For financial securities, this is often contractually arranged at inception.

The Risk of Claims

- Levered equity is the residual claim after the debt has been satisfied. It is riskier than full ownership, which in turn is riskier than the debt.

The Cost of Capital

- Riskier claims almost always have to offer higher expected rates of return. (The exceptions are pathological cases, in which the market beta is very negative.) Normally, levered equity has to offer a higher expected rate of return than outright ownership, which in turn has to offer a higher expected rate of return than debt and other liabilities.

- The *quoted* interest rate on financial debt can not only be much higher than its expected rate of return, but can also be much higher than the *expected* rate of return on equity.
- Assuming that the firm is financed only with debt and equity, the absence of arbitrage implies that the capitalization-weighted average expected rate of return (WACC) is:

$$\text{WACC} = w_{\text{Equity}} \cdot \mathcal{E}(\tilde{r}_{\text{Equity}}) + w_{\text{Debt}} \cdot \mathcal{E}(\tilde{r}_{\text{Debt}}) = \mathcal{E}(\tilde{r}_{\text{Firm}}) \quad (16.2)$$

where the weights w_{Equity} and w_{Debt} are the values of equity and debt when quoted as a fraction of the overall firm value *today*.
- The project's WACC remains the same, no matter how the firm is financed. It is determined by the underlying projects.

One more factoid: Expected (i.e., required) rates of return on equity can be very high if leverage is very high.

If the firm's debt ratio is very high and the firm has enough collateralizable assets (meaning its debt remains almost risk free), then it is also not uncommon to see very high expected rates of return on the equity—multiple times that of the firm's WACC. For example, if the risk-free rate is 5% and a firm with a 10% cost of capital were to increase its debt to 95% of the firm's value, the residual equity would have a seemingly astronomical cost of capital,

$$\begin{array}{ccccccc} 5\% \cdot \mathcal{E}(\tilde{r}_{\text{Equity}}) & + & 95\% \cdot 5\% & = & 10\% & \Longrightarrow & \mathcal{E}(\tilde{r}_{\text{Equity}}) = 105\% \\ w_{\text{Equity}} \cdot \mathcal{E}(\tilde{r}_{\text{Equity}}) & + & w_{\text{Debt}} \cdot \mathcal{E}(\tilde{r}_{\text{Debt}}) & = & \mathcal{E}(\tilde{r}_{\text{Firm}}) & & \end{array}$$

(Of course, this also happens to be the same case in which the debt's promised [stated] interest rate is usually astronomically higher than its expected interest rate.)

SOLVE NOW!

Q 16.17 Is a firm that uses a weighted average cost of capital that is lower than the interest rate that it has to pay to the bank making a mistake?

Q 16.18 If a firm has a 5% cost of debt capital, a 10% cost of project capital, and a 20% cost of equity capital, what is its debt/equity ratio?

Q 16.19 How can it be possible for a firm with a positive cost of project capital to have a negative cost of equity capital? How high can the cost of project capital be in this case?

16.6 NONFINANCIAL AND OPERATIONAL LIABILITIES AND THE MARGINAL COST OF CAPITAL

Firms have many nonfinancial liabilities.
➤ Table 15.1, p. 555

In Table 15.1, you saw that IBM's total liabilities were about three times as large as its financial debt. This is typical for many U.S. companies. Does the M&M proposition—that firm value is not influenced by capital structure and thus that capital structure is irrelevant—still apply in the presence of nonfinancial claims?

16.6A VALUE IRRELEVANCE

The logic of the perfect-markets M&M proposition.

The argument is actually somewhat subtle. Start by recalling the logic of the M&M perfect-markets argument: The value of the firm's financing does not depend on how it is divided between debt and equity. The proof was by contradiction. If a firm instituted a capital structure with a dumb debt covenant—that is, one that forced it to pay all its future cash flows to charity—could this firm be worth less than a more intelligently financed firm? No! A horde of arbitrageurs would immediately compete to purchase all these bad claims (at their presumably lower value) and undo the dumb capital structure. Therefore, this dumb capital structure could not trade for a lower price than the optimal capital structure. It would have the same value as the best capital structure, but it would exist for only half an instant before it was undone. The perfect market provided two aspects important to the M&M argument:

1. The capital market is perfectly elastic. All financial claims that the firm could dream up would be snatched up by a perfect capital market at an appropriate price.
2. There is no link between the firm's operations and the financial claims that a firm is able to take on. (In the original M&M paper, the authors assumed that all operating decisions were already made.)

Nonfinancial financing can add value. Thus, M&M breaks down. In effect, its financing now takes on the characteristics of its nonfinancial market imperfections.

These two assumptions can fail on nonfinancial liabilities. Let me give you two respective examples:

1. **Income tax liabilities:** If you do not pay your taxes until April 15 (tax day), you can use your tax liability for your own investment purposes. Your effective cost of capital on these funds is zero. However, you cannot raise more funds at will at this same zero interest rate from Uncle Sam. You also cannot return this financing to the provider at a fair market cost of capital. If you prepay your taxes, Uncle Sam will not credit you with interest for early payment.
2. **Trade credit:** It is not uncommon for suppliers to give firms 0% financing as trade credit. This is *not* the perfect-market appropriate price for financing and you would want to take as much of this trade credit as possible. However, this trade credit is usually only available to you if you purchase more of the underlying good. Your supplier would not provide you more trade credit in order to pay your rent if you did not buy his goods. Consequently, if you were to buy your supplier's goods, a capital structure with more trade credit would be better than one without. Conversely, you may not even buy these goods without trade credit.

➤ Formula 16.1, p. 579

Now think back to how the value of your firm was determined by the net present values of your project. Formula 16.1 stated that

$$\text{Firm Value} = \text{Project Value} + \text{(Trade Credit) Financing Value}$$

Under M&M, the financing NPV was always zero. However, your trade credit in this example would be a positive-NPV project in itself. The consequence is that you might choose different real operations (purchasing the supplier's goods) if you were financed with trade credit than if you were financed without trade credit. The separation between operations and financing is broken. On the contrary, if trade credit is a bargain, it now makes sense to think of a bundle that includes the project and the project-specific financing that comes with it.

It is possible to put forth a perfect-markets scenario for operations that unlinks their nonfinancial claims in order to get a full M&M proposition also for nonfinancial claims. However, this is not particularly useful for two reasons: First, we are interested primarily in finance, not in operations. Second, nonfinancial markets are generally far from perfect—much more so than financial markets—and many operational choices are irreversible once made. With such a large discrepancy between the necessary perfect-markets conditions and reality, such a proposition would not be very helpful in thinking about real-world problems.

M&M for operations and nonfinancial liabilities would be less plausible and not very useful.

But you do need to understand how to think of the firm's financing claims in a broader perspective. And you must remember that if a firm has nonfinancial liabilities and its operations are not yet fixed, then the original M&M proposition was not really about the firm; it was only about the firm's financial claims. In sum, if the operations of the firm have not yet been set in stone, then:

The logic of perfect-market M&M still applies to the financial claims.

- In the absence of a perfect market for operations and nonfinancial liabilities, the ordinary M&M proposition states only that the value of the firm's *financial claims* is indifferent to its arrangement between debt and equity.
- The ordinary M&M proposition does *not* state that the value of the firm (i.e., all financial and nonfinancial claims) is indifferent to its arrangement between financial and nonfinancial claims.

SOLVE NOW!

Q 16.20 In a world of perfect financial markets, is the value of the firm independent of how it is financed if there are also nonfinancial liabilities?

Q 16.21 In a world of perfect financial markets, is the value of the firm's financial claims independent of how it is financed?

16.6B THE MARGINAL AND WEIGHTED AVERAGE COSTS OF CAPITAL

There is one more important issue that you did not yet have to worry about in the M&M world. The **marginal cost of capital** applies to the next dollar of capital the firm would raise; the **average cost of capital** is the financing cost for all of the firm's existing projects. As a manager, you ultimately want to learn your projects' marginal costs of capital, because it is these rates that you would then compare to your projects' marginal rates of return. The firm's average cost of capital is really quite irrelevant. Fortunately, under M&M, the two are the same. Thus, if you compute the weighted average cost of capital, you know the marginal cost of capital for raising one more dollar.

Perfect world: The average cost of capital *is* the marginal cost of capital.

Unfortunately, in the real and imperfect world, the average and marginal costs of capital can be different. For example, it could be that the first dollar of financing that the firm obtains is internal and thus cheaper than the billionth dollar of financing if the firm had to search for investors first. Thus, when you compute a WACC from a firm's existing capital providers (and published in the financial data), be aware that even if the project is typical for the firm, it may only be your average cost of capital—not the marginal cost of capital that you may need.

Real world: The two costs of capital can be different.

The natural definition of the firm's WACC with nonfinancial liabilities.

Now recall that the firm's weighted average cost of capital is

$$\text{Firm's Average Cost of Capital} = \text{Sum of Value-Weighted Claims' Costs of Capital}$$

➤ WACC with nonfinancial liabilities, Section 22.1D, p. 824

In the context of a firm financed only with financial capital (debt and equity), this is

$$\text{Firm's Average Cost of Capital} = w_{\text{Debt}} \cdot \mathcal{E}(\tilde{r}_{\text{Debt}}) + w_{\text{Equity}} \cdot \mathcal{E}(\tilde{r}_{\text{Equity}})$$

The original M&M proposition states that this cost of financial capital is not affected by shifting w_{Debt} to w_{Equity}. A convenient way to think about the cost of capital is that neither debt nor equity are positive- or negative-NPV projects. Thus, shifting between them does not change the value of the firm.

Unfortunately, most nonfinancial liabilities are not zero NPV.

In the presence of nonfinancial liabilities (NFL), the definition of the firm's weighted average cost of capital expands into

$$\text{Firm's Average Cost of Capital} = w_{\text{NFL}} \cdot \mathcal{E}(\tilde{r}_{\text{NFL}}) + w_{\text{FL}} \cdot \mathcal{E}(\tilde{r}_{\text{FL}}) + w_{\text{Equity}} \cdot \mathcal{E}(\tilde{r}_{\text{Equity}})$$

where FL are the financial liabilities. Unfortunately, you cannot expand or contract the nonfinancial liabilities at will. Consequently, even if you finance and operate your projects optimally, you will probably not face the same risk-adjusted cost of capital on the margin for your nonfinancial liabilities as you will for your financial liabilities. Think back to the income tax liabilities. They have an interest rate of 0% if you delay paying until April 15 (the tax due date). But you cannot expand the amount borrowed from Uncle Sam. Thus, you have a fixed and nonexpandable amount of financing at a cost of capital of 0% until you reach your tax liabilities, and an infinite cost of capital thereafter. Put differently, your average cost of capital would increase if you shifted financing from w_{NFL} to w_{Debt} or w_{Equity} by paying your taxes unnecessarily early.

Nonfinancial liabilities should be used until their costs of capital reach those of the financial claims.

The firm's best financing strategy now is to select the lowest-cost marginal source of financing.

Nonfinancial sources of funding tied to the firm: Step up the ladder.

- If your source of financing is tied to the firm (but not to particular projects), it may not influence your selection of projects. In this case, you should first finance projects with the lowest cost of capital (e.g., delay paying income taxes and/or pensions) before you proceed to more expensive sources of financing. Eventually, once you have gone up the ladder of financing costs, you reach the cost of financing via financial claims. Assuming debt and equity exist in a perfect capital market, you can then raise as much capital as you wish at their appropriate marginal costs of capital.

Nonfinancial sources of funding tied to the project: Potentially include NPV of nonfinancial funds in the project.

- If your cheapest source of financing is tied to a particular project, it may be best to include it in the costs and benefits of the project. For example, if a retail branch can be financed with trade credit from suppliers, and if this is cheaper than financial capital, then you could count the trade-credit NPV as part of the retail store project NPV. If trade credit is not cheaper, you would not use it and rely on the perfect capital market instead. (In the real world, you may have the extra complication that it is difficult to measure the cost of capital. For example, what is the cost of capital of accounts payable, given that delaying payment can cost you goodwill among your suppliers?)

Note that in both cases, you use the cheapest nonfinancial sources of funds until you reach the cost of your financial capital. At this point, you rely solely on the perfect-markets financial capital as your source of marginal funding. The financial cost of capital then becomes your firm's marginal cost of capital.

IMPORTANT:

- If a source of low-cost (nonfinancial) financing is tied to a specific project, it is usually convenient to consider it as part of the project. You would include the financing's net present value in the project's return.
- If financing is not tied to specific projects, firms should first use up all sources of capital that are cheaper than what the financial capital markets are demanding.
- If the financial capital markets are perfect, and if the firm has already exhausted all cheaper sources of financing from the imperfect nonfinancial markets, then the firm's *marginal* cost of capital is determined by the cost of capital of debt and equity. In other words, for a firm that has optimized its nonfinancial sources of funding,

$$\text{Optimized Firm's Marginal Cost of Capital} = \text{Firm's Cost of Financial Capital}$$
$$= w_{\text{Debt}} \cdot \mathcal{E}(\tilde{r}_{\text{Debt}}) + w_{\text{Equity}} \cdot \mathcal{E}(\tilde{r}_{\text{Equity}})$$

  You would compare this marginal cost of financial capital to the rate of return of your marginal product.
- You can still use the original M&M proposition, but only within the context of financial claims—that is, the value of the firm's *financial* claims is indifferent to whether the firm is financed by debt or equity.
- This *marginal* cost of *financial* capital is also the *average* cost of *financial* capital in a perfect capital market. However, it is decidedly *not* the firm's *overall average* cost of capital. The firm's average cost of capital is lower, because nonfinancial financing that the firm would accept would have to come with a lower cost of capital.

Again, don't get too carried away. The M&M propositions are helpful only for thinking about the subject of capital structure. They are not intended to be realistic. They are thought experiments. In the real world, capital structure can matter, and you have to think about how your cost of capital changes with different capital structures, whether it is financial claims or nonfinancial claims. This is the subject of the next chapters.

Don't think these propositions are too realistic.

SOLVE NOW!

Q 16.22 If you observe a firm with nonfinancial claims that have a zero marginal cost of capital (such as delayed income tax obligations), does it make sense to compute a cost of capital based only on the firm's financial capital (debt and equity)?

SUMMARY

This chapter covered the following major points:

- Managers should want to maximize firm value, not shareholder value. If they do not, they would lose value. In a perfect market, managers who do not act in this way would be replaced with managers who do.
- Entrepreneurs have an incentive to set up a capital structure that maximizes firm value, not equity value. This is because capital providers know that entrepreneurs later would want to behave opportunistically.
- The Modigliani-Miller (M&M) capital structure proposition states that it makes no difference in a perfect market whether a firm finances itself with debt or equity.
  - Competitive arbitrageurs can buy all cash flow and control rights if they purchase all debt and equity.
  - Arbitrageurs can instantly eliminate and undo any bad capital structure choices (and/or any bad project choices).
  - Arbitrageurs would compete to bid up the value of any bad capital structure to the value of the firm under the optimal capital structure (and/or optimal operating policy).
  - The value of all claims under *any* capital structure is therefore that of the value under the *best* capital structure.
  - The firm's cost of capital is therefore invariant to the split between debt and equity. It is always equal to the same weighted average cost of capital (WACC).

  An even simpler version assumes that project choices were already fixed and are now immutable. The M&M propositions are interesting not because they are realistic, but because they are benchmarks that point out when capital structure (and/or operating policy) would not matter.
- More debt does not imply that the overall cost of capital increases, even though both debt and equity become riskier.
- The bank may demand an interest rate that is higher than the expected cost of capital on the equity. This does not mean that the cost of debt capital is higher than the cost of equity capital.
- The CAPM is compatible with the M&M perfect-markets point of view. It can provide costs of capital for financial debt and equity. However, it cannot provide costs of capital for other liabilities that do not originate in a perfectly competitive market, such as tax obligations. Such loans could even be interest-free.
- The marginal and average costs of capital are the same for claims that arise in a perfect market.
- Nonfinancial liabilities usually do not arise in a perfect capital market. Thus, their average costs of capital are often lower than their marginal costs of capital.
- When cheap financing (such as special trade credit) is tied to a particular project, it is often convenient to combine it with the project.

- If an optimizing firm has exhausted all its lower-cost nonfinancial sources of funding, then the infinitely elastic perfect capital markets' financial funding becomes the marginal source of capital.

KEY TERMS

SOLVE NOW! SOLUTIONS

Q 16.1 Ex-ante means "before the fact"; ex-post means "after the fact." To the extent that the original owner-entrepreneur can set up a situation (charter) that encourages best (i.e., from the perspective of the firm) ex-post behavior, the ex-ante value (for which the firm can be sold right now) is maximized. However, if the situation (charter) is such that the owner himself or his managers will later try to expropriate capital providers, or such that the managers will make bad decisions in the future, then the ex-ante value today for which the firm can be sold would be less.

Q 16.2 Yes, an ex-post maximizing choice can be bad from an ex-ante perspective. The example of the \$3-for-\$1 transaction in the text shows that you would want to restrain yourself.

Q 16.3 Clearly, managers in the future would want not to pay debt if they can avoid doing so. However, such behavior could have repercussions for their future attempts to borrow money. The firm would have to weigh the gains from reneging on this particular loan (and the ethical implications of doing so!) against the costs of a lost creditor relationship and thus more expensive credit in the future.

Q 16.4 The idea is to explain it really simply. Milk, cream, pizza, and pockets are handy metaphors.

Q 16.5 Capital structure does not matter in a perfect market: No transaction costs, perfect competition, no taxes, and no differences in opinion and information.

Q 16.6 The risk-neutrality assumption really buys nothing. We do not need it. We only use it because it makes the tables simpler to compute.

Q 16.7 Work out the following:

$$\begin{array}{lrcrcl} \text{Bad Luck:} & d \cdot \$55 & + & e \cdot \$5 & = & \$0 \cdot 5\% \\ \text{Good Luck:} & d \cdot \$55 & + & e \cdot \$105 & = & \$66 \cdot 5\% \end{array} \Longrightarrow (\$105 - \$5) \cdot e = (\$66 - \$0) \cdot 5\%$$

$$\Longrightarrow \begin{array}{rcl} d & = & -0.003 \\ e & = & +0.033 \end{array}$$

You would purchase 3.3% of the LD equity and sell (issue) 0.3% of the equivalent of the LD debt. The equity would cost you $e \cdot \$50 = \$1.65$; the debt issue would give you \$0.15 in proceeds. Your net cost would thus be \$1.50—as it should be, because purchasing 5% of the MD equity would have cost you 5% of \$30, which also comes to \$1.50.

Q 16.8 No. The "homemade leverage restructuring" argument misses the aspect of control rights.

Q 16.9 Yes, they can destroy shareholder value. If existing management gives away debt claims at too low a price, creditors will own more of the firm having paid less money. New management cannot undo this, because the contract cannot be renegotiated. Giving away debt too cheaply would not change the value of the firm. It only changes who owns more or less of the firm.

Q 16.10 To work out the firm's equity cost of capital and the debt's promised rate of return, imitate the payoff tables from the text (dollars are in millions):

		Scheme AE	Scheme DE	
		100% Equity	Bond (promises \$100)	Levered Equity (after \$100 obligation)
$\mathcal{P}rob = 1/3$	\$50	\$50	\$50	\$0
$\mathcal{P}rob = 1/3$	\$150	\$150	\$100	\$50
$\mathcal{P}rob = 1/3$	\$400	\$400	\$100	\$300
$\mathcal{E}$ Future Payoff		\$200	\$83.33	\$116.67
Price P Today		\$181.82	\$79.37	\$102.45
$\mathcal{E}$ Rate of Return ($\mathcal{E}(\tilde{r})$)		10%	5%	13.88%

The debt's promised rate of return is $\$100/\$79.37 - 1 \approx 26\%$.

Q 16.11 You need to recall the standard deviation formula (Formula 8.1) on page 204:

$$\text{Full Ownership:}\quad \mathcal{S}dv = \sqrt{0.20 \cdot (-73.81\% - 10\%)^2 + 0.80 \cdot (+30.95\% - 10\%)^2} \approx 41.9\%$$

$$\text{Debt:}\quad \mathcal{S}dv = \sqrt{0.20 \cdot (-20\% - 6\%)^2 + 0.80 \cdot (+12.5\% - 6\%)^2} = 13\%$$

$$\text{Levered Equity:}\quad \mathcal{S}dv = \sqrt{0.20 \cdot (-100\% - 11.95\%)^2 + 0.80 \cdot (+39.93\% - 11.95\%)^2} \approx 55.97\%$$

Q 16.12 Most likely, you can fund the project. In a perfect market, you can hold low-risk debt that has first dibs on all proceeds.

Q 16.13 Please rework the examples for yourself. For example, for the promised debt of \$50,000: If the weight is 53.72%, then the expected rate of return on the debt should be $4.053\% + 5.947\% \cdot 53.72\% \approx 7.25\%$.

Q 16.14 For the example from page 589, in which the debt promises \$75,000, to confirm that the weight of the debt in the capital structure is 77.14%, construct the full payoff table:

		100% Equity	Bond (promises \$75,000)	Levered Equity (after \$75,000 obligation)
$\mathcal{P}rob$(Sunshine) = 80%	\$100,000.00	\$100,000.00	\$75,000.00	\$25,000.00
$\mathcal{P}rob$(Tornado) = 20%	\$20,000.00	\$20,000.00	\$20,000.00	\$0.00
$\mathcal{E}$ Future Payoff		\$84,000.00	\$64,000.00	\$20,000.00
$\mathcal{E}$ Rate of Return ($\mathcal{E}(\tilde{r})$)		10%	8.64%	14.59%
Price P Today		\$76,363.64	\$58,910.16	\$17,453.48
Capital Structure Weight (Security Price/Firm Value)			77.14%	22.86%
Promised Rate of Return (Bond Promise/Bond Price – 1)			27.31%	

Q 16.15 No. Firm A need not have a higher overall cost of capital than firm B. The example in the "How Bad Are Mistakes?" section illustrates this fallacy. The relative weights of debt and equity also change, therefore falsifying this claim.

Q 16.16 The solution proceeds the same way as in the text on page 396 (Chapter 12):

(a) The project should have an appropriate rate of return of $\mathcal{E}(\tilde{r}) = 3\% + 4\% \cdot 0.5 = 5\%$. It is immediately obvious that the project's cost of capital of 5% is below its internal rate of return of $\$11/\$10 - 1 = 10\%$. The net present value of the project is $-\$10 + \$11/1.05 \approx \$0.48$ million. Yes, the firm should take it.

(b) If the firm uses a cost of capital based on its beta of 3, it would conclude that the value is $\mathcal{E}(\tilde{r}) = 3\% + 4\% \cdot 3 = 15\%$. Thus, with its 10% expected rate of return as its internal hurdle rate, a misguided firm would not take this project. This means that the firm loses \$0.48 million in value it could have otherwise gained, simply because the firm managers are making the mistake of not taking the positive-NPV project. This is because they do not understand that projects should be evaluated by the projects' own costs of capital, not the firm's cost of capital.

(c) The value of the new project today is $\$11/1.05 \approx \$10.48$ million. The value of the old projects was given as \$100 million. Thus, the value of a combined firm with all projects would be about \$110.48 million.

(d) To raise \$10 million, the firm needs to give up $\$10/\$110.48 \approx 9.05\%$ of the combined firm to new shareholders.

(e) \$10.48 million would be from the new project. \$100 million would be from the old project. Thus, $\$10.48/110.48 \approx 9.49\%$ of the firm value would be in the new project. The remaining 90.51% would be in the old projects.

(f) The market beta of the combined firm would be $90.51\% \cdot 3 + 9.49\% \cdot 0.5 \approx 2.763$.

(g) The average cost of capital would now be $3\% + 4\% \cdot 2.763 \approx 14.05\%$.

In sum, the value of the firm would jump by the net present value of the new project, that is, by \$0.48 million. No more calculations are necessary. However, you can also do this by computing the discount on the entire firm. First, to be worth \$100 million at a cost of capital of 15%, the expected payoffs next year have to be \$115 million. The future value of the combined firm is therefore $\$115 + \$11 = \$126$ million, and its present value is $(\$115 + \$11)/(1 + 14.05\%) \approx \$110.48$ million.

Q 16.17 No, it is quite possible that the weighted average cost of capital is lower than the interest rate that it has to pay to the bank. After all, the bank rate is promised, not expected.

Q 16.18 In a perfect market, the cost of capital under a 100% equity financing strategy with cost 10% must be the same as it is under a mixed debt and equity strategy. Therefore, $w_{\text{Debt}} \cdot 0.05 + (1 - w_{\text{Debt}}) \cdot 0.2 = 0.1 \Longrightarrow w_{\text{Debt}} = 2/3$. This firm is 2 parts debt, 1 part equity, so the debt/equity ratio is 2.

Q 16.19 Though obscure, a firm with a very negative beta can indeed be in this situation. It must be the case then that the firm's project cost of capital is lower than the risk-free rate. (For example, a firm may have 90% debt at the risk-free rate of 5%, 10% equity at a rate of −1%, and a WACC of 4.4%—this is indeed less than the risk-free rate.)

Q 16.20 No, the value of the firm may be linked to its financing, because its financing is linked to its projects. You also need to break the link between nonfinancial liabilities and operations.

Q 16.21 Yes, the value of the firm's *financial* claims is independent of how the financial claims are arranged in an M&M world. This is because no financial security offers a positive or negative NPV—all financial securities are fairly priced.

Q 16.22 Yes, it may still make sense to compute a cost of capital based only on the firm's financial capital (debt and equity) if the firm has exhausted all its nonfinancial low-cost sources of capital. It is then an estimate of the marginal cost of another dollar of capital raised, which is now financial capital.

PROBLEMS

The *indicates problems available in* myfinancelab

Q 16.23 Explain when "shareholder maximization" is the right goal and when it is the wrong goal for management.

Q 16.24 Comment on the following statement: "New shareholders would be worse off if management destroyed wealth by capturing the board and paying themselves much higher executive compensation without better performance."

Q 16.25 In a world that is not perfect but risk neutral, assume that the firm has projects worth \$100 in the down-state, \$500 in the up-state. The cost of capital for projects is 25%. However, if you could finance it with 50-50 debt, the cash flow rights alone are enough to make the cost of capital a lower 20%. Managers are intransigent and do not want to switch to this new capital structure. You only have \$60 of capital and cannot borrow more to take over the firm. What can you do?

Q 16.26 A firm can be worth \$100 million (with 20% probability), \$200 million (with 60% probability), or \$300 million (with 20% probability). The firm has one senior bond outstanding, promising to pay \$80 million. It also has one junior bond outstanding, promising to pay \$70 million. The senior bond promises an interest rate of 5%. The junior bond promises an interest rate of 26%. If the firm's projects require an appropriate cost of capital of 10%, then what is the firm's levered equity cost of capital?

Q 16.27 If a change in capital structure increases the risk of the firm's equity and the risk of the firm's debt, and there are no other financial claims, does it imply the firm's risk has increased?

Q 16.28 Work the example from page 590 if the debt promises \$65,000. Confirm that the weight of the debt in the capital structure is 67.85%.

Q 16.29 When both debt and equity become riskier due to an increase in the firm's leverage, the firm remains worth exactly the same and stays exactly as risky (in a perfect market). Conceptually, what would it take for the firm to become worth more and/or safer even when both debt and equity become riskier due to an increase in the firm's leverage?

Q 16.30 Compute a graph similar to Figure 16.1. Use a spreadsheet. Your firm will be worth either \$50,000 or \$100,000 with equal probabilities. The cost of capital on your debt is given by the formula $\mathcal{E}(\tilde{r}_{\text{Debt}}) = 5\% + 10\% \cdot w_{\text{Debt}}$—but only if the debt is risky. (Hint: The risk-free rate of return is 11.85%. What is the WACC of the firm if it is 100% debt financed?)

Q 16.31 Show how a firm can increase its cost of equity capital and its cost of debt capital, and still come out with an overall cost of capital that is unchanged.

Q 16.32 Does the standard M&M proposition apply to nonfinancial liabilities?

Q 16.33 In a world of perfect financial markets, is the cost of capital of the firm's financial claims independent of how it is financed?

Q 16.34 In a world of perfect financial markets (but not necessarily product markets), is the cost of capital of the firm independent of how it is operated and financed?

17

The Weighted Cost of Capital and Adjusted Present Value in an Imperfect Market with Taxes

THE CORPORATE INCOME TAX ADVANTAGE OF DEBT

Now that you understand how financing works in a perfect world, it is time to move on to the real and imperfect world. The presence of corporate income taxes is an important violation of the M&M perfect-market assumptions in the real world. This chapter shows that you can create value through intelligent capital structure policy that reduces these taxes. There are even formulas that help you compute the explicit tax-value consequences for different leverage structures. The most popular are the adjusted present value (APV) formula and the tax-adjusted weighted average cost of capital (WACC) formula. These techniques are in such wide use that they deserve a lot of airtime—and why this chapter is kept separate from the following one, which will discuss other market imperfections.

Note that this chapter is concerned only with *corporate* income taxes, and not investors' *personal* income taxes. For now, if it makes your thinking easier, just assume that all shareholders are tax-exempt pension funds. The next chapter will consider both corporate and personal income taxes.

17.1 RELATIVE TAXATION OF DEBT AND EQUITY

A basic corporate example with equal taxation.

Let's discuss a simple hypothetical firm with the following parameters:

Investment Cost in Year 0	\$200
Before-Tax Return in Year 1	\$280
Before-Tax Net Return from Year 0 to Year 1	\$80
Corporate Income Tax Rate (τ)	30%
Appropriate Cost of Capital from 0 to 1	12%

Your goal is to understand the value of this firm under different tax regimes.

17.1A HYPOTHETICAL EQUAL TAXATION AND CAPITAL BUDGETING

This short section's unrealistic tax code.

If the firm faces the same tax rate on debt and equity, no matter how it is financed, what is its value? In the real world, this assumption is entirely unrealistic. (Instead, only interest payments are tax deductible). This scenario is useful only to show that investors care about "after corporate income tax" returns, not about "before corporate income tax" returns.

Taxes mean that the after-tax rate of return is lower than the before-tax rate of return.

Under this tax regime, consider financing your firm entirely with equity. With \$280 in before-tax earnings on the \$200 investment, you have a before-tax internal rate of return of (\$280 − \$200)/\$200 = 40%. But, with taxes to the tune of 30% on the net return of \$80, Uncle Sam collects \$24. Your firm's after-tax net rate of return is therefore only (\$256 − \$200)/\$200 = 28%.

Investors receive an after-corporate-income-tax rate of return from the "black-box" firm.

Now hold your investors' other opportunities in the economy constant. What is the influence of a change in the corporate income tax that is applicable only to your firm? From the perspective of your firm, you are a "price-taker" when it comes to raising capital. This means that you are too small to make a difference. After all, you are competing with many other firms for the capital of many competitive investors. Ultimately, these investors care only about the cash that you will return to them. Let us assume that firms of your risk class (market beta) must offer an after-corporate-income-tax rate of return of $\mathcal{E}(\tilde{r}_{\text{Firm}}) = 12\%$ to attract investors. This 12% is the equivalent of a 17.14% before-tax rate of return, because $17.14\% \cdot (1 - 30\%) = 12\%$. Put differently, you can invest \$100 in equally risky projects elsewhere, expect to receive back \$117.14, pay Uncle Sam \$5.14 in taxes on \$17.14 in earnings, and keep \$12. (In this chapter, we again omit time subscripts if there is little risk of confusion.) How exactly do taxes matter to the rate of return that your projects must generate?

Projects with more tax liability must create more value before taxes to be on equal footing after taxes.

Your investor-owners really do not care what happens inside the firm, only what your firm can pay them in the end. It is all the same to them if:

- your projects earn 12% before tax and you manage to avoid all corporate income taxes;
- your projects earn 24% but you have to pay half of it in corporate income taxes;
- your projects earn 600%, of which 98% is confiscated by the government ($600\% \cdot (1 - 98\%) = 12\%$); or
- your projects face a 30% corporate tax rate, and your own projects earn 17.14% in before-tax rate of return in order to generate for your investors 12% in actual rate of

ANECDOTE Special Tax Breaks and Corporate Welfare

"Special income tax provisions" are tax breaks enacted by Congress for specific activities, often on behalf of a single corporation. These special income tax provision amounts are commonly estimated to be about $1 trillion a year—more than the total amount of federal discretionary spending! These provisions are a main reason why corporations—large corporations, really—have paid less and less in income taxes relative to the rest of the population and relative to other OECD countries. In 1965, corporate income taxes were 4.1% of U.S. GDP; in 2000, about 2.5%; and in 2002, about 1.5%. For comparison, in 2000, Germany's rate was 1.8%, and Canada's rate was 4.0%.

It would be wonderful if the low U.S. corporate income tax rate would attract businesses to locate into the United States and to create jobs. Alas, because the low effective corporate income tax rates come about through strange corporate tax shelters (often through relocation of headquarters into foreign countries), the United States often ends up with the worst of both worlds: Both incentives for companies to move out of the United States and low corporate income tax receipts. The only president in recent history to buck the trend may have been Ronald Reagan, who slashed both the corporate income tax and the ability of companies to circumvent it.

Source: "Testimony of Robert S. McIntyre" (http://www.ctj.org), Director of Citizens for Tax Justice.

return. Of course, this is the same calculation we already made. Your investment of $200 turns into $234.28, you pay Uncle Sam 30% in taxes on income of $34.28 for a total income tax of $10.28, and you are left with $224 to return to your investors after the corporate income tax is paid.

The NPV formula is well equipped to handle corporate income taxes. However, as already explained in Chapter 10, you must calculate the present value using after-tax quantities in both the numerator and denominator. For example, the "$280-before-corporate-income-tax" firm, with its 12% required after-corporate-income-tax cost of capital, has a PV of:

Investors demand a proper (risk-adjusted) rate of return, regardless of how the firm gets there.
➤ Taxes in NPV, Section 10.4C, p. 325

$$\text{PV} = \frac{\mathcal{E}(C_{\text{after-corp-tax}})}{1 + \mathcal{E}(\tilde{r}_{\text{after-corp-tax}})} = \frac{\$280 - \$80 \cdot 30\%}{1 + 12\%} = \frac{\$256}{1 + 12\%} \approx \$228.57$$

There are some simple mistakes you must avoid here. You cannot usually find the same result if you work with before-tax expected cash flows and before-tax required rates of return. And you would definitely get a very wrong result if you used after-tax expected cash flows and then compared them to a cost of capital obtained from investments that have not yet been taxed at the corporate level.

SOLVE NOW!

Q 17.1 Assume a 30% corporate income tax. Show that a project that returns 17% before-tax would have a negative NPV if it cost $100 today and if the appropriate after-tax cost of capital is 12%.

17.1B REALISTIC DIFFERENTIAL TAXATION OF DEBT AND EQUITY

Let's move on to a model of a tax code that reflects reality better. In many countries—the United States included—individuals and corporations face similar tax treatments, tax schedules, and tax rates. Although tax code details vary from year to year, country

Tax codes worldwide violate the M&M no-tax assumption.

to country, state to state, county to county, and even city to city, most tax codes are pretty similar in spirit. Thus, the tax concepts in this book apply relatively universally.

Tax codes subsidize borrowing: Firms pay interest from before-tax income but pay dividends from after-tax income.
➤ Introduction to taxes, Section 10.4, p. 321

Section 10.4 described how the form of payout matters. Firms pay taxes on their earnings *net of interest payments*. That is, unlike dividend distributions or money used to repurchase shares or money reinvested, the IRS considers interest payments to be a cost of your operations. Therefore, it allows the payment of interest to be treated as a before-tax expense rather than as an after-tax distribution of earnings. The result is that a corporation saves on taxes when it distributes its earnings in the form of interest payments. For example, if PepsiCo's operations really produced \$100, and if \$100 in interest was owed to creditors, then Uncle Sam would get nothing and the creditors would get the entire \$100. However, if not paid out in interest, Uncle Sam would first collect corporate income taxes, say, 30%. PepsiCo could only keep (or distribute) the \$70 that would be left over. The point of this chapter is to show how an astute CFO can best exploit this difference in relative tax treatment.

Preview: With too much debt, other not-yet-explained forces may increase the cost of capital.

At this point, you may be wondering why you would not always finance your firm with as much debt as possible. The short preview answer is that if you were in a world in which corporate income taxes were the only distortion, then having as much debt as possible would indeed be ideal. However, there is more going on. If you take on too much debt, eventually other forces raise the firm's cost of capital to the point that further increases in debt are no longer value-increasing. These forces are the subject of the next chapter. But you must first understand how managers should go about capital budgeting if there are only corporate income taxes, and no other taxes or perfect-market distortions.

SOLVE NOW!

Q 17.2 A debt/equity hybrid security would like to pay out \$500 to its holders. The firm is in the 33% corporate income tax bracket. How much would the firm have to earn if the IRS designates the payment an interest payment? How much would the firm have to earn if the IRS designates the payment a dividend distribution?

17.2 FIRM VALUE UNDER DIFFERENT CAPITAL STRUCTURES

Introducing an interest tax subsidy leads to a corporate preference for debt.

In a perfect world, firms are indifferent between debt and equity. In the real world, Uncle Sam subsidizes firms that pay interest, relative to firms that retain earnings, pay dividends, or repurchase shares. Therefore, *on corporate tax grounds*, firms should have a preference for debt. What is the exact value of the firm in the presence of this tax subsidy for debt interest payments?

If the firm is debt financed, then there is more money that can be paid to the owners. This is money that the IRS does not get.

To answer this question, begin with Table 17.1. It works out the value of one hypothetical firm in two financing scenarios.

An equity-financing (EF) scenario: In the all-equity scenario, the firm does not exploit the help of the IRS. It earns \$280 on an investment of \$200. At a 30% corporate income tax rate, it will pay corporate income taxes of $30\% \cdot \$80 = \$24$. It can then pay out the remaining \$56 in dividends.

TABLE 17.1 TWO FINANCING SCENARIOS FOR A SAFE 1-YEAR FIRM

Both scenarios assume:		
Investment Cost in Year 0		\$200.00
Before-Tax Return in Year 1		\$280.00
Before-Tax Net Return from Year 0 to Year 1		\$80.00
Corporate Income Tax Rate (τ)		30%
Appropriate Average Cost of Capital from 0 to 1 [a]		12%
Scenario EF: 100% equity financing.		
Taxable Profits Next Year		\$80.00
Corporate Income Taxes Next Year (30% of \$80)		\$24.00
Owners Will Keep *Next Year*		\$56.00
Scenario DF: \$200 debt financing at 11%. The rest is levered equity.		
Interest Payments		\$22.00
Taxable Profits Next Year		\$58.00
Corporate Income Taxes Next Year (30% of \$58)		\$17.40
Equity Owners Will Keep Next Year		\$40.60
Equity and Debt Owners Will Keep *Next Year*	\$22.00 + \$40.60 =	\$62.60

a. As in the example in Section 17.1A, in order to clear its cost-of-capital hurdle rate of 12%, the firm's projects must earn a rate of return of 17.14% before the firm pays out corporate income tax. With a 30% corporate income tax rate, Uncle Sam would confiscate 30% · 17.14% ≈ 5.14%, from the firm itself and corporate investors would receive a rate of return of 12%.

A debt-financing (DF) scenario: In the debt-financing scenario, the firm borrows \$200 today at an interest rate of 11% for interest payments next year of \$22. Therefore, its corporate profits will be \$80 − \$22 = \$58, on which it would have to pay Uncle Sam \$17.40. This permits owners (creditors and shareholders—and a person may be both) to receive \$62.60, the sum of \$22 for its creditors and \$40.60 for its equity holders.

Relative to the 100% equity-financed case (in which owners keep \$56.00), the debt-financed case (in which owners keep \$62.60) increases the firm's after-tax cash flow by \$6.60. A quicker way to compute the tax savings is to multiply the tax rate by the interest payments: If the IRS allows the firm to deduct \$22 in interest payments, the firm will save \$22 · 30% = \$6.60 in corporate income taxes. This \$6.60 in tax savings will occur next year, and it will therefore have to be discounted back. It is common (but not necessarily unique or even correct) to use the firm's cost of capital to discount the tax shelter for a growing firm. This chapter's appendix explains the appropriate discount rate in greater detail, but just realize that whether you discount the much smaller tax shelter of \$6.60 by the low cost of capital on debt (11%) or by a higher one, say, 15% (the firm's cost of capital), it would only make a difference of \$5.95 − \$5.74 = \$0.21. On a \$280 expected cash flow, this is not big, especially

ANECDOTE The RJR Buyout Tax Loophole

In a **leveraged buyout** (LBO), the firm's indebtedness can increase dramatically—and this can significantly reduce corporate income taxes. In 1988, First Boston's plan to take over RJR Nabisco relied on an esoteric tax loophole just about to be closed. By "monetizing" its food operations (a fancy way to increase indebtedness), the deferring of taxes would have saved an estimated \$3–\$4 billion of RJR's corporate income taxes—which would have increased the annual federal U.S. deficit by 2%! Ultimately, First Boston lost its bid, and this scenario did not come about.

compared to our other uncertainties in our cash flow estimate, our CAPM model use, our rate of return model estimate, and so on. We are done: Relative to the EF capital structure, the DF capital structure created just under \$6 in present value.

SOLVE NOW!

Q 17.3 A \$1 million construction project is expected to return \$1.2 million in 1 year. Your company is in a 45% combined federal and state marginal income tax bracket.

(a) If you finance the project with cash, how much will you pay in taxes?

(b) If you finance the project with an \$800,000 mortgage at an interest rate of 5%, how much will you pay in taxes?

(c) If the appropriate project interest rate is 8%, what is the present value of the tax savings from financing the project with a mortgage?

17.3 FORMULAIC VALUATION METHODS: APV AND WACC

We need formulas that work for any intermediate debt ratios.

Are there formulas that allow you to compute the firm value today not only for the current financing arrangement but also for other debt ratios that you might contemplate? Yes. There are essentially three methods. This section explains two of them, the APV and WACC:

1. You can compute an **adjusted present value** (APV), which adds back the tax subsidy. (This is basically the calculation from the previous section.)
2. You can generalize the **weighted average cost of capital** (WACC) formula to reflect the preferential treatment of debt by suitably lowering the cost of debt capital.

Method #3 is called "flow-to-equity."

➤ Valuing after-tax cash flows, Section 13.3, p. 466

The next section explains a third method to value the tax benefits. This "flow-to-equity" method constructs the financials for the firm in the new hypothetical capital structure and then values the after-tax cash flows directly. (Without describing it as such, you have actually already done this in Chapter 13, and you will do it again in Chapter 20, where you will have to create a pro forma.) Properly applied, all three methods should provide similar—though not necessarily the exact same—answers.

Before you get into the nitty-gritty, it is important that you realize that the tax model is just that—a model. You are working out the debt-related tax savings for a company that faces a fixed marginal income tax rate. The model further ignores many other possibly important tax issues, such as delayed income tax payments, tax-loss carryforwards, recapture of past tax payments, different marginal corporate income tax rates at different income levels, the possibility of default on income tax payments, state taxes, foreign taxes, special tax incentives, transfer pricing, or even outright tax evasion and fraud. Most of the time, our model works fairly well, but do not get carried away with excessive accuracy after the decimal point.

Keep our simplifications in perspective.

17.3A ADJUSTED PRESENT VALUE (APV): THEORY

APV decomposes the value of the firm into two components:

The main idea of APV: Value an all-equity firm, then add the tax subsidy.

1. The value of the firm as if it were *all equity-financed and fully taxed*
2. An additional tax subsidy for each dollar that can be named "interest" rather than "dividend"

In our example from Table 17.1, the expected cash flow of the firm if it is 100% equity-financed is \$280 return minus \$24 in corporate taxes for a net of \$256. The APV method then adds the tax subsidy depending on the firm's debt ratio. For example:

Zero interest payments: If the firm is all equity-financed, the tax subsidy is zero.

High interest payments: If the firm has interest payments of \$80, the IRS would believe that the firm had not earned a penny. Therefore, the owners could keep an extra \$24 above the \$256 all-equity scenario *next year*.

Normal interest payments: If the firm has interest payments of, say, \$19, the IRS would see \$280 − \$19 = \$261 in return minus \$200 investment cost for a net return of \$61. The IRS would therefore collect 30% · \$61 = \$18.30, which is \$5.70 less than the \$24 that the IRS would have collected if the firm had been 100% equity-financed. Alternatively, you could have directly calculated the expected tax savings as $\tau \cdot (\mathcal{E}(\tilde{r}_{\text{Debt}}) \cdot \text{Debt}) = 30\% \cdot (\$19) = \$5.70$. This \$5.70 is the APV tax subsidy next year.

We only need to make a formula out of this method. Your first step to a more general valuation formula in the presence of corporate income taxes is to relate the amount of debt today to the interest payments next year. Let's return to our example, in which you borrow \$200 at an interest rate of 11%. The expected interest payment is now

Tax savings are the product of the tax rate and the interest paid (debt level times interest rate).

$$\text{Expected Interest Payment} = 11\% \cdot \$200 = \$22$$

$$\text{Expected Interest Payment} = \mathcal{E}(\tilde{r}_{\text{Debt}}) \cdot \text{Debt}$$

One important error to avoid is that you must use the *expected* debt interest rate (11%), not the *quoted* bank interest rate (which could be considerably higher than 11%). (This would not matter for large firms with little debt, but it could matter for smaller or more highly indebted firms.) Continuing, the future tax savings *relative to an all-equity-financed firm* is the amount of corporate income tax that the firm will *not* have to pay on the interest.

$$\text{Expected Tax Savings} = 30\% \cdot [11\% \cdot \$200] = \$6.60$$
$$\text{Expected Tax Savings} = \tau \cdot [\mathcal{E}(\tilde{r}_{\text{Debt}}) \cdot \text{Debt}]$$

In words, Uncle Sam would expect to receive $6.60 less from the owners of the project, because $22 in profit repatriation is designated as "interest."

APV discounts these tax savings and adds them to an "all-equity type" hypothetical firm.

The $6.60 in tax savings still has to be discounted, because it will occur next year. The APV formula computes the discounted value of an all-equity-financed firm (with after-tax cash flows of $256 next year) and then adds back the *discounted* tax savings:

($200 debt at 11% interest, i.e., $22 interest payment discounted at 11%)

$$\text{APV} = \frac{\$256}{1+12\%} + \frac{30\% \cdot \$22}{1+11\%} \approx \$234.52$$
$$\text{APV} = \frac{\mathcal{E}(C)}{1+\mathcal{E}(\tilde{r}_{\text{Firm}})} + \frac{\tau \cdot [\mathcal{E}(\tilde{r}_{\text{Debt}}) \cdot \text{Debt}]}{1+\mathcal{E}(\tilde{r}_{\text{Debt}})}$$
$$\text{APV} = \text{Value as if 100\% Equity-Financed} + \text{Tax Subsidy from Interest Payments}$$

As described at length in the chapter appendix, you could also reasonably use the firm's cost of capital to discount the tax savings:

($200 debt at 11% interest, i.e., $22 interest payment discounted at 12%)

$$\text{APV} = \frac{\$256}{1+12\%} + \frac{30\% \cdot \$22}{1+12\%} \approx \$234.46$$
$$\text{APV} = \frac{\mathcal{E}(C)}{1+\mathcal{E}(\tilde{r}_{\text{Firm}})} + \frac{\tau \cdot [\mathcal{E}(\tilde{r}_{\text{Debt}}) \cdot \text{Debt}]}{1+\mathcal{E}(\tilde{r}_{\text{Firm}})}$$
$$\text{APV} = \text{Value as if 100\% Equity-Financed} + \text{Tax Subsidy from Interest Payments}$$

The difference of 6 cents is obviously trivial in any real-world application.

APV is easily generalized to more periods.

APV generalizes easily to multiple years: Just compute the tax savings for each year and add them up, the same way that you would add up present values. You will work such a multiperiod example in the next section.

IMPORTANT: The adjusted present value (APV) formula computes an "as if all-equity-financed" PV (i.e., after corporate income tax) and then adds back the tax subsidy:

$$\text{APV} = \begin{matrix}\text{Value as if Firm is 100\%} \\ \text{Equity-Financed and Fully} \\ \text{Taxed}\end{matrix} + \begin{matrix}\text{Tax Subsidies} \\ \text{from Interest} \\ \text{Payments}\end{matrix}$$

If the project lasts for only one period, omitting tedious and obvious time subscripts, this translates into

$$\text{APV Today} = \frac{\mathcal{E}(\text{Future } C)}{1 + \mathcal{E}(\tilde{r}_{\text{Firm}})} + \frac{\mathcal{E}\overbrace{(\tau \cdot \overbrace{\tilde{r}_{\text{Debt}} \cdot \text{Debt}}^{\text{Interest Payment}})}^{\text{Tax Shield}}}{1 + \mathcal{E}(\tilde{r}_{\text{Debt}})}$$

The cost of capital on the second term (but not the first term) may or may not be correct. Because the second term is small, it rarely makes much difference if $\mathcal{E}(\tilde{r}_{\text{Firm}})$ is used instead of $\mathcal{E}(\tilde{r}_{\text{Debt}})$.

APV: Application to a 60/40 Debt-Financing Case

An APV example: Value a firm financed with 60% debt.

In the example, the firm with \$200 debt is worth \$234.46 today. This comes to a debt ratio of \$200/\$234.46 ≈ 85%. Now assume that the firm instead considers a new capital structure in which it would borrow only \$139.16. The firm has determined that this lower-debt capital structure would reduce its debt cost of capital to 9% per annum—after all, at such low levels, the debt is risk free, so risk-averse investors would be willing to accept a lower *expected* rate of return. What would the firm's value then become?

Problem solved.

According to the APV formula, you begin with the value of a 100%-equity firm, which is \$256/1.12, and add back the tax subsidy. Interest payments on \$139.16 of debt will be 9% · \$139.16 ≈ \$12.52 *next year*. Taxes saved will be 30% · \$12.52 ≈ \$3.76 *next year*. Discounted at 9%, this is worth \$3.45 *today*. Therefore,

$$\begin{aligned}
\text{APV} &= \frac{\$256.00}{1 + 12\%} + \frac{30\% \cdot 9\% \cdot \$139.16}{1 + 9\%} \\
&\approx \$228.57 + \$3.45 = \$232.02 \\
\text{APV} &= \frac{\mathcal{E}(C)}{1 + \mathcal{E}(\tilde{r}_{\text{Firm}})} + \frac{\tau \cdot \mathcal{E}(\tilde{r}_{\text{Debt}}) \cdot \text{Debt}}{1 + \mathcal{E}(\tilde{r}_{\text{Debt}})} \\
&= \text{“As if All-Equity-Financed” Firm} + \text{Tax Subsidy}
\end{aligned}$$

If you prefer discounting the expected tax shelter with the firm's cost of capital, use

$$\begin{aligned}
\text{APV} &= \frac{\$256.00}{1+12\%} + \frac{30\% \cdot 9\% \cdot \$139.16}{1+12\%} \\
&\approx \$228.57 + \$3.36 = \$231.93 \\
\text{APV} &= \frac{\mathcal{E}(C)}{1+\mathcal{E}(\tilde{r}_{\text{Firm}})} + \frac{\tau \cdot \mathcal{E}(\tilde{r}_{\text{Debt}}) \cdot \text{Debt}}{1+\mathcal{E}(\tilde{r}_{\text{Firm}})} \\
&= \text{“As if All-Equity-Financed” Firm} + \text{Tax Subsidy}
\end{aligned} \quad (17.1)$$

(Again, the cost of capital on the tax shelter makes little difference, here only $3.45 − $3.36 = $0.09.) This is the APV answer: In the presence of corporate income taxes, a firm financed with $139.16 in debt would be worth about $232.

17.3B TAX-ADJUSTED WEIGHTED AVERAGE COST OF CAPITAL (WACC) VALUATION: THEORY

To show that WACC and APV are similar, we derive the tax-adjusted WACC formula from the APV formula.

The second method for computing the value of the firm uses a tax-adjusted weighted average cost of capital formula. If you start with the APV formula and manipulate it, it will be apparent that the two methods can yield the same value, at least if you start from Formula 17.1. Therefore, stick with the same parameters: 60/40 debt/equity financing, a 30% corporate income tax rate, a 9% cost of debt capital, and $280 before-tax return ($256 after-tax return in the all-equity case). As before, the firm borrows $139.16 at a 9% interest rate for net interest payments of $12.52. The corporate income tax shield is 30% of $12.52, or $3.76. The APV formula (Formula 17.1) values the firm at

$$\text{PV} = \frac{\$256}{1+12\%} + \frac{\overbrace{30\% \cdot \overbrace{(9\% \cdot \$139.16)}^{\approx \$12.52}}^{\approx \$3.76}}{1+12\%} \approx \$231.93$$

$$\text{PV} = \frac{\mathcal{E}(C)}{1+\mathcal{E}(\tilde{r}_{\text{Firm}})} + \frac{\tau \cdot [\mathcal{E}(\tilde{r}_{\text{Debt}}) \cdot \text{Debt}]}{1+\mathcal{E}(\tilde{r}_{\text{Firm}})}$$

The main difference between APV and WACC is that whereas APV works with dollar values of debt and interest payments, the WACC method expresses debt as a ratio of firm value,

$$\begin{array}{lcl}
60\% \approx \$139.16/\$231.93 & & \$139.16 \approx 60\% \cdot \$231.93 \\
w_{\text{Debt}} = \text{Debt/PV} & \Longrightarrow & \text{Debt} = w_{\text{Debt}} \cdot \text{PV}
\end{array}$$

Substitute the debt expression into the APV formula,

$$\text{PV} = \frac{\$256}{1+12\%} + \frac{30\% \cdot [9\% \cdot (60\% \cdot \$231.93)]}{1+12\%} \approx \$231.93$$

$$\text{PV} = \frac{\mathcal{E}(C)}{1+\mathcal{E}(\tilde{r}_{\text{Firm}})} + \frac{\tau \cdot [\mathcal{E}(\tilde{r}_{\text{Debt}}) \cdot (w_{\text{Debt}} \cdot \text{PV})]}{1+\mathcal{E}(\tilde{r}_{\text{Firm}})}$$

You now have PV on both sides of the equation, so you want to solve for PV. This requires a few algebraic steps.

1. Multiply both sides by $[1 + \mathcal{E}(\tilde{r}_{\text{Firm}})] = (1 + 12\%) = 1.12$ to make the denominator disappear:

$$(1 + 12\%) \cdot \$231.93 \approx \$256 + 30\% \cdot [9\% \cdot (60\% \cdot \$231.93)]$$
$$[1 + \mathcal{E}(\tilde{r}_{\text{Firm}})] \cdot \text{PV} = \mathcal{E}(C) + \tau \cdot [\mathcal{E}(\tilde{r}_{\text{Debt}}) \cdot (w_{\text{Debt}} \cdot \text{PV})]$$

2. Move the second term on the right side over to the left side:

$$(1 + 12\%) \cdot \$231.93 - 30\% \cdot [9\% \cdot (60\% \cdot \$231.93)] \approx \$256$$
$$[1 + \mathcal{E}(\tilde{r}_{\text{Firm}})] \cdot \text{PV} - \tau \cdot [\mathcal{E}(\tilde{r}_{\text{Debt}}) \cdot (w_{\text{Debt}} \cdot \text{PV})] = \mathcal{E}(C)$$

3. Pull out the PV:

$$\$231.93 \cdot [1 + 12\% - 30\% \cdot 9\% \cdot 60\%] \approx \$256$$
$$\text{PV} \cdot [1 + \mathcal{E}(\tilde{r}_{\text{Firm}}) - \tau \cdot \mathcal{E}(\tilde{r}_{\text{Debt}}) \cdot w_{\text{Debt}}] = \mathcal{E}(C)$$

4. Divide both sides by the PV multiplier:

$$\$231.93 \approx \frac{\$256}{1 + 12\% - 30\% \cdot 9\% \cdot 60\%} \approx \frac{\$256}{1 + 10.38\%}$$
$$\text{PV} = \frac{\mathcal{E}(C)}{1 + \mathcal{E}(\tilde{r}_{\text{Firm}}) - \tau \cdot [\mathcal{E}(\tilde{r}_{\text{Debt}}) \cdot w_{\text{Debt}}]} = \frac{\mathcal{E}(C)}{1 + \text{WACC}} \quad (17.2)$$

My intuition for the WACC formula.

This is the tax-adjusted WACC valuation formula. Its big idea is to discount the "as if 100%-equity-financed and fully taxed" cash flows (of $\mathcal{E}(C) = \$256$), not with the plain cost of capital $\mathcal{E}(\tilde{r}_{\text{Firm}}) = 12\%$, but with a reduced interest rate that comes from the corporate income tax subsidy on interest payments. The term that does this—relative to our earlier no-tax WACC formula (Formula 16.2)—is $\tau \cdot w_{\text{Debt}} \cdot \mathcal{E}(\tilde{r}_{\text{Debt}}) = 30\% \cdot 60\% \cdot 9\% = 1.62\%$. Therefore, your revised discount rate is $1 + 12\% - 30\% \cdot 9\% \cdot 60\% = 1 + 10.38\%$. The 10.38% is the (tax-adjusted) WACC—lower than your all-equity cost of capital of 12%.

➤ Perfect-markets WACC, Formula 16.2, p. 599

The more common form of WACC breaks out the equity cost of capital.

The WACC formula is often slightly rearranged. Split $\mathcal{E}(\tilde{r}_{\text{Firm}})$ into its cost of equity and cost of debt components, $\mathcal{E}(\tilde{r}_{\text{Firm}}) = w_{\text{Debt}} \cdot \mathcal{E}(\tilde{r}_{\text{Debt}}) + w_{\text{Equity}} \cdot \mathcal{E}(\tilde{r}_{\text{Equity}})$. In our example, to keep the weighted-average firm cost of capital at the constant $\mathcal{E}(\tilde{r}_{\text{Firm}}) = 12\%$, solve $\mathcal{E}(\tilde{r}_{\text{Firm}}) = w_{\text{Debt}} \cdot \mathcal{E}(\tilde{r}_{\text{Debt}}) + w_{\text{Equity}} \cdot \mathcal{E}(\tilde{r}_{\text{Equity}}) = 60\% \cdot 9\% + 40\% \cdot \mathcal{E}(\tilde{r}_{\text{Equity}}) = 12\%$, and find $\mathcal{E}(\tilde{r}_{\text{Equity}}) = 16.5\%$. Substitute this into Formula 17.2, and you get the more common version of the WACC formula,

$$\text{PV} = \frac{\$256}{1 + 10.38\%} = \frac{\$256}{1 + 40\% \cdot 16.5\% + (1 - 30\%) \cdot 60\% \cdot 9\%}$$
$$\text{PV} = \frac{\mathcal{E}(C)}{1 + \text{WACC}} = \frac{\mathcal{E}(C)}{1 + w_{\text{Equity}} \cdot \mathcal{E}(\tilde{r}_{\text{Equity}}) + (1 - \tau) \cdot w_{\text{Debt}} \cdot \mathcal{E}(\tilde{r}_{\text{Debt}})}$$

The tax-adjusted WACC generalizes the perfect-markets WACC from the previous chapter.

➤ WACC in a perfect world, Formula 16.2, p. 599

Your new WACC formula generalizes the old M&M WACC formula from the previous chapter. If the corporate tax rate τ is zero, the tax subsidy is useless, and the tax-adjusted WACC formula simplifies to your older and simpler WACC formula. This works for about half of all publicly traded firms in the United States, which indeed have a marginal tax rate of zero (e.g., due to tax-loss carryforwards or due to clever tax shelters). For these companies, the use of debt does not provide a useful tax shelter. They can use the simplified M&M version of the WACC formula, which ignores the tax subsidy of interest. But for highly taxed firms, you don't have a choice. You need the new WACC formula, which can also handle firms with positive corporate income tax rates.

Alas, in practical use—though convenient and intuitive—WACC is often difficult to apply.

Unfortunately, you can only use the WACC formula in a multiperiod setting *if* the cost of capital, the firm's debt ratio, and the firm's tax rate all stay constant. In this case, a present value formula would look something like

$$\text{PV} = \frac{\mathcal{E}(C_{\text{Time 1}})}{\{1 + [w_{\text{Equity}} \cdot r_{\text{Equity, Time 1}} + w_{\text{Debt}} \cdot \mathcal{E}(\tilde{r}_{\text{Debt, Time 1}}) \cdot (1-\tau)]\}^1} + \frac{\mathcal{E}(C_{\text{Time 2}})}{\{1 + [w_{\text{Equity}} \cdot r_{\text{Equity, Time 2}} + w_{\text{Debt}} \cdot \mathcal{E}(\tilde{r}_{\text{Debt, Time 2}}) \cdot (1-\tau)]\}^2} + \cdots$$

If these quantities are not all constant, no one knows how to compute a proper WACC. It is not unusual for firms to plan on high debt financing up front that they pay back later on. Unfortunately, this is a situation that the WACC formula cannot handle. Moreover, WACC is difficult to use if there are nonfinancial liabilities with marginal costs of capital that are different from those on financial liabilities. In general, the WACC formula is best applied in real life as a quick and useful approximation. The APV method is often more flexible than the WACC method.

➤ WACC with nonfinancial liabilities, Section 16.6B, p. 601

IMPORTANT:

- The (tax-adjusted) weighted average cost of capital (WACC) formula discounts the future cash flows with a lower cost of capital that reflects the corporate income tax shelter:

$$\text{PV} = \frac{\mathcal{E}(C)}{1 + \text{WACC}}$$

where

$$\begin{aligned} \text{WACC} &= \mathcal{E}(\tilde{r}_{\text{Firm}}) - \tau \cdot \mathcal{E}(\tilde{r}_{\text{Debt}}) \cdot w_{\text{Debt}} \\ &= w_{\text{Equity}} \cdot \mathcal{E}(\tilde{r}_{\text{Equity}}) + w_{\text{Debt}} \cdot \mathcal{E}(\tilde{r}_{\text{Debt}}) \cdot (1-\tau) \end{aligned} \quad (17.3)$$

The expected cash flows must be the cash flows "as if the firm were all-equity-financed and fully taxed."

- This formula is a generalization of the WACC formula from the perfect M&M world. Therefore, it is this formula that is usually called the WACC formula.
- It is not clear how to use the WACC formula in a multiperiod setting.

The WACC formula is so common that it is worth memorizing.

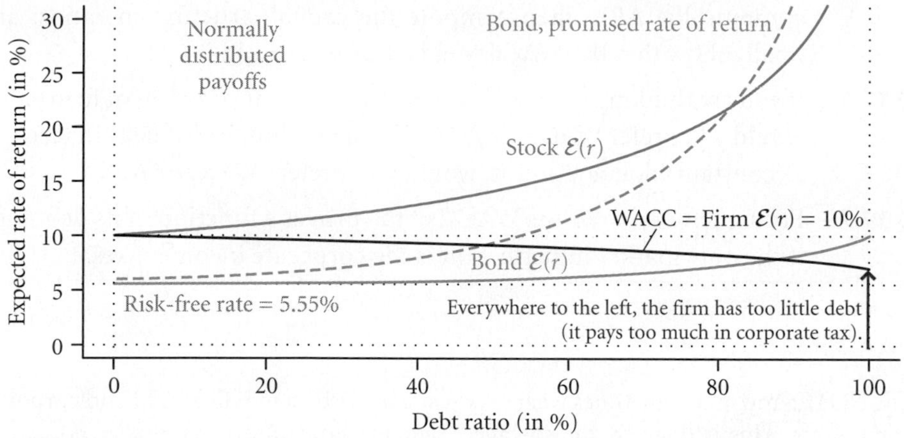

This figure is the equivalent of Figure 16.2, except that debt has a corporate income tax advantage. This means that the firm's overall cost of capital declines with the firm's debt ratio. However, as before in the perfect world, both the cost of debt capital and the cost of equity capital increase with firms' leverage ratios. And, again, note how much higher the firm's promised rate of return on debt is than its expected rate of return. It is again possible that, even though the firm's cost of capital on debt is always less than its cost of capital on equity, the promised rate of return on debt is higher than the firm's cost of equity capital.

FIGURE 17.1 The Cost of Capital in a Corporate Tax-Imperfect World

Now recall Figure 16.2 from the previous chapter. It showed that the cost of capital remains the same 10%, regardless of the firm's capital structure. Is this still the case in the presence of corporate income taxes? No! Figure 17.1 shows that the tax subsidy pushes the firm's cost of capital down for high debt ratios. Indeed, if there were no other issues to consider, the optimal capital structure would be for the firm to have as much debt as possible, a full 100%.

The optimal capital structure without other forces is 100% debt.

SOLVE NOW!

Q 17.4 Consider a 25/75 debt/equity financing case for your firm. Your firm will produce a before-tax return of \$280, the investment costs \$200, the tax rate is 30%, the overall opportunity cost of capital (in other taxable projects) is 12%, and when the firm is 25% debt-financed, debt must offer an expected rate of return of 8%. (If you think of your opportunity cost of capital as the best your firm can achieve elsewhere, then these cost-of-capital numbers are your before-tax costs of capital from other projects before they would be taxed, too. If you think of your opportunity cost of capital as provided by your investors, who [like you] are also taxed, then it is the rate of return before their personal income taxes. The cost of capital for your personal investors is the subject of the next chapter.) First compute the WACC, then compute the debt as 25% of the WACC value, and show how the APV yields the same result.

Q 17.5 Consider financing your firm with \$100 debt: The before-tax return is \$280, the investment cost is \$200, the tax rate is 30%, the overall cost of capital is 12%, and this debt must offer an expected rate of return of 8.7%. (These are again before-tax opportunity rates of return.) First compute the APV, then compute the capital structure in ratios, and finally show that the WACC yields the same result.

Q 17.6 If you are thinking of debt in terms of a (constant) fraction of firm value, would you prefer WACC or APV? If you are thinking of debt in terms of a (constant) dollar amount, would you prefer WACC or APV?

Q 17.7 From memory, draw the WACC of the firm as a function of its debt ratio if the only market imperfection is the corporate income taxes.

SIDE NOTE: You may sometimes wish to adjust a firm's beta to reflect debt and corporate income taxes. This is done by the so-called Hamada Equation, $\beta_{\text{With Debt}} = \beta_{\text{Unlevered}} \cdot \left[1 + (1 - \tau) \cdot (\text{Debt/Equity})\right]$. We shall not use this formula any further.

How Bad Are Mistakes?

APPLYING APV AND WACC TO THE CURRENT CASH FLOWS

Make sure you use the correct project cash flow for APV and WACC.

Unfortunately, both WACC and APV are often used incorrectly. Analysts frequently forget that the correct expected cash flow in the present value numerator is the "as if fully-equity-financed and fully taxed" cash flow (\$256 in our example). It is neither the before-tax project cash flow (\$280 in our example), nor the after-tax cash flow under the current financing scheme (e.g., $\$280 - 9\% \cdot \$139.16 \approx \$267.48$). If you have worked through the examples in this chapter, you should understand why this would provide the wrong answer. Unlike errors in the discount rate applied to the tax shelter—which is a modest error—using the wrong cash flow is a big error.

IMPORTANT: WACC and APV operate with expected "as if 100%-equity-financed and after-corporate-income-tax" cash flows, not the firm's *current* cash flows (which depend on the *current* debt/equity financing).

SOLVE NOW!

Q 17.8 A firm in the 20% marginal tax bracket is currently financed with \$500 debt and \$1,000 equity. The debt carries an interest rate of 6%; the equity's cost of capital is 12%. The risk-free rate is 4%; the equity premium is 3%. What is the firm's beta? The firm is pondering a recapitalization to \$1,000 debt, which would increase the debt's interest rate to 8%.

The firm will exist for only 1 more year. What would the new equity be worth?

Q 17.9 A firm in the 40% income tax bracket has an investment that costs \$300 in year 0, and offers a before-tax return (cash flow) in year 1 of \$500. Assume that the firm's before-tax opportunity cost of capital, as provided by the external capital markets, is approximately 20%. Its debt cost of capital is $\mathcal{E}(\tilde{r}_{\text{Debt}}) = 15\% + w_{\text{Debt}} \cdot 5\%$. Compute the APV, WACC, and a WACC-based value if the firm borrows \$50 to finance it. Repeat if the firm borrows \$100.

17.4 A SAMPLE APPLICATION OF TAX-ADJUSTED VALUATION TECHNIQUES

Let's value a pro forma firm.
➤ Table 13.6, p. 458

Let's move on to a more realistic example. You are actually already familiar with it: It is the hypothetical machine from Chapter 13, Table 13.6. To make the example more useful, add the following parameters:

- The appropriate debt interest rate is 20%, so a loan of \$25 must offer an expected \$5 in interest per annum.
- The appropriate overall cost of capital for the firm is 30%.
- The corporate income tax rate is 40%.

Table 17.2 shows all you need to know. Shareholders pay in \$26 and receive a total of \$137 in dividends. Bondholders invest \$25 and receive \$25 in total interest payments. Your firm follows an odd capital distribution policy, but so be it. What is it worth?

17.4A THE FLOW-TO-EQUITY DIRECT VALUATION FROM THE PRO FORMA FINANCIALS

The third valuation method is flow-to-equity.

The main point of the more involved example is to show you the third method to handle the tax subsidy. This **flow-to-equity** method works directly with a "pro forma." For now, think of a pro forma simply as a forward projection of the financial statements. (Pro formas will be discussed in detail in Chapter 20.) We will demonstrate all three methods now: flow-to-equity, APV, and WACC.

Method #1: Direct cash flows, already after-tax, from the financials.
➤ Project cash flows, Formula 13.4, p. 477

The project cash flow formula (Formula 13.4) tells you that the project cash flows for your NPV valuation are:

Computing Project Cash Flows, \$25 Debt Financing

	Year	1	2	3	4	5	6
	Total Operating Activity	\$46	\$53	\$53	\$43	\$33	\$33
+	Total Investing Activity	−\$75	−\$75	—	—	—	—
+	Interest Expense	—	\$5	\$5	\$5	\$5	\$5
=	**Project Cash Flows**	−\$29	−\$17	+\$58	+\$48	+\$38	+\$38

We need a discount factor for these after-tax cash flows. (This is very difficult to assess accurately, but fortunately the precise discount rate here does not matter too much.

TABLE 17.2 INCOME STATEMENT OF HYPOTHETICAL MACHINE

	Year	1	2	3	4	5	6
	Gross Sales (Revenues)	$70	$70	$70	$70	$70	$70
–	Cost of Goods Sold (COGS)	$5	$5	$5	$5	$5	$5
–	Selling, General & Administrative Expenses (SG&A)	$5	$5	$5	$5	$5	$5
=	EBITDA (Net Sales)	$60	$60	$60	$60	$60	$60
–	Depreciation	$25	$50	$50	$25	$0	$0
=	EBIT (Operating Income)	$35	$10	$10	$35	$60	$60
–	Interest Expense	$0	$5	$5	$5	$5	$5
=	EAIBT (or EBT)	$35	$5	$5	$30	$55	$55
–	Corporate Income Tax (at 40%)	$14	$2	$2	$12	$22	$22
=	**Net Income**	$21	$3	$3	$18	$33	$33

Excerpts from the Cash Flow Statement

	Year	1	2	3	4	5	6
	Net Income	$21	$3	$3	$18	$33	$33
+	Depreciation	$25	$50	$50	$25	$0	$0
=	**Total Operating Activity**	$46	$53	$53	$43	$33	$33
+	Capital Expenditures	–$75	–$75	—	—	—	—
=	**Total Investing Activity**	–$75	–$75	—	—	—	—
+	Financing Cash Flow	—	—	—	—	—	—
+	Net Equity Issue	$26	—	—	—	—	—
+	Dividends	—	—	–$53	–$43	–$33	–$8
+	Net Debt Issue	$25	—	—	—	—	–$25
=	**Total Financing Activity**	$51	—	–$53	–$43	–$33	–$33
=	**Net Change in Cash**	+$22	–$22	$0	$0	$0	$0

The chapter appendix explains this better.) We will be using the same 30% cost of capital for the firm. Now discount these cash flows on the overall firm:

$$\text{NPV} = \frac{-\$29}{1.30} + \frac{-\$17}{1.30^2} + \frac{+\$58}{1.30^3} + \frac{+\$48}{1.30^4} + \frac{+\$38}{1.30^5} + \frac{+\$38}{1.30^6} \approx \$28.95 \qquad (17.4)$$

You would be willing to pay $28.95 *today* for the right to buy (and finance) the firm, which will initiate *next year* with this exact capital structure. But wait: Did you not forget about the tax shelter that came with the debt? No, you did not! The pro forma itself had already incorporated the correct interest expense. The interest payments had already reduced the corporate income tax and thereby appropriately increased your project's cash flows.

17.4B APV

The second method to value this firm is APV. But be careful: The cash flows in Formula 17.4 are *not* the cash flows that you need for the APV analysis, because these are not the cash flows *as if 100% equity financed*. APV states that you can only add back the tax shield to the *as-if-100%-equity-financed* cash flows. If you used the cash flows in Formula 17.4 and then added the tax shield (due to the interest payment designation), you would mistakenly count the tax shield twice. You must therefore start over to find the correct expected cash flows as if the firm were fully equity-financed, in which case the tax obligation would be higher. By how much? You can intuit this even before you write down the full financials. In years 2–6, the taxable net income would be $5 more, so at your 40% corporate income tax rate you would have to pay not $2, but $4 in taxes. This means that you would have to pay an extra $2 in taxes each year.

Method #2, APV, demands a detour: You must construct *as-if-100%-equity-financed* financials.

To make sure this intuition is correct, construct the financials of a 100%-equity-financed firm:

Here are the 100%-equity-financed cash flows.

Abbreviated Income Statement, 100% Equity-Financed

	Year	1	2	3	4	5	6	
=	EBIT (Operating Income)	$35	$10	$10	$35	$60	$60	
−	Interest Expense	$0	$0	$0	$0	$0	$0	
=	EAIBT (or EBT)	$35	$10	$10	$35	$60	$60	
−	Corporate Income Tax (at 40%)	$14	$4	$4	$14	$24	$24	← note higher tax obligation than with some debt financing
=	**Net Income**	$21	$6	$6	$21	$36	$36	

Abbreviated Cash Flow Statement, 100% Equity-Financed

	Year	1	2	3	4	5	6
	Net Income	$21	$6	$6	$21	$36	$36
+	Depreciation	$25	$50	$50	$25	$0	$0
=	**Total Operating Activity**	$46	$56	$56	$46	$36	$36
+	Capital Expenditures	−$75	−$75	—	—	—	—
=	**Total Investing Activity**	−$75	−$75	—	—	—	—

You can now reuse our present value cash flow formula on the 100%-equity-financed version of our firm:

Computing Project Cash Flows, 100% Equity-Financed

	Year	1	2	3	4	5	6
	Total Operating Activity	$46	$56	$56	$46	$36	$36
+	Total Investing Activity	−$75	−$75	—	—	—	—
+	Interest Expense	$0	$0	$0	$0	$0	$0
	Project Cash Flows	−$29	−$19	+$56	+$46	+$36	+$36

Comparing this to the equivalent table on page 623, you can see that the project cash flows in your 100%-equity-financed firm have indeed lost the tax shelter of $2 in each of years 2–6. The intuition was correct!

Return to the main task: APV valuation.

Now discount these "as-if-100%-equity-financed" total project cash flows with the firm's appropriate cost of capital, which is assumed to be 30%. Standing at time 0, this gives you

$$\text{NPV}_{\text{Project, 100\% Equity-Financed}} = \frac{-\$29}{1.30} + \frac{-\$19}{1.30^2} + \frac{+\$56}{1.30^3} + \frac{+\$46}{1.30^4} + \frac{+\$36}{1.30^5} + \frac{+\$36}{1.30^6} \approx \$25.20$$

The APV formula states that you now need to add back the expected tax shield from the debt. The interest tax shields in years 2–6 are the interest payments ($5 per year) multiplied by the corporate tax rate (40%), or $2 per year. What is the value of this tax shelter?

$$\text{NPV}_{\text{Tax Shelter}} = \frac{\$0}{1.30} + \frac{+\$2}{1.30^2} + \frac{+\$2}{1.30^3} + \frac{+\$2}{1.30^4} + \frac{+\$2}{1.30^5} + \frac{+\$2}{1.30^6} \approx \$3.75$$

Therefore, the APV method tells you that the firm value is

$$\text{APV} \approx \$25.20 + \$3.75 = \$28.95$$

This is the same answer that you found in Formula 17.4.

17.4C WACC

Method #3: WACC. The debt is about 35% of the firm's financing.

The third method to value the firm is WACC. Start again with the firm's cash flows, as if 100% equity-financed.

Computing Project Cash Flows, 100% Equity-Financed

Year	1	2	3	4	5	6
Project Cash Flows	−$29	−$19	+$56	+$46	+$36	+$36

The idea is to use an appropriate tax-adjusted WACC to discount these cash flows. But there is another tricky issue: What is the firm's debt ratio? That is, WACC requires $w_{\text{Debt}} = (1 - w_{\text{Equity}})$ as an input. In the real world, you could just look up the current firm values. In our example, I am sparing you the details of working out that the debt is about 35% of the firm's value today. You know the other two remaining inputs that you need to compute WACC, which are the overall corporate cost of capital at 30%, and the debt cost of capital at 20%.

Return to the main task: WACC valuation.

You can now compute the firm's weighted average cost of capital as

$$\text{WACC} = 30\% - 40\% \cdot 35\% \cdot 20\% = 27.2\%$$

$$\text{WACC} = \mathcal{E}(\tilde{r}_{\text{Firm}}) - \tau \cdot w_{\text{Debt}} \cdot \mathcal{E}(\tilde{r}_{\text{Debt}})$$

Under the incorrect but hopefully reasonable assumption that the debt ratio remains at 35%,

$$\text{NPV} = \frac{-\$29}{1.272} + \frac{-\$19}{1.272\%^2} + \frac{+\$56}{1.272\%^3} + \frac{+\$46}{1.272\%^4}$$

$$+ \frac{+\$36}{1.272\%^5} + \frac{+\$36}{1.272\%^6} \approx \$29.55$$

This is a (modest) 60 cents off the value of the APV formula. Most of the difference comes from the fact that the fraction of debt in the capital structure is 35% in the first year but a different proportion of the value in subsequent years. As noted on page 620, the WACC method really does not apply in this case. However, in the real world, this error would be dwarfed by errors in what you have assumed about the tax code and by your uncertainty about the expected cash flows and costs of capital that such projects would carry.

SOLVE NOW!

Q 17.10 Construct a pro forma for the following firm: A 3-year project costs \$150 in year 1 (not year 0) and produces \$70 in year 1, \$60 in year 2, and \$55 in year 3. (All numbers are year-end.) Depreciation, both real and financial, is straight line over 3 years. Projects of this riskiness (and with this term structure of project payoffs) have an 18% before-tax opportunity cost of capital. The marginal corporate income tax rate is 40%.

(a) Assume that the firm is 100% equity-financed. Construct the pro forma and compute expected project cash flows.
(b) Compute the project IRR.
(c) Compute the project NPV.
(d) Assume that this firm expects to receive an extra bonus of \$2 in years 2 and 3 from a benevolent donor. What would be the project's cash flows and IRR now?

For the remaining questions, assume that the firm instead has a capital structure financing \$50 with debt raised in year 1 at a 10% (expected) interest rate. There is no interest paid in year 1, just in years 2 and 3. The principal is repaid in year 3.

(e) Construct the pro forma now. What is the IRR of this project?
(f) From the pro forma, what is the NPV of the debt-financed project?
(g) Compute the NPV via the APV method.
(h) Via the APV method, how much would firm value be if the firm would have taken on not \$50, but \$40, in debt (assuming the same debt interest rate of 10%)?
(i) Does the debt ratio of the firm stay constant over time? Is this firm a good candidate for the WACC method?

TABLE 17.3 PEPSICO'S INCOME STATEMENT (REVISITED), DOLLARS IN MILLIONS

	Income Statement	Dec. 2000
=	Revenue	\$25,479
	COGS	\$10,226
	+ SG&A	\$11,104
	+ Depreciation and Amortization	\$147
	+ Unusual Expenses	\$184
–	= **Total Operating Expenses**	\$21,661
=	**Operating Income**	\$3,818
+	Net Interest Income	\$–57
=	**Income before Tax**	\$3,761
–	Income Tax	\$1,218
=	**Income after Tax**	\$2,543
–	Extraordinary Items	\$0
=	**Net Income**	\$2,543

Source: Courtesy of PepsiCo

17.5 THE TAX SUBSIDY ON PEPSICO'S FINANCIAL STATEMENT

Can you apply your newfound theoretical knowledge of how to handle corporate income taxes to a real-world firm—in fact, to the PepsiCo example from Chapter 13? What is the tax subsidy in PepsiCo's income statement, reproduced in Table 17.3?

You can easily infer PepsiCo's tax subsidy from its corporate financial statements.

In 2000, PepsiCo had \$3.818 billion in operating income, but only had to pay income taxes on \$3.761 billion. With income taxes of \$1.218 billion, PepsiCo's average corporate income tax rate was about 32.4%. If PepsiCo had been purely equity-financed, it would have had to pay taxes on its operating income of \$3.818 billion, or about \$1.237 billion. Thus, by having \$57 million in interest, relative to a hypothetical dividend payout of \$57 million, PepsiCo enjoyed a tax shield in 2000 from its interest payments of

$$\begin{aligned} \text{PepsiCo's 2000 Debt Tax Shield} &= 32.4\% \cdot \$57 \text{ million} \approx \$18.5 \text{ million} \\ \text{Tax Shield} &= \tau \cdot \text{Interest Payments} \end{aligned}$$

Note that you did not need to compute $\mathcal{E}(\tilde{r}_{\text{Debt}}) \cdot \text{Debt}$, because you could read the interest payments directly off the financials. The model's other assumption, that the marginal tax rate is fixed, probably works well in this case. For companies like PepsiCo with high income, the marginal and the average tax rates are practically the same, so you can assume that PepsiCo would have had to pay its average tax rate of 32.4% if it had paid out the \$57 million interest in dividends instead. (Of course, the model here still ignores the many more complex tax issues, such as deferred taxes.)

SOLVE NOW!

Q 17.11 Compute the 2001 tax shield for Coca-Cola, using the information on page 488.

17.6 CONTEMPLATING CORPORATE TAXES

You now understand how managers should adjust to the presence of corporate income taxes. But there are a number of other tax-related issues that are still worth discussing, if only because you may wonder about them in the future.

17.6A WHICH TAX-ADJUSTED VALUATION METHOD IS BEST?

None of the three methods always dominates.

Which of the three valuation methods is best: flow-to-equity, APV, or WACC? They are all in use because each has its advantages and disadvantages.

Estimated values should be similar.

Of course, the three methods should usually come out if not with the same, then at least with very similar, results—otherwise, something would be wrong. As the example in Section 17.4 showed, if suitably applied, the differences are usually modest. This is especially true if you compare valuation-method differences to the errors that you will inevitably introduce in your assessments of future expected cash flows, your estimate for the appropriate costs of capital, and the necessary simplification of the tax code.

Compare the advantages and disadvantages of the methods.

Here is how I see the three methods:

Flow-to-equity: The advantage of the flow-to-equity method is that it is lucid and makes it less likely that you will use an incorrect expected cash flow. The disadvantage of the flow-to-equity method is that it requires a lot more effort (you have to construct full financials!), and that it does not break out the tax advantage of debt explicitly. This makes it more difficult to think about the tax-induced consequences of contemplated capital structure changes.

APV: The APV formula makes it relatively easy to determine how an extra dollar of debt increases firm value. When thinking of a specific addition or project with a specific cost, this may be the easiest formula to use.

WACC: The WACC formula makes it relatively easy to determine how an extra percentage in debt increases firm value. When thinking of a target ratio change in capital structure policy, this may be the easiest formula to use.

My advice: APV is often simplest.

In many common cases, APV is easier to work with than WACC. For example, APV makes it much easier to think about projects that add debt capacity only at some stage in their lives. What drives project debt capacity? The simple answer is that more tangible (collateralizable) projects tend to add more debt capacity, because your bank will find it easier to repossess and resell tangible assets. A research and development (R&D) project may require an equity investment up front, followed by the construction of a laboratory that can be debt-financed. The laboratory adds debt capacity, the R&D does not. APV makes it easy to add in the debt capacity only in later stages. APV also makes it easier to assign different discount factors to the firm's projects and to the firm's tax shields.

WACC is often most difficult for multiyear projects.

WACC is probably the most difficult method. No one knows how to do multiyear compounding with time-varying WACCs. Therefore, the method can only be applied if the firm's debt ratio remains roughly constant in future years. Of course, if you know that this is the case, WACC may be easier to use than APV. However, in all other cases, WACC usage errors could become important. The empirical evidence suggests that publicly traded corporations rarely keep constant debt ratios, often rendering WACC a less preferable method. On a more technical note, WACC also leans more heavily on the assumption that borrowing rates are competitive and thus zero NPV. Therefore, WACC works only in "normal" situations in which creditors are paid the appropriate cost of capital on the debt. WACC cannot deal with "below-market" or "above-market" unfairly priced loans—much like the plain version of the CAPM cannot. (You already know that you need to use a certainty equivalent form of the CAPM in this case.)

➤ Certainty equivalence, Section 9.6, p. 281

REPEAT: THE ONE IMPORTANT MISTAKE TO AVOID

Same warning again: Please don't ever adjust current non-100% equity cash flows via APV or WACC.

The one big mistake you should never commit is to use the wrong expected cash flows for APV or WACC. Using the wrong discount rate on the tax shelter or tax liability is forgivable (within bounds); using the wrong expected cash flows is not. Let's reemphasize what you must do. In the flow-to-equity method, you already have both the projected debt cash flows and the projected equity cash flows, so your life is simple. You can just use these pro forma cash flows, which already take the debt tax shield into account. In contrast, in both the APV and WACC methods, you must not use the expected cash flows of the firm under the current capital structure (much less the expected cash flows of the current equity), but the cash flows that would accrue if the firm were fully equity-financed.

17.6B A QUICK-AND-DIRTY HEURISTIC TAX-SAVINGS RULE

Why bother with such small 1-year tax savings?

Do not confuse the question of whether tax savings are important with the question of whether the right discount factor for the tax savings is important. The former is much bigger than the latter. But aren't the tax savings too small to bother with altogether? Before you draw this conclusion, realize that the firm need not invent anything new or work extra hard to obtain the tax savings. In addition, tax savings materialize year after year after year. In fact, this constancy provides a nice back-of-the-envelope heuristic of what the firm can gain in value from one dollar extra in debt.

The tax savings will repeat. A rule of thumb: Each perpetual dollar of debt increases firm value by the corporate income tax rate.

Start with the APV formula. If a large firm today takes on and maintains an extra \$1 billion in debt rather than an extra \$1 billion in equity, the interest is on the order of about 6%, or \$60 million per year. The tax rate for many corporations is about 40%, leading to a savings of \$24 million—this can pay for a nice executive bonus. But this is only the first year. The \$24 million per year savings is a perpetuity. If the cost of capital on the tax shelter is the cost of capital on the debt (6%), then you can compute the total value increase to the firm today to be \$24/6% = \$400 million.

$$\text{Value Increase} \approx \frac{40\% \cdot 6\% \cdot \$1 \text{ billion}}{6\%} = \$400 \text{ million}$$

$$\text{Value Increase} \approx \frac{\tau \cdot \mathcal{E}(\tilde{r}_{\text{Debt}}) \cdot \text{Debt}}{\mathcal{E}(\tilde{r}_{\text{Debt}})} \approx \tau \cdot \text{Debt}$$

This is a nice shortcut: For every dollar extra in eternal debt, the value of the firm increases by the tax rate of the firm. This formula is so easy that you can often compute it in your head. For example, compare financing a $1 million project with 50% debt (rather than all-equity), in which a firm in the 40% marginal tax bracket plans not to repay any of the debt principal or to take on new debt. The tax savings would be $40\% \cdot \$500{,}000 = \$200{,}000$.

It is important that you recognize that the $\tau \cdot$ Debt formula for the tax savings is not an exact calculation. It is only a heuristic—that is, a rule that gives you a good but not a perfect estimate very quickly. For example, it has made at least two assumptions that are never perfectly satisfied. The first is that the appropriate discount rate on the tax shelter is exactly the same as the cost of capital on debt. The second is that the debt and its tax shelter are truly perpetual, with constant cash flows and discount rates. Still, the formula is very useful to quickly get a handle on the long-term benefits of additional debt.

Two small problems with this heuristic are the discount rate and the perpetuity assumptions.

17.6C ARE INVESTMENT AND FINANCING DECISIONS SEPARATE NOW?

In the perfect M&M world, investment and financing decisions can be made independently: Managers can focus on production choices and leave the financing to the nerds in the finance department. Unfortunately, if debt is tax advantaged, or if there are other market imperfections, this is no longer the case.

If the world is not perfect, projects with different financing options can offer different values. Thus, financing and investment decisions must be considered together, not separately.

For example, consider two projects with equal costs, equal payoffs, and equal costs of capital. (Alternatively, just consider their NPVs to be the same.) The first project is a research and development project; the second is a building. In the real world, it is difficult to find a bank to lend money for R&D: After all, if the firm fails to pay its interest payments, there is often little that the bank can collect and resell. Buildings, on the other hand, are easy to repossess. Therefore, the building offers more **debt capacity** (and income tax shelters) than the R&D project. This can make it more valuable than the otherwise equally promising R&D project. Managers cannot choose among projects without taking into consideration how each project aids the debt capacity of the firm.

IMPORTANT: In an imperfect world, unlike the M&M world, managers cannot ignore or delay financing decisions when making real investment decisions. The two decisions are intertwined.

A second complication derives from the fact that the value of the debt capacity can depend on who the owner is. Although most profitable and older firms are in the same highest tax bracket, some younger, growing, and unprofitable firms are in lower tax brackets. To these younger firms, the debt capacity is worth a lot less than it is to a large firm like PepsiCo (which can immediately use the tax deduction).

The same complication you saw in Chapter 10 is at work here, too: The value depends on the owner's identity.

17.6D THE AVERAGE AND MARGINAL COST OF CAPITAL

In Section 16.6B, you already encountered the distinction between the average and the marginal costs of capital. Beware that in our current chapter, we have been computing only the *average* cost of capital. Unfortunately, as manager, you are often more interested in your *marginal* cost of capital on the next dollar of financing, because you want to compare it to the marginal rate of return on your next project. When the

Different projects can have different financing.

➤ Marginal versus average cost of capital, Section 16.6B, p. 601

world is imperfect, the average cost of capital is usually lower than the marginal cost of capital. For example, your firm may have been able to finance its existing plants with tax-preferred debt, but lenders may not want to provide debt for the R&D that it wants to undertake now. Nevertheless, to help you estimate your marginal cost of capital, it is often still quite useful to learn your average cost of capital. If nothing else, it gives you a lower bound.

Of course, the distinction between the two costs of capital does not change any of the calculations in this chapter. Our chapter is concerned with valuing the firm's tax shelter if you keep the same projects and have the ability to take on different levels of debt. The income tax shelter has an influence on the marginal cost of capital, just as it has on the average cost of capital.

17.6E LESSER EVILS: COMBINING TAX-ADJUSTED WACC WITH THE CAPM

Formally, it is wrong to use the CAPM in a world of taxes.

Let me tie up one final loose end. Formally speaking, the CAPM is a perfect-markets model and does not hold in an imperfect world. But the theoretical advice not to use it does not help you much in the real world. What can you use in the real world?

Informally, you often have no better alternative for the cost of equity capital.

One answer is that you can be a pragmatist and just use the CAPM anyway. You could combine the tax-adjusted WACC formula with a cost of equity capital estimated from the CAPM:

$$\mathcal{E}(\tilde{r}_{\text{Firm}}) = w_{\text{Equity}} \cdot \mathcal{E}(\tilde{r}_{\text{Equity}}) + (1-\tau) \cdot w_{\text{Debt}} \cdot \mathcal{E}(\tilde{r}_{\text{Debt}})$$

$$\approx w_{\text{Equity}} \cdot \left\{ r_{\text{F}} + [\mathcal{E}(\tilde{r}_{\text{M}}) - r_{\text{F}}] \cdot \beta_{\text{Equity}} \right\} + (1-\tau) \cdot w_{\text{Debt}} \cdot \mathcal{E}(\tilde{r}_{\text{Debt}})$$

This use of the CAPM to estimate a cost of equity capital, $\mathcal{E}(\tilde{r}_{\text{Equity}})$, is widespread. After all, we do not have a much better model. The quality of this approximation depends on how good the CAPM is in our real and imperfect world—and it is imperfect not only with respect to corporate income taxes but also with respect to other distortions explained in the next chapter (such as personal income taxes). Users generally hope that the CAPM cost of capital reasonably reflects all these other market imperfections. For example, if Treasuries must also offer relatively higher rates of return to compensate investors for higher personal income taxes on interest receipts—say, 5% taxable instead of 3.5% tax-exempt—your firm and your CAPM risk-free parameter should use the 5%, too. Thus, the personal income tax has made it into the historical parameter estimates of your CAPM model. As a corporation, this extra compensation payable to investors is part of your cost of capital that you have to pay to your investors, too. After all, your investors also suffer this tax imperfection.

Debt cost of capital: Maybe you can use historical average excess rates of return for bonds in the same rating category.

➤ Components of expected rates of return on corporate bonds, Figure 10.1, p. 332

For the term on the right, the cost of debt capital, $\mathcal{E}(\tilde{r}_{\text{Debt}})$, practice is more varied. Again, you want to estimate your *expected* interest rate (cost of capital). Unfortunately, the CAPM may not be a good model for bond pricing. The risk premium that is the main subject of the CAPM is often modest for bonds. Instead, it is liquidity and other imperfect market premiums (also elaborated on in the next chapter) that can be quite important. You may have to be more pragmatic here. One common practice is to estimate the historical average realized spread over Treasury that was earned by bonds of similar credit ratings, and use it to adjust the interest rate that you are quoted by your bank.

Of course, you should never rely on such a *quoted* interest rate on corporate debt, either your own debt or for bonds of similar credit ratings—because doing so would ignore the default premium—even if some analysts mistakenly do so. Fortunately, if you commit this error for very large, publicly traded corporations, you are only making a modest error. They rarely default. Unfortunately, for small firms, this may not be the case.

Do not forget about the difference between expected and promised returns!

➤ Expected versus promised yields, Section 6.2C, p. 147

17.6F SOME OTHER CORPORATE TAX AVOIDANCE SCHEMES

Wall Street and Main Street employ armies of tax experts to help their clients avoid taxes, but this is really an arms race between the IRS (Congress) and investors. Investors keep looking for new tax avoidance schemes, and the IRS tries to close these new loopholes. There are a large number of both past (now closed) and current tax avoidance schemes. Some of the more noteworthy remaining tax reduction schemes are as follows:

There are too many tax avoidance schemes in existence to list in just one book. They are also changing all the time. Here are some examples.

- Sometimes, high-tax firms may be able to purchase low-tax firms, and thereby immediately use the acquired firm's existing **net operating losses (NOLs)**.

  For example, the *Financial Times* reported on February 10, 1994, that the £2.5B GKN Corporation made a hostile bid for the £300M Westland Corporation, solely because GKN needed Westland's NOLs to reduce its own corporate taxes due.

- Compared to purchasing on credit, **leasing** can be a tax-advantageous arrangement. If the borrower does not have enough income to use efficiently the interest deduction, someone else should be the official owner of the asset and "lease" it to the borrower, thereby capturing the full benefit of the interest deductibility.

- Multinational corporations can shift difficult-to-value profitable assets from a high-tax country to a low-tax country. For example, corporate income taxes in Switzerland (federal and canton) can be as low as 7.8% (for holding companies) and as high as 25%. This contrasts with state and federal corporate income tax rates as high as 45% in the United States. Now consider a company that has just developed a patent worth \$10 million per year. If the U.S. branch owns the patent, the firm would retain only $(1 - 45\%) \cdot \$10 = \$5.5$ million per year. If the Swiss branch owns the patent, the firm would retain up to $(1 - 7.8\%) \cdot \$10 \approx \$9.2$ million per year. Why stop at \$10 million? If the Swiss branch charges the U.S. branch \$20 million per year, the firm's U.S. tax obligations (resulting from profits from other businesses) would decrease by \$9 million per year ($45\% \cdot \$20$ million), but Swiss tax obligations would increase by \$1.56 million per year ($7.8\% \cdot \$20$ million). Still, this is a healthy \$7.4 million net gain per year. (Relative to a situation in which the Swiss branch would change nothing).

  This tax-efficient capital transfer can also be accomplished with capital structure. For example, if the Swiss branch lent funds to the U.S. branch at an interest rate of 36% per year, rather than 6% per year, the effect would be a reduction of the firm's tax liabilities. For every \$1,000 in excess interest paid (at the 36% instead of the 6% rate), the company would retain an extra $(45\% - 7.8\% = 37.2\%)$ \$372 in profits. Companies can play similar, but less drastic, tax games by choosing the U.S. state and municipality in which they are headquartered.

The IRS is very much aware of these issues. For example, the *Wall Street Journal* reported on June 24, 2002, that the IRS is trying to prevent firms from shifting intellectual property, such as patents, to other countries in which corporations would have fewer taxes to pay. It's a tough cat-and-mouse game.

- Many firms move their headquarters to different states or even countries (to avoid most U.S. taxes on their worldwide income altogether). Question: Where does Microsoft sell its software from? If you answered "Seattle, Washington," you are wrong. Corporate software sales are located in Nevada, where there is no corporate tax. This saves Microsoft over $50 million per year. Question: Where do you think Dell Computer is located? If you answered "Texas," you are wrong. Dell moved its worldwide headquarters to Singapore in January 2007.

Should the government prevent corporate tax avoidance?

Before such corporate tax avoidance schemes outrage you too much, you should realize that you may even benefit when tax lawyers and Congress help many U.S. companies succeed in escaping some of their tax burdens. First, corporations are just vehicles owned by investors. Corporate income taxes are ultimately paid by the investors—often small dispersed investors like you. Second, the United States has no monopoly on corporate locations. If U.S. taxes are too high, some corporations may just leave the United States; others may never come. Many financial services firms have already done so. U.S. disclosure and tax laws and regulations have built strong financial service centers in places like the Bermudas, the Cayman Islands, and Switzerland. Greenwich, Connecticut is the financial services center that the New York tax code built. See, these days, all the hedge funds have located themselves in Greenwich, a town just across the border from New York that was formerly a place for vacation homes. They did so to avoid N.Y. state and city taxes. (And, in a twist of irony, all these hedge fund managers now own vacation homes in New York City.) Many European countries have even stronger regulations than the United States, and many are in fact experiencing dramatic capital flight right now. (I do not have statistics, but I would guess that the tiny *Isle of Man* may have as many corporations today as the entire *United Kingdom* proper.) Of course, this does not mean that the U.S. system cannot be improved. The current lawyer-plus-accountant-plus-lobbying-for-legislative-pork methods are not rational and efficient ways to run an economy.

Many large firms pay almost no taxes.

Taking into account debt and other shelters, what are the tax rates that publicly traded companies ultimately pay? John Graham (from Duke University) reported that a large number of firms—but not all—are fully aware of how to manage their taxes effectively. In fiscal year 2001, about 6,000 firms had effective tax rates of 5% or less! Between 1,500 and 2,000 firms had tax rates between 5% and 30%. And about 4,000 firms had tax rates between 30% and 40%. These are, of course, *average* tax rates, and not the *marginal* tax rates that would apply to one more dollar earned. But the nature of the distribution of tax rates (at the two extremes) suggests that the marginal tax rates are probably close to the average tax rates. That is, low-tax firms would likely continue to manage paying low taxes on any extra dollar earned, while high-tax firms would likely continue to pay high taxes.

ANECDOTE Stanley Works and Foreign Domiciles

In mid-2002 Stanley Works, a 100-year-old prominent Connecticut-based global manufacturer of tools, was in the process of locating its headquarters to Bermuda. Relocating would have allowed Stanley's *foreign* subsidiaries to escape U.S. income taxes. (A U.S. corporation pays U.S. income taxes on all worldwide income. A foreign corporation pays U.S. income taxes only on its U.S. income.) In the end, unusually strong media attention, public outcries, and the threat of special legislation prevented Stanley's departure.

SOLVE NOW!

Q 17.12 A firm has expected before-tax earnings of \$20 per year forever, starting next year. The firm is in the 25% tax bracket.

(a) If the firm is financed with half debt (risk-free, at 5% per year) and half equity (at 10% per year), and this is eternally maintained, then what is its NPV?

(b) If this firm took on \$50 in debt and maintained its debt load at \$50 forever (i.e., not the 50/50 debt/equity ratio), then what would this firm's value be?

SUMMARY

This chapter covered the following major points:

- In the imperfect real world, the U.S. tax code favors debt over equity. Managers should take this corporate income tax advantage into account.
- The calculation of the income tax advantage can be done through the APV method, the tax-adjusted WACC method, or the flow-to-equity method (a full pro forma employing a financing scenario that subtracts the interest and thereafter corrects for the reduced tax burden).
- Both the APV and the WACC method begin with cash flows *as if fully equity-financed and fully taxed*, which is why they need to put back the tax advantage derived from the presence of debt.
  - APV does so by adding back the tax benefit:

$$\text{APV} = \frac{\mathcal{E}(C)}{1 + \mathcal{E}(\tilde{r}_{\text{Firm}})} + \frac{\overbrace{\mathcal{E}(\tau \cdot \overbrace{\mathcal{E}(\tilde{r}_{\text{Debt}}) \cdot \text{Debt}}^{\text{Interest Payment}})}^{\text{Tax Shield}}}{1 + \mathcal{E}(\tilde{r})}$$

  For the discount rate $\mathcal{E}(\tilde{r})$ applicable to the right term (the expected tax shelter), the following guidelines (explained in the appendix) may help: If the firm's debt ratio will decline over time, use the debt cost of capital. If it will remain constant, use the firm's overall cost of capital. If it will increase, use the equity cost of capital.

- WACC does so by lowering the cost of debt capital:

$$\text{PV} = \frac{\mathcal{E}(C)}{1 + \text{WACC}}$$

$$\text{where} \quad \text{WACC} = \mathcal{E}(\tilde{r}_{\text{Firm}}) - \tau \cdot \mathcal{E}(\tilde{r}_{\text{Debt}}) \cdot w_{\text{Debt}}$$

$$= w_{\text{Equity}} \cdot \mathcal{E}(\tilde{r}_{\text{Equity}}) + w_{\text{Debt}} \cdot \mathcal{E}(\tilde{r}_{\text{Debt}}) \cdot (1 - \tau)$$

- These methods usually arrive at similar but not exactly identical valuations. We are rarely sure about the appropriate discount rate that should be applied to the future tax benefits in the APV formula. The WACC formula cannot deal with changing costs of capital or debt ratios over time at all. However, the errors that an incorrect discount rate on the tax shield would cause are usually dwarfed by other simplifications and uncertainty in expected cash flows and discount rates.
- The one error you should never commit is to use the wrong expected cash flows. That is, never add the APV tax subsidy or lower tax-adjusted WACC cost of capital when the cash flows are not "as if fully equity-financed and after having been fully taxed."
- The following heuristic is often convenient: A constant extra dollar of debt *forever* increases the value of the firm by the firm's marginal income tax rate. For example, a \$100 eternal debt increase will create \$30 in value for a firm in the 30% marginal income tax bracket.
- In the imperfect real world, financing and investment decisions can no longer be separated: Projects that add more debt capacity may add value through the financing channel.
- In the imperfect real world, the WACC is not the marginal cost of capital.
- It is common and reasonable to combine the WACC formula or APV formula with the CAPM formula, even if this is not entirely correct.

KEY TERMS

adjusted present value, 614
APV, 614
debt capacity, 631
flow-to-equity, 623
LBO, 614
leasing, 633
leveraged buyout, 614
net operating losses, 633
NOLs, 633
WACC, 614
weighted average cost of capital, 614

SOLVE NOW! SOLUTIONS

Q 17.1 This 17% and 12% scenario is the example in the text, slightly amplified: NPV $= -\$100 + (\$117.00 - \$17.00 \cdot 30\%)/1.12 \approx -\$0.09 < 0$.

Q 17.2 For this debt/equity hybrid, the firm has to earn \$500 if the security is designated as debt with an interest payment. But if the security is designated as equity with a dividend distribution, then it would have to earn

$500/(1 − 0.33) ≈ $746, because only $500 of the $746 will be left after the firm has paid its corporate income taxes.

Q 17.3 For the $1 million construction project:

(a) With a $200,000 return, Uncle Sam would receive $200,000 · 45% = $90,000 if you pay out cash.

(b) If you finance with 80% debt, you will have $800,000 · 5% = $40,000 in interest to deduct from the $200,000 return. Thus, you would pay taxes only on $160,000. This lowers your tax bill to $160,000 · 45% = $72,000. (*Side advice:* If you borrow $800,000, you may have to invest your $800,000 elsewhere. If you do not choose tax-exempts, Uncle Sam may receive more taxes from your additional income on the $800,000.)

(c) The net subsidy is $90,000 − $72,000 = $18,000 next year. At an appropriate cost of capital of 8%, this is a PV of $18,000/1.08 ≈ $16,667.

Q 17.4 For the 25/75 debt/equity financing, the WACC valuation is

$$\text{PV} = \frac{\mathcal{E}(C)}{1 + w_{\text{Debt}} \cdot \tau \cdot \mathcal{E}(\tilde{r}_{\text{Debt}})} = \frac{\$256}{1 + 12\% - 25\% \cdot 30\% \cdot 8\%} \approx \$229.80$$

The firm has $229.80 · 25% = $57.45 of debt (and $172.35 in equity value today). Its APV is

$$\text{APV} = \frac{\$256}{1 + 12\%} + \frac{30\% \cdot 8\% \cdot \$57.45}{1 + 12\%} \approx \$229.80$$

$$\text{APV} = \frac{\mathcal{E}(C)}{1 + \mathcal{E}(\tilde{r}_{\text{Firm}})} + \frac{\tau \cdot \mathcal{E}(\tilde{r}_{\text{Debt}}) \cdot \text{Debt}}{1 + \mathcal{E}(\tilde{r}_{\text{Firm}})}$$

Q 17.5 For the $100 debt financing, the APV valuation is

$$\text{APV} = \frac{\$256}{1 + 12\%} + \frac{30\% \cdot 8.7\% \cdot \$100}{1 + 12\%} \approx \$230.90$$

$$\text{APV} = \frac{\mathcal{E}(C)}{1 + \mathcal{E}(\tilde{r}_{\text{Firm}})} + \frac{\tau \cdot \mathcal{E}(\tilde{r}_{\text{Debt}}) \cdot \text{Debt}}{1 + \mathcal{E}(\tilde{r}_{\text{Firm}})}$$

Therefore, the $100 debt is 43.3% of the firm's value today. The WACC valuation is

$$\text{PV} \approx \frac{\$256}{1 + 12\% - 43.3\% \cdot 30\% \cdot 8.7\%} \approx \$230.90$$

Q 17.6 You would prefer to use WACC if you follow a constant ratio-based debt target, and APV if you follow a dollar-based debt target. Look at the previous two questions. You cannot figure out the APV in the first question before you determine the WACC, and the opposite is true in the second question.

Q 17.7 Figure 17.1 draws the WACC as a function of the debt ratio with only corporate income tax distortions.

Q 17.8 The firm's overall cost of capital today is 6% · 1/3 + 12% · 2/3 = 10%. Because 4% + 3% · β = 10%, the beta is 2. The easy way is to recognize that the firm is sheltering $500 · 6% = $30 through interest payments. If it refinanced with $1,000, it could now shelter $1,000 · 8% = $80. Uncle Sam would see an additional $50 less in income, which means that the firm would pay $50 · 20% = $10 less in income tax *next year*. Now you need to determine the appropriate discount rate for $10 in tax savings. For convenience, use the debt cost of capital: 8%. This means that our recapitalization increases firm value by $10/1.08 ≈ $9.26. (If you prefer to use the overall firm cost of capital, you would obtain $9.09.) The question intentionally gave additional irrelevant information about the firm's future existence.

Q 17.9 This project will offer $200 before-tax profit in year 1. Discounted back at the firm's cost of capital (don't worry if this is exact), the NPV without taxes is −$300 + $500/1.2 ≈ $116.67. But, if equity-financed, the

IRS will declare taxes due on \$200 of profit, or \$80. Therefore, the NPV with taxes and all equity-financed is $-\$300 + \$420/1.2 = \$50$.

Now, right after the investment, the firm has a value of $\$420/1.2 = \$350$. With debt of \$50 (\$100), the firm carries a debt load of around $\$50/\$350 \approx 14.3\%$ (28.6%). Let's round this to 15% (30%). The cost of debt capital formula given in the question suggests that $\mathcal{E}(\tilde{r}_{\text{Debt}}) = 15\% + 15\% \cdot 5\% = 15.75\%$ (16.5%). (Note: The question is a bit ambiguous in that it does not tell you what to use as firm value. The 15% and 30% debt ratios are reasonable values, though.)

Interest payments on \$50 (\$100) at a cost of capital of 15.75% (16.5%) are \$7.88 (\$16.50) *next year*. Facing a tax rate of 40%, Uncle Sam would thereby subsidize the project to the tune of $40\% \cdot \$7.88 \approx \$3.15$ (\$6.60), which in today's value would be worth around $\$3.15/1.2 \approx \$2.63$ (\$5.50). Therefore, under APV, if financed with \$50 in debt, the project is worth $\$50 + \$2.63 = \$52.63$. (With \$100 in debt, the APV is $\$50 + \$5.50 = \$55.50$).

The equity cost of capital, if 15% of the firm is financed by debt at a rate of 15.75%, is the solution to $15\% \cdot 15.75\% + 85\% \cdot \mathcal{E}(\tilde{r}_{\text{Equity}}) = 20\% \Rightarrow \mathcal{E}(\tilde{r}_{\text{Equity}}) = 20.75\%$. Therefore, the WACC is given by the formula, $w_{\text{Equity}} \cdot \mathcal{E}(\tilde{r}_{\text{Equity}}) + w_{\text{Debt}} \cdot \mathcal{E}(\tilde{r}_{\text{Debt}}) \cdot (1-\tau) = 85\% \cdot 20.75\% + 15\% \cdot 15.75\% \cdot (1-40\%) \approx 19.06\%$. Similarly, if \$100 is borrowed, $\mathcal{E}(\tilde{r}_{\text{Equity}}) = 21.5\%$, and $\text{WACC} = w_{\text{Equity}} \cdot \mathcal{E}(\tilde{r}_{\text{Equity}}) + w_{\text{Debt}} \cdot \mathcal{E}(\tilde{r}_{\text{Debt}}) \cdot (1-\tau) = 70\% \cdot 21.5\% + 30\% \cdot 16.5\% \cdot (1-40\%) \approx 18.02\%$. The WACC-based value with \$50 in debt is thus $-\$300 + \$420/1.1906 \approx \$52.76$. (With \$100 in debt, it is $-\$300 + \$420/1.1802 \approx \$55.87$.) Note that you have made enough little assumptions and approximations that it would make little sense to worry now about being off by a little in the APV and WACC computations (\$52.76 and \$52.63).

Q 17.10 For our 3-year project firm:

(a) The pro forma for a 100% equity-financed firm is shown below.

Income Statement

		Year 1	Year 2	Year 3
	EBITDA (= Net Sales)	\$70	\$60	\$55
−	Depreciation	\$50	\$50	\$50
=	EBIT (= Operating Income)	\$20	\$10	\$5
−	Interest Expense	\$0	\$0	\$0
−	Corporate Income Tax (at 40%)	\$8	\$4	\$2
=	**Net Income**	\$12	\$6	\$3

Cash Flow Statement

		Year 1	Year 2	Year 3
	Net Income	\$12	\$6	\$3
+	Depreciation	\$50	\$50	\$50
=	**Operating Cash Flow**	**\$62**	**\$56**	**\$53**
+	Capital Expenditures	−\$150	\$0	\$0
=	**Investing Cash Flow**	**−\$150**	**0**	**0**

Economic Project Cash Flows (Operating C+ Investing C+ Interest)

	Year 1	Year 2	Year 3
Project Cash Flows	**−\$88**	**+\$56**	**+\$53**

(b) The IRR of our project solves

$$\frac{-\$88}{1+\text{IRR}} + \frac{+\$56}{(1+\text{IRR})^2} + \frac{+\$53}{(1+\text{IRR})^3} = 0$$

Thus, the IRR of a purely equity-financed project is 15.69%.

(c) The NPV of the purely equity-financed project is

$$\text{NPV} = \frac{-\$88}{1.18} + \frac{+\$56}{1.18^2} + \frac{+\$53}{1.18^3} \approx -\$2.10$$

This is in line with the fact that the project IRR of 15.69% is less than the 18% cost of capital.

(d) The cash flows would increase to −\$88, +\$58, and +\$55. The IRR would increase to 18.61%.

(e) The debt-financed pro forma would now be as follows:

Income Statement

		Year 1	Year 2	Year 3
	EBITDA (= Net Sales)	\$70	\$60	\$55
−	Depreciation	\$50	\$50	\$50
=	EBIT (= Operating Income)	\$20	\$10	\$5
−	Interest Expense	**\$0**	**\$5**	**\$5**
−	Corporate Income Tax (at 40%)	\$8	\$2	\$0
=	**Net Income**	\$12	\$3	\$0

Cash Flow Statement

		Year 1	Year 2	Year 3
	Net Income	\$12	\$3	\$0
+	Depreciation	\$50	\$50	\$50
=	**Operating Cash Flow**	**\$62**	**\$53**	**\$50**
+	Capital Expenditures	−\$150	\$0	\$0
=	**Investing Cash Flow**	**−\$150**	**0**	**0**

Economic Project Cash Flows
(Operating C + Investing C + Interest)

		Year 1	Year 2	Year 3
	Project Cash Flows	−\$150 + \$62	\$53 + \$5	\$50 + \$5
=		**−\$88**	**+\$58**	**+\$55**

The Economics of Financing

	Year 1	Year 2	Year 3
Debt Flow	+\$50	−\$5	−\$55
Equity Flow	+\$38	−\$53	\$0

Not surprisingly, these are the same as the aforementioned cash flows, with a \$2 income tax subsidy in years 2 and 3. The IRR is again 18.61%.

(f) The NPV of the debt-financed firm is

$$\text{NPV} = \frac{-\$88}{1.18} + \frac{+\$58}{1.18^2} + \frac{+\$55}{1.18^3} \approx +\$0.55$$

With the tax subsidy, this project becomes worthwhile.

(g) The APV of this project would start with the as-if-100%-equity-financed value. This was computed above as

$$\frac{-\$88}{1.18} + \frac{+\$56}{1.18^2} + \frac{+\$53}{1.18^3} = -\$2.10$$

For APV, now add the discounted tax subsidies in years 2 and 3. These have a value of

$$\text{Tax Subsidy} = \frac{\$2}{1.18^2} + \frac{\$2}{1.18^3} \approx \$2.65$$

Therefore, the APV would be $-\$2.10 + \$2.65 = \$0.55$.

(h) By APV, the expected tax subsidy would shrink from $\tau \cdot \mathcal{E}(\text{Interest Payment}) = 40\% \cdot \$5 = \$2$ per year to $\tau \cdot \mathcal{E}(\text{Interest Payment}) = 40\% \cdot \$4 = \$1.60$ per year. The expected value of the tax subsidy would therefore be

$$\text{Tax Subsidy} = \frac{\$1.60}{1.18^2} + \frac{\$1.60}{1.18^3} \approx \$2.12$$

The net project value would be about $0.02.

(i) You can see that after year 2 and before year 3, the debt is expected to be 100% of the capital structure. However, in year 1, with debt contributing $50, it is obviously not 0% of the firm. Thus, its weight in the capital structure is drastically changing. This firm is not at all a good candidate for using WACC. *P.S.: Please do not try to compute a weighted average cost of capital from the debt and equity internal rates of return (10% and 40%, respectively). If the debt would be at 57% of the firm's capital structure, then the appropriate rate of return of equity would have to be around 30% so that the weighted cost of capital would come out to* $\mathcal{E}(\tilde{r}_{\text{Firm}}) = w_{\text{Debt}} \cdot \mathcal{E}(\tilde{r}_{\text{Debt}}) + w_{\text{Equity}} \cdot \mathcal{E}(\tilde{r}_{\text{Equity}}) = 18.6\%$. *This is much lower than the equity IRR of 40% (which is the same as its expected rate of return from year 1 to year 2), because from year 2 to year 3, the equity becomes a much smaller part of the firm. What bites you in this case is the fact that you have a strong term structure of investment weights.*

Q 17.11 In 2001, with $1,691 million in taxes on $5,670 million income before the corporate income tax, Coca-Cola was in a 30% income tax bracket. The $289 million that Coca-Cola paid in interest therefore cost Uncle Sam about $86.7 million in reduced taxes.

Q 17.12 For the $20 earnings firm in the 25% tax bracket:

(a) The weighted average cost of capital (WACC) is

$$\text{WACC} = 50\% \cdot 5\% \cdot (1 - 25\%) + 50\% \cdot 10\% = 6.875\%$$

$$\text{WACC} = w_{\text{Debt}} \cdot \mathcal{E}(\tilde{r}_{\text{Debt}}) \cdot (1 - \tau) + w_{\text{Equity}} \cdot \mathcal{E}(\tilde{r}_{\text{Equity}})$$

The numerator of the NPV calculation has to be after corporate income tax; therefore, it is $(1 - 25\%) \cdot \$20 = \$15$. This is an annuity, therefore the NPV is $\text{PV} = \$15/6.875\% \approx \$218.18$.

(b) The cost of capital for a fully equity-financed firm without a tax subsidy would be 7.5%, because it had 50% debt at 5% and 50% equity at 10%. Therefore, the as-if-fully-equity-financed value is $\text{PV} = \$15/7.5\% = \$200.00$. Now, you need to add back the tax subsidy. With $50 in risk-free debt and therefore with an interest rate of 5%, the interest payments would be $\mathcal{E}(\tilde{r}_{\text{Debt}}) \cdot \text{Debt} = \$2.50$ per year. The tax savings would be $\tau \cdot \$2.50 = \$0.625$, which is an eternal cash flow. At the interest rate of 5%, the value of the tax subsidy today is $\$0.625/0.05 = \$12.50$. Therefore, the value of this firm is $\$200 + \$12.50 = \$212.50$.

PROBLEMS

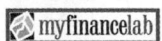

The ▇ indicates problems available in myfinancelab

Q 17.13 Assume a 20% corporate income tax. Does a project that returns 16% before-tax have a negative NPV if it costs $100 today and if the appropriate after-tax cost of capital is 11%?

Q 17.14 A firm will have before-tax cash flows of $3 million. It can invest in equally risky cash flows that earn a before-tax expected rate of return of 14%. What assumption do you have to make to allow yourself to work with before-tax present values?

Q 17.15 If there are no market imperfections except for corporate income taxes, what should the firm's optimal capital structure be?

Q 17.16 Your firm is in a 40% combined federal and state marginal income tax bracket. Your annual income is $500,000 per year for 2 years. If you finance some project with a $1,300,000 mortgage at an interest rate of 8%, how much will Uncle Sam receive? If you finance the project with cash, how much will Uncle Sam receive? If other equivalent firms are offering investors expected rates of return of 10%, what is the PV of the tax savings from financing the project with a mortgage?

Q 17.17 You can take a $1 million project. However, this kind of project is ordinary income for you, and it will produce either nothing or $3 million next year, both with equal probabilities. Assume that your taxable opportunity cost of capital is 10% and your combined tax rate is 35%. Your after-tax cost of capital is thus 6.5%.

(a) What is the project worth? Assume that you could fully use tax losses to offset other income taxed at 35%, too.
(b) How would your answer change if you could not use the tax losses elsewhere?

Q 17.18 A firm would have to invest $1 million to earn a net return of $500 million next year. The firm estimates its debt cost of capital to be $\mathcal{E}(\tilde{r}_{\text{Debt}}) = 5\% + 10\% \cdot w_{\text{Debt}}^2$. (This may be the case for different reasons covered in the next chapter.) The firm is in the 25% marginal tax bracket.

(a) If the firm is fully equity-financed, what is its value?
(b) Using APV, if the firm is financed with equal amounts of debt and equity today, what is its value?
(c) Using WACC, if the firm is financed with equal amounts of debt and equity today, what is its value?
(d) Does this firm have an optimal capital structure? If so, what is its APV and WACC?

Q 17.19 A multibillion-dollar corporation is undertaking an R&D project. It costs $1 million in R&D. Because it is risky, the appropriate cost of capital for R&D is 15%. Next year, if it succeeds (probability of 80%), the firm can build a factory for $10 million that can be financed with an $8 million mortgage, and it will earn $20 million the following year. It has no risk, so the cost of capital is only 6%.

(a) Assume taxes in the economy do not exist. What is the value of this firm?
(b) Assume there are taxes now. The firm is in the 33% tax bracket. The after-tax opportunity costs of capital are therefore 10% and 4%, respectively. The cash outflows of $1 million and $10 million are not tax deductible when they are incurred, but capital losses are fully tax deductible at the same corporate income rate. (Hint: What is the income that Uncle Sam works with in either case? What kind of effective tax credits does this mean from the perspective of the firm?) If the firm is fully equity-financed, what is the value of this project in the presence of taxes?
(c) Using APV, what is the value of this project if the factory is fully financed with risk-free debt?

Q 17.20 Construct a pro forma for the following firm: A 4-year project costs $150 in year 1 (not year 0) and produces $70 in year 1, $60 in year 2, $50 in year 3, and $40 in year 4. (All numbers are year-end.) Depreciation, both real and financial, is straight line over 4 years. Projects of this riskiness (and with this term structure of project payoffs) have a 15% taxable cost of capital. The marginal corporate income tax rate is 33%.

(a) Assume that the firm is 100% equity-financed. Construct the pro forma and compute expected project cash flows.
(b) Compute the project IRR.
(c) Compute the project NPV.

For the remaining questions, assume that the firm instead has a capital structure financing $100 with debt raised in year 1 at a 10% (expected) interest rate. Interest is paid out in each year. Principal and interest are paid out in the final year. Money in excess of interest payments is paid out as dividends.

(d) Construct the pro forma now. What is the IRR of this project?
(e) From the pro forma, what is the NPV of the debt-financed project?
(f) Compute the NPV via the APV method.
(g) Via the APV method, how much would firm value be if the firm would have taken

on not \$100, but \$40, in debt (assuming the same interest rate of 10%)?

(h) Does the debt ratio of the firm stay constant over time? Is this firm a good candidate for the WACC method?

Q 17.21 Chapter 13 Appendix on page 488 contains the financials for Coca-Cola. What were the tax shields that debt provided in 2001, 2000, and 1999?

Q 17.22 Compute the 2005 tax shield for PepsiCo, using information from Yahoo! *Finance*.

Q 17.23 Estimate how PepsiCo's value would have changed in 2003 if it had announced that it planned to take on and maintain an additional \$10 billion in debt in order to repurchase equity. Assume that corporate income taxes are the only market imperfection and that its marginal tax rate would not have been affected.

Q 17.24 Estimate how PepsiCo's value would have changed in 2003 if it had announced that it planned to increase its debt-asset target by an additional 5% and that it would use the generated funds to repurchase equity. Assume that corporate income taxes are the only market imperfection and that its marginal tax rate would not have been affected.

Q 17.25 Can you use the CAPM with the tax-adjusted WACC formula?

Q 17.26 A firm has a current debt/equity ratio of 2:3. It is worth \$10 billion, of which \$4 billion is debt. The firm's overall cost of capital is 12%, and its debt currently pays an (expected) interest rate of 5%. The firm estimates that its debt rating would deteriorate if it were to refinance to a 1:1 debt/equity ratio through a debt-for-equity exchange, so it would have to pay an expected interest rate of 5.5%. The firm is solidly in a 35% corporate income tax bracket. The firm reported net income of \$500 million. On a corporate income tax basis only, ignoring all other capital structure–related effects, what would you estimate the value consequences for this firm to be? When would equity holders reap this benefit? What would be the stock's announcement price reaction?

CHAPTER 17 APPENDIX

Advanced Material

17.7 THE DISCOUNT FACTOR ON TAX OBLIGATIONS AND TAX SHELTERS

On page 613, I stated that it is common to use the firm's cost of capital in discounting the tax shelter. Let me explain why. Start with the firm in Table 17.1. The example is rigged to make it simple. The debt is risk free. We need the equity to be risky, because we can get different appropriate discount rates only with different levels of risk. The firm's beta is assumed to be positive, so the firm's equity cost of capital exceeds its debt cost of capital. The revised scenario is in Table 17.4.

➤ Two financing scenarios, Table 17.1, p. 613

What should you use as the appropriate discount rate (cost of capital) for the future tax obligation ($24 in EF, $17.40 in DF) or for the relative tax shelter (the difference of $6.60)? Assume that the value of the firm with $280 in expected profits will be either $250 (bad) or $310 (good) with equal probability. Therefore, the $200 debt at 11% interest is risk free. Because it is constructed in this way, you know that you can use the debt's (risk-free) cost of capital of 11% for any cash flow that does not covary with the firm's outcome. And you would use a higher discount rate for any cash flow that covaries positively with the firm's outcome.

We know the future tax-related cash flows. How do you discount them? Let's work a simple example with risky payoffs.

The bottom panel in Table 17.4 shows that the income tax obligation is risky and covaries with the firm's return under either financing scenario. Uncle Sam is basically a co-owner, partaking in the good and the bad times. Consequently, you should intuitively know that you need to use a discount rate on the tax *obligation* that is higher than the risk-free rate.

The tax *payment* is as risky as the firm. Thus, it warrants a higher cost of capital than the debt cost of capital.

But what is the cost of capital for the tax *shelter*? Table 17.4 shows that the tax shelter (because of the debt) remains the same $6.60, regardless of the firm's performance. Indeed, the example was constructed so that it would be easy to see that the debt payment, and with it the tax shelter that the owners get from the presence of debt, does not depend on the firm's fortunes. The tax shelter is as safe as the firm's debt. Thus, you should use a discount rate on the tax *shelter* that is the same as the one you use on the firm's debt.

The tax *shelter* is safer than the firm. Thus, it warrants a lower cost of capital than the firm's cost of capital.

Nevertheless, it is common practice to apply the firm's cost of capital and not the debt's cost of capital to the firm's tax obligation. Is this an invitation to deliberately use incorrect discount factors in general? No, but it is a good and convenient working assumption in this particular context of discounting the tax shelter. Let me explain why.

Why use the firm's cost of capital also on the tax *shelter*?

1. In general, it is more important to get the discount rate right on larger amounts. If you wanted to get discount rates on individual component cash flows 100% right, why stop with the corporate tax shelter? Why not also determine individual discount rates for every other component of the company (taxes, depreciation, SG&A, marketing, advertising, furniture, paper clips, and so on)? This is not only impractical but also beyond anyone's capabilities. More importantly, if you want to allow yourself to use a possibly incorrect discount factor, you have to convince yourself that any added valuation precision would be very modest.

Worry more about the correct discount factor on big amounts.

TABLE 17.4 TWO FINANCING SCENARIOS FOR A RISKY 1-YEAR FIRM

Scenario EF: All-equity financing.

	$\mathcal{E}$(Value)	Bad	Good
Before-Tax Return Next Year	\$280.00	\$250.00	\$310.00
Taxable Profits Next Year	\$80.00	\$50.00	\$110.00
Corporate Income Taxes ($\tau = 30\%$) Next Year	\$24.00	\$15.00	\$33.00
Owners Will Keep Next Year	\$56.00	\$35.00	\$77.00

Scenario DF: \$200 debt today at 11% for promised repayment of \$222. The remainder is levered equity.

	$\mathcal{E}$(Value)	Bad	Good
Before-Tax Return Next Year	\$280.00	\$250.00	\$310.00
Interest Payments	\$22.00	\$22.00	\$22.00
Taxable Profits Next Year	\$58.00	\$28.00	\$88.00
Corporate Income Taxes ($\tau = 30\%$) Next Year	\$17.40	\$8.40	\$26.40
Equity Owners Will Keep Next Year	\$40.60	\$19.60	\$61.60
Equity+Debt Owners Will Keep Next Year	\$62.60	\$41.60	\$83.60

Tax Savings (scenario EF versus scenario DF):

	$\mathcal{E}$(Value)	Bad	Good	
Before-Tax Return Next Year	\$280.00	\$250.00	\$310.00	↔ Risky
Scenario 1 Corporate Income Taxes	\$24.00	\$15.00	\$33.00	↔ Risky
Scenario 2 Corporate Income Taxes	\$17.40	\$8.40	\$26.40	↔ Risky
Relative Net Tax Savings Next Year	\$6.60	\$6.60	\$6.60	↔ Safe

How big is the tax shelter relative to the cash flows? The cash flows are \$280, the debt is \$200. (This is unusually large. More typically, firms have debt ratios around 30%.) The interest paid is 11% thereof, or \$22. You need to multiply this further by your corporate income tax rate of 30% to obtain the tax shelter of \$6.60. And now your "big" question is whether to discount this by the firm's cost of capital (say, 15%) or by the firm's debt cost of capital (say, 11%). This makes the difference between \$5.95 and \$5.74, which is only 21 cents today on cash flows of \$280 next year.

Yes, you should definitely worry about the correct discount rate for the project's cash flows of \$280. Yes, the presence and amount of the tax shelter are important. Yes, it would be nice to use the correct discount factor on the tax shelter, too. But, no, it will not make much difference whether you apply the firm's cost of capital or the debt cost of capital to the tax shelter.

Most normal firms adopt a corporate debt policy that induces the tax shelter to grow when the firm grows.

2. The firm's overall cost of capital may in fact be more correct than the debt cost of capital, because the risk-free tax-shelter intuition does not easily generalize from the simple 1-period scenario to many periods. The reason is that if your firm value doubles by next year, you can probably borrow twice as much then and thus enjoy

higher tax savings henceforth. If your firm follows such an intelligent dynamic borrowing strategy, the tax shelter obtained by debt financing will not remain constant but will increase with the firm value, too. To compute the lifetime tax shelter afforded to your firm by its ability to take on more debt, you must therefore realize that intelligent capital structure policies will induce the dollar amount of debt (and thus the tax shelter) to also covary positively with firm value. This is why it is often sensible to discount the tax shelter not with the debt's cost of capital but with the firm's cost of capital (or a discount rate somewhere in between).

This is details about details—how it works.

Because this is a nerd appendix, let's go through the argument with a numerical example. Think of a firm that operates for 1 year and either doubles or disappears in the following year. It follows a dynamic debt policy so that its 1-year debt and 1-year-ahead tax shelter is always risk free. Assume the risk-free rate on the debt is 10%. Further assume the firm's expected tax shelter is \$22 next year. If it doubles, both its risk-free debt and tax shelter will double, too. If it disappears, it will have no tax shelters.

How does the dynamic aspect influence the 2-year-ahead discount rate for the tax shelter? It would be wrong to discount the stream at the risk-free rate of 11% as $\$22/1.11 + \$22/1.11^2 \approx \$37.68$. Instead, the firm's stream of tax-shelter value today is

$$\frac{\$22}{(1+11\%)} + \left[1/2 \cdot \frac{\$44}{(1+11\%)\cdot[1+\mathcal{E}(\tilde{r})]} + 1/2 \cdot \frac{\$0}{(1+11\%)\cdot[1+\mathcal{E}(\tilde{r})]}\right]$$

What is $\mathcal{E}(\tilde{r})$? Because the shelter cash flows of \$0 or \$44 depend on the firm's performance in the first period, it cannot be the risk-free rate. Instead, $\mathcal{E}(\tilde{r})$ must be related to the firm's cost of capital.

Reasonable discount rates for the tax shelter depend on the dynamic debt policy.

Figure 17.2 should help you to think about reasonable choices for the discount rate on the tax shelter. Assume that you are dealing with a typical firm, which tends to grow over time (upper-left graph).

A decreasing debt target: The upper-right graph shows a firm that plans to reduce its debt ratio over time. This is the case if a growing firm wants to retain the same absolute dollar interest payments. Such a firm would expect to save about the same dollar amount in taxes each year, regardless of firm performance. In this case, you should use some rate close to the debt cost of capital ($\mathcal{E}(\tilde{r}_{\text{Debt}})$).

A constant debt target: The lower-left graph shows a firm that plans to keep a constant debt target. (Many CFOs pay lip service to targeting constant debt ratios.) Firm growth will translate into more and more debt and thus into higher and higher dollar interest payments. Consequently, the tax shelter will grow and shrink with the value of the firm, which means that it will be exposed to about the same risk as the firm overall. In turn, this means that you should use some rate close to the firm's overall cost of capital ($\mathcal{E}(\tilde{r}_{\text{Firm}})$).

An increasing debt target: The lower-right graph shows two firms with increasing debt targets. (This kind of debt policy is rare.) The firm with the discontinuous debt target might be a typical R&D project, which will initially provide no debt capacity

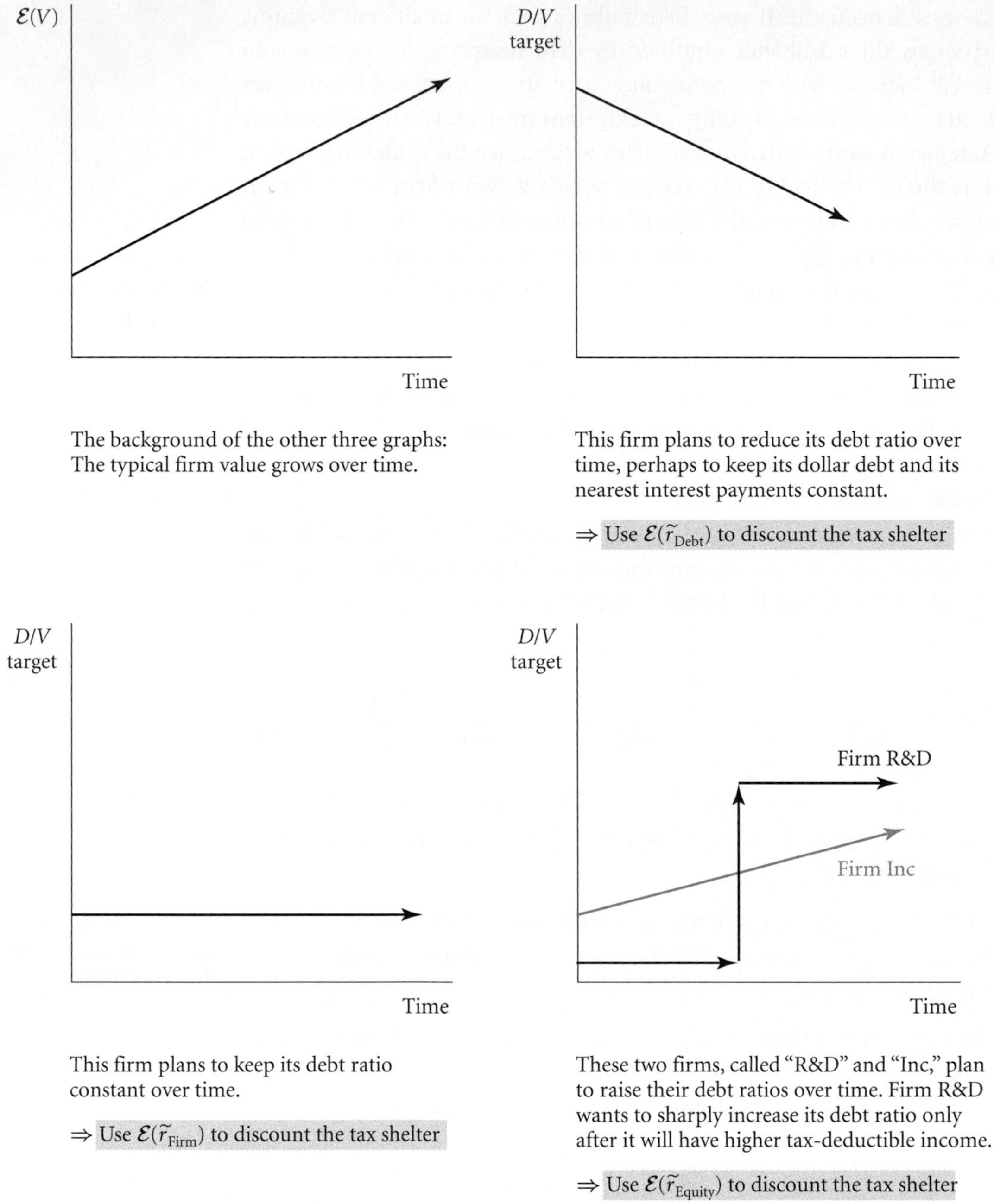

𝓔(V)
Time
The background of the other three graphs: The typical firm value grows over time.
D/V target
Time
This firm plans to reduce its debt ratio over time, perhaps to keep its dollar debt and its nearest interest payments constant.
⇒ Use 𝓔(r̃Debt) to discount the tax shelter
D/V target
Time
This firm plans to keep its debt ratio constant over time.
⇒ Use 𝓔(r̃Firm) to discount the tax shelter
D/V target
Firm R&D
Firm Inc
Time
These two firms, called "R&D" and "Inc," plan to raise their debt ratios over time. Firm R&D wants to sharply increase its debt ratio only after it will have higher tax-deductible income.
⇒ Use 𝓔(r̃Equity) to discount the tax shelter

V is the firm's value. D is the firm's debt. D/V is the firm's debt ratio.

These scenarios illustrate cases in which the firm's debt ratio changes over time, which in turn influences the discount rate that should be applied to the tax shelter. For example, if the firm wants to keep a constant debt ratio over the years, then it will have more debt and therefore a higher debt tax shelter if the firm experiences good times in the first year. This means that the value of the future tax shelter covaries positively with the firm value in the first year. It is therefore not close to risk free (as it was in our example in which the firm existed only for 1 year) but more risky (in fact, almost as risky as the firm is in its first year).

Fortunately, although it would be a first-order error to compute the wrong tax shelter, it is often a second-order error to use the wrong discount factor on the tax shelter. Yes, you should try to get it right anyway, but realize that getting other quantities right is often more important than agonizing whether you should use $\mathcal{E}(\tilde{r}_{\text{Firm}})$, $\mathcal{E}(\tilde{r}_{\text{Debt}})$, or even $\mathcal{E}(\tilde{r}_{\text{Equity}})$.

FIGURE 17.2 Thinking about Proper Discount Rates for the Tax Shelter

and thus no debt tax shelter. Thereafter, if the R&D pays off, the firm has positive cash flows and can take on debt financing. The blue continuous line is a firm that wants to become smoothly more aggressive in its debt policy over time. The values of these tax shelters are even more highly correlated with the value of the firm than if the target had been constant. Therefore, the tax shelter should be discounted even more aggressively. You should use some rate above the firm's overall cost of capital, perhaps something close to the equity cost of capital, $\mathcal{E}(\tilde{r}_{\text{Equity}})$.

It is useful to think about the appropriate discount rate on the tax shelter, but don't torture yourself to get it perfect.

In sum, I hope you are convinced that your overall project valuations will be robust with respect to moderate variations or errors in the choice of discount rate on the tax shelter. (I typically use whatever is most convenient, although I try to keep track of whether I think my assumptions overestimate or underestimate the true firm value.) You should worry primarily about the amount of the tax shelter, and only secondarily about whether the precise discount factor is the firm's cost of capital or the debt cost of capital. Please, give yourself a break!

IMPORTANT:

- The discount rates on the tax obligations and on the tax shelters are usually not exact but just reasonable and convenient approximations. The value consequences of reasonable errors are minor.
- It is common and usually reasonable to value tax *liabilities* at a discount rate equal to the firm's overall cost of capital ($\mathcal{E}(\tilde{r}_{\text{Firm}})$).
- For the tax *shelter*, assuming that the firm will grow over time, it is common and usually reasonable to do the following:
  - Use the debt cost of capital ($\mathcal{E}(\tilde{r}_{\text{Debt}})$) if the firm plans on decreasing its debt ratio.
  - Use the firm's cost of capital ($\mathcal{E}(\tilde{r}_{\text{Firm}})$) if the firm plans on keeping its debt ratio constant.
  - Use the equity cost of capital ($\mathcal{E}(\tilde{r}_{\text{Equity}})$) if the firm plans on increasing its debt ratio.

Important: Estimating the tax shelter well (the numerator) is important; estimating its cost of capital precisely (the denominator) is less important.

Do not forget that this entire discussion—that you can allow yourself some latitude on errors—applied only to the discount factor. The (expected) amount of the tax shelter itself is not unimportant. This also applies to the idiosyncratic risk in the expected tax shelter, a quantity that figures into the present-value numerator of the tax shelter, not the denominator (the discount rate). For example, an R&D project may not generate any tax shelter half the time—in which case, the expected tax shelter (in the PV numerator) to be discounted would be something like

$$\text{Expected Tax Shelter} = 50\% \cdot \left(\begin{array}{c} \text{Tax Shelter if R\&D is Successful} \\ = \text{Tax Rate} \cdot \text{Interest Paid} \end{array} \right) + 50\% \cdot \$0$$

PROBLEMS

The ▬ *indicates problems available in* myfinancelab

Q 17.27 For a firm without default, are the tax *savings* from debt a risky asset?

Q 17.28 For a firm without default, are the tax *obligations* from debt a risky asset?

Q 17.29 If you wanted to be more exact about the appropriate discount rate for the tax shelter in APV, what kind of discount rate would you apply to a firm with a decreasing debt target? What would you apply to a firm with an increasing debt target?

18

More Market Imperfections Influencing Capital Structure

PERSONAL TAXES, BANKRUPTCY COSTS, INSIDE INFORMATION, AGENCY COSTS, AND BEHAVIORAL ISSUES

As a corporate manager, you should consider corporate income taxes to be an important determinant of capital structure—but not the only one. This chapter will show that you can increase firm value and lower the firm's cost of capital if you also optimize your firm's capital structure with respect to such factors as personal income taxes, financial distress, agency considerations, and others.

18.1 WHAT MATTERS?

Investors should care only about value today.

What is really value relevant? (P/E ratios, for instance, are not.)

What could prevent a firm from taking on too much debt to minimize its corporate income tax liabilities?

Let's first think about a hypothetical firm in a Modigliani-Miller world without any market imperfections. It has \$100 in value, must earn 10%, and indeed earns exactly this \$10. Consider two capital structures:

All-equity: The firm's price/earnings ratio is \$100/\$10 = 10.

\$80 in 6% debt: With \$80 in safer debt (which therefore has a lower interest rate), 6% · \$80 = \$4.80 will go to the creditors, and \$5.20 will go to the equity. With \$20 in equity and \$5.20 in earnings, this firm's price/earnings ratio is 3.8.

Should the maintenance of a high price/earnings ratio therefore push the firm away from having debt? Obviously not. In an M&M world, structure does not matter. Therefore, whether the price/earnings ratio is 10 or 3.8 is not important. All that should matter to firm owners is value, and it is unchanged by the price/earnings ratio. Other factors that should be irrelevant to firm value include, for example, whether the debt or the equity is riskier or safer. In fact, you already know that with more debt, both debt and equity become riskier, but this need not be of any value consequence.

Look for real value-relevant causes, not incidental by-products.

Corporate income taxes alone would suggest that firms should be 100% debt-financed. To counteract this, there would have to be some value-relevant forces pulling the optimal capital structure toward equity. For example, if the firm were to get extra cash only if (and because) it is equity financed, then this would create an optimal capital structure that is not 100% debt. Any resulting changes to equity risk, earnings dilution, and all sorts of other financial ratios would be coincidental only. These changes would not in themselves effect what ultimately matters: the change in the overall value of the firm.

Owners are smart enough to care about value, not P/E.

Fortunately, the capital markets are smart enough to know what really matters—money to investors. There is good empirical evidence that financial markets indeed appreciate money—such as money that comes from lower income taxes. Investors reward managerial tax-reduction schemes with higher market values. (The cost of capital, being a measure of future cash flows relative to the value today, is often a one-to-one alternative measure of value. If an action lowers the cost of capital, it usually raises the firm's present value.)

SOLVE NOW!

Q 18.1 Is the high debt risk and equity risk when the firm has too much debt a force away from debt and toward equity? Can this higher risk counterbalance the corporate income tax benefits of debt?

18.2 THE ROLE OF PERSONAL INCOME TAXES AND CLIENTELE EFFECTS

Firms can reduce their costs of capital if they can reduce their investors' taxable personal incomes.

Let's continue where we left off. The corporate income taxes discussed in the previous chapter are just one side of what Uncle Sam receives: He also wants his share from investors' income. As a corporate manager, does this mean that you need to think about your investors' personal income taxes? Yes! In effect, your corporate owners pay both your corporate income tax and their own personal income taxes. Take an extreme hypothetical example in which personal taxes on interest are 99%, personal taxes on dividends are 0%, and corporate income taxes are 40%. As the corporate CFO, should you pay out earnings as interest or as dividends?

- You can pay out \$100 in interest payments. This means your company can avoid all corporate taxes and pay out the full \$100 from before-tax earnings as interest. As the CFO, you have sheltered *all* corporate income from taxes. Congratulations?! No—you have failed your clients. Your investors would have to pay \$99 in taxes and therefore be left with only \$1 to consume.
- You can pay out \$100 in dividend payments. This means your company has to pay \$40 in corporate taxes. Does this mean that you have failed in your job as CFO? No! Your investors would receive the dividends tax-free and therefore get to consume a full \$60.

You would have done good by your investors in choosing the equity-based capital structure, in which payments become dividends, relative to the debt-based capital structure, in which payments become interest. Even though financing with debt would have saved your firm on corporate income taxes, it would have been a terrible overall financial strategy. (As you will learn later, your investors would demand a very high cost of debt capital under this tax code, which would make you as a manager come to the conclusion that debt is not as good a method of financing as equity.)

Investor clienteles and firm clienteles play important roles.

As a CFO, you therefore need to understand how your investors' personal income taxes can influence the optimal corporate capital structure. This chapter explains that there is a subtle interplay between personal and corporate taxes, which creates both investor clienteles and firm clienteles, each with different tax profiles and different strategies, all evolved to reduce the overall tax payment to Uncle Sam. In the real world, we should see the following:

Firm clienteles: Small-growth firms should have more equity in their capital structures than large, cash-rich firms.

Investor clienteles: Highly taxed individual investors should invest more in equity-financed firms, and tax-exempt investors should invest more in bonds.

Let me show you how this works.

SOLVE NOW!

Q 18.2 Why should a CFO be concerned with taxes that he and his firm are not paying?

18.2A BACKGROUND: THE TAX CODE FOR SECURITY OWNERS

The type of income matters: Capital gains income is better than interest income for taxable investors.

➤ Introduction to taxes, Section 10.4, p. 321

First let's review our investors' tax situations. Recall that investors care about the type of income they receive:

Ordinary income is taxed at relatively high ordinary income tax rates (up to 35%), and it is very difficult to shelter from taxes.

Interest income is basically taxed like ordinary income.

Dividend income is taxed at a lower rate. If a domestic corporation has already paid taxes on its earnings, its dividends are considered "qualified," which reduces the personal tax rate imposed on the dividend recipients. Individuals in the 10% and 15% ordinary income tax brackets pay a 5% dividend tax, while individuals in higher tax brackets pay a 15% dividend tax. Giving investors credit for dividends paid from earnings that have already been taxed is similar to how the United Kingdom and many other countries have taxed dividends for a long time. However, in the United States, a lower dividend tax rate (more similar to the long-term capital gains tax rate) was instituted as recently as the Bush tax cuts of 2003.

Capital gains income is generally the most tax-advantaged form of income. Although short-term capital gains are taxed at the (high) ordinary income tax rate (where short-term usually means 1 year or less), long-term capital gains on financial securities are taxed at the same statutory rate as qualifying dividends (i.e., 15% for high-income tax investors). The tax advantage of capital gains is not limited only to its relatively low statutory tax rate, however. There are two more advantages:

Capital gains are not incurred on an annual basis, but only when they are realized. And, unlike interest or dividend income, capital gains can be offset by capital losses. Therefore, the best form of income for investors remains long-term capital gains.

We are ignoring tax code details.

This perspective is simplistic. For example, the U.S. tax code contains many special rules that can apply to certain forms of income depending on the exact payor and recipient. For example, unlike individuals, corporations as security holders still pay a 35% capital gains tax rate. Furthermore, there are some very intricate tax rules on how capital gains income and interest income on bonds must be computed. Generally, these regulations are designed to prevent firms from paying out cash in a form that counts as interest payments for them and as capital gains for their investors. In addition, there are hundreds of special clauses in the tax code—some pure corporate subsidies, some targeted at only one qualifying company, and others penalizing particular situations. The tax code is not static, either, but changes every year! And all this ignores state and sometimes local taxes, Social Security and Medicare contributions, and the like.

You must understand the logic and principles, not the specifics.

The tax treatment of financial securities and the reaction of corporations is an ongoing cat-and-mouse game. You must first learn how to think about taxes, before you learn how our specific tax code works at the moment. Any details will likely be outdated within 10 years—if not sooner.

SOLVE NOW!

Q 18.3 What kinds of income do investors like and dislike from a tax perspective?

Q 18.4 Explain the (personal and corporate) tax treatments if a company pays out its operating cash flow through interest payments, repurchased shares, or dividend payments.

18.2B THE PRINCIPLE SHOULD BE "JOINT TAX AVOIDANCE"

The owners do not care where taxes are paid (corporate or personal), just that as little as possible is paid in total.

The main point of this entire chapter is in the sketch of Figure 18.1: Managers, who want to best represent corporate owners, should consider not only their own corporate income taxes, but also other issues affecting their investors. To understand the logic, pretend that you are the sole owner of a corner shop ("the corporation") and you are also its manager. Do you care whether the IRS taxes you right at the cash register of your corporate business or taxes you personally when you move the cash from the corporate register into your own pocket? Or do you care instead about how much you can ultimately put into your pocket? The finance premise is that you care only about the money in your pocket that you have left over *after* Uncle Sam has had his dip from both. You want to reduce the net tax obligation both at the cash register (the corporate tax) and in your own pocket (the personal tax). Corporate investors are no different from your corner shop. They really should not care about the earnings of the corporation. They should only care about spendable after-tax personal income that these earnings ultimately translate into. It should not matter whether the corporation paid taxes or they themselves paid taxes.

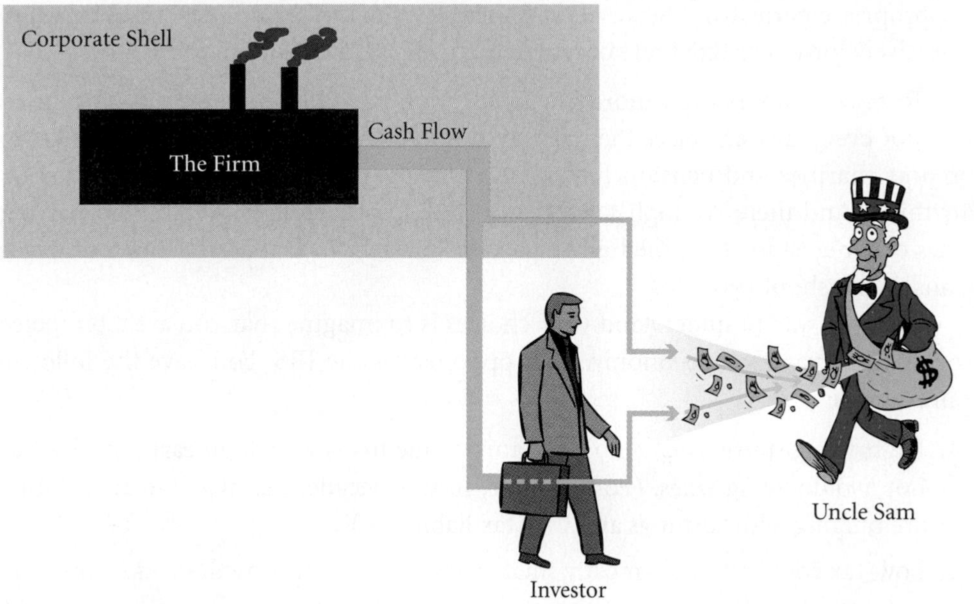

FIGURE 18.1 Illustrative Figure: Uncle Sam Gets Taxes from Two Spigots: First from the Firm, Then from the Investor

IMPORTANT:

- Both corporate and personal taxes that can be avoided translate into cash that the owners can keep.
- Reducing the total taxes ultimately collected by Uncle Sam (now and in the future) at either the corporate or the personal level can increase the value of the firm to its owners.

18.2C TAX CLIENTELES

YOUR PROBLEM: HOW CAN YOU MINIMIZE TOTAL IRS RECEIPTS?

Distributions in interest help the paying firm, but not (taxable) recipient investors. Distributions in capital gains save investors tax money, but not firms.

As a manager acting on behalf of your corporate owners, your corporate goal should be to minimize overall taxes paid, not just corporate taxes paid. You can shift tax burdens from your company to your investors (and vice versa) through your corporate financing and payout policies. Recall that your investors cannot shelter interest income, can modestly shelter dividend income, and can easily shelter capital gains income. So you face a trade-off:

- If you plan to pay out cash as interest income, you will save on your own corporate income tax—but your investors will receive cash as interest payments and thus face the full brunt of Uncle Sam. Thus, your bond investors should demand a relatively higher expected rate of return.
- If you plan to reinvest retained earnings, which means that your earnings will become capital gains for your investors, you will pay a lot more in corporate income taxes—but your investors will receive almost-untaxed capital gains instead of taxable interest. This allows them to avoid most personal income taxes. Thus, relative to the

appropriate perfect-markets rate of return, your equity investors should demand a relatively lower expected rate of return than your equivalent bond investors.

An important complication is that different investors face different personal tax rates.

To make matters even more interesting, you have to be concerned that, in real life, not every investor faces the same tax rate. There are low-tax investors, like tax-exempt charities and pension funds, who pay low or no personal income taxes on anything. And there are high-tax investors, like most retail investors, who pay high taxes on interest income, medium-high taxes on dividends, and low taxes on capital gains. What should you do?

SimCity Live: Let's arrange firms and investors to minimize tax liabilities.

The best way to understand your choices is to imagine that you are a puppeteer, controlling the private economy. Your opponent is the IRS. You have the following game pieces:

1. High-tax corporations—mostly mature value firms with high earnings that cannot avoid paying taxes. (For example, in this decade, PepsiCo and RJR Nabisco are bulging with earnings and thus tax liabilities.)
2. Low-tax corporations—mostly smaller and often high-growth firms. (You would not have heard of most of these companies, but let me give you an example, anyway. In 1985, *Itar* was a shell company that consisted of nothing except large tax-loss carryforwards on net operating losses. Therefore, any earnings it would create [e.g., after a merger with a profitable company] would not be taxed.)
3. High-tax investors—like retail investors earning over $100,000 per year.
4. Low-tax or tax-exempt investors—like pension funds or money in tax-advantaged 401K retirement accounts.

This is not a perfect classification, because even low-tax investors must eventually pay some taxes, and even low-tax corporations may run out of tax shelters (or they can immediately use up all their tax credits and thereby become high-tax companies!). But it serves us well in thinking about the problem. How would you arrange your pieces? Would you have the high-tax corporation finance itself with debt or equity? Would you have the low-tax investor own the high-tax corporation or the low-tax corporation?

Your Solution: Arrange Clienteles

Who should own what is only interesting if tax-exempt investors are not in practically unlimited supply—or else they would own everything.

Clearly, you would not face a difficult problem if 99% of all investors were tax exempt—you could make all taxed corporations issue lots of debt (and thereby avoid corporate income taxes). In this case, neither corporations nor the almost entirely tax-exempt investor sector would end up owing taxes. Corporations would not have to worry about, or compensate, their investors for their (nonexistent) personal income taxes. Corporations could offer bonds with the same yield as equivalently risky but tax-exempt entities.

In the real world, low-tax investors are not in infinite supply.

However, low-tax investors are not in unlimited supply. The NYSE's *Factbook* reports that there was $11 trillion in total equities outstanding in 2002, of which 49.8% was held by all institutional investors, 36% by retail investors, and 11% by foreign investors. Almost half of the institutional money—a total 21.5% of the equities market—were tax-exempt pension funds. Thus, tax-exempt institutions are indeed a force, although a limited one.

ANECDOTE Tax Reductions for the Needy? For-Profit Companies with No Tax Obligations

Are all cash-cow corporations in high marginal tax brackets? *The Washington Post* reported a study by the Institute on Taxation and Economic Policy that showed that 41 companies not only owed no taxes but received money back in at least 1 of the 3 years studied (1996–1998). These firms reported a total of $25.8 billion in before-tax profits. In 1998 alone, 24 companies—nearly 1 in 10 studied—received tax rebates, including such household names as Texaco, Chevron, PepsiCo, MCI WorldCom, Goodyear Tire & Rubber, and General Motors. Texaco, for example, received a tax rebate of $67.7 million, which meant that it paid taxes at a rate of negative 37.2% on the $182 million in profit it reported in 1998. In dollar terms, the study found that tax breaks enabled the companies collectively to reduce their taxes by $98 billion over the 3 years, with 25 companies receiving almost half of that amount. General Electric topped the list, with $6.9 billion in breaks, which cut its tax bill by 77% over the 3 years. A G.E. spokesman also questioned the report's methodology, noting that of the $6.9 billion in breaks cited, $2.4 billion was deferred taxes "that we will pay."

The 24 profitable companies that paid less than nothing in federal income taxes in 1998 are presented in the following table. (Profit and Tax columns are in millions.)

Company	Profit	Tax	Rate
Lyondell Chem	$80.0	−$44.0	−55.0%
Texaco	$182.0	−$67.7	−37.2%
Company	Profit	Tax	Rate
Chevron	$708.0	−$186.8	−26.4%
CSX	$386.6	−$102.1	−26.4%
Tosco	$227.4	−$46.7	−20.6%
PepsiCo	$1,583.0	−$302.0	−19.1%
Owens & Minor	$46.1	−$7.9	−17.1%
Pfizer	$1,197.6	−$197.2	−16.5%
JP Morgan	$481.1	−$62.3	−12.9%
Saks	$83.0	−$7.9	−9.5%
Goodyear	$400.7	−$33.2	−8.3%
Ryder	$227.5	−$16.4	−7.2%
Enron	$189.0	−$12.5	−6.6%
Colgate-Palmolive	$348.5	−$19.6	−5.6%
MCI WorldCom	$2,724.2	−$112.6	−4.1%
Eaton	$478.8	−$18.0	−3.8%
Weyerhaeuser	$405.0	−$9.5	−2.3%
General Motors	$952.0	−$19.0	−2.0%
El Paso Energy	$383.7	−$3.0	−0.8%
WestPoint Stevens	$142.6	−$1.2	−0.8%
MedPartners	$49.6	−$0.4	−0.7%
Phillips Petroleum	$145.0	−$1.1	−0.7%
McKesson	$234.0	−$1.0	−0.4%
Northrop Grumman	$297.7	−$1.0	−0.3%

So what is your best strategy? As master puppeteer with a limited number of tax-exempt investors, and with the task of minimizing Uncle Sam's take and maximizing your private sector take, you should sort your pieces into the following clienteles:

"Clientele effects" mean different firms attract different investors. If carried to extremes, they may prevent Uncle Sam from getting large amounts of tax revenue.

High-tax, profitable firms: Make your "cash-cow" value firms in the highest tax bracket issue debt, so that their cash flows can be paid out as interest, thereby avoiding the high corporate income tax.

High-tax, profitable firms should pay out via interest (thus, have debt).

Low-tax investors: Make your tax-exempt investors hold this corporate debt, so that the interest receipts remain untaxed at the recipient level. (If you instead made your high-tax investors hold this debt, Uncle Sam would be better off, and you and your investors would be worse off.)

Low-tax investors should hold this debt.

Uncle Sam therefore sees little cash from either of these two. You still have low-tax firms and high-tax investors to allocate. What can you do with them?

High-tax investors should hold equity.

High-tax investors: Make your high-tax individual investors hold stocks instead of bonds. They will then either receive capital gains (taxed very little) or dividends (taxed just a little more). This way, your high-tax investors will suffer only fairly low tax penalties, too.

Low-tax, unprofitable firms should pay out via share repurchases or dividends (thus, have equity).

Low-tax firms: Make your growth firms and other firms in the lowest corporate tax bracket finance themselves with equity, not with debt. You need this arrangement to satisfy the demand for equity by your high-tax investors. You can make your low-tax firms use their cash flows to reinvest in the corporation, repurchase their shares, or pay dividends. In any case, it would allow these firms' predominantly high-tax investors not to suffer much in taxes. (If you instead made your low-tax firms finance themselves with debt, the firms would have little use for the corporate income tax shelter provided by debt, at least compared to high corporate tax firms—and your high-tax investors would have no equities to buy.)

Again, Uncle Sam therefore sees little cash from either of these two.

We make up some tax rates to illustrate our best clientele allocations.

Figures 18.2 and 18.3 try to illustrate the best puppeteering choices for firms and investors—and Uncle Sam's consequent take. All the numbers and tax rates are illustrative only and not exact. For simplicity, let's assume that the world is risk neutral, so that you do not have to worry about higher costs of capital for equity than for debt. Our tax rate assumptions roughly follow the U.S. tax code:

- High-tax corporations can pay interest from before-tax earnings.
- High-tax corporations pay taxes at a rate of 40% on earnings. They can then use after-tax earnings to repurchase shares or pay dividends.
- High-tax corporations pay taxes at a rate of 20% on earnings *if the earnings are reinvested*. This is because they can designate some reinvestment as a cost of operations (advanced "maintenance") and/or because there are often investment tax credits of some form or another.
- Low-tax corporations pay one-tenth the effective corporate income tax as high-tax corporations (i.e., 4% on earnings and 2% on reinvested earnings). This reflects the fact that they may face positive tax rates in the distant future, after they have exhausted all their tax-loss carryforwards. That is, using up tax-loss carryforwards is not "free."
- High-tax investors pay a tax rate of 40% on interest receipts.
- High-tax investors pay a tax rate of 20% on dividend receipts.
- High-tax investors pay a tax rate of 10% on capital gains. This tax rate (which is lower than the dividend tax rate) sketches a situation in which capital gains are better than dividends, because capital gains can be deferred and offset by losses.
- Low-tax investors pay one-tenth the effective personal income tax as high-tax investors. This means tax rates of 4%, 2%, and 1% on interest, dividends, and capital gains, respectively. The tax rates are not zero, because not all low-tax investors are nonprofit organizations and pension funds.

Let's consider what happens if either type of firm has $100 at its disposal.

Work out the high-tax firm first.

Figure 18.2 shows that the high-tax firm can pay debt from before-tax earnings without incurring any tax penalty. Investors would receive interest, on which they would have to pay the full 40% ordinary income tax rate that is also applicable to interest income. If the firm reinvests all cash, it would manage to get some maintenance or investment tax credits, so it would face a 20% effective corporate income tax rate. Investors would therefore get $80 in the form of capital gains (a higher value of their shares). If these are high-tax investors, they suffer only a 10% income tax rate on this gain, for a net personal tax obligation of $\$80 \cdot 10\% = \$8$. If the firm instead uses the money to repurchase shares or pay dividends, it would do so from after-corporate-income-tax cash. If the firm chose to repurchase shares, investors would pay 10% capital gains tax on $60 in share repurchases (i.e., $6) and twice this on dividends ($12). If you look at the last column ("net effect"), you can see that the best arrangement here is the top line—the clientele effect we discussed earlier, in which the IRS receives only $4.

Now work out the low-tax firm.

Figure 18.3 shows the low-tax firm. It can no longer use our low-tax investors—our economy has already used them up to help high-tax firms avoid corporate income taxes (in Figure 18.2). In addition, we still need to find our high-tax investors (like most ordinary retail investors) some investment opportunities. We therefore need to consider them only. If the low-tax firm pays interest, our high-tax investors would suffer a punitive $40 interest tax. Yikes! If the low-tax firm reinvests, it must pay $2 in corporate income taxes. High-tax investors still suffer 10% as their effective personal income tax on capital gains, but this still leaves the IRS with only $11.80 and investors with $88.20. A choice that is just a little worse would be for the low-tax firm to repurchase its stock. The firm would pay a little more in corporate income tax ($4 instead of $2), and high-tax investors would still pay 10% ($9.60). Dividend payments still don't make much sense, because dividends are not as good as share repurchases for investors. (In fact, in the real world, because the low-tax firm has not paid enough in taxes, a special personal income tax rule applies, which taxes dividends at the ordinary income tax rate, instead of at the lower dividend tax rate.)

Can you do better? No.

Now put the two figures together. Our proposed solution leaves Uncle Sam with $\$4 + \$11.80 = \$15.80$ in receipts and the rest of the economy with $\$200 - \$15.80 = \$184.20$. Can you find a combination that is better? No! This is the best puppeteering that you can do!

Market Prices as Puppeteers

Extreme tax avoidance is interesting. But there is no puppeteer. Or is there?

But you are not a puppeteer, so why does any of the above matter? Is there a puppeteer in real life? Actually, there is. The puppeteer is the financial market! This is what capitalist markets are really good at—they allocate resources to their best uses, and the best use of capital here is where capital avoids paying taxes. The puppeteer's strings are the required costs of capital on debt and equity. They induce investors and firms to sort themselves to where the (tax-loss) frictions are the lowest. (If the market did not sort everything well, arbitrageurs could find a way to make money from rearranging firms and investors better to save on aggregate taxes.)

The puppeteer is the set of market prices that induce firms and investors to do the right thing.

Let me show you an example of how this might work. Let's work with the same example as before, in which $100 in before-tax cash is all that either type of firm has to decide on. However, to make it really simple, assume further that there is no uncertainty. What would happen if the financial market demanded a 10% interest rate as appropriate compensation for debt holders and a 7% capital gains rate as appropriate compensation for equity holders?

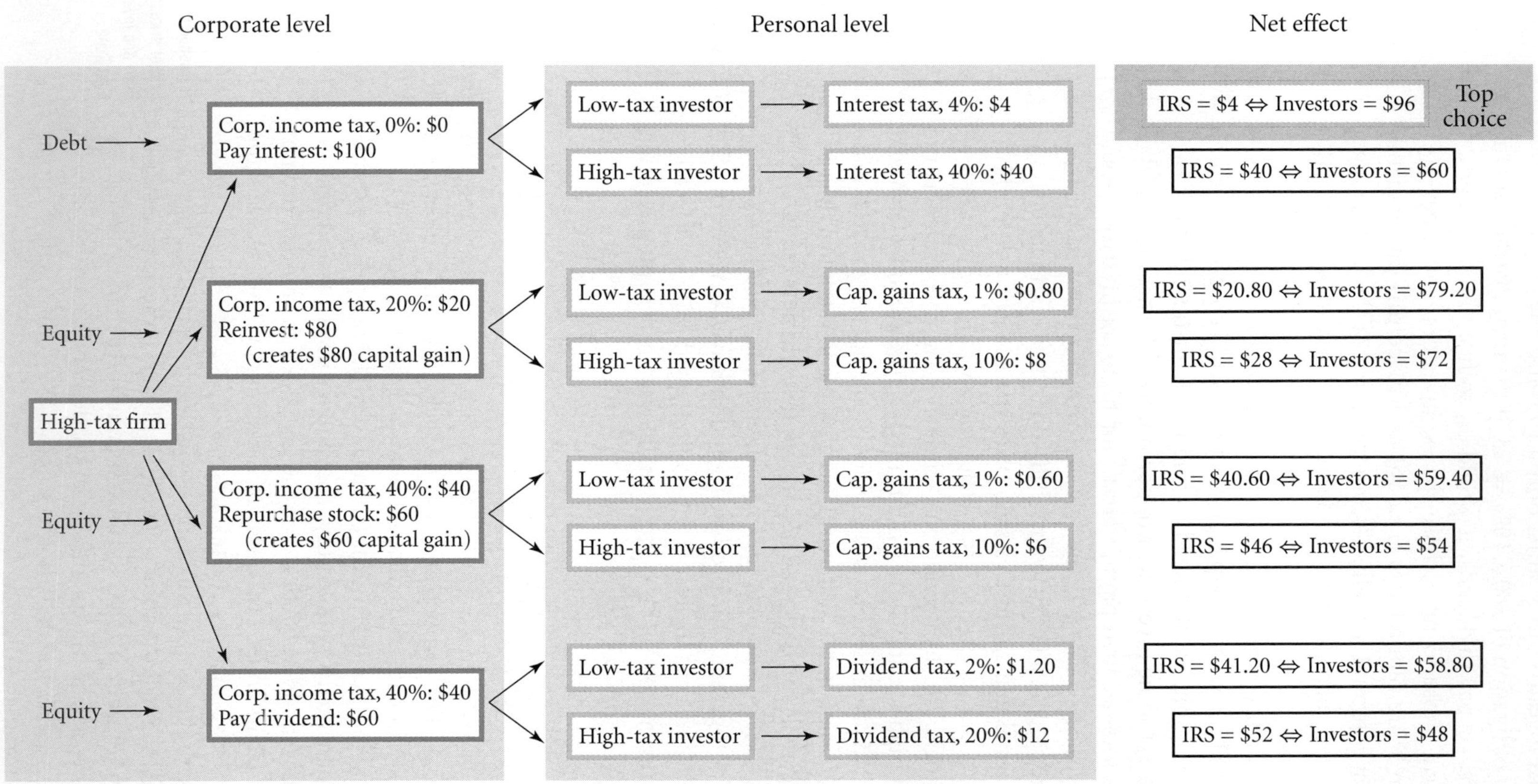

A high-tax firm may be a value firm with lots of earnings and few deductions, such as RJR Nabisco. A high-tax investor may be a typical retail investor. A low-tax investor may be a tax-exempt pension fund. The low-tax investor is assumed to have an effective tax rate that is 1/10 that of a high-tax investor.

FIGURE 18.2 Taxation Chain of a High-Tax Firm with $100 to Distribute

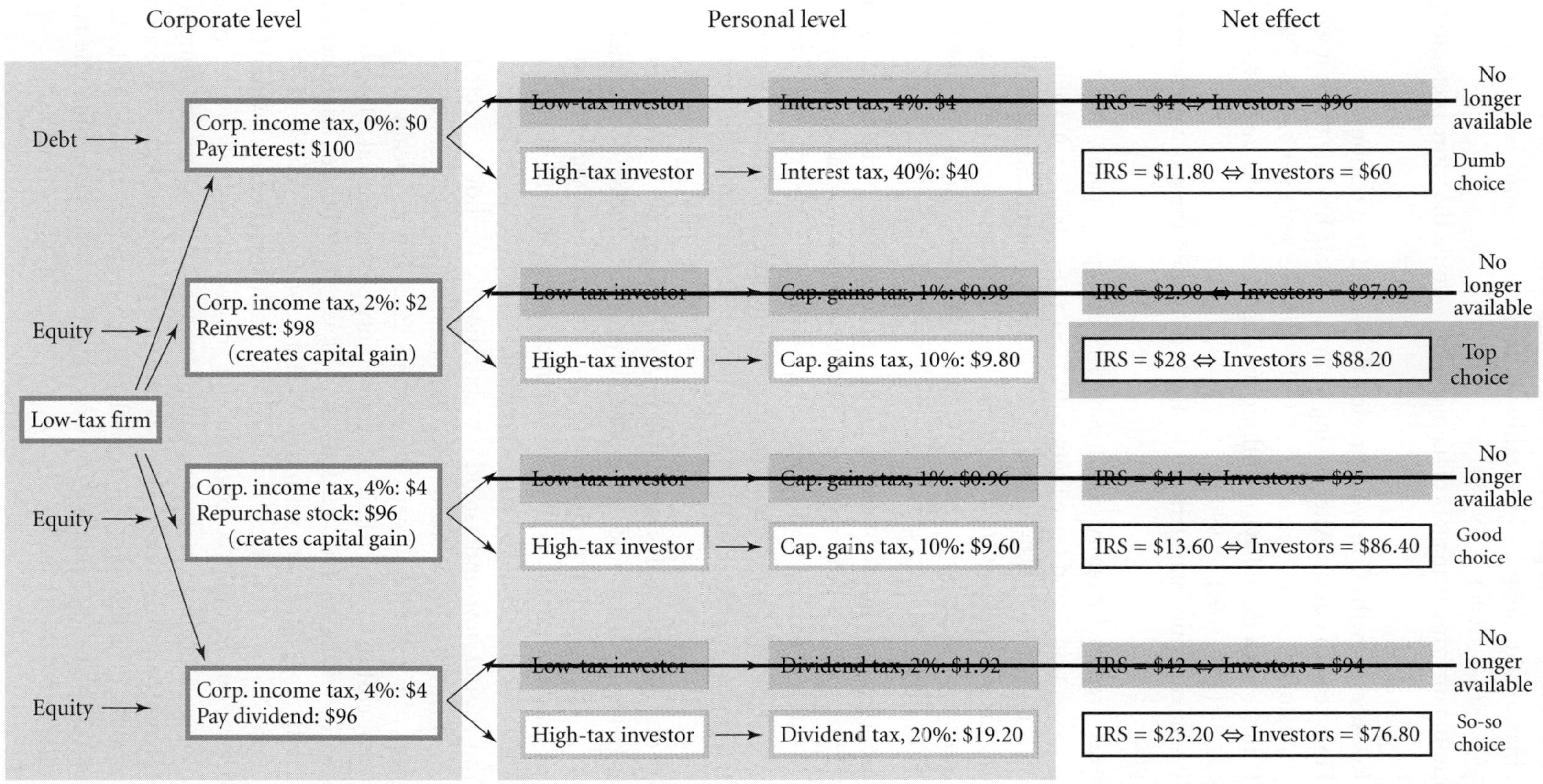

A low-tax firm may be a firm with a lot of tax-loss carryforwards or a growth firm that is unlikely to earn a profit for many years to come. The dark boxes in this figure (and "no longer available" lines) indicate that we have already used up our low-tax investors on high-tax firms, so that there are few or no low-tax investors left.

Side note: A more realistic model would recognize that the Bush tax cuts of 2003 require the firm to have paid enough in tax, so that their investors qualify for the lower personal dividend tax rate. Because the low-tax firm here has not paid enough in taxes, investors may be taxed at the full rate of 40%. This 40% tax rate on $96 in income would result in a $38.40 dividend tax, on which the $4 of corporate income tax credit is applied. This means that the investor would have to pay a true dividend tax of $34.40, not $19.20.

FIGURE 18.3 Taxation Chain of a Low-Tax Firm with $100 to Distribute when Only High-Tax Investors Remain

The high-tax (cash-cow) firm with \$100 of income would realize that it had two options:

1. **Finance with equity:** After paying \$40 in corporate income taxes, it would offer its investors a capital gain of \$60, which would be worth $\$60/(1 + 7\%) \approx \$56.07$.
2. **Finance with debt:** Paying nothing in corporate income taxes, it would be worth $\$100/(1 + 10\%) \approx \$90.91$.

Value-maximizing managers of high-tax firms would therefore prefer to finance with debt.

The low-tax (growth) firm would realize that it had two options:

1. **Finance with equity:** After paying \$2 in corporate income taxes, it would offer its investors a capital gain of \$98, which would be worth $\$98/(1 + 7\%) \approx \$91.59$.
2. **Finance with debt:** Paying nothing in corporate income taxes, it would be worth $\$100/(1 + 10\%) \approx \$90.91$.

Value-maximizing managers of low-tax firms would therefore prefer to finance with equity.

High-tax (retail) investors could earn 7% in capital gains. After 10% in capital gains taxes, this would leave them with $7\% \cdot (1 - 10\%) = 6.3\%$ in after-personal-income-tax returns. Or they could earn 10% in interest income. After 40% in interest taxes, this would leave them with 6% in after-personal-income-tax returns. They will therefore prefer to invest in the equity of low-tax firms and not in the debt of high-tax firms.

Low-tax (pension fund) investors could also earn 7% in capital gains. This would leave them with a little under 7% in after-personal-income-tax returns. Or they could earn 10% in interest income. After 4% in interest taxes, this leaves them with $10\% \cdot (1 - 4\%) = 9.6\%$ in after-personal-income-tax returns. They will therefore prefer to invest in the debt of high-tax firms and not in the equity of low-tax firms.

As you can see, every party gravitated toward the choice that was most tax efficient—just as I claimed they would. It happened because I set the before-tax yields on interest above their perfect-market equivalents, and the before-tax yields on equity below their perfect-market equivalents. If there was uncertainty, then these required yields would of course also be affected by risk premiums.

Clienteles mitigate tax effects.

You should now understand the tax rationale for how expected rates of return will sort firms and investors to minimize taxes. From your perspective as a corporate manager, the presence of personal income taxes has magically worked to increase your debt cost of capital relative to your equity cost of capital. However, relative to a nonclientele situation, clientele self-sorting has reduced the effective personal income tax penalty on debt. Clienteles mitigate your debt cost of capital.

The real world resembles this model sketch.

There is good empirical evidence that such tax-clientele ownership effects are important. For example, corporate bonds are overwhelmingly owned by tax-exempt institutions. Of course, in the real world, tax avoidance is just one (important) force at work, so the world is not as neat as our model. For instance, tax-exempt investors may want to diversify across many different companies, and not just hold exclusively the debt of high-tax, cash-cow corporations. The clientele net income tax reduction is not the only force at work.

SOLVE NOW!

Q 18.5 Would Uncle Sam be better off if our puppeteer forced the low-tax firm to be financed with debt and the high-tax firm with (share-repurchasing) equity? Refer back to Figures 18.2 and 18.3.

Q 18.6 Would Uncle Sam be better off if our puppeteer forced low-tax investors to hold equity and high-tax investors to hold debt? Refer back to Figures 18.2 and 18.3.

Q 18.7 From a tax perspective, would you expect large, stable firms to be predominantly held by pension funds or by high-tax individuals? Would you expect young, growing firms to be predominantly held by pension funds or by high-tax individuals?

Q 18.8 Is it more critical for the high-tax firm or the low-tax firm to finance itself correctly?

Q 18.9 In a risk-neutral world, would a high-tax investor be satisfied with a lower rate of return on capital gains?

18.2D HOW TO THINK ABOUT DIFFERENT TAX CODES

It is better to know how to analyze tax systems than to know just the current U.S. one.

Although this chapter has focused on the U.S. tax system, many other countries have similar tax codes, so the concepts remain universal. However, thinking about how taxes shape the optimal capital structure can help sharpen your understanding of the subject—and itself can be economically important. After all, there is no guarantee that the U.S. tax code won't be radically different in 10 years, or even that you will be working in the United States in 5 years. So let's consider the effects of two tax code changes:

1. Standing in 2002, what would you have expected the effect of the Bush tax cuts of 2003 to be? Recall that these tax changes lowered the effective tax rates on qualified dividends.
2. How should German firms behave, given that there are practically no tax-exempt investors?

How would either change your analysis?

The Effects of a Reduction in Individual Dividend Taxes—Bush 2003

The Bush dividend tax cuts would have dropped the required rate of return on equity.

From an abstract capital structure perspective, you can think of lowering the dividend tax rate as the equivalent of lowering the effective personal income tax rate on equity. For argument's sake, assume an extreme perspective:

- Your investors demand an expected after-personal-income-tax rate of return of 6%.
- Ignore the fact that even before 2003 corporations often avoided all personal income taxes on dividends by repurchasing shares or by reinvesting earnings. Instead, assume that dividend tax cuts reduced the effective taxation from 50% to 25%.

Compared to 2002, at what rates were corporations expected to be able to finance projects in 2003?

Corporations should have taken on more equity in their capital structures, because they could now pay more in dividends with less of a tax penalty.

Before 2003, your investors would have held your shares only if the expected equity rate of return was $\mathcal{E}(r_{\text{Equity}}) = 12\%$, of which they got to keep 6%. At the newly lowered personal income tax rate, they should be equally pleased to hold your equity at the lower 8% before-personal income tax rate of return, because $(1 - 25\%) \cdot 8\% = 6\%$. Consequently, from the perspective of your corporation, the necessary and appropriate equity cost of capital, $\mathcal{E}(r_{\text{Equity}})$, in the valuation formulas would have dropped from 12% to 8%. (Of course, this is a simplification. The tax cuts may also have changed the economy and with it other alternatives available to investors. They could have attracted more firms and investors into this market, too, which could have forced an appropriate equilibrium after-tax expected rate of return on equity that was not exactly 6%.) For most firms, such a drop would mean that they should shift from debt financing to equity financing—and that they should take more projects, given the now lower cost of capital.

The Effects of a Reduction in Tax-Exempt Investors—Germany

Germany has no tax-exempt investors.

Our second example of a different tax code is the situation in Germany, a country without tax-exempt investors. If the absence of such investors is the only difference, how would you advise the management of a German firm about its optimal capital structure?

From the firm's perspective, tax-exempt investors (in the United States) reduce the cost of capital on debt.

➤ Corporate tax-adjusted WACC, Formula 17.3, p. 620

First note that the WACC formula itself remains the same:

$$\text{WACC} = w_{\text{Equity}} \cdot \mathcal{E}(\tilde{r}_{\text{Equity}}) + w_{\text{Debt}} \cdot \mathcal{E}(\tilde{r}_{\text{Debt}}) \cdot (1 - \tau)$$

After all, the formula was never qualified with "only if there are at least x tax-exempt investors." But the absence of tax-exempt investors could have an influence on its inputs—most of all the cost of debt capital. The U.S. tax-clientele sorting had tax-exempt pension funds invest in corporate bonds and taxable retail investors invest in corporate stock. The presence of tax-exempt investors in the United States effectively reduced the cost of capital of debt financing. Even though the previous chapter did not say so explicitly, this was the principal reason why high-tax corporations in the United States enjoyed net tax savings by issuing bonds—why the effective corporate income tax subsidy to debt financing was so high and the cost of capital to debt was so low. Tax-exempt investors kept the cost of debt capital, $\mathcal{E}(\tilde{r}_{\text{Debt}})$—and with it $(1 - \tau) \cdot \mathcal{E}(\tilde{r}_{\text{Debt}})$—low relative to the cost of equity capital, $\mathcal{E}(\tilde{r}_{\text{Equity}})$. This favored debt financing over equity financing.

Without tax-exempt investors, it could be that the optimal tax solution is for firms to be all-equity-financed (if interest income is sufficiently badly taxed for taxable investors).

Without tax-exempt investors, financial market investors would demand a higher interest rate for corporate debt, $\mathcal{E}(\tilde{r}_{\text{Debt}})$. After all, taxable investors (which must also hold the corporate debt) care about their after-personal-tax rates of return, not their before-personal-tax rates of return. Investors would suffer especially high personal income taxes if they held corporate debt. Thus, they would demand a relatively higher $\mathcal{E}(\tilde{r}_{\text{Debt}})$. The result is that the overall corporate WACC in Germany, unlike in the United States, may not decline with w_{Debt}. It may even be that $\mathcal{E}(\tilde{r}_{\text{Debt}}) \cdot (1 - \tau)$ is higher than $\mathcal{E}(\tilde{r}_{\text{Equity}})$ for even low corporate debt levels. Though algebraically correct, the tax-advantaged WACC formula would now be unimportant: The minimum WACC could even occur at a $w_{\text{Equity}} = 1$ if investors' personal taxes on received interest income are higher than the tax deductions that firms receive on paid interest.

Thinking more broadly about foreign tax codes, what should matter for the optimal capital structure is the relative effective tax rate of investors and corporations.

Our tax-shifting SimCity arrangements now depend more on the relative taxes that investors versus corporations would have to pay.

- If the effective tax rate is higher for individuals than it is for corporations, then the better tax arrangement is for corporations to pay the taxes—there would be no net tax advantage to debt. Corporate debt would not be subsidized, but rather penalized by the foreign tax code. Firms should be financed with equity, which allows investors to avoid tax liabilities.
- If the effective tax rate is higher for corporations than it is for individuals, then the better tax arrangement is for the investors to pay the taxes—there would be a net tax advantage to debt. Firms should now be financed heavily with debt, which forces the tax liability onto investors. This is conceptually similar to the U.S. solution, with a U.S.-style WACC formula, except that $\mathcal{E}(\tilde{r}_{\text{Debt}})$ could be fairly high.

Debt versus equity is still a mechanism to shift the tax liability, and low-tax firms should still finance with more equity than high-tax firms should.

However, even if corporate taxes are high and personal taxes are low, one feature of the U.S. situation would likely survive in other countries. Companies are heterogeneous, and debt remains a mechanism to shift tax liabilities from the firm to investors. Thus, there would still be some low-tax firms and some high-tax firms. Low-tax firms would find that their optimal capital structure would still be primarily equity, because they would not gain anything from the tax deductibility of interest. In contrast, high-tax firms would have to decide to finance with either debt or equity, and this decision would depend on their own marginal corporate income tax rates relative to the investors' marginal personal income tax rates. Their managers would obtain this information by looking at the relative costs of debt and equity financing offered to them in the financial markets. In sum, low-tax firms would want to keep the tax liability (by remaining equity-financed) rather than hand the tax liability to their investors. We cannot say what the optimal choice of high-tax firms would be. If the corporate income tax rate is lower than the personal income tax rate, then even high-tax firms may want to finance themselves with equity.

SOLVE NOW!

Q 18.10 In Atlantis, all firms are tax exempt. Only investors pay income taxes. How should firms be financed? How would the WACC formula work?

18.3 OPERATING POLICY: BEHAVIOR IN BAD TIMES (FINANCIAL DISTRESS)

Personal income taxes are not the only reason why firms should limit their indebtedness, despite all the saved corporate income taxes. Too much debt can make it more likely that a firm will not be able to meet its repayment obligations and go bankrupt—creating a whole new can of worms. This means that firms may limit the amount of debt that they take on for these reasons, too.

TABLE 18.1 ILLUSTRATION OF DEADWEIGHT COSTS IN FINANCIAL DISTRESS

		Bad Luck	Good Luck		
	Prob:	1/2	1/2	Expected Value	PV(r = 10%)
Project	Firm	\$60	\$160	\$110	\$100
	Capital Structure LD: Bond with Face Value \$55				
Bond	Debt	\$55	\$55	\$55	\$50
Equity	Equity	\$5	\$105	\$55	\$50
Capital Structure MD: Bond with Face Value \$94 and \$10 Deadweight Costs When in Distress					
		Distressed State			
Bond	Debt	\$60 − \$10 = \$50	\$94	\$77 − \$5 = \$72	\$70 − \$4.55 = \$65.45
Equity	Equity	\$0	\$66	\$33	\$30

The cost of capital in this example is 10% for all securities, which is equivalent to assuming risk neutrality. Capital structure MD faces \$10 financial distress costs in the bad luck state.

18.3A THE TRADE-OFF IN THE PRESENCE OF FINANCIAL DISTRESS COSTS

Start with the perfect-market example from Table 16.1 on page 580.

A firm that has debt in its capital structure is more likely to experience financial distress or even go bankrupt. Table 18.1 shows how such financial distress can matter. If the firm has less debt, as in capital structure LD with its face value of \$55, the firm can always fully meet its debt obligations. Consequently, we assume that it will not experience financial distress, and our LD scenario still matches our perfect world from Table 16.1. However, if the firm has more debt, as in capital structure MD with its face value of \$94, the firm may not pay creditors all it has promised. If the world were perfect, as it had been in Table 16.1, this bankruptcy condition would merely change the payoff pattern. Everyone (including bondholders) would have known that the firm would be transferred to bondholders, who would liquidate a full \$60. The firm value would not be impacted by the financial distress and would therefore still be \$100.

➤ Perfect-world house payoffs, Table 16.1, p. 580

Deadweight distress costs can make low-debt structures better.

However, bankruptcy matters if we introduce deadweight losses—such as legal fees—that are triggered in financial distress. In the lower part of Table 18.1, we assume that these deadweight bankruptcy costs amount to \$10. How does this matter?

- If you choose LD, you would borrow \$50 and promise \$55. Your cost of capital would be 10%. Your firm value would be \$100 today.
- If you choose MD, you would borrow \$65.45 and promise \$94, for an interest rate of 43.6%. The expected rate of return to creditors would not change—it would still be 10%. (Every investment has to offer 10% in our risk-neutral world.) However, the deadweight bankruptcy cost increases *your* cost of capital. You are giving up what *should have been* \$60 or \$94 (because it is now only an expected value of \$77) in exchange for a payment of \$65.45. Thus, you could sell your firm only for \$65.45 + \$30 = \$95.45, not for \$50 + \$50 = \$100. Relative to its potential of \$110, your cost of capital would have increased from \$110/\$100 − 1 = 10% to \$110/\$95.45 − 1 ≈ 15.2%!

From your perspective, capital structure MD is worse than capital structure LD, in which the firm could never go bankrupt. The important insight with respect to bankruptcy is that it is not bankruptcy per se that is the problem, but only the deadweight losses in and around financial distress that matter.

Who ultimately bears the cost of bankruptcy—you as the entrepreneur selling the firm, or the creditors providing capital? It would be you, because creditors demand fair compensation up front. How would you want to structure your firm if you face both taxes and bankruptcy losses? You should now try to reduce not only the deadweight loss from taxes but also the deadweight losses from financial distress:

Owners may trade off debt's expected tax savings against its deadweight bankruptcy cost increases.

- Too little debt, and you lose too much in taxes.
- Too much debt, and you lose too much in bankruptcy costs.

Therefore, an amount of debt not too high and not too low maximizes the value of your firm today.

The rest of this section describes other forms of deadweight losses in financial distress. These deadweight losses can be more important than any legal fees in formal bankruptcy. For example:

Deadweight distress costs can come in various forms.

1. The firm may have to spend money to avoid formal bankruptcy.
2. Fear of bankruptcy may prevent the firm from taking a positive-NPV project. If the firm does not take otherwise optimal NPV projects, this would count as a deadweight loss.
3. Concern about bankruptcy may lead customers and suppliers to demand different terms.

The latter two issues are often called **indirect bankruptcy costs**, because they do not involve direct cash outlays. In any case, it does not matter whether the deadweight costs are direct or indirect. They all have the same effect in the end—they increase the firm's cost of capital and decrease the firm's value today. Note that the financial distress itself never needs to actually occur—the probability that it may occur in the future is enough to reduce the firm value today. The higher the probability of financial distress, the higher the costs.

IMPORTANT: Financial distress costs usually favor equity over debt as a cheaper financing vehicle.

SOLVE NOW!

Q 18.11 Do deadweight bankruptcy costs favor debt or equity? Why?

18.3B DIRECT LOSSES OF FIRM VALUE

THE PROCESS

Although the process and history of bankruptcy, both in the United States and worldwide, are fascinating, the full legal details of bankruptcy are beyond the scope of this book. In the United States, there are two legal forms of bankruptcy: **Chapter 7 liquidation** and **Chapter 11 reorganization**. Larger firms almost always petition to enter

Chapter 7 liquidation and Chapter 11 reorganization. Firm owners internalize creditor costs.

Chapter 11 (not Chapter 7), which gives them a stay from creditors trying to seize their vital assets. If the court determines that the business is still viable, the firm can reorganize its financial claims and emerge from bankruptcy if its creditors vote to agree to the reorganization. Otherwise, the case is converted into Chapter 7 and the firm is liquidated. Both forms are supervised by a federal judge (and/or a federal bankruptcy trustee) and last on average about 2–3 years. In real life, creditors in Chapter 11 sometimes agree to modest violations from the absolute priority rule —which we have always used to construct our state-contingent tables—in order to reduce running bankruptcy costs. The firm typically has to pay for most of the legal fees of all creditor classes—but even if it does not, creditors will ask for compensation for their expected legal fees up front. In one way or another, the firm's owners today have to carry the expected costs of bankruptcy in the future.

➤ Absolute priority rule, Section 15.2A, p. 545

Direct and Indirect Costs

Direct legal and administrative bankruptcy costs are easily visible. But bankruptcy also has non-cash-outlay costs.

The direct fees—the legal fees that the bankruptcy process consumes—are just the most obvious costs. There are also hours spent by management, employees, and experts to deal with the running process. But much of the cost of financial distress is indirect and on the real business side. For example, it may become more expensive to produce (e.g., because suppliers may charge more, fearing delayed or no payment), more difficult to focus (e.g., management may become distracted with bankruptcy and talented employees may leave), more expensive to sell products (e.g., customers may flee due to loss of confidence), and more expensive to sell assets (e.g., liquidation sales may mean low fire-auction prices). All these costs reduce the value of the firm, and they are real welfare losses caused by financial distress. These costs can also arise even before formal bankruptcy. Many of these costs originate from the fact that firms can shed promised claims in bankruptcy, even if they would like to commit themselves today (ex-ante) to not shedding them in the future. This inability to commit causes a loss of value when future distress is possible. Consider the following examples:

If a computer firm could disappear, customers become unwilling to purchase its computers—making this a self-fulfilling prophecy.

- **When products require customer investments, customers may be reluctant to purchase the products and invest, knowing that their investments could turn out to be wasted if the firm were to disappear.** For example, the value of a computer is determined not only by its hardware but also by the manufacturer's continued provision of hardware and software support and development. End-of-life hardware or software, no matter how good, is often close to worthless. Even if the firm promises to continue development of faster hardware to preserve its customers' software investments, if the firm is liquidated, it would not be able to keep such a promise. The inability of the firm to commit to honoring its promises in the future hurts its sales to customers today—and may even cause the bankruptcy itself.
- **When product sales require promises of future contact, customers may be reluctant to purchase the product, given that the future promised rebate may fail to materialize.** For example, airlines depend on frequent flier plans to attract business travelers. When the promise of future free flights loses its credibility, an airline becomes severely handicapped. In effect, any firm whose products require warranties should weigh whether issuing debt might not alarm its customers. Such products

may require future service, and customers may be reluctant to purchase the product, knowing that the service may become unobtainable in the future.

- **When product quality is difficult to judge, customers become afraid that companies may cut corners in order to avoid financial distress.** Have you ever wondered whether an airline in financial distress cuts corners on airplane maintenance? (You should next time you are booking a ticket!) The capital structure influence here is not that maintenance would be cheaper but rather the fear of customers that the firm may cut corners. Consequently, the price at which such an airline can sell tickets may be below that of a financially solid airline. Similarly, wholesalers will not deliver their goods to near-bankrupt retailers unless they are assured of payment. Because bankrupt retailers may no longer be able to purchase credit, the costs of their goods may increase—and their competitive advantage may erode.

Without trustworthy warranty programs, competing in some businesses is very difficult.

- **If suppliers fear that the retailer can go bankrupt, they may not extend trade credit.** Some businesses rely on **trade credit**, in which suppliers sell their goods to buyers in an open credit arrangement. (It is in effect a credit line that is limited to the specific goods the supplier sells.) In some cases, not having access to trade credit can hamper business operations to the point where it can itself cause the onset of bankruptcy.

➤ Trade credit, Section 16.6, p. 600

- **If buyers fear that the seller cannot provide service once bankrupt, they may not buy any goods to begin with.** When Aloha and ATA Airlines went bankrupt in early 2008, customers who believed they had purchased flights instead ended up owning only worthless pieces of paper. Even passengers who had already flown to their destination found themselves stranded without a return ticket. While this may not have been bad for Aloha and ATA (essentially owning passenger money without having had to provide service), many other airlines now face far more skeptical customers. Smaller airlines with more debt that are more likely to go bankrupt now may find customers hard to come by—and therefore go bankrupt.

Financial Distress Costs as Transaction Costs?

But there is a limit to the importance of bankruptcy costs. We can muster an argument similar in spirit to the M&M proof: If financial distress costs are too high, you could purchase all debt and equity—an action that would immediately eliminate any financial distress costs caused by too much debt. You would own an entire firm that suffers no more debt-caused distress costs. In the real world, if the transaction costs to purchase all securities are an extra $100, it must be that the value reduction caused by the financial distress costs is less than $100. Otherwise, you and every other arbitrageur around would clamor to take over the firm.

One upper limit to the importance of financial distress costs is the cost of turning debt back into equity.

So, how much extra (above the true value) could it possibly cost an arbitrageur to purchase all securities? Remarkably, this could be more than just the normal financial transaction costs. The reason is a **holdout** problem. Put yourself in the shoes of a single bondholder. Let's assume your bond promised to pay $100, but the firm is now worth so little that your bond is worth only $50. Some arbitrageur has just offered you and every other bondholder a buyout for $55. Would you take this offer? You would if you held all the bonds. But if you are just a small bondholder among many, you could refuse to sell, hoping that the arbitrageur will be so exasperated that he will offer you the $100 just to get rid of you. The extra $45 won't make or break the

Buying back debt and issuing equity should be cheap, but creditor holdout problems could imply that they are not.

ANECDOTE Fear and Relief

Here are some real-world examples of how companies in financial distress lose customers because they are in financial distress, which worsens their financial distress—a self-fulfilling prophecy. A capital structure with more equity and less debt would often have avoided such problems in the first place.

First, here is an example in which actual financial distress has reduced the value of the underlying operations. On March 3, 2008, the *Associated Press* reported how gift cards had become worthless when The Sharper Image filed for bankruptcy. The gift card business was among its most profitable operations, constituting about $32 million of outstanding credit. How many customers do you believe will buy gift cards from The Sharper Image in the future? One customer noted, "With the uncertainty today, I didn't want my aunt's gift to be only a card."

Second, here is an example in which merely the fear of financial distress has led to the de facto collapse of the entire firm. On Thursday, March 13, 2008, the 85-year-old Bear Stearns investment bank closed at $57.07 per share, a market value of about $8 billion. Half an hour after Friday's stock market opening, rumors emerged that some of Bear Stearns' sources of short-term capital were drying up. (These are the equivalent of suppliers in the financial services industry.) As a consequence, Bear Stearns had trouble not only finding other short-term capital suppliers but also in executing financial trades with counterparties (the equivalent of customers). Both suppliers and customers feared that Bear Stearns could go bankrupt. Bear Stearns' stock price fell to $31.54—a level that it maintained for the rest of Friday. However, these developments caused even more short-term capital providers and trading counterparties to jump ship. Over the weekend, the same withdrawal dynamic continued, and on Saturday morning, the Federal Reserve coopted JP Morgan for a bailout of Bear Stearns. JP Morgan announced that it had agreed to acquire Bear Stearns for—hold on to your hat—$2 per share. This is an extreme example of how a "run on the bank" can become self-fulfilling. Chances are that both suppliers and customers would not have jumped ship if they had not feared other suppliers and customers jumping ship. A capital structure with less debt, more equity, and more cash would have prevented this meltdown.

offer, and your continued presence as a creditor (e.g., in the courts) could make the arbitrageur's life a nightmare. Unfortunately, every other little creditor would realize this, too, and would prefer to hold out and be bought off. Given such bargaining complications, the transaction costs of acquiring all the debt could be very high, which means the firm may end up running down the rest of its true economic value rather than being efficiently reorganized. (One justification for the U.S. Chapter 11 reorganization procedure is that it allows a judge to force all creditors to participate and thus eliminates the holdout problem.)

If all creditors are in the same creditor class and own equity, too, they would not hold out.

➤ Unit securities, Section 15.2A, p. 550

One attempt to reduce the transaction cost is for firms to bundle their financial claims into **units** (unit securities) of debt and equity. Each creditor would also be a shareholder. If the firm fails to pay interest in the future, creditors would be more inclined to compromise in order to avoid financial distress—after all, there is little reason to force bankruptcy in order to collect assets from oneself.

Assessing the Magnitude of Direct Bankruptcy Costs

For most Fortune 500 companies, expected financial distress costs are small.

In small firms, future financial distress is always a possibility, and legal fees can quickly consume their assets. Managers of such firms need to be careful not to take on too many liabilities. But what about the average Fortune 500 company? What would be a good estimate for its expected direct bankruptcy costs? We can do some back-of-the-envelope calculations. Say you run a typical healthy Fortune 500 company today, worth $10 billion. Fewer than five Fortune 500 companies enter financial distress (either formal or informal) in a given year. Quadruple this number to get an estimate of 4% probability of bankruptcy at the outset of the year. To be among them, your company would have to drop by, say, about 70% of its market value. In other words, it is unlikely for you to run into real distress unless your firm value dropped to about $3 billion. (Year-to-year changes of plus or minus 30% [$3 billion] are common occurrences.) Finally, let's estimate the deadweight financial distress losses if you run into trouble. Assume that your bankruptcy costs would be 5% of the value of your distressed Fortune 500 company *when you enter bankruptcy*. Again quadruple this number to assume a 20% distress cost. For example, say you run a $10 billion company today. Say it has a 4% chance to drop to $3 billion in value, setting off financial distress and legal costs amounting to 20% · $3 billion = $600 million in distress costs. (Yes, $600 million in distress costs is a lot of money for bankruptcy lawyers to fight over *if* your firm goes bankrupt.) Yet, in expectation today, for your $10 billion firm this is only

$$4\% \quad \cdot \quad 30\% \quad \cdot \quad 20\% \quad = \quad 24 \text{ basis points}$$

$$\text{Distress Probability} \cdot \text{Value if Distressed} \cdot \text{Deadweight Loss} = \textit{High Expected Distress Costs Estimate}$$

or $24 million. This is not a whole lot when compared to the potential tax savings of debt if you are currently a healthy $10 billion firm in the 35% tax bracket and you are thinking about taking another loan. In sum, for the average healthy Fortune 500 firm today, bankruptcy costs do not seem large enough to prevent them from taking on more debt.

The fact that some firms used to go bankrupt "regularly" suggests that they had relatively low bankruptcy costs.

This argument does not, of course, apply to each and every firm. Which firms are likely to suffer high deadweight losses in bankruptcy? We know that many U.S. railroads have declared bankruptcy dozens of times, without interruption in service. Even large retailers, like Federated Department Stores (Macy's and Bloomingdales), have been in and out of bankruptcy several times. Airlines have some easily transferable and collaterizable assets (airplanes) and thus may have fewer deadweight losses—many airlines have ceased operations with their planes sold, repainted, and turned around for another carrier. Airlines' bankruptcy deadweight losses may be bearable. In contrast, firms with mostly intangible assets (such as reputation or name recognition) need to be more concerned with reducing the probability of future bankruptcy. For example, if Chanel were to go bankrupt, Chanel No. 5 might acquire the odor of death, rather than the odor of high style, and the entire business might disappear. Chanel should therefore choose a capital structure that is not too liability-heavy in order to avoid the loss of prestige that a bankruptcy could bring about.

In sum, expected bankruptcy costs are probably small for healthy, large companies.

The importance of bankruptcy costs as an important determinant of capital structure remains an empirical issue. The current academic consensus is that bankruptcy costs matter for some firms and some industries, particularly during recessions. They can easily be very large, but for most healthy Fortune 500 firms, the expected deadweight costs are probably small—some exceptions notwithstanding. (P.S. The Fortune 500 firms Enron and Arthur Andersen did not go bankrupt because they had too much debt.)

SOLVE NOW!

Q 18.12 What do U.S. managers usually mean by Chapter 11 and Chapter 7?

Q 18.13 Give examples of bankruptcy costs. Distinguish between direct and indirect costs.

18.3C OPERATIONAL DISTORTIONS OF INCENTIVES

A second set of financial distress costs arises from the fact that shareholders' incentives diverge from bondholders' incentives if the firm gets close to financial distress.

UNDERINVESTMENT

When there is more debt than assets, equity holders may not take proper care of the assets.

The **underinvestment** problem is the bondholder concern that managers will not make necessary investments if the promised debt payments end up being too large. That is, owners may prefer to pay out cash to shareholders rather than spend their money on maintenance and repair (or other projects). This may be in their interest if the project proceeds would more than likely go to bondholders than to themselves. Ex-ante, underinvestment reduces the payoffs bondholders expect to receive, which increases the price at which bond purchasers would be willing to lend money to the firm today.

Would "underwater" shareholders want to take all profitable projects?

For example, assume a firm has only \$50 in cash and no projects. Worse, it owes creditors a promised \$100 in a couple of years. Fortunately for the shareholders, in our simple example, the firm can pay \$50 in dividends and leave the bondholders with nothing. Yet, suddenly, managers find an unexpected opportunity. They can pay the \$50 to start a project that will yield either \$60 or \$160 by the time the debt is due. The firm should undertake this project, because it is a positive-NPV project. But would managers acting in the interest of shareholders be willing to do so?

Ex-ante, entrepreneurs internalize the cost of future inefficient behavior.

Table 18.2 shows that the answer is no. Managers would prefer to pay out \$50 to shareholders rather than take this positive-NPV project. Most of the benefit of the project would go to cover the "debt overhang," which is something that managers who act on behalf of shareholders would not care much about. Again, this "underinvestment problem" is a cost of debt to the firm. If the firm had chosen a zero-debt capital structure ex-ante, such profitable future investments would not be ignored, which in turn would increase the value at which our hypothetical owner can sell the firm today.

IMPORTANT: Ex-post reluctance to do the right thing (such as additional maintenance investment) favors equity over debt as the cheaper financing vehicle.

RELUCTANCE TO LIQUIDATE

Managers may not want to liquidate the firm, even if they should. If the firm is underwater, this can even hurt creditors.

A similar problem is **reluctance to liquidate**. Managers acting on behalf of equity holders may not always wish to liquidate the firm when it has fallen onto hard times, even if doing so would maximize firm value. Equity holders always prefer more risky payoffs because equity is essentially like an option. If there is even a small chance of improvement and even if deterioration is more likely, equity holders are better off to take their chances than to give up their options and liquidate. For example, assume

TABLE 18.2 ILLUSTRATION OF UNDERINVESTMENT DISTORTIONS

Initial condition: The firm has $50 in cash, no projects, but has an outstanding bond with a $100 face value. It pays out $50 in cash to shareholders and waits.

	Prob:	1/2	1/2	Expected Value	PV(r = 10%)
Project	Firm	$0	$0	$0	$0
Bond	Debt	$0	$0	$0	$0
Equity	After $50 dividend payout today	$0	$0	$0	$0

New development: A positive-NPV project comes along that costs $50 and pays either $60 or $160.

Managerial choice #1: Pay $50 to shareholders today. Default on the debt that comes due in the future.

Managerial choice #2: Use the firm's $50 to take the project today. When the project finishes, the debt obligation with $100 face value is due, which the firm must then honor.

	Prob:	1/2	1/2	Expected Value	PV(r = 10%)
Project	Firm	$60	$160	$110	$100
Bond	Debt	$60	$100	$80	$72.73
Equity	Equity	$0	$60	$30	$27.27

This firm is considering a positive-NPV project, which it should take. The management is assumed to act on behalf of shareholders, and not on behalf of the overall firm. The cost of capital in this example is 10% for all securities. Will the managers take this project?

that the $60 represents the liquidation value of the factory, and the MD debt is due in 2 years rather than in 1 year. Further, assume that managers can continue running the factory, in which case it will be worth either $100 or $0 with equal probability. The optimal unconflicted behavior would be to liquidate the factory. Unfortunately, shareholders prefer to continue operating—they would get nothing in liquidation, but perhaps $6 if the factory were to be worth $100. In effect, equity holders have an option on the firm. They would often even make running interest and principal payments in order to keep their option alive! This inefficient behavior, caused by the presence of debt in the capital structure, reduces the value of a firm with both debt and equity *today*.

IMPORTANT: Ex-post reluctance to liquidate *by managers not acting on behalf of the overall firm but on behalf of equity* can favor equity as the cheaper financing vehicle.

However, reluctance to liquidate can also hurt equity.

So far, we have assumed that management acts on behalf of shareholders. They indeed typically care more about equity than about debt, which we just argued may induce them to exploit the debt on behalf of equity. However, managers can also act on behalf of themselves, especially if shareholders would be best served by corporate liquidation, too. Managers may run down the firm's equity substance in order to keep their jobs instead of returning the money to the owners. To reduce the incidence of such behavior, firms may add debt to the capital structure. Debt can limit the ability of managers to run down the entire firm and force them to liquidate and disgorge some of the remaining assets. This can benefit both debt and equity.

IMPORTANT: Ex-post reluctance to liquidate *by managers not acting on behalf of the overall firm but on behalf of themselves* can favor debt over equity as the cheaper financing vehicle.

We discuss agency problems between managers and owners in the next section and in Chapter 24. Such agency issues tend to be more dramatic in good times. But you should realize that conflicts of interest can occur in financial distress, too—in which case the presence of more debt could be as good a cure to discipline unwilling managers as it often is in good times.

SOLVE NOW!

Q 18.14 Give an example of an underinvestment problem.

Q 18.15 What kinds of firms are most likely to be influenced by underinvestment costs when choosing a capital structure?

Q 18.16 Give an example of a reluctance-to-liquidate problem. Is this an issue that could hurt only the creditors, or only the shareholders?

Q 18.17 What kinds of firms are most likely to be influenced by possible reluctance-to-liquidate costs when choosing a capital structure?

18.3D STRATEGIC CONSIDERATIONS

Debt can change the nature of the competition in the product market.

Finally, there are some theories in which debt is a strategic commitment device. This argument is perhaps easiest to understand by analogy. Consider playing a game of chicken (two cars driving toward one another; the first to "chicken out" and get out of the way loses). How can you make sure you win? If you can tie down your steering controls, remove the steering wheel, and throw it visibly out the window, any smart opponent would surely chicken out! The trick is to commit yourself visibly to not giving way. (Some people have suggested that driving an old, large, and apparently unstable Oldsmobile is the equivalent of throwing out the wheel; other cars will be in a hurry to get out of the way.)

This is an argument that debt can make firms more aggressive (commit to fight entrants), thereby making the firm itself better off.

➤ Risk shifting, Section 18.5A, p. 676

The same argument has been made for debt—that by having debt, firms can commit to squash potential entrant competitors in their product markets. Assume for a moment that a monopolist has borrowed a lot of money. Consider the decision of a potential market entrant who knows this. The market entrant also knows that it is in the interest of the shareholders to increase risk—they will gain more of the upside than the downside. A price war is riskier than accommodation—so the monopolist's managers (acting on behalf of equity holders) may prefer the more risky strategy of a price war over accommodation. Consequently, the potential entrant may chicken out, and the monopolist may never have to start the price war. (Of course, if the market entrant is too stupid to understand the message, both players—the monopolist and the entrant—will be hurt badly. The two cars will end up crashing head-on.)

Empirically, the argument of intentional value-enhancing self-commitment seems not too important. On the contrary: Debt may make firms less competitive and worse off.

This argument is clever, but it may not be a first-order factor in the real world. We do know that industry matters—for example, financial services companies tend to rely on a lot of debt. However, it is not clear whether managers have strategic intent in mind when they pursue capital structure change. There is not much evidence that managers of companies with more debt have relatively more of a tendency to act in a more risk-seeking fashion in the product market. There is not much evidence that they choose a price war strategy. And there is even less evidence that they consciously increase their debt ex-ante *in order to* commit themselves to a price war. Some empirical research has actually found that more debt tends to hurt firms in the product market. Owners tend to take on more debt when they are severely cash constrained, and this may prevent them from competing effectively. Indeed, there is some evidence that supermarkets that dramatically increased their leverage were systematically attacked by their competitors with price wars and failed to compete as effectively. In the aforementioned Sharper Image bankruptcy in 2008, the *Associated Press* writes, "Bankrupt businesses also face the risk that card holders left in the cold could defect to other stores just when struggling merchants need their customers the most . . . Sharper Image's rival, Brookstone, is capitalizing on the situation. It announced last week that it would exchange Sharper Image gift cards for 25 percent off any purchase, no matter the amount of the gift card or the cost of the item." To the extent that high leverage can cause weakness in the product markets, it would count as a direct cost of debt. The subject of product-market related strategic capital structure choice is still under active investigation, and the final word has not been spoken.

➤ The Sharper Image, p. 667

IMPORTANT: The competitive product-market environment of the firm could favor either equity or debt.

SOLVE NOW!

Q 18.18 Is debt always a strategic advantage? Describe the arguments on both sides.

18.4 OPERATING POLICY: AGENCY ISSUES AND BEHAVIOR IN GOOD TIMES

In most of the previous section, debt was usually worse than equity, because it made it more likely that the firm would enter financial distress. Just as too much debt can cause the firm to make poor operating decisions when financial distress looms, too little debt can also cause the firm to make poor operating decisions when the business is going well.

You already met agency conflicts in Chapter 12. We will cover them again in great detail in Chapter 24 (the corporate governance chapter). A less academic name for an agency conflict is a **conflict of interest**. A more academic name is **moral hazard**, although this term is also in common use in the insurance industry.

Agency conflicts also play important roles in capital structure theory:

Managers like building empires and receiving perks; debt restrains them.

Free cash flow: Managers usually prefer spending money internally on their pet projects instead of returning money to shareholders. For example, in the 1980s, many large oil companies continued exploring for oil even though it was well known that oil companies could be bought on the stock exchange for significantly less than the expected cost of finding equivalent oil reserves. Free cash flow issues are especially problematic in declining industries—faced with shrinking markets, managers often desperately search for alternative investing ventures that are not their competitive advantage, rather than returning the money to the rightful owners. How can capital structure counterweigh this tendency? Debt requires coupon payments, which force managers to perform. Managers who fail to generate enough income to pay the coupons are subject to bankruptcy and (as has been shown empirically) almost always lose their jobs. Therefore, managers who have more debt will spend less wastefully, which makes such firms worth more *today*.

Managers might steal: Debt restrains their ability to do so without being discovered.

Theft (and verification): Another important problem of too much equity instead of debt is implicit or explicit **theft**.If you are a passive partner, you are dependent on true and accurate reporting of what profits really are. The active partners or the managers, however, might try to avoid reporting large profits: They might rather use corporate cash to build more of an empire, to compensate themselves better, or just to outright steal it! Debt has the advantage that the creditor may not even need to know what the profits are: If the agreed-upon payments are not made, the creditor can force bankruptcy.

Employees or other critical stakeholders may hold up the firm's shareholders for more of its money. Creditors are much less forgiving.

Stakeholder holdup: Higher potential hold-up costs are another important drawback of equity. When a company, especially a public company, rolls in cash, anyone who has the power to hold up the business will try to extort more of a share of these profits. (This is called **rent seeking**.) For example, a supplier who delivers an important input, a wholesaler who is an important distributor, or any key employees who can bring production to a stop may want to pressure the firm to renegotiate their deals and gain more of the riches. Airlines, for example, suffer greatly from this problem. A strike by any one of its unions can render billions of dollars in airplanes useless and destroy much of the customer goodwill (though airlines have almost none these days). If the airline has the cash to afford it, it will have no choice but to give in. Yet if such a company is financed more via debt than equity, these third parties will recognize that there is less cash to expropriate. After all, if the company does not pay the debt, it can go bankrupt. Thus, in a company with more debt, the equity earnings (which parties can renegotiate) are smaller.

When management owns more of the levered equity, possible only with a lot of debt, then management may be less conflicted.

Higher effective managerial stake: More debt amplifies the effects of managerial equity holdings. For example, if managers have enough wealth to own \$5 of a \$100 firm, it would mean that they owned 5% of the firm. A decline in the value of projects from \$100 to \$80 would cost them \$1. In contrast, if the firm were financed with \$60 in debt, managers' \$5 in shares would be a $\$5/\$40 = 12.5\%$ stake in the

ANECDOTE Airlines, Unions, and Shareholders

In September 2002, American Airlines (AMR) operated over 1,000 airplanes, and owned about half of them. It had assets valued at about $30 billion and debt valued at around $15 billion. Still, its equity market value was only $800 million—about the price of 3 of its 40 top-of-the-line Boeing 777 airplanes. And it is not clear if American was worth even this $800 million: Bankruptcy was imminent for all other major U.S. carriers (except Southwest).

In 2002, American lost a significant amount of money in its operations. If it is ever to make positive profits again, its unions will surely capture the lion's share. After all, it only takes one of its unions (pilots, flight attendants, or mechanics) to ground a fleet worth $30 billion and to wreck customer loyalty. If there was only one union, it would ultimately make sure that shareholders would receive just enough for them not to kill the golden goose. Three unions, all trying to get the most for their members, may yet end up killing the goose. For AMR's owners, debt is the only chance that it has to resist union demands.

As of May 2008, AMR's profit outlook continues to be negative. Yet AMR's equity is worth $2.3 billion—and even this low value is a mystery to me. Airlines should not exist as public corporations, but should instead be owned by their unions.

firm, and a drop from $100 to $80 would wipe out half of the value of their equity. Thus, managers would lose not $1 but $2.50. Chances are that with more debt, managers would be much less inclined to take bad projects that reduced firm value from $100 to $80.

IMPORTANT: Free cash flow and agency concerns favor debt over equity as the cheaper financing vehicle.

Agency conflicts are very important, especially in large, stalwart firms. But be careful: Just because these agency conflicts are important, and although it is true that the presence of debt helps control agency conflicts, it is not automatically true that real-world companies will have more debt. If managers were already to have taken effective control of the corporate board (by stacking it with insiders and friends), they will be the "agents in charge," and they will act in their own interests and structure the firm to carry more equity and *not* more debt.

A more sinister view of the corporation: Firms have equity not because it is value-enhancing, but because managers in charge like it.

➤ Do future capital needs protect shareholders?, Section 24.1D, p. 903

IMPORTANT: Uncontrolled free cash flow and agency concerns can mean that firms have more equity than debt financing, even if this is not value maximizing.

In the real world, it comes down to how good the corporate governance of the firm is. Chapter 24 explains that a good independent board, a large external equity owner, or a set of potential external acquirers can sometimes exert enough pressure on management to issue more debt when it is optimal to do so. (One could argue that this is the role that **private equity** firms are playing.) Unfortunately, strong corporate governance by shareholders over managers is the exception and not the rule in Fortune 500 firms. Thus, you should not be surprised that there are also many large blue-chip firms that could benefit substantially from exchanging their equity for more debt, but their management has chosen to keep the firm fairly unlevered.

Corporate governance breakdown in many large Fortune 500 companies could explain excessive equity in their financing.

SOLVE NOW!

Q 18.19 Give some examples of perks that management might have to give up if they work at a firm with more debt.

Q 18.20 Do managerial agency concerns induce firms to be more debt-financed or more equity-financed?

18.5 BONDHOLDER EXPROPRIATION

If there is debt, equity shareholders may want management to expropriate these debtors. This has bad ex-ante value consequences.

You already know that entrepreneurs should structure the firm *at the outset* (ex-ante) so as to make it in their interest to optimize firm value in the future. In order to raise debt at an attractive interest rate, managers must also take into account that bondholders know that managers might later want to weasel out of their obligations. They would prefer to transfer value from bondholders to shareholders. After all, creditors realize that it is the shareholders who vote managers into office, not the bondholders. This section shows that managers can expropriate bondholders on behalf of shareholders in two ways:

1. They can increase the risk of the firm's projects (a change in operating policies).
2. They can issue more bonds of equal or higher priority. (Bonds that pay cash earlier are de facto higher priority.)

If potential bondholders believe that they can be expropriated, they will demand a higher cost of capital today. Let me explain this better.

18.5A PROJECT RISK CHANGES

Risk-shifting: Adding a risky, but negative, NPV project changes the state-contingent payoffs.

➤ Table 18.1, p. 664

The first expropriation risk that creditors face is called "risk-shifting." Table 18.3 returns to our firm with an LD capital structure from Table 18.1 but allows managers to add project "New" after the original debt has been raised. The new project is independent of the old project and pays either +\$50 or −\$60 with equal probability. It is a negative-NPV project, so it would not be too hard for managers to find such projects—any Las Vegas casino provides better investment opportunities. Why would a negative-NPV project matter? Would the managers not reject this negative-NPV project?

The shareholders gamble with the bondholders' money. Ex-post, shareholders will be better off.

The lower half of the table shows that if the new negative-NPV project is taken, the value of the equity would increase from \$50 to \$57.95. If shareholders are in firm control of their managers and vote them into and out of office, managers would indeed take this project *despite the bad consequences for the firm overall*! In essence, the new project would eliminate \$50 − \$37.50 = \$12.50 of bondholder value, waste \$4.55, and hand \$7.95 extra value to shareholders. The intuition is that this risky project gives existing shareholders relatively more of the upside and existing bondholders relatively more of the downside.

Ex-ante, entrepreneurs should prevent it to reduce their cost of debt capital.

Everyone—managers, shareholders, and bondholders—recognizes that taking the project will be in the interest of the managers if a bond with a face value of \$55 was originally sold. Although this is good for equity holders ex-post, ex-ante it is bad for them (and the firm). Skeptical creditors will assume that the debt payoff is only \$41.25 (not \$55) and thus pay no more than \$37.50. The firm would have to pay a cost of capital of $\$55/\$37.50 - 1 \approx 46.7\%$, even if it wanted to finance itself with debt.

TABLE 18.3 THE EFFECT OF RISK-SHIFTING ON DEBT AND EQUITY VALUE

		Bad Luck	Good Luck		
	Prob:	1/2	1/2	Expected Value	PV(r = 10%)
Project	Firm	$60	$160	$110	$100
		Capital Structure LD: Bond with Face Value			
Bond	Debt	$55	$55	$55	$50
Equity	Equity	$5	$105	$55	$50

Adding Risky Project "New"

		Bad Luck		Good Luck			
	Prob:	1/4	1/4	1/4	1/4	Expected Value	PV(r = 10%)
Project	Firm	$60	$60	$160	$160	$110	$100.00
Project	New	$50	–$60	$50	–$60	–$5	–$4.55
Total Projects		$110	$0	$210	$100	$105	$95.45
		Capital Structure LD: Bond with Face Value $55					
Bond	Debt	$55	$0	$55	$55	$41.25	$37.50
Equity	Equity	$55	$0	$155	$45	$63.75	$57.95

The cost of capital in this example is 10% for all securities, which is equivalent to assuming risk neutrality.

Note that the real problem is not that creditors receive less but that managers would have the incentive to destroy firm value in the process of reducing their liabilities in the future. If they did not destroy any value—if it were just reallocation of the payoffs in different states—both equity and creditors could simply recompute the appropriate fair value of their contingent claims up front, pay appropriate claims prices, and the overall firm value today would be unaffected. As before, an ex-post issue has consequences ex-ante.

Ex-ante, the real problem is value reduction (taking negative-NPV projects)—not the state reallocation.

If you now conclude that it is good for the corporation to commit itself not to take other projects, you would be wrong. This could backfire, too. If a new zero-cost project were to come along that either pays off –$60 or +$500, it would have a highly positive NPV. If creditors had negotiated a commitment at bond issue, they would insist that the project not be taken, because their wealth would still decline. But this would prevent the firm from taking great projects. Therefore, a wholesale ex-ante commitment not to take any more projects is not necessarily a good thing for the value of the overall firm.

Unfortunately, committing not to shift risk could prevent positive-NPV projects—also costly.

SOLVE NOW!

Q 18.21 Return to a project similar to the firm in Table 18.3. The risk-neutral required interest rate is 10%. The firm is worth either $100 or $120. The bond promises $90. We shall consider two cases: one in which the bond is convertible into 75% of the firm's equity, and one in which it is not.

1. Work out the value of the firm. For the bond, create three rows for each state:
   (a) If bondholders never convert (which is also the value for the nonconvertible bond);
   (b) If bondholders always convert;
   (c) If bondholders convert only if it is optimal for them (which is also the value for the convertible bond).

   Does the convertibility feature have any value?
2. Now a new and independent project "BAD" becomes available. It will pay off either +\$50 or −\$60 with equal probabilities.
   (a) If the bond is not convertible, is it in the interest of shareholders to undertake "BAD"?
   (b) If the bond is convertible (into 75% equity), is it in the interest of shareholders to undertake "BAD"? Would you expect to see many conversions if this were the case? How does frequency of actual conversion empirically relate to the value of convertibility?

Managers can also exploit bondholders by issuing more debt of equal or higher priority.

18.5B ISSUANCE OF BONDS OF SIMILAR PRIORITY

There are also other expropriation risks that creditors face. The first is the issuance of more bonds of equal or higher priority. (Paying out some cash before the original bond comes due is in effect higher priority.) Table 18.4 shows an example, in which the firm issues another bond with a face value of \$20 that has equal priority. In bankruptcy (the bad state), the old bond would have to share proceeds with the new bond of equal priority. Being equal, the "spoils" would often be allocated according to face value within bonds of the same priority. Because the \$20 bond represents $\$20/(\$20 + \$55) \approx 27\%$ of the debt claim, it would receive $27\% \cdot \$60 \approx \$16$; and the \$55 bond would receive the remaining $73\% \cdot \$60 \approx \$44$. This means that when the firm announces the issuance of the new bond, the old bond would immediately drop by $\$50 - \$45 = \$5$ in value. Would this be in the interest of the equity? It now receives nothing in the bad state and \$85 in the good state—plus the one-time dividend of \$16.36. In total, by issuing new debt of equal priority, equity holders would have increased their wealth from \$50 to $\$38.64 + \$16.36 = \$55$.

Again, fearing expropriation, the entrepreneur has to pay a higher interest up front to potential bondholders.

This expropriation is not as bad as our risk-shifting example, in that managers need not destroy firm value. But it can force a certain capital structure dynamic on the firm. The first creditors will again assume that they will be expropriated, and therefore they will demand a higher interest rate today. They would demand a quoted interest rate of $\$55/\$45 - 1 \approx 22.2\%$. To recoup this higher interest rate, the managers will have no choice but to indeed issue more bonds that expropriate these first bond purchasers later. In effect, before deciding on any capital structure, the firm has two choices: Either issue no bonds or be dragged into a capital structure that will require expropriating existing debt more and more (by issuing more and more new debt).

The problem is again that it requires contortion by the firm (negative-NPV projects) to expropriate creditors after the fact.

A similar but even more benign form of creditor expropriation could be as follows: If creditors were always to receive $x\%$ of what they were promised, they would simply incorporate this into the interest rate they demand. The overall firm value

TABLE 18.4 THE EFFECT OF ISSUANCE OF EQUAL-SENIORITY OR SHORTER-TERM BONDS ON DEBT AND EQUITY VALUES

		Bad Luck	Good Luck		
	Prob:	1/2	1/2	Expected Value	PV(r = 10%)
Project	Firm	$60	$160	$110	$100
Capital Structure LD: Bond with Face Value $55					
Old Bond	Debt	$55	$55	$55	$50
Equity	Equity	$5	$105	$55	$50

Adding an Equal-Priority Bond with Face Value $20

		Bad Luck	Good Luck		
	Prob:	1/2	1/2	Expected Value	PV(r = 10%)
Project	Firm	$60	$160	$110	$100
Capital Structure LD Plus: an Equal-Priority Bond					
Old Bond(Face Value $55)	Debt	$73\% \cdot \$60 \approx \$44$	$55	$49.50	$45.00
New Bond(Face Value $20)	Debt	$27\% \cdot \$60 \approx \$16$	$20	$18	$16.36
Equity	Equity	$0	$85	$42.50	$38.64

The cost of capital in this example is 10% for all securities, which is equivalent to assuming risk neutrality. 73% is the proportional allocation of the old debt, $\$55/(\$55 + \$20) \approx 73\%$.

would not change. This is actually quite relevant in the real world. In bankruptcy, the agreed-upon absolute priority rule (in which bondholders are supposed to be paid in full before equity holders receive anything) is often not followed. Fortunately, such deviations from promised absolute priority are expected and simply change the contingent payoffs and thus the effective values of the securities. They do not reduce the total value of the pie (the firm). Relative to strict APR, for a given probability of financial distress and expected nonadherence to APR, the value of bonds at issue is just lower by the amount that the value of the equity is higher.

➤ Absolute priority rule, Section 15.2A, p. 545

SOLVE NOW!

Q 18.22 Describe the two basic mechanisms whereby unprotected bondholders can be expropriated by shareholders. Can you illustrate your arguments with numerical examples?

18.5C COUNTERACTING FORCES AGAINST EXPROPRIATION

Bondholders demand a premium ex-ante that they would not demand if the firm could commit not to expropriate them ex-post. The premium may prevent the firm from raising debt at fair interest rates and thus tilt the optimal capital structure more toward equity. Even managers with the best intentions not to act against bondholders may not be able to shield themselves from the pressures of expropriating creditors later. Who ultimately loses? To the extent that smart bond investors anticipate their

If the entrepreneur can commit to not expropriate creditors later, he can enjoy lower interest rates.

fate, they will demand and receive fair compensation. Ultimately, it is the firm that suffers. Its inability to commit to not expropriating creditors may prevent it from issuing debt at fair prices—which would mean it may have to forgo debt's other advantages (such as tax savings).

Mechanisms that help align managerial interests with those of prospective bondholders.

In the real world, there are a number of mechanisms that can help to reduce the fears of bondholders, thereby allowing the firm to issue debt at higher interest rates—which thereby often lowers the firm's overall cost of capital.

Managers dislike going bankrupt, so they are probably not inclined to gamble unless the firm is already in terrible distress.

Managerial risk aversion: We noted earlier that shareholders like increases in project risk, because they help them at the expense of bondholders. However, it is not clear if managers really act on behalf of shareholders and thus like higher risk, too. After all, if the project fails and the firm enters financial distress, they might get fired themselves. Thus, managerial risk aversion is a natural counterbalance to the shareholders' incentives to increase risk.

Bond covenants reduce exploitational opportunities in the future—but at a cost in flexibility.

➤ Covenants, Section 10.2B, p. 313

Bond covenants: A variety of bond covenants have developed to mitigate bondholder skepticism.

- Many bonds prohibit excessive dividend payouts.
- Many bonds prohibit large new debt issues, especially of shorter term and of equal priority.
- Many bonds require the maintenance of certain financial ratios. For example, covenants may mandate maximum debt/equity ratios, maximum payout ratios, minimum earnings retention ratios, minimum liquidity ratios, and so on. These ratio restrictions can all help prevent the firm from taking on riskier projects.

If the covenant is broken, creditors can sue or demand their money back. Covenants are never perfect. It is just impossible to enumerate all the things managers can do. In addition, if the firm enters Chapter 11 bankruptcy, the law says that any new debt issued will automatically receive higher priority, no matter what the covenants of the original bond stated.

Bonds with strong covenants often have a "call" feature that allows the firm to retire the bond before maturity at an agreed-upon price—and thereby free itself of the covenant requirements.

And, again, covenants reduce the flexibility of the firm to take advantage of other opportunities. Sometimes, reputation can substitute for covenants.

Corporate reputation: Covenants are inflexible, so they impose costs, too. For example, if the firm happens to come across a project with +$1 billion in NPV, the covenants could prevent the firm from taking it. Again, a firm that fails to take all profitable projects in the future is worth less today. One alternative to formal covenants is for firms to build a less formal "reputation." This is not easy to do, but firms may realize that it is in their interest not to exploit current bondholders because any future bondholders would henceforth definitely assume the worst behavior. Put differently, if managers were to take advantage of creditors today, then future financing costs would be so much higher that managers would rather not do so. Reputation is not perfect, though, especially if the advantage that can be taken of creditors today becomes very large. The most prominent example of broken reputation is possibly RJR Nabisco. In the 1980s, it was generally believed to be a safe investment for bondholders. However, when it was bought out in 1988 (in the largest leveraged buyout of its time), RJR tripled its debt overnight, its out-

➤ RJR Nabisco and other large LBOs, Section 23.1G, p. 867

standing bonds went from investment grade to speculative grade, and bondholders experienced an announcement-month loss of 15%.

Convertible bonds or strip financing: Another mechanism is to try to allow creditors to partake in the upside of equity. The most common such financing vehicles are **convertible bonds**. Again, they can limit the ex-post expropriation of bondholders while still preserving the firm's option to accept new projects. Instead of straight bonds with strong covenants, "convertible bonds" with weak covenants allow creditors to participate if a great new project were to come along. This reduces the risk expropriation problem. **Strip financing**, in which individuals purchase debt and equity in equal units, is a similar idea—it eliminates the incentives of shareholders to exploit each other (i.e., themselves).

Convertible bonds allow bondholders to participate in the upside, and reduce exploitational incentives in the future.

Units: The same idea is behind the use of units. A unit is a combination of securities. It can consist of a debt security and an equity security. Thus, there is no difference in identity between shareholders and bondholders. However, if the firm pays interest, it shifts its tax burden to the unit owners. If the firm pays dividends, it shifts this tax burden to itself. More important, unless the buyers unbundle the units, it does not matter to them if the firm expropriates bondholders at the expense of shareholders. Every bondholder is a shareholder! Note that this also puts a stark limit on the amount that bondholder expropriation may possibly destroy. After all, if it were that important, someone could just purchase the securities and resell them as inseparable units. This cannot be too expensive, so ex-ante bondholder expropriation costs cannot be too much in equilibrium.

If shareholders are also the creditors, there would be little use for them to expropriate themselves.

➤ Units of debt and equity, Section 18.3B, p. 665

In the real world, firms have to undertake a delicate balancing act. When they issue debt, it can only be issued at favorable terms when the firm can promise not to exploit bondholders after the bonds are issued. Even if such promises can be credibly made, they cause a loss of flexibility, which can be expensive. This can mean that the firm cannot issue debt—and thus that it has to forgo some other beneficial effects of debt (such as tax advantages).

Recap: Entrepreneurs internalize the cost of future inefficient behavior.

IMPORTANT:

- Bondholders and other creditors can lose value if either of the following occurs:
  - The firm later undertakes riskier projects.
  - The firm adds more debt of equal or higher priority.
- Creditors demand higher interest rates if they fear such expropriation. Thus, it is in the interest of the owners to assure creditors that they will not do so. The prime mechanisms to accomplish this are
  - Loan covenants
  - Reputation
  - Bond convertibility

SOLVE NOW!

Q 18.23 Does managerial risk aversion mitigate or exacerbate the fear of creditors to be expropriated in favor of shareholders?

Q 18.24 In a market in which bond covenants are priced at what they are worth, can their presence still increase firm value? When could covenants reduce firm value?

Q 18.25 What is an advantage of adding a convertibility feature to a bond?

18.6 INSIDE INFORMATION AND ADVERSE SELECTION

New potential partners (shareholders) have less information than current managers and owners.

Our next important determinant of capital structure is inside information. Typically, firm managers (acting on behalf of the old owners) have better information than new investors. New investors should be careful that they are not exploited. As the old adage says, "Never bet with someone better informed than yourself."

If owners want partners rather than lenders, the project may not be as good.

Consider this scenario: You are a potential investor in an oil well, and you know that the current owner/manager (who has to raise new capital) already knows whether or not there is oil. You do not know. You have to ask yourself the following questions:

- What will you believe about the oil well if the present owner offers to make you a full partner who shares in all future profits?
- What will you believe about the oil well if the present owner asks you for a loan to be paid back that she is willing to collateralize with her present assets?

➤ Winner's curse, Section 21.7, p. 806

If you are offered partnership, you should be reluctant to believe that there is oil. If, however, the present owner wants to keep the profits and simply borrow, she probably knows that the project is profitable. This is sometimes called the **winner's curse**, **adverse selection**, or simply the **lemon problem**. If you receive the offer to become partner, it does not help you very much. (There won't be oil in the ground.) If you do not receive the offer to become partner, you would be better off if you had indeed received it. (There will be oil in the ground.)

A numerical example of the inside information problem.

This analogy is directly transferable to capital structure. Sharing in the firm's equity is the equivalent of becoming a partner. Table 18.5 again considers our example, but it adds the knowledge of owners and your beliefs as a potential investor.

If you also know project quality: Not surprisingly, if the project is good and you believe this, the owners end up with \$160 next year. Similarly, if the project is bad, the owners end up with \$60 next year. Unfortunately, you do not know this.

If you believe either project quality is equally likely: This implies that you are willing to purchase equity based on the expected project payoff of \$110 (worth \$100 today). Thus, you would provide \$50 in exchange for half the firm. Is this a rational belief?

Consider what a current owner would do. If he knew the project was good and financed through debt, he would be better off (\$160) than if he financed through equity (\$135). Not a single good-project owner would thus finance with equity. (Only bad-project owners would.) Thus, your belief that project quality is equally likely is false.

TABLE 18.5 INSIDE CALCULATIONS

	Prob:	1/2	Bad Luck 1/2	Good Luck Expected Value	PV($r = 10\%$)
Project	Firm	$60	$160	$110	$100

Firm is Truly	If Debt Financed, Financier-Owners Will Keep	Outside Investors Believe Firm is	PV of Firm	Percent of Equity Sold to Raise $50	If Equity Financed, Financier-Owners Will Keep	Is Belief Sensible?
Good	**$160**	Good	(⇒ $145.45)	$50/$145.45 = 34.375%	$55 + 65.625% · $160 = **$160.00**	No: Bad guys would issue equity, too.
Bad	$60	Good	(⇒ $145.45)	$50/$145.45 = 34.375%	$55 + 65.625% · $60 ≈ **$94.38**	
Good	**$160**	50-50[a]	(⇒ $100.00)	$50/$100.00 = 50%	$55 + 50% · $160 = $135.00	No: Only bad guys would issue equity.
Bad	$60	50-50[a]	(⇒ $100.00)	$50/$100.00 = 50%	$55 + 50% · $60 = **$85.00**	
Good	**$160**	Bad	(⇒ $54.55)	$50/$54.55 ≈ 91.667%	$55 + 8.333% · $160 ≈ $68.33	Yes: Only bad guys issue equity.
Bad	**$60**	Bad	(⇒ $54.55)	$50/$54.55 ≈ 91.667%	$55 + 8.333% · $60 = **$60.00**	

a. 50-50 means that outside investors believe there is an even chance that the firm is either good or bad.

The cost of capital in this example is 10% for all securities, which is equivalent to assuming risk neutrality. The financier-owners want to raise $50 today. They can do so by issuing debt or equity. Outside investors have to guess what type of firm they are dealing with, based on what they can see (the financing method of the financier-owners). In equilibrium, investors are not stupid: Their expectations should be bornr out by what will happen. To understand the lower panel, consider, for instance, the first rows:

- The original financier-owners can sell debt for $50 and invest it in Treasuries. Next year, they receive $55 from the Treasuries. If the firm is good (or bad), they will receive $160 (or $60) from the project. They pay their creditors the $55, and keep the project cash flows of $160 (or $60). Note that the creditors always receive the full $55 repayment regardless of what type the firm truly is. Thus, investors' beliefs are irrelevant when it comes to debt financing.
- If the financier-owners want to sell equity, then it matters what their outside investors believe. If they believe that the firm is good, then they should believe that it will yield $160, which means that this firm is worth $160/1.1 ≈ $145.45 today. Consequently, the original financier-owners can sell investors 34.375% of the $145.45 firm today in exchange for cash of $50. For the original owners, this $50 in cash will turn into $55 next year. In addition, the original owners retain 1 − 34.375% = 65.625% of the firm, which will yield them $160 · 65.625% = $105. In sum, under these investor beliefs, good firms end up with $160 when they issue equity.
- Because good firms are no worse off if investors believe all equity issuers are good, the good firms would be willing to participate.
- Unfortunately, it is not a rational belief that all firms that issue equity are good: Indeed, all bad firms would claim to be good firms, too, because the $94.38 that they receive when they pretend they are good is more than the $60 that they receive when they tell the truth.

Bold is the preferred choice (either debt or equity) in each row. Looking over all rows, the only equilibrium that is feasible is one in which investors believe that all good guys finance themselves with debt. That is, investors believe that all firms financing themselves with equity must be bad guys. Indeed, in equilibrium, all good guys prefer to finance with debt rather than equity. (The bad guys are indifferent between issuing debt and equity, so we can assume that they use debt.)

If you believe equity-financed projects are bad: Would this belief be rational? Yes—all good firms have wandered off to the debt market, and only the bad projects remain.

The "pecking order": Issuing more equity-like (partner-like) shares reveals bad news. Thus, new equity shares can only be sold at low prices.

New equity investors are not inclined to assume that the project is good. They will assume that their new claims are on a project that will eventually develop problems. Thus, when existing owners announce a new equity offering, it releases information that the firm's projects are worse than generally believed, and the new equity can only be sold for a very low price. This is again an example of adverse selection—only companies fearing the future would want to share their prospects. In real life, we indeed observe that when firms announce that they plan to raise about $1 by issuing new equity, their old public equity value declines by about 10 cents. But this argument extends not only to equity but to other claims as well. The more risky the securities are that insiders want to sell rather than keep, the worse are their beliefs in their projects. Sharing in more junior (risky) bonds is the equivalent of the present owners making you a "little partner," when they are not willing to collateralize their loans. Consequently, the announcement of a risky junior security releases information that the firm's projects are not too great, but not too bad, either. In contrast, the new issue of a collateralized loan (or a risk-free senior bond) will indicate that the firm's projects are better than expected. The outcome is that the better the firm's projects are, the more senior the security the managers will offer for sale. This leads to a **pecking order** view of capital structure: The best projects are financed by the most senior debt, worse projects by junior debt, and the worst projects by equity.

Firms may want to avoid issuing equity to avoid signaling bad news.

What does this imply about the optimal capital structure? Consider a firm that cannot issue debt easily because it has little collateral or because additional debt would unduly increase expected bankruptcy costs. If it cannot issue equity because of these insider concerns, such a firm may have to pass up on some good (but perhaps not stellar) projects, simply because owners do not want to sell their projects at the price of the worst possible scenario. A publicly traded firm thus may take on too much debt (incurring financial distress costs) or ration its projects, failing to take at least some of its positive-NPV projects.

IMPORTANT: The presence of inside information concerns (investors fearing the worst) favors debt over equity as the cheaper financing vehicle.

If managers can convey all they know, the adverse selection penalty would disappear.

When could a firm issue equity without an insider penalty?

- If there is a mechanism—for example, a detailed audit—by which insiders with good projects can credibly convey the true quality of the project, it would be in their interest to do so. Indeed, if such a mechanism is known to exist and owners do not undertake it, potential investors should immediately assume that current owners are not doing so because they know that the outcome will be bad.
- If current owners can convince potential investors that they have invested all of their own money, that they have maxed out their personal credit cards, and that they just cannot put any more personal capital at risk than they already have, then there is no bad inside information in the fact that they are trying to raise equity capital. In this

case, external investors can assume that the project is not necessarily bad. Indeed, no venture capitalist will ever invest in a start-up in which the current owners do not have most of their personal wealth at stake.

The inside information and the free cash flow (agency) theories have a very close family relationship. The former says that when firms issue equity, managers signal that they believe that the future will be worse. The latter says that when firms issue equity, managers will make the future worse—they will waste the money. In both cases, issuing equity sends signals to investors about bad futures. Therefore, both create pecking orders in which appropriate skepticism of investors should induce the ordinary manager to prefer issuing debt to equity. The main difference between the two theories is that the agency explanation is more causal than the inside information explanation.

Agency costs and inside information are closely related—both create a pecking order.

SOLVE NOW!

Q 18.26 A house up for auction can be worth either $500,000 or $1,000,000 with 50-50 probability. The other bidders know the true value; you do not. If you bid for the house in an auction, what should you bid? If you bid $750,000, what is *your* expected rate of return?

Q 18.27 What is the pecking order? (Thinking question: In a real-world firm, will a pecking order lead to a **financing pyramid**, in which firms tend to be financed mostly by debt [the bottom of the pyramid] and by very little equity [the top of the pyramid]?)

Q 18.28 Does concern with inside information suggest that firms should issue debt or equity? Why?

18.7 TRANSACTION COSTS AND BEHAVIORAL ISSUES

Transaction costs have played an important role in all capital structure examples above: If transaction costs had been zero, external pressures would force management to choose the best capital structure. But if transaction costs are high, managerial mistakes are difficult or impossible to correct for outsiders. It is not just enough for an outsider to purchase shares and then sell them. The appropriate corrective action requires accumulating enough shares and pressuring management to improve the situation. Without the discipline of external pressure, managers and investors can commit mistakes. They may take too much debt or too much equity, and the market may not be able to correct it.

Transaction costs are everywhere. They can definitely prevent optimal capital structure adjustment.

Transaction costs can also play a direct role. For example, the reporting requirements and liabilities imposed by the *1933 Securities Act* for publicly traded equity securities can be much larger than those for private borrowing. The recent *Sarbanes-Oxley Act* (explained in Chapter 24) has raised the costs of public equity even further. Other evidence further shows that issuing new equity has direct transaction costs of around 5–15% of the issue. For many small companies, these costs of equity may be

The transaction costs of maintaining public equity can be quite large, especially for tiny firms. Equity-issuing costs are also expensive.

➤ Sarbanes-Oxley, Section 24.6C, p. 935

large enough to warrant a capital structure consisting not of public equity but exclusively of private securities and bank debt.

Transaction costs could also prevent firms from issuing debt.

➤ Issuing costs, Figure 23.4, p. 875

Another example of how marketwide transaction costs may affect individual capital structures depends on the absence of certain markets. For example, many institutions are not allowed by law to hold securities with too low of a credit rating. Firms with a credit rating lower than BBB cannot tap the large commercial paper market, either. This could create a situation in which the cost of capital of debt is low only for small debt ratios (where the corporation can issue high-rated debt), but it rises dramatically if the firm takes on too much debt. On a more basic level, it is not cheap to trade a specific company's corporate debt for retail investors. If mutual funds cannot facilitate such access, it could further raise the cost of issuing debt.

IMPORTANT: Transaction cost considerations could favor either debt or equity.

Transaction costs "cause" behavioral finance concerns.

➤ Behavioral finance, Section 11.2, p. 350

Section 11.2 has already explained the link between high transaction costs and behavioral finance. When transaction costs are high—which means that one cannot easily correct mistakes—then behavioral finance considerations are likely to play important roles. Such conditions are indeed common in the corporate finance context. It is simply too expensive to take over a firm in order to correct a capital structure that should have, say, 10% more debt.

Unfortunately, behavioral theory is often hard to use, perhaps because we are just getting started on it.

Behavioral considerations can explain a lot of managerial behavior, which is otherwise difficult to explain. For example, we know that managers like to imitate their peers, perhaps too much so. Unfortunately, on a vague level, without a further description of what the specific behavioral mistakes are, behavioral finance is less prescriptive than the earlier theories of capital structure optimality. That is, we do not yet fully understand the guidance that the behavioral finance theory gives managers in deciding on an optimal capital structure in a world in which they, and others, can make all sorts of mistakes.

Specific behavioral errors can have specific implications.

➤ Behavioral biases, Section 12.7, p. 418

Behavioral finance is the most promising new direction in corporate finance. But it is probably still too early to tell where and how it will help us better understand the world. Some early insights suggest that there are certain behavioral mistakes that are more common than others. For example, we now believe that **overconfidence** and **overoptimism** are common traits among both managers and investors. If managers are overoptimistic, it may aggravate agency concerns (they may take some negative-NPV projects) and reluctance-to-liquidate concerns, but alleviate underinvestment problems. If investors are overoptimistic, issuing equity may not be as disadvantageous as the inside information argument suggests. Investors may not necessarily believe the worst—and there is some evidence that such was the case during the Internet bubble at the turn of the millennium. Although it is less likely that markets rather than managers are committing mistakes, there is good evidence that financial markets may be imperfect, too. If markets indeed misvalue securities—either because they are irrational or imperfect—it would be rational for managers to try to find the best time to issue equity.

IMPORTANT: Behavioral considerations could favor either debt or equity.

SOLVE NOW!

Q 18.29 Give an example of transaction costs that favor more equity in the capital structure. Give an example of transaction costs that favor more debt.

18.8 STATIC CAPITAL STRUCTURE SUMMARY

The static forces are summarized in Table 18.6.

Table 18.6 gives a summary of all capital structure effects discussed so far. The four major forces that pull the firm toward equity are uncontrolled agency issues (managers like equity, because it makes their lives easier and allows them to purchase other firms more easily), financial distress costs, personal income taxes, and debt expropriation—ordered by my assessment of their relative importance in many large firms. The three major forces that pull the firm toward debt are corporate income taxes, mitigating agency conflicts, and inside information issues—in my view, all very important and difficult to rank. Tugging against one another, these forces pull firms toward their capital structures. From a value maximization perspective:

- Too much debt, and the firm would expect to lose too much in financial distress handling, impose too much in personal taxes on its owners, and suffer too many creditor trust issues.
- Too little debt, and the firm would pay too much in corporate income taxes, suffer from too much rent-seeking by management, employees, and possibly others, and not signal enough confidence about the future.

As noted, unmitigated agency conflicts can instead pull the firm toward having too much equity and too little debt, because managers in charge prefer it that way.

SOLVE NOW!

Q 18.30 List the main effects pulling capital structures toward equity. List the main effects pulling capital structures toward debt. Are all these forces working through the desire of entrepreneurs and managers to maximize firm value?

18.9 THE EFFECT OF LEVERAGE ON COSTS OF CAPITAL AND QUOTED BOND YIELDS

With more forces than just corporate income taxes, there could be an interior optimal debt ratio now.

This chapter described the effect of the many countervailing forces on firm value and on optimal debt/equity financing. But how do these forces influence the firm's effective WACC? The firm value and the cost of capital are mirrors of one another, so higher costs of capital mean lower firm values, and vice versa. Just think of the value of the firm today as the expected future cash flows of given projects, divided by one plus the cost of capital. Holding expected cash flows (projects) constant, when the firm's cost of capital increases, its present value decreases, and vice versa. What

TABLE 18.6 SUMMARY OF IMPORTANT CAPITAL STRUCTURE FORCES AND EFFECTS

Managers Maximizing Their Own Welfare Pull the Firm Toward . . .	
Unmitigated Agency Conflicts	Equity
Managers like shareholders' equity and the flexibility it provides, and they dislike debt and the discipline it imposes. Here, the presence of equity *reduces* the value of the firm.	
Entrepreneurs Maximizing the Firm Value Pull the Firm Toward . . .	
Financial Distress Costs	Equity (usually)
Includes inefficient operations, underinvestment problems, supplier and customer incentives, failure to liquidate or sell at appropriate prices, predatory policies by competitors, and so on.	
Personal Income Taxes	Equity
Interest receipts are tax-disadvantaged from investors' points of view.	
Debt Expropriation	Equity
Includes costs arising from the interaction of borrower credibility and borrower flexibility. Includes complete contract specification costs. Possibly less important than other forces in this table.	
Corporate Income Taxes	Debt
Interest payments are tax-deductible by the corporation.	
Too Much Cash Flow (Mitigating Agency Conflicts)	Debt
Sometimes called moral hazard. Includes empire building, free cash flow, excessive managerial perks, verification, and so on.	
Inside Information	Debt
Sometimes called adverse selection or even the lemon problem. (Sometimes, adverse selection is mistakenly called "pecking order"—inside information issues indeed create a pecking order, but so can other forces.)	
Behavioral Finance	Situation-Dependent
Transaction Costs	Situation-Dependent

With the exception of the first effect, it is overall value maximization that should push firms toward financing themselves with the security that is described in the right column.

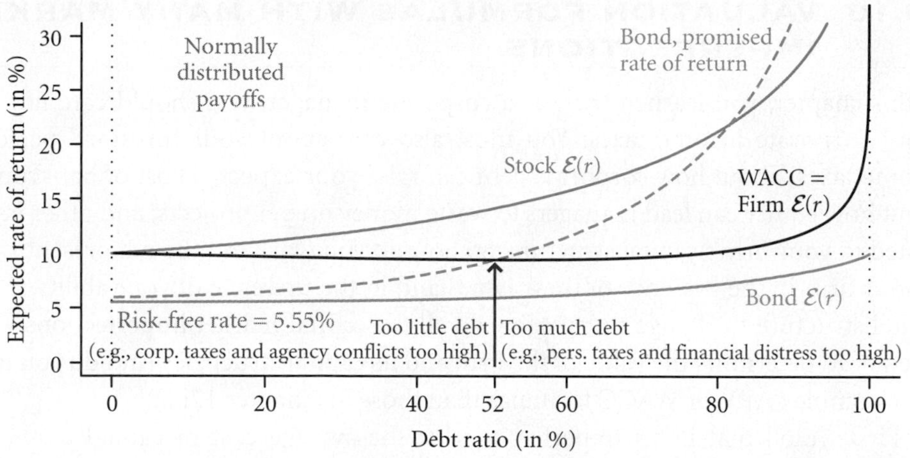

This figure is the equivalent of Figure 17.1 on page 621, except that debt now has some drawbacks, too—bankruptcy costs. This results in an optimal leverage ratio for the firm, below which the firm pays too much in taxes, and above which the firm's cost of financial distress is too high.

FIGURE 18.4 The Cost of Capital in an Imperfect World

does the firm's cost of capital look like as a function of its debt ratio? You have already seen it in a perfect world (Figure 16.2) and in a world in which there were corporate income taxes (Figure 17.1). Figure 18.4 shows how it looks when there are multiple capital market imperfections, in which the optimal capital structure balances many forces. The cost of equity capital and the cost of debt capital are now both influenced by these forces. As drawn in the graph, the resulting WACC function has a minimum at a debt ratio of 52%. It is also quite flat, so in this case the firm would not make a big mistake being off by, say, 10% in its ratio.

➤ The cost of capital in a perfect world, Figure 16.2, p. 594

➤ The cost of capital in a world with corporate income taxes, Figure 17.1, p. 621

IMPORTANT: For many (but not all) firms, the optimal capital structure seems quite flat. That is, small deviations in their debt ratios from the optimum, one way or the other, do not seem to have large influences on firm value. If there are high transaction costs to change debt into equity, or vice versa, taking no action may be the best choice, even when the firm is not at its otherwise best debt/equity ratio.

Of course, this is not always the case. There are firms in which the effective cost of capital is considerably more curved, in which case a suboptimal capital structure would destroy a lot more value. So, make sure you focus on what the important first-order effects are for the specific company that you are involved with, not those minor effects that do not cause much curvature in the firm's cost of capital.

SOLVE NOW!

Q 18.31 If the firm is not in an M&M perfect-markets situation, how will this be reflected in the relation between its cost of capital and its leverage?

18.10 VALUATION FORMULAS WITH MANY MARKET IMPERFECTIONS

How should you think of corporate valuation formulas in the presence of market imperfections?

In this chapter, you learned that, as a corporate manager, you should care not just about corporate income taxes. You must also care about your investors' personal income taxes, about how corporate debt can raise your expected cost of bankruptcy, about how equity can lead managers to waste money on pet projects, and other issues related to your firm's capital structure. So how do you work out the net present value of your firm in the presence of these issues and in the presence of your ability to use capital structure to change them? How do all the capital market imperfections work together to determine the value of the firm and its capital structure? And do you need more complex APV or WACC formulas than those in Chapter 17?

In an imperfect market, don't think the average and the marginal costs of capital are the same.

➤ Marginal and average cost of capital, Section 16.6B, p. 601

First, recall that in an imperfect market the average cost of capital is not the marginal cost of capital that you would want to compare to your next project's internal rate of return. The cost of raising or retiring one more dollar in external financing can be substantially different from your cost of raising or retiring a billion dollars. The existing cost of capital that you can read from your balance sheet is just a historical number, and not what you need. Nevertheless, the average cost of capital can often be very useful to learn, if only because the same forces that influenced the average cost of capital in the past likely also influence the marginal cost of capital today. For many large firms, the average cost of capital may not be too far from the marginal cost of capital.

Figure 18.5 is a conceptual graph that shows how different costs of debt and equity flow into the APV formula.

Figure 18.5 illustrates how you can think about valuing your firm (or just your next project) from different perspectives. The firm's value would be \$100 in a perfect market, but it is only \$80 because of market imperfections. (The flow-to-equity approach works directly with cash flows and costs of capital that are reduced by the \$20 worth of imperfections.) Although the tax shelter created by the tax deductibility of interest plays a special role in the algebraic formulation of APV (and WACC), the other factors can be just as important. This is shown in the last row, where \$5 worth of corporate income tax mitigation is broken out. Yet, this is not because corporate income taxes were the only, or even the most important, factor. Only \$5 of the \$20 reduction is due to corporate income taxes. The remaining \$15 of market imperfections is more important, but it enters value by flowing directly into the \$75 present value of cash flows. Alternatively, you could think of an APV-type approach to other imperfections, too: You would work with \$70 of value under extreme market imperfections if they remained totally unmitigated and then you would add back the \$10 in value that your clever capital structure has mitigated. This is rarely a useful method. Let me explain why.

18.10A DO YOU NEED OTHER VALUATION (APV OR WACC) FORMULAS?

APV and WACC are "as-if-bad but remedied." You can compute the exact corporate income tax remedy.

➤ WACC and APV, Section 17.3, p. 614

Think back. In the previous chapter, you learned that you could handle corporate income taxes in one of the following ways:

1. You could work with expected cash flows and costs of capital "as if fully taxed" and then add back the debt shelter–created remedy that reduces the corporate income tax. This was the principle behind the first two methods, WACC and APV.

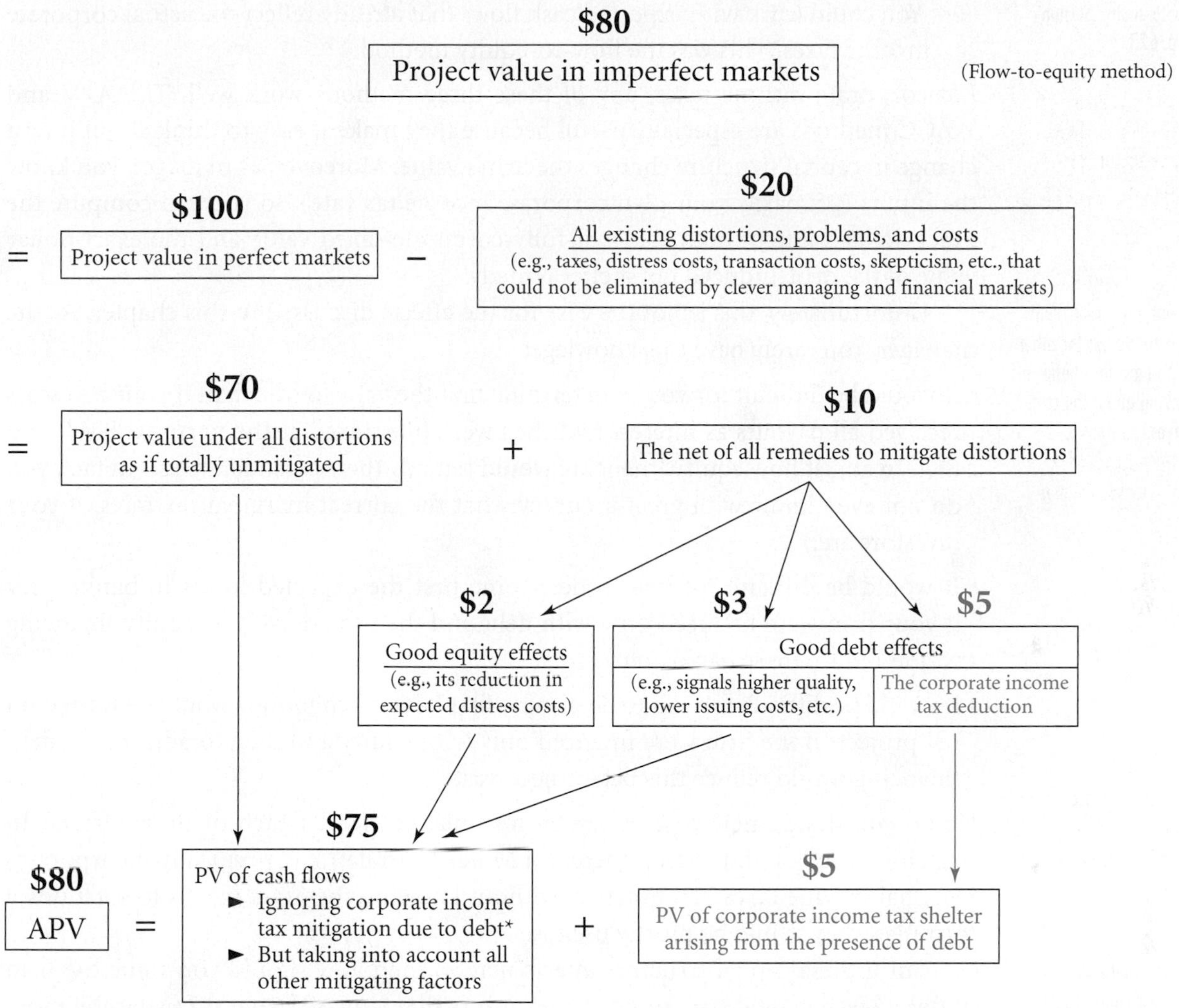

This figure provides a conceptual basis for thinking about capital structure in imperfect markets. All dollar numbers are made up to facilitate this explanation.

- Consider a project that is worth $100 in a perfect world. Market imperfections, such as corporate income taxes and financial distress costs that cannot be avoided, reduce this value to $80. This is the true imperfect-market value of the firm.
- You can think of this firm in another way, though. For example, consider a firm that has a capital structure that gets the worst of all worlds—it suffers market imperfections left and right, and does nothing to remedy it. This firm might be worth only $70. It follows that all imperfect market remedies together must save this firm $10.
- Now think about the potential remedies to market imperfections. There may be corporate taxes that can be avoided (e.g., by having debt and taking advantage of other tax loopholes). There may be ways to signal that the firm is worth more (e.g., by having more debt). There may be ways to reduce distress costs or to reduce personal income taxes (e.g., by having more equity). These increase the value of the firm relative to the $70 value.
- APV breaks out just one part of these remedies. It works with the value of the firm as if all noncorporate tax parts have been remedied as much as they can be remedied (here, $75). APV then adds back the corporate tax part (here, $5).
- Note how in the real world, you still have to come up with the $75 number—the value of the firm assuming all other remedies. This includes all other net effects, such as personal income tax effects, financial distress costs, and so on. You must think about how debt and equity change this number.

* This means that cash flows are computed as if no interest payments are tax deductible.

FIGURE 18.5 Conceptual Framework for Capital Structure Effects and Formulas

➤ Flow-to-equity, Section 17.4A, p. 623

2. You could work with expected cash flows that already reflect the actual corporate income taxes. This was the flow-to-equity method.

For corporate income taxes, any of these three methods work well. The APV and WACC methods are especially useful because they make it easy to think about how a change in capital structure changes the firm's value. Moreover, as manager, you know the inputs (primarily your own corporate income tax rate), so you can compute the exact dollar value of both the as-if-fully-corporate-taxed value and the exact dollar value of the debt-induced tax shelter remedy.

You do not have equivalent precise input values for other effects. You are thus better off just thinking about the costs themselves.

Unfortunately, this is not the case for the effects discussed in this chapter. As the manager, you rarely have this knowlege:

- It would be difficult for you to determine first the value of the firm if your investors received all payouts as interest and thus were fully taxed at the personal level, and then to adjust how equity financing would remedy their personal taxes. (In fact, you do not even know with great accuracy what the correct marginal tax rates of your investors are.)
- It would be difficult for you to determine first the expected losses in bankruptcy if your firm were financed only with debt and then to adjust how equity financing would reduce these bankruptcy costs.
- It would be difficult for you to determine first how much money would be wasted on pet projects if the firm were financed only with equity and then to adjust how debt financing would reduce this pet-project waste.

Could you design new cost-of-capital formulas to handle each of these effects? In principle, you could. (In fact, there is a Miller formula that specifically incorporates personal income taxes.) In practice, without knowing the exact inputs to such novel formulas, they would be mostly useless.

The cost-of-capital inputs for debt and equity in the valuation formulas reflect the effects from this chapter, not a new remedy term.

But if these capital structure effects matter, then how should you value the firm under a given capital structure? The answer is that you are better off using the more direct equivalent that a flow-to-equity–like method provides. You would have to reflect all other capital structure influences in your inputs (expected cash flows and costs of capital).

- If you can reduce your investors' personal income taxes on certain types of claims, then your own corporate cost of capital on these claims would be lower. The reason is that your investors will want to give you their money at lower expected rates of return. (You may want to ask your investment banker by how much.)
- If you can reduce your probability of bankruptcy, your expected cash flows would go up (and your cost of capital may go down).
- If you can reduce inefficient pet projects by adding more debt, again your expected cash flows would go up (and your cost of capital may go down).

And so on. In sum, all the factors discussed in this chapter enter your cost-of-capital formula, but they do so through their influence on your inputs in the existing formulas, not through a new term in a new formula. (In Figure 18.5, they flow into determining the $75.)

No formula does not mean less important or "no thinking required."

It is important for you to understand that just because you have no new formulas does not mean you can think less about the factors discussed in this chapter. On the contrary, personal income taxes, bankruptcy costs, and so on, are not any less important than corporate income taxes just because they do not have their own formulas. (Figure 18.5 gives you such an example.) As the CFO, you can create value for your investors and reduce your cost of capital not only by reducing your corporate income taxes but also by taking into account all the effects discussed in this chapter. You must think about how your actions and your capital structure maximize firm value. More than likely, because you can rarely easily compute exact magnitudes of these market imperfections, you may have to spend more time to understand them, not less. In the end, as you learned in Section 17.6E, if you can reduce market imperfections, your firm will ultimately enjoy lower costs of capital. From a managerial perspective, you can turn this around, too: If you can minimize your expected costs of capital, you will have also optimized your firm against all the market imperfections explained in this chapter.

➤ CAPM as a WACC input in an imperfect world, Section 17.6E, p. 632

IMPORTANT:

- Corporate income taxes are just one factor influencing firm value. This chapter explained many other factors.
- Corporate income taxes are often handled through the specialized WACC and APV formulas presented in Chapter 17, because managers usually have the quantitative inputs readily available. (These two inputs are the value of the firm as if it were fully taxed and the value of the corporate tax shelter due to debt.)
- Corporate income taxes could also be handled through a flow-to-equity approach, which relies on actual estimated costs of capital—not tax-adjusted costs of capital.
- Other capital structure influences are better handled through a similar direct cost-of-capital estimate. This is analogous to the flow-to-equity method. Market imperfections enter the valuation through their influence on the expected cash flows and/or costs of capital. Deriving formula extensions, where these factors would receive their own formula terms, would rarely, if ever, be useful.
- The fact that only corporate income tax has its own valuation formula and that other factors do not, does not mean that corporate income taxes are more important than other factors.
- Good managers think about the value effects of other capital structures! They often use market intelligence to obtain good estimates of their after-all-effects expected cash flows and their after-all-effects costs of capital.

SOLVE NOW!

Q 18.32 Does the lack of a personal income tax rate in the APV and WACC formula mean that the personal tax rate does not matter to the valuation of the firm?

18.11 CAPITAL STRUCTURE DYNAMICS

Executing the value-optimizing strategy may not be possible.

Of course, we have not covered *everything* about capital structure in our chapter, but you now have a very good grasp of the most important factors to think about. Still, the real world is considerably more complex. First of all, the many forces are not as surgically isolated as they were presented above. Usually, many forces are pulling at the same time and in different directions. Second, the world is not static. In the description you have read, management looks at its projects and the forces determining the optimal capital structure, sets the capital structure once, and then everything goes its course. Alas, this is not realistic. Instead, managers are usually confronted with many issues, and not just this year but every year. This can raise altogether novel issues. The presence of one problem—or attempts to reduce it—may worsen another.

Should the firm trade off distress costs against tax benefits?

For example, there are often significant costs to move from a suboptimal to an optimal capital structure. Let us start with the simplest capital structure trade-off scenario: You own a firm in which you need to balance financial distress costs against the tax benefit of corporate debt. In a static scenario, you would choose an intermediate level of debt.

Why not get the best of both worlds?

But why could you not optimize the capital structure dynamically? That is, instead of a medium debt/equity ratio, could you not keep a high debt ratio while the firm is healthy and lower it if and when bad news arrives? This way, your firm could take advantage of the tax deductions if it earns high profits, and avoid the financial distress costs if it does not. It would be the best of both worlds!

Conflict among different interest groups can prevent optimal solutions.

In reality, this may not be so easy. It is true that if a firm is close to bankruptcy, issuing equity could avoid or reduce bankruptcy costs, which in turn would increase firm value. But the infusion of more equity may mostly benefit bondholders, so equity holders may not agree to put in more equity. Individual creditors might hold up a reorganization, too. Thus, even when a new start could install a better capital structure, you would still have to solve many problems to get there, given the current capital structure.

IMPORTANT: Interaction effects can make it difficult to adjust capital structure optimally in the future. This can favor a more flexible capital structure (more equity and financial slack) today.

Can we avoid the debt-or-equity dilemma by writing innovative dynamic contracts up front?

But what prevents the firm from arranging contracts ex-ante, so that the optimal rearrangements happen automatically ex-post? For example, an ex-ante bond covenant could force the firm to issue equity automatically, so there could be no reluctance by equity holders ex-post. Or the firm could execute a simple tax arbitrage. It could give a major equity owner a bond in exchange for shares and simultaneously execute a forward contract that will reexchange the bond into the same number of shares in 1 year. The payments during the year to this equity (now bond) owner would now be called interest payments, and thus they would be tax deductible from the corporation's point of view. Nothing other than extra corporate tax savings (during the most likely healthy next year) would have occurred. Under both mechanisms, shareholders and bondholders would pay a fair price for their securities—but the sum total of these security values would be higher, because the firm has increased its tax savings without raising its financial distress costs. Yet few firms seem to engage in such practices.

Perhaps the reason is that our setup is not applicable to most firms. One premise was that we wanted to stave off financial distress, but equity infusions to stave off bankruptcy may not always be value maximizing. For example, equity infusions could allow the firm to continue to burn its remaining assets instead of optimally liquidating them. Financial distress could also be the best or only mechanism for firing bad managers; and if managers could avoid financial distress at will, then debt would lose its function in the control of agency issues. Raising more equity to eliminate financial distress costs might thus facilitate the *wrong* managerial behavior.

Equity infusions may not always be so good, either.

Another important issue that can come up in a repeated, multiperiod setting is reputation. Reputation can lower financing costs, improve certain incentives, and increase firm value. Do you remember our earlier example in which the presence of an ex-post ability of managers to expropriate bondholders hurt the firm today? If managers had a reputation for not taking such bad projects, perhaps overly restrictive covenants could be avoided, in effect lowering financing costs ex-ante. More importantly, the example assumed that everyone knew exactly what expropriation opportunities existed and what their probabilities were. But despite restrictive covenants, bondholders will always have the nagging suspicion that they may be expropriated, after all, when unforeseen opportunities appear. Thus firms are often well advised to build trust and reputation to mitigate such suspicions.

Sometimes, owners are best off building a corporate reputation, which can help alleviate investor worries.

Do investors trust managers? *Can* investors trust managers? *Should* investors trust managers? When is it worthwhile for a manager/firm to build such a reputation? How can this effectively be accomplished? These are difficult questions to answer empirically, but they are important in the real world.

To trust or not to trust!

Ultimately, the trick to being a good manager is to judge and weigh the plethora of marginal costs and marginal benefits of projects, of debt, and of equity, and to have sound judgment in deciding on a good combination thereof. Choosing a good capital structure remains as much an "art" as it is a "science." This is good news for today's business students: Capital structure choices are unlikely to be taken over by a computer program anytime soon.

Choosing the best capital structure is a combination of art and science.

If you have the time, then this would be a good time to read two optional chapters that relate to the capital structure issues we just covered. Chapter 21 explains the dynamic process that determines corporate capital structures (including the role of investment bankers and the role of mergers and acquisitions). Chapter 22 explains the actual historical evidence describing corporate capital structures in the United States.

SOLVE NOW!

Q 18.33 A cash-cow firm, susceptible to agency issues, might hit short-term financial difficulties in a recession. What kind of financial security would maximize the firm's value?

SUMMARY

This chapter covered the following major points:

- One managerial objective should be to minimize the overall tax burden—the sum of taxes paid by the corporation and its investors.
- Investor clientele effects arise because they reduce overall tax payments. These effects are illustrated below.

Choice	Low-Tax Investors (e.g., pension funds)	High-Tax Investors (e.g., high-income individuals)
Good	Hold bonds (or very-high-dividend stocks)	Hold (low-dividend) stocks with high capital gains
Bad	Hold (low-dividend) stocks with high capital gains	Hold bonds (or very-high-dividend stocks)

Choice	High-Tax Corporations (e.g., "cash cows")	Low-Tax Corporations (e.g., "growth firms")
Good	Finance with bonds	Finance with stocks (pay out with share repurchases instead of dividends)
Bad	Finance with stocks	Finance with bonds

  It is the market prices for the cost of capital that incentivize smart firms and smart investors to arrange themselves in this clientele fashion to reduce overall taxes.

- There are numerous other tax-reduction schemes that firms can undertake—way too numerous to enumerate.
- Capital structure can influence managerial behavior in good times and in bad times, and both positively or negatively.
- Equity has an advantage in that it reduces the likelihood of financial distress, and with it deadweight bankruptcy costs in bad times. This includes both direct costs (such as legal fees) and indirect costs (such as underinvestment, reluctance to liquidate, and excessive risk taking).
- Debt has an advantage in that it imposes discipline on managers and thus reduces money wasting in good times. Managers and employees tend to work harder if poor performance can lead to bankruptcy.
- Equity has an advantage in that it does not tempt managers to expropriate creditors. If bondholders fear expropriation from subsequent increases in corporate risk or from the issuance of more debt with earlier payments or payments that are equal or higher in priority, they demand a higher cost of capital.
- Debt has an advantage in that it signals confidence. If owners—or managers acting on behalf of owners—prefer to sell partnership shares rather than debt, they probably believe that the project's true quality is worse. Thus, the cost of raising equity is high, because new partners will assume the worst.

- If agency conflicts are unmitigated, managers may not choose an optimal capital structure, but rather a relatively equity-heavy one.
- Section 18.8 summarizes the effects of different forces on firm value and cost of capital. It also summarizes how you should think of cost-of-capital formulas.
- Figure 18.5 illustrates how different forces enter valuation formulas.
- You do not need a more complex formula than WACC or APV from Chapter 17. The reason is that all market imperfections are better addressed with a flow-to-equity–like approach. That is, these factors should determine your expected cash flows and cost-of-capital inputs into the formula.
- Not needing a formula for other forces does not mean that these forces are any less important. You must think about (and often effectively estimate) how these forces influence your expected cash flows and costs of capital on both debt and equity.

KEY TERMS

SOLVE NOW! SOLUTIONS

Q 18.1 Higher debt and equity risk when the firm is more levered is not necessarily a force against leverage. Even in an M&M world with unchanging firm value, debt and equity have higher risk when the firm takes on more risk. See Section 16.4C on page 591. Consequently, higher risk in itself is usually not a counteracting force to the beneficial corporate income tax consequences of debt.

Q 18.2 A CFO should be concerned with the taxes that his investors are paying because he is supposed to act on behalf of the owners of the firm. This includes the task of minimizing any taxes that these owners are paying.

Q 18.3 Investors like capital gains best, then dividend income, then (equally) ordinary income and interest income.

Q 18.4 The firm must pay corporate income tax on cash used for repurchases and dividends, but it can use before-tax cash to pay interest. When the firm repurchases shares, investors receive the gains as capital gains (or, equivalently, an increase in the percentage of the firm that they own). Investors can easily shelter most of these payouts because they are capital gains, which face a lower statutory tax rate and which can be delayed until opportune. In contrast, investors face the full brunt of Uncle Sam on cash that comes to them in the form of interest payments. Dividend payments receive a treatment that is in between the two (impossible to delay, but subject to a lower statutory tax rate).

Q 18.5 If the puppeteer forced low-tax firms to finance with debt, and high-tax firms to finance with equity:

- The IRS would collect no corporate income tax from the low-tax firm. Low-tax investors who do not mind interest receipts would preferentially sort themselves toward the low-tax firms. With a 4% tax on $100 interest receipts, the IRS would collect $4 from them.
- The IRS would collect a full $40 from the high-tax firm. High-tax investors who like equity gains would preferentially hold their shares. The $60 paid out to investors would face a 10% capital gains tax rate, for another IRS take of $6. In sum, Uncle Sam ends up with $46.

The total tax payment would therefore be $4 + $40 + $6 = $50. This is much higher than the $15.80 tax in our proposed best solution. So the answer to our original question is yes—Uncle Sam would be better off if he could eliminate the tax deduction of interest for high-tax firms.

Q 18.6 Assuming that the high-tax firm still borrows and pays out $100, and the low-tax firm still finances with equity and pays out $98 (the answer is qualitatively the same if you assume that they pay out $96), if the puppeteer forced low-tax investors to hold equity and high-tax investors to hold debt:

- The high-tax investors would receive $100 (from high-tax firms) but pay $40 for interest receipts to the IRS.
- The low-tax investors would receive $98 (from low-tax firms) and pay 1% ($0.98) in capital gains tax.

The net payment of $40 + $2 + $0.98 = $42.98 is higher than the $15.80 in our proposed solution. So the answer to our original question is yes—Uncle Sam would be better off if he could force interest receipts on high-tax investors.

Q 18.7 Old, stable firms typically have large profits and would issue debt to minimize their tax liabilities. Because pension funds are largely tax exempt, they like the interest receipts that they receive from bonds. Young, growing firms should use a lot of equity financing. The tax deductibility of interest payouts would be of little use to them. Thus, their investors would gain primarily from capital gains. This is of value primarily to high-tax individuals who want to avoid highly taxed inflows.

Q 18.8 It is usually more critical for the high-tax firm to do the right thing, because it has to try to avoid its own corporate income taxes.

Q 18.9 Yes—a high-tax investor would be willing to accept a lower rate of return on capital gains in a risk-neutral world. The alternative is to receive interest income, which would be too heavily taxed.

Q 18.10 In Atlantis, investors should never receive the tax liability. Firms should therefore be always fully equity-financed. In the WACC formula, τ would be equal to zero, and $\mathcal{E}(\tilde{r}_{\text{Debt}})$ would be relatively higher than $\mathcal{E}(\tilde{r}_{\text{Equity}})$, so $\mathcal{E}(\tilde{r}_{\text{Firm}})$ would increase with w_{Debt}.

Q 18.11 Deadweight bankruptcy costs, both direct and indirect, favor equity: In the extreme, with no debt, the firm would never incur them.

Q 18.12 U.S. managers usually mean the chapters of the bankruptcy code: Reorganization is Chapter 11; liquidation is Chapter 7.

Q 18.13 Direct bankruptcy costs are legal fees and management time. Indirect costs are, for example, reluctance of customers to purchase goods from firms that could go bankrupt (e.g., if the good requires future contact or offers a warranty) and reluctance of suppliers to extend trade credit.

Q 18.14 As an example of an underinvestment problem, think of neglected maintenance that reduces the value of assets relative to the first-best behavior.

Q 18.15 To be influenced by underinvestment issues, assets must be very maintenance intensive (such as boats), and the firm must be reasonably likely to go bankrupt so that underinvestment considerations could come into play.

Q 18.16 Here are two examples of reluctance-to-liquidate problems:

- Entrenched managers may not want to sell off the remaining assets, because they would rather run down the firm and keep their jobs. This can hurt shareholders.

- Shareholders may not want to liquidate and sell the firm if it is "underwater," even if the offer is more than the firm is worth. The reason is that the benefits would go primarily to the creditors. The shareholders may prefer to gamble with the creditors' money on high-risk ventures instead. Note that this problem now helps shareholders, whereas in the previous case it hurt them.

Thus, this reluctance-to-liquidate issue is never good for creditors, but it can either hurt or help shareholders depending on the situation.

Q 18.17 Firms in declining industries are more likely to suffer reluctance-to-liquidate problems, especially if their managers are well entrenched.

Q 18.18 Debt is not always a strategic advantage. It could commit the firm to undertake more risky projects. In some cases, this could deter competitive entry into the firm's markets. However, debt could also make it more difficult for the management of a company to respond effectively.

Q 18.19 Management in firms with a lot of debt to service may have to forgo corporate airplanes, large headquarters, and/or large staff.

Q 18.20 It depends. If the firm is not yet under the firm control of management—for example, if it is under the control of a large value-maximizing shareholder-entrepreneur—then this entrepreneur would want the firm to be more debt-financed to keep management in check. However, if the firm is already under the firm control of conflicted management, then these managers will likely push to move away from debt and toward equity.

Q 18.21 1. For the firm worth \$100 or \$120 with debt promising \$90:

			Bad Luck	Good Luck		
		Prob:	1/2	1/2	Expected Value	PV($r = 10\%$)
	Project	Firm	\$100	\$120	\$110	\$100
	Convertible Bond with Face Value \$90					
(a)	Bond is Never Converted	Debt	\$90	\$90		
(b)	Always Converted (to 75% Equity)	Debt	75% · \$100 = \$75	75% · \$120 = \$90		
(c)	If Optimal Conversion Choice	Debt	\$90	\$90	\$90	\$81.82
	Equity	Equity	\$10	\$30	\$20	\$18.18

With these project payoffs, it is optimal for bondholders never to convert. Therefore, the conversion feature has no value.

2. With the new project "BAD" (which pays +\$50 or −\$60 with equal probabilities, independent of the original project), the payoffs are:

		Bad Luck		Good Luck			
	Prob:	1/4	1/4	1/4	1/4	Expected Value	PV($r = 10\%$)
Project	Firm	\$100	\$100	\$120	\$120	\$110	\$100.00
Project	BAD	\$50	−\$60	\$50	−\$60	−\$5	−\$4.54
Total Projects		\$150	\$40	\$170	\$60	\$105	\$95.45

We can now consider the two scenarios:

(a) In this case, the bond is nonconvertible.

Straight Bond with Face Value $90

		Bad Luck		Good Luck			
	Prob:	1/4	1/4	1/4	1/4	Expected Value	PV(r = 10%)
Total Projects		$150	$40	$170	$60	$105	$95.45
Bond	Debt	$90	$40	$90	$60	$70	$63.64
Equity	Equity	$60	$0	$80	$0	$35	$31.82

Yes, in this case, the shareholders want this project to be undertaken, because $31.82 is more than $18.18.

(b) In this case, the bond with $90 face value is convertible into 75% of the firm's equity.

		Bad Luck		Good Luck			
Prob:		1/4	1/4	1/4	1/4	Expected Value	PV(r = 10%)
Total Projects		$150	$40	$170	$60	$105	$95.45
Bond	Debt	$90	$40	$90	$60		
If Converted (to 75% Equity)	Debt	$112.50	$30	$127.50	$45		
If Optimally Converted	Debt	$112.50	$40	$127.50	$60	$85	$77.27
Equity	Equity	$37.50	$0	$42.50	$0	$20	$18.18

The shareholders are now no longer better off if project "BAD" is undertaken, because they now receive $18.18 either way. (If we made the debt convertible into 75.1% of the firm's equity, then the shareholders would be outright worse off.) Therefore, the convertibility adds value, even though we would never observe an actual conversion taking place. The convertibility would have deterred shareholders from taking bad projects in the first place.

Q 18.22 First, shareholders can expropriate bondholders by issuing other claims that have an earlier or equal priority on the firm's cash flows in distress. This could be other bonds of equal or higher priority, or a straight-out dividend payment. Second, shareholders could induce the firm to take on more risky projects. Numerical examples illustrating these two mechanisms are in the text.

Q 18.23 Managerial risk aversion usually mitigates the fear of creditors that they will be expropriated by risk shifting because managers dislike the same kind of risk. After all, if the firm were to go bankrupt, these managers would lose their jobs.

Q 18.24 Bond covenants can help reduce the incentives of equity shareholders to expropriate bondholders. This can increase the firm value if it prevents managers from taking negative-NPV projects whose main purpose was to shift value from bondholders to shareholders. However, covenants can also decrease the firm value if they prevent managers from taking positive-NPV projects that would trigger the bond covenant.

Q 18.25 The convertibility feature can reduce the need for some bond covenants and thus give the firm more flexibility in case a great project were to appear suddenly. Bondholders would be happy because they would benefit, too. (Of course, bondholders get more if the firm does well, and shareholders get a lower interest rate, but this is just state reallocation. The important aspect here is that the net effect of the alignment of interests would be a reduction in the firm's overall cost of capital.)

Q 18.26 You should not bid anything above $500,000 for this house. If you bid $750,000, then you will get the house only if it is worth $500,000, and you would therefore earn $500,000/$750,000 − 1 =−33%. The other half of the time, you would not be the highest bidder so your rate of return would be 0%. Thus, your expected rate of return would be 50% · (−33%) + 50% · 0% = −16.7%.

Q 18.27 The "pecking order" refers to a scenario in which firms first issue as many senior securities (debt) as they can, before they issue more junior securities (equity). As to the thinking question, in a real-world firm, a pecking order may or may not lead to the firm being more debt-financed over time, however. The reason is that the projects of many firms are profitable, which increases the value of the equity of the firm over time, too.

Q 18.28 Firms that are concerned about inside information issues (i.e., that investors infer the quality of the projects from their behavior) should issue debt, because issuing equity would send a bad signal about the value of their projects.

Q 18.29 An example of transaction costs favoring equity is market segmentation in the corporate debt market that might prevent selling corporate debt cheaply to many institutions and retail investors. An example of transaction costs favoring debt are high regulatory costs and exchange fees for listing the company's shares in the public market.

Q 18.30 See Table 18.6 for these forces. Not all forces are value optimizing for the overall firm (e.g., unmitigated agency conflicts).

Q 18.31 In an imperfect market, the costs of debt and equity capital (and thus of the firm's capital) can be affected by the firm's leverage ratio. Thus, the WACC function is no longer a horizontal line.

Q 18.32 No, the personal income tax rate is still value relevant. However, it works through its influence on the cost of capital that enters the WACC formula, not through its own term.

Q 18.33 A cash-cow firm would best be financed by something that looks like a bond until a recession comes around. You could design a novel kind of bond that has the ability to cancel or delay bond payments *if, and only if,* the official GDP or unemployment numbers state that there is a recession. The presence of agency issues makes it better if the contract does not allow managers to delay payments at their own discretion under normal circumstances.

PROBLEMS

The ▭ *indicates problems available in* myfinancelab

Q 18.34 Is the negative effect of debt on the price/earnings ratio a force that pushes firms toward equity?

Q 18.35 Go to the IRS website. Look up the highest marginal income tax rates for investors and corporations today on the different types of income that they might earn.

Q 18.36 From a joint income tax perspective, how should a high-tax value firm be financed? How should a low-tax growth firm be financed?

Q 18.37 From an income tax perspective, what kind of investments should a high net-income investor hold? What should a tax-exempt pension fund hold?

Q 18.38 Let's work a problem that shows how investors and firms sort themselves. Assume that taxable and tax-exempt firms each earn $1 of income. Assume that the financial markets offer 8% for tax-exempt income and 10% for taxable income. Assume that taxable firms and taxable investors are both taxed at 33.3%. Show what each type of firm and investors would do. Assume that capital gains are entirely untaxed. How would the arrangement change if the financial markets offered 9% for tax-exempt income?

Q 18.39 What does a corporate manager have to do to assign high-tax investors to his equity securities and low tax investors to his debt securities?

Q 18.40 In Nirvana, all investors are tax exempt. Only firms pay income taxes. How should firms be financed? How would the WACC formula work?

Q 18.41 When is financial distress neutral, with regard to capital structure? When is it not neutral?

Q 18.42 In what types of firms would you imagine financial distress costs to be high?

Q 18.43 Does it appear as if financial distress costs should be a significant determinant of Fortune 100 firms' capital structures? What about for small growth firms?

Q 18.44 A firm has debt with a face value of \$100. Its projects will pay a safe \$80 tomorrow. Managers care only about shareholders. A new quickie project comes along that costs \$20, earns either \$10 or \$40 with equal probabilities, and does so by tomorrow.

(a) Is this a positive-NPV project?
(b) If the new project can only be financed with a new equity issue, would the shareholders vote for this? Would the creditors?
(c) Assume the existing bond contract was written in a way that allows the new projects to be financed with first collateral (superseniority with respect to the existing creditors). New creditors can collect \$20 from what the existing projects will surely pay. Would the existing creditors be better off?
(d) What is the better arrangement from a firm-value perspective?

Q 18.45 Rent and watch the movie *Other People's Money.* Pay close attention to Danny DeVito's speech at the shareholders' meeting. What capital structure–related issue is he talking about? What kind of security would have reduced this problem?

Q 18.46 What kind of firms are most likely to be influenced by free cash flow issues when choosing a capital structure?

Q 18.47 A firm has debt with a face value of \$100. Its projects will pay a safe \$80 tomorrow. Managers care only about shareholders. A new quickie project comes along that costs \$30, earns either \$0 or \$70 with equal probabilities, and does so by tomorrow.

(a) Is this a positive-NPV project?
(b) If the new project can only be financed with a new equity issue, would the shareholders vote for this? Would the creditors?
(c) Assume the existing bond contract was written in a way that allows the new projects to be financed with first collateral (superseniority with respect to the existing creditors). New creditors can collect \$30 from what the existing projects will surely pay. Would the existing creditors be better off?
(d) What is the better arrangement from a firm-value perspective if the old bondholders have veto power?

Q 18.48 What are the advantages and disadvantages of unit offering bundles?

Q 18.49 ADVANCED: A firm has \$100 in cash and debt of \$80. Assume that the time value of money is zero. A novel project comes along that costs \$60 and that will either deliver \$0 or x with equal probabilities.

(a) What is the value of debt and equity without the project?
(b) What is the x value above which the project would be positive NPV? Call this xh.
(c) What is the x value above which the shareholders want the firm to take the project? Call this xl.
(d) Divide the possible regions into those below xl, those between xl and xh, and those above xh. More specifically, pick $xl - \$10$, $(xl + xh)/2$, and $xh + 10$ as your returns in the good state. In these three cases:
   1. If the debt can convert into 80% of the post-conversion equity, what would the debt and equity be worth? Would existing equity want to take the project?
   2. If the debt can convert into 0% of the post-conversion equity (i.e., if it is not convertible), what would the debt and equity be worth? Would existing equity want to take the project?
   3. If the debt can convert into 40% of the post-conversion equity, what would the debt and equity be worth? Would existing equity want to take the project?

(e) What conversion rate would you recommend to maximize the value of the firm today?

Q 18.50 Are shareholders better off if they can expropriate bondholders?

Q 18.51 A stake in an oil field is for sale. It can be worth either \$500 or \$1,000 with equal probabilities. It costs \$250 to develop. The seller knows the true value; you do not. The seller has no personal sources of funds. In an otherwise perfect market with no time value of money, what can the seller expect to raise and at what price?

Q 18.52 Repeat the last question but now assume that this seller has personal savings of $200. With this extra capital and bargaining power, what can the seller expect to raise and at what price?

Q 18.53 If investors are rational and managers are overoptimistic, how would the value of the firm change if management were to raise more money for new projects? Would it be worse if the firm raised equity?

Q 18.54 When private equity firms take over publicly traded firms, they usually increase the leverage tremendously. Discuss what effect this capital structure policy should have on the firm's value and why.

Q 18.55 Explain three forces that can make debt cheaper than equity for corporate financing.

Q 18.56 Explain three forces that can make equity cheaper than debt for corporate financing.

Q 18.57 If the firm maximizes its *value* in an imperfect financial market, how would this change its *cost of capital*?

Q 18.58 What forces can change the shape of the graph of cost of capital versus leverage?

Q 18.59 Where do agency considerations appear in the WACC formula? Do agency costs influence the firm's WACC?

Q 18.60 If you could design a novel security at the inception of a growth firm that you expect to turn into a cash-generating value firm in 5 years, what would it look like?

Q 18.61 Is the ability of a firm to stave off financial distress always optimal from the firm-value perspective?

19

Equity Payouts: Dividends and Share Repurchases

DOES PAYOUT POLICY MATTER?

As a CFO, you can do four things with the money the corporation has earned: You can keep it in the company (spend or reinvest it), you can pay off liabilities, you can use it to pay dividends, or you can use it to repurchase shares. The latter two courses of action increase the debt/equity ratio and send money from inside the firm to the outside, thereby shrinking firm size. They are the primary mechanisms by which equity shareholders receive a payback on their investment, and thus they are of interest in themselves. In addition, they are under regular and easy discretion of management. The board can decide on these payouts almost every quarter. This is why they warrant their own chapter—although a short one.

19.1 BACKGROUND

A short retrospective where you have seen dividends before.

You have already seen cash dividends in previous chapters. Let me recap for you.

➤ Separation of consumption and investment choices, Section 4.1A, p. 68

➤ Tax clienteles and dividends, Section 18.2, p. 650

In the context of perfect markets, you learned that as an investor, you can always sell your shares, thereby breaking the link between when the project generates cash and when you need it. Cash dividends do not destroy or generate value, because they do not fall like manna from heaven.

In the context of imperfect markets, you learned that dividends are not a tax-efficient way to distribute cash, because investors cannot shelter dividend payments from the IRS as easily as they can shelter repurchase payouts or capital gains. However, vis-à-vis managers spending money on themselves, a dividend payout can reduce agency conflicts.

➤ Issuing and firm size, Section 21.1B, p. 788

You can also think of equity payouts as the opposite of equity share issuing activity. In this sense, the arguments from all previous capital structure–related chapters apply just as well to equity payouts. An equity issue increases the firm size and decreases the debt/equity ratio. Both cash dividends and share repurchases reduce the firm size and increase the debt/equity ratio. However, the empirical evidence suggests that dividends and share repurchases are not very important in terms of changing the debt/equity ratio in the typical U.S. company.

➤ Debt/equity ratios and dividends, Section 22.3A, p. 836

19.1A DIVIDEND MECHANICS

The institutional basics of ordinary and special dividends.

A **dividend** is a distribution from the firm to its investors. If not qualified, this usually means a **cash dividend**. These come in one of two forms: regular dividends or special dividends. In 2004, about one in four publicly traded companies (usually large earnings-rich stocks) paid a regular dividend, typically once per quarter. Special dividends are designated to be one-time payouts and can be considerably larger than ordinary dividends. Although the whole point of a special dividend is that investors should not expect it to be repeated, many companies repeat special dividends over and over anyway.

The two important dates: the announcement and the cum-/ex-dividend date.

There are two important dates when it comes to the execution of a dividend:

1. On the **declaration date**, the board of directors votes to pay a dividend on a particular date—usually a couple of weeks later. This is usually when the market first learns of the payment, although many dividends are so regular that investors practically know it in advance.
2. The **cum-dividend date** is the last date on which a share still has the right to receive the dividend. Shares traded the following day, the **ex-dividend date**, are without the payment of the dividend.

There are also two administrative bookkeeping dates: The *record date* on which share ownership is ascertained (to determine where to send the check) and the *payment date* on which the firm actually sends the money.

DRIPs—a tax liability in the mail?!

One odd creature in which money does not change hands is the **dividend reinvestment plan (DRIP)**. In a DRIP, participating shareholders agree to reinvest automatically any dividend payments into more shares of the company. Consequently, investors do not receive any cash. All that they receive is a tax obligation at the end of the year for the dividends that they presumably received. If the company had just kept all the money, its investors would not have received this obligation to pay personal income taxes on the dividend. To complicate matters further, if set up with the corporation itself rather than through a brokerage firm, many DRIPs reimburse investors with shares at a discount or at a rate that is not the current market value. (The average value over the most recent quarter is common.) In this case, the company effectively hands its investors a personal income tax liability, but compensates them for it. Thus, the firm pays much of the tax penalty itself (with the shareholders' money, of course).

Stock dividends and splits are not payouts, but changes in numeraire.

A rarer type of dividend is the **stock dividend**. This is not an equity payout at all—no cash is involved. Instead, each share owner receives more shares. For example, if a $1 billion company whose shares are trading for $100 per share issues a 1-share stock dividend for every 10 outstanding shares, then its 10 million shares would just become 11 million shares. In a perfect market, each share would be worth $90.91. No money has changed hands, and all shareholders own the same fraction of the firm as they did before. A stock dividend is really more like a small **stock split**. An example of a 2-for-1 stock split is when the firm converts its 10 million shares, each worth $100, into 20 million shares, each worth $50. Again, there is no cash changing hands. Every shareholder owns exactly the same fraction of the company before and after. A **reverse stock split** is a similar exchange, but the number of shares declines and the price of the shares increases.

SOLVE NOW!

Q 19.1 What are the two important dates when it comes to dividends?

Q 19.2 What should be the stock market reaction to the announcement of a split in a perfect market?

19.1B SHARE REPURCHASE MECHANICS

The institutional basics of auction-based and open-market share repurchases.

Share repurchases allow corporations to buy back their own stock. You can think of them as the opposite of equity issues. There are two main ways to repurchase stock:

Auction-based repurchases: In a typical auction-based repurchase program, shareholders receive an offer by the firm wanting to purchase a fixed number of shares at a fixed-price premium (typically around 15% to 20%) from its investors, or a notice that the firm wants to buy shares from those sellers willing to part with them at the lowest premium. If there is too much shareholder interest, the firm usually repurchases shares **pro rata** (i.e., in proportionally fair allocations).

Rare but big.

Auction-based repurchases are fairly rare. In a typical year in the late 1990s, all publicly traded firms together announced only about $5 to $10 billion worth of auction-based repurchases. They are used primarily when a company wants to purchase large quantities of its shares quickly. This means that they usually occur when a firm faces a proxy fight or is targeted by outside hostile acquirers.

➤ Resistance to a hostile takeover, Section 23.3B, p. 883

Open-market repurchases: The more common way for firms to repurchase their shares is through open-market repurchases. Such a program is approved by the corporate board, and then must be disclosed publicly (because it is material news). However, the SEC imposes no filing requirements or progress disclosures. After its announcement, the firm can then purchase shares at its own discretion. There are no fixed limits on program size or duration. Typically, firms announce that they want to repurchase around 5% of their share base and that the repurchase program will last for 2 to 3 years.

Repurchases could face or avoid price manipulation charges.

Before 1982, one problem that corporations could run into was that their actual repurchasing activity could violate the SEC rules against price manipulation (the well-known **Rule 10b-5**). Fortunately, in 1982, the SEC issued a clarification, (**Rule 10b-18**), which provides a **safe harbor**. (This safe harbor means that the SEC will not file price manipulation charges against companies repurchasing shares on the open market. Perhaps more important, because qualifying behavior is deemed reasonable by the SEC, it makes it harder for other investors to win a lawsuit against the firm for doing so, too.) Firms are in the clear if they use only one broker, do not execute the repurchase at market opening or during the last half hour of trading, do not pay unusual prices, and do not purchase more than 25% of average daily trading volume over the past 4 weeks. In addition, these limits do not apply to shares repurchased on behalf of an employee stock ownership plan (ESOP) and do not apply to negotiated off-market trades. And finally, the SEC has relaxed even these rules—for example, right after the 1987 stock market crash. Despite all these exceptions, it is common for firms to stay only within the spirit of Rule 10b-18, but not within the letter of the law.

Open-based repurchases are very common, but often small.

Open-based repurchase programs are very common. In a typical year in the late 1990s, publicly traded firms together announced about $150 to $200 billion worth of such repurchasing. About 70% to 80% of S&P 500 firms had a share repurchase program going at any given point in time, and roughly one in four S&P 500 companies announced a new multiyear share repurchase program in a given year. The programs themselves are very flexible—firms may never purchase *any* shares if they so desire.

With no disclosure requirements, repurchase programs are difficult to study.

Unfortunately, because firms also do not need to disclose the outcome, researchers can only guess what happens from bits and pieces of evidence that have surfaced informally. Our best estimates are that firms repurchase about three-quarters of their announced share repurchase target over a period of 3 years. (Of course, at the same time, corporations can issue many shares, e.g., in connection with ESOPs.) Nevertheless, in the aggregate, open-market announced repurchase programs are clearly much more important than auction-based programs.

SOLVE NOW!

Q 19.3 What are the two kinds of repurchase programs?

Q 19.4 Could a firm undertaking an open-market repurchase program be accused of manipulating its stock price?

19.2 PERFECT-MARKET IRRELEVANCE

In a perfect world à la M&M, dividends neither destroy nor create value.

Corporate payout policy should not matter in a perfect-market setting. This is the second Modigliani-Miller proposition. From the corporate perspective, if managers pay $1 in dividends, this money has to come from somewhere. Dividends do not fall like manna from heaven, so no value is created or destroyed when firms pay dividends. Money that was previously owned by investors but held inside the corporate shell is just being moved to the same investors, so that it is now outside the corporate shell. The owners do not have any more or any less wealth because of the dividend payment. You can use an M&M arbitrage argument to give this statement more perspective. If managers undertook a dividend policy that destroyed value, then any investor could step in to purchase the firm, fire the management, institute the better dividend policy, and resell the firm for the difference. Therefore, the value of the firm cannot be a function of its dividend policy.

The M&M logic helps us think about our imperfect real world.

Like the point of the M&M capital structure proposition, the point of the M&M dividend proposition is not to argue that dividends do not matter. It is to point out what perfect-market violations must be in place for dividend policy to matter, and how much these violations can matter. For example, if it costs a round-trip premium of $10 million to purchase and then resell a firm, then it cannot be that the wrong dividend policy destroys more than $10 million. If it did, you could make money even in this specific imperfect world.

The situation today: Dividend yields are generally low. Dividend increases are on average value-enhancing.

As of 2008, the average dividend yield of large firms was around 1% of firm value per year. This is probably so low that the real-world transaction costs are much larger than what you could earn by taking over a firm to correct a poor dividend policy. That is, if the optimal payout were actually 0% or 2% instead of 1%, the value gain is probably even less than this 1% value increase. You would not bother stepping in to correct it. As you will learn later in this chapter, there is good evidence that the M&M assumptions are indeed violated in this context: When firms announce dividend increases, their values usually go up; and when they announce dividend decreases, their values usually go down. Can you speculate which M&M assumption is most likely violated? Most finance professors believe that paying dividends sends a credible signal from management about the firm's future prospects and good managerial behavior (that managers will not waste the money on themselves). This violates the M&M assumption that everyone has the same information: In the real world, managers have inside information that investors do *not* have—even if it is only about how much money they may waste in the future.

Some common fallacies to set straight.

Before we move on to a more realistic world, we can use perfect-market thinking to dispense with some naïve conceptions that are obviously wrong.

Dividends eat as much substance as share sales do!

1. **Dividends do not eat "investment substance," whereas selling shares does.** False. It makes no sense to argue that dividends are paid because investors "need" money or that share sales (repurchases by the firm) do not eat equal substance. It is true that if you hold 100 shares worth $4,000, and the company pays you a dividend of $200, you can use the dividends to spend if you so choose. You would have $3,800 worth of shares left. Yet, if the company reinvested the money instead of paying dividends, if you had sold 5 shares for $200 on the stock exchange, you would similarly have been left with $3,800 in shares and $200 in cash. Your "substance" (i.e., your remaining investment) would have been the same, either way.

All investors gain from share repurchases.

2. **Only tendering shareholders gain from share repurchases.** False. Share repurchases benefit not only shareholders who tender their shares into the repurchase, but all investors. This is the same situation as with dividends. When firms repurchase shares at a fair price in a perfect world, participating and nonparticipating investors prosper equally. Participating investors get cash; nonparticipating investors get to own a higher fraction of the firm. Here is an example. A firm with 100 shareholders, each owning $10 worth of shares, could pay $50 worth of dividends ($0.50 to each shareholder), and the firm would be worth $950. Each shareholder would have a share worth $9.50 and $0.50 in dividends. If the firm repurchased $50 worth of shares, the firm would be left with 95 shareholders, each owning $10 worth of shares. Both tendering and nontendering investors have neither gained nor lost.

   In sum, the following simple table illustrates some of what the firm can do with cash it has earned:

FIRM'S ACTION	RESULT
Reinvest cash	All investors receive (unrealized) capital gains.
Repurchase shares	Some investors realize capital gains. Other investors own more of the firm.
Pay dividends	All investors receive taxable dividends.

Therefore, it also makes sense to compare dividends to the alternative of capital gains.

It is an important assumption in this example that the price paid for shares is fair. If it is not, then the remaining shareholders could be better off (if the firm repurchased the shares for less than their true value) or worse off (if the firm repurchased the shares for more than their true value). Indeed, the latter sometimes happens. In a **targeted repurchase**, management makes an offer to purchase shares at an above-market price only to specific shareholders. (For example, in the 1980s, it was common for management to "buy off" potential acquirers.) In this case, the stock value of the remaining shareholders goes down. Buying shares above fair value destroys value for the remaining shareholders.

➤ Greenmail, Section 23.3B, p. 883

3. **Share repurchases increase EPS.** False. It is correct that a repurchase reduces the number of shares outstanding. But the cash paid out also reduces the amount of money that is reinvested. Thus, it depends on whether the cash reinvested would have produced more or less earnings (in proportion). For example, if the firm pays out cash by selling its most profitable and riskiest projects, then its expected earnings per share should go down. As long as the price received is fair, this does not create or destroy value. Conversely, if the cash had been sitting in safe Treasuries and not in riskier projects with higher expected earnings, then the firm's expected EPS should go up. Of course, doing so does not generate value by itself. The firm's earnings will go up, but so will its risk. After all, Treasuries are zero-NPV projects.

   More usefully, you should think of firm value (not EPS). In a share repurchase, value increases if the firm avoids taking negative-NPV projects that it would have otherwise undertaken.

Share repurchases do not necessarily increase EPS. You should think of firm value rather than EPS.

To the extent that financial markets are close to perfect, real life should not be too different, so the above statements should hold more or less. Nevertheless, they do not need to hold perfectly. In an imperfect financial market, these statements may not necessarily be plain fallacies. However, to make this argument in an imperfect market requires a much more sophisticated train of thought. For example, retail investors receiving dividends who need spending money may save on transaction costs if they do not have to sell shares. Thus, a dividend may leave them with a little more substance than a share repurchase. This may not be plausible, but it is logically possible. For another example, a repurchase could increase a firm's EPS if it reduces agency conflicts and money wasting by managers.

In an imperfect world, very mild forms of the above fallacies could be true, though this is not likely.

In sum, in a perfect market, thinking about dividends and share repurchases is easy. They are irrelevant from a value perspective. *In the perfect M&M world, without taxes, **all** shareholders are equally well off with or without either a repurchase or a dividend payment.* It does not matter, either, where the funds for the payout come from. The firm could either raise new funds from new creditors or from new shareholders in order to pay out cash to existing shareholders (which many corporations do), or it could use its retained earnings, or it could sell some of its operations. What really matters instead is that the company takes all its projects with positive NPVs. The sum-total value of its projects is the value of the firm. If this were not the case, someone would take over the company and make it so.

Dividends and repurchase policy are irrelevant in the M&M world. Money can come from anywhere and go to anywhere.

The remainder of this chapter therefore focuses on the more interesting question of how dividends and share repurchases function in the real world—in an imperfect financial market.

SOLVE NOW!

Q 19.5 In a perfect market, if a normal investor cannot participate in a share repurchase program, would she be better off with a dividend payout than with a share repurchase?

Q 19.6 Consider a firm with 80 shareholders, including yourself, who each own $10 worth of shares. In addition, I own 20 shares (for a firm total of 100 shares) and I am trying to fire the management. To appease me, the management has offered to purchase my shares at $15 per share. How would this change the value of your shares?

Q 19.7 Under what circumstances do share repurchases increase the firm's EPS?

19.3 DIVIDENDS AND SHARE REPURCHASES

The "payout versus no payout" is the opposite of the "issue versus no issue" argument discussed in the previous chapters.

➤ How to invest if you know more than the market, Section 11.6C, p. 372

You already know the answer to the question of whether paying out cash creates or destroys value in imperfect capital markets. There is nothing new here: The answer is based on exact analogs of the arguments in the capital structure section. Ultimately, it comes back to the question of whether, as CFO, you should put your investors' cash to use in your company or whether you should return it to them. If you pass up positive-NPV projects because you pay out cash, then you destroy value. If you pass up negative-NPV projects because you pay out cash, then you create value. The same market imperfections that determined capital structure are at play in determining payout policy, too. For example:

Corporate taxes: If you pay dividends or repurchase shares by issuing more debt, future payouts will be tax advantaged. In this case, equity payouts can create value.

Personal taxes: If you pay dividends or repurchase shares, your investors will have a bigger tax liability on these receipts than if you reinvest the money. This can destroy value.

Financial distress: If you pay dividends or repurchase shares when the company is cash constrained, it can increase the probability that the firm will go bankrupt. This can impose direct and indirect bankruptcy costs, which can destroy value.

Agency and signaling: If you pay dividends or repurchase shares when the temptation is to use the cash on pet projects, empire building, or managerial perks—all of which are negative-NPV projects—you can create value.

And so on.

The more novel question concerns the decision of whether you should pay out cash in the form of dividends or in the form of share repurchases. The most obvious differences between dividend payments and share repurchases are those related to personal income tax treatment, so let's cover personal income taxes first.

SOLVE NOW!

Q 19.8 Can you think of dividend payouts and equity share repurchases as the opposite of issuing equity shares? If so, do the forces from Table 18.6 page 688 apply here, too?

19.3A PERSONAL INCOME TAX DIFFERENCES AND INVESTOR CLIENTELES

The clientele diagrams in Section 18.2 illustrated a basic fact: From a personal income tax perspective, dividends are worse than share repurchases. Share repurchases remain the smarter way to pay out cash, even though the Bush dividend tax cut of 2003 has largely eliminated the differences in statutory personal income tax rates between capital gains and dividends. In a share repurchase, nonparticipating investors face no tax consequences, and participating investors face only potential capital gains taxes. The remaining advantages of repurchases, then, relate to the fact that dividends are taxed every year, whereas capital gains are only taxed when an investor realizes them.

Today, dividends are almost as good as capital gains from a tax perspective.

➤ Tax clienteles, Section 18.2, p. 650

Accumulating taxation: For example, if a firm were to offer capital gains of 20% per year, then a \$100 investment would earn you $\$100 \cdot 1.2 \cdot 1.2 = \$144$ over 2 years. (The same would apply if your benefit [from the repurchase] came not from a value increase but from each of your shares representing a larger fraction of the firm.) Assuming a 50% tax rate, you would keep \$22. In contrast, if the \$20 were dividend payments, then you would receive a 10% after-tax interest rate every year and thus keep only $\$100 \cdot 1.1 \cdot 1.1 - \$100 = \$21$. The \$1 difference between dividend payments and repurchase payments is due to the fact that Uncle Sam can earn interest on a part of your dividend receipts that were paid out after 1 year. The example is overstated, because the statutory tax rate is much lower than 50%—but over many years, the forgone return on intermediate taxes can accumulate and make a difference.

➤ Tax timing, Section 10.4D, p. 328

Capital loss offsets: Capital losses can be used to offset the benefits of any capital gains resulting from reinvestment or share repurchases. It is at the discretion of each investor to determine when she has enough capital losses elsewhere not to suffer capital gains taxes. In contrast, capital losses (mostly) cannot be used to offset dividend payments. Moreover, dividends are forced upon each and every investor, possibly in relatively inopportune years from a particular investor's perspective.

Clienteles: Repurchases allow retail clienteles to develop—a fact that helps to take some bite out of capital gains tax. Among retail investors, there will be some who purchased the stock at a high price and others who purchased it at a low price. When the firm repurchases shares, those investors with low accumulated capital gains (having purchased the stock at a relatively high price) can participate in the share repurchase without much of a capital gains consequence. This allows other investors with higher accumulated capital gains to delay/avoid realization and suffer no tax consequences.

Share repurchases are just a little better than dividends from a tax perspective nowadays.

Tax clienteles among retail investors with different unrealized capital gains are good at taking a bite out of the tax penalty on repurchases but not out of the tax

ANECDOTE Pre-Bush Tax Cuts: Ralph Nader and Microsoft

On January 4, 2002, Ralph Nader wrote an open letter to William H. Gates III, Chairman of Microsoft, that began as follows:

> We are writing to ask Microsoft to change its practice of not paying dividends to shareholders. Our reasons are as follows.
>
> 1. The quantitative failure to pay dividends year after year is an inappropriate and we believe unlawful device to shelter Microsoft earnings from federal income taxes.
>
> By not paying dividends, wealthy Microsoft shareholders such as yourself avoid paying the top marginal tax rate of 39.6 percent that would apply to income distributed as dividends. By taking earnings entirely through stock sales, wealthy shareholders lower their tax rate to the maximum 20 percent that applies to capital gains. According to the most recent SEC reports on insider trades, you personally sold more than $2.9 billion in Microsoft stock last year, benefiting enormously from the lower tax rate that applies to stock sales.

This letter does not even point out that 20% is an overstatement: Gates is taxed only on *realized* capital gains! If he does not sell his shares, he suffers zero taxes on increases in his wealth over the years. And, with the Republicans' elimination of the estate tax, neither do his heirs suffer any taxes. In defense of Gates, most of his wealth has gone into a foundation that promotes global health.

The Bush tax reforms of 2003 have further significantly reduced the taxes on dividend payments. Microsoft promptly started paying dividends in 2003—many billions' worth.

Here is an interesting question: Is it the fault of Bill Gates (who is also a prolific political campaign donor) or is it the fault of the U.S. government that Gates has suffered only minimal tax obligations on his wealth gains over the last 20 years?

penalty on dividends. However, other clienteles potentially can: Zero-tax retail investors or tax-exempt investors, such as pension funds or low-income investors, could take a bite even out of dividend taxes. They can not only hold bonds to shelter interest taxes, but also hold stocks to shelter dividend taxes. This is especially effective if it needs to occur only around the cum-/ex-dividend date (which determines whether an investor receives the dividend). However, the evidence suggests that low-tax investors are in short supply, and some IRS rules are making this special form of 1-day tax arbitrage illegal. Thus, dividend tax arbitrage is not perfect. The tax-exempt investor clienteles have only reduced the penalty of dividends relative to share repurchases—they have not eliminated it. Thus, the presence of pension funds cannot explain why firms pay dividends from a tax perspective: Share repurchases remain better, because they can de facto avoid almost *all* personal income taxes. From a pure tax perspective, share repurchases simply dominate dividends.

An IRS rule against using share repurchases over dividends is largely irrelevant.

There may be one final minor wrinkle. The IRS could in principle declare a share repurchase as the equivalent of a dividend. However, enforcement of this provision has been weak or nonexistent in *publicly traded* corporations—in fact, I don't know of *any* recent instances. With some proper care to evade specific IRS tests, this is not a biting constraint for public firms.

Empirical historical evidence about typical dividend yields and dividend changes. Repurchases and dividends are now approximately equally important.

If you want to understand historical equity payout patterns, you need to know that dividends used to be treated much worse than repurchases from a tax perspective. Figure 19.1 plots the historical tax rates on dividends and capital gains. Until 2003, the tax rate on dividends was the same as the ordinary income tax rate (35% in 2002), not the 15% capital gains tax that it is in 2008. (The 35% still applies to foreign corporations' dividends and to some nonqualifying dividends if a domestic company has not

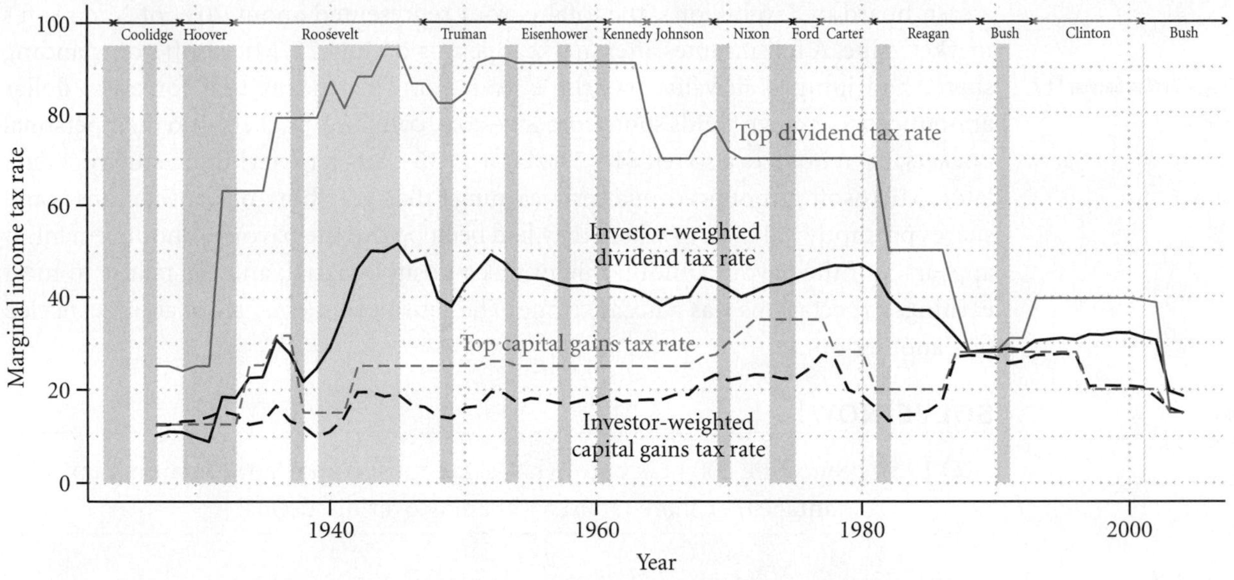

The blue lines show the marginal tax rates on dividends and capital gains for an investor in the top income bracket. Because not all investors were in this bracket, the black lines are investor-weighted, taking investors in all tax brackets into account. The capital gains taxes are an overstatement, because they can be washed against capital losses and realized at the investor's discretion. The pink background represents recessions; the blue background represents World War II.
Source: Sialm (2006). Reprinted with permission of the author.

FIGURE 19.1 Capital Gains and Dividend Tax Rates, 1927–2004

paid appropriate income taxes.) Before the Reagan *Tax Reform Act of 1986*, it was yet worse again, because dividends suffered tax rates of 50% (just like ordinary income). Between World War II and 1965, the government practically confiscated dividend payments to investors in the top income bracket! You may find it difficult to understand why corporations pay out cash in dividends today—but it is merely a minor puzzle. Yet 30 years ago, the academic community was really at a total loss trying to understand why any firm would want to pay dividends. Fortunately, education helped. A generation of business school–educated students eventually moved into corporate headquarters, and more and more companies followed the academics' advice, paying out more and more through share repurchases rather than through dividends. The empirical evidence shows that since the 1980s, many firms have been shifting away from dividend payments and toward share repurchases as a means to return money to shareholders. (It helped that other forces such as the 1982 10b-15 ruling and executive self-interest also pulled managers toward more share repurchases—discussed in more detail below.)

Microsoft's dividend initiation in 2003 is a good example of the effect of the 2003 dividend tax rate cut.

A good number of firms responded to the Bush dividend tax cut of 2003 in the logical way: They started paying dividends for the first time. The most prominent was Microsoft (MSFT). After the market closed on July 20, 2004, it announced a \$32 billion special dividend, plus a \$30 billion share repurchase, plus an increase in ordinary dividends from 16 cents to 32 cents per share (a yield increase from 0.56% to 1.12%). With a market capitalization of about \$300 billion (a P/E ratio of about 20 [based on forward-looking earnings] or 37 [based on recent earnings], and a cash hoard of $56 billion), the total payout represented about 20% of Microsoft's market value. A few minutes after market opening on July 21, Microsoft's outstanding shares had jumped in value by a little over 3%. This means that for every dollar announced to change hands soon from investors' company pockets into their personal pockets, shareholders also felt $\$1 \cdot 3\%/20\% = 15$ cents happier! Interestingly, 2 days later, Microsoft announced quarterly earnings that fell short of expectations—and shares promptly fell back to where they had been before the payout announcement. It appears as if the payout announcement was a positive signal, and the failure to meet earnings expectations was a negative one. These two event effects just about canceled one another out.

➤ Event studies, Section 11.7, p. 375

SOLVE NOW!

Q 19.9 Since the 2003 tax cuts, what is the most important remaining tax advantage that share repurchases enjoy over dividends?

19.3B NONTAX DIFFERENCES

There are still some nontax differences between dividends and share repurchases.

With the reduction of the personal income tax differences, other differences between dividends and share repurchases have become relatively more important. Here they are, ranked by my assessment of their importance.

Dividends are stickier.

1. **Dividend smoothing:** Many share repurchases used to be done fairly irregularly. In contrast, ordinary dividends informally oblige management to continue them. This was first noted in 1956 by John Lintner. He found that firms were reluctant to cut dividends, instead preferring to slowly increase them over time. This behavior is called **dividend smoothing**. It still holds today, though it is no longer as strong as it once was. In the mid-1990s, out of 100 firms that paid dividends, 10 would increase them every quarter, 89 would continue them, and 1 would cut them. (Lintner also documented a second fact: Companies had a target dividend/earnings payout ratio, to which they smoothly tried to adjust. This does not seem to be the case anymore.)

   This stickiness of dividends leads to a whole range of interesting behavior patterns. For example, there is an interesting signaling game that could ensue: Shareholders expect dividends to continue. This, in turn, may itself be the reason why managers tend to oblige. If they believe that an earnings shock is transitory, they would probably pay out cash via a share repurchase. They would use a dividend payment only if they believe it is permanent. The reason is that if they increased dividends because of a one-time positive shock to earnings, then they might have to cut their dividends in the future. This risks disappointment of the financial markets—and possibly their own jobs. A dividend increase therefore implies that managers signal more optimism about the future than they would signal with an equal share repurchase.

   (The regularity difference is not perfect, though. Many companies have semiregular share repurchase programs, which make repurchases almost as regular as dividend payments. And many other companies pay "special dividends" [or bond dividends] that signal their one-time nature to investors. Such special dividends are as much "one-time" as share repurchases.)

2. **Executive stock options:** Executives often receive **executive stock options** in the company, whose value depends on the share price. (You can find an estimate of their value in the financial statement footnotes. Chapter 26 explains how this value is computed.) A dividend is bad for any call option owner, because the share price drops when it is paid. For example, if a manager of a $60 company has an option that allows her to purchase shares at $50, then the manager would be reluctant to pay $20 in dividends—after all, the share price would drop to about $40, making the right to purchase at $50 much less valuable. Therefore, managers with many options prefer repurchases to dividend payments.

Executives holding options prefer capital gains.

3. **Executive ownership:** Executives and insiders are often not permitted to tender their shares in share repurchase offers. Thus, they will own relatively more of the company after a repurchase than after an equivalent dividend payment.

Repurchases increase inside ownership.

4. **Investor preferences:** There is some "behavioral finance" evidence that small retail investors simply "like" dividends better than share repurchases—although it is a great mystery why this is so. You already know that the argument that investors like dividends "because they need cash" does not hold water. Selling a fraction of the shares in stocks that pay zero dividends provides physical cash, too—except that the investor would not have had to pay as much in personal income taxes. Indeed, personal tax considerations suggest that investors would likely end up with more if they sold shares. Still, it seems that many investors—especially less sophisticated ones—wrongly think only of share sales but not of dividend receipts as reductions in their "investment substance." Given the existence of such shareholders, companies may respond appropriately by paying dividends.

   Fortunately, the tax penalty of dividends is lower today than it was in the past, so the mystery is smaller and less significant. The behavior of small investors is under active academic investigation. My guess is that the answer will likely be that these individual investor preference effects are real and irrational but that they are not universal, and ultimately not overly important.

Some investors just like dividends.

5. **Fund charter exclusion clauses:** Some institutional shareholders are obliged by their charters to hold *only* dividend-paying stocks. This provision excludes them from holding stocks such as Microsoft prior to 2003, that is, before Microsoft initiated dividend payments.

Some funds cannot hold firms that pay no dividends.

SOLVE NOW!

Q 19.10 What are the differences, other than personal income tax differences, between a share repurchase and a dividend payment?

19.4 EMPIRICAL EVIDENCE

You now know the factors at play when it comes to dividends and repurchases. But in what form, and how much, did firms actually pay cash to their shareholders historically?

19.4A HISTORICAL PAYOUT PATTERNS

Dividend/earnings ratios have been at a constant 50% for large firms.

Dividend ratios: Figure 19.2 graphs the payout patterns over the last century. Graph (a) shows that S&P 500 firms paid out about half of their earnings in dividends. (This **dividend/earnings ratio** is sometimes just called the **dividend/payout ratio.**) This payout ratio has been fairly stable for large firms, at least since World War II.

Dividend/price ratios have fallen.

Graph (b) shows that dividend payouts have become a smaller fraction of the share price (invested money), at least after 1980. Nowadays, S&P 500 corporations have **dividend yields** (or **dividend/price ratios**) that are below 2% of their stock market values. The two top graphs are consistent, because stock prices relative to earnings (P/E ratios) are higher today than they used to be.

For NYSE firms, net payout ratios have not changed much.

Total net payout (dividends, repurchases, and equity issues): As you know, dividends are not the whole payout picture. Corporations can also repurchase and issue shares. You can think of the latter as the opposite of the former. Although graph (c) comes from a different set of firms (all NYSE firms, including smaller firms), chances are that this is not important. It appears that the overall net corporate payout has not changed much. Graph (c) shows that there was no clear trend in whether firms paid out more than they raised in equity. However, there are time-period differences. Until the 1980s, corporations paid out more than they raised. In the 1980s, firms began to raise equity capital much more aggressively, but by the 1990s the net-payout pattern had gone back to normal. The two big outliers were 1929 and 1930 (right after **Black Tuesday**—the stock market crash that began the *Great Depression*). In these 2 years, corporations paid out *much more* than they raised. (Although you cannot see this in the annual data, in the weeks after the October 1987 stock market crash, companies similarly repurchased their own shares aggressively.)

Other evidence: Share repurchases have increased in importance.

Dividends versus repurchases: A 2000 paper by Grullon and Michaely compared equity share repurchases and dividends for all publicly traded firms. They found that companies' expenditures on share repurchase programs increased from 4.8% of total earnings in 1980 to 50.1% in 1998. Furthermore, although share repurchase expenditures grew at an average annual rate of 28.3% from 1980 to 1998, dividends only grew at an average annual rate of 7.5%. As a consequence of these large differences in growth rates, share repurchases—which were only 13.1% of dividends in 1980—exceeded dividends by 1998. Specifically, industrial firms spent $181.8 billion on share repurchases versus $174.1 billion on dividend payments. However, be warned that many of these shares were just repurchased, not retired, so they may not have been true payouts that reduced firm size. Instead, they were immediately given out again in employee and/or executive compensation.

Was the 1982 10b-18 SEC ruling a structural shock?

The Grullon and Michaely paper suggests that the main reason why firms increased their repurchases in the 1980s was not primarily the personal income tax penalty (though it mattered), but the 10b-18 SEC ruling. Before 1982, the risk of violating the antimanipulation provisions of the *Securities Exchange Act of 1934* simply deterred most corporations from repurchasing shares. Just 1 year after the approval of Rule 10b-18, the aggregate amount of cash spent on share repurchase programs tripled.

Fewer and fewer firms were paying dividends until 2000 . . .

Disappearing dividends: Another 2000 paper by Fama and French documented that the fraction of firms paying dividends had declined from 67% in 1978 to 21% in

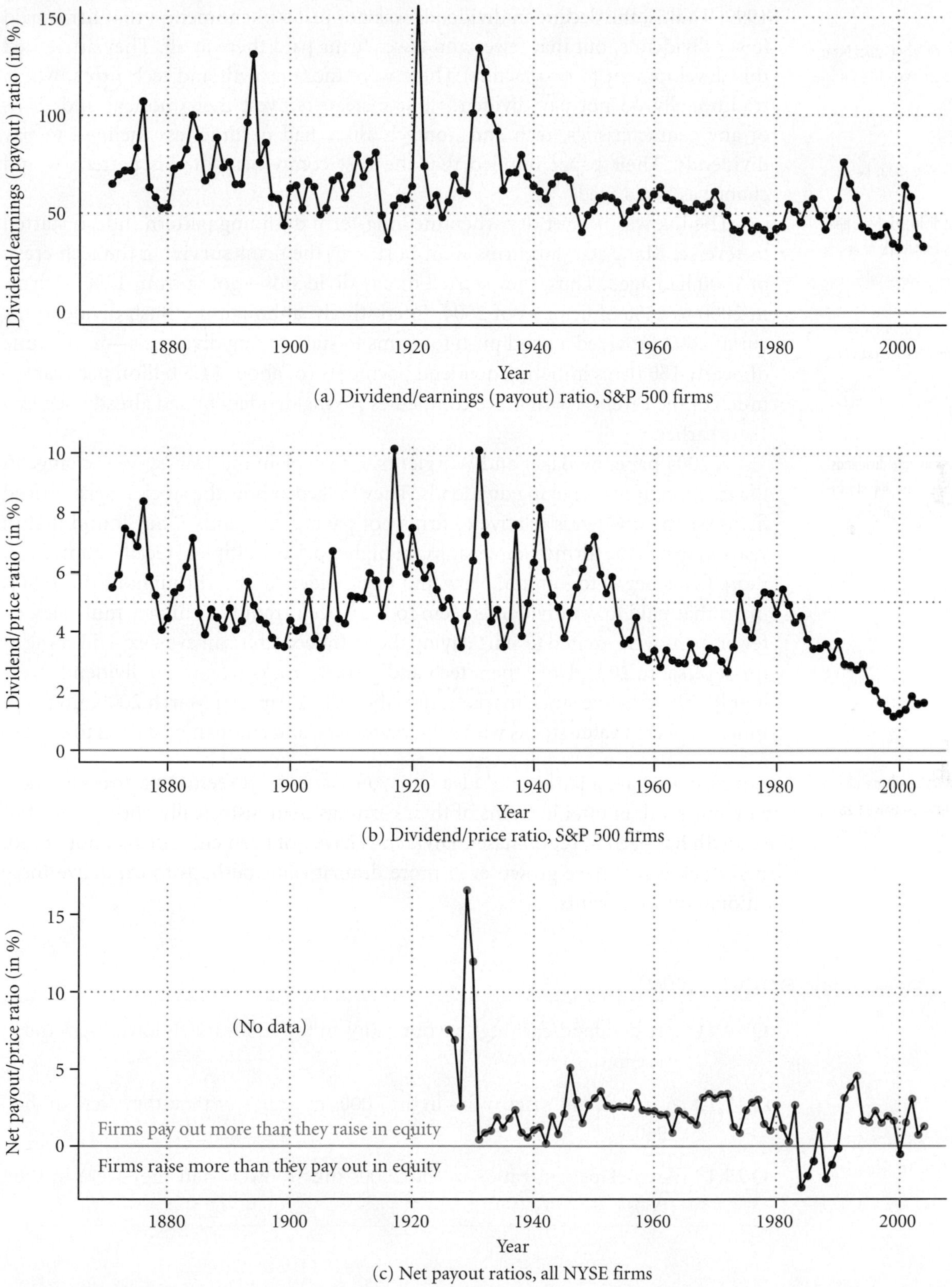

Graph (a) shows the percent of earnings that are paid out as dividends. Graph (b) shows dividends as a percent of stock price. Graph (c) shows dividends plus share repurchases minus share issuing, as a percent of stock price.

FIGURE 19.2 Historical Dividend Payout Patterns, 1870–2004

1999. That is, the decline in dividends was not just a phenomenon that firms paid lower dividends, but that fewer and fewer firms paid them at all. They attributed this development to two factors: There were more growth and tech firms, which traditionally do not pay dividends but instead reinvest their money; and firms of any characteristics, tech and nontech alike, had become less inclined to pay dividends. Their paper implied that the first component of this pattern would change as firms aged.

. . . but dividends have been making a comeback after 2000.

The ink was not yet dry when the long-term declining pattern indeed started to reverse. Many start-up firms went bust, and the firms surviving the tech crash of 2000 had aged. Thus, they started to pay dividends—going from 17% of firms in 2000 to 25% of firms as of 2004. Interestingly, although the Bush dividend tax cut of 2003 provided a good push for firms to start paying dividends—to the tune of nearly 150 firms initiating dividend payments (of about $1.5 billion per year)—much of the reverse (with more companies paying dividends) had already begun 3 years earlier.

More firms initiate dividends when dividend-paying stocks trade at higher multiples.

A 2004 paper by Baker and Wurgler tries to explain the year-by-year change in the fraction of firms paying dividends. They looked at how the stock market priced firms paying dividends relative to firms not paying dividends. They found that in years in which the former were trading at higher price multiples (recall Chapter 14), more firms began to join the party and pay dividends. But throughout the 1990s, firms that paid lower dividends seem to have been trading at higher multiples, so fewer firms were excited to start paying them. Indeed, this can even explain some of the reversal in 2000. Until then, tech and growth stocks paying no dividends were highly valued by the stock market. After the tech collapse of March 2000, investors much preferred value stocks with solid dividends, and companies started to oblige.

The empirical evidence of payout patterns summarized.

In sum, we have a fairly good idea of payout patterns. It seems that firms are now paying out more in total in terms of their earnings than historically, though most of the growth has been in repurchases. Dividends have not been cut, but also not raised. Firms' stock values have grown even more dramatically, perhaps to capitalize these additional future payouts.

SOLVE NOW!

Q 19.11 Are dividend/earnings payout ratios in the 2000s much lower than they were in the 1960s?

Q 19.12 Are dividend/price ratios in the 2000s much lower than they were in the 1960s?

Q 19.13 Are net-payout ratios in the 2000s much lower than they were in the 1960s?

19.4B MARKET REACTIONS

➤ Event studies, Section 11.7, p. 375

In addition to looking at how corporations pay cash to shareholders, we can also look at how the stock market responds to these payouts.

Announcement Response

If an efficient stock market considers a dividend payment to be value-relevant news, any consequent reaction must occur when the market first learns about the dividend, that is, on or before the declaration date. *The reaction must not occur on the later cum- or ex-dividend date.* After all, every investor learns on the declaration date when the stock will go ex-dividend. Consequently, it should not be possible to use such dated information to earn excess profits. Similarly, you should not expect dividend continuation dates to be great news—most firms are expected to continue, so the news is only mild (that dividends are not lowered or raised). In contrast, because dividend initiations are far more difficult to forecast, we should expect them to be associated with considerably higher returns.

Any reaction must appear as soon as investors learn of the news. Usually, this is on the *declaration* date, not thereafter.

Figure 19.3 shows what happens when a firm declares a quarterly dividend. The graph represents over 200,000 ordinary dividend declarations. However, because the dividend could have been declared during or after market closing, the stock price effect could have occurred either on the declaration day or on the following day. Moreover, the figure does not distinguish between continuations and initiations. Graph (a) shows that the share price increased by about 24 basis points around the declaration days. This is a large number. A typical firm with a dividend yield of 2% would only declare a quarterly dividend of about 50 basis points (0.5%). Thus, for every dollar that a firm declares in dividends, the value of shares increases by $24/0.5 = 48$ cents! (Shareholders get the dollar of dividends later, too.) However, graph (b) is a histogram that shows that this is not the experience of any one given firm, just an average of many firms' announcement returns. Even though 24 basis points is a large increase, there are many firms that experience much higher or much lower returns. There are even many firms that declare a dividend and promptly drop by 500 basis points on the same day, often for entirely different reasons, though.

Empirically, dividend payment announcements have been good news.

Though not in the charts, we can also look at how the market responded to different types of dividend announcements. When firms continue their dividends, their share price increases by only about 15 to 20 basis points. When firms meaningfully increase their dividends (10 or more basis points in the dividend yield increase), their stock price declaration response is a much larger 60 basis points. For new dividend initiations, the average increase is a much larger 300 to 400 basis points.

Dividend initiations have huge value effects.

We can also look at the dividend declaration market response by firms' market capitalizations. At the declaration, large firms (more than $8 billion in market cap) increased by about 14 basis points, whereas tiny firms (less than $30 million) increased by about 37 basis points. Thus, a dividend payment is even better news if the firm is small. However, be warned that you cannot interpret this to mean that you should pay dividends if you are the CFO for a small firm. The 37 basis points were for a particular set of small firms that considered paying dividends to be a good thing to do, perhaps because they did not have any good projects.

Dividend announcements are also stronger news for small firms than for large firms.

There is another intriguing related puzzle brought up in a paper by Benartzi, Michaely, and Thaler about how we should interpret the announcement reaction. Do managers change their dividends when they suddenly anticipate a better future, or do they change them after they have experienced good times in the past? In other words, do dividends send a new signal of the future, or do they merely reflect the past? The answer is likely "both." We know that managers do not increase dividends

Do dividends predict the future, or are they predictable history (which investors should already know)?

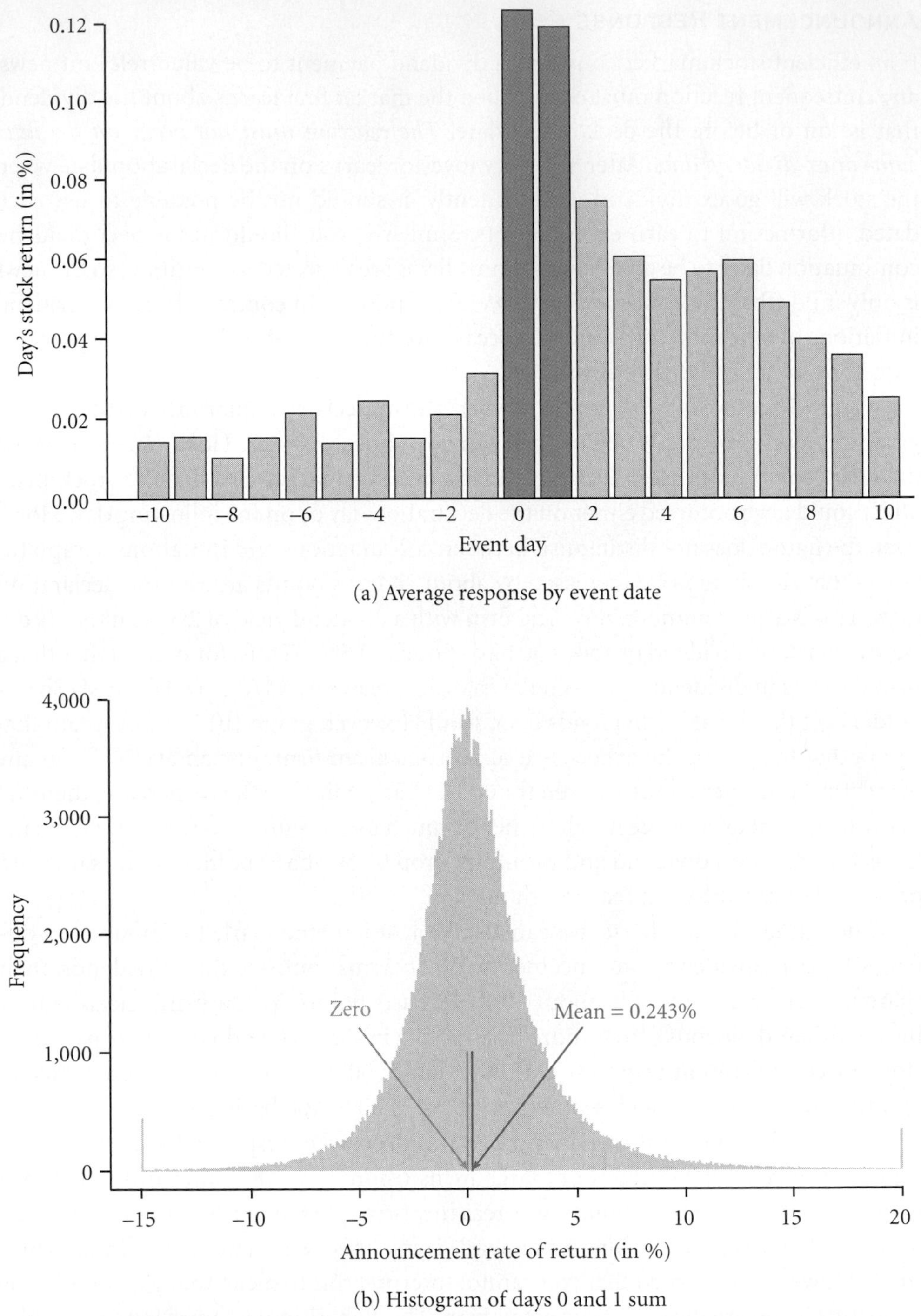

Note that a 2- to 4- basis-point increase per day is average for common stocks. In graph (a), day 0 is the declaration day, and day 1 is the following day. In graph (b), the announcement rate of return is the sum of the rates of return on the declaration day (about 12 bp) and the following day (another 12 bp, for about 24 bp total).

FIGURE 19.3 All Ordinary Dividend Declaration Stock Responses, 1980–2000

unless they believe that the future will continue to be good. This means that they pay out earnings both when they have them and when they are confident that they will continue. (Another recent paper suggests that dividends signal not so much higher future earnings, but rather a lower market beta.) Finally, the market also learns from the declarations that managers are inclined to pay them, and continue to pay them—good news in itself.

Why would there be an announcement response if dividend changes contain no news?

The puzzle is not why firms pay dividends, but why they are such good news to the financial markets. They should only be good news if they tell investors something about the future (such as the permanence of good times). The fact that the market can infer from past good times that managers are likely to increase dividends should not matter. The financial markets should already have taken the latter into account; it should not have been news, and you should not have been able to trade profitably on it. Yet some evidence seems to suggest that the past is as, or more, important than the future in explaining why the stock market reacts so positively. However, because managerial dividend choices are so intertwined with both the past and the future, this is intrinsically not an easy question to answer. This question is still under active investigation—the jury is still out.

Tax Trading and the Cum-to-Ex Dividend Stock Response

In a perfect market, the cum-to-ex stock price drop should equal the dividend.

Although it is not news after the declaration date that a stock will soon trade without the dividend (i.e., the day on which the stock will go from *cum* into *ex* status is known in advance), there should still be a stock *price* reaction. Here is why. Consider a perfect market. The expected stock return should be just about zero (or only a few basis points). This means that the expected stock price change is not zero, because shares are worth more with the dividend. For example, if a \$50 stock pays \$1 in dividends, it should be trading for \$49 on the following day. If shares fell only to \$49.10, then you could earn a \$0.10 profit: Buy at \$50, earn the dividend of \$1, and sell at \$49.10. In sum, although the expected rate of return should be just about zero, the capital gain should be negative by just about the amount of the dividend payment.

➤ Capital gains versus net returns, Section 2.3, p. 15

Tax arbitrage if you have a low tax rate: Buy on the cum-date, sell on the ex-date.

In an imperfect world, the capital loss on the ex-date becomes more interesting: It should depend on investors' personal income tax rates. Consider again the \$50 stock that pays a \$1 dividend. If the drop is from \$50 to \$49, then the stock is priced as if investors suffer no personal income tax penalties. If the drop is from \$50 to \$49.50 instead, then the stock is priced as if investors faced a 50% personal income tax rate. Here is why. Ignore transaction costs, capital gains tax consequences, and IRS regulations for a moment. Concentrate only on the personal income tax rate consequences and the fact that an investor should not earn unusual rates of return overnight. Every investor with a tax rate below 50% should buy the stock on the afternoon of the last cum-day from investors with higher tax rates and then sell it on the morning of the following ex-day. For example, a tax-exempt institution could pay \$50, receive \$1 in dividends, and then resell at \$49.50 for an instant profit of \$0.50 per share. This would be an overnight rate of return of just about 1%. Do this every trading day of the year (there are 255 trading days in a year), and you end up with a rate of return of more than 1,000% per annum! An investor with a higher tax rate, say, 60%, should not hold onto the stock. Starting with \$50, the investor gets to keep only \$0.40 in dividends and \$49.50 in stock—a perfectly predictable wealth loss of 10 cents.

Such an investor should not want to hold the stock. Note that normal retail investors could even hold dividend-paying stocks for 251 out of 255 trading days of the year without paying any dividend taxes. They would just sell them to institutions on the cum-day, and repurchase them on the ex-day.

Competition among (tax-exempt) investors for the best investment opportunities should bring down the *effective* tax rate.

There is more than just one tax-exempt institution in the market. Consequently, these institutions should compete to bid up the cum-price from \$50 to something more. This would mean that the effective income tax rate should come down to something more modest than 50%. In the real world, however, the tax arbitrage competition is limited by transaction costs, IRS rules, capital gains consequences, and overnight holding risk. If this were not the case, even the presence of a few smart tax-exempt investors would drive the cum-price to \$50.50 and the effective tax rate to zero. In real life, some such tax arbitrage indeed happens. Tax-exempt funds compete to purchase these shares, driving up the share prices before the ex-dividend date. Such transactions are known as **bed-and-breakfast deals** for equity, and **bond-washing** for bonds—even though both the IRS and the Bank of England have specifically prohibited such tax arbitrage. The latter has imposed a 1-week holding period for tax-free institutions purchasing around dividend dates. Naturally, there is more tax arbitrage if the dividends are bigger (e.g., when it comes to large special one-time dividends).

The price drop from the cum- to the ex-date allows us to infer the effective marginal income tax rate.

Now return to our hypothetical drop from \$50 to \$49.50. As noted, it is only an investor with a tax rate of 50% who would be indifferent between buying and selling. Anyone with a higher tax rate should sell; anyone with a lower tax rate should buy. The formula to compute this marginal investor's **effective dividend tax rate** is set by the fact that the overnight rate of return should be close to zero.

$$0 = \frac{\$49.50 - \$50 + (1-\tau)\cdot\$1}{\$50} \Leftrightarrow \tau = \frac{\$1 + \$49.50 - \$50}{\$1} = 50\%$$

$$r = \frac{P_{\text{ex}} - P_{\text{cum}} + (1-\tau)\cdot D}{P_{\text{cum}}} \Leftrightarrow \tau = \frac{D + P_{\text{ex}} - P_{\text{cum}}}{D}$$

With this formula, you can now use the capital loss to determine the marginal investor's tax rate for dividend-paying stocks on the dividend cum-/ex-days. For example, if the share price drop is from \$50 to \$49.25, the stock is priced as if the marginal investor suffered a [\$1 + (\$49.25 − \$50)]/\$1 = 25% tax rate.

The marginal tax rate measures a market imperfection: The inability of tax-exempt investors to exploit the tax arbitrage fully.

Although we know that some tax arbitrage does happen, the question is still how much. On a typical *quarterly* dividend day, a \$50 stock with a 2% dividend yield would pay only \$1/4 = \$0.25. Subtract round-trip transaction costs, and take into account that the IRS won't look kindly on immediate purchases and sales by tax-exempt investors, that tax-exempts want to remain diversified, and that there are only a limited number of tax-exempt investors. Given all these complications, is the competition among tax-exempt investors—subject to transaction costs—enough to compete away the dividend tax penalty?

The empirical evidence suggests that the effective tax rate is close to the personal income tax rate. Tax-exempt investors seem to make little dent in eliminating the tax arbitrage.

Figure 19.4 shows that the answer is no. The marginal tax rate was historically closer to the prevailing personal income tax rate than it was to the tax-exempt rate of zero. The figure shows that in the early 1980s, it was around 50%. After the *Tax Reform Act of 1986*, it dropped to about 25%, from which it slowly crept up, roughly in line with the increase in personal income tax rates during the George H.W. Bush

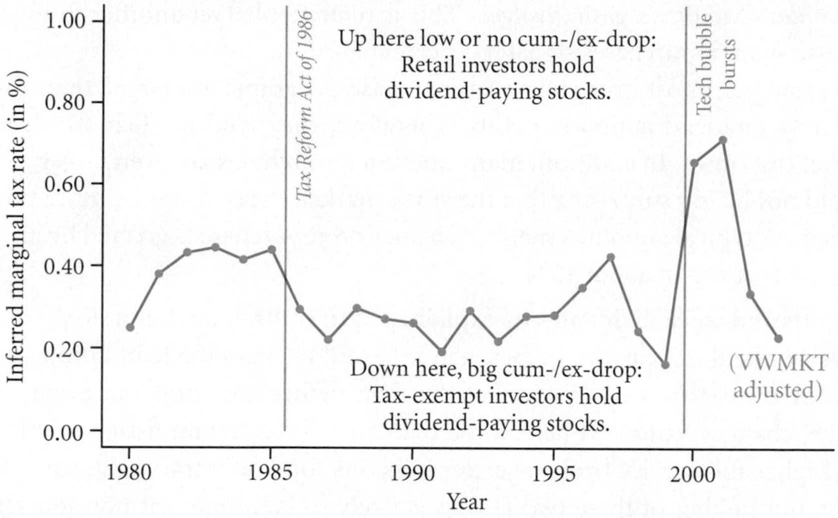

FIGURE 19.4 Implied Tax Rates from the Cum-/Ex-Drop from Ordinary Dividends, 1980–2004

and early Clinton years. Interestingly, during the tech boom of the late 1990s, retail investors seem not to have held many dividend payers (Internet and similar stocks were "in"). And after the tech crash of 2000 (these stocks were "out"), retail investors were so eager to hold dividend payers that they practically ignored the tax penalty and put the same value on stocks cum-dividends and ex-dividends. The implied tax rate shot up to above 60%. An inferred tax rate this high—beyond all actual tax rates—also suggests that there is more going on than just tax effects. Most likely, with dividend yields very low, the transaction costs may have prevented ordinary investors from this tax arbitrage. Of course, this does not answer the question as to who would have been willing to sell shares on the cum-date or buy shares on the ex-date, rather than vice versa. Fortunately, by 2003, the implied marginal tax rate had declined again to more normal levels, although 20%+ still seems high, given the Bush dividend tax cut.

Here is yet another financial mystery: There are countries in which dividends are not taxed, so the effective marginal tax rate should be zero. There should be a one-to-one drop of the share price with the dividends on the ex-date, or buying on the cum-date and selling on the ex-date would be a great trading strategy. Yet, even in these countries, there is a positive total rate of return on such days. Why would anyone sell such shares on the cum-date and why would anyone purchase such shares on the ex-date (rather than the cum-date)? It makes no sense. This evidence should caution us not to overinterpret the U.S. cum-to-ex price drop as a pure marginal tax effect. We may not understand this drop as well as we think.

Maybe there is more going on than just taxes on the cum-/ex-drop?!

Other Important Empirical Evidence

Share repurchase announcements: Unfortunately, there is no clear announcement of how much firms will repurchase. They can announce that they plan to repurchase and then decide never to do so. This fuzziness makes empirical work much more challenging. Nevertheless, from what we know, it appears that the stock market response to a share repurchase seems roughly similar to that for a dividend payment

Share repurchases tend to experience similar market responses as dividends do.

for similar amounts of cash involved. This is remarkable (yet another mild puzzle), because share repurchases signal less permanence.

Big repurchases naturally have bigger responses.

However, most open-market repurchase programs are larger than ordinary quarterly dividend announcements. Therefore, they tend to elicit stronger stock market responses. In addition, many auction repurchases are even larger, and so it should not be too surprising that the stock market responds much more positively to them. A typical announcement of an auction repurchase is greeted by an instant stock price jump of about 15%.

Stock splits and stock dividends: As explained at the outset, neither a stock split nor a stock dividend is a payout. In fact, neither event changes the firm's projects. Every investor owns the same fraction of the firm before and after the event, and no money changes hands. (It used to be that there were certain listing requirements and higher full-service brokerage commissions for stocks trading around $30 per share, but neither of these two factors is likely to be important nowadays.) Stock splits and stock dividends are good "null" benchmarks with which to compare dividend declarations and share repurchase announcements. We should expect just about a zero response to the announcement of either.

The market also responds to stock splits.

Alas, on average, investors seem to respond positively when firms announce a split, where the number of shares increases and the stock price drops. This suggests that the market considers a split to be good news—it must increase its assessment of the net present value of the firm's underlying project. Indeed, many firms that split often produce better earnings after the stock split. In a reverse split, the firm merges shares. For example, two shares each worth $5 become one share worth $10. Again, no money changes hands—and, again, the stock market responds. In this case, upon the announcement, the share price usually drops.

Long-term reaction: In an efficient market, we would expect stock prices to incorporate all relevant information at the announcement. There should be no slow long-term stock market reaction after the news has been released. However, there is evidence that there may indeed be a strategy that allows you to earn abnormal returns: Firms that pay out more in dividends and repurchases tend to perform better in the long run—not just in terms of their earnings (which you would expect) but also in terms of their financial market values (which you would not expect if the market had taken all available information into account as soon as it had the information). Firms that increased their dividends seemed to outperform those firms that decreased their dividends. The cumulative stock return difference was about 10% per year. Conversely, firms that issue equity tend to underperform over the following years.

➤ Relevance of empirical history, Section 7.1E, p. 189

However, before you invest all your money into firms that have recently raised their payout, be aware that long-term returns are quite difficult to measure reliably, and we do not know if the historical experience will continue in the future.

SOLVE NOW!

Q 19.14 If the stock price is not expected to drop from the cum-day to the ex-day, what is the marginal income tax rate?

Q 19.15 What is the implied tax rate suggested by the real-world cum-/ex-drop?

Q 19.16 Should a stock split create value? Does it?

Q 19.17 Do stock price announcement responses to dividend initiations (or dividend eliminations) tend to be underreactions or overreactions?

19.5 SURVEY EVIDENCE

What do the decision makers believe?

Instead of researching in the data as to what CFOs are actually doing, we can also just try to ask them. A 2004 paper by Brav, Graham, Harvey, and Michaely does exactly this, surveying 384 financial executives. This kind of evidence is not a substitute for, but a complement to, the empirical evidence. Managers may respond to immediate financial market pressures and incentives without fully realizing their underlying causes. The proverbial grain of salt is appropriate.

Here are their opinions that make sense.

The CFOs in this study have some very definite and interesting opinions:

- They state that they pay dividends because they are trapped by history. They do not want to cut existing dividends, but given the choice, they would not begin paying dividends in the first place. In fact, their desire not to cut dividends goes so far that they claim that they would not only raise more external capital, but even pass up positive-NPV projects to pay them. They claim not to care at all about investment opportunities when it comes to dividends.
- In contrast, CFOs do care about investment opportunities and residual cash left over when it comes to share repurchases. In fact, they seem to think of their own stock as an investment opportunity in that they try to earn money by attempting to "time" their own stock, buying more shares when the price seems low.
- 40% of these executives want to attract institutional investors with dividends—but they also believe that they can accomplish this with share repurchases.
- 40% of these executives target a dividend-per-share ratio (and 27% target changes therein), 28% target a dividend-to-earnings (payout) ratio, and 14% target a dividend-to-price ratio. When it comes to share repurchases, they tend to target a dollar value of repurchases, not any particular ratio.
- Repurchases are often related to option or stock compensation plans, providing the firm with the shares needed to satisfy their employee obligations.
- Repurchases offer a flexibility that dividends do not. Managers perceive this to be a good thing and would argue that it creates value for the company.
- However, managerial answers to surveys are in line with what one would expect if they were agency conflicted—that is, interested first in helping themselves. This is not to say that executives deliberately plot how to enrich themselves, but that over time their views tend to evolve toward what is in their own best interests. Although reinvestment increases the share price and firm size, payout only helps anonymous investors far away from the firm, who own less of the firm after the payout, and this diminishes the share price and firm size. Thus, payouts are less salient to managers.

➤ CFO survey, Section 22.5, p. 846

- Further evidence of an agency conflict is that dividend-paying financial executives state that they would most like to use the money saved by a hypothetical dividend elimination not for a share repurchase (the obvious substitute) but for paying down debt. Avoiding bond-rating downgrades and retaining financial flexibility are important to CFOs. (Note again that high bond ratings and financial flexibility reduce external pressure on management, even if they do not create value.)

Here are their opinions that are more difficult to understand.

So far, so good. Now it becomes a bit stranger. Only one-third of the respondents contemplate personal income tax consequences, though 40% realize the relevant repurchase advantage. However, if they recognize it, they rarely consider their investors' personal income tax consequences to be important to their payout decisions. This finding may not be too strange, because differential tax consequences are rather modest today.

Here are their two opinions that seem incomprehensible.

However, here is where it gets *truly* strange:

- Many CFOs believe that repurchases automatically increase earnings per share, as if money paid out would not otherwise create more earnings. This is contrary to what you learned on page 709.
- Clearly, dividends are related to the stability of future earnings, and CFOs recognize this fact. They also know that they take future earnings into account when they decide on dividends. Alas, they then claim that there is no additional discipline imposed by dividend payments, and they claim that dividends and repurchases convey similar information. This is inconsistent. Moreover, they believe that it is unimportant that payouts, and especially dividends, convey information to the market. Again, this is odd, because they state that they pay out dividends depending on their opinions about the future. Why would the market not learn their inside perspectives from their dividend payout choices?

SOLVE NOW!

Q 19.18 Do CFOs feel more pressure to continue dividends or share repurchase programs?

SUMMARY

What payout policy should a company choose? The most important recommendation is that a company should pay out cash when the alternative uses for it are not positive-NPV projects. Interestingly, Warren Buffett (from Berkshire Hathaway) has stated publicly something similar to this philosophy: "We will pay either large dividends or none at all if we can't obtain more money through reinvestment [of those funds]." Of course, many other managers do not like to hear this advice or they assert that all of their projects are high NPV, whether this is true or not. They would rather govern large firms with much financial flexibility—firms that are unconstrained by debt or payout requirements. Compared to the question of whether the firm should pay out or not pay out, the question of whether the form of payout should be dividends or share repurchases is of secondary importance nowadays, given the small residual differences between them. Their differences mattered more in the past, before the double taxation of dividends was reduced in 2003. Dividends signal more long-term confidence, but they cost investors more in personal income taxes.

This chapter covered the following major points:

- Equity payouts come in two forms: dividends and share repurchases. Share repurchases are either auction based or open market. Dividends are either ordinary or special. (Stock dividends are not payouts, but more like stock splits.)
- In a perfect market, it does not matter whether the firm pays out or reinvests, or how it pays out.
- Dividends and share repurchases have equal effects in terms of "eating substance" for investors.
- In a share repurchase, both tendering and nontendering shareholders benefit.
- Share repurchases do not necessarily raise EPS.
- An equity payout is the opposite of issuing. Thus, all factors discussed in the earlier capital structure chapters apply here, too.
- Share repurchases are better than dividends from a personal income tax perspective, but no longer greatly so.
- Unlike share repurchases, ordinary dividends are regular and steady. This behavior is called dividend smoothing. The financial market expects dividends to continue, which pushes managers to continue them, which in turn makes the market expect them.
- Executives with stock options benefit relatively more from a share repurchase than from a dividend payout.
- Since World War II, dividend/earnings ratios have remained stable at around 50%.
- Dividend/price ratios have declined from 4–5% in the 1980s to about 2% today.
- The net-payout ratio—dividends plus share repurchases minus share issuing—has not declined systematically over the last 20 years.
- Repurchases and dividends are about equally important today.
- In 1980, one in two firms paid dividends. Today, only one in four do so. However, as firms have matured, the trend is now back on the upswing. When the market places higher multiples on dividend payers, more firms seem to want to start paying dividends.
- Firms experience a positive stock price response when they declare a dividend. The effect of the initial dividend declaration is a stunning 2–4%.
- There is mild evidence that the effect is similar for a repurchase *for a similar amount of cash*. For large repurchases, often auction based, the response can be very large—15% on average.
- The market response from the cum- to the ex-date allows us to infer the marginal investor's tax rate. For ordinary dividends, it tends to be fairly close to the tax rate of retail investors. This leaves room for tax-exempt investors to earn excess returns.
- When asked, financial executives feel trapped by their dividend history. They would rather not pay dividends but feel that they have to—even when paying dividends forces them to pass up good projects. They try to trade profitably on their own stock price when they repurchase. Their answers are broadly consistent with what is in

their own best interests. Strangely, many believe incorrectly that repurchases always raise EPS, and they dispute that dividends carry useful information and/or discipline to the market.

KEY TERMS

SOLVE NOW! SOLUTIONS

Q 19.1 The two important dividend dates are the declaration date (when the dividend payment is announced) and the cum- versus ex-dividend date (when the stock trades with versus without dividends).

Q 19.2 In a perfect market, a stock split should not change anything value-wise. It is merely a change in numeraire, which does not affect anything fundamental about the company (such as earnings, cash flows, etc.). Thus, the stock market response should be zero.

Q 19.3 The two kinds of programs are auction-based repurchases and open-market repurchases.

Q 19.4 Yes, a firm undertaking an open-market repurchase program could be accused of manipulating its stock price. This is why the SEC has laid down rules (i.e., Rule 10b-18) that allow firms to escape such lawsuits.

Q 19.5 No! Even a normal investor is as well off with a share repurchase as with a dividend payout in a perfect market. Neither a share repurchase nor a dividend payout changes the investor's wealth. (The "wealth increase" in a share repurchase comes from an increase in the fraction of the firm that each share now owns.)

Q 19.6 The firm was worth \$1,000, so shares are currently worth \$10 each. If the firm repurchases my shares, it pays out $20 \cdot \$15 = \$300$ and has \$700 left, to be split among 80 shares. Thus, the remaining shares are now worth only $\$700/\$80 = \$8.75$ each. The moral of the story is that when a firm offers to purchase shares for more than they are worth, the nonparticipating shareholders suffer.

Q 19.7 If the firm uses money for share repurchases that previously was used to fund negative-NPV projects, then the firm's EPS should go up.

Q 19.8 Basically, yes: Dividends and share repurchases are indeed mostly the opposite of equity issuing. They reduce the equity investment in a firm—the opposite of what equity issues accomplish. Therefore, virtually all arguments made in Chapters 17 and 18 apply to dividends and repurchases in reverse.

Q 19.9 The remaining tax advantage of share repurchases comes from the fact that capital gains can be realized mostly by those investor clienteles who face low capital gains taxes, perhaps because they have low income and statutory rates, or perhaps because they have losses elsewhere. This allows the shareholders in the aggregate to escape most repurchase payout taxation. The remaining investors are not taxed in the interim—their money continues to bear fruit for them, and not for the IRS.

Q 19.10 The remaining differences are as follows: Dividends tend to be more regular than share repurchases; executives and insiders may often not tender into a repurchase, but they will enjoy the relatively higher share price from a repurchase through executive compensation that is linked to the share price; some retail investors like dividends; some funds cannot hold stocks that do not pay dividends.

Q 19.11 No. D/E ratios in the 2000s are generally similar to what they were 40 years ago.

Q 19.12 Yes. D/P ratios in the 2000s are generally lower than they were in the 1960s. D/P ratios have declined to about 1–2%.

Q 19.13 Definitely no. Net-payout ratios are not very different in the 2000s than they were in the 1960s.

Q 19.14 If the stock price is the same on the cum-day and the ex-day, then the marginal income tax rate is $\tau = 100\%$, because every investor who would purchase the stock on the cum-day afternoon and sell it on the ex-day morning would get to keep "for free" whatever part of the dividend is not taxed. (I am ignoring the small daily upward drift of stock prices.)

Q 19.15 The tax rate implied by the average drop from the cum-date to the ex-date seems to be about 20%.

Q 19.16 A stock split should not create value in a perfect market. Logically, it is just a change in numeraire. It should make no difference to investors whether they own 1 stock worth $100 or 2 stocks worth $50 each. However, stock splits do seem to signal that the future is brighter, because the stock price usually responds positively to stock split announcements, and may therefore create value in the real world.

Q 19.17 The stock price does not seem to react fully to dividend initiations (or dividend eliminations), because the positive (negative) instant reaction is followed by more of the same, on average. Thus, they are underreactions.

Q 19.18 In a survey, CFOs indicated that they feel more pressure to continue dividends.

PROBLEMS

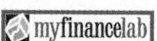

The ▇▇ *indicates problems available in* myfinancelab

Q 19.19 Search the Web to find a company that has recently announced a stock split. What happened to its stock price on the day of the announcement?

Q 19.20 Use a financial website to identify the company with the highest dividend yield today. What is it?

Q 19.21 Use a financial website to identify three firms that are currently undertaking an auction-based repurchase program. What fraction of the shares are they repurchasing?

Q 19.22 Consider a firm with 80 shareholders, including yourself, who each own 1 share worth $10. In addition, I own 20 shares (for a firm total of 100 shares) and I am trying to fire the management. To appease me, the management has offered to purchase my 20 shares at $9 per share. How would this change the value of your share?

Q 19.23 Can the firm's EPS go down if the firm takes on a positive-NPV project?

Q 19.24 How would the value change if a firm decides to increase its dividend payout, and if financial distress and agency/signaling costs are the only relevant concerns?

Q 19.25 Considering the differences other than personal income taxes, what companies should pay dividends rather than repurchase shares? How important is the right choice between the two?

Q 19.26 Think about the non-tax-related differences between share repurchases and dividends.

Describe the firms in which each difference would be relatively more important.

Q 19.27 Do more or fewer firms pay dividends in the 2000s than in the 1970s? Is this a trend?

Q 19.28 In an efficient market, when should the stock price react to the value consequences of a dividend change? Discuss the effect both on the total return and on the capital gain. Which should be larger?

Q 19.29 Comparing the dividend announcement effect of 24 basis points to a typical daily standard deviation (80 basis points) and round-trip transaction costs (about 30 basis points) suggests that firms should not bother with dividends. Discuss.

Q 19.30 Would you expect trading volume to be higher for dividend-paying stocks on the declaration date or around the cum-date/ex-date?

Q 19.31 If the stock price drops on average by 0.65% from the cum-day to the ex-day when dividends of 1% of the firm are paid, then what is the marginal income tax rate?

Q 19.32 What are the dividend targets that different U.S. corporations seem to try to peg? If you cannot ask the executives, can you learn from the behavior of the firm what they peg their dividend targets to?

Q 19.33 How do managers view dividends and share repurchases differently? Which do they seem to prefer?

Q 19.34 What is the survey evidence that there is an agency conflict between shareholders and managers when it comes to dividends? Can it be interpreted differently?

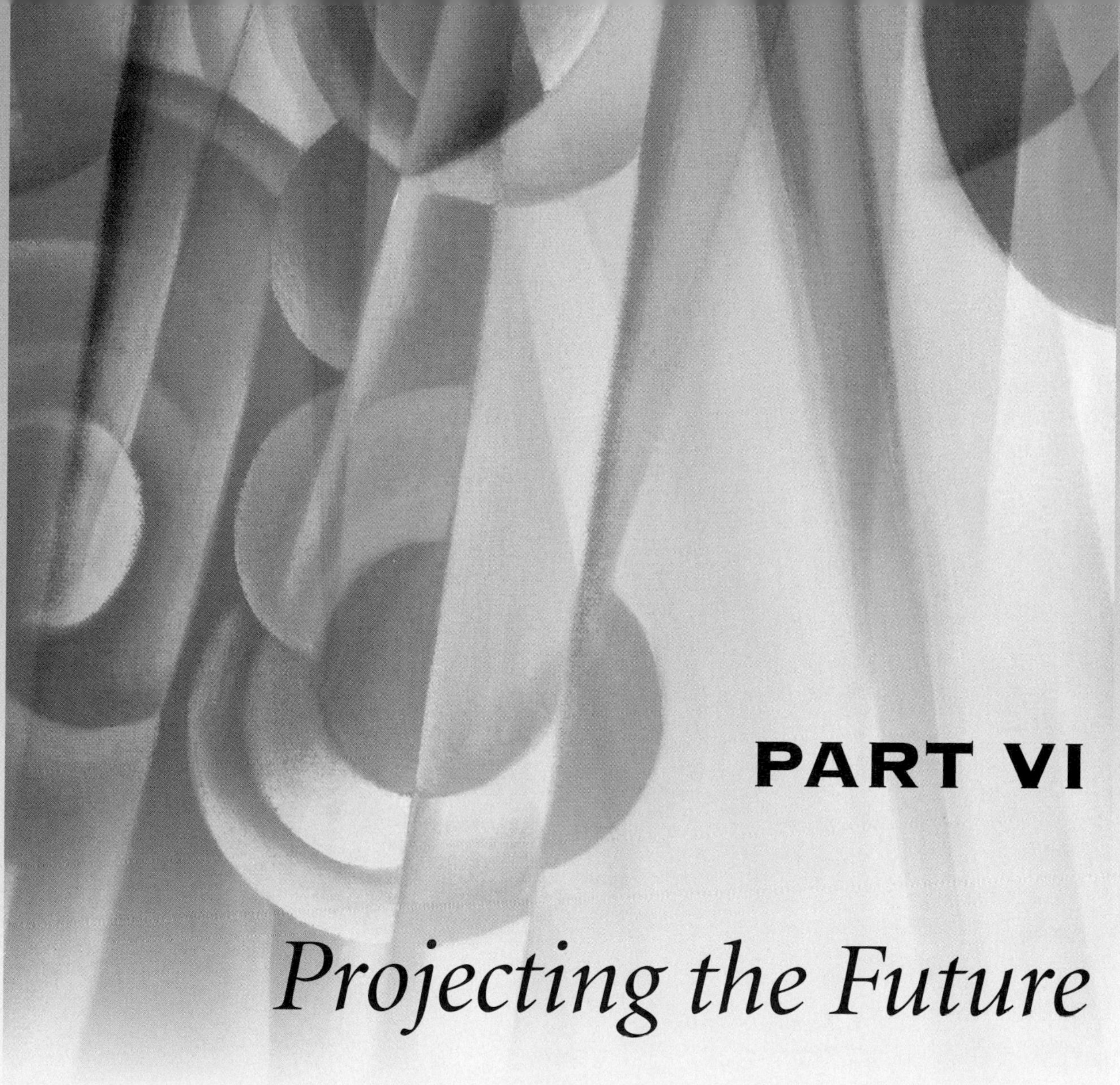

PART VI

Projecting the Future

THE "BUSINESS WAY"

In any formal setting, financial professionals propose new projects through pro formas—whether it is the expansion of a factory building within a corporation, or a new business for presentation to venture capitalists. A good pro forma is a combination of financial expertise, business expertise, and intuition. Both art and science go into its construction. The book's synthesis chapter is the creation of such a pro forma. It combines all the ingredients from earlier chapters—capital budgeting, taxes, the cost of capital, capital structure, and so on.

20

Pro Forma Financial Statements

FOR VALUE, FINANCIAL STRUCTURE, AND CORPORATE STRATEGY ANALYSIS

According to Merriam-Webster, *pro forma* is a Latin term meaning "for form." Its use dates from around 1580. Pro forma has two definitions: "provided in advance to prescribe form or describe items;" and "made or carried out in a perfunctory manner or as a formality." In our context, a pro forma is a model of a hypothetical future scenario, and specifically the financial performance in this scenario. (Hopefully, your model will be more like the first definition in Merriam-Webster and less like the second.)

In a sense, pro formas are what much of corporate finance is all about—the standard business approach to contemplate financing or investing. For example, if you want to propose a new project to your boss, to the board of directors, or to an external venture capitalist, you will almost surely be asked to produce a business plan. The most critical part of this business plan will have to be your "pro forma" financials. These financials will then be used as the baseline for discussion and evaluation of your proposed project.

Managers and entrepreneurs are not the only producers of pro formas. Analysts for major investment banks or for firms seeking acquisitions or mergers also have to produce pro formas to back up their analyses of corporate value. Their task is both easier and harder than that of the entrepreneur: Analysts can often rely on corporate history upon which to base their pro formas, but they also often lack the detailed knowledge of the business internals and corporate intentions that the internal managers and entrepreneurs would have.

Every business is different, and thus every pro forma is different. Still, this chapter tries to give you some guidance regarding the process of creating pro formas. Specifically, you will learn how to produce pro forma analyses of PepsiCo. These pro formas will be from a number of different perspectives—that of an analyst valuing it as if it were a privately traded company and had no market value, that of an investment banker proposing a capital structure change, and that of an economist who has the advantage of hindsight.

20.1 THE GOAL AND LOGIC

Pro formas are more detailed than simple cash flow projections. This helps you think about the economics of business.

To repeat, a **pro forma** is a model of financial performance in a hypothetical future. Creating a pro forma is a challenge similar to what you encountered in earlier chapters, where you had to estimate a project's present value. There, you needed to understand a whole variety of issues—the expected cash flows, the appropriate costs of capital, the corporate and capital structures, the agency conflicts, and so on. The main novelty here is that you need to do this in the context of the financial statements rather than just in the context of isolated formulas. Creating a full pro forma is not an empty exercise: It will help impose some discipline and structure on your thinking about the design and value of your proposed project. It forces you to think about important "details," such as what you believe sales and costs will be, how you will manage working capital, how quickly earnings and cash flows will turn positive, whether taxes will be an important factor, and so on.

Forecasting pro formas is both hard and different from business to business.

No finance professor would dispute the importance of pro formas, but we are often reluctant to teach much about them. The cynical view is that constructing a pro forma is difficult and that we finance professors naturally prefer the "easy" tasks! The less cynical view is that there are at least three good reasons for our reluctance:

1. **Idiosyncracy:** In contrast to the many beautifully simple, elegant, and universal theoretical concepts in finance (such as present value or the capital asset pricing model), financials and pro formas are messy and unique for each business. Forecasting the financials for a new cancer drug is different from forecasting the financials for a new toy fad, which is different from forecasting the financials for a retail store, which is different from forecasting the financials for aluminum mining, and so on. Many of the guidelines for creating good pro formas are necessarily less universal and more ad hoc.
2. **Relativity:** The difficulties in making good financial projections for a specific project are often tremendous. It is important that you realize the limits of what you can and cannot do. You should be able to do it better than your peers—a *relative* rather than an *absolute* standard. Looking in retrospect at what later actually happened in relation to what you predicted in your pro forma is often a great lesson in humility. You are not alone in this predicament.
3. **Learning by doing:** The best way to learn how to do a pro forma is to struggle with designing one. Such an active case-based approach is considerably more effective than a passive listening approach. After reading this chapter, your next step in learning pro formas should be working through and critiquing many case studies—necessarily more of a trial-and-error-and-experience process than a tutorial process.

Still, this chapter seeks to prepare you at least a little. It will give you some general guidance, because, in the end, you must learn how to design good pro formas if you want to be an effective entrepreneur, manager, or analyst. You must be able to produce your own pro formas, and you must be able to analyze critically the financial pro formas of others.

SOLVE NOW!

Q 20.1 What does a full pro forma analysis force you to do that a simpler projection would not?

20.1A AN EXTERNAL ANALYST'S VIEW VERSUS AN ENTREPRENEUR'S VIEW

Pro formas put together by outsiders are often used to value the business—and potentially acquire it.

There are two distinctly different users and consumers of pro formas. The first set are outsiders, such as external analysts, who have to construct a pro forma for a privately traded firm with an unknown market value. Such a perspective is also taken by analysts of private equity buyout firms, who try to assess whether the market value of a publicly traded company seems too low. If their pro forma value estimates are much higher than the market value, then the company deserves a closer look as a potential buyout candidate. This perspective is also what much of this chapter is about.

Pro formas are often used by insiders to plan the business.

The second set of users are insiders, such as entrepreneurs, who often create pro formas to assess value. However, they face some unique problems of their own:

Working capital: Entrepreneurs usually must worry about working-capital projection and management for the sake of policy design. A small entrepreneurial firm could lose its entire business if it were to run out of cash, even if only temporarily and even if the underlying economics of its real business were sound. In contrast, working-capital projections to assure financial viability are fairly unimportant for PepsiCo. PepsiCo is so big, stable, and currently with so few liabilities and so little financial debt that it can easily borrow more capital if it were ever to need more. (Managing working capital well can be important even for large firms in the sense that better handling can cut costs. In this case, it is an operational-efficiency problem, not a forecasting problem to avoid financial distress.)

Inside knowledge: Entrepreneurs often know the operational details of the proposed project in great detail. In contrast, external analysts (and sometimes even venture capitalists considering funding start-up projects) rarely do—and neither do you for PepsiCo.

Start-up versus mature phase: Entrepreneurs usually do not have a long prior history of operations that can give good guidance. If everything goes according to plan, then their cash flows will often start with a sharp initial business growth curve, to be followed only later by a more stable period. As firms mature and grow, they become less likely to default. This later decline in credit risk allows their promised rates of return to decline. In addition to having to pay higher default premiums, many young, small firms also have to pay higher expected rates of return. The reasons are that they tend to be especially vulnerable to downturns in economy-wide conditions—which reflects itself in higher betas and higher costs of capital—and the fact that their capital markets are less perfect. In contrast, PepsiCo is an established company, and its projects have long prior histories.

➤ Entrepreneurial finance, Section 10.5, p. 328

You will learn in a moment that the end of the start-up growth phase is often a natural break. It is often a good choice for T, the break of your pro forma into a detailed projection period and final market value. But PepsiCo is already in its mature, stable state and, as an outsider, you have no detailed knowledge of how the next year will be different from what will happen in 10 years. Therefore, you could even just work out a terminal value right now and dispense with the initial detailed-projection phase altogether. Nevertheless, we will work out the detailed projections to illustrate the process.

PepsiCo is an imperfect example, because it could be done a lot more simply.

We cannot illustrate all the issues discussed above in this chapter: PepsiCo will not run out of cash, we have no special knowledge of PepsiCo operations, and PepsiCo is mature. Moreover, we shall construct the pro forma as if we stand at the end of 2001. This will allow us later to use hindsight knowledge to "autopsy" how good or bad our forecasts turned out.

SOLVE NOW!

Q 20.2 What are usually the two most important projection goals for a pro forma analysis for an entrepreneur?

20.2 THE TEMPLATE

You decide on a detailed projection phase and a terminal value.

The standard method for creating a pro forma separates the future into a "detailed projection" time period, for which you forecast the financials in great detail, and a **terminal value**, which you can think of as the "then market value" of the business—a going-concern value of the business if you were to sell it at this point in the future. You have to decide for how many years you want to project financials in detail before capping your value analysis with your terminal value.

Here is the template of what you need to do.

➤ PepsiCo's financial statements, Tables 13.1 through 13.4, p. 449

As our guinea pig, let's use PepsiCo, because you have already studied its historical financials in Chapter 13. Your goal now is to construct a good pro forma as of December 2001 to estimate PepsiCo's market value, presuming you already know the 2001 financials. The construction template is in Table 20.1. It shows the three big areas you must work on:

1. A choice of horizon T that separates the initial and terminal phases
2. The detailed financials during the initial projection phase, from time +1 (next year) to time $T - 1$
3. A terminal market value at time $T - 1$, which is a stand-in for the cash flows from time T to eternity

SOLVE NOW!

Q 20.3 What are the three main components of a pro forma that you need to work out?

20.3 THE LENGTH OF THE DETAILED PROJECTION PERIOD

How many years of detailed financials should you project?

Your first goal is to understand how to choose a suitable value for the horizon choice T in Table 20.1. Remember that the horizon is the span of time up to which you project

TABLE 20.1 THE PRO FORMA PROBLEM FOR PEPSICO

		Pro Forma Income Statement							To be determined ↘
Year	−2	−1	0	+1	+2	+3	···	+T	Terminal Value
	1999	2000	2001	2002	2003	2004	···		
Net Sales	$25,093	$25,479	$26,935	Projected year by year					
− COGS	$10,326	$10,226	$10,754	Projected year by year					
⋮				Projected year by year					
− Net Interest Expense	−$792	$57	−$8	Projected year by year					
⋮				Projected year by year					
= Net Income	$2,505	$2,543	$2,662						
		Pro Forma Cash Flow Statement							
Net Income	$2,505	$2,543	$2,662	Projected year by year					
+ Depreciation	$1,156	$1,093	$1,082	Projected year by year					
⋮				Projected year by year					
= Operating Cash Flow	$3,605	$4,440	$4,201	Projected year by year					Wholesale PV projection
⋮				Projected year by year					
=Investing Cash Flow	−$1,172	−$1,996	−$2,637	Projected year by year					Wholesale PV projection
= Economic Cash Flow	$1,641	$2,501	$1,556	Projected year by year					Wholesale PV Projection

The numbers for PepsiCo's income statement were taken from Table 13.3 on page 451. Economic cash flows can be computed from Formula 13.4 on page 477. All net sales include bottling operations. The numbers for PepsiCo's cash flow statement were taken from Table 13.4 on page 452. (Small note: You may recall that PepsiCo actually earned interest in 1999 and 2001, which is rather unusual. Most corporations pay net interest.) Your goal will be to determine a good break for T, and to project future cash flows—T periods' worth of detailed financials—followed by a wholesale market value estimate of the remaining cash flows until eternity.

detailed financials and beyond which you substitute your "wholesale" terminal value estimate.

As an initial step, let us take a brief detour into forecasting. There are two surprising and key insights to note:

The very long run may not be any more daunting than the intermediate run. Although future cash flows may be equally uncertain, their present values could be less uncertain.

1. You may be able to project future cash flows in the very long term as accurately as in the intermediate term.
2. At some point, your cash flows are not very likely to grow that fast anymore. This is not to say that they won't grow at all—just that your expected value forecasts today no longer grow very steeply and/or reliably.

These issues imply that you would be able to estimate the *present* value of long-term cash flows *better* than that of intermediate-term cash flows. This is best explained by example.

An example of "constant" uncertainty, which does grow with horizon.

If you have to forecast the temperature in 2 hours, your (short-term) forecast will be pretty good, and much better than your 6-month forecast. But how would your 6-month forecast compare to your 50-year forecast? Most likely, both your prediction and level of accuracy would be similar. For example, your temperature forecast for August of next year should probably be the same 80 degrees, plus or minus 10 degrees, as your forecast for August in 50 years. Thus, if the environment is stable, then your uncertainty is not likely to grow with your horizon after some point. (A stable environment is often a bigger assumption than you may realize—think about what global warming could do, for example.)

When you discount the long-term uncertainty, it may be less problematic from an NPV perspective.

Now say you want to value an ice cream store. How does your temperature forecast affect your store's estimated present value? The effect of temperature uncertainty for August of next year is less discounted and thus more important than the effect of temperature uncertainty in August in 50 years. If your store expects to earn \$100,000, and a 10-degree temperature difference can cause you to earn anything between \$75,000 and \$125,000, then the temperature uncertainty for August of next year can cause a present value difference of about $\$50{,}000/1.15^1 \approx \$43{,}478$ at a 15% discount rate (cost of capital). But the same temperature uncertainty in 50 years causes only a present value difference of about $\$50{,}000/1.15^{50} \approx \$46$. Consequently, to estimate your store's value today, your intermediate-term uncertainty should worry you more than your long-term uncertainty.

Economics and strategy: Scarce resources create rents for (existing) shareholders!

The role of intermediate-term versus long-term uncertainty generalizes beyond ice cream stores, because knowledge of economics and strategy allows you to put reasonable bounds on long-term future profitability (in 20 or 50 years). At such far-out horizons, you should not expect businesses to still have unusually large growth rates and to earn **economic rents**, where economic rents are defined as investment rates of return that are much higher than the costs of capital. Economic rents can only be achieved when a firm has assets and capabilities that are scarce, valuable, and difficult to imitate. Examples of such scarce resources are the presence of a unique and excellent manager (e.g., Steve Jobs at Apple Computer), economies of scale (e.g., Microsoft's computer software or Wal-Mart's mass logistics and buying power), unduplicable corporate reputation (e.g., Sony's brand name), legally protected intellectual property (e.g., Glaxo's retroviral drug patents or Disney's Mickey Mouse), or consumer switching costs (e.g., Comcast's cable television). In the long run (i.e., over decades) scarce resources tend to become less scarce as new technologies and consumers make old advantages obsolete. In 2004, I first wrote here that Wal-Mart seemed like an unbeatable juggernaut but that it would almost surely not remain such in 20 years. It surely would not have the scarce and unique resources that would allow its shareholder owners to continue earning rates of return much above their investments' costs of capital. I had to wait less than I expected—as of 2008, Wal-Mart had already lost much of its glamour. Its share price had dropped from \$60 in 2004 to below \$50 in mid-2008.

You should think about barriers to potential competition. The forces of economics have worked on products historically, too.

To determine how long it might take before a product becomes a commodity and thus produces only normal profits, you need to apply economic thinking to your specific business knowledge. If the company owns few unique resources and there are few entry barriers, then it may only take a couple of years before unusually high corporate growth rates slow down and there are no more economic rents. For example, there are few entry barriers to flat-screen television technology today. Consequently, you can count on the industry that produces flat-screen televisions to earn few excess rents within 10 years. (If you do not believe this, think back to 1997, when the average DVD player sold for $800. Today, all entry barriers have disappeared, and you can purchase a DVD player for $20.) Other products, however, can enjoy more scarcity and entry barriers for longer periods of time. For example, if you can get a patent on an effective cancer drug, you will be able to earn economic rents for 15 to 25 years—although better competitors' drugs will eventually come onto the scene and your patent will eventually run out.

Don't get caught up in today's perspective.

Your first reaction might be to dismiss such a long-term perspective. Google may just seem too good in 2008 for you to believe in its eventual slowdown or even demise. But like most of us, you are just letting your present-day experience color your long-term forecasts. Look back 50 years and ask yourself whether the fast-growing, exciting companies operating then are still the same. Or just look back 25 years. Can you even name the companies from the 1980s that still earn large economic rents? If you had picked two companies that looked similar in 1985, are both companies still around? For example, Dell may still be doing well, but Gateway looked just as good in 1985—and there are literally dozens of now-bankrupt mail-based computer retailers that looked no different then, either. Standing in 1985, you should not have expected to earn large economic rents if you had bet on any one computer hardware vendor then.

The discipline of business strategy asks: What factors delay the erosion of economic rents?

The perspective of the economist lends insight into a good choice for T. The economics that helps you decide on when a firm is likely to settle into a lower economic growth rate is taught in great detail in business strategy courses and carries different labels (e.g., Porter's Five Forces). To determine when economic rents are likely to dry up, strategy suggests you ask questions such as:

- How long before your entry barriers will erode?
- How long before your success will be mimicked by the competition?
- How long before you will be squeezed by suppliers or customers?

The first consideration for setting T: business economics.

One good guideline for choosing your horizon T is to consider the underlying firm economics. It should be around the point when the company will earn only "ordinary profits." This is where long-run economic forces will have eroded most of the economic edge of the company—where growth will return from the initial but unsustainably high short-term rates to sustainable, ordinary long-term rates. At this point, a terminal value is relatively easy to forecast. Your goal, then, should be to capture the initially rapid and possibly unstable growth phase with detailed financial forecasts, and the stable period with the terminal value. Another way to say this is that a good T is the point in time when you expect the present value of growth opportunities (PVGO) to be low (or even zero).

➤ PVGO, Section 14.2B, p. 497

The second consideration for setting T: discount factors.

But there is also a second consideration to your choice of T. You want to pick a horizon such that the discount factor is high enough so that the precise choice of T would not matter *too* much. For example, at a 10% discount rate, $1 in 5 years is still worth 62 cents today. An incorrect terminal value would make a big difference to your NPV estimate. If you were to use 20 or even 30 years, $1 would be worth only about 15 cents or 6 cents in present value, respectively. Such high discount factors can help plaster over the errors that your terminal value estimate will inevitably commit. And when it comes to exit values on horizons that are so far away, the best you can hope for is a *halfway* reasonable estimate of market value, anyway.

Typical values for T: 5 to 10 years. We "cheat" for PepsiCo and use just 3 years.

For most businesses, you would pick a terminal phase about 3 to 20 years out, with 5 to 10 years being most common. Let's apply economic intuition to choose a T for PepsiCo. PepsiCo is a very stable company, so it is not necessary to project 20 years of financials in great detail. You can instead "lump" the value created in all future years into one terminal market value fairly soon. A short period is a relief—it saves you from guessing detailed numbers for many initial projection years about which you (as an outsider) have little clue. Thus, for expositional convenience, let us choose a horizon of $T = 3$ years. That is, you should try to project in detail from 2002 to 2004, and then summarize all cash flows from 2005 to eternity with one value estimate as of the end of 2004.

IMPORTANT: The choice of break point T between a detailed projection period and a terminal market value is often dictated by two considerations:

1. A desire to distinguish between an upfront strong growth phase and a subsequent mature and stable phase
2. A desire to have a small discount factor on the terminal market value to reduce the present value importance of estimation errors

In practice, most pro formas choose a T between 5 and 10 years.

SOLVE NOW!

Q 20.4 Is it usually easier to predict the growth rate of earnings (or cash flows) of new businesses in 2 years or in 20 years?

Q 20.5 What considerations would push you toward a longer detailed projection horizon?

20.4 THE DETAILED PROJECTION PHASE

In real life, you must use all your economic knowledge to make a good projection.

You have now dealt with the first goal of choosing the horizon T. Your second goal is to determine your expected cash flows during the beginning growth period, from next year up to the year of your terminal forecast. The good news is that if you were an actual analyst, you would probably know your business quite well and thus be able to reasonably predict the immediate future. You could use PepsiCo's historical cash flows for some guidance about future cash flows. Of course, to do this well, you would still have to understand a lot about the underlying economics of the business, and you would still have to make many assumptions. In this process, you would want to use additional information that we have mostly ignored so far—such as the specific industry economics or the current and historical corporate balance sheets.

Initial growth projections are highly product-specific.

Unfortunately, illustrating this process in a textbook is difficult. There are no clear rules that apply to all companies, and this book is not about PepsiCo or the soda industry. You probably do not know much about PepsiCo's business—and even if I could fully explain and analyze PepsiCo's many businesses for you, it would not help you elsewhere. Pharmaceutical drug research, aluminum mining, fad toys, and a new stamping machine each have their own unique business, financial, and accounting patterns. There is little generality here. In contrast to the terminal value, long-run economic forces are unlikely to bite forcefully in the projection-phase period.

Even though we lack specific information, we must not simply brush over the initial growth phase. Accurate, detailed forecasts have a significant impact on project wealth through two channels. First, these forecasts for the first 3 years have a direct contribution to today's present value. Second, the terminal value itself is (usually) estimated relative to a baseline expected cash flow from the last year of the initial phase. If your baseline is wrong, your terminal value will also be wrong.

IMPORTANT: Your detailed projections will also influence your terminal values.

We are going to have to make up some estimates to illustrate the process. Be warned: Our financial projections for PepsiCo are necessarily very naïve. Again, because you know very little about PepsiCo's business or the plans of its managers, accuracy is not the goal—illustration is.

Warning: Don't expect precision in any pro forma—especially in ours.

The two primary methods of projecting financials are explained in the next two subsections:

Projecting economic cash flows directly (almost a cheat) or indirectly (via detailed financials).

1. Direct extrapolation of the accounting component that you are interested in (i.e., the economic NPV cash flows for the project, though sometimes also the earnings)
2. Detailed financial modeling of all, or most, items in the financial statements

The first is a drastic shortcut, used by analysts only when time and knowledge are severely limited. We actually used this trick in the earlier parts of the book, where cash flow forecasts fell like manna from heaven. In real life, the second method is much more common. Incidentally, computer spreadsheets were originally invented primarily to facilitate the projections in pro formas. They are the preferred tool for designing pro formas.

SOLVE NOW!

Q 20.6 Assume that it is easier in your business to forecast the long-run growth rate than it is to forecast the growth rate over the next 5 years. Further assume that 80% of the present value will sit in the terminal value. Is it still important to get good intermediate projections?

20.4A FAKING IT: DIRECT EXTRAPOLATION OF HISTORICAL CASH FLOWS

The first method is really a "cheat": It is a shortcut that avoids having to do the full-blown financial pro forma analysis. It directly projects the historical cash flows forward, for example, by assuming a constant growth rate forever. Applying Formula 13.4 for project cash flows to PepsiCo from 1999 to 2001 you can compute the cash flows (from Table 20.1) that accrued to both debt and equity:

You could directly project the final cash flows themselves forward. Here (and probably often elsewhere), it gives bad results.

➤ Economic cash flows, Formula 13.4, p. 477

$$\text{Asset Cash Flow}_{1999} = \$3{,}605 + (-\$1{,}172) + (-\$792) = \$1{,}641$$

$$\text{Asset Cash Flow}_{2000} = \$4{,}440 + (-\$1{,}996) + (+\$57) = \$2{,}501$$

$$\text{Asset Cash Flow}_{2001} = \$4{,}201 + (-\$2{,}637) + (-\$8) = \$1{,}556$$

$$\text{Economic Project Cash Flow} = \text{Operating Cash Flow} + \text{Investing Cash Flow} + \text{Interest Expense}$$

Warning: You really need to understand the business. Mechanical extrapolation rarely works well.

➤ Table 13.4, p. 452

Over the 3 years, PepsiCo showed a cash flow decline of about $\$1{,}556/\$1{,}641 - 1 \approx -5.2\%$. This comes to an annual decline of about $(\$1{,}556/\$1{,}641)^{1/2} - 1 \approx -2.6\%$. Over the most recent 12 months, asset cash flows even dropped by one-third! You could assume that PepsiCo's cash flows will continue to decline at this rate forever. But does this make sense? If you investigate PepsiCo's cash flow statement in Table 13.4 further, you can see that much of PepsiCo's decline was due to a heavy increase in (other) investing activity, not a decline in its business (sales). Some of it was due to the acquisition of Quaker, which PepsiCo hopes will eventually pay off in *more* cash, not less cash. This tells you how hazardous simplistic extrapolation of cash flows can be: You really need to know more about the business itself and the reasons behind the financial trends. Purely mechanical rather than economic models of the business usually just don't work well. Again, always remember that valuation requires much economic and common sense, and that it is as much an art as a science. For lack of a better estimate of cash flow growth due to higher investment spending, let us assume a growth rate of 10%. Table 20.2 shows the cash flows if you adopt this projection.

You could project earnings instead of cash flows—which has advantages (e.g., smoothness) and disadvantages (e.g., not used for NPV).

Although it is not as much the case for PepsiCo, the typical lumpiness of cash flows when the firm makes acquisitions (such as when PepsiCo bought Quaker) often makes the forecasting of cash flows very difficult. But there is an alternative. In Chap-

TABLE 20.2 PRO FORMA: DIRECT PROJECTIONS (IN MILLIONS)

10% Growth Cash Flow Projections

	Known			"Detailed" Model Growth at 10%			Terminal Value (see next section)	
	1999	2000	2001	2002	2003	2004	2005	
	Year −2	Year −1	Year 0	Year +1	Year +2	Year +3	Year +4	4 to ∞
Cash Flows	$1,641	$2,501	$1,556	$1,712	$1,883	$2,071	$2,278	?

3% Growth of Earnings Projections

	Known			"Detailed" Model Growth at 3%			Terminal Value (see next section)	
	1999	2000	2001	2002	2003	2004	2005	
	Year −2	Year −1	Year 0	Year +1	Year +2	Year +3	Year +4	4 to ∞
Earnings	$2,505	$2,543	$2,662	$2,742	$2,824	$2,909	$2,996	?

In the top panel, we are simply projecting that cash flows will grow 10% per year, due to current investments, until at least 2005. In the bottom panel, we are simply extrapolating the 2-year historical earnings growth rate of 3% into the future.

ter 14, you worked with earnings rather than cash flows, and for the same lumpiness-of-cash-flows reason. In the very long run, earnings and cash flows should be roughly equal—after all, earnings "just" shift the time-series accruals. The question here is whether historical net income growth or historical cash flow growth represents the present value of the future cash flow growth stream better, given that you have to work with time-truncated forecasts.

Net income (earnings): On the positive side, earnings are smoother than cash flows, because the accountants have reflected likely future cash flows in current earnings. On the negative side, the discount factors are wrong, because you are applying them not to real cash but to a combination of real cash and future cash. Moreover, the human intervention also means historical net income could have been more easily manipulated than historical cash flows.

Cash flows: On the positive side, cash flows are the gold standard *if you can project them out accurately to infinity*. On the negative side, if you have to truncate your forecast in the future or rely on a finite number of cash flows as representative of the future, it is not clear whether or not your history paints an accurate picture of the future.

For example, if you have a plant that costs \$20 million and produces \$15 million that same year as well as the following year, the cash flow stream would suggest huge growth (from −\$5 million to +\$15 million). You could even be tempted to predict another \$20 million in growth (i.e., \$35 million) for the following year if you based your analysis on extrapolated historical cash flows. In contrast, with 2-year linear depreciation, the earnings stream would be a more sensible \$15 − \$10 = \$5 million of income followed by another \$15 − \$10 = \$5 million of income the next year (suggesting a zero growth rate). At least, you would not predict the same runaway growth.

Let's work a PepsiCo forecast based on earnings, not cash flows.

So let's also create a growth rate projection for earnings. PepsiCo had earnings of \$2,662 million in 2001, having grown at rates of 1.5% and 4.7% over the 2 prior years. If PepsiCo were to grow its earnings by 3% per year, you would find the earnings trend at the bottom of Table 20.2. As you can see, earnings would reach nearly \$3 billion by 2005. This estimate is much higher than the equivalent cash flow projection for 2005.

What should you use? Earnings forecasting tends to be better than cash flow forecasting.

In some cases, cash flow–based forecasting is better; in other cases, earnings-based forecasting is better. Academic research has shown that earnings-based terminal value projections are superior to pure cash flow–based terminal value projections *on average for publicly traded corporations*. You could also try other approaches. For example, you could try to distinguish between lower cash flows due to investment (which should create higher future cash flows) and lower cash flows due to lower sales or higher costs (which should not create higher future cash flows).

SOLVE NOW!

Q 20.7 If you do a direct projection, is it usually better to project cash flows or earnings based on the last 3 years of data?

20.4B THE REAL THING: DETAILED FINANCIAL PRO FORMA PROJECTIONS

The more sophisticated method attempts to model the complete financial statements, not just the "end product of" economic cash flows (or earnings). (This is the real pro forma analysis.)

The second and more common method of projecting economic cash flows during the initial period is to project complete financial statements. This requires providing individual components for the economic cash flows you ultimately seek. Doing so is often (but not always) better than projecting economic cash flows directly for three reasons:

1. As just noted, neither cash flow nor earnings forecasts are particularly reliable. Cash flows are difficult to project directly, because they tend to be volatile and lumpy. Net income is smoother but contains many fictional accounting accruals that are not true cash. You are caught between the proverbial rock and hard place.
2. The full projection method can make it easier to incorporate your knowledge of the underlying business into the economic cash flow estimates. For example, you may happen to know that unusual expenses will be zero next year, or that a new payment system may speed the collection of receivables. By forecasting the individual items, you can integrate such economic knowledge into your cash flow estimates.
3. The full projection method can help you judge other important information—such as working capital availability, suitable debt/equity ratios, and your interest rate coverage. Especially for entrepreneurs who are often in danger of a liquidity crisis, such information can be just as important as the economic cash flows themselves. In fact, *all* ratio analyses, such as those exploring the financial health and profitability ratios, are often more useful when applied to pro forma financials than when applied to current financials. Ratio analysis can thereby help you judge whether the firm is on a sound or critical path.

➤ Financial ratios, Section 14.4B, p. 523

THE INCOME STATEMENT: SALES

The baseline for detailed pro formas is sales prediction.

The detailed projection method usually starts by forecasting future sales in the income statement. *Your sales forecast is the single most critical aspect of any pro forma,* because it becomes the baseline number from which many other financial item forecasts will follow. For example, in PepsiCo's case, you could use a mechanistic model that extrapolates sales growth from historical financials. Table 20.3 allows you to compute that PepsiCo sales grew at an annualized rate of $(\$26{,}935/\$25{,}093)^{1/2} - 1 \approx$ 3.61% from 1999 to 2001. Let's assume that PepsiCo sales will continue in 2002 at the same growth rate. Therefore, you could project PepsiCo sales in 2002 to be $\$26{,}935 \cdot (\$26{,}935/\$25{,}093)^{1/2} \approx \$26{,}935 \cdot (1 + 3.61\%) \approx \$27{,}906$ million.

Pro formas should explain all assumptions!

Like every other pro forma line item, the sales forecast should have a footnote (in Table 20.3) to explain the basis behind the estimate. Admittedly, the footnotes in Table 20.3 are mostly perfunctory. For example, note "a" does not even explain where the 3.6% came from. In the real world, you would carefully explain the background assumptions behind each and every critical component of your pro forma—sometimes with many paragraphs and additional tables.

You can use more information and even subjective judgments!

Do not believe that sales forecasting is always as simple as this. You could, and should, use an economic model that uses detailed business intelligence. For example, as a real-world analyst, you might use your knowledge as to

TABLE 20.3 A POSSIBLE PEPSICO PRO FORMA INCOME STATEMENT MODEL FOR 2002 (IN MILLIONS)

	Income Statement	December 1999	2000	2001	Estimated 2002	2003	. . .
=	Sales [a]	\$25,093	\$25,479	\$26,935	\$27,906	. . .	. . .
	+ COGS [b]	\$10,326	\$10,226	\$10,754	\$10,762	. . .	. . .
	+ SG&A [c]	\$11,018	\$11,104	\$11,608	\$12,279	. . .	. . .
	+ Deprec./Amort. [d]	\$193	\$147	\$165	\$168	. . .	. . .
	+ Unusual Expenses [e]	\$73	\$184	\$387	\$279	. . .	. . .
−	**= Operating Expenses** [f]	\$21,610	\$21,661	\$22,914	\$23,486	. . .	. . .
=	**Operating Income** [g]	\$3,483	\$3,818	\$4,021	\$4,420	. . .	. . .
+	Net Interest Income [h]	\$792	−\$57	\$8	\$0	. . .	. . .
=	**Income before Tax** [i]	\$4,275	\$3,761	\$4,029	\$4,420	. . .	. . .
−	Corporate Income Tax [j]	\$1,770	\$1,218	\$1,367	\$1,591	. . .	. . .
=	**Income after Tax** [k]	\$2,505	\$2,543	\$2,662	\$2,828	. . .	. . .
−	Extraordinary Items [l]	\$0	\$0	\$0	\$0	. . .	. . .
=	**Net Income** [m]	\$2,505	\$2,543	\$2,662	\$2,828	. . .	. . .

Explanations (notes) are applicable to the 2002 figures:

a. Grows by historical 3.6%
b. \$3,506 + 26% · $\mathcal{E}$(sales)
c. 44% · $\mathcal{E}$(sales)
d. 3-year historical average
e. 1% · $\mathcal{E}$(sales)
f. Sum the above, rounded
g. Subtract the above
h. Too ignorant and lazy
i. Sum the above
j. 36% · $\mathcal{E}$(IBT)
k. Subtract the above, rounded
l. Too ignorant and lazy
m. Subtract the above

- whether PepsiCo is about to launch many exciting new products or whether it has few new projects in the pipeline;
- whether PepsiCo paid less in dividends in order to reinvest its earnings into operations, which eventually will turn into more sales or profitability;
- whether there is a recession or a boom on the horizon for 2002;

and so on. This would help you adjust your sales estimates for a more accurate projection. In a real pro forma where your money is on the line, it would be outright reckless to forecast sales through a mechanistic model without an economic model!

THE INCOME STATEMENT: OTHER COMPONENTS

How to estimate other financial line items. You could extrapolate them by themselves, but the better way is often to project them in relation to (as a fraction of) sales.

You would then go down item by item on the income statement. Your next estimate would be for COGS. You have a whole range of options, including but not limited to a plain growth forecast (similar to what we used for sales). Here are five possible methods (and keep in mind that the following income statement figures are in millions):

1. **A plain growth forecast:** You could repeat the sales exercise with COGS: A pure growth model would project that COGS' historical growth rate of $(\$10{,}754/\$10{,}326)^{1/2} - 1 \approx 2.05\%$ will continue in 2002. If applied to the year 2001 COGS

of \$10,754, your 2002 COGS forecast would thus be $\$10{,}754 \cdot (1 + 2.05\%) \approx \$10{,}975$.

2. **A pure proportion of sales forecast:** You can forecast COGS not only relative to its own history but also relative to your already-projected sales of \$27,906 for 2002. You also know the historical relationship between COGS and sales, which you can use to predict a relationship between 2002 sales and 2002 COGS. For example, PepsiCo's COGS was $\$10{,}326/\$25{,}093 \approx 41.15\%$ of sales in 1999, 40.14% of sales in 2000, and 39.93% of sales in 2001. The simplest sales-based model might just project that COGS would be a slowly declining fraction of sales in 2002. In this case, your COGS forecast might be

$$\begin{aligned}\mathcal{E}(\text{COGS}_{2002}) &\approx 0 + 39.5\% \cdot \mathcal{E}(\text{Sales}_{2002}) \\ &= \quad 39.5\% \cdot \quad \$27{,}906 \quad \approx \$11{,}023\end{aligned}$$

3. **An economies-of-scale forecast:** A more sophisticated model might pose economies of scale. In this case, COGS would not go up proportionally with sales. Instead, COGS would have both a "fixed component," whose cost would not change with sales (e.g., some necessary maintenance costs or salaries), and a "variable component," whose cost would increase with sales (e.g., the cola syrup) but at a rate of less than one to one. You might try to plot COGS against sales for 1999–2001 and determine visually that a good line fit would be

$$\begin{aligned}\mathcal{E}(\text{COGS}_{2002}) &= \$3{,}500 + 25\% \cdot \mathcal{E}(\text{Sales}_{2002}) \\ &= \quad a \quad + \quad b \cdot \mathcal{E}(\text{Sales}_{2002})\end{aligned}$$

This says that \$3,500 (remember we are working in millions) is an unalterable factory cost, but for each extra dollar of sales, you have to purchase only 25 cents of syrup. Substituting in our estimated 2002 sales of \$27,906, you would project COGS for 2002 to be

$$\mathcal{E}(\text{COGS}_{2002}) \approx \$3{,}500 + 25\% \cdot \$27{,}906 \approx \$10{,}477$$

Or, you could use heavier statistical artillery and run a regression relating PepsiCo's COGS to sales over its most recent 3 years. (Don't worry if you do not know what this is.) Such a regression suggests that a better line fit would be

$$\mathcal{E}(\text{COGS}_{2002}) \approx \$3{,}506 + 26\% \cdot \mathcal{E}(\text{Sales}_{2002})$$

so your prediction would change to

$$\mathcal{E}(\text{COGS}_{2002}) \approx \$3{,}506 + 26\% \cdot \$27{,}906 \approx \$10{,}762 \qquad (20.1)$$

More sophisticated methods can use more information than just sales—for example, they can use industry benchmarks or the company's own depreciation.

4. **An industry-based forecast:** You could draw on information from other firms, such as Coca-Cola. In 2001, Coca-Cola had COGS of \$6,044 on sales of \$20,092 (a ratio of 30%), which is much lower than PepsiCo's ratio. This may not only suggest that Coca-Cola's business is different but also that PepsiCo may be able to

lower its COGS in the future to meet "better practice" standards. Thus, you might want to lower PepsiCo's COGS estimate from $10,762.

5. **A disaggregated forecast:** If you were even more sophisticated, you could recognize that COGS contains some depreciation. Thus, the history of PepsiCo's past capital expenditures could also influence your COGS estimate. You could throw past capital expenditures into your statistical regression, too, to come up with a better predictive formula.

The sky—your economic and econometric background knowledge—is your limit. For illustration's sake, let's adopt $10,762 from Formula 20.1 as our predicted COGS in Table 20.3.

Other financial line items in the table may follow other models.

You can repeat these forecasting processes to predict other income statement items. Again, you have many options. Like COGS, SG&A contains both fixed and variable expenses, as well as depreciation that relates to past investments. SG&A might thus be modeled as a combination of a fixed component, plus a sales-variable component, plus a past capital expenditure–based component. There is also no need to remain consistent across different items—you could use one method to estimate COGS and another to estimate SG&A (or any other financial statement item, for that matter). For example, you could relate net interest income to how much debt PepsiCo currently has and what you know current interest rates are and what you believe future interest rates will be. But because no money (only scarce book space) is at stake, for the rest of the income statement, let's play it simple. The footnotes in Table 20.3 describe the method of projection for each item. Clearly, if your money were at stake, you would want to know as much as possible about the business and use this knowledge to come up with better models for the relationships between PepsiCo's financial variables. Again, the limit is only your knowledge—and for our PepsiCo example, it is obviously very limited, indeed.

SIDE NOTE: In the appendix to this chapter, there are similar formulas for many pro forma components estimated with data from the universe of publicly traded companies. These can be used "in a pinch"—or even to help you gain some intuition about how important the fixed and variable components are in a particular data item. However, the formulas there are mechanistic and therefore definitely not particularly reliable in any individual case—so be careful.

THE CASH FLOW STATEMENT

Your cash flow statement model would rely on your income statement model.

Next, you would model the cash flow statement. Table 20.4 is our attempt for PepsiCo. It starts by transferring the projected net income from the pro forma income statement model into the pro forma cash flow statement model. For the remaining cash flow items, our estimates remain perfunctory—after all, this is only an illustration. We really have no idea about PepsiCo's depreciation and depletion (or about PepsiCo's plants, for that matter), but a number on the order of $1,100 million looks "reasonably reasonable," given the stability of PepsiCo's prior history of depreciation and capital expenditures. (We also ignore the fact that some parts of depreciation have already

TABLE 20.4 A POSSIBLE PEPSICO PRO FORMA CASH FLOW STATEMENT MODEL (IN MILLIONS)

	Cash Flow Statement	December 1999	2000	2001	Estimated 2002	
	Net Income [a]	$2,505	$2,543	$2,662	$2,828	. . .
+	Depreciation and Depletion [b]	$1,156	$1,093	$1,082	$1,100	. . .
+	Deferred Taxes [c]	$573	$33	$162	$300	. . .
+	Noncash Items [d]	−$708	$355	$211	$0	. . .
+	Cash Contributed by Changes in Working Capital [e]	$79	$416	$84	−$200	. . .
=	**Total Operating Activity** [f]	$3,605	$4,440	$4,201	$4,028	. . .
−	Capital Expenditures [g]	$1,341	$1,352	$1,324	$1,300	. . .
+	Other Investing [h]	$169	−$644	−$1,313	$0	. . .
=	**Total Investing Activity** [i]	−$1,172	−$1,996	−$2,637	−$1,300	. . .
	Operating Plus Investing				$2,728	. . .

Explanations (notes) are applicable to the 2002 figures:

a. Transfer from IS (Table 20.3)
b. Eyeballed
c. 15%–20% of corporate income tax, rounded
d. Too ignorant and lazy
e. ≈ −20% of revenue *increase*
f. Sum of above
g. Eyeballed
h. Too ignorant and lazy
i. Sum the above

Note that changes in working capital that contribute positively to the cash flows are decreases in the amount of net working capital on the balance sheet.

been modeled into components of items in the income statement; you really should check the internal consistency of your forecasts—something we shall not do here.)

A quick rundown of other cash flow statement components.

Working down the cash flow statement, you must adopt a ratio for your model for deferred taxes that fits the history reasonably well—let's go with around 18% of PepsiCo's income taxes. You know nothing about noncash items, and PepsiCo's history does not suggest a clear pattern, so choose zero. Changes in working capital are more noteworthy, because their relation to sales contains interesting economics. We know that it is not the absolute level of sales but sales growth that determines the working capital that the business consumes—but not one to one. For example, you may have to carry more inventory to satisfy sales growth, although economies of scale may allow you to grow inventory less than one to one. Your receivables collection policies and technologies (and your willingness to sell to dubious customers) may influence how much your receivables should grow with sales. Your willingness to pay your suppliers may influence your payables, and so on. With a projected sales increase for 2002 of just under $1 billion, it would suggest that PepsiCo will need more working capital. Yet PepsiCo also grew in prior years, and it still managed to pull working capital out of the business rather than put it in! This is rather unusual and may hint at some interesting choices PepsiCo has made. We could dig further to find out; but without further knowledge, and after (not much pretend) analysis of the underlying business, just assume that PepsiCo will reverse its recent trend and put $200 million into the business to finance its sales growth. The outcome of all this handwaving is a forecast of operating cash flow of $4 billion. Finally, after equally long consideration of PepsiCo's business, and equally long interviews with PepsiCo management, let's assume that you determine PepsiCo is planning to invest \$1.3 billion into capital expenditures, and nothing into other activities. Thus, the outcome of operating plus investing cash flows is \$2.7 billion.

Financing Policy, the Balance Sheet, and Linkages

One step that we have mostly bypassed is to think more about your financing policy. It would influence not only the remainder of your cash flow statement (the financing cash flows) but also your balance sheet (debt and equity positions) and even your income statement (interest payments). In fact, depending on what you assume, you may have to go back to the income statement and go through your forecasts again. Other linkages will arise, too. For example:

The four financial statements have other linkages, which we omit for lack of space.

- What you assume about financing cash flows will influence your end-of-period cash position on your balance sheet, because the cash position next year is the cash position this year plus the net of all cash flows.
- What you assume about how your technology will change your inventory or your collection abilities will influence both your current assets and current liabilities on your balance sheet, as well as your consumption of working capital on your cash flow statement.

Of course, you would also need to provide detailed projections for the remaining detailed projection period, 2003–2005. The principles are the same as they were for your projection of 2002. We will skip all these for lack of space.

Future years—more work and trouble.

SOLVE NOW!

Q 20.8 What financial statement line item plays the role of a "base forecast" off of which many other forecasts are often derived?

Q 20.9 How do economies of scale manifest themselves in line item forecasts?

Q 20.10 Are the income statement and the cash flow statement linked?

20.4C RATIO CALCULATIONS AND POLICY WITH PRO FORMAS

After you have also projected the other two financial statements—the balance sheet and the statement of owners' equity—up to the terminal value, T, what can you do with these numbers?

Economic Project Cash Flows

The first important use of the pro forma is project value analysis. Having guesstimated the components of the cash flow statement for 2002, you can now compute the economic cash flow for your NPV analysis, using the basic cash flow formula (Formula 13.4). Economic project cash flows for PepsiCo are the sum of operating cash flows and investing cash flows minus interest income (from Table 20.3). Subtracting interest income is the same as adding interest expense. This comes to around \$2,728 million—much higher than your \$1,712 million direct projection in Table 20.2. This is not because the forecasting technique is different but primarily because you now projected other investing activity to be zero. (It implicitly accounted for around \$1

The projected cash flows for PepsiCo are now much higher, due to our "other investing" assumptions.

➤ Economic cash flows, Formula 13.4, p. 477

➤ Table 20.2, p. 742

billion of consumed cash in 2001.) Without detailed knowledge of PepsiCo's business, you cannot resolve which of the two assumptions—investing activity at $0 or $1 billion—seems more reasonable.

Ratio and Soundness Analysis

Pro formas allow for ratio or financial health analyses.

➤ Financial ratios, Section 14.4, p. 519

A second common use for detailed financial projections is forward-looking ratio analysis to judge whether the business remains viable and sound. Such an analysis can serve to check the reasonableness of your forecasts—and the viability of the firm in your scenario. For example, if a start-up firm were to end up with a very high debt/equity ratio and very little cash, the implied future interest coverage ratio should set off an alarm. Or, a growth path may have an interim negative cash position—which could doom an otherwise healthy firm. The firm may be on a collision course with reality, and management should change course to preserve cash before the entire firm evaporates. However, because most ratio analysis requires aspects of the financials that we do not have space to model—specifically, the financing policy on the cash flow statement and the full balance sheet—we will not discuss this any further. Once you have the full pro forma model, the ratio analysis principles and soundness principles remain exactly the same as they were in Chapter 14.

➤ Other financial ratios, Section 14.4, p. 519

Corporate Policy Changes

Historical projections work only if the economic environment is stable.

Pro forma projections depend not only on external factors—for example, whether the economy is going into a recession—but also on many choices that managers make. For example, managers must make decisions about how quickly to pay or collect outstanding bills, how much to invest into new projects versus how much to pay out in dividends, how much to finance with debt versus how much to finance with equity, and so on. You have to be careful to realize that historical extrapolations may no longer work if either the external environment or the corporate policy is changing.

If the firm is changing its own policy, then the world would likely no longer be stable—and history may no longer be a good guide for projecting.

This is even more important to recognize when you are not an external analyst but a manager constructing a pro forma in order to contemplate a corporate policy change. For example, if you invest more in new factories, all sorts of relationships—some of them nonobvious—may change. For instance, the relationship between COGS and sales may change if the consumers of your product ask for more or less complementary products from other producers, which in turn may change the cost of raw materials that you require for production. Just be careful not to think too mechanistically about the effect of changes in one policy on other items in your financials.

SOLVE NOW!

Q 20.11 Does ratio analysis make sense in the context of a pro forma?

20.5 THE TERMINAL VALUE

After you have decided on T and the cash flows up to T, you can work on the terminal value.

➤ Growing perpetuity, Formula 3.1, p. 43

Your third goal is to determine the firm's terminal market value. Conceptually, the terminal value is your best estimate of what you believe the firm could be sold for at future time T. Practically, it is most commonly estimated with the growing perpetuity formula (Formula 3.1). You would start with your detailed estimated value of cash flows for time T, assume that it will grow forever at some sustainable long-term growth rate $\mathcal{E}(g)$, and discount it back:

$$\mathcal{E}(\text{Terminal Value}_{T=2004}) = \frac{\mathcal{E}(\text{Cash Flow}_{T=2005})}{\mathcal{E}(r) - \mathcal{E}(g)}$$

For illustration's sake, the remainder of the chapter relies only on the direct cash flow forecasts from Table 20.2 (i.e., $\mathcal{E}(\text{Cash Flow}_{T=2005}) = \$2{,}278$) in the numerator. You still need estimates for the eventual (stable and eternal) growth rate, $\mathcal{E}(g)$, and for the future cost of capital, $\mathcal{E}(r)$, or at least for the difference between them, $(\mathcal{E}(r) - \mathcal{E}(g))$. Let's look at the future cost of capital first.

➤ Table 20.2, p. 742

20.5A THE COST OF CAPITAL

You would probably rely on the CAPM to determine the cost of capital for PepsiCo as of late 2001. Because PepsiCo was publicly traded, you could use its own historical return data. If the thought experiment is that PepsiCo is not yet publicly traded, then you could use information from one or more comparables, such as Coca-Cola, instead. Table 20.5 gathers a couple of years of (dividend-adjusted) stock prices from Yahoo! *Finance* for the S&P 500, PepsiCo, and Coca-Cola.

Estimate an appropriate expected rate of return. You might use the CAPM on PepsiCo stock—or a firm that is similar.

You could now compute historical rates of return from historical prices to obtain the following table:

The PepsiCo example: historical beta estimates.

Date	S&P 500	PEP	KO	$\tilde{r}_{S\&P\ 500}$	$\tilde{r}_{PEP}$	$\tilde{r}_{KO}$
30-Jan-98	980.28	\$32.86	\$58.87	1.015%	−0.3639%	−2.919%
27-Feb-98	1,049.34	\$33.20	\$62.39	7.045%	1.0347%	5.979%
31-Mar-98	1,101.75	\$38.95	\$70.56	4.995%	17.3193%	13.095%
...						

(For example, $r = 1{,}101.75/1{,}049.34 - 1 \approx 4.995\%$). With these rates of return, you can compute (or trust me with) the relevant historical statistics:

Statistic	$\tilde{r}_{S\&P\ 500}$	$\tilde{r}_{PEP}$	$\tilde{r}_{KO}$
Mean	0.49%	1.08%	−0.21%
Variance	27.77%%	67.03%%	84.46%%
Standard Deviation	5.27%	8.19%	9.19%
Cov with $\tilde{r}_{S\&P\ 500}$	27.77%%	19.30%%	12.76%%
Corr with $\tilde{r}_{S\&P\ 500}$	100%	45%	26%

These statistics make it easy to calculate the historical equity beta of PepsiCo and Coca-Cola:

$$\beta_{PEP,\,S\&P\ 500} \approx \frac{0.001930}{0.002777} \approx 0.70 \quad \text{and} \quad \beta_{KO,\,S\&P\ 500} \approx \frac{0.001276}{0.002777} \approx 0.46$$

$$\beta_{i,\,S\&P\ 500} = \frac{Cov(\tilde{r}_i, \tilde{r}_{S\&P\ 500})}{Var(\tilde{r}_{S\&P\ 500})}$$

TABLE 20.5 FOUR YEARS OF HISTORICAL STOCK PRICES

Date	S&P 500	PEP	KO	Date	S&P 500	PEP	KO
Dec-97	970	$32.98	$60.64	Jan-00	1,394	$31.94	$53.21
Jan-98	980	$32.86	$58.87	Feb-00	1,366	$30.07	$45.05
Feb-98	1,049	$33.20	$62.39	Mar-00	1,499	$32.79	$43.65
Mar-98	1,102	$38.95	$70.56	Apr-00	1,452	$34.49	$43.94
Apr-98	1,112	$36.22	$69.12	May-00	1,421	$38.25	$49.64
May-98	1,091	$37.24	$71.40	Jun-00	1,455	$41.92	$53.58
Jun-98	1,134	$37.70	$78.04	Jul-00	1,431	$43.22	$57.19
Jul-98	1,121	$35.64	$73.48	Aug-00	1,518	$40.23	$49.11
Aug-98	957	$25.52	$59.44	Sep-00	1,437	$43.54	$51.59
Sep-98	1,017	$27.06	$52.73	Oct-00	1,429	$45.85	$56.51
Oct-98	1,099	$31.02	$61.82	Nov-00	1,315	$42.95	$58.78
Nov-98	1,164	$35.56	$64.24	Dec-00	1,320	$47.06	$57.19
Dec-98	1,229	$37.70	$61.43	Jan-01	1,366	$41.84	$54.43
Jan-99	1,280	$35.97	$59.88	Feb-01	1,240	$43.75	$49.77
Feb-99	1,238	$34.64	$58.57	Mar-01	1,160	$41.86	$42.53
Mar-99	1,286	$36.26	$56.42	Apr-01	1,249	$41.59	$43.51
Apr-99	1,335	$34.18	$62.56	May-01	1,256	$42.63	$44.64
May-99	1,302	$32.85	$62.97	Jun-01	1,224	$42.23	$42.55
Jun-99	1,373	$35.94	$57.13	Jul-01	1,211	$44.55	$42.17
Jul-99	1,329	$36.17	$55.80	Aug-01	1,134	$44.91	$46.02
Aug-99	1,320	$31.70	$55.11	Sep-01	1,041	$46.48	$44.30
Sep-99	1,283	$28.44	$44.59	Oct-01	1,060	$46.68	$45.27
Oct-99	1,363	$32.35	$54.53	Nov-01	1,139	$46.61	$44.57
Nov-99	1,389	$32.23	$62.36	Dec-01	1,148	$46.80	$44.75
Dec-99	1,469	$32.99	$53.96				

All prices were obtained from Yahoo! *Finance* and were from the last day of each month. They are adjusted for stock splits and dividends. It would have been better to compute a beta from daily stock returns, but there were too many to print them in a table here. For space reasons, S&P 500 quotes were rounded.
Source: Reproduced with permission of Yahoo! Inc. © 2008 by Yahoo! Inc. YAHOO! and the YAHOO! logo are trademarks of Yahoo! Inc.

(Of course, it would have been better to use a few years of daily stock returns.) What would be your best estimate of PepsiCo's future equity beta?

- You could just adopt PepsiCo's historical equity market beta of 0.7 (assuming you knew the historical return data for PepsiCo).
- You could assume that equity betas should be shrunk toward the average beta in the market, which is $\beta_{M,M} = 1$. In this case, you might want to choose a market beta of $\beta_{PEP,S\&P\ 500} = (0.7 + 1)/2 = 0.85$.

➤ Beta shrinking, Section 8.3B, p. 216

- You could compute an industry beta, which might be more reliable than even PepsiCo's own beta. After all, PepsiCo's data can be noisy because it relies on just one historical outcome for this single firm. (Well, you do not have industry information here, so let's skip this option.)

- You could assume that Coca-Cola is similar to PepsiCo, which gives you information about PEP's future market beta, too. You might then choose a market beta of 0.46, or an average between PepsiCo's and Coca-Cola's market betas. This would give you an equity beta estimate of around 0.6.

Convert the equity beta into the asset beta.

Let's say you adopt $\beta_{\text{PEP, S\&P 500}} = 0.7$ as your equity beta. But this is not the beta you need. You want to value PepsiCo's assets, not its equity. About 10% of PepsiCo's total market value was in financial and nonfinancial liabilities, which likely would have had market betas close to zero. Therefore, with an equity beta of 0.7, PepsiCo's asset beta would likely have been lower. Your asset beta estimate would be $\beta_{\text{PEP (Firm)}} \approx 90\% \cdot \beta_{\text{PEP (Equity)}} + 10\% \cdot \beta_{\text{PEP (Debt)}} \approx 90\% \cdot 0.7 + 10\% \cdot 0 \approx 0.6$. Henceforth, let us assume that your best asset beta estimate for PepsiCo is $\beta_{\text{PEP, S\&P 500}} = 0.6$. (For convenience, we omit subscripting the asset beta differently from the equity beta—the difference for PepsiCo is tiny.)

Estimate the other (economy-wide) CAPM inputs.

➤ CAPM inputs, Section 9.4, p. 257

To use the CAPM, you also need estimates of the economy-wide risk-free rate and equity premium.

The risk-free rate: At the end of 2001, the 5-year Treasury yield was about 4.4%, and the 20-year Treasury yield was about 5.7%, both holding pretty steady throughout 2001. Given that PepsiCo is likely to be around for a while, maybe a 10-year interest rate would be a good choice. You could choose a rate of around 5% per annum, perhaps plus or minus 1–2%.

(Oy vey.)

The equity premium: It is more difficult to settle on an appropriate equity premium. Pretend that the board of PepsiCo and the management team have unanimously declared that 3% per annum is the standardized estimate.

Okay, we now have a cost-of-capital estimate for PepsiCo.

Putting the three inputs (asset beta, risk-free rate, and equity premium) together yields a CAPM cost-of-capital estimate for PepsiCo—the firm (not the equity)—of

$$\text{Asset Cost of Capital:} \quad \mathcal{E}(\tilde{r}_{\text{PEP}}) \approx 5\% + 3\% \cdot 0.6 = 6.8\%$$
$$\mathcal{E}(\tilde{r}_{\text{PEP}}) = r_F + [\mathcal{E}(\tilde{r}_M) - r_F] \cdot \beta_{\text{PEP, S\&P 500}}$$

Let's just round this to 7%—the CAPM is not a model with accuracy after the decimal point, anyway. Reasonable variations on the estimate for PepsiCo's market beta, for the risk-free rate, and for the equity premium could easily justify other cost-of-capital estimates, say, between about 5% and 10%.

SOLVE NOW!

Q 20.12 When would you want to use asset betas, and when would you want to use equity betas?

Q 20.13 What is the most common model used to estimate the cost of capital in pro formas?

Q 20.14 You should always worry about something you have overlooked or that does not fit together. In Section 20.5A on page 751, for example, PepsiCo's bonds were rated A+ in 2001. Such bonds carried an average interest rate of 7.5%.

(a) Would it be better to use 7.5% in the CAPM formula to obtain PepsiCo's cost of capital?
(b) Estimate PepsiCo's historical average interest rate. Use the income statement's interest expense and the balance sheet's debt (short-term and long-term). Is such an estimate in line with the prevailing interest rate on A+ bonds?
(c) Does it make sense for bonds to have a higher cost of capital than equity? In light of the 7.5% interest rate on A+ bonds, should you change your 7% estimate for PepsiCo's cost of capital?

20.5B THE COST OF CAPITAL MINUS THE GROWTH RATE OF CASH FLOWS

It is easy to come up with a (uselessly) wide range for $\mathcal{E}(g)$.

To compute your terminal value estimate with the perpetuity formula, you still need an estimate of the eternal expected growth rate of cash flows, ($\mathcal{E}(g)$), or at least of the cost of capital, $\mathcal{E}(r)$, minus this growth rate. It is easy to come up with *high* upper bounds on sustainable growth rates. For example, $\mathcal{E}(g)$ cannot be above the firm's cost of capital, or PepsiCo's value would be infinite. You would also not expect $\mathcal{E}(g)$ to be much above the growth rates of GDP—you would not expect the economy to eventually consist of nothing but PepsiCo. In sum, a number like 5–6% is probably an upper bound on PepsiCo's $\mathcal{E}(g)$. You can also think of *low* lower bounds. Although it is not impossible to imagine PepsiCo fading away, this is unlikely to happen quickly, so you might want to choose an estimated growth rate of no less than, say, −1% per annum. Sometimes, it is more intuitive to think of such changes not in terms of nominal growth rates, but in terms of real growth rates. With an assumption of an inflation rate of 2% per annum, the −1% nominal growth rate would correspond to a real rate of about −3% per annum.

It is difficult to come up with a (usefully) narrow range for $\mathcal{E}(g)$. Subjective judgment is needed, yet again.

But you need to do better than these very wide limits. Otherwise, your valuation range would just be too wide to be useful. To improve on your eternal growth rate estimate, you can draw on information from two sources:

1. **Internal company information:** For example, you can assume that managers will not drastically overinvest or underinvest forever. This means you should be consistent in your choice of expected cash flows and the expected growth rate of your cash flows. Would you really want to assume that PepsiCo will invest 20% of its value each year forever, but that this investment will grow its cash flows by only 1% forever? Probably not.

   In PepsiCo's case, cash flow from investing activity was \$2,637 million in 2001. This was a reinvestment rate of around 3% per annum. Admittedly, this required a peak at PepsiCo's asset market value of \$100 billion to compute \$2,637/\$100,000 ≈ 3%. But you could have instead used other base rates. For example, you could start with a reasonable growth rate, then use the value estimate that your pro forma produces, then check your reinvestment rate, then reestimate your value, and so on, until you end up with a consistent number. Consequently, a number in the 3% vicinity for $\mathcal{E}(g)$ would make sense.
2. **Industry or comparable firm information:** For example, you can analyze the publicly traded Coca-Cola to better understand PepsiCo. (Coca-Cola's financials are in Tables 13.11 and 13.12.) Coca-Cola's economic cash flows were described

on page 488. It had earnings (in millions) of \$2,431 in 1999, \$2,177 in 2000, and \$3,969 in 2001. Its economic cash flows (in millions) were \$799, \$2,867, and \$3,211, respectively—driving home yet again how lumpy cash flows are compared to earnings! Moreover, Coca-Cola was valued throughout 2001 at just about \$100 billion.

➤ Coca-Cola's financials and economic cash flows, Section 13.7, p. 488

If you think of Coca-Cola in 2000 or 2001 as comparable to a then-stable PepsiCo as of 2005, you can back out an estimate of $\mathcal{E}(r - g)$ from Coca-Cola's value of about \$150 billion. For example,

$$\$150{,}000 \approx \frac{\$3{,}211}{\mathcal{E}(r - g)} \Rightarrow \mathcal{E}(r - g) \approx 2.1\%$$

$$\text{Terminal Value}_{2000} \approx \frac{C_{2001}}{\mathcal{E}(r) - \mathcal{E}(g)}$$

This contains a small error: It is the estimate for 2000, not for 2001. However, this error is minor compared to the real problem: If you had computed this just 2 years earlier, the same calculation would have yielded not 2.1% but 0.8%! Clearly, the lumpiness of cash flows makes backing out eternal growth rates hazardous. This is why many analysts prefer to use the smoother earnings as a stand-in for cash flows, which is exactly analogous to why many analysts do comparables in terms of earnings rather than in terms of cash flows. Unfortunately, even Coca-Cola's earnings were lumpy, too. In 2000, they were only \$2,177; in 2001, they were \$3,969. Thus, alternative estimates for $\mathcal{E}(r - g)$ could be either 1.5% or 2.6%, respectively.

➤ Comparables with earnings versus cash flows, Section 14.2A, p. 496

Nevertheless, most of these estimates are not too different, suggesting you should settle on an eternal growth rate of around 2–4% per annum. (Such agreement is, unfortunately, quite rare.) Moreover, this is about 1–2% above the inflation rate and roughly in line with generally predicted long-run real growth rates of GDP. This gives us some confidence in our estimates (or, more likely, overconfidence).

Wow—this is novel! We do not have too bad of a dilemma for PepsiCo with respect to the eternal growth rate.

You can now combine the estimate of your eternal growth rate with your estimate for the cost of capital. At an appropriate expected rate of return at 7%, you would expect $\mathcal{E}(r - g) = \mathcal{E}(r) - \mathcal{E}(g) = 7\% - 3\% = 4\%$ per annum. Your cash flow estimate for 2005 was \$2,278 million (from Table 20.2). All together, your estimate of the terminal value for all cash flows from 2005 to eternity could be a 2004 value of (per Table 20.7

Still, you could have used other estimates.

➤ Table 20.2, p. 742

$$\text{Terminal Value}_{2004} \approx \frac{\$2{,}278}{\mathcal{E}(r) - \mathcal{E}(g)} = \frac{\$2{,}278}{4\%} = \$56{,}950$$

$$\text{Terminal Value}_{T-1=2004} \approx \frac{C_{T=2005}}{\mathcal{E}(r) - \mathcal{E}(g)}$$

in millions of dollars, which rounds to about \$57 billion. Again, this terminal value represents the 2004 value of all future cash flows that PepsiCo will create from 2005 to eternity—your assumed market value if you had to sell PepsiCo at the end of 2004. You still need to discount this back to 2001, of course. One issue we will not have to confront in PepsiCo's case is that of time-changing costs of capital. In start-up firms, the early discount rate would often be higher than the long-run discount rate (used in the growing perpetuity formula). The reason is that there is more uncertainty and market dependence before the firm reaches its more stable phase, causing a higher cost of capital early on. In contrast, for PepsiCo, the market risk is probably the same in 2001 as it is after 2005, so you can use the same discount rate. Therefore, you can just adopt the same $\mathcal{E}(r)$ for both early and late years. Discount the \$57 billion in 2004 back to 2001 at the 7% cost of capital, and you find that PepsiCo's terminal value contributes about $\$57/1.07^3 \approx \$46.5$ billion in present value.

How Bad Are Mistakes?

HOW ROBUST IS YOUR VALUATION?

How much does your growth estimate matter?

Immediately after you have estimated your terminal value, you should wonder how robust it is. Recall that your cost-of-capital estimate could easily have been 10% instead of 7%, which would have implied $\mathcal{E}(r - g) = 10\% - 3\% = 7\%$ per annum on the high end; or it could have been 5%, which would have implied $\mathcal{E}(r - g) = 5\% - 3\% = 2\%$ or even $5\% - 4\% = 1\%$ per annum on the low end. Would it have made a difference if you had used a different cost of capital or a different eternal growth rate for earnings? Should you worry about it?

Differences in estimates of $\mathcal{E}(r - g)$ matter even for a company as large as PepsiCo—and PepsiCo is not a growth firm for which almost all its earnings power is far in the future.

Unfortunately, the answer is yes. The uncertainty in your $\mathcal{E}(r - g)$ estimate not only is wide but it also has a significant influence on your valuation. (This is often the case in the real world, too.) Table 20.6 shows the influence of your terminal value estimate on your overall present value if you vary the denominator.

Thus, for reasonable $\mathcal{E}(r - g)$ estimates from 2% to 6% and $\mathcal{E}(r)$ estimates from 5% to 9%, you get present value estimates between \$98 billion and \$29 billion. Unfortunately, the discount factor has not worked miracles and plastered over differences in the denominator $\mathcal{E}(r - g)$; the value difference remains large.

How can you deal with the sensitivity to your assumptions? Unfortunately, you can only use your judgment (and biases) in the end.

You clearly face a problem. Your uncertainty about the difference between the cost of capital and the appropriate eternal growth rate has a big impact on your valuation. What should you do now? In real life, you would probably entertain a range of possible

TABLE 20.6 TERMINAL AND PRESENT VALUES BASED ON DIFFERENT COST OF CAPITAL ESTIMATES

Growth $\mathcal{E}(g)$	Cost of Capital $\mathcal{E}(r)$	$\mathcal{E}(r - g)$	Value of Cash Flows from 2005 to ∞: Terminal Value in $T = 2004$	Present Value in $T = 2001$
3%	4%	1%	$\$2.278/1\% \approx \$228$ billion	$\$228/1.04^3 \approx \$203$ billion
3%	5%	2%	$\$2.278/2\% \approx \$114$ billion	$\$114/1.05^3 \approx \$98$ billion
3%	6%	3%	$\$2.278/3\% \approx \$76$ billion	$\$76/1.06^3 \approx \$64$ billion
3%	7%	4%	$\$2.278/4\% \approx \$57$ billion	$\$57/1.07^3 \approx \$46$ billion
3%	8%	5%	$\$2.278/5\% \approx \$46$ billion	$\$46/1.08^3 \approx \$36$ billion
3%	9%	6%	$\$2.278/6\% \approx \$38$ billion	$\$38/1.09^3 \approx \$29$ billion
3%	10%	7%	$\$2.278/7\% \approx \$33$ billion	$\$33/1.10^3 \approx \$24$ billion

values, do more research, and pick estimates based on the purpose for which you wanted to use the pro forma. If you wanted to sell the company, you would pick a low discount and a high growth rate to make the value appear large. If you wanted to buy the company, you would want to claim a high discount and a low growth rate in your negotiations with the seller. Yes, you would probably choose whatever suits you. It's not all science!

SOLVE NOW!

Q 20.15 Are your present value estimates (usually) sensitive to your assumption about the eternal growth rate of earnings or cash flows, assuming that they are used only in the terminal value forecast?

20.6 SOME PRO FORMAS

You now have the ingredients necessary to produce a pro forma with a market value: economic cash flow forecasts, a terminal value based on the cost of capital and the eternal growth rate, and discount factors. Let's put it all together.

20.6A AN UNBIASED PRO FORMA

Here is a first pro forma value estimate for PepsiCo. It is only $50 billion.

➤ Table 20.2, p. 742

Table 20.7 uses one specific set of assumptions. It starts with the projected asset cash flows from Table 20.2: $1,712, $1,883, $2,071, and $2,278 (million) from 2002 through 2005. Next, we adopt one particular terminal market value estimate based on an eternal cost of capital of 7%, an eternal growth rate of cash flows of 3%, starting from a 2005 base of $2,278 million. According to Table 20.6, this gives a terminal value for cash flows from 2005 to eternity of $57 billion as of 2004. Add to this the 2004 $2.1

TABLE 20.7 AN UNBIASED PRO FORMA BASED ON DIRECT ECONOMIC CASH FLOW PROJECTIONS AND ASSUMING CASH FLOW GROWTH OF 10% PER YEAR

Pro Forma Cash Flow Statement

2000 Year −1	2001 Year 0		2002 Year +1	2003 Year +2	2004 Year +3	2005 Year +4	to ∞
$2,501	$1,556	Projected Annual Asset Cash Flows	$1,712	$1,883	$2,071	$2,278	see next row
					$\frac{\$2,278}{7\%-3\%}$		
		Terminal Market Value in 2004 for Cash Flows from 2005 to Eternity at $\mathcal{E}(g) = 3\%$:			≈$57 billion		
		Total Cash Flows	$1,712	$1,883	≈ $59 billion		
		Discount Factor ($\mathcal{E}(r) = 7\%$)	$1/1.07^1$	$1/1.07^2$	$1/1.07^3$		
		2001 Present Value of Cash Flows	$1.6 billion	$1.6 billion	$48 billion		
		Total Present Value in 2001 of Asset Cash Flows from 2002 to Eternity:				≈ $50 billion	

This pro forma estimates the total firm value of PepsiCo (i.e., not merely value to shareholders) using the direct cash flow projections from Table 20.2 The terminal value is obtained by assuming a 3% eternal growth rate and a 7% cost of capital. Final numbers are generously rounded to prevent giving the impression that there is much accuracy here. Unless noted as billions, dollar values are in millions.

billion in cash flows and you get a 2004 value of about $59 billion. Discount all cash flows (beginning in 2002) with a 7% cost of capital, and you find a present value of about $50 billion. Of course, this is not the only estimate that we could have produced. We could have reasonably relied on different forecasts and obtained possibly very different values.

20.6B A CALIBRATED PRO FORMA

As an investment banker, you need a pro forma to propose a capital structure change. If PepsiCo is public, then you can incorporate more information about its market value in your pro forma.

Now switch your perspective to someone who is analyzing not the hypothetical privately held company but the actual publicly traded PepsiCo. Why would you even want to create a pro forma for a firm for which you already have a public market value? You already know one such scenario—you are considering purchasing shares in PepsiCo and want to learn whether PepsiCo's market value is lower than its underlying fundamental value. But there is another common scenario: You may not just be a passive analyst but an investment banker who wants to suggest a capital structure change. Such a change not only might increase PepsiCo's value, but, more importantly, would also generate banker fees for you. The pro forma is the language of proposing such corporate changes.

Most important, compare our pro forma value and the market value.

Because the firm is public, it is easy to check whether your pro forma value is in line with the actual market value. It turns out that PepsiCo's actual stock market value in 2001 was around $87.4 billion (plus about $3 billion of financial debt and another $10 billion in nonfinancial liabilities), yielding a total asset value of about $100 billion. This suggests that our pro forma value estimate of $50 billion would have been *way too low*. (In Section 20.9, we will look at PepsiCo's subsequent performance to try to find out why.)

➤ Hindsight analysis of PepsiCo, Section 20.9, p. 767

Modify your pro forma to reflect the public market value information, or you will look silly.

Naturally, to propose a capital structure change, you will have to present our pro forma to PepsiCo's management. What would happen if you showed them our pro forma statement? PepsiCo's management would likely be so displeased with our low pro forma value estimate that they would not even listen to any of your proposals. Besides, it would also be silly for you to claim that PepsiCo is worth only $50 billion when it is trading for $100 billion.

You need to "calibrate" your model to the current market value. Calibrate = Fudge.

Before you can go in front of management, you must come up with a pro forma with a value estimate that fits the actual market value of PepsiCo. You must find reasons why PepsiCo is worth more than what our original pro forma suggested. You must find reasons to change the inputs to your model. Although this could be called model "fudging," the technical term is model **calibration**.

You can tinker with all pro forma input numbers.

You basically have three tools at your disposal that can increase the pro forma value so that it will reach the market value: Change the cash flows, change the cost of capital, or change the growth rate.

Change the growth rate of your cash flow estimates.

1. **Detailed projections:** You can depart from our current projected cash flow path. Our original pro forma relied on the direct-projection cash flows that assumed a growth rate of 10%. If you alter the cash flow growth rate, you get two important effects: You change the initial-period cash flow projections and you change the 2005 cash flow projection of $2,278 million, upon which our terminal value was based.

You can justify higher cash flows by arguing for higher sales, lower expenses, higher future cash flows, and the like. This can create a faster growth path for directly projected cash flows. For example, your calibrated model can assume that PepsiCo should be valued off of cash flows that grow faster than 10%—say, 15%:

Projected @ 15% Growth	2001 Year 0	2002 Year +1	2003 Year +2	2004 Year +3	2005 Year +4
(Economic) Cash Flows	$1,556	$1,789	$2,058	$2,366	$2,721

Another way to increase value is to work off the detailed financials from Table 20.4 rather than the direct projections, because the former were higher, reaching $2,728 million as early as 2002.

➤ Table 20.4, p. 748

Yet another way is to shift your focus to earnings, either from the detailed financials or from the direct projection. You know that in the very long run, discounted earnings and discounted cash flows should be roughly equal—after all, earnings "just" shift the time-series accruals. You also know that earnings may be more suitable to a growing-perpetuity valuation, because they are less affected by temporary and possibly lumpy investment patterns. Perhaps PepsiCo accelerated its investments from 1999 to 2001, sacrificing immediate cash flows for higher future cash flows. Relying on earnings growing at 3% per annum, you have the following revised figures:

Try earnings forecasts, instead.

Projected @ 3% Growth	2001 Year 0	2002 Year +1	2003 Year +2	2004 Year +3	2005 Year +4
Earnings (not cash flows)	$2,662	$2,742	$2,824	$2,909	$2,996

Or, you can rely on the detailed earnings projections in Table 20.3, which were even higher, reaching $2,828 million as early as 2002.

➤ Table 20.3, p. 745

2. **Cost-of-capital projections:** You can reduce your estimate of PepsiCo's cost of capital from 7% to a lower number. This again has two effects: It makes future cash flows more valuable, and it increases your estimated terminal market value. The first effect is relatively unimportant—you already know that present values over short horizons are reasonably robust to modest changes in the cost of capital. It is the second effect that gives you a lot of valuation "bang for the buck." Referring back to Table 20.6, you can see that reducing the cost of capital by just 1% can give you an extra $20 billion in present value. Reducing the cost of capital by 2% can give you an extra $50 billion in present value.

➤ Table 20.6, p. 756

3. **Eternal earnings growth projections:** You can increase PepsiCo's eternal earnings growth rate estimate $\mathcal{E}(g)$, thereby changing its growth profile. Doing so would assume that PepsiCo has more of the characteristics of a growth firm than a value firm. Increasing the eternal growth rate is just as powerful as reducing the long-term cost of capital, because g and r enter only as a difference in the perpetuity formula.

TABLE 20.8 A CALIBRATED PRO FORMA ASSUMING CASH FLOW GROWTH OF 15% PER YEAR, 3.5% ETERNAL GROWTH, AND 6% COST OF CAPITAL

Pro Forma Cash Flow Statement

2001 Year 0		2002 Year +1	2003 Year +2	2004 Year +3	2005 Year +4	to ∞
\$1,556	Projected Annual	\$1,789	\$2,058	\$2,366	\$2,721	see next row
				$\frac{\$2,721}{6\%-3.5\%}$		
	Terminal Market Value in 2004 for Cash Flows from 2005 to Eternity at $\mathcal{E}(g) = 3.5\%$:			≈ \$109 billion		
	Total Cash Flows	\$1,789	\$2,058	≈ \$111 billion		
	Discount Factor ($\mathcal{E}(r) = 6\%$)	$1/1.06^1$	$1/1.06^2$	$1/1.06^3$		
	2001 Present Value of Cash Flows	\$1.7 billion	\$1.8 billion	\$93 billion		
	Total Present Value in 2001 of Asset Cash Flows from 2002 to Eternity:			≈ \$100 billion		

This repeats Table 20.7, but with more aggressive assumptions that are intended to match the actual market value of around \$100 billion of PepsiCo in 2000. Unless noted as billions, dollar values are in millions.

Voila! With enough fudging, our pro forma value matches the market value.

In the real world, you would probably choose a combination of all three tools. Table 20.8 contains one calibrated version of the PepsiCo pro forma that makes the following adjustments:

1. It increases the initial cash flow growth rate from 10% to 15%.
2. It reduces the cost of capital from 7% to 6%.
3. It increases the eternal growth rate of cash flows from 3% to 3.5%.

Together, these changes push the market value from \$50 billion to \$100 billion—and you could fudge our assumptions a little more to increase the value further. If you do this, PepsiCo's management will likely be pleased with our calibrated pro forma—it would indicate to them not only that their market value is justified but that even better times may be ahead. (Of course, to keep them happy, you should not show them our original uncalibrated pro forma.)

Be cognizant of what you are doing when you are "calibrating" the inputs!

What is most important here is that you remain conceptually clear about what you are doing when you are calibrating a pro forma: You are "fudging" input estimates to make the outcome fit a market value. You are adopting a "deus ex machina"—a number that is dropped on you from another part of the stage (the financial markets), even though you may not fully understand it. But don't be appalled: This is not so different from what we have always done. Calibration is the equivalent of conducting a *relative* valuation that accepts known market value as a good baseline. After all, every financial concept in this book is based on valuation relative to known market values—though usually only of comparable companies, not of the same company. Calibration is often a justifiable and reasonable procedure because the financial market value of PepsiCo is likely efficient and probably much better than our own pro forma estimate.

How should you look at our private attempt to come up with a pro forma value versus the actual value?

Finally, how would an investor in 2001, reading your analyst's report, have looked at our unbiased pro forma? He would have done an "intuitive" calibration. Most of his faith would have been in the market value of PepsiCo, not in our pro forma value analysis. He would not have trusted our ability to forecast the economics. However, if we had more knowledge of the underlying sales dynamics, our value analysis might have raised enough doubts in him to believe that PepsiCo might be a little overvalued. After all, any public market value is the clearing price where the bears and bulls on PepsiCo are in equilibrium—and our analysis would have led him to join the bears. But he would have kept it all in proper perspective—he would have found it unreasonable to believe that the pro forma value of $50 billion was the appropriate market price of PepsiCo when he could see that the market value was $100 billion. A reasonable synthesis of the PepsiCo value estimates would instead have concluded a value closer to the market value than to the pro forma value—say, a synthesis of $95 billion.

SOLVE NOW!

Q 20.16 What exactly does the technical term "calibration" mean in the context of a pro forma?

Q 20.17 What are your three main calibration tools?

20.7 ALTERNATIVE ASSUMPTIONS AND SENSITIVITY AND SCENARIO ANALYSES

What should you learn from this chapter? Perhaps most importantly, do not trust any single pro forma estimate. And when someone else is handing you a calibrated pro forma, be afraid—be very afraid.

In terms of your own pro formas, you should try to understand how robust your estimates actually are. Such analyses are usually easiest to perform in spreadsheets because they allow you to try out different assumptions and alternative scenarios relatively painlessly.

You need sensitivity analysis—try different inputs.

20.7A FIDDLING WITH INDIVIDUAL ITEMS

Always keep your ultimate goal in mind—you want to find the best value estimate for your business. Your goal is not an exercise in NPV analysis. It is not beauty or simplicity, either. Although both are nice to have, you cannot neglect important value drivers just because the outcome is messier. Use your imagination, your head, and your good common sense!

You want to find a best estimate of value—not the simplest or most complex, easiest or hardest, or even most conceptually beautiful pro forma.

You should always pay attention to other information—and even your personal intuition. For example, in the PepsiCo valuation, our estimated expected cash flow for 2005 was $2,278 million (or $2,996 million if you use earnings). If you had good reason to believe that this was a low estimate, you could adjust ("fudge") it. For example, if you believed that a new drink was going to hit the market and give cash flows a one-time upward value transition of $500 million, then you could use $2,800 million or even $3,500 million. Your estimate does not have to be based on formal, scientific forecasting. Of course, the consumer of your pro forma may not agree with your estimate, so you should be ready to mount a good and credible defense for your number.

You can use ad hoc assumptions if you believe they offer better estimates.

You can also use alternative methods to estimate your terminal value.

Similarly, there are no laws that say that you have to use the growing perpetuity formula on cash flows to obtain your terminal market value. Instead of using the assumption that growth will remain eternally the same (say, 3% per year), you could develop another formula that assumes high growth rates for a few years (say, 5% next year), followed by growth-rate declines until the growth rate reaches the inflation rate (say, 2% per year). Or, you might deem it best if you avoided all formulas and instead assumed that you could find a buyer for PepsiCo who will be paying $200 billion in 2005—ultimately, it is this quantity that you seek to model with your terminal value. Again, you'd better be ready to argue why your $200 billion is the best estimate.

Scenario analysis can help to determine expected (rather than just most likely) cash flows.

Modeling the pro forma as a spreadsheet also allows you to consider specific future scenarios. (Computer spreadsheets were invented precisely to make such analyses relatively easy.) For example, what would happen if the new product were to be wildly successful, or if it were to fall on hard times? What would happen in a recession, based on what has happened in past recessions? What would happen if sales were to decline by 5% next year rather than grow by 3.6% per year? What would happen if sales were to decline for a number of years, not just for 1 year? How bad would one, or many, inputs have to be for you to regret having bought into the project in the first place? And, of course, you can ask the venerable payback question: How long will it take before you get your money back? Admittedly, with more time, technology, and printing space, you should look at many different modified scenario analyses to understand our PepsiCo pro forma better. A detailed pro forma analysis of even one company, such as PepsiCo, could easily consume a few books all by itself. The sky is the limit. There is no point at which you know you have it perfectly nailed. More likely, at some point, you realize that you are not getting any more precise, so you might as well stop.

SOLVE NOW!

Q 20.18 What is the main computer tool for building pro formas?

20.7B DO NOT FORGET FAILURE

The biggest problem: A pro forma is usually one scenario, not an expected value! Overall failure is often not considered.

➤ Typical versus expected values, Section 12.2B, p. 391

The biggest problem in most pro formas, however, is not even in the details. It is the fact that a pro forma is just one particular scenario, and usually a reasonably optimistic one. Many pro formas model just a "typical" or median outcome (recall Section 12.2B). This would not be dissimilar to an average outcome, *but it is conditional on the project not being aborted altogether*.

Entrepreneurial ventures—especially tech ventures—often have almost all value in their terminal value estimates.

Obviously, this is more important for entrepreneurial ventures or start-ups than it is for PepsiCo. For example, if someone pitches you a new magazine, most of the time the pro forma will project a mildly optimistic scenario—*on condition that the magazine succeeds*. It probably does not take into account the fact that 50% of all new magazines fold within a year. It is your task as the consumer of the pro forma to determine for yourself the probability of overall magazine failure, or you will end up misled. (Immediate death does not matter for our PepsiCo pro forma. PepsiCo is likely to stay around for a few more years.)

SOLVE NOW!

Q 20.19 What may be the biggest common mistake in contemplating most pro formas?

20.7C ASSESSING THE QUALITY OF A PRO FORMA

Can you assess the robustness and quality of our pro forma?

By now, you should have realized that the question "Which PepsiCo pro forma is correct?" is not a good one. *No* pro forma is correct! A better question is, "Which PepsiCo pro forma is better?" This is not an easy question, either. Even if you know the ex-post outcome, you will still never know for sure what the best ex-ante pro forma would have been. Even a lousy pro forma forecast will occasionally beat a good pro forma forecast. (Even a stopped clock is correct twice a day.) It often remains a judgment issue, but there are clearly pro formas that rely on better assumptions, are better reasoned, and are more likely to come true than others. Perhaps the best question is, "How can I judge how good a pro forma is?" Or better, "How can I judge how good *my* pro forma is?" There is no easy answer, either. Here are some relevant issues you might contemplate, however.

An interesting diagnostic: What fraction of the value comes from the final value estimate?

➤ Table 20.7, p. 757

➤ Table 20.8, p. 760

You should definitely contemplate your uncertainty about each input. Often, the most influential source of uncertainty is the long-run value. For PepsiCo, it came into play in our terminal value. An interesting statistic is, therefore, what fraction of the value comes from the terminal value. In Table 20.7, the present value estimate of $50 billion was driven mostly by the $57 billion in terminal value. In Table 20.8, the present value estimate of $100 billion was driven mostly by the $111 billion in terminal value. So most of our PepsiCo pro forma value was buried in our terminal value estimate. To the extent that you do not trust our estimate of the present value embodied in the very-long-run future, you should be particularly careful. Of course, if you had stretched T, more value would have been part of the detailed period rather than in the terminal value—but this would not mean that our forecast would have had more reliability. Consequently, the fraction of terminal value in the overall value is only one interesting statistic. Often, this is just how it is, and there is little you can do about it. The terminal value is commonly large even for established companies. However, for start-up companies, it is often almost all of their values. The typical business plans that venture capitalists see have 80% to 95% of their present value (despite a high discount rate) in this "dark-gray box" called terminal value. Watch out!

Monte Carlo analysis may help, too.

➤ Monte carlo analysis, Section 12.10, p. 441

Are there any tools that can help? Even though a spreadsheet is the right tool for presenting and playing with one pro forma at a time, it does not allow you to incorporate your uncertainty in a more systematic way. Your input into each cell of your pro forma spreadsheet should contain not just one number for your best estimate but also a second number that tells you how reliable you deem your best estimate to be. This requires an even more sophisticated method of analysis called **Monte Carlo simulation**. It allows you to associate your uncertainty with each cell in your pro forma spreadsheet. The Monte Carlo procedure then simulates a whole range of possible scenarios (NPV values) and gives you a distribution of outcomes. You can think of it as systematic, automated sensitivity analysis. But this is beyond the scope of a first textbook in finance. (However, Monte Carlo analysis is explained in the advanced web chapter on real options.)

SOLVE NOW!

Q 20.20 If you produce a pro forma for a firm in which 60% of the value sits in the terminal value and one in which 90% of the value sits in the terminal value, which pro forma is more reliable?

20.8 PROPOSING CAPITAL STRUCTURE CHANGE

Play investment banker to propose a capital structure change.

Return now to the scenario in which you are an investment banker seeking to propose a capital structure change. Equipped with our calibrated pro forma, you can now go in front of PepsiCo's management and present two capital structure scenarios—the current structure and your proposed change. Your exposition will rely on our calibrated pro forma. (It would have to include the full balance sheet and financing section on the cash flow statement, which I omit for space constraints in this textbook.)

The current capital structure situation.

➤ PepsiCo's balance sheet, Table 13.1, p. 449

Let's begin by evaluating PepsiCo's current capital structure and tax liabilities. In 2001, its balance sheet shows that its asset market value of over \$100 billion consisted of \$87 billion in equity, \$354 in short-term debt, \$2,651 in long-term debt, and other liabilities and deferred income taxes of \$5,372. Its income statement shows that it paid \$219 in interest and \$1,367 in corporate income taxes. With \$4,029 in before-tax earnings, this is a 34% average tax rate.

Judge the reasons for, and against, different capital structures.

With so little financial debt, the only question of real interest (pun intended) is whether it would make sense for PepsiCo to take on more debt. To decide, you must weigh the various capital structure rationales from Chapters 17 and 18—and ask questions such as:

- How much could PepsiCo save in corporate income taxes if it takes on more debt?
- How likely is PepsiCo to go into financial distress if it borrows more money?
- How important are agency-related free cash flow problems? Would more debt create more efficient operations, and if so, how much value would this add? What would investors infer about PepsiCo if the funds were used to repurchase shares or to finance other operations?

And so on.

To sell a capital structure change to PepsiCo, you must estimate the cost of debt.

➤ Credit rating categories, Table 6.1, p. 148

In PepsiCo's case, many of these questions are relatively easy. For example, the probability that PepsiCo will experience financial distress if it took on a couple of billion dollars in extra debt is very low. Moody's rated PepsiCo's current debt an A1, Standard & Poor's rated it an A+. To pitch a new debt issue, you would have to inform PepsiCo what you believe its cost of debt would be if it took on more debt. You would probably begin by looking at the credit ratings of other companies. For example, Table 20.9 gives some relevant statistics for firms with different credit ratings, debt ratios, and interest coverages. (These are not great statistics, but they were all I could find. Thus, we shall have to work with the same ratios.) In 2001, PepsiCo had a book value–based long-term debt/assets ratio of $\$3{,}005/\$21{,}695 \approx 14\%$, and its EBIT/interest ratio was about 25. Looking at the table, PepsiCo seemed like an outlier—its S&P rating should have been AA, not just A+.

Let's speculate on debt interest rates under alternative capital structures.

Table 20.9 suggests that firms with long-term book debt ratios of about 33% and an EBIT/interest ratio of 5–7 still tended to rank as "investment grade," a category

TABLE 20.9 CHARACTERISTICS OF FIRMS BY S&P BOND RATINGS, DECEMBER 2001

		Investment Grade			Speculative Grade		
		AA	A	BBB	BB	B	C
Long-Term Debt / Book Assets	Mean	23%	26%	34%	43%	54%	62%
	Median	20%	26%	33%	42%	52%	56%
	Std. Dev.	15%	16%	16%	20%	26%	56%
	Quartile 1	11%	15%	23%	30%	36%	22%
	Quartile 3	32%	37%	44%	53%	67%	86%
EBIT / Interest	Mean	17	11	7	5	4	1
	Median	14	7	5	3	1	0
	Std. Dev.	15	15	11	14	25	4
	Quartile 1	6	4	3	2	0	−1
	Quartile 3	24	12	8	5	3	1

PepsiCo had an equivalent total long-term liabilities-to-assets ratio of ($8,023)/$21,695 ≈ 37%, and an equivalent operating income over interest ratio of $4,021/$219 ≈ 18. Assets are book value based. For an old firm such as PepsiCo, this book value method usually understates the true value of assets—often quite dramatically.

that many investment professionals consider an important break. How much more debt could PepsiCo take on and not get too close to the speculative-grade level? PepsiCo had a book value–based debt ratio of 37% on assets of $21,695 million. Its EBIT/interest ratio looked great, though. This suggests that it could take on another $1 billion and remain investment grade. Let's contemplate a debt-for-equity exchange in which PepsiCo issues $1 billion in debt and repurchases $1 billion in equity.

Here is a good estimate of our interest cost of capital.

With about $1 billion additional debt, and even if PepsiCo had to pay an 8% interest rate, it would still likely remain BBB rated. A quick look at prevailing interest rates on financial websites further reveals that AAA bonds promised to pay about 7% and BB bonds about 7.95% on average. Consequently, a PepsiCo with $3.5 billion in debt may have to promise an interest rate of about 7.7% (which seems high relative to our cost of capital, but this is a promised rate, not an expected rate). Of course, in order to convince PepsiCo, you should spend many more hours researching a good interest rate estimate for PepsiCo's new debt.

The point of releveraging is to produce long-term and short-term tax savings. Here is how big the savings could be.

You should advise management to weigh the potential benefits of more debt against these (and potentially other) costs of debt. What would the benefit of more debt be on PepsiCo's value? Fortunately, you even have formulas to help you assess the tax savings. For each extra dollar in debt rather than in equity financing *forever*, the corporate income tax avoided would be equivalent to a present value of $\tau \cdot$ Debt, or about 34% $\cdot$ $1 billion ≈ $340 million. Computed in detail, with an interest rate of 7.7% on $1 billion of new debt, PepsiCo's interest payments would increase by $77 million. At its $\tau = 34\%$ tax rate, this would create a net present value of tax not paid

➤ Tax savings rule, Section 17.6B, p. 630

to Uncle Sam of about $26 million in the first year alone—about 0.65% of net income. If PepsiCo maintained the $1 billion of extra debt in perpetuity, the present value of these tax savings would come to about $340 million—not bad for a day's work.

Other efficiency-related savings.

It is more difficult to judge the operational savings that more debt could bring. For example, PepsiCo's unions might see a seemingly less-profitable company (lower earnings), which might make them more willing to accept lower wages. Management might work harder, too—perhaps even cut a few corporate airplanes. In deciding whether it would make sense value-wise to relever, you would add these tax savings to any efficiency gains from debt and subtract any deadweight losses.

You can return the cash to shareholders either as dividends or in a repurchase. This makes sense primarily if you do not believe that shares are already overvalued.

➤ Optimal capital structure if overvalued, Section 11.6C, p. 372

Another cost of a debt-for-equity exchange is that if the firm is overvalued, management should issue more shares, not repurchase shares. After all, overvalued shares allow you to raise capital at very low expected rates of return. But to take advantage of the tax savings, the money would need to be returned to shareholders—or else PepsiCo would merely earn more taxable net income. It is not clear whether a share repurchase (or dividend payment) would truly be in the interest of existing shareholders. If you were the owner and manager, and you believed the firm was overvalued and underlevered, the right behavior would be clear: You should have the corporation borrow money and use it to repurchase your personal shares. But management may not want to do this. They have another conflict of interest—why would they want to help existing shareholders and then be saddled with shareholders who purchase the newly issued shares but will be unhappy later when the share price returns to its fundamental value?

Will the management be convinced if all you argue about is "shareholder value"?

This brings up your real problem. As a junior investment banker looking to create value for PepsiCo shareholders, how could you convince PepsiCo's management that more debt is good for *management* itself? Would it be enough to tell management that if they raised $1 billion in debt to repurchase $1 billion in equity, they would probably create an instant corporate value increase of, say, around $300 million—more than just 1 year's $26 million savings but less than the $340 million perpetuity income tax savings?

Unfortunately, probably not. Management has its own interests.

➤ Unmitigated agency conflicts and capital structure, Section 18.4, p. 673

Unfortunately, this is unlikely to sway management. First, on an equity value of $87 billion, even $300 million in more value is only about 0.3% of PepsiCo's stock market value. (Later, you will find out not only that PepsiCo maintained its capital structure but also continued to incur tax obligations of around $1.4 billion every year.) Second, with more debt and less equity, management would have less ability to take over other companies, start new projects, purchase corporate airplanes, or build corporate empires. (They would probably explain it differently—that more equity was good for the company to have more flexibility to take advantage of new opportunities and that it was good to have higher credit ratings.) In thinking about how to pitch to PepsiCo's management, you would have to ask yourself—what's in it for them?

A common solution—suggest a merger that requires levering up!

Clearly, as an investment banker hungry for business, you would have an uphill struggle on your hands, even though a debt-for-equity issue would just as clearly create shareholder value. Any productive answer for you would most likely have to lie in the compensation package of management. Managers tend to get higher compensation when they run larger firms. Consequently, you might want to identify other potential candidate firms that PepsiCo could take over—not only would this create issuing fees for debt necessary to finance the takeover, but it would also create additional M&A advisory fees! (And you may even find acquisitions that would create value for the acquirer, too!) In sum, your best shot may be to convince PepsiCo to take over another company and lever up in the process.

Your final alternative is less workable: You could try to convince a third party to take over PepsiCo and relever. Unfortunately, this is not very attractive in this case, because PepsiCo may already have been overvalued by the market, if you believe our original pro forma.

Or, play the M&M game: Take over the firm, relever it, capture the gain, and resell it.

SOLVE NOW!

Q 20.21 Can capital structure issues affect the numbers in your pro forma?

Q 20.22 How can you estimate the required stated cost of capital on debt if you were to change the firm's leverage ratio?

20.9 OUR PRO FORMA IN HINDSIGHT

Let's now switch perspectives again. This time, you will get to look at your preceding analysis as an analyst. As a manager, it is always a good idea to look back and study your earlier analysis after the future has played out—how you ended up being right, being wrong, and just plain lucky or unlucky. If you do not learn from your own past, you are destined to repeat your mistakes. With hindsight, why was this actual market value so much higher than our original unbiased pro forma estimate? Were the financial markets too optimistic, or were we too pessimistic?

We analyzed PepsiCo from a few years ago. Thus, we can use hindsight to do an autopsy!

Before we delve into what happened to PepsiCo from 2002 to 2005, you should realize that the actual realized ex-post performance would not necessarily have been the best ex-ante forecast. The outcome contains subsequent and possibly unexpected developments. For example, if you had believed defense contractors to be poor investments in 2000, it might have been the right forecast, but the events of, and following, September 11, 2001 would have proven you wrong. (Knowing that you were right may, however, have been of little consolation if your bet had lost you a lot of money.) Nevertheless, on average, the best forecast is more likely to be borne out by the events of the future. Analyzing one realization of the subsequent events does not give you a perfect assessment of what you should have predicted—but it is informative. In our case, PepsiCo's actual 2002–2005 performance may indicate why the financial markets in 2001 were more optimistic than our pro forma was. An autopsy can therefore give you a guess—but not a perfect explanation—as to where our forecast went wrong.

You can learn from an autopsy, but you can never know for sure what the best ex-ante estimates would have been, even with perfect hindsight.

Our pro forma forecast would have been too low if our initial-period forecasts were too pessimistic. Unfortunately, there is a minor nuisance: You cannot directly compare the historical numbers to future numbers. PepsiCo sold its Quaker Foods division and two international Frito-Lay divisions, and made other accounting changes that affected the reporting of sales and COGS. This means that PepsiCo even revised its historical numbers for 2000 and 2001. Instead of looking at realized levels, you will therefore have to look at year-to-year changes. Table 20.10, then, shows our predictions were generally too low.

Here is what you learn: We may have been pessimistic because PepsiCo's actual growth was faster than our predicted growth.

Net sales: PepsiCo's sales actually increased from 2001 to 2002 by about $1,600 million. This is much more than the projected $971 million sales growth (from $26,935

TABLE 20.10 ACTUAL (HINDSIGHT) VERSUS FORECAST ESTIMATES OF SALES, CASH FLOWS, AND EARNINGS FOR PEPSICO (IN MILLIONS)

	Known			Actual or Estimated		
Year	1999	2000	2001	2002	2003	2004
Known Historical Sales	$25,093	$25,479	$26,935			
Sales, Direct Projection (Table 20.3)				$27,906		
Change Therein				**+$971**		
Actual Sales, *Revised*		$22,337	$23,512	$25,112	$26,971	$29,261
Change Therein				**+$1,600**	+$1,859	+$2,290
Actual Economic Cash Flow	$1,641	$2,501	$1,556	$4,242	$2,169	$2,817
Projected, Direct (Tables 20.2 and 20.7)				$1,712	$1,883	$2,071
Projected, Detailed (Table 20.4)				$2,728		
Actual Net Income	$2,505	$2,543	$2,662	$3,000	$3,568	$4,212
Projected, Direct (Table 20.2)				$2,742	$2,824	$2,909
Projected, Detailed (Table 20.3)				$2,828		

The 2002 detailed projected cash flow of $2,728 omits interest paid and is therefore a little too low. Blue numbers are forecasts.

➤ Table 20.1, p. 737

million to $27,906 million) in our detailed pro forma forecast from Table 20.1. Sales grew generally faster than predicted also in subsequent years.

Cash flows: PepsiCo confirms what you already knew—cash flows are too lumpy to be well suited to direct projections. Selling off its subsidiaries, PepsiCo produced a one-time cash windfall. Added to ordinary cash flows, PepsiCo had over $4.2 billion in 2002, again much higher than our predicted $1.7 billion or $2.7 billion. However, in 2003 PepsiCo invested more than usual, and its cash flows dropped back to just above $2 billion. Still, our forecasts were generally too low.

Earnings: The PepsiCo earnings grew more smoothly than cash flows—but again much faster than what we had projected. By 2004, actual earnings were almost 50% higher than our direct forecast.

No wonder that our pro forma value estimate was too pessimistic: Almost all of PepsiCo's higher profits and earnings came from sales increases that were much higher than what we predicted. Our method of mechanistic projection models from past financial data is rarely very accurate, and the PepsiCo case was no exception. Unless we had known the business and market well enough to forecast sales this high, we would have stood no chance estimating the value as well as the financial market forecast it!

Our cost-of-capital estimate was also too low, but our cost of capital minus the growth estimate looks okay.

You can also autopsy the pro forma estimate of $\mathcal{E}(r - g)$. As of mid-2005, PepsiCo had an asset market cap of $100 billion ($87 billion in equity) on earnings of $4.3 billion, plus another $300 million in interest payments. Consequently, in mid 2005, it was capitalized at about $\mathcal{E}(r - g) = \mathcal{E}(CF)/\text{PV} = \$4.6/\$100 = 4.6\%$—in line with our own forecasts. Next, autopsy the forecast for $\mathcal{E}(r)$, again as of 2005. PepsiCo had a lower beta of only about 0.35—closer to the optimistic historical 0.7 beta than the pessimistic, shrunk beta of 0.85. Interest rates also turned out to have remained low, so the 2005 cost-of-capital estimate might be

$$\mathcal{E}(r) = 5\% + 3\% \cdot 0.35 \approx 6\%$$

which is lower than our unbiased 7% cost-of-capital estimate. Together with the $\mathcal{E}(r - g) = 4.6\%$, this implies that PepsiCo is capitalized as if its earnings were to grow only by about 1.4% per year—not a very optimistic valuation, and indeed even lower than both the 2005 rate of inflation and the estimate in our unbiased pro forma. So, we did not do too badly on our $\mathcal{E}(r - g)$ forecast.

PepsiCo should have been an "easy" pro forma—and we were still off by a factor of two.

In sum, hindsight shows that the primary driver of PepsiCo's higher value was its higher sales from 2002 to 2005. Let this be a lesson in humility: Even for a large and established company with a solid history, valuation is difficult and suffers from plenty of uncertainties—though economic knowledge could have done much to improve our estimates. And for start-up projects, even more of the value is uncertain and lies far off in the future. Don't find the uncertainties too discouraging. Just as the CAPM is the premier model for the cost of capital, the pro forma is the premier model for writing business plans—*simply, there is no better alternative*. Forecasting the future is the tough job that economic value is all about. Fortunately, you do not even need to be able to forecast *well*. All that matters is that you can forecast *better* than the rest of us. If you can, you will become rich.

SOLVE NOW!

Q 20.23 Where did our forecast of PepsiCo's value go wrong?

20.10 CAUTION—THE EMPEROR'S NEW CLOTHES

Do not instinctively trust pro formas! They can look very professional, and still be utterly not credible.

➤ Table 20.3, p. 745
➤ Table 20.4, p. 748

Did our projections seem arbitrary to you? They should have, because they *were* arbitrary—and this chapter made a point of telling you so throughout. But look back at our financial projections in Tables 20.3 and 20.4. If you did not round, but quoted a few more digits (for pseudo-accuracy), if you expanded the footnotes with some more mumbo jumbo, and if you added a few more columns of future years, a naïve reader might be fooled into thinking that you were a sophisticated analyst who knew what you were doing! A well-written pro forma can easily convey an image of professional knowledge even where there is none. (Form over content may work here!) It is important that you do not end up being such a naïve consumer of pro formas. In the case of pro formas, even the best emperor wears only a bathing suit.

Do not lose the forest and discuss only mini-details.

Another danger for the unwary pro forma reader is falling into the trap of looking at the trees rather than the forest. You can easily get involved in endless discussions of a particular projected item in someone else's pro forma. In real life, most pro formas rely on plenty of heroic assumptions—in some cases, there are just one or two critical assumptions; in other cases, there may be many. You must look at the big picture as well as at the minor assumptions. There is devil in both the details and in the sum total.

With all the problems, a pro forma may still be the *best* tool you have at your disposal.

I hope I have not been sounding dismissive of pro formas. On the contrary—again, you have *no* alternative. Forecasting the future is inherently a difficult, but important, task. The universal use of heroic assumptions does not mean that there is no difference between a good and a bad pro forma. You can distinguish a good one from a bad one. *On average*, if you do, you will come out ahead. A good pro forma pitched to a sophisticated audience must use solid economics and have detailed footnotes explaining and justifying just about every important line item. It is a starting point for a good discussion, not an end in itself.

Closing the circle—valuation is more art than science.

Ultimately, finance is about value, so it must revolve around projections, and pro formas are good tools to organize projections. Projecting is very hard. Remember how the book started? I told you then that valuation is both an art and a science. The formulas are easy; the application is hard. I trust that you believe me now. Welcome to the club of financiers!

SOLVE NOW!

Q 20.24 How trustworthy are business pro formas?

SUMMARY

This chapter covered the following major points:

- The purpose of pro formas is to project financials, which are then often used to compute a project's NPV today. You can also use pro formas to perform a ratio analysis to test the financial soundness of a business plan or to analyze a project's working capital requirement.
- Pro formas are usually split into a detailed forecast period and a terminal value.
- A good horizon choice for the detailed forecast period depends on the prevailing discount rate and the economics of the business. The detailed projection period is often applied to the initial strong-growth period, while the terminal value is often applied to the stable no-more-growth phase.
- A quick-and-dirty pro forma analysis may just project the line items of direct use. A more complete and detailed pro forma analysis can try to project many intermediate components.
- A useful distinction is to think of fixed versus sales-variable forecasts for individual components.
- Scenario analysis helps you to better understand the uncertainty in your pro forma.
- Calibration is the deliberate manipulation of inputs to meet the observed valuation in the financial markets.
- Pro formas are often idiosyncratic and not very reliable. But you have no better alternative. Use caution in constructing and interpreting pro formas.

KEY TERMS

calibration, 758
economic rents, 738
Monte Carlo simulation, 763
pro forma, 734
terminal value, 736

SOLVE NOW! SOLUTIONS

Q 20.1 A full pro forma analysis forces you to think more about the economics of your business, and about issues such as working capital and cash management.

Q 20.2 Entrepreneurs are inside analysts. They are often primarily interested in working capital management and secondarily in a present value analysis.

Q 20.3 The three components that you need to work out are your choice of horizon, your detailed financial projections, and your terminal market value estimate.

Q 20.4 The growth rate of earnings or cash flows is probably easier to predict in 20 years, when it is likely to be "normal." It is in the start-up phase (i.e., in 2 years) that most new businesses have unusual uncertainty. (Of course, if the business were to go bankrupt, your growth rate projection in 20 years is as good as any other—multiplying zero by your number will still give zero.)

Q 20.5 You would choose a longer detailed projection horizon if your growth phase is longer before you get to a stable business phase. You would also choose a longer horizon if your discount rate is smaller.

Q 20.6 The intermediate projections are still very important, because your terminal projection is based off of the intermediate projections.

Q 20.7 It is usually better to forecast earnings than cash flows because earnings are more smooth.

Q 20.8 The "base forecast" for pro formas is usually sales. It will in turn influence COGS, SG&A, and so on.

Q 20.9 Economies of scale manifest themselves in a coefficient that is not one to one with sales. For costs, (e.g., COGS) this means a smaller coefficient; for gains (e.g., earnings), this means a larger coefficient.

Q 20.10 Yes, the income statement and cash flow statement are linked. The latter even begins with net income. In addition, there can also be many other relevant linkages that you would expect a reasonable model for the firm to satisfy. For example, bill collection technologies could influence both cash management and earnings.

Q 20.11 Yes, ratio analysis does make sense—indeed, it may make *more* sense in a pro forma context than it does in a historical context.

Q 20.12 You would want to use asset betas if you are trying to determine the value of the firm. You would want to use equity betas if you are trying to determine the value of the equity. This in turn depends on whether you care about (buying) the firm or the equity. For discounting the equity cash flows, use a cost of capital based on the equity beta; for discounting the asset cash flows, use one based on the asset beta.

Q 20.13 The most common model to estimate the cost of capital in pro formas is the CAPM.

Q 20.14 (a) No, it would not be better to use PepsiCo's rate of 7.5% as the CAPM risk-free rate. The CAPM requires the risk-free rate, not PepsiCo's expected interest rate (and definitely not its promised interest rate, either).
(b) PepsiCo had an interest expense of $219 in 2001 on balance sheet short-term borrowings of $354 and long-term debt of $2,651. This interest/debt ratio suggests a nominal interest rate of $219/($354 +

$2,651) ≈ 7.3%. However. you do not know whether some of the interest expense went to pay for other liabilities, when PepsiCo contracted its debt, or what the interest rate would be if it could refinance in 2001. This rate is indeed reasonably in line with the 7.5% typical for A+ rated bonds.

(c) Yes, it makes sense. Realize that PepsiCo's asset cost of capital also includes liabilities that are interest free (such as taxes payable). More importantly, the 7.5% A+ bond yield is based on promised rates of return, not on expected rates of return. It contains a default premium, as well as a risk premium and a liquidity premium. So, 7% is not necessarily crazy as an overall cost of capital, but it definitely appears to be on the low side.

Q 20.15 Yes, unfortunately, present value estimates (usually) remain sensitive to the assumption about the eternal growth rate of earnings or cash flows.

Q 20.16 Calibration occurs in the context of publicly traded corporations. It means that you are changing your estimates to obtain a value that is in line with the actual observed market value.

Q 20.17 Your three main calibration tools are to change your three inputs of the pro forma analysis: the cash flow forecasts in the initial period (themselves based on sales and other items), the cost of capital, and the eternal growth rate.

Q 20.18 A computer spreadsheet is the main tool to help you build pro formas. If you are very sophisticated, you might consider a Monte Carlo simulator, too (explained in Section 20.7C).

Q 20.19 The biggest common mistake in contemplating pro formas may be forgetting about the probability of total failure and business shutdown.

Q 20.20 You cannot infer from the percentage of the value that sits in the terminal value which of the two pro formas is more reliable! For instance, you can put more or less into the terminal value by stretching the number of years in the initial projection phase, but this does not mean that you have fed more information into your forecast.

Q 20.21 Yes, capital structure can influence the numbers in your pro forma. You need to take your capital structure into account when projecting the pro forma inputs because the world is not a perfect M&M world. Therefore, your choice of capital structure affects your project's present value, most directly (but not only) through your corporate income taxes.

Q 20.22 You can estimate the required stated cost of capital on debt by relating variables such as interest coverage ratios to the firm's credit ratings, which in turn would give you a good estimate of the required interest rate.

Q 20.23 Our forecast of PepsiCo's value went wrong primarily in our sales forecasts that were not optimistic enough.

Q 20.24 Usually, pro formas are not very trustworthy. They may look professional, but no one has a true crystal ball for complex businesses.

PROBLEMS

The ▒ *indicates problems available in* myfinancelab

Q 20.25 Are internal pro formas or external pro formas usually more accurate?

Q 20.26 What are common and reasonable detailed projection period horizons?

Q 20.27 What are the problems with a simple projection of historical sales growth rates?

Q 20.28 Look over a general income statement and balance sheet. Make a good guess and justify which financial statement items are likely to increase more than one to one with sales, which are likely to increase less than one to one with sales, and which are likely to move one to one with sales?

Q 20.29 What specific methods can you use to forecast individual financial statement items, such as SG&A? Discuss.

Q 20.30 In a detailed projection, does it make sense to project the cash flow statement before you project the income statement?

Q 20.31 How can you obtain a discount rate for use in your financial analysis?

Q 20.32 Can you compute the market beta of PepsiCo prevailing in early 2002 based on 3 years of daily stock returns? (You can download the data from Yahoo! *Finance*.) Would your beta estimate be different from the 0.70?

Q 20.33 If your course covered this: What would be the alternative to using the CAPM for determining the appropriate cost of capital? Look back at the appendix of Chapter 9. Can you compute the cost of capital with this alternative, following the recipe?

Q 20.34 When would you want to calibrate your pro forma model to available market data? Do you believe most pro formas are calibrated, whether they state it or not? Is caution advisable?

Q 20.35 When would you want to use only one of your three calibration tools? When would you want to use all three?

Q 20.36 Can agency issues affect the numbers in your pro formas?

Q 20.37 When would you believe pro formas in real life to be objective, and when would you believe them to be tailored to what the audience wants to hear?

Q 20.38 Come up with a pro forma for a company assigned by your instructor. (This makes a good final project for a corporate finance course.)

Q 20.39 Pick any publicly traded corporation today. Have yourself and a number of your friends work out three types of pro formas: one if you are a bidder for the corporation, one if you are the owner of the corporation, and an unbiased one. Compare the results. (Note: Often, the average value estimate is a good estimate. Who came closest?)

CHAPTER 20 APPENDIX

In-a-Pinch Advice: Fixed versus Variable Components

What is fixed? What is variable? Some advice.

Is it possible to predict *in general* how firms' income statements and cash flow statements are likely to develop in the future? Is depreciation better modeled as consisting of both fixed and variable components, or is it better modeled as a fixed component only, or perhaps as a variable component only? Is COGS more sales-variable or more stable? What about dividends? Of course, every business is different, so there are no uniform answers here. Some firms rely more on fixed-cost technologies, others on variable-cost technologies. However, rather than not providing any guidance, I will now describe how corporate financials have evolved *on average* in publicly traded companies. Our specific interest is whether particular accounting items have been better explained by their own history or by sales growth. Although such knowledge of how the average publicly traded firm has evolved can sometimes help you in a pinch (when you need something quickly and without much thought), it is better if you regard this section as a "jump start" to get you to do more economic thinking about, exploration of, and business modeling for your particular company.

IMPORTANT: If you can, ignore the crutches provided for you in this section. Instead, execute your modeling based on specific and sound intelligence about your business.

Our projections consist only of a fixed component and a variable (sales-related) component.

Our basic public company financial item prediction model will be

$$\mathcal{E}(X_{t+1}) \approx \gamma_{\text{Fixed}} \cdot X_t + \gamma_{\text{Variable}} \cdot \left\{ X_t \cdot \left[\frac{\mathcal{E}(\text{Sales}_{t+1})}{\text{Sales}_t} \right] \right\}$$

where X is a financial statement number, such as COGS or SG&A, and t is a year index. For example, statistical history suggests that

$$\begin{aligned} \mathcal{E}(\text{SG\&A}_{t+1}) &\approx 36\% \cdot \text{SG\&A}_t + 68\% \cdot \left\{ \text{SG\&A}_t \cdot \left[\frac{\mathcal{E}(\text{Sales}_{t+1})}{\text{Sales}_t} \right] \right\} \\ &= \gamma_{\text{Fixed}} \cdot \text{SG\&A}_t + \gamma_{\text{Variable}} \cdot \left\{ \text{SG\&A}_t \cdot \left[\frac{\mathcal{E}(\text{Sales}_{t+1})}{\text{Sales}_t} \right] \right\} \end{aligned} \tag{20.2}$$

This says that the typical firm's SG&A was about one-third related to its own past SG&A value and two-thirds related to SG&A adjusted for sales growth. How would you use this prediction in our PepsiCo pro forma? In 2001, PepsiCo had SG&A of \$11,608 million, and sales of \$26,935 million. Projected 2002 sales were \$27,906 million for a 3.6% increase. Thus, Formula 20.2 suggests (dollars are in millions)

$$\begin{aligned}\mathcal{E}(\text{SG\&A}_{2002}) &\approx 36\% \cdot \$11{,}608 + 68\% \cdot \left[\$11{,}608 \cdot \left(\frac{\$27{,}906}{\$26{,}935}\right)\right] \\ &\approx 36\% \cdot \$11{,}608 + 68\% \cdot [\$11{,}608 \cdot (1 + 3.6\%)] \\ &\approx 36\% \cdot \$11{,}608 + 68\% \cdot \$12{,}026 \approx \$12{,}357\end{aligned} \tag{20.3}$$

The left part of the formula measures the "fixed effect," that is, the degree to which SG&A remains the same as last year's SG&A, independent of PepsiCo's 2002 sales growth. The right part of the formula measures the "variable effect," that is, how SG&A has to increase with sales growth in 2002.

SIDE NOTE: The reason why the coefficients in Formula 20.3 do not add up to 1 is that SG&A increased on average in the sample—perhaps due to inflation. If γ_{Fixed} is 1 and γ_{Variable} is 0, then the best prediction of X next year is the same as X this year. If γ_{Fixed} is 0 and γ_{Variable} is 1, then the best prediction of X next year is obtained by multiplying last year's X by the observed or predicted sales increase from this year to next year.

Again, use these estimates only for basic intuition and guidance, and—if need be—as stand-ins, but do not believe they fit *your* project well.

It is important that you do not believe that the precise coefficient estimates of 36% and 68% are applicable to *your* company. They are based on mechanical statistical models, which rely only on historical information for publicly traded companies that may be totally unrelated to your own and which depend on a time period that is ancient history. The coefficient estimates can serve only as "quick-and-dirty" stand-ins until you use your skills and smarts to produce something better. They are here only to help give you some initial guidance in your own economic exploration of whether a particular financial item in your firm tends to be more fixed or more variable.

Again, projection formulas can definitely be hazardous to your wealth. Watch it.

Moreover, keep in mind that most of the time you will be asked to create a pro forma when the company contemplates a change in policy or when you want to propose a new project. The historical behavior of large publicly traded companies is unlikely to be a good representation of what will happen in such circumstances. Instead, your pro forma forecasts must be specific in addressing the contemplated policy changes. So, please do better than the formulas below.

Enough words of caution. Here are some nuggets of forecasting advice:

Sales: This is the most important variable. You must forecast this number as diligently as you possibly can. Other variables below can depend on this critical estimate. For illustration, we shall forecast PepsiCo's 2002 sales to be \$27,906 million, which means that PepsiCo's 2002 sales growth is $\$27{,}906/\$26{,}935 - 1 \approx 3.6\%$.

COGS: In our average publicly traded companies,

$$\mathcal{E}(\text{COGS})_{t+1} \approx 6\% \cdot \text{COGS}_t + 95\% \cdot \left\{\text{COGS}_t \cdot \left[\frac{\mathcal{E}(\text{Sales}_{t+1})}{\text{Sales}_t}\right]\right\}$$

Coefficients so close to 0 and 1, respectively, suggest that cost of goods sold is best explained as a constant ratio of sales (unless the firm deliberately shifts production into different [fixed cost] production). Like all other formulas below, this formula is based on the history of reasonably large publicly traded U.S. firms (and thus is neither necessarily applicable to smaller firms nor to the future).

To use this formula to forecast PepsiCo's COGS for 2002, you would compute (dollars are in millions)

$$\mathcal{E}(\text{COGS})_{2002} \approx 6\% \cdot \text{COGS}_{2001} + 95\% \cdot \left\{\text{COGS}_{2001} \cdot \left[\frac{\mathcal{E}(\text{Sales}_{2002})}{\text{Sales}_{2001}}\right]\right\}$$

$$\approx 6\% \cdot \$10{,}754 + 95\% \cdot \{\$10{,}754 \cdot [1.036]\}$$

$$\approx \$11{,}229$$

SG&A: Selling, general, and administrative expenses was used as an illustration earlier (Formula 20.2).

Unusual expenses: No particular advice.

Operating income: Either construct this from the items above (i.e., use the accounting identities), or forecast it as

$$\mathcal{E}(\text{Oper. Inc.}_{t+1}) \approx -41\% \cdot \text{Oper. Inc.}_{t} + 120\% \cdot \left\{\text{Oper. Inc.}_{t} \cdot \left[\frac{\mathcal{E}(\text{Sales}_{t+1})}{\text{Sales}_{t}}\right]\right\}$$

Note that operating income is extremely sensitive to sales growth: Any extra sales on the margin have more than a one-to-one effect on operating income. This is why the first coefficient is negative and the second is above 1. It makes economic sense: Operating income goes positive only above some break-even sales point. (A strong sensitivity to sales growth also appears in some other variables below.) However, there is one unusual feature of this formula that you should understand: The two coefficients sum up to considerably less than 100%. This means that the formula indicates a strong "drift" of operating income toward zero. For example, for PepsiCo,

$$\mathcal{E}(\text{Oper. Inc.}_{2002}) \approx -41\% \cdot \text{Oper. Inc.}_{2001} + 120\% \cdot \left\{\text{Oper. Inc.}_{t} \cdot \left[\frac{\mathcal{E}(\text{Sales}_{2002})}{\text{Sales}_{2001}}\right]\right\}$$

$$\approx -41\% \cdot \$4{,}021 + 120\% \cdot \{\$4{,}021 \cdot [1.036]\}$$

$$\approx \$3{,}350$$

You would estimate declining operating income even in the face of increasing sales! This also occurs in a number of formulas below. You must watch out for this—and think about whether such a drift toward zero would make sense for your particular company and pro forma!

Interest income/payments: Either construct these from debt and/or the previous year's interest payments, or forecast them as

$$\mathcal{E}(\text{Interest Inc.}_{t+1}) \approx 22\% \cdot \text{Interest Inc.}_{t} + 67\% \cdot \left\{\text{Interest Inc.}_{t} \cdot \left[\frac{\mathcal{E}(\text{Sales}_{t+1})}{\text{Sales}_{t}}\right]\right\}$$

Remember: If a change in capital structure policy is contemplated, this item needs to reflect it. For PepsiCo,

$$\begin{aligned}\mathcal{E}(\text{Interest Inc.}_{2002}) &\approx 22\% \cdot \text{Interest Inc.}_{2001} + 67\% \cdot \left\{\text{Interest Inc.}_{2001} \cdot \left[\frac{\mathcal{E}(\text{Sales}_{2002})}{\text{Sales}_{2001}}\right]\right\} \\ &\approx 22\% \cdot \$8 + 67\% \cdot \{\$8 \cdot [1.036]\} \\ &\approx \$7\end{aligned}$$

Income before tax: Either construct this from the items above, or forecast it as

$$\mathcal{E}(\text{Inc. bef. Tax}_{t+1}) \approx -32\% \cdot \text{Inc. bef. Tax}_t + 116\% \cdot \left\{\text{Inc. bef. Tax}_t \cdot \left[\frac{\mathcal{E}(\text{Sales}_{t+1})}{\text{Sales}_t}\right]\right\}$$

For PepsiCo,

$$\begin{aligned}\mathcal{E}(\text{Inc. bef. Tax}_{2002}) &\approx -32\% \cdot \text{Inc. bef. Tax}_{2001} + 116\% \cdot \left\{\text{Inc. bef. Tax}_{2001} \cdot \left[\frac{\mathcal{E}(\text{Sales}_{2002})}{\text{Sales}_{2001}}\right]\right\} \\ &\approx -32\% \cdot \$4{,}029 + 116\% \cdot \{\$4{,}029 \cdot [1.036]\} \\ &\approx \$3{,}553\end{aligned}$$

Income tax: Either construct this from the items above, or forecast it as

$$\mathcal{E}(\text{Income Tax}_{t+1}) \approx -55\% \cdot \text{Income Tax}_t + 123\% \cdot \left\{\text{Income Tax}_t \cdot \left[\frac{\mathcal{E}(\text{Sales}_{t+1})}{\text{Sales}_t}\right]\right\}$$

For PepsiCo,

$$\begin{aligned}\mathcal{E}(\text{Income Tax}_{2002}) &\approx -55\% \cdot \text{Income Tax}_{2001} + 123\% \cdot \left\{\text{Income Tax}_{2001} \cdot \left[\frac{\mathcal{E}(\text{Sales}_{2002})}{\text{Sales}_{2001}}\right]\right\} \\ &\approx -55\% \cdot \$1{,}367 + 123\% \cdot \{\$1{,}367 \cdot [1.036]\} \\ &\approx \$990\end{aligned}$$

Income after tax (but before extraordinary items): Either construct this from the items above, or forecast it as

$$\mathcal{E}(\text{Inc. aft. Tax}_{t+1}) \approx -30\% \cdot \text{Inc. aft. Tax}_t + 113\% \cdot \left\{\text{Inc. aft. Tax}_t \cdot \left[\frac{\mathcal{E}(\text{Sales}_{t+1})}{\text{Sales}_t}\right]\right\}$$

For PepsiCo,

$$\begin{aligned}\mathcal{E}(\text{Inc. aft. Tax}_{2002}) &\approx -30\% \cdot \text{Inc. aft. Tax}_{2001} + 113\% \cdot \left\{\text{Inc. aft. Tax}_{2001} \cdot \left[\frac{\mathcal{E}(\text{Sales}_{2002})}{\text{Sales}_{2001}}\right]\right\} \\ &\approx -30\% \cdot \$2{,}662 + 113\% \cdot \{\$2{,}662 \cdot [1.036]\} \\ &\approx \$2{,}318\end{aligned}$$

Extraordinary items: No specific advice.

Net income: Either construct this from the items above, or forecast it as

$$\mathcal{E}(\text{Net Inc.}_{t+1}) \approx -42\% \cdot \text{Net Inc.}_t + 114\% \cdot \left\{ \text{Net Inc.}_t \cdot \left[\frac{\mathcal{E}(\text{Sales}_{t+1})}{\text{Sales}_t} \right] \right\}$$

For PepsiCo,

$$\begin{aligned}\mathcal{E}(\text{Net Inc.}_{2002}) &\approx -42\% \cdot \text{Net Inc.}_{2001} + 114\% \cdot \left\{ \text{Net Inc.}_{2001} \cdot \left[\frac{\mathcal{E}(\text{Sales}_{2002})}{\text{Sales}_{2001}} \right] \right\} \\ &\approx -42\% \cdot \$2{,}662 + 114\% \cdot \{\$2{,}662 \cdot [1.036]\} \\ &\approx \$2{,}026\end{aligned}$$

Depreciation and depletion: Either construct this from the items above, or forecast it as

$$\mathcal{E}(\text{DD}_{t+1}) \approx 42\% \cdot \text{DD}_t + 62\% \cdot \left\{ \text{DD}_t \cdot \left[\frac{\mathcal{E}(\text{Sales}_{t+1})}{\text{Sales}_t} \right] \right\}$$

For PepsiCo,

$$\begin{aligned}\mathcal{E}(\text{DD}_{2002}) &\approx 42\% \cdot \text{DD}_{2001} + 62\% \cdot \left\{ \text{DD}_{2001} \cdot \left[\frac{\mathcal{E}(\text{Sales}_{2002})}{\text{Sales}_{2001}} \right] \right\} \\ &\approx 42\% \cdot \$1{,}082 + 62\% \cdot \{\$1{,}082 \cdot [1.036]\} \\ &\approx \$1{,}149\end{aligned}$$

Deferred taxes: Very strongly related to sales growth and/or capital investment.

Noncash items: Very sticky, but negatively related to sales growth.

➤ Working capital, Section 13.4, p. 469

Changes in working capital: In Section 13.4, we discussed that changes in working capital can use up cash quite quickly, especially when the firm is growing fast. Consequently, this is one of the cases where a negative coefficient on the sales growth–adjusted term makes sense. And, indeed, we find that a decent model for large firms is

$$\mathcal{E}(\Delta WC_{t+1}) \approx 46\% \cdot \Delta WC_t + (-43\%) \cdot \left\{ \Delta WC_t \cdot \left[\frac{\mathcal{E}(\text{Sales}_{t+1})}{\text{Sales}_t} \right] \right\}$$

For PepsiCo,

$$\begin{aligned}\mathcal{E}(\Delta WC_{2002}) &\approx 46\% \cdot \Delta WC_{2001} + (-43\%) \cdot \left\{ \Delta WC_{2001} \cdot \left[\frac{\mathcal{E}(\text{Sales}_{2002})}{\text{Sales}_{2001}} \right] \right\} \\ &\approx 46\% \cdot \$84 + (-43\%) \cdot \{\$84 \cdot [1.036]\} \\ &\approx \$1\end{aligned}$$

Capital expenditures: Capital expenditures seem to be strongly related to sales growth:

$$\mathcal{E}(\text{Cap. Exp.}_{t+1}) \approx 0\% \cdot \text{Cap. Exp.}_t + 100\% \cdot \left\{ \text{Cap. Exp.}_t \cdot \left[\frac{\mathcal{E}(\text{Sales}_{t+1})}{\text{Sales}_t} \right] \right\}$$

For PepsiCo,

$$\mathcal{E}(\text{Cap. Exp.}_{2002}) \approx 0\% \cdot \text{Cap. Exp.}_{2001} + 100\% \cdot \left\{\text{Cap. Exp.}_{2001} \cdot \left[\frac{\mathcal{E}(\text{Sales}_{2002})}{\text{Sales}_{2001}}\right]\right\}$$

$$\approx \quad 0\% \cdot \$1{,}324 \quad + \quad 100\% \cdot \{\$1{,}324 \cdot [1.036]\}$$

$$\approx \quad \$1{,}372$$

(Note: If a change in capital expenditures policy is contemplated, this item needs to reflect it.)

Other investing: Very sticky, but negatively related to sales growth.

Total cash flows from investing activity:

$$\mathcal{E}(\text{CF-Inv}_{t+1}) \approx (-320\%) \cdot \text{CF-Inv}_t + 340\% \cdot \left\{\text{CF-Inv}_t \cdot \left[\frac{\mathcal{E}(\text{Sales}_{t+1})}{\text{Sales}_t}\right]\right\}$$

For PepsiCo,

$$\mathcal{E}(\text{CF-Inv}_{2002}) \approx (-320\%) \cdot \text{CF-Inv}_{2001} + 340\% \cdot \left\{\text{CF-Inv}_{2001} \cdot \left[\frac{\mathcal{E}(\text{Sales}_{2002})}{\text{Sales}_{2001}}\right]\right\}$$

$$\approx (-320\%) \cdot (-\$2{,}637) + \quad 340\% \cdot \{-\$2{,}637 \cdot [1.036]\}$$

$$\approx \quad -\$850$$

Very strongly related to sales growth.

Financing cash flow items: No useful relationship.

Dividends: Very sticky, but negatively related to sales growth.

$$\mathcal{E}(\text{Dividends}_{t+1}) \approx 159\% \cdot \text{Dividends}_t + (-82\%) \cdot \left\{\text{Dividends}_t \cdot \left[\frac{\mathcal{E}(\text{Sales}_{t+1})}{\text{Sales}_t}\right]\right\}$$

This estimated formula often does not make much economic sense: Why would dividends go down if sales go up? It is not altogether impossible, of course. For example, if the firm experiences great sales surprises, it may decide that it needs the money to cover working capital or that it wants to reinvest the money rather than pay it out as dividends. However, you should consider this on a case-by-case basis. You might be better off just assuming last year's dividends.

Net stock issuing: No useful relationship. Strongly related to sales growth.

Net debt issuing: Strongly related to sales growth.

$$\mathcal{E}(\text{Debt-Issue}_{t+1}) \approx (-192\%) \cdot \text{Debt-Issue}_t + 195\% \cdot \left\{\text{Debt-Issue}_t \cdot \left[\frac{\mathcal{E}(\text{Sales}_{t+1})}{\text{Sales}_t}\right]\right\}$$

Total cash flows from financing activity: Mildly related to sales growth.

$$\mathcal{E}(\text{CF-Fin}_{t+1}) \approx (-7\%) \cdot \text{CF-Fin}_t + 25\% \cdot \left\{\text{CF-Fin}_t \cdot \left[\frac{\mathcal{E}(\text{Sales}_{t+1})}{\text{Sales}_t}\right]\right\}$$

For PepsiCo,

$$\mathcal{E}(\text{CF-Fin}_{2002}) \approx (-7\%) \cdot \text{CF-Fin}_{2001} + 25\% \cdot \left\{\text{CF-Fin}_{2001} \cdot \left[\frac{\mathcal{E}(\text{Sales}_{2002})}{\text{Sales}_{2001}}\right]\right\}$$

$$\approx (-7\%) \cdot (-\$1{,}919) + \quad 25\% \cdot \{-\$1{,}919 \cdot [1.036]\}$$

$$\approx \quad -\$363$$

Foreign exchange effects: Sticky.

$$\mathcal{E}(\text{FX}_{t+1}) \approx 75\% \cdot \text{FX}_t + (-52\%) \cdot \left\{\text{FX}_t \cdot \left[\frac{\mathcal{E}(\text{Sales}_{t+1})}{\text{Sales}_t}\right]\right\}$$

For PepsiCo,

$$\mathcal{E}(\text{FX}_{2002}) \approx 75\% \cdot \text{FX}_{2001} + (-52\%) \cdot \left\{\text{FX}_{2001} \cdot \left[\frac{\mathcal{E}(\text{Sales}_{2002})}{\text{Sales}_{2001}}\right]\right\}$$

$$\approx \quad 75\% \cdot \$0 \quad + \quad (-52\%) \cdot \{\$0 \cdot [1.036]\}$$

$$\approx \quad \$0$$

This is not the most important item for PepsiCo.

Total net cash flows:

$$\mathcal{E}(\text{Net CF}_{t+1}) \approx 272\% \cdot \text{Net CF}_t + (-267\%) \cdot \left\{\text{Net CF}_t \cdot \left[\frac{\mathcal{E}(\text{Sales}_{t+1})}{\text{Sales}_t}\right]\right\}$$

Here is an example of an estimated formula that serves as a warning: A negative coefficient on the sales growth–adjusted number probably makes little sense for most large companies. Yes, it could be that the company does consume more working capital as it grows, but it just does not seem to be applicable in many cases—such as PepsiCo. You might just want to avoid this formula.

DIGGING DEEPER

The formulas were estimated using "regression analysis." For you super nerds: All variables were normalized by sales, regressions were run firm by firm, and the coefficients were then averaged over firms. Even more sophisticated modeling assumptions and techniques did no better than the simple regression approach adopted here.

In conclusion, do not trust these formulas. They are merely tools that you can use for constructing a first draft of your pro forma—they are not good blueprints. Forecasting the performance of any business, but especially a new business, remains an art that relies on the underlying sciences of economics, statistics, accounting, and finance. Don't just rely on statistics alone. Use common sense. Use good knowledge of the economics of the business and the industry. Document your reasoning in informed and detailed footnotes. And then—pray!

PROBLEMS

The ▬ *indicates problems available in* myfinancelab

Q 20.40 Complete the 2002 forecast in the cash flow statement model in Table 20.4 on page 748. Create a forecast for 2003. (Iterate on depreciation and investing to determine sensible inputs into both.)

Q 20.41 Does it make sense for the net income coefficient to have a negative coefficient on the first term?

Q 20.42 In the in-a-pinch models, is the expected growth rate of each financial data item *plus one* a linear function of the expected growth rate of sales *plus one*?

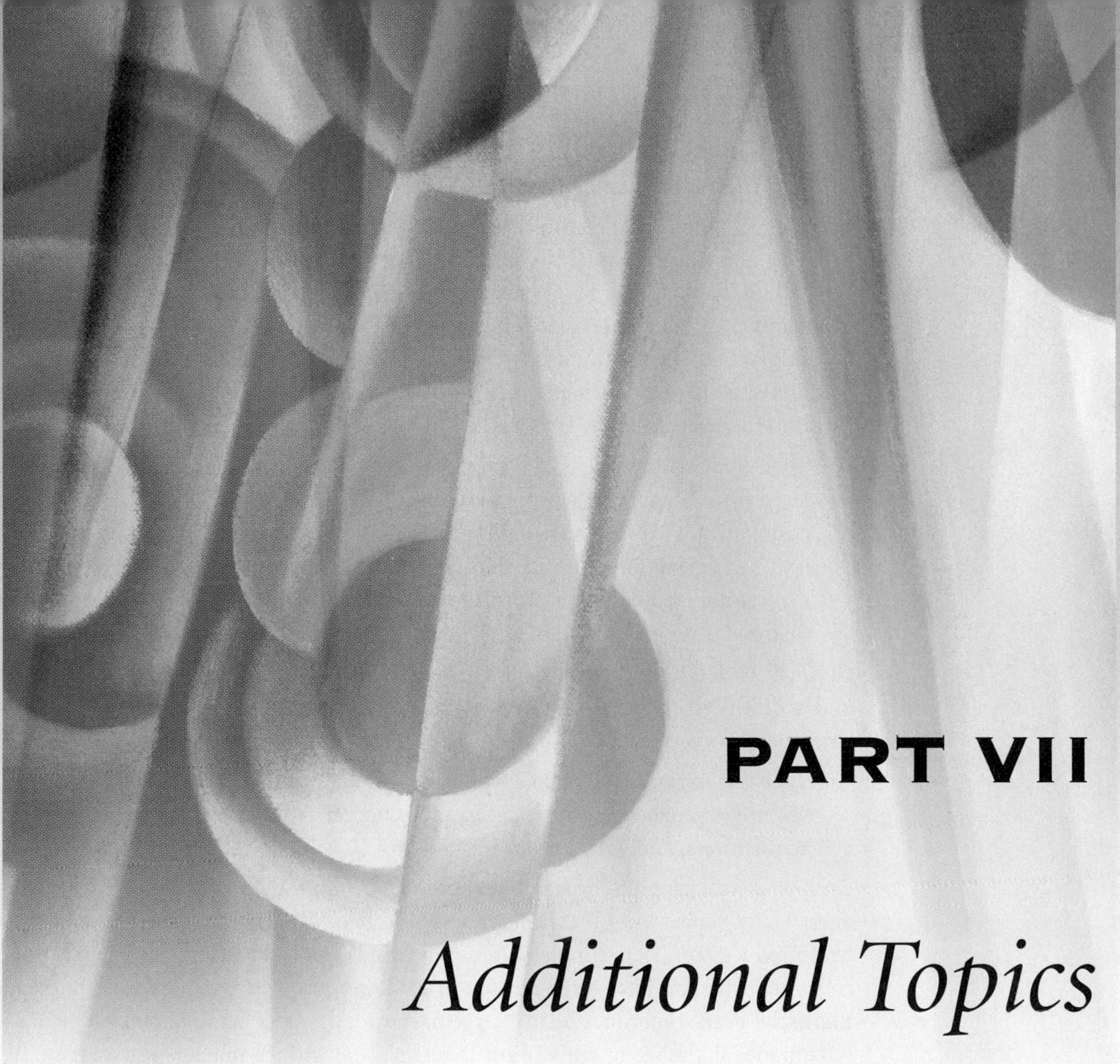

PART VII

Additional Topics

WHAT YOU WANT TO LEARN IN THIS PART

This part covers many topics that most introductory classes unfortunately just won't have time to cover. They are important, though. These chapters are stand-alone, meaning that there is no particular order in which you should read them.

- Chapter 21 shifts the emphasis from capital structure *levels* to capital structure *changes*. It explains how managers should be thinking about effecting change in their capital structures (and firm sizes).

  Typical questions: What mechanisms can managers use to change capital structure and firm size? How do the pecking order view of capital structure (which you learned earlier) and the financing pyramid view of capital structure relate to one another? What happens if managers act suboptimally? How are actual offerings typically structured? Are initial public offerings different from ordinary offerings by established publicly traded companies?

- Chapter 22 describes the empirical capital structure evidence in the United States. That is, it does not explain what capital structure *should* look like, but what it typically *does* look like. The first part of the chapter describes how easily the IBM financials from Chapter 15 generalize to other types of firms, big and small. The second part explains both the corporate motives for capital structure change and the mechanisms by which it happens. This means it looks at capital structure changes through the lens of the theories discussed in earlier chapters.

  Typical questions: How have firms' current capital structures come about? Are large firms' capital structures different from those of small firms? What are the companies with the most debt and the least debt? How important are equity issues in determining the debt/equity ratio of the typical company? Do managers use capital structure to minimize corporate income taxes or to avoid financial distress?

- Chapter 23 describes the role of investment banks and makes a detour into mergers and acquisitions (M&A)—an area in which investment bankers are playing a major role, too.

  Typical questions: What do investment bankers really do? Who are the top investment bankers? How much do they charge? How common are mergers and acquisitions, and why do they occur?

- Chapter 24 focuses on corporate governance in more detail. It explains how managers really behave (not just how they should behave) and how firms should be set up to reduce conflicts of interest between professional managers and shareholders. In some firms, this has become a "fox in the henhouse" problem, because managers themselves can sometimes be in charge of setting up these arrangements. Corporate governance is the set of control mechanisms that induce managers to satisfy their obligations to the ultimate owners: the creditors and shareholders. Corporate governance is often mistakenly confused with good management.

  Typical questions: How can managers steal or waste the firm's money in their own interests? What can creditors, shareholders, the legal environment, and the public do to rein in such behavior? How effective is corporate governance in publicly traded U.S. corporations today?

- Chapter 25 explains the role of currency translations and international market segmentation for both investments and corporate budgeting purposes. It is a throwback to earlier chapters, in that it carefully works out a detailed example to make it crystal clear how it really works.

  Typical questions: If your firm has operations in South Africa, Great Britain, and the United States, and you want to raise debt capital on the London Stock Exchange, and most of your debt capital providers are from Kuwait, what is your cost of capital?

The above chapters are primarily corporate finance chapters, although the international chapter contains a lot of information relevant in an investments context. There is one chapter that is primarily an investments topic:

- Chapter 26 returns to the perfect-market scenario. It works out how financial options should be priced. An option is the right (but not the obligation) to buy or sell a security for a predetermined price to someone who has agreed to be the counterparty (in exchange for money upfront).

  Typical questions: What is the value of one option to purchase IBM shares for 6 months at a so-called strike price of $50 per share? What is the relationship between calls and puts? What is the Black-Scholes formula?

21

Capital Structure Dynamics

AND THE FINANCING PROCESS

In the real world, you rarely have the luxury of thinking about the optimal capital structure and the optimal firm size from scratch. Instead, you are saddled with a situation caused by the firm's history. You have a set of tools at your disposal, and a set of goals you want to accomplish. You must learn how to decide on your goals and how to get from here to there. This is the role of this chapter. It connects the theories of capital structure *levels* to *changes* in capital structure and firm size, both on a conceptual level and on an institutional-detail level.

Along the way, this chapter covers two subjects that occasionally receive their own treatments: working capital management and initial public offerings.

21.1 CAPITAL STRUCTURE AND FIRM SCALE

What are your tools? What are your capital structure targets?

Say you are the CFO of a large firm who wants to maximize shareholder wealth. Your current capital structure was determined in your firm's past—you are not starting from scratch. Some of the future changes are under your control, some are not. Faced with your current situation, what questions and issues should you ponder? What tools do you have at your disposal? What can trip you up?

21.1A THE KEY DECISION QUESTIONS

The two important questions: Can you offer your investors great project opportunities, and do your investors understand this?

There are a lot of actions you can take, such as paying out cash, raising more cash, expanding your operations, and so on. If you are a manager who wants to act on behalf of the firm's owners, then you should always keep two key questions in mind when you make decisions:

1. Can you invest your investors' money better through your firm than what your investors could find as investment opportunities elsewhere?

If not, you should return their money to them. After all, it is not *your* money, but your corporation's investors' money, that you are working with. They should own the earnings the firm generates.

2. Do your investors share your beliefs that your actions will increase value—that the additional money will be well spent?

   If your investors agree with your managerial judgment, as they would in a perfect market, then you have no problem. However, if your investors disagree with you—as they may in an imperfect market—then you may have a problem. For example, if you know that investing in a new technology is highly worthwhile but requires cutting your dividends, then your investors (the market) may interpret this negatively. This means that all your current investors would be taking a hit on their market value right now, just as they would if you had thrown away their money. If you are correct, however, then your investors will eventually realize the value gain, and thus your share price will appreciate again. But this is little consolation to those investors who have to sell their shares this year. Should you represent your current investors or your future investors? There is no easy answer to this difficult question. (Incidentally, many agency researchers are skeptical about managers' claims that they weigh the choices and decide to represent the long-run investors—researchers tend to believe that such claims are only excuses for managers to represent *themselves*. But everyone agrees that good communication from managers to investors can only help.)

You must worry about operations and disclosure.

The latter dilemma shows that capital structure has intricate links to your firm's project opportunities, corporate governance, and disclosure policy. If your firm has great opportunities, if your managers are well motivated, and if your firm can convince investors of these great opportunities, then the answer to both of the above questions is often yes. You can then create value even by reducing dividends and share repurchases and by raising more equity. If the answer to both questions is no, then the firm should not issue equity and instead seek to increase dividends and share repurchases. And if the answers to both questions are contradictory or fuzzy—*as they often are*—then you have tough judgment calls to make.

SOLVE NOW!

Q 21.1 What should be your two main questions when deciding on capital structure actions?

21.1B MECHANISMS INFLUENCING CAPITAL STRUCTURE AND FIRM SIZE

Most actions have two-dimensional outcomes: capital structure and firm scale (size).

Let's presume that you have worked out what is in the interest of your investors. You know what capital structure and firm size you want to get to. Most capital structure tools at your disposal have consequences for firm size (and vice versa). If you issue equity or debt, your firm becomes larger. If your firm grows in a good year, not only does the equity of your firm increase, but your leverage goes down as well. As CFO, you must use your tools carefully, keeping an eye on both outcomes—capital structure and firm size.

TABLE 21.1 NONOPERATING CAPITALIZATION AND CAPITAL STRUCTURE INFLUENCES

Debt/Equity Ratio	Firm Value (Firm Size)		
	Decreases	Constant	Increases
Decreases	• **Debt repurchase (e.g., sinking fund and interest payment)** • **Repayment of principal or interest** • Debt call	• Debt-into-equity conversion • Equity-for-debt exchange (more equity, less debt)	• **Firm value increases** [a] • **Primary seasoned equity issue in M&A context** • **Share creation for employee compensation purposes** • Primary seasoned equity issue outside M&A context • Warrant exercise
Could Be Either	• Simultaneous debt/equity payout • **Sale of assets (e.g., carve-out)**		• Simultaneous debt/equity issue • **Hybrid security issue** **Purchase of assets (e.g., M&A)**
Increases	• **Firm value drops** [a] • **Share repurchase** • **Cash dividend**	• Debt-for-equity exchange (more debt, less equity)	• **Debt issue**

a. Firm value changes can be exogenous to the firm (e.g., investors change their preferences, or government or nature intervenes) or endogenous (e.g., the firm returns earnings or wastes funds).

Boldfaced changes are common, though not necessarily of equal quantitative importance. Non-boldfaced changes are much rarer. Note that this table ignores the complex interactions with existing capital structure. In particular, if the firm is 100%-equity-financed, an increase or decrease in firm value, an equity issue or equity repurchase, and a dividend payment have no influence on the firm's debt/equity ratio—it will remain at 0%.

Let's look more systematically at the tools at your disposal. Table 21.1 organizes some available mechanisms by their effects on both outcomes. Many of these mechanisms are what you already suspected. For example, when a firm issues debt, both the firm size and the debt ratio increase. Most, but not all, of the changes listed in the table contain transactions that are due to active financial market intervention orchestrated by you, the manager.

Many mechanisms work as you would expect—and they are under management's control.

If you now think that you can easily deduce which firms today have higher leverage just by a quick naïve glance at their historical financial debt and equity issuing activities, then you are mistaken. There are a number of disconnects, some of which you have already seen in the case of IBM's capital structure (in Chapter 15). Here are some issues to ponder:

Working debt ratios are not so simple.

Nonfinancial claims: Nonfinancial claims on the firm are often as large as financial debt and equity. Corporate operations can increase both your assets and your liabilities (e.g., pension claims or accounts payable), just like your financial claims. You therefore cannot ignore your firm's real operations when thinking about indebtedness.

Nonfinancial liabilities can arise from your operations, intentionally or unintentionally.

Existing leverage: Your existing capital structure plays an important role in the effect that issuing has on the capital structure. When a $200 million firm with a 100%

Debt ratios are not linear in debt and equity.

equity structure issues $100 million in new equity shares, it does not change its debt ratio. But when another equally large firm with a $180/$200 = 90% debt ratio issues the same $100 million in new equity, the effect of this issue is a dramatic reduction in leverage to $180/$300 = 60%.

Could a firm that issues $400 million in debt and $100 million in equity actually *lower* its leverage ratio? (Yes—if the firm had $900 million in debt and $100 million in equity prior to the issues, its financial debt ratio would drop from 90% to 87%.)

Debt and equity issuing activity can be simultaneous and merger-related.

➤ Mergers & acquisitions, Section 23.3, p. 877

Simultaneous issues: Equity issuing often occurs jointly with debt issuing. Most importantly, new equity (and debt) tends to come in dramatically when a firm acquires another firm. Thus, it may even be that when firms issue large amounts of equity, it is precisely the time when their debt ratio goes up—not because of the equity issuing, but because of their simultaneous other activity.

Stock returns may not fully be under the control of management.

➤ IBM value changes, Section 15.4B, p. 561

Value changes: There are firm value changes (aka stock returns) that affect both the scale and the debt/equity ratio of the firm. For example, a $100 firm that is financed 50-50 by risk-free debt and equity and that doubles in value to $200 would see its debt/equity ratio change to 50-150, unless managers do something to counteract this decline. You have already seen the effects of stock returns in IBM's case—when its stock price tumbled from $121 to $78 per share, its equity lost over one-third of its value. This, in turn, dramatically reduced IBM's size and increased IBM's debt ratio.

What factors might cause firm value changes? Some factors are beyond the manager's control. For example, investors could become more risk averse and therefore may no longer be willing to pay $121 per share for IBM with its level of risk. Other factors that can change IBM's value would be unexpectedly good news (e.g., large orders for video game machine CPUs) or bad news (e.g., an earthquake). Of course, some parts of such value changes *are* under the manager's control. Your firm may pay out a lot of equity in dividends to shareholders, or you may run the firm poorly.

(Chapter 22 will show you that IBM was not unusual. A considerable proportion of most firms' current debt/equity ratios are determined by such firm value changes, which are reflected most obviously in the firm's stock price.)

There are also the effects of bond price changes, which we ignored. When economy-wide interest rates rise or the firm's credit rating deteriorates, then the debt usually declines in value—although in many cases, so does the equity. Conversely, when economy-wide interest rates drop or the firm's credit rating appreciates, then the debt usually increases in value—though again, so might the equity. Thus, the effect of changing interest rates on the debt/equity ratio is usually ambiguous. (Moreover, there are situations in financial distress in which the debt wrests power from the equity—there would be no change in overall capitalization, but a good change in the firm's debt/equity ratio.)

In sum, my point is simple: Don't make the common mistake of equating debt issuing or equity issuing causally with the typical directional changes in your leverage ratio. Yes, they are linked, but they are not linked one to one. Issuing activity does not add to or subtract from capital structure the same simple way that one number adds to or subtracts from another.

THE MULTI-CONSEQUENCE AND MULTI-MECHANISM VIEW

Don't think "dividends, yes or no?" Think instead of capital inflows versus outflows and of debt versus equity consequences.

As a manager, there are some mechanisms that you cannot influence and there are some mechanisms that you have at your disposal, and you need to target both a capital structure ratio and a firm size. For example, recall that Table 21.1 showed the following:

Scale: Dividend payments, bond coupon payments, debt and equity repurchasing, and debt and equity issuing are *all* mechanisms for transferring cash from inside the corporation to the outside owners, or vice versa.

Debt ratio: Equity issues, debt repurchases, and interest payments are *all* mechanisms for lowering the firm's debt/equity ratio.

You need to think about all of these mechanisms simultaneously. How?

An example of a firm in an M&M world.

Here is an illustration. For simplicity's sake, start by assuming you are still in the perfect-market world of Modigliani-Miller (M&M). Consequently, the mix of financing does not influence total firm value. Your firm is currently worth $1 billion, of which $400 million is outstanding debt (including nonfinancial liabilities). Let's say you choose to raise $100 million in new equity, raise $200 million in new debt, pay out $30 million to retire old debt (principal and interest), pay out $20 million in dividends, and repurchase $50 million of the firm's own equity shares. De facto, your firm has done the following:

1. Transferred $\$100 + \$200 - \$30 - \$20 - \$50 = \$200$ million of cash from the outside to the inside, and thereby increased its value from $1 billion to $1.2 billion
2. Increased its debt/equity ratio from $\$400/\$600 \approx 67\%$ to $\$570/\$630 \approx 90\%$

The same firm in a non-M&M world.

Of course, the real world is not M&M perfect. This means that you need to reconsider your choices, because investors will react to them. For example, if investors believe that your corporation suffers badly from agency conflicts (i.e., that you will waste their money), then they may react negatively to the $200 million increase in extra cash available to managers. On the other hand, if investors believe that the higher debt/equity ratio will save the corporation relatively more in corporate income taxes, then they may react positively to the increase in the debt/equity ratio. In fact, as CFO, you should consider each and every value effect that we discussed in Chapters 16–18. Without knowing more about our particular firm, it would be hard to guess whether the financial markets would look fondly or not so fondly on these capital structure changes. Why does this matter? If your capital structure rearrangement created $100 million extra in value, for example, it might well be that the outcome is not $1.2 billion in value and a debt/equity ratio of $570/$630, but, say, $1.3 billion in value and a debt/equity ratio of $570/$730. (The web chapter describes in detail how U.S. financial markets have responded to corporate issuing and dividend activity.)

www.prenhall.com/welch

IMPORTANT: Managers cannot view capital structure as a simple one-dimensional process. It is closely linked to firm size. It is the outcome of many forces, and only some are under the control of managers.

An ignored secondary effect: Dividends are stickier and thus send a signal.

➤ Dividends versus repurchases, Section 19.3, p. 710

Before we move on, there is one last interesting capital structure effect worth noting. The differences between repurchases and dividends were discussed in Section 19.3. Of interest in an imperfect world is the fact that your investors would draw some inferences from the fact that your firm paid out only \$20 million in dividends but repurchased \$50 million in shares. The reason is that dividends tend to be stickier than share repurchases, and thus the fact that your firm pays out more in repurchases than in dividends may send a mixed signal—are the managers worried about the firm's ability to pay out cash again next year?

SOLVE NOW!

Q 21.2 Describe the financial mechanisms that can change capital structures and firm sizes.

Q 21.3 When do firms usually experience their most dramatic changes in capital structure?

Q 21.4 Is the level of corporate debt under the complete control and at the discretion of management?

Q 21.5 A \$500 million firm is financed by \$250 million in debt and \$250 million in equity. If the market value does not change, describe some actions that managers can undertake to increase firm size to \$600 million and change its debt/equity ratio to 5:1.

Q 21.6 What is the effect of a share repurchase on the firm's size and the firm's debt ratio in a perfect market?

21.2 THEORIES OF CAPITAL STRUCTURE LEVELS, CHANGES, AND ISSUING ACTIVITY

The pecking order is partly a rerun. It is a theory about *change*.

➤ Pecking order, Section 18.6, p. 682

Given that firms in the real world rarely start from scratch, it is no surprise that our theories of capital structure *levels* spawned versions tailored to capital structure *changes*. The most prominent theory has its own name—the **pecking order** theory. You have already seen it in Section 18.6, but it is well worth elaborating here.

21.2A THE PECKING ORDER

Pecking order: (1) Firms prefer funding with more-senior claims; (2) Firms' values drop on average when they announce that they will fund with less-senior claims.

The pecking order theory is the name for two connected empirical implications:

1. Firms decline more in value when they announce issuance of more-junior securities.
2. Firms are reluctant to issue more-junior securities (such as equity instead of debt).

The second implication should not be surprising, given the first. Managers who want to increase firm value should not issue securities that reduce their firms' values.

Whence the name?

The name "pecking order" comes from the insight that this implies that firms fund new projects in a specific order. They first fully exhaust funding projects with the most senior claims that they have available to them. Only after these are exhausted will they proceed to the next class of more-junior claims. In the extreme, if they can, firms may never issue equity to fund new projects.

Deeper Causes for Pecking Orders

The pecking order applies in situations in which issuing more-junior securities is more expensive than issuing more-senior securities. Clearly, if your firm already has more equity than is optimal, then issuing even more equity would be detrimental to firm value.

Q: What capital structure *level* theories can cause a pecking order?

In Chapters 17 and 18 you learned the forces that pull firms toward a capital structure in which having more debt is better than having more equity. You can go through these chapters and realize that every force that favors debt over equity can pull a firm toward following a pecking order (assuming absence of other forces). Here are some examples:

A: Any theory in which debt is cheaper than equity can cause a pecking order.

➤ Summary of capital structure forces, Table 18.6, p. 688

1. **Inside information:** When your company wants to raise more financing, it is in your interest to convince investors that managers and owners are confident in the firm's future. Put differently, as existing owners and managers, you want to signal your confidence in the firm by remaining as heavily invested yourself as you possibly can. If your firm were to issue equity, investors would infer the worst and your firm value would drop. It follows that managers should not like to issue equity. (Historically, it was in the context of inside information theory that the pecking order theory first emerged.)
2. **Agency considerations:** This is quite similar, except that the future is now under the manager's control. The idea is that when you want to raise more financing, it is in your interest to convince investors that you will not waste money. The more junior the security that you are issuing, the more free cash flow you could waste without likely penalty in the future. Thus, if you want to invest money profitably instead of wasting it, you will not mind the more stringent requirements that come with newly issued senior securities. The end effect is the same as it was in story number 1: If you were to issue equity, firm value would drop. Thus, managers do not like to issue equity.
3. **Issuing costs:** It may simply be much more expensive to issue more-junior claims. Issuing equity is more expensive than issuing debt, which in turn is more expensive than funding projects internally. (This is empirically true, and it could be due to legal liability, regulations, difficulties in finding/costs of convincing investors to buy more-junior securities, etc.)

There are also other theories that explain why senior securities can add value. Of course, for the pecking order to apply to a particular firm, the net of all factors favoring issuing debt must outweigh the net of all factors favoring issuing equity. Otherwise, firms would experience a positive response if they issued more equity—they should then be eager to do so, and the pecking order would not apply.

Gradations of Seniority

The pecking order also works in gradations of seniority.

Here is a novel fact to the pecking order theory. As you already know, the definition of a more junior security is that it is paid off in bankruptcy only after the more senior securities are paid off. Equity is (usually) the most junior security. Debt is more senior. But there are also seniority differences within the firm's debt financing. Some examples:

- Bonds with stronger covenants are safer than bonds with weaker covenants.
- Short-term bonds are safer than long-term bonds. (Creditors in the former are likely to get their money back long before the firm can run into trouble in the more distant future.)
- Collateralized bonds are safer than ordinary bonds. Again, creditors can lay claim to the collateral even before ordinary bonds are paid.
- Factored receivables (that is, accounts receivable that are sold off) are often short term and can be safer than the debt of the firm itself. By taking the firm out of the repayment process, receivables can become safer.

So far so good. But you may be surprised to learn what the most senior claim is: If the firm already has funds (as retained earnings), it does not even need to issue any new claims. In comparison, even the most senior debt is more junior than retained earnings, because it may not be fully repaid if the firm suffers a catastrophic loss. (This makes such debt junior to funds that the firm in effect raises from itself.)

You can restate the pecking order with more seniority classes.

With so many different seniority gradations, the pecking order theory therefore states that a firm should prefer to fund new projects from its own cash first until this funding source is exhausted. Then it should issue the most senior, short-term debt next, until that is exhausted, too. And so on. In sum, the more junior the funding source, the more reluctant managers should be. If managers instead carry out with a more junior offering anyway, the firm's value should drop more on its announcement.

How about corporate taxes? They can explain a debt/equity pecking order, but not an internal funds pecking order.

Chapter 17 showed that one important force pulling firms toward debt is the presence of corporate income taxes. If the firm is highly taxed, issuing debt rather than equity can reduce the firm's tax burden. Thus, high-tax firms would experience a worse stock-price response to a new equity issue than they would to a new debt issue. Consequently, such firms should be reluctant to issue more equity. Corporate taxes can therefore explain a pecking order between debt and equity. However, the corporate income tax does not offer a reason why internal funds are better than debt (using retained cash is not tax-preferred to paying out cash and issuing senior debt to finance projects).

Empirical Evidence

The empirical evidence largely supports a pecking order explanation.

What is the empirical evidence? The academic consensus is by and large that many large publicly traded corporations are underlevered. This suggests that such firms should follow a pecking order, in which they should be reluctant to issue more-junior securities. Indeed, the empirical evidence suggests that this is the case, too. Equity issues are rare among such firms, and when they do happen, they are usually associated with a decline in firm value. Moreover, internal funding tends to be used before debt is. In the United States, such large publicly traded firms cover about 50–90% of their funding needs with retained earnings. (The remainder is usually predominantly debt-financed, and preferentially with short-term notes and collateralized debt rather than with general-obligation junior debt.)

SOLVE NOW!

Q 21.7 What is the financing pecking order?

Q 21.8 Evaluate: If a theory predicts that issuing equity is more expensive than issuing debt, a pecking order should naturally arise.

21.2B ALTERNATIVE NON-PECKING-ORDER FINANCING ARRANGEMENTS

Not all companies (should) choose pecking order–type financing.

Not all firms are best off following the pecking order prescription of funding projects with the most senior securities possible. For example, there are many small high-tech firms that start out with a lot of debt. Depending on the particulars of the situation, many such firms can gain value if they issue equity instead of debt. Similarly, many utilities firms are often better off if they issue equity instead of debt due to the way their cost of capital is computed by their government regulators.

LBO firms often do not signal their confidence in their portfolio firms. This violates the spirit of the pecking order.

A less obvious example of behavior that is not pecking-order-like applies to many private-equity firms. For example, the typical leveraged-buyout firm owns a number of acquired firms, each called a portfolio company. The inside information version of the pecking order theory states that an LBO firm should issue more-senior securities because it should want to keep as much of the upside as possible, which signals its confidence in its own company. It should issue claims that are less safe only if it is absolutely unavoidable. However, it turns out that LBO firms purchase a number of companies, but keep each of them in its own insulated shell. Thus, if one portfolio company goes bankrupt, it does not bring down the other portfolio companies. (This arrangement provides good incentives to the management in each individual company. A mistake by a portfolio company's management could be deadly!)

Lenders' perspective of non-pecking-order capital structures.

The lenders know that they will not be able to lay claim to any other portfolio companies if the management of one were to perform poorly. And they know that the LBO firm was not confident enough in the quality of each particular acquisition to pledge its remaining portfolio companies to the lenders. If the LBO firm had followed the intuition of the adverse selection/pecking order, it should have been willing to stake all its projects as collateral when it borrowed money for each portfolio company. Because it failed to do so, lenders demand significantly higher interest rates from individual portfolio companies than they would otherwise have demanded. Therefore, the LBO firm has to pay the price in a higher total cost of capital than it otherwise would have. LBO firms believe that the net benefits of this insulation strategy outweigh the net costs, and they therefore do not follow the pecking order prescription.

21.2C THE FINANCING PYRAMID

The "financing pyramid" suggests that firms should have more senior securities than junior securities.

Historically, the pecking order theory was taught together with the so-called **financing pyramid**. A financing pyramid is a name for a capital structure in which most of the funding sits in the most senior claims (at the bottom), presumably short-term, collateralized notes. Less funding would sit in more-junior, ordinary, long-term debt. Even less funding would be convertibles, and very little funding would be equity. This is illustrated in Figure 21.1.

➤ Financing pyramid, Solve Now! Q18.27, p. 685

The pecking order can lead to a financing pyramid, but it does not have to.

There is a natural connection between the pecking order and the financing pyramid. If the firm does nothing but issue financial claims, and nothing else happens then pecking order behavior would build up a financing pyramid (because firms would

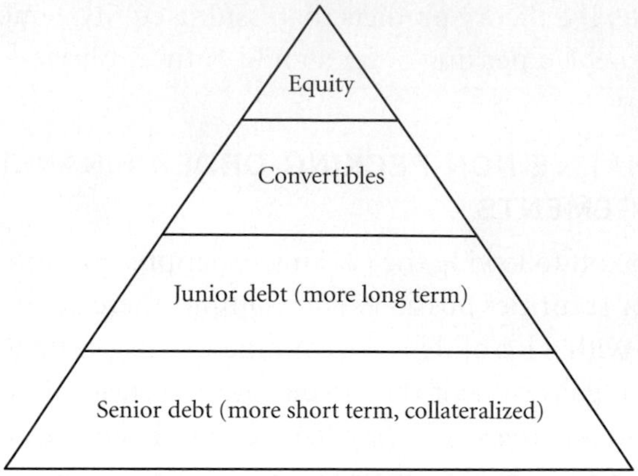

This figure illustrates the capital structure of a firm that follows a financing pyramid. It has more senior debt outstanding than junior debt, more junior debt than convertibles, and more convertibles than equity.

FIGURE 21.1 A Hypothetical Financing Pyramid

prefer issuing securities further down in the pyramid). However, a financing pyramid is not a necessary consequence of a pecking order, and vice versa. The most important wedge between the two is changes in the value of the firm. Over time, many firms operate, pay down debt, and gain in value. Thus, once publicly trading, a firm can follow a perfect pecking order in its issuing activities—raising funds only internally or through debt—and yet be financed with much more equity than debt. (It could also be that many firms follow this pyramid financing arrangement, not because they actively issued debt, but because they incurred many operating liabilities along the way.) Empirically, some firms' capital structures indeed look like a financing pyramid, but most capital structures do not. (In particular, convertibles are fairly rare relative to equity.) Chapter 22 will show that the actual capital structure of a firm is determined more by its industry, past performance, and M&A activity than by its past issuing policies.

SOLVE NOW!

Q 21.9 What is the financing pyramid? Is it a good description of empirical reality?

Q 21.10 Does the pecking order necessarily imply that firms are financed like a financing pyramid?

21.2D THE INFLUENCE OF STOCK RETURNS ON OPPORTUNISTIC ISSUING

Capital structure can come about "passively."

From the above and from IBM's example in Chapter 15, you know that stock returns have a direct influence on capital structure, just like active equity or debt-issuing activities have influence. We could call this influence the "direct" effect of stock returns: A firm that is financed by $1 billion in debt and $1 billion in equity and that loses one-quarter of its value ($500 million) will experience a debt/equity ratio increase from 1:1 to 2:1. (If so desired, managers can counteract this effect by issuing more equity and retiring some debt.)

But stock returns and value changes could have a second entirely different conduit by which stock returns can influence capital structure. Although it is tied directly to past stock returns, it is not automatic. Instead, it is about how managers respond through issuing to market returns. There is some evidence that CFOs believe and act as if they can predict ("time") the financial markets. This is not too surprising. Most managers' sense of their firm's value is based on the corporate internals, not on how the financial markets have moved recently. If the financial markets have moved up, managers' internal beliefs do not catch up immediately, so they now believe that they can raise equity relatively cheaply at high market valuations. They feel that their stock is relatively more overpriced. Note that this mechanism suggests exactly the opposite behavior to what would be required for the firm to return to its original debt/equity ratio. If the firm wanted to keep a particular debt/equity ratio, it would have to repurchase equity after it has gone up and issue more equity after it has gone down. If the firm instead wanted to time the market, it would do just the opposite: Repurchase equity after the stock has gone down, and issue more equity after it has gone up. Moreover, there is even better evidence that managers seem to try to time general interest rates and the (Treasury) yield curve. If interest rates are higher (lower) than they were in the past, companies tend to avoid bonds, and vice versa. If the yield curve is steep by historical standards, corporations tend to borrow more at short-term interest rates and issue fewer long-term bonds. In an efficient financial market, there should be little benefit to attempts at market timing, but also no cost to doing so. You can look at this attempt at market timing as just another investment, which is a fairly harmless attempt by managers to make profitable investments.

Managers seem to believe they know when prices are high or low.

➤ Overconfidence, Section 12.7, p. 418

However, what is surprising is not the fact that managers have tried to time financial markets *but the empirical evidence that this has actually turned out to be profitable*! Even stranger, managers have been good not only in predicting their own stock price level but also in predicting the overall stock market level—an incredibly difficult feat. (In fact, why bother being a corporate manager if you have this ability? You could get rich much more easily.) There is academic controversy as to whether this success has been the result of coincidence or real timing ability. For example, one counterargument is that this seeming timing ability is merely survivorship bias: Firms that failed in their timing disproportionally disappeared. It could also just be that when the financial markets go up, more and more firms raise external funds, and this stops when financial markets go down. Thus, even though managers cannot predict the financial markets, when economists look at when firms raised funds, they will find that they did so before the market went down. Either of these two theories could explain seeming market-timing ability where there is in fact none. Hopefully, by the time the next edition of this book appears, we will understand corporate market timing better than we do today.

Weird—market timing should not have worked. Nevertheless it seems to have worked.

➤ Survivorship bias, Section 11.5B, p. 366

21.3 CAPITAL MARKET PRESSURES TOWARD THE OPTIMAL CAPITAL STRUCTURE

Finding the best capital structure is not easy. Why should you make your life so difficult by trying to determine the best capital structure? Why can you not simply copy the existing capital structures of similar comparable (and often competitor) firms?

Is imitation of similar firms a cheap way to learn what is optimal?

Intriguing evidence: Why are firms not more proactive in responding to stock-caused changes in capital structure?

Unfortunately, simple imitation is often a bad idea. The empirical evidence suggests that firms are very slow to counteract what stock market changes do to them, even when stock market changes have caused very large changes in their debt/equity ratios. Your comparable (and you!) may have a 30% debt ratio one year and a 70% debt ratio the following year. This finding has led to an academic debate (still unresolved) about what this implies:

1. Are the transaction costs too high to make it worthwhile for managers to readjust their capital structures? (If this is true, all our earlier arguments about what should drive capital structure are relatively unimportant. The best advice would be to do nothing to avoid paying issuing or repurchasing costs.)
2. Does the optimal capital structure itself change one to one with the firm's market value? (If this is true, we should not see firms change their capital structures. Whatever it happens to turn out to be is also likely the optimal capital structure.)
3. Are firms making mistakes by failing to optimize their capital structures? (If this is true, then copying comparable capital structures would be a bad idea.)

Poor capital structures can persist, because the (arbitrage) forces toward optimality are too weak.

Let's evaluate the third perspective. Such a conclusion should hinge on your belief in a reasonably efficient market for corporate control. If you believe that an outside investor can make money by fixing a bad capital structure, as in a perfect market, then you would also believe that current capital structures in the market are more than likely fairly close to optimal. Unfortunately, the perfect-markets scenario may be too far away from reality in this context. To "arbitrage" an incorrect financing choice, you would have to mount a corporate takeover. A typical takeover requires a premium of 15% to 30% above the current market price, plus another percentage point to pay in fees to the investment banker. To recapture such a large control premium, rectifying an incorrect capital structure would have to create large tangible benefits. But capital structure corrections are not likely to do so. A more reasonable estimate for the value increase when moving from a bad capital structure to the optimal capital structure is typically on the order of 1% to 3% per annum. Even capitalized over many years, this rarely reaches the 15–30% control premium.

➤ Costs versus benefits of takeovers, Section 24.5C, p. 928

Existing managers can, and should, fix bad capital structures.

Does the fact that outside investors cannot easily rectify capital structure mistakes mean that capital structure is irrelevant? No. The situation for inside managers is different, because they do not have to pay a control premium. They are already in charge. For them, 1–3% is not an inconsequentially low amount—especially because it is annual and because it requires almost no effort or investment to fix. For a company like IBM, which is worth several hundred billion dollars, the value created may be "only" a couple of billion dollars per year—certainly enough to cover your consulting fee! In sum, the fact that external shareholders cannot easily bring much pressure to bear on managers does not mean that internal managers should not try to get it right.

The empirical evidence is *not* prescriptive, telling you what to do. It is only descriptive.

Returning to our original question, can you find your own optimal capital structure by copying your comparables? There are several arguments against imitation:

- Whatever capital structure the comparables chose is not necessarily the outcome of competitive market pressures, in which only the best capital structure could have prevailed. Instead, there can be a whole range of capital financing arrangements that could persist in the economy—including poor ones—and no one but the managers in charge can fix them.

- You also know that managers' incentives differ from those of the shareholders. Managers like free cash flow, financial flexibility, and control over large firms. Do you want to learn how to maximize firm value, or how to maximize managerial comfort?
- Comparables are never perfectly comparable. You already know from Chapter 14 that "comparable" may be an oxymoron, because most seemingly similar firms ultimately tend to be very different upon closer inspection.
- Maybe there is value to being different from your competitors. For example, if all of them are very indebted, you might want to remain unlevered to speculate that a recession might wipe out all your competition. (The low-debt capital structure would be a strategic option—most likely not a good idea, but nevertheless there would be states of the world where it could be fabulously successful.)

➤ Strategic options, Section 12.6, p. 413

In sum, unlike stock market values where you can believe in reasonably efficient markets, capital structure and corporate control are not as efficiently determined. Thus, as manager, you cannot have blind faith in the "magic of markets" to get the capital structure right. Some modest faith may be appropriate, though. Knowing what other managers are doing can still be helpful. Just take this knowledge with a big grain of salt.

SOLVE NOW!

Q 21.11 Are existing capital structures necessarily optimal?

21.4 WORKING CAPITAL MANAGEMENT AND FINANCIAL FLEXIBILITY

How to manage working capital: First and foremost, do not run out of money!

Much day-to-day capital structure management has to do with working capital management. Corporate growth usually consumes working capital. Customers buy goods, but they do not pay immediately. (Terms are often 30 days until payment.) This delay can create short-term cash problems, especially for small and fast-growing firms. There are many intrinsically profitable companies that have had to fold because of poor liquidity management. As the CFO of such a firm, long-run capital structure is not as important as **cash management**—and fortunately, unlike capital structure where your target was murky, this one is easy and straightforward.

> **IMPORTANT:** As a manager, you would not want to let your company run out of cash. From a firm value maximization perspective, this is usually, but not always, the case, too. (This will soon become clearer.)

Of course, I do not mean cash in the register but rather cash necessary to pay creditors. Your company does not have to have lots of cash on hand. It is enough if you can borrow with ease and rapidity to satisfy creditors when payments are due. It is not unusual for firms to refinance principal payments on loans with new loans.

Lack of funds can quickly become a self-fulfilling prophecy.

But problems can arise when your firm operates too close to the brink of its financial flexibility. In this instance, it is quite possible that either of two self-fulfilling prophecies ("equilibria") can occur:

1. Lenders are not worried about the company. The company borrows and operates profitably. Lenders see their beliefs confirmed and are repaid.
2. Lenders are worried about the company and are unwilling to extend credit. Without money, the company goes bankrupt. Lenders see their beliefs confirmed that it was wise not to have extended more credit.

The prominent collapse of the investment bank Bear Stearns in March 2008 was probably just such a self-fulfilling prophecy.

Financial flexibility (credit lines, low debt ratios, matching inflows and outflows) helps, but it is expensive.

What can you do to avoid the second, disaster equilibrium? You have a number of options, though all of them are costly:

Match assets and liabilities: You can try to match expected future cash coming in with cash going out. For example, say you want to take out a loan to pay for a new factory. The factory will produce income in 3 years. You could then take out a loan that requires interest and sinking fund payments beginning in 3 years. Matching future inflows to expected outflows is easier if your cash flows are relatively more predictable and if they occur sooner. Moreover, if you borrow with longer-term debt, you may have to pay higher liquidity premiums, risk premiums, and credit premiums. Note also that matching inflows and outflows makes more sense on a firm-wide basis, and less sense on a project-by-project basis.

Pay for flexibility: You can pay a commercial bank for an irrevocable credit line. However, although it is often cheap to get a credit line in sunny times, it is often expensive to get one that will hold up (not be revoked) in rainy times. Even IBM's $15 billion credit line is subject to various bond covenants—and if IBM were to get into trouble and needed this credit, it might no longer be available.

➤ IBM's credit line, Section 15.4A, p. 555

Hold liquid investments: You can invest cash in assets that have fairly safe values and allow for relatively quick and cheap liquidation. Unfortunately, unless your company is a Treasury bond fund, your business is not likely to need such assets as much as it needs the kinds of assets that are risky and hard to liquidate. For example, your half-constructed laboratory or half-finished R&D would be very difficult to resell quickly, but these are precisely the types of assets that will allow you to create value.

Adjust capital structure: You can keep liabilities low relative to your equity cushion. In this case, it is likely that your future cash flows will easily cover your future debt obligations. Moreover, if you have a low debt ratio and high interest rate coverage, you will have an easier time borrowing more cash if you ever need more. Of course, both liquid investments and a low debt ratio are costly in themselves. For instance, both would likely increase the corporate income tax obligation of your firm.

In real life, managers really care about having cash.

When CFOs are surveyed, they state that they pay close attention to their "financial flexibility"—they care very much about their interest coverage ratios and bond ratings. Such concerns may be good for firm value from a liquidity perspective. With high bond ratings and a lot of cash to pay for interest, firms are unlikely to go

> **ANECDOTE How Bond Ratings Doomed Trust-Preferred Securities and Created ECAPS**
>
> In 2005, investment bank Lehman Brothers introduced a new debt hybrid called an **ECAPS** (enhanced capital advantaged security). These are securities that have tax-deductible interest payments (which the IRS does not allow for any perpetual bonds), but they are also very long term and allow for interest-payment postponement. Therefore, these bonds are risky and in many ways more like equity than bonds. This is a very efficient tax innovation: Firms effectively get interest-payment tax deductibility on an equity-like security.
>
> Yet an earlier incarnation of such bonds (known as trust-preferred securities) had stalled because Moody's and S&P had not determined how to treat these securities. The ECAPS deal succeeded because Moody's assigned it into its "Basket D," which counted ECAPS as 75% equity and 25% debt. Therefore, with the extra cash inflow and its (according to Moody's) modest debt increase, an ECAPS would not likely impact the issuer's rating negatively.

bankrupt, which can save on expected bankruptcy costs. Is this managerial concern a good sign of benign intent?

Unfortunately, the drawback to too much cash is that managers waste it.

Not necessarily. There is also a *very* dark side to this flexibility. From the manager's perspective, having more cash is always better than having less cash. Yet, especially in large and slow-growing firms, access to all that cash "lying around" tempts managers to waste money or undertake ventures that they should not and otherwise probably would not undertake. Your investors may not even be all that thrilled if management is insulated from financial default because of its great working capital management—this ability can lead management to be satisfied with a status quo of inefficient operations. Both management and employees would likely work harder if they knew that the company would go bankrupt if they performed poorly. Consequently, if the company has great working capital management and enough of a financial buffer, it may never go bankrupt, but it may also remain stuck with poor management and unmotivated employees.

SOLVE NOW!

Q 21.12 How can managers reduce the likelihood that they will run out of cash?

21.5 DEBT AND DEBT-HYBRID OFFERINGS

Debt is less sexy than equity but it is often more important.

We first turn to firms' debt-issuing activities. Debt offerings are much more frequent than equity offerings. In fact, except in the context of acquisitions where both equity and debt offerings are common, large publicly traded firms tend to finance almost all of their projects through either retained earnings or debt offerings. Debt offerings are the bread and butter for both firms and investment banks.

21.5A DOES FAIR PRICING IMPLY IRRELEVANCE?

Contract provisions are "priced into" interest rates.

➤ Bond flavors, Section 15.2A, p. 545

➤ IBM's long-term and short term liabilities, Table 15.2, p. 557

➤ Table 15.3, p. 559

Section 15.2A explained how to think about the many bond flavors available to you. Recall all the features and variables involved: seniority, security, covenants, collateral, conversion, callability, putability, maturity, duration, fixed or floating, and so on. IBM's debt structure, described in Tables 15.2 and 15.3, is a good example of the variety of debt claims a single firm may have outstanding. For most bond features, as for all other financing methods, the basic finance mantra holds: You get what you pay for. For example, if as CFO you give bond buyers more rights (e.g., a conversion feature), you get to pay a lower interest rate. If you want to keep more rights (e.g., write in a call feature), you must pay a higher interest rate. Despite the just mentioned empirical behavioral finance evidence on timing to the contrary, by and large it seems unlikely that managers can guess very precisely what features the market generally overvalues or undervalues, and of course whether interest rates will go up or down.

Important: Fair pricing does not mean that all security features are equally good or irrelevant.

But fair pricing does not mean that you cannot add value by choosing debt securities that employ the features that are most appropriate to your own firm. Recall the example (from page 581), that required changing the CEO every week. Or consider a bond feature that says that all factories will be permanently closed if the AFC team wins the Super Bowl. In a competitive market, you will get a fair price for these bonds and any other securities that you might issue, but these are not a great security to issue if you want to maximize market value. The point is that you should offer bonds that have features that are well suited to your company. But if you stay within the limits of ordinary and frequent bond features (say, choosing a convertibility or callability feature), it is often true that it will matter only modestly which exact features your bonds are offering.

21.5B ASSEMBLING THE BUILDING BLOCKS OF A BOND OFFERING

Real-world debt issues are complex enough that you need an investment banker to manage the issuing process.

So far, you have enjoyed the à la carte approach to bond features—each by itself, one at a time. Let's now have a full-course dinner. How do large, publicly traded corporations really borrow money? The most common way for many mid- to large-cap companies to borrow is to obtain a bank credit facility and issue multiple bonds ("term debt") at the same time. The typical financing package consists of two parts, the revolver and the term debt:

The revolver (i.e., a revolving credit line) is a line of credit on which the company can borrow and repay, and borrow again, until a termination date/maturity. The bank offering the revolving credit line also receives a fee for the unused/undrawn portion of the revolver.

The term debt is structured in one or more **tranches** (French for "slices"). The principal payment schedule and maturity date are different for each of the tranches. Tranche A would begin to amortize right away and would have the shortest term to maturity. The tranche B term loan would amortize and mature after the tranche A term loan but before the tranche C term loan, and so on.

The revolver and tranche A loan usually carry the same interest rate spread over LIBOR (the London Interbank Offer Rate) and are marketed as a package. The tranche B and C lenders receive wider spreads over LIBOR to compensate creditors for the added credit risk of having a longer-term loan to maturity.

The selling agent is typically an investment bank.

Who sells these instruments? If the bond issue is large, a "lead" investment banker ("underwriter") syndicates a large part of the corporate bond to other investment banks to make it easier to place the bond. (Lead underwriters are often the big-money banks, such as JP Morgan Chase or Citibank.) The deal itself is brought to the capital markets (potential investors) with proposed pricing by the syndicate lead, but it is ultimately priced at whatever price (interest rate) clears the market.

Who are the investors in these multiple loan instruments (all issued simultaneously)? Because institutions and mutual funds are not set up to provide revolving credit, the "pro rata" revolver piece and tranche A loan are often purchased by commercial banks. The market for subsequent tranches of term debt is more liquid, and these bonds are typically purchased by mutual funds, commercial banks, hedge funds, and the like.

The typical investor buyer is a bond fund.

Smaller companies usually borrow in simpler ways. They often have a relationship with either a smaller syndicate of commercial banks or perhaps a regional bank in the case of a very small company. The structure would in all likelihood be less complex—a revolver and only one tranche of term debt, or perhaps even only a revolver. In terms of pricing, their bonds must offer premium pricing to compensate the lenders for the added credit risk of lending to a small company and for holding a less liquid financial claim. (The price is negotiated between the borrower and lender.)

Smaller companies often do simpler borrowing.

21.5C POST-ISSUE PLACEMENT AND BOND LIQUIDITY

As with all securities, issuers can raise financing at lower costs if they can give potential investors more information and the ability to liquidate their investments quickly. Equity securities are usually bought and sold on stock exchanges after the original offering. The two most important exchanges in the United States are NASDAQ and the NYSE. Bonds, on the other hand, often do not trade on any exchange (such as the **New York Bond Exchange**). And when they do trade, the markets tend to be not very liquid. (The bond trading volume on exchanges is very low.) Instead, most bonds are traded **over the counter**, that is, by large investors who call up individual investment banks' desks. The transaction price is usually not disclosed in such cases, and trading is fairly rare. Because the vast majority of bond transactions take place between dealers rather than on an exchange, accurate bond prices are difficult to come by. (As an individual investor, you are better off staying away from purchasing individual corporate bonds. Buy a mutual fund that holds corporate bonds instead.) Over the last few years, however, a financial market has developed that is a close substitute for the corporate bond market—the credit default swap (CDS). Instead of purchasing a corporate bond on IBM, an investor can purchase a Treasury bond and sell a CDS. The two strategies are almost exactly alike.

Corporate bonds are usually illiquid—and, when they do trade, they trade "over the counter."

➤ Over the counter, Section 7.2B, p. 192

➤ CDS, Section 6.2F, p. 151

21.5D COERCIVE BOND EXCHANGE OFFERS

Most bonds include contract provisions by which covenants can be changed. However, such provisions are usually difficult to invoke, except in financial distress. For the most part, firms must live with whatever covenants they write up front.

Most of the time, bond covenants are inflexible (whatever they are when written).

But there are two mechanisms that allow creditors to change the terms that public bondholders have negotiated. The first is bankruptcy, a process in which the judge can change the terms. The second is the **exchange offer**. These days, exchange offers are rare, because creditors have learned to protect themselves against such "offers." Still, the basics of this mechanism are worth knowing.

But beware of exchange offers (and bankruptcy).

➤ The bankruptcy process, Section 18.3B, p. 665

Consider a firm that had earlier sold only one class of bond with a face value of \$1,000 to 100 creditors. You are one of the creditors and you hold one bond. Each bond is a claim to \$10. Unfortunately, the firm value has already dropped to \$500, so your bond is now worth only \$5. Would you agree to reduce the face value of your

A coercion works in scenarios in which the firm is underwater.

bond from \$10 to \$6 now? If you were to agree, and if the firm later had some luck increasing its value from \$500 to, say, \$1,000, you would not receive anything more than \$6.

Here is how you can take advantage of uncoordinated bondholders.

It turns out that the firm can "make you an offer that you cannot refuse." Let's say that the firm offered each creditor the option to exchange the \$10 bond into a \$6 bond that is more senior. Now consider what *is* in your interest:

- If no other creditor accepts the exchange offer, and neither do you, then your unexchanged \$10 bond is worth \$5. If you accept the exchange, your senior bond is paid before the other bonds, so your bond's value increases from \$5 to \$6.
- If all other 99 creditors accept the exchange offer, then they would have claims on $99 \cdot \$6 = \$594$ of the firm worth \$500. Your own \$10 bond is more junior, so you would get nothing.

P.S. This is a so-called prisoner's dilemma.

It is in the interest of each bondholder to participate, but that means they will collectively end up worse off. Thus, the bond exchange offer works by playing off creditors against one another—the firm cannot play the same game if one single creditor (a bank) holds the entire bond issue. To eliminate such coercive bond exchange offers, many bond covenants now require firms to obtain approval by majority or supermajority vote before they can exchange any bonds (or waive covenants). In our example, every bondholder would vote against the exchange offer, and thereby all bondholders would come out better off.

SOLVE NOW!

Q 21.13 How does a coercive bond exchange offer work?

21.6 SEASONED EQUITY OFFERINGS

Seasoned equity offerings are rare for large firms.

➤ How securities appear, Section 7.2D, p. 195

Most publicly traded shares appear on an exchange in the context of a public equity offering. A **seasoned equity offering** is the sale of shares in an already publicly traded company. Seasoned equity offerings are rare events for large, publicly traded corporations, except in connection with M&A activity. Remarkably, in contrast to bonds, liquidity is often not a big problem for after-market stock investors. Over 10,000 large U.S. firms now have their common stock traded on a major public stock exchange, such as the NASDAQ or the NYSE. There, any investor can easily purchase and sell shares, and closing prices for the previous day can readily be found in most newspapers. Not all shares are first issued and sold on an exchange. Some shares may simply be granted to employees or managers. These shares sometimes come from the **treasury stock**, which are the shares that the company itself has repurchased.

There is a way to avoid the long SEC IPO process.

The institutional process required to sell new shares in a public offering is lengthy and unwieldy. (For initial public offerings, it is an outright ordeal.) Fortunately, firms with fewer than 100 investors that do not try to sell their claims to the public are not (or are at least less) regulated by the SEC and thus can avoid the long process. (In a famous incident, Google ran into the constraint that it had more than 100 entities owning shares, so it had no choice but to go public, even though it did not need external funds.) Many smaller companies and hedge funds would simply be overwhelmed by the costs of navigating the SEC processes and requirements.

Public firms can issue seasoned equity through various mechanisms. Three are most important:

Here are three methods of selling (seasoned) equity.

1. **A standard issue:** For example, a firm with 50 million shares representing $400 million in outstanding equity (i.e., $8/share) may announce that its board of directors has approved the issuance and sale of another 10 million shares in 3 months. The shares are to be sold into the market at the then-prevailing stock price 3 months later. If the stock price will be $10/share at the time of the offering, the firm value will be $500 million just before the offering and $600 million just after the offering. Both immediately before and after the offering, each old shareholder will still own a claim of $10/share.

Ideally, old shareholders would come out the same.

2. **A shelf offering (Rule 415 offering):** For new equity shares registered with the SEC under Rule 415, the firm does not set one specific date at which the shares are to be sold into the market. Instead, the firm can put the shares "on a shelf" and sell them over a period of up to 2 years, at its own discretion and without further announcements.

Shelf offerings can be "lazy."

3. **A rights offering:** Yet another way to sell new equity shares is a **rights offering**. These are rare in the United States, but they are popular in some other countries (e.g., the United Kingdom). Instead of issuing new shares to anyone willing to purchase them, the company grants existing shareholders the right to purchase 1 additional share of equity at $2/share. If all 50 million shareholders participate, the company will raise $100 million. Each shareholder will own 2 shares, so there will now be 100 million shares to represent $600 million in assets. Each share will be worth $6, and each old investor will have invested $12 for 2 shares.

First, rights offerings' mechanics.

So far, there is no difference between the rights offering and the plain cash offering: Both facilitate the raising of $100 million without loss for existing shareholders. However, what happens to a shareholder who does not participate? This shareholder will then own 1 share, for which she will have paid $10 and which will now only be worth $6. This nonparticipating shareholder will have been expropriated. Therefore, rights offerings allow the firm to leave existing shareholders with no reasonable choice but to participate in the offering. (Of course, if a shareholder does not have cash, selling the shares to someone else for a fair price—or, if possible, the unbundled rights—solves such liquidity constraints.)

Rights offerings can force participation.

Like bond offerings, equity offerings are usually orchestrated by an underwriter.

➤ Underwriting, Section 23.1A, p. 855

You also need to know what **primary shares** and **secondary shares** are. These are confusing names, because they do not describe the distinction between shares from an initial public offering and a seasoned offering. Instead, primary shares are shares that are newly minted and sold by the firm itself. The proceeds go to the firm itself. (These are really the kinds of offerings that we just discussed.) Secondary shares are shares that are sold by an investor in the firm (e.g., by the founder). The company does not receive the issue proceeds. Secondary offerings are more like insider sales, so they are also often smaller than primary offerings. But they are usually greeted especially negatively by the market: An owner who wants to abandon ship and sell

Primary shares are newly created, and their proceeds flow into the company. Secondary shares are really just insider sales.

➤ Insider sales, Section 18.6, p. 682

out is not good news. Because our book focuses on the firm's capital structure, we are concentrating on primary offerings.

SOLVE NOW!

Q 21.14 Assume that there is a rights offering for a firm that is worth $500 million and that offers its shareholders the right to buy 1 extra share for each share they already own. The "discount" price for the new shares is 1/5 the price of the current shares. Assume that half the investors do not participate. What is the loss to nonparticipating investors (shares) and the gain to participating investors (shares)?

Q 21.15 How could a coercive seasoned equity rights offering work?

21.7 INITIAL PUBLIC OFFERINGS (IPOs)

IPOs are special. Their shares are much riskier, there is no existing market price, and the issuer faces many special regulations.

In contrast to a seasoned equity offering, an **initial public offering** is the *first* public sale of shares. There are many features that are unique to IPOs:

1. There is no established price, so it is considerably more difficult and risky to place IPO shares than SEO shares. Moreover, without an existing public price, we cannot measure how the financial market responds to the announcement of an IPO.
2. There are many unusual regulations governing the issuance of IPOs. For example, the issuer and the underwriter are liable not just for false statements but even for "material omissions."
3. Until recently, shares had to be sold at a fixed price that, once set, could not be adjusted upward if demand for shares was strong, or downward if demand for shares was weak. Most IPOs are still conducted this way, although it is now possible for strong issuers to auction their shares into the public markets. (The 2004 IPO of Google was the most prominent auction.)

The institutional process.

In a typical IPO, the issuer must provide audited financials for the most recent 3 years. Thus, unless the firm is so new that it has no recent history, or unless the firm has carefully planned its IPO years ahead, many firms must go back and create audited financials for activities that happened long ago. Similarly, firms often have a lot of other housecleaning to do—folding in or laying out subsidiaries, untangling relationships between the private owners and the firm, and so on. The real IPO process starts when the firm selects an underwriter (usually after competitive presentations by several investment bankers). It is the underwriter who orchestrates the offering, who shepherds the institutional process, and who markets the offering to generate interest among potential investors. Together with the auditor and legal counsel, the underwriter and the firm create a preliminary offering prospectus and file it with the SEC. They then give a set of "road show" presentations to solicit interest among potential investors. But neither the firm nor the underwriter is legally allowed to make statements beyond those in the preliminary prospectus. The preliminary prospectus also does not usually name one fixed price, only an estimate (a price range). The range itself is estimated via the methods you have already learned, specifically, through NPV and comparables. However, the exact assumptions used to come up with the range are not explained in the prospectus in order to avoid legal liability if the projections turn out to have been overly optimistic. Finally, the underwriter can informally collect a list of interested parties but is not allowed to take firm buy orders. This process is called "book-building," and the information in the book is ultimately used both to set the final offering price and to decide on who receives what shares.

IPO underpricing is the typical first-day appreciation of about 10–15%.

Usually within 48 hours after the SEC approves the prospectus, the offering goes live. The final offer price is set on the morning of the offering, based on investor demand reflected in the book. Remarkably, IPOs are usually priced to create excess demand among investors, so shares become rationed. The average IPO experiences a jump of about 10–15% in 1 day (not annualized!), called **IPO underpricing**. During the 1999–2000 bubble, however, average underpricing reached as high as 65%, a remarkable rate of return for just 1 day! There are a number of theories that help explain why IPO underpricing occurs, and in real life, they probably all carry some degree of truth:

Popular explanations for IPO underpricing.

Winner's curse: If you are an uninformed investor and ask for allocations, you will likely be stuck disproportionately with shares in the hard-to-sell offerings. For example, if half the offerings earn +10% and are oversubscribed by a factor of 2, and half the offerings earn −10% and are undersubscribed, it would be 0% on average, but you would most likely receive an allocation of only half as many shares in the +10% offering as in the −10% offering, so your average rate of return would be

➤ Winner's curse, Section 18.6, p. 682

$$\underbrace{50\%}_{\text{\% Underpriced Offerings}} \cdot \overbrace{0.5}^{\text{Expected Share Allocation}} \cdot \underbrace{(+10\%)}_{\text{Underpricing}} + \underbrace{50\%}_{\text{\% Overpriced Offerings}} \cdot \overbrace{1.0}^{\text{Expected Share Allocation}} \cdot \underbrace{(-10\%)}_{\text{Overpricing}} = -2.5\%$$

Consequently, if shares on average earn a 0% rate of return, you and others like you should not participate. Your return will be negative. To keep you in the market, underwriters must underprice their IPOs.

Information extraction: How can underwriters get you to tell them what you think, so that they can build an accurate book (of preliminary orders)? Without a financial incentive to tell the truth, you and others like you would tell the underwriter that you believe that the offering is not worthwhile, hoping to get them to price the offering lower. With underpricing as the currency of compensation, the underwriters can pay you to tell truthfully your otherwise private reservation price. The underwriter must then reward the more enthusiastic investors with more (and just mildly) underpriced shares. It has been shown that such a strategy can actually maximize the offering proceeds.

Good taste in investors' mouths: How can firms signal that they are in the game for the long run, rather than just a fly-by-night fraud? The best way is to show patience and to give you a relatively good deal in the IPO. It would create "goodwill" among investors and thus make it easier to place subsequent offerings. A bad or fraudulent issuer would not want to play this game, because the fraud would likely collapse before the goodwill ever pays off.

Cascading, highly elastic demand: As an investor, you can probably learn a lot from how excited other investors are about the IPO. If investors all eye one another, and if shares are just fairly priced, any IPO could end up either a tremendous success or an utter failure, depending on where the investor herd is stampeding. From the perspective of the underwriter, the demand for shares would be both very elastic and very noisy. In this case, underwriters may prefer to ensure success by underpricing. This creates enough enthusiasm and avoids the risk of failure.

Agency conflicts (underwriter selling effort): Underwriters do not like to work very hard to sell difficult-to-place, fairly priced shares. However, the issuer cannot easily learn how hard the banker is trying to work the crowd. Thus, it is often more efficient for the issuer simply to underprice shares to make selling easier than it is for the issuer to price the shares correctly and then try to ascertain whether the underwriters are doing their best to place the offering.

Agency conflicts (additional underwriter compensation): Although it may not be in the interest of the issuer, underwriters use IPO underpricing as "currency" to reward their best brokerage customers. This requires that the underwriter be in the driver's seat, not the issuer (and for the issuer to acquiesce to give away money). (In my opinion, this was probably the best explanation for the extremely high underpricing during the tech boom of the late 1990s.)

➤ IPO share allocation, Anecdote, Section 7.2C, p. 194

Firms typically only sell about one-third of the firm to the financial markets. Therefore, to the entrepreneur, 10% underpricing of one-third of the firm translates only into about 3% in terms of value. Clearly, the entrepreneur would be better off to keep this 3% than to donate it to external investors, but the loss is modest. It is outright small compared to the potential diversification benefits experienced by many entrepreneurs, who are often very undiversified. Thus, many of them are less worried about 3% underpricing and instead more eager to successfully "cash out" to enjoy some of their wealth and to become less dependent on the fortunes of their single company.

Post-IPO, the investment banker provides some more services.

➤ Market makers, Section 7.2B, p. 192

After the firm is publicly trading, the underwriter often tries to promote the firm and maintain reasonably stable pricing and trading volume in the after-market. Indeed, for most smaller offerings, the underwriter usually also becomes the NASDAQ market maker, providing investors that want to buy and sell shares with the appropriate liquidity.

Some other interesting and important IPO empirical regularities.

Underpricing is just one among a number of interesting phenomena for IPO firms. We do not yet fully understand all of them, but here is an interesting selection of findings about IPOs:

- On average, IPO firms drastically underperform similar benchmark firms, beginning about 6 months after the IPO and lasting for about 3 to 5 years. (A conservative estimate is a risk-adjusted underperformance of about 5% per annum relative to the overall stock market.) However, it is not only the IPO firms themselves that seem to perform poorly after the IPO, but also firms that are similarly sized and in the same industry. No one really knows why. We do know that this downward drift is considerably stronger for firms that are relatively more aggressive in the reporting of their financials at the IPO. (A similar downward drift occurs after firms issue seasoned equity.)

  Who would be foolish enough to hold onto shares of a firm that has issued equity for more than the first 6 months? Because academic researchers cannot find out

ANECDOTE The Analyst Recommends: Buy!

The number of analysts' **buy recommendations** outnumbers the number of **sell recommendations** by a ratio of about 5:1; when limited to **strong buy** and **strong sell** recommendations, this ratio changes to over 10:1.

The primary reason for this imbalance is a conflict of interest. Most brokerage firms—and by extension their analysts—are owned by investment banks. (They are even called "sell-side" analysts, even though their "advice" goes to investors!) The investment banks are well aware that a sell recommendation is likely to induce the targeted firms not only to exclude the particular analyst from obtaining further information about the firm but also to induce the targeted firm to select a different underwriter. Therefore, the investment banks discourage their analysts subtly and not so subtly from issuing sell recommendations. Although this analyst bias was always widely recognized by professional investors, it had received scant attention in the press and little recognition by small investors—until 2001, when it suddenly became a public scandal. (It is still somewhat of a mystery why then, but not before.) In April 2003, ten of the largest investment banks settled a lawsuit by setting aside funds for making independent research available to brokerage clients and promising a separation of their brokerage analysis from their investment banking functions. It is not yet clear how effective these reforms have been. Recent financial market issues have overshadowed and diverted attention from these issues.

where equity shares are located (most stock holdings are confidential), we cannot fully study this phenomenon. The "word on the street" is that many of these shares end up in the accounts of very unsophisticated investors, such as "trust accounts" for widows and orphans.

- Underwriters' analysts routinely issue "buy" recommendations on their IPOs. This is not surprising. What is surprising is why this still seems to matter. Why would any investor pay attention to these obviously conflicted analysts' opinions?
- Insiders routinely sell their shares as soon as a pre-agreed lock-up period (typically, 6 months) expires. When the lock-up expiration week comes around, the IPO stock price predictably goes down by about 2%. This is a financial mystery: Who would want to hold IPO shares the day before the lock-up expiration?
- IPOs either happen in droves or do not happen at all. When the overall stock market and the firm's industry have recently performed well, IPOs tend to pour in. Professionals call this an "open IPO window." When the opposite occurs, the window is closed and there are zero IPOs. IPOs are not just reduced in price or scale, but they are typically withdrawn completely. Why?
- It is not surprising that the average IPO pays 7% in underwriting commission—the maximum allowed by the National Association of Securities Dealers (NASD)—though many issuers find some backdoor mechanisms to raise the underwriter commissions further. But it is surprising that *virtually every* IPO pays 7% commission. In such a competitive market, why do underwriters not compete more fiercely on the commission front?

These are all interesting questions for future research.

SOLVE NOW!

Q 21.16 Evaluate: IPOs should be underpriced by about 10–15%, because the average rate of return on the stock market is about 10–15%, too.

Q 21.17 Here is another winner's curse example. A painting is up for auction. There are 5 bidders, you among them. Each bidder has a private signal (opinion) about the value of the painting. One of them overestimates the value by 20%, another by 10%, another estimates its value correctly, and two underestimate the value by 15%.

(a) Is the average private value equal to the expected painting value?

(b) You do not know the value of the painting, but believe it to be worth $150. The distribution of bidders' relative valuations is still 20%, 10%, 0%, −15%, and −15%. What should be your absolute maximum bid before you expect to lose money?

(c) ADVANCED: What should you bid in a real-world auction in which each investor has a normally distributed signal with mean of $100 (the true value) and standard deviation of $10? (In real-world applications, you must judge the reasonable uncertainty that each bidder has around the true value.) Your spreadsheet can draw such a normally distributed random value with **norminv(rand(), 100, 10)**. In each row, have five such entries (columns A–E), one for each of the five bidders in the auction. In column (F), write down how much the maximum bidder believes the painting to be worth. (Hint: Use **max (A:E)** in this column.) Create 1,000 such rows, and compute the average highest bid. How biased is it? What would you expect to earn if you bid your private opinion? (You could repeat this with more or fewer bidders and graph the estimate of the winning unbiased bid against the true value—what should you bid on eBay, where there may be a thousand bidders?)

Q 21.18 If shares in successful IPOs are oversubscribed by a factor of 3, and if offerings are equally likely to either appreciate or depreciate by about 15% on the first day of trading, what would you expect your rate of return to be without IPO underpricing, assuming fair rationing?

Q 21.19 What fraction of the firm is usually sold in an IPO?

Q 21.20 What are various reasons why IPOs are underpriced?

Q 21.21 What are the main empirical regularities about IPO pricing and stock returns?

Q 21.22 What is a good predictor for future IPO waves?

21.8 RAISING FUNDS THROUGH OTHER CLAIMS AND MEANS

Think of hybrid securities as a mix of debt and equity.

Debt and equity are not the only claims that corporations can issue to raise funds, but they are the broadest categories and the best studied. Investment banks regularly help firms to issue all sorts of debt/equity hybrids, and for the most part, you can think of many hybrids as combinations somewhere along a continuum. For example, a bond may be straight, or it may have a conversion feature only at a very high firm value (in which case it is almost like a straight bond), or it may have a conversion feature at a very low firm value (in which case it is almost like equity). The aforementioned ECAPS is a good example.

➤ ECAPS Anecdote, Section 21.4, p. 801

There are also alternative money providers outside the financial markets.

Firms can obtain financing not only from public markets with the help of an investment bank but also from plain old commercial banks—and most large publicly traded corporations do. (Most smaller firms rely on banks almost exclusively as their loan providers.) But insurance companies, pension funds, mutual funds, foundations, venture capital funds, private equity funds, and even a multitude of government support programs have also jumped into the fray and may help provide specific companies with needed capital.

There are ways to avoid financial markets for raising money altogether.

Firms can also obtain funds by the issuing of hedging contracts (which may promise future delivery of a good in exchange for cash today), securitization (in which the firm sells off assets such as its accounts receivable instead of retaining its assets), and so on. (The firm can also reduce its cash needs through transactions in which it leases instead of buys, through divestitures, etc.)

Working capital is often a surprisingly powerful method to raise funds.

➤ Trade credit, Section 16.6, p. 599

An often-important method of obtaining (or granting) financing is trade credit, in which the seller of a good allows the buyer to delay payment. (The typical publicly traded firm has just a little less in accounts payable than it has in all its financial debt together.) A customer firm may even raise financing unilaterally simply by not paying bills on time. But small and shaky firms are not always alone in stretching payments. Even large firms may earn an important competitive advantage through better working capital management. For example, Wal-Mart has often been accused of squeezing its suppliers (i.e., by not paying them for a very long time). It can afford to do so because its suppliers dare not risk losing Wal-Mart's large market distribution. From 2000 to 2005, the very large British retailer Tesco increased its accounts payable by £2.2 billion while its inventory stock increased by only £700 million—prompting the British Office of Fair Trading to open an investigation as to whether this was due to unfair pressure on suppliers or merely an efficiency gain in working capital management (though one does not exclude the other). Amazon actually has negative working capital—it first receives customer payments before it obtains the goods, thereby having capital with which it can either run its business and/or earn a financial rate of return.

These are all plausible and common methods to finance operations—whether they are wise or not depends on the situation and the firm.

SOLVE NOW!

Q 21.23 What is trade credit? Can trade credit be an important source of funding for firms?

21.9 THE CAPITAL MARKET RESPONSE TO ISSUE (AND DIVIDEND) ANNOUNCEMENTS

An important question: How do financial markets react?

As CFO, an important question on your mind will be how your stock price would respond if you decided to issue equity or debt (or the opposite, if you decided to retire equity, pay a dividend, or retire debt). By and large, if your actions raise firm value, then your stock price should increase. If your actions decrease firm value, then your stock price should fall. Beware, however, that it is only "by and large," because it may not be your actions themselves that would necessarily be responsible. Recall the second question at the outset of the chapter, which asked whether your investors understand why your actions are good for the firm. For example, it could be that an equity issue is truly in the interest of your investors, but they incorrectly believe that your issuing equity signals that you plan to waste the money. Or, it could be that your equity issue saves your firm from catastrophic bankruptcy and thereby adds value, but your investors had not realized how bad the situation was. Even though your equity issue adds value, the announcement of the equity offering would then be associated with a value drop in outstanding shares.

What can you learn from other firms?

As a manager, you should therefore be quite interested to find out what you can learn from the announcement price reaction of other firms having done similar things. Moreover, are your actual issuing costs the sum of the announcement price reaction and the issuing fees? If it costs you $10 million in fees to issue equity, and your stock price increases by $10 million upon the announcement, does this mean that the equity issue neither adds nor subtracts value? We also have an academic interest in this question: A more negative reaction to the issuance of more-junior securities is the prime assumption underlying the pecking order. Are these reactions really negative for many firms?

21.9A WHAT ANNOUNCEMENT VALUE CHANGES MEAN

The announcement capital market reaction (dilution) is a measure of the overall net cost/gain of an issue in perfect markets. The costs are borne by *old* shareholders, not new shareholders.

First, let's work out how issuing costs (such as investment banking fees and your time) relate to the stock price reaction when the firm announces an offering. Start with a perfect market in which a $100 million firm raises $50 million and pays the underwriter $30 million in commissions. Who ultimately pays for these commissions? It is the old shareholders. The new shareholders participate only if they can buy at the appropriate price. Because the post-offer firm will be worth $120 million, new shareholders demand $50/$120 ≈ 41.7% of the firm in exchange for their $50 million contribution, or they will balk. Old shareholders therefore experience an announcement price drop:

Existing Outstanding Equity Value	
Pre-Announcement Value:	100% · $100 million = $100 million
Post-Announcement Value:	58.3% · $120 million ≈ $70 million
⟹ Issuing Announcement Drop:	30%

➤ Dilution, Section 15.2A, p. 547

A common measure of the cost of an offering is the ratio of the announcement drop over the amount of equity raised, called **dilution**—and here 60% (30% of $50 million). Put differently, the firm value increased by only 40% of the $50 million issue. The rest was dissipated.

Do not add dilution and fees together for a total cost.

Some CFOs add the dilution cost ($30 million) to the underwriting fee ($30 million) to come up with a total cost of issuing. You should now understand why this is a mistake. The dilution (the announcement drop) is *not* a measure of additional cost but a measure of total inclusive cost. Adding the two would be double-counting.

You can back out the value of all other effects.

If you were now to observe that the value of outstanding equity had dropped from $100 million to $60 million instead of to $70 million, then the firm must have lost another $10 million in value through the issuing of the equity not explained by fees. In contrast to the direct fees, you usually do not immediately know the causes for the extra $10 million in remaining dilution. You have to make an educated guess. It could be that existing owners believe that the firm gave away too much in features, or that it chose the wrong securities features, or that the firm or shareholders will now pay more in taxes, or that shareholders learned the bad news that management was doing poorly and needed to raise more money. Actually, the announcement effect is more likely not just one or the other but the sum of all of these value effects. In the end, the point is that the extra loss of $10 million is a cost, just like the direct cost of $30 million paid to the underwriter. Note that this $10 million cost is merely associated with the offering, not necessarily caused by it. For example, as already mentioned twice, it could be that the market merely reacted negatively because it learned that the firm had run out of money—something that would have happened sooner or later even if the firm had never issued any equity. Not issuing equity would not have helped—in fact, it could have made things far worse.

Dilution can be positive or negative, depending on value created/destroyed.

The converse also works. If the value of outstanding equity had dropped from $100 million to $80 million, the issue must have cost the $30 million in commissions but created $10 million in value elsewhere. In the extreme, if the firm value increased upon the announcement from $100 million to $110 million (and we know that some firms do, in fact, increase in value upon the announcement of a new issue), you would know that the issue cost $30 million in underwriting fees but created $40 million in value.

IMPORTANT:

- A firm that seeks to maximize shareholder value should minimize all costs of issuing—whether underwriter/related costs or deadweight costs (such as taxes)—and maximize all value created by issuing.
- In an efficient and perfect market, the instant dilution at the announcement includes the costs and benefits of an issue. Never add dilution and issuing costs together to come up with a total cost of issuing.
- Some dilution is correlated with issuing activity but not caused by it. For example, investors may learn to expect a worse future if the firm issues equity, and the stock price may drop. This does not mean that the act of issuing equity itself reduced the value of the firm. In the extreme, it could even be that the alternative of not issuing could leave the firm bankrupt and worthless.

A real-life difficulty is that we cannot measure anticipation that well, meaning our announcement response is only partial.

In real life, why can you not just look at the announcement reaction and then decide whether you want to issue equity? Unfortunately, when you consider whether to issue, you have not announced it yet, and so you do not know the exact stock price reaction. How about the following strategy, instead: Could you announce your intent and wait to see what the value consequence is—and if it is negative, then couldn't you just announce that you have changed your mind and not go forward? Unfortunately, if the market can anticipate that you are just floating a trial balloon, then the stock price may not react at all. If the market response is a function of what it believes you will do, and if what you will do is a function of what you believe the market will do, then the blind may be leading the blind. The outcome could be anything. If the market believes you will carry through an equity offering, it could respond negatively, and you would cancel the issue. Interestingly, sometimes managers do cancel offerings if the stock market reaction is especially violent. In this case, the stock price usually shoots up again. The net value effect is not as bad as it would have been had they carried through with the bad issue—but the empirical evidence also suggests that it is still worse than if they had never announced an issue to begin with.

SOLVE NOW!

Q 21.24 In an efficient market, when would you expect the issue announcement price drop to occur—at the instant of the issue announcement or at the instant of the issue?

Q 21.25 If you know that offering more equity will reduce the value of your firm, does this mean that issuing such equity would be harmful to the firm?

21.9B THE EXACT EMPIRICAL ESTIMATES

Equity offerings are bad news. Debt offerings are not much news.

➤ Event studies, Section 11.7, p. 375

Before you mistake this for a cliff-hanger in which you will never learn how the U.S. stock market reacts to announcements, let me tell you the historical event study evidence. (The web chapter describes it in much greater detail.)

Equity offerings: *On average,* when firms raise more external equity capital, it is bad news and the stock price drops. For publicly traded firms in the United States from 1980 to 2000, the 2-day announcement price change for an equity issue (increasing firm size and decreasing debt/equity ratio) was a drop of about 1.5–2.0%, with a standard deviation of about 6%.

➤ Gross spread, Figure 23.4, p. 875

Because offerings are much smaller than the outstanding capitalization, the average dilution was about 15%. This 15% is the total cost of issuing. It includes the direct fees. Figure 23.4 shows that these direct equity issuing costs are around 5%, so they can explain only about one-third of the 15% dilution. Thus, the evidence suggests that investors either infer that management will not use the extra money productively, destroying another 10% in value, or that the firm can no longer produce as much money as they thought it could (which investors would have found out sooner or later anyway).

Debt offerings: *On average,* the announcement of a new debt issue seems to be neither particularly good nor bad news. The equivalent announcement price change for the typical debt issue was about +0.2%, with a standard deviation of about 3%. Though statistically significant, this is a very modest drop. You can almost consider it to be about zero.

Debt-for-equity exchanges: On occasion, some firms have replaced debt with equity, or vice versa, keeping the firm size unchanged. *On average,* when firms moved toward debt, their stock prices generally increased. Conversely, when they moved toward equity, their stock prices generally decreased.

Dividends: On average, the market likes dividend increases. The equivalent announcement price change for a dividend announcement in our sample was a price gain of about 0.25%, with a standard deviation of about 4%.

Remarkably, the size of the issue or the size of the firm seems to have mattered little. However, bigger dividends and dividends issued by smaller firms were greeted with a relatively more favorable response. In all of these announcements, there was also considerable heterogeneity. For example, some firms issuing equity were greeted with very positive market reactions.

SOLVE NOW!

Q 21.26 What do you expect the price reaction to be on the day that the new seasoned equity offering shares are *sold* into the market? (This is not the announcement day.)

21.9C EXTRAPOLATING THE AVERAGE EMPIRICAL EVIDENCE TO YOUR COMPANY

What should you conclude?

As a CFO, what can you learn from what other corporations have experienced in the same situation? How can you interpret these market reactions? Should you apply them as a prediction for your own firm?

The evidence suggests that shareholders like managers to have less cash at their discretion.

Recall that both debt issues and equity issues increase the size of the firm, but they have opposite effects on firms' debt ratios. Taken together with the empirical announcement price evidence, this suggests the following:

- Increases in firm size are bad news. Payout of capital is good news.
- Increases in debt ratios are good news. Increases in equity ratios are bad news.

For debt issues, the two effects roughly cancel each other out; for equity issues, they act in the same (negative) direction.

A level deeper: The financial market gets very suspicious when a publicly traded firm wants to raise more equity cash.

Thinking further, this suggests that the market believes that, for the *average* publicly traded company, tight finances (with high debt burdens and little free cash flow) enhance corporate efficiency. This supports the agency perspective of capital structure. (The evidence is also consistent with a corporate tax perspective and an inside information perspective, but not with a financial distress costs perspective.)

But be careful not to overread this evidence.

There are also a number of caveats why you should not overread the evidence. The event studies have definite limits: They try to isolate an effect from very noisy stock prices; they suffer from the fact that investors may have anticipated the offering; and they rarely apply directly to any one given company. (The average company in the market is unlikely to be a good comparable for *your* company.) For example, even the very pronounced equity announcement drop of 2% still allows about 40% of all firms to experience a positive announcement reaction—this could be your company! In sum, yes, the evidence is useful and informative, but you must also think about your own firm. Other firms' experiences can only take you so far.

If you want to understand these issues better, please read the web chapter on capital market responses.

SOLVE NOW!

Q 21.27 Are activities that increase firm size through issuing usually good news from a firm value perspective? Are increases in debt ratios usually good news from a firm value perspective? What about from a CFO's perspective?

SUMMARY

This chapter covered the following major points:

- Both capital scale and capital structure dynamics are influenced by factors under management's immediate control (such as debt issuing or share repurchasing) and factors beyond management's immediate control (such as value changes, a.k.a. stock returns).
- A CFO should consider a comprehensive view of capital policy. Many activities and external factors influence both the firm scale and the debt/equity ratio.
- Appropriate cash management should be a primary concern in many firms, especially in small high-growth firms.
- Many firms follow a "pecking order" financing scheme, in which they finance projects first with retained earnings, then with progressively less senior debt, and finally with new equity (as a last resort).
- There is empirical evidence that many managers try to "time" the financial markets. Remarkably, this has often turned out to be profitable, although we do not yet fully understand why.
- Debt offerings come in many varieties, and although we have surgically dissected their features, the actual debt offerings are often complex packages.
- Seasoned equity offerings are rare, especially among large, publicly traded corporations. They can be standard, shelf-registered, or rights offerings. Secondary shares are more insider sales than corporate capital structure events.
- Initial public offerings tend to appear in waves within certain industries and at certain times. The average 1-day IPO underpricing is about 10–15%, but IPOs begin to underperform the market beginning about 6 months after the offering for about 3 to 5 years.
- Ordinary financial debt and equity are not the only venues for raising financing. There are other methods, for example, stretching out the payment of bills.
- The financial markets respond negatively to the announcement of an equity issue, neutrally to the announcement of a debt issue, and positively to the announcement of dividends. However, there is considerable heterogeneity across firms in this response.
- The typical firm drops about 2% when it announces a new equity issue. This corresponds to a 10–20% dilution cost for existing shareholders. Dilution costs and underwriting fees must not be added to determine the total cost of an offering.

KEY TERMS

buy recommendation, 809
cash management, 799
dilution, 812
ECAPS, 801
exchange offer, 803
financing pyramid, 795
initial public offering, 806
IPO underpricing, 807
New York Bond Exchange, 803
over the counter, 803
pecking order, 792
primary shares, 805
revolver, 802
rights offering, 805
Rule 415, 805
seasoned equity offering, 804
secondary shares, 805
sell recommendation, 809
strong buy, 809
strong sell, 809
tranche, 802
treasury stock, 804

SOLVE NOW! SOLUTIONS

Q 21.1 From a value perspective, your two main questions when deciding on capital structure actions should be: (1) Can you invest your investors' money better than they can? (2) Do your investors understand this?

Q 21.2 Table 21.1 describes the financial mechanisms that can change capital structures and firm sizes:
(a) Debt ratio increases, firm size decreases: Exogenous value drop, share repurchase, cash dividend.
(b) Debt ratio decreases, firm size decreases: Debt repurchase, principal repayment, debt call.
(c) Debt ratio increases, firm size increases: Debt issue.
(d) Debt ratio decreases, firm size increases: Firm value increase, seasoned equity offering, ESOP share issuance, warrant exercise.

Q 21.3 Firms usually experience their most drastic capital structure changes when they take over other firms.

Q 21.4 The answer to whether the level of corporate debt is under the complete control and at the discretion of management is ambiguous. Firms that operate may incur liabilities, so in this sense the answer is no. Moreover, economy-wide interest rate increases could reduce the value of the firms' financial debt. However, firms could change their operations or refinance their liabilities by raising equity.

Q 21.5 To have a 5:1 debt/equity ratio with $600 million in overall value, the firm needs to have $500 million in debt and $100 million in equity. One way to accomplish this is to issue $250 million in debt and repurchase $150 million in equity. (New firm size = $250 debt + $250 debt + $250 equity – $150 equity = $600 total.)

Q 21.6 A share repurchase decreases the firm size and increases the firm's debt ratio.

Q 21.7 The pecking order states that managers prefer issuing higher-priority (safer) securities first, before proceeding to lower-priority, less safe alternatives. Therefore, they prefer to finance first from cash, then from collateralized debt, then from senior debt, then from junior debt, then from convertible debt, and finally from equity.

Q 21.8 True: If a theory predicts that issuing equity is more expensive than issuing debt, then a pecking order would arise naturally.

Q 21.9 The "financing pyramid" states that companies are financed predominantly by safer securities. Equity would be the small part of the pyramid at the top. The traditional view of the financing pyramid does not apply to many successful companies, because the equity would have grown over time.

Q 21.10 No, the pecking order does not fully imply that firms have to follow a financing pyramid. Equity can change in value (and debt can accumulate during operations). Many firms follow a financing pecking order, but their capital structures do not look like a financing pyramid.

Q 21.11 No, existing capital structures may not be optimal. The market pressures that force poorly financed companies to their optimal capital structures are too weak. In addition, other firms' managers may not even want to optimize the firm's capital structure—they may be more interested in making their own situations as pleasant as possible.

Q 21.12 Managers can reduce the likelihood of running out of cash by matching cash inflows and outflows, paying for an irrevocable credit line, holding liquid investments, or reducing their liabilities relative to their equity.

Q 21.13 A coercive bond exchange offer gives existing bondholders the right to exchange their bonds for more senior bonds with lower face values. Bondholders who do not participate are effectively expropriated.

Q 21.14 Assume that the shares are \$10 each. You can then purchase shares for the 1/5 price mentioned in the question, that is, \$2 each. Of 50 million shares, 25 million will participate. You will raise an extra \$50 million. Thus, total corporate assets will be \$550 million. There are now 75 million shares in total. Therefore, each share will be worth \$7.33. Participating investors will own 2 shares worth \$14.66, for which they will have paid \$12. This represents a 22% gain. Nonparticipating investors will own 1 share worth \$7.33, for which they will have paid \$10. This represents a 26.7% loss.

Q 21.15 A coercive seasoned equity rights offering could give existing shareholders the right to purchase more shares at a price below the market value of shares. Investors who do not participate are effectively expropriated.

Q 21.16 False. The 10–15% IPO underpricing is not an annualized figure, unlike the stock market, which has a rate of return of about 10% *per annum.* IPO underpricing is a 1-day figure. Thus, the IPO 10% magnitude is enormous.

Q 21.17 For the painting:

(a) Yes, the average private value is equal to the expected painting value, because $(20\% + 10\% + 0\% - 15\% - 15\%)/5 = 0\%$.

(b) You should assume you are the one that had the 20% overestimate. Thus, if you know that there is exactly one bidder with the highest overestimate, it being exactly 20% of the value, then you should shave 20% off your bid. In this example, if you have drawn \$150, then you should offer no more than \$150/1.2 = \$125.

(c) When you follow the instructions, you will find that with five bidders, your expected winning painting bid is about \$111.7. So you should bid no more than \$100/\$111.7 ≈ 89.5% of your private value estimate. Here are more expected values of the top bid as a function of the number of bidders:

	Number of Bidders									
	1	2	3	4	5	10	20	100	1,000	∞
1,000-Row Average of Top Bid	\$100	\$105.7	\$108.7	\$110.2	\$111.7	\$115.4	\$118.6	\$124.8	\$132.3	\$138.4

Q 21.18 This is an example of the winner's curse in the IPO context. An uninformed investor would expect to be rationed if the offering is underpriced. For every share requested, fair rationing means that she would only receive 1/3 of a share (due to the oversubscription by a factor of 3). Thus, this investor would earn $\frac{1}{2} \cdot \frac{1}{3} \cdot (+15\%) + \frac{1}{2} \cdot 1 \cdot (-15\%) = -5\%$.

Q 21.19 The typical IPO sells off about one-third of the firm.

Q 21.20 There are a number of explanations for IPO underpricing—such as the winner's curse, payment to investors for revealing information, the intent to leave goodwill for future offerings, highly elastic cascade-related after-market demand, and agency conflicts between the firm and the underwriter.

Q 21.21 On average, IPO shares appreciate by 10–15% from the offer price to the first after-market price and then lose about 5% per annum over the following 3 to 5 years. (Other regularities are described in the text.)

Q 21.22 The performance of an industry in the stock market is a good predictor for future IPO waves.

Q 21.23 Trade credit is extended by a firm's supplier in the form of delayed payment due dates. That is, the firm is not required to pay for the goods upon receipt. Therefore, the firm has some time to sell the goods that it purchased via trade credit. This gives it an alternative source of funds—the supplier rather than, say, a bank. The empirical evidence suggests that trade credit and accounts payable are very important sources of financing for firms—for many firms they are as important as their financial debt financing.

Q 21.24 Recall from Section 11.7 on page 375 that any value drop must occur at the instant of the issue announcement. Otherwise, you could profitably trade on your advance knowledge of the already-announced event that will occur in the future.

Q 21.25 Issuing such equity would not necessarily harm the firm—it could even rescue it. The negative reaction may come from your investors learning (possibly correctly) that something bad has recently happened—for example, your R&D has failed. To rescue the firm's valuable projects, your best choice would still be to obtain more funding despite the negative reaction.

Q 21.26 The price reaction on the actual issue day should be about zero, because the share sale is an event that was announced earlier and thus should have been almost perfectly anticipated. If the market did not use this information efficiently, and the share price were to go down on the day of the offering, you could short the equity shares the day before the offering, and repurchase them the day after the offering for a profit.

Q 21.27 From a firm value perspective: The answers are no and yes. The empirical evidence suggests that increases in funds and thus firm size are usually *bad* news for the firm. Increases in debt ratios are usually *good* news. (The deeper explanation is consistent with a view that investors see equity issues as more opportunities for managers to waste money.) From the perspective of a CFO, it would probably be the opposite—recall the agency conflict discussion in Section 12.8 on page 420. (It will also be taken up again in Chapter 24.) Managers usually like to reside over big empires (managers of larger firms also usually earn more) and like to enjoy financial flexibility that makes life easy for them.

PROBLEMS

The ▭ indicates problems available in myfinancelab

Q 21.28 What are the two important questions that a CFO acting on behalf of shareholders should ask?

Q 21.29 Is it possible that issuing new equity to take a positive-NPV project reduces the value of the firm?

Q 21.30 Give an example of one financial mechanism each in a perfect market that (a) increases the debt ratio of the firm and decreases the firm size; (b) decreases the debt ratio of the firm and decreases the firm size; (c) increases the debt ratio of the firm and increases the firm size; (d) decreases the debt ratio of the firm and increases the firm size.

Q 21.31 Name some examples of financial and nonfinancial liabilities.

Q 21.32 A firm issues $50 in new debt and $200 in new equity. Does this mean that its debt/equity ratio decreases?

Q 21.33 Does the debt/equity ratio of a firm change only with the firm's issuance and retirement of debt and equity?

Q 21.34 A $500 million firm is financed by $250 million in debt and $250 million in equity. It issues $150 million in debt and repurchases $50 million in equity. The market believes the $100 million increase in value will result in wasteful spending by managers, which costs $5 million in NPV. However, the higher $150 million in new debt will also create $20 million in additional tax shelter NPV. What is the firm's new value and new debt/equity ratio?

Q 21.35 What is the effect of a repayment of debt on the firm's value and on the firm's debt ratio in a perfect market?

Q 21.36 If the world is not perfect, what is the likely effect of an equity issue on the firm's value and on the firm's debt ratio? How does it compare to the perfect-market scenario?

Q 21.37 If the pecking order holds perfectly, would managers ever issue equity?

Q 21.38 What are the theories that can explain why firms may follow a pecking order when issuing securities?

Q 21.39 Do all firms follow capital structures that were created through a pecking order?

Q 21.40 Would a firm that has followed only a pecking order after its IPO in its capital-issuing decision end up with more debt than equity in its capital structure?

Q 21.41 Explain the difference between the financing pyramid and the pecking order. Which leads to which?

Q 21.42 Empirically, do managers seem to act as if they believe that they can time the *overall* stock market (not just their own stock)? Are they doing so successfully?

Q 21.43 Is it a good idea to follow the same capital structure as other firms in your industry?

Q 21.44 How can a firm manage its cash to avoid running into financial distress? What are the drawbacks?

Q 21.45 From a firm value perspective, should managers always strive to make financial flexibility a main goal, as they claim in surveys?

Q 21.46 Evaluate the following statement: If a firm faces an efficient bond market, then this firm can issue any bond it likes—it does not matter as far as firm value is concerned.

Q 21.47 What are the components in a typical corporate bond issue?

Q 21.48 Do corporate bonds trade very actively? If so, where do they trade? If not, why not?

Q 21.49 Give an illustration of a coercive bond offer.

Q 21.50 How does a rights offering differ from a shelf offering?

Q 21.51 Your firm has $200 million of debt outstanding (held by 600 creditors) and $300 million of equity outstanding (held by 300,000 shareholders). Construct a coercive rights offering to raise $100 million in new equity. How does your example change if you have no debt outstanding? How does your example change if you want to raise $200 million?

Q 21.52 Explain the winner's curse. Does it apply only to IPO shares, or could it also apply to an auction for a one-of-a-kind painting?

Q 21.53 What are the possible reasons for IPO underpricing?

Q 21.54 What is the empirical evidence on the long-run performance of IPOs?

Q 21.55 Evaluate: Everyone knows that analysts are conflicted and not trustworthy when evaluating IPOs that their own firm issues. Therefore, because no investor would pay serious attention, analysts do not publish recommendations to buy or sell shares in their own bank's IPO firms.

Q 21.56 What typically happens to the IPO share price when the lock-up period expires?

Q 21.57 What is an "open IPO window"?

Q 21.58 What is the typical underwriting commission for IPOs?

Q 21.59 Can a firm raise financing through its management of accounts payable?

Q 21.60 How would you measure the whole cost of issuing, including deadweight costs that capital structure changes create, direct fees, and everything else? Should you add the dilution costs and the underwriter fees?

22

Capital Structure Patterns in the United States

THE EMPIRICAL EVIDENCE

We are now returning to the question of how, in broad strokes, publicly traded corporations in the United States have financed themselves over the last few decades. (There is very little data and research on how private firms are financed.) You have already learned basic patterns from our discussion of IBM in Chapter 15. This chapter tries to do this more systematically and to reconcile some of our theoretical insights with the empirical evidence.

You should realize that this chapter is at the cutting edge of research. There are different interpretations of the data, so it is unavoidable that what you are reading is my interpretation of the evidence. My goal is to give you a taste of what we know—and what we do not know.

22.1 HOW TO MEASURE LEVERAGE

We first need to decide on a good summary measure of how indebted a company is. You may need it not only to assess how likely it is that a firm will fall into financial distress, but also if you want to compute the weighted average cost of capital. So let's look at leverage ratios in some more detail.

We need to measure indebtedness to assess financial precariousness and to compute WACC.

➤ WACC, Section 17.3, p. 614

22.1A BOOK OR MARKET VALUE?

By definition, a firm is

$$\underbrace{\text{Total Liabilities}}_{\text{Senior}} + \underbrace{\text{Equity}}_{\text{Junior}} = \text{Assets}$$

Should you measure equity value (and total asset value) as book value or market value?

Alas, one complication arises immediately. How should you measure the value of equity (which is also a component of the value of total assets)? Should it be the market value of equity or the book value of equity? The market value has the advantage that it is based on economic value, not on accounting value, and it is my favorite. However, reasonable people can disagree and prefer the book value instead. The main advantage of book value is that it varies less year to year, and thus many contracts and bond covenants are written with respect to the book value and not the market value. Most, but not all, of the discussion in this chapter works with the equity value. In the typical publicly traded U.S. firm, the market value of equity is about twice as large as the book value of its equity—and the older the firm is, the higher is the discrepancy on average. However, there are many firms in which this ratio reverses—and there are even firms that have negative book values of equity.

Using the book value for debt is (more) reasonable.

You rarely have to worry about book value versus market value with respect to liabilities. You cannot use the market value of liabilities, simply because you usually do not have it. Thus, you have no choice. Fortunately, this is not too bad—for liabilities, book values and market values are often fairly similar (unless the firm is in such dire straits that its liabilities become very risky, too).

22.1B TOTAL LEVERAGE: THE TOTAL-LIABILITIES-TO-TOTAL-ASSETS RATIO

Here is how you compute IBM's leverage ratios.

The formula above suggests that our first leverage ratio should be total liabilities (i.e., the senior claims) divided by total assets (i.e., all claims). Let's use IBM to illustrate this leverage measure. You can find the data you need to compute the liabilities-to-asset ratio in Table 15.1 (all quoted in millions):

➤ IBM's capital structure, Table 15.1, p. 555

		2001	2002	2003
Total Liabilities	TL	$66,855	$73,702	$76,593
Market Value of Equity	MVE	$208,437	$133,484	$157,047
Book Value of Equity	BVE	$23,448	$22,782	$27,864
Market Value of Assets	TL+MVE	$275,292	$207,186	$233,640
Book Value of Assets	TL+BVE	$90,303	$96,484	$104,457

A convenient way to compute the market value of assets is to start with the book value of assets on the balance sheet, and then to subtract the book value of equity and add the market value of equity (e.g., for 2001: $90,303 − $23,448 + $208,437 = $275,292).

Measure #1: Liabilities-to-assets

Therefore, IBM's total-liabilities-to-assets ratios were

		2001	2002	2003
Total-Liabilities-to-Assets, Market Value	TL/(TL+MVE)	24%	36%	33%
Total-Liabilities-to-Assets, Book Value	TL/(TL+BVE)	74%	76%	73%

You should not be surprised that the market-based debt ratios are much lower—after all, and as is common for older firms, the market value of IBM's equity is much larger than its book value. If you are a newspaper reporter and you want to hype how high IBM's corporate leverage ratio is, you will report the latter. If you are the CEO and you want to brag about how modest your leverage is, you will report the former. For us, a more sensible approach would be to put IBM's leverage ratio into context, by comparing it to those of other similar firms (such as Hewlett-Packard) and to its historical ratios, rather than looking at IBM's leverage ratios in absolute terms.

A closely related ratio is the liabilities-to-equity ratio. It uses the same two inputs (liabilities and equity), but the denominator is not their sum. You can always translate a liabilities-to-equity ratio into a liabilities-to-assets ratio, and vice versa. (For example, if you have a 3-to-1 liabilities-to-equity ratio, you know you have a 3-to-4 liabilities-to-assets ratio). However, a big problem with equity-denominated ratios is that the book value of equity can be very small or even negative, which can easily make the liabilities-to-equity ratio seem unreasonably large. A second problem is that in the WACC computations, you need a ratio that is denominated by the sum (i.e., here, assets). More below.

You can use TL/E instead of TL/(TL+E), but it can be difficult to interpret—and it may not be what you want, anyway.

SOLVE NOW!

Q 22.1 In 2004, IBM's financials reported total assets of $111,003 and total liabilities of $79,315. Its market value of equity was $155,459. What was its liabilities-to-assets ratio, in book and market value?

22.1C FINANCIAL LEVERAGE: THE FINANCIAL-DEBT-TO-FINANCIAL-CAPITAL RATIO

The liabilities-to-asset ratio includes nonfinancial claims such as accounts payable (as well as some liabilities that are not even real but invented by accountants). Therefore, a second common measure of leverage ignores nonfinancial liabilities. The financial-debt-to-capital ratio breaks out the financial claims (long-term debt and debt in short-term liabilities) from the firm's total liabilities.

Measure #2: Financial debt-to-capital.

$$\underbrace{\text{Nonfinancial Liabilities} + \overbrace{\text{Financial Liabilities}}^{\text{Financial Capital}}}_{\text{Senior}} \overbrace{+ \underbrace{\text{Equity}}_{\text{Junior}}} = \text{Assets}$$

In the typical publicly traded firm, financial capital is typically about one-half to one-third of the firm's total liabilities. Our second financial leverage measure, then, divides the financial debt by **financial capital**, defined as the sum of financial debt plus equity. Again, Table 15.1 has all the information you need:

		2001	2002	2003
Financial Debt	FD	$27,151	$26,017	$23,632
Market Value of Equity	MVE	$208,437	$133,484	$157,047
Book Value of Equity	BVE	$23,448	$22,782	$27,864
Market Value of Financial Capital	FD+MVE	$235,588	$159,501	$180,679
Book Value of Financial Capital	FD+BVE	$50,599	$48,799	$51,496

Therefore, the financial-debt-to-capital ratios are

		2001	2002	2003
Financial Debt-to-Capital, Market Value	FD/(FD+MVE)	12%	16%	13%
Financial Debt-to-Capital, Book Value	FD/(FD+BVE)	54%	53%	46%

This requires a small correction to my earlier remark—if IBM's CEO wanted to brag about modest debt, he would probably cite the financial-debt-to-capital ratio, not the liabilities-to-assets ratio.

Short-term debt ratios.

➤ IBM's short-term liabilities, Table 15.3, p. 559

When you want to explore the financial stability or precariousness of firms, you may find it sometimes helpful to use measures that use firms' short-term liabilities, and especially short-term financial debt. For IBM, this was $6,646 in 2003. You might then compute the ratio of short-term liabilities to cash holdings, or to equity, or to assets. We shall ignore these ratios.

Enterprise value defined.

Many analysts subtract cash and short-term holdings from financial debt. After all, this cash could presumably be used to immediately reduce this debt. The sum of the market value of equity and financial debt, that is, financial capital at market value, minus cash and short-term holdings is called the **enterprise value**.

You can compute FD/E instead of FD/(FD+E).

And, as was the case for the liabilities-to-equity ratio, the financial-debt-to-equity ratio has the same two inputs and can act as a stand-in for the financial-debt-to-capital ratio. However, it too can suffer from nonsensibly small equity values and is not what we shall need below to compute the weighted average cost of capital.

SOLVE NOW!

Q 22.2 (Continued from Q 22.1) In 2004, IBM's financials reported financial debt of $22,927. What was its financial-debt-to-capital ratio, in book value and market value?

22.1D COMPARING TOTAL AND FINANCIAL LEVERAGE RATIOS—AND WACC

Cousins.

What is the difference between the liabilities-to-assets ratio and the debt-to-capital ratio? Conceptually, the two ratios are cousins, and it is often the case that firms within the same industry have a similar rank ordering regardless of which measure is used. Mechanically, the big difference is that the liabilities-to-assets ratio includes nonfinancial liabilities (such as pension liabilities and accounts payable), which the debt-to-capital ratio ignores.

Claimants become so by providing assets, the same for both financial or nonfinancial liabilities.

This raises the question: How are nonfinancial claims different from claims that financial creditors and shareholders receive? Think about what a claim is and how it comes about. Someone provides assets to the firm and receives a claim in exchange. For financial claimants, such as bondholders and shareholders, it is a direct money contribution. For nonfinancial claimants, there is an equivalent contribution, but it is usually not in money. For example, how did IBM's pension fund become a claimant? Employees made a contribution to the firm, which has not been fully paid by the firm yet. The firm still owes the pension claim, which is money to be paid that is still part of IBM's assets.

Many nonfinancial liabilities also require regular payments and often even on timetables that are as rigid as those on financial debt. And, as is the case for financial liabilities, failure to pay nonfinancial liabilities has sanctions and can force bankruptcy. Moreover, for both financial and nonfinancial liabilities, all payments are made from funds *before* corporate income tax is computed.

Nonfinancial liabilities also have similar payment schedules, sanctions, and tax treatment.

This perspective suggests that nonfinancial liabilities should be included in a leverage ratio—that is, that you should use the broader liabilities-to-assets ratio and not the debt-to-capital ratio. The liabilities-to-assets ratio would be better for measuring the firm's precariousness in many circumstances. Ignoring the nonfinancial liabilities would seem to be a mistake.

TL/A is often better to assess precariousness.

However, there is also a very good reason to use the financial-debt-to-capital ratio. It was first explained in Section 16.6B. Financial debt is often the *marginal* source of funding, which the firm would have to pay on the next dollar that the corporation could raise. Consequently, it is the financial claims' cost of capital that you should compare to the productivity of your next project. After all, many nonfinancial claims cannot be expanded or contracted at will. Moreover, even if this were not the case, how would you even measure the marginal cost of nonfinancial capital accurately? For example, if you do not pay off your accounts payable for a while, you can indeed earn interest on the cash you retain. However, your delaying payment may deprive your firm of better suppliers and raise your future prices on your inputs. Although this additional cost due to delay is conceptually the same as an interest payment, it is impossible to measure accurately in practice. Not knowing the cost of capital on nonfinancial liabilities means that it would not be easy to compute a weighted average cost of capital that includes your nonfinancial liabilities.

FD/C is often better for estimating the marginal cost of capital.

➤ Marginal and average costs of capital, Section 16.6B, p. 601

In contrast, it is relatively easy to compute the WACC if you use the financial-debt-to-financial-capital ratio. For example, for IBM in 2003, all you need is the cost of capital on debt and equity. You would not use the cost of capital on nonfinancial liabilities. IBM was unlikely to go bankrupt, so its stated interest rate was probably close to its expected interest rate. On page 561, we guessed that its debt cost of capital was around 2.8%. (Admittedly, it was only the average cost of debt capital; the marginal cost could be higher.) The cost of its equity may have been around 7%—a number I obtained from a CAPM-type estimation. You can then compute the WACC:

Here is an easy estimate of IBM's WACC.

➤ Estimating the cost of capital in WACC, Section 17.6E, p. 632

$$\text{WACC} = 13\% \times 2.8\% + 87\% \times 7\% \approx 6.5\%$$

$$\text{WACC} = 13\% \times \begin{pmatrix}\text{Expected}\\ \text{Int. Cost}\end{pmatrix} + 87\% \times \begin{pmatrix}\text{Expected Equity}\\ \text{Cost of Capital}\end{pmatrix}$$

$$\text{WACC} = \begin{pmatrix}\text{Debt-to-}\\ \text{Capital Ratio}\end{pmatrix} \times \begin{pmatrix}\text{Expected Financial}\\ \text{Debt Int. Rate}\end{pmatrix} + \left[1 - \begin{pmatrix}\text{Debt-to-}\\ \text{Capital Ratio}\end{pmatrix}\right] \times \begin{pmatrix}\text{Expected Equity}\\ \text{Cost of Capital}\end{pmatrix}$$

This 6.5% is an estimate of the cost of capital on funds that IBM could have raised or retired relatively quickly—that is, on the financial funds that most likely best represent IBM's marginal cost of raising funds. It is this 6.5% that IBM's executives may have wanted to use as a hurdle rate for projects. Of course, this applies only to projects like IBM's typical projects in 2003.

➤ Projects–specific costs of capital, Section 12.3, p. 393

Now, can you please compute what the WACC is when you include nonfinancial liabilities? (As for me, I simply have no idea how I could do this, because I do not know what the cost of capital on nonfinancial liabilities is.)

How Bad Are Mistakes?

FINANCIAL DEBT-TO-ASSETS

In common use, but conceptually flawed: A financial-debt-to-assets ratio.

You may on occasion encounter the ratio of financial debt divided by the value of assets as a measure of leverage. For example, using book values of assets,

		2001	2002	2003
Financial Debt	FD	\$27,151	\$26,017	\$23,632
Book Value of Assets	TL+BVE	\$90,303	\$96,484	\$104,457
Financial Debt-to-Assets	FD/(TL+BVE)	30%	27%	23%

The reason why such a ratio makes no sense as a leverage ratio is that a firm can *reduce* its leverage ratio by *increasing* its nonfinancial liabilities. If IBM had taken on another \$100 billion in accounts payable or was hit with an additional income tax obligation of \$100 billion, everything else being equal, its 2003 financial-debt-to-assets ratio would have fallen from $\$23.6/\$104.5 \approx 23\%$ to $\$23.6/\$204.5 \approx 12\%$, even though its indebtedness would have become worse, not better. In real life, some debt covenants are written on the financial-debt-to-asset ratio, and thus some CFOs may care about it—but it is not a sensible measure of leverage.

SOLVE NOW!

Q 22.3 Are firms partly financed by their nonfinancial liabilities? If so, how do you incorporate this into the firm's WACC?

22.1E A FLOW-BASED APPROACH: THE INTEREST COVERAGE RATIO

Perhaps we should measure indebtedness and precariousness from flows, not from stocks.

➤ Interest coverage ratio, Section 14.4B, p. 523

Another altogether different approach to measuring indebtedness is through the running obligations incurred by the debt relative to the money coming in, that is, not through the *levels* of liabilities, debt, or equity. The natural flow-based summary ratio is the interest coverage ratio. It measures how much of the firm's operating income is consumed by debt service, principally interest payments. The idea is that it measures whether the firm will encounter financial distress because it cannot meet its running debt obligations. The problem with interest coverage ratios is that flow measures can be very volatile from year to year. Specifically, corporate earnings can be highly variable or even negative for 1 or 2 years. In this case, the interest coverage ratio can look unnecessarily dire. In addition, principal repayment obligations are often more stringent than interest payment obligations, and firms must also meet their nonfinancial obligations. Still, the interest coverage ratio gives a good different perspective on the leverage of a firm.

I think you realize by now that characterizing capital structure cannot be accurately accomplished with just one indebtedness ratio. Instead, capital structure must be seen from multiple angles.

SOLVE NOW!

Q 22.4 What are the drawbacks to using the interest coverage ratio as a measure of indebtedness?

22.2 EMPIRICAL CAPITAL STRUCTURE PATTERNS

Obviously, we cannot look at all publicly traded companies at the same level of detail as we did for IBM in Section 15.4. Still, you probably want to know about not just the needle but also the haystack. Is IBM a representative firm, or is it the exception? What are the debt ratios of companies of different sizes? Are there any patterns?

➤ IBM's capital structure, Section 15.4, p. 554

You can measure indebtedness in a number of ways:

Financial debt or total liabilities? Book value or market value? Asset ratios or equity ratios?

- You can see indebtedness narrowly or widely: narrowly in terms of the firm's financial indebtedness (long-term debt plus debt in current liabilities), or widely in terms of all liabilities (which includes nonfinancial obligations such as payables, pensions, and other liabilities, for example).
- You can see equity in terms of market value or book value. Although I prefer the former, the latter is also often used in practice, especially by creditors who are interested in assets that they can repossess in case of bankruptcy. (Book value is often a more conservative measure of value if a firm is dismembered.)
- You can see indebtedness in terms of equity ratios or sum-total ratios: Equity ratios divide debt only by the value of equity, as in a debt-to-equity ratio. Sum-total ratios divide by a bigger number, as in a liabilities-to-assets ratio or a debt-to-capital ratio, where capital is the sum of debt and equity. Reasonable sum-total ratios should be between 0% and 100%. Thus, it makes sense to divide total liabilities by total assets (market value or book value); and it makes sense to divide financial debt by the sum of financial debt and equity.

We shall look at different measures at different times so that you get used to the multidimensional variety here.

22.2A THE LARGEST U.S. FIRMS IN 2005

Let me start by showing you the capital structures of the 28 U.S.-traded firms on Yahoo! *Finance* at the end of 2005 that had more than $100 billion in enterprise value—making this an exercise that you can easily repeat yourself *today*. Table 22.1 shows both their book and market values, but our focus is primarily on market value–based ratios.

The 28 largest firms in 2005.

Of these 28 companies, 11 were primarily in finance-related businesses, 1 was a large conglomerate, 2 were in car manufacturing and their financing, and 14 were in other businesses. (IBM was among the latter.) The table shows that, just like IBM,

Financial firms tend to have high debt-to-equity ratios. Nonfinancial U.S. firms not in financial distress and not involved in M&A had low debt ratios.

TABLE 22.1 FINANCIAL-DEBT-TO-CAPITAL RATIOS FOR U.S. FIRMS WITH AT LEAST $100 BILLION IN ENTERPRISE VALUE, DECEMBER 2005

Ticker	Company	Total Enterprise Value	Debt (FD)	Equity (MVE)	Debt : Equity FD:MVE	Debt : Equity FD:BVE
	Primarily Financial and Insurance Firms					
FNM	Fannie Mae	985	940	47	20.2:1	42.7:1
FRE	Freddie Mac	713	716	46	15.5:1	26.2:1
BAC	Bank of America	311	425	188	2.3:1	4.2:1
AIG	Amer Intl Group (AIG)	238	116	176	1:2	1.3:1
WFC	Wells Fargo & Co	180	102	107	1.0:1	2.6:1
C	Citigroup	177	516	249	2.1:1	4.7:1
WM	Washington Mutual	143	115	43	2.7:1	4.6:1
WB	Wachovia	114	123	83	1.5:1	2.6:1
SLM	SLM (Sallie Mae)	111	89	23	3.9:1	27.5:1
USB	US Bancorp	108	59	56	1.1:1	3.0:1
AXP	American Express	102	44	65	1:2	4.5:1
	Car Manufacturers and Conglomerates, Incl. Large Financing Arms					
GE	General Electric	722	360	374	1.0:1	3.2:1
GM	General Motors	274	278	11	26.1:1	12.4:1
F	Ford Motor	140	142	15	9.6:1	10.4:1
	Firms with Primarily Nonfinancial Operations					
XOM	Exxon Mobil	338	8	354	2%	8%
MSFT	Microsoft	244	0	282	0%	0%
WMT	Wal-Mart Stores	236	38	202	19%	76%
MO	Altria Group	177	25	159	16%	72%
PFE	Pfizer	176	12	177	7%	18%
JNJ	Johnson & Johnson	168	2	181	1%	7%
PG	Procter & Gamble	161	30	139	21%	228%
IBM	IBM	144	21	131	16%	71%
INTC	Intel	143	1	157	0%	2%
CVX	Chevron	131	14	128	11%	23%
VZ	Verizon Comm.	122	39	85	47%	101%
GOOG	Google	118	0	127	0%	0%
BRK-A	Berkshire Hathaway	105	15	136	11%	17%
T	AT&T Inc.	103	23	81	29%	60%

All numbers are from Yahoo! *Finance*. FD is financial debt (long-term debt plus debt in current liabilities), measured in book value. Equity is market value. The enterprise value is the sum of financial capital (financial debt plus the market value of equity) minus cash and short-term holdings. (This ignores all nonfinancial liabilities.) In the top two panels, instead of reporting high percentages (e.g., 4,270%), most of these financial-debt-to-equity ratios are reported in ratios (e.g., 42.7:1). Ford and General Motors include their large financing companies that facilitate leasing.

Conclusion: Among large firms, financial firms tend to have the highest leverage. Very profitable companies, like Microsoft, Exxon, Intel, and Google, have very low leverage.

most of these large firms had market values that were 2 to 3 times their book values. A quick glance suggests the following:

Some financial firms had very high debt ratios. The most extreme examples were Fannie Mae and Freddie Mac mortgage lenders, which are also the world's largest firms. Fannie Mae had outstanding debt obligations of $940 billion—20 times its equity capitalization. (In turn, most of its assets were mortgage loans to homeowners.) (In June 2008, they suddenly ran into trouble and became quite [in-]famous.) But many other financial companies also had more debt than equity.

Car manufacturers also had relatively high debt/equity ratios and for two reasons. First, the two remaining public U.S. car manufacturers (General Motors and Ford) have been in real economic distress for decades. This is why their equity market values were not multiples of their book values—in fact, GM's book value was above its market value! This is a rarity among large old U.S. companies. Second, they are actually no longer car companies but primarily financial service companies. Most of GM's and Ford's assets today are the loans and leases extended to customers who are purchasing vehicles. Of course, this relative reallocation of value came about by the same process that rendered them distressed.

Nonfinancial firms (i.e., many of the remaining large U.S. firms) had market-based debt-to-equity ratios that were low—11 out of 14 had ratios of less than 20%. The two outliers were Verizon and AT&T, both of which had recently made large acquisitions. (Verizon bought MCI; SBC purchased AT&T and changed its name to AT&T.) IBM did not seem unusual, but it was also among the more indebted companies. (IBM also has a large financing subsidiary, which may explain this.)

General Electric is a conglomerate that is hard to classify. It has a large financing subsidiary, too.

Looking at more large firms: Recent performance and industry seem to matter.

You can easily explore debt ratios further on Yahoo! *Finance*. For example, when I looked at all 416 nonfinancial firms with more than $10 billion in enterprise value, I noticed the following: As to firms with substantial debt, there were only 12 firms with debt ratios above 90%. Four firms were airlines (United, Delta, Northwest, American); three were car manufacturers or suppliers (GM, Ford, Goodyear); three were energy-related firms (Calpine, CMS Energy, Mirant); the final two were Charter Cable and Owens-Corning (which had been forced into bankruptcy by its asbestos liabilities). All of them had experienced dramatic declines in their equity values in the prior 2 years and were either close to, or already in, bankruptcy. A quick glance at other highly indebted firms shows that this pattern continues. Among the next 40 firms with the highest debt ratios, three-quarters were in energy—a sector that had suffered a terrible year in 2004. (The sector did great after 2006, however. As of 2008, these firms had become among the most profitable in the world.) Of the remaining one-quarter, the majority of firms were car-related. I also looked at the 191 financial firms. These had a median debt ratio of 55%—much higher than the 40% for the 416 nonfinancial firms that I just mentioned. As to firms with very little or zero debt, Microsoft, Google, Intuit, and other software manufacturers were particularly prominent, with a sprinkling of biotech and some other firms (such as Bed Bath & Beyond) thrown in.

22.2B PUBLICLY TRADED U.S. FIRMS IN 2003

We want to learn about leverage patterns by firm size.

Even the large companies mentioned above are not representative of companies in the U.S. economy. There are thousands of smaller firms. Unfortunately, it is impossible to look at their individual capital structures one by one. We need to use a quantitative database of firms to summarize the information. I only had data from S&P's Compustat data service until 2003. Fortunately, this has a number of advantages. First, it allows you to check that the capital structure patterns were as similar in 2003 as they were in 2004 and 2005. The year 2003 was also interesting in that, on average, small publicly traded firms barely broke even, but many large firms had already escaped the recession and had solid earnings. (Still, the same findings would have held up if I had chosen 2001 instead of 2003. However, there is no guarantee that these numbers will still be accurate in 2010.) Second, it allows you to compare the IBM numbers you saw in the previous sections to the overall universe of firms. Third, it gives you more freedom to look at different types of firms.

Indebtedness ratios are often drastically different from one another.

We will look at three measures:

FD/(FD+MVE), the financial indebtedness ratio, which we define as long-term debt plus debt in current liabilities, divided by the firm's financial securities' market value. The latter is again long-term debt plus debt in current liabilities, plus the market value of equity. Overall, publicly traded U.S. firms had a median of 17% and a mean of 25% on this ratio in 2003.

TL/(TL+MVE), a broad market value–based total indebtedness ratio, which we define as total liabilities, divided by the sum of total liabilities plus the market value of equity. Overall, publicly traded U.S. firms had a median of 38% and a mean of 42% on this ratio in 2003.

TL/(TL+BVE), a broad book value–based total indebtedness ratio, which we define as total liabilities, divided by the book value of assets (the sum of total liabilities plus the book value of equity). Overall, publicly traded U.S. firms had both a median and a mean of 57% on this ratio in 2003.

As with IBM, how you define indebtedness matters to what numbers you get and whether they seem high or low. Financial and market-based debt ratios are generally lower than broader liability and book value–based debt ratios. (This is less problematic when you compare firms within the same industry on the same leverage ratio, because they usually have similar rankings on both measures.)

INDEBTEDNESS RATIOS

Larger firms ⇒ more debt.

Table 22.2 categorizes firms by firm size. The tiny firms had market capitalizations of less than \$100 million, small firms between \$100 million and \$1 billion, medium firms between \$1 billion and \$10 billion, and large firms more than \$10 billion. (The equivalent categories for their book values were \$100 million, \$500 million, \$2.5 billion, and \$10 billion, respectively.) A clear pattern emerges: No matter how you sort, no matter what indebtedness ratio you choose, and no matter whether you use the median or the mean, *larger firms tended to be more indebted*. However, within each category, firms were not homogeneous. Quite the opposite—there was a lot of

TABLE 22.2 INDEBTEDNESS RATIOS, BY FIRM SIZE IN 2003

Sorted by:	FD / (FD+MVE)			TL / (TL+MVE)			TL / (TL+BVE)		
MV of Assets	Mean	Median	25–75%	Mean	Median	25–75%	Mean	Median	25–75%
1,321 Tiny	19.6	7.8	0–30	36.5	30.8	14–54	51.8	47.3	25–77
2,142 Small	22.8	12.3	0–40	39.7	30.9	12–69	51.5	47.9	27–78
1,580 Medium	29.2	24.3	10–46	46.4	43.6	24–71	62.5	63.3	46–84
594 Large	33.0	28.5	13–48	53.8	55.4	32–79	70.6	73.4	57–90
Conclusion:	Larger firms have higher debt ratios.								

Sorted by:	FD / (FD+MVE)			TL / (TL+MVE)			TL / (TL+BVE)		
BV of Assets	Mean	Median	25–75%	Mean	Median	25–75%	Mean	Median	25–75%
1,744 Tiny	16.1	3.8	0–24	30.9	22.7	9–47	47.8	41.6	22–72
1,458 Small	22.0	11.5	0–37	38.7	29.2	14–63	50.6	46.6	27–74
1,365 Medium	30.9	26.5	11–48	49.7	46.8	26–78	63.2	63.7	46–88
628 Large	34.2	30.8	15–50	53.5	52.1	35–77	68.6	70.3	56–87
448 Largest	37.6	35.9	17–54	60.6	62.8	41–83	74.6	77.2	62–91
Conclusion:	Larger firms have higher debt ratios.								

FD is financial debt (long-term debt plus debt in current liabilities); TL is total liabilities; MVE is the market value of equity; BVE is the book value of equity. All numbers are quoted in percent. The total-liabilities-to-asset ratios are "broader" total leverage ratios. 25–75% is the interquartile range—that is, it tells you the difference between the 25th percentile and the 75th percentile (it measures how heterogeneous firms are).

variation. For example, it was not at all unusual to have broad market value–based liabilities of 54% for a tiny firm and 32% for a large firm.

Lots of heterogeneity.

PROFITABLE AND UNPROFITABLE FIRMS IN 2003: INDEBTEDNESS RATIOS

More profitable firms ⇒ more debt.

Another good question is whether more profitable companies have systematically different capital structures. Table 22.3 shows that more profitable firms tended to have higher indebtedness ratios. This is not as strong a pattern in terms of their financial debt ratios as it is in terms of their total liabilities ratios.

INDEBTEDNESS RATIOS BY INDUSTRY IN 2003

Industry may have mattered, too.

Table 22.4 categorizes firms by industry in 2003. There does seem to be some heterogeneity in debt ratios, although it is mild. Consumer-goods firms (drugs, soap, perfumes, tobacco), machinery and business equipment makers, and mining and mineral companies tended to have lower debt ratios (market value–based). Utilities, steel, and automobile companies tended to have higher financial debt ratios. Financial services companies are interesting—they tended to have higher financial debt ratios but relatively lower, broader total indebtedness ratios. (Their high financial debt ratios are

TABLE 22.3 INDEBTEDNESS ASSET RATIOS BY PROFITABILITY IN 2003

Sorted by: Earnings/Sales	FD/(FD+MVE) Mean	FD/(FD+MVE) Median	FD/(FD+MVE) 25–75%	TL/(TL+MVE) Mean	TL/(TL+MVE) Median	TL/(TL+MVE) 25–75%	TL/(TL+BVE) Mean	TL/(TL+BVE) Median	TL/(TL+BVE) 25–75%
1,688 Unprofitable (< 0%)	24.3	10.4	0–42	38.7	31.5	12–63	55.2	54.0	28–83
1,207 Low (< 5%)	26.9	21.9	6–42	44.8	43.9	27–61	56.1	57.1	41–72
977 Medium (< 10%)	20.2	14.5	2–31	36.5	30.7	17–52	52.6	52.6	34–71
582 High (< 15%)	24.6	15.4	2–43	41.6	33.6	14–74	57.2	59.4	33–87
1,189 Huge (> 15%)	27.9	24.3	1–47	50.0	53.0	15–83	62.8	72.7	35–91

Conclusion: The most profitable firms had higher debt ratios. Otherwise, inferences are measure dependent.

(This table uses the same definitions as Table 22.2.)

partly at fault for the liquidity crisis of March 2008, in which Bear Stearns required rescuing.) Note also that there was great variability across firms—the standard deviation was very high. Even within an industry, some firms had very high debt ratios, while others had very low ones. (Of course, these industry definitions are still very broad. It is quite possible that many smaller industries had their own unique debt ratios. But even if we use much finer industry definitions, we would find great heterogeneity.)

➤ Bear Stearns financial distress, Section 18.3B, p. 665

Guessing industry causes.

Where do these patterns come from? Even before we entertain more formal theories, we can speculate. For utilities, high debt ratios are likely driven by government regulations. For financial companies, high leverage is part of the business. For transportation companies, such as airlines, it is partly hard times and partly the fact that airplanes are easy to collateralize, which makes debt easier to obtain. In contrast, biotech companies tend to have low financial debt ratios, perhaps because R&D is difficult to collateralize. Drug development is either hit or miss. In fact, any debt extended to a smaller biotech firm may almost be called equity, because if the drug fails, chances are that creditors will receive nothing—the same as equity holders.

MEASURES AND COMPONENTS FOR SMALL AND LARGE FIRMS IN 2003

With the Compustat database, we can also take a closer look at other relevant ratios and measures of indebtedness. As in the previous section, you should be interested primarily in ballpark figures—details change from year to year and from sample to sample. We rely on the market value–based criteria we used in Table 22.2. We shall compare the averages against the IBM estimate, so that you can intuitively compare magnitudes and judge whether the IBM number was representative.

Small firms had less financial debt.

You have already seen that you can base debt ratios on only financial debt or on total liabilities. How big is financial debt, usually, relative to total liabilities?

Financial debt to total liabilities: In 2003, IBM had $23.632 billion in financial debt, out of total liabilities of $76.593 billion. Thus, just over 30% of its debt was financial. Was IBM representative, at least among larger firms?

TABLE 22.4 INDEBTEDNESS ASSET RATIOS BY INDUSTRY, IN 2003

	FD / (FD+MVE)			TL / (TL+MVE)			TL / (TL+BVE)			
	Mean	Median	SDV	Mean	Median	SDV	Mean	Median	SDV	N
1 Food	27%	23%	23%	24%	19%	19%	24%	21%	21%	122
2 Mining and Minerals	15%	6%	6%	13%	7%	7%	16%	12%	12%	94
3 Oil and Petroleum Products	26%	23%	23%	19%	13%	13%	19%	15%	15%	196
4 Textiles, Apparel	25%	16%	16%	27%	19%	19%	24%	21%	21%	89
5 Consumer Durables	27%	18%	18%	31%	22%	22%	27%	23%	23%	119
6 Chemicals	29%	24%	24%	26%	21%	21%	21%	19%	19%	93
7 Drugs, Soap, Perfumes, Tobacco	11%	5%	5%	11%	8%	8%	22%	18%	18%	221
8 Construction	31%	25%	25%	32%	25%	25%	27%	23%	23%	106
9 Steel Works, etc.	38%	34%	34%	34%	26%	26%	22%	20%	20%	62
10 Fabricated Products	33%	25%	25%	32%	25%	25%	26%	22%	22%	33
11 Machinery and Business Equip.	15%	6%	6%	19%	13%	13%	26%	21%	21%	693
12 Automobiles	29%	21%	21%	33%	28%	28%	29%	26%	26%	65
13 Transportation	35%	30%	30%	29%	22%	22%	25%	22%	22%	169
14 Utilities	47%	47%	47%	29%	25%	25%	17%	15%	15%	133
15 Retail Stores	23%	14%	14%	28%	21%	21%	29%	25%	25%	293
16 Banks, Insurance, Financials	39%	40%	40%	18%	11%	11%	29%	19%	19%	151

(This table uses the same definitions as Table 22.2.) N is the number of firms in each industry. The industry definitions were put together based on Standard Industry Codes (SIC) by Fama and French. The original SIC data came from the Compustat financial database.
Conclusion: The table shows that financial debt ratios are low for mining, drugs, and machinery; and financial debt ratios are high among utilities, financials, and steel. There are no strong industry patterns on total indebtedness measures.

Financial Debt / Total Liabilities	Tiny	Small	Medium	Large	IBM
Median, 2003	24%	21%	41%	38%	31%
25th–75th Percentile Range	0–53%	1–52%	15–63%	21–55%	

This shows that IBM's 30% ratio was relatively small among large companies. More typically, large firms tended to have just under half of their total liabilities in financial debt. In contrast, small firms tended to have relatively more nonfinancial liabilities. (And many small firms tended to have *no* financial liabilities.)

Small firms rely more on trade credit.

If it is not through financial debt, then how did small firms borrow? Did they use more "day-to-day" borrowing than large firms, and, in particular, more trade credit? Yes, they did:

Short-term liabilities to total liabilities: Of IBM's $76.593 billion in total liabilities, $37.9 billion was short term.

Short-Term Liabilities / Total Liabilities	Tiny	Small	Medium	Large	IBM
Median, 2003	77%	64%	37%	37%	49%
25th–75th Percentile Range	49–98%	36–90%	22–59%	23–51%	

IBM sat on the high end among large companies. More typically, large firms had only about one-third of their total liabilities in short-term liabilities. In contrast, small firms tended to have two-thirds of their liabilities in short-term liabilities. Small firms, indeed, seemed to live more precariously than large firms.

Accounts payable to total liabilities: IBM had $8.46 billion in accounts payable.

Payables / Total Liabilities	Tiny	Small	Medium	Large	IBM
Median, 2003	19%	18%	12%	11%	11%
25th–75th Percentile Range	9–34%	7–39%	5–30%	5–30%	

Here, IBM was typical for large firms. In contrast to such large firms, many small firms indeed financed themselves relatively more aggressively through trade credit.

Equity Value Measures

Book values are typically lower than market-values.

I already mentioned at the outset of this chapter that book values of equity tend to be less than market values of equity. So, what is the effect of quoting equity in terms of market or book values? If all firms have similar book-to-market value ratios, then a market value–based debt ratio would always be the same fraction of a book value–based debt ratio, and the indebtedness rank of a company relative to other companies would not depend on whether you quote book-based or market-based ratios. Unfortunately, there are usually systematic differences in book-to-market ratios:

Book value to market value of equity: IBM had a market value of equity of $157.047 billion, and a book value of $27.864 billion.

Book Equity / Market Equity	Tiny	Small	Medium	Large	IBM
Median, 2003	46%	50%	44%	43%	18%
25th–75th Percentile Range	16–91%	28–74%	29–61%	26–62%	

IBM was relatively low on its book-to-market ratio—firms with especially low ratios are sometimes called "growth firms." But book values tended to be below market values for all types of firms. Importantly, there was much variation across firms even within size categories. Thus, it is likely that firms rank differently in terms of indebtedness depending on whether you quote their ratios in terms of book value or market value.

SOLVE NOW!

Q 22.5 Roughly and on average, what were the liabilities ratios of firms—large and small—on various measures?

Q 22.6 Did profitable firms have higher or lower indebtedness ratios than unprofitable firms?

Q 22.7 What industries were characterized by very high debt ratios? Which were characterized by very low debt ratios?

22.2C INTERNATIONAL INDEBTEDNESS RATIOS

Some international evidence. Countries are tough to compare.

We can try to extend our analysis from the United States to other countries. Unfortunately, this is not easy. For example, in South Korea, there are four large companies, the so-called *chaebol* (Samsung, Hyundai, Daewoo, and Lucky Goldstar). There are very few medium-sized companies. In Finland, it is even more extreme: Nokia is the only large global company. Is Nokia then better compared to the single-largest U.S. company or to the top 10% of U.S. companies? (There is no clear answer.) But even in countries with many small- and medium-sized companies, data is tough to come by. And even if data exists, it is not even clear what it means. Debt and liability ratios may not be comparable because international accounting rules are often different from those elsewhere. (For example, German companies record "financial reserves" as liabilities, although these may be more like equity than debt. In many other countries, deferred taxes may never come due and thus may not be booked as liabilities. Of course, M&A activity can also change the book value of equity drastically. And what subsidiaries are consolidated into the main financials in different countries is a science in itself.)

U.S. firms tended to be on the low side in 1991, but not extremely so.

Table 22.5 describes the data in one study of the capital structure of large firms in 1991. Despite the comparability problems, the capital structure picture seemed broadly similar in all these highly developed countries. The Anglo-Saxon countries may have had somewhat lower indebtedness ratios, but the differences were mild. The authors additionally observed that companies in all countries displayed substantial heterogeneity—heterogeneity that was usually as large as the reported medians; and that Germany was the only country in which larger firms tended to have lower indebtedness ratios.

TABLE 22.5 INDEBTEDNESS RATIOS IN OTHER COUNTRIES, MEDIANS IN 1991

		US	UK	Canada	Japan	Germany	France	Italy
Liabilities to Assets	TL/(TL+MVE)	44%	40%	49%	45%	69%	64%	70%
Liabilities to Assets	TL/(TL+BVE)	58%	54%	56%	69%	73%	71%	70%
Fin. Debt to Fin. Claims	FD/(FD+MVE)	28%	19%	35%	29%	23%	41%	46%
Fin. Debt to Fin. Claims	FD/(FD+BVE)	37%	28%	39%	53%	38%	48%	47%

Conclusions: The table shows that the three Anglo-Saxon countries tended to have lower debt ratios than the other four countries.
Source: Rajan and Zingales, *The Journal of Finance*, 1995. Reprinted with permission.

SOLVE NOW!

Q 22.8 In 1991, were U.S. firms more or less indebted than their British counterparts?

22.3 MECHANISMS VERSUS CAUSES

What determines the ways by which capital structure can change? Layers of causality.

Our next question is how the debt/equity ratios of publicly traded companies have evolved over time. First, a short lesson in metaphysics. You can examine phenomena at different layers of causality—you can always drill deeper and deeper. Eventually, if you dig deep enough, you will find yourself in the world of philosophy and theology. For example, say you want to know what makes a car fast. The first layer of causality may be that its speed is due to lots of power, low weight, and low wind resistance. But *why* is there a lot of power? This question brings you to a deeper layer of causality, with questions such as how many cylinder and intake valves your engine has. You can then drill down into yet another layer of causality. Why is this particular number of cylinders/valves more powerful? Yet another deeper layer of causality emerges with questions such as why and how gasoline combusts. If you continue this long enough, you end up with questions about why nature's physical constants are the way they are—it can even become a question of theology. Moreover, it is often the case that when you drill deeper, you become less and less able to explain the specific phenomenon, here the speed of the car (because you must necessarily work with simplifying models). All of this diversion applies just as much to corporate capital structure choice as it does to cars.

Two layers of causality: mechanisms and forces.

We are going to explore the dynamics of debt/equity ratio changes on two levels:

➤ Capitalization and capital structure changes, Table 21.1, p. 789

1. We can call our first, somewhat shallow layer the "mechanistic layer": How important are the various mechanisms through which debt/equity ratios can evolve? These mechanisms are basically the cells you have already seen in Table 21.1, such as debt and equity issuing and repurchasing.
2. The second, deeper layer is more causal and explores the variables, characteristics, and economic forces that induce firms and financial markets to engage these mechanisms in the first place. As in our car example, you cannot expect these forces to work as well in explaining capital structure choice as the mechanisms.

There is one factor that could be classified either in the first or second level—the role of stock value changes. You can think of value changes either as a mechanism that shifts capital structure around or as an economic force that lies partly inside and partly outside the domain of the mechanisms that managers can use to change capital structure.

22.3A MECHANISMS: HOW DOES CAPITAL STRUCTURE CHANGE COME ABOUT?

Stock returns and long-term debt issuing are the most important factors changing debt/equity ratios.

Let's begin with the big-picture mechanisms. In the real world, what is the relative importance of the various mechanisms that you learned about in the previous chapter? That is, has the typical company's debt/equity ratio been driven more by the firm's value or by the CFO's net issuing activities (which include issuing, repurchasing, and

TABLE 22.6 RELATIVE IMPORTANCE OF FACTORS DETERMINING CAPITAL STRUCTURE CHANGES OVER 5 YEARS

All Net Issuing (with Dividend Activity)			69%
All Net Issuing (without Dividend Activity)			66%
All Net Debt Issuing Activity		40%	
Convertible Debt Only	4%		
Short-Term Debt Only	14%		
Long-Term Debt Only	32%		
All Net Equity Issuing Activity		16%	
Direct Effect of Stock Returns on Existing Capital Structure			40%

These values measure how much of the change in capital structure from today to 5 years from now that you could explain if you had perfect foreknowledge of each component. Net issuing means issues net of retirements. The samples were all publicly traded U.S. stocks from 1964 to 2003. (The numbers need not add up to 100%, because one component can have information about the other components.) The equity is measured by its market value.
Source: Welch, 2004.

dividends)? This question can be phrased as, "If you knew in advance how much every firm would issue over the next x years, net of all repurchases, what fraction of the change in capital structure could you explain?" Table 22.6 answers this question for 5-year horizons.

NET DEBT AND EQUITY ISSUING ACTIVITY

The first row of Table 22.6 shows that CFOs were by no means inactive in the capital markets. If you had known perfectly how firms had issued and retired debt and equity and paid in and paid out funds, you could have explained 69% of firms' total capital structure changes over a 5-year horizon. The remaining 31% were necessarily corporate value changes that were not directly influenced by managerial issuing and repurchasing. Omitting dividends dropped the explanatory power from 69% to 66%, so dividends could explain only a meager 3% of capital structure changes—as far as comparative debt/equity ratio dynamics in publicly traded corporations are concerned, dividends were a sideshow.

Net debt issuing was important.

Net debt issuing: The third row in Table 22.6 tells you that 40% of all capital structure changes over 5 years were due to firms' net debt issuing activity. The next three rows tell you that long-term debt alone could account for 32% of changes in debt/equity ratios, that short-term debt was somewhat less important, and that convertible debt was fairly unimportant. It would be interesting to break these debt issuing activities into their components—issuing and repurchasing—and to break the repurchasing in turn into sinking fund payments, interest payments, and principal repayments, so that we could understand better what part of the mechanism really drives capital structure. Remarkably, despite the obvious importance of debt issuing activity, no one has yet worked out this decomposition.

Net equity issuing was not even half as important as net debt issuing.

Net equity issuing: The seventh row in Table 22.6 shows that net equity issuing could explain about 16% of changes in firms' debt/equity ratios, and therefore was less

TABLE 22.7 TYPICAL EQUITY SHARE ACTIVITY AMONG S&P 100 STOCKS, 1999–2001

Total Seasoned Equity Offering Activity	+ 3.77%
M&A Related	3.68%
Not M&A Related	0.09%
Executive Compensation	+ 1.05%
Convertible Debt	+ 0.14%
Warrant Exercise	+ 0.05%
Share Repurchases	− 1.44%
= Changes in Equity Outstanding	+ 3.57%

Categories describe equity issued in conjunction with an activity. Equity share activity is measured per annum and as a fraction of total assets. For scale, changes in total liabilities were about 10.07% of assets, and changes in retained earnings were about 1.37% of assets.
Source: From Eugene F. Fama and Kenneth R. French, "Finance Decisions: Who Issues Stock?" Journal of Financial Economics, Volume 76, Issue 3, June 2005, Pages 549–582. Reprinted with permission of the authors.

important than net debt issuing as a determinant of capital structure. Nevertheless, equity issues are more glamorous, so economists have studied them a lot more.

SEOs outside M&A were rare. Executive compensation and share repurchases were important.

Table 22.7 decomposes equity issuing (this time, not net of equity repurchasing) into its components, though only for the very large S&P 100 firms. (Unfortunately, there is no equivalent information for smaller firms.) The table dispels the popular myth that most shares occur through plain seasoned equity offerings (SEOs). Instead, from 1999 to 2001, equity shares appeared most commonly through equity offerings in connection with corporate acquisitions. (We cannot conclude that firms' debt/equity ratios declined during acquisitions. We also know that firms commonly issue not only equity but also debt to finance acquisitions and that leverage ratios are nonlinear, too. Outside an acquisition, seasoned equity offerings were exceedingly rare. We also saw these patterns in IBM's case in Section 15.4—IBM did not issue equity, repurchased some shares into its treasury, and then used equity shares from its treasury in its acquisition of PwCC Partners and in its funding of employee stock option plans.

SEOs are rare in smaller firms, too.

Moreover, evidence from other papers similarly suggests that, even including M&A activity, public equity offerings are rare. The 10,000 or so firms trading on the NYSE and NASDAQ conducted only about 12,000 equity offerings from 1990 to 2000, of which about half were initial public offerings and about half were seasoned equity offerings. With only 300 SEOs in an average year, you can work out that a typical publicly traded firm would have issued equity only about once every 20 years.

FIRM VALUE CHANGES AND STOCK RETURNS

Value changes are proxied by stock returns.

➤ Issuing mechanisms, Section 21.1B, p. 788

The final row in Table 22.6 shows the direct effect of stock returns on capital structure. Recall that this is the change in the debt/equity ratio that a company experiences when it increases or decreases in value—a $200 million firm with $100 million in debt and $100 million in equity, which doubles in value from $200 million to $400 million, experiences a drop in its debt/equity ratio from 1:1 to 1:3. As mentioned earlier, corporate stock returns can be viewed both as a mechanism (itself influenced by deeper forces) and as an external force that tugs on firms' debt/equity ratios.

Value changes can account for a little less than half of capital structure changes.

Table 22.6 shows that if you had known perfectly how stock returns would turn out over the next 5 years, you could have explained 40% of firms' total capital structure changes. (Note how all issuing was able to explain 69%, so a good part of variation must have been explainable by either issuing activity or stock returns—suggesting that the two are linked.) The fact that stock returns are a major factor should not come as a big surprise to you. If you recall our IBM example from Section 15.4, it was changes in the stock price that first reduced IBM's equity value by one-third from 2001 to 2002 and was the primary cause of its debt/equity ratio's increase from 0.31 to 0.55.

➤ IBM capital structure, Section 15.4, p. 554

Apparently, managers did not fully rebalance.

Importantly, you can think of these stock returns as the "relevant" changes that were not undone by managers. If firms had undone the value changes and rebalanced through issuing equity after negative stock returns and repurchasing after positive stock returns, then knowing the stock returns would not have helped in explaining changes in capital structure. Our empirical evidence therefore suggests that even over a 5-year horizon, firms do not fully rebalance their capital structures.

Market timing is probably only a secondary concern.

You may wonder whether some part of this 40% could also have been due to managers trying to "time" the market (issuing more equity as the stock price went up). However, other empirical evidence suggests that, even if present, market timing is likely to be only a small factor. The reason is that, in response to stock price increases, firms issue not only equity but also debt, and they tend to pay out more in dividends. Therefore, the timing effect on net debt/equity ratios is fairly modest. The 40% that we see is almost entirely the direct value effect of stock returns on debt/equity ratios.

In perspective: Observed capital structure today is strongly related to past corporate performance.

Explaining 40% of something that is as variable and firm-specific (as corporate debt/equity ratio changes are) is quite robust—even though our explanatory variable is conceptually on a fairly shallow level of causality. Consequently, if you want to know why some firms have high debt/equity ratios today and why other firms have low ones, a part of your first explanation has to be not just that the former issued a lot of debt and the latter issued a lot of equity, but that the former had experienced negative stock returns and the latter had experienced positive stock returns.

Firm size (scale) is also not deliberate.

Managers also typically do not pay out large value gains or raise more funds in response to large value losses. Therefore, like debt/equity ratios, firm scale has a large external component too—firms that are large today may not be large primarily because they raised a lot of funds, but rather because they appreciated in value. In sum, few firms seem to deliberately choose their target scale and target debt/equity ratios, and then act to retain these targets.

A life cycle? Zero debt for most old large firms? Maybe not.

This relationship between stock returns and capital structure would suggest a natural debt/equity life cycle for firms. Firms could start out being highly levered—the owner must borrow to finance the firm. Eventually, as the firm survives and accumulates equity, its scale should increase and its liabilities and debt ratio should decline. Can we see this in the data? Do large firms have smaller debt ratios? You have already seen relevant evidence in Section 22.2B:

➤ Indebtedness ratios, Table 22.2, p. 831

1. Many of the nonfinancial giant companies indeed seem to have very low debt ratios, often in the single digits. This is supportive.
2. Depending on the precise measure of debt ratio, large firms have debt/equity ratios around 40%. This is nothing even close to zero. This is not supportive.

Most importantly, larger publicly traded firms today tend to have higher debt ratios. Thus, the answer as to whether large firms have smaller debt ratios is no. But this is not the last word. An important data factor is "survivorship bias"—that is, the average publicly traded firm in the United States lasted for only about 5 years before it went bankrupt, was bought by another company, or merged into an entirely new entity. This makes it difficult to track the long-run evolution of firms' capital structures. The firms you see today are not the firms you would have wanted to follow over the years. In sum, the relative importance of the mechanisms that have created the diversity of firms' capital structures today is still not fully understood.

➤ Survivorship bias, Section 11.5B, p. 366

DIGGING DEEPER

Stock returns are good proxies for the value changes we discussed in Section 21.2D. Theoretically, however, stock returns could miss some of the change in the underlying asset values, if these changes benefited or hurt debt holders by making debt repayment more or less likely. However, unless the firm is in—or close to—financial distress, almost all of a firm's own value change goes to equity owners. In the extreme, risk-free debt would not be affected *at all* by firm value changes, and stock returns *would be exactly equivalent to* the value change. In any case, we do not mean that debt value changes cannot occur, just that they tend to be so much smaller that our proxy of stock returns will capture most of how firms differ from one another in terms of value changes at any given point in time. Besides, we do not have good market value data for corporate debt, so we could not really measure the whole change in value even if we wanted to.

SOLVE NOW!

Q 22.9 What are the most important financial mechanisms influencing capital structure changes over 5-year horizons?

Q 22.10 Is dividend activity a major factor in determining capital structure changes in U.S. firms—explaining why some firms have high debt ratios and other firms have low debt ratios?

Q 22.11 Is long-term net debt issuing a major factor in determining the capital structure changes of U.S. firms—explaining why some firms are increasing their debt ratios and other firms are lowering their debt ratios?

Q 22.12 How important is seasoned equity issuing activity that does not occur in the context of M&A activity, at least for S&P 100 firms?

Q 22.13 If many equity shares appear in the context of M&A activity, does this imply that the firm's debt/equity ratio is likely to go down?

22.4 WHAT ARE THE UNDERLYING RATIONALES FOR CAPITAL STRUCTURE CHANGES?

What forces determine how managers operate their mechanisms?

You know how important the mechanisms that change debt/equity ratios are, but you do not yet know *why* firms use them. You also know that if you had a choice, you would want to learn first what drives net debt issuing (especially long-term debt), because it seems most important for capital structure changes, then what drives net equity issuing and net short-term debt issuing, and only finally what drives convertible debt issuing and dividends—in that order. You can usefully think of these mechanisms as "channels" through which other forces can operate—forces that are one layer deeper in terms of causality. You can now ask the main question for each of the six channels:

1. What makes firms change their nonfinancial liabilities?
2. What makes firms issue debt?
3. What makes firms retire debt?
4. What makes firms issue equity?
5. What makes firms retire equity (or pay dividends)?
6. What makes firms experience good/bad corporate value performance? (As noted earlier, you might classify value changes as deeper than a managerial mechanism, though.)

Again, these questions are getting at the deeper issue of *why* capital structure is what it is. Thus, you cannot expect them to work as well as the above mechanisms in terms of explaining capital structure. But the deeper reasons are also more interesting than the mechanics discussed earlier. (No pain, no gain.)

The debt ratio outcomes are based on all forces and mechanisms.

If a variable strongly influences one channel, this influence will likely—but not necessarily—percolate into an influence on the overall capital structure. For example, if solar flares were to make firms issue debt, then we would also expect solar flares to increase firms' debt/equity ratios. However, this is not a necessary outcome. If solar flares had a strong positive influence on debt/equity ratios through one channel and a strong negative influence through another, then solar flares could end up having no influence on overall capital structure. Moreover, you learned earlier that it is possible for a variable to explain a lot of equity issuing, yet have no influence on typical debt/equity ratios. If the firms that are subject to this variable are already 100% financed by equity, the firm will still remain all-equity. The opposite can also be the case. Some variable could have only a weak influence through every single channel and we would be tempted to discard it as too weak, but if it worked for all six channels, it could end up having a strong influence on the firms' overall debt/equity ratios.

22.4A A COMPREHENSIVE EMPIRICAL STUDY

The best of what we know.

A recent large-scale empirical study by Hovakimian, Opler, and Titman (2001)—let's call them HOT—explores how different variables exert influences on four of the above channels over 1-year horizons. The authors document that there are a multitude of variables that seem to have played statistically significant roles—*but all of these variables together could explain only a few percentage points of the total variation in capital structures across firms*. For the most part, there are no smoking guns. We can explain only a small fraction of firm behavior, that is, of what is driving their corporate financing choices.

The big findings.

The study did not look at the first channel (nonfinancial liabilities) or the last channel (stock returns), but it did look at the others:

Debt issuing: asset performance and industry benchmarks.

The debt issuing channel: For the second channel, HOT found that firms issued more *long-term* debt if they had high market/book ratios, if they had good recent stock market performance, and if they had much of their existing debt coming due soon.

Firms issued more *short-term* debt if they had poor recent asset performance and if they had less short-term debt than their industry peers. In both cases, though, the relationship was very weak: These causes could explain only 2% to 3% of its cross-sectional variation (called R^2)—a miniscule proportion. In sum, it is still largely a mystery why firms issued debt.

Debt retirement: industry benchmarks and recent performance.

The debt retirement channel: For the third channel (debt retirement), HOT found that firms reduced their debt if they were above their industry peers in terms of their debt ratios and if they had good recent stock market, but bad accounting, performance. Interestingly, these actions were thus the opposite of what it would have taken to rebalance to the previous debt/equity ratio. How important were these causes? Here we get a much better 12% in explanatory power (R^2)—not good, but better.

Equity issuing and repurchasing: recent performance.

The equity issuing and retiring channels: The fourth and fifth channels are where most of the academic research has focused. There are three good reasons for this: First, we have robust theories here, specifically the pecking order theory, which seems to be reasonably consistent with some of the evidence. Second, the announcement of market-related equity issuing and dividend activity plays a prominent role in the financial press. And third, we have a lot of publicly available data here. Nevertheless, dozens of earlier studies have informed us that equity issuing and retiring activity also remain a mystery.

HOT's evidence seems to suggest that firms first and foremost did not like to issue equity—consistent with a pecking order. When firms did announce that they would issue equity, it was on average greeted with a negative return on its outstanding stock. (This is the subject of the web chapter.) On balance, firms tended to issue equity (rather than debt) if they had worse accounting performances and better stock market performances. (Although firms also tended to issue debt in response to positive stock returns, their tendencies to issue equity were stronger—possibly evidence that managers tried to "time" the stock market.) Especially firms with higher tax obligations preferred issuing debt over equity.

www.prenhall.com/welch

Altogether, the authors could explain 3% of the variation in firms' equity repurchasing activity and 15% of firms' equity issuing activity.

The most important factors explaining capital structure choice, IMHO.

Putting this (and other) evidence together, here is my overall impression of what factors play important roles in influencing capital structure outcomes, roughly in order of their importance:

Direct stock performance influence: If you classify stock returns as a cause rather than a mechanism, then it is by far the most important variable in nonfinancial firms. Because firms do not counteract stock returns, firms with good stock price performances tend to end up with lower debt ratios, while firms with poor stock price performances tend to end up with higher debt ratios. (You may want to dig deeper and ask what causes stock performance, but this would again be a difficult predictive exercise.)

➤ Pecking order, Section 21.2A, p. 792

Equity issuance avoidance: Firms seem to want to avoid issuing equity. A seasoned equity offering is a rarity, and even more so outside of an M&A transaction. Given that the costs of an equity issue are high (including the often negative market reaction), this is not surprising behavior.

Peer similarity: Firms not only seem to end up with capital structures similar to those of their industry peers due to their commonality in industry stock returns, but they also seem to *like* being similar, often issuing or retiring debt or equity to come closer to their peers. Some industries (R&D heavy with few tangible assets) have avoided debt financing altogether. (You may want to ask what determines peers' ratios, and why firms want to be similar to their peers, but this is an even deeper level of causality—one that is still mostly beyond our current knowledge.)

Corporate income taxes: Firms with high corporate income tax rates tend to actively issue debt and retire equity, that is, increase their debt ratios.

Nevertheless, many high-tax firms have *low* debt ratios. How can this be? The reason is that good performance translates not only into high profits and therefore high corporate taxes, but also into positive stock price performance. The latter directly reduces the firm's debt ratio. Although the end effect can be complex, on average, net issuing activity is usually not enough to undo the direct stock return effect.

Accounting performance: Firms prefer net debt issuing over net equity issuing if they have better accounting profitability and more tangible assets (which can be easily collateralized). But as with taxes, good accounting profitability correlates strongly with higher stock prices, which in turn correlates strongly with *lower* debt ratios.

M&A activity: Much debt and much equity are issued in connection with M&A activity, although proportionally more debt is issued than equity. M&A activity may be the most important reason why most well-performing nonfinancial firms do not end up with practically zero debt. However, because firms usually start acquiring firms after good stock price performances, the overall capital structure effect can be complex. Good operating performance can lower the debt ratio through the value increase but then increase the debt ratio through acquisitions.

Financial distress: Firms that are in dire straits have no choice but to retire some debt and issue equity. This seems to be an unusually solid net issuing influence, but only for firms close to the verge of bankruptcy.

Credit ratings: To access the commercial paper market, firms need to have a reasonable credit rating. To maintain it, many firms tend to borrow less, especially if they are close to the margin where more or less debt could make a big difference (i.e., if they have an AA− or A+ rating, or a BBB rating).

➤ Credit ratings, Section 6.2D, p. 148

Active market timing: Firms that experience stock price increases tend to issue more securities—through both debt and equity, so the capital structure consequence is not too strong. Moreover, such firms also tend to pay out more in dividends, so even the net equity issuing effect is not yet clear. Nevertheless, when surveyed, CFOs claim that they do watch their stock market value, and respond to it—perhaps even try to time it. In any case, active market timing is the newest and thus the most interesting factor to explore—as more research comes forth, we may learn that we underestimated or overestimated its importance.

➤ Market timing, Section 21.2D, p. 796

Uncertainty: Firms with more volatile underlying assets tend to have less debt in their capital structures.

I also believe that managers in many old, large, publicly traded companies, in which corporate governance has broken down, have equity in their capital structures even if this is not optimal for the firm—simply because managers like equity more than debt. However, it is difficult to measure whether these firms have a lot of equity because corporate governance has broken down, or whether corporate governance has broken down because there is a lot of equity.

SOLVE NOW!

Q 22.14 How good is our knowledge about what deeper determinants create the empirically observed capital structure patterns?

Q 22.15 Firms with large tax obligations are known to be more inclined to issue debt and retire equity. Does this mean that firms with high tax obligations usually have high debt ratios?

Q 22.16 What deeper characteristics help explain corporate debt/equity ratios?

22.4B THEORY VERSUS EMPIRICS

We learn from what we can measure.

The above variables are interesting, but they are not exactly what the theories were asking for. For example, an interest coverage ratio is often used as a proxy to measure the proximity to financial distress—but it is not exactly the same financial distress. Some firms have low interest payments relative to earnings and are in distress; other firms have high interest payments relative to earnings and are financially sound. Yet ultimately, we study such specific variables only because they are relatively easy to measure empirically. We would have preferred direct measures of our theories of capital structure, but such measures are usually not as easily available. Most of the time, our variables are a compromise between empirical availability and theoretical construct, and we then try to interpret our empirical findings through the lenses of our theories. From our proxies, we can draw two basic conclusions about the theories: First, it appears that agency concerns, pecking order concerns, financial distress (in very few companies), and corporate taxes all matter in some ways, at least a little. Second, there are some other variables that matter, for which the reason is still mysterious. For example, why do firms not counteract market influences very strongly, and why do they seem to "like" capital structures similar to those of their industry peers? Future research will tell us the answers.

Why do our variables explain so little?

You now know that we do not yet fully understand the factors that are driving firms to actively change their capital structures. It seems to be a complex process, possibly with a lot of idiosyncratic behavior. Our variables are statistically significant, but they leave much to be explained. You can read this situation in a number of ways:

1. Our variables may not matter much, because they are poor proxies for our theoretical constructs (e.g., for tax savings or bankruptcy costs). With more research, we may eventually find better proxies that will improve our understanding of capital structure.
2. There are other theories and factors not yet understood that may be more important than those that we have now.

3. Our variables may not matter much, because capital structure choice is practically irrelevant. Whatever managers may be acting on—whether based on, say, book-market ratios or their horoscopes—may have only minimal value consequences. You could think of this as an empirical validation of Modigliani-Miller.
4. Managers may just act poorly and erratically (or in their own self-interests), and there is nothing outsiders can do to correct it.

The lack of explanatory power may also reflect a little of each of the above reasons. Right now, capital structure is an especially fertile area for behavioral finance, because idiosyncratic managerial behavior seems important and because there is no easy way for financial markets to arbitrage misbehavior. Empirical capital structure remains an exciting field of research. We are definitely making progress in learning *how* managers behave, but we also have a long way to go.

➤ Behavioral finance, Section 18.7, p. 685

SOLVE NOW!

Q 22.17 Why do our theories of capital structure explain relatively little of firms' capital structures?

22.4C MANAGERIAL LESSONS

What can practical executives learn from the empirical evidence?

What can CFOs learn from the empirical evidence? A lot! First, the evidence that (partly) external stock returns have a long-lasting effect on capital structure is solid. What can you conclude from this?

- ***Is** the fact that managers do not rebalance their sizes and their debt/equity ratios evidence that they make bad decisions?* Absolutely not. It might well be that the optimal firm size increases and the optimal debt/equity ratio decreases as the firm's underlying business becomes more valuable. In this case, managers should be happy with their capital structures. Or it might be that such rearrangements are fairly expensive, relative to the costs. In this case, managers may be unhappy with their capital structures, but it would not be profitable for the firm to fix it.
- ***Could** the fact that managers do not rebalance their sizes and their debt/equity ratios be evidence that managers make bad decisions?* Yes, it could be—but it does not need to be. In some firms, the evidence that managers are miscapitalized is fairly suggestive. In other firms, we are not so sure. There is lively academic controversy surrounding this question.
- *Does this mean that you should not worry about capital structure or appropriate corporate scale?* Absolutely not. Even if many other managers are passive and/or do not do the right thing, you still can! Your managerial choices should remain intelligent and dynamic.
- *Does this mean that you cannot rely on the capital structures of other companies to judge what the capital structure of your own firm should be?* Probably yes. Their capital structures are less indicative of deliberate designs than they are of their historical performances.

SOLVE NOW!

Q 22.18 If firms fail to readjust their capital structure, does this mean that learning about capital structure theories is a waste of your time?

22.5 SURVEY EVIDENCE FROM CFOs

Let's ask the CFOs.

There is another way to approach the question of how managers choose capital structures—just ask them. Of course, we should not blindly believe that just because CFOs publicly proclaim a motive that it really *is* their motive. Graham and Harvey (2001) surveyed 392 CFOs to find out what they proclaim makes them issue equity or debt. Graham and Harvey found not only interesting, but also some rather puzzling, results.

CFOs recognize taxes and financial distress costs.

➤ Summary of capital structure effects, Table 18.6, p. 688

First, the good news: CFOs do care about the tax benefits of corporate debt, at least moderately. But they seem more concerned about their credit ratings. We know that credit ratings are closely related to interest coverage ratios (interest payments divided by earnings) and are good proxies for possible financial distress costs. Managers seem cognizant of the basic trade-off between taxes and financial distress.

CFOs do not recognize our other theoretical suggestions. They seem to like financial flexibility (more money ⇒ more free cash flow!) and dislike dilution.

Now for the bad news, at least from the perspective of some of our theories:

1. Many of our other capital structure arguments seem unimportant to managers, from personal income taxes borne by their shareholders, to expropriation concerns by their creditors, to strategic product market factor considerations, to deliberate control of free cash flow incentives, to intentional signaling of good or bad news (inside information), to transaction cost considerations.

   On the one hand, this may not be as bad as it appears. Managers may still care about these considerations, because their cost of capital itself reflects these considerations. (For example, if a firm's investors face higher tax consequences, it increases the firm's cost of capital, and we know that managers do care about their costs of capital.) On the other hand, if a firm does not need to raise money, managers may not compute the correct hurdle rates for their projects. If they do not take these factors into consideration when estimating the cost of capital that the market would be charging, they could set too high or too low of a project hurdle rate.
2. Managers like "financial flexibility," which means that they like having cash around and having untapped debt capacity for possible future activities. Liking this kind of flexibility makes perfect sense from the manager's perspective—but it also hints that free cash flow is a real problem. Managers seem to like this "flexibility" primarily in order to take over other companies—a move that is often not value enhancing for their shareholders. With almost no chance of bankruptcy in many large companies, it is unlikely that fear of a cash crunch is the driving concern behind the desire for flexibility.
3. Managers worry about lower earnings per share (called **earnings dilution**) if they issue more equity. This makes little sense in itself, because the newly raised funds would presumably also produce earnings.

4. Even managers who claim to target a debt ratio tend not to retire equity if their equity has recently increased in value, and tend not to issue more equity if their equity has recently fallen. This makes little sense because this is exactly what is required in order to target a debt ratio.
5. Managers believe that they can time the financial markets.
   - About two-thirds of managers feel that the stock market undervalues their firm—a fact that restrains many from issuing equity. When their stock market values have recently increased, then managers feel that they have a "window of opportunity" for equity issues. In other words, they believe that they can forecast their stock prices, and the stock market's usual pessimism will be appropriately corrected in due course.
   - Even more remarkable, CFOs believe that they can time overall market interest rates: They issue more debt when interest rates fall or have fallen.

   Amazingly, although it seems almost absurd to believe that they have this ability, there is some new and actively debated empirical evidence that managers have indeed collectively shown some ability to time the market. To explain such corporate issuing activity *and its success*, it appears that we have to look more toward the field of behavioral finance.

The survey on payout policy.

➤ Brav et al. 2004 dividend survey, Section 19.5, p. 725

You already read about another survey in Section 19.5. CFOs generally see the question of dividends versus repurchases as one of desirable flexibility—dividends being steady, share repurchases being paid "as available." Their other answers mirror those in the Graham and Harvey survey. Here, too, managers pretty much considered personal income taxes on dividends to be fairly irrelevant both to themselves and to the preferences of their shareholders. They also believed that dividends tended to attract more individual retail shareholders than large institutional tax-exempt investors. If the CFOs are correct, it is investors who are acting irrationally. Once again, this seems like a fruitful area of future research for behavioral finance.

SOLVE NOW!

Q 22.19 Managers frequently state that they like sound finances with plenty of financial flexibility. Is financial flexibility also always good for shareholders?

SUMMARY

What we know.

Before the usual point-by-point summary, let me reemphasize that it is important that you keep the empirical evidence in proper perspective. We *do* know that our theories can explain at least some of the behavior of corporations. We should not dismiss them as determinants of observed capital structure. There is a good chance that further refining of our theories and proxies will explain quite a bit more about how firms behave. We also *do* know that we *do not* know why our theories explain relatively little about the differences in behavior across companies. There is a good chance that there are other systematic factors that we do not yet fully understand (probably in the domain of behavioral finance). There is also a good chance that much corporate behavior is just erratic and will never be explained. We should keep an open mind.

Why torture you in this chapter with something that we do not fully understand? The reason is that capital structure is an important area, and you must be aware of what we do not yet know! As a manager, you will meet many investment bankers mustering arguments about what other firms have been doing, and offering advice as to what you should do. As an investment banker, you should know not only what factors influence firms' capital structures but also how important or unimportant individual factors are—and how you can measure them to find new potential clients. As a policy maker, you should know how authoritative the capital structure outcomes and choices of firms really are.

It is important that you are aware of what you do not know.

But perhaps most importantly, the empirical evidence does not suggest that our theories are worthless. For example, does our empirical evidence mean that just because other firms do not exploit the corporate income tax advantage of debt that you should ignore it, too? Absolutely not! You can still think about how important a corporate income tax advantage is to *your* firm, and what this means for *your* optimal capital structure. Perhaps more importantly, if many firms are ignoring the factors that they should pay attention to, then over time some will end up with very poor capital structures. In this case, you can think about how you can come in and change these existing firms to increase their values. You can effect change from many different directions: You can work in the firm itself and argue for a capital structure change; you can become an investment banker and advise clients on better capital structures; or you can even buy some companies. Maybe you will start the next wave of leveraged buyouts, which usually create much value by increasing the target's leverage.

The empirical evidence is not about the normative implications of the theories—in fact, it may help you to determine where you can make money.

➤ Takeover activity waves, Section 23.1, p. 854

➤ LBO's, Section 23.3A, p. 879

Back to the point-by-point summary. In this chapter, we first discussed how to measure leverage.

- Indebtedness ratios can be measured in many different ways. The most common leverage ratios are total leverage (liabilities-to-assets) and financial leverage (debt-to-capital). It often matters greatly whether equity is measured in book value or equity value. An altogether different flow-based way of measuring leverage is the interest coverage ratio.
- The financial leverage ratio is commonly used to estimate the marginal cost of capital via the WACC formula.

We then examined a database of publicly traded firms in 2003 and surveyed some conclusions from the academic literature. The following patterns stand out:

- Industry matters. Many financial firms have very high debt ratios. Many pharmaceutical and computer companies have very low debt ratios.
- Distressed firms and firms that have recently acquired other firms often have high debt ratios.
- Large firms not in the preceding two categories can have very low debt ratios—as low as the single digits. Nevertheless, on average, large firms tend to have higher debt ratios.

- Typical financial debt ratios (divided by financial capital, market value–based) are around 10–15% for small firms and 25–35% for large firms.
- Typical liability ratios (divided by assets) are around 30% for small firms and 50% for large firms if assets are quoted in terms of market value.
- Typical liability ratios (divided by assets) are around 50% for small firms and 70% for large firms if assets are quoted in terms of book value.
- There is wide heterogeneity in how individual firms are financed.
- Large firms tend to have relatively more of their total liabilities in financial obligations (45%) than small firms (20–25%).
- Large firms tend to have relatively less of their total debt in short-term obligations (35–40%) than small firms (60–70%). Small firms rely disproportionally more on trade credit (20% versus 10%).
- Book-based debt-asset ratios are often two or three times as high as market-based debt-asset ratios. (The reason is that book values of equity are on average less than half the market values of equity.)
- We can explore both the mechanisms of capital structure change and the underlying forces (causes). These forces can work through multiple mechanisms.
- Over a 5-year horizon, the two most important mechanisms affecting capital structure are stock returns and net debt issuing activity. Both can explain about 40% of the changes in debt/equity ratios.
- Long-term debt can explain about 30% of the changes in debt/equity ratios, short-term debt and equity issuing can both explain about 15%, and both convertible debt and payout policy can explain less than 5%.
- Among the S&P 100 firms, seasoned equity offerings are rare, and they appear almost always in the context of acquisitions. (Executive compensation is remarkably high, and about as important as share repurchasing activity.)
- We know a number of statistically significant forces (potential causes), but they can explain only a very small percentage of capital structure dynamics. Among the more important influences are these:
  - Stock returns
  - A reluctance to issue equity
  - A desire to imitate industry peers
  - Corporate income taxes
  - Accounting performance, such as profitability
  - M&A activity
  - Financial distress
  - Credit ratings
  - Market timing
  - Uncertainty

  In addition, executives of large, old, publicly traded corporations probably like equity even if it is not value enhancing.
- In surveys, CFOs claim to be very concerned about their credit ratings and financial flexibility. Together with often largely untapped debt capacity, these findings can be

evidence of significant free cash flow problems. CFOs also claim not to care about taxes borne by their investors or many other factors suggested by the theories, but they do believe that they can "time" the market.

- Even if firms do not seem to act according to the theories, the capital structure theories still offer good guidance about how you can add value by doing things differently.

KEY TERMS

earnings dilution, 846 enterprise value, 824 financial capital, 823

SOLVE NOW! SOLUTIONS

Q 22.1 IBM's *market* value of assets in 2004 was $79,315 + $155,459 = $234,774. This means that its book liabilities-to-assets ratio was $79,315/$111,003 ≈ 71%; its market liabilities-to-assets ratio was $79,315/$234,774 ≈ 34%. The former is higher than the latter, because IBM's market value was more than twice its book value.

Q 22.2 You must use the information from Q 22.1. First note that the book value of equity is the difference between total assets and total liablities, that is, BVE = $111,003 − $79,315 = $31,688. Financial capital and financial debt add together to arrive at $31,688 + $22,927 = $54,615 in book value. The market value of equity was given in Q 22.1 as $155,459, so the financial capital is $155,459 + $22,927 = $178,386 in market value. This means that its book financial-debt-to-capital was $22,927/$54,615 ≈ 42%; its market financial-debt-to-capital was $22,927/$178,386 ≈ 13%.

Q 22.3 Yes, virtually all firms are partly financed by at least some nonfinancial liabilities, too. However, the nonfinancial liabilities may not allow arbitrary use on the margin. Thus, the financial debt may be the marginal method to finance projects. Therefore, we usually do not consider nonfinancial liabilities when we compute the WACC.

Q 22.4 A drawback to using an interest coverage ratio is that the operating profit of a firm can vary greatly from one year to the next. The interest coverage ratio therefore moves around a lot. In some years, it may even be negative. This can render the coverage ratio meaningless. The interest coverage ratio also does not take required principal repayments into account. Finally, it does not reflect the firm's nonfinancial liabilities. This is why the interest coverage ratio—like other ratios—should not be used as an exclusive measure.

Q 22.5 Measured in market values, small firms had median financial debt ratios of about 10–15%; large firms of about 25–35%. Small firms had median total liability ratios of about 30%; large firms of about 50%. Book values tended to be another 15–20% higher.

Q 22.6 Profitable firms tended to have higher indebtedness ratios.

Q 22.7 High debt ratios: Utilities and banks had high financial debt ratios, though not necessarily high broader total indebtedness measures. Steel and automobiles are more indebted on broader measures. Low debt ratios: Mining, drugs, and machines had low financial debt ratios. Mining and oil had low broader indebtedness ratios.

Q 22.8 In 1991, U.S. firms were slightly more indebted than their British counterparts.

Q 22.9 Over 5-year horizons, the most important financial mechanisms were (a) debt net issuing and (b) the direct influence of stock returns. Both accounted for about 40% of the variation in debt/equity ratios. Beyond this, (c) long-term debt net issuing accounted for about 30%, and short-term debt and equity net issuing accounted for about 15%.

Q 22.10 No, dividend activity is typically fairly unimportant from a larger capital structure perspective. Table 22.6 suggests that dividends explain only about 69% − 66% = 3% of capital structure changes.

Q 22.11 Yes, long-term debt net issuing activity is important. It can explain over 30% of the variation in 5-year changes.

Q 22.12 On average, seasoned equity issuing activity outside M&A is trivial.

Q 22.13 No. For example, in the context of M&A activity, although it is correct that many equity shares appear, generally even more debt offerings appear. This can increase or decrease the debt ratio.

Q 22.14 Our knowledge about the deeper determinants is not very good. We can only explain a small part of the variation of capital structure with proxies for deeper causes such as financial distress or agency costs.

Q 22.15 Firms with large tax obligations may not have high debt ratios, because these are often the same kinds of firms that were highly profitable—which would have increased the value of their equity.

Q 22.16 The important deep factors seem to be direct stock performance, equity issuance avoidance, peer similarity, corporate income taxes, accounting performance, M&A activity, financial distress, credit ratings, active market timing, and uncertainty.

Q 22.17 Theories of capital structure may explain relatively little of firms' capital structures for the following reasons: Our variables may be poor proxies, our theories may have guided us to the wrong forces, capital structure policy may be irrelevant, and managers may act poorly and/or erratically.

Q 22.18 It could be a waste of time if we got the theories wrong and missed the most important ones. However, it is more likely that our capital structure theories would still be useful. If firms do not readjust their capital structure, the capital structure theories (forces) may mean that there is a lot of money left on the table by managers. If you can join such a firm, you may be able to optimize its capital structure and thereby save the firm a lot of money.

Q 22.19 No, financial flexibility could be bad for shareholders. If managers have a lot of money lying around, they can often do as they please. They can build empires, avoid being fired if they make bad decisions (because the firm will not run into financial distress), and so on. Thus, financial flexibility is great for managers but not necessarily for shareholders, given the firm's profitability. Of course, it is better for firms to have more cash rather than less, and there could also be some beneficial effects (e.g., distress avoidance).

PROBLEMS

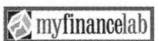

The ▬ *indicates problems available in* myfinancelab

Q 22.20 Roughly and on average, what is the typical ratio of the market value over the book value for a large firm? For a small firm?

Q 22.21 Is it inconsistent to use the market value of equity but the book value of liabilities? If they are inconsistent, would it make sense to use them as inputs in the same ratio?

Q 22.22 In 2005, IBM's financials reported total assets of $105,748 million, total liabilities of $72,650 million, and financial debt of $22,641 million. Its market value of equity was $129,463 million. (a) What was its liabilities-to-assets ratio, in book and market value? (b) What was its financial-debt-to-capital ratio, in book value and market value?

Q 22.23 What is "enterprise value"? What does it omit?

Q 22.24 Why might you want to use the financial-debt-to-capital ratio rather than the broader total-liabilities-to-assets ratio?

Q 22.25 Is the financial-debt-to-assets ratio a good measure of firm leverage? If yes, please compute it for IBM for 2005, using information from the preceding questions. If no, please explain why.

Q 22.26 What are your main choices for measuring leverage when you want to describe a firm's capital structure?

Q 22.27 What debt ratio characteristics did the largest firms in 2005 have? What firms had very high debt ratios?

Q 22.28 Roughly and on average, what were the liabilities ratios of firms—large and small—on various measures?

Q 22.29 Did profitable firms have higher or lower indebtedness ratios than unprofitable firms?

Q 22.30 What industries in 2003 were characterized by very high debt ratios? Which were characterized by very low debt ratios? Is it still the same today?

Q 22.31 Roughly and on average, how much of very large and very small firms' total liabilities were financial debt?

Q 22.32 Roughly and on average, how much of very large and very small firms' total liabilities were short term in nature?

Q 22.33 How did book and market values of equity compare for firms of various sizes?

Q 22.34 Were Anglo-Saxon firms more indebted than their foreign counterparts in 1991?

Q 22.35 Are value changes (stock returns) a major factor in determining the capital structure changes of U.S. firms—explaining why some firms have higher debt ratios and other firms have lower debt ratios?

Q 22.36 Is seasoned equity issuing net of repurchasing activity (excluding M&A activity) a major factor in determining the capital structure changes of U.S. firms? That is, does it explain well why some firms increase their debt ratios and other firms lower their debt ratios?

Q 22.37 How did most new equity shares for large S&P 100 firms enter the financial markets?

Q 22.38 What are the important deeper causes for firms' capital structures?

Q 22.39 If our empirical knowledge about the deeper determinants of capital structure is modest, does this mean that capital structure theories are irrelevant?

Q 22.40 What do CFOs claim they care about when thinking about the best capital structure?

Q 22.41 Are answers from managers "prescriptive" (i.e., giving good guidance as to what corporations should do)?

CHAPTER 22 APPENDIX

A List of Some Recent Empirical Capital Structure–Related Publications

Unlike many other subjects of our book—where our knowledge has solidified over several decades—empirical capital structure remains a largely unresolved but actively researched area. Much of what I know seems to be unusually fluid and has only recently appeared. My summary in this chapter is my *own* subjective reading thereof.

You will eventually find references to papers, past and current, for all chapters on the book website. However, to allow you to make up your own mind on this very unsettled area, I will now break the rule that references are not in the book but only on the website. (Having this list is not a sign of the greater importance of capital structure evidence. On the contrary, it should signal our shortcomings in fully understanding the phenomenon.) Here is a short list of papers published after the turn of the millennium. These papers will in turn reference many related, older, but equally (or possibly more) interesting and relevant papers.

www.prenhall.com/welch

- Franklin Allen and Roni Michaely, 2003. "Payout Policy." *North-Holland Handbook of Economics,* ed. Constantinides, Harris, and Stulz.
- Malcolm Baker and Jeffrey Wurgler, 2002. "Market Timing and Capital Structure." *The Journal of Finance* 57(1): 1–32.
- Alon Brav, John R. Graham, Campbell R. Harvey, and Roni Michaely, 2005. "Payout Policy in the 21st Century." *Journal of Financial Economics* 77(3): 483–527.
- Raj Chetty and Emmanuel Saez, 2005. "Dividend Taxes and Corporate Behavior: Evidence from the 2003 Dividend Tax Cut." *Quarterly Journal of Economics* 120(3): 791–833.
- Eugene F. Fama and Kenneth French, 2004. "Financing Decisions: Who Issues Stock?" *Journal of Financial Economics* 76(3):549–582.
- John R. Graham, 2003. "Taxes and Corporate Finance: A Review." *Review of Financial Studies* 16:1074–1129.
- John R. Graham and Campbell R. Harvey, 2001. "The Theory and Practice of Corporate Finance: Evidence from the Field." *Journal of Financial Economics* 60(2–3):187–243.
- Armen Hovakimian, Timothy C. Opler, and Sheridan Titman, 2001. "The Debt-Equity Choice." *Journal of Financial and Quantitative Analysis* 36:1–24.
- Brandon Julio and David L. Ikenberry, 2004. "Reappearing Dividends." Working Paper, UIUC.
- Mark T. Leary and Michael R. Roberts, 2004. "Do Firms Rebalance Their Capital Structures?" *The Journal of Finance* 60(6): 2575–2619.
- Peter MacKay and Gordon M. Philips, 2004. "How Does Industry Affect Firm Financial Structure?" *Review of Financial Studies* 18(4): 1433–1466.
- Ivo Welch, 2004. "Capital Structure and Stock Returns." *Journal of Political Economy* 112(1): 106–131.

Investment Banking and Mergers & Acquisitions

THE CORPORATE FINANCIAL SECTOR

Investment banks are the most important intermediaries between large firms and the public capital markets. (They will also be plum employers of many readers of this book.) Simply put, an investment bank is pretty much the same animal as an ordinary consumer bank, except that its services are focused not on retail but on corporate clients. Like consumer banks, investment banks engage in two primary functions:

Capital intermediation: They lend capital and act as agents on behalf of both firms and other capital providers. They also orchestrate the process and handle many of the legal aspects of the capital-raising process. Collectively, these functions are called **underwriting**.

Advice and facilitation: Investment banks offer advice—solicited and unsolicited—and assistance. This matters most when firms want to undertake large investments, such as mergers and acquisitions (familiarly known as M&A).

This chapter will go over these functions in more detail. This also gives us an excellent opportunity to take a more detailed look at the capital-issuing and M&A processes themselves.

23.1 THE INVESTMENT BANKING BUSINESS

Let's take a closer look at the investment banking industry. Let me first explain what its two business functions (underwriting and advice) really entail. Then we will look at one investment bank in more detail, and the industry in general. In the final two sections, we will look at these processes more from the point of view of the corporate client.

23.1A WHAT EXACTLY IS UNDERWRITING?

Underwriting means guaranteeing the proceeds. However, this is no longer important.

The first major business of investment banks is the underwriting of financial securities. Almost all debt and equity offerings by exchange-traded firms are underwritten by investment banks. The term **underwriter** originally came from the guarantee of the issuing proceeds by the banker to the issuing client, similar to the underwriting of a policy by an insurance company. This mattered greatly in an era when communications traveled by horse, investors were dispersed over thousands of miles, sales had to be made by foreign agents, and it took weeks to place the shares. Times have changed. Communication is now instantaneous around the globe, and every underwriter knows almost every important large investor. A few dozen large institutional funds are so big that they could easily absorb hundreds of offerings. Given today's financial information environment, the underwriter knows quite well on the day of the offering at what price the issue can be sold for. If the issuer were to refuse to accept this price point, the underwriter would not bring the issue to the market in the first place. Thus, the actual underwriting guarantee itself, which is granted only on the morning of the offering, also has become unimportant.

Underwriting today is an agency business. Underwriters help corporations sell securities to third-party investors.

Instead, the main functions of underwriters today are different:

Issue origination: Underwriters must have the expertise to handle the legal and operational processes.

Issue placement: Underwriters must maintain and tap their investor networks to find the investors desired by issuers. (Many issuers prefer institutional investors; others prefer dispersed ownership.)

Reputation and signaling: Underwriters vouch for the integrity of the process and the quality of the issuer to the investors.

➤ Analysts' conflict of interest, Anecdote, Section 21.7, p. 809

Underwriters also help throughout the process in ways that are not as formal. For example, many investment banks have large brokerage arms. After the offering, the banks' analysts will continue to provide helpful information to institutional and retail investors on an ongoing basis. (For IPOs, they can also help spread "positive hype" through optimistic analyst reports on behalf of the issuer.) This presumably increases the demand for investment in the company and is thus good for selling more shares and debt in the future. Underwriters are allowed by a special SEC exception to "stabilize" (i.e., manipulate) the price.

Syndicates and lead underwriters.

Although every major bank nowadays has plenty of contacts to place even the largest issues on its own (and plenty of capital so as not to have to fear the risk of a failed offering), another historical aspect of the underwriting process that has survived is that almost all offerings are brought to market by a **syndicate** of banks put together for each deal. Syndicates typically contain between two and six lead underwriters. Syndicates are led by **book runners** and **lead managers**, with the former in charge of assembling the book of investors interested in purchasing shares (actually, a spreadsheet), and the latter in charge of handling the due diligence and the technical and legal aspects of the process. Normally, lead underwriters are also the book runners. Sometimes, different book runners are in charge of different market segments, such as domestic versus foreign placements. Offerings also used to have many co-underwriters who helped to place shares, but this feature has largely disappeared in the last decade.

Underwriter reputation is often measured by ranking.

Investment banks care greatly about "bragging rights" (more formally called "reputation"). For example, banks consider it important to be named a lead underwriter, because it helps their rankings. The two main providers of these rankings are Thomson Financial and Deal Logic. Historically, before rankings became widely available, the location, placement, and font size of the underwriter's name in the printed financial advertisement of an offering (the so-called **tombstone** advertisement) was another important sign of the relative prestige of an investment bank. However, tombstones are rapidly becoming extinct.

SOLVE NOW!

Q 23.1 What are the most important services and functions of underwriters today?

Q 23.2 How good and unbiased are brokerage analysts' buy recommendations?

23.1B WHAT EXACTLY IS M&A ADVICE?

Advisory services are basically an agency business. Think "personal real estate agent" on a larger scale.

The second major business of investment banks is the handling of M&A transactions. This business is easiest to visualize if you think of a good common real estate broker—the two jobs are really quite similar. They differ primarily in scale. Here is what a good advisor typically does:

- The advisor identifies his own potential clients, or vice versa. Sometimes, the client initiates the contact when she wants to buy or sell a target business. At other times, an investment banker has an idea that he brings to the client.
- The advisor offers valuation services for potential targets. (This was the subject of most of this textbook. You already know that this is not an easy task.)
- If working for a potential target, the advisor helps to position the business so that it can be sold. This may be a simple or a complex task. It could involve hiring new personnel, restating the financials in a light that makes them look more favorable, helping to advertise the business, and so on.
- The advisor helps to find potential acquirers or targets. This is often not just an intelligence-gathering function. Many good advisors also have personal and/or business connections to potential counterparties that make an approach much easier.

➤ Agents: Who works for whom? Anecdote, Section 10.3A, p. 315

- The advisor has expertise in negotiation, which the client may lack. Advisors have a great incentive not to let negotiations break down. (However, this is not necessarily good. Advisors are often less willing than the principal client to walk away from deals if the terms are not right.)
- The acquirer's advisor can help conduct **due diligence** (i.e., a minimal amount of scrutiny) to locate gaping problems in the target or transaction that would otherwise be overlooked. Most of the time, however, this has become just a legal requirement that must be satisfied.
- The advisor can help with the tax structure of a deal. This can be a hugely important aspect, saving the parties as much as 20% of the deal compared to a worse structure. (For example, a seller is often better off not taking a consulting role in the merged

entity. Such a position would have cash flows taxed at high ordinary income tax rates, rather than at lower capital gains tax rates.)

- The advisor can often arrange the financing needed to complete an acquisition. Indeed, most acquirers do not have enough cash on hand, so the investment bank also often provides **bridge financing** to facilitate the acquisition. As the name suggests, the intent is for the acquirer to liquidate some corporate assets right after the acquisition to repay this loan.
- The advisor knows how to navigate the legal aspects of the process, everything ranging from state laws to SEC regulations.

These are difficult tasks that require expertise that few acquirers or targets have themselves—thus, the role of the investment banker.

23.1C THE GLOBAL MARKET

It would be a mistake to consider the topic of investment banking in isolation. It exists in the context of a larger and global banking market. Nowadays, banks from all over the world compete to provide capital to institutions not only in the United States but also in Europe, Asia, and everywhere else. Moreover, many large global banks not only can act as intermediaries for most of their clients' credit needs, but can also satisfy these needs with loans from their own capital base.

Banking is a global and wider business than U.S. investment banking.

Before we look at U.S. investment banking, let's look first at the broader context:

The (commercial) banking sector at large: Table 23.1 lists the 25 biggest global banks in 2007. The United States and United Kingdom together are still very prominently represented, but some other European, Japanese, and even Chinese banks have joined the list of banks with deep pockets. As noted, many of these banks are not so much intermediaries as principal lenders. Other banks on this list are both.

(Commercial) banks can lend as principals, too—unlike investment banks, which just facilitate funding by other investors.

Size alone is not necessarily an asset. (Bad pun.) In many foreign countries, these banks are seen as national resources, or as threats to public welfare, and are therefore highly regulated. This can make it difficult for them to compete in the world market.

There are many interesting facts not reported in the table. For example, the U.S. and U.K. banks are considerably more profitable than their foreign competitors when measured against their Tier 1 capital. Out of the top 1,000 banks, the top 200 U.S. banks accounted for about 28% of the profits, while the top 300 banks from the European Union accounted for about 40% of the profits. (Europe was dragged down by the 100 German banks, which were only marginally profitable.)

The global investment banking market: The market in which banks act primarily as intermediaries rather than as principal lenders is not just domestic, either. The United States and Europe still have the largest financial markets in the world, though Asia (including China) is clearly coming on strong. Market sizes and market shares in 2007 for seasoned equity offerings (SEOs), initial public offerings (IPOs), debt offerings, and M&A advice are shown in Table 23.2.

By size of the capital market, the United States is now only *primus inter pares* (first among equals).

Don't take these numbers too literally. Not only do they change year to year, but it is not even clear any longer what is issued and who is holding what. For example, a Latin American company may issue securities in the United States that are bought by Japanese banks that are owned by Kuwaiti investors. Which region's

TABLE 23.1 THE LARGEST 25 GLOBAL COMMERCIAL BANKS IN 2007

	Bank	Country	Tier 1 Capital			Market Value			Client Assets		
•	Bank of America	USA	$91,065	1	↑	$220,379	2	–	$1,459,737	10	↑
•	Citigroup	USA	$90,899	2	↓	$261,270	1	–	$1,882,556	4	↓
•	HSBC	UK	$87,842	3	–	$214,934	3	–	$1,860,758	5	–
	Credit Agricole	France	$84,937	4	↓			↓↓	$1,818,341	6	↓
•	JP Morgan Chase	USA	$81,055	5	↑	$168,585	5	↑	$1,351,520	11	↑
	Mitsubishi UFJ	Japan	$68,464	6	↓	$126,676	9	↓	$1,579,390	8	↓
	ICBC	China	$59,166	7	↑	$209,060	4	↑↑	$961,576	20	↑
	Royal Bank of Scotland	UK	$58,973	8	–	$119,808	10	↓	$1,710,703	7	↑
	Bank of China	China	$52,518	9	↑	$157,343	6	↑↑			
	Santander	Spain	$46,805	10	↑	$114,095	12	↑	$1,098,213	17	↑
	BNP Paribas	France	$45,305	11	↓	$109,388	13	↓	$1,896,935	3	↑
•	Barclays	UK	$45,161	12	–	$94,732	15	↓	$1,956,786	2	↑↑
	HBOS	UK	$44,030	13	↑	$76,249	25		$1,160,245	16	↑
	China Construction Bank	China	$42,286	14	↑	$132,224	7	↑↑			
	Mizuho	Japan	$41,934	15	↓	$84,970	22	↓↓	$1,235,443	14	↓↓
•	Wachovia	USA	$39,428	16		$101,312	14				
	UniCredit	Italy	$38,700	17		$91,876	17		$1,084,267	18	↑
	Wells Fargo	USA	$36,808	18		$117,492	11				
	Rabobank	Netherlands	$34,757	19					$732,708	25	
	ING Bank	Netherlands	$33,958	20					$1,178,697	15	
•	UBS	Switzerland	$33,212	21	↓	$128,331	8	↓	$1,963,870	1	↑
	Sumitomo	Japan	$33,177	22	↓↓				$826,599	22	↓↓
•	Deutsche Bank	Germany	$32,264	23	↓↓			↓↓	$1,483,248	10	↓
	ABN Amro	Netherlands	$31,239	24		$90,526	18		$1,299,966	12	
	Credit Mutuel	France	$29,792	25							
	Intesa	Italy				$92,563	16				
	Bank of Communications	China				$88,122	19				
•	Credit Suisse	Switzerland				$87,168	20		$1,029,219	19	↓
	Societe Generale	France				$85,755	21		$1,260,162	13	
	BBVA	Spain				$84,142	23				
	Sberbank	Russia				$81,700	24				
	Fortis	Belgium							888,570	21	
	Commerzbank	Germany							801,184	23	
	Dexia	Belgium							746,402	24	

All dollars are in millions. Tier 1 Capital (also called **core equity**) is common stock, disclosed reserves, and retained earnings. Although based on book value and therefore unreliable, it is the most common regulatory definition for bank capitalization. Market value is the market value of equity, as of early 2008. Arrows indicate how the bank changed since 2003 (but indicated only if the information was available). Two arrows imply bigger moves. The • symbol on the far left means that the bank was among the most prominent investment banks active in the United States in 2007.

Source: *The Banker*, 2008.

TABLE 23.2 GLOBAL MARKET SIZES AND MARKET SHARES IN UNDERWRITING

Market Shares	Equity				
	SEO	IPO	All	Debt	M&A
United States	23%	15%	27%	58%	42%
Europe (Middle East, Africa)	33%	41%	33%	37%	40%
Asia	31%	28%	26%		7%
Australia	6%	2%	4%		4%
Japan	4%	2%	3%		3%
Latin America	3%	12%	6%		2%
World Market Share in 2007, in billion US dollars	$362	$304	$844	$6,226	$4,482

Source: Thomson Financial

capital market would you give credit to? Nevertheless, the table does give some insight into how large capital markcts in different regions are. Overall, the United States is still the largest financial market in the world. Yet it is no longer the largest equity market. That honor now belongs to Europe and will soon belong to Asia. This should not be too surprising. The demand for capital in other countries is expanding: Firms in Asia and Eastern Europe are just beginning to go public. Similarly, the supply of capital by other countries has been expanding (principally the capital from Asia). Thus, it is easy to predict that the rest of the world will continue to catch up with the United States. There is just too much capital and economic development happening outside our borders.

Still, the United States remains the top dog.

However, as you will learn below, thc world's principal investment banking operations of most global banks are still headquartered in New York City. Most also have a strong satellite office in London, perhaps another in Hong Kong, Singapore, Tokyo, or Shanghai, and one in their home country. Thus, the United States still deserves special treatment in this chapter.

Here is where you can find updated statistics on the current investment banking markets.

Inevitably, by the time you read this, the information here will be outdated. However, Thomson Financial publicly posts updated "League Tables" at http://www.thomsonreuters.com/products_services/financial/league_tables, which not only provide other related information (such as fee revenues), but also slice and dice the data in all sorts of other interesting ways. The Thomson League Tables are free and highly recommended for browsing.

SOLVE NOW!

Q 23.3 Can you name some of the leading global commercial banks from memory? Roughly how much Tier 1 capital, market value, and client assets do the top 25 banks have?

Q 23.4 Where are the biggest capital markets for placing securities? Roughly, how do they compare in size?

23.1D THE INVESTMENT BANKING HISTORY IN THE UNITED STATES

Due to U.S. regulations, investment banks have a unique history in the United States.

In the United States, the distinction between investment banking and ordinary banking has not just been a conceptual one. Investment banking has had a rather unusual history here. During the Great Depression, many banks that had invested depositors' money in the stock market collapsed. Thus, Congress passed the **Glass-Steagall Act of 1933**, which prohibited the mixing of retail business—the taking of deposits from retail investors—and investment banking. Glass-Steagall therefore made it impossible for large consumer banks, such as Citibank or Chase Manhattan Bank, to compete effectively in the investment banking sector. Many other countries never made such a distinction—they just had one type of bank that performed both consumer/commercial and investment banking. It was our unusual laws that made the United States unique in fostering a large number of relatively small investment banks.

After 1999, this uniqueness disappeared, and commercial banking empires quickly emerged.

Over the decades, Glass-Steagall was augmented with other laws, first strengthening it and later weakening it. It was finally repealed in November 1999. With the legal separation between ordinary and investment banking gone, the investment banking sector rapidly began to consolidate. For example, Citicorp and Travelers Group merged in 1998 to become Citigroup. In the same year, Smith Barney purchased Salomon Brothers to become Salomon Smith Barney. A year later, with Glass-Steagall fully repealed, Citigroup then purchased Salomon Smith Barney, so the five formerly independent financial services providers are now all just parts of one large financial conglomerate. Similarly, Chase Manhattan purchased JP Morgan in 2000, then merged with Bank One Corporation (a large credit card issuer) in 2004. CSFB is the combination of Credit Suisse, a very large Swiss bank, and First Boston, an old U.S. investment bank. And so on.

SOLVE NOW!

Q 23.5 What was the Glass-Steagall Act?

23.1E AN EXAMPLE: GOLDMAN SACHS

Getting information from investment banks is like pulling teeth.

Unfortunately, it is not easy to find much information about financial firms. (Hedge funds are even worse than investment banks in this regard.) Generally, financial firms consider information their competitive advantage, so it is usually impossible to convince them to part voluntarily with any data. (Trust me: I have tried.) Fortunately, SEC disclosure requirements allow us to get a limited glimpse into their operations. The SEC requires investment banks that facilitate issues of other firms (e.g., in the public issuing process of securities), to disclose certain information. Moreover, because investment banks are publicly traded firms, they have to disclose certain information about themselves in their own annual reports. This information is easiest to come by if the U.S. investment bank is not just a small part of a larger empire. There are only a

ANECDOTE An Investment Banking Job?

In a 2008 *Journal of Finance* article called "The Making of an Investment Banker," Paul Oyer tracked Stanford MBA graduates from the classes of 1960 through 1997. Investment bankers enjoyed between $2 million and $6 million in discounted lifetime income (in real 1996 dollars). This is much higher than what they would have earned if they had entered other professions. Fifteen years after graduation, the average I-banker earned 60% more than the average management consultant at graduation, and 300% more than the average Stanford MBA graduate. (Today, it is not uncommon for investment bankers to earn $1 million per year or more.)

More interestingly, Oyer found that stock market conditions at graduation time played a big role not only in obtaining a first job in I-banking but also in the probability that an individual would *ever* end up on Wall Street. (And, equally remarkable, many of the individuals graduating in bear years ended up as entrepreneurs!)

Oyer concludes that random factors beyond talent are very important in determining individuals' lifetime paths and compensation—and that there is a very deep pool of potential I-bankers in any given Stanford MBA class.

few major U.S. investment banks left today for which this is the case (and even these are much more than investment banks, as you will soon see).

Goldman's history.

One of these banks is Goldman Sachs. It is perhaps the most prominent investment bank in the world today. It was founded in 1869 by Marcus Goldman as a *commercial paper* business. In 1896, Goldman's son-in-law, Samuel Sachs, joined the firm, which was then renamed Goldman Sachs. It became a member of the New York Stock Exchange the same year. In 1999, it converted from a partnership into a publicly traded corporation via an IPO. As of November 2007, Goldman Sachs conducted business in 25 countries: 43% of its employees were outside the United States, 49% of its net revenues and 57% of its earnings were from outside the Americas, and its clients were companies and individuals worldwide. (Despite its obvious Jewish heritage, Goldman Sachs even received a license in January 2008 to operate in Saudi Arabia.)

➤ Commercial Paper, Section 15.2A, p. 545

➤ IPOs, Section 21.7, p. 806

Goldman's most important resource by any measure is its employees.

In 2007, Goldman had 30,522 employees (17,383 in the United States), plus another 4,572 employees in affiliated businesses. About 6% of these were managing directors, which is the highest job title that Goldman conveys. Investment banking hierarchies are usually fairly flat, with only four or five ranks: analyst, associate, vice president, director, and managing director. (You may also find it interesting that Goldman Sachs was among the pioneers recruiting MBAs and PhDs from many business schools.) Investment banks are unusual businesses in that their main resources walk out of their buildings every night (though it may often be after midnight). Keeping its best employees happy is perhaps Goldman's main business challenge. Many successful Goldman employees have left to join government (such as Goldman's ex-CEO, Henry Paulson, U.S. Treasury Secretary under George W. Bush) and hedge funds (such as Goldman's ex-head of prime brokerage, Emmanuel Roman, now co-CEO of GLG Partners). To fight against the departures of valuable employees, Goldman paid out $20.2 billion in employee compensation in 2007. (Nonemployee costs were only $8.2 billion.) The $20.2 billion comes to an average of just over $600,000 per employee, most of which was in the form of bonus payments. The distribution of compensation is highly skewed. For example, three traders (aged 35 to 40) who pushed Goldman

How Goldmanites were compensated in 2007.

into a profitable bet against subprime were paid between $5 and $15 million each. Interestingly, on Wall Street, the top earners in any given year need not be the CEO. It could equally well be the traders with the best performance. In 2007, however, it was Goldman's CEO, Lloyd Blankfein, who took home $100 million. Four other top executives also earned between $30 and $60 million.

Goldman's culture.

Goldman prides itself on a more collaborative atmosphere than its competitors. To foster this atmosphere, its annual bonus and retention evaluation scheme takes into account how collaboratively an employee behaves. On the flip side, like many other investment banks, Goldman has a policy of laying off 5% of its worst-performing staff every year.

Does bank size really matter?

But look back at Table 23.1: Where was Goldman Sachs? *It was not on the list of the top 25 global commercial banks*. Neither were some other prominent U.S. investment banks, such as Merrill Lynch, Lehman Brothers, or Morgan Stanley. Yet these U.S. investment banks are active and nimble competitors, quite capable of being leading investment banks worldwide, even without access to the large capital bases of the banks from Table 23.1. If you have read the preceding carefully, you probably understand why the limiting resource is not financial capital (though having more capital definitely helps) but expertise and human talent. As long as Goldman and other U.S. and U.K. banks still excel in attracting and retaining the best talent from all over the world (and they still do), they will remain the global leaders in investment banking.

Goldman's profitability and market value.

Let's move on to Goldman's actual business. During 2007, Goldman's equity market value fluctuated between $70 and $100 billion. It had earnings of $11.7 billion—a little more than half of Goldman's $20.2 billion employee compensation. Remarkably, unlike most of its competitors, Goldman had dodged the subprime liquidity crisis of 2007 by placing a well-timed (and subsequently well-publicized) bet against subprime mortgages that ultimately contributed $4 billion in profit to its 2007 earnings—recommended by the three aforementioned traders.

Of Goldman's three main business lines, investment banking is actually the smallest.

Goldman's business itself consists of three divisions:

Division Name	Net Revenues	Operating Expenses	Before-Tax Earnings
Trading and Principal Investments	$31,226	$17,998	$13,228
Asset Management and Securities Services	$7,206	$5,363	$1,843
Investment Banking	$7,555	$4,985	$2,570
Total	$45,987	$28,383	$17,604

P.S.: Goldman's numbers on page 57 of its 2007 annual report do not add up.

The trading and principal investments arm is basically an investments arbitrage business in fixed income, currencies, commodities, equities, and private equity (with investments in China and Japan). Goldman's asset management arm specializes in institutional clients and high-net-worth individuals, although it also entertains some retail clients. It had about $868 billion under management (of which $151 billion was in alternative investments, such as hedge funds, private equity, real estate, currencies, commodities, and asset allocation strategies), $255 billion in equity, $256 billion in fixed income, and $206 billion in money markets. The asset management arm also contains its prime brokerage business.

➤ Prime brokerage, Section 7.2A, p. 191

The focus of our chapter is the investment banking arm. Look carefully: Even though Goldman is still called an investment bank, the term has become somewhat of a misnomer. Goldman is now primarily a trading and arbitrage firm (with little regulatory oversight) and no longer primarily an investment bank these days. Trading is what consumes most of Goldman's resources: its capital, value at risk, talent, bonus pool, and so on. Of course, investment banking is still a nontrivial aspect of the business, and appropriately a prime concern in our corporate finance textbook. In the case of Goldman and many other investment banks, investment banking consists of the same two roughly equal parts that we have already discussed:

Our focus is the investment banking business, which has two components: restructuring advice and underwriting.

Financial advisory: The advisory branch works mostly on M&A-related consulting, although it also includes restructuring advice, acquisition financing, and cross-border structuring expertise (which is mostly a tax-planning service). M&A advising also links into other services offered by the firm, especially its bridge loan facilitation. As a sidenote, you may find it interesting that Goldman Sachs is unusual in that it has historically specialized in helping management defend itself against unfriendly takeovers. Most likely, this policy was not instituted for moral reasons (i.e., to help poor victim CEOs) but rather to protect its other business.

In 2007, Goldman earned $4.222 billion (of its $7.555 billion in investment banking) in advising on approximately $1.5 trillion in about 400 transactions. Goldman's advice cost about $7.5 million per deal on average ($10 million per deal in the United States). Two-thirds of its advisory business was still in the United States.

Underwriting: The underwriting branch helps client firms issue securities, principally debt and equity.

In 2007, Goldman earned $1.382 billion on underwriting about $71 billion worth of proceeds in over 200 equity transactions. It earned approximately $1.951 billion on underwriting about $312 billion worth of proceeds in about 700 debt transactions. About half of Goldman's underwriting business was in the United States. (Note that much of its debt issuing activity is not on behalf of corporate clients but on behalf of foreign countries, federal credit agencies, mortgage-backed securities, municipal debt, and so on).

These figures tell you that underwriting as an activity was less profitable than M&A advice in 2007. It turns out that 2007 was a banner year for the M&A industry. In many earlier years, the two businesses were more balanced. For example, in 2000, advisory earned $2.592 billion while underwriting earned $2.779 billion. However, it has always been the case that an equity underwriting deal is more profitable than a debt underwriting deal. In Goldman's case, it earned more in equity underwriting, even though it underwrote four times as much debt as equity.

Usually advisory and underwriting are roughly equal. In 2007, however, advisory was much more important.

Unfortunately, Goldman's financials do not break out much more information. Thus, we have to look at some other data sources, which cannot be perfectly reconciled with the information in Goldman's annual report. Nevertheless, they still allow

Goldman has significant market shares in its investment banking services, both global and domestic.

you to get a few more glimpses. Thomson Financial reports how competitive and important Goldman was in its markets. Goldman's market shares were as follows:

	Market Share	
Activity	Deal Size	Fees
U.S. Equity	9.0%	11.2%
Worldwide Equity	5.6%	8.1%
Worldwide Debt	4.9%	4.3%
High-Grade Corporate		9.1%
Worldwide Debt and Equity	5.6%	4.8%
U.S. M&A Advice		10.6%
Worldwide M&A Advice		7.1%

You can see that Goldman is a major player in the markets it competes in, with worldwide and domestic market shares between about 5% and 10%. It also charges a premium for its participation in equities: Its market share of equity fees is higher than its market share in equity deal sizes.

SOLVE NOW!

Q 23.6 What was the approximate average compensation of a Goldman Sachs employee in 2007? What would you guess the average seasoned investment banker earned?

23.1F THE UNDERWRITING BUSINESS

Our main data provider for the industry at large is Thomson. What does the market for debt underwriting look like?

Now that you understand one investment bank in some detail, let's look at the investment banking industry more broadly. Thomson Financial is more or less the standard data provider in this industry. It reported that in 2007 global debt underwriting fees topped $19 billion (on over $6 trillion in issuing proceeds), and global equity underwriting fees topped $22 billion (on about $1.5 trillion in proceeds). You already know how much of this Goldman earned, but who "owned" the rest of this market? And what kind of securities were underwritten?

Lots and lots of government debt, still a good deal of investment-grade debt, and some non-investment-grade debt.

➤ Investment grade, Section 6.2D, p. 148

Table 23.3 shows how the largest investment banks in the United States divided the pie from 2005 to 2007. The most important debt issuers are the three U.S. government agency bonds: the two home-loan agencies—Freddie Mac and Fannie Mae—and the Federal Farm Credit System. They accounted for a staggering 75% of the bond market. In the remaining 25% segment, most bond issues are of investment-grade quality. Non-investment-grade debt is fairly rare—though even the most reputable investment banks underwrite in this market. This relative rarity is easy to explain: It is often cheaper for smaller firms to borrow from commercial banks instead of going to the public market. (This market for original high-yield junk bonds was invented in the early 1980s by Michael Milken of Drexel-Burnham-Lambert.) Underwriters charge about three times as much for issuing non-investment-grade securities (fees are about 1.3%) as they charge for investment-grade securities (fees are about 0.5%). The government agencies paid the lowest fees—only 0.1% on average. (After their

➤ High-yield (junk) bonds, Appendix B, p. B-3

TABLE 23.3 U.S. NONCONVERTIBLE CORPORATE DEBT UNDERWRITING, 2005 TO 2007

	Government Agency			Investment Grade			Speculative Grade		
Underwriter	Proceeds	Fees	N	Proceeds	Fees	N	Proceeds	Fees	N
JP Morgan	$108,348	0.1%	655	$147,385	0.4%	585	$11,354	1.3%	47
Citigroup	$46,779	0.1%	255	$160,556	0.6%	549	$8,705	1.5%	37
Merrill Lynch	$92,972	0.2%	1,336	$106,762	0.6%	354	$5,889	1.6%	16
Goldman Sachs	$73,635	0.2%	287	$143,902	0.4%	354	$2,468	1.4%	12
Lehman Brothers	$93,557	0.2%	568	$100,968	0.4%	301	$3,998	1.4%	23
Morgan Stanley	$59,407	0.1%	398	$116,239	0.4%	346	$4,336	1.4%	15
UBS	$127,920	0.1%	1,086	$28,144	0.6%	177	$1,833	0.8%	9
Bank of America	$55,949	0.1%	418	$103,482	0.4%	428	$4,370	1.2%	28
Deutsche Bank	$84,482	0.1%	416	$33,870	0.4%	181	$3,578	1.1%	21
CFSB	$35,173	0.1%	397	$58,388	0.4%	190	$3,080	1.3%	23
HSBC	$49,347	0.1%	315	$57,501	0.3%	125			
Wachovia	$57,048	0.2%	568	$63,164	0.5%	285	$1,779	1.0%	14
Barclays	$57,048	0.1%	362	$32,586	0.5%	190	$954	0.7%	6
Bear Stearns	$41,662	0.2%	505	$17,914	0.4%	44	$610	1.7%	5
All Others	$265,837	0.2%	9,244	$86,393	0.4%	477	$2,584	1.3%	15
Grand Sum	$1,209,505	0.1%	16,810	$1,257,254	0.5%	4,586	$55,540	1.4%	271

Source: Gerard Hoberg's website (http://www.rhsmith.umd.edu/faculty/ghoberg/byuw.html), based on data from Thomson Financial. The proceeds statistics are averages for offerings for which the underwriter identity, proceeds, and gross spread were known. (The gross spread is the amount of money the underwriter receives from the issuing proceeds, and represents the lion's share of the issuer's payment to the bank.) When U underwriters led an offering, each underwriter was credited with $1/U$ of the proceeds. (This means that these statistics are less than those touted by the underwriters themselves.) Proceeds are measured in millions of U.S. dollars (e.g., JP Morgan issued $108 billion in agency debt). Quoted fees are the proceeds-weighted average of gross spread, quoted as a fraction of proceeds. N is the number of lead underwriters in offerings. (Because an offering can have more than one lead underwriter, this number is larger than the number of offerings.) This table was put together based on an original data source with just under 35,000 offerings from 2005 to 2007 in the Thomson securities issuing database. The government agencies were Freddie Mac, Fannie Mae, and the Federal Farm Credit System. (Not all debt issues had full data available, especially underwriter spreads. We are also omitting offerings without a debt rating.)

highly publicized troubles in 2008, their fees will surely go up.) These figures naturally varied with the specific underwriter, the specific issuer, and the specific market conditions.

The market for equity underwriting is smaller, but underwriter fees are higher.

Table 23.4 is the equivalent table for equity underwriting activity. Compared to the corporate debt issuing market, the equity issuing market is only about half the size in terms of number of offerings, and even less in terms of proceeds raised. (This is not even counting government bonds.) However, as you have already seen in Goldman's case, equity underwriting fees are much higher than those for debt. Thus, equity underwriting is the more profitable of the two markets. From the perspective of investment banks, bonds are the bread and butter, equity is the gravy.

TABLE 23.4 U.S. CORPORATE EQUITY UNDERWRITING, 2005 TO 2007

	Convertible			Preferred Equity			Seasoned Equity			IPOs		
Underwriter	Proceeds	Fees	N	Proceeds	Fees	N	Proceeds	Fees	N	Proceeds	Fees	N
JP Morgan	$1,995	2.4%	14	$2,778	2.6%	19	$17,129	3.2%	125	$8,086	6.1%	81
Citigroup	$3,438	1.8%	11	$8,404	2.6%	36	$18,057	3.3%	127	$21,234	5.3%	92
Merrill Lynch	$2,030	2.0%	12	$7,888	2.9%	42	$20,810	3.7%	151	$24,149	4.9%	117
Goldman Sachs	$5,242	1.9%	11	$5,202	2.7%	18	$16,675	3.2%	91	$8,781	6.1%	71
Lehman Brothers	$3,072	1.5%	13	$4,237	2.1%	27	$19,645	2.8%	132	$6,972	6.1%	68
Morgan Stanley	$1,438	2.5%	8	$3,863	2.9%	33	$18,365	3.2%	109	$13,853	5.6%	87
UBS	$1,167	2.4%	9	$1,749	2.9%	23	$15,900	3.7%	156	$9,180	5.6%	61
Bank of America	$698	2.2%	5	$2,897	2.0%	15	$7,253	3.7%	80	$4,449	6.3%	44
Deutsche Bank	$2,670	2.3%	10	$697	2.7%	9	$8,067	3.3%	74	$3,719	6.3%	39
CFSB	$2,452	2.1%	16	$1,745	2.6%	9	$10,957	3.6%	85	$7,743	6.2%	71
HSBC				$825	3.1%	3	$110	4.9%	2	$600	4.7%	1
Wachovia	$1,012	1.5%	5	$6,989	3.1%	47	$6,211	3.4%	79	$12,657	4.8%	36
Barclays	$200	2.2%	1	$15	2.0%	1						
Bear Stearns	$233	0.8%	2	$1,237	2.9%	18	$6,333	3.9%	61	$3,088	5.5%	27
All Others	$1,607	3.4%	8	$3,980	2.4%	44	$23,260	4.8%	466	$21,478	6.1%	323
Grand Sum	$27,255	2.1%	125	$52,515	2.7%	344	$188,771	3.5%	1,738	$145,989	5.6%	1,118

Source: Gerard Hoberg's website (http://www.rhsmith.umd.edu/faculty/ghoberg/byuw.html), based on data from Thomson Financial. The proceeds statistics are averages for offerings for which the underwriter identity, proceeds, and gross spread were known. When U underwriters led an offering, each underwriter was credited with $1/U$ of the proceeds. (This means that these statistics are less than those touted by the underwriters themselves.) Proceeds are measured in millions of U.S. dollars. Quoted fees are the proceeds-weighted average of gross spread, quoted as a fraction of proceeds. N is the number of lead underwriters in offerings. (Because an offering can have more than one lead underwriter, this number is larger than the number of offerings.)

Convertibles and preferred are both hybrids with riskiness in between debt and equity; seasoned equity is riskier; IPOs are riskiest. Underwriter spreads follow the same ordering.

➤ Preferred equity, Section 15.3, p. 552

➤ Origins of new equity shares in S&P 100 firms, Table 22.7, p. 838

Convertibles and preferred stock are hybrids, having both equity- and debt-like characteristics—and both are fairly rare. The average issuing proceeds are roughly similarly sized, but underwriter spreads are on average higher for preferred equity (at 2.6%) than they are for convertible debt (at 2.1%). The SEO issuing market and even the IPO issuing market are much larger. They also tend to involve the same firms: In the life cycle of firms, more equity issuing ocurrs relatively early in firms' lives when the firms are still small. Not shown in the table, about one in four IPO issuers returns for more funding within a few years, which means that a good fraction of the SEOs shown here are conducted by firms that have gone public fairly recently. From the perspective of underwriters, both are important markets, because the spread in SEOs reaches 3.5% and that in IPOs reaches 5.6%. These are proceeds-weighted fees, thus emphasizing the fees in larger offerings more. (Smaller offerings command higher underwriter spreads.) Like the debt underwriting market, the equity underwriting market seems highly competitive, with many active players, none of which control more than 10% of the market.

Why underwriters charge more for bringing risky offerings to market.

Underwriters have good reason to charge more for placing riskier securities:

1. Investors can be found a lot more easily for safer securities. In the extreme, safe short-term investment-grade corporate bond issues could almost be substitutes for Treasury bonds, so investors are not very concerned about risk analysis, which means that investors are easy to find.
2. Due diligence is much more difficult to do for a small high-yield issuer than for, say, a high-grade debt offering for General Electric.
3. Underwriters put their own reputation capital on the line. For example, when an underwriter takes a firm public in an IPO that later goes bankrupt, it will not play well with the investors that the bank had solicited. After a couple of such bankruptcy repeats, the underwriter will probably no longer be able to find IPO investors easily. Therefore, when companies first sell shares in an initial public offering—which is the most risky investment banking business around—the underwriting costs are usually highest. Table 23.4 shows this fact quite nicely.

In addition, IPOs require unusually cumbersome legal procedures and impose extra legal liabilities on underwriters, above and beyond what is required for other offerings. They also require significantly more marketing to investors than ordinary SEOs.

SOLVE NOW!

Q 23.7 Is the underwriting very competitive or dominated by a small number of firms?

Q 23.8 Why is it more expensive to place equity than debt?

23.1G THE MERGER & ACQUISITION ADVICE BUSINESS

Let's move on to M&A activity. Again, our main interest is to determine how much of a market was served by investment banks. Advice for the typical deal can cost the transacting firms anywhere between 0.5% and 1% of the acquisition size.

The history of M&A activity: Global M&A waves appeared during U.S. bull markets. The United States accounts for about one-quarter of the worldwide M&A activity.

M&A activity can be measured in many different ways: as all completed and attempted offerings (or just completed acquisitions), as full or partial acquisitions (in which the target remains an independent publicly traded entity), as U.S. or worldwide acquisitions, and so on. Fortunately, the trends tend to be similar no matter what measures are used. However, the absolute magnitudes can be quite different. With this caveat, Figure 23.1 gives you a first impression of M&A activity over the decades. The top graph shows that successfully completed M&A activity, adjusted for inflation, peaked in the United States just before the turn of the millennium. (This graph includes partial acquisitions, in which the target or parts of it could remain publicly traded. If we require full acquisitions, the reported activity roughly halves.) This graph represents over $1 trillion in acquisitions—a staggering amount by any measure. The color of the bars indicates the performance of the stock market in each year. It shows that takeover activity is procyclical—there are more acquisitions in bull markets than in bear markets. (Although not shown, takeover activity also relates to interest rate

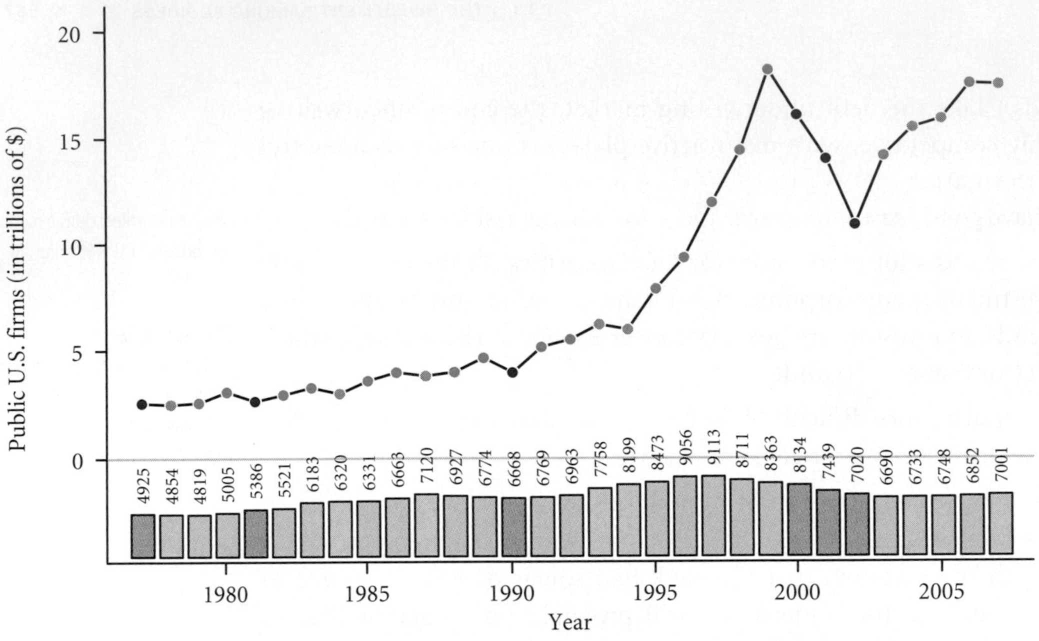

Equity Capitalization and Number of All Publicly Traded U.S. Firms

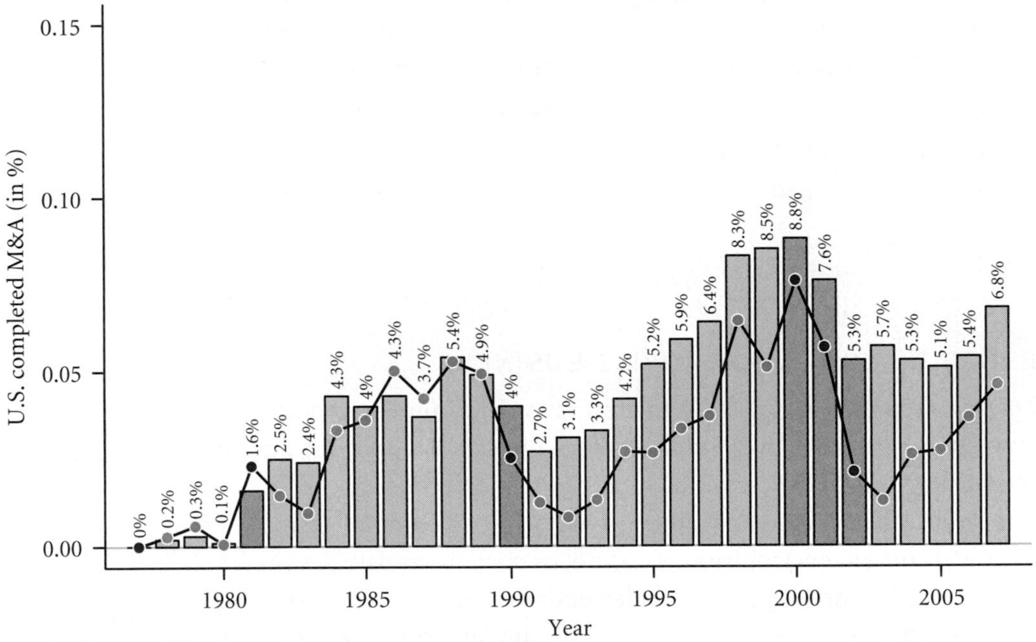

Completed Takeover Activity as a Fraction of Public Equity Market Capitalization

These graphs put U.S. M&A activity in the context of the size of the U.S. public equity markets. Years in which the S&P 500 declined are drawn in magenta. Years in which it increased by more than 10% are drawn in blue. Years in which the S&P 500 did not decline, but did not increase by more than 10%, are drawn in gray. The bars are statistics about the number of firms; lines are statistics about the value of target firms (in 2000 dollars).

The top graph shows the number and inflation-adjusted dollar value of publicly traded U.S. firms. For example, the number of publicly traded firms peaked at 9,113 in 1997. The dollar value peaked at $17.6 trillion in 1999.

The bottom graph shows that takeover activity was generally higher in bull markets than in bear markets. For example, by the measures used here, about 8.8% of all publicly traded firms were targeted in 2000, representing about 7.6% of the public equity value. (**Warning #1:** These fractions may be understating the ratio, because deal value includes both debt and equity of the acquirer, and the denominator here is all publicly traded equity only. **Warning #2:** These fractions may be overstating the ratio, because they include activity that did not result in a full takeover of the target. Other published estimates have included only full acquisitions [and used different definitions and data vendors] and reported numbers only about half this large.)

Sources: Thomson Financial and CRSP.

FIGURE 23.1 M&A Activity in Perspective, from 1970 to 2007

conditions. When interest rates are low, there are more acquisitions.) The bottom graph expands your perspective to foreign target acquisitions and includes attempted but not completed acquisitions. The United States typically accounts for about a quarter of worldwide acquisition activity *in dollar value*. Foreign and U.S. acquisitions seem to move in sync. (Incidentally and not reported, firms' equity issuing activity also synchronizes with the acquisition activity.)

To give some more perspective on the magnitude of takeover activity, the top graph in Figure 23.2 provides important background: It shows the value and number of all publicly traded firms in the U.S. markets. Figure 23.1 shows that in 2007, there were about 7,000 publicly traded firms with over $18 trillion in equity market capitalization. (U.S. GDP was under $14 trillion in 2007, which came to $44,000 per capita). The bottom graph of Figure 23.2 is our real interest: Was takeover activity an important economic activity or merely a sideshow? The graph shows that there were three peaks of M&A activity:

M&A activity was large enough that it is an important economic activity in a broader economy-wide context, too, especially at wave peaks.

1. The late 1980s (the most prominent takeover of the era was the RJR Nabisco hostile acquisition by Kohlberg Kravis Roberts (KKR)).
2. The turn of the millennium (the most prominent takeovers involved Internet firms, especially the acquisition of Time Warner by AOL). At this peak, all or partial acquisitions involved just under 10% of the public equity markets.
3. The mid-2000s (which included the acquisition of Chrysler by Cerberus).

Again, if we restrict ourselves to full rather than partial acquisitions, the numbers roughly halve. Yet even if only, say, 2–5% of all publicly traded firms are acquired, one would still be inclined to conclude that acquisition activity would qualify as an important economic phenomenon. Furthermore, Figure 23.1 shows that both market capitalization and takeover activity tend to increase in bull markets. Is the fraction of firms acquired higher or lower in bull markets? Figure 23.2 shows that *even relatively* more firms are acquired in bull markets. That is, acquisition activity is procyclical.

Hostile Acquisitions

Of particular interest are **hostile acquisitions**—those that are made without the consent of the target's board and management. Hostile acquisitions in the United States are the subject of Figure 23.3. First, you should notice that they are very rare. In a typical year, there are only a handful of them. Second, you should notice that they can be quite large. In particular, 1999 saw the hostile takeover of Warner-Lambert by Pfizer for just under $90 billion. With this one exception, hostile activity was far more common from 1983 to 1989 than in other years. This is also visible in the lower graph, where hostile activity is expressed in terms of all publicly traded firms. Hostile leveraged buyouts (LBOs) started with the advent of high-yield bonds in the early 1980s—invented by Michael Milken at Drexel Burnham Lambert. It peaked with the takeover of RJR Nabisco by KKR. (The book *Barbarians at the Gate* explains this takeover much better than I ever could. It is also highly entertaining.) It then took about 5–10 years for targets to learn how to better defend themselves against such unwanted approaches. Once this happened, and with the onset of the recession and bear market of the early 1990s, hostile activity declined again. Table 23.5 shows that, contrary to public perception, hostile takeovers are *not* principally a U.S. phenomenon. In

Hostile acquisitions are very rare. Though pioneered in the United States, they are *not* primarily a U.S. phenomenon.

➤ Takeovers, Section 24.5C, p. 928

➤ LBOs, Section 23.3, p. 877

➤ Target resistance, Section 23.3B, p. 883

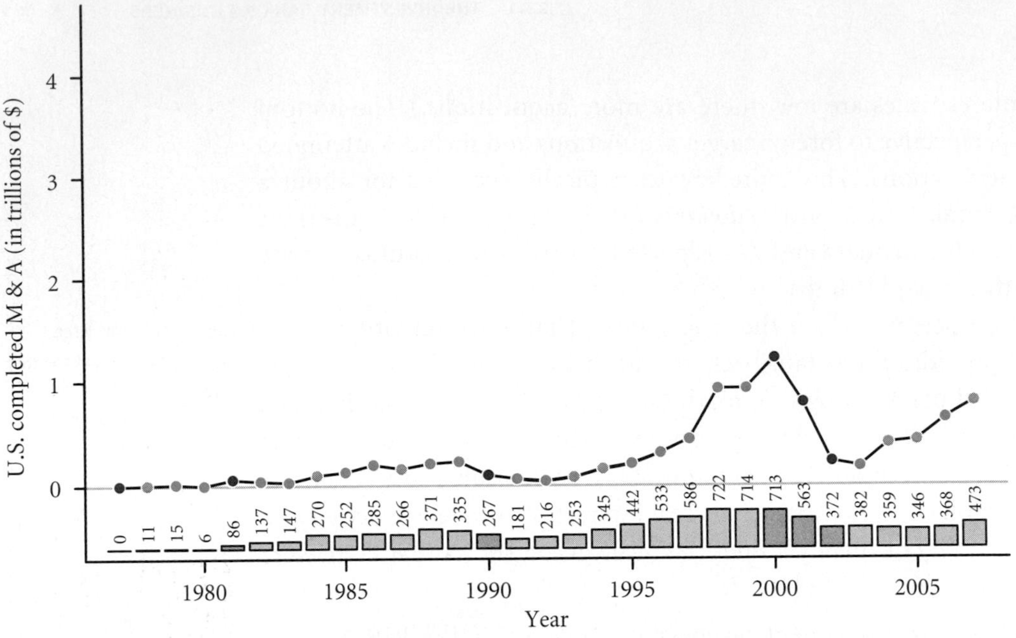

U.S. M&A Activity, Completed

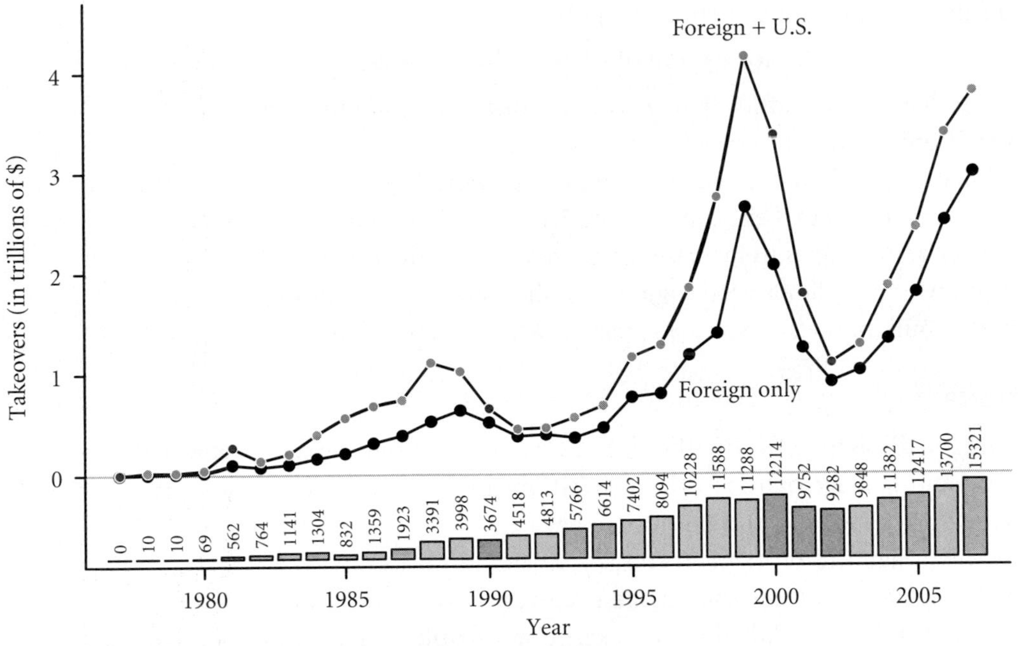

Global M&A Activity, Attempted and Completed

These graphs show M&A activity from 1970 to 2007. Dollar values are in trillions, adjusted to 2000 levels using the CPI. Years in which the S&P 500 declined are drawn in magenta. Years in which the S&P 500 increased by more than 10% are drawn in blue. Years in which the S&P 500 did not decline, but did not increase by more than 10%, are drawn in gray. Bars indicate the number of deals; lines indicate dollar values of deals.

The top graph shows completed U.S. M&A activity. (Targets need not be fully acquired, however. Some of the parts may remain publicly traded.) For example, in 1998, the number of transactions peaked at 722. In 2000, the value of transactions peaked at just over $1 trillion. The bottom graph shows all foreign M&A activity, including transactions that were not concluded. In addition, it relies on the dollar value of activity in global markets, not just in the U.S. markets. The graph shows that foreign acquisition activity is in sync with U.S. activity, and that U.S. activity accounts for about a quarter of worldwide activity. For example, in 1999, there were 11,288 foreign completed or attempted deals, with about $2.5 trillion in value. Adding the equivalent U.S. activity brings this number to over $4 trillion.

Source: Thomson Financial.

FIGURE 23.2 Mergers & Acquisitions, from 1970 to 2007

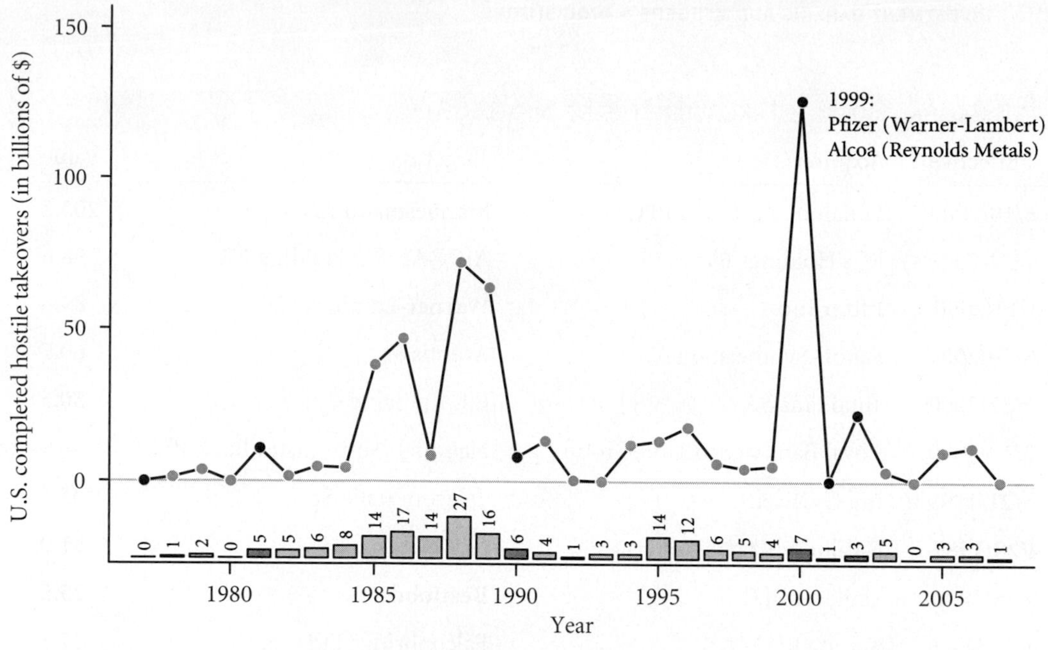

Absolute Number and Value of Completed Hostile U.S. Acquisitions

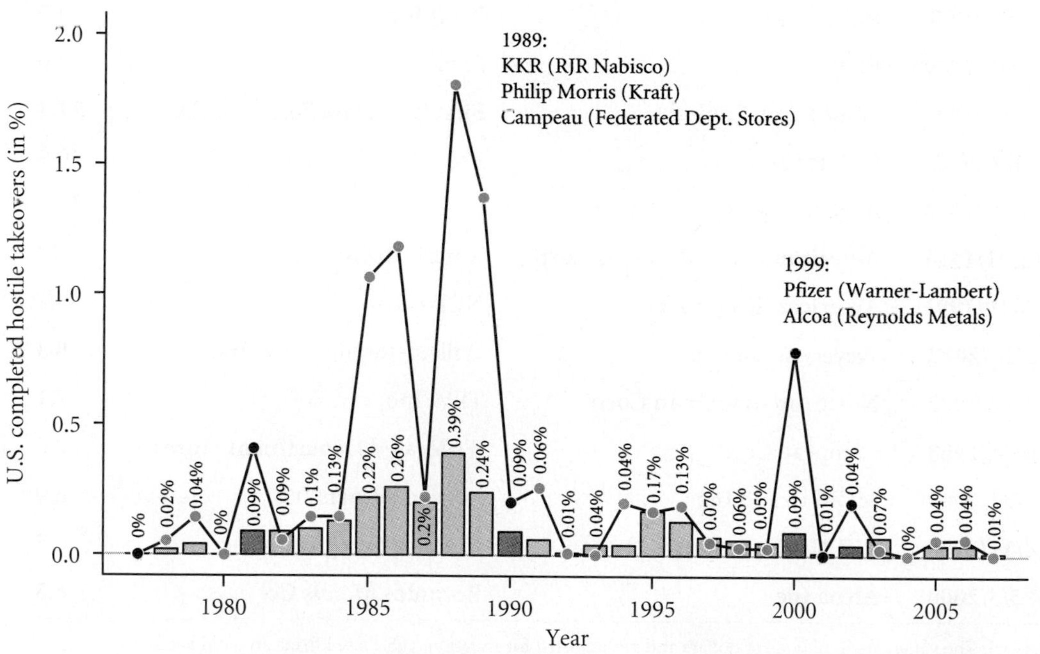

Relative to U.S. Publicly Traded Equity Market Capitalization

These graphs show hostile M&A activity in the United States. Years in which the S&P 500 declined are drawn in magenta. Years in which it increased by more than 10% are drawn in blue. Years in which the S&P 500 did not decline, but did not increase by more than 10%, are drawn in gray. The bars are statistics about the number of firms; lines are statistics about the value of target firms (in 2000 dollars).

The top graph shows that hostile acquisitions were quite rare. The number of hostile takeovers in the United States peaked at 27 in 1988. The value peaked in 1999 at around $130 billion, primarily because of Pfizer's hostile acquisition of Warner-Lambert for $89.6 billion.

The bottom graph shows this hostile takeover activity in the context of all publicly traded companies. Hostile activity was generally high in the 1980s. Thereafter, only 1999 stood out due to the aforementioned Pfizer acquisition of Warner-Lambert.

sources: Thomson Financial and CRSP.

FIGURE 23.3 Hostile Takeover Activity in the United States

TABLE 23.5 Top 25 Global Hostile Takeovers (as of Mid-2008)

Announced	Effective	Acquirer	Target	Value
11/14/1999	6/19/2000	Vodafone AirTouch PLC	Mannesmann AG	203.2
4/25/2007	11/2/2007	RFS Holdings BV	ABN-AMRO Holding NV	98.6
11/4/1999	**6/19/2000**	**Pfizer Inc**	**Warner-Lambert Co**	**89.6**
1/26/2004	8/20/2004	Sanofi-Synthelabo SA	Aventis SA	60.7
7/5/1999	3/27/2000	Total Fina SA	Elf Aquitaine	50.5
11/29/1999	3/13/2000	Royal Bank of Scotland Group	National Westminster Bank PLC	38.9
2/20/1999	5/21/1999	Ing C Olivetti	Telecom Italia SpA	35.2
10/24/1988	**4/28/1989**	**Kohlberg Kravis Roberts**	**RJR Nabisco Inc**	**31.0**
5/2/2000	**10/4/2000**	Unilever PLC	**Bestfoods**	**25.5**
5/15/2006	8/25/2006	Xstrata PLC	Falconbridge Ltd	17.8
8/11/2006	11/3/2006	Cia Vale do Rio Doce SA	Inco Ltd	17.6
1/20/1995	**5/1/1995**	**Glaxo Holdings PLC**	**Wellcome PLC**	**14.7**
10/17/1988	**12/7/1988**	**Philip Morris Inc**	**Kraft Inc**	**13.9**
3/9/1999	8/6/1999	BNP	Paribas SA	13.0
10/18/1995	**4/1/1996**	**Wells Fargo Capital Corp**	**First Interstate Bancorp, CA**	**11.4**
6/6/2003	**1/7/2005**	**Oracle Corp**	**PeopleSoft Inc**	**10.9**
9/14/1999	1/13/2000	Assicurazioni Generali SpA	INA	10.6
8/2/1994	**12/21/1994**	**American Home Products Corp**	**American Cyanamid Co**	**10**
12/2/1990	**9/19/1991**	**American Telephone**	**NCR Corp**	**8.3**
11/13/2000	**3/14/2002**	**Weyerhaeuser Co**	Willamette Industries Inc	**8.3**
2/22/2002	**12/11/2002**	**Northrop Grumman Corp**	TRW Inc	**7.1**
1/24/1988	**6/24/1988**	Campeau Corp	**Federated Department Stores**	**7.0**
2/22/2000	**5/31/2000**	**MGM Grand Inc**	**Mirage Resorts Inc**	**6.9**
10/16/1985	**4/17/1986**	**BCI Holdings Corp**	**Beatrice Companies Inc**	**6.5**
8/11/1999	**5/3/2000**	**Alcoa Inc**	**Reynolds Metals Co**	**6.5**

Source: Thomson Financial. The values are in billions of dollars and *not* adjusted for inflation. U.S.-based firms are boldfaced.

fact, the largest two hostile acquisitions ever did not even involve U.S. firms on either side. Of the top ten, only two involved U.S. firms. However, for practical purposes, the United States can claim to have pioneered them.

SOLVE NOW!

Q 23.9 Describe how global M&A activity changed over the last four decades.

Q 23.10 Are hostile takeovers just a U.S. phenomenon?

23.2 UNDERWRITING SERVICES FROM THE FIRM'S PERSPECTIVE

Now let's look at investment banking services from the perspective of the client firm—starting with underwriting. For most publicly traded firms, there is no way around hiring an underwriter for placing public securities. The expertise and contacts required are too much for most firms.

Underwriters are conflicted agents.

But how should a CFO think about and work with her investment bank? How much should she pay? As I have already hinted, it would be naïve for CFOs to consider investment banks as unconflicted agents working on their behalf. Investment banks make money from transactions. Thus, they will push their clients to engage in activity even if it is value-decreasing (though this is not their goal). Of course, a good investment bank can work hard and create value for its clients by identifying value-increasing acquisitions. Just don't attribute ulterior motives to the advisor (or the client), and remain aware of the conflicts involved.

23.2A UNDERWRITER SELECTION

Depending on context, underwriters are selected by different methods.

How should you select an underwriter? How do firms usually select underwriters? It is useful to distinguish between the following three situations:

Regulated offerings: Certain firms—principally utilities—are obliged to select underwriters for each offering through a competitive process.

The IPO market is competitive. Industry expertise and matching are important.

Initial public offerings: Firms engaging in IPOs typically interview a number of competing underwriters to select the best one for their particular situation. There is a natural matching process, in that large underwriters (with their higher cost bases) tend to charge higher fees, which makes them worthwhile only for large IPOs. Industry expertise is also very important. Such expertise can help the underwriter navigate the process more smoothly, communicate and better understand the concerns of top management, connect the firm to the right potential investors, and offer the services of specialized analysts who can help cover the offerings after the IPO. For offerings less than $100 million in size, underwriters compete less on a fee basis—they all charge about 7.0% gross spread—and more on a "package basis." This package includes such services as stabilizing the post-IPO trading price, post-IPO market making, marketing, process managing, share placing to particular types of investors, and so on. The firm then selects the team it likes best.

SEO underwriter selection is either by inertia, or, in rare instances, by competition.

Seasoned offerings: As long as the underwriter's expertise and size still match the firm, most of the time firms will select underwriters by simple inertia: They tend to go with the investment bank that they have always done business with. The most common reason for separation between a firm and its "house underwriter" is when the firm "outgrows" its historical underwriter and now needs to select a bigger one. When this happens, the selection process is often similar to that in the initial public offering. Managers will usually investigate the available options and select a team that is best for the firm (and themselves, of course).

Why don't issuers ask for a few competing bids from different underwriters?

However, there is a puzzle. There is empirical evidence that suggests that regulated utilities (and on rare occasions also some nonutilities) find it cheaper to ask several investment banks to compete for the underwriting of an issue—but most firms don't bother. They just continue to use their old investment banks. Why do ordinary firms not encourage greater competition in their underwriter choice? There are a number of possible reasons:

- Utilities firms could be intrinsically different. If more regular firms tried competitive bidding, most would end up paying more than they do when they just use standard noncompetitive bidding methods.
- Firms could be willing to pay more because the hired investment banks provide better ongoing service along other dimensions than the lowest-cost bidder. For example, services such as analyst coverage could be very important to clients. Smaller firms are especially willing to pay more for such coverage, which they can only do by paying generously for other investment banking services and maintaining a relationship over time. Moreover, it may take less management time if the existing underwriter is already well informed about the company through previous interactions.
- A more cynical view is that managers select their underwriters based on convenience and personal relationships.
- The most cynical view is that executives are personally conflicted. For example, they may like underwriters who help them personally. For instance, they may give them better and cheaper *personal* banking services (such as valuable allocations to underpriced shares in other initial public offerings). Investment banks may also provide a job-placement network that helps executives move to another company. After all, an investment banker who barely knows a CFO, except in the context of tough negotiations that minimize the bank's profits, is not likely to recommend an executive to a bigger and better company.

➤ IPO allocations to personal executive accounts, Section 24.2A, p. 905

These reasons are not mutually exclusive. In real life, there can be offerings in which fees seem high but they are actually low given the deal characteristics; offerings in which underwriters provide extra services; and still others in which underwriters get business by taking advantage of breakdowns in governance (managerial agency issues) inside their clients' corporations—the subject of our next chapter.

SOLVE NOW!

Q 23.11 What factors are important when firms select underwriters?

23.2B DIRECT UNDERWRITING FEES AND COSTS

The size distribution of different types of issues.

You already know approximately how much specific underwriters charge on average for debt and equity. But this does not tell you how much it will cost you to issue, say, \$50 million of a security. Figure 23.4 illuminates the underwriter spread as a fraction of proceeds. The numbers on the lines show the frequency upon which segments of each curve are based. For example, the most frequent IPO and SEO proceeds were around \$150 million (with 378 and 628 observations), the most frequent investment-grade offering proceeds were around \$300 million. Convertible and preferred offerings and speculative-grade offerings were all fairly rare.

Safer and larger offerings tend to have lower spreads.

Figure 23.4 shows that the same rank ordering of spreads from Tables 23.3 and 23.4 applies more generally: The more risk an offering has for sale, the higher the underwriting spread. There is usually more value at risk in a \$10 million equity

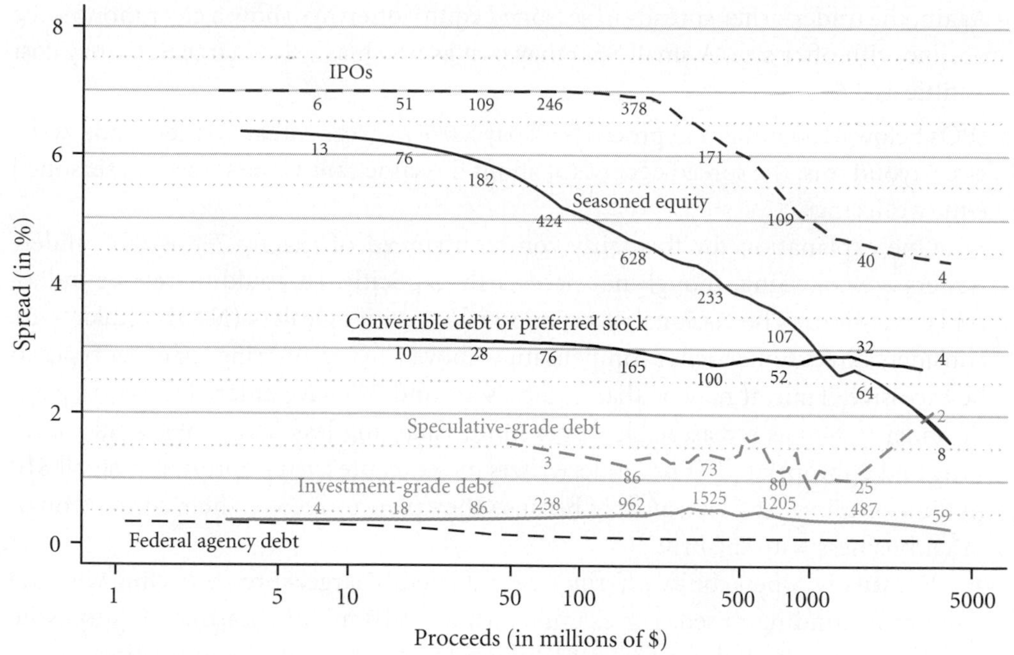

This figure shows the gross spread charged by the underwriter. The numbers on the lines describe the number of observations used to compute segments of these curves.
Source: Gerard Hoberg's website (http://www.rhsmith.umd.edu/faculty/ghoberg/byuw.html), based on data from Thomson Financial.

FIGURE 23.4 Typical U.S. Underwriter Spreads, 2005–2007

offering than in a $100 million bond offering. Thus, underwriting costs on the former are often higher even in absolute dollar terms (not just in percentage terms) than they are on the latter.

Underwriter spreads on different types of issues can be summarized as follows:

Here is a summary of all the findings. Read it!

- Remarkably, there is a strong robust relation between the offering size and the underwriter spread only for equity offerings. The underwriter spread appears fairly unrelated to the amount of proceeds for debt offerings.
- Federal agency–issued debt enjoys the lowest issuing costs, especially when the offering size is over $50 million. Spreads of about 0.1% to 0.2% of proceeds are normal.
- The cost of an investment-grade debt issue is within a narrow band (0.4% to 0.6%).
- Issuing speculative-grade debt is more expensive than issuing investment-grade debt. However, the relation between fees and proceeds is otherwise not too clear, because we have too few issues. Numbers between 0.8% and 2% are reasonable estimates for the underwriter spread, and around 1.5% seems to be a good average.
- There are also too few convertibles and preferred stock to draw strong conclusions, so I have lumped them together. From Table 23.4, you know that convertibles are about the same size, but tend to command a slightly lower underwriter spread than preferred stock. Spreads of around 3% seem about right. Interestingly, spreads are mostly unaffected by offering size; however, for the very largest offerings there does seem to be a small decline in spread.

- Again, the underwriter spreads in seasoned equity offerings show a clear monotonic decline with offer size. A small SEO may cost as much as 6%. A large SEO may cost as little as 2%.
- IPOs below $100 million in proceeds all pay 7.0% in gross spread to their underwriters. Beyond this, the spread declines at about the same rate as the spread on seasoned equity offerings.

  One explanation for this fairly common spread of exactly 7% is that underwriters are colluding, though not necessarily explicitly. (It could merely be industry convention.) The National Association of Securities Dealers (NASD) Rule 97-81 considers direct underwriter compensation above 7.5% in offerings of other types to be excessive. Thus, it may be that numbers around 7% have entered the conscience of underwriters as a reasonable upper limit: Charging less than 7.5% would seem "safe and appropriate." Thus, underwriters may execute even unprofitable small $10 million offerings at 7%, but only because they plan to recoup their costs through other business with the firm.

  Eventually, when equity offerings get sufficiently large, spreads decline with the amount of funding raised. For example, while a $10 million seasoned equity issue requires a spread of about 6%, a $1 billion seasoned equity issue requires only a spread of about 3%.

There are other costs than just underwriter spreads, too.

The underwriter spreads plotted in Figure 23.4 are not the only costs that issuers incur:

1. The spread does not include other direct costs. A 1996 paper by Lee, Lochhead, Ritter, and Zhao reported that from 1990 to 1994, direct costs other than the underwriter spread added about $0.5 million for small offerings and up to $2 million for large offerings. (Nowadays, these figures may have quadrupled.)
2. The spread does not account for the time and focus that management spends on the issuing process, which could otherwise have been spent more productively (an opportunity cost). The effort is relatively more modest in safer bond offerings, but for IPOs, it is a very lengthy and time-consuming task. In addition, any time delay in funding could itself be very costly, too. These costs are conceivably just as important as the underwriter spread, but we cannot assess them because we have no data on the costs of management time and project delay.
3. There are potentially other indirect costs and benefits that the revised capital structure itself creates—the subject of our earlier Chapters 17 and 18 and of Section 21.9. These would manifest themselves in more dilution.

➤ Opportunity costs, Section 1.1A, p. 2

➤ Dilution, Section 21.9A, p. 812

Bond Rating Costs

Bond rating agencies again.

➤ Bond ratings, Section 10.2B, p. 313

There is one additional direct cost to issuing debt that is worth mentioning. You already learned about bond rating agencies in Section 10.2B. Issuers can pay Moody's, Standard & Poor's, or Fitch to rate their bonds. This typically costs $5,000 to $25,000 per bond issue. Having a public bond rating helps potential investors gauge the risk. Indeed, many institutions are prohibited from buying any unrated bond, making ratings a necessity for many large bond offerings. Only the largest and most stable firms can issue investment-grade bonds, and having this rating is also a requirement to participate in the much shorter-term commercial paper market. All other firms

ANECDOTE Legal Monopolies: Bond Ratings

Prior to 2003, federal securities laws had just three "nationally recognized statistical rating organizations" (NRSRO): Moody's, Standard & Poor's, and Fitch. (In 2003, the SEC added Dominion; in 2005, it added A.M. Best; as of 2007, there were about 10 organizations.) In the second half of the twentieth century, the SEC began to rely on ratings to determine what sort of securities certain regulated financial institutions could own. The raters had not always enjoyed such privileged status. At the beginning of the twentieth century, they were simply investment service agencies that provided investors with research for a fee. In the 1970s, the revenue model changed, and Moody's and S&P (by far the larger and more important agencies) began to charge issuers instead of investors.

In 1994, the Jefferson County School District No. R-1 of Colorado decided not to obtain a Moody's ranking. To their surprise, Moody's decided to publish an unsolicited and unusually detailed "Special Comment" anyway. It was a negative rating that downgraded the school district, and interestingly, it occurred on the day of the pricing of the bond. Although Jefferson County sued, a judge later ruled that Moody's was protected by the First Amendment's *freedom of speech* clause.

This legal protection also helped the three major credit rating agencies in Enron's case. Most other service providers were sued by investors—investment bankers and auditors, in particular. But all three credit rating agencies had received substantial fees from Enron, too. Nevertheless, even when Enron was already trading at $3 per share and the market was aware of Enron's trouble, all three major agencies still failed to respond and instead held onto investment-grade ratings for Enron's debt for a while.

On June 4, 2008, the *Wall Street Journal* reported that the bond firms had finally agreed with the New York attorney general to reform their payment structure to make "agency shopping"—whereby issuers would select and pay only when receiving a good rating—more difficult. Now, agencies would have to require payment *before* issuing a rating. As of 2008, various government agencies and financial publications continue to scrutinize the rating agencies' practices.

can only issue speculative-grade bond, that is, bonds rated BB or worse. To get a better impression of issuing activity, please browse the issuing calendar in the *Wall Street Journal*, as well as *Moody's Bond Record* or the *S&P Bond Guide* in your local library. (The Moody's descriptions are now published by Mergent, a sister company of Moody's.)

➤ Table 6.2, p. 149

SOLVE NOW!

Q 23.12 A firm wants to raise $200 million. Compare the costs of issuing $20 million in seasoned equity versus those of issuing $100 million in speculative-grade debt and $100 million in seasoned equity. Which one is more expensive? Why?

23.3 MERGERS & ACQUISITIONS (M&A) FROM THE FIRM'S PERSPECTIVE

The second main function of investment banks—advice—arises principally in the context of mergers and acquisitions. A **merger** occurs when two corporations agree to marry on an equal basis. An **acquisition** occurs when one company purchases another. Conceptually, the two are sufficiently similar that most analysts commonly use the terms interchangeably. (Note that buyers can be smaller than the targets, especially if buyers rely on leverage to finance the acquisition.) The typical method of execution is the **tender offer**, which simply invites shareholders to present their

The M&A functions of investment bankers are advice and facilitation.

ANECDOTE RJR, Ego, and Overpayment

The bestseller *Barbarians at the Gate*, also made into a movie, describes the epic takeover battle for RJR Nabisco between Kohlberg Kravis Roberts and RJR management (supported by Shearson Lehman [now Lehman Brothers]). In October 1988, RJR's CEO Ross Johnson and his predecessors had mismanaged the company long enough to allow him to offer RJR shareholders the premium price of $17.6 billion in a leveraged management buyout. Because of a conflict of interest, Johnson had to resign from the board when it contemplated Johnson's buyout offer. This, in turn, opened the door to a $20.6 billion counteroffer by KKR. Eventually, KKR purchased RJR for $25 billion, and Johnson got a $53 million golden parachute. This takeover was also probably KKR's biggest miscalculation, in that it overpaid for RJR. The prime reasons were personal egos and animosities, which fueled an irrational bidding war—all to the benefit of RJR shareholders.

➤ Table 22.7, p. 838

shares in exchange for cash or stock. Its execution can be contingent on enough shares being tendered. The role of the investment bank is not only to advise, but also to facilitate and handle the legal parts of the M&A processes. These M&A functions also overlap with the world of underwriting, because much issuing—and almost all seasoned equity issuing by older Fortune 100 companies—occurs in M&A contexts. However, successful M&A advising does not require an underwriting department. There are some prominent M&A advisors that have no underwriting business—most prominently, the two boutique firms of Lazard and Rothschild.

Leveraged buyouts allow small firms to swallow large firms.

➤ High-powered leverage, Section 6.4E, p. 161

➤ Corporate governance and M&A, Section 24.5C, p. 928

One particular form of acquisition is the **leveraged buyout** (**LBO**), in which the acquirer is financing the buyout mostly with debt. Thus, the acquirer usually ends up owning only a small slice of the firm in the form of very high-powered equity. Consequently, even modest post-LBO underperformance could result in a total investment loss for the LBO buyer. This gives the acquirer enormous incentives to get everything right. Indeed, it is generally believed that the two most important sources of value in a leveraged buyout are these:

1. Better control of agency conflicts.
2. The reduction of corporate income tax obligations through the use of debt (explained in Chapter 17).

There are many **private equity** firms that specialize in leveraged buyouts. The most prominent firm of the 1980s was Kohlberg Kravis Roberts (having purchased, among many other firms, RJR Nabisco). The most prominent firm today may well be Cerberus Capital (having purchased, among many other firms, Chrysler). In the typical LBO, the acquirer either fires existing management or completely restructures the existing management-compensation contracts in order to dramatically improve managerial incentives. In a **management buyout** (**MBO**), the existing management itself becomes the LBO buyer.

Hostile acquisitions are rare but especially interesting.

The overwhelming majority of mergers and acquisitions are friendly, that is, they are solicited by or occur with the blessing of target management. However, this is not always the case. In a hostile takeover (formally called an **unsolicited bid**), a **corporate raider** makes a tender offer to purchase shares in order to obtain either the whole firm or a voting majority. If the acquirer succeeds, he can appoint new board members. They in turn can oust management, allowing the acquirer to take control.

23.3A REASONS FOR MERGERS & ACQUISITIONS

Managers are often enthusiastic about acquiring more companies. It is often not a necessary condition (though usually a welcome one) that the acquisition benefit the acquirer's shareholders. As far as managers are concerned, running a bigger company usually means more prestige and more compensation down the line. In some cases, however, this enthusiasm is short-lived. If an acquirer underperforms significantly in the years after the acquisition, existing management may face a larger risk of being ousted. If an acquisition is bad enough, it can contribute to such poor performance and thus management dismissals. In contrast, target managers are often reluctant participants. They often lose not just their independence but also their jobs. Thus, unless adequately "bribed," target management naturally often wants to resist (the subject of the next section)—even if their shareholders would be better off.

Acquiring management usually likes acquisitions. Target management rarely likes acquisitions (unless suitably bribed).

An extreme example of this conflict of interest was the merger between Chase and Bank One. The *Wall Street Journal* reported:

One of my favorite corporate tales . . .

➤ JP Morgan Chase and Bank One, Anecdote, p. 424

> The negotiation took place between the Bank One CEO, Dimon, and JP Morgan Chase CEO Harrison, both of whom wanted to become CEO immediately. The original plan was for Dimon to succeed Harrison after two years. Dimon offered to sell Bank One at a zero premium if he just were to become the merged company's CEO immediately. Harrison rejected this offer, and instead paid a $7 billion premium from Chase shareholders to Bank One shareholders in order to retain his post for these two extra years.

Let me rephrase this for you: Dimon offered to pay $7 billion of Chase shareholders' money to Bank One shareholders simply for the privilege of not having to wait just 2 years before becoming CEO—and, not to be outdone, Harrison refused to accept the $7 billion on behalf of Bank One's shareholders in order to be the boss for just 2 more years! The conflicts of interest between shareholders and managers are the subject of the next chapter.

VALUE CHANGES

The fact that managers like acquisitions does not mean that M&As are value neutral or exist only for the benefit of acquiring managers. M&A transactions can create or destroy value for shareholders, too. The combined or acquired entity could be worth more than the two original units. The most important causes of corporate value gains (though not in order of importance) are the following:

Here is a laundry list of where potential value gains in acquisitions can come from.

Scale synergies: The merging of systems, skills, structures, departments, and staff can improve operating efficiency. Efficiency gains due to economies of scale can result from a number of sources:

➤ Synergies and the economics of project interactions, Section 12.4, p. 401

- Elimination of duplicate departments and fixed overhead can lower operating costs. For example, headquarters, legal, human resources, and IT departments may be combinable.
- Production and distribution efficiencies, for example, in the merging of ATM networks, can attract more bank customers.
- Reduction of market imperfections: Smaller firms may also find it easier to tap the public financial markets and thus gain financing efficiencies by linking with other firms. (From 1996 to 1999, so-called **rollups** were popular, in which multiple

small firms were combined into one entity that was then large enough to be taken public.) More generally, by reducing the idiosyncratic risks, some mergers may also reduce bankruptcy costs, information disagreements, share illiquidity, and so on, thereby making the financial market more perfect.

Reduction of competition: The elimination of the target from competition with the acquirer can make it easier to raise prices.

Expertise: An acquirer may find it easier to purchase a firm than to build up the expertise of the target. Although this may not raise the overall value of the new entity, doing this could still be the cheapest option for the acquirer. (This was the prime reason in the attempted Yahoo takeover by Microsoft described in Section 23.3D.)

Elimination of poor target management: It may simply be that current management is running the firm into the ground, and replacing it (kicking and screaming) could provide value gains.

Shutdown efficiencies: Sometimes it is better to shrink or liquidate a firm, but the current management is unwilling or unable to execute drastic measures. A takeover by individuals with less of an institutional history often makes this easier.

➤ Breaking loyalty when doing so increases firm value, Section 24.2B, p. 908

Expropriation: A transfer of management can allow breaking implicit promises that firms have made but not put into writing. All companies rely on at least some employee loyalty, and all employees rely on at least some company loyalty. It is impossible to contract out every small promise that employers make to employees, and vice versa. Usually, this is a fair, efficient, and trustworthy arrangement.

But it also leaves firms vulnerable, because a takeover can generate value by breaking implicit promises. For example, consider a company that, although it pays lower salaries than the rest of the industry, attracts employees by implicitly promising long-term employment stability and generous pension and health benefits. This makes early operations especially profitable. Yet as the company and its workers age, these liabilities can become quite significant, and a takeover could allow new management to save money by firing now older and more expensive employees or by replacing an overfunded pension fund and health care plan with a less costly and less safe alternative. (In the 1980s, there were some prominent examples in which the substitute low-cost insurance provider then promptly went bankrupt.)

It is also often difficult to distinguish expropriation from shutdown efficiencies. If an older worker has foregone better opportunities elsewhere in order to receive a pension, is his firing and the elimination of his pension an expropriation or efficient (value-enhancing) governance?

The tax benefits and corporate governance improvement are often two extremely important sources of value.

There are two more *very important* value gains that come about through the higher leverage often assumed in acquisitions, especially in leveraged or management buyouts:

➤ Firm value and corporate taxes under different capital structures, Section 17.2, p. 612

Tax benefits: Higher debt ratios reduce the amount of taxes collected by the IRS.

Better governance: The need to service debt usually makes it easier to convince both managers and employees that they have to work harder and spend less on pet projects—or the firm will go bankrupt. Ironically, management buyouts are often contemplated by the most wasteful managers, who themselves have the incentives to make their own corporations look bad, so that they can buy them cheaply and then magically improve them.

All of these can be important M&A value drivers, though not equally important in each and every takeover. In some takeovers, the important driver may be primarily synergies; in others, it may be primarily better governance.

But acquisitions can also destroy value.

However, many takeovers also fail in delivering value enhancements. The most common negatives when a larger company takes over a smaller company are less focus, more bureaucracy, and poorer management. (The canonical example here may be Quaker's acquisition of Snapple for $1.7 billion in 1994 and its resale for only $300 million just 2 years later. You can read sordid tales by googling for the history of this acquisition.) There is good evidence that takeover activity in the 1960s and 1970s was driven by the desires of managers to increase firm size and form conglomerates, many of which were then run more poorly after the acquisition than before. That is, a company that suffers from poor governance may see its managers purchase other companies for management's sake rather than for the shareholders' sake. As noted at the outset of this section, acquiring managers can benefit by the following:

➤ Acquisitions by uncontrolled management, Section 24.1D, p. 903

Idiosyncratic risk reduction: Takeovers naturally increase the scale of the firm. This typically reduces the idiosyncratic risk of the firm and increases the firm's revenues and earnings. However, this need not create any value. Risk reduction can be achieved by investors themselves holding the shares of both companies; and they would just as well hold their shares of the combined firm's revenues and earnings.

Larger empire: Acquiring managers tend to like running bigger firms not only because it makes them more important but also because managers of bigger firms usually receive more compensation.

➤ Empire building, Section 12.8, p. 420

Ironically, in the 1980s, the situation reversed: Many of these large conglomerates were themselves taken over by smaller firms and promptly dismembered. However, it is not without cost when smaller firms take over larger firms, either. The most common negatives are the loss of the benefits of easy access to more capital (meaning that projects are cut back if they do not generate cash to service debt in the immediate future), and the lack of diversification by the new owner. Many LBOs will cut positive-NPV projects, especially if they are risky and long-term—risk-shifting incentives notwithstanding.

➤ Risk shifting, Section 18.5A, p. 676

SOLVE NOW!

Q 23.13 If the firm fires workers that cost more than they are producing, is this always a sign of better governance that is in the interest of society?

Q 23.14 What are the main sources of value generated in most mergers & acquisitions? Are all of them in the interest of society as a whole?

VALUE-CHANGE BENEFICIARIES

Which shareholders gain? This depends on the purhcase price.

I have not yet answered one important question: Who benefits from the net value changes (hopefully positive value gains)—the acquiring shareholders or the target shareholders? Conceptually, this is easiest to think of in terms of an efficient market, in which the target was priced as if the acquirer had not yet appeared:

➤ Unexpected and expected value changes, Section 11.7, p. 375

- If the acquirer purchases the target at the original market price, then all gains and losses that the acquisition itself produces would accrue to the acquirer.
- If the acquirer purchases the target at a price above the previously prevailing one, then some merger benefits would accrue to target shareholders.
- If the price fully includes the value of all net benefits, only the target shareholders gain from the net benefits, and the acquiring shareholders end up indifferent.
- If the price is even higher, the acquiring shareholders lose money to the target shareholders.

Here is an extreme example of the issues involved. The poster child for the end of the LBO wave of the 1980s was Campeau's 1988 purchase of Federated Department Stores (which owns Macy's and Bloomingdales) for $7.67 billion. Before the buyout, it had traded for $4.35 billion. Thus, Campeau paid a $3.32 billion windfall to target shareholders. They did well. However, Campeau did not. When Campeau emerged from bankruptcy in 1992, it became clear that Campeau had created value—just not for itself. It had managed to raise Federated's value from $4.35 to $5.85 billion (adjusting for market movements over the same period)—a $1.5 billion value increase during a recession! Unfortunately for Campeau, this was still well below the $7.67 billion purchase price.

Target shareholders almost always gain, while acquiring shareholders often come out even or lose.

Of course, a single anecdote is not systematic evidence. However, it appears that the Campeau evidence is extreme, but not isolated. The empirical evidence suggests that *on average* (i.e., not in each and every takeover), the following holds:

Target shareholders: They almost always make out like bandits. The average takeover premium seems to be around 20–30% above the public pre-takeover price. A study by Ernst and Young showed that this premium even shot up to between 40% and 50% from 1996 to 2000. Moreover, when target management succeeded in scuttling the takeover attempt, the target's average share price usually declined significantly, often back to the original pre-takeover price.

➤ Price effect of Microsoft dropping its Yahoo offer, Section 23.3D, p. 886

Acquiring shareholders: With acquiring managers eager to take over other companies, it should perhaps not come as a surprise, then, that most of the takeover value gains have not accrued to the acquirer's shareholders. On the contrary, many acquirers have been overpaying. A study by Moeller, Schlingemann, and Stulz (2005) looked at publicly trading acquirers. They found that the average acquirer from 1980 to 1998 lost about 1.6 cents in value for every acquisition dollar. From 1998 to 2001, this shot up to 12 cents per acquisition dollar. As usual, there was a lot of heterogeneity across M&As. Much of the 12 cent figure was driven by some *really* bad outlier acquisitions. Again, this was an average. There were also many acquisitions that were greeted positively by the share price of the announcing acquirer. You have to judge acquisitions on a one-by-one basis.

The evidence on net gains is mixed.

With large average gains to the usually smaller target and small average losses to the usually larger acquirer, is there a net loss or a net gain? Such evidence could speak to the question about whether there are synergies or efficiency gains. The evidence is mixed. Net in net, the dollar benefit to target shareholders plus the dollar cost to acquiring shareholders (the acquirer is usually larger!) seems to be just about zero. Again, be warned that there is great heterogeneity here.

SUMMARY

In sum, target managers are almost always worse off if the acquisition succeeds (absent any side payment to them personally); acquiring managers are often, though not always, better off if the acquisition succeeds. The opposite appears to be the case for shareholders. Target shareholders are almost always better off; acquiring shareholders may be worse off. If there ever was a situation rife with agency conflicts between managers and shareholders, M&As are it.

Acquisitions are rife with agency conflicts (and solutions to them) left and right.

Before we leave the subject of who gains and who loses, let's mention that there are also some other parties involved in takeover transactions. First, there are the investment banks. They make good fees both from M&A financing and from M&A advice. Naturally, they are eager to push potential acquirers into such transactions. Other investment banks make money by "defending" the target. They, too, can earn good fees. Second, there are other stakeholders in the firm: employees, suppliers, customers, and so on. It is not clear whether they tend to gain or lose. It is correct that they are often squeezed in the initial stages of a completed takeover, but if a target is better managed after the acquisition, it may actually grow more in the long run. In some cases, the long-run beneficial effects can be much higher than the short-run pain.

Investment bankers love M&As; few other stakeholders in the firms do, though this is not always the case.

SOLVE NOW!

Q 23.15 Can an acquisition that is value increasing be a bad deal for the acquirer?

Q 23.16 Why do many firms like to acquire other firms?

23.3B RESISTANCE TO CORPORATE CONTROL ACTIVITY

Target management is not helpless. On the contrary, when approached by an unwelcome outsider, they can resist a hostile takeover through so-called **shark repellents**. Among the more prominent defenses are the following:

Management can resist being acquired with some very powerful tactics.

Greenmail: Management uses shareholders' money to "buy off" the shares of a potential acquirer at a premium. This has become rare due to bad publicity.

Golden parachute: Management lets itself be bought off with a large bonus by the acquirer. (It is a defense only if it is large enough to deter the acquirer.)

Acquisitions: The target management buys other companies, because a bigger company is more difficult to take over. (This is called the "blowfish" defense.)

Scorched earth: Management can threaten to sell off corporate assets that are of particular interest to the acquirer.

Poison pill: When triggered, a poison pill entitles other shareholders to purchase more shares at a discount. The potential raider would then have to repurchase these shares at the acquisition price, too. The emergence of poison pills in the 1990s essentially shut down all hostile acquisition activity.

New share issuance (without the poison pill): Management issues more shares to employees and themselves. Similar alternatives are accelerating the vesting of existing shares and options, and promising high severance packages for any employees wanting to leave if the firm is taken over. The acquirer would then have to repurchase more shares and pay employees more.

Fair value provision: A fair value provision forces an acquirer to pay every shareholder the same price, that is, the highest price at which *any* share can be acquired. In other words, the effective share acquisition price changes from the lower average price to the higher marginal price.

Supermajority rule: An acquirer is required to obtain more than just a majority of votes to replace the board. (Moreover, Delaware law [where most large publicly traded firms are incorporated] restricts what raiders can do if they control between 15% and 85% of the shares for up to 2 years.)

Litigation: Management can delay a potential takeover in the courts, especially if the potential acquirer is in the same industry, in which case antitrust litigation issues can come into play.

Staggered boards virtually eliminate all hostile takeovers.

➤ Delaware, p. 915

However, by far the most effective takeover prevention strategy is the following:

Staggered board: Each year, only a fraction of the directors are up for reelection. (Another Delaware provision requires this fraction to be at least one-third). Therefore, even an outsider owning 100% of the shares on the day of the annual shareholder meetings cannot take control of the board. Only one-third of the board will be replaced; the other two-thirds will remain in office. This means that the company will continue to be under the control of the existing board for at least 1 more year, during which the existing management can do a lot of harm.

The refinement in defensive weaponry is probably the prime reason why hostile takeovers have become so infrequent after the 1990s.

The Indirect Effects of (the Possibilities of) Attack and Defense

Resistance can be good—especially if it is futile.

Not all managerial resistance by the target is necessarily value reducing. For example, resistance can, and often has, forced acquirers to pay more for the firm. To the extent that target management resists, it has often forced the acquirer to sweeten the offer—a good thing for target shareholders if it raises the price, a bad thing for target shareholders if it leads the acquirer to abandon the offer.

Is a golden parachute a good thing?

Acquirers also have other tools at their disposal. To get target management to cooperate—to make it "friendly"—acquirers usually pay a (perfectly legal) personal bribe to target management, called a **golden parachute**. But even the golden parachute has often been argued to be a good thing for target shareholders. If it is not too large, it may help induce target management not to resist to the point where the acquisition is aborted. (The moral argument that target managers deserve it because they have invested so much of their human capital in the firm rings hollow, though. The same management rarely insists on the same kinds of golden parachutes for their ordinary long-term employees, many of whom are unceremoniously laid off without fanfare or extra compensation after the acquisition.) Unfortunately, despite much research, it is still not clear when the presence of a golden parachute is good on average and when it is bad for shareholders.

(Is a golden parachute morally appropriate?)

It is also important that you realize that even if hostile takeovers are rare and even if defense mechanisms are rarely triggered, they set a much broader stage for the company. (Think about how nuclear weapons were never used in Europe but still determined how the Cold War between the United States and the Soviet Union played out.) First, they dictate the attitudes in negotiations between the parties for potential friendly acquisitions. The target is well aware that the acquirer could become a lot more nasty; the acquirer is well aware that the target could trigger defenses. This influences the outcome of the negotiations—or the lack of negotiations—depending on the relative strengths of the parties. Second, even if target management ultimately wins (or is never approached by an outside offer to begin with), it may still have to shape up—for example, by making a competing tender repurchase offer for its own shares or by paying more of its free cash back to shareholders (e.g., in the form of a repurchase or extraordinary dividend).

The fallback option of a hostile takeover attempt can have a strong influence on how firms behave—even if they are themselves rare.

➤ Extraordinary dividends and repurchases, Section 19.1, p. 704

SOLVE NOW!

Q 23.17 What can an executive do to resist a takeover?

Q 23.18 Is it true that if hostile takeovers are rare, they should not matter very much?

23.3C PROXY CONTESTS AND SHAREHOLDER RESOLUTIONS

If target management is not helpless, neither is the potential raider. In addition to the outright assault of a hostile takeover attempt, raiders have some other weapons. In a **proxy contest**, a large shareholder (with enough shares to care to spend a lot of time and money) can actively solicit other shareholders to vote against management's own board slate and in favor of an alternative board slate. Often, a hostile would-be acquirer launches both a hostile offer and a proxy contest to eliminate the board and any charter provisions that would prevent him from purchasing all shares. The most prominent recent proxy contest may be Hewlett-Packard's in 2002 and Yahoo's in 2008, which is narrated below. Very few proxy contests without a simultaneous takeover are ultimately successful, and though they are cheaper than a full-blown takeover, they are still not cheap.

Proxy contests seek votes to change management and the board.

➤ Costs of proxy contests, Section 24.5C, p. 930

➤ HP proxy contest, Section 24.5C Anecdote, p. 930

A more modest and dirt-cheap form of the proxy contest is the **shareholder proposal**. Any shareholder can put forth a shareholder proposal for vote by all shareholders. The SEC judges whether shareholder proxy suggestions are appropriate for a shareholder vote. (The rules by which the SEC accepts or rejects shareholder proposals are explained at http://www.sec.gov/interps/legal/cfslb14.htm.) Shareholder proposals are usually not binding and can therefore be ignored by the board. The Delaware court has declared that if a shareholder resolution were binding, it would infringe on the board's prerogatives, which therefore would allow the board to exclude the resolution from a vote altogether. To avoid triggering this clause, shareholder proposals must not be binding.

Shareholder proposals are odd creatures and nonbinding . . .

Nevertheless, shareholder proposals carry both moral sway and signaling value: If a large number of shares vote in favor of a proposal, it is more difficult for the board to pretend that this proposal is not in the shareholders' interest. Moreover, if a majority

. . . but they can still carry quite a punch.

of shareholders votes in favor, chances are that a full-blown proxy contest revisiting the same question would succeed. Any sane management would naturally fear that a positive outcome would encourage such a proxy contest, and thus many boards have followed some of the recommendations of shareholder proposals, even though they were not binding.

- Shareholder proposals have been particularly useful in removing antitakeover defenses. The most frequent shareholder proposal concerns the staggering of the board. This can set the stage for later takeovers if the management continues to perform poorly. For example, Lucian Bebchuk (a leading corporate governance researcher from Harvard) offered a shareholder proposal in March 2008 that Safeway change its bylaws to limit its poison pills. In response, Safeway adopted the provision and Bebchuk withdrew the proposal.
- Other boards have ignored shareholder proposals. For example, in May 2007 and again in May 2008, shareholders holding 40% of Exxon's shares voted for a resolution that Exxon invest in alternative energy and separate the position of chairman and CEO. The chairman and CEO, Rex Tillerson, promptly announced that he would ignore the resolution, defending his action with the public remark that Exxon already paid 49% of its earnings to tax authorities. (This is a bizarre defense: Wasting 49% of shareholders' money through poor tax management is not a good argument against either better investment policies or better corporate governance.)
- Many other shareholder proposals are brought by special interest groups, such as churches or labor unions, and are not necessarily in the interest of shareholders. They are almost always voted down. For example, in May 2008, Google shareholders voted down proposals about instituting a board on human rights and doing business in China.

Nowadays, many less-than-friendly takeovers begin with shareholder proposals a few years prior and/or immediate proxy contests that seek to eliminate the takeover defenses.

SOLVE NOW!

Q 23.19 What are some of the reasons why the fear of proxy and takeover contests may not control all CEOs?

Q 23.20 How is a shareholder proposal different from a proxy contest?

23.3D MORE EMPIRICAL EVIDENCE ABOUT M&A ACTIVITY

I love this tale. It has all the elements of a good movie.

Before we look at the systematic empirical evidence, let's have some fun and start with a juicy tale. The *Wall Street Journal* featured an article in its Weekend edition (January 19–20, 2008, p. B16) called "Yahoo's Ripe for Shake-Up":

> Yahoo chief Jerry Yang recently summarized a plan to turn the company around by becoming the start page for every Internet user across the globe. What Mr. Yang failed to provide, however, was a convincing solution to Yahoo's existential crisis. The Hamlet of the Web won't succeed by simply trying to become a start page. Yahoo is navigating the waters of Internet advertising like a goldfish evading

a shark, in the form of Google. Activist investors ought to take heed—Yahoo is ready for a shake-up.

Yahoo, based in Sunnyvale, Calif., has many ingredients that make it a tantalizing target for uppity investors. There's a discredited management team, a corporate strategy in need of a makeover, stock-price underperformance, a large free float with no controlling shareholder, cash on the balance sheet and many moving parts whose values don't appear to be adequately reflected in the Yahoo share price—particularly its investments in two hot Asian Internet firms.

Consider the management question. A month after Mr. Yang, a Yahoo founder, took over from former Hollywood studio boss Terry Semel in June, he promised action to turn around the flailing Internet titan within 100 days. Nearly 200 days later, there is little sign of this. Since he took over, Yahoo stock has dropped 23%, while Google's has added roughly 10%. In the past two years, the company's value has been halved, so it is hard to see how investors would oppose a management shake-up.

On strategy, Yahoo has many strengths, but its primary weakness remains in search, where its U.S. market share has dropped to 17% from 22% a year ago, despite investing mightily to catch up to Google. An activist would almost certainly pressure Yahoo to swallow its pride and hand its search traffic over to Microsoft, or even Google, for a fat fee. Outsourcing search could boost Yahoo's revenue from the business by at least 30% to $3.5 billion, according to some analyst estimates.

Then there are Yahoo's stakes in Yahoo Japan and Alibaba. Although they fluctuate in value, they currently are valued at $8.4 billion and $4 billion, respectively. If monetized, the two stakes, which represent a huge chunk of Yahoo's $28 billion of market value, could provide a windfall for the company's shareholders. But there is a problem: Yahoo would incur steep capital-gains taxes in a sale.

That is, unless Yahoo gets creative with its finances. And this may be where an activist with a little corporate finance up his sleeve could make a big difference. According to Sanford Bernstein analyst Jeffrey Lindsay, the company could, for example, employ what is known as a reverse Morris Trust structure. This would essentially allow Yahoo to put the stakes into a new listed entity, let's call it Yahoo Asian Investment Co. (Yaico), which could then be spun off to Yahoo's shareholders tax-free.

Given Yahoo's low share price, an external offer was a real possibility. Remarkably, when it came, it was not from an acquirer seeking to break it up to improve its operations. Instead, it came from an unexpected corner.

On February 1, 2008, Microsoft extended an unsolicited (i.e., hostile) acquisition offer for Yahoo at $31 per share ($44.6 billion for the company)—a 62% premium over Yahoo's $19 stock price before the offer. For Microsoft, Yahoo was worth more than just its breakup value. It was the potential synergy that a quick acquisition could provide in Microsoft's attempt to take on Google on the World Wide Web.

Google was obviously less than thrilled. A Microsoft merger with Yahoo could resuscitate the latter as a Web competitor. Thus, just one day after the announcement, a Google executive blogged that "a Microsoft-Yahoo merger could threaten the openness on which the Internet is based." Despite a history of a cold and competitive relationship vis-à-vis Yahoo, Google CEO Eric Schmidt even called Jerry Yang to offer help—most probably in the form of a partnership between the companies, in order to thwart Microsoft.

By February 11, Yahoo had rebuffed the Microsoft offer as being too low. In a letter to shareholders, Yang was claiming a value for Yahoo of at least $40 per share. It also began a search for a "white knight." (A **white knight** is a company that offers a friendly takeover to another company under threat of a hostile takeover from an unwelcome bidder, sometimes known as a **black knight**.) It began talks with News Corp, but almost exactly one month later, News Corp had dropped out.

After having informed Yahoo that it was willing to raise its offer to $33 per share, Microsoft withdrew its bid on May 4 when Yahoo demanded $37. At the opening of the stock market on May 5, Yahoo's price dropped in value by about $8.5 billion (a 20% drop, from $29 to $23). On the other hand, Microsoft's stockholders were ecstatic: Microsoft's share price increased by about $5 billion (2%). Remarkably, Google was another big winner—its equity value also increased by about $4 billion (also 2%).

On May 3, Carl Icahn (a well-known corporate raider) announced that he had begun to accumulate shares with the goal of forcing Yahoo to sell out to Microsoft. He started a proxy contest, proposing his own slate of directors for the next Yahoo shareholder meeting, set for August 1, and then also proposed firing Yahoo's Jerry Yang as CEO. At the same time but independently, a large shareholder filed suit in Delaware against the board (*Police and Fire Retirement System of the City of Detroit v. Yahoo, CA3561*). On June 3, 2008, the Delaware court refused to keep papers sealed that revealed that Microsoft had in fact offered $40 per share in January. Apparently, Yang had also effectively torpedoed the Microsoft offer by insisting that all employees receive a severance plan that would incentivize them to quit rather than stay on under different management. (This applied even more so to Yahoo executives.) The pension fund then amended its suit, because this severance plan could also be triggered if Icahn were to take control of the board first. On June 13, Yang announced that all continuing talks with Microsoft had ended, because Microsoft had withdrawn from the $47.5 billion offer that it had put on the table the previous month. Yahoo also announced a search partnership with Google that it hoped would raise its advertising revenue. On these news announcements, Yahoo shares dropped 3.6%, and Microsoft shares increased 1.9%.

On July 25, Icahn and Yahoo came to a surprising agreement: Icahn and two of his associates would join the 11-member Yahoo board, but Yang would continue to control the board. This new board was elected (with some shareholder grumblings) on August 1. It is anybody's guess at this point what will happen next.

More about Takeover Characteristics and the Role of Investment Banks

Statistics about issuer and advisor characteristics for 15,000 deals from 1980 to 2003.

Let's learn more about the systematic characteristics of deals and investment banking fees now. Table 23.6 presents the key table from a recent academic study. It gives detailed statistics for (almost) all domestic acquisitions that involved a publicly traded corporation between 1980 and 2003. It classifies deals by the quality of advisor (within

TABLE 23.6 AVERAGE CHARACTERISTICS OF U.S. M&A TRANSACTIONS FROM 1980 TO 2003

	Tier of Acquirer Advisor				Tier of Target Advisor			
	Top	Middle	Bottom	All	Top	Middle	Bottom	All
Firm Value (in millions)	$7,642	$5,084	$1,020	$4,916	$2,106	$1,237	$265	$1,395
Median (in millions)	$1,765	$711	$213	$736	$440	$251	$65	$241
Acq and Tgt in Same Industry	63.6%	62.7%	65.9%	64.0%	49.0%	45.5%	60.5%	52.2%
Proportion of Public Acquirers					64.5%	62.0%	72.0%	66.6%
Proportion of Public Targets	58.5%	50.4%	43.3%	51.3%				
Deal (Tgt) value (in millions)	$1,357	$659	$127	$761	$1,821	$663	$126	$840
Median (in millions)	$275	$132	$37	$120	$403	$138	$48	$127
Proportion of Tender Offers	19.7%	17.7%	9.7%	16.1%	24.9%	23.1%	15.3%	20.8%
Proportion of Hostile Deals	3.6%	3.9%	0.8%	2.9%	10.4%	5.3%	2.0%	5.7%
Number of Acquirer Advisors	1.20	1.11	1.03	1.12	0.84	0.67	0.49	0.66
Number of Target Advisors	0.90	0.77	0.59	0.76	1.34	1.16	1.06	1.18
Probability of Completion	88.9%	89.2%	91.8%	90.0%	73.6%	79.5%	85.6%	79.8%
Days to Completion	116	100	102	106	141	132	148	141
Proportion of All-Cash Deals	37.6%	38.3%	32.8%	36.3%	42.8%	48.6%	42.8%	44.5%
Proportion of All-Stock Deals	28.8%	27.8%	39.1%	31.6%	23.4%	22.1%	38.9%	28.9%
Percentage of Cash	47.3%	48.7%	42.2%	46.2%	53.0%	58.2%	48.8%	53.0%
Percentage of Other	14.5%	14.3%	10.1%	13.1%	16.1%	14.0%	6.4%	11.8%
Percentage of Stock	38.1%	36.9%	47.7%	40.7%	30.9%	27.8%	44.8%	35.2%
Fees Paid to Advisors (in millions)								
Mean	$4.83	$2.65	$0.77	$2.89	$6.47	$2.79	$0.97	$3.06
Median	$2.38	$1.00	$0.25	$1.00	$3.70	$1.40	$0.44	$1.13
Deal Value (in millions)								
Mean	$2,494	$1,092	$208	$1,345	$2,177	$749	$150	$899
Median	$416	$195	$55	$177	$525	$181	$58	$144
Fees Paid, as Percentage of Deal Value								
Mean	0.91%	0.90%	0.93%	0.91%	0.87%	1.13%	1.15%	1.06%
Median	0.47%	0.58%	0.52%	0.52%	0.67%	0.80%	0.82%	0.76%
Number of Observations (N)	733	672	591	1,996	1,124	1,113	1,695	3,932

Rows report means (except where noted otherwise) and can be based on different numbers of observations. In the top and middle panels, there are typically about 15,000 acquisitions. These are roughly equally split across categories. However, in the bottom panels, there is fee information for only about 6,000 acquisitions, and the distribution is somewhat biased, which is why N is reported in the last row, and why the deal values here do not match deal values above.

Source: Walter, Yawson, Young, "The Role of Investment Banks in M&A Transactions: Fees and Services," table 1 (June 2005).

the industry in which the takeover occurred). Still, this data is not as complete as our earlier data. There were many mergers and acquisitions among firms that were not public, and even for the roughly 15,000 acquisitions involving a public corporation, they had good data on advisory fees for only 6,000 acquisitions.

Targets are usually one-quarter the size of the acquirer. Many acquisitions are within an industry.

Table 23.6 shows that the typical acquirer in this sample was about three to four times as large as the typical target. Also, the mean firm size was much larger than the median firm size, suggesting some disproportionally large firms were in the sample. About one-half to two-thirds of M&As occurred between firms in the same industry (classified by the "two-digit SIC [standard industry classification] code"). About one-half to two-thirds of M&As involved public acquirers or targets.

Deal characteristics: The typical target was $800 million in size. Statistics about methods of acquiring control, methods of payment, and successful completion rates.

The average deal size was about $800 million, but the top-tier investment banks advised on disproportionally larger deals. About 1 in 5 takeovers occurred through a tender offer (the alternative being a negotiated merger with the target, not involving an offer to shareholders). Only a small fraction of all deals were classified as hostile, where the target management resisted. (Acquisitions are also often classified by whether the acquirer pays with cash [a **cash offer**] or with the corporation's shares as currency [a **stock offer**].) About one-third to one-half of all deals were paid for in "all cash," and about one-third were paid for with "all stock" (in which the acquirer paid target shareholders with its own shares). Somewhere between about 10% and 15% of acquisitions were abandoned. If successful, it took the typical deal about 4 months to complete. Note that when the deal was hostile, a much larger fraction of targets seem to have engaged top-tier advisors.

Typical advisory fees were 0.5–1% of the target size.

The median advising fees were just about 0.5 1% of the amount of the transaction (usually the target size), on average. The mean fee was much larger, suggesting that there were a few large fee outliers. Remarkably, top-tier investment bankers charged about the same proportional fees as their lower-tier brethren—the reason why they earned more fees is simply that their deals were larger.

SOLVE NOW!

Q 23.21 What are the two main payment methods in acquisition offers?

Q 23.22 How large is the typical acquirer relative to the typical target?

Q 23.23 What is the typical commission for M&A advice that investment bankers earn? How does it differ across the tier of investment bank retained, and across acquirer and target?

SUMMARY

This chapter covered the following major points:

- Investment banking consists of underwriting and advisory services. Many so-called investment banks are engaged more in non-investment-banking services (such as proprietary trading and asset management) than in investment-banking services.

- Nowadays, securities underwriting is primarily the facilitation of public offerings. A typical underwriter syndicate may have a handful of participants.
- Advisory services are mostly about the facilitation of mergers & acquisitions—from start to finish.
- The investment banking market is an agent market. It contrasts with ordinary commercial banking, in which loans are made by the bank itself.
- The equity capital markets in the United States, Europe, and Asia are now about equal in equity size. The debt market in the United States is still larger than that in Europe or Asia.
- The U.S. investment banks are still the top dogs, primarily because of their ability to attract the best talent from all over the world. Commercial banking is more diffuse.
- No investment bank has more than a 10% share of the market. In 2007, in the United States, a typical top 15 investment bank may have underwritten about $70 billion in investment-grade bonds, $20 billion in non-investment-grade bonds, $80 billion in government bonds, $10 billion in seasoned equity, and $8 billion in IPOs.
- Equity underwriting is a more profitable activity than debt underwriting. The securities are riskier, and due diligence and placement are more difficult. Somewhat unusual, for many investment banks, M&A advice was a lot more profitable than underwriting in 2007.
- M&A activity comes in waves—more when the stock market has gone up. It reached its highest peak around 2000, though 2006 was close.
- Hostile acquisitions are very rare. Still, they are important because they set the stage for managerial behavior. Hostile acquisitions are no longer primarily a U.S. phenomenon.
- Competitive bidding seems to result in lower underwriter spreads. However, few firms bid out their issuing.
- Underwriter spreads can be characterized as follows:
  - Remarkably, there is a strong relation between the offering size and the underwriter spread only for equity offerings. The underwriter spread seems unrelated to offering size for debt offerings.
  - For IPOs smaller than $100 million in proceeds, it is almost always 7%. Other direct costs can add 2–3%. IPOs above $100 million have lower underwriter spreads reaching down to 5%.
  - Larger SEOs have lower spreads. The range is from about 6% for $20 million offerings to 3% for $1 billion offerings.
  - Convertible debt and preferred stock command underwriter spreads of around 3%.
  - Speculative-grade bonds command underwriter spreads of about 1.5%.
  - Investment-grade bonds command underwriter spreads of about 0.5%.
- M&As can create shareholder value through scale synergies, reduction of competition, provision of expertise, elimination of poor management, shutdown efficiencies, better corporate governance, stakeholder expropriation, and/or tax benefits.

It can destroy value if governance and operations become worse. Absent a golden parachute for target managers, acquiring managers tend to end up better off than target managers.

- Most of the value gains tend to accrue to target shareholders, not acquiring shareholders. In many cases, acquiring managers overpay for targets. However, there is a lot of heterogeneity.
- Target management can resist acquisitions through various shark repellents, such as greenmail, excessive golden parachutes, acquisitions by the target itself, scorched earth strategies, poison pills, new share issues, fair value provisions, supermajority rules, litigation, and staggered boards.
- Even though shareholder resolutions are not binding (as full-blown proxy contests are), they are much cheaper. In addition, they often nudge management into doing the right thing.
- Based on information from M&A deals among publicly traded corporations between 1980 and 2003, one study found that:
  - Average advisory fees are about 1% of the target (transaction) size.
  - Median advising fees are about 0.5–0.7% of the transaction size.
  - The 80–90% of proposed deals that ultimately carry through take about four months to complete.
  - Fewer than 5% of acquisitions are hostile (and most of these occurred in the 1980s).
  - The typical acquirer is about three or four times larger than the target.
  - Between one-half and two-thirds of acquisitions are within the same industry.
  - About one-third to one-half of acquisitions are paid for with all cash, and about one-third are paid for with all stock.

The next chapter will discuss the role of corporate governance. Not surprisingly, corporate control activity and M&A activity play an important role in that chapter, too.

KEY TERMS

SOLVE NOW! SOLUTIONS

Q 23.1 The three important functions of underwriters today are issue origination, issue placement, and reputation and signaling. There are also a host of less formal tasks (such as analyst coverage).

Q 23.2 This is actually from Section 21.7: Most brokerage analysts' recommendations are not to be trusted blindly, as evidenced by the fact that most recommendations are "buy." Favorable recommendations help investment bankers attract corporate clients.

Q 23.3 See Table 23.1 for the top commercial banks worldwide. The so-called eyeball scientific method suggests that the typical bank in this list had around $50 billion in Tier 1 capital, $100 billion in market value, and $1.2 trillion in client assets.

Q 23.4 The United States is still the biggest capital market for securities, but Europe and Asia are no longer far behind. When it comes to equity, they have even surpassed the United States on some measures.

Q 23.5 The Glass-Steagall Act of 1933 prevented retail banks from doing investment banking. When it was repealed in 1999, a number of financial institutions merged to become larger financial conglomerates.

Q 23.6 The average compensation of a Goldman Sachs employee was about $600,000. It was highly skewed, though, with many individuals earning double-digit million-dollar salaries. Given that Goldman also has an administrative staff, which did not earn as much, a safe guess is that the average seasoned investment banker earned a seven-figure compensation.

Q 23.7 It seems rather competitive to me.

Q 23.8 There is more capital at risk, which in turn means that the underwriter has to put more of its reputation on the line and work harder to place the securities. In the extreme, if the debt is risk free, it should be very easy to place.

Q 23.9 Figure 23.2 shows that M&A activity rose gradually in the 1980s, starting from scratch and ending just below 4,000 transactions per year. Over the next 10 years, the number roughly tripled and the dollar amount quintupled. From 2000 to 2003 it crashed, but then recovered by 2007 to levels seen in 2000. Not shown here, in 2008, the activity level crashed again.

Q 23.10 Hostile takeovers are not just a U.S. phenomenon, but have also appeared outside the United States. In fact, the biggest two hostile takeovers ever (Mannesmann and ABN-Amro) were foreign target acquisitions by foreign raiders.

Q 23.11 Firms often just use the same underwriter that they have used in the past. Firms also switch underwriters when they "outgrow" their previous underwriters. In this case, industry expertise and other services (such as analyst coverage) matter. There could be personal issues at work, ranging from very positive ones (such as trust) to neutral ones (such as limited time) to negative ones (such as personal bribes).

Q 23.12 Look at Figure 23.4. The $100 million seasoned equity offering would cost about 5% in spread. The $100 million speculative-grade debt offering would cost about 1.5%. The total underwriter spread would be 3.25% ($6.5 million). Issuing $200 million in seasoned equity would cost around 4.5%, which comes to about $9 million. The reason why the all equity offering would be more expensive is because it would be riskier and harder to place.

Q 23.13 Yes and no. Clearly, the firm could operate more productively by replacing these workers. However, it could be that these fired workers had implicit promises that they did not have to be as productive in their old age. This would be a form of expropriation.

Q 23.14 Sources of value in M&A are synergies, reduction of competition, acquisition of expertise, elimination of poor management, shutdown efficiencies, expropriation, tax benefits, and improved corporate governance. Not all are in the interest of society—expropriation and tax reduction, in particular, could help the firm but not society as a whole.

Q 23.15 Yes, even if the net value gain is positive, if the acquirer overpays, the acquirer's shareholders can lose.

Q 23.16 Firms may want to acquire other firms either because it is in the interest of the firm (creating value), or because it is in the interest of managers (and advising bankers).

Q 23.17 The list of resistance measures in takeovers can be found in Section 23.3B: greenmail, golden parachutes, acquisitions, scorched earth strategies, poison pills, new share issues, fair value provisions, supermajority rules, litigation, and staggered boards.

Q 23.18 Even though hostile takeovers are rare, they matter greatly. They are the fallback position if "friendly" negotiations fail. A hostile offer is the (quiet) gorilla in the backroom that can always be called out.

Q 23.19 It is very costly to execute a proxy and takeover contest. A typical takeover premium may be as high as 20%—worthwhile only if the current management commits the most egregious breach of appropriate behavior. A proxy contest costs "only" a few million dollars to execute.

Q 23.20 With a few legal exceptions, shareholder proposals are not binding. (If they were binding, they would fall under the management authority of the board of directors, who therefore would have the power to exclude them from being voted on. To get a proposal on the ballot, the proposing shareholder therefore needs to give up the right for the proposal to be binding.)

Q 23.21 The two main methods of payments in acquisitions are cash offers and stock offers.

Q 23.22 The typical acquirer is about three to four times as large as the target.

Q 23.23 The mean M&A advising commission is about 1% (0.9% for acquirer, 1.1% for target). The median is about 0.6% (0.5% for the acquirer, 0.8% for the target). The differences across tiers and between target and acquirer seem fairly small.

PROBLEMS

The ▇ *indicates problems available in* myfinancelab

Q 23.24 How important is the guarantee of securities placement success that underwriters provide their clients?

Q 23.25 What are the most important services and functions of underwriters today?

Q 23.26 Look up five recent IPOs. (Google is your friend.) How many book runners and underwriters can you identify?

Q 23.27 Describe the functions of M&A advisory services.

Q 23.28 How do client assets under management and Tier 1 capital translate into market value? That is, are U.S. and U.K. banks relatively more valuable than their foreign competitors?

Q 23.29 In relative terms, how important is the American market in equity underwriting compared to the European market?

Q 23.30 Is it appropriate to call Goldman Sachs principally an investment bank? Why?

Q 23.31 How are underwriting and M&A linked? Do investment banks have to have both?

Q 23.32 Look at the Thomson Financial League tables on the Web (http://www.thomsonreuters.com/products_services/financial/league_tables). Who are the top debt underwriters, top equity underwriters, and top M&A advisors this year?

Q 23.33 In the context of all takeovers, are hostile takeovers rare?

Q 23.34 How are the interests of investment banks different from those of their clients (investors and firms)?

Q 23.35 What is the main institutional difference between equity issues by regulated utilities firms and equity issues by nonregulated ordinary firms? Which of these two types of firms seems to raise capital at a cheaper rate?

Q 23.36 Do competitive bids for underwriting services end up cheaper or more expensive than noncompetitive bids? Which one is more prevalent and why?

Q 23.37 A firm wants to raise $500 million. Compare the costs of issuing $500 million in convertible equity versus those of issuing $250 million in speculative-grade debt and $250 million in seasoned equity.

Q 23.38 Look up the debt ratings for Goldman Sachs. Is all its debt ranked identically?

Q 23.39 Search the financial websites to determine what the biggest three acquisitions in the last 12 months were. Can you describe each deal in a page or less? Where does the value come from?

Q 23.40 Research Cerberus Capital's portfolio companies on the Web. When did Cerberus take these companies over? Did interest rates seem to have had an effect on Cerberus's takeover activities?

Q 23.41 What are the main sources of value generation in most mergers and acquisitions? Are all of them in the interest of society as a whole?

Q 23.42 What sources of value in an acquisition are strongest in leveraged buyouts? Is this different from ordinary acquisitions?

Q 23.43 On average, do acquiring or target shareholders gain more from the acquisition? On average, does acquiring or target management gain more from an acquisition?

Q 23.44 What has been the most effective antitakeover device? Explain how it works, and why it works so well. What does a raider have to do to take over a company that has deployed this device?

Q 23.45 Is a golden parachute always/never in the interest of shareholders? Explain.

Q 23.46 Is there a moral dilemma when it comes to golden parachutes? Do long-standing workers who lose their jobs also deserve and receive golden parachutes?

Q 23.47 When one firm acquires another, what form of payment do the shareholders of the target firm usually receive?

24

Corporate Governance

AGENCY CONFLICTS GALORE

For the most part, we have assumed that managers act on behalf of owners and maximize firm value. This fits conveniently into a perfect-market-perspective, but there are situations in which this is not a good representation of reality. Like everyone else, managers are self-interested. This causes agency conflicts. You already learned a good deal about them in Chapters 12 and 18. We now drill deeper into this conflict between corporate investors (the "owners," usually shareholders and sometimes also the creditors) and those in day-to-day control of the company (the corporate board and its managers).

You already know the theory: Debt should be paid first, equity should receive the residual, and managers should be compensated according to their marginal contribution to the value of the firm. But we have not yet asked the simplest of all questions: Why do managers in charge return *any* money to investors? After all, what do investors contribute *after* the corporation has their money? What harm would come to the managers if they simply ignored investors? Outside the United States, large shareholders often control the firm. In such cases, why do they allow the firm to return any money to small shareholders?

These questions fall into the domain of **corporate governance**, which concerns itself with the conflict of interest between those who control the corporation and those who provide the capital and thus own it. James Madison's words are as applicable to firms today as they were to governments in the eighteenth century:

> If men were angels, no government would be necessary. If angels were to govern men, neither external nor internal controls would be necessary. In framing a government which is to be administered by men over men, the great difficulty lies in this: You must first enable the government to control the governed; and in the next place oblige it to control itself.

It is also important for you to understand what corporate governance is *not*—it is not good management. Instead, governance is the set of mechanisms that can discipline management *if* it wanted to become bad. If the sanctions are strong enough or if management is good enough, then governance sanctions may never have to spring into action. Of course, controls are never free. Better governance has its cost. Remarkably, many good managers—even those who are intent on, and good at, maximizing firm value—argue reflexively and publicly against tougher governance controls. They do not point out that governance is costly (which is a good argument); rather, they argue that they are good at what they are doing and that the very presence of controls would damage their integrity (which is not a good argument). Perhaps they believe themselves to be angels—but even if they are (and many are), their successors may not be!

24.1 SEPARATION OF OWNERSHIP AND CONTROL

Firms typically start out tightly controlled but eventually become professionally managed.

A **conflict of interest** is a situation in which different parties have competing interests. Most companies start out with few such conflicts—if only because the entrepreneur owns the entire firm, provides most capital, works alone, and makes all decisions. (One cannot be self-conflicted in our sense.) Eventually, the founder's personal role begins to fade. Management becomes more and more "professional" in the sense that it becomes a contracted resource. Unfortunately, professional managers bring with them not only novel qualifications and specialization benefits but also new problems. They are only **agents** who have a position of trust that requires them to act on behalf of the owners. Yet, like everyone else, they want to maximize their own wealth, not necessarily the wealth of the owner. This is called an **agency problem** or a **principal-agent problem**. (The entrepreneur is the firm's **principal**.) It is in the principal's self-interest to oversee management.

Ownership also changes in character over time—entrepreneurs sell off claims to raise funds.

Eventually, most entrepreneurs want to raise more funds to expand operations or enjoy the riches. This usually happens in the form of debt. Eventually, they also get older and are no longer able to run the firm and control managers. Thus, many owners sell shares to external investors, who share the principal's role with the entrepreneur. Together, the principals appoint a corporate board, which is supposed to coordinate the desires of shareholders, especially vis-à-vis managers. Over time, in many firms, external shareholders become the majority owners of the firm.

➤ Corporate boards, Section 24.5A, p. 921

Multiple owners are good at providing capital, but they are not good at supervising managers.

Unfortunately, as the separation between those who provide capital, those who oversee management, and those who manage the firm itself grows over time, so do the conflict-of-interest problems. Multitudes of shareholders are just not capable of constantly voting and communicating their desires to their agent-managers, much less checking over what their managers are doing day to day. The same may apply to multitudes of different creditors—and creditors and shareholders may not always see eye to eye, either. Managers are quite aware of this situation, too.

Owners may even squabble among themselves.

Even if managers are purely altruistic, it may not always be easy for them to act based on one entrepreneur's wishes. It may be outright impossible for them to act based on the interests of many different shareholders. The reason is that conflicts of interest can develop not just between owners and managers, but also among owners themselves. Even two or three co-owners can squabble, but when there are thousands of shareholders, as in a publicly traded company, the coordination problems take on an entirely new dimension. Fortunately, even if they agree on little else, most investors agree that they prefer more money to less money. Thus, maximizing their investors' wealth is the marching order for management in most publicly traded corporations in the United States. Outside the United States, this is usually true, too, although in some European countries, managers are also legally obliged to look after the interests of employees and other stakeholders of the firm.

Outside the United States, managers are often beholden to large controlling shareholders.

In general, the conflict between managers and shareholders looms as the most important governance problem in the United States. Shareholders of all types and sizes are typically in the same boat. Outside the United States, the voting rights in many firms are held in a way that gives one or just a few large shareholders a lot of influence. In these cases, large shareholders often control the managers—or become the managers themselves. In turn, this means that the conflict between investors and managers turns primarily into a conflict between the large investors—in control of the corporate board and management—and other smaller investors.

24.1A CONTROL RIGHTS AND CORPORATE DESIGN

Entrepreneurs internalize bad governance.

➤ Corporate design to maximize value, Section 16.1, p. 573

Let's start at the beginning. When an entrepreneur needs to raise more outside capital, he wants to do so at terms that leave him well off. If you recall Chapters 17 and 18, you learned why it is ultimately the entrepreneur who bears the price of a bad capital structure. In a competitive market, new investors have many other opportunities. To attract them, the entrepreneur's price must be appropriate, given whatever structure he sets into place. This applies not only to the capital structure—where a better debt/equity ratio allows the entrepreneur to sell the firm for a higher price— but also to a better governance structure. Simply put, if an entrepreneur designs a firm in which he (or his managers) can later steal all of the external investors' money, no investors would want to provide capital in the first place. Ultimately, this would leave the entrepreneur worse off.

IMPORTANT: Investors would not be willing to provide capital at favorable terms if they are not well protected. The entrepreneur ultimately internalizes any potential future failures caused by an inadequate corporate design today. Thus, to raise money on good terms in the first place, entrepreneurs want to design the firm and its governance structure so that investors will be protected.

Control rights make fund-raising possible.

To be able to induce investors to part with their cash, the entrepreneur must create a corporate charter and install safeguards that satisfy potential investors, legal requirements, and common practice. Solemn promises alone of both corporate value maximization and eventual profit participation are simply not enough. So, how will investors be able to coerce the agents—appointed by the entrepreneur (first, the entrepreneur himself, later the corporate board and management)—to honor their promises? The answer is that entrepreneurs can give investors power by granting them **control rights**. It is these control rights that later allow investors to get their due. Again, it is in the interest of entrepreneur-owners to grant new investors strong control rights, because these rights improve the terms under which they can obtain capital in the first place.

➤ Control rights and cash flow rights, Section 15.1A, p. 543

You already know that debt and equity are different in terms of their **cash flow rights**. (Debt has first dibs on the promised payments; equity owns the residual.) Their control rights are very different, too:

Control rights differ for debt and equity.

Equity: Shareholders are (usually) the nominal owners of the firm. Their primary power is their ability to vote and appoint the **corporate board**, usually once a year during the annual meeting. During the year, the corporate board is an agent that is supposed to act on behalf of the firm's owners, which are the principals in economic terms. (Legally, it is the board that is the principal of the corporation.) Most importantly, the board has the power to hire and fire managers.

Debt: Creditors enjoy the right to demand performance and payments on terms specified when the debt is originally extended. The bond contract not only specifies how much the firm obligates itself to repay in the future, but also specifies the immediate legal remedy if the lender fails to pay or fails to meet any number of prespecified covenants. This often means that the lender receives possession of the firm or specific collateral to satisfy her claims—(almost) no ifs, ands, or buts.

How *not* to find investors.

A firm that has no independent corporate board control may not find investors willing to purchase equity shares. A firm in which a large shareholder can influence the firm to "tunnel" assets from the public corporation into her private pockets may not find minority shareholders willing to contribute capital. A firm that does not give creditors the right to force bankruptcy upon default may not find any creditors willing to lend money.

Real-world outcomes are usually "second best," with unavoidable managerial self-enrichment.

But control rights are not all black-and-white. If the firm does not offer perfect protection to its capital providers, it may still be able to obtain capital. However, this would be on worse terms that would require the surrender of a higher percentage of the firm's shares or the payment of a higher interest rate. In real life, control rights are never perfect. It would be impractical to protect capital providers *perfectly*, because the cost of preventing all managerial opportunism would be prohibitive. It would not maximize firm value if the firm spent \$10 in audits to prevent \$1 in fraud. Thus, by necessity, corporations and capital providers must live with **second-best outcomes**, in which there is a constant tension between investor protection and managerial self-enrichment.

Self-control fails if the entrepreneur can wiggle out, if owners have no more control themselves, or if managers no longer need to raise funds.

The rest of this section explains why governance incentives and mechanisms are strong when entrepreneurs first want to raise external capital. Briefly, their desire to raise capital is the most important reason why they want good corporate governance. But it also explains when corporate governance is likely to weaken or break down:

1. It can break down after the entrepreneur has already received the funds and finds a loophole to wiggle out of his obligations to external capital providers. Of course, if an entrepreneur still needs to sell a lot of shares, treating existing investors badly will not make it easy to attract new ones.
2. As decades go by and firms grow, professional management eventually wrests more and more control from owners. Managers' desire to obtain reasonable costs of capital may no longer be enough to restrain their self-interests. After all, once they have taken control, they may care more for themselves than for the wealth of the owners. In this case, they may not even care if they have to give away a larger fraction of the firm from the pockets of the existing shareholders in order to get control of more money (from new shareholders).

3. Older companies often have enough projects generating cash so that they may not even need to tap the capital markets any longer. If shareholders cannot effectively challenge managerial control, managers could simply spend this internal cash on themselves rather than return it to their shareholders.

The last two points suggest that managers in old firms are no longer constrained by their needs to raise capital at advantageous rates (as was the case for the entrepreneur). Thus, any limits to what managers will do most likely would have to come from their desire not to lose control.

SOLVE NOW!

Q 24.1 What are the main control rights of debt and equity?

24.1B THE ENTREPRENEUR'S ORIGINAL INCENTIVES

Example parameters.

Let's assume you are the owner of an invention that requires a \$25 million investment. If undertaken, its present value is \$100 million. If you could borrow or had \$25 million in cash, you would not need to raise any external funds and have to deal with any governance issues. Your net project wealth contribution would be \$75 million.

Here are progressively worse scenarios confronting the entrepreneur:

Governance comes into play only if you have some good reason to raise external money. In our example, we assume that if you cannot sell shares to raise the money to start the project, then you cannot undertake the project and you have nothing. Consequently, you can enjoy large gains only if you can find investors. This is why companies go public to begin with: The gains from diversification for the owner and the provision of external capital outweigh the costs of agency conflicts. Now let's consider different scenarios:

Perfect commitment

- What if your investors believe that you will not act opportunistically? In this case, they would be satisfied with your promise of 25% of the company (worth \$25 million), leaving you with 75%, worth \$75 million.

Imperfect commitment

- What if your investors believe that your incentives will change the moment that you have their money? For example, you could pay yourself an excessive executive salary of \$30 million. Let's call this theft, even if it is not so in the legal, criminal sense. Assume you cannot restrain yourself from stealing this \$30 million. Actually, this is still not a problem. Potential investors now believe the firm's value is \$70 million. They would part with \$25 million in exchange for $\$25/\$70 \approx 35.7\%$ of the firm. You would keep 64.3% of the firm. In total, you would have 64.3% of \$70 million (\$45 million), plus the \$30 million you would have "stolen" in salary. You would still end up with the full \$75 million.

Imperfect commitment with waste

- What if you will have to waste an additional \$10 million when the time comes to hide your \$30 million of theft? For example, you may have to hire expensive compensation consultants, spend your time "engineering" your corporate board instead of finding good projects, and perhaps even change the firm's projects to make you indispensable. Would your outside investors still be satisfied with a 35.7% stake in the company for their \$25 million investment? No! Again, they expect you to steal the money when the time comes. But now they value the company only at $\$100 - \$30 - \$10 = \$60$ million. Raising \$25 million requires you to part with

$25/$60 ≈ 41.7% of your company now, not 35.7%. Unfortunately, your net worth is now only 58.3% · $60 ≈ $35 million, which you will own in stock, plus the $30 million that you can steal. This $65 million is $10 million less than what you could have gotten if you could have committed yourself not to steal in the future. The lesson is that it is *you* who must carry the full brunt of your inability to commit yourself not to steal. You have effectively "internalized" the $10 million in waste.

The same argument applies to any managerial agency problems other than theft—the more you can limit future agency costs, the more your firm is worth today. To the extent that you cannot fully restrain yourself from destroying value in the future, you are worth less than $75 million today. Nevertheless, you may not have another alternative. You may just have to grin and bear it. You are still better off taking money from investors at unfavorable terms (41.7% for $25 million, leaving you with $65 million) than you would be with $0 if you could not raise *any* external funding.

Imperfect commitment with waste, future managers, and inability to contract fully with future management

- What if your project's duration exceeds your lifetime and you must hand the firm to professional managers (who will also waste the $10 million in pursuit of higher compensation)? In this case, the $30 million in excessive compensation will go to them. Your 58.3% remaining stake will still only be worth $35 million. In a perfect market, you could charge the new management $30 million for the right to run the firm. Unfortunately, in the real and imperfect market, this may not be possible. If you can charge your management successors only $10 million in reduced future salary and they keep the right to expropriate $30 million, then you would own 58.3% · $60 + $10 ≈ $45 million—even less than the $65 million worked out above.

The worst case—imperfect commitment and too much to steal.

- What if you can steal more than $75 million from the $100 million project in the future? Assuming you cannot borrow and you cannot sell more than 100% of the firm, then no investor would give you the $25 million in the first place. In this worst case, you would not be able to take the project, and would lose it all.

The example shows that entrepreneurs internalize all failures of corporate governance.

In sum, if corporate governance is costless and (thus) perfect, you are in a **first-best outcome** in which you have instituted perfect corporate governance. You are worse off if you cannot commit yourself to avoid future wasteful conflicts of interest. You may be even worse off if you cannot commit your firm's future managers to prevent future wasteful conflicts of interest. And you may be worst off if you cannot raise the funds to be able to take the project. The main insight from this example is that, from the perspective of a 100% owner-entrepreneur, the better you control all future agency conflicts, the more you are worth today.

SOLVE NOW!

Q 24.2 Reconsider the example in which you have to waste $10 million in order to get $30 million in loot. External shareholders receive 41.7% of the firm in exchange for $25 million in funding. Would it be in your interest *after the fact* (ex-post) to avoid the $10 million deadweight loss and thus forego the $30 million in theft, if your investors do not fully trust you?

Q 24.3 When are the incentives to control agency conflict strongest? Why? Can you give a numerical example?

24.1C COSTS VERSUS BENEFITS OF THE ENTREPRENEUR'S CONTROL INCENTIVES

To what extent would 100% owner-entrepreneurs write contracts up front (ex-ante) in the real world to control all possible future agency conflicts? There are definitely some limiting factors:

Governance may be too costly (or outright impossible).

1. **Ex-ante cost of governance:** You can use our example to think about the role of the costs of control. If it costs \$1 million to commit yourself not to steal and you thereby avoid wasting \$10 million, you should pay for it. Your net wealth would be \$74 million—less than the \$75 million that you could have if governance were free but more than the \$65 million that you could have if you could not commit yourself. On the other hand, if the control were to cost \$12 million, you may as well live with the theft and the waste of \$10 million.

   In the real world, you would prevent only some conflicts of interest. As a practicing economist, you know that you should balance the marginal cost of each control against its marginal benefit. Your new investors would demand more shares to compensate them for those agency conflicts that you have not prevented.

   As Shakespeare put it: *What a piece of work is man! How noble in reason! How infinite in faculty!*

   In the extreme, it could even be infinitely expensive to institute control. It may be impossible to write contracts for all future contingencies that prevent you from enriching yourself, especially insofar as future managerial schemes are concerned—the human mind can be very creative. Indeed, the typical firm charter does not even try to account for all future contingencies—most are simple boilerplate. Worse, many agency control clauses could even end up being counterproductive if they rob the firm of flexibility that managers could use to *increase* the firm's value under unforeseen circumstances in the future.

   One alternative to detailed formal governance provisions and clauses, which prescribe what managers can and cannot do, is to rely on laws or mechanisms that do not specify a lot of details but allow shareholders to regain control if management gets really bad. Of course, once in charge, managers would have all the incentives to try to eliminate these mechanisms.

The control of in-the-distant-future agency problems is rarely worthwhile.

2. **Ex-ante magnitudes of far-away conflicts:** Even if you can write perfect preventative contracts, your incentive to do so may sometimes be surprisingly modest. In particular, few companies are designed at the outset for greatness in the far future. When Walt Disney designed the corporate charter of Disney in 1957, he probably did not do so with an eye toward Disney managers in the twenty-first century. Indeed, most companies that go public will never face any large agency problems—most will simply end up acquired or bankrupt!

   How important is it for the entrepreneur to prevent agency conflicts in the distant future? A quick back-of-the-envelope calculation may help you see that it cannot be too important. Assume that only 1 out of 100 firms becomes large enough to indulge significant agency conflict of, say, 0.5% of firm value. This 0.5% of a \$100 billion company is \$500 million (say, a 10% perpetuity of \$50 million a year in excessive managerial compensation, theft, or mismanagement). However, from the original entrepreneur's perspective, in *ex-ante terms*, this imperfect control represents only a cost of $1/100 \cdot 0.5\% \approx 0.005\%$ of the firm's net worth.

This argument has assumed that investors are perfectly rational and would be willing to pay the entrepreneur this 0.005% more if the contract is designed to prevent bad behavior. More likely, entrepreneurs would not even capture this 0.005% by writing anticipatory contracts. Would real-world investors fully understand better corporate governance controls and be willing to pay for them? How many investors would have paid Walt Disney more money for their shares in the year 1957 if he had put better incentives into place for the year 2000? Even the most sophisticated investors may not have bothered to understand fully the far-off repercussions. If anything, with detailed covenants and controls that go far beyond the ordinary, investors may even think they "smell a rat" (wondering whether they should infer something about the entrepreneur's character and designs) and demand more, not less, compensation.

SOLVE NOW!

Q 24.4 What limits are there to writing a corporate charter that eliminates future agency conflicts?

24.1D DO FUTURE CAPITAL NEEDS PROTECT SHAREHOLDERS?

Our focus so far has been about agency controls when a 100% owner first raises capital. This has created the incentive for the entrepreneur to protect investors. It was in his interest (even if only mildly so). But does the need to raise capital protect the current shareholders after the firm is already public?

What about firms in which the entrepreneur has been long since dead?

Unfortunately, no. In fact, quite the opposite can happen. Let me demonstrate. Revise our scenario by assuming that the entrepreneur is no longer both the decision maker and the sole shareholder. Instead, assume the opposite for a \$60 million firm: You are the manager firmly in charge and are the one benefitting from agency conflicts, but you own zero shares. Let's say you now come across a project that costs \$50 million, which produces cash flows of \$30 million in shareholder value plus \$10 million in perks for you. (Actually, the example would also work with \$10 in perks.) Would you raise \$50 million in capital to fund this miserable project?

The difference between an entrepreneur-in-charge and management-in-charge is that the former owns the firm, too.

Without the new project, the firm is worth \$60 million. If you raise funds and take the new project, shareholders will own a claim on a \$90 million firm—\$30 million of new project plus \$60 million of old project. To raise \$50 million in capital requires issuing them shares worth $\$50/\$90 \approx 55.6\%$ of the company. These shares are sold into the market at the appropriate price, and new shareholders always pay only the fair price. However, your previous shareholders now own only $1 - 55.6\% \approx 44.4\%$ of the company for a net of $44.4\% \cdot \$90 \approx \$40$ million in the new firm, down from \$60 million. In effect, your \$10 million in perks is paid for with \$20 million from your existing shareholders. This example may even understate the problem. In fact, fearing similar expropriation in the future, the new shareholders may demand even more than 55.6% of the company—and you have the incentive to give your new shareholders even larger stakes in order to get your \$10 million of perks.

The need to raise capital would not constrain management from taking a really bad project.

In sum, the need to raise capital is not a guarantee that the management of a publicly traded corporation will want to control agency problems. On the contrary,

The need/ability to raise capital may hurt existing shareholders if it facilitates negative-NPV projects.

raising capital can become yet another mechanism that helps managers extract shareholder wealth for themselves. Old capital in effect allows new capital to be raised and thereby allows managers to expand the firm again and again. Even if managerial theft has reduced the value of $10 million of old equity into just $1 million now, managers might still want to raise another $1 million in capital for their personal consumption by promising 51% of the new firm, leaving old shareholders with only $490,000.

There are real-world companies that had high growth, yet negative stock returns.

This behavior is not as absurd as you might believe. There are some fairly prominent companies that have grown tremendously and yet have not delivered for their shareholders. For example, firm growth (in terms of market capitalization) and stock price performance for four such companies were as follows:

Company	From/To	Growth (in billions)	Shareholders' Rate of Return
Rite-Aid	1987–2007	from $1.486 to $2.218	−59%
Reebok	1989–2007	from $0.003 to $3.722	−50%
AOL (Time-Warner)	1999–2007	from $1.163 to $2.962	−59%
Del Monte	1999–2007	from $0.644 to $1.898	−21%

Of course, growth that results in poor performance could also have been an accident, although it would not change the fact that managers would not have ended up as badly as their shareholders.

Managerial ownership can solve this problem, but can make other problems worse.

If you now think that having management own a large share of the company (like an entrepreneur holding 100% of the company) reduces this problem, you are right and wrong. You are right because a larger share indeed mitigates managers' desire to waste funds. You are wrong because it creates a novel problem that could be just as bad or even worse: It could create a situation in which other shareholders are even less likely to ever wrest control of the firm away from misbehaving management. This is effectively the situation in many foreign countries, in which a large external shareholder is solidly in charge of the firm. Such shareholders can then use this control to siphon funds from the firm into their own pockets.

➤ Tunneling, Section 24.2A, p. 906

IMPORTANT: The theory suggests the following:

- The firm's incentives to control conflicts of interest are probably strong at the outset. The need to raise capital at favorable terms protects shareholders early on.
- As the firm gets older, corporate control generally deteriorates. The need to raise capital loses its power as a managerial-control device. Managers become restrained primarily by their desires not to lose this control.

The empirical evidence generally supports these predictions. We rarely hear of governance breakdowns in young firms that have strapped cash flows and that still have large shareholders with a control influence that is separate from those of management.

SOLVE NOW!

Q 24.5 Assume that the CEO is firmly in charge of a $100 million firm. The CEO finds a new project that costs $30 million and returns $25 million next year. The CEO can only raise equity to fund this project.
(a) Is it possible that the CEO wants to take such a project?
(b) If the CEO does take this project, what will happen to the voting power of the existing shareholders?
(c) Would existing shareholders be better off if the CEO were to finance this new project with debt instead of equity?
(d) Does the need to raise equity always impose a "capital market discipline" on the CEO?
(e) Under what circumstances could the need to raise equity impose a "capital market discipline" on the CEO?

24.2 MANAGERIAL TEMPTATIONS

The human mind's aptitude for scheming is infinite.

Although the legal fiction is that managers act solely on behalf of the firm and that shareholders own the firm after creditors are paid off, the fact is that all parties act primarily in their own interests. But exactly how do managers enrich themselves? Unfortunately, there is a whole battery of tactics managers can employ to enrich themselves at the expense of shareholders, and to understand governance, you need to know what they are. Don't believe that such behavior is necessarily common in the real world—the point is to recognize the possibilities. We will then discuss the institutions and mechanisms that seek to restrain much of it.

24.2A ILLEGAL TEMPTATIONS

Let's first consider some criminal acts, in order of their complexity, starting with the simplest.

THEFT

Simple theft is rare, but it does occur.

The simplest method is theft. For example, in April 2004, 58-year-old C. Gregory Earls, head of an investment company called USV Partners, was convicted for simply funneling investor money into a trust fund for his children. What prevents corporate managers from taking corporate diamonds out of the corporate safe? For the most part, it is the law, which criminalizes simple theft. Therefore, such behavior is fairly rare. (Mr. Earls could compete for a Darwin prize for the "dumbest criminal"—it is hard to leave a paper trail any clearer than his.)

FRAUD

Fraud is more common and illegal . . .

The next step up is fraud. It is more complex and therefore more difficult to detect and prove. For example, in 2003, Hop-on Wireless claimed to sell disposable cell phones. It turns out that the prototypes were Nokia phones with plastic cases around them. The CEO raised funding, promising not to take a salary—but promptly used the funds to pay off his credit card debts (see theft above) and gave a company he owned a $500,000 contract (see transfer payments below).

. . . and earnings management can even be both legal and appropriate.

➤ Earnings management, Section 13.5, p. 473

➤ GAAP, Section 13.1A, p. 447

Usually, fraud involves manipulation of financials. Unlike Hop-on's extreme case, many accounting choices are not so black-and-white—the line between illegal accounting manipulation and legal earnings management can be more of a gray spectrum. Corporate executives have to make many judgment calls. For example, there is empirical evidence that *legal* corporate earnings management is particularly aggressive just before the corporation issues more equity, for obvious reasons (and also that firms that are more aggressive in their accounting perform worse later on). Even conservatism may or may not be in the interest of existing owners. Painting *too* bleak a picture may make the business collapse. And what prevents rosy picture painting? Again, it is mostly the law and regulations. GAAP and SEC scrutiny limit the discretion of managers to legally manipulate the financials. And again, there are criminal penalties against fraud.

Insider Trading

Insider trading is very common.

➤ Market efficiency and insider trading, Section 11.2B, p. 353

One more step up—and a surprisingly common form of agency conflict—is insider trading. For example, a well-publicized insider trading scandal in late 2001 involved Sam Waksal, CEO of ImClone (IMCL). Waksal received advance bad news about clinical tests of an ImClone cancer drug and proceeded to tip off his family and friends (including Martha Stewart) that they should immediately sell their shares. (Waksal began serving his 7-year prison term in 2003. Martha Stewart followed in September 2004.)

Some insider trading is legal and should be allowed—but how do you tell which is which?

Like earnings management, insider trading can be either legal or illegal—and again, there is a wide gray spectrum. Managers almost always have more information than shareholders. They would love to trade on it before the public learns of it, and naturally, this would not make other shareholders better off. Yet it would be unwise to prohibit all insider trading, because insiders do need to be able to sell and buy shares just like the rest of us, if only to diversify some of their wealth. Formally, it is illegal for them to trade on information that is not yet public. In real life, illegal trading is only easy to prove if the situation entails an impending news release. (It is surprising how someone as smart as Waksal could have made such a big mistake, because his illegal trades were so easy to detect and prove.) More often, the information that executives have is "soft." The empirical evidence shows that they indeed do well in their private, legal insider trading. They generally tend to buy before the firm gets better and sell before the firm gets worse.

Tunneling

Complex theft through transfers is more common.

The next step up in criminal acts is yet more difficult to detect and prove. Since the 1990s, the colloquial (and also academic) name for transfers of assets from the corporation to an insider (such as to management or to a large or controlling stakeholder) is **tunneling**. The idea is that the insiders of a public company can own other private companies that do business with the public company on very favorable terms. As long as the tunneling is not excessive and the corporate board is informed and has consented, it is very difficult to prove. It is only occasionally that the terms become *so* egregiously favorable that they warrant criminal indictment. This was the case, for example, for Andrew Fastow, former CFO of Enron. On May 1, 2003, the U.S. Department of Justice alleged that "in 1997, Fastow conspired with others, including his wife, to create an [entity owned by the Fastows] in order to reap for themselves the prof-

ANECDOTE Board Courage at Citigroup

The PBS series *Frontline* episode "The Wall Street Fix" (www.pbs.org) illuminates many of the conflicts of interest between ordinary shareholders and larger stakeholders. It details how Jack Grubman, star analyst for the investment bank of Salomon Smith Barney, hyped WorldCom in 2000 to its brokerage's small retail investors. At the same time, the CEO of WorldCom, Bernie Ebbers, held a personal $1 billion mortgage from Travelers. Both SSB and Travelers are owned by Citigroup. Ebbers' wealth (and therefore his $1 billion mortgage) was closely tied to the WorldCom stock value. (In 2005, Ebbers was convicted of corporate fraud.)

In a display of less-than-extraordinary courage, after the indictment of Citigroup for a variety of such questionable activities, the Citigroup board voted its full support and confidence in its CEO, Sandy Weill. *Business Week* was not so generous: In January 2003, it ranked Sandy Weill as the worst manager in America.

its generated by certain Enron wind farms, while simultaneously enabling Enron to fraudulently receive government financial benefits to which it was not entitled." Naturally, the smarter the manager, the more complex the tunneling arrangements, so that the true costs and true benefits to the public company are more difficult to assess. Again, criminal prosecution of such schemes is fairly rare, especially if the corporate executive has followed legal procedures to the letter.

Note that tunneling must not necessarily be to the manager himself. It can also be made to "friends" of management or to large shareholders, who then owe more loyalty to the CEO. The ambiguous role of large shareholders in corporate governance will be explained in Section 24.5B.

➤ Large shareholders, Section 24.5B, p. 925

BRIBES

Yet another way for executives to get rich at the expense of shareholders, and again one step more difficult to detect, is that of bribes. Managers of publicly traded companies need not even solicit them: They practically come to them. For example, during the 1998–2000 technology bubble, receiving IPO share allocations was almost like getting free money. (Normal first-day rates of return were around 50%. Ordinary brokerage clients would rarely receive any allocations.) In one infamous example, Citigroup was eager to do investment-banking business with WorldCom, a publicly traded telecom company. Citigroup allocated $17 million in 21 offerings into WorldCom CEO Bernie Ebbers's *personal* account. In one IPO (Rhythms Net Connections) alone, Ebbers was allegedly handed $16 million. Ebbers was in effect "courted" to direct the business of the shareholders of the publicly traded company WorldCom to Citigroup. (If he had not been conflicted, he could have solicited the shares on WorldCom's behalf instead.)

Bribing the executive personally can be an effective way to win corporate business contracts.

➤ Initial public offerings and the 1998–2000 bubble, Section 21.7, p. 806

➤ How underwriters are selected, Section 23.2A, p. 873

Preferential allocations to, and treatment of, executives' personal accounts have been, and continue to be, common practice. Ebbers was an extreme case, but not a rare one. Lesser methods of bribing executives are so commonplace that they are considered almost ordinary. For example, there is evidence that competitive bids for high-level professional services (such as the hiring of a search firm or the placement of a bond or equity issue) usually result in better contract terms than negotiated contracts for the firm—and yet most companies negotiate rather than bid out contracts. Although negotiation can be better for other reasons, more commonly the reason lies elsewhere: Executives of smaller firms naturally want to be on the candidacy list to become executives of bigger companies. It is therefore in their interests to form good

Third parties bribe managers all the time.

➤ Underwriter selection, Section 23.2A, p. 873

relationships with investment banks and executive search firms. An executive who uses competitive bids, which minimize the profits of the professional service firms, and who constantly switches from one low bidder to the next, is unlikely to build much loyalty and subsequent quid pro quo support.

24.2B LEGAL TEMPTATIONS

Most managers are not criminals.

If you now have the impression that fraud, theft, insider trading, tunneling, and bribes are the most important agency conflicts between shareholders and managers, then you are wrong. The most important conflicts arise in the day-to-day execution of business and are of a type in which managerial misbehavior is not illegal. Even more so, there are many decisions that are judgment calls and not even outright unethical—few CEOs actively seek out behavior that is obviously unethical, and almost none seek out behavior that is obviously illegal or criminal. Simply put, many executives are really the "good guys" and want to be seen as such.

Your previous encounter with legal temptations.

➤ The agency view of capital structure, p. 675

You have already encountered a number of legal temptations. For example, in Section 18.4, you learned that managers like capital structures that are biased toward equity, because this reduces the pressure for them to perform and the likelihood of going bankrupt or being fired. It also makes it easier for them to take over other firms. Let's look at common agency conflicts that are not illegal and arise in the ordinary course of business.

Misallocation of Resources and Empire Building

Unnecessary corporate growth is probably most costly to U.S. shareholders.

Many academics believe that the highest agency costs in American companies today (in terms of expected costs to shareholders) have to do with the failure to direct corporate assets toward the activities that maximize shareholder wealth. These agency costs are particularly high for firms that have lots of cash and cash flow (e.g., from prior profitable activities) but few good new growth opportunities. Thus, it is no accident that I am first listing the sin of **empire building**—the tendency to acquire greater resources.

➤ Empire building, Section 12.8, p. 420

Most managers want to grow the firm.

Most managers see it as their natural task to grow, or at least prevent the shrinking of, the firm's business. Unfortunately, corporate growth is not necessarily shareholder value–maximizing. For example, many airlines have been notorious money sinks for investors for decades. Every time an airline has enjoyed a brief spike in profitability, its three unions (pilots, flight attendants, and mechanics) have negotiated higher pay packages that quickly eliminated the profits. For years, these airlines have stumbled from one calamity to the next. The shareholders of many big airlines would have been better off if management had just decided to sell off all the airplanes and landing slots, and return the funds to investors. Instead, the typical such airline just ran down all the available funds until there was nothing left worth liquidating.

➤ Eastern Airlines, Anecdote, Section 15.2, p. 545

Managers are often paid for growth—or believe they are.

From the managers' perspective, it may also seem counterintuitive that the best course of action is to sell off assets and return more to shareholders than the normal trickle of cash that the firm pays out in ordinary dividends. Generally, managers believe that they are paid for operating the company well—executing difficult tasks such as handling employees and customers, growing the firm, and acquiring other companies. It must seem odd to a manager that her best actions might be to drastically shrink the firm, sell off the assets, or be taken over by another company. Would selling off the firm's assets not admit personal defeat—that someone else can do better with the assets than the current management?

Bigger firms ⇒ more compensation and more status.

Note that it is also all too human for managers to convince themselves that what is most in their own interest is also in the best interest of the company. Although the reward for shrinking the firm could well be unemployment, the reward for growing it is running a bigger company. Executives of bigger companies are more prominent, have higher social status, and usually receive more compensation. Some decades ago, this was even explicit: Managerial compensation schemes were often directly tied to sales, not earnings.

You should measure spending of too much money relative to the optimal investment (which could be negative for dying firms).

These issues apply both to healthy and to dying companies. Dying companies may use up all their assets in futile attempts to rescue failing businesses. Healthy, profitable companies may use their plentiful internal cash to enter new businesses or acquire other firms. Recall from Section 23.3A that acquiring shareholders typically do not gain in M&A.

➤ Losers in acquisitions, Section 23.3A, p. 881

Conflicts: Friendship, Loyalty, and Ethics

Favoring friends and employees over abstract shareholders is understandable.

Almost all managers are less loyal to an abstract, ever-changing shareholder than they are to what they see as their very real company, with flesh-and-blood employees that they talk to every day. Like all human beings, they become friends with those whom they are working with. Managers prize such loyalty and return the favor. Few managers like to be surrounded by gadflies, naysayers, adversaries, or, worse, potential replacements. Critics who would likely fire existing management are rarely welcome on corporate boards. Natural human tendencies and self interest promote nepotism (in the broad sense) that is not in the interest of capital providers.

Ethical dilemmas: Who should pay for loyalty?

Even managers of the highest ethical integrity often face difficult choices. For example, as a manager, should you feel any loyalty toward employees, customers, and suppliers that used to be, but are no longer, important to shareholders? This includes the town in which your factories are located, the workers who spent their whole lives working for the company, the charitable and worthwhile causes the company contributed to, and so on. Do managers have the right (or perhaps even the moral duty) to donate explicitly or implicitly the shareholders' money, especially when those good causes seem more ethical and worthwhile than the paying of dividends? If you still don't see the problem, consider what you should do if you can make your shareholders richer if you break some contracts that your firm has made in the past. Or if you can sell misleading, inferior, defective, or dangerous products. Is it really your duty to act purely in the interests of shareholders without concern for anything else of moral value?

➤ Breaking contracts as a source of value in M&A, Section 23.3A, p. 879

We are all good at rationalizing things we like.

If not forced, most managers would likely put the interests of diffuse and remote shareholders not only behind their own interests, but also behind the interests of their friends and coworkers. If need be, they can also probably come up with some good excuse as to why, in their executive judgments, it would be in the interests of shareholders to reward their friends and coworkers (and, of course, most of all themselves).

Could governance mechanisms protect managers?

In a sense, strong governance mechanisms that leave managers no choice may even save them from the temptations of harsh moral dilemmas. (Incidentally, this is also the reason why professors like to have no influence over university admissions.)

Entrenchment

Taking projects where one's expertise will be irreplaceable.

Not surprisingly, managers and employees also like to be indispensable. If they decide to take projects for which they will be indispensable, their own personal value to the firm, and therefore their compensation, will likely go up. If they decide to build redundancy—that is, hire someone who can step in for them, thereby making themselves dispensable—their own value to the firm will likely go down. In fact, they may even be replaced by the board. On the other hand, if they make themselves very difficult to replace, their ability to "hold up" the company will force the company to compensate the managers very generously. The board will have no choice but to retain the executive and will award high compensation packages quite "voluntarily."

Bureaucracies can be barriers to entry for new executives.

Bureaucracy often helps promote entrenchment. It can discourage shareholder wealth maximization but help managers become indispensable (knowledgeable of the internal processes). It can even lead firms to undertake opaque and bizarre projects, internally justified by "proper procedure." In contrast, fighting bureaucratization on behalf of shareholders is a painful and never-ending process, with few rewards for the executives involved (unless the firm is in such dire straits that the executives fear for their own jobs).

Corporate Perks

Perks are "goodies" for managers that managers order the firm to buy.

One step higher on the ladder of actions that are nothing but self-interest are expenses on corporate perks. For example, consider a public company that may buy a corporate jet that costs shareholders $100 million and that increases productivity of management by the equivalent of $10 million. This is obviously a bad deal. However, if avoiding public airports and flying in style gives the CEO a lot of extra pleasure—worth, say, the equivalent of $1 million in salary—then he may direct the company to buy the jet anyway. Plush corporate headquarters, fleets of corporate aircraft, and lavish expense accounts are usually "symptoms" of publicly traded companies, especially in slow-growth industries in which firms are flush with cash. Excessive spending on corporate perks is extremely common, but fortunately the amount of money spent on them is usually much less than the amount of money that can be wasted in operational issues, such as futile attempts to build empires.

Work Incentives and Perverse Incentives

Poor work ethics are probably rare.

Some economists' models assume that executives prefer working less (called **shirking**). However, others (including myself) believe that lack of work ethics among executives is rarely a problem in the real world. It is not uncommon for many executives to work 80 hours a week.

On even rarer occasions, managers may even *prefer* low firm values.

➤ The RJR Nabisco LBO, Section 23.2, p. 873

In exceedingly rare circumstances, managers can even have the incentive to drive down firm value. They can then negotiate better incentive compensation contracts or even buy the firm, either of which is often followed by seemingly miraculous turnarounds. The most prominent example is that of the attempted management buyout of RJR Nabisco by its CEO Ross Johnson. His actions are chronicled in the best-selling book, *Barbarians at the Gate*.

24.2C THE BIGGEST LEGAL TEMPTATION: EXECUTIVE COMPENSATION

Naturally, executives are most conflicted when it comes to higher pay for themselves. However, in the United States, there are some legal limits as to how much influence they are allowed to exert in this respect. For example, the corporate board's executive compensation committee must consist of independent directors.

EMPIRICAL MAGNITUDES

Executive pay: Salaries, bonuses, and stock/option grants are most visible.

Executive compensation comes in many forms: salaries, bonuses, stock grants, option grants, retirement benefits, perks, and severance packages. The most visible components are salary and bonus compensation and stock and option grants. For example, Forbes reported that the average CEO of America's largest firms earned over $15 million in 2006, about half of which was due to stock or option gains. The latter component is responsible for some of the fantastic salaries of the highest paid executives: Steve Jobs earned $647 million in 2006—and arguably, he deserved every penny of it, having single-handedly transformed the once moribund Apple Corporation into the most admired brand in the world today. On the other hand, Ray Irani of Occidental Petroleum earned $322 million in pay, but the increased oil price that raised Occidental's value was hardly his personal accomplishment. Not surprisingly, when firms have performed poorly, executive compensation is only salary and bonus. For example, from 2000 to 2006, H. Lee Scott, CEO of Wal-Mart, earned $63 million while Wal-Mart shareholders earned a 7-year stock return of under 1% (less than inflation); Kevin Sharer of Amgen earned $98 million while Amgen shareholders earned less than 7%; and Sidney Taurel of Eli Lilly earned $50 million while shareholders lost 21%.

Executive pay: Fringe benefits, gross-ups, retirement benefits, and parachutes are more obscure.

Other components of executive compensation are often less visible. For example, in December 2005, the *Wall Street Journal* reported that the income taxes on corporate perks (e.g., cars, jets, loan forgiveness) that many CEOs receive are often paid by the corporations and reported only as relatively obscure "tax gross-ups." (More than half [52%] of companies report some gross-ups.) Other recent empirical evidence from Lucian Bebcuk at Harvard shows that pension packages *that usually escape public scrutiny* are often larger than reported executive compensation. Finally, the majority of managers even get paid for poor performance. In 2001 and 2002, the average exit golden parachute in the United States when a manager was terminated "for cause" was $16.5 million.

Why are executives paid so well?

Why is executive pay so high? This question should be divided into two issues: First, is the average level of compensation, regardless of corporate performance, (too) high? Second, is the link between corporate performance and managerial compensation, often called the "slope," (too) high? Let's tackle these issues one at a time.

PAY LEVEL

Simple demand and supply?

In a perfect market, demand and supply should determine executive pay levels. An economist's first question would be: How much better is the current manager than the next-best potential replacement, and how much would this replacement cost? This points to the following first two explanations:

1. Being CEO could be a much harder job than being second-in-command. Thus, high compensation is required to find willing candidates. Empirical evidence suggests that the difference between the top CEO and her immediate employees (who are more likely to leave and thus under high pressures, too) is so large that this explanation seems unlikely. Executive pay packages do not seem low enough to leave CEOs relatively indifferent. Indeed, anecdotal evidence suggests that internal candidates would likely accept the CEO position even if it did not come with a pay raise.

Superstar pay?

2. Executive talent could be scarce—that is, the supply could be very limited. Even though there may be hundreds of potential CEOs, the specific challenges in a specific company and industry may limit viable candidates to just a few. Moreover, the marginal impact of a CEO could be huge. Let me explain: It would not matter much whether the firm hires an assistant who can type 10% faster than another one. The firm could simply pay the slower typist 10% less. The pay per unit of performance would be the same. In contrast, a CEO with just a little higher ability could have a huge marginal impact on the performance of the entire firm. In such cases, the economics of superstars (or, if you wish, rock stars or NBA players) applies to CEOs, too. The best performer may be just a little better than the second-best performer and yet play a very different role and command a lot more compensation.

   Competitive pricing is likely to be a good explanation in cases where the firm first needs to attract a new CEO from the outside. It is also likely to be a good explanation in cases such as Apple's Steve Jobs, in which the next-best alternative would probably be much worse.

   (However, even here, there are some puzzles. First, is Jobs the exception or the norm? Second, if Apple paid Jobs only $200 million instead of $650 million, would he have left? Did shareholders really have to pay so much to get Jobs to perform well for them?)

Efficient excess pay?

➤ Economic rents, Section 20.3, p. 736

In the above two explanations, CEO compensation does not contain pay that goes beyond the normal. (Economists call such excess pay "rent.") Instead, executive pay is simply fair and appropriate. However, there are also economic explanations that allow for excessive CEO compensation on the grounds of economic efficiency:

3. Becoming a CEO could be a prize for which everyone is competing. It motivates everyone below the CEO position to work hard in order to become the CEO. Thus, the marginal effect of the CEO's pay is not just its effect on the CEO's work, but also on many other executives' work.
4. CEOs need something to lose in order to care about the future, to not commit mistakes, and to not defect to the competition and spill the beans. This "something" is their (high) future wages. In economics, this is called an **efficiency wage**.

But why is executive pay so much lower in other countries?

These are all sound economic arguments. Unfortunately, there is one fact that is difficult to reconcile with these arguments: Executives in Europe, Singapore, Australia, and Japan earn a lot less (often merely 10%) than their counterparts in the United States. It is hard to believe that being CEO is much harder in the United States, that executive talent is much scarcer, that CEOs matter more, that becoming a CEO is more needed as a prize, and that CEOs here would be relatively more careless than their foreign counterparts if not in fear of losing their future wages.

Excess pay as bad outcomes?

There are other explanations as to why CEO compensation in the United States is so much higher than that elsewhere:

Worse corporate governance over managers in the United States?

5. It could be that American CEOs are operating in a governance structure that has allowed them to receive higher salaries than their foreign counterparts. Indeed, there are at least three important differences:
   - CEOs in the United States are more likely to obtain control over their corporate boards. The United States is unusual in the fact that the CEO is also commonly the chairman.
   - It is more common for foreign companies to have a large, active, and possibly controlling shareholder. This is consistent with the view that the important governance problem elsewhere is not so much the self-interest of the CEO as the self-interest of large, controlling shareholders.
   - The cultural, ethical, and legal constraints on managerial compensation in other countries are different from those in the United States. Of course, from a shareholder perspective, those social norms and regulations also have a flip side. For example, in Europe, it is more difficult for managers to take drastic actions on behalf of shareholders (e.g., when it comes to downsizing and employee layoffs).

➤ Chairman and CEO, Section 24.5A, p. 921

6. It could be a simple error that is not corrected by the market for executives—this market may simply not be perfect. Maybe foreign companies have it wrong and are simply paying their CEOs too little. Or maybe Americans have it wrong and are simply paying their CEOs too much.

   The truth probably has aspects of all six points to it.

Pay Slope: Pay-for-Performance Sensitivity

Pay for company performance? Yes.

How much more are CEOs of publicly traded companies rewarded when they perform better for their shareholders? There is clear evidence that managers earn higher bonuses, and receive more in valuable shares and options, when the firm does better. We also know that if the corporation performs extremely poorly, managers are more likely to be fired. Moreover, this slope is probably higher in the United States than it is in many foreign countries.

Or pay for manager performance? No!

Yet there is an important puzzle in the slope, too. Most executive compensation in the United States does not even make an attempt to distinguish between firm performance to which the CEO has not contributed and firm performance for which the CEO is primarily responsible. One easy way to reward only the latter would be to tie executive compensation to the corporation's performance relative to its industry. Instead, even executive stock and option grants are always tied to the firm's unadjusted share price. This means that stocks and options reward not only the executive's leadership but also external factors beyond the CEO's control. For example, Lee Raymond, CEO of Exxon, earned $400 million as a retirement package in 2005, primarily because Exxon had earned $36 billion in profit in 2005. Yet it was hardly Mr. Raymond's leadership ability that made the oil price triple in 2005. If Raymond's compensation had been about Exxon's performance relative to the oil price or Exxon's share price performance relative to those of other oil companies, his compensation would have almost surely be an order of magnitude lower. Similarly, a manager who avoids the worst in bad times, perhaps earning negative returns that are less negative than peer companies, should really earn more pay, not less.

Or just hiding pay levels?

An alternative view of shares and options is that they are a form of compensation that is easier to defend from a public relations perspective or that is more advantageous from a tax perspective. In 2006, a number of firms were caught having granted to their CEOs backdated options *after* the stock price had already gone up. This made it appear (wrongly so) that the CEO received pay for executive performance, when it really was just pay. As of 2008, a number of executives have been indicted for backdating, and the SEC now requires firms to disclose their incentive compensation schemes up front.

➤ The options backdating scandal Anecdote, p. 1010

PRIVATE EQUITY COMPENSATION BENCHMARKS

Firms taken private: Good managers earn even more.

Does the evidence suggest that managers are overpaid, or that managers are not paid appropriately for performance? Compelling evidence comes from firms that were taken private in a leveraged buyout. In this context, you can think of private equity funds as a large shareholder wresting control back from management, thereby significantly reducing the agency conflict between shareholders and managers. When a public firm is taken over, the private equity owners usually tie the executive compensation even more closely to the corporate performance than ever before. Indeed, if the firm does well, executives of newly private firms are paid *even more* than they ever were when the firm was still publicly traded. This suggests that the big problem is not so much that executives in publicly traded firms are overpaid, but that they are not rewarded enough for good performance and not penalized enough for bad performance. (However, an alternative explanation for more equity participation is that it makes more sense for managers to share the risk in privately held companies.)

SOLVE NOW!

Q 24.6 What are possible explanations for high CEO pay?

Q 24.7 Describe the main illegal and legal temptations that managers face in their duty to maximize shareholder wealth.

24.3 THE ROLE OF SOCIAL INSTITUTIONS

Society-wide constraints.

We now turn to the institutions that reduce these conflicts of interest. In this section, we look at the most basic social economic institutions that aid entrepreneurs in setting up their corporate governance. In the next two sections, we will look at contracted rights that are more specific to creditors and shareholders, respectively.

Property rights are the underlying basics.

The most basic provision a functioning capitalist economy conveys on its subjects is the right to write and enforce contracts. This creates **property rights**, which can be transferred from one party to another. In addition, society also imposes limits on what managers can do, both formal (laws and regulations) and informal (ethical considerations, social norms, and potential adverse publicity). Unlike the contractual agreements that are discussed in the next sections, many of these social and legal constraints are difficult to escape. (But it is not impossible. For example, a firm could reincorporate itself in a foreign country.)

24.3A THE FORMAL ENVIRONMENT: LAWS AND REGULATIONS

In the United States, investors are protected by a set of federal and state laws, many regulations, and appropriate legal enforcement—both criminal and civil. Yet, most of our body of law has come about not through formal legislation but through court rulings and judicial precedence. The evidence suggests that our mixed process seems to have more flexibility to evolve than its counterparts that rely purely on statutory laws. In civil-law countries, like France or Belgium, where almost all regulations are legislated from the top, investor protections tend to be worse and less flexible.

U.S. law is more flexible than its foreign counterparts.

STATE REGULATIONS, ESPECIALLY IN DELAWARE

In the United States, it is the individual states that set most of the rules under which both public and private companies operate. The majority of large U.S. corporations are incorporated in the state of Delaware, which has developed an impressive set of case laws and expertise in resolving corporate issues in the courts. The **Delaware General Corporation Law** prescribes such arrangements as follows:

The most important regulations are U.S. state regulations, especially those in Delaware.

- The role of directors and officers
- Meetings, elections, voting, and notice
- How to amend the charter
- How to execute mergers, consolidation, conversions, asset sales, and so on
- How to handle insolvency (bankruptcy itself is handled by the federal code, however)
- Suits against corporations, directors, officers, or stockholders

Not surprisingly, most novel governance issues often play out in the Delaware courts.

Shareholders' single most important and broadest legal protection is management's legal **fiduciary responsibility** to act on behalf of the shareholders. Black's *Law Dictionary* defines a fiduciary relationship as one "in which one person is under a duty to act for the benefit of the others." The seminal opinion on fiduciary duty was written by the New York Court of Appeals in 1984:

Shareholders are protected by *fiduciary responsibility*. It limits self-dealing by managers and large shareholders.

> Because the power to manage the affairs of a corporation is vested in the directors and majority shareholders, they are cast in the fiduciary role of "guardians of the corporate welfare." In this position of trust, they have an obligation to all shareholders to adhere to fiduciary standards of conduct and to exercise their responsibilities in good faith when undertaking any corporate action. Actions that may accord with statutory requirements are still subject to the limitation that such conduct may not be for the aggrandizement or undue advantage of the fiduciary to the exclusion or detriment of the stockholders.
>
> The fiduciary must treat all shareholders, majority and minority, fairly. Moreover, all corporate responsibilities must be discharged in good faith and with "conscientious fairness, morality and honesty in purpose." Also imposed are the obligations of candor and of good and prudent management of the corporation. When a breach of fiduciary duty occurs, that action will be considered unlawful and the aggrieved shareholder may be entitled to equitable relief.

In other words, fiduciary responsibility is intended to limit excessive self-dealing, especially transactions between those in charge of a public company and the public company itself. It does not extend to ordinary business decisions that do not preferentially enrich the parties in control. In fact, the **business judgment rule** protects the corporate board and in turn its managers against lawsuits if they make poor choices in the execution of most other company affairs. (Otherwise, the litigious climate in the United States would paralyze them!) Virtually every U.S. state has legislated both a fiduciary responsibility and a business judgment rule.

OTHER MECHANISMS: FEDERAL LAW, ENFORCEMENT, AND PRIVATE LAWSUITS

Federal laws and regulations apply primarily to publicly traded corporations.

➤ SEC, Section 7.2D, p. 195

➤ FASB, Section 13.2A, p. 457

Federal law applies primarily to publicly traded companies, not privately owned companies. It mostly concerns itself with regulating appropriate information disclosure, although it does contain some self-dealing and insider-trading restrictions, too. Congress has delegated most of the day-to-day handling of these laws to the Securities and Exchange Commission (SEC). The SEC has further delegated some of its tasks to professional associations (for example, the National Association of Securities Dealers, NASD), stock exchanges, bond rating agencies, the Financial Accounting Standards Board (FASB), and private auditing firms. In addition to congressional law, the U.S. Constitution gives the federal government control over all bankruptcies, both personal and corporate.

Legal enforcement is important to give laws bite.

The importance of *enforcement* of laws (rather than just what is on the books) is not to be overlooked, either. The United States has strong civil (financial) and criminal penalties and enforcement. (Although the wheels of American justice are not perfect and only grind slowly, usually taking years to resolve even clear-cut cases, they do grind.) In contrast, some other countries have stronger laws but weaker enforcement. For example, by a common governance measure, Indonesia has theoretical protections and self-dealing restrictions that are just as good as those in the United States—yet it takes over four times as long to enforce one's rights (e.g., collecting on a bounced check) in Indonesia as it does in the United States.

If you are looking for perfection, stop.

Of course, if an executive has no scruples, even the best legal and corporate system is unlikely to succeed in curbing all misbehavior. This applies to society just as it applies to corporations. The system still needs vigilance, the ability to respond to new crimes, and prisons, despite all the laws against bad behavior.

Private class-action lawsuits can also influence managers.

Firms also have to try to avoid class-action lawsuits (by shareholders or customers), which have bankrupted more than one company. The desire to reduce the frequency of lawsuits could play a beneficial role from a corporate governance perspective. Firms can be sued in any state in which they are operating. Being sued has become so common in some states that it is now considered part of the ordinary cost of doing business. Nevertheless, despite some positive aspects, the corporate costs of class-action lawsuits likely outweigh their governance benefits.

SOLVE NOW!

Q 24.8 Does the rule of law have limited ability to control the CEO?

Q 24.9 Could there be good corporate governance in the absence of government rules and regulations?

24.3B THE INFORMAL ENVIRONMENT: ETHICS, PUBLICITY, AND REPUTATION

Fortunately, managers are like many other social groups. Most managers are ethical, but there is a great deal of heterogeneity among them. Thus, for most CEOs, social norms and ethical standards are also important constraints. They want to do well for themselves but also remain within the bounds of what is considered normal, ethical, and acceptable. Staying "normal" also reduces the chance that behavior will draw negative publicity and create legal liability for violation of fiduciary duty.

Managers are self-interested, but most are not criminal or unethical.

Yet ethical standards and norms are themselves defined by CEOs as a group. If a practice is commonplace, it is unlikely to violate a manager's sense of appropriateness. Naturally, these standards change over time. On some dimensions, the race seems to have been to the bottom. For example, 100 years ago, the financier J. P. Morgan argued that *no* CEO should make more than 20 times what the average company employee earns. By 2000, the *average* CEO earned 525 times the average worker's pay. Consequently, being paid 500 times an average worker's pay would not violate the ethical boundary of any CEO today—on the contrary, it may prove executive acumen and convey more social prestige through the power that wealth brings.

Ethical standards are relative and also changing.

Social norms can be different for different constituencies. Although excessive compensation may be something worth bragging about to other executives at the local country club, managers rarely find it desirable to broadcast it to the press. Their desire to avoid negative publicity seems to be one constraint on executive compensation. Indeed, managerial compensation has come to consist of ever more complex components, which render them rather opaque to analysts. Researchers are often similarly bewildered when they try to determine whether high pay is primarily due to the need to retain or incentivize a manager, or to the fact that a manager has fired all critics and taken control of the corporate board and so is merely enriching himself. Both may matter, but there is some empirical evidence that intentional obfuscation—which points toward the latter—is important. For example, consider the following:

Lack of transparency and other practices hint that large executive pay packages are constrained more by publicity than by corporate board discipline.

- The more obscure parts of executive pay packages (retirement packages, golden parachutes, sign-on bonuses, etc.) are often higher than the more transparent and publicly reported parts of the compensation packages (salary, bonus, and options) that are printed in popular business magazine rankings.
- Boards often change the terms of executive options after the fact if they would otherwise expire worthless.
- A number of companies were caught backdating option grants in a way that increased CEO compensation without risk but made it appear as if it were performance pay.

These facts indicate that the structure of many pay packages is determined more by the desire to pay large sums and still avoid public scrutiny, and less by the need to incentivize executives.

In some cases, managerial reputation can be a useful corporate governance mechanism, too. For example, a manager may not want to treat shareholders badly if she is running only a small company and has her sights set on being selected manager of a larger company in the future. To receive a higher call (with more opportunities to become richer), the manager must constrain her self-interest for a while. One problem

Reputation concerns sometimes constrain managers.

ANECDOTE The Fox Guarding the Henhouse: The NYSE

Until 2005, the New York Stock Exchange (NYSE) was a "mutual" that was owned by its members, primarily by investment banks like Goldman Sachs. These members were appointed to the NYSE board. (Nowadays, the NYSE is a publicly traded firm.)

The NYSE is an odd creature in one other respect. It is both a stock exchange and a regulatory agency, because the SEC relies on the NYSE to execute some corporate governance rules. This is the case both for the NYSE members and its traded firms, which represent almost all large U.S. corporations (with the exception of the technology sector).

As guardian of good corporate governance, the NYSE should have been a beacon of good arrangements—but it was remarkably conflicted. The NYSE board decided on its chairman's compensation package. The chairman regulated its members. The NYSE members appointed the board. The board appointed the chairman and set the chairman's pay package. The chairman regulated the members who appointed the board. The board paid the chairman. The governance chain was circular! (And, to an extent, it still is.)

In August 2003, the media found out that NYSE Chairman Richard Grasso held a retirement package worth $140 million—about four times the annual profits of the NYSE. The media later found an additional $48 million in pay, which Grasso then publicly and graciously declined. (But he never did so in writing.) After more press digging, it was revealed that Grasso also helped pick the executive compensation committee. Many large institutional shareholders then joined the chorus, publicly demanding Grasso's resignation. On September 17, 2003, Grasso finally bowed to the board's discontent—but he did not resign outright. Meeting with his lawyers, he learned that by forcing the board to terminate him (rather than by resigning), he would receive an additional $57.7 million on top of the $140 million deferred compensation—which he did.

In 2004, Grasso sued the NYSE for $50 million more, because his contract of 2003 contained a clause that forbade exchange executives from making any statement against Grasso if he left the NYSE. In March 2005, Grasso further sued the former chairman of *his* compensation committee for having overseen the approval of Grasso's pay package. Ultimately Grasso received $193 million in compensation and pension benefits. (In other litigation, the New York attorney general sought to recover $100 million from Grasso as "excessive compensation.") As of 2008, the suits were still continuing.

with reputation as an agency control mechanism is that managers close to retirement tend not to care as much about their reputations as they care about their severance packages. Most CEOs retire, rather than graduate to bigger companies.

SOLVE NOW!

Q 24.10 What are some of the reasons why ethical standards may have a limited ability to control the CEO?

24.4 DEBT: THE RIGHT OF CREDITORS TO FORCE DEFAULT

Contractual protections.

The governance constraints in the previous section arise more or less by default, and they are not easy to evade. However, entrepreneurs can also create specific contractual protections, and, like the legal constraints, these rights usually differ across different types of securities. This section starts with the easy one: debt.

Debt has an easy task: Collect promised amounts or seize assets.

Creditors do not need to play a large role in the day-to-day operations of the company in order to receive their due. Ascertaining the value of collateral is cheap and easy most of the time. If a firm fails to pay principal or interest when promised—regardless of whether it is because the market environment is bad, because management has performed poorly, or because management just hides assets—the company falls into automatic default (usually bankruptcy).

Moreover, we have already learned (in Chapter 15) that creditors usually demand and receive covenants, by which the firm must live. Covenants may include collateral, priority, the naming of an auditor, the specification of limits on financial ratios (for example, on dividend payout ratios), and many more terms. Default occurs when covenants are not met. Importantly, coordinated creditor action upon delinquency is not required, because such mechanisms are designed at inception. In the case of a public bond, the covenants designate a trustee to oversee performance of these covenants. The trustee has the obligation to declare a bond in default when the covenants are not met. (The process is mechanical.) In the case of a single large bank creditor, this is not even necessary. Therefore, lenders do not commonly suffer from free-rider problems, where one wants to shift the work of enforcement to the other.

Credit covenants can reduce or avoid creditor free-riding problems in enforcement.

➤ Bond covenants, Section 15.2A, p. 545

After some institutional delay, caused primarily by Chapter 11 bankruptcy protection, creditors usually can take control of the company and/or the collateral. Therefore, creditors need not spend much time or money investigating managers in ordinary circumstances. In many, but not all, OECD countries, creditor protection is even stronger than it is in the United States. For example, there is no Chapter 11 bankruptcy protection for firms in Germany, liquidation is often instantaneous, and violations of the absolute priority rule are almost unheard of. Even in the United States, management typically avoids default on debt as if it were the plague. The reason is not just that equity owners (on whose behalves managers supposedly act) lose the firm's future projects, but more importantly, that corporate management is replaced in virtually all bankrupt companies. Looming bankruptcy gives management strong incentives to maximize firm value.

Fear of bankruptcy is very effective, perhaps even more so outside the United States.

➤ OECD countries, Section 25.1, p. 944

➤ Absolute priority rule, Section 15.2A, p. 545

Creditor Expropriation

Although there are some escape mechanisms that permit management to manipulate the covenants, these are rare and slow. The first such mechanism is a "forced exchange offer," in which managers set up a "prisoner's dilemma" that makes it in the interest of every bondholder to exchange their current bonds for bonds that are worth less but have higher seniority—even though it is not in the bondholders' collective interest. The second mechanism is a covenant amendment, which must be approved by the bond trustee and voted on by bondholders. The third mechanism is asset sales or divisional splits. They require major corporate surgery and are often produced by bond covenants. For example, when Marriott Corporation announced that it would split into two companies (hotel operator Marriott International and a real-estate investment trust Host Marriott) in 1992, its share price rose by 10%. Marriott's bondholders sued, however, because the old Marriott debt now would be owed only by one descendent, Host Marriott.

Escaping bondholders' rights is possible, but it is not easy.

➤ Coercive bond exchange offers, Section 21.5D, p. 803

The fourth mechanism is bankruptcy. The costs of enforcing their claims in bankruptcy and delay or violations of APR could leave creditors less well off. In the United States, management can file for Chapter 11 protection, which can delay the turning over of assets to creditors. This option does not exist in many other countries. For example, in Germany, creditors can practically force immediate liquidation of the

In other countries, it is even more difficult to evade creditors.

ANECDOTE Would You Lend Your Money to a Country or a State?

There is very little other than a country's desire for a good name and its foreign assets that prevents it from simply repudiating its debt. For example, Argentina owed about $220 billion in 2001, with required repayments of $22 billion a year—during the worst economic crisis the country had ever experienced. It repudiated its debt in a very interesting fashion. In July 2000, an Argentinian judge named Jorge Ballestero sent down an intriguing ruling on the foreign debt: The ruling attributed responsibility for the debt to the civil servants during the previous dictatorship *and co-responsibility* to international organizations like the IMF, which approved the loans—now declared illegal and fraudulent.

However, don't think this is just a foreign phenomenon. There have been instances in the past in which individual U.S. states have repudiated their debt. For example, the Arkansas state constitution even has a specific clause that repudiates repayments for its 1868 bonds, in effect making it impossible for creditors to reverse this default by legislation. Creditors have no legal recourse in this case—the federal courts will not intervene.

Source: http://odiousdebts.org.

firm upon nonpayment. As a result of strong creditor protection (and poor shareholder protection), many German companies are heavily creditor-financed: It is far more difficult for German companies to find shareholders than it is to find creditors. Many of the largest German companies remain financed by the families who founded them.

Creditor expropriation is rare. Discipline imposed by creditors could be indirectly beneficial for shareholders, too.

In sum, creditor violations are the exceptions rather than the rule. It is generally hard for management to escape bondholder discipline. In turn, this could even help shareholders—even though liquidation almost always hurts shareholders, the threat of future liquidation upon poor managerial performance can motivate managers and thereby help dispersed public shareholders from an ex-ante perspective.

Large creditors could try to exploit the firm. This is rare for banks.

Although we have discussed primarily the case in which creditors cannot trust corporations, the opposite could also be the case. (And it can just as much prevent a firm from asking for debt financing.) A creditor may be able to turn the tables, pull its line of credit, and thereby threaten management or expropriate the firm's equity (receiving control of the firm). Banks would often be in a strong position to pull this off, but if they did, they would acquire a reputation for doing this, which would make it more difficult for them to find new borrowers.

SOLVE NOW!

Q 24.11 Why does management usually want to avoid bankruptcy?

24.5 EQUITY: THE RIGHT OF SHAREHOLDERS TO VOTE

Equity faces far more interesting corporate governance challenges.

The more challenging governance issues confront equity. The value of equity, unlike that of debt, is highly sensitive to project cash flows and to managerial performance. Consequently, when managers waste money, it is primarily coming from the top—off shareholders' hides. Moreover, shareholders may not even know whether management is acting in their interests unless the firm is transparent and releases a lot of information and the owners do a lot of verification and checking. And even if shareholders are firmly in charge of the firm and have all the information possible, they still have the unenviable task of determining whether any poor performance is the fault of management, the market, or both. In sum, most of the tough questions in corporate governance are primarily in the domain of equity.

24.5A THE CORPORATE BOARD

As already noted, the majority of publicly traded corporations are incorporated in Delaware. Delaware law and stock exchange regulations set down the basic rules for the relationship between companies and their shareholders.

Corporate boards are required by law.

Firms must have a **corporate board**, which is the ruling body of the firm. This board is supposed to represent the owners, principally the shareholders. Normal boards meet about 5 to 10 times during the year for 1 day each. It is the board's responsibility to appoint management and to oversee it—to ensure that management is acting in the best interests of shareholders. Although in economics we deem the investors as the principals of the firm, it is the board that is the principal of the corporation from a legal perspective. Legally, the board is the backbone of our system of corporate governance.

The corporate board is supposed to represent shareholders (and control managers).

The most important control right that entrepreneurs (must) grant shareholders is the **right to vote** on the appointment of the board. This happens normally once a year at the **annual meeting**, which is itself orchestrated by the existing board.

The right to vote for the board is required by law.

THE ROLE OF THE CHAIRMAN OF THE BOARD

The most important individual on the board is the **chairman of the board**. He controls the board's meeting agenda and directs management to produce the necessary information. Of course, the chairman ultimately has to rely on management to receive the right information to present for discussion. The power to set the agenda and filter the information flow should not be underestimated. After all, with only a couple of days per year on the job, and with their own full-time jobs elsewhere to attend to, board members cannot possibly know the business in great detail. Having thousands of pages of reading as preparation for a board meeting is just about as useful to board members as having zero pages. And board members know that if they do not stick to the specific agenda, they run the risk that the discussion will degenerate into long-winded, unfocused conversations. Not surprisingly, boards with more than a dozen members are usually not very effective.

The agenda and information available are important sources of real power for the chairman of the board.

In theory, the board appoints the management and then oversees and protects shareholders against conflicting interests by the management. If the CEO acts in her self-interest, the board can dismiss her. Unfortunately, in practice, corporate boards rarely play such a role under ordinary circumstances. The reason is simple: *In most U.S. corporations, the CEO is also the chairman of the board*. For example, here is the breakdown of the 30 Dow Jones Industrial Average companies as of April 2008:

Most corporations have no independent chairman to oversee the CEO.

➤ Dow Jones, Section 9.4A, p. 257

- In 24 cases, the CEO was also the chairman of the board.
- In three cases (AIG, Citigroup, and Disney), a separation of the two positions occurred recently because of scandals and shareholder revolts.
- In one case (McDonald's), the CEO and chairman of the board died of a sudden heart attack in 2004. His successor, an avid McDonald's eater himself, died of colon cancer at the age of 44 within the year.

- In two cases (Microsoft and Wal-Mart), corporate control was effectively still in the hands of the firm's founders, who remained large, concentrated shareholders.

Clearly, if the CEO is also the chairman of the board, it makes it highly unlikely that the chairman will objectively evaluate, control, and, if necessary, discipline or even fire the CEO. Who wouldn't like to have himself as a boss?

Board Constitution

The definitions of inside and outside (independent) directors.

Of course, the chairman of the board is not alone in making decisions. The other board members could potentially outvote the chairman and oust both the chairman and management. Thus, you should understand how the rest of the board is typically constituted. Nowadays, the most common board composition is about one-third "inside directors" and two-thirds "outside directors."

Inside directors are typically other managers at the firm itself (i.e., employees under the direct day-to-day control of the CEO). Obviously, it is rare that a direct subordinate of a chairman-CEO would revolt or undermine her—if the coup fails, this subordinate would almost surely lose his job.

Outside directors (independent directors) are individuals who have no current or recent material relationship with the company. (However, although independent directors are not allowed to have a relationship with the company, they are allowed to have a relationship with the CEO or the chairman. For example, from 1993 to 2002, Disney's CEO Michael Eisner appointed his children's primary-school teacher to Disney's board. In 2001, four of Disney's independent directors had relatives employed by Disney. The head of Disney's compensation committee was Eisner's personal lawyer.)

Usually, in real life, the existing board can appoint the next board.

Presumably, it is not the former but the latter who would serve as a control function. Let's look at their independence in more detail. How does the typical corporate board come about? The existing board first creates a subcommittee of independent board members, which then identifies suitable candidates. The most common qualification is being an executive at a similarly sized company. The second most common qualification is based on political considerations—almost all boards of large corporations have minority and women representation. Finally, there are firms in which large and active shareholder-investors (often from the founding family) or creditors have representatives. (I am not aware of even a single case in which a board member was recruited from the ranks of known public advocates for the rights of small shareholders or advocates for stricter corporate governance.) Nominated board candidates must then be approved by the full board, including the chairman and inside directors. After the existing board is comfortable with its planned next incarnation, a complete slate is put forth for an up-or-down vote at the annual shareholder meeting. Many corporate board elections are about as democratic and thrilling as elections in North Korea. However, after 2006, a number of companies have voluntarily improved their bylaws and now require individual directors to be approved, too. (Unfortunately, these are rarely the companies with the worst boards to begin with.)

CEOs as a group largely set CEO compensation.

Executive compensation must be determined by a committee of independent directors. However, most members of such committees are themselves CEOs. In effect, as a group, CEOs mostly determine their compensation themselves. As a CEO, would

ANECDOTE Board Composition, Board Perpetuation, and Executive Compensation (IBM)

The CEO-chairman has considerable influence over which board members should retire and who the next board members should be. Of course, these board members in turn nominate the executive compensation committee, who in turn decide on the CEO-chairman's compensation.

The Corporate Library's study of compensation committee membership found that when a director sits on executive compensation committees of multiple firms, these firms tend to have similar executive severance pay packages. There are at least some anecdotes of exit package imitation and possibly mutual back-scratching in the CEO community:

- Charles Knight was the CEO of Emerson Electric Co. from 1973 to 2000 and chairman from 1974 to 2004. David Farr first succeeded him as CEO, then as chairman. (Farr was probably not opposed to nice exit packages for his predecessor from both jobs.) Remarkably, Knight's exit package was not only unusually generous, but it also contained unusual provisions that were similar to those in Jack Welch's package from General Electric.

  Here is where it gets interesting: Knight was the chair of IBM's compensation committee in 2002, when IBM CEO Lou Gerstner retired. Would you expect Gerstner's exit package to have been similar in both generosity and unusual provisions to Knight's own exit package? (The answer is that it was indeed so.)
- Ivan Seidenberg, CEO of Verizon, was singled out by the report for enjoying one of the most egregious severance packages. Seidenberg sits on Honeywell's compensation committee. How do you think the report judged Honeywell's CEO's exit package? Yes, it was also singled out for being among the most egregious.

Source: "You're Fired. Congratulations," http://www.thecorporatelibrary.com.

you be inclined to believe that CEOs should be dearly compensated or held on a short leash? And, as CEO, would you like to argue to your own board that you should be paid more if you have recently been involved (on the executive committee) in cutting the compensation of the CEO of a comparable company? It is not clear if it would be better to require non-CEO directors to determine the compensation, simply because such directors may depend more on the current CEO for their appointment and reappointment to the board. There is no easy solution here.

EMPIRICAL EVIDENCE OF BOARD CONSTITUTION AND EFFECTIVENESS

Empirical studies point to very little board independence.

There are only a few studies of board effectiveness—perhaps because it is so difficult to find something that is not there. Michael Weisbach studied 495 corporate boards from 1974 to 1983 and classified directors as insiders if they were full employees of the company. This would necessarily put them under the direct control of the CEO. This was an era in which only about one-half of the 495 NYSE corporate boards even had a majority of outside directors! Only 128 had boards with clear majorities of outside directors, though many of these had their own dealings with the company and were thus also conflicted. Although no one has repeated this study, the majority of directors in most corporations these days would be outsiders.

Boards tended not to fire poorly performing managers anyway.

In the Weisbach study's 10-year period, the probability that a CEO would depart was about 5% per year. It increased to 6% when a company lost 33% (!) of its stock market value (adjusted for general market movements)—and the causality in these cases may even have been the reverse. That is, the CEO may have acted worse because she was planning her retirement for the following year. What was the effect of an independent board? Firms with more than 60% outside directors had an additional 1% resignation frequency if they had this high of a loss. However, for firms that lost "only" 10% to 25% of their values, the presence of a majority of outside directors did not increase the CEO resignation frequency at all.

Management ≈ Board. CEO ≈ Chairman.

In sum, there is little reason to believe, and little evidence to support, the hypothesis that most corporate boards are effective monitors on behalf of shareholders in the ordinary conduct of business. Indeed, in most of this chapter, and most of the press, the use of the term "management" and "board" are just as interchangeable as the term "CEO" and "chairman."

The Positive Role of the Board

Corporate boards are not always useless. They do serve important control functions, mostly in unusual situations.

When it comes to proactive control of managerial misbehavior, most corporate boardrooms in the United States today are more theatrical stages than effective corporate control mechanisms. It is usually the case that it is not the board that controls the CEO, but the CEO who controls the board. This is not to say that corporate boards never serve a useful control function:

1. When there is a large influential and active shareholder to whom some board members owe independent loyalty, these board members could take sides and vote against the CEO-chairman.
2. When the CEO-chairman is fairly new and has not yet taken full control of the board, the board may have enough residual independent directors who could constitute a threat to the new CEO-chairman.
3. When a CEO-chairman unexpectedly disappears, the board can often take charge and select the successor. A good successor can make it less likely that the firm will have to deal later with many more agency conflicts.
4. When an external offer to buy shares at a much higher price arrives, the board has the legal obligation to weigh the offer in the interest of shareholders. In such an extreme situation, some boards split into factions between those who support the incumbent management and those who believe that shareholders are entitled to the windfall gain even if current management is displaced.
5. When the CEO's performance or misbehavior is so egregious that board members begin to fear negative publicity and personal legal liability, they can and have engineered successful coups.

Boards can also serve other roles—but they are rarely governance organs.

Boards can also serve other useful noncontrol functions. They can advise executives, they can signal a commitment to diversity, they can help build relationships with suppliers and customers, and they can help to run the firm if the current CEO unexpectedly "evaporates."

Better corporate board control could be costly.

The discrepancy between the supposed and the actual control role for many boards is so large that many reform ideas focus on trying to improve the independence of corporate boards. If legal reform could reduce the cozy relationship between board and management, management would indeed be better controlled—but it would come with a cost. It might allow large shareholders to extort more value for themselves at the expense of small shareholders, it might reduce other beneficial functions of the board (e.g., better relations with suppliers), and it could even destroy the company if the relationship between management and the board were to degenerate into a cold war.

SOLVE NOW!

Q 24.12 What are some of the reasons why corporate boards have limited ability to control the CEO? What other roles may boards serve?

24.5B LARGE SHAREHOLDERS AND FOUNDERS

Only large shareholders could possibly step in to control management.

At this point, you should wonder about the natural next question: Why do shareholders not vote to oust poor boards? The main reason is that fights between (small) shareholders and the corporate board and management are unfair contests. While the board and managers have all the incentives in the world to spend a lot of time engineering the ballots and lining up the votes in a way that makes their choices likely to pass, and all the corporate resources at their disposal to sway specific shareholders with favors, individual shareholders have only their own votes. For small, diverse shareholders, it would not be worth the time to attempt to vote and/or to influence management. The costs of meaningful action and coordination are too high, and the benefits to each individual small shareholder are too low. This is an example of the **tragedy of the commons**, in which each individual acts in his or her own personal interest, preferring that other individuals would band together to correct the problems that they all jointly face. Instead, it is in the interest of all individuals to "free-ride," and the hope of every shareholder that others will put in the effort inevitably ends up in vain.

➤ Swaying shareholders with favors, Section 24.5C, Anecdote, p. 930

THE BENEVOLENT ROLE

The influence of large shareholders (mostly activist pension and hedge funds) is limited in most firms.

The only kinds of shareholders who could reasonably play a role in the governance of publicly traded firms are large-block shareholders. They could have enough value at stake to take an active interest and enough votes to scare management. However, their influence is limited, too:

1. To become a large shareholder and/or increase share holdings is costly, because it foregoes the benefit of risk diversification—and the larger the firm, the more costly it is to become a large shareholder. Not surprisingly, in large firms, the stakes of the largest outside shareholders are usually much smaller than they are in small firms. Holding everything else equal, this means that management tends to be less restrained in large firms. Not surprisingly, the empirical evidence suggests that in large firms in which shareholders are more widely dispersed, agency problems are more severe.
2. Even if large shareholders have some incentives to control management, it is still usually not enough. A shareholder who owns 5% of a firm suffers 100% of the cost of any effort to influence management, yet she reaps only 5% of the benefit.
3. If the large shareholder is a mutual fund, it cannot actively seek to influence corporate behavior. If it did, it could run into insider trading regulations when it wanted to divest itself of its stake upon learning negative information. Therefore, most large institutional shareholders abstain from actively seeking corporate influence.

➤ Large and old firm governance versus small and young firm governance, Section 24.1D, Important, p. 904

ANECDOTE CalPERS Top-10 List

The most visible corporate governance activist in the United States is the California Public Employees' Retirement System (CalPERS) with about $240 billion in assets. CalPERS publishes an annual list of worst corporate governance companies (in its portfolio). Among its 2008 winners were the restaurant chain the Cheesecake Factory, the home builder Standard-Pacific, insurance broker Hilb Rogal, and furniture maker La-Z-Boy. (These firms experienced underperformance relative to their peers of at least 40%. In response, their boards focused on establishing rules that made a takeover impossible, such as through staggering the director elections. The detailed corporate governance shortcomings listed by CalPERS make juicy reading.)

But even CalPERS rarely takes on Fortune 100 companies (which are most prone to suffer from agency conflicts). The reason may be not only political but also due to the fact that CalPERS' ownership share in Fortune 100 companies is too low to make much of a difference.

➤ Value-reducing takeovers, Section 23.3A, p. 881

There is evidence that it is only primarily public pension funds, like CalPERS (see the anecdote above), that systematically play a beneficial role. Their very presence seems to deter management from undertaking value-reducing takeovers. Newer anecdotal evidence suggests that some individuals and hedge funds also have begun to play such a role. (Other evidence suggests that private pension fund managers and mutual funds do not play such a role. This may be because the incumbent board may tunnel business to these managers and their allied investment banks.) Moreover, there is also evidence that firms with 5% external owners tend to perform better than firms without such owners. There is also evidence that managers in poorly performing companies are more often replaced when there are large shareholders.

4. Votes are not anonymous: Managers know exactly how their shareholders vote and can seek retribution later on. If the shareholder is linked to an investment bank, insurance company, or independent pension fund manager, it is unlikely that any corporate business would ever flow to these parties again.

Fortunately, the presence of passive shareholders can help.

Thus, the primary beneficial governance role of large, passive, institutional shareholders is that they are likely to vote their shares *against* management if a third party were to seek an active influence. The concentrated presence of large blocks of shares, which could potentially overwhelm the voting power held by management and its allies, is a low-level but constant restraint on management.

The Malevolent Role

A large shareholder could take over (i.e., become) the management and then expropriate other shareholders.

Generally, when small and large shareholders sit in the same boat, the presence of large shareholders is beneficial for small shareholders. Unfortunately, this is not always the case. The interests of large shareholders can differ from those of smaller shareholders. With enough voting shares, a large, active shareholder can in effect pressure, appoint, or even become management. This means that many (though not all) of the conflicts of interest that apply to management then apply to a large shareholder, too. From the perspective of minority shareholders, with control of enough votes, the cure (new management acting on behalf of one other shareholder) could be worse than the disease (independent management acting on behalf of themselves).

Fortunately, such conflict between a large shareholder and small shareholders is rarely the most important governance issue in the United States. First, most shares are in the hands of passive funds, which usually have to abstain from active influence. Second, not only management, but also large shareholders, explicitly suffer legal fiduciary duty to *all* shareholders under U.S. state laws, which makes such expropriation more difficult and easily challengeable in court.

Fiduciary duty restrains management in the United States.

Of course, even in the United States, it is still not in the interest of executives to pick fights with their largest shareholders. Most corporate executives seek a cordial arrangement with their large shareholders. Special treatment of large shareholders is usually more effective than confrontation. Such "VIP" goodies can include special access to information, the sharing of corporate perks (such as golf outings), and special deals (such as sweetheart deals for the firm—or even a private deal for the manager of a mutual fund who is controlling votable public shares of other investors). A noteworthy (and legal) form of preferential treatment of large shareholders, especially threatening ones, is **greenmail** (formally, a **targeted share repurchase**), in which company management uses shareholder money to repurchase pesky investors' shares at a higher price. This has become rare in light of the negative publicity that it has attracted.

Large shareholders may not seek better governance but rather better treatment for themselves: VIP treatment, greenmail, and business with the company. Most corporate boards seek to accommodate large shareholders.

➤ Greenmail, Section 23.3B, p. 883

In many other countries, however, large shareholders are typically not as benevolent. Small shareholders fear not so much that the managers will expropriate all shareholders, but that large shareholders will expropriate small shareholders. The most prominent method of such expropriation is the aforementioned *tunneling*. For example, in Europe and Asia, small numbers of families often control large corporate pyramids in which firms often trade with one another. If a family owns 100% of one company and 10% of another company, and it controls both managements, it can engineer the sale of a $100 million factory from the latter to the former in exchange for a sweetheart price of $20 million. This enriches the first company by $80 million, and the large shareholder family nets $72 million.

In other countries, the problematic role of large shareholders is a more important governance issue than runaway management.

This is not to say that tunneling never happens in the United States. An example that caught public attention occurred in 2001. Ronald Perelman owned a 35% stake in M&F Worldwide Group (MFW), a publicly traded tobacco ingredient company. Perelman also owned 7.3 million shares of Panavision, trading for about $4 per share. The M&F board then voted to approve a purchase of Perelman's stake in Panavision at $17 per share. (MFW shares fell by 25% throughout this transaction, but so did the market.) After more than a year in court with a minority shareholder (a hedge fund that had to pay for its own court costs), Perelman graciously agreed to reverse the transaction.

Okay, on occasion, this happens in the United States, too.

The conflict between a large shareholder and many small shareholders in the United States is usually a factor only when the founding family is still in charge. Many founders not only hold enough shares to control the company but also still consider the firm to be their own property. Sometimes this is good; more often it is bad. There is empirical evidence suggesting that founders are often detrimental to shareholders *on average*: When the founder of a company suddenly dies, the stock price of the company usually goes up, not down! In perspective, the best control of agency problems caused by a founding large shareholder may be his managerial

Specifically, in the United States, corporate founders are often both insiders and large shareholders. Oy vey!

➤ Event studies, Section 11.7, p. 375

retirement and death. Founders are also usually suspicious enough not to allow the next manager to have as strong a level of control as they themselves enjoyed.

Benevolent or Malevolent?

There are pluses and minuses.

On the one hand, large block shareholders can incentivize managers to be more eager maximizers of share value. Their stakes make it worthwhile for them to maintain some checks on the actions of the board. This can benefit small shareholders. On the other hand, large shareholders or founder-managers, who both hold a good voting block and are effectively appointing management, may win any shareholder vote. They can use this power to lift everyone's boat, or they can abuse this power to enrich themselves at the expense of small shareholders.

Some large shareholders help; other large shareholders hurt.

Not surprisingly, in some firms large shareholders serve a useful role in constraining management, thereby aiding small shareholders. In other firms, large shareholders can use their power to help themselves to corporate assets, thereby hurting small shareholders. This is more common in many foreign countries than in the United States, where strong legal protection makes such expropriation relatively more difficult.

SOLVE NOW!

Q 24.13 What are some of the reasons why large shareholders may have limited ability to control the CEO?

24.5C TAKEOVERS, PROXY CONTESTS, AND SHAREHOLDER PROPOSALS

The private market for corporate control—that is, external raiders—can restrain management.

The most effective mechanism for controlling corporate management in older firms may well be (the fear of) external corporate control activity. It could displace them. In Chapter 23, we already looked in detail at mergers & acquisitions, so we will describe them only briefly here, and more from a corporate governance perspective. (However, you should also keep in mind that not all acquisitions are driven by poor target management—on the contrary, many are driven by poor acquirer management.)

There are essentially three control mechanisms to pressure an existing board and management. In order of the audacity (and cost) of the attempt, they are corporate takeovers, proxy contests, and shareholder proposals.

Corporate Takeovers

Hostile takeovers and their threat can be a powerful constraint.

In a **corporate takeover**, an external shareholder amasses enough shares, votes, or support to take over the firm. If the management resists, it is called a "hostile"—or at least a "neutral"—takeover, and it is primarily these types that are likely to discipline poor management. If the raider succeeds, he can then oust the board and its management. Of course, some takeovers are classified as friendly, only because target management recognizes that a raider could win and they can get better exit packages if they cooperate. It is important that you realize not only that it is the actual takeovers that discipline management, but also that their mere threat can have a significant positive effect on how incumbent boards operate.

Unfortunately, corporate takeovers are very expensive and thus somewhat rare. It is not uncommon for an acquirer to have to pay a premium of 20–30% above the share price just before the takeover is announced. If executive compensation abuse costs the firm "only" 10% of its value—that is, "only" $10 billion for a $100 billion company—it would still not be enough to make a takeover worthwhile.

Poor management must be extreme to make a takeover worthwhile.

Nevertheless, there is evidence that even though they are uncommon, the threat of hostile takeovers has helped to discipline management, at least in certain time periods. Figure 23.3 shows that the era of hostile acquisition was the 1980s. Many of these LBOs created shareholder value through better control of agency problems. The evidence suggests that most of the value gains went to the existing target shareholders in the price they received for tendering their shares. Moreover, the sheer visibility, novelty, and threats of such takeovers were big enough to convince many firms in the 1980s to correct their shortcomings.

Has takeover activity ever mattered? . . .

➤ U.S. hostile takeover activity, Figure 23.3, p. 871

➤ Leveraged buyouts (LBO), Section 23.2, p. 873

However, Figure 23.3 also shows that hostile activity declined significantly in the 1990s. There are a number of reasons for this:

. . . Yes in the 1980s. No in the 1990s.

1. Many public firms had curbed their worst agency excesses, which raised their values and thus made a hostile takeover less important. It became harder and harder for raiders to find companies that could be purchased cheaply and then improved.
2. Market valuations generally increased in the 1990s. In addition, a number of high-profile LBOs from the 1980s had failed, inducing lenders to tighten the spigot. Higher interest rates made takeovers of public companies by smaller private acquirers more difficult to engineer.
3. Companies learned how to institute better takeover defenses—especially poison pills and staggered boards—that were too expensive for potential acquirers to overcome.

➤ Managerial resistance, Section 23.3B, p. 883

Thus, throughout the 1990s and early 2000s, corporate governance through external takeovers and leveraged buyouts faded into the background. After 1990, the hostile takeover threat generally receded and was no longer the proverbial sword of Damocles hanging over—and thereby controlling—corporate management.

It took 20 years—until the mid-2000s—before (friendly) leveraged buyouts experienced a renaissance. With nominal costs of capital at historic lows and public sentiment having swung against many managers in the wake of a number of management and executive compensation scandals, private equity firms again began taking over many large publicly traded firms. It became more difficult for boards to fend off offers that were significantly higher than their share prices. In addition, to soften their resistance, most incumbent executives received generous golden parachutes to sweeten the blow of their loss of control. Few companies seemed to be too large to be acquired. In 2005, over $130 billion flowed into such acquisitions. Neiman-Marcus, Toys "R" Us, Sunguard, Hertz, and a host of firms worth double-digit billions are now under the control of private equity firms. The most prominent, though not the largest, may have been the Chrysler buyout by Cerberus Capital. The credit crisis of 2008, however, put an abrupt end to most of this LBO activity.

. . . Maybe yes again in the early and mid-2000s. No in 2008.

ANECDOTE Bribing Shareholders in Proxy Fights

Perhaps the most prominent proxy contest involved Hewlett-Packard (HP) in 2002. It is also a good example of how management can muster all the resources of the firm against a large external shareholder, even to the point of giving away shareholder assets to other parties in order to achieve its goal.

The subject of the proxy vote was the proposed acquisition of Compaq by HP. Walter Hewlett, a corporate director and son of co-founder William Hewlett, was holding 18% of HP. He challenged this acquisition in a proxy fight. However, he lost the proxy vote against the merger after Deutsche Bank (DB) switched 17 million of the 25 million shares it controlled in favor of the $22 billion merger. (Incidentally, these were not shares owned by DB but shares owned by DB clients and held in the DB asset management division.) DB decided to vote for the HP-Compaq merger only after it had become the co-arranger of a new multibillion-dollar line of credit.

In August 2003, the government fined DB $750,000 for having failed to disclose another apparent conflict of interest to DB's asset management client. In a memo to the CEO of DB in the midst of the fight, HP head Carly Fiorina had suggested HP do something "extraordinary" for DB and another firm. HP paid DB's investment banking arm $1 million for "market intelligence," with another $1 million contingent upon success. DB's investment banking arm then helped to convince DB's asset management group of DB's interest—and rightly so. During a conference call with DB money managers, Fiorina then reminded DB that their votes would be "of great importance to our ongoing relationship."

Some other institutional shareholders held shares in the target, Compaq, and therefore also voted in favor. (CalPERS, the prominent pension fund and advocate of better corporate governance mentioned in the previous anecdote, voted with Hewlett.) In all, 838 million shares voted in favor of the deal, 793 million shares voted against it. Hewlett alleged that HP spent roughly $150 million of shareholders' money on the proxy fight against him (18% of which he had to effectively pay for).

It is little consolation for Walter Hewlett that he was proven right. The acquisition indeed turned out to be a failure. Carly Fiorina was fired by the board in 2005.

PROXY CONTESTS AND SHAREHOLDER PROPOSALS

A proxy contest is a "takeover lite."

➤ Proxy contests, Section 23.2, p. 873

In a **proxy contest**, a pesky shareholder does not seek to take over a firm by himself. Instead, he solicits the votes of other shareholders—most of all, the votes of other large-block shareholders. Although proxy contests are much cheaper than takeovers, they are neither cheap nor likely to succeed. For example, Institutional Shareholder Services (a consulting firm advising on votes) reported that there were 17 proxy contests in the first 8 months of 2003, of which only 4 resulted in dissident victories. The average dissident's cost per proxy contest was about $1 million. (The highest cost was over $5 million.) Let's put this in perspective. If management pays itself $100 million too much in a $10 billion firm (for a 1% loss), would a shareholder owning a large block of $200 million in shares find it worthwhile to launch a proxy contest? She would expect to gain $1\% \cdot \$200 = \$2$ million with a $4/17 \approx 25\%$ chance of success. Multiply this to calculate a net expected gain of about $500,000. Therefore, she would not find it worthwhile to undertake a proxy contest this year. And the following year, existing management could even vote a shiny new $100 million block of shares against her proxy. Consequently, to launch a proxy contest, there would have to be a financial reason more weighty than just ordinary excessive executive compensation. Such an example occurred in 1988, the year in which Karla Scherer led the *only* successful proxy contest of a major U.S. publicly held company, Scherer Corporation, founded by her father in 1933. As a result, the company was sold in June 1989 at a price more than double the value of each shareholder's investment the year before, when the proxy contest began. Clearly, the value gains from dislodging management in the Scherer case were large enough to justify the battle.

Losing a proxy contest is problematic for a board.

In sum, "modest" governance problems, such as excessive executive salaries worth \$1 billion in a \$30 billion company (3% of value), are just not enough to make the expense of a full-blown proxy fight worthwhile for any external party. Nevertheless, the small success ratio could be misleading, because even the threat of a shareholder proxy contest can cause management to seek a compromise to rectify some of the problems. Executives are worried about a sudden cascade of dissent, in which all shareholders suddenly believe that the board will be ousted, which could then become a self-fulfilling prophecy. And, compared to hostile takeovers, proxy contests are outright cheap.

A proxy contest is often preparation for a hostile takeover.

The most important use of proxy contests nowadays is as tools to facilitate a hostile takeover attempt. The proxy contest seeks to remove the takeover defenses put in place to protect the board and its management. The hostile takeover can then follow.

A shareholder proposal is a "proxy contest lite."

➤ Shareholder proposals, Section 23.3, p. 877

There is an even more modest form of the proxy contest: shareholder proposals. These are fairly cheap but usually not binding. Their most common use is to try to induce management to eliminate the toughest takeover defense—the staggered board provision. Corporate boards follow many such suggestions, even if they are not binding. Some are never even brought to a vote—upon receiving the notice, boards sometimes prefer accommodating the request instead of risking a cascade of public dissent.

SOLVE NOW!

Q 24.14 What is an LBO? How common are LBOs?

24.5D THE LINK BETWEEN MECHANISMS

Our surgical approach to individual governance sanctions may have painted a misleading picture.

There are also many interactions between corporate control mechanisms. For example, if the board is very poor, it will be more difficult for large shareholders to influence it. If there are no potential raiders, the presence of large shareholders will not have an effect—management will not worry that it could lose control. If there are no large independently owned share blocks, a hostile acquisition will have a lower chance of success. If the board is dominated by the CEO-chairman, she can institute effective antitakeover defenses. This could prevent potential outside acquirers from stepping in. In turn, this could make the stock less attractive for institutions to acquire blocks. And so on.

24.6 THE DESIGN AND EFFECTIVENESS OF CORPORATE GOVERNANCE SYSTEMS

Unavoidable behavior is not necessarily right.

So far, we have mostly taken the perspective of entrepreneurs who operate within an existing system of corporate governance. Firms trade off the advantages of being public (such as access to more capital and better diversification) against the disadvantages (the internalized costs of managerial misbehavior). This is not to condone the latter: Just because some shoplifting may be unavoidable does not mean it is either ethically justifiable or efficiency enhancing.

Good governance is a matter of national competitiveness.

We now take the perspective of engineers of corporate governance systems. How good is our corporate governance system? Arguably, a country that has better corporate governance is likely to match entrepreneurs and funds better, induce management to take more value-enhancing projects, and generally allow it to outcompete other countries. It is a matter of great importance to a nation's economic competitiveness to have a good system. Of course, no governance system is ever perfect. It is impossible to design a system in which corporate contracts and arrangements result in first-best outcomes. In the real and imperfect world, the outcomes are usually second-best. In equilibrium, the system must trade off the costs of governance regulations (such as regulatory costs, administrative costs, compliance costs, enforcement costs, a reduced willingness by managers to take risks, extortion by politicians, etc.) against the benefits (better access to financing by entrepreneurs, less agency waste, etc.).

24.6A RUNAWAY DYNAMICS, SELF-REGULATION, AND THE MARKET

Can markets do it all?

As practicing economists (i.e., business men and women), our first inclination is to ask whether the free market can be put in charge of coming up with a good governance system or whether government intervention is warranted. There is much empirical evidence that governmental supervision often has strong drawbacks, ranging from inflexibility as circumstances change, to useless bureaucracy, to capture of the regulatory agency by the incumbents supposed to be regulated, to the ability of regulators and politicians to shake down regulated firms. Most economists intuitively prefer less government intervention. So, is corporate governance a domain in which we want more or less government intervention than what we have at the moment?

Our theory predicted: Yes, the free market works well for young and upstart firms.

➤ Large and old firm governance versus small and young firm governance, Section 24.1D, Important, p. 904

Our theory also predicted that the free market probably does not work for mature firms.

In the very first section of this chapter, you learned that theory predicts that young, upstart companies should be fairly well governed. Thus, society can probably rely on the free market in these cases: It is in the interests of entrepreneurs to write good constitutions that will work well for the first few years after the IPO. It is unlikely that bureaucratic government regulations from the top could do any better.

However, the theory also predicts that many diffusely held, large, old, cash-rich companies are poorly controlled. The problems should be especially bad if the corporate board and management have enjoyed long tenure and there are no large external shareholders willing and able to step in. Neither the entrepreneur's design nor the need to raise capital would play much of a role in shareholders' control over management.

The real-world situation is actually worse (for old firms): Managers will exploit any chink in the armor.

The situation may actually be even worse than I insinuated. A good metaphor for the point that I want to make now is that corporate governance is like a dam holding back a water reservoir. If there is even a tiny crack in the dam, the water's energy focuses quickly on widening this crack. Analogously, if there is even a small crack in the ability of the board to control its manager, this manager can use this crack in order to perpetuate it and to create further weaknesses. For example, once the CEO has appointed a few of his friends to the corporate board, then appointing more friends to the corporate board generally becomes easier. A manager who controls the board can institute stronger takeover defenses to avert external control challenges. A manager who succeeds in obtaining a large executive share grant has more shares to vote in the following year.

But what about the many good CEOs? In this context, they don't matter. This is about governance, not good management. If the manager's intent is intrinsically good, it will make little difference whether the firm has good or bad governance. Such managers won't spend much time searching for chinks in the armor. It is only when the manager is bad and harbors an intent to enrich himself that he will spend a lot of his time on weakening the governance structures that restrain his self-interest. Thus, it is precisely when management is most self-seeking that poor corporate governance really hurts owners the most. Its the "perfect storm."

Self-selection means that the free market works well only for firms that don't need governance—an umbrella only for sunshine.

Given that just a brief lapse in governance can lead to perpetual control of management, it should not come as a surprise that it may not even be possible to design a good charter. Even if it mattered greatly to the entrepreneur to institute a corporate charter that controlled future managers in the long run (which you know is not the case), it probably wouldn't work. No matter what mechanisms an entrepreneur may create, in the long run, management will find ways to neuter them. Ultimately, internal governance provisions, such as the corporate charter alone, can offer only weak protection, because management can amend it.

The "crack in the dam" can be very small. However, once it's there, the CEO will chip at it to make it grow.

➤ Benefits of long-run control to entrepreneur, Section 24.1C, p. 902

This runaway dynamic suggests that it is difficult to rely on companies themselves to maintain a balanced governance structure. It also suggests the same two outcomes that the theory in Section 24.1D predicted:

The crack-in-the-dam theory has the same implication: Old firms are poorly controlled.

- Young, small firms have good governance
- Old, large, cash-rich firms do not have good governance

Both theories imply that early in their lives, firms will be fairly well controlled. They have large shareholders interested in wealth maximization, corporate boards that share the goal of maximizing the owner's welfare, and firm sizes that could make them appetizing targets if they are not well run. Over time, management will seek to gain more and more control. At some point, incumbent management will become powerful enough to systematically dismantle most remaining charter protections. At this point, only laws and regulation that cannot be circumvented—such as fiduciary duty, legal limitations on takeover defenses, and statutory requirements (e.g., shareholder votes)—can be firmly relied upon as defenses against bad management.

The new implication is that the only good protections are those that cannot be dismantled by management.

Casual observation suggests that when we hear about breakdowns in governance for publicly traded corporations, it is often exactly in the kinds of firms where we would expect them—large, old firms with lots of free cash flow. Although this may not have been a big problem for entrepreneurs and early investors in these companies decades ago (such as Walt Disney in 1957), it could be a big problem from a social perspective. Firms like Disney constitute an important part of our economy, employing millions of people and controlling hundreds of billions of dollars. As an economy and as a society, we do have an interest in keeping these firms running well.

Large firm breakdowns are not as much a problem for entrepreneurs as they are for society.

24.6B MY OPINION: WHAT WORKS AND WHAT DOES NOT WORK IN THE UNITED STATES

Fortunately, corporate governance in the United States still seems to work better than it does in many other countries. Nevertheless, it seems broken in many large, publicly traded, old companies. Even when governance is broken, if the management is intrinsically good, the consequences of bad governance may be modest.

Corporate governance in the United States has both light and shade.

Poor corporate governance is a national problem.

Capitalism in the United States will not collapse because of managerial theft and misbehavior, even though our corporate governance system has undeniable problems—perhaps because theft and mismanagement can only be *so* large. Our problems are not even big enough to destroy most of the wealth created by many of our multibillion-dollar publicly traded companies. But in terms of the wealth siphoned off from the corporate sector into individual pockets and in terms of bad decisions taken, the problem may not be so modest. Again, we are talking not only about billions of dollars but also about millions of jobs. And even though U.S. capitalism will not collapse over poor corporate governance, individual companies could fail and the U.S. economy could fall behind global competitors.

My own opinion about what works.

Like the agency problems themselves, the solutions to agency problems are complex. All governance systems rely on a combination of mechanisms. You already know that today's mechanisms involve the combination of legal obligations, informal and ethical obligations, and corporate contractual obligations. Although they all need one another, we can wonder what really works. Of course, there is much disagreement on a subject as broad as that of corporate governance. It does require judgment, and here is my own.

Internal governance: Corporate board governance is not an effective control mechanism in many companies. It cannot be relied on. It works only in extreme cases.

External market for corporate control: External raiders in the United States are sophisticated and have deep pockets. Laws strongly influence this channel. On the plus side, U.S. corporate laws have made it difficult for boards to isolate themselves *completely* against bids. Thus, external threats continue to be powerful restraints. On the minus side, our corporate laws have also given boards very powerful tools to prevent most takeovers. Moreover, macroeconomic financial market conditions are not always suitable for takeovers.

Informal social constraints: Social norms and the press continue to be important, although the standards of appropriate behavior have shifted over time.

Formal legal constraints: Laws are perhaps our most important bedrock protection, not only because they lay the foundation for private contracting but also because they are least susceptible to being changed over time if a bad corporate board wants to institute rules that give it more and more power.

The best protections in old companies are only those that management cannot dismantle.

IMHO, legal protections in the United States are investors' best friends. Not originating from the firm itself, they are simply more difficult for management to dismantle. Our laws do not allow the board to declare shares void, dilute existing shareholders away, eliminate all outside directors, or even to schedule shareholder meetings only once every decade. Delaware and other state laws prescribe that firms have to have directors and an annual meeting, that managers have a fiduciary legal responsibility, and so on. Moreover, as noted, it is our laws and regulations that generally still make it possible for an external shareholder in the typical publicly traded corporation to acquire a majority of shares and take control of the firm even against the will of an incumbent board. This possibility of an external takeover is still among the important restraints on management of old publicly traded corporations. Yet although managers cannot circumvent the law and its regulations completely, many boards can and have

ANECDOTE Investor Rights Outside the United States

If you believe that the U.S. corporate governance situation is imperfect, consider the situation in other countries, such as Germany or Russia.

Germany: In Germany, insider trading was legal until 1994. Disclosure standards are still modest. Minority shareholders have few rights against self-dealing by majority shareholders which are themselves often other corporations. Executives have legal obligations not only to shareholders but also to employees. This means that they may be legally forced to spend investors' money on behalf of the employees instead of returning it to investors. (Would you invest in a business in which a large part of your profits would have to go to employees by law?)

But perhaps most amazing is the fact that many German firms are owned by complex webs of other firms, which in turn are owned by yet other sets of firms, which in turn own themselves. Ultimately, most large, publicly traded German firms are owned by the banks. The banks in turn are owned by . . . themselves! Deutsche Bank holds voting rights for 47.2% of its shares, Dresdner for 59.25%, and Commerzbank for 30.29%. *Source*: Charkham (1994).

Russia: Germany looks like investor heaven relative to Russia. In Russia, shares can be declared void by the board at any time, majority share owners cannot force an issue onto the corporate agenda, and even physical threats against pesky shareholders are not unheard of. (And do not look to courts and police for protection: Judicial and political corruption in Russia is legendary.)

managed to blunt it. For example, a staggered corporate board effectively eliminates the possibility of a hostile takeover. There has not been a single successful unfriendly takeover of a firm with a staggered board. It would take an external raider at least a year of suffering from value destruction by an existing hostile board before he could take control of the firm.

➤ Managerial defense mechanisms, Section 23.3B, p. 883

In sum, it seems to be the legal structure in the United States that is our saving grace. Our standard of disclosure; our requirement of fiduciary responsibility; our effectively enforced prohibition of theft, fraud, and insider trading; our personalized legal liability; our strong enforcement of laws; and our facilitation of some external pressure by raiders all contribute to a viable governance framework. Surprisingly, this is enough to rank the United States at the top of locales for equity investors.

Legal protection as a corporate governance mechanism carries a real danger. Still, in this case, it may be needed.

This situation is perplexing to me as an economist. Most economists' perspective (or call it our gut instinct) is usually that much of what the government touches comes out for the worse. Private contracting usually tends to do better. Yet it seems that the legal structure in the United States is our most effective mechanism for corporate governance. All in all, I deem it appropriate for the government to take a (more) active role in corporate affairs, despite the drawbacks and risks that government intervention carries. *You may disagree.*

24.6C WHERE ARE WE GOING?

A good corporate governance system cannot be static.

One might be tempted to just leave a system alone that seems to have worked for decades. (In fact, economists are very good at arguing that a current system, whatever it happens to be, is efficient.) But this system has never been static, either. Bad managers have always found new ways to profit, and new mechanisms, regulations, and court rulings have always come about to push them back. There is a real danger that if no action is taken and the balance between the costs and benefits of corporate governance shifts without a good response, then investors (and firms) may leave the United States for greener pastures in other countries.

Third parties have offered many best-practice suggestions.

I am not the only analyst who feels this way. A whole range of institutions and temporary commissions have proposed "**best practice**" guidelines for corporate governance over the years. The most prominent are the *GM Board Guidelines* (since 1994), the *American Law Institute Principles* (since 1992), the *Business Roundtable Principles* (since 2002), the *National Association of Corporate Directors Report* (since 1996), the *Conference Board Recommendations* (since 2002), the *CalPERS Principles/Guidelines* (since 1998), the *Council of Institutional Investors Principles and Positions* (since 1998), the *TIAA-CREF Policy Statement* (since 1997), the *AFL-CIO Voting Guidelines* (since 1997), and the *OECD Principles/Millstein Report* (since 1998).

In fact, there are too many.

➤ FASB and GAAP, Section 13.1A, p. 447

One big problem with the credibility of these recommendations is that there is not a single authoritative one. My sarcastic view of our situation is that "the nice thing about our standards is that everyone can pick his own." FASB works so well because it is the only official recommender of "generally accepted accounting principles." We really need one clear authoritative standard, not many.

Sarbanes-Oxley

The specific corporate scandals of 2001–2003 ironically were not the result of corporate governance laws that failed to prohibit them.

Recent corporate scandals in the United States, especially the Enron scandal of 2001, caused a public outcry that brought with it a number of corporate governance reforms. Ironically, these scandals are not what needed remedy. They were the results of already criminal actions, and many of their perpetrators have ended up in prison under the old laws. Of course, no reform can eliminate all scandals in the future: Just as bank robberies exist despite laws against bank robbery, so will illegal managerial behavior continue despite laws against it.

The most important new regulation in decades is the Sarbanes-Oxley Act.

The **Sarbanes-Oxley Act of 2002** (popularly dubbed **SOX**) was the most important law passed in the wake of a number of spectacular corporate collapses. SOX builds on our multitiered system of corporate regulation (e.g., the SEC, FASB, and direct legal corporate requirements). Most of its provisions seek to strengthen the independence and function of the corporate board, especially insofar as the audit, executive compensation, and nomination committees are concerned. Some are improvements over existing rules, in that they are cheap and eminently sensible. For example:

A list of SOX changes to corporate governance. The good ones first.

- There is now a clear definition of what an independent director is: An independent director is an individual who has no current or recent material relationship with the company. (But note that independent board members can still have close relationships with the CEO.)
- Independent directors must meet among themselves in regularly scheduled executive sessions without management.
- Companies can select the members of their executive compensation committee and board-nominating committee, but these committees must be majority independent (NASDAQ) or fully independent (NYSE).
- Section 302 prescribes that the CEO and CFO must certify to the audit committee the accuracy of the company's financial reports/condition. (Interestingly, this was not really a novel feature of SOX. Executives were responsible for the reported fi-

nancials of their companies even before its enactment. It made for good television, though.)

- Attorneys must alert the SEC if they learn of credible evidence of breaches of fiduciary duty or of securities law.
- A large part of SOX pertains to the audit committee, as the act itself was sparked by accounting scandals:
  - The audit committee, which checks over the company's financial reports, must consist entirely of independent directors. There are additional special rules for the audit committee pertaining to large shareholders.
  - The audit committee must have choice of, oversight of, and compensation responsibility for the company's auditors. It can engage additional advisors, and it must institute procedures to handle both complaints and whistle-blowers.
  - The audit committee must identify which of its members is a financial expert, and at least one expert is required.
  - The audit committee has "code of ethics" responsibility.
- External auditors are now limited in the amount of consulting work they can do for companies. Historically, this has been a great source of conflict for public auditors. In addition, the audit committee must approve any remaining nonaudit consulting work by the auditor.

The following SOX provisions could be quite harmful to our corporate system.

With the possible exception of the prohibition of consulting work by auditors, none of the above prescriptions are expensive from a corporate perspective and most make common sense. However, other SOX requirements are more controversial because they have increased corporate costs quite significantly:

- Auditors must be rotated on a regular basis in order to reduce the tendencies of relationships between firms and auditors to become too cozy. This may or may not be a good idea—the jury is still out. New auditors have to learn more about the firm first, and they may be *less* adept at detecting unusual behavior. Moreover, there are now only four big accounting firms competing for Fortune 100 business. In real life, a corporation may only be able to ask for bids for work from three other (busy) accounting firms.
- **Section 404** is SOX's most controversial requirement. It prescribes that the annual report has to explain the internal controls and attest to their effectiveness. (Actual implementation was delegated to the SEC.) Of course, being a part of the internal report, this part has to be audited—and the evidence suggests that this has doubled annual audit fees. Although Section 404 is costly for firms of all sizes, the smaller the firm, the more burdensome this seems to be. Auditing fees are not insignificant for small, publicly traded corporations. It is common for their audit fees to exceed their annual earnings—only the hope of future growth keeps them going. The extra burden may push many of them over the cliff.
- SOX has also added record-keeping requirements that are often not clear how to interpret. Sections 103 and 802 require that all audit-related information be retained for a period of not less than 7 years—any electronic messages, emails, and the like.

This can be broadly constructed to apply to almost everything and will be a bonanza for IT departments and consulting firms (and later for trial lawyers) for years to come.

BETTER ALTERNATIVES?

SOX was not a great law—it seems more like a knee-jerk reaction. It is expensive and only modestly effective.

Was SOX a good reform? In my opinion, probably not:

A good system of corporate governance should be cheap and effective.

SOX is neither. Even its authors Michael Oxley and Paul Sarbanes admit that they would write the act differently today, according to *The Economist* ("Five Years Under the Thumb," 7/26/2007). SOX was passed too quickly under tremendous public outcry in the wake of corporate scandals. Although well intended and not devoid of positive aspects, it is probably a good example of how corporate governance should *not* be legislated. For the most part, SOX focused on process over outcome. It added a lot of new compliance and paperwork. Some have even called it the "accountants' windfall profit act"—ironic, because it was accountants' failure that contributed greatly to many of the scandals in the first place. Since 2003, the remaining four accounting firms have enjoyed banner years of high profitability.

The benchmark for SOX should be the right changes, not no changes.

My opinion is not so much that SOX was terrible—though the jury is still out on how the more expensive provisions will hinder young, small firms' access to capital. It could even be that SOX's reforms were a net positive relative to what preceded it. However, my opinion is that the appropriate benchmark should be the law and reforms that could have been passed in SOX's stead. Here are my views on what should have been.

Our politicians should recognize that the SEC has morphed into our primary economic corporate regulator, not just a legal enforcement agency that happens to regulate the corporate sector.

My first reform suggestion would not even require a law. Today, the SEC is not only a legal enforcement agency (of insider trading) but also our premier corporate regulatory agency. It is charged with putting general legislation into practice with specific rules and often with giving advice and perspective to Congressional committees. However, the SEC has traditionally been run by a lawyer. Lawyers are by nature more inclined to emphasize the legal process and more focused on the first task, enforcement. Instead, we need more emphasis on the second task, regulation, and on instituting effective mechanisms that have low compliance costs. It's time to appoint an economist as SEC chair.

It is better to rely on a carrot-and-stick "safe harbor" approach than to force regulation on each and every firm.

➤ Safe harbor for SEC Rule 10b-18, Section 19.1B, p. 706

Next, the SEC should institute an authoritative independent board, somewhat similar to FASB, that recommends best practice for corporate governance. By placing best practice in the hands of a government-endorsed independent institution, the system would hopefully remain flexible and unpoliticized enough to make changes when the environment demands it. Firms, boards, and managers that follow best practice should receive "safe harbor" legal consideration against regulatory action and investor lawsuits. Having definitive recommended best-practice regulations would also put appropriate legal and moral pressure on firms to follow these practices. However, the system should allow firms to ignore certain recommendations when it makes great financial sense for them. A more flexible "safe harbor nudge" instead of a strict legal requirement can accomplish this.

Here is what I think are the most important specific changes that would make U.S. governance better.

I also have a list of what I believe a governance board should recommend as best practice—but these are really better decided by a group than by me alone:

- The position of chairman of the board should be separate from that of chief executive officer. (This was strongly championed by Ira Millstein.) It should be obvious that if the chairman is also the CEO, at best, independent corporate board directors can only struggle to maintain a little influence over management, rather than oversee management in the interest of shareholders. Today, in executive circles, a company that has a separate chairman is viewed as not trusting its CEO. It must become the accepted corporate norm for these two positions to be separate.

  The argument against separation, mustered by many CEOs, is that it would cost them time and effort to deal with a separate chairman. One can view this argument as stating that a benign dictator is better than checks and balances. This is true—checks that always determine that the CEO has acted the right way may be a waste. However, good governance does not come for free. It can cost money if management is good. Good governance can save money to prevent management from turning bad—which is, after all, the whole point of governance. Again, good governance is not good management. Good governance is the mechanism to prevent management from turning to the dark side.

- Inside directors should be allowed to be members, but they should not be allowed to vote on corporate board decisions. This would also help clarify the pecking order and enhance separation between the board overseeing management and management running the firm.

- Directors should be required to be individually approved, not just as part of a slate. This would impose a discipline on the types of directors that boards would propose and allow disgruntled shareholders to express dissent in a manner painful to the board. Many S&P 500 companies have recently voluntarily instituted this. (Presumably this includes few companies where it would really be needed.)

- Staggered board provisions should require extra scrutiny. For example, they could be required to receive approval by 2/3 of all (and not just voting) shareholders.

- Shareholders should have a "say on pay"—that is, a (possibly nonbinding) opportunity to express their views, similar to what shareholder proposals accomplish.

- Any insider trading should be disclosed a few days *before* a trade, not after it. The cost of such a rule would be that it makes it less desirable for a CEO to own shares. In some situations, this can be a negative. However, anyone who is in favor of restrictions on insider trading should probably also be in favor of upfront disclosure.

- Large, publicly traded companies with more than $100 million in market capitalization should be forced to disclose their tax financials. This would reduce their incentives to overstate earnings. The cost is that companies might lose a competitive edge if they had to disclose more information. However, the same critique applies equally well to all GAAP disclosures.

I believe the above changes could be effective at modest cost—unlike SOX, which is not effective and has high costs. Again, individual firms that find them too expensive could opt out at their own risk.

The free market would never institute these reforms. Only a systemwide implementation could bring them about.

In my opinion, these suggestions cannot be implemented by individual companies. There are three reasons:

ANECDOTE The Corporate Governance Consulting Industry

A recent phenomenon is the emergence of corporate governance consultants. For example, Georgeson publishes an interesting year-end wrap-up of shareholder proposals and proxy contests. Unfortunately, some corporate governance consultants not only publish ratings of how well publicly traded companies are governed but also sell "advice services" to companies. Not surprisingly, following the consultants' advice, the client tends to improve in the consultants' rankings. It is clear that the corporate governance consulting industry has some serious corporate governance issues itself!

1. Single firms compete for managerial talent. They cannot go against the arrangements that are common in other firms. (Over time, this competition for managerial talent may even have created a "race to the bottom" in which firms are competing on the least governance.)
2. Having a system different from that of other firms would be viewed with deep suspicion. Do unusual and stricter controls signal something about the board and its desire to institute better rules, or something about the trust that the board has in its own managers?
3. Voluntary restraints would work in precisely the kind of firms that do not need them—those with good CEOs. In firms in which bad management has taken charge, the dynamic has set in that would again eliminate these constraints.

Thus, it is my view that governance improvements generally work better if they are systemwide.

Be critical, both of the existing system and of my own views.

Most importantly, you should not adopt my view without your own critical consideration of the corporate governance situation in the United States today. Many of my views and suggestions are quite radical, and none are without cost. This means that intelligent people can strongly disagree with my opinions. You should contemplate whether you want to be one of them.

SOLVE NOW!

Q 24.15 What are the main SOX reforms?

SUMMARY

This chapter covered the following major points:

- Control rights are necessary components of any security in order to defend investors' cash flow rights. Debt can force bankruptcy in case of violations of covenants or nonpayment. Equity can elect the corporate board.
- It is in the interest of the entrepreneur to set up the firm so that it will not suffer a subsequent breakdown of governance. This increases the value of the firm when first sold. Unfortunately, this incentive to "set it up right" is strong only at the outset when the firm is first taken public.
- Once a firm is public and diffusely held, a "runaway" long-run dynamic can set in: Management will want to exploit any gaps in governance to wrest even more control

of governance away from shareholders. Thus, the primary governance sanctions working well in old, cash-rich companies are those that are not at the discretion of the board and management itself.

- Managers have the incentive to act in their own self-interests, not necessarily in the interests of shareholders and creditors. Among the issues that governance must be concerned with are illegal temptations (such as theft, fraud, insider trading, tunneling, and bribes) and legal temptations (such as empire building, entrenchment, corporate perk consumption, excessive executive pay, ethical conflicts, or misaligned incentives).
- There are many mechanisms that reduce or rein in managerial misbehavior. The most prominent are corporate boards, corporate takeovers, the presence of large shareholders, the legal environment (especially that in Delaware), social norms and ethics, and debt (that forces management to perform or go bankrupt).
- The most prominent change in the corporate governance landscape in decades was the Sarbanes-Oxley Act of 2002. However, relative to possible other alternatives, it instituted measures that were very costly for corporations but that improved actual governance only very mildly.

KEY TERMS

agency problem, 897
agents, 897
annual meeting, 921
best practice, 936
business judgment rule, 916
cash flow right, 899
chairman of the board, 921
conflict of interest, 897
control right, 898
corporate board, 899, 921
corporate governance, 896
corporate takeover, 928
Delaware General Corporation Law, 915
efficiency wage, 912
empire building, 908
fiduciary responsibility, 915
first-best outcome, 901
greenmail, 927
independent director, 922
inside director, 922
outside director, 922
principal, 897
principal-agent problem, 897
property right, 914
proxy contest, 930
right to vote, 921
Sarbanes-Oxley Act of 2002, 936
second-best outcome, 899
Section 404, 937
shirking, 910
SOX, 936
targeted share repurchase, 927
tragedy of the commons, 925
tunneling, 906

SOLVE NOW! SOLUTIONS

Q 24.1 For debt, the main control right is the right to force bankruptcy if covenants are violated or payments are not made. For equity, the main control right is the right to elect the corporate board at the annual meeting.

Q 24.2 It would not be in your interest to avoid wasting the \$10 million. If you did not try to steal the \$30 million, you would own 58.3% of \$100 million, that is, \$58.3 million. This is less than the \$65 million that you receive if you proceeded with the loot-and-waste plan.

Q 24.3 The incentives to control agency conflicts are strongest around the time the firm goes public. The entrepreneur internalizes all future agency conflicts. To the extent that money will be diverted from owners in the future, these owners will be willing to pay less for the firm today. For a numerical example, see the text.

Q 24.4 The following are limits to how charters can eliminate all future agency conflicts: First, there is the cost of eliminating future conflict. It may even be impossible (infinitely costly): Who can think of all future contingencies that could happen and that should be considered in the charter? Second, reasonable entrepreneurs care primarily about agency conflicts soon after the IPO and pretty much ignore what may happen many decades later. The magnitude of far-away conflicts, in the unlikely case that the firm will still exist, is just too small for them to bother with.

Q 24.5 For the \$100 million firm with the \$30 million project that will return \$25 million:

(a) Yes, it is possible that the CEO wants to take this project if she gets personal control benefits.

(b) The voting power of existing shareholders will go down. They will no longer hold 100%. New shareholders will demand $\$25/[\$125/(1+r)]$, leaving old shareholders with $1 - \$25/[\$125/(1+r)]$ of the firm's shares. (This assumes that the new shareholders do not believe something like this will happen to them later, too. If they do, old shareholders are even worse off.)

(c) No. Equity holders would still bear the brunt if the CEO took a bad project. It would still be the existing equity that would pay for the folly of this project. New creditors would simply get a fair value. In the end, it is not the process of raising external equity that destroys value, but the taking of negative-NPV projects.

(d) No, raising equity does not always impose market discipline that controls management, as this example shows.

(e) If the CEO is not fully entrenched, the need to execute such bad transactions may induce the board or an external raider to come into action and get rid of the CEO. This is especially likely if the project is very bad and the capital markets are not willing to provide favorable financing terms. Alternatively, if the CEO owns a large stake in the firm (effectively making her equivalent to the entrepreneur in our examples), the CEO may not want to take projects that have a negative value impact on her existing ownership stake.

Q 24.6 Possible explanations for high CEO pay are (1) the job is enormously more difficult (implausible); (2) talent is scarce, and even a little more CEO talent can make a lot of value difference; (3) becoming CEO is a prize that motivates everyone; (4) high salary is required to ensure that CEOs care; (5) the CEO has "captured" the board; and (6) it is an error that an imperfect market has not corrected.

Q 24.7 Illegal: theft, fraud, insider trading, tunneling, bribes. Legal: empire building, friendship and loyalty, excessive entrenchment, perks and the incentives to drive down the firm value in order to purchase the company on the cheap. Executive pay is particularly prominent.

Q 24.8 The rule of law (regulations, laws, rulings, etc.) regulates only the most egregious violations of fiduciary duty. It does not extend to "business judgment" calls.

Q 24.9 Probably not: Without laws that allow the enforcement of written contracts, for example, no corporation would be able to contract with anyone.

Q 24.10 The standards are themselves set by the behavior of CEOs as a group. Moreover, ethical standards tend to be higher when information is publicly available, but not all managerial actions are publicly reported.

Q 24.11 Even if the company continues to exist (Chapter 11), management is usually replaced.

Q 24.12 The CEO knows the firm the best and, through judicious choice of information, controls the agenda. The CEO is often the chairman of the board. Elections for the board are often by slate and rarely contested. Inside directors are under the control of the CEO. Independent directors are often CEOs themselves. Corporate boards also have other roles: advice, a commitment to diversity, the building of corporate relationships, as well as support and backup during management successions.

Q 24.13 In large, widely held publicly traded corporations, even large shareholders typically hold only a small fraction of the shares. Thus, they will not invest too much effort, because they do not receive 100% of the benefits from lobbying. Some types of shareholders will not invest any activist effort to avoid insider trading regulations. Moreover, management will find out whether a shareholder voted against them.

Q 24.14 An LBO is a leveraged buyout, that is, one that is financed with a significant amount of debt. They were very common in the 1980s. They receded in the 1990s but made a small comeback in the mid-2000s. With the credit crisis of 2008, they disappeared again.

Q 24.15 Independent directors are now clearly defined. They must meet by themselves regularly without management. Rules concerning the audit committee and the independence of auditors were beefed up. The CEO and CFO must certify the accuracy of the company's financial reports. Attorneys must report certain breaches of fiduciary duty or securities laws. The executive compensation and board-nominating committees must be majority independent. There are also some other reforms that seem to be less beneficial.

PROBLEMS

The ▬ *indicates problems available in* myfinancelab

Q 24.16 Go to Edgar, the SEC's website. Look up *El Torito*'s S-4 filing on 2004-06-09. Describe the covenants and requirements to which *El Torito* is obligated. (Note: This may take a while, but reading this S-4 will introduce you to how these agreements look in the real world. If you already did this exercise in Chapter 10, pick another company of your choice.)

Q 24.17 Thomas Edison took General Electric public in the 1880s. Would it have been in his interest to write a charter that would prevent a self-serving CEO 100 years later to pay himself 1% of the firm's value as compensation? Would it have been possible?

Q 24.18 Should society worry that executives would unduly enrich themselves, or can society rely on the entrepreneurs' incentives to write corporate charters that prevent this? Under what circumstances does either of these two perspectives seem more powerful?

Q 24.19 In the example in Section 24.1D, the manager of a $60 million firm takes a $30 million project that costs $50 million, just because it produces $10 million in managerial perks. Let's presume this project produces no perks, but managerial compensation is 1% of firm size, every year. This means, for example, that the manager earns $600,000 without the project. Would the manager still want to take this project?

Q 24.20 Does the desire to raise equity capital always control managerial agency conflicts? That is, does it induce managers to do the right thing?

Q 24.21 Are all de facto "bribes" of executives illegal?

Q 24.22 Search the Web to find the executive compensation of the 10 highest-paid executives last year. In which cases would you attribute the salary to superior performance of the executives themselves?

Q 24.23 Make the argument why managers in the United States are paid appropriately.

Q 24.24 Make the argument that managers in the United States are paid too much.

Q 24.25 Discuss the pros and cons of the government taking a more active role in determining the corporate governance rules by which corporations operate.

Q 24.26 Search the Web to find 10 bankruptcies that occurred about 3 years ago. In how many cases is the CEO still in charge today? What happened to the CEO afterward—did this CEO get a good job elsewhere?

Q 24.27 Search the Web to identify any 30 Fortune 500 companies. In which of these firms is the CEO also the chairman of the board? What fraction of the board are employees of the company who are reporting directly to the CEO?

Q 24.28 Under what circumstances would you expect the sudden appearance of large shareholders to be good for minority shareholders? When would their appearance be good for independent executives?

Q 24.29 Can you recommend other corporate governance reforms that were not described in this chapter? Discuss the pros and cons of your suggestions. Under what circumstances do you think the pros would outweigh the cons, and vice versa?

International Finance

WITH FOCUS ON THE CORPORATE PERSPECTIVE

This chapter provides a brief introduction to international finance as viewed from the perspective of a domestic CFO, who is dealing (at relative arms-length) with subsidiaries, sales, or the raising of capital in other countries. When a U.S. firm goes multinational, many issues can become more complex. For example, marketing to customers, hiring employees, dealing with suppliers, and accounting rules can all be different in other countries. These issues are not principally the domain of corporate finance, and thus we shall ignore them in this chapter. Similarly, foreign managers of foreign corporations can face a whole slew of novel corporate finance issues that we will also ignore—for example, in some European countries, managers are legally obliged to maximize not just shareholder value, but a broader stakeholder value.

Ultimately, for the financial (but not the operational) side of U.S. firms expanding abroad, there is one primary complication: currencies. Otherwise, you can treat foreign subsidiaries located in other highly developed countries pretty much the same as you treat domestic operations. The problems and solutions look very much alike. Of course, currency issues can pervade multiple areas of finance—exchange rates for trading, foreign investment, capital budgeting, and hedging. These are the subject of our chapter.

25.1 CURRENCIES AND EXCHANGE RATES

The United States is the largest financial market, followed by Europe and Japan.

The financial markets of the United States are the largest in the world. About half of the world's stock market capitalization and bond market capitalization is in the United States. Europe accounts for about one-quarter, and Japan accounts for about one-eighth. (It is likely that southeast Asia, including China, will soon play a more prominent role.) Corporate borrowing is even more lopsided: U.S. corporations account for about 75% of the world's corporate bond issues.

Throughout this chapter, we want to look at the United States vis-à-vis a broad set of other countries. To refer to richer nations with open capital markets, we shall follow the common practice and just call them the OECD countries. (The OECD is the Organization for Economic Cooperation and Development and includes many North American and European countries, Australia, Japan, and Korea.) The most important conceptual difference between a financial transaction within the United States and a financial transaction with another OECD country is often that of currency exchange rates. Thus, this is our first order of business.

For OECD countries, the biggest novel aspect are currencies.

25.1A EXCHANGE RATES AND CURRENCY-DEPENDENT RATES OF RETURN

An **exchange rate** is the price of one unit of some country's currency in terms of one unit of another country's currency. It is really no different than the price of a good. For example, your grocery store really posts "exchange rates," too: for example, 0.25 $/apple or 4 apples/1$.

Every price is really an exchange rate.

There are standardized currency quoting conventions. For example, one convention is to quote the yen-dollar exchange rate (e.g., 105 ¥/$) rather than the dollar-yen exchange rate; and another convention is to quote the dollar-euro exchange rate (e.g., 1.55 $/€) and the dollar-pound exchange rate (e.g., 1.95 $/£). Be careful: The dollar depreciates either when the ¥/$ rate decreases (fewer yen per dollar) or when the $/€ rate increases (more dollars per euro).

Convention: Yen/U.S. dollar but U.S. dollar/euro and U.S. dollar/British pound.

The exchange rate that you pay when you travel and need physical cash, for example, from your hotel or an airport exchange booth, is usually rather unfavorable. But the *financial* currency markets, whose exchange rates apply to large financial transactions, are the most liquid and competitive markets in the world, with very low transaction costs and bid-ask spreads. Although there are no solid statistics, the typical currency trading, including forward and futures trading, is around $1.5 trillion a day. To put this into perspective, this is more than 10 times the typical daily trading volume in equities and about 10% of the *annual* U.S. gross domestic product (GDP). In such liquid and active financial markets, it makes sense to believe in market efficiency. Few, if any, investors should have an unusual ability to predict the exchange rates better than the market itself.

Financial exchange rates are almost frictionless when no physical cash is involved.

25.1B CURRENCY FORWARDS AND INTEREST RATE PARITY

Corporations can hedge the risk caused by exchange rate fluctuations by trading currency contracts. The most familiar contract is a **spot contract**, which is for an immediate exchange of a fixed amount of currency based on the **spot currency rate**—the current exchange rate.

The spot rate is the current exchange rate.

FORWARDS VERSUS FUTURES

In addition to spot transactions, traders can engage in transactions that are based on future spot rates. A **forward contract** is an agreement to exchange a fixed amount of currency on a fixed date in the future at a price that is locked in today. These contracts are usually structured so that they are a fair exchange between parties, and neither party needs to pay anything at the outset. For example, a contract between a buyer

A forward (contract) is an agreement to exchange currency in the future.

and a seller may state a mutual agreement to swap \$1.5 million for €1 million in 3 years.

Unlike forwards, futures are daily settled.

However, currencies (and many other assets) trade not only as forward contracts but also as **futures contracts**. A future differs from a forward in that it settles up contract value changes *every day*. For example, assume you have purchased a futures contract today that commits to exchange (your) \$200 for the receipt of (someone else's) £100 next year. Let's say that the dollar depreciates tomorrow and the futures exchange price changes from 2 \$/£ to 3 \$/£. Your £100 committed receipt is now worth \$300. Instead of waiting, the futures contract immediately requires an interim settlement: The seller of your futures contract must pay you the \$100 at the end of the same day. After each daily settlement, the contract value of a future (but not of a forward) always resets to zero.

Futures have the advantage that it is almost never worthwhile for either party to skip town.

This immediate settlement arrangement reduces the counterparty credit risk, that is, the probability that one side accumulates losses big enough to default on the contract. This idea of immediate futures settlement has a long history. They were common on the Amsterdam securities exchange as early as the 17th century. This is no accident: Avoiding credit risk is especially important in exchange markets, where all kinds of investors can participate anonymously. Nowadays, currency futures are primarily traded on exchange markets, such as the Chicago Mercantile Exchange. This also means that the prevailing spot and futures currency exchange rates are publicly posted and easily accessible (e.g., on www.barchart.com).

Forwards are party-to-party contracts.

➤ Over-the-counter markets, Section 7.2B, p. 192

In contrast to futures, forwards are typically bought and sold in an over-the-counter (OTC) market. As in most OTC markets, there is no such thing as one unique forward rate. Corporations and other interested parties call up various banks, which will quote them forward rates for their desired horizons—taking into account such factors as the credit risk of the transacting parties and the sophistication of the person on the other end of the telephone line. Therefore, forward rates are similar, but not identical, from bank to bank and from corporation to corporation. The forward market is much larger than the futures market.

The price difference between a future and a typical forward is small.

There is usually a small difference in the pricing of equivalent futures and forwards. For example, on March 26, 2008 (around 10:00 am for reference), the euro stood at 1.5725 \$/€. The average 6-month forward stood at 1.5570 \$/€, while the 6-month future stood at 1.5575 \$/€. This 0.0005 \$/€ difference was driven by issues such as the credit risk in the forward and the fact that the along-the-way daily settlement of futures has implications as to which party is likely to receive interim cash (with its consequent interest receipts). For currency traders, the price difference between the future and the forward can matter. For purposes of illustrating corporate finance, however, we can ignore the difference and treat futures and forwards alike.

Covered Interest Rate Parity

Covered IRP is a round-trip transaction, which fixes the currency forward rate based on the spot rate and the two interest rates.

How are spot and forward rates related? Here is an example of the spot and futures euro versus dollar currency rates on August 22, 2003:

Currency	Spot	Forwards		Futures				
	(Aug 03)	6 Months	1 Year	Sep 03	Dec 03	Mar 04	Jun 04	Sep 04
(\$/€)	1.0886	1.0823	1.0783	1.0878	1.0850	1.0825	1.0803	1.0783

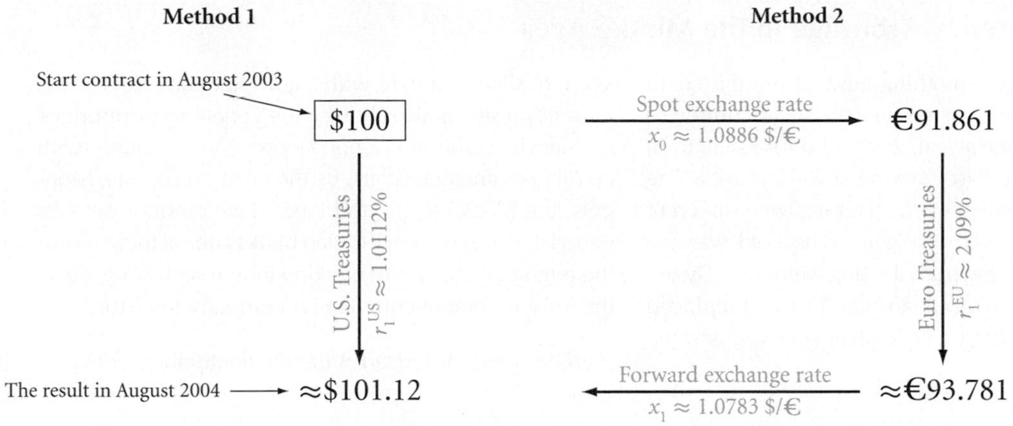

All numbers are known today, at time 0 (August 2003): The 1-year U.S. Treasury interest rate of 1.12%, the 1-year Euro Treasury interest rate of 2.09%, the current exchange rate of 1.0886 $/€, and the 1-year forward exchange rate of 1.0783 $/€ are known and contractible in August 2003. Note that we do not use—and thus do not need to know—the future spot exchange rate.

FIGURE 25.1 Covered Interest Rate Parity: Two Methods to Earn a 1.12% Dollar Interest Rate

You could receive 1.0886 dollars for each euro "on the spot." Or you could commit to a dollar-euro forward exchange 12 months later, which would only get you 1.0783 dollars for each euro. Why? Does this mean that the euro will depreciate against the dollar? Not necessarily. There is an arbitrage condition called **covered interest rate parity** (**IRP**), which ties together the currency spot rate, the currency forward rate, and the country Treasury interest rates. (We pretend that the futures price is also the forward price.) Let's call "right now" time 0, and August 22, 2004, time 1.

A sample round-trip law-of-one-price arbitrage condition.

Figure 25.1 illustrates covered interest rate parity by showing two methods that lead to the same result. On August 22, 2003, the 1-year U.S. dollar Treasury interest rate was 1.12%. The 1-year European Central Bank interest rate was 2.09%. (Each currency has its own yield curve. You can find many such yield curves on financial websites, e.g., at www.bloomberg.com.) The left part of the figure shows that you could save $100 at the U.S. Treasury interest rate of 1.0112% to receive $101.12 in 1 year. The right part of the figure shows that you could instead exchange $100 into €91.861 at the spot rate, invest the euros at the Euro Treasury interest rate of 2.09% to receive €91.861 · 1.0209 ≈ €93.781 in 1 year, and lock in the 1-year-ahead forward exchange at the rate of 1.0783 $/€ to translate your future €93.781 back into 1.0783 $/€ · €93.781 ≈ $101.12.

If there were no transaction costs and IRP did not hold, you could get rich.

What if the 1-year forward $/€ rate had been different? For example, what should you have done if the current forward rate had been 1.0886 $/€ (like the spot rate) instead of the actual 1.0783 $/€? You should have exchanged into euros today and locked in the exchange rate of future euros back into dollars in order to earn the interest rate in euros. Specifically, you could have exchanged your $100 into €91.861 and earned the 2.09% interest to end up with €93.781, with a lock back into the reverse currency exchange for a net of €93.781 · 1.0886 $/€ ≈ $102.09. This is $0.97 more than the $101.12 that you would have received if you had invested in U.S. Treasuries. The U.S. Treasury rate would have been inferior—an inadmissible arbitrage opportunity that would have violated the law of one price.

ANECDOTE Currency Arbitrage in the Middle Ages

Currency arbitrage is nothing new. In the thirteenth century, Venetian bankers speculated in currencies on a grand scale. Twice a year, 20 to 30 ships sailed from Venice to the Middle East carrying silver and returning with gold. The gold/silver exchange rates were different in Europe than they were in Egypt. (The gold was exported from China to Egypt by looting Mongols.) By the fourteenth century, the Venetians had in effect replaced the Eastern gold standard with a silver standard and the Western silver standard with a gold standard. Their large currency reserves also allowed the Venetians to introduce cashless bank transfers among merchants' accounts, with credit lines and overdrafts. By the fifteenth century, Mongols, the Black Death, and large-scale creditor defaults ended the dominance of Italian banks and set the stage for the reign of the German banking family of the Fuggers—the most dominant commercial company in history.

Partial source: American Almanac September 1995.

The round-trip as the IRP formula.

You can write covered interest rate parity as a formula. Call the \$/€ exchange rate today x_0. Call the forward exchange rate that you can lock in August 2003 for an exchange in August 2004 x_1. The arbitrage relationship is

$$\$100 \cdot (1 + 1.12\%) \approx [\$100/(1.0886\ \$/€)] \cdot (1 + 2.09\%) \cdot (1.0783\ \$/€)$$
$$I \cdot (1 + r_1^{\text{US}}) = I \cdot 1/x_0 \cdot (1 + r_1^{\text{EU}}) \cdot x_1$$

Simplify and rearrange this formula into the more standard way to write the interest rate parity equation, and you get Formula 25.1.

IMPORTANT: Covered interest rate parity is an arbitrage condition that implies that currency spot and forward exchange rates are linked to the country interest rates via

$$\frac{x_1}{x_0} = \frac{(1 + r_1^{\text{US}})}{(1 + r_1^{\text{EU}})} \quad \left(= \frac{f_1}{s_0}\right) \tag{25.1}$$

The exchange rate x is defined in \$/€. x_1 is the forward exchange rate at time 0 for an exchange at the future time 1. In our example, 1.0783 \$/€/1.0886 \$/€ $\approx 1.0112/1.0209$. (The formula is easy to remember: Dollar and euro interest rates are in the same order as the exchange rate: dollar on top, euro on bottom. For extra clarity, the right side repeats the left side, but with f as the name for the forward rate and s as the name for the spot rate.)

Uncovered IRP is an economic hypothesis, not an arbitrage condition.

➤ Expectation or risk compensation in forward interest rates, Section 5.4, p. 111

Is the forward exchange rate the expected future spot exchange rate? The answer is "not necessarily." The question is analogous to whether forward interest rates are expected future spot interest rates. Recall that you learned in Section 5.4 that there are two possible explanations for high forward interest rates: The expected future interest rate could be higher than today's interest rate, or investors may require risk compensation to be willing to hold longer-term bonds. In our currency context, the forward exchange rate could be different from the spot exchange rate for the same two reasons:

1. The future spot exchange rate could be expected to be different from today's spot rate.
2. One side of the futures contract must be compensated for being willing to carry risk.

It is only if you believe that there is no risk compensation that the exchange rate future today would be the best expectation of the future spot exchange rate. This is called **uncovered interest rate parity**. In this case, you can replace the forward rate in the covered interest parity with the expected future spot rate: The prevailing forward rate f_1 would be an unbiased predictor of the unknown future spot rate s_1: $f_1 = \mathcal{E}(s_1)$. There is no reason to believe that this is usually the case.

SOLVE NOW!

Q 25.1 On Friday, August 22, 2003, the Mexican peso forward currency rates were as follows:

	Cash Spot	1-Year Forward
$/peso	0.09230	0.08660

In other words, 1 peso = $0.0923. The 1-year U.S. Treasury note offered a yield of 1.12%. Explain what interest rate a 1-year Mexico Treasury investment in 1,000,000 pesos would earn.

Q 25.2 Does the forward rate necessarily give you the best forecast of the future expected exchange rate in x months? Can it tell you how it will differ from the current spot rate?

Q 25.3 If the ¥/€ forward rate is at a **forward premium** relative to the spot rate (i.e., the forward rate is higher than the spot rate), is the nominal interest rate in Japanese ¥ or in European € higher?

25.1C PURCHASING POWER PARITY

Why are interest rates different across countries?

Forward exchange rates are exactly determined by interest rates through an arbitrage condition. But there is a deeper question here: Why is the interest rate in euros higher than the interest rate in U.S. dollars in our example?

The question is not just about money, but about all goods. Should they cost the same in different places? If they do, you have PPP.

Economists are not sure, and here is why. The most important question is whether **purchasing power parity (PPP)** holds. The PPP theory of exchange rates posits that prices of identical goods should be the same in all countries, differing only in the costs of transport and duties. But does PPP hold? Does $108.86 buy the same amount of goods—say, apples—that €100 buy? If an apple costs $1.0886 in the United States and €1.00 in Europe, then PPP holds. What if it does not hold? What if, for example, an apple costs $1.00 in the United States and €1.00 in Europe? Then we should export cheaper U.S. apples to Europe, sell them for €1, and earn a profit of about $0.09/apple. Transport costs and import/export barriers (such as tariffs) are probably too high to permit an apple "arbitrage," but there are other more easily transportable commodities, ranging from diamonds to gold to gasoline. As economists, we expect prices for easily exportable and tradeable commodities to obey PPP. But other goods need not obey PPP: Land in France is not the same as land in Manhattan and it cannot be exported. Concrete is too costly to transport because shipping costs are too high. Raspberries spoil too easily to transport long distances. Maple syrup has little demand in Europe. A work hour by a Czech hair stylist is not the same as a work hour by an American hair stylist. And so on. Indeed, PPP does not even hold inside one country: Apartments and plumbers cost more in Manhattan than they do in New Jersey. Gas costs more in San Francisco than in San Antonio. The reasons why PPP does not hold *inside* a country are the same as the reasons why PPP does not hold *across* countries. But, if after taking transport costs into account, gas is still too expensive in San Francisco relative to San Antonio, someone will likely start shipping it from San Antonio to San Francisco—and sooner rather than later.

➤ Arbitrage and its limits, Section 11.4, p. 360

If PPP always holds, differential interest rates are determined by differential inflation rates.

Still, let us assume for a moment that PPP does hold—that is, that goods in Europe and goods in the United States cost the same—and that PPP will also hold in the future. This assumption allows us to determine relative inflation rates. For example, consider an apple that costs \$1.0886 in the United States today and that costs €1 in Europe today. If the U.S. dollar inflation rate is 2%, then the apple will cost $\$1.0886 \cdot 1.02 \approx \$1.1104$ next year. We can lock in a forward exchange rate of 1.0783 \$/€, which means that next year's U.S. apple will be worth $\$1.1104/1.0783 \approx$ €1.0298. Thus, a euro apple that costs €1 today will cost €1.0298 next year, which means that the euro inflation rate would have to be 2.98%.

PPP implies that *real* interest rates should be the same across countries.

Another consequence of purchasing power parity is that *real* interest rates must be equal. (A real interest rate is just an inflation-adjusted nominal interest rate.) After all, you can think of money as a good like apples, although it loses value through inflation and gains value through interest earnings. Therefore, in our context, the PPP claim is that

$$\frac{1.0209}{1.0298} \approx \frac{1.0112}{1.02}$$

$$\frac{(1 + r_1^{\text{EU}})}{(1 + \pi_1^{\text{EU}})} = \frac{(1 + r_1^{\text{US}})}{(1 + \pi_1^{\text{US}})} \tag{25.2}$$

where r is the nominal interest rate and π is the inflation rate.

Don't forget: PPP is a strong assumption that may not hold in the real world.

Clearly, purchasing power parity is a strong assumption. Real-world import-export "arbitrage" is likely to make PPP hold well for goods that trade in perfect markets and that are easy to move from one location to the other, and less well for those goods that do not. It is also more likely to hold in the long run than in the short run, because it takes time to set up import/export busineses.

The Fisher hypothesis states that PPP should hold in the long run (in expectational terms).

➤ Expectation or risk compensation in forward interest rates, Section 5.4, p. 111

There is also a weaker form of the PPP formula (Formula 25.2), which replaces *actual* inflation rates with *expected* inflation rates. The **Fisher hypothesis** (or **Fisher effect**) states that *expected* real rates of return should be equal across countries. There is no arbitrage reason that forces this relationship to hold, either. Aside from the basic question of which goods the inflation rate refers to, it could again be that investors on one of the two sides earn extra compensation for sharing the risk of currency movements.

ANECDOTE Yale's Most Famous Economist

Irving Fisher, inventor of the Fisher hypothesis, easily ranks among the best economists ever. But he was also an eccentric, colorful (and flawed) human being. When Irving Fisher wrote his 1892 dissertation, he constructed a mechanical machine equipped with pumps, wheels, levers, and pipes in order to illustrate his price theory. (You can google for images of his first and second prototypes on a number of websites.) Socially, he was an avid advocate of eugenics and health food diets. He made a fortune with his visible index card system—known today as the rolodex—and advocated the establishment of a 100% reserve requirement banking system. His fortune was lost and his reputation was severely marred by the 1929 Wall Street crash, when just days before the crash, he was reassuring investors that stock prices were not overinflated but rather had achieved a new, permanent plateau. Even financial geniuses can be humbled by the markets.

Source: http://cepa.newschool.edu/het/profiles/fisher.htm.

IMPORTANT:

- If PPP holds, then goods should cost the same in different countries. In turn, this means that interest rate differentials should be driven by inflation rate differentials.
- The Fisher hypothesis states that *expected* real rates of return should be the same across countries.

In the real world, different goods follow PPP to varying degrees. For gold, for which there is no import duty between the European Union and the United States, PPP holds very well. For many other commodities, the answer may be a "maybe." It depends on how perfect the underlying real-goods market is. Moreover, few noncommodity goods are exactly alike, and the reported inflation rate is itself based on an arbitrary bundle of goods, usually the Consumer Price Index (CPI). What about the empirical evidence? Do countries with higher "average" inflation rates experience depreciating currencies, as they should under PPP? The answer is "only very weakly" over horizons of 1–5 years. But in the long run, 5–20 years, there are many arbitrageurs (called "import/export firms") that are hard at work to help make PPP come true—or at least to limit deviations from PPP. The same evidence that suggests almost no PPP over shorter horizons suggests that PPP holds much better over 10- to 20-year horizons. Market forces are on the side of PPP!

PPP holds well for easily transportable goods, but not for other goods or services. PPP holds better over longer periods.

➤ Inflation definition, Section 5.2, p. 97

SOLVE NOW!

Q 25.4 According to the *CIA World Factbook*, in early 2007, China had an inflation rate of 1.5%, while the United States had an inflation rate of 3.7%. The exchange rate was 7.61 yuan per U.S. dollar. How would you have expected the exchange rate to change in 2007?

Q 25.5 What factors can prevent arbitrage from kicking in if PPP does not hold?

Q 25.6 What is the Fisher effect?

Q 25.7 If PPP holds for "Small Macs," and the 1-year U.S. inflation rate is 1% per annum, and the Small Mac in Mexico costs the equivalent of $2.12

today, how much would you expect the Small Mac to cost next year in pesos? Again, assume a 1.12% U.S. Treasury rate, a 7.78% peso interest rate, and a spot rate that is 0.09230 peso/$.

Q 25.8 How does interest rate parity differ from purchasing power parity?

Q 25.9 Is it possible that PPP holds for some goods but not others?

25.2 INVESTMENTS IN FOREIGN FINANCIAL MARKETS

We need to understand our investors' opportunities to find our opportunity cost of capital.

Now that you understand currencies, our next subject is a necessary prelude to determining the corporate cost of capital in an international context. If you recall the logic of the corporate cost of capital, managers have to determine the opportunities that in-

ANECDOTE Purchasing Power Parity and the Big Mac Index

The price of the Big Mac has become such a popular measure of PPP among economists that it is published at least once a year (with updates) in *The Economist*. In July 2008, the Big Mac Index stood as follows:

Country	PPP of U.S. $	Rel. Value
United States	$3.57	—
Argentina	$3.64	+2%
Australia	$3.36	−6%
Brazil	$4.73	+33%
Britain	$4.57	+28%
Canada	$4.08	+14%
China [a]	$1.83	−49%
Egypt	$2.45	−31%
Euro Area	$5.34	+50%
Hong Kong [a]	$1.71	−52%
Japan	$2.62	−27%
Mexico	$3.15	−12%
Norway	$7.88	+121%
Philippines	$1.96	−45%
Russia	$2.54	−29%
Singapore	$2.92	−18%
Saudi Arabia	$2.67	−25%
South Africa	$2.24	−37%
South Korea	$3.14	−12%
Sweden	$6.37	+79%
Switzerland	$6.36	+78%
Thailand	$1.86	−48%
Turkey	$4.32	+21%

a. China and Hong Kong have pegged their currencies to the U.S. dollar at exchange rates that are generally believed to be too low. This makes it cheap for them to export and expensive to import. Both countries are, however, slowly raising their exchange rates.

If you plan to retire on your U.S. Social Security check, Europe looks financially a lot less attractive than the Asian countries—at least, if you like to eat Big Macs.

Of course, one Big Mac alone is not a representative consumption basket. On August 29, 1993—a time when management gurus predicted that the Japanese model was destined to rule the world—the *New York Times* reported the following violations from PPP:

Item	Manhattan	Tokyo
Doughnut	$0.75	$1.06
Rice	$0.89	$2.71
Kirin Beer	$1.50	$2.12
Big Mac	$2.99	$3.66
Häagen Daz	$2.99	$8.18
Movie Ticket	$7.50	$17.33
Sony Walkman, AM/FM Cassette	$39.99	$209.92
Round-Trip Economy Airfare, Tokyo–NYC	$1,360.45	$3,832.45
Apartment, per sq.ft. Purchase Price	$309.00	$715.67

How times have changed . . .

vestors have elsewhere (in the financial markets) and then infer the cost of capital for their own corporate projects relative to these opportunities. So we must first discuss foreign investment opportunities. Although they are conceptually like investments in domestic financial securities, they do have some novel components—especially those related to market access and the local currency and exchange rate.

25.2A LOCAL VERSUS FOREIGN RETURNS AND HOME BIAS

Recall that the CAPM suggests that investors hold the (value-weighted) market portfolio. This portfolio should consider all investable assets, domestic and foreign. The CAPM therefore states that investors should invest not just in the U.S. market but also in all foreign markets. Of course, even if the CAPM does not hold, thinking about diversification across all possible dimensions—including international opportunities—is a good thing to do.

In a perfect market, the world market portfolio should be the relevant one . . .

However, the empirical evidence suggests that investors tend to have a strong **home bias**—a tendency to prefer domestic securities. U.S. investors tend to overweight U.S. stocks; European investors tend to overweight European stocks; Japanese investors tend to overweight Japanese stocks; and so on. In fact, many investors hold nothing but domestic securities. This home bias holds up even after we adjust for differential transaction costs and the following currency complications.

. . . but investors tend to have a "home bias."

Currencies matter because investment rates of return themselves depend on the currency in which they are earned. For example, Volkswagen AG started 2002 with a price of €52.30 and ended 2002 with a price of €34.50. Therefore, its *local currency rate of return* was $€34.50/€52.30 - 1 \approx -34\%$ (incorrectly ignoring dividends). But the euro started 2002 at 0.90 \$/€ and ended 2002 at 1.05 \$/€, a 16.7% appreciation of the euro against the dollar. To a U.S. investor, the Volkswagen shares therefore cost $€52.30 \cdot 0.90\ \$/€ = \$47.07$ and returned $€34.50 \cdot 1.05\ \$/€ \approx \$36.23$ for a more favorable Volkswagen *U.S. dollar rate of return* of −23%. Most U.S. investors in Volkswagen are more concerned with the dollar rate of return; most German investors in Volkswagen are more concerned with their local currency rate of return.

Stocks have different rates of return for locals and foreigners due to exchange rate movements.

Let's look at more examples of how local rates and dollar rates of return can differ. The Morgan Stanley Capital International (MSCI) indexes provide rates of return on country-based investing activities, as well as a "world index" of all stock markets in MSCI's database. The following are the historical rate-of-return statistics, from 1970 to 2005, in percent per month:

Some historical statistics. The world index had lower risk.

					Market Beta with Respect to the	
Index	Currency	Type of Investor	Mean	Sdv	U.S. Market	World Market
MSCI World Index	in Dollars	World-Savvy U.S. Investor	0.92	4.18	0.80	1.00
United States Index	in Dollars	Home-Biased U.S. Investor	0.95	4.46	1.00	0.92
German Index	in Dollars	German-Savvy U.S. Investor	**1.02**	6.19	0.64	0.93
German Index	in Euros	Home-Biased German Investor	**0.79**	5.70	0.65	0.78

Before we get to our real point, note that both the U.S. stock market and the world market experienced average price increases of about 0.95% per month (which comes to about 11% per year). But the MSCI world index had much lower volatility—due to extra diversification. A home-biased U.S. investor would have missed out on this free risk reduction.

The U.S. investor would have been able to obtain both a higher mean and more risk diversification by investing a little in the German market.

How would a German investor and how would an American investor think about the reward and risk contribution of investing in the German stock market? For a German investor, the average rate of return was 0.79% (around 9.5% per annum) in euros. Of course, the beta with respect to the German market was 1. But for a U.S. investor, because the dollar depreciated, the euro investment component was more profitable, thereby earning a higher 1.02% (around 12.2% per annum) in dollars. Furthermore, the risk contribution of Germany for our U.S. investor would have depended on whether our investor was home-biased or fully globally diversified (world savvy). If our U.S. investor had held the world portfolio, then investing a little more in Germany would have contributed to the overall portfolio risk with a market beta of 0.93. However, if our U.S. investor was home-biased and held primarily the U.S. stock market, then adding a little investment in Germany would have contributed with a market beta of 0.64—much better diversification benefits. The first dollar of investment in Germany really helped!

Corporations can add value through foreign investments if their investors suffer a home bias.

This leaves us with an important conceptual question: As corporate executives of a U.S. corporation, what shall we assume about our investors when we judge our opportunity costs of capital? In line with empirical reality, we will assume that most of our investors are domestic and home-biased, and that they consume and therefore care about their investment returns in dollars. It is in this context that we will evaluate the effect of adding any foreign investments to our firm. Therefore, we are primarily interested in the expected rate of return in dollars and in the beta of our foreign investment with respect to the U.S. market portfolio—not with respect to the world market portfolio. (Of course, the simplest such investment could even be the purchase of a future on a foreign currency, although an investment in a foreign stock market would likely add more in diversification benefits.) But keep in mind that this home-bias scenario need not apply to every country and company—and that it may change in the future if stock market investors become more globally diversified.

SOLVE NOW!

Q 25.10 If a U.S. investor in the U.S. stock market experiences a negative rate of return, is it possible for a French investor with the same investment to experience a positive rate of return?

Q 25.11 Why is it useful to look at the risk contribution of foreign stock markets with respect to the U.S. stock market index, rather than to the world market?

Q 25.12 Should we consider the rate of return of the British stock market in terms of British pounds or in terms of U.S. dollars?

25.2B HISTORICAL INTERNATIONAL INVESTMENT PERFORMANCE

From 1970 to 2005, correlations were modest, so diversification would have helped.

From a U.S. investor's perspective, how did investment into the stock markets of different countries perform historically? Table 25.1 describes the performance of various MSCI stock market returns from 1970 to 2005 and from 1986 to 2005. It also shows

TABLE 25.1 MONTHLY REWARD, RISK, AND U.S. BETA OF MORGAN STANLEY CAPITAL INTERNATIONAL INDEXES (RETURNS IN DOLLARS)

		1970–2005			1986–2005		
Country	Code	Mean	Sdv	Beta	Mean	Sdv	Beta
Australia	aus	1.00	7.0	0.76	1.29	6.5	0.70
Austria	aut	1.08	6.0	0.24	1.23	6.8	0.33
Canada	can	0.96	5.5	0.89	0.96	5.2	0.88
France	fra	1.12	6.5	0.72	1.31	6.1	0.81
Germany	ger	1.02	6.2	0.64	1.16	6.7	0.83
Hong Kong	hkg	1.84	10.8	0.84	1.48	8.2	0.95
Italy	ita	0.86	7.4	0.48	1.26	7.3	0.59
Japan	jpn	1.07	6.5	0.44	0.74	7.0	0.50
Netherlands	net	1.21	5.3	0.73	1.27	5.1	0.77
Scandinavia	sca	1.29	5.9	0.73	1.51	6.4	0.91
Singapore	sng	1.27	8.5	0.91	0.96	7.8	0.95
Switzerland	swi	1.12	5.4	0.62	1.35	5.3	0.64
United Kingdom	uk	1.13	6.6	0.78	1.13	5.1	0.76
United States	us	0.95	4.5	1.00	1.07	4.5	1.00
Equal-Weighted	E	1.14	4.5	0.70	1.39	4.4	0.71
MSCI World	W	0.92	4.2	0.80	0.97	4.3	0.80

The returns are monthly U.S. dollar returns from December 1969 or December 1986 through May 2005 on index-type broadly diversified stock market investments. The table shows, for example, that the U.S. financial market returned about $0.95\% \cdot 12 \approx 11.4\%$ annualized over the entire 36 years, and about 12.8% annualized over the 20-year span. (The average U.S. index percent price changes, i.e., the return without dividends, would have been around 3% lower.) The beta is the country rate of return with respect to the U.S. stock market—that is, the covariance of returns in the two stock markets, divided by the variance of the rate of return in the U.S. stock market, with both returns quoted in U.S. dollars.
Dollar returns are relevant if we are assuming that investors care about consuming and therefore performance in dollars. Betas with respect to the U.S. stock market are relevant if we are assuming that investors are home biased and from the United States.
Source: Morgan Stanley Capital International indexes.

the performance of two more global indexes: the equal-weighted index of the preceding 14 countries in the table, and the MSCI world index.

Reward: Even though 1970–2005 were terrific years for the U.S. stock market, it appears that foreign stock markets performed almost as well, if not better. (An important factor is, of course, that the dollar generally depreciated over these years.) Scandinavia and Hong Kong beat the U.S. market handily. Not all countries did, however—Canada, Singapore, and Japan beat the United States only over the full 36-year horizon, but not over the shorter 20-year horizon.

Risk contribution: All foreign stock markets had betas with respect to the U.S. stock market below 1. Austria and Japan were particularly helpful in diversifying U.S. market risk; Scandinavia, Hong Kong, and Singapore less so.

Over the full 36 years, the equal weighted index of the countries also performed better than the U.S. stock market, although with equal volatility. The MSCI world index was safer than the U.S. stock market, although it sacrificed a tiny 3 basis points per month performance. In the second half, both world indexes had lower risk, but only the equal-weighted portfolio outperformed the U.S. stock market.

Risk contribution relative to the reward: Would investing in these countries' stock market portfolios have offered U.S. investors a high enough rate of return to make at least a small investment in international stock markets worthwhile? To answer this question, we use a U.S. CAPM formula. The market beta of each country's stock market with respect to a U.S. stock market index is the measure of how much reward our foreign stock market has to offer for its risk contribution/diversification. To use a CAPM formula, we need an estimate for the appropriate risk-free rate in U.S. dollars. Reasonable choices would be about 0.4% per month (5% per annum) over the 36-year period, and 0.3% per month (4% per annum) over the 20-year period. Therefore, the ex-post CAPM in the United States was something like

$$1970\text{–}2005:\quad \mathcal{E}(\tilde{r}_i) \approx 0.4\% + (0.95\% - 0.4\%) \cdot \beta_i$$

$$1986\text{–}2005:\quad \mathcal{E}(\tilde{r}_i) \approx 0.3\% + (1.07\% - 0.3\%) \cdot \beta_i$$

Foreign countries were a good investment from a U.S. investor's CAPM perspective.

Using these formulas, how did our specific countries perform for a U.S. investor? The majority outperformed! For example, according to our U.S. CAPM, Austria should have earned about $0.3\% + (1.07\% - 0.3\%) \cdot \beta_{aut} \approx 0.55\%$ per month from 1986 to 2005. Instead, it offered about twice this average return. Only Canada and Singapore did not outperform. Even Japan, which had the lowest average stock market returns, still outperformed because its U.S. beta was so low.

But recently, global stock markets have covaried quite a bit more. International diversification works less well than it has in the past.

Moreover, although the sample suggests that international diversification has worked quite well and that the OECD country indexes in Table 25.1 had low betas with respect to the U.S. stock market, this empirical relationship seems to have changed in recent years. The OECD countries' stock indexes seem to be covarying more strongly with the U.S. stock market nowadays—perhaps a sign of increasing financial integration. Nevertheless, even if international diversification no longer works as well as it has historically, chances are that it is still not a bad financial choice.

Careful—we have ignored taxes and transaction costs, and historical data is only indicative.

➤ Will history repeat itself?, Section 7.1E, p. 189

Of course, we have ignored taxes and transaction costs. (Dividends from foreign stocks are taxed at a higher personal income tax rate under U.S. tax law than those from domestic stocks.) And you already know that you should always be cautious when it comes to historical data: The *ex-post* actual distribution may not be representative of the future. Much of the strong historical performance of foreign markets was due to the weakening of the dollar (a mean effect, which will not necessarily repeat). Fortunately, variances and covariances are generally more stable, so the international diversification benefits are likely to continue. Finally, it could also matter a little as to what specific stock market index and risk-free rate you are using for each country, just as it could matter as to which exact sample period and foreign stock market indexes you use to look at the historical performances.

In sum, the evidence suggests that investing in OECD countries' equity markets offered decent diversification benefits—but also that they have become less useful as more investors have taken advantage of them. And fortunately, widely available international mutual funds have made it very easy and cheap to partake in the diversification benefits. Nevertheless, many investors are not taking advantage of them.

Diversification across OECD countries is easy, but perhaps only of modest use.

The jury is still out on the diversification benefits and expected rates of return from investments in "emerging markets" (developing countries). Many of these emerging markets did not exist, or were not easy to access, for U.S. investors just 20 years ago and have only recently become available in a form that a typical U.S. retail investor can take advantage of (i.e., with ADRs or country-specific mutual funds).

Diversification across emerging countries is harder, but perhaps of great use.

➤ ADRs and funds, Section 7.2C, p. 194

SOLVE NOW!

Q 25.13 How did investment in foreign stock markets perform in our sample? What explains this performance?

Q 25.14 From the perspective of a U.S. investor, does an investment in foreign countries carry with it a beta above 1 or a beta below 1?

25.3 CAPITAL BUDGETING WITH FOREIGN CASH FLOWS

We now turn to our main corporate finance question: What is the corporate cost of capital for our foreign projects? We always start by determining other appropriate market opportunities for our investors as our benchmark. Finance theorists would immediately point out that our investors *should* be investing globally. Their best trade-off would then be determined by the world market index. As corporate executives, we should therefore be thinking in terms of how our projects reduce the risk in the global market index. This should determine our project's cost of capital. Unfortunately, this would most likely be bad advice. The reason is that *even though it should be so, it is not so.* Most investors suffer from a home bias. If we are a U.S. firm listed on the U.S. exchange, most of our investors are likely to be U.S. investors. And our investors are most likely holding portfolios that look much more like the S&P 500 than they look like a global market index. Thus, thinking about how our (foreign) operations reduce the risk in our investors' U.S. portfolio holdings is probably still better than thinking about how our operations fit into investors' global market CAPM trade-off.

Conceptually, as of 2008, it is probably better to think of foreign projects in the context of a domestic U.S. CAPM.

So let's now consider the practical problem of finding the cost of capital for a foreign subsidiary. For example, if you are the manager for a U.S. corporation—say, the National Football League (NFL)—and you care about helping your domestic investors earn expected rates of return above what they could earn in similar-risk investments domestically, should you set up a German football league (or syndicate U.S. television rights to Europe)? What should your capital budgeting rule be?

An example—investing in Europe.

25.3A THE GENERAL PERSPECTIVE: CERTAIN AND UNCERTAIN CASH FLOWS

As with any domestic project, the capital budgeting principle is easy; the implementation is tough. You "just" need to know the expected cash flows and discount rates to

Capital budgeting is always easy if cash flows are certain.

work out the net present value of your project. Your task is easy if your foreign cash flows are certain. For example, in August 2003, how would you value the television rights if they provided €100 (million) in August 2004 for sure?

1. You could execute a currency forward contract today to lock in an exchange rate of 1.0783 $/€ for August 2004. This means that you would have €100 · 1.0783 $/€ ≈ $107.83 million for sure. You can discount this safe dollar cash flow with the U.S. 1-year Treasury rate of 1.12% per annum to obtain a project present value of $107.83/1.0112 ≈ $106.64 million.
2. You could discount the certain cash flow of €100 at the euro Treasury rate of 2.09% into €100/1.0209 ≈ €97.95 million today. Using the spot currency exchange rate, you emerge with €97.95 · 1.0886 $/€ ≈ $106.63 million. (The $0.01 difference is rounding error.)

The two alternatives are equivalent under covered interest rate parity.

Capital budgeting is always hard if cash flows are uncertain.

However, your task is more difficult if your cash flows are uncertain. For example, say your cash flows could be either €50 or €150. You cannot lock in the appropriate future exchange rate, because you do not know how much cash flow you need to lock for. You need to go back to basics. You need to determine two inputs: the expected cash flows of your project *in dollars* when the cash flows materialize, and the appropriate discount rate (based on dollar rates).

Expected cash flows are difficult to estimate, but forecasting foreign ones is just like forecasting domestic ones. Currency uncertainty is just another piece to the puzzle.

You already know that it is usually both more important, and more difficult, to estimate expected cash flows accurately. This is probably especially true for foreign projects, for which you may not have a long history and/or many easy comparable international projects. In addition, there is the uncertainty about future spot rates, the risk of political expropriation (e.g., having operations nationalized [stolen] by foreign governments), international tax issues, and so on. Yet all in all, there is little conceptual novelty to estimating expected foreign cash flows. The main difficulty is in the practice, just as it is for domestic projects.

But currency uncertainty can make the opportunity cost of capital estimation more complex.

Estimating the appropriate discount rate for your project, however, does add one important novelty. You want to know the beta of your project's rate of return with respect to the U.S. stock market, again post–exchange rate (i.e., as a U.S. dollar rate of return). There is one sense in which this is the same (difficult) task of determining the beta of *any* new project: You need to have a good feel for how your dollar cash flow returns will covary with the U.S. stock market. The interesting novelty is that you can conceptually decompose this estimation into its components—a fact that makes your task a little easier. Our next subject is therefore figuring out how a U.S. firm's European operations covary with the U.S. stock market.

25.3B VALUING A FOREIGN PROJECT WITH UNCERTAIN CASH FLOWS

Build a model to mimic domestic and foreign stock market movements and exchange rate movements.

First, you need some intuition of how correlations of exchange rates and local market projects matter. Let's make up a simple example. As a representative of the NFL, living in a U.S. CAPM world, you are considering investing in the creation of a German Football League (GFL). You want to determine the appropriate cost of capital for this project, taking into account currency movements. Moreover, the empirical evidence is that project returns are typically linked to their local stock markets more than to the U.S. stock market. (This is *very* common.) We shall assume the following macroeconomic scenario:

- The U.S. market can go up 16% or down 8% (expected rate of return: +4%).
- The spot rate is 1.0886 \$/€. The 1-year forward currency rate today is 1.0783 \$/€. In addition, we now assume that the actual exchange rate will be either 1.0000 \$/€ or 1.1566 \$/€ next year, averaging to 1.0783 \$/€. It is important that we assume that currency movements are independent of stock market movements.
- The German stock market index, the DAX, returns whatever the U.S. market returns (adjusted for forward/spot rate movements), plus or minus 10%. For example, if the U.S. market appreciates 16%, then the German market is expected to appreciate by 7.1% or 27.1%. (I have not assumed that it will be exactly 7.0% or 27.0%, because of the expected currency rate change embedded in today's forward rate. The extra 0.1% is not an important factor here. Just trust me and don't worry about this one.)

The model empirically matches market and exchange rate movements.

With two outcomes each, there are eight scenarios. We assume that they are equally likely. Figure 25.2 illustrates these scenarios. Actually, this is not a bad macroeconomic model: It has reasonably realistic annual rates of return, exchange rates, standard deviations, and correlations. When the U.S. stock market increases by 16%, the German stock market is expected to increase by (27.1% + 7.1%)/2 = 17.1% (in euro returns!). When the U.S. stock market decreases by 8%, the DAX is expected to change by (2.9% − 17.1%)/2 = −7.1%. So the DAX moves about one to one with the S&P 500—although the DAX rates of return are in euros and the S&P 500 rates of return are in dollars. (More recent historical data suggests that this relationship is empirically higher than the 0.65 that I reported in the table on page 953, perhaps now closer to this 1.0 that we are using here.) And, also in line with our example, there is good empirical evidence that currency movements are empirically *not* correlated with stock market movements.

Here is our project with its known German beta, which follows a German CAPM.

Now consider our German project. Starting the German Football League costs €100 (million) today. We presume it has a German beta with respect to the German stock market, quoted in euros, of 1.5. The expected rate of return on this project is assumed to be

$$\mathcal{E}(\tilde{r}_{\text{P}}) \approx 2.09\% + [\mathcal{E}(\tilde{r}_{\text{M}}^{G}) - 2.09\%] \cdot \ 1.5$$

$$\mathcal{E}(\tilde{r}_{\text{P}}) = \ r_{\text{F}}^{G} \ + \ [\mathcal{E}(\tilde{r}_{\text{M}}^{G}) - r_{\text{F}}^{G}] \ \cdot \beta_{\text{p},\text{M}^G}^{G} \qquad \text{(all in euros)}$$

The GFL follows a German CAPM with a German market beta of 1.5 and a euro risk-free rate of 2.09%. For example, if the DAX were to return 7.1% *in euros*, the GFL would be expected to return 2.09% + (7.1% − 2.09%) · 1.5 ≈ 9.6% *in euros*. This is not what you need to know, though: You are not representing a German corporation with German investors—you are representing a U.S. corporation with U.S. investors. What should be the project's appropriate cost of capital and value *for you*?

A detailed explanation of Figure 25.2.

Figure 25.2 works through the necessary calculations (and it's easier than it looks). The €100 project costs you \$108.86 today. Just work through one of the branches (marked in yellow in the table): What happens if the U.S. stock market increases by +16%, if the exchange rate goes from 1.00886 today to 1.1566 next year, and if the DAX increases by 7.1%? Your project would then have a euro rate of return of

Macroeconomics			Our Project				
U.S. Mkt in $	Xchg Rate in $/€	Ger Mkt in €	Rate of Return in €	Return in €	Return in $	Rate of Return in $	
+16%	1.0000	+27.1%	+39.6%	€139.62	$139.62	+28.26%	*Project Return: Mean ≈ $134.38 (+23.44%)*
		+7.1%	+9.6%	€109.62	$109.62	+0.70%	
	1.1566	+27.1%	+39.6%	€139.62	$161.48	+48.34%	
		+7.1%	+9.6%	€109.62	$126.79	+16.47%	
Project Cost: €100.00 ≈ $108.86							
−8%	1.0000	+2.9%	+3.3%	€103.28	$103.28	–5.13%	*Project Return: Mean ≈ $95.19 (–12.56%)*
		–17.1%	–26.7%	€73.28	$73.28	–32.69%	
	1.1566	+2.9%	+3.3%	€103.28	$119.45	+9.73%	
		–17.1%	+26.7%	€73.28	$84.75	–22.15%	
Mean: +4%	1.0783	+4.99%	+6.45%	€106.45	$114.78	5.44%	

Macroeconomics: There are eight equally likely scenarios, resulting from the combinations of the U.S. stock market going up or down, the German stock market going up or down, and the dollar/euro exchange rate going up or down. The U.S. market will be either −8% or +16%. The German market is the U.S. market plus or minus 10%, plus a little adjustment for the forward exchange rate (that you could lock in today); +16% in the U.S. will associate either with +27.1% or with +7.1% local currency return in Germany. The exchange rate of 1.0886 $/€ will either move to 1.0000 $/€ or to 1.1566 $/€.

Our Project: Our German project, the GFL, costs €100 today, and has a German beta of 1.5. Specifically, it is expected to return $2.09\% + (\tilde{r}_M^G - 2.09\%) \cdot 1.5$. Thus, if the German market appreciates by 27.1%, our German project will return $2.09\% + (27.1\% - 2.09\%) \cdot 1.5 \approx 39.6\%$.

The easiest way to understand this graph is to follow one scenario—say, the one in yellow, in which the U.S. stock market will increase by 16% (in dollars), the exchange rate will be 1.1566 €/$, and the German stock market will increase by 7.1% (in euros). Our project costs €100 = $108.86 today. With a beta of 1.5 and a German market rate of return of 7.1%, our project will have a euro-based rate of return of $2.09\% + (7.1\% - 2.09\%) \cdot 1.5 \approx 9.62\%$. Thus, it will be worth €100.00 × (1 + 9.62%) ≈ €109.62.

At the 1.1566 $/€ exchange rate, this is €109.62 · 1.1566 €/$ ≈ $126.79. Thus, your $108.86 ended up with $126.79, a $126.79/$108.86 − 1 ≈ 16.47% rate of return in U.S. dollars.

FIGURE 25.2 The German Project from the U.S. Corporation's Perspective

$2.09\% + (7.1\% - 2.09\%) \cdot 1.5 \approx +9.6\%$. Having cost €100, your project would now be worth €109.62. At the 1.1566 $/€ exchange rate, this would be $126.79, equivalent to a dollar rate of return of 16.47% on your $108.86 investment.

The U.S. market beta can be drawn: project rate of return on the y-axis, market rate of return on the x-axis.

To determine the U.S. market beta, we need to find out what we can expect when the U.S. market goes up versus when the U.S. market goes down. The table tells us that your average return is $134.38 (or +23.44%) if the U.S. market increases by 16%, and $95.19 (or −12.56%) if the U.S. market decreases by 8%. If you draw a line between the points $(X, Y) = (+16\%, +23.44\%)$ and $(X, Y) = (-8\%, -12.56\%)$, you will find that the slope is

$$\beta_{P,\,S\&P\;500} = \frac{23.44\% - (-12.56\%)}{16\% - (-8\%)} = 1.5$$

This is our main point: *If the German stock market moves about one to one with the U.S. stock market (both in local currency, and even in the presence of extra volatility in the German market), and if exchange rate movements are uncorrelated with stock market movements, then the German project beta with respect to the DAX (quoted in euros) is about the same as the project beta with respect to the S&P 500 (quoted in dollars).*

We find that the U.S. dollar beta is also 1.5.

A conceptual question: Although we assumed that our GFL project follows the German CAPM, does it also follow the U.S. CAPM? The U.S. CAPM would predict

We find that the German project also follows the U.S. CAPM.

$$\begin{aligned} \mathcal{E}(\tilde{r}_P) &= 1.12\% + (4\% - 1.12\%) \cdot 1.5 = 5.44\% \\ &= r_F^{US} + \left[\mathcal{E}(\tilde{r}_M^{US}) - r_F^{US}\right] \cdot \beta_P^{US} \end{aligned}$$

Figure 25.2 shows that the expected rate of return on our project is [23.44% + (−12.56%)]/2 = 5.44%. It appears that we can indeed use our U.S. CAPM. Projects are fairly priced; the world is in good order. Hooray!

Recap of the Decomposition

What should you learn from this example? The answer is that you can mentally decompose the foreign project's beta with respect to the U.S. market (which determines its attractiveness to your U.S. investors) into three factors:

The U.S. beta of a foreign project has three components:

1. **Our foreign project's exposure in its own, foreign market:** For us, this is the German stock market beta of our foreign GFL project with respect to its own foreign stock market index (the DAX), with both rates of return quoted in euros.

   (1) The foreign project's beta against its foreign country market index, both in foreign currency units.

   This local beta is a number that you must estimate. In many cases, you may have useful information from your U.S. experience. For example, gadget sales may have the same beta in the foreign country with respect to the foreign stock market (in foreign currency units) as gadget sales have in the United States with respect to the U.S. stock market (in U.S. dollars). There may be comparables in the foreign market that are similar to your foreign subsidiary—for example, the Taiwanese stock market lists many computer manufacturers that could be similar to your computer manufacturing division. Of course, mechanics without intuition rarely works well. Other businesses may be different in other countries and you may have no good comparables. Use your intuition to fit your specific business needs.

2. **The foreign market's exposure with respect to our U.S. market:** For us, this is how the U.S. stock market and the German DAX stock market move together, both still quoted in terms of euro rates of return.

   (2) The foreign market index's beta with respect to the U.S. market index.

   In general, if a foreign stock market index has a high beta with respect to the S&P 500, then each time the U.S. stock market moves, the foreign stock market moves even more—and with it, the foreign operations (through the project's local market beta). This would mean a higher U.S. beta for your project. Conversely, if the foreign stock market has no correlation with the U.S. stock market, then the foreign operation—which comoves with the foreign stock market—would show little or no correlation with the U.S. market.

As was the case in our example, the beta of the German stock market with respect to the U.S. stock market is actually just a little below 1 nowadays. (However, the correlation between the German and the U.S. stock markets is only around 50%, so the two indexes can diverge quite substantially. This is because both indexes have their own idiosyncratic volatilities.) Many OECD countries have similar market betas with respect to the S&P 500.

(3) The foreign currency exchange rate beta with respect to the U.S. market index.

3. **The currency exchange rate's exposure with respect to our U.S. market:** This considers whether the euro exchange rate changes (and with it your dollar receipts) systematically when the U.S. stock market changes.

   For example, if financial asset markets and currency exchange rates tend to move together, you will need to adjust the beta upward. If every time the S&P 500 moves up, the euro appreciates, and every time the S&P 500 moves down, the euro depreciates, then any S&P 500 fluctuations will be amplified in the value of the project through the currency channel.

   But as it turns out empirically, there is almost no correlation between currency movements and stock market rates of return. This is not to say that exchange rates are not a source of risk. They are—but primarily of idiosyncratic risk, which the CAPM considers irrelevant. It is only the systematic risk that matters to diversified U.S. investors. For many practical purposes, the empirical evidence allows us to assume that currency fluctuations do not influence your U.S. beta and therefore can be benignly ignored. (Besides, you could lock in some of the variation in future exchange rates through forward contracts, and you could also hedge the currency risk, which is explained in the next section.)

German market betas, all in all, are probably similar to American betas, because euro exchange rate movements are uncorrelated with the U.S. market. Also, the German market itself has a U.S. market beta of about 1.

In our specific example, because the German stock market has a U.S. market beta of about 1, and because the euro/dollar exchange rate is almost uncorrelated with stock market performance, we have discovered that the German (euro) operation would have a similar beta with respect to the U.S. stock market as an equivalent American (dollar) operation would have with respect to the U.S. stock market.

DIGGING DEEPER

There is also an international CAPM (also named **ICAPM**), a close relative of the intertemporal CAPM or APT (page 292). (The international CAPM identifies the relevant factors for you.) In this model, investors care not only about the performance of the U.S. stock market but also about currency performance. For example, if investors already have half their wealth in the U.S. stock market and the other half in euro cash, then they may not like it if a corporation adds more euro exposure. The CAPM formula would then be modified to have one additional term,

$$\mathcal{E}(\tilde{r}_i) = r_F + \left[\mathcal{E}(\tilde{r}_M) - r_F\right] \cdot \beta_i + [\gamma] \cdot \beta_{i,X \text{ in } €/\$}$$

where γ is some constant (like the equity premium), and $\beta_{i,X \text{ in } €/\$}$ would measure the exposure of the project with respect to euro exchange rate movements. The γ could be either a positive or a negative constant, and functions just like the equity premium in the CAPM formula. The empirical evidence suggests that gamma is very small, so this extension of the CAPM is not too important—at least for OECD countries.

SOLVE NOW!

Q 25.15 As a U.S. corporation, assuming your own investors are domestic, can you evaluate foreign projects in terms of their expected rate of return and market beta with respect to the U.S. market?

Q 25.16 If foreign stocks follow their local CAPM, and U.S. stocks follow a U.S. CAPM, and U.S. and foreign stocks can be bought by both investors, is it likely that these foreign stocks obey a U.S. CAPM?

Q 25.17 Into what components can you decompose the U.S. market beta of a foreign project?

Q 25.18 Assume that the local stock market beta of a Japanese project is 1.5. Assume that the beta of the Japanese stock market with respect to the U.S. stock market is 0.5. Assume that the market beta of $/¥ exchange rate movements is 0. What would you expect the U.S. market beta of this Japanese project to be?

25.4 CORPORATE CURRENCY HEDGING

There are other types of firms that can be hurt by euro depreciation (dollar appreciation).

A corporation like the NFL thinking about building a German subsidiary is not the only type of firm worried about declines in the value of the euro. In fact, there are three types of firms that are concerned:

1. U.S. firms thinking about establishing a foreign subsidiary or selling products in foreign markets—like our NFL example.
2. U.S. exporters. For example, Boeing builds aircraft in the United States, so its costs are mostly in dollars. It sells aircraft in Europe, and these aircraft may be sold in euros. If the euro appreciates, it is good news when it is time to deliver. Instead of $108 million per plane, Boeing might receive $116 million per plane. But if the euro depreciates, it is bad news for Boeing. It might receive only $100 million per plane. In this case, it may not even be able to cover its costs any longer. (Note that currency volatility might not necessarily be bad for Boeing from an ex-ante perspective. If it can expand its operations when the euro appreciates, then currency fluctuations would give it a valuable real option.)
3. European importers. For example, Danone of France (known as Dannon in the United States) buys organic yogurt from Stonyfield Farms in dollars and resells it in France in euros. If the euro depreciates, Danone's U.S. dollar inputs become more expensive.

➤ Real options, Section 12.6, p. 413

In Section 26.5C, we discuss risk management and hedging in the context of any types of risks (not only currency risks). For example, gasoline distributors can use crude oil forward contracts to hedge the risk of adverse oil price movements. Aluminum manufacturers can hedge the price of electricity. Currency risk is just one among many hedgeable risks.

In some cases, currency movements may influence both sides of the balance sheet and therefore not influence cash flow volatility—for instance, it could be that Danone can raise its selling prices in line with yogurt input costs, so it may not face any cash flow volatility—but this is fairly rare. Our question now is: What can firms that are worried about currency movements do to reduce their exposures?

SOLVE NOW!

Q 25.19 What kinds of firms are negatively affected by an appreciation of the Swiss franc?

25.4A HEDGING WITH CURRENCY FORWARDS

The hedge sells off our *future* euro receipts *today*.

One answer to reducing currency risk is *hedging* of the euro receipts. A **hedge** is a simultaneous investment that moves in an opposite direction and thereby reduces risk. Here is our $108.86 investment example from Figure 25.2 again. Reorganize our eight scenarios (possible project outcomes).

Scenario	U.S. Mkt ↑ Ger Mkt ↑	U.S. Mkt ↑ Ger Mkt ↓	U.S. Mkt ↓ Ger Mkt ↑	U.S. Mkt ↓ Ger Mkt ↓	Average	
Euro depreciates to 1.0000 $/€:	$139.62	$109.62	$103.28	$73.28	$106.45	−2.22%
Euro appreciates to 1.1566 $/€:	$161.48	$126.79	$119.45	$84.75	$123.12	13.10%

➤ Forward contracts, Section 25.1B, p. 945

The idea of a currency hedge is to sign a contract that will yield cash if the exchange rate moves against the real operations profits. We can use a forward contract to accomplish this. What would happen, for example, if Boeing engaged in a forward contract to deliver €100 in exchange for receipts of $107.83?

Scenario	Pay	Receive	€100 is Worth	"Profit" (Relative to Value)
Euro depreciates to 1.0000 $/€:	€100	$107.83	$100.00	+$7.83
Euro appreciates to 1.1566 $/€:	€100	$107.83	$115.66	−$7.83

If the euro depreciates to 1.0000 $/€, the contract will still deliver $107.83, even though the €100 would really be worth only $100.00—it would have earned $7.83. If the euro appreciates to 1.1566 $/€, the contract will oblige us to exchange €100 for $107.83, even though the €100 is really worth $115.66—it would have lost $7.83.

The hedge reduces our currency uncertainty and thus total uncertainty, but does not eliminate uncertainty.

Now consider the project and forward contract together. You just need to add the $7.83 gain from the future to the project proceeds if the euro depreciates, and subtract it if the euro appreciates:

Scenario	U.S. Mkt ↑ Ger Mkt ↑	U.S. Mkt ↑ Ger Mkt ↓	U.S. Mkt ↓ Ger Mkt ↑	U.S. Mkt ↓ Ger Mkt ↓	Average	
Euro depreciates to 1.0000 $/€ (+$7.83):	$147.45	$117.45	$111.11	$81.11	$114.28	+4.98%
Euro appreciates to 1.1566 $/€ (−$7.83):	$153.65	$118.96	$111.62	$76.92	$115.29	+5.91%

The (currency-related) volatility of the GFL project plus the currency contract is lower than the (currency-related) volatility of the GFL alone, *because the returns on the currency forward and those on the project move in opposite directions*. In fact, the forward contract has almost neutralized the effect of exchange rate movements: Instead of the average rates of return of −2.22% and +13.10%, they are now +4.98% and +5.91%.

(In Question 25.20, you will be asked to increase the scale of the currency contract to eliminate even this residual currency risk.) Of course, the currency contract has *not* eliminated other sources of uncertainty. For example, if a fourth scenario comes about, the net revenues are either \$81.11 or \$76.92, both of which are significant losses relative to the \$108.86 investment.

This forward contract reduces cash flow volatility because our firm is paying for its corporate expenses in dollars and is receiving its corporate revenues in euros. The currency contract is like an insurance hedge because it gains if the euro goes down and loses if the euro goes up. Who would buy the other side of our currency forward contract? There are three natural candidates:

The forward contract's other side is needed by other corporations.

1. A European firm, like L'Oréal, building a plant in the United States is the exact opposite of the U.S.-based NFL starting up a German football league.
2. Airbus is the exact opposite of Boeing. It builds airplanes in Europe, so its costs are primarily in euros, and it sells many of its airplanes to U.S. airlines.
3. American importing firms that pay for inputs in euros and sell their products in dollars are just like L'Oréal or Airbus. If the euro appreciates, the input costs rise—a bad situation.

Thus, these types of firms naturally take the other side of the Boeing currency forward contract.

Most corporations with substantial foreign sales or operations use currency hedges of one kind or another. They usually just want to reduce their currency risks. Few companies want to fully eliminate it for a number of reasons:

Full hedging is often both difficult and impractical.

- It is not easy for a corporation to determine how the value of a German operation changes if this operation has cash flows not only next year but for, say, 50 years. What exactly are the expected cash flows in 50 years that are to be hedged?
- Currency hedges can have detrimental accounting implications. Currency contracts have to be "marked to market" while the underlying hedged assets may not be. This can lead to interim problems (such as violations of bond covenants).
- There are many cases in which the full currency hedge would be multiples of the firm value—and it is neither easy nor especially advisable for a company worth \$1 billion to have open currency forward hedges for, say, \$10 billion.

Therefore, instead of exact hedging of each future cash flow in every year (for a complete NPV hedge), most corporations hedge only cash flows or some component of earnings occurring over the next few years.

SOLVE NOW!

Q 25.20 The example used a €100 ↔ \$107.83 currency contract to drop the risk from a range of about 15% to a risk of about 1%. Can you do better? What kind of currency forward contract would improve the hedge against exchange risk?

ANECDOTE Metallgesellschaft's Hedging

In late 1993, Metallgesellschaft (a very large, 100-year-old German company) experienced a major crisis: Owning a set of gas stations, Metallgesellschaft had agreed to purchase 2 billion barrels of oil at a price of \$16 to \$18 per barrel. The claimed intent was to "hedge" its input costs. Unfortunately, not only did the oil price move against the hedge (having fallen to \$15 by the fall of 1993), but its gas stations had also performed poorly, and it did not need as much oil any longer. In addition, it had made some hedging mistakes in matching the duration of its gas station assets and its hedging liabilities, and this triggered various bond covenants that pushed Metallgesellschaft into default. Not surprisingly, the market value of all shares in Metallgesellschaft fell from about 3.7 billion DM to 1.5 billion DM.

25.4B HEDGING WITH REAL OPERATIONS

Matching inputs and outputs in foreign operations is a natural hedge.

Forward contracts are not the only method of currency hedging. For example, we know that a company that purchases inputs in its home currency and has sales in a foreign country can be hurt by a rise in its home currency against the foreign currency. If it sets up a foreign operation, which can then also purchase its inputs in the foreign market in foreign currency, then its currency exchange risk will be much lower—both costs and revenues will occur in the same currency. Further, such international operations often create a "real option," whereby companies can shift some production from the high-cost country to the low-cost country when exchange rates shift. (By the way, this can also create important tax implications that require armies of tax experts to understand.) Automakers, in particular, have invested heavily in such strategies: Most Toyota Camrys for the United States are produced in Georgetown, Kentucky. (Many are now reexported to Japan. Ironically, it is not inconceivable for the United States to become the top exporter of Japanese cars in the future if the dollar continues to depreciate.) BMW has manufacturing facilities in Georgia, Illinois, and California. Ford and General Motors have large European subsidiaries.

➤ Real options, Section 12.6, p. 413

25.4C HEDGING WITH FOREIGN FINANCING

Financing in foreign currency is another method of hedging.

Yet another method of hedging for corporations is to match assets and liabilities: If a firm has an asset (such as a foreign operation) that has a net present value of €100, then it can create a liability that is also worth €100. The easiest way to do this is to raise the financing for the asset not in U.S. dollars (as we did in Figure 25.2) but in euros. If an operation has borrowed €100 and is worth €100, the currency risk on the assets itself almost disappears: Currency risk remains only in the earnings performance of the euro subsidiary. If you recall Table 15.2, IBM was an example of a firm that extensively borrowed in foreign currencies.

➤ IBM's capital structure, Table 15.2, p. 557

Host country financing (foreign bonds) can hedge political risk.

If we raise this capital in the foreign host country itself, it may also mitigate **political risk**: If a revolution were to occur in Russia and our Russian operations were nationalized, chances are that we would not be liable to pay Russian investors and lenders. This type of hedge is often accomplished with **foreign bonds**, which have been around for at least 100 years. They are issued by corporations foreign to the host country in which they are issued and denominated in host country currency. They are named differently in different countries: **Yankee bonds** in the United States (i.e., issued by a non-U.S. corporation), **samurai bonds** in Japan, **matador bonds** in

Spain, and **bulldog bonds** in Great Britain. For example, when Ford Motors issues a Japanese-yen bond in Tokyo, it would be a samurai bond.

EUROBONDS AND THE ISSUE-AND-SWAP MARKET

Eurobonds are bonds issued by corporations foreign to the host country in which they are issued, but in contrast to foreign bonds, they are denominated in the currency of a *nonhost* country. They are neither necessarily denominated in euros nor traded in Europe. For example, when Ford issues a dollar-denominated bond in Japan, it is a Eurobond, despite the name. (As you saw above, when Ford issues a yen-denominated bond in Japan, it would be called a foreign bond.) Therefore, depending on the currency that they are issued in, such bonds may or may not serve a hedging role. The name "Eurobond" is a historic term. The first important *public* Eurobond issue was an 1822 bearer bond, issued by Russia, denominated in British pounds, and payable at Rothschild Bank offices anywhere in the world. The first corporate Eurobond was issued by Petrofina in 1957.

The foreign market: Eurobonds are denominated in the currency of the nonhost country.

The Eurobond market accounts for a much larger share of borrowing than foreign bonds today, roughly by a factor of 5. It is also larger now than the U.S. bond market. The annual nominal issuing value had reached around $1 trillion by 2000, with outstanding debt of over $4 trillion. By 2006, issuing activity was $2 trillion. For U.S. companies issuing in Europe or Japan, the Eurobond market is often less a mechanism to hedge currency risk (many of their issues are denominated in U.S. dollars) than it is a mechanism to escape the regulation and supervision of the SEC. The institutional customs and features of Eurobonds are more flexible and somewhat different from those that apply to ordinary U.S. bonds. (The typical issue costs are about 25 to 50 basis points of the market price.)

Eurobonds are far more important than foreign bonds.

Another very large market for corporate financing is the **issue-and-swap market**, where a firm issues a bond and immediately swaps its payments with a counterparty. For example, a company like Disney may feel that its name recognition in the United States allows it a better borrowing rate in the United States than in Japan, even though it really wants to issue yen debt; while a company like Matsushita may feel that its Japanese name recognition allows it a better borrowing rate in Japan than in the United States—even though it really wants to issue dollar debt. An investment bank arranges for these firms to raise capital in their host countries, where it is cheap for them, and then sets up a swap. In this swap, Matsushita pays Disney's debt service and Disney pays Matsushita's debt service. The complication is that, although the obligations are a fairly close match at the outset, over time, one loan may become more valuable than the other. To reduce the risk of default, a large AAA rated company (such as an insurance company) guarantees performance in exchange for an upfront payment. If Matsushita were to go bankrupt and could no longer pay for Disney's debt, Disney would then no longer pay for Matsushita's debt, either, and the difference would have to be picked up by the AAA guarantor.

Issue-and-swap explained.

SOLVE NOW!

Q 25.21 What methods of foreign currency hedging can firms consider?

Q 25.22 What kind of foreign bonds might U.S. companies issue? What are the alternatives?

25.4D SHOULD FIRMS HEDGE?

Two strong perfect-market arguments suggest that hedging adds little value.

➤ Why hedge?, Section 26.5C, p. 1005

Hedging can reduce the volatility of cash flows. But does this add shareholder value? Maybe, but it is probably not a first-order effect for two reasons. First, our shareholders should care little about the idiosyncratic currency risk our corporation faces because they are heavily diversified. As long as the foreign currency does not comove with the (U.S.) stock market, any extra currency risk should not change the U.S. market beta. For our investors' portfolios, currency fluctuations across many different companies—some net exporters, some net importers—should mostly wash out. Second, if our shareholders dislike the risk of losing money when the euro goes up or down, then they can themselves buy the proper currency forward hedges to neutralize any such risks.

Possible reasons for hedging—second-order effects due to market imperfections.

Still, many corporations do hedge currency fluctuations. Why? There are a number of possible explanations. Most are exact analogs of the arguments in Chapter 18 as to why capital structure can influence firm value. Here are some examples:

- If adverse currency fluctuations could lead a firm to incur financial distress, the resulting costs to handle the financial distress are quite real. In this sense, hedging is really just like capital structure policy—the first-order effect should be that firms should be worth what the underlying operations are worth, which should not strongly depend on how the firm is financed. But if a firm is close to financial distress, too much debt can cost value.
- Managerial and corporate performance may be easier to evaluate if the firm can reduce the effects of unexpected currency fluctuations. This can reduce agency problems.
- Managers may just not like the uncertainty of currency fluctuations and may try to neutralize this risk even if it does not increase value. This could be a sign of an unmitigated agency conflict.

Sadly, some firms "hedge" because their traders believe they can outguess the financial markets and thereby increase their profits. This is often a sign of poor internal controls because the compensation of the employees who handle the hedging often implicitly or explicitly depends on the profitability of their hedges. Therefore, these employees often participate more in the upside than in the downside of their contracts. Thus, they may be quite willing to gamble with shareholders' money. The first lesson of good risk management should be to manage the risk of those managing the risk. Lack of such controls has led to a number of very high-profile corporate failures.

SOLVE NOW!

Q 25.23 Why is it that corporate hedging is unlikely to create much shareholder value?

Q 25.24 How can foreign currency hedging create value?

25.5 WHO ARE YOU WORKING FOR?

The previous section assumed you care only about the U.S. CAPM trade-off.

I have allowed our corporation to be multinational, but I have silently sneaked in one big assumption—that you are a U.S. corporation living in a U.S. CAPM world and working on behalf of U.S. shareholders who consume in U.S. dollars. This is a reasonable assumption if your shareholders (owners) are all Americans who are not otherwise internationally diversified, perhaps because they have a strong home bias that makes them hold a U.S. stock market portfolio exculsively. These investors naturally like projects that help them reduce the U.S. stock market risk—and in the end, they care only about consuming in U.S. dollars. This was the scenario that you worked out above.

But what if your investors are not Americans who are concerned only with their opportunities in the U.S. financial markets? What if your U.S. company shares are held by Chinese investors, and you are now considering an investment in a German plant? How should you think about the risk contribution of your investment projects now?

What if you have foreign investors and foreign opportunities?

The answer is surprisingly clear. Ultimately, as a corporation, you exist for the benefit of your owners. Your goal is to earn a rate of return on the money handed to you that exceeds the opportunity cost of capital otherwise available to your investors. This is how your corporation adds value. If your owners are Chinese investors who otherwise have access only to the Chinese stock market (plus your firm's shares now) and who only consume in Chinese yuan, then your appropriate cost of capital would be determined by the Chinese stock market. You would have to compute the beta of the German plant opportunity with respect to the overall Chinese stock market, measuring the returns produced in euros after translation into yuan.

Your cost of capital arises from alternative opportunities available to your investors, often in *their* stock markets.

Now consider a more complex scenario to test your conceptual understanding: Your Chinese investors want to consume all their returns in British pounds, but they still remain restricted to investment in the Chinese stock market, plus your single firm. In this case, your opportunity cost of capital is still determined by the alternative investments (the Chinese stock market), but all calculations—including measurement of the expected rate of return in the Chinese stock market—should now be done in British pounds. After all, this is what your investors care about in the end.

See if you understood this: Our investors' consumption choices should determine the currency returns that we should care about.

Let me add another complexity: What if Chinese investors are not allowed to invest in American companies? Like investors in many countries, Chinese investors suffer from capital controls. And, even when there are no formal capital controls, investors in many countries fail to diversify themselves internationally. Even U.S. investors are often not diversified, although international diversification is no longer difficult: There are U.S.-traded funds that hold foreign stocks. If your U.S. investors have "forgotten" about foreign investment opportunities, the market is essentially segmented: Not all investors are taking advantage of the same markets. In this case, your U.S. corporation might still be able to add value by expanding domestic investors' opportunity sets through their foreign operations.

Segmentation of what investors are holding, legal or de facto, may mean that our foreign operations can offer really unique opportunities to our investors.

That is, if your investors cannot or do not hold foreign investments, then foreign subsidiaries *should* help in expanding your U.S. investors' opportunities. After all, the foreign operation produces cash flows in foreign currency, which in an efficient stock market should always be appropriately valued in the firm's stock price. The total firm should just become the portfolio of a domestic operation and a foreign operation. Thus, even if the firm is only traded in the United States, the stock of the combined firm *should* covary with both the return in the U.S. financial market and the return in the foreign financial markets. Unfortunately, empirical evidence suggests that this is not as much the case as it should be—firms tend to covary too much with the index

Foreign operations can add diversification for home-biased investors.

on the stock market on which they are trading and too little with the foreign stock market indexes where their underlying holdings are. This puzzle is linked to a number of related puzzles: Closed-end mutual funds that trade on the NYSE and that hold foreign country stocks tend to covary more with the S&P 500 than with their foreign country's stock market; and real estate investment trusts (REITs) seem to covary more with the S&P 500 than with the value of the underlying real estate.

In the real world, determining who our investors are may not be easy for a large public corporation.

So, in the real world, as a corporate manager, you now understand that you must think of the opportunity costs of capital for your underlying corporate owners when you decide on projects. You need to learn who your investors are and what they care about. This is no longer simple. In the domestic CAPM, you could just assume that they cared about the portfolio with the highest expected rate of return, given minimal overall portfolio risk. Now you may have Chinese investors who care about the best Chinese yuan portfolio in the context of the Chinese financial markets but who ultimately want to consume in Canadian or U.S. dollars. Or you may have British investors who care about the best British pound portfolio in the context of the British financial markets but who ultimately want to consume some goods sold in/priced in euros and other goods priced in British pounds. Or you may have other investors who are represented by funds and are thus totally anonymous. In short, the possibilities are endless. What opportunity sets are your investors really facing, and how can your projects improve them? In what currency should you determine the optimal alternative investments? What kind of CAPM world—with an international or a domestic market portfolio—do you live in? These are difficult questions. Most managers focus only on the project opportunities that they are providing to their domestic investors. Given investors' home biases, this could be a reasonable assumption, even if this is not perfectly correct. Fortunately, I am just an academic and therefore have escaped having to make such difficult decisions!

SOLVE NOW!

Q 25.25 Assume you are a corporate manager in Germany. You are thinking of listing on the Brazilian stock exchange. If Brazilian investors are only allowed to invest in Brazil, and all Brazilian investors spend all their money to pay their children's tuition in the United States, then how should you think about investing in a Czech plant?

SUMMARY

This chapter covered the following major points:

- An exchange rate is the price of one unit of a country's currency in terms of units of another country's currency. The spot rate applies to an immediate exchange of money.

- Currency spot markets and futures markets are linked by covered interest rate parity (IRP), an arbitrage condition based on the law of one price.

- Uncovered IRP states that forward exchange rates are also expected exchange rates. This holds only if there is no risk compensation component in the pricing of the forward.

- In the real world, the prices of goods can vary across countries—a phenomenon known as deviation from purchasing power parity (PPP). To the extent that the market for a particular good is not perfect, PPP is not likely to hold.

- The Fisher hypothesis is a consequence of PPP. It posits that *expected* real rates of return are the same across countries. (It does not hold if there are risk premiums.)

- Investors can analyze their risk and reward from investing in foreign stock markets in a CAPM-like framework. Foreign stocks seem to add at least some diversification benefits.

- Market segmentation can make the portfolio problem conceptually more complex. One important cause of market segmentation is investor "home bias."

- Corporate managers should continue to think of capital budgeting in terms of their investors' opportunity cost of capital in an international framework.

  In the context of a U.S. CAPM, they can think of foreign projects as contributing both risk and reward. To measure the risk contribution—the project's U.S. market beta—managers can mentally decompose it into three components:
  (a) The foreign project's beta with respect to its foreign market index (with rates of return quoted in the foreign currency)
  (b) The beta of the foreign market with respect to the U.S. market (both measured in the foreign currency)
  (c) The correlation of exchange rate movements with the U.S. market

  For many OECD countries, the foreign market beta in local currency is likely to be similar to the U.S. market beta in dollars because many international stock markets tend to move together one to one, and currencies do not tend to move with the equity markets.

- Corporate managers can hedge exchange risk through currency forward contracts, by creating foreign operations, or by matching foreign assets with foreign liabilities. This is a form of risk management, which can add value if the financial market that the firm is facing is not perfect.

- You can determine the currency and market that you should use to compute your cost of capital by thinking about who your investors are.

KEY TERMS

SOLVE NOW! SOLUTIONS

Q 25.1 To compute the peso interest rate, use Formula 25.1:

$$\frac{0.08660\ \$/\text{Peso}}{0.09230\ \$/\text{Peso}} \approx \frac{(1+1.12\%)}{(1+r_1^{\text{MX}})}$$

$$\frac{f}{S_0} = \frac{(1+r_1^{\text{US}})}{(1+r_1^{\text{MX}})}$$

Therefore, the peso interest rate would be $1.0112/(0.08660/0.09230) - 1 \approx 7.78\%$. In English: Think about starting with 1 peso. Change it into \$0.0923 dollars at the spot rate. Earn the 1.12% U.S. dollar interest rate so that you have $\$0.0923 \cdot 1.0112 \approx \$0.0933$ after 1 year. Convert it back into pesos at the forward rate to get \$0.0933/0.0866 Peso/\$ ≈ Peso 1.0778. This is the 7.78% interest rate.

Q 25.2 The forward rate is not necessarily the expected exchange rate. There is also a risk compensation component in the forward rate, which drives a difference between the best expected future spot rate and the forward rate. Instead, the spot and forward rates are linked through arbitrage via the interest rate differential. So the forward rate tells you only about the interest rate differential. To the extent that there is a forecast of a future exchange rate, it should be reflected in today's exchange rate, too.

Q 25.3 Let's work through an example in which the ¥/€ forward rate is at a forward premium. Think of a spot rate of 100 ¥/€ and a forward rate of 200 ¥/€. If the interest rate in euros is 0%, and the interest rate in yen is 100%, you would indeed be indifferent. You can invest €1 and have €1 next year, or you can invest ¥100 today, earn 100% interest, which comes to ¥200, and exchange it for €1. Thus, the interest rate in Japan is higher.

Q 25.4 Given the *CIA World Factbook* information, the yuan should have appreciated by $1.037/1.015 - 1 \approx 2.2\%$ in 2007. In real life, the yuan ($\overline{\pi}$) appreciated from 7.97 $\overline{\pi}$/\$ to 7.61 $\overline{\pi}$/\$, or 4.7%. One important reason is that China has a soft peg on its currency to the U.S. dollar, meaning that they actively manipulate it. Thus, the Chinese currency was significantly undervalued at the start of 2007. (This is also why the *Factbook* listed China's GDP at purchasing power parity as \$7.043 trillion, but as \$3.249 at the official exchange rate.) Another way to look at this problem is to work it this way: \$1 in 1 year has a purchasing power of $\$1/1.037 \approx \$0.96432$ today; 7.61 yuan in 1 year has a purchasing power of $\overline{\pi}7.61/1.015 \approx \overline{\pi}7.4975$; so the future exchange rate differential in today's terms would be $\overline{\pi}7.4975/\$0.96432 \approx 7.7749\ \overline{\pi}/\$$. This is an increase in the expected currency exchange rate of $(7.7749\ \overline{\pi}/\$ - 7.61\ \overline{\pi}/\$)/(7.61\ \overline{\pi}/\$) \approx 2.2\%$.

Q 25.5 PPP arbitrage is prevented primarily by transaction costs, transport costs, and import barriers—all problems related to imperfect markets. In addition, different tastes could also play a role.

Q 25.6 The Fisher effect is the claim that real interest rates should be the same in different countries.

Q 25.7 The peso inflation rate can be computed as $(1 + 1.12\%)/(1 + 1\%) \approx (1 + 7.78\%)/(1 + \pi) \Longrightarrow \pi \approx 7.65\%$. At the current spot rate, the Small Mac, which costs \$2.12, goes for about 23.00 pesos. Thus, if PPP holds, we would expect the Small Mac to cost 24.76 pesos in 1 year.

Q 25.8 Interest rate parity is the relation between interest rates and forward rates. Arbitraging violations require only financial market transactions and are therefore very easy. This ensures that IRP holds quite well. Purchasing power parity is the relation between the prices of goods and currencies. Arbitraging violations require importing/exporting and are therefore very difficult. This means that PPP holds only in the very long run.

Q 25.9 Yes, PPP holds for some, but not all, goods. It almost always holds for gold but rarely holds for, say, cars. The former is easier to import/export than the latter.

Q 25.10 Yes. For example, if the U.S. stock value drops from \$100 to \$75 per share but the U.S. dollar doubles in euros, then the French investor would experience a positive euro rate of return of 50%.

Q 25.11 The reason for looking at the risk contribution of a foreign stock market with respect to the U.S. stock market is that investors are home biased. Therefore, U.S. investors are primarily invested in the U.S. stock market, and they benefit if foreign investments help them diversify.

Q 25.12 If you are a U.S. investor who is mostly consuming in U.S. dollars, you are interested in the U.S. dollar rate of return. If you are a British investor, you are interested in the British pound rate of return. So, the kind of currency return that you are interested in depends on who you are.

Q 25.13 Foreign stock market investments outperformed U.S. stock market investments, primarily because the dollar depreciated during this period.

Q 25.14 The beta was below 1 for all foreign countries.

Q 25.15 Yes, you can evaluate foreign projects in terms of their expected rate of return and market beta with respect to the U.S. market. From your perspective, a foreign project is just like any other project. Risk is valued by your model of what expected rates of return should be, regardless of whether it comes from drug development or currency movement.

Q 25.16 Yes. If a project follows its local CAPM, it is also likely to follow a U.S. CAPM, as illustrated by our German example.

Q 25.17 You can decompose the U.S. market beta of your foreign project into three parts: (1) The beta of the project's cash flows with respect to the foreign financial market, measured in foreign currency; (2) the beta of foreign exchange movements (usually 0); and (3) the beta of the foreign stock market with respect to the U.S. stock market (usually a little below 1).

Q 25.18 Think simple. If the U.S. stock market performs +20% better than expected, the beta of 0.5 means that the Japanese stock market performs +10% better than expected. If the Japanese stock market performs +10%, the local (Japanese) project performs $1.5 \cdot 10\% = +15\%$ better. Thus, for a +20% performance in the U.S. stock market, you expect the local Japanese project to perform +15% better. In other words, you are expecting a U.S. market beta for this Japanese project to be $0.5 \cdot 1.5 = 0.75$.

Q 25.19 Firms whose costs are in Swiss francs and whose revenues are in other currencies are negatively affected by Swiss franc appreciation. For example, there could be a Swiss pharmaceutical firm like Novartis, which produces in Switzerland and sells worldwide. The equivalent would be a foreign importer of Swiss goods. Finally, the value of Swiss subsidiaries in foreign countries would decline from the perspective of a Swiss investor.

Q 25.20 Yes, you can improve on the hedge in the text. You need to hedge a little bit more to reduce the remaining \$1.01 difference between \$114.28 and \$115.29 in the two states. Each €100 contract gives you a profit of \$7.83 if the euro depreciates and a loss of \$7.83 if the euro appreciates. To hedge the remaining \$1.01, you need to earn $\$1.01/2 = \$0.505$ more if the euro depreciates. The cost on the other side would be $\$1.01/2 = \$0.505$ less return if the euro appreciates. Thus, you need to increase your contract by $\$0.505/\$7.83 \approx 6.45\%$. Your best hedge would be a forward contract on €106.45. Repeating the table in the text:

Scenario	Pay	Receive	€106.45 is Worth	"Profit" (Relative to Value)
Euro depreciates to 1.0000 $/€:	€106.45	$114.785	$106.45	+$8.335
Euro appreciates to 1.1566 $/€:	€106.45	$114.785	$123.12	−$8.335

Now add the gain and loss of $8.335 into the combined project table:

Scenario	U.S. Mkt ↑ Ger Mkt ↑	U.S. Mkt ↑ Ger Mkt ↓	U.S. Mkt ↓ Ger Mkt ↑	U.S. Mkt ↓ Ger Mkt ↓	Average	
Euro depreciates to 1.0000 $/€:	$147.96	$117.96	$111.62	$81.62	$114.79	+5.45%
Euro appreciates to 1.1566 $/€:	$153.15	$118.46	$111.12	$76.42	$114.79	+5.45%

Q 25.21 Firms can do direct hedging with forwards or futures, hedging by moving the cost centers to the same currency location as the revenue centers, and hedging by financing revenues with debt in the same currency.

Q 25.22 For a U.S. company, there are foreign bonds that are issued by corporations in the foreign host currency. Such bonds include bulldog bonds, matador bonds, samurai bonds, or yankee bonds. There are Eurobonds, which are basically a mechanism to escape SEC supervision. And there is a large issue-and-swap market, in which two firms exchange different types of obligations.

Q 25.23 Investors are widely diversified, so a little exposure to one or the other currency—as long as it remains idiosyncratic—does not matter to them. Besides, if investors care about currency risk, they can easily hedge for themselves.

Q 25.24 Currency hedging can add value only if it reduces market imperfections. For example, hedging can reduce financial distress costs.

Q 25.25 The opportunity cost of your investors' capital are other opportunities in the Brazilian stock market, so you should use the Brazilian interest rates and Brazilian stock market index (as your CAPM market portfolio). Brazilians care about U.S. dollar returns, so you should work only in U.S. dollar returns (including Brazilian bonds and stocks, and your own Czech plant).

PROBLEMS

The *indicates problems available in* myfinancelab

Q 25.26 What is the most common form of quoting the exchange rate between the dollar and the British pound? What is the rate today? What would be the less common form of quoting this exchange rate?

Q 25.27 On September 30, 2007, the following were the prices for the Euro FX Contract:

		Months				
		3	6	9	12	18
	Cash	Dec. 07	March 08	June 08	Sep. 08	Dec. 08
€/$	TBD	1.4293	1.4303	1.4308	1.4311	1.4311

The 3-month U.S. Treasury offered a yield of 3.64% and the 6-month offered 3.91%. The price of USD to EUR was 0.7006€. The yield on the 3-month German federal security was 3.88%.

(a) What was the spot rate?
(b) If there are no market imperfections, was there an arbitrage opportunity here? If so, how would you have exploited it?
(c) What is the most likely reason why you could not get rich?

Q 25.28 If you believe that the euro will be higher in 6 months than it is today, would it be better to purchase the 6-month forward contract instead of the spot rate?

Q 25.29 If the \$/€ forward rate is at a forward discount relative to the spot rate (that is, the forward rate is lower than the spot rate), is the nominal interest rate in Europe or in the United States higher?

Q 25.30 Explain the difference between covered and uncovered interest rate parity.

Q 25.31 In 2007, according to the *CIA World Factbook,* Zimbabwe had an inflation rate of 976% per annum—the world's undisputed inflation leader. Botswana, its neighbor to the east, had an inflation rate of 11.4%. If PPP holds, how would you expect their currency exchange rates to move over the next 12 months?

Q 25.32 If everyone expects a currency exchange rate in 6 months to be higher than it is today (so that it will come back to PPP), would this be reflected in the differential between today's spot rate and the forward rate?

Q 25.33 What kind of characteristics of goods are most likely to obey PPP (and drive diverging economies back toward it)?

Q 25.34 Would you expect import and export firms to help make interest rate parity come true?

Q 25.35 Look up where the Big Mac index stands today. Where is the United States relative to other countries? Which are the most expensive and which are the cheapest countries? How would this index suggest that the U.S. dollar should move relative to these currencies in the future if you believed in long-run PPP?

Q 25.36 The Australian firm CommSec has recently created the iPod Index. What are its conceptual advantages and disadvantages relative to the Big Mac Index? Search the Web to find where the two indexes stand relative to one another.

Q 25.37 Construct a textbook price index. That is, take some of your school textbooks and see how their prices differ in five countries of your choice. Do textbooks obey PPP? Can you arbitrage the price differences?

Q 25.38 In your assessment, do real-goods markets or financial capital markets have more influence on exchange rates? Why?

Q 25.39 Download the most recent 3 years of historical daily stock returns for various international stock market indexes from Yahoo! *Finance.* Compute the beta of these stock markets with respect to the S&P 500 market index. What do your market betas suggest about the diversification benefits of these markets?

Q 25.40 Redraw Figure 25.2, but do so assuming a 6-month period and a currency exchange rate that is in line with those from March 2008: The euro stood at \$1.57, and the 6-month forward rate stood at \$1.55. Work with an equal probability of an up-movement to \$1.50 or a down-movement to \$1.60.

Q 25.41 Assume that the local stock market beta of a British project is 3. Assume that the beta of the British stock market with respect to the U.S. stock market is 0.75. Assume that the market beta of \$/£ exchange rate movements is 0. What would you expect the U.S. market beta of this British project to be?

Q 25.42 Why do firms in the real world not hedge all foreign exchange risk? Is this necessarily a bad thing for their investors?

Q 25.43 Suppose you are a U.S. oil company thinking about investing in Russia. (The Kremlin has a track record of changing contracts after the fact.) How would you finance your Russian operations?

Q 25.44 Search the SEC's Edgar database for a 424(b)(5) filing by KfW on 2007/09/28. What kind of bond is this?

Q 25.45 Assume you are a corporate manager in the United Kingdom. You are thinking of listing on the NYSE. If British investors are primarily investing in the United States, and British investors mostly consume in Britain, then how should you think about investing in a new plant in China?

CHAPTER 25 APPENDIX

Prominent International Institutions

The **International Monetary Fund** (http://www.imf.org) is a United Nations nonprofit agency established in 1946 with 38 members and currently made up of 185 member nations (in 2008). Its prime purpose is to encourage the smooth functioning of money flows and to aid in the stability of currencies (e.g., by preventing runs on country currencies or by facilitating information disclosure). The IMF's operations consist of "surveillance, financial assistance, and technical assistance." (For example, in September 2002, it lent $30 billion to Brazil to dispel doubts that Brazil might default on its foreign debt.) Member countries' voting power is determined by their contributions to the IMF capital pool. The IMF's board of governors consists of finance ministers and central bank heads. Day-to-day operations are performed by a 24-person executive committee. Eight countries have permanent representations, while the remaining 16 rotate. The IMF headquarters is in Washington, D.C. In early 2008, the IMF had about $362 billion at its disposal, from which it could make temporary loans.

The **World Bank** (http://www.worldbank.org) is also a United Nations nonprofit agency (really five closely associated institutions). It was also established in 1946, and is made up of the same 185 member countries. (World Bank members must be members of the IMF.) The World Bank was set up to reduce poverty in developing nations. It both extends loans itself and attempts to coordinate third-party private and bilateral loans. The World Bank raises financing through World Bank bonds (it has an AAA rating) and passes the resulting low interest rates onto developing country client loans. The World Bank headquarters is in Washington, D.C. About 20% of the $23 billion raised by the World Bank in 2006 was used for outright grants (not loans) to poor countries.

The **World Trade Organization** (http://www.wto.org) was set up in 1995 to deal with the global rules of trade between nations, set out in the General Agreement on Tariffs and Trade (GATT). In 2007, the WTO had 150 member countries, accounting for over 97% of world trade. Its main function is to ensure that trade flows as smoothly, predictably, and freely as possible. It handles trade disputes, administers WTO trade agreements, offers a forum for trade negotiations, monitors national trade, and provides some technical assistance and training for developing countries. The WTO headquarters is in Geneva. Its 2007 budget was 182 million Swiss francs.

➤ OECD countries, Section 25.1, p. 944

The **Organization for Economic Cooperation and Development** (http://www.oecd.org), founded in 1961, grew out of the Marshall Plan for reconstruction after World War II. In 2007, its 30 member countries produced about 2/3 of the world GDP. (Another 70 countries had informal links.) The OECD is a sort of think-tank agency and/or meeting place and/or information agency that seeks to aid economic cooperation among like-minded, democratic, well-developed, and mostly open economy countries. It is common to refer to the developed countries as OECD countries. The OECD headquarters is in Paris. Its 2008 budget was €343 million.

ANECDOTE Free Trade—Where Convenient

The OECD nations are generally proponents of free trade. Most economists would agree that free trade generally helps all nations develop. Unfortunately, the OECD countries show little consistency. On one hand, for example, their farmers have enormous domestic voting power, which has made OECD countries erect high trade barriers against potentially competitive agricultural imports from Third World countries. On the other hand, they subsidize their farming industries and regularly get into mutual disputes as to which nation (among them) is "most unfair." Unfortunately, the Third World just does not have enough power to demand a level playing field. Naturally, the OECD nations will press and penalize Third World nations if they erect trade barriers against their goods. A particularly egregious example is the fact that the United States presses other nations not to tax American tobacco and cigarette companies.

But thinking of this as a self-interested conspiracy is too simplistic. For example, the United States and Europe have permitted Southeast Asian (especially Japanese and Chinese) imports aplenty, even when the playing field has not been level for U.S. industries (some of which thereby suffered huge job losses or destruction). In reality, trade policy is a rather incoherent and highly politicized area.

ANECDOTE Protesting World Bank Policies

Despite their seemingly uncontroversial missions and intents, all these international agencies have been widely criticized. The critics make strange bedfellows—there are, for example, both analytical economists and political activists with Molotov cocktails. This is not a light matter: The decisions of these financial organizations decide not only the fortunes of billions of people but the very lives of millions of people in the developing world. (Personally, I think it is fair to say that both the international organizations and their critics have good intentions, but the issues themselves are so complex that there is tremendous disagreement about what is right and what is wrong. There are no easy and obvious answers.)

On the lighter side, one of the more unusual political soap operas was instigated by World Bank chief economist Josef Stiglitz (former professor of economics at Stanford) in late 1999. It began when Stiglitz sharply criticized the IMF and its former managing director, Stanley Fischer (former professor of economics at MIT). In turn, Larry Summers (professor of economics and a former president of Harvard), tried to influence the World Bank to quiet Stiglitz's view. The World Bank president refused—only to find Stiglitz starting to publicly criticize the World Bank, too. Eventually, Stiglitz resigned with a big splash in an attempt to bring more attention to his policy views.

Partial source: http://www.globalpolicy.org.

KEY TERMS

International Monetary Fund, 976
Organization for Economic Cooperation and Development, 976
World Bank, 976
World Trade Organization, 976

26

Options and Risk Management

. . . AND SOME OTHER DERIVATIVES

This chapter provides a brief introduction to the most important aspects of the area of options. It covers options basics, arbitrage relationships, put-call parity, the Black-Scholes formula (and binomial option pricing), and corporate applications of option pricing ideas and methods—but all in a very condensed form. You may prefer to resort to a full book on options and derivatives if this chapter is too telegraphic for you.

Most of the concepts in the world of financial options rely on arbitrage, which is primarily a perfect-market concept. Fortunately, for large financial institutions, the market for options seems fairly close to perfect. For smaller investors, transaction costs and tax implications can play a role. In this case, the arbitrage relations discussed in this chapter hold only within the bounds defined by these market imperfections.

26.1 OPTIONS

Base assets and contingent claims (derivatives).

Options are examples of **derivatives** (also called **contingent claims**). A derivative is an investment whose value is itself determined by the value of some other underlying base asset. For example, a $100 side bet that a Van Gogh painting—the base asset—will sell for more than $5 million at auction is an example of a contingent claim, because the bet's payoffs are derived from the value of the Van Gogh painting (the underlying base asset). Similarly, a contract that states that you will make a cash payment to me that is equal to the square of the price per barrel of oil in 2010 is a contingent claim, because it depends on the price of an underlying base asset (oil).

Voluntary contracting ⇒ both parties are better off *ex-ante*. Only one party is better off *ex-post*.

As with any other voluntary contract, both parties presumably engage in a derivatives contract because doing so makes them better off *ex-ante*. For example, your car insurance is a contingent claim that depends on the value of your car (the base asset). Ex-ante, both the insurance company and you are better off contracting to this

ANECDOTE A Brief History of Options

Options have been in use since Aristotle's time. The earliest known such contract was, in fact, not a financial but a real option. It was recorded by Aristotle in the story of Thales the Milesian, an ancient Greek philosopher. Believing that the upcoming olive harvest would be especially bountiful, Thales entered into agreements with the owners of all the olive oil presses in the region. In exchange for a small deposit months ahead of the harvest, Thales obtained the right to lease the presses at market prices during the harvest. As it turned out, Thales was correct about the harvest, demand for oil presses boomed, and he made a great deal of money.

Many centuries later, in 1688, Joseph de la Vega described in *Confusion de Confusiones* how options were widely traded on the Amsterdam Stock Exchange. It is likely that he actively exploited put-call parity, an arbitrage relationship between options discussed in this chapter. In the United States, options have been traded over the counter since the nineteenth century. A dedicated options market, however, was organized only in 1973. In some other countries, option trading is banned because it is considered gambling.

Source: Wisegeek's "What Are Futures?"

contingent claim than either would be without the insurance contract. This does not mean that both parties expect to come out even. *On average*, your insurance company should earn a positive rate of return for offering you such a contract, which means that you should earn a negative expected rate of return. Of course, ex-post, only one of you will come out better off. If you have a bad accident, the insurance was a good deal for you and a bad deal for the insurance company. If you do not have an accident, the reverse is the case.

26.1A CALL AND PUT OPTIONS ON STOCK

Call and put options are contingent claims.

➤ Limited liability, Section 6.4, p. 155

Options are perhaps the most prominent type of contingent claim. And the most prominent option is simply the choice to walk away from an unprofitable position without retaining any obligation. A **call option** gives its holder the right to "call" (i.e., to buy) an underlying base security for a prespecified dollar amount—called the **strike price** or **exercise price**—usually for a specific period of time. A **put option** gives its holder the equivalent right to "put" (i.e., to sell) the security. Naturally, the values of these rights depend on the value of the base asset, which can fluctuate over time. Let's look at these options in more detail.

CALL OPTIONS

Example #1: Call options give the right to buy—upside participation.

Table 26.1 shows a number of options that were trading on May 31, 2002. For example, you could have purchased a July IBM stock call option with a strike price of $85, thereby giving you the right to purchase one share of IBM stock at the price of $85 anywhere between May 31 and July 20, 2002. Call options increase in value as the underlying stock appreciates and decrease in value as the underlying stock depreciates. If on July 20, 2002, the price of a share of IBM stock was below $85, your right would have been worthless: Shares would have been cheaper to purchase on the open market. (Indeed, exercising would have lost money: Purchasing shares that are worth, say, $70, for $85 would not be a brilliant idea.) Again, the beauty of owning a call option is that you can just walk away. However, if on July 20, 2002, the price of a share of IBM stock was above $85, then your call option (purchase right) would have been worth the difference between what IBM stock was trading for and your exercise price of $85. You

TABLE 26.1 SOME IBM OPTION PRICES ON MAY 31, 2002

Underlying Base Asset		Expiration T	Strike Price K	Call Price	Put Price
IBM	$80.50	July 20, 2002	$85	$1.900	$6.200
		Different Strike Prices			
IBM	$80.50	July 20, 2002	$75	$7.400	$1.725
IBM	$80.50	July 20, 2002	$80	$4.150	$3.400
IBM	$80.50	July 20, 2002	$90	$0.725	$10.100
		Different Expiration Dates			
IBM	$80.50	Oct. 19, 2002	$85	$4.550	$8.700
IBM	$80.50	Jan. 18, 2003	$85	$6.550	$10.200

The source of these prices was OptionMetrics. July 20 was about 0.1333 years away. (IBM's closing price at 4:00 pm EST was 5 cents lower than what the website reported.) The prevailing interest rates were 1.77% over 1 month, and 1.95% over 6 months. For up-to-date option prices on IBM options, see, for example, http://finance.yahoo.com/q/op?s=IBM, or optionmetrics.com.

Source: Reproduced with permission of Yahoo! Inc. © 2008 by Yahoo! Inc. YAHOO! and the YAHOO! logo are trademarks of Yahoo! Inc.

should have exercised the right to purchase the share at $85 from the call writer. For example, if the price of IBM stock turned out to be $100, you would have enjoyed an immediate net payoff of $100 − $85 = $15. The relationship between the call value and the stock value an instant before the call option expires is

$$C_T(K = \$85,\ \text{at } T \text{ on July 20, 2002} \Leftrightarrow \text{ remaining time } t = 0\,) = \max(0,\ S_T - \$85)$$

$$C_T(K, t = 0) = \max(0,\ S_T - K)$$

where C_T is the value of the call option on the final date T, given the (pre-agreed) strike price K. If the stock price at expiration, S_T, is above K, the option owner earns the difference between S_T and K. If S_T is below K, then the option owner will not exercise the option and earn zero. (The max function means "take whichever of its arguments is the bigger.") Note that, like other derivatives, an option is like a side bet between two outside observers of the stock price. Neither party necessarily needs to own any stock. Therefore, because the person owning the call is paid $\max(0,\ S_T - K)$ at the final date (relative to not owning the call), the person having sold the call must pay $\max(0,\ S_T - K)$ (relative to not having written the call).

The upfront price of the option compensates the option writer.

Why would someone sell ("write") an option? The answer is "for the money up front." Table 26.1 shows that on May 31, 2002 (when IBM stock was trading for $80.50), an IBM call with a strike price of $85 and an expiration date of July 20, 2002, cost $1.90. As long as the upfront price is fair—and many option markets tend to be close to perfect—neither the purchaser nor the seller comes out for the worse. Indeed, as already noted, because both parties voluntarily engage in the contract, they should both be better off ex-ante. Of course, ex-post, the financial contract will force one side to pay the other, making one side financially worse off and the other side financially better off, relative to not having written the contract.

Call options are often used by shareholders to sell off some of the upside. For example, the following are common motivations for participants:

What could be the participants' deeper motives?

The buyer: Why would someone want to purchase a call option? It's just another way to speculate that IBM's stock price will go up—and it is very efficient in terms of its use of cash up front. In May 2002, the option to purchase IBM at $90 until July 20, 2002, cost only $0.725 per share, much less than the $80.50 that one IBM share cost at the time.

The seller: As a large IBM share owner, you may have decided that you wanted to keep the upside until $90 but did not care as much about the upside beyond $90 (or you believed that the IBM share price would not rise beyond $90 by July 20, 2002). In this case, you might have sold a $90 call option today. This would have given you an immediate payment of $0.725. You could have invested this anywhere (including into more IBM shares or Treasuries). The extra cash of $0.725 would have boosted your rate of return if the IBM stock price had remained below $90. But if IBM had ended up at $120, you would have participated only in the first $9.50 gain (from $80.50 to $90). (Of course, you would also have kept the upfront option payment.) The remaining $30 of the IBM upside would have gone to your call option purchaser instead of to you.

If you write an option on a stock that you are holding, it is called "writing a covered option." Effectively, this is like a hedged position, being long in the stock and short in the call. Thus, if properly arranged, its risk is modest. However, there are also some sellers that write options without owning the underlying stock. This is called naked option writing. (I kid you not.) Lacking the long leg of the hedge, this can be a very risky proposition. In our extreme $120 example, the option buyer would have had a rate of return on the option alone of $(\$30 - \$0.725)/\$0.725 \approx 4{,}038\%$. Thus, the option seller would have lost 4,038%. (You can exceed −100% because your liability is not limited to your investment.) Writing naked out-of-the-money options is sometimes compared to picking up pennies in front of a steamroller—profitable most of the time, but with a huge risk.

Do you want to be caught naked?

PUT OPTIONS

In some sense, a **put option** is the flip side of a call option. It gives the owner the right (but not the obligation) to "put" (i.e., sell) an underlying security for a specific period of time in exchange for a prespecified price. For example, again in May 2002, you could have purchased a put option for the right to sell one share of IBM stock at the price of $75 up until July 20, 2002. This option would have cost you $1.725, according to Table 26.1. Unlike a call option, a put option speculates that the underlying security will decline in value. If the price of a share of IBM stock had remained above $75 before July 20, 2002, the put right would have been worthless: Shares could be sold for more on the open market. However, if the price of a share of IBM stock was below $75 on the expiration date, the put right would have been worth the difference between $75 and IBM's stock price. For example, if the IBM share price had been $50, the put owner could have purchased one share of IBM at $50 on the open market and exercised the right to sell the share at $75 to the option writer for an immediate net payoff of $25. The relationship between the put value and the stock value at the final moment when the put option expires can be written as

Example #2: Put options give the right to sell—downside protection.

$$P_T(K = \$75, \text{ at } T \text{ on July 20, 2002} \Leftrightarrow \text{remaining time } t = 0) = \max(0, \$75 - S_T)$$
$$P_T(K, t = 0) = \max(0, K - S_T)$$

A common use of a put is protection (insurance).

Put options are often purchased as "insurance" by investors. For example, if you had owned a lot of IBM shares when they were trading at \$80.50/share on May 31, 2002, you may have been willing to live with a little bit of loss, but not a lot. In this case, you might have purchased put options with a strike price of \$75. If IBM were to have ended up at \$60 per share on July 20, 2002, the gain on your put option (\$15/put) would have made up for some of the losses (\$20.50/share) on your underlying IBM shares. Of course, buying this put option insurance would have cost you money—\$1.725 per share to be exact.

SOLVE NOW!

Q 26.1 How is owning a call option the same as selling a put option? How is it different?

26.1B MORE INSTITUTIONAL STOCK OPTION ARRANGEMENTS

American options can be exercised *before* expiration. European options can be exercised only *at* expiration.

There are a variety of other option contract features. One common feature is based on the time at which exercise can occur. An **American option** allows the holder of the option to exercise the right any time up to, and including, the expiration date. The largest financial market for trading options on stocks is the **Chicago Board Options Exchange** (**CBOE**) and its options are usually of the American type. A less common form is called a **European option**. It allows the holder of the option to exercise the right only at the expiration date. The popular S&P index options are of the European type.

Splits and dividends?

What happens to the value of a CBOE stock option when the underlying stock pays a dividend or executes a stock split? In a stock split, a company decides to change the meaning, but not the value, of its shares. For example, in a 2-for-1 split, an owner who held 1,000 shares at \$80.50/share would now own 2,000 shares at \$40.25 per share (at least in a perfect market). Splitting itself should not create shareholder value—it should not change the market capitalization of the underlying company.

➤ Stock splits, Section 19.1A, p. 705

ANECDOTE Geography and Options

The origin of the terms "European" and "American" is a historical coincidence, not a reflection of what kind of options are traded where. Although no one seems to remember the origins of these designations, one conjecture is that contracts called "primes" were traded in France. These could only be exercised at maturity—but they were not exactly what are now called European options. Instead, the option owner either exercised (and received $S - K$) or did not exercise and paid a "penalty" fee of D called a "dont" (not "don't"). There was no upfront cost. (The best strategy for the prime owner was to exercise if $S - X > -D$.) Because these contracts could only be exercised at maturity and because American options could be exercised at any time, the terminology may have stuck.

Incidentally, "Bermuda options," or "Atlantic options," can be exercised periodically before maturity but not at any other time. They are so named not because they are used in Bermuda, but because Bermuda (and of course the Atlantic Ocean) lies between Europe and America.

Although such a split should make little difference to the owners of the shares ($80,500 worth of shares, no matter what), it could be bad news for the owner of a call option. After all, a call with a strike price of $75 would have been **in-the-money** (i.e., the underlying share price of $80.50 was above the strike price) before the split. If the option were American, the call would be worth $5.50 per share if exercised immediately. After the split, however, the call would be far **out-of-the-money** (i.e., the underlying share price of $40.25 would be far below the strike price of $75). Fortunately, the option contracts that are traded on most exchanges (e.g., the CBOE) automatically adjust for stock splits, so that the value of the option does not change when a stock split occurs: In this case, the option's effective strike price would automatically halve from $75 to $37.50 and the number of calls would automatically double from 1 to 2. (Completing the options terminology, not surprisingly, **at-the-money** means that the share price and the strike price are about equal.)

Most options are adjusted for splits.

But common options are typically *not* adjusted for dividend payments: If the $80.50 IBM share were to pay out $40 in dividends, and unless dividends fall like manna from heaven, then the post-dividend share price would have to drop to around $40.50. Therefore, the in-the-money call option would become an out-of-the-money call option. Consequently, if your call was American, you might decide to exercise your call with a $75 strike price to net $5.50 just before the dividend date.

But options are usually not adjusted for dividends.

➤ Dividend ex-day price drop, Section 19.4B, p. 721

IMPORTANT: When you purchase/value a typical financial stock option, the contract is written in a way that renders stock splits but not dividend payments irrelevant.

There are other important institutional details that you should know if you want to trade options. First, because the value of options can be very small (e.g., 72.5 cents for each IBM call option), they are usually traded in bundles of 100. This is called an **option contract**. Five option contracts on IBM are therefore 500 options (options on 500 shares), which in the example would cost $\$0.725 \cdot 500 = \$362.50$. Second, CBOE options typically expire on the Saturday following the third Friday of each month, which is where our 20th of July came from. Third, published option prices can be mismatched to the underlying stock price. The CBOE closing price is at 4:00 pm CST (5:00 pm EST), which is 1 hour later than the closing price from the NYSE (4:00 pm EST). This sometimes leads to seeming arbitrages in printed quotes, which are not really there. Instead, what usually happens is that the underlying stock price has changed between 4:00 pm and 5:00 pm and the printed quotes do not reflect the change. (In addition, the closing price may be a recent bid or recent ask quote, rather than the price at which you could actually transact.)

One option contract is (a bundle of) 100 options.

SOLVE NOW!

Q 26.2 An option is far in-the-money and will expire tonight. How would you expect its value to change when the stock price changes?

Q 26.3 In a perfect market, would a put option holder welcome an unexpected stock split? In a perfect market, would a put option owner welcome an unexpected dividend increase?

26.1C OPTION PAYOFFS AT EXPIRATION

Payoff diagrams describe (European) options.

➤ Payoff diagrams in the building and capital structure context, Section 6.4, p. 155

It is easiest to gain more intuition about an option by studying its payoff diagram (and payoff table). You have already seen these in the building and capital structure contexts. They show the value of the option as a function of the underlying base asset at the final moment before expiration. Figure 26.1 shows the payoff tables and payoff diagrams for a call and a put option, each with a strike price of $90. The characteristic of any option's payoff is the kink at the strike price: For the call, the value is zero below the strike price, and a +45-degree line above the strike price. For the put, the value is zero above the strike price, and a −45-degree line below the strike price.

OPTIONAL: MORE COMPLEX OPTION STRATEGIES

Some common complex option strategies.

Payoff diagrams can also help you understand more complex option-based strategies, which are very popular on Wall Street. Such strategies may go long and/or short in different options at the same time. They can allow you to speculate on all sorts of future developments for the stock price—for example, that the stock price will be above $60 and below $70. In many (but not all) cases, it is not clear why someone would want to engage in such strategies, except for speculation.

Payoff diagrams for spreads and combinations.

Two important classes of complex option strategies are **spreads**, which consist of long and short options of the same type (calls or puts), and **combinations**, which consist of options of different types.

A **simple spread** is a position that is long one option and short another option, on the same stock. The options here are of the same type (puts or calls) and have the same expiration date but different strike prices. For example, a simple spread may purchase one put with a strike price of $90 and sell one put with a strike price of $70. Figure 26.2 plots the payoff diagram for this position.

A **complex spread** contains multiple options, some short, others long. You will get to graph the payoff diagram of a so-called butterfly spread in Question 26.6.

A **straddle** may be the most popular combination. It combines one put and one call, both either long or short, often with the same strike price and with the same time to expiration. You will get to graph the payoff diagram in Question 26.25.

In sum,

Option Strategy	Version A	Version B
Simple Spread	Long Call, Short Call	Long Put, Short Put
Combination	Long Call, Short Put	Short Call, Long Put
Straddle	Long Call, Long Put	Short Call, Short Put

$Stock_T$	$Call_T$	Put_T	$Stock_T$	$Call_T$	Put_T
\$0	\$0	\$90	\$100	\$10	\$0
\$25	\$0	\$65	\$125	\$35	\$0
\$50	\$0	\$40	\$150	\$60	\$0
\$75	\$0	\$15	\$175	\$85	\$0

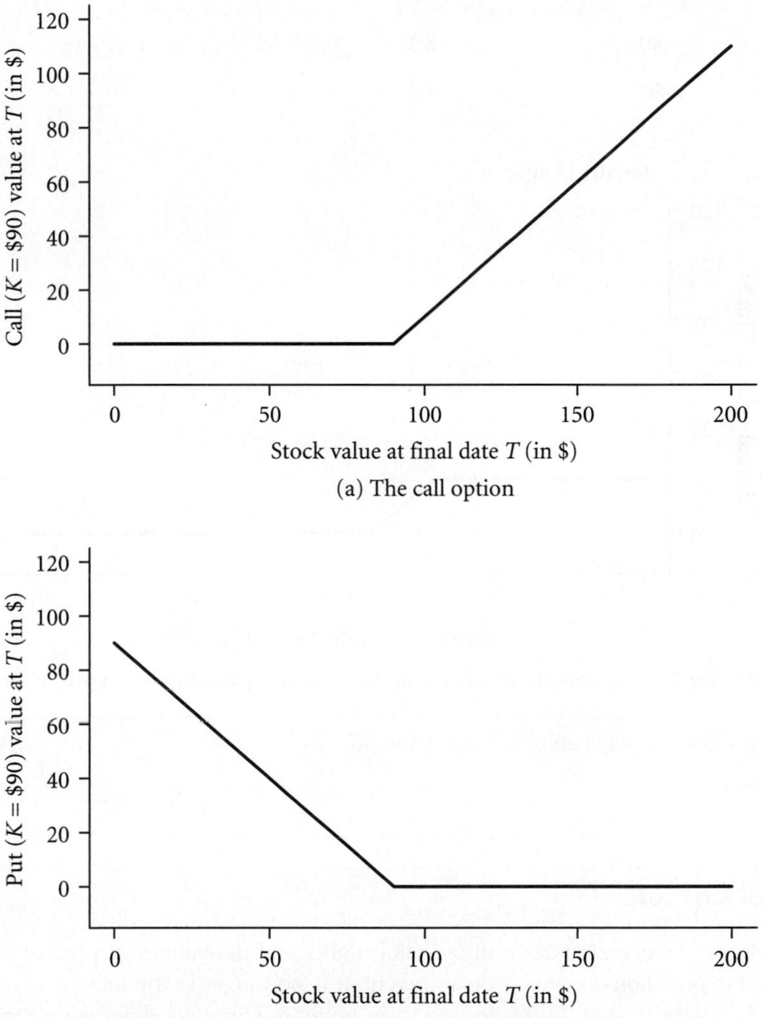

(b) The put option

Note: In Figure 26.3, we will graph the value of an option *prior to* expiration.

FIGURE 26.1 Payoff Table and Payoff Diagrams of Options with Strike Price $K = \$90$ on the Expiration Date T

Payoff Table

$Stock_T$	Long Put($K = \$90$)	Short Put($K = \$70$)	Net
\$50	\$40	−\$20	\$20
\$60	\$30	−\$10	\$20
\$70	\$20	\$0	\$20
\$80	\$10	\$0	\$10
\$90	\$0	\$0	\$0
\$100	\$0	\$0	\$0

Payoff Diagram

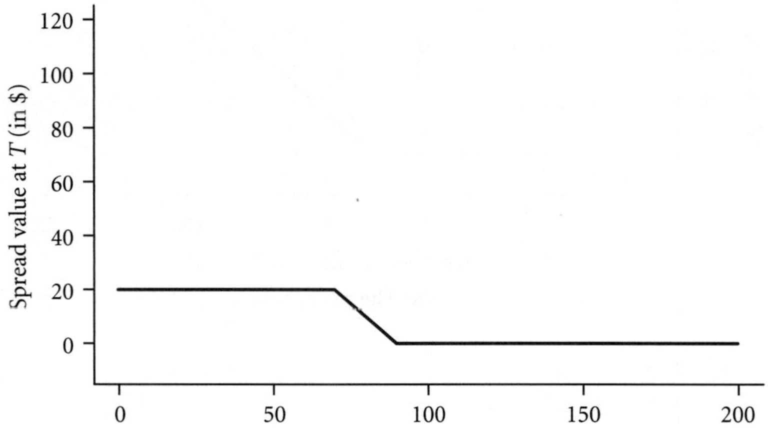

This spread is long 1 put option with a strike price of \$90 and short 1 put option with a strike price of \$70.

FIGURE 26.2 Payoff Diagram of a Simple Spread

ANECDOTE Environmental Options

Publicly traded options extend beyond stocks. For example, there is an active market in pollution options, which give option owners the legal right to spew out emissions such as CO_2. Experts generally agree that despite some shortcomings, the system of permitting trading in pollution rights and derivatives has led to a cleaner environment. It is no longer in the interest of a polluter to maximize pollution: Shutting down an old plant and selling the right to pollute can be more profitable than operating the plant.

A rarer strategy is the **calendar spread**, which is a position that is long one option and short another option, on the same stock. The options are of the same type (puts or calls) and have the same strike prices but different expiration dates. Therefore, they do not lend themselves to easy graphing via payoff diagrams because payoff diagrams hold the expiration date constant.

SOLVE NOW!

Q 26.4 Write down the payoff table and draw the payoff diagram (both at expiration) of a portfolio consisting of 1 call option with a strike price K of \$60 and 1 put option with a strike price K of \$80.

Q 26.5 Write down the payoff table and draw the payoff diagram (both at expiration) of a portfolio consisting of 1 call *short* with a strike price K of \$60 and 1 put *short* with a strike price K of \$80.

Q 26.6 Graph the payoff diagram for the following butterfly spread:
- 1 long call option with a strike price of \$50
- 2 short call options with strike prices of \$55
- 1 long call option with a strike price of \$60

26.2 STATIC NO-ARBITRAGE RELATIONSHIPS

There are very few pricing bounds on underlying asset prices.

How easy is it to value an underlying stock? For example, to value the shares of IBM, you have to determine all future cash flows of IBM's underlying projects with their appropriate costs of capital. You already know that this is very difficult. I cannot even tell you with great confidence that the price of an IBM share should be within a range that is bounded by a factor of 3 (say, between \$50 and \$150).

But there are good pricing bounds on their derivatives.

In contrast, it is possible to find very good pricing bounds for options. Intuitively, the law of one price works quite well for them. The reason is that you can design a clever position—consisting of the underlying stocks and bonds—that has virtually the same payoffs as a call (or a put) option. Thus, the price of the call option should be very similar to the price of the securities you need to create such a call-mimicking position. This is a no-arbitrage argument. *The price of an option should be such that no arbitrage is possible.*

➤ Arbitrage, Section 11.4, p. 360

26.2A SOME SIMPLE NO-ARBITRAGE REQUIREMENTS

The value of the option depends on the stock, which makes the option price easier to determine.

Let us derive the first pricing bound: A call option cannot be worth more than the underlying base asset. For example, if IBM trades for \$80.50 per share, a call option with a strike price of, say, \$50 cannot cost \$85 per option. If it did, you should purchase the share and sell the call. Today, you would make \$85 − \$80.50 = \$4.50. In the future, if the stock price goes up and the call buyer exercises, you deliver the one share you have, still having pocketed the \$4.50 net gain. If the stock price goes down and the call buyer does not exercise, you still own the share plus the upfront fee. Therefore, lack of arbitrage dictates that the value of the call C_0 today must be (weakly) below the value of the stock S_0,

$$C_0 \leq S_0$$

This is an upper bound on what a call can be worth. It improves your knowledge of what a reasonable price for a call can be. It may be weak, but at least it exists—there is no comparable upper bound on the value of the underlying stock!

Selected (obvious) static no-arbitrage relations.

There are many other option pricing relations that give you other bounds on what the option price can be today. For notation, call $C_0(K, t)$ the call option price today,

K the strike price, (lowercase) t the time to option expiration, and P_0 the put option price today. Here are some more pricing bounds:

- Because the option owner only exercises it if it is in-the-money, an option must have a nonnegative value. Therefore,

$$C_0 \geq 0, \quad P_0 \geq 0$$

- It is better to own a call option with a lower exercise price. Therefore,

$$K_{\text{High}} \geq K_{\text{Low}} \Longleftrightarrow C_0(K_{\text{Low}}) \geq C_0(K_{\text{High}})$$

- It is better to own a put option with a higher exercise price. Therefore,

$$K_{\text{High}} \geq K_{\text{Low}} \Longleftrightarrow P_0(K_{\text{Low}}) \leq P_0(K_{\text{High}})$$

American options, which can immediately be exercised, enjoy further arbitrage bounds:

- The value of an American call today must be no less than what you can receive from exercising it immediately. Therefore,

$$C_0 \geq \max(0, S_0 - K)$$

- The value of an American put today must be no less than what you can receive from exercising it immediately. Therefore,

$$P_0 \geq \max(0, K - S_0)$$

- It is better to have an American call option that expires later. Therefore,

$$t_{\text{Longer}} \geq t_{\text{Shorter}} \Longleftrightarrow C_0(t_{\text{Longer}}) \geq C_0(t_{\text{Shorter}})$$

- It is better to have an American put option that expires later. Therefore,

$$t_{\text{Longer}} \geq t_{\text{Shorter}} \Longleftrightarrow P_0(t_{\text{Longer}}) \geq P_0(t_{\text{Shorter}})$$

These are commonly called **no-arbitrage relationships**, for obvious reasons.

26.2B PUT-CALL PARITY

Put-call parity via example.

There is one especially interesting and important no-arbitrage relationship, called **put-call parity**. It relates the price of a European call to the price of its equivalent European put, the underlying stock price, and the interest rate. Here is how it works. Assume the following:

- The interest rate is 10% per year.
- The current stock price S_0 is \$80.

TABLE 26.2 SAMPLE PUT-CALL PARITY VIOLATION

Today			**At Final Expiration Time T**				
		Covering S_T Range:	$S_T < \$100$		$S_T = \$100$	$S_T > \$100$	
Execute	Cash Flow	Price S_T is:	\$80	\$90	\$100	\$110	\$120
Purchase 1 call with strike price $K = \$100$	−\$30.00 $-C_0(K)$	You can exercise	\$0 \$0	\$0 \$0	\$0 $S_T - K$	+\$10 $S_T - K$	+\$20 $S_T - K$
Sell 1 put with strike price $K = \$100$	+\$50.00 $+P_0(K)$	Your buyer can exercise	−\$20 $S_T - K$	−\$10 $S_T - K$	\$0 $S_T - K$	\$0 \$0	\$0 \$0
Sell 1 share (= short 1 share):	+\$80.00 $+S_0$	The short is closed	−\$80 $-S_T$	−\$90 $-S_T$	−\$100 $-S_T$	−\$110 $-S_T$	−\$120 $-S_T$
Save money, to pay the PV of the strike price	−\$90.91 $-\text{PV}_0(K)$	You get your money back	+\$100 +\$K	+\$100 +\$K	+\$100 +\$K	+\$100 +\$K	+\$100 +\$K
Net =	+\$9.09	Net =	\$0 \$0	\$0 \$0	\$0 \$0	\$0 \$0	\$0 \$0

The net arbitrage profit is

$$(-\$30) + (+\$50) + (+\$80) + (-\$90.91) = (+\$9.09)$$

$$-\ C_0(K) + P_0(K) + S_0 - \text{PV}_0(K) = \text{This is not } \$0. \Rightarrow \text{This is a put-call parity arbitrage violation.}$$

- A 1-year European call option with a strike price of \$100 costs $C_0(K = \$100) = \$30$.
- A 1-year European put option with a strike price of \$100 costs $P_0(K = \$100) = \$50$.

Further, assume that there are no dividends (which is important). Because the options are European, you only need to consider what you pay now and what will happen at expiration T. (Nothing can happen in between.) If this were the situation, could you get rich? Try the position in Table 26.2. (You can check the sign, because any position that gives you a positive inflow today must give you a negative outflow tomorrow, or vice versa. Otherwise, you would have a security that always makes, or always loses, money.)

The prices in the table violate put-call parity ⇒ arbitrage.

Table 26.2 shows that you could sell one put for \$50 and short one share (for proceeds of \$80 from the buyer). You would use the \$130 in cash to buy one call for \$30 and deposit \$90.91 in the bank. This leaves you with your free lunch of \$9.09. The table also shows that regardless of how the stock price turns out, you will not have to pay anything. This is an arbitrage. Naturally, you should not expect this to happen in the real world: One of the securities is obviously mispriced here. Given that the risk-free interest rate applies to all securities, and given that the stock price is what it is, you can think of put-call parity as relating the price of the call option to the price of the put option, and vice versa—and in this example, either the call is too cheap or the put is too expensive.

Put-call parity via algebra.

As usual, the algebraic formulas are just under the numerical calculations. The table shows that put-call parity means that the world is sane only if

$$-\ C_0(K) + P_0(K) + S_0 - \mathrm{PV}_0(K) = 0 \Leftrightarrow C_0(K) = P_0(K) + S_0 - \mathrm{PV}_0(K)$$

➤ Table 26.1, p. 980

Let's apply put-call parity to the option prices in Table 26.1. An IBM put with a strike price of \$85, expiring on July 20, 2002, costs \$6.200. The expiration was 34 out of 255 trading days away ($34/255 \approx 0.1333$ years), or, if you prefer, 50 out of 365 actual days ($50/365 \approx 0.137$ years)—this is rounding error that makes little difference. The prevailing interest rate was 1.77% per annum. Thus, the strike price of \$85 was worth $\$85/(1 + 1.77\%)^{0.133} \approx \$84.80$. Put-call parity implies that the call should cost

$$\begin{aligned} C_0(K) &\approx \$6.20 + \$80.50 - \$84.80 = \$1.90 \\ C_0(K) &= P_0(K) + \quad S_0 \quad - \mathrm{PV}_0(K) \end{aligned}$$

This was indeed the call price in the market, as you can see in Table 26.1.

IMPORTANT: Given an interest rate and the current stock price, the prices of a European call option and a European put option with identical expiration dates and strike prices are related by put-call parity,

$$C_0(K) = P_0(K) + S_0 - \mathrm{PV}_0(K) \qquad (26.1)$$

The stock must not pay dividends before expiration.

SOLVE NOW!

Q 26.7 Write down the put-call parity formula, preferably without referring back to the text. What are the inputs?

Q 26.8 A 1-year call option with a strike price of \$80 costs \$20. A share costs \$70. The interest rate is 10% per year.

(a) What should a 1-year put option with a strike price of \$80 trade for?

(b) How could you earn money if the put option with a strike price of \$80 traded in the market for \$25 per share instead? Be explicit in what you would have to short (sell) and what you would have to long (buy).

26.2C THE AMERICAN EARLY EXERCISE FEATURE

Although put-call parity applies *only* to European options, it has the interesting and clever implication that American call options should never be exercised early. (Again, keep in mind that the underlying stock must *not* pay dividends.) Here is why: If an American call option is exercised immediately, it pays $C_0 = S_0 - K$. If the call is not exercised immediately, is the live option price more or less than this? Well, you know that the American option cannot be worth less than an equivalent European, because you can always hold onto the American option until expiration:

Assuming no dividends on the stock, put-call parity implies that an American call is never exercised early.

$$\text{American Call Value} \geq \text{European Call Value}$$

Put-call parity tells you that the European call price is

$$\text{European Call Value} = C_0 = P_0(K) + S_0 - \text{PV}_0(K)$$

$P_0(K)$ is a positive number and $\text{PV}_0(K)$ is less than K, which means that

$$\begin{aligned}\text{American Call Value} &\geq \text{European Call Value}\\ &= P_0(K) + S_0 - \text{PV}_0(K)\\ &\geq S_0 - \text{PV}_0(K)\\ &\geq S_0 - K\end{aligned}$$

Therefore, the prevailing value of a live, unexercised American call is always at least equal to what you could get from its immediate exercise $(S_0 - K)$. If you need money, sell the call in the market (at its arbitrage-determined value) and don't exercise it! By the way, you can also see from Table 26.1 that the American call price was higher than what you could have gotten from immediate exercise. For example, the July 20, 2002, call with a strike price of $75 would have netted you only $80.50 − $75 = $5.50 upon immediate exercise, but $7.40 in the open market.

➤ Table 26.1, p. 980

In sum, the value of the right to exercise early an American call option on a non-dividend-paying stock is zero. Therefore, an American call option—even though it can be exercised before expiration—is not worth more than the equivalent European call option:

Thus, such an American call is like a European call.

$$\text{American Call Value} = \text{European Call Value}$$

> **IMPORTANT:** Assuming that the underlying stock pays no dividends, put-call parity implies that the value of an American call option is higher alive than if it is immediately exercised. Therefore, the American right to exercise early is worthless, and the price of a European call option is the same as the price of an American call option.

However, you may want to exercise other American options early.

However, there are cases when early exercise can be valuable, and in this case, American options are worth more than European options. Consider extreme examples for two cases:

Calls on dividend-paying stocks: If the underlying stock pays a liquidating dividend, and the call is in-the-money, it definitely becomes worthwhile for the American call option holder to exercise the call just before the dividend is paid.

Put options: If you have a 100-year put option with a strike price of \$1 on a stock that trades for \$100 today, it is worthwhile to exercise the option, collect \$99, and invest this money elsewhere to earn interest. Given that stocks appreciate on average, waiting 100 years to expiration reduces your payoff.

SOLVE NOW!

Q 26.9 Under what conditions can a European option be worth as much as the equivalent American option?

Q 26.10 Compare the direct value of exercising an American put that is in-the-money (you get $K - S_0$) to the value of the put in the put-call parity formula $P_0(K) = C_0(K) + \left[\text{PV}_0(K) - S_0\right]$. Under what conditions is it better not to exercise the American put?

26.3 VALUING OPTIONS FROM UNDERLYING STOCK PRICES

Without the put price, put-call parity does not give you the call price (and vice versa).

Put-call parity gives you the value of a call option if you know the value of the equivalent put option (or vice versa). Unfortunately, if you don't know the value of either the put or the call, you cannot pin down the value of the other. To determine the price of either, you need a formula that values one of them if all you have is the underlying stock price.

Finding the call price without the put. An intuitive explanation for binomial pricing.

Valuing an option from just the underlying stock (and risk-free bonds) requires a new idea—*dynamic arbitrage*. It asks you to construct a mimicking portfolio consisting of the underlying stock and borrowed cash, so that the call option and your mimicking portfolio always change by the same amount over the next instant. In our example, IBM stock trades for \$80.50. Now presume that it can either increase by 1 cent to \$80.51 or decrease by 1 cent to \$80.49. (This is why this method is called binomial pricing.) How much would the value of the IBM call with a strike price of \$85 change? The answer turns out to be about 0.3371 cents. Thus, your mimicking portfolio would invest about 33.71% · \$80.50 ≈ \$27.14 into IBM stock. In addition, you would have to take into consideration that you may have to pay the strike price, which is essentially handled by borrowing the appropriate amount of cash. If you do this right, then the mimicking portfolio and the call option will respond to a 1-cent change over one instant in the price of underlying IBM stock in exactly the same way. The law of one price then means that the IBM call and the mimicking portfolio (consisting of IBM stock and borrowing) should cost the same amount. Unlike static arbitrage (where you can establish a position once and then wait until expiration), dynamic arbitrage does not allow you to sit back. After this first instant, you will have to change your stock and borrowings again. If IBM goes up, then you will have to establish a stock position different from the one where IBM goes down.

Why you see a formula drop from the sky.

The details of the binomial pricing method are explained in more detail in the chapter appendix. The bad news is that it is very tedious—you have to work out all possible stock price paths until expiration. The good news is that it is a mechanical method—well suited to computer programming—and that it is very flexible. It can handle all kinds of options (even American puts and dividend-paying stocks). The best news is that there is one special-case version that gives you a quick formula for the price of a European call option on a stock without dividends. It is called the Black-Scholes formula (named after Fischer Black and Myron Scholes for their 1973 article). This formula, and the dynamic arbitrage concept on which it is based, rank among the most important advances of modern finance. Its inventors were justly honored with half an economics Nobel Prize in 1997. (The other half went to Robert Merton for his set of no-arbitrage static relationships that you already learned above.) Let me show you how to use this formula.

26.3A THE BLACK-SCHOLES FORMULA

The Black-Scholes formula is not perfect, but it works quite well in pricing real-world options.

Unlike the CAPM, which provides only modestly accurate appropriate expected rates of return, the Black-Scholes formula is usually very accurate in practice. The reason why it works so well is that it is built around an arbitrage argument—although one that requires constant dynamic trading. It turns out that, as a potential arbitrageur, you can obtain the exact same payoffs that you receive from the call if you purchase the underlying stocks and bonds in just the right proportion and trade them infinitely often. (This is explained in detail in the chapter appendix.) In other words, if the call price does not equal the same price, then you could get rich in a perfect market. In an imperfect real world, the call price can diverge a little from the Black-Scholes price, but not much beyond transaction costs. In contrast, if the CAPM formula is not satisfied, you may find some great portfolio bets—but there are usually no arbitrage opportunities.

26.3B AN EXAMPLE USE OF THE BLACK-SCHOLES FORMULA

The best way to understand how to use Black-Scholes is to use it once.

Although the Black-Scholes formula may look awe-inspiring, it is not as daunting as it appears at first sight. Let's use it to determine the price of a sample call option:

Stock Price Today	S_0	\$80.50
Agreed-Upon Strike Price	K	\$85.00
Time Remaining to Maturity	t	0.1333 years
Interest Rate on Risk-Free Bonds	r_F	1.77% per year
Volatility (Standard Deviation) of the Underlying Stock	σ	30% per year

Your task is to determine the Black-Scholes call value:

$$C_0(S_0 = \$80.50,\ K = \$85,\ t = 0.1333,\ r_F = 1.77\%,\ \sigma = 30\%) = ?$$

IMPORTANT: The **Black-Scholes** formula gives the value of a call option on a stock not paying dividends:

$$C_0(S_0, K, t, r_F, \sigma) = S_0 \cdot \mathcal{N}(d_1) - \text{PV}_0(K) \cdot \mathcal{N}(d_2)$$

where you compute $$d_1 = \frac{\ln[S_0/\text{PV}_0(K)]}{\sigma \cdot \sqrt{t}} + 1/2 \cdot \sigma \cdot \sqrt{t}$$

and $$d_2 = d_1 - \sigma \cdot \sqrt{t}$$

The five inputs are as follows:

S_0	is today's stock price.
t	is the time left to maturity.
K	is the strike price.
$\text{PV}_0(K)$	is the present value of K that depends on r_F (the risk-free interest rate input, which is used only to compute $\text{PV}_0(K)$).
σ	is the standard deviation of the underlying stock's continuously compounded rate of return, and it is often casually called just "the stock volatility." It is very similar to the stock's rate of return standard deviation, $\mathcal{S}dv$ (from Chapter 8). However, each rate of return must first be converted into its continuously compounded equivalent (from Section 5.11 on page 130) by calculating the natural log of one plus the rate of return. For example, if the two simple rates of return are +1% and −0.5%, you would compute the standard deviation from $\ln(1 + 1\%) \approx 0.995\%$ and $\ln(1 - 0.5\%) \approx -0.501\%$. The returns (and therefore $\mathcal{S}dv$ and σ) are similar if rates of return are low.

Note that the three parameters t, r_F, and σ have to be quoted in the same time units. (Typically, they are quoted in annualized terms.) These are the two functions:

$\ln(\cdot)$	is the *natural* log.
$\mathcal{N}(\cdot)$	is the **cumulative normal distribution** function. (Spreadsheets call this the "**normsdist()**" function.) You can also look up its values in a table in the book appendix on page A-8.

This requires five steps:

1. Compute the present value of the strike price. For the approximately 7 weeks left, the interest rate would have been $(1 + 1.77\%)^{0.1333} - 1 \approx 0.2342\%$. Therefore, the $\text{PV}_0(\$85) \approx \$84.80$.
2. Compute the input d_1, which is needed later as the argument in the left cumulative normal distribution function:

$$
\begin{aligned}
d_1 &= \frac{\ln(S_0/\text{PV}_0(K))}{\sigma \cdot \sqrt{t}} + 1/2 \cdot \sigma \cdot \sqrt{t} \\
&= \frac{\ln[\$80.50/\text{PV}_0(\$85)]}{30\% \cdot \sqrt{0.1333}} + 1/2 \cdot 30\% \cdot \sqrt{0.1333} \\
&\approx \frac{\ln(\$80.50/\$84.80)}{30\% \cdot 0.365} + 1/2 \cdot 30\% \cdot 0.365 \\
&\approx \frac{\ln(0.949)}{10.95\%} + 1/2 \cdot 10.95\% \\
&\approx \frac{-0.052}{10.95\%} + 5.48\% \\
&\approx -47.52\% + 5.48\% \\
&\approx -42.04\%
\end{aligned}
$$

(My calculations could be a little different from yours because I am carrying full precision.)

3. Compute d_2, the argument in the right cumulative normal distribution function:

$$
\begin{aligned}
d_2 &= d_1 - \sigma \cdot \sqrt{t} \\
&\approx -42.04\% - 30\% \cdot \sqrt{0.1333} \\
&\approx -42.04\% - 10.95\% \\
&\approx -53.00\%
\end{aligned}
$$

4. Look up the standard normal distribution for the d_1 and d_2 arguments in Table A.1, or use the spreadsheet **normsdist**() function:

➤ Cumulative normal distribution probabilities, Table A.1, p. A-8

$$\mathcal{N}(-0.4204) \approx 0.3371, \mathcal{N}(-0.5300) \approx 0.2981$$

5. Compute the Black-Scholes value:

$$
\begin{aligned}
&C_0(S_0 = \$80.50, K = \$85, t = 0.1333, r_F = 1.77\%, \sigma = 30\%) \\
&= S_0 \cdot \mathcal{N}(d_1) - \text{PV}_0(K) \cdot \mathcal{N}(d_2) \\
&\approx \$80.50 \cdot \mathcal{N}(-0.4204) - \$84.80 \cdot \mathcal{N}(-0.5300) \\
&\approx \$80.50 \cdot 0.3371 - \$84.80 \cdot 0.2981 \\
&\approx \$27.14 - \$25.28 \\
&\approx \$1.86
\end{aligned}
$$

In sum, a call option with a strike price of \$85 and 0.1333 years left to expiration on a stock with a current price of \$80.50 should cost about \$1.86, assuming that the underlying volatility is 30% per annum and the risk-free interest rate is 1.77%

per annum. Trust me when I state that the empirical evidence suggests that 30% per annum was a reasonably good estimate of IBM's volatility in 2002. If you look at Table 26.1, you will see that the actual call option price of just such an option was \$1.90, not far off from the theoretical Black-Scholes value of \$1.86.

➤ Table 26.1, p. 980

SOLVE NOW!

Q 26.11 What is the value of a call option with infinite time to maturity and a strike price of \$0? Use the parameters of the example: $S_0 = \$80.50$, $r_F = 1.77\%$, and $\sigma = 50\%$.

Q 26.12 Price a call option with a stock price of \$80, a strike price of \$75, 3 months to maturity, a 5% risk-free rate of return, and a standard deviation of 20% on the underlying stock.

26.3C THE BLACK-SCHOLES VALUE FOR OTHER OPTIONS

B-S can be used to price certain types of options, but not others.

The Black-Scholes formula prices European call options for stocks that pay no dividends. How can you apply the Black-Scholes formula to other options? First, the good news:

➤ No early exercise, Section 26.2C, p. 991

American calls on stocks without dividends: Because you would never exercise such a call before expiration, the value of an American call is equal to the value of a European call. Therefore, the Black-Scholes formula prices such American call options just as well as European call options.

➤ Put-call parity, Formula 26.1, p. 990

European puts: If you know the value of the European call option, you can use put-call parity to determine the value of a *European* put option with the same strike price and maturity as the call option. In our example,

$$P_0 \approx \$1.86 - \$80.50 + \$84.80 = \$6.16$$

$$P_0 = C_0 - S_0 + \text{PV}_0(K)$$

This happens to be close to, but not exactly equal to, the real-world (though American) put price of \$6.20 in Table 26.1.

Now the bad news: For other options, although there are sometimes ways to bend the Black-Scholes formula, you generally have to use the more complex binomial valuation technique explained in the chapter appendix to get an exact solution. This applies to American calls on dividend-paying stocks and to American puts.

SOLVE NOW!

Q 26.13 Price an IBM put option with a strike price of \$100, using the parameters of the example in the text: $t = 0.1333$, $r_F = 1.77\%$, $\sigma = 30\%$, $S_0 = \$80.50$.

(a) What is the price if the option is European?

(b) What is the price if the option is American? Would you continue holding onto it?

26.3D SYNTHETIC SECURITIES

A different way to look at arbitrage relationships is to recognize that they define securities. That is, even if a put option were not available in the financial markets, it would be easy for you to manufacture one (assuming minimal transaction costs, of course). For example, return to the put-call parity relationship. It states that European options have the relationship

How can you make a put option yourself?

$$C_0(K) = P_0(K) + S_0 - \text{PV}_0(K) \iff P_0(K) = C_0(K) - S_0 + \text{PV}_0(K)$$

Instead of purchasing one put option, you can purchase one call option, short one stock, and invest the present value of the strike price in Treasuries. You would receive the same payoffs as if you had purchased the put option itself. Therefore, you have manufactured a synthetic put option for yourself.

Creating synthetic securities has become a big business for Wall Street. For example, a client company owning gas stations may wish to obtain an option to purchase 10,000 barrels of crude oil in 10 years at a price of \$50 per barrel. A Wall Street supplier of such call options models the price of oil and determines the appropriate value of a synthetic call option. The gas station company then sells the call option to the firm for a little more. But would the Wall Street firm now not be exposed to changes in the oil price? Yes—but it would in turn try to hedge this risk away. In this example, the Wall Street firm could undertake a (usually dynamic) hedge—the same idea that underlies the Black-Scholes formula. That is, it would first determine its hedge ratio, which is the amount by which the value of a synthetic 10-year call option with a strike price of \$50 per barrel changes with the underlying oil price today. Say this value is 0.08. In this case, the Wall Street firm would purchase a forward contract for $10{,}000 \cdot 0.08 = 800$ barrels of oil. If the price of oil increases, then the Wall Street firm's own position in oil increases by the same amount as its obligation to the gas station company. This way, the Wall Street firm has low or no exposure to changes in the underlying oil price. And it has added value to its clients through its better ability to execute and monitor such dynamic hedges than the clients themselves.

Making and selling synthetic securities is big business on Wall Street.

➤ Hedge ratio, Section 26.4B, p. 999

➤ Forward contracts, Section 25.1B, p. 945

26.4 THE BLACK-SCHOLES INPUTS

Let us now look a bit more closely at the five ingredients of the Black-Scholes formula.

26.4A OBTAINING THE BLACK-SCHOLES FORMULA INPUTS

The first four inputs, S_0, K, t, and r_F, either are given by the option contract (the strike price K and time to expiration t) or can be easily found online (the current stock price S_0 and the risk-free interest rate r_F [required to compute $\text{PV}_0(K)$]). Only one input, σ, the standard deviation of the underlying stock returns, has to be guesstimated. There are two methods to do so.

Only σ, the standard deviation of the rate of return on the underlying stock, is difficult to estimate.

1. The old-fashioned way uses, say, 3–5 years of historical stock returns and computes the standard deviation of daily rates of return:

$$\sigma_{\text{Daily}} = \sqrt{\frac{\text{Sum from Day 1 to } N\text{: } (r_t - \overline{r})^2}{N - 1}}$$

➤ Continuous compounding, Section 5.11, p. 130

➤ Annualization and *sdv* time scaling, Question 8.35, p. 236

(To be perfectly accurate, the rates of return that you should be using here are continuously compounded, not simple rates of return.) Then, this number is annualized by multiplying it by $\sqrt{255}$, because 255 is the approximate number of trading days. For example, if the daily standard deviation is 1%, the annual standard deviation would be $\sqrt{255} \cdot 1\% \approx 16.0\%$. (Annualization is done by multiplying a standard deviation by the square root of the number of periods.)

2. If other call option prices are already known, it is possible to extract a volatility estimate using the Black-Scholes formula itself. For example, assume that the price of the stock is \$80.50 and the price of a July call with a strike price of \$80 is \$4.15.

$$C_0(S_0 = \$80.50,\ K = \$80,\ t = 34/255,\ r = 1.77\%,\ \sigma = ?) \approx \$4.15$$

What is the volatility of the underlying stock that is consistent with the \$4.15 price? The idea is to try different values of σ until the Black-Scholes formula exactly fits the known price of this option.

Start with a volatility guess of 0.20. After tedious calculations, you find that

$$C_0(S_0 = \$80.50,\ K = \$80,\ t \approx 0.1333,\ r = 1.77\%,\ \sigma = 0.20) \approx \$2.70$$

Option values increase with uncertainty, so this was too low a guess for σ. Try a higher value—say, 0.50:

$$C_0(S_0 = \$80.50,\ K = \$80,\ t \approx 0.1333,\ r = 1.77\%,\ \sigma = 0.50) \approx \$6.18$$

Too high. Try something in between. (Because \$4.15 is closer than \$2.70 than it is to \$6.18, try something a little bit closer to 0.20—say, 0.25.)

$$C_0(S_0 = \$80.50,\ K = \$80,\ t \approx 0.1333,\ r = 1.77\%,\ \sigma = 0.25) \approx \$3.27$$

Too low, but pretty close already. After a few more tries, you can determine that $\sigma \approx 0.325$ is the volatility that makes the Black-Scholes option pricing value equal to the actual call option price of \$4.15.

You can now work with this **implied volatility** estimate as if it were the best estimate of volatility, and use it to price other options with the Black-Scholes formula. Unlike the historical estimated volatility, the implied volatility is forward-looking! That is, it is the market guess of what volatility will be like in the future.

Obtaining an implied volatility is such a common procedure that many Web pages provide both the option price and the implied volatility. For instance, Table 26.3 shows OptionMetrics' reported implied volatilities. For the specific \$80 July call, OptionMetrics computed an implied volatility of 32.58%—just about the 32.5% that we computed ourselves.

Sometimes, this implied volatility is even used interchangeably with the option price itself. That is, instead of reporting the Black-Scholes call price, traders might just report that the option is priced at a "32.5% vol." This makes it sometimes easier to compare different options. Table 26.3 shows that the \$75 July call has a price of \$7.40, while the \$85 January put has a price of \$10.20. How do you

TABLE 26.3 ADDING IMPLIED VOLATILITIES TO TABLE 26.1

Underlying Base Asset		Expiration T	Strike Price K	Option Type	Option Price	Implied Volatility	Option Type	Option Price	Implied Volatility
IBM	\$80.50	July 20, 2002	\$85	Call	\$1.900	30.38%	Put	\$6.200	29.82%
		Different Strike Prices							
IBM	\$80.50	July 20, 2002	\$75	Call	\$7.400	34.89%	Put	\$1.725	34.51%
IBM	\$80.50	July 20, 2002	\$80	Call	\$4.150	32.58%	Put	\$3.400	31.67%
IBM	\$80.50	July 20, 2002	\$90	Call	\$0.725	29.24%	Put	\$10.100	29.18%
		Different Expiration Dates							
IBM	\$80.50	Oct. 19, 2002	\$85	Call	\$4.550	31.32%	Put	\$8.700	31.61%
IBM	\$80.50	Jan. 18, 2003	\$85	Call	\$6.550	31.71%	Put	\$10.200	31.40%

The source of both prices and implied volatilities was OptionMetrics on May 31, 2002. July 20 was 0.1333 years away. The prevailing interest rates were 1.77% over 1 month, and 1.95% over 6 months.

compare the two? Quoting them as volatilities—34.89% versus 31.40%—makes them easier to compare.

The volatility "smile," an empirical regularity, suggests that B-S prices for deep-out-of-the-money options are too low.

The Black-Scholes formula is not the only option pricing formula, although it is by far the most common and also usually the easiest to use. It is pretty accurate. However, there are similar formulas based on the same dynamic trading concept that can price options just a little better. In particular, they can explain what would be an anomaly from the perspective of the Black-Scholes formula: The real-world prices of options that are far out-of-the-money—both calls and puts—are typically higher than what the Black-Scholes formula suggests. Put differently, according to the Black-Scholes formula, out-of-the-money options are priced as if their volatilities are higher than that of options that are at-the-money. If you draw the implied volatilities as a function of strike price, you get a so-called **volatility smile**—which is exactly what this empirical regularity is called by traders. One explanation for the smile is that there is a rare probability of a large stock price shock that is ignored by the Black-Scholes model. This may indeed be why far-out-of-the-money options are more expensive in the real world than in the model. It is especially plausible for puts, which can serve as insurance against a stock market crash, but perhaps less plausible for calls. For hardcore option traders, this opens up another question: If there is no longer just one implied volatility for a stock but different ones depending on the strike price, then which of these should you use? To predict future volatility, the recommendation here is to use at-the-money options. Historically, they have tended to predict volatility better than out-of-the-money options.

26.4B COMPARATIVE STATICS FOR THE BLACK-SCHOLES FORMULA

How the B-S formula changes with its inputs.

If you have solved all the exercises from the previous section (as you should have before proceeding!), you have already seen how the Black-Scholes call option value changes with its inputs. Specifically:

➤ Arbitrage, Section 26.2A, p. 988

Current stock price (S_0)—***positive*:** A call option is worth more when the stock price today is higher. This was also a static no-arbitrage relationship, and the Black-Scholes formula obviously must obey it. Furthermore, not only do you know that the Black-Scholes formula increases with S, but you can even work out by how much. Look at the Black-Scholes formula:

$$C_0(S, K, t, r_F, \sigma) = S \cdot \mathcal{N}(d_1) - PV_0(K) \cdot \mathcal{N}(d_2)$$

The stock price appears at this very high level, separate from the strike price K, and multiplied only by $\mathcal{N}(d_1)$. It turns out that $\mathcal{N}(d_1)$ is how the value of the call changes with respect to *small* value changes in the underlying stock price. For example, if $\mathcal{N}(d_1) \approx 0.3371$, then for a 10 cent increase in the value of the underlying stock, the value of the call option increases by 3.371 cents. Put differently, if your mimicking arbitrage position is long 100 shares and short 33.71 options, then your overall portfolio will not be affected one way or the other when the underlying stock price increases (or decreases) by 1 cent. You are said to be hedged against small changes in the stock price; that is, your portfolio is insured against such changes. For this reason, $\mathcal{N}(d_1)$ is also called the **hedge ratio**. Option traders also call it the **delta**. $\mathcal{N}(d_1)$ is the number of stocks that you need to purchase in order to mimic the behavior of your one option. For example, if right now the value of your call option increases by about $0.0025 when the underlying stock price increases by $0.01, then your hedge ratio is 0.25. If you own four of these call options, your position would change in value by the same $0.01 amount that it would change if you owned one stock. (In addition, option traders often want to know how quickly the delta [the stock position] itself changes when the underlying stock price changes. This is called the **gamma** of the option. You can think of it as the delta of the delta.)

Strike price (K)—***negative*:** A call option is worth more when the strike price is lower. Again, this was also a static arbitrage relationship.

Time left to maturity (t)—***positive*:** A call option is worth more when there is more time to maturity. Again, this was also a static arbitrage relationship. (The change in the price of the option as time changes is commonly called **theta**.)

Interest rate to maturity (r_F)—***positive*:** A call option is worth more when the interest rate is higher. This comparative static is not as intuitive as the three previous "comparative statics." My best attempt at explaining this intuition is that as the call option purchaser, you do not need to lay out the cash to cover the strike price immediately. You live on "borrowed" money. The higher the interest rate, the more value there is to you, the call owner, not to have to pay the strike price up front.

This is most obvious when the option is far in-the-money. For example, take a 1-year option with a strike price of $40 on a stock with a price of $100. Assume that the volatility is zero. If the interest rate is zero, the value of the call option is $60: With no volatility, you know that the option will pay off $60, and with an interest rate of zero, the value of the future payoff is the same as its present value. However, if the interest rate is 20%, then you can invest the $40 in bonds for 1 year. Therefore, the value of the option is $60 (at exercise), plus the $8 in interest earned along the way—a total of \$68. (The change in the price of the option as the risk-free rate changes is commonly called **rho**.)

Volatility to maturity (σ)—*positive*: A call option is worth more when there is more volatility. When the underlying stock increases in volatility, the call option holder gets all the extra upside, but does not lose more from all the extra downside (due to limited liability). This increases the value of the option. If this comparative static is not obvious, then ask yourself whether you would rather own an option with a strike price of \$100 on a stock that will be worth either \$99 or \$101 at expiration, or on a stock that will be worth either \$50 or \$150 at expiration. Holding everything else constant, an option on a more volatile asset is worth more. (The change in the price of the option as volatility changes is commonly called **vega**.)

There is one counterintuitive feature of the Black-Scholes formula: The expected rate of return on the underlying stock plays no role. This is because the other inputs, most of all the stock price (but also the interest rate and volatility), already incorporate the expected rate of return on the stock and therefore all the necessary information that you need to price an option. (Different purchasers can even disagree as to what the expected rate of return on the stock should be and still agree on the appropriate price on the option.)

But where is the expected rate of return on the stock in the B-S formula?

SOLVE NOW!

Q 26.14 What is the delta of an option? Does it have another name, too?

Q 26.15 In words, how does the value of a call option change with the Black-Scholes inputs?

26.4C VALUE PRIOR TO EXPIRATION

The Black-Scholes formula allows you to determine the price of a call option not only *on* the final expiration date, but also *before* the final expiration date. Figure 26.3 plots the Black-Scholes value of a call option with a strike price of \$90, an interest rate of 5%, and a standard deviation of 20% for three different times to expiration. The figure shows that the Black-Scholes value is always strictly above $\max(0, S_0 - K)$—otherwise, you could arbitrage by purchasing the call option and exercising it immediately. Moreover, you also already know that calls must be worth more when the underlying stock value is higher and when there is more time left to expiration. The figure nicely shows all of these features.

The B-S value can be used to plot values prior to expiration.

➤ Final date payoffs, Section 26.1C, p. 984

26.4D OPTION RISKINESS

You can now ask another interesting question: What are the advantages and disadvantages of call options with different strike prices? The answer is that different options provide different risk profiles. For example, say the stock was trading at \$100, 3 months prior to option expiration, the annual interest rate was 5%, and the annual standard deviation of the stock's underlying rates of return was 20%. According to Black-Scholes, a call option with a strike price of \$50 would have cost \$50.61. A call option with a strike price of \$90 would have cost \$11.65. And a call option with a strike

Options with different strike prices have different risk profiles.

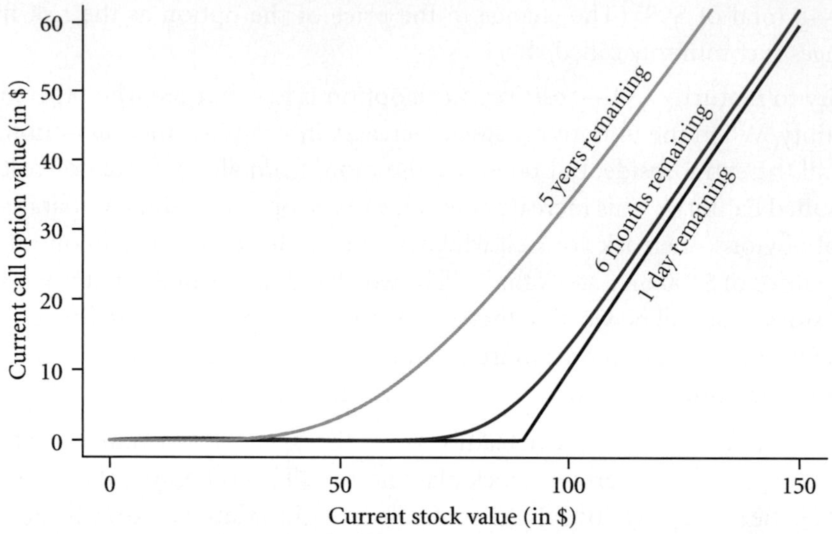

In this example, the time to expiration is either 1 day, 6 months, or 5 years. In all cases, the strike price is K = \$90, the annual interest rate is 5%, and the annual standard deviation is 20%.

FIGURE 26.3 Black-Scholes Values Prior to, and at, Expiration

price of \$120 would have cost \$0.20. All are fair prices. But consider what happens if the stock were to end up either very, very high or very, very low. If the stock price ends up at \$70, the \$50 option is the only one worth exercising, providing its holder with a \$20 payoff. This is equivalent to a rate of return of (\$20 − \$50.61)/\$50.61 ≈ −60%. Figure 26.4 shows this calculation as well as a couple more. The call with the strike price of \$50 is relatively safe compared to those with higher strike prices: It is in-the-money in both cases. The call with the strike price of \$90 has roughly a 50-50 chance of losing everything—but it provides more "juice" for each dollar invested *if* it expires in-the-money. Finally, the call with the strike price of \$120 is very likely to be a complete loss—but if the stock price were to exceed the strike price even by a little, the rate of return would quickly become astronomical. The rates of return on the four call options are graphed in Figure 26.4.

26.5 CORPORATE APPLICATIONS

Actually, the current chapter is not the first time you have encountered options. On the contrary.

26.5A DÉJÀ VU: SECURITIES AS FINANCIAL OPTIONS

Limited liability building ownership is a call option.

➤ Table 6.3, p. 159

The first time you worked with options was when you learned about uncertainty. In Section 6.4, you computed the value of levered equity ownership under limited liability. Limited liability is, at its heart, an option—the option to walk away without owing anything else.

Let's put the example from Table 6.3 of levered equity in a building into option's lingo. If you owe a \$25,000 mortgage, then your levered equity ownership is in effect a call option with a strike price of \$25,000. If your building ends up being worth more

Call Option	Price Today	Stock Will End at $70		Stock Will End at $130	
Strike Price	Payoff at T	Payoff at T	Return	Payoff at T	Return
Call (Strike = $0)	$90.00	$70−$0	−22%	$130−$0	+44%
Call (Strike = $50)	$50.61	$70−$50	−60%	$130−$50	+58%
Call (Strike = $70)	$30.85	$70−$70	−100%	$130−$70	+94%
Call (Strike = $90)	$11.65	$0	−100%	$130−$90	+243%
Call (Strike = $100)	$4.60	$0	−100%	$130−$100	+552%
Call (Strike = $120)	$0.20	$0	−100%	$130−$120	+4,900%
Call (Strike = $130)	$0.02	$0	−100%	$130−$130	−100%

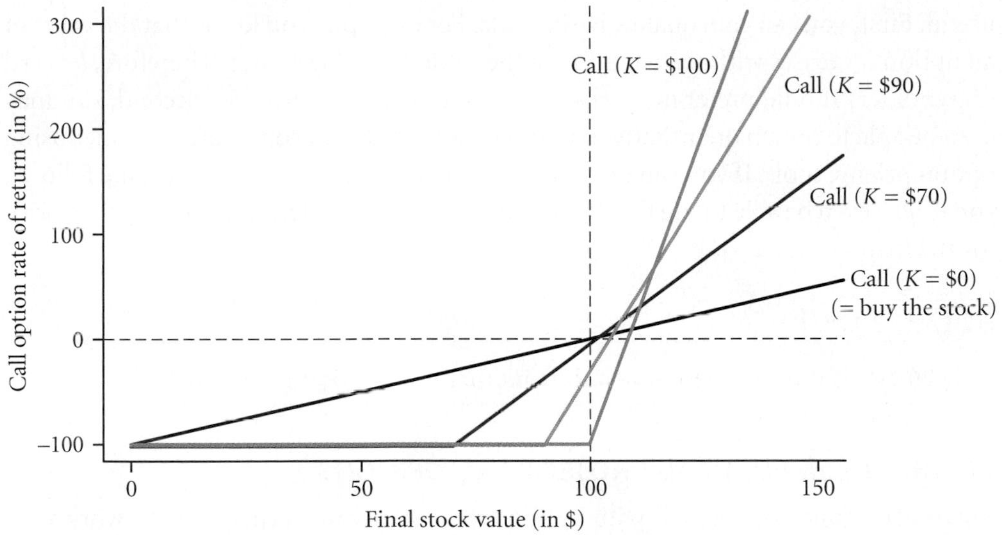

In all cases, the current stock price is $100, the option is 3 months before expiration, the interest rate is 5%, and annual volatility is 20%.

FIGURE 26.4 Rates of Return on Call Option Investments

than $25,000 (at loan expiration), it is in your interest to pay off the mortgage and keep the rest. If your building ends up being worth less than $25,000, you walk away and end up with $0. Alternatively, by put-call parity, you can think of equity *with* limited liability as being the same as a portfolio of equity *without* limited liability plus a put option with a strike price of $25,000, plus $25,000 in a loan. If the building ends up being worth only $20,000, you exercise the put. This means that you sell your $20,000 house and the put gives you the $25,000 − $20,000 = $5,000 profit. You use the $20,000 + $5,000 to pay off the $25,000 loan.

Levered equity (stock) is a call option.

➤ Levered equity (shares), Section 15.1A, p. 543

We expanded on the building example in Section 15.1A. Equity holders in corporations are also limited liability owners. They are in-the-money only *after* the corporate debt is paid off. Like a building owner, a stockholder has the option to walk away without having to make up further losses to creditors. Therefore, shareholders' levered equity is essentially an option on the value of the underlying base asset, which is the firm. You can even see the equivalence of a financial option and levered equity by comparing their payoff diagrams in Figures 15.1 and 26.1, respectively. Conversely, corporate debt is like a portfolio of risk-free bonds plus a put option sold to equity owners:

- If the firm is worth a lot, the shareholders pay the face value of the bonds. This is the horizontal line in the payoff diagram.
- If the firm is worth very little, the shareholders walk away from the firm: They exercise their right to sell the firm to the creditors for the face value of the corporate debt. Creditors lose an amount that increases with the difference between the face value of the debt and the actual value of the firm. This is the diagonal line in the payoff diagram.

Option pricing techniques can help you understand and value corporate securities.

➤ Risk-shifting, Section 18.5A, p. 676

The direct-options perspective on the cash flow rights of securities can be quite useful. First, you can gain qualitative insights. For example, you know that the value of an option increases with the volatility of the underlying base asset. Therefore, levered shareholders should prefer more risky projects to less risky projects. Second, you may even be able to obtain quantitative solutions for the value of corporate securities using option pricing tools. If you can learn what process the firm's underlying value follows, you might even be able to use the Black-Scholes formula to derive an appropriate price for the firm's levered equity.

SOLVE NOW!

Q 26.16 Is it possible to have a security that is an option on an option?

26.5B DÉJÀ VU: REAL PROJECTS AS OPTIONS

A real option depends not on an underlying financial asset (such as a stock), but on an underlying real asset.

➤ Real options, Section 12.6, p. 413

The second time you worked with options was when you learned how to work with "real options" in Section 12.6. Recall that I explained that it is important to recognize the real options features of your projects and to value them properly. A real option is really the value of your flexibility to respond to changing environments in the future. For example, if you have the ability to shut down production if the market price of your output product were to fall, then you have an option on a base asset that is the market price of your output product. Your option's strike price would be equal to the output price at which production becomes profitable.

Sometimes, you can even use the B-S formula to value a real option.

➤ Real options, Section 26.6, p. 1017

In Section 12.6 we used a tree approach for valuing a number of these real options. It is almost the same approach as the binomial approach explained in this chapter's appendix. The difference is that in the tree framework of the earlier chapter, you had to provide probabilities of up and down movements, and then use standard discounting over time. In the binomial framework in this chapter, you do not have to guess the discount rate. (The underlying base asset is a traded stock. Recall also that the Black-Scholes formula does not ask you for an expected rate of return as an input.) This is a nice advantage, but not a big one. The main difficulty is writing down the tree payoffs in the first place and working out what the optimal operating policy is (as a function of different state variables). Unfortunately, compared with the wealth of options embedded in real projects and their value dependence on many underlying factors, even complex financial options seem like child's play. It is rare that you can use the same financial option tools, like the Black-Scholes formula, to value a real option—more commonly, a tree approach using CAPM-type (or even risk-neutral) discounting makes your task simpler. Fortunately, the approach to valuing real options remains conceptually very similar, so once you understand one, the other is much easier.

(This book also has a complete web chapter dedicated to real options valuation. Even this dedicated chapter can only scratch the surface. Other authors have written entire books on the subject.)

www.prenhall.com/welch

SOLVE NOW!

Q 26.17 You have received an offer to buy a lease for 1 week's worth of production (100 ounces) in a particular gold mine. This lease will occur in exactly 18 months. It is an old mine, so it costs \$400/ounce to extract gold. Gold is trading for \$365/ounce today but has a volatility of 40% per annum. The prevailing interest rate is 10% per year. What is the value of the gold mine?

Q 26.18 Now assume that you own this mine. If the mine is inexhaustible, but can only extract 100 ounces per week, and the production cost increases by 20% per year (starting at \$400 next week, your first production period), how would you value this mine? (Do not solve this algebraically. Just think about the concepts.)

26.5C DÉJÀ VU: RISK MANAGEMENT

Risk management is the manipulation of the firm's exposure to risk.

➤ Currency hedging, Section 25.4, p. 963

The third time you worked with derivatives (though not with options) was in Chapter 25, which showed you how a firm can hedge its exchange rate exposure. For example, consider an American corporation that has just sold its product to a German corporation for payment in euros in 6 months but that must pay its suppliers for its own inputs in U.S. dollars. It can lock in today's dollar value of its future euro receipts by selling some euro futures. This is a form of **risk management**, the deliberate manipulation of the risk exposure that the corporation faces. (For most companies, risk management means lowering risk exposure.) Risk management is worth covering in more generality. For example, a firm may also purchase liability insurance to protect it against occasional random mishaps. Or it may want to hedge its credit risk or oil risk exposures. Options and other derivatives are natural tools that can help to manage corporate risk, which is why we cover risk management in this chapter.

WHY HEDGE?

Risk management is irrelevant in a perfect market.

➤ Corporate consequences of market efficiency, Section 11.6A, p. 370

In a perfect market, there is no value to risk management. You learned in Section 11.6A that if investors can freely do or undo a transaction, it cannot add value. If the firm sells euros for dollars at the appropriate price, investors can easily undo this by taking the offsetting position (buying euros). Investors' return would again be based only on the value of the unhedged firm. Equivalently, if the firm were not to hedge the currency, investors could hedge for themselves. They could sell euros, and their return would come from the unhedged firm plus the value of the hedge. This argument is really the same as the Modigliani-Miller indifference proposition in the

➤ Modigliani-Miller propositions, Section 16.2, p. 576

context of capital structure. Indeed, hedging risk is often the equivalent of a capital structure activity—the company can often share its risk either by selling equity or by hedging.

Risk management can be useful in an imperfect market.

It is only in an imperfect market that risk management matters. In this case, you have to think about all the capital structure issues raised in Chapters 17 and 18:

- Can risk management change the taxes paid by the corporation or its investors?
- Can it reduce deadweight financial distress costs?
- Can it worsen or alleviate conflicts between bondholders and stockholders?
- Can it induce the manager to work harder and make better decisions, or work less and make worse decisions?

And so on. The considerations in favor of risk management are usually the same as those in favor of having more equity and less debt. For example, an airline company could avoid the financial distress that rising fuel prices could cause if it were to purchase fuel futures. If the fuel price were to rise, its flight operations would turn unprofitable, but its fuel hedge would make money. Such a fuel hedge could add value if it avoids the collapse of an otherwise valuable underlying business. But it could also subtract value if it prevents the managers (the agents of the owners) from shutting down the airline and selling its assets if this were the value-maximizing action.

How to Hedge

The firm can hedge different types of risks with many tools—not just with derivatives.

The basic idea of risk management through hedging is simple: The firm reduces a source of risk that it otherwise faces. The firm has a number of risk-management tools at its disposal:

- It can buy a policy from an insurance company that may specialize in, and thus understand and manage, the risk better. This works especially well if the risks are idiosyncratic—for example, the risk of a firm being sued or the risk of a firm's building collapsing. Insurance policies may work—but often less well—for more systematic risks, such as industry risks, commodity price risks, exchange rate risks, or interest rate risks. (In the credit crisis of 2008, investors that had purchased insurance against the credit risk in bonds suddenly learned that their main risk was not that just the underlying issuer would go out of business. Rather, it was also that many low-credit bonds could default at the same time and the insurer itself could go out of business. In other words, these investors mistook a true systematic risk for idiosyncratic risk and thus used the wrong tool [insurance policies] as protection.)
- It can execute or not execute certain projects. For example, it can take fewer projects or reduce its risk by preferentially taking more projects that have a lower correlation with its existing operations. This is the diversification intuition we used for the CAPM, except that the firm uses it here to reduce its own firm risk and not its investors' portfolio risks.
- It can buy or sell contracts in the financial markets. For example, it can buy or sell options (or futures or stocks) to shift the risk to another party. This is especially popular if the risk is systematic and economy-wide. (In some cases, both contract parties may experience a decline in risk. For example, an oil producer may want to sell the oil futures that an oil consumer would want to buy. In other cases, there may

be firms that specialize in absorbing risks. [This is one of the roles of funds, especially hedge funds.] The risk management of such firms is to *increase* their corporate risk, although preferably in a very deliberate fashion.)

Hedging goods, exchange rates, interest rates, etc.

Because this is a chapter on options, we shall focus primarily on buying and selling contracts in the financial markets. The three most common risks that companies hedge are the prices of input or output goods (especially commodities), currency exchange prices, and interest rates. Hedging them is conceptually the same, so we can cover all of them together:

1. In the real world, the firm decides what it wants to hedge (e.g., its costs, sales, or income) and then determines its exposure to this risk.

   Some firms know their exposures from the operations of their actual businesses. For example, in 2005, Southwest Airlines spent about \$1.3 billion on jet fuel, about 20% of its operating expenses. Thus, it knew that a 5% rise in fuel prices would increase its operating expenses by \$65 million.

   Other businesses have to estimate their risks. For example, even a domestic U.S. firm may find that its U.S. customers tend to buy less of its product when the yen becomes cheaper. In this case, it must first determine its exposures. This is often done through a historical regression in which the firm's sales are explained by the underlying base asset (here, the exchange rate). For example, our firm may have run a regression of monthly sales on the exchange rate to find

$$\text{Sales (in Millions)} = \$10 - \$0.05 \cdot (¥/\$) + \text{Noise} \tag{26.2}$$

   This suggests that if the current exchange rate is 100 ¥/\$, expected sales should be around $\$10 - \$0.05 \cdot (100) = \$5$ million. More importantly, it suggests that if the exchange rate increases to 101 ¥/\$ (that is, the yen becomes cheaper because you get more yen per dollar), sales would be expected to decline to \$4.95 million. Thus, this firm has a sales exposure of \$50,000 for each 1-yen change in value. This is exactly what the 0.05 regression coefficient gives you—it is your hedge ratio, the same as the delta in the Black-Scholes formula.

2. The firm decides how much of its risk it wants to hedge. Reducing risk has not only an upside but also a downside. For example, if an airline buys jet fuel today, it is a great hedge against future fuel price increases, but it will hurt its profitability if the fuel price decreases. An airline may also suffer other maladies and may not need as much fuel as it originally anticipated. And there is a cost to executing fuel hedges. Then there are strategic considerations—if the airline is very different from its competitors, it may go out of business in the most likely scenario, but it could really pounce and gobble up its competitors if the less likely scenario occurs. Thus, hedging can create a real option!

A real-world example: Southwest's lucky fuel hedging program.

Firms do not need to disclose all their hedges. Indeed, hedging operations are often so complex and multifaceted that it may not even be possible to disclose them fully within the confines of a typical financial statement. Although we do not have full knowledge of how firms are hedging, we do have some data from certain industries. Research by Carter, Rogers, and Simkins shows that about two-thirds of U.S. airlines engaged in active hedging programs from 1992 to 2003. But during that time

ANECDOTE 223 years of Barings; 1 year of Leeson

Derivatives can be powerful hedging tools. But they can also be powerful speculation tools. In 1994, Barings was a venerable 223-year-old London investment bank. It had financed the Napoleonic Wars and the Louisiana Purchase. However, Barings was not equipped to handle its own 28-year-old trader Nick Leeson in its Singapore branch office. Leeson lost $1.3 billion—the entire assets of Barings—in a series of bets using options on forwards on the Nikkei index. (Like any other derivatives, these Nikkei options can be used either for hedging or for speculation.) The lesson from Barings is that inadequate oversight of financial traders—who usually earn bonuses on trading profits—can easily make the risk of a firm worse, not better. *Firms need good risk management for their risk management.* The lesson from Leeson is that becoming notorious is not a bad way to earn large fees on the after-dinner speaking circuit.

Source: BBC.

no airline hedged even 1 full year of jet fuel consumption. They typically hedged only about 15% of their annual fuel purchases. The two most active hedgers were Southwest and JetBlue, which hedged 43% of their annual fuel purchases. (By 2005, Southwest had significantly scaled up its fuel hedging operations—and to its good fortune. In 2005, it yielded a positive $892 million inflow vis-à-vis its $1.3 billion fuel cost.) Of course, even if an airline hedges its entire fuel budget for 1 year, if fuel prices rise, it would likely affect not only the next year but many years thereafter. This means that its lifetime operating costs would still remain quite exposed to fuel price risk. In this long-run sense, most corporate hedging programs seem conservative.

We have only scratched the tip of the iceberg—the devil is in the details.

This is only a small taste of risk management. In the real world, there are many other complications. For example, firms need to consider what exactly they should hedge—operating costs may not be the right target. After all, it could be that firms can charge customers higher prices when their input costs are higher. Higher input costs may not be detrimental—in fact, some financially strong firms may even benefit from otherwise adverse economic price developments if their competitors are forced out of business. Another hedging consideration is more technical: What firms want to hedge may not be linearly related to the underlying commodity, as it was in Formula 26.2. This can often be dealt with through dynamic trading (the same concept underlying the Black-Scholes formula). Yet another common problem is that the commodity available for hedging may not be the exact commodity that the firm wants to hedge. (It may only have short-term crude oil futures to trade, while it would really want to buy long-term jet fuel.) This can create all sorts of mismatching trouble. In any case, the firm may have to make some interim payments on its hedges and so has to worry about having enough liquidity before its own investments mature. This can also have certain accounting reporting obligations, which could in turn trigger certain bond covenants.

SOLVE NOW!

Q 26.19 Assume that oil is trading for $50 per barrel today. The oil price can go down by 33% or up by 50% per year. That is, it can sell for either $33.33 or $75.

(a) You own a refinery. It is worth more if the oil price is higher. Intuitively, what kind of oil transaction would reduce your risk?

(b) Your refinery can produce profits of $1.5 million if oil trades for $33.33, and profits of $3 million if it trades for $75. If you write a contract to sell 30,000 barrels of oil for $50/barrel next year, how would your risk exposure change?
(c) If you want to be fully hedged, how many barrels of oil should you be selling?

Q 26.20 Is it possible for a small firm to hedge the risk of overall stock market (S&P 500) movements? That is, could a firm with a market beta of 1.5 change its market beta to 0? If so, have you seen its hedge ratio (delta) before?

26.5D EMPLOYEE STOCK OPTIONS

Employee options differ from ordinary financial options.

Many firms have managerial and **employee stock option plans** (ESOP) in order to better motivate their workforce. The main idea is that options are more sensitive to changes in the underlying value of the firm than stock, so employees will be especially motivated to work hard if they own options. There are many unusual details to these employee options:

- They tend to be very long term (often as long as 10 years).
- They often vest only after several years (meaning that if the employee leaves the firm before that time, he loses the option).
- They are actually misnamed. If exercise triggers the creation of new underlying shares by the firm, then the proper name for such a claim would be a **warrant**, not an option. This is the case here: Almost all employee stock options are dilutive.
- Because of tax rules, most of these options must have a strike price equal to the current underlying stock price.
- Most importantly, they cannot be sold or bought, and because employees are often not allowed to short the firm's stock or own put options on it, these options cannot be easily hedged by employees. This should not be surprising—after all, the very reason the firm gives its employees these options is to leave them exposed to the fortunes of the firm.

➤ Warrants and dilution, Section 15.3, p. 552

The last feature means that employee stock options are very different from other financial options. There is no hedge that forces their value. On the contrary—they are worth less to employees than they would be to third parties. To say it again: The firm gives its employees a security that costs more than what employees value it for. In the extreme, if employees are extremely risk averse, they may not place any value ex-ante on these options. Moreover, employees should exercise their options as soon as they can in order to diversify their wealth away from being too linked to this one company. From the perspective of the company, early exercise reduces the options' effective costs when compared with a hypothetical issue of freely trading warrants to external investors. But early exercise also robs the firm of the options' incentive effects sooner—which was, after all, the whole point of granting these options. Our tools, like the Black-Scholes formula or put-call parity, are definitely not applicable in this context.

ANECDOTE 2006 GAAP Change in the Treatment of Executive and Employee Options

Executive options seemed particularly attractive to firms prior to 2006, because U.S. GAAP did not require firms to expense these options. Thus, these options did not have a negative influence on firms' financial statements upon granting—they were almost invisible as far as the firms' financials were concerned. (Of course, this was highly misleading. Even if not exercised, options can have tremendous value at issue time. They are *not* free to the corporation.) The adoption of this option-expensing rule by FASB in 2004 provoked strong complaints by many firms, especially high-tech firms. Even the U.S. Senate did some grandstanding with a motion to strike down this rule.

However, this storm of indignation died down in the wake of another scandal. Articles by David Yermack (from New York University) and others showed that many of these executive options were (illegally) backdated. That is, many corporate boards claimed to have granted options to their executives a number of days earlier when/if the stock price was lower in order to artificially increase the option value.

Employee and executive option grants can be very big, especially, but not only, in high-tech firms.

Executive options are not small potatoes. For example, in April 2002, *Business Week* reported that Larry Ellison, CEO of Oracle, had pocketed $706 million from the exercise of long-held stock options—more than the GDP of Grenada! "Fortunately," Oracle stock was off 57% that year, or Ellison's options would have been worth $2 billion more. That same year, Dennis Kozlowski, CEO of Tyco, hit #3 on the executive payoff list. However, he wound up in jail, partly for criminally looting $600 million from Tyco. (Maybe he should have received more options!)

SUMMARY

This chapter covered the following major points:

- Call options give the right (but not the obligation) to purchase underlying securities at a predetermined strike price for a given period of time. Put options give the right (but not the obligation) to sell underlying securities at a predetermined strike price for a given period of time. American call options give this right all the way up to the final expiration; European call options give this right only at the final expiration.
- Option payoffs at expiration and complex option strategies are best understood by graphing their payoff diagrams.
- A number of static no-arbitrage relationships limit the range of prices that an option can have.
- The most important no-arbitrage relationship is put-call parity, which relates the price of a call to the price of a put, the price of the underlying stock, and the interest rate.
- Put-call parity implies that American call options are never exercised early, and therefore that American calls are worth the same as European options. (This assumes no dividends.)
- The Black-Scholes formula relates the price of a call to five input parameters. The Black-Scholes value increases with the stock price, decreases with the strike price, increases with the time left to maturity, increases with the volatility, and increases with the risk-free interest rate.

• Options techniques and insights have found applications in the valuation of corporate securities, in capital budgeting of projects that allow for future flexibility (real options), and in risk management. They are less easy to apply in the context of employee and executive stock option plans.

KEY TERMS

SOLVE NOW! SOLUTIONS

Q 26.1 Owning a call option is similar to selling a put option in that both are bullish bets. However, they have *very* different payoff patterns (tables). For example, the owner of a call option enjoys limited liability and thus can, at most, lose the money paid for the call. The seller of a put option can lose an unlimited amount.

Q 26.2 An option that is far in-the-money and expiring soon will change in value about one to one with the underlying stock price. After all, it will almost surely pay off.

Q 26.3 A put option holder is indifferent to the stock split in a perfect market because the contract is such that the option would be adjusted. However, the unexpected dividend increase would be good news for a put holder. In a perfect market, there would be no value change to the dividend announcement, but the post-dividend price at expiration would be lower.

Q 26.4 The long call option with a strike price of \$60 pays off if the stock price ends above \$60; the long put option with a strike price of \$80 pays off if it ends up below \$80:

Stock_T	Pfio_T	Stock_T	Pfio_T
\$0	+\$80	\$70	+\$20
\$20	+\$60	\$75	+\$20
\$40	+\$40	\$80	+\$20
\$60	+\$20	\$90	+\$30
\$65	+\$20	\$100	+\$40

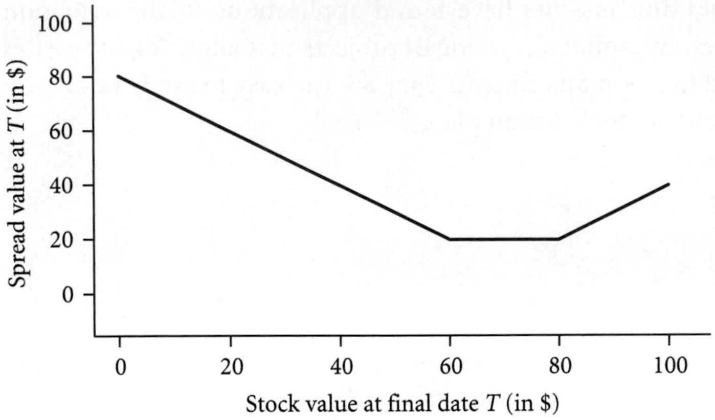

Q 26.5 The short call option with a strike price of \$60 costs money if the stock ends up above \$60; the short put option with a strike price of \$80 costs money below \$80:

$Stock_T$	$Pfio_T$	$Stock_T$	$Pfio_T$
\$0	−\$80	\$70	−\$20
\$20	−\$60	\$75	−\$20
\$40	−\$40	\$80	−\$20
\$60	−\$20	\$90	−\$30
\$65	−\$20	\$100	−\$40

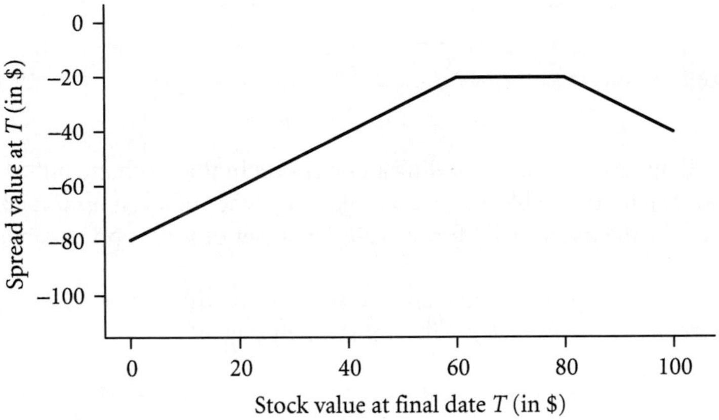

Q 26.6 The butterfly spread (1 long call $K = \$50$, 2 short calls $K = \$55$, 1 long call $K = \$60$):

$Stock_T$	1 Long Call $K = \$50$	2 Short Calls $K = \$55$	1 Long Call $K = \$60$	Net
⋮				
\$40	\$0	\$0	\$0	\$0
\$50	\$0	\$0	\$0	\$0
\$52	\$2	\$0	\$0	\$2
\$53	\$3	\$0	\$0	\$3
\$55	\$5	\$0	\$0	\$5
\$57	\$7	−\$4	\$0	\$3
\$58	\$8	−\$6	\$0	\$2

\$60	\$10	−\$10	\$0	\$0
\$65	\$15	−\$20	\$5	\$0
\$70	\$20	−\$30	\$10	\$0
⋮				

The payoff diagram of this butterfly spread is

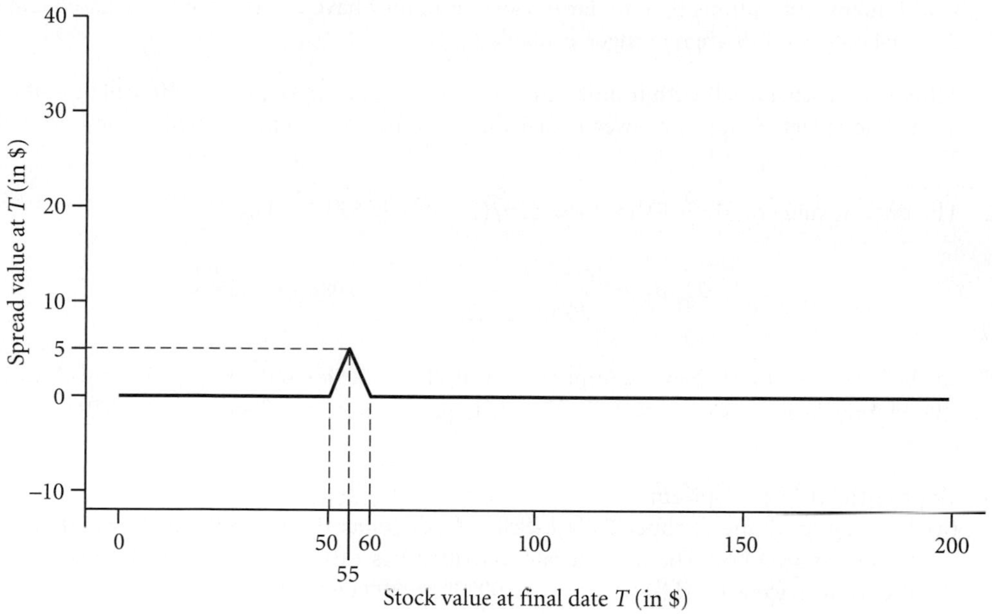

Q 26.7 Put-call parity is the formula $C_0(K) = P_0(K) + S_0 - \text{PV}_0(K)$. The price of a call option today, the price of the same put option (strike price and expiration time) today, the stock price, and the present value of the strike price are the inputs.

Q 26.8 (a) Put-call parity states that $C_0(K) = P_0(K) + S_0 - \text{PV}_0(K)$. Therefore, $P_0(K) = C_0(K) + \text{PV}_0(K) - S_0 = \$20 + \$80/1.10 - \$70 \approx \$22.73$.

(b) The put option should cost \$22.73, but it indeed costs \$25.00. Therefore, it is too expensive, and you definitely need to short it. To cover yourself after shorting it, you now need to "manufacture" an artificial put option to neutralize your exposure. Put-call parity is $P_0(K) = C_0(K) + \text{PV}_0(K) - S_0 \approx \$22.73$. Loosely translated, a long put is a long call, a long present value of a strike price, and a short stock. Try purchasing one call (outflow today), saving the present value of the strike price (outflow), and shorting the stock (inflow today):

		Stock Price at Expiration T Will Be				
		$S_T < \$80$		$S_T = 80$	$S_T > \$80$	
Execute	Today	\$60	\$70	\$80	\$90	\$100
Purchase 1 Call ($K = \$80$):	−\$20.00	\$0	\$0	\$0	\$10	\$20
Sell 1 Share:	+\$70.00	−\$60	−\$70	−\$80	−\$90	−\$100
Save to Pay Strike Price PV_0 (\$80):	−\$72.73	+\$80	+\$80	+\$80	+\$80	+\$80
Sell 1 Put ($K = \$80$):	+\$25.00	−\$20	−\$10	\$0	\$0	\$0
Net	+\$2.27	\$0	\$0	\$0	\$0	\$0

You would earn an immediate arbitrage profit of \$2.27.

Q 26.9 A European option can be worth as much as the equivalent American option if there is no value to early exercise. This happens if the option is a call option on a stock that pays no dividends.

Q 26.10 To compare the value of a live put to a dead put, compute the net value of a live put $(C_0(K) + [PV_0(K) - S_0])$ minus that of a dead put $\{(K - S_0)\}$. It is $\{C_0(K) + [PV_0(K) - S_0]\} - \{(K - S_0)\}$. This can be simplified into $C_0(K) + [PV_0(K) - K]$. This expression is worth more if the call is worth more (the stock price is high relative to the strike price) and if the interest rate is low. It is under those circumstances that you should not exercise the American put because it is worth less dead than alive. (In the real world, many put options that are far out-of-the-money have already been purchased *and* exercised before the final date, so they are no longer available.)

Q 26.11 Think about what a call with infinite time to maturity and strike price of \$0 really is—it is simply the stock itself. The (Black-Scholes) answer is that this must be equivalent to owning the underlying stock itself. Therefore, $C_0 = S_0 = \$80.50$.

Q 26.12 The present value of \$75 is $\text{PV}(\$75) = \$75/(1.05^{1/4}) \approx \$74.09$. Thus,

$$d_1 \approx \frac{\ln(\$80/\$74.09)}{20\% \cdot \sqrt{0.25}} + \frac{1}{2} \cdot 20\% \cdot \sqrt{0.25} \approx 0.817,$$

so $\mathcal{N}(0.817) \approx 0.793$. Next, compute $d_2 = 0.817 - 20\% \cdot \sqrt{0.25} \approx 0.717$ and $\mathcal{N}(0.717) \approx 0.763$. Therefore, $\text{BS}(S_0 = \$80,\ K = \$75,\ T = 1/4,\ r_F = 5\%,\ \sigma = 20\%) = \$80 \cdot 0.793 - \$74.09 \cdot 0.763 \approx \$6.89$.

Q 26.13 To price the IBM put option:

(a) First compute the European Black-Scholes call value: $\text{BS}(S = \$80.50,\ K = \$100,\ r_F = 1.77\%,\ t = 0.1333,\ \sigma = 30\%)$. The interest rate to maturity is $1.0177^{0.1333} \approx 1.00234$. Thus, the present value of the strike price is $\text{PV}(\$100) \approx \$100/1.00234 \approx \$99.767$. Next,

$$d_1 \approx \frac{\ln(\$80.50/\$99.767)}{30\% \cdot \sqrt{0.1333}} + \frac{1}{2} \cdot 30\% \cdot \sqrt{0.1333} \approx -1.9589 + 0.05477 \approx -1.904$$

and $\mathcal{N}(d_1) \approx 0.02845$. Then $d_2 \approx -2.0136$ and $\mathcal{N}(d_2) \approx 0.02202$. The call price is therefore about $\text{BS}(\$80.50, \$100, 0.1333, 1.77\%, 30\%) \approx \$80.50 \cdot 0.02845 - \$99.767 \cdot 0.02202 \approx \$2.289 - \$2.196 \approx \$0.0928$. Therefore, the European IBM put would be worth $\$0.0928 - \$80.50 + \$99.767 \approx \$19.36$. (Your answer may vary slightly due to rounding.)

(b) If you hold onto the put if it is American, you have an asset worth \$19.36. If you exercise it, you receive an immediate $\$100 - \$80.50 = \$19.50$. Therefore, you would be better off exercising immediately!

Q 26.14 The delta of an option is the number of stocks that you need to purchase in order to mimic the option. Delta is also called the hedge ratio.

Q 26.15 The value of a call option increases with higher share prices, longer lengths to maturity, more volatility, and higher interest rates; it decreases with higher strike prices.

Q 26.16 Not only is it possible to have a security that is an option on an option, but the fact is that almost all common financial options are such. This is because the stock on which they are written is itself an option on the underlying firm value. Thus, CBOE options are essentially options on options.

Q 26.17 Let's price the lease in 18 months. Assume that you must decide to produce at the start of this week. If you see that the price of gold is above \$400, then you extract gold. Otherwise, you do not. You can now value the gold mine as if it were 100 Black-Scholes call options, each with current price \$365, strike price of \$400, interest rate of 10%, volatility of 40% per annum, and 18 months to expiration. You can calculate this. The present value of the strike price is $\text{PV}(K) = \$400/1.1^{1.5} \approx \$346.71$. $\ln[S/\text{PV}(K)] \approx \ln(\$365/\$346.71) \approx 0.0514$. The Black-Scholes value of such a call is about $\text{BS}(S = \$365,\ K = \$400,\ t = 1.5,\ r = 0.1,\ \sigma = 0.4) \approx \$79.51$. Thus, 100 calls should be worth \$7,951.

Q 26.18 The value of the mine would be the sum of many such options. The production cost per ounce increases by about $20\%/52 \approx 0.35\%$ per week. It would increase the strike price from \$400 to \$401.40, then to \$402.81, and so on.

$$\begin{aligned}\text{Value} = \quad & \text{BS}(S = \$365,\ K = \$400,\ t = 1,\ r = 10\%,\ \sigma = 40\%) \\ & + \text{BS}(S = \$365,\ K = \$401.40,\ t = 2,\ r = 10\%,\ \sigma = 40\%) \\ & + \text{BS}(S = \$365,\ K = \$402.81,\ t = 3,\ r = 10\%,\ \sigma = 40\%) + \cdots\end{aligned}$$

Q 26.19 Given this process on the price of oil:

(a) Selling oil would reduce your risk.

(b) If you have agreed to sell 30,000 barrels of oil for \$50/barrel, you would receive \$1.5 million. If the oil price were to be \$33.33/barrel, you can buy 30,000 barrels for \$1 million. This would give you a net profit of \$0.5 million. If the oil price were to be \$75/barrel, you can buy the barrels for \$2.25 million. This would give you a net loss of \$0.75 million. Putting this together with your refinery, your payoffs would now be $\$1.5 + \$0.5 = \$2$ million if oil goes down, and $\$3 - \$0.75 = \$2.25$ million if oil goes up. Your risk is much lower now.

(c) If you contract on 36,000 barrels of oil, your net is \$2.1 million in either case:
- If oil drops to \$33.33, the gain on your hedge is $(\$50 - \$33.33) \cdot 36{,}000 = \$600{,}120$. Thus, your payoffs would be $\$1.5 + \$0.6 \approx \$2.1$ million.
- If oil rises to \$75.00, the loss on your hedge is $(\$75 - \$50) \cdot 36{,}000 = \$900{,}000$. Thus, your payoffs would be $\$3 - \$0.9 \approx \$2.1$ million.

The 36,000 ($x = 36$) was obtained by solving $\$1{,}500 + (\$50 - \$33.33) \cdot x = \$3{,}000 - (\$75 - \$50) \cdot x$.

Q 26.20 A firm could easily hedge its S&P 500 risk by shorting the stock market. This is cheaply done by trading S&P 500 futures or forwards. If the firm is worth \$100 million and has a beta of 1.5, shorting \$150 million in this future should do the trick. The hedge ratio is really the market beta itself!

PROBLEMS

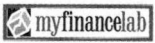

The ▬ indicates problems available in myfinancelab

Q 26.21 Is writing a call the same as buying a put, provided both have the same strike price and same expiration date? That is, do they give the same payoffs in future states of the world?

Q 26.22 An option is far out-of-the-money and will expire tonight. How would you expect its value to change when the stock price changes?

Q 26.23 Would a call option writer welcome an unexpected stock split? Would a call option writer welcome an unexpected dividend increase? (Assume a perfect market in both scenarios.)

Q 26.24 Write down the payoff table and draw the payoff diagram (both at expiration) of a portfolio consisting of one *short* call with a strike price $K = \$60$ and one *long* put with a strike price $K = \$80$.

Q 26.25 Graph the payoff diagram for the following straddle: one long call option with a strike price of \$50 and one long put option with a strike price of \$60.

Q 26.26 How could you earn money in the put-call parity example in Section 26.2B if the 1-year put option traded in the market for \$25 per share, the stock price were \$80, the equivalent 1-year call cost \$30, and the interest rate were 10% per year?

Q 26.27 A 1-year put option with a strike price of \$80 costs \$25. A share costs \$70. The interest rate is 8% per year. What should a 1-year call option with a strike price of \$80 trade for?

Q 26.28 List and describe the simple no-arbitrage relationships, preferably both in words and in algebra.

Q 26.29 How would you cook up a numerical example in which you would want to exercise an

American put before expiration? Is your American put in-the-money or out-of-the-money?

Q 26.30 What is the value of a call option with a strike price of $0 and 6 months to expiration? Use the parameters of the example: $S_0 = \$80.50$, $r_F = 1.77\%$, and $\sigma = 50\%$.

Q 26.31 Write a computer spreadsheet that computes the Black-Scholes value on row 4 as a function of its five inputs (in the first two rows). This will teach you more about the Black-Scholes formula than all the pages in this book. Recall that the normal distribution function is **normsdist**.

Q 26.32 Use your spreadsheet from Question 26.31 to price a call option with a stock price of $80, a strike price of $75, 3 months to maturity, a 5% risk-free rate of return, and a standard deviation of return of 20% on the underlying stock. Check it against the solution in Question 26.12.

Q 26.33 Price the earlier call option but with a higher *strike price*. That is, price a call with a stock price of $80, a strike price of $80, 3 months to maturity, a 5% risk-free rate of return, and a standard deviation of return of 20% on the underlying stock.

Q 26.34 Price the earlier call option with a higher *interest rate*. That is, price a call with a stock price of $80, a strike price of $75, 3 months to maturity, a 10% risk-free rate of return, and a standard deviation of return of 20% on the underlying stock.

Q 26.35 Price the earlier call option with a higher *volatility*. That is, price a call with a stock price of $80, a strike price of $75, 3 months to maturity, a 5% risk-free rate of return, and a standard deviation of return of 30% on the underlying stock.

Q 26.36 Price a *European put option* with a stock price of $80, a strike price of $75, 3 months to maturity, a 5% risk-free rate of return, and a standard deviation of return of 20% on the underlying stock.

Q 26.37 Price a *European straddle*: one call and one put option on a stock with a price of $80, both with strike prices of $75, a 5% risk-free rate of return, and a standard deviation of return of 20% on the underlying stock.

(a) What is the price of the position if there are 3 months to maturity?
(b) What is the price if nothing changed and there is only 1 month left to maturity?
(c) What is the price at expiration?

Q 26.38 ADVANCED: There are numerous calculators on the Web that will calculate an implied volatility for you. Fortunately, it is not difficult to write one yourself in a computer spreadsheet, using the built-in equation solver. Write a computer spreadsheet program that uses this equation solver to back out a volatility estimate, given a call price and the five Black-Scholes inputs. Use it to confirm the implied volatilities in Table 26.3. Then use your spreadsheet and data from a financial website to compute the implied volatility of IBM today. Be clear about what inputs you are using.

Q 26.39 Are the deltas of options with different strike prices different?

Q 26.40 Using the computer spreadsheet you created in Question 26.31, graph the Black-Scholes value as a function of today's stock value for options with two different interest rates: 5% and 20%. That is, repeat Figure 26.4 for a 3-month option with strike price $K = \$90$, 3 months to expiration, and a 20% volatility.

Q 26.41 Using the computer spreadsheet you created in Question 26.31, graph the Black-Scholes value as a function of today's stock value for options with three different volatilities: 20%, 80%, and 160%. That is, repeat Figure 26.4 for a 3-month option with strike price $K = \$90$, 3 months to expiration, and a 5% interest rate.

Q 26.42 In words, how does the value of a call option change with the Black-Scholes inputs?

Q 26.43 Should employees and firms value employee stock options using the Black-Scholes formula?

CHAPTER 26 APPENDIX

The Ideas behind the Black-Scholes Formula

In the previous sections, you learned how to use the Black-Scholes formula. However, it descended on you out of the ether. If you are wondering where the formula actually comes from, then this section is for you.

26.6 MODELING THE STOCK PRICE PROCESS AS A BINOMIAL TREE

Assume at each instant, the stock prices go up by u or down by d.

The basic building element for the Black-Scholes formula is the assumption that over one instant, the stock price can only move up or down. (This is called a **binomial process.**) So you must first understand how to work in such a world. Over two instants, the stock price can move up twice, move up once and move down once, or move down twice. Use the letter u to describe the stock price multiplier when an up move occurs, and d to describe the stock price multiplier when a down move occurs. You can represent the stock price process with a binomial tree—where one branch represents a price-up movement and the other a price-down movement. For example, if $d = 0.96$ (which means that on a down move, the stock price declines by 4%) and $u = 1.05$ (the stock price increases by 5%), the stock price is as follows:

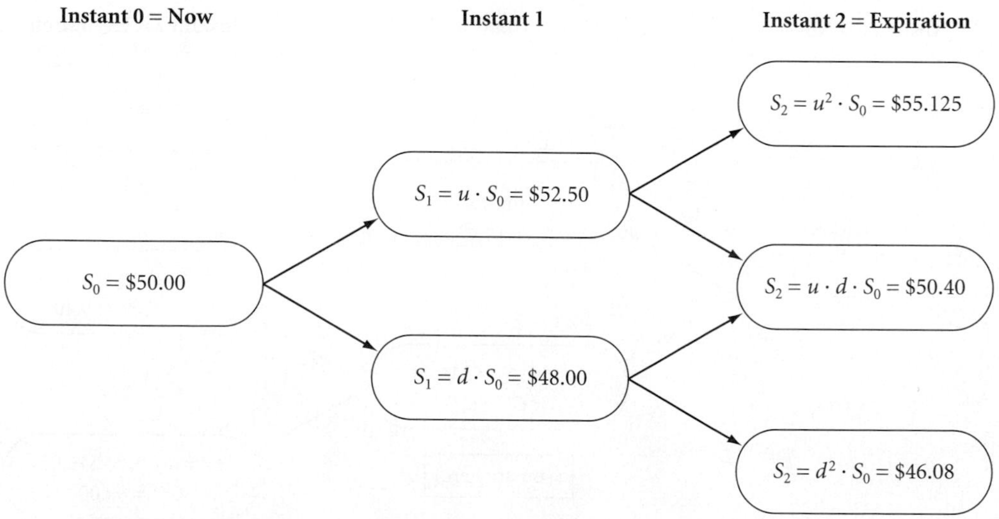

There are more outcomes (i.e., higher probability of reaching the nodes) in the middle of a binomial tree than at the edges.

➤ Bell shaped distributions and binomial trees, Section 26.8, p. 1020

Note that at instant 2, the middle outcome occurs on two possible paths, while the two extreme outcomes occur only on one path each; $u \cdot d \cdot S_0$ can come about if there is one u followed by one d, or if there is one d followed by one u. This is already a statistical distribution that shares with a bell-shaped (normal) distribution the feature that middle outcomes are more likely than extreme outcomes. (With many more binomial tree levels, you indeed end up with a continuous distribution that looks a lot like a bell-shaped curve.)

26.7 THE OPTION HEDGE

First, set out your goal: Find the value of an option two instants before expiration.

If you know that your stock follows this binomial process, and you know u and d, can you price a call option with a strike price of \$50? On inspection of the tree, realize that the call option pays \$0 if the stock price moves down twice, \$0.40 if the stock price moves up once and down once (or vice versa), and \$5.125 if the stock price moves up twice.

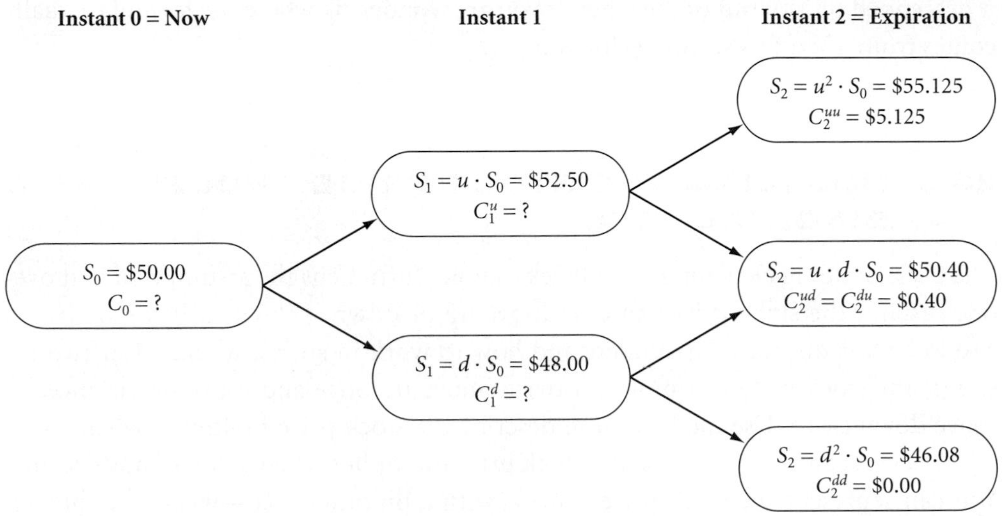

Price the call in the down state (C_1^d).

Your ultimate goal is to determine the call price at the outset, C_0. First place yourself into the position where the stock price has moved down once already, that is, where the stock price stands at \$48.00.

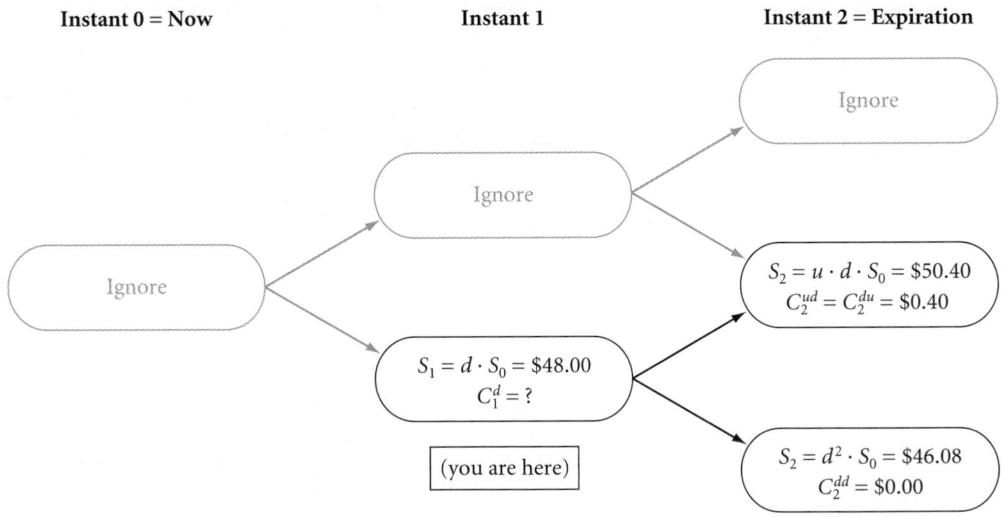

Simplifying the pricing with formulas.

Your immediate goal is to buy stocks and risk-free bonds so that you receive \$0 if the stock moves down and \$0.40 if the stock moves up. Assume you purchase δ stocks and b bonds. Bonds increase at a risk-free rate of $1 + 0.1\%$ each instant. If you own δ stock and the stock price goes up, you will own $\delta \cdot u \cdot S_0$ stock. If you own δ stock and the stock price goes down, you will own $\delta \cdot d \cdot S_0$ stock. Can you purchase a particular δ amount of stock and a particular b amount of bonds to earn exactly the same as your call option? Solve for b and δ so that

$$\delta \cdot 0.96 \cdot \$48 + b \cdot (1.001) = \$0.00$$
$$\delta \cdot 1.05 \cdot \$48 + b \cdot (1.001) = \$0.40$$
$$\delta \cdot d \cdot S_0 + b \cdot (1+r) \quad = \quad C_d$$
$$\delta \cdot u \cdot S_0 + b \cdot (1+r) \quad = \quad C_u$$

The solution is

$$\delta = \frac{\$0.40 - \$0.00}{1.05 \cdot \$48 - 0.96 \cdot \$48} \approx 0.0926 \quad \text{and} \quad b \approx -\$4.262$$

If you purchase a portfolio of 0.0926 shares (which costs $0.0926 \cdot \$48 \approx \$4.444$) and borrow \$4.262 (for a net outlay of \$0.182 today), then in the next period, this portfolio will pay off \$0 in the downstate and \$0.40 in the upstate. Because this is exactly the same as the payoff on the call option, the C_1^d call option should also be worth \$0.182. This is the law of one price (absence of arbitrage) in action.

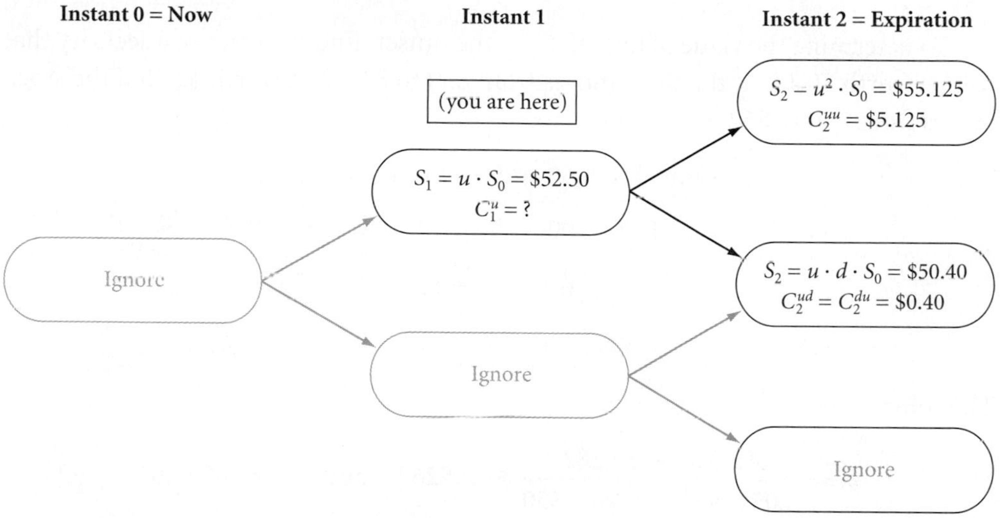

Now repeat the same exercise where the stock price stands at \$52.50 and next instant you can end up with either \$0.40 in the downstate or \$5.125 in the upstate. In this case, solve

Repeat the option pricing in the up state (C_1^u).

$$\delta \cdot 0.96 \cdot \$52.50 + b \cdot (1.001) = \$0.400$$
$$\delta \cdot 1.05 \cdot \$52.50 + b \cdot (1.001) = \$5.125$$
$$\delta \cdot d \cdot S_0 + b \cdot (1+r) \quad = \quad C_d$$
$$\delta \cdot u \cdot S_0 + b \cdot (1+r) \quad = \quad C_u$$

And the solutions are

$$\delta = \frac{\$5.125 - \$0.40}{1.05 \cdot \$52.50 - 0.96 \cdot \$52.50} = 1.00 \quad \text{and} \quad b \approx -\$49.95$$

If you purchase 1.00 shares (at a price of \$52.50) and borrow \$49.95 (for a net portfolio cost of \$2.550), you will receive \$5.125 if the stock price goes up and \$0.40 if the stock price goes down. Therefore, after the stock price has gone up once to stand at \$52.50, the C_1^u call option has to be valued at \$2.550, too.

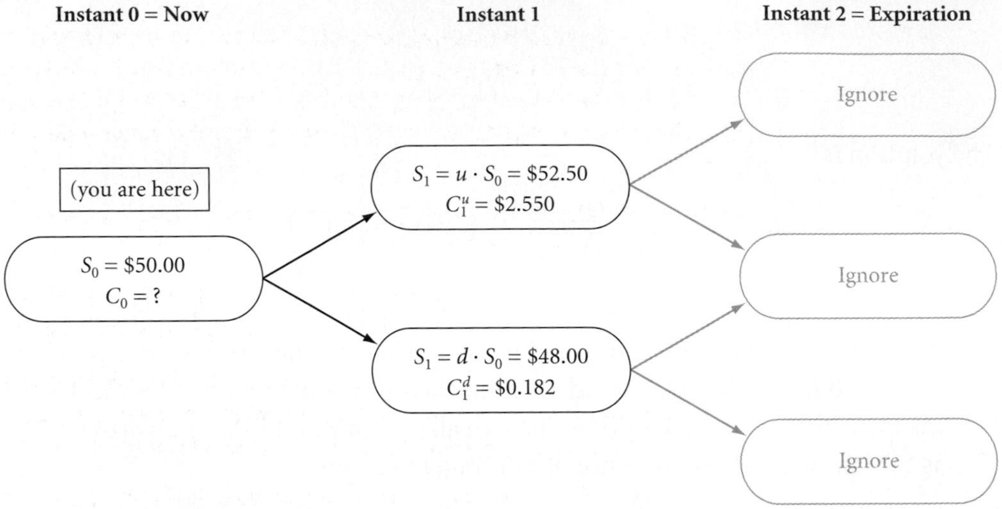

Repeat the option pricing today (C_0).

To determine the value of the call C_0 at the outset, find the price of a security that will be worth \$0.182 if the stock moves from \$50 to \$48, and worth \$2.55 if the stock moves from \$50 to \$52.50:

$$\delta \cdot 0.96 \cdot \$50.00 + b \cdot (1.001) = \$0.182$$

$$\delta \cdot 1.05 \cdot \$50.00 + b \cdot (1.001) = \$2.550$$

$$\delta \cdot d \cdot S_0 + b \cdot (1 + r) = C_d$$

$$\delta \cdot u \cdot S_0 + b \cdot (1 + r) = C_u$$

The solution is

$$\delta = \frac{\$2.550 - \$0.182}{1.05 \cdot \$50 - 0.96 \cdot \$50} \approx 0.5262 \quad \text{and} \quad b \approx -\$25.05$$

You have to purchase 0.5262 shares (cost today: \$26.31), and borrow \$25.05 dollars. Your portfolio's total net outlay is \$26.31 − \$25.05 ≈ \$1.26. Therefore, it follows that, by arbitrage, the price of the call option C_0 must be about \$1.26 today.

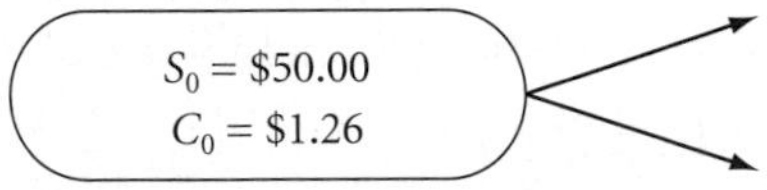

26.8 MATCHING A STOCK PRICE DISTRIBUTION TO A BINOMIAL TREE AND INFINITE-LEVEL PRICING

In real life, the stock price can move many more times than just twice. You need a tree with many more levels, so you need to generalize this binomial process to more levels. For example, if there are 10 instants, what would be the worst possible outcome? Ten instant down movements mean that the stock price would be

$$\text{Worst-Case Scenario:} \quad d^{10} \cdot S_0 = 0.96^{10} \cdot \$50 \approx \$33.24$$

The second-worst outcome would be one instant of up movement, and nine instants of down movement.

$$\text{Second-Worst-Case Scenario:} \quad d^9 \cdot u^1 \cdot S_0 = 0.96^9 \cdot 1.05^1 \cdot \$50 \approx \$36.36$$

Although the worst scenario can only occur if there are exactly 10 down movements, there are 10 different ways to fall into the second-worst scenario, ranging from *duuuuuuuuu*, *uduuuuuuuu*, . . . , to *uuuuuuuuud*. This should bring back bad memories of "combinations" from your SAT test: These are the 10 possible combinations, better written as

$$\binom{10}{1} = \frac{10!}{1! \cdot 9!} = 10$$

$$\binom{N}{i} = \frac{N!}{N! \cdot (N-i)!}$$

Therefore, with N levels in the tree, the stock price will be $u^i \cdot d^{N-i} \cdot S_0$ in $\binom{N}{i}$ paths. The probability of exactly 1 in 10 up movements, if the probability of each up movement is 40%, would be

$$\mathcal{P}rob(1\ u's,\ 9\ d's) = \binom{10}{1} \cdot 0.4^1 \cdot (1-0.4)^{10-1} \approx 4\%$$

$$\mathcal{P}rob((i)\ u's,\ (N-i)\ d's) = \binom{N}{i} \cdot p^i \cdot (1-p)^{N-i}$$

Still, is it enough to work with such an unrealistic binomial tree process, given that the stock price from today to expiration is more likely to have a continuous bell-shaped distribution? Put differently, how realistic is this binomial stock price process? Figure 26.5 plots a distribution of prices at the end of the tree if there are up to 500 nodes, if up and downs are equally likely, and if $u = 1.02$ and $d = 1/u \approx 0.98$. This binomial process looks as if it can generate a pretty reasonable distribution of possible future stock price outcomes.

With many nodes, a binomial tree becomes a log-normal distribution.

If you assume that the stock prices can only move up or down each instant and that there are an infinite number of instants, then the underlying stock price distribution follows a **log-normal distribution**, with \$0 as the lowest possible outcome. The rate of return follows a log-normal distribution with −100% as the lowest possible outcome. (The log-normal name comes from the fact that if a variable P follows a log-normal distribution, then $\log(P)$ follows a normal distribution.)

How the distribution works in the limit with infinitely many levels.

A practical question is how to select u, d, and q (where q is the true probability of an up movement) in a simulated tree to match an empirically observed stock price distribution. Assume you have a historical rate of return series to provide you with a reasonable mean and a reasonable variance for the expected rate of return. Call dt a really tiny time interval, call m the mean that you want to match, and s the standard deviation. Then select u and d as follows:

$$u = m \cdot dt + s \cdot \sqrt{dt} \quad \text{and} \quad d = m \cdot dt + s \cdot \sqrt{dt}$$

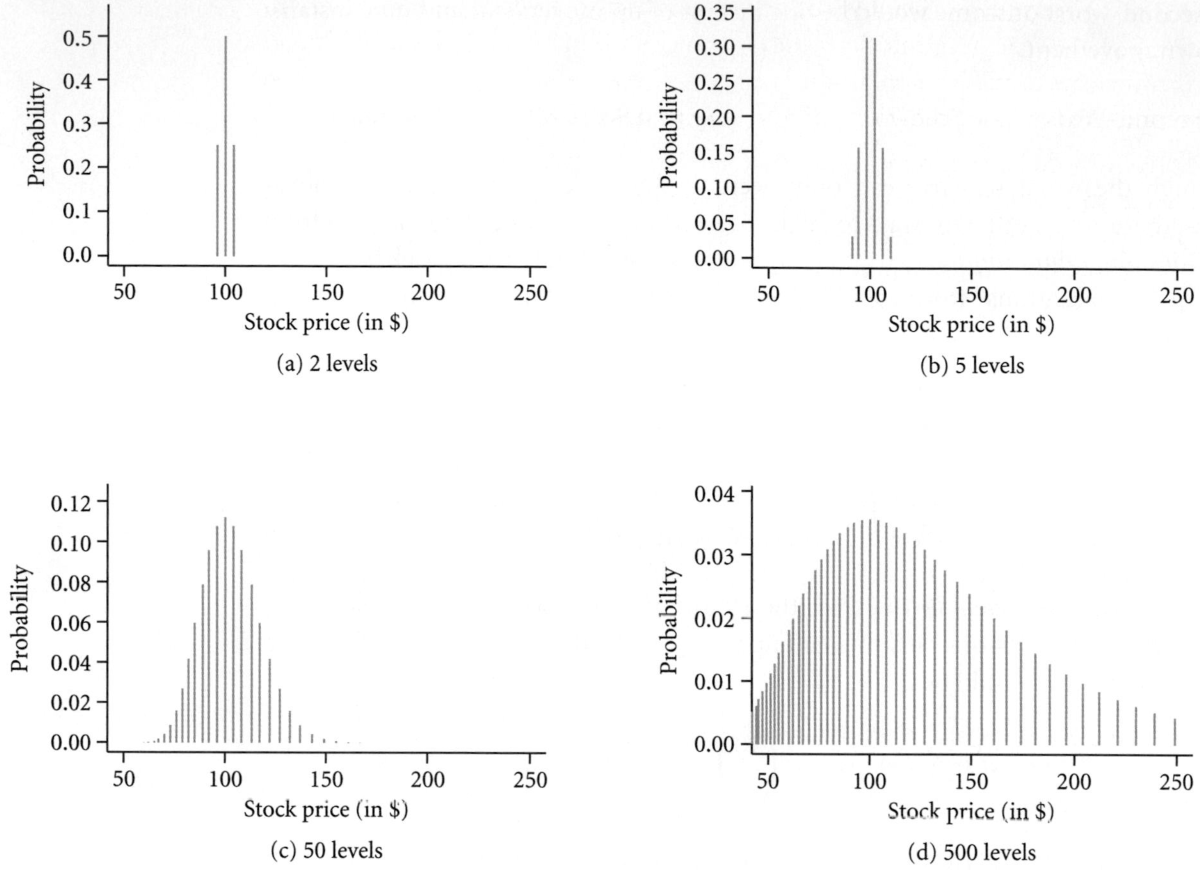

The probability of an up movement at each tree node is 50-50. The value multiplier is $u = 1.02$ if an up movement occurs, $d = 1/1.02$ if a down movement occurs. The stock price is \$100. The graphs differ in the number of levels in the tree: 2, 5, 50, and 500.

FIGURE 26.5 Stock Price Processes Simulated via Binomial Processes

In the limit, these choices create a log-normal distribution, which is completely characterized by its mean and variance, with mean m and standard deviation s.

26.9 BINOMIAL PRICING AND THE BLACK-SCHOLES FORMULA

B-S is a tree with infinitely many of these nodes.

In sum, the process to price options is as follows:

1. Determine the real-world stock price distribution to expiration—most importantly, the stock volatility.
2. Compute the u and d that you need in order to build your tree with a great many levels to expiration—the more the better—to match the real-world stock price distribution.
3. After you have written down your tree, write down the payoff of your option as a function of the underlying stock on the final nodes.
4. Work your way backward through the binomial tree.

5. At the origin node, you can read off the amount of stock (delta) that you need to purchase in order to mimic your option. You can buy the underlying stock and borrow some funds so as to mimic exactly how your option can change in value over the next instant, and your net cost determines the value of the option.

Computers can do this extremely quickly. You can also use this technique to price options that you could not otherwise price. For example, to price an American put option, work your way backward through the tree, asking yourself at each node whether exercising your put option would yield greater profits than keeping it. If it would, assume you would exercise at this node, and use this higher value while working backward thereafter.

To find the Black-Scholes formula, there are no more novel concepts or intuition. You only need a lot of (tedious) algebraic manipulation and simplification. You let the number of levels in the tree go to infinity—of course, adjusting u and d in a way that continues to match the real-world stock volatility from now to expiration. After this messy algebra, the Black-Scholes formula pops right out. The amount of stock you need to purchase for your mimicking portfolio, which is δ in our binomial notation, becomes $\mathcal{N}(d_1)$ in this limit. Done.

KEY TERMS

binomial process, 1017

log-normal distribution, 1021

PROBLEMS

The [ ] *indicates problems available in* myfinancelab

Q 26.44 Price an American call option with a strike price of $53 over the last two instants before expiration.

Q 26.45 Price a European put option with a strike price of $53 over the last two instants before expiration. How does its value differ from an American Put option? (Hint: for the American put, consider at each node whether you would want to exercise the put or continue to hold it.)

Epilogue

AFTERTHOUGHTS AND OPINIONS

You have traveled a long distance with me through this book. We have now reached the epilogue, where by tradition, I am allowed to voice my own personal opinions—in effect, to pontificate. I want to leave you with some of my thoughts on finance theory versus practice, business and finance education, business school rankings, finance research, and what I hope you will take with you after having read this book.

E.1 THEORY OR PRACTICE?

By nature, academic finance is very closely related to its practice. In our discipline, Yogi Berra's famous quote does not hold:

In theory, there is no difference between theory and practice. In practice, there is.

Finance theory and practice are ruled by the same ideas. As an academic myself, I am proud to claim that the majority of financial management ideas were either invented or developed in academia first *before* they crossed over into practice.

E.1A ACADEMIC RESEARCH—AN ACADEMIC QUESTION?

But finance research is not just for aspiring academics: Management consultants and economics consultants are basically researchers. Firms like McKinsey, Booze-Allen, or Boston Consulting Group (BCG) may have different audiences, production speeds, team systems, and publication and evaluation processes, but they research the same issues that academics do and with the same methods. Similarly, many proprietary trading and asset-management firms are really best characterized as "academic research departments in disguise." There is also much cross-fertilization: Many professors work regularly with major consulting or asset-investment firms—and some have even quit academia altogether to quadruple their pay. (If you want to become a management consultant or investment manager, my advice to you would be to try to work for a professor as a research assistant, paid or unpaid. Chances are you will learn as much or more from working on a research project as you have learned in your classes.)

Because finance is by nature such an applied discipline, after reading this book, you should not need anything else to understand finance research today. In an ideal world, you should be able to read the current state-of-the-art research right now. Unfortunately, there is one little problem: Academic finance journals love intimidating jargon. (They also prefer algebra to our numerical examples as the means for expressing ideas.) Thus, you may need some extra training in "language" if you want to read original-source academic papers. Nevertheless, if you were to decide to learn just a little bit more jargon, you would probably have the background to understand the most cutting-edge and interesting research ideas in finance journals today. Let me point you to some good initial sources to browse: Start with top academic journals (such as the *Journal of Finance*), top practitioners' journals (such as the *Financial Analysts Journal*), or good working-papers sites (such as SSRN.com). References in their articles can in turn direct you to other good journals and resources.

E.1B HOW MUCH CAN WE REALLY KNOW?

So, do we really understand finance? Certainly not fully. I have stated several times throughout the book that finance is as much an art as it is a science. All three parts of finance—valuation, investments, and financing—have simple conceptual underpinnings, but their applications in real life are difficult. And for all three of them, there is no alternative: Finding the proper value, the proper portfolio, and the proper capital structure may be tough, but this is what it is all about.

Given our deficiencies—given that all our methods have their errors—what should you do? My best advice to you is to use common sense, to employ a number of different techniques to come up with a range of possible answers, and to then make a judgment at the end of the day as to what estimate appears most reasonable in light of different models. As I have noted many times, finance is art based on science.

If we research finance long enough, will we ever fully understand it? The answer is again no. It is the nature of the beast. Most financial economics is a social science. When there are no arbitrage conditions, then behavior and prices can and will deviate from the theory. On occasion, this leads some to conclude that finance is less worthy of study or even a lesser science than, say, physics. This is a mistake:

- The questions are different. Finance is not interested in the big bang, and physics is not interested in the behavior of CFOs or investors. The study of one is not necessarily more or less worthy than the study of the other. We just have to bring the best tools to each question we want to study.
- Moreover, the perception that there is always more science and accuracy in physics is a misunderstanding, too: Some questions permit more precise answers than others. In physics, some systems (e.g., the weather or earthquakes) are by nature chaotic and difficult to predict, while others (e.g., Newtonian mechanics or planetary orbits) are more exact. It is the same in finance: Some questions are difficult to answer (e.g., the appropriate equilibrium rate of return on a stock), while others are relatively precise (e.g., option and fixed-income pricing).

- Economics and finance ask many questions to which the answers are more difficult and complex than those often pondered in mathematics and physics. For example, economic agents can react to economic forecasts, which makes predicting the stock market even harder than predicting the weather. Imagine how much more difficult it would be for meteorologists to forecast if the weather could read its own forecast and then change its behavior *because* it read the weather forecast!
- Physics and finance even share another property: Real-world constraints may prevent us from doing certain research. In physics, particle colliders have become so expensive that physicists can no longer study certain particles. In finance, our financial institutions have come to consider their data to be their proprietary competitive advantage. They also fear the legal liability that public disclosure and study could bring—and given the litigiousness of U.S. society, justly so. Sadly, as in physics, many interesting questions in finance may therefore no longer be researchable or answerable.

The fact that we do not have all the answers is both good news and bad news. The bad news is that we will never fully understand financial markets and individuals. The good news is that our knowledge will continue to improve and that there is plenty of space for new and exciting research in finance. For me, this means finance is still intellectually challenging enough to remain "fun." For you, if you go into practice, this means there is enough art involved so that computers will only help you, but never replace you.

E.1C OTHER POINTS

Before I end my monologue on research, let me mention that I have written about a number of other related issues on my own website at http://welch.econ.brown.edu/:

- I wrote a description of what I think our profession has accomplished over the last few decades and what challenges lie ahead.
- I described alternative finance degree choices, such as undergraduate finance education or master's degrees. You could even consider getting a Ph.D. It is not as monastic as you may think—in fact, the starting salary for many finance professors is now around $200,000 per year. (Because it takes more than 5 years on average to get a finance PhD, it is still not an NPV-maximizing choice, however.) I also explained how you should think of academic departments if you want to pursue a PhD program in financial economics.
- I explained why being a finance professor is a 60-hour-per-week job—the 20 hours of teaching that you see consumes only one-third of the time of a full-time finance professor. The other two-thirds are consumed in roughly equal parts by research (to come up with the ideas that make it into books like mine), service to the university (to run the school), and service to the academic profession at large (to help weed out good ideas from bad ideas). Of course, part-time professors often have the luxury of focusing only on the teaching part.

E.2 THOUGHTS ON BUSINESS AND FINANCE EDUCATION

Let me move on to some thoughts about how we teach. I began teaching in 1989. Since then, I believe the gap between faculty and MBA students has slowly but steadily grown. First, I must admit that we faculty are at least partly to blame. We are often guilty in not selling our ideas to our students. Sometimes, we think that our ideas are too difficult to communicate, or we have simply not yet worked them out well enough for ourselves. Of course, the dense curriculum rarely leaves us much time to talk about current academic research in the classroom, too.

But allowing this to happen has been a mistake. After all, excitement about new knowledge and research is exactly what has drawn us academics to business schools rather than to practice—with the opportunity to convey our ideas to our students and to the world at large. If we do not incorporate our current academic research into the curriculum, too, then we should not be surprised if our students sometimes wonder about its value. *As a profession, we need to do better.*

I am as guilty as others. However, I have tried to take some steps in the right direction. In addition to sneaking in many novel ideas into this book, I have tried to find the time to give a special final lecture in my own classes: I pick five current working papers from my department and talk about the questions they address and the answers they provide. Every time, even those students who were dead bored by me in my other lectures woke up and started asking questions, often coming up with interesting and different interpretations themselves. This last class session has always been the most fun both for myself and for my students. Maybe you can suggest such a class session to your instructor.

E.2A VOCATIONAL TRAINING?

Over the years, the common lack of exposure to (and thus appreciation for) research has made some students wonder what their education is all about. There is one view that holds that business schools exist primarily to enhance job opportunities, and as such, they should provide a "vocational education." In this model, teachers ideally share plenty of war stories, vouch for the importance of their own teaching in their past business environments, and may even help some students to get jobs with their own or their friends' businesses. This model—teaching job-specific skills—is one that works for many community colleges. It is not a model that can work for a good business school. A good business school is a center of thought and research. If you expect primarily vocational training from your business school, your finance education will be a rather unrewarding experience.

Good business schools should provide a predominantly intellectual experience. Such an experience allows students to take a fresh look at the world, to explore other business areas for the first time, to learn how to think in economic and business terms, to consider the intellectual foundations of business, and to learn about the most novel ideas—those that have not yet permeated practice. Yes, real-world CFOs have a lot of knowledge and great skill that neither finance professors nor you possess. But do you really want to learn *only* what current CFOs know *today*? Chances are that many of their practices are based on what they learned in their own education *20 to 30 years ago*. Here is an example that should make this clear. In October 2003, the UK's City & Guilds Institution released its study of 405 random financial directors. One in seven needed help switching his or her computer on and off. One in five struggled to save a document. More than one in five needed assistance in printing. And a quarter could not understand spreadsheets—invented almost 25 years earlier for the purpose of financial analysis. You should not aspire to learn just what CFOs do know—instead, you should aspire to learn also what they do not know!

So what should business schools teach you? In my opinion, the answer is that we need to focus on subjects that we can teach better than practitioners can. If we do it right, you have to be patient: You should not receive much job-specific training from us. You should realize that this is not a problem. If you get a job in Goldman's fixed-income department, Goldman will explain in its own training program the specialized fixed-income and institutional knowledge that it will require. If you get a marketing job at Pfizer, its orientation program (and your partnered salespeople) will show you how to "market" Lipitor. I am not belittling sales. Selling products (or ideas) is a skill of first-order importance. However, even if we could teach such subjects in business schools, firms can simply teach them better and faster than we can. It's not what we in business schools do best. Rather, our job must be to provide businesses with students who are smart, flexible, open-minded, and suitably critical, with a solid understanding of fundamental ideas—of forests, not of trees. Table E.1 is my perspective on who does what better. In closing, please do not expect to learn *everything* you need for success only from practice or only from school. If you do, you will be disappointed.

But, but, but . . . What about Finding a Job?

Naturally, like most students, you probably feel a great deal of anxiety about your first job prospects. Should you select your classes based on how "practical" you think they are? Is this not the "practical knowledge" that your recruiters expect?

Actually, the answer is mostly no. In my experience, recruiters are rarely looking for specific business practice knowledge. Employers first and foremost want to hire smart, curious, and enthusiastic individuals who are solid on the basic concepts *and who can think how to apply them to new situations*. To quote Hannibal Lecter, what matters is, "First principles. Simplicity. Read Marcus Aurelius. Of each particular thing ask: What is it in itself? What is its nature?" If you can take a business scenario and simplify it—analyze it in the context of the theories that you have learned—you will do well. This process is really very similar to what this book has been trying to teach. I did not write my book as training for an interview—it is just that the skills that I consider to be important are also the skills that are important in the interview process. On the flip side, if you try to skip the basics in favor of more "applied classes," my guess is that you will fail your interviews.

Your value, as an MBA graduate—even to your first employer—is not your immediate business knowledge. Instead, your value is your intellectual ability and flexibility; your knowledge of the fundamentals, of the basic theories, of their application, and of cutting-edge ideas; your human skills, team skills, and sales skills; and so on. Some of these skills are innate, but most can be taught or at least improved upon by studying. In the end, it is your versatility and curiosity, your ability to generalize and synthesize,

TABLE E.1 ADVANTAGES AND DISADVANTAGES OF BUSINESS SCHOOLS OVER BUSINESS PRACTICE

Some Examples of: What Business School Teaches Better Than Practice	What Practice Teaches Better Than Business School
General, universal knowledge	Job-specific knowledge
Concepts of business	The specific business
General tools (statistics, data, economics, etc.)	Specific tools (e.g., a particular accounting system)
Marketing methods	The company's specific product or service marketing
Method of thinking	Methods of *this* company's practice
Concepts of ideas for the next 20 years	Implementation of ideas from the last 10 years
Knowledge for a lifetime	Knowledge tailored to this year's business climate
Leadership principles and theories	Learning how to lead a particular set of people
Source of conflict	Conflict resolution with a specific person
Learning by study	Learning by doing
Reflection	Action
Selling principles	Selling the company's specific product or service
Negotiation principles	Negotiating with specific customers
"Forests"	"Trees"

your ability to apply theories to practice, and your talent for bringing a novel perspective to specific problems that will allow your MBA to be of value for many years to come.

E.2B YOUR FIRST FINANCE COURSE AND STUDENT HETEROGENEITY

There is another issue in your introductory finance class that may initially make you unhappy—and it is important that you realize why this is so. Chances are that you will find yourself in a classroom with considerable heterogeneity in student preparation. Many students will find the tempo of the first finance course too slow, and other students will find it too fast. The reason is that as many as half the students in business school may come from a finance-related job background. Usually, their work experience will not have left them with knowledge solid enough that they can skip the finance core course. Still, their background makes it much easier for them to take in new finance-related teaching. Other students may not have seen an equation for many years in their work. It will be a challenge for such students simply to keep up. If you are one of them, you will inevitably at first feel overwhelmed by your class experience. (And you will likely not do as well on the early exams—the world is simply not fair.) But let me advise patience, practice, and reflection: Your new knowledge will eventually fall into place, and you can do well *in the end*. Some of my best and brightest students felt frustrated during the course, but they kept at it, studied twice as hard, and ended up at the top of their classes. Struggling and anxiety along the way are necessary, maybe even desirable, and in the end, unavoidable.

Before you blame your instructor for all your early frustrations, please contemplate how you would gear the introductory finance class toward the different kinds of students in your class. There are no easy solutions. It is generally agreed that teaching introductory finance in a business school is among the most difficult assignments an instructor can take on. There are different levels of student preparedness, and there is a large amount of material that absolutely cannot be skipped. Again, recruiters expect students to have a solid grasp of the finance basics and often ask questions that could go right onto the midterm or final. As an instructor, after having blamed the situation, let me not disavow our biggest responsibility: It is our duty to make the first finance course a surmountable challenge for *all* motivated students, regardless of background. Every unprepared student must be able to acquire a solid finance background; every prepared student must still find the class to be useful. It is not our duty to be entertaining or even to be liked. In fact, a recent study at the U.S. Air Force Academy has shown that students randomly enrolled in classes did better in subsequent courses if their first instructor was less generous in grading and less well liked.

E.3 THE BUSINESS SCHOOL RANKINGS

Now indulge me for a moment. If you are an MBA student, you are surely familiar with the biannual influential *Business Week* (*BW*) rankings, first published in 1998. This rankings issue has become one of *BW*'s top sellers. Unfortunately, the quality of the *BW* rankings is only mediocre. Worse, their influence on business education has been both enormous and negative.

The not-so-secret sauce in *BW* rankings is what they describe as "customer satisfaction" measures of students and recruiters. But do these measures really make sense for a ranking?

- Is student happiness really an appropriate measure of student education? For example, consider another prominent survey: *Playboy*'s party school rankings. How do you think students at a perennially top-rated school (California State University at Chico) would respond? They would probably rate their educational satisfaction very highly—but this does not necessarily make Cal State Chico a great school.
- Is recruiter evaluation the appropriate measure of student education? Most recruiters are themselves alums of *one* of the schools they are asked to rank. (They also see themselves reflected in the students from their own alma maters.) Most business school alums have never studied at any school other their own—a fact that naturally makes them relatively ill-equipped to make comparisons. Because larger schools have more alums that are sampled, the size of the pool of alums ends up being the primary predictor of "recruiter opinion" in the *BW* survey. The result is inevitable: The average recruiter ranks his or her own alma mater highest (or at least very highly). As a consequence, the correlation between the historical size of a school's graduating classes and its *BW* ranking is very high.
- Can *BW* expect truthful answers? It turns out that all schools, students, and alums are now catering to and manipulating the *BW* rankings. Students and alums now know that if they do not rank their own schools highly, the values of their degrees

will go down. And at almost every school, some faculty member will explain this to those students who have not yet understood this basic fact.

At best, I would consider the *BW* rankings today to be measures of familiarity and size. But as a measure of educational quality, I can hardly imagine a worse methodology. Still let's pretend for a moment that this is not the case. There is an even more fundamental error in these rankings: They treat education as if it were a consumption good sold by (business school) vendors. *It is not!* Instead, education is something that is coproduced by the school *and the student*.

See, the usefulness of the MBA degree is largely determined by the depth of engagement of the student. A student who coasts through classes that were selected to be easy and entertaining will learn little, no matter how good the school is. Yes, there are some quality differences, but the *BW* rankings do not fairly reflect them and they are not very large. Nowadays, most business schools teach similar curricula. In my opinion, my book is just as suitable to the #1-ranked school as it is to the #100-ranked school. My personal guess is that the educational quality difference (and average student quality difference) between the #1 school and the #10 school is quite small (as it would be between #10 and #30, or between #30 and #100). In contrast, there is great variation among students in the same school. *The variation in what any one individual gets out of an MBA program within one particular school just swamps the average quality variations across schools.*

Ultimately, it is up to you to make your education top-ranked. Fortunately, although deciding on the right school is a tough problem, there are really many good choices to pick from. Many schools that never show up in these rankings offer excellent business educations today. Again, by selection of classes and instructors, you can easily get a better business education at the #100 school than many students get at the #1 school.

But not all is well. One worrisome trend is that in their quest to improve on their *Business Week* rankings, many schools have begun to make curriculum changes that I deem to be counterproductive. They are tempted to substitute happiness over content, at least at the margin—but good teaching is neither necessarily an entertainment nor necessarily a popularity contest. The material has to be tough and challenging, even if it makes the experience less fun. Perhaps as a result of curriculum changes over time, I have begun to hear complaints from more and more top recruiters these days that a good undergraduate or master of finance student can be as good at finance as the (twice-as-expensive) MBA counterpart. This needs to change. The answer must be to make the MBA curriculum tougher and more rigorous again. If MBA students want to get paid twice the money, they have to be twice as good! We can't have cake, and eat it, too.

E.4 BON VOYAGE

Our book has covered the principles of finance in some depth and breadth. You should be very well prepared now for the next steps in your finance/business education. You can probably choose your next courses á la carte: investments, derivatives, advanced corporate finance, fixed income, financial institutions, international finance, or something else. If you are still curious to learn more from or about me, then you can also visit the book's website at www.prenhall.com/welch, or my own website at http://welch.econ.brown.edu.

By now you should no longer be surprised by one of my more quirky obsessions. It was as important to me to try to teach you how to approach problems as it was to teach you finance. When you are confronted with a new problem, please think in terms of the easiest numerical example that you can come up with. Only gradually work your way up. That is, address your full problem only after you have understood simpler examples. Hey, you may not even have to remember any of the formulas in this book—given time, you should now be able to "reinvent" them. This would be my greatest victory.

I have enjoyed writing this book in the same way that I enjoy writing my academic research papers, and pretty much for the same reason: It has been like solving an intriguing puzzle that no one else has figured out in quite the same way—a particular way to see and explain finance. Of course, writing it has taken me far longer than I had anticipated—5 years and still counting just for the first edition!

But it will all have been worth it if you have learned from it. If you have studied the book, you should now know about 90% of what I know about finance. Interestingly, there were a number of topics that I thought I had understood, but had not—and it was only my having to explain them to you that clarified them for me, too. And this brings me to a key point that I want to leave you with—never be afraid to ask questions, even about first principles. To do so is not a sign of stupidity—on the contrary, it is often a sign of deepening awareness and understanding.

I have no illusions: You will not remember all the fine details in this book as time passes—I know I won't. But more than the details, I hope that I will have left you with an appreciation for the big ideas, an arsenal of tools, a method for approaching novel problems, and a new perspective. You can now think like a financier.

—Ivo Welch
Brown University
September 2008

Appendix A
Background

Links to websites are listed on the book's website at www.prenhall.com/welch.

A.1 GENERAL MATHEMATICAL AND STATISTICAL BACKGROUND

- Finding a base:

$$3^2 = 9 \quad \Leftrightarrow \quad 3 = 9^{1/2}$$
$$x^a = b \quad \Leftrightarrow \quad x = b^{1/a}$$

  A power of 1/2 is also equivalent to the square root operation.

- Finding an exponent:

$$3^2 = 9 \Leftrightarrow 2 = \frac{\ln(9)}{\ln(3)}$$
$$a^x = b \Leftrightarrow x = \frac{\ln(b)}{\ln(a)}$$

  (Instead of the natural log ln, you could use any other log, too.)

- Summation notation:

$$\sum_{i=1}^{N} f(i) = f(1) + f(2) + \cdots + f(N)$$

  This should be read as the "sum over all i from 1 to N." There are N terms in this sum. i is not a real variable: It is simply a dummy counter to abbreviate the notation. When 1 and N are omitted, it usually means "over all possible i."

- Summation rules:

$$\sum_{i=1}^{N} [a \cdot f(i) + b] = [a \cdot f(1) + b] + [a \cdot f(2) + b] + \cdots + [a \cdot f(N) + b]$$
$$= a \cdot \left[\sum_{i=1}^{N} f(i)\right] + N \cdot b$$

Here is an illustration:

$$\sum_{i=1}^{3}\left[5 \cdot i^i + 2\right] = [5 \cdot 1^1 + 2] + [5 \cdot 2^2 + 2] + [5 \cdot 3^3 + 2] = 7 + 22 + 137 = 166$$

- Linear functions: A function $\mathcal{L}(\cdot)$ is called a linear function if and only if $\mathcal{L}(a + b \cdot x) = a + \mathcal{L}(b \cdot x) = a + b \cdot \mathcal{L}(x)$, where a and b are constants.

  Here is an illustration. The (weighted) average is a linear function. For example, start with (5, 10, 15) as a data series. The average is 10. Pick $a = 2$ and $b = 3$. For averaging to be a linear function, it must be that

$$\text{Average}(2 + 3 \cdot \text{Data}) = 2 + 3 \cdot \text{Average}(\text{Data})$$

Let's try this—the left-hand side (LHS) would become the average of 17, 32, 47, which is 32. The right-hand side (RHS) would become $2 + 3 \cdot 10 = 32$. It works: Averaging indeed behaves like a linear function. In contrast, the square root is not a linear function, because $\sqrt{-2 + 3 \cdot 9} \neq -2 + 3 \cdot \sqrt{9}$. The LHS is 5, the RHS is 7.

Linear functions are very important in financial economics:

- Similar to averaging, expected values are linear functions. This is what has permitted us to interchange expectations and linear functions:

$$\mathcal{E}(a + b \cdot \tilde{X}) = a + b \cdot \mathcal{E}(\tilde{X})$$

  This will be explained in the next section.

- The rate of return on a portfolio is also a linear function of the investment weights. For example, a portfolio rate of return may be $r(x) = 20\% \cdot r_x + 80\% \cdot r_y$, where r_x is the rate of return on the component into which you invested \$20. For $r(x)$ to be a linear function, we need

$$2 + 3 \cdot r(x) = r(2 + 3 \cdot x)$$

$$a + b \cdot r(x) = r(a + b \cdot x)$$

  Substitute in

$$2 + 3 \cdot (20\% \cdot r_x + 80\% \cdot r_y) = 20\% \cdot (2 + 3 \cdot r_x) + 80\% \cdot (2 + 3 \cdot r_y)$$

  Both sides simplify to $2 + 60\% \cdot r_x + 240\% \cdot r_y$, so our statement is true and a portfolio return is indeed a linear function.

However, not all functions are linear. The variance is not a linear function, because

$$\mathcal{V}ar(a + b \cdot \tilde{X}) \neq a + b \cdot \mathcal{V}ar(\tilde{X})$$

You will confirm this in the next section.

SOLVE NOW!

Q A.1 If $(1 + x)^{10} = (1 + 50\%) = 1.5$, what is x?

Q A.2 If $(1 + 10\%)^x = (1 + 50\%) = 1.5$, what is x?

Q A.3 Are $\sum_{i=1}^{N} x_i$ and $\sum_{s=1}^{N} x_s$ the same?

Q A.4 Write out and compute $\sum_{x=1}^{3}(3 + 5 \cdot x)$. Is x a variable or just a placeholder to write the expression more conveniently?

Q A.5 Write out and compute $\left(\sum_{y=1}^{3} 3\right) + 5 \cdot \left(\sum_{x=1}^{3} y\right)$. Compare the result to the previous expression.

Q A.6 Is $\sum_{i=1}^{3}(i \cdot i)$ the same as $\left(\sum_{i=1}^{3}\right) \cdot \left(\sum_{i=1}^{3} i\right)$?

A.2 LAWS OF PROBABILITY, PORTFOLIOS, AND EXPECTATIONS

Let's go over the algebra of probabilities and portfolios, which you had to use in the investments chapters. It is presented in a more mathematical fashion than it was in the chapters, which you may find easier or harder, depending on your background.

A.2A SINGLE RANDOM VARIABLES

The **laws of expectations** for single random variables are as follows:

- Definition of expectation

$$\mathcal{E}(\tilde{X}) = \sum_{i=1}^{N} \mathcal{P}rob(i) \cdot [\tilde{X} = X(i)]$$

An expectation is basically a probability-weighted average.

- The expected value of a linear transformation (a and b are known constants):

$$\mathcal{E}(a \cdot \tilde{X} + b) = a \cdot \mathcal{E}(\tilde{X}) + b \tag{A.1}$$

To see this, consider a fair coin that can be either 1 or 2. Say $a = 4$ and $b = 10$. In this case, the LHS is $\mathcal{E}(a \cdot \tilde{X} + b) = \mathcal{E}(4 \cdot \tilde{X} + 10) = 0.5 \cdot (4 \cdot 1 + 10) + 0.5 \cdot (4 \cdot 2 + 10) = 0.5 \cdot 14 + 0.5 \cdot 18 = 16$. The RHS is $4 \cdot (0.5 \cdot 1 + 0.5 \cdot 2) + 10 = 16$. This all worked because expectation is a linear operator. (It is a fancy way of saying that it is a summation, which allows you to regroup the summation terms of the linear combination $a \cdot \tilde{X} + b$ inside the expectation, which is also a probability-weighted linear combination.) A little more generally, you could rename $\tilde{X}$ as $f(\tilde{X})$, so

$$\mathcal{E}[a \cdot f(\tilde{X}) + b] = a \cdot \mathcal{E}[f(\tilde{X})] + b$$

However, you cannot always "pull" expectations in, so $\mathcal{E}(f(\tilde{X}))$ is not always $f(\mathcal{E}(\tilde{X}))$. For example, if $f(x) = x^2$, it is the case that

$$\mathcal{E}(\tilde{X} \cdot \tilde{X}) \neq \mathcal{E}(\tilde{X}) \cdot \mathcal{E}(\tilde{X})$$

To see this, reconsider the fair 1 or 2 coin. The LHS is $\mathcal{E}(\tilde{X}^2) = 0.5 \cdot (1 \cdot 1) + 0.5 \cdot (2 \cdot 2) = 2.5$, but the RHS is $[\mathcal{E}(\tilde{X})]^2 = (0.5 \cdot 1 + 0.5 \cdot 2)^2 = (1.5^2) = 2.25$.

- Definition of variance:

$$\mathcal{V}ar(\tilde{X}) = \mathcal{E}\left(\left[\tilde{X} - \mathcal{E}(\tilde{X})\right]^2\right)$$

It is sometimes easier to rewrite this formula as $\mathcal{V}ar(\tilde{X}) = \mathcal{E}(\tilde{X}^2) - [\mathcal{E}(\tilde{X})]^2$. Let me show you that this works. For our fair 1 or 2 coin example, the variance according to the main formula is $0.5 \cdot (1 - 1.5)^2 + 0.5 \cdot (2 - 1.5)^2 = 0.25$. For the second formula, we just computed $\mathcal{E}(\tilde{X}^2) = 2.5$ and $[\mathcal{E}(\tilde{X})]^2 = 2.25$. Subtracting these terms yields the same 0.25.

- Definition of a standard deviation:

$$\text{Standard Deviation}(\tilde{X}) = \sqrt{\mathcal{V}ar(\tilde{X})}$$

- The variance of a linear combination (where a and b are known constants):

$$\mathcal{V}ar(a \cdot \tilde{X} + b) = a^2 \cdot \mathcal{V}ar(\tilde{X}) \tag{A.2}$$

For our fair 1 or 2 coin example, with $a = 4$ and $b = 10$, the LHS is $0.5 \cdot [(4 \cdot 1 + 10) - 16]^2 + 0.5 + 0.5 \cdot [(4 \cdot 2 + 10) - 16]^2 = 0.5 \cdot [-2]^2 + 0.5 \cdot [2]^2 = 4$. The RHS is $4^2 \cdot 0.25 = 4$.

Here is an extended illustration. A coin, outcome called $\tilde{X}$, has 4 and 8 written on the two sides. These two outcomes can be written as $4 \cdot i$ where i is either 1 or 2. Therefore, the expected value of $\tilde{X}$ is

$$\begin{aligned}
\mathcal{E}(\tilde{X}) &= \sum_{i=1}^{2} \mathcal{P}rob[\tilde{X} = (4 \cdot i)] \cdot (4 \cdot i) \\
&= \mathcal{P}rob(\tilde{X} = 4) \cdot (4) + \mathcal{P}rob(\tilde{X} = 8) \cdot (8) \\
&= 50\% \cdot 4 + 50\% \cdot 8 \qquad = 6 \\
\mathcal{V}ar(\tilde{X}) &= \sum_{i=1}^{2} \mathcal{P}rob[\tilde{X} = (4 \cdot i)] \cdot [(4 \cdot i) - 6]^2 \\
&= \mathcal{P}rob(\tilde{X} = 4) \cdot (4 - 6)^2 + \mathcal{P}rob(\tilde{X} = 8) \cdot (8 - 6)^2 \\
&= 50\% \cdot 4 + 50\% \cdot 4 \qquad = 4
\end{aligned}$$

The standard deviation is the square root of the variance, here 2.

$\mathcal{E}(\tilde{X}^2)$ is, of course, not the same as $[\mathcal{E}(\tilde{X})]^2 = [3]^2 = 9$, because

$$\begin{aligned}
\mathcal{E}(\tilde{X}^2) &= \sum_{i=1}^{2} \mathcal{P}rob[\tilde{X} = (2 \cdot i)] \cdot (2 \cdot i)^2 \\
&= \mathcal{P}rob(\tilde{X} = 2) \cdot (2^2) + \mathcal{P}rob(\tilde{X} = 4) \cdot (4^2) \\
&= 50\% \cdot 4 + 50\% \cdot 16 = 10
\end{aligned}$$

Now work with a linear transformation of the X, say, $\tilde{Z} = \$2.5 \cdot \tilde{X} + \$10$. This is a fundamental operation in finance, because the rates of return on portfolios are such linear transformations. For example, if you own 25% in A and 75% in B, you will earn $0.25 \cdot \tilde{r}_A + 0.75 \cdot \tilde{r}_B$. Thus,

Prob	Coin	$\tilde{X}$	$\tilde{Z}$
1/2	Heads	4	\$20
1/2	Tails	8	\$30

You want to convince yourself that the expected value of $\tilde{Z}$, defined as $\$2.5 \cdot \tilde{X} + \$10$, is $\$2.5 \cdot \mathcal{E}(\tilde{X}) + \$10 = \$25$. First, compute by hand the expected value the long way from $\tilde{Z}$,

$$\begin{aligned}
\mathcal{E}(\tilde{Z}) &= \sum_{i=1}^{2} \mathcal{P}rob[\tilde{X} = (4 \cdot i) \text{ same as } \tilde{Z} = \$2.5 \cdot \tilde{X} + \$10] \cdot (Z_i) \\
&= \mathcal{P}rob(\tilde{X} = 4 \text{ same as } \tilde{Z} = \$20) \cdot (\$20) \\
&\quad + \mathcal{P}rob(\tilde{X} = 8 \text{ same as } \tilde{Z} = \$30) \cdot (\$30) \\
&= 50\% \cdot \$20 + 50\% \cdot \$30 = \$25
\end{aligned}$$

Unlike the mean (the expected value), the variance is *not* a linear function. The variance of $\tilde{Z} = \$2.5 \cdot \tilde{X} + \$10$ is *not* $\$2.5 \cdot \mathcal{V}ar(\tilde{X}) + \$10 = \$2.5 \cdot 4 + \$10 = \$20$. Instead, $\mathcal{V}ar(\tilde{Z}) = \mathcal{V}ar(a \cdot \tilde{X} + b) = a^2 \cdot \mathcal{V}ar(\tilde{X}) = (\$2.5)^2 \cdot \mathcal{V}ar(\tilde{X}) = \$\$6.25 \cdot 4 = \$\$25$. You can confirm this working with $\tilde{Z}$ directly:

$$\begin{aligned}
\mathcal{V}ar(\tilde{Z}) &= \sum_{i=1}^{2} \mathcal{P}rob[\tilde{X} = (4 \cdot i)] \cdot \left[(\tilde{Z}_i) - \mathcal{E}(\tilde{Z})\right]^2 \\
&= \mathcal{P}rob(\tilde{X} = 4 \text{ same as } \tilde{Z} = \$20) \cdot (\$20 - \$25)^2 \\
&\quad + \mathcal{P}rob(\tilde{X} = 8 \text{ same as } \tilde{Z} = \$30) \cdot (\$30 - \$25)^2 \\
&= 50\% \cdot (\$5)^2 + 50\% \cdot (\$5)^2 = \$\$25
\end{aligned}$$

The standard deviation of $\tilde{Z}$ is therefore $\sqrt{\$\$25} = \$5$.

Let us quickly confirm Formula A.1 for $\tilde{Z} = \$2.5 \cdot \tilde{X} + \$10$:

$$\begin{aligned}
\mathcal{E}(\tilde{Z}) &= \mathcal{E}(a \cdot \tilde{X} + b) = a \cdot \mathcal{E}(\tilde{X}) + b \\
\$25 &= \mathcal{E}(\$2.5 \cdot \tilde{X} + \$10) = \$2.5 \cdot \mathcal{E}(\tilde{X}) + \$10 = \$2.5 \cdot 6 + \$10 = \$25
\end{aligned}$$

Let us also quickly confirm Formula A.2:

$$\begin{aligned}
\mathcal{V}ar(\tilde{Z}) &= \mathcal{V}ar(a \cdot \tilde{X} + b) = a^2 \cdot \mathcal{V}ar(\tilde{X}) \\
\$\$25 &= \mathcal{V}ar(\$2.5 \cdot \tilde{X} + \$10) = (\$2.5^2) \cdot \mathcal{V}ar(\tilde{X}) = \$\$6.25 \cdot 4 = \$\$25
\end{aligned}$$

SOLVE NOW!

Q A.7 What is the expected value and standard deviation of a bet $\tilde{B}$ that pays off the number of points on a fair die, squared? For example, if the die lands on 3, you receive \$9.

Q A.8 Assume that you have to pay \$30, but you receive twice the outcome of the bet $\tilde{B}$ from Question A.7. This is a new bet, called $\tilde{C}$. That is, your payoff is $\tilde{C} = -\$30 + 2 \cdot \tilde{B}$. What is the expected payoff and risk of your position? (Suggestion: Make your life easy by working with your answers from Question A.7.)

A.2B PORTFOLIOS

Portfolios are defined as follows:

$$\tilde{r}_{\text{P}} = \sum_i w_{\text{i}} \cdot \tilde{r}_{\text{i}}$$

where w_{i} is the known investment weights in security i, and $\tilde{r}_{\text{i}}$ is the security return on security i. Unlike the simpler definitions above, portfolios are the weighted sum of multiple random variables.

- Portfolio expectations:

$$\mathcal{E}\left(\sum_i w_{\text{i}} \cdot \tilde{r}_{\text{i}}\right) = \sum_i w_{\text{i}} \cdot \mathcal{E}(\tilde{r}_{\text{i}})$$

  Although the weights are fixed and known constants, they cannot be pulled out of the summation, because they are indexed by i (each could be different from the others).

- Portfolio riskiness:

$$\mathcal{V}ar\left(\sum_i w_{\text{i}} \cdot \tilde{r}_{\text{i}}\right) = \sum_{i=1}^{\text{N}} \left\{ \sum_{j=1}^{\text{N}} \left[w_{\text{i}} \cdot w_{\text{j}} \cdot \mathcal{C}ov(\tilde{r}_{\text{i}}, \tilde{r}_{\text{j}}) \right] \right\}$$

$$= \sum_{i=1}^{\text{N}} \sum_{j=1}^{\text{N}} \left[w_{\text{i}} \cdot w_{\text{j}} \cdot \mathcal{C}ov(\tilde{r}_{\text{i}}, \tilde{r}_{\text{j}}) \right]$$

Here is an illustration. A coin toss outcome is a random variable, $\tilde{T}$, and it will return either \$2 (heads) or \$4 (tails). You have to pay \$2 to receive this bet. This looks like a good bet: The mean rate of return on each coin toss, $\mathcal{E}(\tilde{r}_{\text{T}})$, is 50%. The variance on *each* coin toss is

$$\mathcal{V}ar(\tilde{r}_{\text{T}}) = 1/2 \cdot (0\% - 50\%)^2 + 1/2 \cdot (100\% - 50\%)^2 = 0.25$$

Therefore, the standard deviation of each coin toss is 50%.

Now, bet on two independent such coin toss outcomes. You have \$10 invested on the first bet and \$20 on the second bet. In other words, your overall actual and unknown rates of return are

$$\text{Actual:} \qquad r = \sum_{i=1}^{2} w_i \cdot r_i$$

$$\text{Random Unknown:} \quad \tilde{r} = \sum_{i=1}^{2} w_i \cdot \tilde{r}_i$$

(The second formula is in random variable terms.) Assume that your investment portfolio consists of the following investments:

$$w_1 = \frac{\$10}{\$30} \approx 0.33 \quad \text{and} \quad w_2 = (1 - w_1) = \frac{\$20}{\$30} \approx 0.67$$

We can now use the formulas to compute your expected rate of return ($\mathcal{E}(\tilde{r})$) and risk ($\mathcal{S}dv(\tilde{r})$). To compute your expected rate of return, use

$$\begin{aligned}\mathcal{E}(\tilde{r}) = \sum_{i=1}^{2} w_i \cdot \mathcal{E}(\tilde{r}_i) &= w_1 \cdot \mathcal{E}(\tilde{r}_1) + w_2 \cdot \mathcal{E}(\tilde{r}_2) \\ &= 1/3 \cdot (50\%) + 2/3 \cdot (50\%) = 50\%\end{aligned}$$

(Recall that an expectation is a linear operator, that is, a summation. A portfolio is a summation, too. Because both are ultimately nothing but summations, you can regroup terms, which means that the above formula works.) To compute your variance, use

$$\begin{aligned}\mathcal{V}ar(\tilde{r}) &= \sum_{i=1}^{2}\sum_{j=1}^{2} w_i \cdot w_j \cdot \mathcal{C}ov(\tilde{r}_i, \tilde{r}_j) \\ &= w_1 \cdot w_1 \cdot \mathcal{C}ov(\tilde{r}_1, \tilde{r}_1) + w_1 \cdot w_2 \cdot \mathcal{C}ov(\tilde{r}_1, \tilde{r}_2) \\ &\quad + w_2 \cdot w_1 \cdot \mathcal{C}ov(\tilde{r}_2, \tilde{r}_1) + w_2 \cdot w_2 \cdot \mathcal{C}ov(\tilde{r}_2, \tilde{r}_2) \\ &= w_1^2 \cdot \mathcal{C}ov(\tilde{r}_1, \tilde{r}_1) + 2 \cdot w_1 \cdot w_2 \cdot \mathcal{C}ov(\tilde{r}_1, \tilde{r}_2) \\ &\quad + w_2^2 \cdot \mathcal{C}ov(\tilde{r}_2, \tilde{r}_2) \\ &= w_1^2 \cdot \mathcal{V}ar(\tilde{r}_1) + 2 \cdot w_1 \cdot w_2 \cdot \mathcal{C}ov(\tilde{r}_1, \tilde{r}_2) \\ &\quad + w_2^2 \cdot \mathcal{V}ar(\tilde{r}_2) \\ &= (1/3)^2 \cdot \mathcal{V}ar(\tilde{r}_1) + 2 \cdot w_1 \cdot w_2 \cdot 0 + (2/3)^2 \cdot \mathcal{V}ar(\tilde{r}_2) \\ &= (1/9) \cdot \mathcal{V}ar(\tilde{r}_1) + (4/9) \cdot \mathcal{V}ar(\tilde{r}_2) \\ &= (1/9) \cdot 0.25 + (4/9) \cdot 0.25 \qquad \approx 0.1389\end{aligned}$$

The standard deviation is therefore $\sqrt{0.1389} \approx 37.3\%$. This is lower than the 50% that a single coin toss would provide you with.

TABLE A.1 CUMULATIVE NORMAL DISTRIBUTION TABLE

z	$\mathcal{N}(z)$	z	$\mathcal{N}(z)$	z	$\mathcal{N}(z)$	z	$\mathcal{N}(z)$	z	$\mathcal{N}(z)$	z	$\mathcal{N}(z)$
−4.0	0.00003										
−3.5	0.00023										
−3.0	0.0013	−2.0	0.0228	−1.0	0.1587	0.0	0.5000	1.0	0.8413	2.0	0.9772
−2.9	0.0019	−1.9	0.0287	−0.9	0.1841	0.1	0.5398	1.1	0.8643	2.1	0.9821
−2.8	0.0026	−1.8	0.0359	−0.8	0.2119	0.2	0.5793	1.2	0.8849	2.2	0.9861
−2.7	0.0035	−1.7	0.0446	−0.7	0.2420	0.3	0.6179	1.3	0.9032	2.3	0.9893
−2.6	0.0047	−1.6	0.0548	−0.6	0.2743	0.4	0.6554	1.4	0.9192	2.4	0.9918
−2.5	0.0062	−1.5	0.0668	−0.5	0.3085	0.5	0.6915	1.5	0.9332	2.5	0.9938
−2.4	0.0082	−1.4	0.0808	−0.4	0.3446	0.6	0.7257	1.6	0.9452	2.6	0.9953
−2.3	0.0107	−1.3	0.0968	−0.3	0.3821	0.7	0.7580	1.7	0.9554	2.7	0.9965
−2.2	0.0139	−1.2	0.1151	−0.2	0.4207	0.8	0.7881	1.8	0.9641	2.8	0.9974
−2.1	0.0179	−1.1	0.1357	−0.1	0.4602	0.9	0.8159	1.9	0.9713	2.9	0.9981
										3.5	0.99977
										4.0	0.99997

Normal score (z) versus standardized normal cumulative distribution probability $\mathcal{N}(z)$

SOLVE NOW!

Q A.9 Repeat the example, but assume that you invest $15 into each coin toss rather than $10 and $20, respectively. Would you expect the risk to be higher or lower? (Hint: What happens if you choose a portfolio that invests more and more into just one of the two bets?)

A.3 CUMULATIVE NORMAL DISTRIBUTION TABLE

Table A.1 allows you to determine the probability that an outcome X will be less than a prespecified value x, when standardized into the score z. For example, if the mean is 15 and the standard deviation is 5, an outcome of $X = 10$ is 1 standard deviation below the mean. This standardized score can be obtained by computing $z(x) = [x - \mathcal{E}(x)]/\mathcal{S}dv(x) = (x - 15)/5 = (10 - 15)/5 = (-1)$. This table then indicates that the probability that the outcome of $\tilde{X}$ (i.e., drawn from this distribution with mean 15 and standard deviation 5) will be less than 10 (i.e., less than its score of $z = -1$) is 15.87%.

Figure A.1 shows what the table represents. Figure A.1(a) is the classical bell curve. Recall that at $z = -1$, the table gives $\mathcal{N}(z = -1) = 15.87\%$. This 15.87% is the shaded area under the curve up to and including $z = -1$. Figure A.1(b) just plots the values in the table itself, that is, the area under the graph to the left of each value from Figure A.1(a).

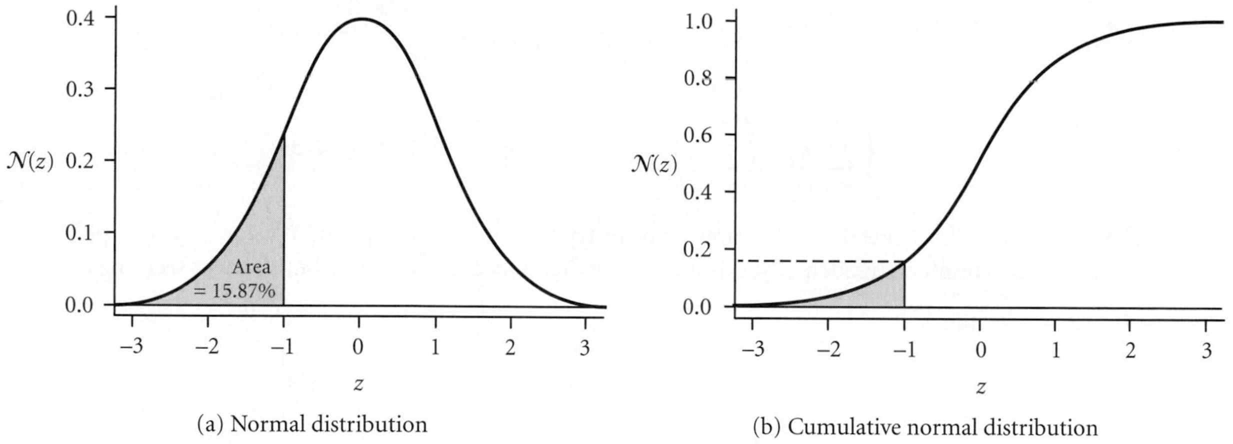

FIGURE A.1 Graphical Normal Distribution Figures

If you ever need to approximate the cumulative normal distribution in a spreadsheet, you can use the built-in function **normsdist**.

KEY TERMS

SOLVE NOW! SOLUTIONS

Q A.1 $x \approx 4.138\%$. Check: $(1 + 4.138\%)^{10} \approx 1.5$.

Q A.2 $x \approx 4.254$. Check: $1.1^{4.254} \approx 1.5$.

Q A.3 Yes! i and s are not variables, but notation!

Q A.4 The expression is

$$\sum_{x=1}^{3}(3 + 5 \cdot x) = (3 + 5 \cdot 1) + (3 + 5 \cdot 2) + (3 + 5 \cdot 3) = 8 + 13 + 18 = 39$$

x is not a variable. It is simply a counter dummy used for writing convenience. It is not a part of the expression itself.

Q A.5 The expression is

$$\left(\sum_{y=1}^{3} 3\right) + 5 \cdot \left(\sum_{y=1}^{3} y\right) = (3 + 3 + 3) + 5 \cdot (1 + 2 + 3) = 39$$

The result is the same. This is an example of why $\sum_i a + b \cdot x = \left(\sum_i a\right) + b \cdot \sum_i x$.

Q A.6 No. The two expressions are

$$\sum_{i=1}^{3}(i \cdot i) \quad = \quad 1 + 4 + 9 \quad = 14$$

$$\left(\sum_{i=1}^{3} i\right) \cdot \left(\sum_{i=1}^{3} i\right) = (1 + 2 + 3) \cdot (1 + 2 + 3) = 36$$

The two are not the same! Thus, be careful not to try to pull out multiplying *i*'s! You can only pull out constants, not counters. Incidentally, this is also why $\mathcal{E}(\tilde{X}^2) \neq \mathcal{E}(\tilde{X})^2$, as stated in the next section.

Q A.7 The expected value is

$$\mathcal{E}(\tilde{B}) = (1/6) \cdot \$1 + (1/6) \cdot \$4 + (1/6) \cdot \$9 + (1/6) \cdot \$16 + (1/6) \cdot \$25 + (1/6) \cdot \$36 \approx \$15.17$$

The variance is

$$\begin{aligned} \mathcal{V}ar(\tilde{B}) = \quad & (1/6) \cdot (\$1 - \$15.17)^2 + (1/6) \cdot (\$4 - \$15.17)^2 + (1/6) \cdot (\$9 - \$15.17)^2 \\ & + (1/6) \cdot (\$16 - \$15.17)^2 + (1/6) \cdot (\$25 - \$15.17)^2 + (1/6) \cdot (\$36 - \$15.17)^2 \\ \approx \quad & \$\$149.14 \end{aligned}$$

The standard deviation is therefore

$$\mathcal{S}dv(\tilde{B}) = \sqrt{\mathcal{V}ar(\tilde{B})} \approx \sqrt{\$\$149.14} \approx \$12.21$$

Q A.8 You expect to receive

$$\begin{aligned} \mathcal{E}(\tilde{C}) &= -\$30 + 2 \cdot \mathcal{E}(\tilde{B}) \approx -\$30 + 2 \cdot \$15.17 \approx \quad \$0.34 \\ \mathcal{V}ar(\tilde{C}) &= \quad 2^2 \cdot \mathcal{V}ar(\tilde{B}) \approx 4 \cdot \$\$149.14 \quad = \$\$595.56 \\ \mathcal{S}dv(\tilde{C}) &= \quad \sqrt{\mathcal{V}ar(\tilde{C})} \quad \approx \$24.42 \end{aligned}$$

Q A.9 Your investment weights are now $w_1 = w_2 = 0.5$. The mean rate of return remains the same 50%. The variance of the rate of return is computed similarly to the example in the text:

$$\mathcal{V}ar(\tilde{r}) = (1/2)^2 \cdot 0.25 + (1/2)^2 \cdot 0.25 = 0.125$$

Therefore, the risk (standard deviation) is 35.35%. This is lower than it was when you put more weight on one of the coin tosses. This makes sense: As you put more and more into one of the two coin tosses, you lose the benefit of diversification!

Appendix B

A Short Glossary of Some Bonds and Rates

This appendix briefly describes a plethora of different interest rates and bonds that you may encounter. More complete finance glossaries can be found at http://www.investopedia.com and *The New York Times Dictionary of Money and Investing* (also available online).

In the real world, there are many different interest rates. Every borrower and every lender may pay a slightly different interest rate, depending on the bond's default risk, risk premium, liquidity, maturity, identity, convenience, and so on. It is impossible to describe every common bond or rate. Section C of the *Wall Street Journal* has a wealth of information on many common and important interest bearing instruments. In addition, futures on interest rates (similar to forward rates) are listed in the B section.

Here are short descriptions of some of the fixed-income instruments and interest rates that are in common use.

Agency bonds: Issued by quasi-governmental companies, such as FannieMae, FreddieMac, the Federal Farm Credit Bank, and SallieMae (all described below). These agencies were originally set up by the U.S. government to facilitate loans for a particular purpose, then bundle the loans and sell them to the financial markets. These companies are huge. Sometimes they are thought to be implicitly backed by the U.S. government, though no explicit guarantees may exist.

APR (annual percentage rate): A measure of interest due on a mortgage loan that accounts for upfront costs and payments. Unfortunately, there are no clear rules about how to compute APR, so the APR computation can vary across companies.

ARM (adjustable rate mortgage): A mortgage with an interest rate that is usually reset once per year according to a then-prevailing interest rate, prespecified by a formula but subject to some upper limit (called a cap), repayable by the borrower.

Bankers acceptances: Loans by banks to importers, used to pay the exporting firm. Backed by the issuing bank if the importer defaults. Usual maturities are 30 to 180 days.

Certificate of deposit (CD): An instrument issued by banks to retail customers willing to commit funds for longer than a day, but still over a short-term or medium-term period. Unlike ordinary savings accounts, CDs are not insured by the government if the bank fails.

Callable bonds: Bonds that the issuer can call back at a prespecified price. Often a feature of convertible bonds.

CMO (collateralized mortgage obligation): A security backed by a pool of real estate mortgages, with specified claims to interest and principal payments. For example, there are **interest only** (**IO**) bonds and **principal only** (**PO**) bonds, which entitle bondholders either only to the interest or the principal income that the pool of mortgages receives.

Collateralized trust bonds: Often issued by corporations, these bonds pledge as collateral the securities owned by a subsidiary.

Commercial paper: Short term bonds issued by corporations to the public markets. Often backed by bank guarantees. Because commercial paper is short term and often backed by assets, it is usually very low risk.

Consumer credit rates: The *Wall Street Journal* lists typical **credit card rates** and **car loan rates**.

Convertible bonds: Bonds that the holder can convert into common equity. Often issued with a call feature.

Debenture: Unsecured general obligation bond.

Discount rate: The interest rate that the Federal Reserve charges banks for short-term loans of reserves.

Equipment obligations: Unlike debentures, these corporate bonds usually pledge specific equipment as collateral.

Eurobond: Bonds issued by the U.S. government outside the domain of the Securities and Exchange Commission (e.g., in Europe) and purchased by foreign investors. Eurobonds need not be denominated in dollars.

Federal funds rate: Banks must hold financial reserves at the Federal Reserve Bank. If they have more reserves than they legally need, they can lend them to other banks. The rate at which they lend to one another overnight is the federal funds rate. It is this interest rate that is primarily under the control of the board of governors of the Federal Reserve.

FannieMae: Originally the Federal National Mortgage Association (**FNMA**), a corporation set up by the government to help facilitate mortgage lending. It holds mortgages as assets. FannieMae and FreddieMac together hold most of the U.S. mortgages, although they sell off claims against these mortgage bundles into the financial markets. The FNMA bonds are themselves collateralized (backed) by the mortgages, but, despite common perception before the 2008 crisis, *not* by the U.S. government. Still, it would be difficult to imagine that the United States would let FannieMae default. FannieMae may simply be too big to fail. To be eligible, an FNMA mortgage cannot exceed a certain limit. In 2008, this was $417,000 for a single-family first mortgage loan.

Federal Farm Credit Banks Funding Corporation: Similar to FreddieMac and FannieMae, but focused on farm lending.

FreddieMac: Originally the Federal Home Loan Mortgage Corporation (**FHLMC**), an agency similar to FannieMae.

GIC (guaranteed investment contract): Usually issued by insurance companies and purchased by retirement plans. The interest rate is guaranteed, but the principal is not.

G.O. bond (general obligation bond): A bond whose repayment is not guaranteed by a specific revenue stream. See also revenue bond.

GinnieMae: The Government National Mortgage Association (**GNMA**) backs loans made by other federal departments (e.g., the Department of Veterans Affairs). GinnieMae securities are the only mortgage bonds guaranteed by the U.S. government and thus cannot default.

High-yield bonds: Sometimes also called **non-investment-grade bonds** or just **junk bonds**, high-yield bonds are bonds (usually of corporations) that have credit ratings of BB and lower.

Home equity loan rate: The rate for loans secured by a home. Usually second mortgages, that is, mortgages taken after another mortgage is already in place.

Investment-grade bonds: Bonds that have a credit rating of BBB or better. This is a common (and important) classification for corporate bonds.

Jumbo mortgage: A mortgage that exceeds the FNMA limit on standard mortgage sizes.

LIBOR (London interbank offer rate): The typical rate at which large London banks lend dollars to one another. Nowadays primarily a benchmark published by the *Wall Street Journal*.

Money market: Cash sitting in a brokerage account and not invested in other assets.

Mortgage bonds: Bonds secured by a particular real-estate property. In case of default, the creditor can foreclose the secured property. If still not satisfied, the remainder of the creditor's claim becomes a general obligation.

Municipal bond: Bonds issued by a municipality. Often tax-exempt.

***N*-year mortgage rate:** The interest rate paid on a fixed-rate loan by the borrower, secured by a house, with standard coupon payments. The published number usually is for standardized mortgages issued through FNMA.

Prime rate: Historically, the prime rate was an average interest rate that banks usually offered their best customers for short-term loans. These days, it is primarily a rate published by the *Wall Street Journal*. The WSJ does not clearly explain its computation, but just states vaguely that it is "the base rate on corporate loans posted by at least 75% of the nation's 30 largest banks." The prime rate is used less and less nowadays. It is being replaced by LIBOR, at least in most commercial usage.

Repo rate: A repo is a *repurchase* agreement, in which a seller of a bond agrees to repurchase the bond, usually within 30 to 90 days, but also sometimes overnight. (Repos for more than 30 days are called *term repos*.) This allows the bondholder to obtain actual cash to make additional purchases while still being fully exposed to, and thus speculating on, the bond.

Revenue bonds: Bonds secured by a specific revenue stream. See also G.O. bond.

SallieMae: Originally **Student Loan Marketing Association** (SLMA). Like FannieMae, an agency (corporation) set up by the U.S. government. It facilitates student loans.

Savings bonds: Issued by the U.S. Treasury, savings bonds can only be purchased from, or sold to, agents authorized by the Treasury Department. They must be registered in the name of the holder. **Series E bonds** are zero-bonds; **series H bonds** are semiannual coupon payers and often have a variable interest feature. In contrast to savings bonds, other bonds are typically **bearer bonds**, which do not record the name of the owner and are therefore easy to resell (or steal).

Tax-exempt bonds: Typically bonds issued by municipalities. Their interest is usually exempt from some or all income taxes. The designation **G.O. bond** means **general obligation bond**, that is, a bond that was not issued to finance a particular obligation. In contrast, a **revenue bond** is a bond backed by specific municipal revenues—but it may or may not be tax-exempt.

Treasury security: The subject of Section 5.3, Treasuries are all bonds issued by the U.S. government's Treasury department to finance the national debt. They come in the form of short-term bills, medium-term notes, and long-term bonds.

Treasury STRIPS: An acronym for *Separate Trading of Registered Interest and Principal of Securities*. Financial institutions can convert each coupon payment and principal payment of ordinary Treasury coupon bonds into individual zero-bonds. The Treasury website has a detailed explanation.

Yankee bonds: U.S. dollar–denominated and SEC-registered bonds by foreign issuers.

Prepayment.

Note: Mortgage (and many other) bonds can be paid off by the borrower before maturity. Prepayment is common, especially if interest rates are dropping.

Glossary

10-K The form that U.S. companies are required to use when filing their annual financial statements with the SEC.

10-Q The form that U.S. companies are required to use when filing their quarterly financial statements with the SEC.

Absolute priority rule (APR) The legal requirement that, in the event of liquidation, senior securities such as bonds are paid before more junior claimants such as stockholders.

Accounts payable A current liability that represents money owed to creditors for goods purchased on credit.

Accounts receivable A current asset that represents money owed to the firm for goods sold on credit.

Accruals Economic transactions that have delayed cash implications—the main difference between income and cash flow.

Acid ratio *See* quick ratio.

Acquisition The act of one company purchasing another.

Adjusted present value (APV) The net present value of a project when financed only by equity plus the present value of the tax subsidy.

ADR *See* American depositary receipt.

Adverse selection A market process in which information asymmetries between buyers and sellers lead to a trading premium for the better-informed participant.

After-tax expenses Expenses that cannot be deducted from gross income to lower the amount of taxes paid.

Agency problem (principal agent problem) The conflict that arises when agents act to maximize their own utility or wealth, not necessarily that of their employer, usually referring to such conflicts between stockholders, bondholders, and firm managers.

Agents Persons or organizations having a position of trust that requires them to act on behalf of others.

Alternative minimum tax (AMT) An IRS calculation that factors some tax-preference items back into adjusted gross income. If the AMT amount is higher than the regular tax liability for the year, the taxpayer pays more than his or her regular taxes.

American depositary receipt (ADR) A unit investment trust representing claims to shares of foreign stocks that makes it easy for domestic investors to trade in a foreign security.

American option An option that can be exercised any time up to, and including, the expiration date.

Amortization The yearly, prorated, tax-deductible decline in accounting (book) value resulting from the allocation of the cost of an intangible asset over time.

AMT *See* alternative minimum tax.

Annual meeting The meeting once a year, required by law, of the corporate board of directors.

Annual report A financial report summarizing the company's business and financial reports, sent to stockholders on a yearly basis.

Annualized rates A convenient per-year unit of measurement for the rate at which money accumulates.

Annuity A stream of equal cash flows for a given number of periods.

APR *See* absolute priority rule.

APT *See* arbitrage pricing theory.

APV *See* adjusted present value.

Arbitrage pricing theory (APT) A financial theory similar to the CAPM but that allows more than one beta (and more than one risk premium).

Ask price The price at which an investor or the exchange's market maker is currently willing to sell shares.

Asset beta The firm beta adjusted for debt.

Asset classes Broad classifications of financial investment opportunities such as cash, bonds, and stocks.

Asset pricing model A formula most often expressed in terms of a required expected rate of return rather than in terms of an appropriate project price.

At-the-money The condition in which an option's exercise price equals the underlying assets price.

Auction market A market in which one designated specialist (assigned for each stock) manages the auction process by trading with individual brokers on the floor of the exchange.

Auction-based repurchase An auction-based share repurchase program in which shareholders receive an offer by the firm wanting to purchase a fixed number of shares at a fixed-price premium (typically around 15% to 20%) from its investors.

Audit In financial accounting, an audit is a required examination of a company's financial statements by an independent third party.

Average (or mean) The probability-weighted average of all possible outcomes.

Average collection period *See* days of sales outstanding.

Average cost of capital The average financing cost for all of the firm's existing projects.

Average rate of return An interest rate average that does not take into account compound interest.

Average tax rate The ratio of taxes paid to taxable income.

Balloon payment Principal or outstanding balance repaid in full amount at maturity.

Bank loan A private debt issue in which there is often only one lender.

Bank overdraft A current liability that represents a negative bank balance.

Base asset *See* derivative.

Bed-and-breakfast deal A tax arbitrage strategy in which tax-exempt funds drive up the share price before the ex-dividend date, sell them, and then buy them back the next day to create a tax loss. Both the IRS and the Bank of England have limited such tax arbitrage with time limits.

Before-tax expenses Expenses that can be deducted from gross income to lower the amount of taxes paid.

Behavioral finance A school of thought that posits that markets sometimes do *not* use all available information due to psychological factors in human behavior.

Berkshire Hathaway A well-known conglomerate holding company based in Omaha, Nebraska, run by chairman and CEO Warren Buffett. It manages numerous subsidiary businesses.

Best practice Recommended guidelines for corporate governance to improve accountability, ethics, disclosure, timeliness matters, etc.

Beta The slope of a line showing the relationship between the independent variable (the x-axis) and a dependent variable (the y-axis).

Bid price The price at which an investor or the exchange's market maker is currently willing to buy shares.

Bid-ask bounce A data illusion in which, without new information, the actual price for a security will vary between the bid and the ask price, depending on whether the trade was initiated by a buyer or a seller, resulting in a small day-to-day price reversals.

Big Board (NYSE) *See* New York Stock Exchange.

Binomial process A discrete probability distribution describing the number of successes and failures that occur in a particular number of independent trials.

Black knight An unwelcome bidder who threatens a hostile takeover of a company.

Black Tuesday October 29, 1929, the last of the three worst days of the stock market crash that began the *Great Depression.*

Black-Scholes A formula that explains the value of a call option on a stock as a function of the underlying stock price, the volatility, the risk-free interest rate, the time period, and the exercise price.

BLS *See* Bureau of Labor Statistics.

Bond covenants Legal restrictions in bond indentures that bind the issuer in various ways to prevent undercutting repayment ability.

Bond duration A weighted measure of how soon bond payments are made or a measure of how sensitive the bond price is to changes in interest rates.

Bond maturity The time to final payback of principal and interest on a bond.

Bond seniority A bond provision that specifies exactly which bondholders are paid first in case of bankruptcy and liquidation.

Bond-washing A tax arbitrage strategy for bonds in which the interest income is changed into a capital gain, thereby getting the lower capital gains tax rate. The IRS "wash sale" rule imposes a 30-day time limit on this practice.

Book runners Managers who lead syndicates and are in charge of assembling the book (list or spreadsheet) of investors interested in purchasing shares of a company.

Book value An accounting valuation of an asset, usually very different from the asset's market value. In particular, the book value of shareholders' equity is more of a "plug-in" number that serves to equalize assets and liabilities than an intrinsically meaningful figure.

Book-equity-to-market-equity ratio The inverse of the book equity–based valuation multiple.

Bridge financing The short-term financing needed to complete an acquisition until a long-term loan can be arranged.

Brownian motion The scientific term for random walks, applied to many different fields, including finance.

Bubble A historical run-up in the stock market, or a runaway market in which rationality has temporarily disappeared.

Bulldog bonds Foreign bonds in Great Britain.

Bureau of Labor Statistics (BLS) The U.S. government agency that determines the compositions of a number of prominent stock and bond indexes and publishes the average

Business judgment rule An American case-law concept that protects the corporate board and its managers against lawsuits if they make poor choices in the execution of company affairs except for obvious self-dealings or fraud.

Buy recommendation A recommendation made by market stock analysts to purchase securities.

Buy-and-hold trader An investor who trades stocks rarely.

Calendar spread An option strategy wherein options are bought and sold on the same stock. The options are of the same type (puts or calls), have the same strike prices, but have different expiration dates.

Calibration Changing the inputs (cash flows, cost of capital, or growth rate) in a pro forma model to make it better fit the actual market value of the company.

Call option The right to buy an underlying base security for a prespecified dollar amount for a specific period of time.

Callability A bond provision that allows the issuer (the firm) to "call in" (buy back) the outstanding bond at a prespecified price.

Capital asset pricing model (CAPM) A model providing the appropriate expected rate of return (cost of capital) for a project when given the project's relevant risk characteristics.

Capital market line The linear tangent line showing the combination of the risk-free assets and a risky portfolio on the efficient frontier.

Capital structure The relative proportions of the total claims on the assets of the firm.

CAPM *See* capital asset pricing model.

Capped A provision that the interest rate on floating-rate debt will never exceed a predetermined ceiling.

Cash (money market) Not only physical dollar bills but also debt securities that are very liquid, very low-risk, and very short-term, such as certificate of deposits (CDs), savings deposits, or commercial paper.

Cash (treasury) management Managing the cash holdings of the firm to maximize profits and prevent insolvency.

Cash Currency and coins.

Cash conversion cycle The sum of the inventory-processing period and the number of days needed to collect receivables, minus the number of days the firm takes to pay its suppliers.

Cash dividend A dividend that comes in one of two forms: regular dividends or special dividends.

Cash flow The net payment streams to debt and equity issues.

Cash flow rights The priority of receiving payment in the event of bankruptcy.

Cash flow statement A financial statement that shows a company's sources and uses of cash during some time period. These sources and uses are broken down into cash flows from operating activities, investing activities, and financing activities.

Cash offer Acquisitions wherein the acquiring firm pays with cash instead of stock.

Cash ratio Similar to the current ratio but with receivables deleted from current assets.

CBOE *See* Chicago Board Options Exchange.

CDS *See* credit default swap.

Certainty equivalence form A formula that rearranges the CAPM formula by reducing the expected value of the future cash flow by some number that relates to the cash flow's covariance with the market. This reduced value can then be discounted with the risk-free rate.

Certainty equivalent The lower certain return on an investment that would leave one indifferent to taking a chance on a higher-return, but more risky, investment.

CFO *See* chief financial officer.

Chairman of the board The most important individual on the board. He or she controls the board's meeting agenda and directs management to produce the necessary information.

Changes in working capital Changes in current assets or current liabilities.

Chapter 11 reorganization A chapter in the current *U.S. Federal Bankruptcy Code* that allows for corporate reorganization of a firm in bankruptcy.

Chapter 7 liquidation A chapter in the current *U.S. Federal Bankruptcy Code* that allows for corporate liquidation of a firm in bankruptcy.

Chicago Board Options Exchange (CBOE) The largest financial market for trading options on stocks.

Chief financial officer (CFO) The top financial officer of a company.

Classical finance A school of thought with a firm belief in efficient markets.

Closed-end fund An investment company that does not redeem fund shares. Instead, those shares are traded like stocks on the open market.

COGS *See* cost of goods sold.

Collared *See* capped.

Collateral Specific corporate assets, also called security, pledged to a specific bond in case of default.

Combination An option strategy that consists of options of different types.

Commercial paper Short-term unsecured debt of larger corporations, often guaranteed by a bank's credit line and therefore almost risk-free to the lender.

Common equity *See* common stock.

Common stock Ownership shares in public corporations, the most common type of equity, also called *ordinary equity* or *common equity.*

Compartmentalization The tendency of people to categorize decisions—a behavioral error that can cause predictable valuation mistakes.

Competitive market A market in which no buyer or seller has the ability to set the price.

Complex spread Contains multiple options, some short, others long.

Computer science The study of the theory and foundations of information and computation methods and how they can be applied to computer systems.

Conflict of interest A situation in which different parties have competing interests or agency conflicts.

Conglomerates Companies with widely diversified and often unrelated business holdings.

Consol bonds Perpetuity bonds that promise a fixed payment forever.

Consumer Price Index (CPI) The most prominent inflation measure, a hypothetical bundle of average household consumption on a monthly basis. It is the official source of most inflation measures.

Contingent claim *See* derivative.

Continuously compounded interest rate An interest rate that compounds as if interest is paid every instant.

Control rights Power given to investors by the entrepreneurs who later allow investors to obtain what they were promised.

Convertibility The most common bond mechanism to allow creditors to partake in the upside of equity that limits the ex-post expropriation of bondholders while preserving the firm's option to accept new projects.

Convertible bond A bond with an option that allows the bond holder to exchange the bond for shares under certain conditions.

Convertible preferred Preferred shares that give the holder the right to convert them into common stock at some future date if the firm succeeds.

Core equity (Tier 1 capital) The book value of the total amount of common stock, disclosed reserves, and retained earnings, the most common regulatory definition for bank capitalization.

Corporate board The legal agent or principal elected by the shareholders that is supposed to act on behalf of the firm's owners. It has the power to hire and fire managers.

Corporate charter The legal document that specifies the basics of the firm's decision powers, governance, contractual matters, amending the charter, etc.

Corporate dividend exclusion rule A provision in the U.S. tax code that reduces a second round of tax for corporate owners on dividend income that was previously taxed.

Corporate governance The system of corporate controls and regulations that manages the problems of accountability and agency conflicts between shareholders and managers.

Corporate raider An acquirer who makes a hostile tender offer to purchase shares in order to obtain control of either the whole firm or a voting majority of shareholders.

Corporate takeover A merger or acquisition in which the ownership and control of a firm changes.

Correlation A unitless statistic indicating how well two variables move together.

Cost of capital The expected rate of return at which the firm can obtain financing. It is dependent on the amount of levered equity ownership.

Cost of goods sold (COGS) The direct costs of producing goods, such as the cost of materials and labor. It excludes indirect expenses such as distribution and sales costs.

Coupon bond A bond that pays a fixed coupon on a regular schedule (usually semiannually) until maturity.

Covariance A statistic which shows how two variables covary together.

Covenants Loan or bond provisions in which lenders grant their creditors additional control rights in the original lending agreement. For example, a loan agreement may specify that the firm must maintain a certain level of liquidity.

Covered interest rate parity (IRP) An arbitrage condition that ties together the currency spot rate, the currency forward rate, and the country Treasury interest rates.

CPI *See* consumer price index.

CPI bonds *See* treasury inflation protected securities.

Credit Default Swap (CDS) A tradable credit derivative contract that transfers the default risk from a bond buyer to a bond seller.

Credit line A loan provision that, like instant debt, permits borrowers to draw down from a loan account and repay at will until a termination date or maturity.

Credit premium *See* default risk premium.

Credit risk premium *See* default risk premium.

Crossing system A method to trade stocks that focuses primarily on matching large institutional trades with one another in an auction-like manner.

Cum-dividend date The last date on which a share still has the right to receive the dividend.

Cumulative normal distribution The probability of a random variable in a normal distribution being less than or equal to some value.

Current assets Short-term assets such as cash assets, marketable securities, accounts receivable, and inventories, etc., that will convert into cash within a year or less.

Current liabilities Short-term liabilities such as accruals, payables, short-term notes, etc., that will be paid within a year or less.

Current ratio The ratio of current assets to current liabilities. It is a measure of short-term liquidity.

Day trader An investor who trades stocks daily.

Days of inventories outstanding Inventory divided by total sales on credit, times number of days outstanding.

Days of payables outstanding (DPO) Accounts payable divided by total sales on credit, times number of days outstanding.

Days of receivables outstanding (DRO) *See* days of sales outstanding.

Days of sales outstanding (DSO) Accounts receivable divided by total sales on credit, then multiplied by the number of days per year.

Debt An amount of money owed to another person or entity.

Debt capacity The maximum borrowing level of a firm at which it is able to repay its debts in a timely manner.

Debt ratio The ratio of total debt (the sum of current liabilities and long-term liabilities) to total assets (the sum of current assets, fixed assets, and any other assets).

Debt rights That part of control rights in which debt has first priority on the promised payments and equity is entitled to any residual value.

Debt/equity ratio The ratio of a firm's total debt to its shareholder equity. The ratio may be calculated using book values, market values, or a combination of book and market values for each component.

Declaration date The date the board of directors votes to for a dividend to be paid at a later date.

Default The act of failing to repay either interest or principal timely and in full.

Default risk (or credit premium or credit risk) The probability of failing to repay either interest or principal timely and in full.

Default risk premium The difference between the promised rate and the expected rate that the lender needs to break even.

Deferred taxes The difference between "IRS real taxes" and "GAAP pretend taxes" that publicly traded firms are required to report on the balance sheet, also called *accumulated deferred taxes.*

Deflation The opposite of inflation, a process in which the general price level falls.

Delaware General Corporation Law A set of historic Delaware state case laws that guide the settlement of corporate conflicts on governance and liability issues.

Delta *See* hedge ratio.

Depletion The yearly, prorated, tax-deductible decline in accounting (book) value resulting from the allocation of the cost of a natural resource over time.

Depreciation The yearly, prorated, tax-deductible decline in accounting (book) value resulting from the allocation of the cost of a tangible asset over time.

Derivative (base asset or contingent claim) A financial security the value of which is determined by the value of some other underlying base asset.

Dilution The drop in ownership value of outstanding shares as a result of new shares of stock being issued by a company.

Discount bond A bond that sells for less than its par or face value.

Diseconomies of scale The case wherein all inputs are increased proportionately but the output increases less than proportionally.

Diversification The mixing of different investments within a portfolio that reduces the impact of each one on the overall portfolio performance.

Dividend A distribution from the firm to its investors that can take the form of cash or shares of stock. If not qualified, this usually means cash.

Dividend payout ratio The ratio of dividends to net income, measuring the percentage of earnings paid out as dividends.

Dividend reinvestment plan (DRIP) A plan whereby participating shareholders agree to reinvest automatically any dividend payments into more shares of the company.

Dividend smoothing Corporate policy that favors a slow increase in dividends over time in order to avoid cutting dividends.

Dividend yield End-of-period dividend / current stock price.

Dividend-earnings ratio *See* dividend-payout ratio.

Dividend-payout ratio The ratio of dividends to net income.

Dividend-price ratio The ratio of dividends to the end-of-period share price.

Dividends Capital distributions in which companies pay some of their earnings in cash to investors.

Dot-com bubble *See* Internet bubble.

Double taxation of dividends The situation wherein company earnings are first taxed at the corporate level, and then individual investors are taxed a second time at the full dividend personal income tax rate.

Dow Jones 30 A popular stock market index consisting of 30 large stocks in different industries.

DPO *See* days of payables outstanding.

DRIP *See* dividend reinvestment plan.

DRO *See* days of receivables outstanding.

DSO *See* days of sales outstanding.

Due diligence A voluntary or legal obligation to investigate some aspect of business performance.

DuPont model ROE = (net profit margin) x (asset turnover) x (equity multiplier), or ROE = (net income / book value of equity) = (net income / sales) x (sales / assets) x (assets / book equity).

Duration A method of measuring the average or *effective* time-length payout pattern of a bond. The simplest duration measure computes the time-weighted average of bond payouts, divided by the sum of all payments. It can also be applied to projects or firms.

EAC *See* equivalent annual cost.

Earnings An accounting measure of company income that equals revenues − (cost of sales + operating expenses + taxes) over a period of time.

Earnings before interest, taxes, depreciation, and amortization (EBITDA) A non-GAAP accounting measure of company income equal to operating revenue − operating expenses + other revenue. It omits interest, taxes, depreciation, and amortization. It is not a measure of cash flow.

Earnings dilution Lower earnings per share resulting from more issuing of equity.

Earnings retention ratio The ratio of the change in retained earnings to either sales, assets, or income.

Earnings yield The reciprocal of the P/E ratio, the percentage of price that is due to current earnings.

EBIT Earnings before interest and taxes. *See also* operating income.

EBITDA *See* earnings before interest, taxes, depreciation, and amortization.

ECAP *See* enhanced capital advantaged security.

ECN *See* electronic communication network.

Economic rents Investment rates of return that are much higher than the cost of capital, stemming from "monopoly" power of some kind, such as having scarce assets or capabilities.

Economies of scale The case wherein all inputs are increased proportionately but the output increases more than proportionally.

EDGAR *See* Electronic Data Gathering, Analysis, and Retrieval.

Efficiency wage An above-market wage high enough to induce agents to more closely align their interests with the firm.

Efficient Adjective term usually given to a financial price if the market has set that price correctly using *all* available information.

Efficient Market Hypothesis (EMH) A financial theory that holds that all securities are priced efficiently and fairly since they incorporate all relevant information.

Electronic communication network (ECN) A computer network that trades the same stocks that exchanges trade and that competes with exchanges in terms of cost and speed of execution, cutting out the specialist and thereby allowing investors to post price-contingent orders themselves. The biggest ECN's are Archipelago and Instinet.

Electronic Data-Gathering, Analysis, and Retrieval (EDGAR) A comprehensive electronic repository of corporate financials, including annual and quarterly reports run by the SEC.

EMH *See* efficient market hypothesis.

Empire building An agency cost in which managers acquire greater resources for themselves and their pet projects at the expense of maximizing shareholder wealth.

Employee stock option plan (ESOP) In the United States, a type of defined contribution benefit plan wherein a company buys and holds company stock for its employees.

Enhanced capital advantaged security (ECAP) A new debt hybrid introduced in 2005 whereby firms effectively get interest payment tax deductibility on an equity-like security.

Enterprise value The sum of the market value of equity and financial debt, or financial capital at market value minus cash and short-term holdings.

Equal-weighted portfolio A portfolio in which the dollar amounts invested are equal among the portfolio securities.

Equity The value of ownership or residual interest in the property or the assets of a firm after subtracting liabilities. Also called *stock*, it is one of the basic building blocks of the firm's financial structure.

Equity beta The firm beta unadjusted for debt.

Equity premium The difference between the expected rate of return on the risky stock market and the risk-free investment, also called *market risk premium.*

Equivalent annual cost (EAC) The equal annual payment that would provide the same NPV as a pattern of unequal payments.

ESO *See* executive stock option.

ESOP *See* employee stock option plan.

ETF *See* exchange-traded fund.

Eurobonds Bonds issued by corporations foreign to the host country in which they are issued and not denominated in the currency of the host country. They are neither necessarily denominated in euros nor traded in Europe.

European option An option that can only be exercised *at* expiration.

Event study An empirical analysis of the effect of some event on stock returns.

Ex-ante Before the fact.

Exchange A centralized location where financial securities are traded at auction.

Exchange offer A (rare) mechanism besides bankruptcy that allows creditors to change the terms that public bondholders have negotiated.

Exchange rate The price of one unit of some country's currency in terms of one unit of another country's currency.

Exchange-traded fund (ETF) A popular unit investment trust, traded like a stock, which typically tries to mimic a market index (such as the S&P 500).

Ex-dividend date The date stock shares are traded without payment of the dividend.

Executive stock option (ESO) A call option to buy company stock, the value of which depend on the share price. Frequently given to management to align firm and company interests.

Exercise price *See* strike price.

Expected rate of return The probability-weighted average of all possible returns.

Expected value The probability-weighted average of all possible future outcomes.

Expense A cash outflow that is "used up" at the time of purchase and is therefore not depreciated over time.

Ex-post After the fact.

Externalities *See* interactions.

Fair bet A bet that costs its expected value. If repeated infinitely often, both the person offering the bet and the person taking the bet would expect to end up even.

Fama-French factors The value and size factors added by Eugene Fama and Ken French to make the CAPM better predict returns.

FASB *See* Financial Accounting Standards Board.

Fiduciary duty *See* fiduciary responsibility.

Fiduciary responsibility A legal responsibility to act on behalf of the firm's shareholders that limits self-dealing by managers and large shareholders.

Financial Accounting Standards Board (FASB) A private, not-for-profit organization designated by the SEC to establish generally accepted accounting principles (GAAP) for public companies in the United States.

Financial capital The sum of financial debt plus equity.

Financial debt The sum of a firm's long-term debt plus its current liabilities.

Financial footnotes Footnotes that accompany a company's financial statements and which explain the details of the liabilities.

Financial reports *See* financial statements.

Financial statements Reports by publicly traded companies of their internal operations to their shareholders through standardized accounting entries. Also called *financials.*

Financials *See* financial statements.

Financing pyramid A capital structure in which the amount of funding correlates with the seniority. Equity funding would be the tip of the pyramid, while the base of the pyramid would be long-term senior debt.

First-best outcome The increased firm value resulting from perfect corporate governance that fully reduces all agency conflicts between investors and management.

Fisher effect *See* Fisher hypothesis.

Fisher hypothesis (Fisher effect) The theory that *expected* real rates of return should be equal across countries.

Fixed-rate debt Fixed-rate bonds that promise to pay a predetermined interest rate over the life of the bond.

Fixed-rate mortgage A loan that promises a specified stream of equal cash payments each month to a lender.

Flight to quality A time in which investors in all markets suddenly seem to prefer only the most liquid securities. In such situations, the spreads on almost all bonds relative to Treasuries tend to widen all at the same time.

Floating-rate debt Floating-rate bonds that offer a spread relative to some other interest rate, usually to *LIBOR* or to the *prime rate,* over the life of the bond.

Flow-to-equity method A valuation method that takes into account the tax subsidy on the interest expense by working directly with a "pro forma" statement of cash flows.

Foreign bonds Bonds issued by corporations foreign to the host country in which they are issued and denominated in host country currency.

Forward contract An agreement to exchange a fixed amount of currency on a fixed date in the future at a price that is locked in today.

Forward premium The condition in which the forward rate is higher than the spot rate.

Forward rate An interest rate that occurs in future periods.

Forward transaction A financial transaction that allows one to lock in the forward rate that is determined by the yield curve today.

Free cash flow = EBIT ? Taxes + Depletion & Depreciation & Amortization ? Capital Expenditures ? Increases in Working Capital.

Fundamental trading Trading based on underlying firm fundamentals such as financial statements, management methods, or market competitiveness.

Funded debt Short-term debt with a maturity of less than 1 year on the corporate balance sheet.

Futures contract A legal financial contract wherein traders agree to purchase or sell a fixed quantity of an item in the future for a prespecified price today. Unlike forward contracts, futures contracts involve exchange trading, standardization, and daily marking-to-market.

GAAP *See* generally accepted accounting principles.

Gamma A measure of how quickly the delta of the stock position changes when the underlying stock price changes.

GDP Deflator A broader inflation measure based on the change in prices of newly produced goods in a country over a specific time period. The deflator is used to convert nominal GDP into real (constant dollar) GDP.

Generally Accepted Accounting Principles (GAAP) The standard rules that go into preparing the public financial statements for companies.

Geometric average An annualized rate that takes into account any compounding over time.

Geometric average rate of return *See* geometric average.

Glass-Steagall Act of 1933 Law that separated commercial and investment banking. It was repealed in 1999 by the Gramm-Leach-Bliley Act.

Golden parachute A legal and lucrative inducement offered to target management in exchange for their cooperation in a merger or acquisition.

Gordon growth model *See* growing perpetuity.

Great bet A vernacular term for risk(y) arbitrage.

Greedy algorithm A common heuristic algorithm that involves solving for the best immediate solution first in the hopes (and with the risk) of eventually getting to an overall optimum solution.

Greenmail (targeted share repurchase) A legal form of preferential treatment of large shareholders, especially takeover-threatening ones, in which company management uses other shareholders' money to repurchase only the threatening investors' shares at a higher price.

Gross profit margin Gross income divided by sales.

Growing annuity formula A special annuity formula often used in the context of pension cash flows that grow for a fixed number of time periods and then stop.

Growing perpetuity A formula that allows the cash flows to increase by a constant growth rate g per period forever.

Growth firms Firms that have higher market values than accounting book values.

Hedge An investment made to lower or even cancel the risk of other investments.

Hedge funds Private trading companies that do not qualify as investment companies in the SEC sense and are therefore exempt from SEC regulation.

Hedge ratio (delta) The number of stocks needed in order to counteract the behavior of one option.

Hedging (corporate) The act whereby firms reduce their overall risk by investing in noncorrelated projects or businesses.

Heuristic A rule of thumb that simplifies decisions, often at the expense of accuracy.

Histogram A graph that has the possible outcomes of a probability distribution on the x-axis and the frequency (or probability) of those outcomes on the y-axis.

Holdout problem The situation in a firm restructuring wherein some bondholders reject the firm's debt buyback offer and "hold out" for more favorable terms for more than just the normal financial transaction costs, thereby disrupting the restructuring process.

Home bias A condition in which investors prefer and overweight domestic securities.

Hostile acquisitions Acquisitions made without the consent of the target's board and management.

Hurdle rate The appropriate discount rate (risk-adjusted cost of capital) used to discount a firm's projects' cash flows.

Hyperinflation A period of highly excessive inflation such as occurred in Germany from 1922–1923.

I/B/E/S Institutional Brokers' Estimate System, a very large database that assembles many different earnings estimates for most U.S. publicly traded companies. It began in 1976 for US equities and 1987 for international equities.

ICAPM *See* intertemporal CAPM.

Impairment rules Standardized schedules over which particular assets are depreciated by accountants.

Implied volatility The estimate of the standard deviation derived from the Black-Scholes formula.

Income tax A tax levied on income, however measured.

Incremental *See* marginal.

Independent A classification for projects that have no mutual interactions.

Independent directors *See* outside directors.

Indirect bankruptcy costs Costs that do not involve direct cash outlays and that occur in financial distress, such as higher capital costs, problems with vendors, losing better employees, etc. In addition, there are agency costs such as the firm acquiring riskier projects or raising dividends at the expense of bondholders.

Inflation A general rise in the price level during which money loses its value.

Inflation-indexed terms Prices that incorporate the inflation rate over time.

Initial public offering (IPO) An event in which a privately traded company first sells shares to retail and institutional investors for the general public.

Inside directors Members of the board of directors who are also owners and/or managers.

Insider trading Trading securities on unreleased specific information, mostly illegal.

Intangible assets Intangible assets that lack physical substance such as patents, copyrights, licenses, goodwill, etc.

Interactions The case in which one project has external influences on other projects—sometimes imposing external costs, and sometimes providing external benefits.

Interest coverage ratio The TIE ratio (EBIT/total interest) is one popular common interest coverage ratio. Many variations exist depending on the definitions used for earnings and interest.

Interest forwards Financial forward transactions that allow speculators to finance today with money coming in when they need it and with money going out when they have it, all in one transaction.

Internal rate of return (IRR) The "interest rate" that makes the NPV of a set of cash flows equal to zero. It is also called a *yield-to-maturity* when calculated for bonds.

Internal Revenue Service (IRS) The federal U.S. agency responsible for collecting taxes on individuals and businesses.

International CAPM A CAPM model in which investors weight not only the performance of the U.S. stock market but also currency performance.

Internet bubble The period from around 1998 to 2000 in which technology stocks experienced a highly abnormal rise in prices.

Intertemporal CAPM (ICAPM) An extension of the ordinary CAPM that explains the CAPM in a dynamic setting with multiple risk factors.

In-the-money The condition in which an option would be profitable to exercise, ignoring the option price.

Inventories Goods and materials that are held readily available in stock at a business.

Inventory turnover The ratio of the cost of goods sold (COGS) to average inventory, a measures that shows how often inventories translate into sales.

Investment companies Important trading companies in the U.S. financial markets, regulated by the SEC. There are three kinds: unit investment trusts (UIT's), mutual funds (open-end funds), and closed-end funds.

Investment grade The top four rating grades for bonds with the lowest risk.

Investment in goodwill A misnomer. It actually refers to cash paid when one firm acquires another firm.

IPO *See* initial public offering.

IPO underpricing The well-known experience of IPOs in which share prices historically have experienced a jump of about 10–15% in 1 day, not annualized.

IRP *See* covered interest rate parity.

IRR *See* internal rate of return.

IRS *See* internal revenue service.

Issue-and-swap market A large market for corporate financing in which a firm issues a bond and immediately swaps its payments with a counterparty.

Junior bond A bond that, in bankruptcy, is paid only after full payment of any senior bonds.

Large-cap stocks *See* S&P 500.

Lead managers Those managers in charge of determining the IPO price and in charge of handling the due diligence and the technical and many legal aspects of the process.

Leasing Using the property of another entity for a periodic payment or rent. Leasing can be a tax-advantageous arrangement.

Lemon problem *See* adverse selection.

Level coupon bond A bond with coupon payments that remain the same for the life of the bond.

Leverage Using debt so that a smaller but riskier equity investment controls a larger asset base.

Leveraged buyout (LBO) The act of obtaining a controlling interest in a company's equity by the use of a high level of leverage (borrowing) to make the purchase.

Levered equity Equity or stock that accrues to the business owner *after* the debt is paid off.

Levered ownership *See* levered equity.

Liabilities Financial obligations arising from *past* transactions that entail the future transfer of assets.

Liabilities/equity ratio The ratio of a firm's liabilities to a firm's shareholder equity. The ratio appears in many variations. For example, the numerator can use long-term debt, financial debt, or all liabilities.

Limit order book The record of as-yet-unexecuted orders from investors to purchase or sell if the stock price changes.

Limit orders Orders to buy or sell securities that ask for execution if the price is above or below a limit that the investor specifies.

Limited capacity A complexity of overhead allocation due to the problem of adding capacity in discrete chunks.

Limited liability A legal limit such that the most investors can lose is their investment.

Linear regression A statistical procedure that fits the best linear relationship between the set of points generated by two variables.

Liquidity premium An extra expected rate of return to compensate the investor for holding an asset that will be difficult to convert into full cash value immediately.

Liquidnet A method of trading stocks that uses peer-to-peer networking—like the original Napster—in order to match buyers and sellers in real time.

Loan *See* debt.

Log-normal distribution The distribution of a random variable whose logarithm is normally distributed.

Long bond 30-year bonds issued by the U.S. Treasury.

Long-term accrual An accrual classification over a period longer than 1 year.

M&M *See* Modigliani-Miller.

Macaulay duration A method to calculate the effective maturity of a bond by weighting the payment times with the present value of the payouts.

Management buyout (MBO) A leveraged buyout of a company by the existing management.

Marginal The concept of decision-making based on incremental gains and losses.

Marginal cost of capital The cost of raising the next dollar of capital.

Marginal tax rate The tax rate on the next dollar of income, usually higher than the average tax rate because of the progressive U.S. tax system.

Market beta A measure of how the rate of return of a project fluctuates with that of the overall market.

Market beta calculation The slope of a line showing the relationship between the independent variable of the market rate and the dependent variable of the individual security's return.

Market efficiency The state in which the market uses all information in setting the price of a financial asset. In a fully efficient market, no available information can be used to predict future returns better than the market can.

Market maker A broker-dealer who continuously matches security buyers and sellers and stands ready to buy or sell shares, thereby creating a liquid and immediate market.

Market model The formula that states that a security's required rate of return is equal to the risk-free rate plus the product of a risk premium multiplied by the security's beta.

Market order An order to buy or sell securities that asks for execution at the current price.

Market portfolio The set of all available investment opportunities in proportion to their market value.

Market risk premium *See* equity premium.

Market-equity-to-book-equity ratio The ratio of the stock's market value to its book or accounting value.

Matador bonds Foreign bonds in Spain issued by a non-Spanish corporation.

Maturity The final payment date of a loan or bond. On that date, all remaining interest and principal is due.

MBO *See* management buyout.

Mean *See* average.

Mean-variance efficient frontier The points on the efficient frontier with the optimal risk-reward portfolios.

Merger The union of two corporations to form a new corporation.

Minimum-variance portfolio The west-most portfolio on the efficient frontier, the portfolio with the lowest risk as measured by variance or standard deviation.

Modigliani-Miller (M&M) The most popular capital structure finance theory with two main versions. The 1958 no-corporate-tax model implies that capital structure does not matter to the value of the firm. The 1963 with corporate-tax model implies that the firm should finance with all debt.

Money market (cash) The market for debt securities that are very liquid, very low-risk, and have very short-term maturities such as certificate of deposits (CDs), savings deposits, or commercial paper.

Monte Carlo simulation *See* simulation analysis.

Moody's One of the two biggest credit rating agencies for corporations that rate the issuer's probability that their bonds will default.

Moral hazard An agency conflict in which a person or institution protected from risk may act less carefully than if they were fully exposed to the risk since they would not bear the full consequences of its actions.

Muni bonds *See* municipal bonds.

Municipal bonds Bonds issued by municipalities such as cities and states. Such bonds are exempt from federal income tax, but they are risky.

Munis *See* municipal bonds.

Mutual funds Investment companies that hold and actively trade shares of other stocks and are open-ended. They do not trade on exchanges but are easily and cheaply accessible through retail brokers.

MVE frontier *See* mean-variance efficient frontier.

NASD *See* national association of securities dealers.

NASDAQ *See* national association of securities dealers automated quotation system.

National Association of Securities Dealers *An* association that operates a semi-OTC market for the stocks of smaller firms that are listed on the so-called pink sheets.

National Association of Securities Dealers Automated Quotation System One of the two most important stock exchanges in the United States, it is the largest electronic equity securities trading market in the United States.

Natural logarithm A logarithm using the natural base e = 2.718.

Natural monopoly The case in which an industry exhibits economies of scale so that the number of low-cost firms is very small and may even be just one.

Natural resources Naturally occurring substances such as soil, trees, petroleum, mineral ores, etc.

Negative interactions The case where one project has a negative influence on the NPV of another project. Therefore, it cannot be valued without taking into account his negative influence—the sum of the parts is worth less than the parts summed individually.

Negotiated debt The opposite of a credit line, in which both the bank and the firm commit to a fixed loan.

Net income The accounting definition of income after taxes have been subtracted, often known as the "bottom line."

Net issuance of debt The difference between debt principal that was raised and debt principal that was repaid as shown on the cash flow statement.

Net operating loss (NOL) A financial loss that occurs when tax-deductible expenses are greater than taxable revenues in an operating year.

Net profit margin (NPM) Net income divided by sales.

Net working capital Current assets minus current liabilities, often just called *working capital* (without the "net" qualification).

New York Board of Trade (NYBOT) A physical commodities exchange known primarily for its "soft" commodity trading. Located in New York City, it became a subsidiary of Intercontinental Exchange (ICE) in 2007.

New York Bond Exchange (NYBE) The part of the NYSE wherein bonds trade on a formal exchange; much smaller than the OTC exchange where most bond trades occur.

New York Mercantile Exchange (NYMEX) The NYMEX is the world's largest physical commodity futures exchange. With physical headquarters in New York City, it maintains an open outcry system.

New York Stock Exchange (NYSE) Known colloquially as "the Big Board," it is the largest stock exchange in the world in terms of dollar volume, and the second largest stock exchange in the world in terms of company listings.

No-arbitrage relationship A condition in which no profit can be made on trading among the calls and puts on a stock, given the risk-free rate and the time period.

Noise traders Traders who do not collect information and who may trade for idiosyncratic reasons.

NOL *See* net operating losses.

Nominal terms Prices or interest rates that are not adjusted for inflation

No-recourse loan A mortgage loan in which the owner could default and the creditor could repossess the asset guaranteeing the loan but not any of the borrower's other assets.

Normsdist The cumulative normal distribution function in a spreadsheet.

Note A short-term bond that is also often callable, a feature that makes it easy for a corporation to expand or contract debt as needed.

NPM *See* net profit margin.

NYBE *See* New York bond exchange.

NYBOT *See* New York Board of Trade.

NYSE *See* New York Stock Exchange.

NYSE Euronext The merged electronic trading exchange of the NYSE, ArcaEx, and Euronext.

Off-the-run bond A similar but not identical bond to an on-the-run bond, perhaps differing in maturity by a few days.

On margin The act of purchasing securities with money borrowed at some interest rate, usually the broker call rate.

On the margin The extra credit/charge to a project and all the externalities that such a project adds to the existing firm.

On-the-run bond The most recently issued Treasury of a particular maturity. Because bond traders and the financial press focus on this particular bond, it is easier to buy and sell.

Open-end UIT A unit investment trust wherein the investors not only can sell their shares to other investors, but can also exchange their UIT shares into the some fraction of the underlying holdings.

Open-market repurchases The most common way for firms to repurchase their shares. The repurchase program is approved by the corporate board and must be disclosed publicly. The SEC imposes no filing requirements or progress disclosures.

Operating activity net of investing activity Total operating activity minus total investing activity.

Operating income (EBIT) An accounting measure of company income equal to operating revenue − operating expenses + non-operating income.

Operating profit margin Operating income divided by sales.

Operations research The area of applied mathematics that employs mathematical models, statistics, and algorithms to compute optimal or next-best solutions to complex problems.

Opportunity cost The next-best alternative foregone when making a choice.

Optimal capital structure The weights of debt and equity that maximize the value of the firm.

Option The most prominent type of contingent claim wherein the buyer has the right but not the obligation to engage in a future transaction.

Option contract A bundle of 100 options, the normal option trading unit.

Ordinary equity *See* common stock.

Origination The process of creating a security issue by a bank or broker that has the expertise to handle the legal and operational processes.

OTC *See* over the counter.

Out-of-the-money The condition in which an option would not be profitable to exercise, ignoring the option price.

Outside directors (independent directors) Individuals who have no current or recent material relationship with the company.

Over the counter (OTC) An electronic securities quotation system with real-time quotes wherein most bonds are traded by large investors who telephone individual investment banks' desks.

Overconfidence The tendency of people to believe that their own assessments are more accurate than they really are—a behavioral error that can cause predictable valuation mistakes.

Over-optimism A trait among investors that can counter the agency cost of a firm issuing equity due to the inside information argument.

P/E ratio *See* price-earnings ratio.

Paper loss A loss shown in accounting terms, not in actual cash terms.

Par value Stated or face value. It is not really a market value, but only a way to quote coupon payment flow patterns for bonds. For stocks, it is practically meaningless.

Payables turnover The ratio of net sales to payables, a measure of how quickly the firm pays its suppliers.

Payback rule A measure used in capital budgeting that calculates the number of periods need to pay back the original capital investment cost.

Payoff diagram A diagram showing the breakdown of cash flow rights to the bondholders and shareholders of a firm.

Payoff table A table that assigns probabilities to a project value in each possible future value–relevant scenario.

Payout ratio The ratio of (dividends + equity repurchasing) to net income.

PE ratio *See* price-earnings ratio.

P-E ratio *See* price-earnings ratio.

Pecking order A theory of capital structure in which firms prefer to finance first with internal equity, second with debt, and last by issuing external equity.

PEG ratio The P/E ratio divided by earnings growth.

Perpetuity A stream of constant cash flows that repeats forever at regular intervals.

Pink sheets The past name for Pink Quote, an electronic quotation system (not a stock exchange). The system lists quotes from broker-dealers for many over-the-counter securities. The companies file almost no financial statements, and most of them are closely held, very small, and are thinly traded. These are very risky investments.

Placement An offer of securities, public or private, to the general public by underwriters who find the investors desired by issuers.

Political risk The chance that a financial investment would suffer in a foreign country due to that country's political structure.

Portfolio risk The standard deviation of the portfolio's rate of return.

Positive interactions The case where one project has a positive influence on the NPV of another project. Therefore, it cannot be valued without taking into account this positive influence—the sum of the parts is worth more than the parts individually.

Post audits Audits of past projects. Such audits evaluate the accuracy of the financial numbers and the quality of the managers' forecasts. The expectation of post audits presumably encourages managers to make more accurate forecasts in the first place.

PPI *See* producer price index.

PPP *See* purchasing power parity.

Preferred equity A claim with both debt and equity characteristics. Preferred dividends are usually paid as a fixed dollar amount per calendar quarter per share, are usually higher than common dividends, and have priority over any common dividend payments in bankruptcy.

Premium bond A bond that sells for more than its par or face value.

Present value of growth opportunities (PVGO) The difference between the present value of a firm with constant growth and the present value of a firm with no growth.

Price-earnings ratio The ratio of the stock price to earnings, often abbreviated as *P-E ratio, P/E ratio,* or *PE Ratio.*

Primary shares Newly created shares in which the proceeds flow directly to the company.

Prime brokers Brokers who only manage the bookkeeping of the investor's portfolio, margin provisions, and shorting provisions.

Principal The entrepreneur (or corporate board or management) of the firm who oversees management and is ultimately responsible for the firm's performance.

Principal The face (par) amount on a bond that is repaid at the bond's maturity. In essence, it is the remaining loan balance.

Principal agent problem *See* agency problem.

Private equity A wide variety of assets composed of equity securities used in companies that are not publicly traded on a stock exchange.

Private equity funds *See* hedge funds.

Pro forma A hypothetical, model of future financial performance, with a detailed projection time period of cash flows and a terminal value.

Probability distribution A list of all possible outcomes and their respective probabilities that define a random variable.

Producer Price Index A common inflation measure which is based on prices of inputs to companies.

Profitability index A measure used in capital budgeting that divides the present value of future cash flows by the project cost.

Promised interest rate Usually published in newspaper and financial publications. It is also called *quoted interest rate* or *stated interest rate.* It is to be distinguished from the expected return.

Promised rate of return *See* promised interest rate.

Property rights The legal ability to own and dispense property in various forms, including the right to transfer property and the right to write and enforce contracts.

Pro-rata A share repurchase in which the firm repurchases shares in proportionally fair allocations based on a Dutch auction.

Proxy contest A hostile takeover in which the would-be acquirer solicits the votes of other shareholders to elect different board members.

Purchasing power parity (PPP) A theory of exchange rates in which prices of identical goods are the same in all countries, differing only in the costs of transport and duties.

Put option An option that gives its holder the right but not the obligation to sell an underlying security for a specific period of time for a prespecified price.

Putability A bond option that allows bondholders to return the bonds to the issuer in exchange for a pre-agreed payment. This is similar to convertibility, except that the conversion is into cash, not into equity.

Put-call parity A no-arbitrage relationship that relates the price of a European call to the price of its equivalent European put, the underlying stock price, and the interest rate.

PVGO *See* present value of growth opportunities.

Quarterly report *See* 10-Q.

Quick ratio similar to the current ratio but with inventories deleted from current assets.

Random variable A variable whose outcome has not yet been determined.

Random walk In finance, the theory that the past movement of a variable (such as a stock price) is of no use in predicting its future movement.

Rational economics A school of thought wherein economic actors are assumed to logically and without emotion compare the costs and benefits of their actions.

Real option The ability to change course in the future, depending on the prevailing economic environment in the future. Such flexibility adds value, but real options do not trade in markets.

Real return The return that removes inflation from the nominal rate, the purchasing power return.

Real terms *See* inflation-indexed terms.

Realizations A series of actual outcomes.

Receivables *See* accounts receivable.

Receivables turnover The ratio of net credit sales to receivables, a measure of how quickly customers are paying.

Redeem Repurchase a bond.

Reinvestment rate The new or changed interest rate at which cash flows can be invested.

Relativism The tendency of people to consider issues of relative scale when they should not—a behavioral error that can cause predictable valuation mistakes.

Reluctance to liquidate An agency conflict in which firm managers, acting on behalf of equity holders, refrain from liquidating the firm in financial distress in order to gamble on risky payoffs.

Rent seeking An act wherein an entity seeks to obtain an uncompensated transfer to itself by manipulating the economic and/or legal system rather than by productive channels of trade or work.

Retail broker A financial securities broker that executes buy or sell orders for stocks for individuals. Examples are *Ameritrade, Charles Schwab,* or *Merrill Lynch.*

Return on (book) assets (ROA) Net income divided by the book value of assets.

Return on (book) equity (ROE) Net income divided by the book value of equity.

Return on sales (ROS) *See* net profit margin.

Revenue (sales) Cash flow to a company from the sale of its goods and services except when the sale is on credit. In the latter case, the revenue is "booked" as a sale, but there is no cash flow *until* the company collects the cash at a later date.

Reverse mergers A way to enter the public financial markets in which a large privately owned company that wants to go public merges with a small company that is already publicly traded. The owners of the big company receive newly issued shares in the combined entity.

Reverse split A merging of a firm's shares, often used to inflate reported earnings. No cash flow occurs since the share price rises to maintain the same total value.

Revolver A revolving credit line without fixed payments on which the company can alternately borrow and repay until a termination date or maturity.

Reward The expected dollar value of an investment.

Rho The measure of the change in the price of the option as the risk-free rate changes.

Right to vote The most important control right that entrepreneurs (must) grant shareholders—the right to vote for the appointment of the board members.

Rights offering A way of selling new equity shares in which the company grants existing shareholders the right to purchase a proportional share of a new issue at a given price in a limited period.

Risk A summary measure of how spread out the possible investment outcomes are.

Risk management The deliberate manipulation of the risk exposure that the corporation faces.

Risk neutral An investor willing to write or take any fair bet.

Risk premium An expected rate of return representing a reward for willingness to absorb risk.

Risk(y) arbitrage A business transaction that may not be risk-free but that still offers above-normal profits given its risk and other characteristics.

ROA *See* return on (book) assets.

ROE *See* return on (book) equity.

Rollup The combining of multiple small firms into one entity large enough to be taken public.

ROS *See* return on sales.

Round-trip costs All the transactions costs involved in buying and later selling an asset.

Rule 10b-18 (safe harbor) A 1982 ruling by the SEC clarifying Rule 10b-5 saying that the SEC will not file price manipulation charges against companies repurchasing shares on the open market.

Rule 10b-5 A pre-1982 SEC rule against price manipulation resulting from repurchasing activity.

Rule 415 The SEC rule that allows shelf registrations of securities to be issued when market conditions are viewed as more favorable by the firm.

Run on liquidity *See* flight to quality.

S&P 500 *See* Standard and Poor's.

Safe harbor *See* Rule 10b-18.

Sales *See* revenue.

Samurai bonds Foreign bonds in Japan issued by a non-Japanese corporation.

Sarbanes-Oxley Act of 2002 (SOX) A Federal law that applies only to public companies with the purpose of strengthening corporate accounting and reporting requirements.

Scenario analysis A numerical simulation that shows how sensitive an estimated value is to reasonable alternative possible outcomes of several other variables simultaneously.

Seasoned equity offering (SEO) An offer by an established public company to sell more shares.

Seasoned equity offering The sale of shares in an existing publicly traded company. They are rare events for large, publicly traded corporations, except in connection with M&A activity.

SEC *See* Securities and Exchange Commission.

Secondary shares Existing stock shares sold to firm investors.

Second-best outcome The reduced firm value resulting from imperfect corporate governance which falls short of reducing all agency conflicts between investors and management.

Section 404 The section of the Sarbanes-Oxley Act requiring the annual report to explain the company's internal controls and attest to their effectiveness. This part requires burdensome and expensive auditing.

Secured bond A bond collateralized by the underlying security.

Securities Financial claims such as debt and equity that often indicate registration with the Securities and Exchange Commission (SEC).

Securities and Exchange Commission (SEC) The U.S. governmental agency responsible for enforcing the federal securities laws and regulating the securities industry.

Security market line (SML) A graphical representation of the CAPM formula that shows the relationship between the expected rate of return of a project and its beta.

Sell recommendations Recommendations made by market stock analysts to sell securities.

Selling, general & administrative expenses (SG&A) Company expenditures that comprise all direct and indirect selling expenses and all general and administrative expenses.

Semistrong market efficiency A market condition in which all public information is reflected in today's stock price, so that neither fundamental trading nor technical analysis can be used to beat the market.

Senior bond A bond that, in bankruptcy, must be paid in full before a subordinated bond (junior bond) is paid.

Sensitivity analysis A numerical simulation that shows how sensitive an estimated value is to reasonable alternative possible outcomes of only one other variable.

SEO *See* seasoned equity offering.

Separate Trading of Registered Interest and Principal of Securities (STRIPS) The U.S. Treasury's own coupon-stripping program.

Separation of decisions The independence of investment decisions from consumption preferences.

SG&A *See* selling, general & administrative expenses

Share repurchases The purchase of a corporation's shares by the issuing corporation. The open market repurchase is the most common way this is done.

Shareholder proposal A more modest and inexpensive form of the proxy contest wherein all shareholders vote on a proposal. Shareholder proposals are usually not binding and can be ignored by the board.

Shareholder wealth maximization A popular financial viewpoint that the goal of firm managers should be to maximize the per share price.

Shark repellants Tactics by target management to resist a hostile takeover.

Shirking The act of working less than agreed, an agency or moral hazard problem.

Short sale The process of borrowing securities, selling them to third parties, receiving the cash, buying back the securities later in the market, and then returning them to the lender of the securities.

Signal-to-noise ratio The ratio of (meaningful) information to (irrelevant) background noise. Financial signals are often small compared to the noise, making it difficult to settle issues such as market efficiency.

Simple spread A position that is long one option and short another option on the same stock. The options are of the same type and have the same expiration date but different strike prices.

Simulation analysis A more advanced form of scenario analysis that varies all variables at once to trace out a probabilistic impact on the dependent variable.

Sinking fund A bond provision that mandates that the firm will repurchase a specified fraction of the bond principal before maturity.

Small Business Administration A United States government agency that provides support to small businesses, mostly in the form of loan guarantees.

SML *See* security market line.

Solvent The financial state of a company wherein it has the ability to pay its debts with available cash and can meet its long-term fixed expenses.

SOX *See* Sarbanes-Oxley Act of 2002.

Specialist A trader usually assigned to the trading of a specific stock.

Speculative grade Or junk grade, the bottom five rating grades for bonds.

Spot contract A contract for an immediate exchange of a fixed amount of currency based on the current exchange rate.

Spot currency rate The current exchange rate.

Spot rate The current interest rate.

Spread The difference between the bid price and the ask price of an asset traded on an auction exchange.

Spreads Option strategies that consist of long and short options of the same type (calls or puts).

Spurious strategies Trading strategies that seemed to have worked historically but disappeared shortly after discovery or that were never real in the first place.

Stakeholder holdup A variant of rent seeking in which anyone who has the power to obstruct ("hold up") a business, especially a profitable public company, will try to extort a share of profits.

Standard & Poor's (S&P) One of the two biggest credit rating agencies for corporations that rate the issuer's bond default probability.

Standard deviation The square root of the average squared deviation from the mean, or the square root of the variance.

State A future value of the firm.

State-contingent claims Financial claims such as debt and equity, the value of which depend on the future state of the firm.

Stock *See* equity.

Stock dividend A dividend paid in the form of more stock shares. No cash is involved, so it is not an equity payout. If more shares are issued to do this, the share price falls so that no extra wealth is created.

Stock offer The tendering of a corporation's own shares to pay for an acquisition.

Stock shareholders *See* stockholders.

Stock split A change in the number of shares of stock with a corresponding change in the stock price so that the total stock value remains the same. No cash flow is involved.

Stockholders An abbreviation for stock shareholders. Stockholders own shares of equity ownership in a joint stock company, either public or private.

Straddle A popular option combination that combines one put and one call, both either long or short, often with the same strike price, and with the same time to expiration.

Straight-line depreciation A common method of depreciation wherein the depreciable cost of the asset is divided by the number of years of its useful life.

Strategic option *See* real option.

Strike price (exercise price) The prespecified price of at which an option can be exercised.

Strip financing A repackaging of debt and equity in equal units to eliminate the incentives of shareholders to exploit each other.

Stripping A process whereby bond buyers clip the coupons from a bond and resell them separately.

STRIPS *See* separate trading of registered interest and principal of securities.

Strong buy A recommendation by a stock market analyst to purchase securities when the buy/sell ratio is about 5:1.

Strong form market efficiency A market condition in which all information, both public and private, is reflected in today's stock price, so that not even private insider information can be used to beat the market.

Strong sell A recommendation by a stock market analyst to sell when the buy/sell ratio is over 10:1.

Subordinated bond *See* junior bond.

Sunk cost An oxymoron. Costs incurred in the past that therefore do not involve opportunities foregone today.

Supervisory board A group of individuals elected by stockholders to serve their interests by hiring and supervising the CEO and company directors.

Survivorship bias A phenomenon in which financial performance is exaggerated because poor-performing investments failed and were excluded from the overall results. Usually occurs in the context of mutual funds.

Syndicate A collection of underwriters who together bring offerings to market.

Synergies The managerial term for positive externalities between an acquirer and a potential acquisition target; an important managerial buzzword.

Tangible assets Assets that have physical substance such as factories, machines, equipment, land, buildings, etc.

Targeted repurchase *See* greenmail.

Targeted share repurchase *See* greenmail.

Taxes payable A current liability that represents money owed for taxes.

Tax premium A higher interest rate premium paid by non-municipal and corporate bonds relative to Treasuries because of the tax-exemption on the latter.

T-bills *See* treasury bills.

Tech bubble *See* Internet bubble.

Technical analysis Trading based solely on historical market data such as price and/or volume patterns.

Tender offer The offer to target shareholders to exchange their shares for cash or stock for a fixed price within a fixed time period.

Term structure of interest rates A graphical representation of time to maturity on the x-axis and the annualized interest rate on the y-axis.

Terminal value The market value of the business as a going-concern at a point in the future, usually beyond the forecast period.

Theft An agency problem in which a larger equity stake leads to exploitation of the more passive debt partners who are dependent on true and accurate reporting of profits.

Theta A measure of the change in the price of the option as time changes.

TIE *See* times interest earned.

Tier 1 capital *See* core equity.

Time premium The pure opportunity cost (interest rate) with no risk or inflation premium.

Times interest earned (TIE) The ratio of earnings before interest (usually also before taxes) to the firm's interest payments.

TIPS *See* treasury inflation protected securities.

Tombstone A printed financial advertisement of a securities offering.

Total investing activity Cash inflows and outflows from investing activities that include the purchase or sale of property, plants, and equipment, as well as the purchase or sale of any investment securities that the firm holds.

Total operating activity Ceeu ash flows from the firm's main business operations, calculated by starting with net income, adding back the non-cash expenses, and adjusting for changes in net working capital.

Trade credit A financial arrangement in which suppliers (vendors) sell their goods to buyers (companies) for later payment in an open credit arrangement limited to the specific goods the supplier sells.

Tragedy of the commons A situation in which each individual acts in his or her own personal interest, resulting in harm to the whole group (e.g., over-grazing by cattle on the Boston commons in the 1630s).

Trailing 12-month method (TTM) A method to adjust flow variables (such as earnings) into a recent annualized equivalent. The timeframe of the past 12 months used for reporting financial figures.

Tranche A classification structure of debt in which the debt is structured so that the principal payment schedule and maturity date are different for each of the issues.

Treasuries Bonds of various maturities issued by the U.S. Treasury.

Treasury bills (T-bills) Bonds issued by the U.S. Treasury with maturities of less than 1 year.

Treasury bonds Bonds issued by the U.S. Treasury with maturities greater than 10 years.

Treasury Inflation Protected Securities (TIPS or CPI bonds) Bonds not affected by inflation in a perfect market.

Treasury management *See* cash management.

Treasury notes Bonds issued by the U.S. Treasury with maturities between 1 and 10 years.

Treasury shares Shares of stock that are repurchased by the issuing company.

Treasury stock Shares of stock repurchased by the issuing company.

True arbitrage A business transaction that offers positive net cash inflows in at least some scenarios, and under no circumstances has a negative net cash flow. Therefore, it is risk-free.

TTM *See* trailing 12-month method.

Tunneling An unethical and sometimes fraudulent transfer of assets from a corporation to an insider such as management or to a large or controlling stakeholder.

Turnover The ratio of sales to another number, usually a component of net working capital.

Two-fund separation theorem The principle that investors would purchase only a combination of the risk-free asset and the risky tangency portfolio, regardless of risk aversion.

U.S. Treasuries yield curve A yield curve using U.S. Treasuries.

Uncovered interest rate parity The theoretical condition in which the exchange rate future today would be the best expectation of the future spot exchange rate because there is no risk premium and investors are risk neutral.

Underinvestment problem An agency conflict wherein bondholders fear that managers will not make necessary investments if the promised debt payments are too large. Ex-ante, such underinvestment reduces the payoffs bondholders expect to receive, which increases current bond interest rates.

Underwriter An investment bank that guarantees the issuing proceeds of an IPO to the issuing client when helping corporations sell securities to third-party investors.

Underwriting The process wherein investment bankers raise capital from investors for securities being issued by corporations and government.

Unfunded debt Debt on the corporate balance sheet with a maturity of more than 1 year.

Unit A bundle of multiple types of financial claims that are sold together. For example, one common type of unit bundles a bond with a warrant.

Unit investment trust (UIT) A passive "basket" investment fund with a fixed termination date that holds stocks and that can be listed on a stock exchange such as American Depositary Receipts (ADR's).

Unit securities A combination of securities consisting of debt securities and equity securities, thereby eliminating the conflict between shareholders and bondholders and thus reducing transaction costs.

Unsolicited bid A hostile takeover attempt of one company by another.

Valuation ratio A ratio of the stock price to some measurable attribute; for example, the P/E ratio.

Value firms Stocks with high accounting book value of equity divided by the market value of equity.

Value-weighted portfolio A portfolio in which the security weights correspond to the market values of the components.

Variance The expected value of the squared deviations from the mean.

Vega A measure of the change in the price of the option as volatility changes.

Volatility The amount of dispersion of a variable from its measure of central tendency. In finance, this is usually measured by the variance or standard deviation.

Volatility smile An empirical regularity in which the implied volatilities as a function of strike price produce a graph concave upward.

WACC *See* weighted average cost of capital.

Warrant A long-lived option issued by a company itself. It is not traded on an exchange, and its exercise is dilutive when it triggers the creation of new underlying shares by the firm.

Weak market efficiency A market condition in which all information in past prices is reflected in today's price so that technical analysis cannot be used to beat the market.

Weighted average cost of capital (WACC) The value-weighted average cost of capital of all the firm's claims.

White knight A company that offers a friendly takeover to another company under threat of a hostile takeover from an unwelcome bidder.

Winner's curse *See* adverse selection.

Working capital *See* net working capital.

Yankee bonds Foreign bonds in the United States issued by a non-U.S. corporation.

Yield curve *See* term structure of interest rates.

Yield-to-maturity (YTM) The "interest rate" that makes the NPV of a set of cash flows equal to zero. It is also called a *yield-to-maturity* when calculated for bonds. Otherwise, it is the same concept as an internal rate of return.

YTM *See* yield-to-maturity.

Zero coupon bonds Bonds that pay only a single lump sum at the maturity of the bond with no interim coupons.

Zero-bonds *See* zero coupon bonds.

Index

Page numbers with an "a" refer to items appearing in Anecdotes. Page numbers with a "d" refer to items appearing in Digging Deeper boxes.

KEY EQUATIONS